Customer Support Information

Plunkett's Health Care Industry Almanac 2008

Please register your book immediately...

if you did not purchase it directly from Plunkett Research, Ltd. This will enable us to fulfill your replacement request if you have a damaged product, or your requests for assistance. Also it will enable us to notify you of future editions, so that you may purchase them from the source of your choice.

If you are an actual, original purchaser but did not receive a FREE CD-ROM version with your book...*

you may request it by returning this form.

____ YES, please register me as a purchaser of the book.
I did not buy it directly from Plunkett Research, Ltd.

____ YES, please send me a free CD-ROM version of the book.
I am an actual purchaser, but I did not receive one with my book. (Proof of purchase may be required.)

Customer Name ________

Title ________________

Organization ___________

Address ______________________________

City ______________________ State ________ Zip ______________

Country (if other than USA) ______________________________

Phone ______________________ Fax ______________________

E-mail ______________________________

Mail or Fax to: **Plunkett Research, Ltd.**

Attn: FREE CD-ROM and/or Registration
P.O. Drawer 541737, Houston, TX 77254-1737 USA
713.932.0000 · Fax 713.932.7080 · www.plunkettresearch.com

* Purchasers of used books are not eligible to register. Use of CD-ROMs is subject to the terms of their end user license agreements.

PLUNKETT'S HEALTH CARE INDUSTRY ALMANAC 2008

The Only Comprehensive Guide to the Health Care Industry

Jack W. Plunkett

Published by:
Plunkett Research, Ltd., Houston, Texas
www.plunkettresearch.com

PLUNKETT'S HEALTH CARE INDUSTRY ALMANAC 2008

Editor and Publisher:
Jack W. Plunkett

Executive Editor and Database Manager:
Martha Burgher Plunkett

Senior Editors and Researchers:
Addie K. FryeWeaver
Christie Manck
John Peterson

Editors, Researchers and Assistants:
Andreea Balan
Brandon Brison
Daniel Jordan
Kara Jordan
Lindsey Meyn
Kristen Morrow
Michael Sheehan
Kyle Wark
Suzanne Zarosky

E-Commerce Managers:
Heather M. Cook
Jared Deter
Emily Hurley
Ian Markham
Lynne Zarosky

Information Technology Managers:
Wenping Guo
Carl Thomsen

Cover Design:
Kim Paxson, Just Graphics
Junction, TX

Special Thanks to:
American Hospital Association
Organisation for Economic Co-operation and Development (OECD)
U.S. Department of Commerce,
Census Bureau,
International Trade Administration,
National Technical Information Service
U.S. Department of Health and Human Services
Centers for Disease Control,
Centers for Medicare and Medicaid Services,
National Center for Health Statistics,
National Institutes of Health
U.S. Department of Labor
Bureau of Labor Statistics
U.S. National Science Foundation

Plunkett Research, Ltd.
P. O. Drawer 541737, Houston, Texas 77254 USA
Phone: 713.932.0000 Fax: 713.932.7080
www.plunkettresearch.com

Published by:
Plunkett Research, Ltd.
P. O. Drawer 541737
Houston, Texas 77254-1737

Phone: 713.932.0000
Fax: 713.932.7080
Internet: www.plunkettresearch.com

ISBN10 # 1-59392-096-2
ISBN13 # 978-1-59392-096-8

Disclaimer of liability for use and results of use:

The editors and publishers assume no responsibility for your own success in making an investment or business decision, in seeking or keeping any job, in succeeding at any firm or in obtaining any amount or type of benefits or wages. Your own results and the job stability or financial stability of any company depend on influences outside of our control. All risks are assumed by the reader. Investigate any potential employer or business relationship carefully and carefully verify past and present finances, present business conditions and the level of compensation and benefits currently paid. Each company's details are taken from sources deemed reliable; however, their accuracy is not guaranteed. The editors and publishers assume no liability, beyond the actual payment received from a reader, for any direct, indirect, incidental or consequential, special or exemplary damages, and they do not guarantee, warrant nor make any representation regarding the use of this material. Trademarks or tradenames are used without symbols and only in a descriptive sense, and this use is not authorized by, associated with or sponsored by the trademarks' owners. Ranks and ratings are presented as an introductory and general glance at corporations, based on our research and our knowledge of businesses and the industries in which they operate. The reader should use caution.

PLUNKETT'S HEALTH CARE INDUSTRY ALMANAC 2008

CONTENTS

Continued on next page

Continued from previous page

Continued on next page

Continued from previous page

A Short Health Care Industry Glossary

10-K: An annual report filed by publicly held companies. It provides a comprehensive overview of the company's business and its finances. By law, it must contain specific information and follow a given form, the "Annual Report on Form 10-K." The U.S. Securities and Exchange Commission requires that it be filed within 90 days after fiscal year end. However, these reports are often filed late due to extenuating circumstances. Variations of a 10-K are often filed to indicate amendments and changes. Most publicly held companies also publish an "annual report" that is not on Form 10-K. These annual reports are more informal and are frequently used by a company to enhance its image with customers, investors and industry peers.

3DCRT: Three dimensional conformal radiotherapy (3DCRT) is a method of radiation therapy whereby PET CAT and other imaging technologies are used to more precisely map tumors or tissues to be treated with radiation. The intent is to better focus the radiation and limit damage to surrounding tissues. (Also, see "IGRT".)

510 K: An application filed with the FDA for a new medical device to show that the apparatus is "substantially equivalent" to one that is already marketed.

Accountable Health Plan: A network of health care providers, such as hospitals and primary and specialty care physicians, that provides care and services and competes with other systems in the region for enrollees.

ADME (Absorption, Distribution, Metabolism and Excretion): In clinical trials, the bodily processes studied to determine the extent and duration of systemic exposure to a drug.

AE (Adverse Event): In clinical trials, a condition not observed at baseline or worsened if present at baseline. Sometimes called Treatment Emergent Signs and Symptoms (TESS).

Alternate Site Care: Health care that was previously provided in general hospitals, but is now offered in less costly, alternate sites. Examples of alternate care include home IV therapy, outpatient surgery centers, rehabilitation units within nursing homes and free-standing centers providing dialysis, radiation therapy and imaging.

Amino Acid: Any of a class of 20 molecules that combine to form proteins.

ANDA (Abbreviated New Drug Application): An application filed with the FDA showing that a substance is the same as an existing, previously approved drug (i.e., a generic version).

Angiogenesis: Blood vessel formation, typically in the growth of malignant tissue.

Angioplasty: The re-opening of a blood vessel by non-surgical techniques such as balloon dilation or laser, or through surgery.

Antibody: A protein produced by white blood cells in response to a foreign substance. Each antibody can bind only to one specific antigen. See "Antigen."

Antigen: A foreign substance that causes the immune system to create an antibody. See "Antibody."

Apoptosis: A normal cellular process leading to the termination of a cell's life.

Applied Research: The application of compounds, processes, materials or other items discovered during basic research to practical uses. The goal is to move discoveries along to the final development phase.

Arthroscopy: The examination of the interior of a joint using a type of endoscope that is inserted into the joint through a small incision. See "Endoscope."

Assay: A laboratory test to identify and/or measure the amount of a particular substance in a sample. Types of assays include endpoint assays, in which a single measurement is made at a fixed time; kinetic assays, in which increasing amounts of a product are formed with time and are monitored at multiple points; microbiological assays, which measure the concentration of antimicrobials in biological material; and immunological assays, in which analysis or measurement is based on antigen-antibody reactions.

Baby Boomer: Generally refers to people born in the U.S. and Western Europe from 1946 to 1964. In the U.S., the total number of Baby Boomers is about 78 million--one of the largest and most affluent demographic groups. The term evolved to include the children of soldiers and war industry workers who were involved in World War II. When those veterans and workers returned to civilian life they started or added to families in large numbers. As a result, the baby boom generation is one of the largest demographic segments in the U.S. Some baby boomers have already started reaching early retirement age. By 2011, millions will begin turning traditional retirement age (65), resulting in extremely rapid growth in the senior portion of the population.

Baseline: A set of data used in clinical studies, or other types of research, for control or comparison.

Basic Research: Attempts to discover compounds, materials, processes or other items that may be largely or entirely new and/or unique. Basic research may start with a theoretical concept that has yet to be proven. The goal is to create discoveries that can be moved along to applied research. Basic research is sometimes referred to as "blue sky" research.

Behavioral Health: The assessment and treatment of mental health and/or substance abuse disorders. Substance abuse includes alcohol and other drugs.

Big Pharma: The top tier of pharmaceutical companies in terms of sales and profits (e.g., Pfizer, Merck, Johnson & Johnson).

Bioavailability: In pharmaceuticals, the rate and extent to which a drug is absorbed or is otherwise available to the treatment site in the body.

Bioequivalence: In pharmaceuticals, the demonstration that a drug's rate and extent of absorption are not significantly different from those of an existing drug that is already approved by the FDA. This is the basis upon which generic and brand name drugs are compared.

Biogenerics: Genetic versions of drugs that have been created via biotechnology. Also, see "Follow-on Biologics."

Bioinformatics: Research, development or application of computational tools and approaches for expanding the use of biological, medical, behavioral or health data, including those to acquire, store, organize, archive, analyze or visualize such data. Bioinformatics is often applied to the study of genetic data. It applies principles of information sciences and technologies to make vast, diverse and complex life sciences data more understandable and useful.

Biologic: Drugs that are synthesized from living organisms. Specifically, biologics may be any virus, therapeutic serum, toxin, antitoxin, vaccine, blood, blood component or derivative, allergenic or analogous product, or arsphenamine or one of its derivatives used for the prevention, treatment or cure of disease.

Biopharmaceutical: That portion of the pharmaceutical industry focused on the use of biotechnology to create new drugs. A biopharmaceutical can be any biological compound that is intended to be used as a therapeutic drug, including recombinant proteins, monoclonal and polyclonal antibodies, antisense oligonucleotides, therapeutic genes, and recombinant and DNA vaccines.

Biosimilar: See "Follow-on Biologics."

Biotechnology: A set of powerful tools that employ living organisms (or parts of organisms) to make or modify products, improve plants or animals (including humans) or develop microorganisms for specific uses. Early uses of biotechnology included traditional animal and plant breeding techniques, based on improving genetic lineage in order to create a plant or animal with desirable characteristics. Early uses also included the use of yeast in making bread, beer, wine and cheese. Today, biotechnology is most commonly thought of to include the development of human medical therapies and processes using recombinant DNA, cell fusion, other genetic techniques and bioremediation. Modern biotechnology uses advanced technologies to modify the genes of cells so they will produce new substances or perform new functions. A good example is recombinant DNA technology, in which a copy of DNA containing one or more genes is transferred between organisms or recombined within an organism.

BLA (Biologics License Application): An application to be submitted to the FDA when a firm wants to obtain permission to market a biological product. It is typically submitted after completion of Phase III clinical trials. It was formerly known as Product License Application (PLA).

Boutique Medicine: A medical practice in which patients receive unlimited access to physicians for an annual retainer fee. Services include same-day or next-day appointments, unrestricted examination times and after-hours access to physicians via pagers or cell phone numbers.

Brachytherapy: A method of internal radiation therapy whereby tiny containers of radioactive material, sometimes referred to as "seeds," are implanted directly in contact with tissue that is afflicted with cancerous tumors. It is a common method of treating prostate cancer and is sometimes used for the treatment of breast cancer. These seeds are never removed from the body. They typically have a radioactive half-life of six months. Eventually, they emit virtually no radiation at all.

Branding: A marketing strategy that places a focus on the brand name of a product, service or firm in order to increase the brand's market share, increase sales, establish credibility, improve satisfaction, raise the profile of the firm and increase profits.

B-to-B, or B2B: See "Business-to-Business."

B-to-C, or B2C: See "Business-to-Consumer."

B-to-E, or B2E: See "Business-to-Employee."

B-to-G, or B2G: See "Business-to-Government."

Business Process Outsourcing (BPO): The outsourcing of non-mission-critical business processes that may include call centers, basic accounting or human resources management, depending on the industry involved. Also, see "ITES (IT-Enabled Services)."

Business-to-Business: An organization focused on selling products, services or data to commercial customers rather than individual consumers. Also known as B2B.

Business-to-Consumer: An organization focused on selling products, services or data to individual consumers rather than commercial customers. Also known as B2C.

Business-to-Employee: A corporate communications system, such as an intranet, aimed at conveying information from a company to its employees. Also known as B2E.

Business-to-Government: An organization focused on selling products, services or data to government units rather than commercial businesses or consumers. Also known as B2G.

CANDA (Computer-Assisted New Drug Application): An electronic submission of a new drug application (NDA) to the FDA.

Capitation: A fee method in which care providers offer a standard, or capped, per-member fee for services to participants in a particular HMO.

Captive Offshoring: Used to describe a company-owned offshore operation. For example, Microsoft owns and operates significant captive offshore research and development centers in China and elsewhere that are offshore from Microsoft's U.S. home base. Also see "Offshoring."

Carcinogen: A substance capable of causing cancer. A suspected carcinogen is a substance that may cause cancer in humans or animals but for which the evidence is not conclusive.

Cardiac Catheterization Laboratory: Facilities offering special diagnostic procedures for cardiac patients, including the introduction of a catheter into the interior of the heart by way of a vein or artery or by direct needle puncture. Procedures must be performed in a laboratory or a special procedure room.

Cardiac Intensive Care Services: Services provided in a unit staffed with specially trained nursing personnel and containing monitoring and specialized support or treatment equipment for patients who (because of heart seizure, open-heart surgery or other life-threatening conditions) require intensified, comprehensive observation and care. May include myocardial infarction care, pulmonary care, and heart transplant units.

Catheter: A tubular instrument used to add or withdraw fluids. Heart or cardiac catheterization involves the passage of flexible catheters into the great vessels and chambers of the heart. IV catheters add intravenous fluids to the veins. Foley catheters withdraw fluid from the bladder. Significant recent advances in technology allow administration of powerful drug and diagnostic therapies via catheters.

CBER (Center for Biologics Evaluation and Research): The branch of the FDA responsible for the regulation of biological products, including blood, vaccines, therapeutics and related drugs and devices, to ensure purity, potency, safety, availability and effectiveness. www.fda.gov/cber

CDC (Centers for Disease Control and Prevention): The federal agency charged with protecting the public health of the nation by providing leadership and direction in the prevention and control of diseases and other preventable conditions and responding to public health emergencies. Headquartered in Atlanta, it was established as an operating health agency within the U.S. Public Health Service on July 1, 1973. See www.cdc.gov.

CDER (Center for Drug Evaluation and Research): The branch of the FDA responsible for the regulation of drug products. www.fda.gov/cder

CDRH (Center for Devices and Radiological Health): The branch of the FDA responsible for the regulation of medical devices. www.fda.gov/cdrh

CFR (Code of Federal Regulations): A codification of the general and permanent rules published in the Federal Register by the executive departments and agencies of the Federal Government. The code is divided into 50 titles that represent broad areas subject to federal regulation. Title 21 of the CFR covers FDA regulations.

Chemotherapy: The treatment of cancer using anticancer drugs, often conducted in association with radiation therapy. See "Radiation Therapy."

Chromosome: A structure in the nucleus of a cell that contains genes. Chromosomes are found in pairs.

Class I Device: An FDA classification of medical devices for which general controls are sufficient to ensure safety and efficacy.

Class II Device: An FDA classification of medical devices for which performance standards and special controls are sufficient to ensure safety and efficacy.

Class III Device: An FDA classification of medical devices for which pre-market approval is required to ensure safety and efficacy, unless the device is substantially equivalent to a currently marketed device. See "510 K."

Clinical Trial: See "Phase I Clinical Trials," along with definitions for Phase II, Phase III and Phase IV.

Clone: A group of identical genes, cells or organisms derived from one ancestor. A clone is an identical copy. "Dolly" the sheep is a famous case of a clone of an animal. Also see "Cloning (Reproductive)" and "Cloning (Therapeutic)."

Cloning (Reproductive): A method of reproducing an exact copy of an animal or, potentially, an exact copy of a human being. A scientist removes the nucleus from a donor's unfertilized egg, inserts a nucleus from the animal to be copied and then stimulates the nucleus to begin dividing to form an embryo. In the case of a mammal, such as a human, the embryo would then be implanted in the uterus of a host female. Also see "Cloning (Therapeutic)."

Cloning (Therapeutic): A method of reproducing exact copies of cells needed for research or for the development of replacement tissue or organs. A scientist removes the nucleus from a donor's unfertilized egg, inserts a nucleus from the animal whose cells are to be copied and then stimulates the nucleus to begin dividing to form an embryo. However, the embryo is never allowed to grow to any significant stage of development. Instead, it is allowed to grow for a few hours or days, and stem cells are then removed from it for use in regenerating tissue. Also see "Cloning (Reproductive)."

CMS (Centers for Medicare and Medicaid Services): A federal agency responsible for administering Medicare and monitoring the states' operations of Medicaid. See www.cms.hhs.gov.

COBRA (Consolidated Omnibus Budget Reconciliation Act): A federal law that requires employers to offer uninterrupted health care coverage to certain employees and their beneficiaries whose group coverage has been terminated.

Coinsurance (Co-insurance): Co-insurance is a practice in some medical coverage plans, homeowners insurance, Medicare and other types of insurance coverage whereby the beneficiary is required to pay a set percentage of costs in certain circumstances. For example, the covered party may be required to pay 20% of costs.

Computed Tomography: See "CT (CAT Scan)."

Concierge Care: See "Boutique Medicine."

Continuing Care Retirement Communities (CCRCs): Communities that provide coordinated housing and health-related services to older individuals under an agreement which may last as little as one year or as long as the life of the individual.

Contract Manufacturer: A company that manufactures products that will be sold under the brand names of its client companies. For example, a large number of consumer electronics, such as laptop computers, are manufactured by contract manufacturers for leading brand-name computer companies such as Dell. Many other types of products are made under contract manufacturing, from apparel to pharmaceuticals. Also see "OEM (Original Equipment Manufacturer)" and "ODM (Original Design Manufacturer)."

Coordinator: In clinical trials, the person at an investigative site who handles the administrative responsibilities of the trial, acts as a liaison between the investigative site and the sponsor, and reviews data and records during a monitoring visit.

Copayment (Co-payment): An amount that is commonly required to be paid by the patient under health care plans including Medicare. For example, the patient may be required to pay $20 toward the cost of a doctor's office visit, or $15 toward the cost of a prescription drug.

COSTART: In medical and drug product development, a dictionary of adverse events and body systems used for coding and classifying adverse events.

CPMP (Committee on Proprietary Medicinal Products): A committee, composed of two people from each EU Member State (see "EU (European Union)"), that is responsible for the scientific evaluation and assessment of marketing applications for medicinal products in the EU. The CPMP is the major body involved in the harmonization of pharmaceutical regulations within the EU and receives administrative support from the European Medicines Evaluation Agency. See "EMEA (European Medicines Evaluation Agency)."

CRM (Customer Relationship Management): The automation of integrated business processes involving customers, including sales (contact management, product configuration), marketing (campaign management, telemarketing) and customer service (call center, field service).

CRO (Contract Research Organization): An independent organization that contracts with a client to conduct part of the work on a study or research project. For example, drug and medical device makers frequently outsource clinical trials and other research work to CROs.

CRT: Conformal radiotherapy. See "3DCRT."

Cryoablation: Cryoablation is a technology based on the use of extremely cold temperatures delivered via a catheter or other device to treat tissues. It is an accepted method of treating cancer of the prostate. It also has applications in the prevention of heart arrhythmia.

Cryosurgery: See "Cryoablation."

CT (CAT Scan): Computed tomography (CT). An imaging method that uses x-rays to create cross-sectional pictures of the body. The technique is frequently referred to as a "CAT Scan." A patient lies on a narrow platform while the machine's x-ray beam rotates around him or her. Small detectors inside the scanner measure the amount of x-rays that make it through the part of the body being studied. A computer takes this information and uses it to create several individual images, called slices. These images can be stored, viewed on a monitor, or printed on film. Three-dimensional models of organs can be created by stacking the individual slices together. The newest machines are capable of operating at 64 slice levels, creating very high resolution images in a short period of time. Eventually, 256 slice technology will be introduced.

Current Procedural Terminology (CPT): The most widely accepted medical nomenclature used to report medical procedures and services under public and private health insurance programs. CPT is also used for administrative management purposes, such as claims processing and developing guidelines for medical care review.

CVMP (Committee for Veterinary Medicinal Products): A committee that is a veterinary equivalent of the CPMP (see "CPMP (Committee on Proprietary Medicinal Products)") in the EU. See "EU (European Union)."

DBA: Doing business as.

Deductible (Insurance Deductible): The initial amount of a loss that must be paid by the insurance policy holder. For example, a typical automobile policy deductible is $500, which means that the first $500 of any loss must be paid by the policy holder before the insurance company will pay for a portion above $500.

Defibrillator: In medicine, an instrument used externally (as electrodes on the chest) or implanted (as a small device similar in size to a pacemaker) that delivers an electric shock to return the heart to its normal rhythm.

Demand Chain: A similar concept to a supply chain, but with an emphasis on the end user.

Demographics: The breakdown of the population into statistical categories such as age, income, education and sex.

Development: The phase of research and development (R&D) in which researchers attempt to create new products from the results of discoveries and applications created during basic and applied research.

Device: In medical products, an instrument, apparatus, implement, machine, contrivance, implant, in vitro reagent or other similar or related article, including any component, part or accessory, that 1) is recognized in the official National Formulary or United States Pharmacopoeia or any supplement to them, 2) is intended for use in the diagnosis of disease or other conditions, or in the cure, mitigation, treatment or prevention of disease, in man or animals or 3) is intended to affect the structure of the body of man or animals and does not achieve any of its principal intended purposes through chemical action within or on the body of man or animals and is not dependent upon being metabolized for the achievement of any of its principal intended purposes.

Diagnostic Radioisotope Facility: A medical facility in which radioactive isotopes (radiopharmaceuticals) are used as tracers or indicators to detect an abnormal condition or disease in the body.

Dialysis: An artificial blood-filtering process used to clean the blood of patients with malfunctioning kidneys.

Dietary Supplements Sold as Food: Legal diet aids that do not require licensing under medical regulations. Typically, dietary supplements sold as food are offered in powder, tablet, pill or capsule form.

Disease Management: The use of programs that closely monitor the condition of a patient on a regular basis while educating and motivating that person about lifestyle and treatment alternatives that will reduce the impacts of certain conditions.

Distributor: An individual or business involved in marketing, warehousing and/or shipping of products manufactured by others to a specific group of end users. Distributors do not sell to the general public. In order to develop a competitive advantage, distributors often focus on serving one industry or one set of niche clients. For example, within the medical industry, there are major distributors that focus on providing pharmaceuticals, surgical supplies or dental supplies to clinics and hospitals.

DNA (Deoxyribonucleic Acid): The carrier of the genetic information that cells need to replicate and to produce proteins.

DNA Chip: A revolutionary tool used to identify mutations in genes like BRCA1 and BRCA2. The chip, which consists of a small glass plate encased in plastic, is manufactured using a process similar to the one used to make computer microchips. On the surface, each chip contains synthetic single-stranded DNA sequences identical to a normal gene.

Drug Utilization Review: A quantitative assessment of patient drug use and physicians' patterns of prescribing drugs in an effort to determine the usefulness of drug therapy.

EBRT (External Beam Radiation Therapy): EBRT (External Beam Radiation Therapy) is the application of radiation to a patient via external sources, such as X-ray, gamma ray or proton beam, in order to kill cancerous cells and shrink tumors.

EC (European Community): See "EU (European Union)."

Ecology: The study of relationships among all living organisms and the environment, especially the totality or pattern of interactions; a view that includes all plant and animal species and their unique contributions to a particular habitat.

E-Commerce: The use of online, Internet-based sales methods. The phrase is used to describe both business-to-consumer and business-to-business sales.

EDI (Electronic Data Interchange): An accepted standard format for the exchange of data between various companies' networks. EDI allows for the transfer of e-mail as well as orders, invoices and other files from one company to another.

EEG (Electroencephalography): Measures electrical activity in the brain.

Efficacy: A drug or medical product's ability to effectively produce beneficial results within a patient.

EFGCP (European Forum for Good Clinical Practices): The organization dedicated to finding common ground in Europe on the implementation of Good Clinical Practices. See "GCP (Good Clinical Practices)." www.efgcp.org

EHR (Electronic Health Record): Refers to digital patient records in the health care industry.

ELA (Establishment License Application): Required for the approval of a biologic (see "Biologic"). It permits a specific facility to manufacture a biological product for commercial purposes. Compare to "PLA (Product License Agreement)."

Electroporation: A health care technology that uses short pulses of electric current (DC) to create openings (pores) in the membranes of cancerous cells, thus leading to death of the cells. It has potential as a treatment for prostate cancer. In the laboratory, it is a means of introducing foreign proteins or DNA into living cells.

EMEA (European Medicines Evaluation Agency): The European agency responsible for supervising and coordinating applications for marketing medicinal products in the European Union (see "EU (European Union)" and "CPMP (Committee on Proprietary Medicine)"). The EMEA is headquartered in the U.K. www.eudraportal.eudra.org

Employee Assistance Program (EAP): A program designed to help employees, employers and family members find solutions to workplace and personal problems.

Endoscope: A tiny, flexible tube-shaped instrument with a fiber optic light and a video camera lens at the end. It is inserted into the body through a natural body opening or a small incision, and has both diagnostic and therapeutic capabilities. Laparoscopic surgery is conducted in a minimally invasive manner using the endoscope to enable the surgeon to see the tissue being operated on. Such surgery is often conducted through an incision as small as one or two centimeters in length. Consequently, patients tend to heal very quickly after such surgery.

Enterprise Resource Planning (ERP): An integrated information system that helps manage all aspects of a business, including accounting, ordering and human resources, typically across all locations of a major corporation or organization. ERP is considered to be a critical tool for management of large organizations. Suppliers of ERP tools include SAP and Oracle.

Enzyme: A protein that acts as a catalyst, affecting the chemical reactions in cells.

ESWL (Extracorporeal Shock Wave Lithotripter): A medical device used for treating stones in the kidney or urethra. The device disintegrates kidney stones noninvasively through the transmission of acoustic shock waves directed at the stones.

Etiology: The study of the causes or origins of diseases.

EU (European Union): A consolidation of European countries (member states) functioning as one body to facilitate trade. Previously known as the European Community (EC), the EU expanded to include much of Eastern Europe in 2004, raising the total number of member states to 25. In 2002, the EU launched a unified currency, the Euro. See europa.eu.int.

EU Competence: The jurisdiction in which the EU can take legal action.

Exclusive Provider Organization: Technically the same as an HMO, with the exception that the organization provides coverage only for services from contracted providers. See “Health Maintenance Organization (HMO).”

Extracorporeal Shock Wave Lithotripter (ESWL): A medical device used for treating stones in the kidney or urethra. The device disintegrates kidney stones noninvasively through the transmission of acoustic shock waves directed at the stones.

FD&C Act (Federal Food, Drug and Cosmetic Act): A set of laws passed by the U.S. Congress, which controls, among other things, residues in food and feed.

FDA (Food and Drug Administration): The U.S. government agency responsible for the enforcement of the Federal Food, Drug and Cosmetic Act, ensuring industry compliance with laws regulating products in commerce. The FDA’s mission is to protect the public from harm and encourage technological advances that hold the promise of benefiting society. www.fda.gov

Fee-For-Service Equivalency: The amount of reimbursement from capitation compared to fee-for-service reimbursement.

Fee-For-Service Reimbursement: The old system of payment under which payments to providers do not exceed the billed charge for each unit of service provided.

Fissure: A long narrow crack or opening.

Follow-on Biologics: A term used to describe generic versions of drugs that have been created using biotechnology. Because biotech drugs (“biologics”) are made from living cells, a generic version of a drug probably won't be biochemically identical to the original branded version of the drug. Consequently, they are described as “follow-on” drugs to set them apart. Since these drugs won't be biochemically the same as the original drugs, there are concerns that they may not be as safe or effective unless they go through clinical trials for proof of quality. In Europe, these drugs are referred to as “biosimilars.”

Formulary: A preferred list of drug products that typically limits the number of drugs available within a therapeutic class for purposes of drug purchasing, dispensing and/or reimbursement. A government body, third-party insurer or health plan, or an institution may compile a formulary. Some institutions or health plans develop closed (i.e. restricted) formularies where only those drug products listed can be dispensed in that institution or reimbursed by the health plan. Other formularies may have no restrictions (open formulary) or may have certain restrictions such as higher patient cost-sharing requirements for off-formulary drugs.

Functional Imaging: The uses of PET scan, MRI and other advanced imaging technology to see how an area of the body is functioning and responding. For example, brain activity can be viewed, and the reaction of cancer tumors to therapies can be judged using functional imaging.

Gamma Knife: A unique type of radiation therapy with tissue-sparing properties. It involves focusing low-dose gamma radiation on a tumor, while exposing only a small amount of healthy, nearby tissue to radiation. It is often used to treat certain brain cancers.

GCP (Good Clinical Practices): FDA regulations and guidelines that define the responsibilities of the key figures involved in a clinical trial, including the sponsor, the investigator, the monitor and the Institutional Review Board. See “IRB (Institutional Review Board).”

GDP (Gross Domestic Product): The total value of a nation's output, income and expenditures produced with a nation's physical borders.

Gene: A working subunit of DNA; the carrier of inheritable traits.

Gene Chip: See “DNA Chip.”

Gene Therapy: Treatment based on the alteration or replacement of existing genes. Genetic therapy involves splicing desired genes insolated from one patient into a second patient’s cells in order to compensate for that patient’s inherited genetic defect, or to enable that patient’s body to better fight a specific disease.

Genetic Code: The sequence of nucleotides, determining the sequence of amino acids in protein synthesis.

Genetically Modified (GM) Foods: Food crops that are bioengineered to resist herbicides, diseases or insects; have higher nutritional value than non-engineered plants; produce a higher yield per acre; and/or last longer on the shelf. Additional traits may include resistance to temperature and moisture extremes. Agricultural animals also may be genetically modified organisms.

Genetics: The study of the process of heredity.

Genome: The genetic material (composed of DNA) in the chromosomes of a living organism.

Genomics: The study of genes, their role in diseases and our ability to manipulate them.

Globalization: The increased mobility of goods, services, labor, technology and capital throughout the world.

Although globalization is not a new development, its pace has increased with the advent of new technologies, especially in the areas of telecommunications, finance and shipping.

GLP (Good Laboratory Practices): A collection of regulations and guidelines to be used in laboratories where research is conducted on drugs, biologics or devices that are intended for submission to the FDA.

GMP (Good Manufacturing Practices): A collection of regulations and guidelines to be used in manufacturing drugs, biologics and medical devices.

GNP (Gross National Product): A country's total output of goods and services from all forms of economic activity measured at market prices for one calendar year. It differs from GDP (Gross Domestic Product) in that GNP includes income from investments made in foreign nations.

Group Practice Without Walls: A "quasi" group formed when a hospital sponsors or provides capital to physicians for the establishment of a practice to share administrative expenses while remaining independent practitioners.

Health Indemnity Insurance: Provides traditional insurance coverage, after a deductible, for specified health care needs. Typically, the patient can go to any physician or any hospital, and there is no aspect of managed care involved.

Health Maintenance Organization (HMO): An insurance entity that provides managed health care services. An HMO functions as a form of health care insurance which is sold on a group basis. The HMO contracts with doctors, hospitals, labs and other medical facilities for low rates in exchange for high volume. For the patient, only visits to professionals within the HMO network are covered in the highest possible amount by the HMO. The patient selects a primary care physician who is approved by the HMO. For care, the patient first visits the primary care physician who may refer the patient to a specialist on an as-needed basis. Also see "Managed Care" and "Preferred Provider Organization (PPO)."

Health Reimbursement Account (HRA): A form of health care coverage plan provided to employees by their employer. Under an HRA, the employer places a given amount of money into a special account each year for the employee to spend on health care. The employer also provides a high-deductible health coverage plan. The employee elects when and how to spend the money in the account on health care. Because of the high deductible, the employee's share of the monthly premium tends to be much lower than under an HMO or PPO, but the employee faces the burden of paying the high deductible when necessary. Unspent funds in the account can roll over from year to year so that the account grows, but the employee loses the fund balance when leaving the employer.

Health Savings Account (HSA): A plan that combines a tax-free savings and investment account (somewhat similar to a 401k) with a high-deductible health coverage plan. The intent is to give the consumer more incentive to control health care costs by reducing unnecessary care while shopping for the best prices. The consumer contributes pre-tax dollars annually to a savings account (up to $2,850 for an individual or $5,650 for a family, as of 2007). The employer may or may not match part of that contribution. The account may be invested in stocks, bonds or mutual funds. It grows tax-free, but the money may be spent only on health care. Unspent money stays in the account at the end of each year. The consumer must purchase an insurance policy or health care plan with an annual deductible of at least $1,000 for individuals or $2,000 for families.

HESC (Human Embryonic Stem Cell): See "Stem Cells."

HHS (U.S. Department of Health and Human Services): This agency has more than 300 major programs related to human health and welfare, the largest of which is Medicare. See www.hhs.gov

HIFU (High Intensity Focused Ultrasound): A method of using sound waves to produce a focused amount of high heat in tumors or tissues in order to destroy them through thermoablation. Target temperature is about 70 to 90 degrees Centigrade (158 to 194 degrees Fahrenheit). This is a noninvasive treatment that is already in wide use in Europe, Asia and Canada for treatment of particular conditions, particularly cancer of the prostate. Late stage clinical trials were being conducted in the U.S. as of 2007. Several additional uses are being studied, including treatment of cancer of the kidney.

HIPAA: The Health Insurance Portability and Accountability Act of 1996, which demands that all billing and patient data must be exchanged electronically between care givers and insurance payors. A major focus of HIPAA requirements is the protection of patient data privacy.

Home Care Agencies: Home health agencies, home care aid organizations and hospices.

Human Resources Outsourcing (HRO): Refers to the practice of hiring an outsourced services provider to manage an organization's day-to-day human resources needs.

ICD9: International Classification of Diseases - Version 9. A government coding system used for classifying diseases and diagnoses.

IDE (Investigational New Device Exemption): A document that must be filed with the FDA prior to initiating clinical trials of medical devices considered to pose a significant risk to human subjects.

IEEE: The Institute of Electrical and Electronic Engineers. The IEEE sets global technical standards and acts as an authority in technical areas including computer engineering, biomedical technology, telecommunications, electric power, aerospace and consumer electronics, among others. www.ieee.org.

IGRT (Image Guided Radiation Therapy): A radiation technique that takes advantage of sophisticated imaging technologies in order to best target radiation therapy. Prostate cancer is often treated with IGRT. To treat that disease, tiny metal markers are implanted in the prostate using an outpatient procedure. The IGRT equipment is then able to locate the position of the prostate exactly by determining the location of the markers in real time. Varian is a leading manufacturer of IGRT equipment. The technology is similar to IMRT, but better enables radiation technicians to use ultrasound, CT or X-ray images to line up the radiation beam with the intended target. Also, see "IMRT (Intensity Modulated Radiation Therapy)."

Imaging: In medicine, the viewing of the body's organs through external, high-tech means. This reduces the need for broad exploratory surgery. These advances, along with new types of surgical instruments, have made minimally invasive surgery possible. Imaging includes MRI (magnetic resonance imaging), CT (computed tomography or CAT scan), MEG (magnetoencephalography), improved x-ray technology, mammography, ultrasound and angiography.

Imaging Contrast Agent: A molecule or molecular complex that increases the intensity of the signal detected by an imaging technique, including MRI and ultrasound. An MRI contrast agent, for example, might contain gadolinium attached to a targeting antibody. The antibody would bind to a specific target, a metastatic melanoma cell for example, while the gadolinium would increase the magnetic signal detected by the MRI scanner.

Immunoassay: An immunological assay. Types include agglutination, complement-fixation, precipitation, immunodiffusion and electrophoretic assays. Each type of assay utilizes either a particular type of antibody or a specific support medium (such as a gel) to determine the amount of antigen present.

IMRT (Intensity Modulated Radiation Therapy): A radiation technology that enables the technician to apply narrowly focused radiation directly toward cancerous tumors. IMRT helps to limit the amount of damage to surrounding tissues. The process includes using multiple beams (typically from seven to 12) aimed at the tumor from various directions. The beams meet at the tumor to administer the desired dosage. Breaking the dose down into multiple beams lessens the level of radiation that healthy tissues are exposed to. The point at which the beams join can be shaped to conform to the exact size, shape and location of the tumor, thus further sparing healthy tissue. Advanced imaging, such as CT, is used to provide precise guidance to the tumor's location. Also see "IGRT (Image Guided Radiation Therapy)."

In Vitro: Laboratory experiments conducted in the test tube, or otherwise, without using live animals and/or humans.

In Vivo: Laboratory experiments conducted with live animals and/or humans.

IND (Investigational New Drug Application): A document that must be filed with the FDA prior to initiating clinical trials of drugs or biologics.

Independent Practice Association (IPA): A legal entity that holds managed care contracts. The IPA then contracts with physicians, usually in solo practice, to provide care either on a fee-for-services or capitated basis. The purpose of an IPA is to assist solo physicians in obtaining managed care contracts.

Indication: Refers to a specific disease, illness or condition for which a drug is approved as a treatment. Typically, a new drug is first approved for one indication. Then, an application to the FDA is later made for approval of additional indications.

Informed Consent: Must be obtained in writing from people who agree to be clinical trial subjects prior to their enrollment in the study. The document must explain the risks associated with the study and treatment and describe alternative therapy available to the patient. A copy of the document must also be provided to the patient.

Infusion Therapy: The introduction of fluid other than blood into a vein. See "Intravenous Therapy."

Initial Public Offering (IPO): A company's first effort to sell its stock to investors (the public). Investors in an up-trending market eagerly seek stocks offered in many IPOs because the stocks of newly public companies that seem to have great promise may appreciate very rapidly in price, reaping great profits for those who were able to get the stock at the first offering. In the United States, IPOs are regulated by the SEC (U.S. Securities Exchange Commission) and by the state-level regulatory agencies of the states in which the IPO shares are offered.

Intravenous Therapy: The introduction of fluid other than blood into a vein. See "Infusion Therapy."

Investigator: In clinical trials, a clinician who agrees to supervise the use of an investigational drug, device or biologic in humans. Responsibilities of the investigator, as defined in FDA regulations, include administering the drug, observing and testing the patient, collecting data and monitoring the care and welfare of the patient.

Iontophoresis: The transfer of ions of medicine through the skin using a local electric current.

IRB (Institutional Review Board): A group of individuals usually found in medical institutions that is responsible for reviewing protocols for ethical consideration (to ensure the rights of the patients). An IRB also evaluates the benefit-to-risk ratio of a new drug to see that the risk is acceptable for patient exposure. Responsibilities of an IRB are defined in FDA regulations.

IRE: Irreversible Electroporation. See "Electroporation."

ISO 9000, 9001, 9002, 9003: Standards set by the International Organization for Standardization. ISO 9000, 9001, 9002 and 9003 are the highest quality certifications awarded to organizations that meet exacting standards in their operating practices and procedures.

ITES (IT-Enabled Services): The portion of the Information Technology industry focused on providing business services, such as call centers, insurance claims processing and medical records transcription, by utilizing the power of IT, especially the Internet. Most ITES functions are considered to be back-office procedures. Also, see "Business Process Outsourcing (BPO)."

Just-in-Time (JIT) Delivery: Refers to a supply chain practice whereby manufacturers receive components on or just before the time that they are needed on the assembly line, rather than bearing the cost of maintaining several days' or weeks' supply in a warehouse. This adds greatly to the cost-effectiveness of a manufacturing plant and puts the burden of warehousing and timely delivery on the supplier of the components.

Laparoscope: See "Endoscope."

Laparoscopic Surgery: See "Endoscope."

Licensed Practical Nurse (LPN): A nurse who has completed a practical nursing program and is licensed to provide basic patient care under the supervision of a registered nurse or physician. Also known as a Licensed Vocational Nurse (LVN).

Ligand: Any atom or molecule attached to a central atom in a complex compound.

Lithotripsy: See "Extracorporeal Shock Wave Lithotripter."

LOHAS: Lifestyles of Health and Sustainability. A marketing term that refers to consumers who choose to purchase and/or live with items that are natural, organic, less polluting, etc. Such consumers may also prefer products powered by alternative energy, such as hybrid cars.

Low-Calorie: Refers to foods with 40 or fewer calories per serving.

Low-Cholesterol: Refers to foods with 20 or fewer milligrams of cholesterol and two or fewer grams of saturated fat per serving.

Low-Fat: Refers to foods with three or fewer grams of fat per serving.

Low-Sodium: Refers to foods with 140 or fewer milligrams of sodium per serving.

Magnetic Resonance Imaging (MRI): The use of a uniform magnetic field and radio frequencies to study tissues and structures of the body. This procedure enables the visualization of biochemical activity of the cell in vivo without the use of ionizing radiation, radioisotopic substances or high-frequency sound.

Managed Care: A system of prepaid medical plans providing comprehensive coverage to voluntarily enrolled members. Managed health care typically covers professional fees, hospital services, diagnostic services, emergency services, limited mental services, medical treatment for drug or alcohol abuse, home health services and preventive health care. The most common systems in managed care are HMOs (Health Maintenance Organizations) and PPOs (Preferred Provider Organizations), but there are other variations on these models. The word "managed" is used to describe this type of coverage because the total cost and extent of a patient's care is carefully managed and controlled by the group's administrators. Part of this management includes limiting the patient's choice to physicians, hospitals and labs that have agreed to provide reduced fees in exchange for high volume. Patients who receive care outside of this network will receive lesser reimbursement from the managed care provider. Also see "Health Maintenance Organization (HMO)," "Preferred Provider Organization (PPO)" and "Utilization Management."

Management Services Organization (MSO): A corporation, owned by a hospital or a physician/hospital joint venture, that provides management services to one or more medical group practices. The MSO purchases the tangible assets of the practices and leases them back as part of a full-service management agreement, under which the MSO employs all non-physician staff and provides all supplies and administrative systems for a fee.

Manufacturing Resource Planning (MRP II): A methodology that supports effective planning with regard to all resources of a manufacturing company, linking MRP with sales and operations planning, production planning and master production scheduling.

Market Segmentation: The division of a consumer market into specific groups of buyers based on demographic factors.

Marketing: Includes all planning and management activities and expenses associated with the promotion of a product or service. Marketing can encompass advertising, customer surveys, public relations and many other disciplines. Marketing is distinct from selling, which is the process of sell-through to the end user.

Medicaid: A federally supported and state-administered assistance program providing medical care for certain low-income individuals and other citizens. Medicaid was initially envisioned as a safety net for the poor. Today, in addition to meeting many of the health needs of low income households, the majority of Medicaid funds go to seniors and the seriously disabled to pay for nursing home care.

Medical Device: See "Device."

Medical Savings Account (MSA): See "Health Savings Account."

Medical Tourism: The practice of patients in countries such as the U.S., Canada and the U.K. seeking inexpensive medical care in foreign countries.

Medicare: A U.S. government program that pays hospitals, physicians and other medical providers for serving patients aged 65 years and older, certain disabled people and most people with end-stage renal disease (ESRD). Medicare consists of two basic programs: Part A covers hospice care, home health care, skilled nursing care and inpatient hospital stays. Part B covers doctors' fees, outpatient care, X-rays, medical equipment and other fees not covered by Part A. Medicare Part C is designed to expand the types of private plans that beneficiaries may choose from, such as PPOs, and allows for the use of medical savings accounts. Prescription coverage was recently added as Medicare Part D.

MEG (Magnetoencephalography): A newer technology derived from both MRI and electroencephalography (EEG). Like EEG, MEG registers brain patterns, but whereas EEG measures electrical activity in the brain, MEG measures magnetic waves, primarily in the cerebral cortex of the brain.

Minimally Invasive Surgery: The use of very small incisions and advanced instruments that may be viewed through microscopes or video. Includes laparoscopy, endoscopy, electrosurgery and cryosurgery. This practice promotes rapid healing.

Minimally-Invasive Surgery: See "Endoscope."

Molecular Imaging: An emerging field in which advanced biology on the molecular level is combined with noninvasive imaging to determine the presence of certain proteins and other important genetic material.

Monoclonal Antibodies (mAb, Human Monoclonal Antibody): Antibodies that have been cloned from a single antibody and massed produced as a therapy or diagnostic test. An example is an antibody specific to a certain protein found in cancer cells.

Nanotechnology: The science of designing, building or utilizing unique structures that are smaller than 100 nanometers (a nanometer is one billionth of a meter). This involves microscopic structures that are no larger than the width of some cell membranes.

National Drug Code (NDC): An identifying drug number maintained by the FDA.

NDA (New Drug Application): An application requesting FDA approval, after completion of Phase III studies, to market a new drug for human use in interstate commerce. Clinical trial results generally account for approximately 80% of the NDA.

Neonatal Intensive Care Services (NICU): A unit that must be separate from the newborn nursery. It provides intensive care to all sick infants, including those with very low birth weights (less than 1500 grams). The NICU can provide mechanical ventilation, neonatal surgery and special care for the sickest infants.

NIH (National Institutes of Health): A branch of the U.S. Public Health Service that conducts biomedical research. www.nih.gov

Nonclinical Studies: In vitro (laboratory) or in vivo (animal) pharmacology, toxicology and pharmacokinetic studies that support the testing of a product in humans. Usually at least two species are evaluated prior to Phase I clinical trials. Nonclinical studies continue throughout all phases of research to evaluate long-term safety issues.

Nurse Practitioner: A registered nurse (RN) who has completed advanced training and licensing. Nurse practitioners may work independent of a physician, or sometimes with a physician's light supervision. They provide direct examination, diagnosis and treatment of patients, and in many states they may write prescriptions and operate clinics.

Nutraceutical: Nutrient + pharmaceutical – a food or part of a food that has been isolated and sold in a medicinal form and claims to offer benefits such as the treatment or prevention of disease.

ODM (Original Design Manufacturer): A contract manufacturer that offers complete, end-to-end design, engineering and manufacturing services. ODMs design and build products, such as consumer electronics, that client companies can then brand and sell as their own. For example, a large percentage of laptop computers, cell phones and PDAs are made by ODMs. Also see "OEM (Original Equipment Manufacturer)" and "Contract Manufacturer."

OEM (Original Equipment Manufacturer): A company that manufactures a product or component for sale to a customer that will integrate the component into a final product or assembly. The OEM's customer will distribute the end product or resell it to an end user. For example, a personal computer made under a brand name by a given company may contain various components, such as hard drives, graphics cards or speakers, manufactured by several different OEM "vendors," but the firm doing the final assembly/manufacturing process is the final manufacturer. Also see "ODM (Original Design Manufacturer)" and "Contract Manufacturer."

Offshoring: The rapidly growing tendency among U.S., Japanese and Western European firms to send knowledge-based and manufacturing work overseas. The intent is to take advantage of lower wages and operating costs in such nations as China, India, Hungary and Russia. The choice of a nation for offshore work may be influenced by such factors as language and education of the local workforce, transportation systems or natural resources. For example, China and India are graduating high numbers of skilled engineers and scientists from their universities. Also, some nations are noted for large numbers of workers skilled in the English language, such as the Philippines and India. Also see "Captive Offshoring" and "Outsourcing."

Oncogene: A unit of DNA that normally directs cell growth, but which can also promote or allow the uncontrolled growth of cancer.

Oncology: The diagnosis, study and treatment of cancer.

Open Access: Typically found in an IPA HMO, this arrangement allows members to consult specialists without obtaining a referral from another doctor.

Original Design Manufacturer: See "ODM (Original Design Manufacturer)."

Original Equipment Manufacturer: See "OEM (Original Equipment Manufacturer)."

Orphan Drug: A drug, biologic or antibiotic designated by the FDA as providing therapeutic benefit for an indication (disease or condition) affecting less than 200,000 people in the U.S. Companies that market orphan drugs are granted a period of market exclusivity in return for the limited commercial potential of the drug.

Orthodontics: A specialized branch of dentistry that restores the teeth to proper alignment and function. There are several different types of appliances used in orthodontics, braces being one of the most common.

OTC (Over-the-Counter Drugs): FDA-regulated products that do not require a physician's prescription. Some examples are aspirin, sunscreen, nasal spray and sunglasses.

Outsourcing: The hiring of an outside company to perform a task otherwise performed internally by the company, generally with the goal of lowering costs and/or streamlining work flow. Outsourcing contracts are generally several years in length. Companies that hire outsourced services providers often prefer to focus on their core strengths while sending more routine tasks outside for others to perform. Typical outsourced services include the running of human resources departments, telephone call centers and computer departments. When outsourcing is performed overseas, it may be referred to as offshoring. Also see "Offshoring."

Paramedical: A person trained to assist medical professionals and supplement physicians and nurses in their activities in order to give emergency medical treatment.

Patent: A property right granted by the U.S. government to an inventor to exclude others from making, using, offering for sale, or selling the invention throughout the U.S. or importing the invention into the U.S. for a limited time in exchange for public disclosure of the invention when the patent is granted.

Pathogen: Any microorganism (e.g., fungus, virus, bacteria or parasite) that causes a disease.

Peer Review: The process used by the scientific community, whereby review of a paper, project or report is obtained through comments of independent colleagues in the same field.

PET (Imaging): See "Positron Emission Tomography (PET)."

Pharmacodynamics (PD): The study of reactions between drugs and living systems. It can be thought of as the study of what a drug does to the body.

Pharmacoeconomics: The study of the costs and benefits associated with various drug treatments.

Pharmacogenetics: The investigation of the different reactions of human beings to drugs and the underlying genetic predispositions. The differences in reaction are mainly caused by mutations in certain enzymes responsible for drug metabolization. As a result, the degradation of the active substance can lead to harmful by-products, or the drug might have no effect at all.

Pharmacokinetics (PK): The study of the processes of bodily absorption, distribution, metabolism and excretion of compounds and medicines. It can be thought of as the study of what the body does to a drug. See "ADME (Absorption, Distribution, Metabolism and Excretion)."

Pharmacology: The science of drugs, their characteristics and their interactions with living organisms.

Pharmacy Benefit Manager (PBM): An organization that provides administrative services in processing and analyzing prescription claims for pharmacy benefit and coverage programs. Many PBMs also operate mail order pharmacies or have arrangements to include prescription availability through mail order pharmacies.

Phase I Clinical Trials: Studies in this phase include initial introduction of an investigational drug into humans. These studies are closely monitored and are usually conducted in healthy volunteers. Phase I trials are conducted after the completion of extensive nonclinical or pre-clinical trials not involving humans. Phase I studies include the determination of clinical pharmacology, bioavailability, drug interactions and side effects associated with increasing doses of the drug.

Phase II Clinical Trials: Include randomized, masked, controlled clinical studies conducted to evaluate the effectiveness of a drug for a particular indication(s). During Phase II trials, the minimum effective dose and dosing intervals should be determined.

Phase III Clinical Trials: Consist of controlled and uncontrolled trials that are performed after preliminary evidence of effectiveness of a drug has been established. They are conducted to document the safety and efficacy of the drug, as well as to determine adequate directions (labeling) for use by the physician. A specific patient population needs to be clearly identified from the results of these studies. Trials during Phase III are conducted using a large number of patients to determine the frequency of adverse events and to obtain data regarding intolerance.

Phase IV Clinical Trials: Conducted after approval of a drug has been obtained to gather data supporting new or revised labeling, marketing or advertising claims.

PHS (Public Health Service): May stand for the Public Health Service Act, a law passed by the U.S. Congress in 1944. PHS also may stand for the Public Health Service itself, a U.S. government agency established by an act of Congress in July 1798, originally authorizing hospitals for the care of American merchant seamen. Today, the Public Health Service sets national health policy; conducts medical and biomedical research; sponsors programs for disease control and mental health; and enforces laws to assure the safety and efficacy of drugs, foods, cosmetics and medical devices. The FDA (Food and Drug Administration) is part of the Public Health Service, as are the Centers for Disease Control and Prevention (CDC).

Physician-Hospital Organization (PHO), Closed: A PHO that restricts physician membership to those practitioners who meet criteria for cost effectiveness and/or high quality.

Physician-Hospital Organization (PHO), Open: A joint venture between the hospital and all members of the medical staff who wish to participate. The PHO can act as a unified agent in managed care contracting, own a managed care plan, own and operate ambulatory care centers or ancillary services projects, or provide administrative services to physician members.

Pivotal Studies: In clinical trials, a Phase III trial that is designed specifically to support approval of a product. These studies are well-controlled (usually by placebo) and are generally designed with input from the FDA so that they will provide data that is adequate to support approval of the product. Two pivotal studies are required for drug product approval, but usually only one study is required for biologics.

PLA (Product License Agreement): See "BLA (Biologics License Application)."

PMA (Pre-Market Approval): Required for the approval of a new medical device or a device that is to be used for life-sustaining or life-supporting purposes, is implanted in the human body or presents potential risk of illness or injury.

Point-of-Service Plan (POS): A managed care plan in which member patients may go outside of the network to be attended by their preferred physicians, but pay a higher deductible if they so choose. Routine care is provided by a primary care physician who also provides referrals to in-network specialists.

Positron Emission Tomography (PET): Positron Emission Tomography (often referred to as a PET scan) is a nuclear medicine imaging technology that uses computers and radioactive (positron emitting) isotopes, which are created in a cyclotron or generator, to produce composite pictures of the brain and heart at work. PET scanning produces sectional images depicting metabolic activity or blood flow rather than anatomy.

Post-Marketing Surveillance: The FDA's ongoing safety monitoring of marketed drugs.

Preclinical Studies: See "Nonclinical Studies."

Preferred Provider Organization (PPO): Insurance entities that provide "managed health care" services. A PPO is a modified version of the HMO model. Generally, patients who are members of PPOs have more flexibility in the personal choice of physicians than do members of HMOs. Patients pay higher premiums than HMOs because of this flexibility. Patients are encouraged to visit physicians who are part of the PPO's system, but may also receive very good reimbursement for visiting physicians who are "out-of-network." Also see "Health Maintenance Organization (HMO)" and "Managed Care."

Premium (Insurance Premium): An insurance premium is the monthly or yearly fee charged for coverage by the insurance underwriter.

Primary Care Network: A group of primary care physicians who pool their resources to share the financial risk of providing care to their patients who are covered by a particular health plan.

Private Fee For Service (PFFS): Insurance provided under Medicare, in which private companies offer Centers for Medicare and Medicaid Services approved plans that allow patients to choose their own doctors and hospitals. PFFS plans provide beneficiaries with all of their Medicare benefits plus any additional benefits the company chooses to provide. Services generally require a co-payment plus, in certain cases, up to 35% of a Medicare-approved amount.

Proton Beam Radiation Therapy (PBRT): The use of a highly advanced technology to deliver external beam radiation therapy (EBRT) to a patient in order to kill cancerous cells and shrink tumors. While traditional radiation therapies rely on photons delivered by X-rays or gamma rays, Proton Beam Radiation Therapy relies on a particle accelerator to create and deliver protons. Protons are high-energy particles that carry a charge. By varying the velocity of the particles at the time that they enter the body, physicists are able to control the exact spot within the body where the radiation is released. The higher the velocity, the deeper within the body the radiation begins to take effect. With traditional radiation (based on photons rather than protons), there is a significant entry dose of radiation that can be harmful to healthy tissues. Proton beam therapy has the ability to better focus the radiation on the exact place of the tumor, significantly cutting down on side effects and damage to surrounding tissues. There are only a handful of proton beam centers in the world. In the U.S., centers are in place or underway at locations including Loma Linda (California) University Medical Center, which is considered to be the pioneer in applying this technology, Boston, Jacksonville Florida, Indiana University and the M.D. Anderson Cancer Center in Houston. The Houston facility was opened in 2006 at a cost of $125 million. PBRT is in wide use in Japan, and centers also are in use in nations such as Germany and Korea.

Psychiatry: A branch of medicine concerned with the study, treatment and prevention of mental, emotional and behavioral disorders. Psychiatrists are doctors and can treat patients using drugs and other physical methods.

Psychology: The scientific study of human behavior and mental processes. Psychologists treat patients using therapeutic methods, including counseling or group work.

QOL (Quality of Life): In medicine, an endpoint of therapeutic assessment used to adjust measures of effectiveness for clinical decision-making. Typically, QOL endpoints measure the improvement of a patient's day-to-day living as a result of specific therapy.

R&D: Research and development. Also see "Applied Research" and "Basic Research."

Radiation Therapy: Radiation therapy is frequently used to destroy cancerous cells. This branch of medicine is concerned with radioactive substances and the usage of various techniques of imaging, for the diagnosis and treatment of disease. Services can include megavoltage radiation therapy, radioactive implants, stereotactic radiosurgery, therapeutic radioisotope services, or the use of x-rays, gamma rays and other radiation sources.

Radio Frequency Ablation (RFA): The use of focused radiowaves to produce high levels of heat within tumors in order to kill cancer. It is typically applied via needles that have been placed in the tumor, using ultrasound or other imaging techniques to insure correct placement. It is often used in the treatment of cancer of the kidney.

Radioisotope: An object that has varying properties that allows it to penetrate other objects at different rates. For example, a sheet of paper can stop an alpha particle, a beta particle can penetrate tissues in the body and a gamma ray can penetrate concrete. The varying penetration capabilities allow radioisotopes to be used in different ways. (Also called radioactive isotope or radionuclide.)

Radiotherapy: The use of doses of high-energy radiation to kill cancer cells and shrink tumors. Radiation may be applied externally, through external beam radiation therapy, or internally through small radioactive implants. Sources of radiation may include X-ray, gamma ray or proton beams.

Radiowave Therapy: See "Radio Frequency Ablation (RFA)."

Registered Nurse (RN): A graduate of an accredited school of nursing who has been registered and licensed to practice by a state authority. A registered nurse (RN) typically has received more formal education than an LPN (licensed practical nurse) or LVN (licensed vocational nurse). An RN often has received a 4-year college degree leading to the bachelors in science-nursing (BSN).

Return on Investment (ROI): A measure of a company's profitability, expressed in percentage as net profit (after taxes) divided by total dollar investment.

RFID (Radio Frequency Identification): A technology that applies a special microchip-enabled tag to an individual item or piece of merchandise or inventory. RFID technology enables wireless, computerized tracking of that inventory item as it moves through the supply chain from factory to transport to warehouse to retail store or end user. Also known as radio tags.

RNA (Ribonucleic Acid): A macromolecule found in the nucleus and cytoplasm of cells; vital in protein synthesis.

Single Nucleotide Polymorphisms (SNPs): Stable mutations consisting of a change at a single base in a DNA molecule. SNPs can be detected by HTP analyses, such as gene chips, and they are then mapped by DNA sequencing. They are the most common type of genetic variation.

SMDA (Safe Medical Devices Act): An act that amends the Food, Drug and Cosmetic Act to impose additional regulations on medical devices. The act became law in 1990.

SNP: See "Single-Nucleotide Polymorphisms (SNPs)."

SPECT: Single Photon Emission Computerized Tomography. A nuclear medicine imaging technology that combines existing technology of gamma camera imaging with computed tomographic (CT) imaging technology to provide a more precise and clear image.

Sponsor: The individual or company that assumes responsibility for the investigation of a new drug, including compliance with the FD&C Act and regulations. The sponsor may be an individual, partnership, corporation or governmental agency and may be a manufacturer, scientific institution or investigator regularly and lawfully engaged in the investigation of new drugs. The sponsor assumes most of the legal and financial responsibility of the clinical trial.

Stem Cells: Cells found in human bone marrow, the blood stream and the umbilical cord that can be replicated indefinitely and can turn into any type of mature blood cell, including platelets, white blood cells or red bl cells. Also referred to as pluripotent cells.

Stereotactic Body Radiation Therapy (SBRT): S "Stereotactic Radiotherapy."

Stereotactic Radiotherapy: The use of precise three dimensional positioning while delivering a high dose of radiation to a tumor. It is often used to treat brain tumors. The procedure involves the bolting of a metallic frame, like a halo, to the patient's head to prevent any movement and to enhance delivery of radiation.

Study Coordinator: See "Coordinator."

Subsidiary, Wholly-Owned: A company that is wholly controlled by another company through stock ownership.

Summary Plan Description: A description of an employee's entire benefit package as required by self-funded plans.

Supply Chain: The complete set of suppliers of goods and services required for a company to operate its business. For example, a manufacturer's supply chain may include providers of raw materials, components, custom-made parts and packaging materials.

Taste Masking: The creation of a barrier between a drug molecule and taste receptors so the drug is easier to take. It masks bitter or unpleasant tastes.

TESS: See "AE (Adverse Event)."

Third-Party Administrator: An independent person or organization that administers the group plan's benefits and claims and administration for self-insured companies.

Tomotherapy: A relatively new method of radiation treatment that combines the use of very sophisticated computer-controlled radiation beam collimation with an on-board computed tomography (CT) scanner to image the treatment site. The intent is to create an enhanced level of accuracy in beam delivery.

Trial Coordinator: See "Coordinator."

Ultrasound: The use of acoustic waves above the range of 20,000 cycles per second to visualize internal body structures. Frequently used to observe a fetus.

Utility Patent: A utility patent may be granted by the U.S. Patent and Trademark Office to anyone who invents or discovers any new, useful, and non-obvious process, machine, article of manufacture, or composition of matter, or any new and useful improvement thereof.

Utilization Management: A system in which utilization case managers (frequently registered nurses with several years of hospital experience) are assigned to each patient who receives hospitalization or extended treatment. These case managers constantly review the amount of care being provided to the patient in question, frequently resulting in significant cost savings. Also see "Managed Care."

Validation of Data: The procedure carried out to ensure that the data contained in a final clinical trial report match the original observations.

Vegan: A person whose diet includes only plant products and excludes all forms of animal products, including meat, fish, poultry, eggs, dairy, gelatin and honey.

Vegetarian: A person whose diet includes only plant products and animal byproducts, such as eggs and dairy, but excludes meat.

Vendor: Any firm, such as a manufacturer or distributor, from which a retailer obtains merchandise.

Videolaseroscopy: A procedure using an endoscope equipped with a laser that is being used in minimally-invasive surgery to excise and or cauterize damaged tissue in the abdomen and lungs.

WHO (World Health Organization): A United Nations agency that assists governments in strengthening health services, furnishing technical assistance and aid in emergencies, working on the prevention and control of epidemics and promoting cooperation among different countries to improve nutrition, housing, sanitation, recreation and other aspects of environmental hygiene. Any country that is a member of the United Nations may become a member of the WHO by accepting its constitution. The WHO currently has 191 member states.

Xenotransplantation: The science of transplanting organs such as kidneys, hearts or livers into humans from other mammals, such as pigs or other agricultural animals grown with specific traits for this purpose.

Zoonosis: An animal disease that can be transferred to man.

Zootechnical Feed Additives: Medicines, such as growth promoters and antibiotics, which are incorporated as additives into feed.

INTRODUCTION

PLUNKETT'S HEALTH CARE INDUSTRY ALMANAC, the tenth edition of our guide to the health care field, is designed to be used as a general source for researchers of all types.

The data and areas of interest covered are intentionally broad, ranging from the costs and effectiveness of the American health care system, to emerging technology, to an in-depth look at the 500 major firms (which we call THE HEALTH CARE 500) within the many industry sectors that make up the health care system.

This reference book is designed to be a general source for researchers. It is especially intended to assist with market research, strategic planning, employment searches, contact or prospect list creation (be sure to see the export capabilities of the accompanying CD-ROM that is available to book and eBook buyers) and financial research, and as a data resource for executives and students of all types.

PLUNKETT'S HEALTH CARE INDUSTRY ALMANAC takes a rounded approach for the general reader. This book presents a complete overview of the health care field (see “How To Use This Book”). For example, Medicare and Medicaid growth and expenditures are provided in exacting detail, along with easy-to-use charts and tables on all facets of health care in general: from where health care dollars come from to how they are spent.

THE HEALTH CARE 500 is our unique grouping of the biggest, most successful corporations in all segments of the health care industry. Tens of thousands of pieces of information, gathered from a wide variety of sources, have been researched and are presented in a unique form that can be easily understood. This section includes thorough indexes to THE HEALTH CARE 500, by geography, industry, sales, brand names, subsidiary names and many other topics. (See Chapter 4.)

Especially helpful is the way in which PLUNKETT'S HEALTH CARE INDUSTRY ALMANAC enables readers who have no business background to readily compare the financial records and growth plans of health care companies and major industry groups. You’ll see the mid-term financial record of each firm, along with the impact of earnings, sales and strategic plans on each company’s potential to fuel growth, to serve new markets and to provide investment and employment opportunities.

No other source provides this book’s easy-to-understand comparisons of growth, expenditures, technologies, corporations and many other items of great importance to people of all types who may be studying this, one of the largest and most complex industries in the world today.

By scanning the data groups and the unique indexes, you can find the best information to fit your personal research needs. The major growth companies in health care are profiled and then ranked using several different groups of specific criteria. Which firms are the biggest employers? Which companies earn the most profits? These things and much more are easy to find.

In addition to individual company profiles, an overview of health care markets and trends is provided. This book's job is to help you sort through easy-to-understand summaries of today's trends in a quick and effective manner.

Whatever your purpose for researching the health care field, you'll find this book to be a valuable guide. Nonetheless, as is true with all resources, this volume has limitations that the reader should be aware of:

- Financial data and other corporate information can change quickly. A book of this type can be no more current than the data that was available as of the time of editing. Consequently, the financial picture, management and ownership of the firm(s) you are studying may have changed since the date of this book. For example, this almanac includes the most up-to-date sales figures and profits available to the editors as of late-2007. That means that we have typically used corporate financial data as of the end of 2006.

- Corporate mergers, acquisitions and downsizing are occurring at a very rapid rate. Such events may have created significant change, subsequent to the publishing of this book, within a company you are studying.

- Some of the companies in THE HEALTH CARE 500 are so large in scope and in variety of business endeavors conducted within a parent organization, that we have been unable to completely list all subsidiaries, affiliations, divisions and activities within a firm's corporate structure.

- This volume is intended to be a general guide to a vast industry. That means that researchers should look to this book for an overview and, when conducting in-depth research, should contact the specific corporations or industry associations in question for the very latest changes and data. Where possible, we have listed contact names, toll-free telephone numbers and World Wide Web site addresses for the companies, government agencies and industry associations involved so that the reader may get further details without unnecessary delay.

- Tables of industry data and statistics used in this book include the latest numbers available at the time of printing, generally through the end of 2006. In a few cases, the only complete data available was for earlier years.

- We have used exhaustive efforts to locate and fairly present accurate and complete data. However, when using this book or any other source for business and industry information, the reader should use caution and diligence by conducting further research where it seems appropriate. We wish you success in your endeavors, and we trust that your experience with this book will be both satisfactory and productive.

Jack W. Plunkett
Houston, Texas
October 2007

HOW TO USE THIS BOOK

The two primary sections of this book are devoted first to the health care industry as a whole and then to the "Individual Data Listings" for THE HEALTH CARE 500. If time permits, you should begin your research in the front chapters of this book. Also, you will find lengthy indexes in Chapter 4 and in the back of the book.

THE HEALTH CARE INDUSTRY

Glossary: A short list of health care industry terms.

Chapter 1: Major Trends Affecting the Health Care Industry. This chapter presents an encapsulated view of the major trends that are creating rapid changes in the health care industry today.

Chapter 2: Health Care Industry Statistics. This chapter presents in-depth statistics on Medicare, Medicaid, hospitals, pharmaceuticals and more.

Chapter 3: Important Health Care Industry Contacts – Addresses, Telephone Numbers and World Wide Web Sites. This chapter covers contacts for important government agencies, health care organizations and trade groups. Included are numerous important World Wide Web sites.

THE HEALTH CARE 500

Chapter 4: THE HEALTH CARE 500: Who They Are and How They Were Chosen. The companies compared in this book (the actual count is 494) were carefully selected from the health care industry, largely in the United States. 56 of the firms are based outside the U.S. For a complete description, see THE HEALTH CARE 500 indexes in this chapter.

Individual Data Listings:

Look at one of the companies in THE HEALTH CARE 500's Individual Data Listings. You'll find the following information fields:

Company Name:

The company profiles are in alphabetical order by company name. If you don't find the company you are seeking, it may be a subsidiary or division of one of the firms covered in this book. Try looking it up in the Index by Subsidiaries, Brand Names and Selected Affiliations in the back of the book.

Ranks:

Industry Group Code: An NAIC code used to group companies within like segments. (See Chapter 4 for a list of codes.)

Ranks Within This Company's Industry Group: Ranks, within this firm's segment only, for annual sales and annual profits, with 1 being the highest rank.

Business Activities:

A grid arranged into six major industry categories and several sub-categories. A "Y" indicates that the firm operates within the sub-category. A complete Index by Industry is included in the beginning of Chapter 4.

Types of Business:

A listing of the primary types of business specialties conducted by the firm.

Brands/Divisions/Affiliations:

Major brand names, operating divisions or subsidiaries of the firm, as well as major corporate affiliations—such as another firm that owns a significant portion of the company's stock. A complete Index by Subsidiaries, Brand Names and Selected Affiliations is in the back of the book.

Contacts:

The names and titles up to 27 top officers of the company are listed, including human resources contacts.

Address:

The firm's full headquarters address, the headquarters telephone, plus toll-free and fax numbers where available. Also provided is the World Wide Web site address.

Financials:

Annual Sales (2007 or the latest fiscal year available to the editors, plus up to four previous years): These are stated in thousands of dollars (add three zeros if you want the full number). This figure represents consolidated worldwide sales from all operations. 2007 figures may be estimates or may be for only part of the year—partial year figures are appropriately footnoted.

Annual Profits (2007 or the latest fiscal year available to the editors, plus up to four previous years): These are stated in thousands of dollars (add three zeros if you want the full number). This figure represents consolidated, after-tax net profit from all operations. 2007 figures may be estimates or may be for only part of the year—partial year figures are appropriately footnoted.

Stock Ticker, International Exchange, Parent Company: When available, the unique stock market symbol used to identify this firm's common stock for trading and tracking purposes is indicated. Where appropriate, this field may contain "private" or "subsidiary" rather than a ticker symbol. If the firm is a publicly-held company headquartered outside of the U.S., its international ticker and exchange are given. If the firm is a subsidiary, its parent company is listed.

Total Number of Employees: The approximate total number of employees, worldwide, as of the end of 2006 (or the latest data available to the editors).

Apparent Salaries/Benefits:

(The following descriptions generally apply to U.S. employers only.)

A "Y" in appropriate fields indicates "Yes."

Due to wide variations in the manner in which corporations report benefits to the U.S. Government's regulatory bodies, not all plans will have been uncovered or correctly evaluated during our effort to research this data. Also, the availability to employees of such plans will vary according to the qualifications that employees must meet to become eligible. For example, some benefit plans may be available only to salaried workers—others only to employees who work more than 1,000 hours yearly. Benefits that are available to employees of the main or parent company may not be available to employees of the subsidiaries. In addition, employers frequently alter the nature and terms of plans offered.

NOTE: Generally, employees covered by wealth-building benefit plans do not *fully* own ("vest in") funds contributed on their behalf by the employer until as many as five years of service with that employer have passed. All pension plans are voluntary—that is, employers are not obligated to offer pensions.

Pension Plan: The firm offers a pension plan to qualified employees. In this case, in order for a "Y" to appear, the editors believe that the employer offers a defined benefit or cash balance pension plan (see discussions below).The type and generosity of these plans vary widely from firm to firm. Caution: Some employers refer to plans as "pension" or "retirement" plans when they are actually 401(k) savings plans that require a contribution by the employee.

- Defined Benefit Pension Plans: Pension plans that do not require a contribution from the employee are infrequently offered. However, a few companies, particularly larger employers in high-profit-margin industries, offer defined benefit pension plans where the employee is guaranteed to receive a set pension benefit upon retirement. The amount of the benefit is determined by the years of service with the company and the employee's salary during the later years of employment. The longer a person works for the employer, the higher the retirement benefit. These defined benefit plans are funded entirely by the employer. The benefits, up to a reasonable limit, are guaranteed by the Federal Government's Pension Benefit Guaranty Corporation. These plans are not portable—if you leave the company, you cannot transfer your benefits into a different plan. Instead, upon retirement you will receive the benefits that vested during your service with the company. If your employer offers a pension plan, it must give you a summary plan description within 90 days of the date you join the plan. You can also request a summary annual report of the plan, and once every 12 months you may request an individual benefit statement accounting of your interest in the plan.

- Defined Contribution Plans: These are quite different. They do not guarantee a certain amount of pension benefit. Instead, they set out circumstances under which the employer will make a contribution to a plan on your behalf. The most common example is the 401(k) savings plan. Pension benefits are not guaranteed under these plans.
- Cash Balance Pension Plans: These plans were recently invented. These are hybrid plans—part defined benefit and part defined contribution. Many employers have converted their older defined benefit plans into cash balance plans. The employer makes deposits (or credits a given amount of money) on the employee's behalf, usually based on a percentage of pay. Employee accounts grow based on a predetermined interest benchmark, such as the interest rate on Treasury Bonds. There are some advantages to these plans, particularly for younger workers: a) The benefits, up to a reasonable limit, are guaranteed by the Pension Benefit Guaranty Corporation. b) Benefits are portable—they can be moved to another plan when the employee changes companies. c) Younger workers and those who spend a shorter number of years with an employer may receive higher benefits than they would under a traditional defined benefit plan.

ESOP Stock Plan (Employees' Stock Ownership Plan): This type of plan is in wide use. Typically, the plan borrows money from a bank and uses those funds to purchase a large block of the corporation's stock. The corporation makes contributions to the plan over a period of time, and the stock purchase loan is eventually paid off. The value of the plan grows significantly as long as the market price of the stock holds up. Qualified employees are allocated a share of the plan based on their length of service and their level of salary. Under federal regulations, participants in ESOPs are allowed to diversify their account holdings in set percentages that rise as the employee ages and gains years of service with the company. In this manner, not all of the employee's assets are tied up in the employer's stock.

Savings Plan, 401(k): Under this type of plan, employees make a tax-deferred deposit into an account. In the best plans, the company makes annual matching donations to the employees' accounts, typically in some proportion to deposits made by the employees themselves. A good plan will match one-half of employee deposits of up to 6% of wages. For example, an employee earning $30,000 yearly might deposit $1,800 (6%) into the plan. The company will match one-half of the employee's deposit, or $900. The plan grows on a tax-deferred basis, similar to an IRA. A very generous plan will match 100% of employee deposits. However, some plans do not call for the employer to make a matching deposit at all. Other plans call for a matching contribution to be made at the discretion of the firm's board of directors. Actual terms of these plans vary widely from firm to firm. Generally, these savings plans allow employees to deposit as much as 15% of salary into the plan on a tax-deferred basis. However, the portion that the company uses to calculate its matching deposit is generally limited to a maximum of 6%. Employees should take care to diversify the holdings in their 401(k) accounts, and most people should seek professional guidance or investment management for their accounts.

Stock Purchase Plan: Qualified employees may purchase the company's common stock at a price below its market value under a specific plan. Typically, the employee is limited to investing a small percentage of wages in this plan. The discount may range from 5 to 15%. Some of these plans allow for deposits to be made through regular monthly payroll deductions. However, new accounting rules for corporations, along with other factors, are leading many companies to curtail these plans—dropping the discount allowed, cutting the maximum yearly stock purchase or otherwise making the plans less generous or appealing.

Profit Sharing: Qualified employees are awarded an annual amount equal to some portion of a company's profits. In a very generous plan, the pool of money awarded to employees would be 15% of profits. Typically, this money is deposited into a long-term retirement account. Caution: Some employers refer to plans as "profit sharing" when they are actually 401(k) savings plans. True profit sharing plans are rarely offered.

Highest Executive Salary: The highest executive salary paid, typically a 2006 amount (or the latest year available to the editors) and typically paid to the Chief Executive Officer.

Highest Executive Bonus: The apparent bonus, if any, paid to the above person.

Second Highest Executive Salary: The next-highest executive salary paid, typically a 2006 amount (or the latest year available to the editors) and typically paid to the President or Chief Operating Officer.

Second Highest Executive Bonus: The apparent bonus, if any, paid to the above person.

Other Thoughts:

Apparent Women Officers or Directors: It is difficult to obtain this information on an exact basis, and employers generally do not disclose the data in a public way. However, we have indicated what our best efforts reveal to be the apparent number of women who either are in the posts of corporate officers or sit on the board of directors. There is a wide variance from company to company.

Hot Spot for Advancement for Women/Minorities: A "Y" in appropriate fields indicates "Yes." These are firms that appear either to have posted a substantial number of women and/or minorities to high posts or that appear to have a good record of going out of their way to recruit, train, promote and retain women or minorities. (See the Index of Hot Spots For Women and Minorities in the back of the book.) This information may change frequently and can be difficult to obtain and verify. Consequently, the reader should use caution and conduct further investigation where appropriate.

Growth Plans/ Special Features:

Listed here are observations regarding the firm's strategy, hiring plans, plans for growth and product development, along with general information regarding a company's business and prospects.

Locations:

A "Y" in the appropriate field indicates "Yes." Primary locations outside of the headquarters, categorized by regions of the United States and by international locations. A complete index by locations is also in the front of this chapter.

Chapter 1

MAJOR TRENDS AND TECHNOLOGIES AFFECTING THE HEALTH CARE INDUSTRY

Major Trends Affecting the Health Care Industry:

The Outlook for Health Care Technology:

1) Introduction to the Health Care Industry

A study released by the Milliken Institute in 2007 found that during the year 2003 (the year on which the study focused), 109 million Americans suffered from one or more of the most common, chronic diseases, including cancer, diabetes, heart disease, pulmonary conditions, mental disorders, stroke or hypertension. This means that more than one-third of all Americans have these conditions to one degree or another. The study estimated that one year's cost of treatment of these conditions at $277 billion, but estimated lost economic productivity to be vastly higher at $1 trillion. In other words, lost work and lost output due to these illnesses is reducing the nation's GDP by about 10%. These burdens could be vastly reduced through better consumer practices and better preventative medicine. For example, obesity, lack of exercise and cigarette smoking are immense contributors to these diseases. The U.S. Surgeon General estimates that obesity alone results in 300,000 American deaths and $117 billion in health care costs each year.

Meanwhile, technology marches ahead relentlessly. Be sure to read our descriptions of such innovations as HIFU, Proton Beam Radiation Therapy and the newest biotech developments in the "Outlook for Health Care Technology" section.

Health Expenditures and Services in the U.S.:

Health care costs continue to rise rapidly in the U.S. and throughout the developed world. Total U.S. health care expenditures were projected to increase from $2.26 trillion in 2007 to $2.77 trillion in 2010, with annual increases averaging about 7%. The health care market in the U.S. in 2007 was made up of hospital care (about $697.5 billion), physician and clinical services ($474.2 billion), prescription drugs ($229.5 billion), nursing home and home health ($190.0 billion), and other items totaling $668.8 billion. Registered hospitals totaled 5,756 properties in 2006, containing 946,997 beds serving 37 million admitted patients.

Medicare, the U.S. federal government's health care program for Americans 65 years or older, provided coverage to 43.3 million seniors in 2007. By 2030, the number of people covered will balloon to about 78.0 million due to the massive number of Baby Boomers entering retirement age. Federal Medicare expenditures, excluding patients' premiums, totaled $378.6 billion in 2006 and were projected to grow to $433.0 billion in 2007.

Medicaid is the U.S. federal government's health care program for certain groups of seniors in nursing homes as well as low-income and disabled persons. The federal government incurred Medicaid expenditures totaling $180.6 billion in 2006, which was projected to grow to $191.9 billion in 2007. Together, Medicare and Medicaid represented 19.2% of the entire 2006 federal budget that was about $2.65 trillion.

State governments incur large expenses for Medicaid benefits as well. According to the Kaiser Family Foundation, total state and federal spending on Medicaid during 2006 was $304.2 billion. The cost in California alone was $34.2 billion.

Health spending in the U.S., at about 16.2% of Gross Domestic Product (GDP) in 2007, will grow to about 19.6% by 2016 unless drastic reforms take place. Health care spending in America accounts for a larger share of GDP than in any other major industrialized country. Despite the incredible investment America continues to make in health care, 15.8% of Americans (46.9 million people) lacked health care coverage for the entire year of 2006. A significant number of the uninsured, 9.2 million, were in households with annual incomes above $75,000.

Clearly, the large number of people with no coverage is a problem, but there is little-to-no agreement as to what to do about it, if anything. As the 2008 U.S. presidential elections near, there is significant debate among potential candidates about extending health care coverage, perhaps to the extent of universal health care. Even if a candidate who advocates universal care is elected to the presidency, agreement among members of Congress as to the advisability, method and funding of such care is far from certain. At the same time, large numbers of Americans are relatively well satisfied their current payors and method of coverage. Likewise, many Americans and their legislators are extremely reluctant to see government take a lager role in the health care system, fearing runaway costs, bloated bureaucracies and less competition in the marketplace. Some feel that it is not the role of government to penalize patients or employers who do not purchase coverage. Others are reluctant to see America follow in the footsteps of socialized medicine in Canada and the U.K., where patients for many types of common treatments are on extremely long waiting lists or find it next to impossible to receive certain types of advanced therapies.

Health Expenditures Globally and in other Developed Nations:

A comprehensive study published by the OECD (Organization for Economic Cooperation & Development), covering 30 nations with the world's most developed economies, found stark contrasts between health costs in the United States and those of other modern nations.

In 2003 (the latest data available), the average of 29 OECD nations, including France, Germany, Mexico, South Korea, Australia, etc., but not including the U.S., spent 8.4% of GDP on health care, compared to 15% in the U.S. Health expenditures per capita (on a population base of 862 million in non-U.S. OECD nations in 2003) averaged $2,192 for 2003, compared to $5,635 in the U.S. Within North America, Canada, with its well-known nationalized health care, spent 9.9% of GDP, or $3,003 per capita. Mexico, in contrast, spent 6.2% of GDP, or $583 per capita. In Western Europe, the U.K., which likewise has a national health system, spent 7.7% of GDP, or $2,231 per capita. Germany spent 11% of GDP, or $2,996 per capita.

Globally, the total prescription drug market was in the $550 billion range in 2007. Total health care expenditures around the world are difficult to determine, but $4.5 trillion would be a fair estimate. That would place health care at about 8% of global GDP, with health care expenditures per capita at about $800. This $4.5 trillion figure breaks down to approximately $2.2 trillion in the U.S., $2.0 trillion in non-U.S. OECD nations, and $0.3 trillion elsewhere around the world. (Outside the U.S. and the rest of the OECD, that would allow $50 per capita per year in lesser-developed nations.) Clearly, there is vast disparity in the availability and cost of health care among nations, as there is with personal income and GDP.

Health Care Costs in the U.S.

Particularly in the U.S., continuous increases in the cost of health care, growing at rates far exceeding the rate of inflation in general, are hammering health consumers and payors of all types. Managed care providers continue to struggle to contain costs. Meanwhile, employers are hit hard by vast increases in the cost of providing coverage to employees and retirees. In 2007, U.S. major employers saw health coverage cost increases of about 6.1%, according to a study conducted by the Kaiser Family Foundation. This increase is more than double the rate of general inflation. (The rate of increase in 2006 was 7.7 %.) At major employers, health care insurance coverage for a typical family cost an average of $12,106 in 2007 (compared to $11,481 in 2006), according to Kaiser. Employees were required to pay $3,281 of that cost (up from $2,973 in 2006), with employers picking up the balance.

Many major employers are utilizing unique new programs in efforts to reduce employee illness, and thereby reduce costs. For example, the use of preventative care programs is growing, as is the use of employee education programs aimed at better managing the effects of diseases such as diabetes.

Smart employers are showing their employees how to use the Internet to obtain better information about diseases and prevention. Insurance providers are jumping on the Internet bandwagon as well. Some employers are even hiring in-house physicians and nurses to provide primary care in the workplace.

Patients and insurance companies are also dealing with sticker shock as the nation's prescription drug bill soars. Other factors edging costs upward include expensive new medical technologies and patients' demands for greater plan flexibility in choosing doctors and specialists at their will. At the same time, hospitals and health systems write off record amounts of revenues to bad debt, which increases costs for bill-paying patients.

In the wake of the tremendous growth of all aspects of the health care industry from the end of World War II onward, efficiency, competition and productivity were, regretfully, largely overlooked. Much of this occurred because federal and state governments paid such a large portion of the health care bill.

Physicians are caught between the desire for quality care and the desire for cost control on the part of payors, including HMOs, Medicare and Medicaid. The cost versus care debate has spawned an energetic movement to improve the quality of health care in the U.S., much of it centered on patients' rights, disease management, preventative health care and patient education.

Another major challenge facing the health care industry is the severely tarnished image of managed care companies in general. Supporters of managed care contend that its structure offers higher-quality care at a lower cost. Critics of managed care argue that the system risks lives by allowing plan managers to question, and sometimes reverse, the decisions made by medical professionals while emphasizing cost control at the expense of quality, thus sabotaging the bond of trust that should exist between doctor and patient. There is also concern among managed care detractors about the trend of mergers creating huge managed care companies. Some metropolitan markets are dominated by as few as two major health plans. Critics are equally concerned about the lack of autonomy of physicians who are forced to deal with the growing power of managed care giants.

While both supporters and critics make valid arguments, sweeping generalizations about the state of managed care are inherently flawed, since no two managed care plans are exactly alike. Neither society nor consumers can afford to turn back the clock to the traditional, considerably more expensive, fee-for-service system in which quality preventive care was largely non-existent, and patient care was generally provided without regard to cost.

The American health care industry faces more challenges than ever, due to a number of significant factors:

- While the advent of managed care appeared to tame health care cost inflation during the early and mid-1990s, costs have been rising very rapidly since then.
- The number of Americans who are underinsured or are without any type of insurance coverage at all remains staggering at more than 43 million.
- The U.S. population is aging rapidly. At the same time, the life expectancy of seniors is extending. Senior citizens will place a significant strain on the health care system in coming years. America's 78 million Baby Boomers begin turning 65 in 2011.
- The future obligations of Medicare and Medicaid are enough to cause vast problems for the federal budget for decades to come. Reforms are vital. Meanwhile, the number of seniors covered by Medicare will continue to grow at an exceedingly high rate, from 43.3 million people in 2007 to 78.0 million in 2030. The recent addition of Medicare prescription coverage will add to this government program's financial challenges.
- Likewise, costs for Medicaid, which is administered at the state level, have grown so rapidly that they are decimating state budgets and causing cuts in education and other vital services.
- The pharmaceuticals industry faces continued financial challenges. Patients' expenditures for pharmaceuticals are skyrocketing, creating a large backlash among health consumers and payors. Patents for money-making, blockbuster drugs are expiring at a rapid rate, increasing competition from makers of generic drugs. Many drug makers are hounded by massive lawsuits. At the same time, the drug industry remains under intense public scrutiny and is facing continued calls for increased government legislation and regulation.

- We are now entering what will long be remembered as the beginning of the Biotech Era. Breakthroughs in diagnostics and drug therapies are occurring at a rapid pace, creating financial and ethical challenges along with opportunities. Personalized medicine is beginning to emerge, but it remains to be seen who will be the early beneficiaries and who will pay the costs.
- Due to rising health care costs, employers large and small are straining under the financial burden of health care coverage expenses for current employees and retirees. The percentage of health costs paid by employees continues to rise.
- Medical Savings Accounts, used by only a small number of Americans (about 3.5 million in late 2006), are getting a renewed push in an effort to put more choice and responsibility in the hands of the patient.
- Physicians, other care providers, pharmaceutical manufacturers and insurers face daunting pressure from litigation and potential claims regarding malpractice and denial of care. Malpractice insurance costs are out of control. Some lawsuit reform legislation has begun, but much more reform is needed.
- Few Americans focus on leading healthy lifestyles that would prevent disease and cut both the amount and the cost of medical care. A 2005 study led by researchers at Michigan State University estimated that 76% of Americans do not smoke, but only 40.1% maintain a healthy weight and only 22.2% exercise for at least 30 minutes, five times per week. Likewise, only 23.3% were found to eat the recommended amount of daily fruit and vegetable servings.
- The three biggest causes of death in the U.S. are heart disease, cancer and stroke. Death rates from cancer and heart disease are about 200 per 100,000 population per year, and stroke deaths are about 50 per 100,000. Nearly one-fourth of America's annual health expenditures go for treatment of these three killers.
- While only a relatively modest amount of money is spent on preventative medicine and health education, about 70% of health care funds are spent on chronic disease.

Source: Plunkett Research, Ltd.

2) Continued Rise in Health Care Costs

Total Health Care Spending: Total U.S. health care expenditures are projected to increase from $2.26 trillion in 2007 to $4.13 trillion in 2016, with annual increases averaging about 6%. Mid-term projections for health care cost growth far exceed those for overall economic growth. Health spending in the U.S., at about 16% of Gross Domestic Product (GDP) in 2006, will grow to about 19% by 2016.

Spending by Employers: Recent years have seen a slowdown in annual percentage increases in employers' health coverage costs. Factors include a steady shift of costs to employees through co-payments and deductibles, fewer hospital stays and the growing use of generic drugs, which cost much less than branded drugs.

In order to find the average cost to employers who provide coverage to their employees, several surveys are conducted each year, including surveys by the consulting firm of Towers Perrin, the U.S. Bureau of Labor Statistics, Mercer Human Resource Consulting and the Kaiser Family Foundation. Results of the studies vary widely depending on methodology. The Kaiser Foundation estimates that an employer's premium cost to cover a typical family was $10,712 per year in 2005 (a 73% increase since 2000), with the typical worker paying 26% ($2,713) of that premium. For 2006, health care insurance coverage for a typical family cost an average of $11,481 for the year, according to Kaiser. Employees were required to pay $2,973 of that cost, on average, with employers picking up the balance. Kaiser's 2007 study found that health care insurance coverage for a typical family cost an average of $12,106. Employees were required to pay $3,281 of that cost.

The catalysts for these repeated rises include the cost of prescription drugs, medical technology innovation and a growing acceptance of higher-premium health plans that offer greater flexibility in the choice of providers. One way in which employers are attempting to control costs is to implement monitoring and preventive care plans for conditions such as diabetes and heart disease.

The U.S. continues to spend more on health care than any other developed nation, whether measured as total spending, spending per capita or spending as a percentage of GDP. Per capita health expenditures in the U.S. were $7,498 during 2007.

Despite per capita health costs that are vastly higher than other nations, Americans have a much higher incidence of obesity than residents of other developed nations, and the average American's life expectancy is slightly lower than that in Japan, Iceland, Sweden and Canada.

Many cash-strapped Americans abandon their increasingly expensive private health care plans and choose not to be insured at all. Unfortunately, patients who are not covered by managed care organizations are typically charged much higher rates for care, because managed care companies insist on negotiated rates. For example, a hospital might charge a set price of $1,200 for a CT scan procedure when billing an individual not covered by a managed care contract, but discount the cost to $400 for someone who is covered.

3) Employers Push Health Care Costs onto Employees

As employers face continued growth in health care costs, they are, in most cases, shifting more of the burden onto employees. In 2007, employees contributed about 27% of the cost for family health care coverage, up from 25% in 2006, according to a survey by the Henry J. Kaiser Family Foundation. While 99% of companies with more than 200 employees offer some type of health care coverage, only 59% of smaller companies provide health benefits, down from 68% in 2000.

In many cases, retirees are also paying significantly higher shares than before. Many employers have taken measures to decrease health care benefits for retirees in order to cut costs. Whether by raising retirees' share of premiums, capping the total amount paid or cutting benefits partially or entirely, employers have been steadily placing more of the financial burden of health care onto their retired employees. For example, in 1993 IBM capped its spending on health insurance premiums for retirees over 65 (and thereby covered by Medicare) to no more than $3,500 yearly. Caterpillar, Inc. cut costs by $75 million in 2002 by raising the premiums paid by retirees. Aetna cut health benefits out of the retirement package for its workers altogether, starting for those who retire in 2004. General Motors (GM) made headlines in late 2005 when the UAW ratified GM's plans to slash health care costs. Under the new plan, retirees receiving more than $8,000 per year in pensions will pay up to $370 per year in health insurance premiums for individuals and $752 per year for families, plus drug co-payments that will rise from $10 to $18. These trends will likely continue over the mid-term, with more and more of the cost of elderly health care being pushed onto retirees and Medicare.

Health coverage premium increases would be much higher except for proactive measures on the part of many employers. Examples include sponsoring wellness or disease management programs for employees and increasing employees' share of premiums, co-payments or deductibles.

Recently, many employers have utilized a co-insurance plan in which the patient pays a fixed percentage of the cost of a drug or procedure, which can add up to a great deal more than a flat co-pay. For example, a co-insurance plan might require the patient to pay 25% to 50% of a drug's cost, where a co-pay might call for a flat $15 towards a drug's cost. Meanwhile, many co-pay amounts are rising. Employers are struggling to deal with drug cost increases.

A notable exception to this trend of employers pushing health care costs onto their employees is a shift in the benefits policy at Wal-Mart. After receiving scathing criticism from the press as well as activists, the retail giant expanded its employee health plan in 2006. The plan, called the Value Plan, offers benefits to part-time as well as full-time employees and their families. The requirement for consecutive months of employment prior to coverage has dropped dramatically. Participating employees pay $23 per month for themselves and $15 per month per child, and can take advantage of co-pays on generic drugs that have been reduced from $10 to $3. The company offers a 20% employee discount on prescription drugs that are not covered in its benefits plan. In addition, Wal-Mart will provide contributions of up to $1,200 and additional match of up to $1,200 to employees' health savings accounts.

An enhancement to the Wal-Mart plan was announced in late 2007. It stipulates that as of January 1, 2008, the company will give each employee or employee family that signs up for coverage a grant of $100 to $500 for health expenses while charging premiums as low as $5 per month. (Plans with the lowest monthly premiums will have the highest annual deductibles.) Hospital deductibles will be eliminated, and 2,400 generic drugs will be available to employees for $4 per prescription (Wal-Mart pharmacies already offer about 1,400 drugs to the public at that price). The firm currently insures slightly less than one-half of its U.S. workers.

4) Medicare and Medicaid Spending Continue to Surge/ Baby Boomers Pass 65 Years of Age Soon

Americans aged 55 years or older are the fastest-growing segment of the population. In fact, 2006 marked the year that the first Baby Boomers turn 60, meaning that many are taking early retirement.

The term "Baby Boomer" generally refers to people born from 1946 to 1964. It evolved to include the children of soldiers and war industry workers who were involved in World War II. When those veterans and workers returned to civilian life, they started or added to families in large numbers. As a result, the Baby Boom generation is one of the largest demographic segments in the U.S. Based on projections within the 2004 national census of the population, these people will make up 11% of the U.S. population by 2010 and 14.1% by 2020.

By 2011, millions will begin turning traditional retirement age (65), which is also the age that Medicare coverage kicks in. This will result in extremely rapid growth in the senior portion of the population. The increased load on Medicare will be immense. At the same time, this surging senior population will put a greater strain on virtually all sectors of the health care system.

Meanwhile, Medicaid, with about 50 million enrollees, is straining under costs that have been soaring over the long-term. Initially, Medicaid was envisioned as a safety net for the poor. Today, while Medicaid covers many of the health needs of low-income households, the majority of Medicaid funds go to seniors and the seriously disabled to pay for nursing home care. In fact, Medicaid pays about 60% of America's total spending on nursing home care, with seniors taking 26% of Medicaid's budget and the disabled taking 43%. Medicaid is administered largely at the state level, with major financial support coming from the federal government. Many states are facing a nearly impossible task in funding their Medicaid systems. For example, for six years through 2005, Florida's spending on Medicaid grew at an average rate of 13% yearly. An estimated one-quarter of Florida's entire state budget goes for Medicaid.

Reforming the Medicaid system is critical to the financial health of the U.S. Florida, already spending $15.5 billion in 2005 to cover 2.2 million low-income residents, is attempting to lead the way with a proposal that would create more competition among providers and more choice and responsibility among patients. Governor Jeb Bush signed a set of reforms in late 2005 under which each participant is assigned a premium to be used to pay for basic and catastrophic care from a state-approved list of options. The premiums are based on the individual's overall health and adjusted to higher levels for those with serious illnesses. HMOs and physician and hospital networks must compete for patients, which (it is hoped) will bring costs down. In addition, the reforms reward patients who follow their doctors' advice (e.g., stop smoking, take medications as prescribed, vaccinate children), earning funds that are deposited in health savings accounts for the extras that are not covered by Medicaid. Florida is continuing Medicaid reform with several initiatives in 2007 including expanded services for children of low-income families and aged and disabled patients starting in three counties: Baker, Clay and Nassau.

When Medicare and Medicaid were first established in 1965, government programs accounted for about 25% of all health care spending in America. By 2014, they will account for about 49%, as the number of senior citizens grows dramatically. The cost to taxpayers will be astounding, and this public spending on health care will draw funds away from other vital public projects, such as education and infrastructure. Recent legislation providing Medicare payments for drugs kicked in during fiscal 2006, placing a much higher financial burden on the system. During 2005, Medicare spending on prescription drugs was $4.5 billion. In 2006, it multiplied more than 15-fold to $69.9 billion.

Medicare has been conducting an experiment since 2004 in which 266 U.S. hospitals are measured on quality of care standards for conditions such as joint replacements, coronary artery bypass grafts, heart attacks, heart failures and pneumonia. Hospitals that rank in the top 20% receive sizable bonuses, the largest being the approximately $744,000 awarded to Hackensack University Medical Center in New Jersey. In all, a total of $8.7 million is being awarded to 115 hospitals based on 30 quality measures. The experiment, which is managed by Premier, Inc., a nonprofit hospital alliance, is an attempt to award hospitals with greater quality of care, with emphasis on patient education and awareness so that recurrences are reduced.

5) Medicare Changes Include Drug Benefits for Seniors/Medicare Advantage Offers Private Fee for Service Plans

In November 2003, Congress passed a $395-billion bill for Medicare reform, the Medicare Modernization Act (MMA). In a largely bi-partisan vote, legislators approved a measure that gave large private insurers a greater role in health care for senior citizens (the Medicare Advantage plan), as well as provided a prescription drug benefit that went into effect in fiscal 2006. The bill includes provisions such as $25 billion for rural hospitals and health care providers; a stipulation that requires wealthy seniors to pay more for Medicare Part B coverage; and substantial support ($70 billion) for corporations that might otherwise eliminate existing coverage for retirees.

The rather convoluted legislation creates a government-subsidized prescription drug benefit, which may vary from plan to plan. Seniors who participate were issued a drug benefit identification card and paid a monthly premium of $37 starting in 2006. (The average premium was declining substantially in 2007 as insurers offered a growing number of competing plans. For example, 2007 monthly premiums dropped to an average of $22.) Beneficiaries in 2008 are typically responsible for the first $275 in yearly drug expenses, and then will pay, on average, a 25% coinsurance until they reach the benefit limit, which is $2,510 in 2008. Once they reach the benefit limit, they will face a gap in coverage in which they will pay 100% of their drug costs up to $5,726.25 in total drug spending. Medicare will then pay 95% of drug costs above that amount.

Low-income Medicare beneficiaries, those with incomes less than 150% of the federal poverty level, including those who receive Medicaid coverage in addition to Medicare, are eligible for varying levels of additional assistance depending on their incomes and assets.

Many health companies are profiting from this new Medicare drug benefit, including drug manufacturers who may have the opportunity to sell more drugs to more seniors and health plan firms that offer supplemental coverage in the form of Medicare Part D prescription drug plans.

Meanwhile, so many health insurers have entered the Medicare Advantage (MA) plans market that competition has become fierce, and a wide variety of plans is available to seniors. In Houston, Texas, for example, companies offering Advantage plans include Humana, WellCare, Aetna and Blue Cross Blue Shield.

The federal government sees Medicare Advantage as a way to inject private competition into coverage for Medicare beneficiaries. MA plans generally provide additional benefits, which may include dental care, vision care, preventative medicine or catastrophic care. As of mid 2007, about 8.4 million people were enrolled in MA plans, or about 20% of all Medicare beneficiaries. Many are paying modest monthly premiums, averaging $22 in 2007, for additional benefits.

Medicare Advantage gives beneficiaries an opportunity to be covered by private insurance companies, typically HMOs or PPOs. A growing category of Medicare Advantage is "private fee for service (PFFS)" a type of plan in which private insurance companies offer Centers for Medicare and Medicaid Services-approved programs that allow patients to choose their own doctors and hospitals. PFFS plans provide beneficiaries with all of their Medicare benefits plus any additional benefits the company chooses to provide, as long as the health care providers are willing to accept these patients. Services generally require a co-payment, plus (in certain cases) up to 35% of a Medicare-approved amount. A typical plan requires the patient to incur out-of-pocket expenses of $180 per hospital stay for up to five days and $15 or $30 for a visit to a physician. Similar plans began in the late

1990s in rural areas where Medicare patients were unlikely to find physicians and hospitals that participated in HMO or PPO networks. As of June 2007, 1.6 million seniors had PFFS plans, according to the Centers for Medicare and Medicaid Services.

PFFS plans can be lucrative for insurers, thanks to the recent increase in government reimbursement. The insurers, in turn, are competing for seniors' business by lowering premium prices enough to make them competitive with those charged for HMOs or PPOs. Humana, Inc., a major U.S. insurance company, offers PFFS plans in 35 states. WellPoint, another large insurance company, planned to offer the coverage in all 50 states in 2007.

PFFS detractors claim that the plans benefit the insurance companies more than the seniors enrolled in them. Others fault the plans for failing to contain health care costs or coordinate care from multiple providers. In early 2007, some Medicare officials warned that PFFS sales agents were attracting clients by marketing the plans as if they work in the same way as traditional Medicare. Some seniors with the coverage are expecting full choice of physician or treatment center but end up being turned away by doctors who do not want to participate. Officials hope to solve the problem in 2008 by requiring PFFS plans to contact all new enrollees to make sure they understand the system and how it works. The U.S. government has also announced plans to contact PFFS providers "under cover" to assess how the plans are marketed.

6) Adoption of Health Savings Accounts and Health Reimbursement Accounts Begins to Slow

A *Health Savings Account (HSA)* is a plan that combines a tax-free savings and investment account, somewhat similar to a 401(k), with a high-deductible health coverage plan. The intent is to give the consumer more incentive to control health care costs by reducing unnecessary care while shopping for the best prices. The consumer contributes pre-tax dollars annually to a savings account—for 2007, the limits were up to $2,850 for an individual or $5,650 for a family. (People over 55 may make higher contributions.) The employer may or may not match part of that contribution. The account may be invested in stocks, bonds or mutual funds. It increases tax-free, but the money may be spent only on health care. Unspent money stays in the account at the end of each year. The consumer must purchase an insurance policy or health care plan with an annual deductible of at least $1,100 for individuals or $2,200 for families. Funds may be withdrawn to pay a broad variety of medical expenses, including cosmetic surgery, dental care and ophthalmologist/optometrist expenses.

A *Health Reimbursement Account (HRA)* is a form of health care coverage plan provided to employees by their employer. It is quite different from a Health Savings Account. Under an HRA, the employer places a given amount of money each year into a special account for the employee to spend on health care. The employer also provides a high-deductible health coverage plan. The employee elects when and how to spend the money in the account on health care. Because of the high deductible, the employee's share of the monthly premium tends to be much lower than under an HMO or PPO, but the employee faces the burden of paying the high deductible when necessary. Unspent funds in the account can roll over from year to year so that the account grows, but the employee loses the fund balance when leaving the employer.

Both HSAs and HRAs have their opponents. Detractors claim that HSAs provide a tax shelter for the young and wealthy and also make it possible for poor or uninformed seniors to make choices that will ultimately harm rather than help them.

From the employer's point of view, HSAs give employees who carefully manage their costs and investments an opportunity to build up a significant savings account. At the same time, since most employers will pay only a specific amount into an HSA each year, the plan may shield the employer from a portion of any increases in health care costs.

From the point of view of covered workers, HSAs may be a real boon, particularly for those who are relatively healthy and generally spend little on health care. However, a participating worker will be at risk for the amount of the high deductible provided in the coverage plan, until the savings account accumulates enough funds to serve as a substantial cushion. Consequently, some observers speculate that HSAs will appeal mainly to more affluent employees. The plans are required to include annual out-of-pocket expense caps of no more than $5,500 for individuals or $11,000 for families. Some workers may opt to pay higher monthly premiums in exchange for lower expense caps.

From the point of view of health planners and health economists, many feel that widespread use of HSAs could create a true turning point in the American health system. Today, under most coverage plans, health consumers give little thought to the amount or price of the care they are receiving. Few covered consumers question expensive tests and other procedures when they are ordered by their physicians. Fewer still ask the price of procedures or shop around for the best care at the best price. Many HRA proponents hope that, as patients are given control of the purchasing process and a vested stake in the balance in the savings account, they will begin demanding better care at lower prices. Ideally, the result would be more cost competition, greater choices for consumers and an end to the continuous upward spiral of health care costs.

For example, some health analysts estimate that 20% to 30% of health care dollars are spent on needless tests or other procedures. Others feel that Americans are over-cared for—particularly those who can receive an endless stream of care at the expense of their health plans. Some surgical procedures, such as a hip replacement, might be eliminated through the use of much less expensive alternate care, such as physical therapy. Eventually, people who indulge in self-destructive behavior such as smoking or excessive weight gain might be motivated to change their habits when they see the actual costs in terms of health care dollars.

How quickly will the use of HSAs spread? By late 2006, the number of workers using an HSA or HRA had risen to about 2.7 million, up from 2005's 2.4 million. Major employers that were early in offering these programs include Intel, Pitney Bowes and Textron. They, along with other employers who offer HSAs, stand to save hundreds of thousands of dollars in savings on payroll taxes since fund placed in HSAs are not subject to Social Security, Medicare and state and federal unemployment deductions. Those savings effectively cover the administrative costs imposed by HSAs.

In order to encourage participants in HSAs to keep up preventative care and regular checkups, many insurers, such as Aetna and UnitedHealthcare, are offering 100% coverage of such visits to the doctor. Other providers are offering disease management and education programs. Some employers are covering 100% of the cost of vital drugs for people with chronic illnesses.

Despite these incentives, health savings plan adoption is slowing. A study by The Kaiser Family Foundation reports that 40% of employees in a consumer-directed plan are participating because it was the only option offered by their employers. In cases where a choice of health care plans is offered, only 19% choose consumer-driven plans. Many participants are finding it difficult to understand how the plans work. They also are having trouble shopping for the best prices for health care procedures themselves. In order for employers to sell HSAs and HRAs to employees, they must do a better job of marketing the plans in a way that they can be more easily understood.

7) Vast Number of Uninsured and Underinsured Americans

The total number of Americans who were without health insurance for the full year in 2006 (the latest data available) was 46.9 million, an increase of 2.18 million from 2005. This figure accounts for 15.8% of the population, up from 15.3% the previous year.

Who are the uninsured? Many are working adults. Not surprisingly, few are elderly or disabled who are generally covered by Medicare or Medicaid. The U.S. Centers for Disease Control & Prevention estimates that of the more than 46.9 million uninsured Americans, more than 8.6 million are children. Minorities have a high rate of uninsurance as well, with Hispanics topping the list.

There are several possible explanations for the large number of uninsured Americans:

- As a result of the 1996 welfare-reform act, millions of people have shifted from welfare to low-wage jobs with employers that either offer no coverage whatsoever or offer plans with co-payments that lower-income workers cannot afford.
- Increases in the cost of health care coverage have outpaced increases in household income, making coverage unaffordable for the many who are self-employed or who do not qualify for employer-provided plans.
- There has been an increasing trend toward alternate employment, such as temporary and part-time work, which seldom offers health care coverage.

In addition to the number of people with no insurance at all, the growing number of underinsured Americans is a problem. In many cases, increased limitations on care covered by payors result in costs shifting to patients in the form of high co-payments, or in the form of very high deductibles which may be unaffordable.

8) Health Care for All Tested in Several States

A small number of U.S. states are experimenting with universal health care initiatives, starting with Maine, which launched its Dirigo Health Reform Act in January 2005. Under the act, a voluntary enrollment of individuals and businesses receive health coverage including subsidies based on need. The program is designed to support itself by enrolling large numbers of young, healthy people who will pay premiums but incur no costs. Dirigo also has provisions to contain costs by requiring that hospitals voluntarily cap price increases at 3% during the first year of the plan, in addition to placing limits on hospital spending. By mid-2007, only 13,500 people had enrolled, bringing the state uninsured rate down from 14.5% to 12.5%. While some of the uninsured are now covered, the state expected to have 31,000 enrollees in its first year and 130,000 by 2009. The shortfall may derail the state's efforts.

Other states implementing similar programs are Massachusetts and Vermont, with California struggling in a closely watched effort to pass legislation for its own initiative as of mid 2007. In Massachusetts, the plan is mandatory. Those who choose not to enroll (and have an annual income deemed high enough by the state) will face a penalty on their 2007 state income tax of about $219, with increased penalties each year. Massachusetts employers are required to contribute to worker coverage, with state subsidies. Vermont's plan has the added twist of financing from a tobacco tax and Medicaid enrollment caps.

Meanwhile, the City of San Francisco, California has established a network, named "Healthy San Francisco", of city and community clinics that offer free or subsidized care to uninsured residents. Initially aimed at people in very low-income brackets, the city planned, by 2008, to open Healthy San Francisco to any resident who had been uninsured for at least 90 days. Patients' co-payments vary according to their income levels. Various funding schemes are being utilized, including a redirection of funds from existing city health programs, a federal grant, co-payments and modest quarterly membership dues for patients who earn above poverty-level incomes. The annual expense is estimated at $200 million.

The complexity of the issue is great, and proponents and detractors each have valid points. While the need for insurance has been well established, some individuals and business owners do not want to have costly insurance forced upon them. Other people who would like insurance (or businesses that would like to offer coverage to their employees) are suddenly finding themselves with an extra bill each month and little or no extra income to cover it.

Some are calling for federal coverage. The U.S. government already picks up an immense tab for health care, thanks to programs such as Medicare and Medicaid. This expense is going to grow dramatically over coming years as baby boomers age. Watch for continued debate on this issue, particularly as the 2008 presidential elections near.

9) Branded Pharmaceutical Costs Soar While Growing Generic Sales Slow Overall Spending

Historically, the drug industry has been one of the world's most profitable business sectors. The U.S. government estimated that $229 billion would be spent on prescription drugs in 2007, and that spending will grow to $497 billion in 2016. Nearly 20% of pharmaceutical revenue is redirected toward discovering new medicines, well above the average of 4% reinvested in research and development in most industries. Advanced technology has allowed drug companies to saturate their development programs with smarter, more promising drugs. R&D (research and development) budgets are staggering. For example, Pfizer invests more than $7.5 billion yearly in R&D. Total spending on R&D by U.S. drug firms $43 billion reached in 2007, according to PhRMA, an industry association.

Growth in total prescription drug outlays slowed to 1% from September 2006 to September 2007. This is down from a 4.4% annual growth rate from 2004 to 2005. This is largely due to consumers switching to generic drugs. Once a patent on a blockbuster drug such as cholesterol treatment Zocor expires, drug companies are allowed to market cheaper generic brands. According to a 2006 Kaiser Family Foundation study, the average branded drug costs three times as much as the average generic drug.

Drug makers are challenged to price their branded drugs in a way that will earn a good return on investment prior to the expiration of patent protection. The current U.S. patent policy grants drug manufacturers the normal 20 years protection from the date of the original patent (which is most likely filed very early in the research state), plus a period of 14 years after FDA approval. Since typical drugs take 10 to 15 years to research, prove in trials and bring to market, this effectively gives the patent holder only 19 to 24 years before low-price competition from generic manufacturers begins. Branded drugs tend to lose 15% to 30% of market share when generic versions come on the market, eventually losing as much as 75% to 90% after a few years.

Another boost to generic drug sales is Wal-Mart's landmark move in 2006 when it began offering a number of generic drugs for a flat $4 per month. Other discount retailers including Target and Kmart jumped on the generic bandwagon with their own deep discounts. In late 2007, Publix, a grocery store chain in the Southeast U.S. with 684 pharmacies, announced a free generic antibiotic program for prescriptions of several common drugs, for up to 14 days.

Then there is the issue of "follow-on" drugs. These are drugs that hold their own patent for therapies similar to or competing with the original breakthrough patent. Follow-on drugs tend to get through regulatory approval much faster, and often are brought to market at much lower prices. Both factors create a significant competitive advantage for follow-on patent owners.

Major drug companies are trying to get on the generic gravy train by quietly creating their own generic drug subsidiaries. Pfizer, for example, has a division called Greenstone, Ltd., which produces generic versions of its blockbuster drugs including Zoloft, an antidepressant that brought in upwards of $2 billion in 2006 sales. Likewise, Johnson & Johnson has a generic subsidiary called Patriot Pharmaceuticals and Schering-Plough created Warrick Pharmaceuticals. Naturally, independent generic drug companies oppose the practice.

Generic drugs accounted for about 63% of all drug purchases (by volume) in the U.S. during 2006, up from 50% in 2005. From 2007 through 2012, patents will expire on branded drugs in the U.S. with about $60 billion in combined annual sales. For example, by 2011 a generic version of cholesterol-controlling Lipitor is expected to be on the market. Lipitor has long been the world's best selling branded drug (selling as much as $13 billion yearly at one time), but sales were declining in mid-2007 thanks to a generic substitute for a competing drug named Zocor; the generic of Zocor costs about 60% less than Lipitor.

Pharmaceutical company profits and research budgets are under pressure due to a wide range of additional challenges. Blockbuster drugs that might provide the high returns needed to bring a drug to market are increasingly difficult to develop. Lawsuits against drug makers abound, and drug safety issues rank among the top challenges faced by the pharmaceutical industry today.

Meanwhile, payors are fighting to reduce the growing amounts that they spend on prescription drugs, and future revenues for drug makers will be impacted by cost-control measures at the individual level. In addition, the U.S. Government's Medicare drug benefit is putting even greater pressure on drug companies to sell drugs at lower prices. Drug makers are reacting to these pressures as best they can. For example, in mid-2007, Johnson & Johnson announced job cuts affecting 4,800 employees in an effort to reduce operating costs.

Highly effective new drug therapies can be incredibly expensive for patients. Take Iressa, a breakthrough treatment for lung cancer. It costs about $1,800 monthly per patient. Likewise, the groundbreaking colon cancer treatment Erbitux can cost as much a $30,000 for a seven-week treatment. A standard treatment of the latest drug regimens for some diseases can run up a $250,000 or higher bill over a couple of years.

The good news is that as the demand for new and improved treatments intensifies, so do the abilities of modern technology. In addition to expediting the process and lowering the costs of drug discovery and development, advanced pharmaceutical technology promises to increase the number of diseases that are treatable with drugs, enhance the effectiveness of those drugs and increase the ability to predict disease, not just the ability to react to it.

More good news is the FDA's announcement in July 2006 of plans to adapt the ways in which some experimental drugs are brought to clinical trial. In the past, the necessary effort and expense to prepare a request for human trials of a new drug amounted to between $500,000 and $1 million. Under the new proposal, the FDA would require less stringent testing (under limited circumstances) in the lab and on animals before being tried on humans. The FDA's willingness to consider adaptive designs is a major shift.

Consumers' voracious appetites for new drugs continue to grow. Insurance companies may raise co-payments for drugs, strike deals with drug companies and employ pharmacy benefit management tactics in an effort to fend off rising pharmaceutical costs. Also, new drugs have very high prices when they initially hit the market, since they have no generic equivalent.

Until recently, pharmaceutical research was focused primarily on curing life-threatening or severely debilitating illnesses. But a current generation of drugs, commonly referred to as "lifestyle" drugs, is transforming the pharmaceutical industry. Lifestyle drugs target a variety of medical conditions, ranging from the painful to the inconvenient, including obesity, impotence, memory loss and depression. Drug companies also continue to develop lifestyle treatments for hair loss and skin wrinkles in an effort to capture their share of the huge anti-aging market aimed at the Baby Boomer generation. The use of lifestyle drugs dramatically increases the total annual consumer intake of pharmaceuticals, and creates a great deal of controversy over which drugs should be covered by managed care and which should be paid for by the consumer alone.

In coming years, taming pharmaceutical costs will be one of the biggest challenges facing the health care system. Prescription drug costs already account for more than 10% of all health care expenditures in the U.S. Managed care must be able to determine which promising new drugs can deliver meaningful clinical benefits proportionate to their monetary costs.

Several developments are fueling the fire under the controversy over drug costs in the U.S. To begin with, it has become common knowledge that pharmaceutical firms tend to price their drugs at vastly lower prices outside the U.S. market. The result is that U.S. consumers and their managed care payors are bearing a disproportionate share of the costs of developing new drugs. Whereas prices in the U.S. are determined by a free market and are mostly limited only by competition, nations such as Australia and Canada put a cap on drug prices that cannot exceed a given amount. Taking advantage of this discrepancy, generally a 30% to 80% difference, border-crossing U.S. citizens have saved bundles of money on prescription drugs by importing them from Canada. Canadian Internet-based drug retailers have been selling to anyone with a credit card and a faxed prescription. Naturally, U.S. drug companies have raised a furor. Many have threatened to limit Canada's supplies so it only meets the demands of Canadians, as well as putting a corporate embargo on any pharmacy or distributor suspected of selling to Internet companies. However, the U.S. Government has decided to stop interfering. In October 2006, U.S. Customs authorities announced that they would no longer seize individual shipments of drugs from Canada to the U.S. if they contained no more than a 90-day supply.

Factors leading to soaring drug costs in the American health care system:

- 78 million Baby Boomers are beginning to enter their senior years. The lifespan of Americans is increasing, and chronic illnesses are increasing as the population ages.
- Medicare Part D, the recently introduced component of Medicare that pays for prescription drugs for seniors, made affordable drugs available to millions of Americans, fueling overall drug sales.
- The drug industry intensified its sales effort over recent years. Direct-to-consumer advertising and legions of sales professionals calling on physicians increased demand for the newest, most expensive drugs.
- Convoluted and uncoordinated lists of drug "formularies" (available drugs, their uses and their interactions) require increased administrative work to sort through, thus forcing costs upward.
- Physicians often prescribe name-brand drugs when a generic equivalent may be available at a fraction of the cost.
- Research budgets are immense. Breakthroughs in research and development are creating significant new drug therapies, allowing a wide range of popular treatments that were not previously available. An excellent example is the rampant use of antidepressants such as Prozac and Zoloft. Meanwhile, major drug companies face the loss of patent protection on dozens of leading drugs. They are counting on expensive research, partnerships and acquisitions to replace those marquis drugs.
- "Lifestyle" drug use is increasing, as shown by the popularity of such drugs as Viagra (for the treatment of sexual dysfunction), Propecia (male baldness) and Botox (facial wrinkles).

Source: Plunkett Research, Ltd.

10) Biotech Drugs Pick Up the Slack as Blockbuster Mainstream Drugs Age

While Big Pharma has concentrated mainly on mass-market drugs that treat a broad spectrum of ailments, biotech companies have largely developed treatments for rare disorders or maladies such as certain cancers that only affect a small portion of the population. For example, biotech pioneers Genentech and Biogen Idec developed Rituxan for the treatment of non-Hodgkin's lymphoma, which had only $1.8 billion in sales in 2005.

Drugs such as Rituxan are commonly referred to as "orphan drugs," which means that they treat illnesses that no other drug on the market addresses. Technically, a drug designated by the FDA with orphan status provides therapeutic benefit for a disease or condition that affects less than 200,000 people in the U.S. Almost half of all drugs produced by biotech companies are for orphan diseases. These drugs enjoy a unique status due to the Orphan Drug Act of 1983, which gives pharmaceutical companies a seven-year monopoly on the drug without having to file for patent protection, plus a 50% tax credit for research and development costs. As of early-2007 there 1,679 drugs designated "orphan," including a few hundred on the market and the balance pending approval.

Meanwhile, blockbuster drugs are becoming more and more difficult to produce. Although drugs such as Zocor, Zoloft and Ambien faced generic competition for the first time in 2006 when their patents expire, new drugs to replace them are slow in coming.

As the wellspring of mainstream Big Pharma blockbusters begins to dry, many big pharmaceutical companies are rushing to develop their own orphan drugs. Pfizer released Sutent, a drug used to treat cancerous kidney and stomach-lining tumors in 2006, long after biotech firm Genentech had four drugs used for cancer on the market. Genentech's colon cancer treatment, Avastin, is expected to reach $6.2 billion in sales in 2009, while Pfizer's Sutent is projected to bring in only $570 million that same year.

Commentary: The challenges facing the biopharmaceuticals industry from 2004-2010

- Working with governments to develop methods to safely and effectively speed approval of new drugs.
- Working with the investment community to build confidence and foster patience in the investors for the lengthy timeframe required for commercialization of promising new compounds.
- Working with civic, government, religious and academic leaders to deal with ethical questions centered on stem cells and other new technologies in a manner that will enable research and development to move forward.
- Overcoming, through research, the technical obstacles to therapeutic cloning.
- Enhancing sales and distribution channels so that they educate patients, payors and physicians about new drugs in a cost-effective manner.
- Emphasizing fair and appropriate pricing models that will enable payors (both private and public) to afford new drugs and diagnostics while providing ample profit incentives to the industry.
- Developing appropriate standards that fully realize the potential of systems biology (that is, the use of advanced information technology and the resources of genetic databases) in a manner that will create the synergies necessary to accelerate and lower the total cost of new drug development.
- Fostering payor acceptance, diagnostic practices and physician practices that will harness the full potential of genetically targeted, personalized medicine when a large base of new biopharma drugs becomes available.

Source: Plunkett Research, Ltd.

11) Critical Lack of Qualified Nurses in the U.S. Continues Despite Federal Efforts

A report by the Joint Commission on Accreditation of Healthcare Organizations in late 2003 stated that of 1,609 types of unexpected problems (including accidental death or serious physical harm) in U.S. hospitals reported between January 1996 and March 2002, 24% took place because of an insufficient number of nurses on duty. Low staffing levels were found to contribute to 50% of ventilator-related incidents, 42% of surgery-related incidents, 25% of transfusion incidents, 19% of medication errors and 14% of patient falls. In 2006, Vanderbilt University's senior associate dean for research estimated the nursing shortage in the U.S. to be as high as 400,000, with the U.S. government projecting that level to reach 800,000 by 2020.

The implications of the staffing shortage are serious indeed. Analysis of data on nurse staffing levels confirms that there is a direct link between the number of registered nurses on staff and the hours they spend with patients. Likewise, it is a determining factor in whether patients develop a number of serious complications or die while in the hospital. Additional factors include the aging population, the growing numbers of patients who will require care in assisted living centers and all-time low enrollment in nursing school.

In response to the situation, the Nurse Reinvestment Act was passed in Congress in 2002 and was signed by President Bush in 2003. The act authorizes $30 million in federal funding for scholarships and loan repayments for nursing students who agree to work in nursing shortage areas after graduation. While this may be a boon to potential nursing school enrollment, there remains the problem of finding enough masters- and doctorate-level nurses who are qualified to teach in nursing schools. Nursing schools are not able to grow quickly enough largely because of a lack of qualified educators. According to the National League for Nursing, nursing schools across the U.S. rejected 147,465 qualified applicants in 2005 because of capacity problems.

A bit of good news in the midst of the nursing shortage crisis is the improving level of job satisfaction among nurses. In a 2001 survey conducted by the Federation of Nurses and Health Professionals, one in five nurses stated their intention to leave the profession within the next five years due to poor working conditions. Stress, irregular hours, low morale and excessive patient loads were all cited as problems serious enough to cause nurses to quit. Since then, job satisfaction has risen to 83%, due to higher salaries and improved perceptions of the importance of nurses in the face of the shortage. For example, salaries for full time registered nurses grew from $52,000 in 2000 to $69,000 in 2006 in California.

Between 2002 and 2005, the number of registered nurses (RNs), which are nurses who have graduated from an accredited school of nursing and have been registered and licensed by a state authority, rose by 185,000. The rise is due to older nurses re-entering the workforce and growing numbers of foreign nurses taking jobs in U.S. hospitals (75,000 were recruited between 2001 and 2004). In addition, in 2005, Congress allocated 50,000 extra green cards with a priority for foreign nurses. The cards were used within 18 months. However, the increase in nurses on the job has not been great enough to fill all of the positions open, and older nurses will soon retire. In 2002, the average age of practicing nurses in the U.S. was 42.1 years, which is projected to rise to 45.4 by 2010. Just 24% of the nursing workforce is under the age of 35, down from 50% in 1985.

In addition to the shortage of qualified nurses, there are significant shortages of radiology technicians, pharmacists and other allied health professionals. Watch for further efforts by the government to boost the number of students in nursing and allied health professions.

12) Patients Are Seeking Quality of Care Data

With rapidly rising health care costs and concerns about the quality of health care, many people are going online for information regarding their conditions and on the doctors and hospitals they may consult for care—call it comparison shopping for health care. There are growing numbers of web sites that track data on hospitals such as the U.S. Department of Health and Human Services' web site, Hospital Compare (www.hospitalcompare.hhs.gov). Hospital Compare uses data from Medicare and Medicaid to track performance at more than 4,000 facilities across the U.S. Most insurers also make hospital data available to members on their web sites. The kind of data usually available compares hospitals to the national average on statistics, such as mortality rates; good practices, such as administering aspirin to heart patients upon arrival and discharge; and counseling on health habits. Data on individual doctors is harder to find, but more information will become available over the near- to mid-term as web sites expand and multiply.

Quantum Health (www.quantumhealthllc.com), a Columbus, Ohio health care coordinator, offers corporate clients comparative health care data plus a laundry list of services that help employees covered by company insurance navigate the often confusing health care system and get the most out of their health benefits. Quantum Health services include informing patients of what questions they should ask their physicians about their conditions, assistance in finding specialists, advice on medical tests that should or should not be taken and education on wellness.

13) Malpractice Suits Are Blamed for Rising Health Care Costs/Tort Reform Is Capping Awards for Damages

Health care costs have become a hot political topic, and many people have pointed at malpractice lawsuits as a primary cause of rising costs. For years, punitive lawsuits for pain and suffering have levied huge settlements from doctors, hospitals and their insurers. In reaction, premiums for malpractice insurance have burgeoned, growing far faster than the costs for any other type of insurance. Doctors and hospitals, in order to offset malpractice insurance premiums, raise rates and conduct extensive, and often unnecessary, tests in order to protect themselves from legal accountability. These factors contribute significantly to the overall cost of health care in the U.S., and a political battle has ensued, particularly between lobbyists for plaintiffs' lawyers and lobbyists for the health care industry.

In addition to adding immense costs to the health care system, malpractice lawsuits have done much to erode the relationship between doctors and their patients. At the same time, fear of malpractice suits can discourage young physicians from pursuing higher-risk specialties, such as obstetrics and surgery, rather than fields where they are much less likely to be sued. Relations between doctors and lawyers have also become strained, with many doctors blaming the situation on some lawyers' willingness to take even the most frivolous cases. Meanwhile, it is common for physicians in higher-risk fields to face annual malpractice insurance premiums of $100,000 or more, while clinics and hospitals are paying astronomical insurance premiums.

Self-interest has caused some physicians to respond. Reports have been published of physicians refusing to treat attorneys, their families or their employees except in cases of emergency. Meanwhile, many would-be patients have learned how hard it can be to get a physician in high-risk fields, such as obstetrics and gynecology, to take a new client.

Many states are tackling the malpractice awards issue through referenda and legislation that limit total damage awards. Texas is a prime example of a state that has limited non-economic damage awards. By 2000, the state had reached a crisis level: One report compiled in October 2002 showed that 52% of all Texas physicians in the state were subjected to malpractice claims during 2000.

Another report found that in the Lower Rio Grande River Valley it was even worse. Claims were growing at 60% per year, and there were 350 claims for every 100 doctors in that area.

In response to situations such as this, Texas, like many other states, passed legislation to limit rewards given to plaintiffs for "non-economic" damages, which include pain, inconvenience, suffering and disfigurement. By early 2003, 26 states had limited non-economic damages in medical malpractice cases, generally to amounts between $250,000 and $500,000 dollars. The statutes also generally limit the amount that lawyers can make off the case via contingency fees, making sure that the plaintiff receives a substantial portion of the reward. Some critics of this move see such laws as contributing to a failure of the justice system. Others feel that a $250,000 to $500,000 award cap is not fair payment for a patient who has been severely disfigured for life.

On the other hand, there may be few limits on the amount of "economic" damages awarded to a patient—that is, loss of earnings due to the inability to function fully at a job or profession. Patients who earn extremely high salaries may seek damages that are proportionately high—even multimillion-dollar amounts. However, attorneys may be discouraged from taking, on contingency, clients who work in low-paying jobs.

California limits the contingency fee that an attorney can collect under a malpractice claim as follows: 40% of the first $50,000; 33.3% of the next $50,000; 25% of the next $500,000; and 15% of any amount above $600,000. These limits apply whether the damages are collected as a settlement out of court, an award under a lawsuit or an award under arbitration.

As in any other legal matter, there are two sides to the story; arguments for and against malpractice award limits abound. California is often named as the poster child for how effective such legislation can be in lowering insurance premiums and health care costs in general. From 1975, when California first passed malpractice reform, to 2002, the state's malpractice insurance premiums rose only 167%, compared to the national average of 505% in the same period. Texas is experiencing a resurgence in the numbers of practicing physicians since malpractice insurance premiums dropped significantly (up to 22% for the state's largest insurance carrier and an average of 13% for other carriers). The number of related lawsuits in Texas has been cut in half.

Meanwhile, the costs and challenges of lawsuits are not limited to physicians. Every sector of the health chain, from equipment makers to hospitals to drug makers, is swamped by lawsuits, and they are forced to pass along the costs of insurance and litigation in the form of higher fees charged to patients.

14) Transplants are Big Business

Recently, there has been a big leap in consumer support for and interest in organ transplants within the U.S. In 2006, the number of deceased organ donors was 8,022, up from 7,593 the previous year and the first time the number surpassed 8,000. This growing number of available donors increased the total number of transplants performed to 28,923, a 2% jump over the previous year. Of course, there are also a small number of organs, such as kidneys, donated by living donors.

While this is terrific progress, it doesn't come close to filling demand. About 95,000 Americans are on waiting lists for transplants at any one time, for anything from hearts to lungs to kidneys. Unfortunately, more than 7,000 die yearly while waiting.

The first heart transplant was performed in Cape Town, South Africa in 1967, making worldwide news. The first liver transplant was in Denver the same year, and the first kidney transplant was in Boston in 1954. While transplants were once considered to be experimental and unlikely to be of long-term benefit, today successful transplant stories abound, and transplants have evolved from medical miracles to everyday occurrences. Consumers are becoming more aware of the trend and more willing to sign donor cards. Meanwhile, the technologies used in transplant procedures and the drugs used to fight rejection have evolved to a very high level. In 2004, more than 2,000 patients received heart transplants in the U.S. alone. History shows that 83% will still be living after one year and 49% will be alive after 10 years. Recipients of liver transplants (a record breaking 6,650 in 2006), and kidneys (more than 17,000 yearly) have even higher success rates. Organs from living donors have the highest success rates.

Other transplanted organs include corneas, lungs, heart valves, pancreas, intestine and bone marrow. On very rare occasions, there have been hand and ovary transplants.

15) Hospitals Are Reengineering

Conventional hospitals are tradition-filled, vertically-integrated monoliths, capable of delivering virtually all possible types of health care under one roof. As with the rest of the health care sector, hospitals are caught up in a swirling world of new technologies and a drive for cost control. As a result, many hospitals are completely reengineering their policies, procedures and technological bases.

Hospitals have long faced industry-wide problems such as improperly distributed medication, post-operation infections and the unfortunate patient death through error. In addition, there are widespread problems of inefficiencies that cost money. Finally, most hospitals could do a lot to make themselves more patient-friendly. Recent studies have found that a great deal can be accomplished to alleviate these problems and others simply through improved lines of communication and chains of command.

Patient safety and elimination of errors are a major focus. By some estimates, medical errors contribute to the deaths of as many as 100,000 patients yearly, while mistakes, misjudgment and general lack of efficiency may account for $500 billion in yearly spending that might be avoided. Many of these problems occur in the 5,756 acute care hospitals registered with the American Hospital Association.

A movement is aimed at reforming hospital care had remarkable success in 2006. The "100,000 Lives" program was led by the Institute for Healthcare Improvement (www.ihi.org) located in Cambridge, Massachusetts. The institute maintains a list of quality and safety issues and communicates with participating hospitals about new systems and procedures that have been proven effective. Approximately 3,100 hospitals joined the movement, which resulted in saving an estimated 122,300 lives through mid-June 2006. Six measures are credited for the improvement, which include rapid-response teams that provide emergency care in all hospital units to patients with a rapid drop in vital signs; checks and re-checks of patient medications; preventive measures such as pre-surgery antibiotics to avoid post-procedural infections. The IHI is following up the program with a new "5 Million Lives" campaign that aims to save millions of lives over the two year period ending December 9, 2008.

Today, payors, such as managed care organizations and major employers, are demanding better results from hospitals—many are insisting that patients visit only hospitals with above average records. Others are willing to pay more to hospitals with records of fewer errors and better outcomes.

Information technology is now a major tool in solving hospital problems. American hospitals invested about $30 billion in IT during 2006 alone. Systems that are rapidly gaining popularity include digital patient records, systems that collect information regarding each patient's prescription drugs and warn when drugs shouldn't be mixed, RFID tags that clearly define drug container contents, wireless wi-fi networks that enable doctors to maintain communication with patient record computers and digital charts available on monitors at the bedside. (For additional information, see "Information Technology and Health Care".)

Hospitals nationwide are focusing on consumer issues. Progressive hospitals are offering better food, luxury in-room amenities such as Internet access, flat-screen TVs and more comfortable surroundings in general. Some new hospitals feature separate hallways for patients and the general public, so they can have some privacy while going to procedures. Visiting hours are becoming more flexible, and special private areas are being built for consultation between doctors, patients and families. For that matter, many new hospitals recognize that family support is an important part of the healing process, and are therefore making family waiting rooms and other facilities more user-friendly.

New standards for hospitals include private single-patient rooms. Once reserved only for the wealthy, private rooms are to become standard in new hospital construction to lower risks of infection and increase the efficiency of space utilization (double rooms often have only one bed filled). According to construction research firm FMI Corp., annual spending on new hospital construction, including the rebuilding of old facilities and construction on new sites, will surpass $30 billion by 2009 (similar construction outlays in 2005 totaled $19.8 billion).

Meanwhile, the number of "specialty hospitals" is increasing rapidly across the nation. These typically are private hospitals that focus on one aspect of care, such as treatment of women, cardiac patients or orthopedic patients. This focus hopefully enables these institutions to provide a higher level of care at lower costs. Patients may benefit as well through more efficient and effective delivery of care.

16) Obesity Sparks Government Action

Obesity is increasing in nearly every country in the world. The problem is at its worst in the U.S., where obesity has doubled in the past 20 years. A study of a sample of 4,115 adult Americans published in the October 9, 2002 issue of the *Journal of the American Medical Association* found that the age-adjusted prevalence of obesity (a much more serious problem than being merely overweight—see the box regarding "BMI" that follows) was 30.5% (the study was actually conducted in 1999-2000). This was a significant increase from 22.9% in the previous study (made during the 1988-1994 period). The number of adults either overweight or obese was estimated at 64.5%, up from 55.9%. These are official studies under a program referred to as NHANES—the National Health and Nutrition Examination Survey. A report issued by the Center for Disease Control and Prevention (CDC) in 2006 states that obesity continues to rise among men and children in the U.S. The percentage of obese men rose from 27.4% in 1999-2000 to 31% in 2003-2004, while the percentage of obese children rose from 14% to 17% in the same periods. The study found that women's percentage for obesity remained steady at 33%.

It is interesting to compare American obesity levels to those of other nations. For example, the government of Mexico conducted a nutrition survey in 2000 which found that approximately 60% of men and 64% of women were either overweight or obese. A 2000 study published in the British Medical Journal found that 26% of China's 1.3 billion population is overweight or obese. The Organization for Economic Cooperation and Development (OECD) reports that Britain and Australia are not far behind the U.S., with obesity rates of 21% and 20% respectively, while the obesity rate in France is only 9.6%, and in Japan it is only 2.9%. However, while the French and Japanese rates are relatively low, they have nonetheless seen significant increases over the past 10 years. The World Health Organization estimated that 300 million people worldwide are classified as obese and 750 million as overweight (in a global population of about 6.7 billion as of early 2007). The latter figure includes 22 million children under the age of five.

Body Mass Index (BMI) as an indicator of health status based on weight:

Underweight = less than 18.5 BMI
Normal weight = 18.5 to 24.9
Overweight = 25 to 29.9
Obese = 30 or more

To calculate Body Mass Index:
First: divide weight (pounds) by height (inches)
Second: divide the result by height again
Third: multiply the result by 703

Internet Research Tip:
For an easy-to-use, online calculator and a full discussion of BMI, see http://nhlbisupport.com/bmi/

Source: National Institutes of Health, National Heart, Lung and Blood Institute

The alarming rise in obesity in the U.S. has brought about significant changes in the latest set of dietary guidelines from the U.S. federal government. Released in January 2005, the new guide emphasizes counting calories and daily exercise over limiting certain foods such as carbohydrates or fats.

The U.S. Surgeon General estimates that obesity results in 300,000 American deaths and $117 billion in health care costs each year. One of the most critical problems of obesity is the onset of diabetes. If obesity rates continue to skyrocket, some experts predict that the number of diabetics worldwide will triple in the years 2000 to 2015 to 320 million people. The impact of these numbers combined with an accompanying rise in heart disease, cancer, high blood pressure and cholesterol levels may wreak havoc on the health care system.

The 2005 federal dietary guidelines are the result of more than a year's work by an anonymous panel of 13 nutrition experts in the fields of pediatrics, obesity, cardiovascular disease and public health. Panel members remain anonymous to avoid lobbying from food industry groups such as the Soft Drink Association, the Wheat Council, the National Dairy Council and the United Fresh Fruit and Vegetable Association. Final results were presented by the U.S. Department of Health and Human Services.

By law, federal dietary guidelines must be revised every five years based on the latest research. Compared to those of 2000, the 2005 guidelines lower the daily servings of bread, cereals, rice and pasta from nine to seven, with whole grain choices making up at least three of those recommended. Servings of fruits and vegetables grew from five to seven per day. Exercise suggestions have been beefed up to a daily 30 minutes of moderate or vigorous activity to prevent weight gain.

Even the USDA's food pyramid, which debuted in 1992, was overhauled, with the new graphic released in the spring of 2005. The new guidelines appear in the form of a "radiant pyramid," which displays food groups fanning from the point at the top of the pyramid to the base rather than stacked one on top of another. In addition, exercise is emphasized by a figure climbing up steps that ascend the side of the pyramid.

The impact of the new guidelines on the food industry is significant. The snack food industry (which tends to make heavily salted snacks) scored a coup in that the 2005 guidelines limit sodium levels to 2,300 milligrams per day (about one teaspoon), down by a mere 100 milligrams from the guidelines published in 2000. This is despite the fact that many in the medical community suggest a far lower daily level. Likewise, the sugar industry benefits from the new guidelines because, although they continue to caution against the consumption of sugary soft drinks, the warning is not as prominently stressed as in 2000.

PepsiCo, Inc. instigated a test program in late 2006 in which healthier versions of its snacks such as Baked Cheetos and Baked Lay's chips are placed in prominent positions in convenience stores in the urban Chicago area. The test comes on the heels of PepsiCo's millions of dollars in investment in the marketing of its lower fat, lower calorie snacks that, in the first six months of 2006, enjoyed a sales growth of 15% compared to a growth of only 5% for core products such as Doritos and Ruffles fried chips.

Portion sizes, in the U.S. especially, are beginning to shrink in response to wide media attention to the evils of extra-large portions. For example, McDonald's Quarter Pounder with cheese, supersized fries and supersized soft drink totaled a whopping 1,550 calories, until the widely anticipated release of a 2004 documentary called *Super Size Me*. The film, which chronicled the filmmaker's experience of a month-long, McDonald's-only diet, attracted hundreds of thousands of moviegoers and likely influenced the fast food giant to discontinue its supersize promotions altogether in the U.S. (Conversely, rival fast food chain Hardee's introduced its 1,400-calorie "Monster Thickburger" that same year.)

Recently, McDonald's has enjoyed tremendous success with healthier, lower-fat items such as salads and fruit. Meanwhile one of the fastest-growing food categories at restaurants in the U.S. is Japanese food, such as that found at Yoshinoya, a Tokyo-based fast food chain that is opening dozens of outlets in California. Japanese food is often conceived by consumers to be healthier and lower in fat.

Only one country has achieved any sort of success rate in combating the obesity epidemic. Singapore, which requires military service of all adults, has instigated an extended six-week training camp for recruits who are obese in addition to its 10-week basic boot camp. After discharge from the service, most Singaporean men and women remain on reserve status, which requires an annual physical and basic fitness test.

Cashing in on Fat: The Weight Loss Industry

Sales of weight loss programs and products such as Weight Watchers, Jenny Craig and Slim-Fast exceeded $30 billion in 2005. Additional revenues generated by gyms, health clubs and weight loss prescriptions raise the total to $40 billion. By the end of 2007, total revenues in the weight loss industry were expected to exceed $48 billion.

Weight Watchers is the top weight-loss company with $1.233 billion in 2006 revenue. Jenny Craig, Inc., a subsidiary of Nestlé, is another top weight loss company. Two popular diet programs that restrict carbohydrates, the Atkins diet and The Zone, are also producing food products such as nutrition bars, baking mixes and meal replacement drinks.

Major food companies are hoping to cash in on the latest diet craze, since watching the growth in sales of carbohydrate restricted products soar from 41.7% in 2002 to 163.8% in 2004, only to fall by 10.5% in 2005. The next fad that these companies are betting on is foods that help control appetite by creating a sense of fullness or satiety. Unilever's SlimFast is selling an "Optima" version of its meal replacement shakes that promises to keep dieters full for up to four hours. Danone SA is selling "Saciactiv" yogurt, which contains a fiber additive that triggers the release of hormones in the stomach to increase the feeling of fullness.

17) Health Care Goes Offshore, Private Clinics Thrive in China and India

Many people might assume that certain professions could never be outsourced, such as the work of health care professionals. This is not entirely true. For example, in a practice called teleradiology, medical technicians and physicians in India and elsewhere are analyzing x-rays and CAT scans performed in the U.S., diagnosing American patients and relaying results back to American hospitals. In fact, telemedicine has advanced greatly in recent years, and certain physicians provide long-distance patient evaluations on a regular basis. While this is typically done for a patient in a difficult-to-reach location, such as a ship at sea or an offshore oil rig, it could just as easily be a pediatrician in Bangalore discussing a toddler in Omaha's symptoms with the mother via teleconferencing.

Meanwhile, certain less-skilled health care tasks are rapidly moving offshore. Most notably, tens of thousands of jobs in medical record transcription have been moved from the U.S. to offshore centers. These workers, who are trained in medical terminology, use the Internet to access the tape-recorded notes of physicians regarding patients in the U.S. Those notes are transcribed into written databases for permanent storage and future access.

Additionally, there's the growing practice of medical tourism. That is, an increasing number of patients who live in places like the U.S., Canada and the U.K. are traveling abroad to undergo serious surgery. In 2005 in India alone, an estimated 150,000 foreigners sought treatment according to consultants McKinsey & Company. (More than 500,000 Americans sought medical attention overseas in 2006.) McKinsey & Company projects that India's medical tourism revenues could reach $2.2 billion by 2012.

Several factors make this a growing trend. First, the price of international travel has become quite reasonable. Next, a procedure like a hip replacement or a triple bypass can be obtained in nations such as India at as little as 10% to 30% of the cost of the same procedure in the U.S. Since many patients in the U.S. are either underinsured or not insured at all, the cost savings sound very appealing. In addition, in nations like Canada and the U.K., where medicine is socialized, the wait to get an appointment with and obtain care from a specialist can be months or even years (and some "elective" procedures are not covered by government payment programs). Consequently, patients are more likely to consider going offshore. Finally, many physicians in India and elsewhere received their training in the finest clinics and hospitals in the U.S., Canada and the U.K. Several of them have returned to their home nations where they are opening clinics specifically for medical tourists.

At the same time, new private clinics are attracting wealthy locals in China and India. In China, for example, residents who can afford it may sign up for care via a private health program offered by Beijing Universal Medical Assistance, at a fee equal to a few thousand dollars yearly. While the fees are vastly higher than those at the state-run public clinics, these private clinics feature luxury surroundings and prompt, quality service for basic health care needs. Look for the number of larger private hospitals in China to grow, with services expanded to acute care.

A new business sector is opening up, one that manages medical tourism. For example, MedRetreat, a medical tourism agency based in Odenton, Maryland, partners with hospitals in Brazil, Thailand, India, Argentina, South Africa and Malaysia to provide cosmetic, dental and medical procedures to U.S. patients. The company schedules procedures, arranges flights and hotel stays and assigns guides to facilitate the process. For 2006, MedRetreat served 250 patients.

Another medical tourism company, IndUSHealth, is based in North Carolina and outsources medical procedures to hospitals, clinics and physicians in India. IndUSHealth focuses on companies rather than individual patients. Specifically, these are companies that self-insure or pay employees' health care costs directly instead of contracting with an insurance provider.

Agencies like MedRetreat and IndUSHealth generate most of their revenue from commissions for booking hotel rooms and taking 20% discounts on treatments offered by the providers for referrals. The potential is enormous since growing numbers of Americans, Canadians and Brits are looking to medical tourism to lower their health care costs. However, there is no regulation of the practice, and lawsuits or severe medical problems that arise as a result of a mishandled procedure could cripple the infant industry. In late 2006, a test case in which an employee of Blue Ridge Paper Products in Canton, North Carolina was set to go to India for a gall-bladder procedure was scrapped when the employee's union, United Steelworkers, raised questions about the quality of overseas health care and medical liability in case something went wrong.

Despite these obstacles, medical tourism agencies are betting that low prices and western-trained practitioners will insure their success. Some analysts predict that global medical tourism could grow into a $40 billion industry by 2010.

Meanwhile, the states of Colorado and West Virginia introduced bills in their state legislatures in 2007 that call for insurance companies that cover state employees to pay for procedures done overseas, including transportation and lodging. The bills call for insurers to offer patients incentives for choosing cheaper overseas care, paying 20% of the cost savings to the patients. The remaining 80% is to be deposited in accounts used to reduce health premiums for all covered employees. It remains to be seen how much controversy such practices may create and whether these bills become law.

18) Disease Management Programs Take Root

A logical way to reduce the cost of care is through disease management, that is, the use of programs that closely monitor the condition of a patient on a regular basis while educating and motivating that person about lifestyle and treatment alternatives that will reduce the impacts of certain conditions. For example, people who suffer from obesity, asthma, diabetes, high blood pressure, chronic pain, high cholesterol and other such conditions are very likely candidates for disease management.

The intent for many patients will be to encourage changes in diet, exercise and other daily habits in order to reduce weight or lower cholesterol. For patients who are suffering from conditions that have become chronic or dangerous, more aggressive disease management may be offered. Remote monitoring of basic signs such as blood pressure may be utilized.

For example, PepsiCo has offered a program that pays its employees a $100 bonus for filling out a health questionnaire covering subjects such as smoking, weight and blood pressure. Employees who are facing obvious health risks are turned over to disease management coaches who work with them on a regular basis to improve conditions. Many benefit managers see this is a great step forward, with excellent cost control potential through preventative medicine, and performance and quality of life improvements for employees.

Companies offering disease management services include Matria Healthcare and Healthways. Also, major health insurance firms and health services providers are developing their own disease management units, including CuraScript (formerly Priority Healthcare), QMed, McKesson and UnitedHealth Group.

19) Clinics Open in Retail Store Settings

More and more in recent years, the delivery of health care is moving away from the hospital into outpatient clinics and surgery centers. Now, consumers in many cities can go to the local discount store or drug store for basic health care.

A Pennsylvania-based firm, Take Care Health Systems LLC, runs clinics in drugstore chains such as Walgreens, which acquired the company in 2007. Competitor MinuteClinic has dozens of locations in CVS drugstores and Target stores and was recently acquired by CVS. RediClinic operates locations in H-E-B, Wal-Mart and Walgreens stores.

Wal-Mart has already learned the importance of offering a diverse range of services within its stores. For example, it has found that adding supermarket departments to Wal-Mart SuperCenter stores has added greatly to the non-food sales in those stores. When customers visit to buy groceries, they are very likely to go into other departments to shop. The same could easily prove true for customers who drop in to visit the in-store clinics. And, if your six-year-old daughter has an ear infection, why not have her treated at the shopping center while you grab a few things for dinner? These clinics should provide a good boost to in-store pharmacies as well, as patients have their prescriptions filled at the pharmacy counter down the aisle.

The in-store clinics offer reasonable costs and great convenience. Also, the setting may seem less intimidating to some consumers than a trip to a medical office center or full-scale clinic building. Visits to these new in-store clinics range from about $20 to $60 in cost. Many of the patients will be people with no health insurance coverage—cost will be a major consideration. However, since charges are generally much less than those of traditional doctors' offices, health insurers will also be pleased with these clinics. Procedures provided tend to be basic, such as flu shots, a quick physical required for participation on a sports team, or treatment for a simple infection or a minor illness. They tend to be staffed by nurse practitioners. These practitioners have extended educations and special licenses that in many states across the nation allow them to treat minor illness and write simple prescriptions. In some states, they must work in conjunction and consultation with MDs, but the MDs need not be present at the time of treatment.

Since its acquisition by Walgreens, Take Care clinics are expected to be in 400 Walgreens stores by the end of 2008. Within Take Care's clinics, advanced information systems will manage the patients' records, collect information about symptoms during consultations and provide suggestions about diagnoses. If a prescription is called for, they will automatically send the prescription to the in-store pharmacy or to the drug store of the patient's choice.

Dentistry has long been offered in retail environments by companies such as Castle Dental Centers, Inc. and Coast Dental Services, Inc. A new twist to retail dentistry is a mobile dental clinic. On-Site Dental is a Las Vegas, Nevada company with $450,000 buses, each containing fully equipped dental clinics with at least two chairs, hygienists and dentists. In 2005, the company took in $3 million in insurance reimbursements for dental procedures, and it has recently signed contracts to provide dental services to U.S. military units, SprintNextel, NetApp and the U.S. Open Cycling Championships.

Companies to Watch—In-Store Clinics

Take Care Health Systems LLC, www.takecarehealth.com

MinuteClinic, www.minuteclinic.com

RediClinic, www.rediclinic.com

The Outlook for Health Care Technology

20) Health Care Technology Introduction

In recent years, the health care industry has capitalized on many remarkable advances in medical technology, including breakthroughs in computing, communications, small-incision surgery, drug therapies, diagnostics and instruments. For example, huge advances are being made in the fields of cardiovascular care, cancer care, diagnostic imaging and testing, organ transplants and minimally invasive surgery.

In the area of drug development, innovative methods, including genome mapping and high-throughput screening, are providing a clearer understanding of the potential of drugs before they are sent into clinical trials. In addition, the FDA has hired legions of employees in recent years to help process applications for new drugs, medical procedures and equipment.

Meanwhile, more emphasis is being placed on the use of computers and advanced telecommunication technology in many phases of hospital operations and patient care, often in conjunction with complex equipment, to diagnose and improve patients' conditions. Investors, well aware of the long term potential growth of the industry, continue to be anxious to fund new health technologies.

The first part of the 21st Century promises to bring even greater milestones in human health as we begin to reap the benefits of new therapies created through biotechnology and genetic engineering. As our understanding of human biology at the molecular level matures, genetically engineered pharmaceuticals and gene therapies will be developed that target diseases at their molecular origins, thus lessening the need for more costly elements of treatment such as invasive surgery and acute care. If applied during the early stages of disease development, these new biotechnologies will extend and improve the quality of life for the patient. If the disease has already caused the failure or malfunction of vital organs or tissue, it may one day be possible for the patient to receive a fully functioning, genetically engineered replacement, grown from cells harvested from the patient's own tissues. Gene mapping and proteomics will allow researchers to halt disease before it becomes symptomatic, and patients may be screened to determine whether they are genetically predisposed to certain diseases. Knowledge obtained from biomedical research will also help to improve the general health of the public by identifying beneficial behavioral changes. Meanwhile, advanced imaging technology, including recently-introduced 64-slice CT scanning, will greatly enhance physicians' ability to diagnose patients and lead to earlier intervention and higher rates of cure.

HIFU, The Next Big Thing?

High Intensity Focused Ultrasound (HIFU) is a noninvasive method of using sound waves to produce a focused amount of high heat in tumors or tissues in order to destroy them through thermoablation. Target temperature is about 70 to 90 degrees Centigrade (158 to 194 degrees Fahrenheit). Thousands of men have been treated for prostate cancer in this manner, particularly in France, Italy, Canada, the U.K., Japan and Korea. Late stage clinical trials were being conducted in the U.S. as of 2007. Several additional uses are being studied, including trials in the U.K. using HIFU for treatment of cancer of the kidney. HIFU may eventually be used as a noninvasive, outpatient therapy for a wide variety of cancers and other conditions. Currently, affluent American men are traveling to HIFU clinics in Canada, Mexico and the Dominican Republic for quick prostate treatments at a cost of about $20,000. The treatment takes about two hours and is typically done with a local anesthetic. Despite the high price, these patients see HIFU as a very desirable alternative to surgery or radiation. Long-term outcome statistics look very promising. Watch for widespread adoption of HIFU in clinics in the U.S., which will make the treatment readily available and will drive the cost down to a reasonable level.

21) Information Technology and Health Care

According to the Pew Internet & American Life Project, 79% of Internet users in the U.S. search for health care information. Studies by other firms have shown that nearly one-half of people seeking online health information do so to research information on a specific disease, while many others are interested in educational services, prescription drug information, fitness and alternative medicine. About 90% of those who searched for health care information online indicated that what they found was reliable.

Internet Research Tip:
According to The Medical Library Association (www.mlanet.org), the top 10 most useful web sites for health care information are:
National Cancer Institute, www.cancer.gov

Centers for Disease Control and Prevention (CDC), www.cdc.gov
FamilyDoctor.org, www.familydoctor.org
Health Finder, www.healthfinder.gov , a service of the U.S. Dept. of Health & Human Services
HIV InSite, http://hivinsite.ucsf.edu
KidsHealth, www.kidshealth.org
Mayo Clinic, www.mayoclinic.com
MEDEM Medical Library, www.medem.com
MEDLINEplus, www.medlineplus.gov
NOAH: New York Online Access to Health, www.noah-health.org

Internet Research Tip—Checking a Web Site's Accuracy Rating:
When researching health care web sites, look for the seal of approval from the Health on the Net Foundation (www.hon.ch), a nonprofit organization based in Geneva, Switzerland. Founded in 1995 at the behest of international medical experts, the foundation approves medical web sites that meet or exceed its guidelines.

The Internet is also radically transforming the relationship between doctor and patient, since patients can obtain information previously not available from traditional resources. Consumers are now demanding the information necessary to help them make educated decisions regarding medical care. The Internet has allowed patients to walk into their doctors' offices with information in their hands that doctors didn't know about or simply wouldn't supply in the past. Patients can obtain straightforward information from the Internet about their diseases. This empowerment forces physicians to treat the patient more like a partner. It is a fundamental shift of knowledge from physician to patient. E-mail discussions between patient and doctor are growing in popularity. Blue Cross Blue Shield of Florida is offering thousands of physicians the option to be paid for consulting with patients online, via a secure web site.

Internet Research Tip—Getting Hospital Ratings Online:
Patients and concerned family members can now use any of several web sites to check on the quality of hospitals before checking in for treatment. Available data typically includes patient outcomes, fees and whether the latest in technology is available. For patients needing specialized care, this knowledge can be a real windfall. Subimo, at www.subimo.com, gets high marks for its ease of use. It sells subscriptions to major employers and health plans, whose members can then log in. Other sites include HealthGrades, www.healthgrades.com, Medicare's Hospital Compare at www.hospitalcompare.hhs.gov and United Healthcare's www.myUHC.com, designed to be used by the millions of patients who are covered by United.

Useful Internet sites can aid patients in finding a specialist, checking to see how a local hospital measures up and obtaining information about prescription drugs. For example, the American Medical Association (www.ama-assn.org) offers a searchable database with information on doctors' educations and specialties. RxList (www.rxlist.com) allows visitors to search for a drug by generic or brand name, learn about its potential side effects, become familiar with warnings and read about clinical studies. One of the most promising health care sites is Medscape.com (www.medscape.com), where consumers can access information on topics ranging from AIDS to women's health.

The Internet is also becoming a source of information for health care insurance matters. One company, Change: Healthcare LLC (www.changehealthcare.com) offers a $25 per month online tool called MedBillManager that organizes medical bills into summaries that make working with insurance companies easier. SmartMedicalConsumer is a similar tool offered free by SmartMC LLC (www.smartmedicalconsumer.com). Other online medical bill managers of note are Revolution Health (www.revolutionhealth.com), which offers a telephone service to answer questions and will fight disputed insurance claims for $129 per year; and Quicken Medical Expense Manager software ($50), from the bookkeeping software company.

The Internet is also becoming a useful tool for medical professionals. For example, a surgeon can obtain clinical information relevant to surgical practice, both from general professional sites and through specialty and sub-specialty sites. The surgeon can also follow links to other sites offering information on updated techniques or research and educational opportunities. Online discussion groups are growing in popularity; these forums are useful for physicians with similar interests who wish to share information. Another exciting development is live surgeries that can be viewed via webcams. Surgeons and students all over the world can watch and learn from surgical procedures from the comfort of their own homes or offices.

A promising service for diabetics has been developed through the combined efforts of the American Diabetes Association and the insurance group Kaiser Permanente. Together they launched a web site for people with diabetes that suggests customized treatment plans. It is based on a complex software program, developed at a cost of several million dollars, that models health care outcomes based on specified criteria such as medication, diet, demographics and exercise. The software accesses a massive database containing years of patient data. The web site, Diabetes PHD, www.diabetes.org/diabetesphd/, could prove a model for web sites for dozens of other diseases and the patients who suffer from them.

Another Internet innovation that assists diabetes patients is the ability for physicians to monitor glucose levels online. Medem, Inc. launched an online service that saves diabetes patients from multiple office visits to check blood-glucose levels, while giving physicians the ability to evaluate patients' blood sugar levels more frequently. The tool links patients' glucose meters to their computers, then transmits information from those meters to a secure server via the Internet.

RFID Inventory Systems: RFID (radio frequency identification) will be a huge breakthrough in hospital inventory management. RFID systems are based on the placement of microchips in product packaging. These chips, continuously broadcasting product identification data, are used with special sensors in handheld devices or on shelves that alert a central inventory management system about product usage and the need to restock inventory. From loading docks to stockroom shelves to the hospital floor, radio frequency readers will wirelessly track the movement of each and every item, replacing bar codes. These systems will lead to fewer out-of-stock situations and the elimination of costly manual inventory counts.

Johns Hopkins hospital adopted RFID in order to track bags of intravenous fluid, one of the thousands of possible applications that could save the medical industry much of the estimated $75 billion a year currently lost due to mistakes in the prescription, storage and delivery of drugs. RFID chips and the scanners that look after them are rapidly becoming smaller and cheaper and will be steadily adopted for more and more items in hospitals and pharmacies as costs fall. Beyond the monetary savings through better inventory control, RFID systems could save some of the many people who die every year due to errors in prescription drug delivery.

RFID tags implanted in the wristbands worn by hospital patients will also reduce patient identification mistakes, thereby reducing instances of errors in treatment. Data gathered electronically from RFID systems will be integrated with enterprise-wide computer systems throughout the hospital.

The U.S. pharmaceutical industry, with the cooperation of the FDA, began voluntary use of RFID tags on containers of prescription drugs in 2005. The FDA is relying on a nonprofit group, EPCglobal, www.epcglobalinc.org, in Lawrenceville, New Jersey, to set standards for the tags, which have the potential to cut down on stolen drugs, counterfeiting of drugs, drug-related fraud and the dispensing of the wrong drugs. If early use of these tags proves satisfactory, use on all drug containers could become mandatory over the mid-term.

Internet Research Tip:
The Medical Records Institute, www.medrecinst.com provides in depth discussion of electronic health records (EHRs) at its web site. In particular, see the "Health IT Library" page.

Advanced Information Technology and Medical Records Technology: There is a strong movement in the United States, the U.K., Canada and elsewhere to implement widespread use of electronic health records (EHRs). A major goal in this movement is to create Continuity of Care Records (CCRs), which would ensure that a patient's health history could be utilized seamlessly by hospitals, primary care physicians and specialists.

In 2006, in a largely bi-partisan vote, both bodies of the U.S. Congress passed a bill to promote the adoption of the computer hardware and software necessary to create and share EHRs. Proponents of the records estimate that they could significantly reduce medical errors, save lives and cut billions in medical spending a year—as much as $80 billion to $160 billion annually—in shortened hospital stays, reduced nursing time, savings on unnecessary drugs (or drugs that could dangerously react to medications already prescribed for a patient) and the reduction of redundant lab tests and paperwork. Physicians, caregivers and researchers could also benefit enormously by tracking clinical data nationwide and learning which treatments are most effective in any given situation.

The Bush Administration hopes to have an EHR for every American by 2014, as part of its Consolidated Health Informatics Initiative (CHI). The information in those records would be shared on a medical Internet called the National Health Information Network, Inc. (NHIN). The government will pick up the tab for building the network's backbone and creating standards for sharing data. Physicians and hospitals are expected to pay for their own computers and software necessary to connect to the network, an undertaking that is estimated to cost as much as $150 billion over five years.

Such an undertaking is a tall order, especially considering the fact that in mid-2006, only 20% of U.S. physicians use EHRs. However, the potential savings in lives and medical costs could help doctors and medical facilities to bear the initial costs.

The reduction of errors in patient care, in addition to financial savings and productivity improvements, is a major impetus for computerizing the entire health system. An estimated 195,000 deaths occur in hospitals each year from medical errors, ranging from simple cases of neglect to giving patients incorrect medications to extreme cases such as performing the wrong surgery. Information technology (IT) is seen by some as a cure for accidental in-hospital mortality rates, as well as the road to the promised land of efficiencies in costs and time. Historically, the health care industry has lagged behind almost all other business sectors in information system spending as a percent of revenues.

Opponents to the adoption of the NHIN voice concerns about privacy, since database security breaches have occurred time and time again. Others, including legislators and physicians, argue that digitizing medical data is only one step to fixing a national health care system that is in crisis.

Standards Adopted at the Federal level for the Consolidated Health Informatics Initiative (CHI)

As part of the CHI initiative, federal departments that deliver health care services—the Department of Health and Human Services (HHS), the Department of Defense and the Department of Veterans Affairs—are working with other federal agencies to identify appropriate, existing data standards and to endorse them for use across the federal health care sector. These include:

- Health Level 7 (HL7) vocabulary standards for demographic information, units of measure, immunizations, clinical encounters and HL7's Clinical Document Architecture standard for text-based reports.
- The College of American Pathologists Systematized Nomenclature of Medicine Clinical Terms (SNOMED-CT) for laboratory result contents, non-laboratory interventions and procedures, anatomy, diagnosis and nursing. HHS is making SNOMED-CT available for use in the United States at no charge to users.
- Laboratory Logical Observation Identifier Name Codes (LOINC) to standardize the electronic exchange of laboratory test orders and drug label section headers.
- The Health Insurance Portability and Accountability Act of 1996 (HIPAA) set standards for transactions and code sets for the electronic exchange of health related information necessary to perform billing or administrative functions. These are the same standards now required under HIPAA for health plans, health care clearinghouses and those health care providers who engage in certain electronic transactions.
- A set of federal terminologies related to medications, including the Food and Drug Administration's names and codes for ingredients, manufactured dosage forms, drug products and medication packages; the National Library of Medicine's RxNORM for describing clinical drugs; and the Veterans Administration's National Drug File Reference Terminology (NDF-RT) for specific drug classifications.
- The Human Gene Nomenclature (HUGN) for exchanging information regarding the role of genes in biomedical research in the federal health sector.
- The Environmental Protection Agency's Substance Registry System for non-medicinal chemicals of importance to health care.

Developments in the U.K.'s public health system will likely spur the American effort to digitize medical records and patient care. In December 2003, England's National Health Service (NHS) announced plans for a $17 billion project to wire every hospital, doctor's office and clinic by 2008. The British government supplied $3.9 billion for a three-year period from 2004 to 2007, to be followed by another $13 billion. When complete, information on each and every one of the 50 million patients registered in the U.K. national system will reside in a central database. Appointments and referrals will be scheduled online, and doctors' orders and prescriptions will be transmitted automatically to other caregivers and pharmacies. The system could serve as the electronic records and digitized patient care model for the rest of the world.

Several U.S. technology companies, including IBM, bid for the lucrative contracts that split the U.K. job into several multi-million-dollar projects. One major contract concerns the national database of patient records. Five additional contracts address regional networks, which will communicate with the central database. An $108 million contract has already been granted to SchlumbergerSema to handle online appointment booking.

In Canada, another ambitious technical initiative is underway. The Canadian government is investing $844 million in EHR systems. The goal is to link 50% of the country's medical community. Experts estimate that an additional $1.07 billion will be necessary to take the project from coast to coast so that all Canadian health records will be digital.

Several major electronic medical claims processors have been established in the U.S. A pioneer was WebMD. MedAvant Healthcare Solutions also provides electronic processing services. The company was initially a coalition by Aetna, Anthem, Cigna, Heath Net, Oxford, PacifiCare and WellPoint Health Systems called MedUnite. Growth in health care transaction processing is still far from over. Billions of transactions occur every year in the U.S., including prescription processing, insurance claims and so on.

The computer industry is also struggling to convert physicians to the use of PCs and Internet devices. For example, there are dozens of competing platforms attempting to get doctors to use wireless Palm-type devices or personal digital assistants (PDAs) to prescribe medications. This practice reduces medical errors, since electronic orders are easily legible and can be checked for conflicts with other medications currently taken by the patient. The PDAs check and notify physicians of drugs not covered by insurance or those to which a patient is allergic. Some systems can transmit physicians' orders directly to a local server, which then generates faxes to pharmacies or clinics. To eliminate fraud, doctors submit electronic signatures for verification, and drug store systems check for recognized fax numbers. In 2007, computer chip manufacturer Intel, Inc. announced the development of a new mobile clinical assistant, the C5, a lightweight, spill-resistant wireless device that displays patient records to nurses during treatment.

As more physicians and clinics digitize, the need for standardization grows. A consortium, RxHub (www.rxhub.net), has created a standard electronic prescription format that is gaining acceptance within the industry. In addition, RxHub maintains a database of patients' medication histories.

Meanwhile, patients can now opt into online databases where they can enter and store personal health information that can be accessed by their physicians and other care providers. Companies offering this service include Medem, Inc. and Access Strategies, Inc. Some major employers, including Cicso Systems, are buying into this concept. The idea is that covered employees can have efficiently-organized, readily-accessed records that they can take with them if they move to another employer.

As hospitals and other major health care providers scramble to digitize, concerns about the quality of patient care have been voiced. As a result, caregivers and insurers have combined forces to monitor the changes brought about by the technological boom. The Leapfrog Group, a coalition of over 170 companies and private organizations that provides health care benefits, was created to improve, among other things, the flow of patient data and benchmarks for patient outcomes at hospitals. Leapfrog has set exacting standards for the health system to strive for in the creation and utilization of digital data. "Leapfrog compliance" is a catch phrase among hospitals, which are rated on the organization's web site (www.leapfroggroup.org) with regard to compliance issues such as computerized prescription order systems and statistics on staffing and medical procedure success rates.

In addition to Leapfrog, in 2006 a joint effort between 22 electronics and health care companies formed to help make high-tech medical tools work better together. This organization, the Continua Health Alliance (www.continuaalliance.org), includes partners such as Nokia, Panasonic, Philips, Samsung, Cisco Systems, Intel, Kaiser Permanente and Medtronic.

Many medical innovations are becoming widespread. For example, "med carts" equipped with computers and bar code scanners allow nurses to scan patients' identifying wristbands to verify identity and medication orders, improving safety and efficiency. These carts will evolve to use RFID instead of bar codes. In addition, examination and operating rooms are now often equipped with wireless laptops that transmit on-the-spot notes and evaluations for each patient to a central information system.

Remote Patient Monitoring: Visicu, Inc., a Baltimore, Maryland medical information technology company, offers an ICU remote monitoring system called eICU. The system is a combination of software, video and audio feeds and real-time patient vital statistics that hooks patients in ICUs in multiple hospitals to central monitoring facilities manned by ICU specialists. A specialist at the central location mans a standing desk outfitted with five monitors that display patient data, including real-time video and audio for up to 70 patients at a time. The system ranks patients according to their conditions and flags gravely ill patients in red so that their progress can be more easily monitored. Indications such as changes in blood pressure alert the specialist who then contacts the nurse or physician on duty to treat the patient accordingly.

As of mid-2006, only 7% of ICU beds were remotely monitored. Cost is one factor, since a system for one ICU goes for roughly $228,000, and insurance and Medicare do not reimburse hospitals for the technology. However, hospitals that do have eICU have experienced significant cost savings since the system cuts the average ICU stay from 4.4 days to 3.6 by lowering the instances of complications such as pneumonia and infections (these conditions generally occur when patients are not closely monitored by ICU specialists). The Leapfrog Group estimates that 54,000 patients per year could be saved if every U.S. ICU were monitored by specialists. Without technology such as eICU, 25,000 specialists would be needed to staff ICUs sufficiently, while there are only 6,000 such specialists currently licensed to practice.

Other remote monitoring systems are allowing patients to be monitored at home or at out-of-the-way care facilities. For example, American Telecare, Inc.'s CareTone Telephonic Stethoscope checks for heart, lung and bowel sounds using a small stethoscope, a phone line and two-way video stations. Cardiocom LLC's Telescale is a telemonitoring device integrated with an electronic scale. The patient steps onto the scale and answers questions using a touch pad about his or her symptoms. The answers and the patient's weight are communicated via two-way messaging to the consulting physician, who is alerted if there is any deterioration in the patient's health. The system also sends alerts back to the patient for follow-up visits or care plan adjustments.

Sales of health monitoring devices reached $461 million in 2005 in the U.S., according to analysts at Parks Associates, a Dallas, Texas research and consulting firm. Annual sales are expected to grow to over $2.5 billion in 2010. The use of remote monitoring in Europe is also growing at a rapid pace. The EU projects that telemedicine will account for 5% of its health care spending by 2010, up from approximately 1% in 2000.

Computer Modeling: In recent times, impressive advances in computer modeling have lead to accurate mapping of very complex systems, including weather, planetary orbits and molecular interaction. Health care is another natural application of these capabilities. Everything from genes to bodily systems could be mapped by computers, allowing scientists to learn more about the complex interactions within the human body. The technology for mapping genes has now been around for quite awhile, but the technology for mapping other biological entities has been sadly absent. However, many scientists have now realized the benefits that could be gained from advanced mapping of the body and all the processes that go on within it. Think of all the innovations computer modeling has brought to the automobile industry, which can now design a car in a matter of months, predict how the car will perform in crashes, how it will react to wind resistance and how it will wear down over time. Now imagine a similar instance in health care: being able to model a complete human body, predict where things might go wrong, or determine how it will react to certain chemicals. Drug development and diagnosis are two obvious areas where health care might benefit from computer modeling.

One of the most promising uses of modeling is in analyzing patient care outcomes to project the best possible treatment for specific diseases and ailments. Patient records are kept in increasingly powerful databases, which can be analyzed to find the history of treatment outcomes. For the first time, payors such as HMOs and insurance companies have vast amounts of data available to them, including answers to questions such as:

- Which procedures and surgeries do and do not bring the desired results?
- Which physicians and hospitals have the highest and lowest rates of cure (or of untimely deaths of patients)?
- What is the average length of stay required for the treatment and recovery of patients undergoing various surgeries?
- How long should it take for the rehabilitation of a patient with a worker's compensation claim for a specific type of injury?

This knowledge will soon be essentially unlimited, and the result will be higher efficiency and increased use of the most effective treatment and rehabilitation regimens.

Scientists at Oxford in England, as well as at the University of California, San Diego and several other universities, have been developing models of the heart, liver and other organs, hoping to eventually build a complete model of the human body. The project to model the heart intends to mimic everything from chemical reactions up through cellular reactions, all coming together to make an almost perfect model of the heart. In this way, scientists can construct a "normal" heart, and then compare it to images of irregular or diseased hearts, in order to find out what goes wrong and, possibly, how to repair it. Novartis, a leading drug manufacturer, is already using a model of the heart to predict how the heart will react to different drugs, hoping to come up with a compound that can keep hearts healthy or heal them after a heart attack.

Internet Research Tip—Body Computer Modeling:
There are now several companies that are working on modeling human systems:
Immersion Medical, Gaithersburg, MD
www.immersion.com/medical (simulation of the human body for training and education)
Insilicomed, La Jolla, CA
www.insilicomed.com (biological models)
Predix Pharmaceuticals, Woburn, MA
www.predixpharm.com (drug discovery)

22) Stem Cells—Controversy in the U.S. Threatens to Leave America Far Behind in the Research Race

During the 1980s, a biologist at Stanford University, Irving L. Weissman, was the first to isolate the stem cell that builds human blood (the mammalian hematopoietic cell). Later, Weissman isolated a stem cell in a laboratory mouse and went on to co-found SysTemix, Inc. (now part of drug giant Novartis) and StemCells, Inc. to continue this work in a commercial manner.

In November 1998, two different university-based groups of researchers announced that they had accomplished the first isolation and characterization of the human embryonic stem cell (HESC). One group was led by James A. Thomson at the University of Wisconsin at Madison. The second was led by John D. Gearhart at the Johns Hopkins University School of Medicine at Baltimore. The HESC is among the most versatile basic building blocks in the human body. Embryos, when first conceived, begin creating small numbers of HESCs, and these cells eventually differentiate and develop into the more than 200 cell types that make up the distinct tissues and organs of the human body. If scientists can reproduce and then guide the development of these basic HESCs, then they could theoretically grow replacement organs and tissues in the laboratory—even such complicated tissue as brain cells or heart cells.

Ethical and regulatory difficulties have arisen from the fact that the only source for human "embryonic" stem cells is, logically enough, human embryos. A laboratory can obtain these cells in one of three ways: 1) by inserting a patient's DNA into an egg, thus producing a blastocyst that is a clone of the patient—which is then destroyed after only a few days of development; 2) by harvesting stem cells from aborted fetuses; or 3) by harvesting stem cells from embryos that are left over and unused after an in vitro fertilization of a hopeful mother. (Artificial in vitro fertilization requires the creation of a large number of test tube embryos per instance, but only one of these embryos is used in the final process.)

A rich source of similar but "non-embryonic" stem cells is bone marrow. Doctors have been performing bone marrow transplants in humans for years. This procedure essentially harnesses the healing power of stem cells, which proliferate to create healthy new blood cells in the recipient. Several other non-embryonic stem cell sources have great promise (see "Potential methods of developing 'post-embryonic' stem cells without the use of human embryos" below).

In the fall of 2001, a small biotech company called Advanced Cell Technology, Inc. announced the first cloning of a human embryo. The announcement set off yet another firestorm of rhetoric and debate on the scientific and ethical questions that cloning and related stem cell technology inspire. While medical researchers laud the seemingly infinite possibilities stem cells promise for fighting disease and the aging process, conservative theologians, many government policy makers, certain ethics organizations and pro-life groups decry the harvest of cells from aborted fetuses and the possibility of cloning as an ethical and moral abomination.

Stem cell research has been underway for years at biotech companies including Stem Cells, Inc., Geron and ViaCell. One company, Osiris Therapeutics, has been at work long enough to have several clinical trial programs in progress. Osiris derives its stem cells from the bone marrow of healthy adults between the ages of 18 and 30 who are volunteers. Prior to harvesting the stem cells, Osiris screens blood samples of the donors to make sure that they are free of diseases such as HIV and hepatitis. Osiris believes that this approach to gathering stem cells places them outside of the embryonic source controversy.

The potential benefits of stem cell-based therapies are staggering. Neurological disorders might be aided with the growth of healthy cells in the brain. Injured cells in the spinal column might be regenerated. Damaged organs such as hearts, livers and kidneys might be infused with healthy cells. In China, physicians in more than 100 hospitals are already injecting stem cells into damaged spinal cords with varying levels of success.

Potential methods of developing "post-embryonic" stem cells without the use of human embryos:

- Adult Skin Cells—Exposure of harvested adult skin cells to viruses that carry specific genes, capable of reprogramming the skin cells so that they act as stem cells
- Parthenogenesis—manipulation of unfertilized eggs.
- Other Adult Cells—Harvesting adult stem cells from bone marrow or brain tissue.
- Other Cells—harvesting of stem cells from human umbilical cords, placentas or other cells.
- De-Differentiation—use of the nucleus of an existing cell, such as a skin cell, that is altered by an egg that has had its own nucleus removed.
- Transdifferentiation—making a skin cell de-differentiate back to its primordial state so that it can then morph into a useable organ cell, such as heart tissue.

HESCs (typically harvested from five-day-old human embryos which are destroyed during the process) are used because of their ability to evolve into any cell or tissue in the body. Their versatility is undeniable, yet the implications of the death of the embryo are at the heart of the ethical and moral concerns.

Meanwhile, scientists have discovered that there are stem cells in existence in many diverse places in the adult human body, and they are thus succeeding in creating stem cells without embryos, by utilizing "post-embryonic" cells, such as cells from marrow. Such cells are already showing the ability to differentiate and function in animal and human recipients. Best of all, these types of stem cells may not be plagued by problems found in the use of HESCs, such as the tendency for HESCs to form tumors when they develop into differentiated cells. However, Thomas Okarma, CEO and President of Geron, argues that stem cells derived from bone marrow and other adult sources are fundamentally limited in their application, because it is nearly impossible to get them to produce anything besides blood cells. This makes it very difficult to harvest organ or nerve cells.

A landmark approval in 2006 of the blood thinning drug ATryn by the European Commission is the first human protein made by a transgenic animal for commercial production. ATryn is made from the milk of genetically modified goats and is approved initially for use in patients with hereditary deficiency of the human protein antithrombin which inhibits blood clotting. Although antithrombin deficiency is relatively rare (industry analysts value the market for these patients at about $50 million in Europe and the U.S. combined), ATryn may also be used to treat burns, coronary artery bypass surgery, sepsis and bone marrow transplants (up to a $700 million global market).

The biggest news lies in studies published in 2006 and 2007 regarding the reprogramming of adult mouse skin cells into stem cells. Initially, Shinya Yamanaka of Kyoto (Japan) University announced that he and coworkers had exposed skin cells harvested from adult mice to viruses carrying four specific genes. Yamanaka had determined that these four genes are apparently responsible for a stem cell's ability to develop into virtually any type of tissue. The technique is easy to replicate, and it was confirmed by additional studies in the U.S. published in 2007. This may be a tremendous breakthrough in stem cell research. However, scientists are still a long way from overcoming daunting technical challenges and adapting this technique for use in humans.

23) Stem Cell Funding Trickles in the U.S. at the Federal Level While a Few States Create Funding of Their Own

The U.S. Government, in August 2001, set strict limits on the use of federal funding for embryonic stem cell research. This action was taken in spite of impassioned testimony regarding the healing potential of stem cells by physicians, researchers and celebrities, such as actor Michael J. Fox on behalf of research for Parkinson's disease, the late actor Christopher Reeve for spinal injury study and former first lady Nancy Reagan on behalf of Alzheimer's research. The use of non-federal funding, however, is not currently restricted, although many groups would like to see further state or federal level restrictions on stem cell research or usage. A major confrontation is underway between American groups that advocate the potential health benefits of stem cell therapies and groups that decry the use of stem cells on ethical or religious terms. Meanwhile, stem cell development is forging ahead in other technologically advanced nations.

Under current U.S. regulations, federal research funds may be granted only for work with the 78 lines of stem cells that existed in 2001. Harvesting and developing new embryonic lines would not qualify. Once a stem cell starts to replicate, a large colony, or line, of self-replenishing cells can theoretically continue to reproduce forever. Unfortunately, only about a dozen of the stem cell lines existing at the time were considered to be useful, and some scientists believe that these lines are getting tired.

This is not to say that federal funds aren't being used in stem cell research at all. In fact, the Office of Management and Budget reports that total National Institutes of Health is providing some funding for stem cell programs, obviously from "existing" lines.

In November 2004, voters in California approved a unique measure that provides $3 billion in state funding for stem cell research. Connecticut, Massachusetts and New

Jersey have also passed legislation that permits embryonic-stem cell research. California already has a massive biotech industry, spread about San Diego and San Francisco in particular. As approved, California's Proposition 71 creates an oversight committee that will determine how and where grants will be made, and an organization, the California Institute for Regenerative Medicine (www.cirm.ca.gov), to issue bonds for funding and to manage the entire program. The money will be invested in research at a rate of about $295 million yearly over 10 years.

However, a pro-life, not-for-profit group called Life Legal Defense Foundation and a taxpayers group called People's Advocate held up the institute's ability to issue the bonds needed to fund the grants. A lawsuit was been filed in Superior Court in Alameda County, California asserting that the institute cannot legally issue state-backed obligations because the institute doesn't operate under direct state control. In April 2006, the court ruled that the law behind Proposition 71 and California's state-funded stem cell effort is constitutional in its entirety.

In June 2007, the California Institute for Regenerative Medicine approved grants totaling more than $50 million to finance construction of shared research laboratories at 17 academic and non-profit institutions. These facilities are scheduled to be complete and available to researchers within six months to two years of the grant awards. This pushed total funding granted to-date by the organization to more than $200 million. The grants will fund dedicated laboratory space for the culture of human embryonic stem cells (HESCs), particularly those that fall outside federal guidelines.

Meanwhile, many members of the U.S. Congress want to see much greater funding of stem cell research from federal coffers. In a dramatic move in the summer of 2005, Senate majority leader Bill Frist (a physician himself) made a statement backing deeper federal involvement in stem cell research, breaking with the well-known views of President Bush. In 2006, a new bill for the expansion of embryonic stem cell research funding was passed in both the U.S. Senate and the House of Representatives. However, President Bush vetoed the bill, the first veto of his administration. The House vote, which was 235 to 193, was not a two-thirds majority, which would have been the necessary number to override a presidential veto. Reform of federally-funded stem cell research is dead for now.

In the private sector, funding for stem cell research has been generous. For example, the Juvenile Diabetes Research Foundation has an $8 million stem cell research program underway and Stanford University has used a $12 million donation to create a research initiative. Likewise, major, privately funded efforts have been launched at Harvard and at the University of California at San Francisco.

24) Stem Cells—Therapeutic Cloning Techniques Advance

For scientists, the biggest challenge at present may be to discover the exact process by which stem cells are signaled to differentiate. Another big challenge lies in the fact that broad use of therapeutic cloning may require immense numbers of human eggs in which to grow blastocysts.

The clearest path to "therapeutic" cloning may lie in "autologous transplantation." In this method, a tiny amount of a patient's muscle or other tissue would be harvested. This sample's genetic material would then be de-differentiated; that is, reduced to a simple, unprogrammed state. The patient's DNA sample would then be inserted into an egg to grow a blastocyst. The blastocyst would be manipulated so that its stem cells would differentiate into the desired type of tissue, such as heart tissue. That newly grown tissue would then be transplanted to the patient's body. Many obstacles must be overcome before such a transplant can become commonplace, but the potential is definitely there to completely revolutionize healing through such regenerative, stem cell-based processes. One type of bone marrow stem cell, recently discovered by scientists at the University of Minnesota, appears to have a wide range of differentiation capability.

It is instructive to note that there are two distinct types of embryonic cloning: "reproductive" cloning and "therapeutic" cloning. While they have similar beginnings, the desired end results are vastly different.

"Reproductive" cloning is a method of reproducing an exact copy of an animal—or potentially an exact copy of a human being. A scientist would remove the nucleus from a donor's unfertilized egg, insert a nucleus from the animal, or human, to be copied, and then stimulate the nucleus to begin dividing to form an embryo. In the case of a mammal, such as a human, the embryo would then be implanted in the uterus of a host female for gestation and birth. The successful birth of a cloned human baby doesn't necessarily mean that a healthy adult human will result. To date, cloned animals have tended to develop severe health problems. For example, a U.S. firm, Advanced Cell Technology, reports that it has engineered the birth of cloned cows that appeared healthy at first but developed severe health problems after a few years. Nonetheless, successful cloning of animals is progressing at labs in many nations.

On the other hand, "therapeutic" cloning is a method of reproducing exact copies of cells needed for research or for the development of replacement tissue. In this case, once again a scientist removes the nucleus from a donor's unfertilized egg, inserts a nucleus from the animal, or human, whose cells are to be copied, and then stimulates the nucleus to begin dividing to form an embryo. However, in therapeutic use, the embryo would never be allowed to grow to any significant stage of development. Instead, it would be allowed to grow for a few hours or days, and stem cells would then be removed from it for use in regenerating tissue.

Because it can provide a source of stem cells, cloning has uses in regenerative medicine that can be vital in treating many types of disease. The main differences between stem cells derived from clones and those derived from aborted fetuses or fertility specimens is that a) they are made from only one source of genes, rather than by mixing sperm and eggs; and b) they are made specifically for scientific purposes, rather than being existing specimens, putting them up to more intense ethical discussions. Cloned stem cells have the added advantage of being 100% compatible with their donors, because they share the same genes, and so would provide the best possible source for replacement organs and tissues. Although the use of cloning for regeneration has stirred heated debate as well, it has not resulted in universal rejection. Most of the industrialized countries, including Canada, Russia, most of Western Europe and most of Asia, have made some government-sanctioned allowances for research into this area.

As a result of government sanction of research and development, some countries have already made progress in the field of regenerative cloning. In an important development in August 2004, scientists at Newcastle University in the U.K. announced that they have been granted permission by the Human Fertilisation and Embryology Authority (HFEA), a unit of the British Government, to create human embryos as a source of stem cells for certain therapeutic purposes. Specifically, researchers will clone early-stage embryos in search of new treatments for such degenerative diseases as Parkinson's disease, Alzheimer's and diabetes. The embryos will be destroyed before they are two weeks old and will therefore not develop beyond a tiny cluster of cells.

The biggest news to hit therapeutic cloning was the claim by South Korean scientist Hwang Woo Suk of Seoul National University announced that he and his team of researchers had created patient-specific stem cells; that is, cells taken from adult patients and then cloned and further manipulated to become stem cells. Backed by the South Korean government, the breakthrough promised the dawn of a new era of stem cell research with Hwang as the star. However, by December 2005, it became clear that the Korean claims were fraudulent. There were, in fact, no cloned stem cell lines at all.

The good news is that several other cloning methods are on the horizon. Markus Grompe, director of the Oregon Stem Cell Center at Oregon Health and Science University in Portland is working on research similar to that at Newcastle University. Adult donor cells are forced to create a protein called nanog, which is only found in stem cells, yet the process is altered in a way that keeps the cells from forming into embryos. At the same time, researchers at MIT are experimenting with defusing CDX2, a gene in the nucleus of a cell taken from an adult, before transferring the nucleus into a donated human egg that has been stripped of its own DNA. The resulting egg could be developed into stem cells, but due to the lack of CDX2, would be unable to develop into an embryo.

25) Stem Cells—A New Era of Regenerative Medicine Takes Shape

Many firms are conducting product development and research in the areas of skin replacement, vascular tissue replacement and bone grafting or regeneration. Stem cells, as well as transgenic organs harvested from pigs, are under study for use in humans. At its highest and most promising level, regenerative medicine may eventually utilize human stem cells to create virtually any type of replacement organ or tissue.

In one recent, exciting experiment, doctors took stem cells from bone marrow and injected them into the hearts of patients undergoing bypass surgery. The study showed that the bypass patients who received the stem cells were pumping blood 24% better than patients who had not received them.

In another experiment, conducted by Dr. Mark Keating at Harvard, the first evidence was shown that stem cells may be used for regenerating lost limbs and organs. The regenerative abilities of amphibians have long been known, but exactly how they do it, or how it could be applied to mammals, has been little understood. Much of the regenerative challenge lies in differentiation, or the development of stem cells into different types of adult tissue such as muscle and bone. Creatures such as amphibians have the ability to turn their complex cells back into stem cells in order to regenerate lost parts. In the experiment, Dr. Keating made a serum from the regenerating nub (stem cells) of a newt's leg and applied it to adult mouse cells in a petri dish. He observed the mouse cells to "de-differentiate," or turn into stem cells. In a later experiment, de-differentiated cells were turned back into muscle, bone and fat. These experiments could be the first steps to true human regeneration. Keating is continuing to make exciting breakthroughs in regenerative research.

The potential of the relatively young science of tissue engineering appears to be unlimited. Transgenics (the use of organs and tissues grown in laboratory animals for transplantation to humans) is considered by many to have great future potential, and improvements in immune system suppression will eventually make it possible for the human body to tolerate foreign tissue instead of rejecting it. There is also increasing theoretical evidence that malfunctioning or defective vital organs such as livers, bladders and kidneys could be replaced with perfectly functioning "neo-organs" (like spare parts) grown in the laboratory from the patient's own stem cells, with minimal risk of rejection.

The ability of most human tissue to repair itself is a result of the activity of these cells. The potential that cultured stem cells have for transplant medicine and basic developmental biology is enormous.

Diabetics who are forced to cope with daily insulin injection treatments could also benefit from engineered tissues. If they could receive a fully functioning replacement pancreas, diabetics might be able to throw away their hypodermic needles once and for all. This could also save the health care system immense sums, since diabetics tend to suffer from many ailments that require hospitalization and intensive treatment, including blindness, organ failure, diabetic coma and circulatory diseases.

Elsewhere, the harvesting of replacement cartilage, which does not require the growth of new blood vessels, is being used to repair damaged joints and treat urological disorders. Genzyme Corp. recently won FDA approval for its replacement cartilage product Carticel. Genzyme's process involves harvesting the patient's own cartilage-forming cells, and, from those cells, re-growing new cartilage in the laboratory. The physician then injects the new cartilage into the damaged area. Full regeneration of the replacement cartilage is expected to take up to 18 months. The Genzyme process can cost up to $30,000, compared to $10,000 for typical cartilage surgery.

In 1997, Carticel (see www.carticel.com) became the first biologic cell therapy licensed by the FDA under accelerated approval. Since then, more than 10,000 patients have been treated with the Carticel method for treating knee pain. Other companies are exploring alternative methods that may be less expensive and therefore more attractive to payors.

In 2007, U.S. Army medical doctors were treating five soldiers with an extracellular matrix derived from pig bladders. The material is found in all animals and shows promise for healing and regenerating tissue (it is already in use by veterinarians to help repair torn ligaments in horses). The five soldiers in the test lost fingers in the war in Iraq and the experiment is to see how the matrix affects the wounds and if regeneration of any kind occurs.

Companies to Watch: StemCells, Inc., in Palo Alto, California (www.stemcellsinc.com), is focusing on the use of stem cells to treat damage to major organs such as the liver, pancreas and central nervous system. ViaCell, Inc., in Boston, Massachusetts (www.viacellinc.com), develops therapies using umbilical cord stems. Also, their ViaCord product enables families to preserve their baby's umbilical cord at the time of birth for possible future use in treating over 40 diseases and genetic disorders. As of late 2007, 130,000 units of cord blood stem cells had been banked.

Internet Research Tip:
For an excellent primer on genetics and basic biotechnology techniques, see:

National Center for Biotechnology Information
www.ncbi.nlm.nih.gov

26) Gene Therapies and Patients' Genetic Profiles Promise a Personalized Approach to Medicine

Scientists now believe that almost all diseases have some genetic component. For example, some people have a genetic predisposition for breast cancer or heart disease. Understanding of human genetics will soon lead to breakthroughs in gene therapy for many ailments. Organizations ranging from the Mayo Clinic to drug giant GlaxoSmithKline are experimenting with personalized drugs that are designed to provide appropriate therapies based on a patient's personal genetic makeup or their lack of specific genes. Genetic therapy involves splicing desired genes taken from one patient into a second patient's cells in order to compensate for that patient's inherited genetic defect, or to enable that patient's body to better fight a specific disease.

For example, drugs that target the genetic origins of tumors may offer more effective, longer-lasting and far less toxic alternatives to conventional chemotherapy and radiation. One of the most noted drugs that target specific genetic action is Herceptin, a monoclonal antibody that was developed by Genentech. Approved by the FDA in 1998, Herceptin, when used in conjunction with chemotherapy, shows great promise in significantly reducing breast cancer for certain patients who are known to overproduce the HER2 gene. (A simple test is used to determine if this gene is present in the patient.) Herceptin, which works by blocking genetic signals, thus preventing the growth of cancerous cells, may show potential in treating other types of cancer, such as ovarian, pancreatic or prostate cancer.

More recent discoveries include tests that predict side effects from colon cancer drug Irinotecan and best dosage levels for patients taking the blood thinner Warfarin. The Mayo Clinic's Irinotecan test was released in late 2005 and is one of several genetic tests marketed by the clinic. It planned to release an additional 12 tests through 2006. Mayo is also marketing a genetic test that determines whether a patient will respond poorly to antidepressants.

One of the fastest-growing genetic tests is marketed by Genomic Health, based in Redwood City, California. Its Oncotype DX test provides breast cancer patients with an assessment of the likelihood of the recurrence of their cancer based on the expression of 21 different genes in a tumor. The test enables patients to evaluate the results they may expect from post-operative therapies such as Tamoxifen or chemotherapy. The test costs about $3,500, and to-date has generally not been covered by health insurance, despite its potential to save treatment costs. The firm is also doing full-scale clinical development on a test to predict the likelihood of recurrence of colon cancer. Such tests will be standard preventative treatment in coming decades.

The scientific community's rapidly improving knowledge of genes and the role they play in disease is leading to several different tracks for improved treatment results. One track is to profile a patient's genetic makeup for a better understanding of a) which drugs a patient may respond to effectively, and b) whether certain defective genes reside in a patient and are causing a patient's disease or illness. Yet another application of gene testing is to study how a patient's liver is able to metabolize medication, which could help significantly when deciding upon proper dosage. Since today's widely used drugs often produce desired results in only about 50% of patients who receive them, the use of specific medications based on a patient's genetic profile could greatly boost treatment results while cutting costs. Each year, 2.2 million Americans suffer side effects from prescription drugs. Of those, more than 100,000 die, making adverse drug reaction a leading cause of death in the U.S. A Journal of the American Medical Association study states that the annual cost of treating these drug reactions totals $4 billion each year.

A second track for use of genetic knowledge is to attack, and attempt to alter, specific defective genes—this approach is sometimes referred to as "gene therapy." Generally, pure gene therapy attempts to target defective genes within a patient by introducing new copies of normal genes. These new genes may be introduced through the use of viruses or proteins that carry them into the patient's body.

China-based Shenzhen Sibiono GeneTech achieved the world's first pure gene therapy to be approved for wide commercial use in October 2003. The drug is sold under the brand name Gendicine as a treatment for a head and neck cancer known as squamous cell carcinoma (HNSC). The drug has proven highly effective in trials, and the company is testing its technology for several other types of cancer, including esophageal, gastric, colon, liver and rectum. As of mid-2007, the drug was available to Chinese patients at the Haidian Hospital in Beijing and to foreign patients at a facility in Shanghai.

Other applications of gene therapy are already in research in the U.S. and elsewhere for treatment of a wide variety of diseases. For example, gene therapy may be highly effective in the treatment of rare immune system disorders, melanoma (a malignant skin cancer for which there is currently no effective cure once the disease has spread to other organs) and cystic fibrosis. In 2006, two male patients suffering from a rare malady called chronic granulomatous disease (CGD), which makes patients terribly vulnerable to infections, were able to cease taking daily antibiotics due to a gene therapy that introduced healthy genes to replace defective ones in their bloodstreams.

Also in 2006, researchers at the National Cancer Institute in Maryland reported exciting results of a targeted gene therapy used on 17 cancer patients who had advanced melanoma to such a degree that they were not expected to live more than a few months. Two of the patients were completely cancer free 18 months after the start of the treatment, which succeeded in either eradicating or shrinking large tumors to the point that they could be surgically removed. This groundbreaking therapy alters immune system cells so that they target cancerous tumors. The technology has the potential to be adapted for use against other specific cancers. For this study, scientists led by Steven Rosenberg, MD, isolated a genetic component, a T-cell receptor, in a previous patient who had responded particularly well to a T-cell infusion. (T-cells are particular white blood cells that mature in the thymus and work as part of the immune system.) This patient's tumors had shrunk by 95%. Dr. Rosenberg's team spliced this receptor into T-cells removed from the 17 patients in the study, multiplied those cells into the billions, and then transfused them into the melanoma patients.

Great strides in potential gene therapy for muscular dystrophy are being made at two major universities. In 2002, scientists at the University of Washington found that, using a virus-delivery model, gene therapy might successfully be used to implant a healthy, protein-producing gene in patients suffering from the disease. Studies in 2005 at the University of Pittsburgh found that a miniaturized version of this gene could be successfully delivered throughout the bodies of mice that are afflicted with the disease, and that the mice showed some improvement. Success of this type could eventually lead to gene therapy programs for use in humans who suffer from muscular dystrophy.

Roche Pharmaceuticals and Affymetrix, Inc. have developed a lab-on-a-chip (the AmpliChip CYP450) that can detect more than two dozens variations of two different genes. These genes are important to a patient's reaction to and use of drug therapies because the genes regulate the way in which the liver metabolizes a large number of common pharmaceuticals, such as beta blockers and antidepressants. A quick analysis of a tiny bit of a patient's blood can lead to much more effective use of prescriptions. Additional chips for specific types of genetic analysis will follow, such as the 2006 launch of a chip that scans for malignant tumor-causing variations of the human p53 gene.

Another gene discovered by scientists appears to play a major role in widespread forms of the more than 30 different types of congenital heart defects, the most common of all human birth defects. Genes that are used by bacteria to trigger the infection process have also been identified, which could lead to powerful vaccines and antibiotics against life-threatening bacteria such as salmonella.

In the area of heart disease, about 300,000 patients yearly undergo heart bypass surgery in an effort to deliver increased blood flow to and from the heart. Clogged arteries are bypassed with arteries moved from the leg or elsewhere in the patient's body. Genetic experts have now developed the biobypass. That is, they have determined which genes and human proteins create a condition known as angiogenesis, which is the growth of new blood vessels that can increase blood flow without traumatic bypass surgery. This technique may become widespread in the near future.

Gene therapy is still in its infancy, and is not without its failures. An 18-year-old patient suffering from a disorder that builds toxic levels of ammonia in the bloodstream died during a clinical trial conducted by the University of Pennsylvania in 1999. The FDA subsequently shut down a number of drug trials. However, the potential for gene therapy and genetic testing used for the choice and dosage of medications is almost limitless. Watch for major investment by pharmaceutical companies over the mid-term in further study and test development.

27) Breakthrough New Drug Delivery Systems Evolve

Controlling how drugs are delivered is a huge business. Sales of drugs using new drug delivery systems was expected to balloon to $30 billion by 2007, up from $9.8 billion in 1998.

Until the biotech age, drugs were generally comprised of small chemical molecules capable of being absorbed by the stomach and passed into the blood stream—drugs that were swallowed as pills or liquids. However, many new biotech drugs require injection (or some other form of delivery) directly into the bloodstream, because they are based on larger molecules that cannot be absorbed by the stomach. Many new drug delivery techniques that provide an alternative to needles are in development.

In the near future, there may be an implantable microchip, controlled by a miniature computer, capable of releasing variable doses of multiple potent medications over an extended period, potentially up to one year. The miniscule silicon chips will bear a series of tiny wells, sealed with membranes that dissolve and release the contents when a command is received by the computer. Chips that can receive commands beamed through the skin are also theoretically possible. This technology would help treatment of conditions such as Parkinson's disease or cancer, where doctors need to vary medications and dosages. This technology must first be tested in animals and then in humans to ensure that the chips are biocompatible. The chips will more likely be used first in external applications, which may facilitate laboratory testing and drug development.

Other potential needle-free drug delivery systems include synthetic molecules attached to a drug, making it harder for the stomach to render the medicine useless before it reaches the blood. High-tech inhalers, which force medicine through the lungs, are also in the works. For the patient, this means less pain and the promise of better outcomes. Needle-free systems may also make toxic drugs safer and give older drugs new life. For example, the painkiller Fentanyl is now available in a lozenge form.

Alkermes and Alza Corp. are developing techniques to encapsulate or rearrange drug molecules into more sturdy compounds that release steady, even doses over a prolonged period. A patch being developed by Alza Corp., a subsidiary of Johnson & Johnson, has a network of microscopic needles that penetrate painlessly into the first layer of the skin. In addition, Alza is in competition with Vyteris to develop a patch that delivers drugs via a small electric current, activated by a button on the patch itself. Vyteris announced an agreement granting Laboratory Corporation of America Holdings rights to represent the first FDA-approved active transdermal patch using electric current for pain relief from blood draws and venipunctures. Another device, made by Sontra Medical Corp., uses ultrasound and gel to agitate and open temporary pores in the skin that can then receive a drug. The same technology can provide continuous, transdermal glucose monitoring. Yet another potential drug delivery system is edible film; quickly dissolving films treated with medication that melt on the tongue. Already in use as a breath freshener (Listerine brand PocketPaks, made by Pfizer), edible film is now the delivery method of choice for Novartis' Triaminic and Theraflu Thin Strips and Gas-X Thin Strips.

28) Advances in Cancer Research and Therapies

Improvements in Chemotherapy: Chemotherapy continues to reduce the need for surgical excision of cancers and treat cancers that are considered inoperable. Improvements in chemotherapy continue to reduce the number and severity of side effects and the length of treatment, boosting a shift from inpatient to outpatient care. For example, scientists in the Netherlands at the University of Leiden and the University of Utrecht developed new compounds for platinum based chemotherapy that could alleviate side effects altogether. Although some cancers show resistance to chemotherapy, researchers have recently discovered a unique gene that causes resistance, so compounds may be added to chemotherapy that will block the gene's ability to resist. In 2007, new research at the Dana-Farber Cancer Institute combined a platinum chemotherapy agent with the diabetes drug rosiglitazone. This combination shrank or halted the growth of mouse tumors as much as three times more effectively than either of the drugs alone. In many cases, chemotherapy is combined with radiation, other drugs and/or surgery. For example, in 2006, the FDA approved Hycamtin, the first drug treatment for late-stage cervical cancer, to be used in combination with chemotherapy.

Novel Drugs: In late 2006, a doctor at the University of Alberta in Edmonton, Canada, tested a new drug called dichloroacetate or DCA on human cells cultured outside the body. Tests showed that DCA killed lung, breast and brain cancer cells but not healthy cells. Cancerous tumors in rats infected with human cancer cells also shrank significantly when exposed to the drug. Cancer cells were thought to lack mitochondria (an element in cells that is responsible for energy production and cellular respiration), and utilize an inefficient process called glycolysis for energy. New research shows that DCA reactivates mitochondria in cancer cells which causes them to wither and die. Although DCA appears to have great potential, it has yet to complete clinical trials.

Advances in Radiation Therapy: Radiation therapy is commonly used in the treatment of cancerous tumors. This technology has been moving toward greater precision in irradiating tumors. Modern x-ray radiation equipment (photon radiation) can focus on and attack tumors while doing less damage to surrounding tissue than previous technologies. State-of-the-art radiation techniques of today involve several different formats. Specific formats have been found to be most effective for specific cancers.

IMRT (Intensity Modulated Radiation Therapy) is a radiation technology that enables the technician to apply narrowly focused radiation directly toward cancerous tumors. IMRT helps to limit the amount of damage to surrounding tissues. The process includes using multiple beams (typically from seven to 12) aimed at the tumor from various directions. The beams meet at the tumor to administer the desired dosage. Breaking the dose down into multiple beams lessens the level of radiation that healthy tissues are exposed to. The point at which the beams join can be shaped to conform to the exact size, shape and location of the tumor, thus further sparing healthy tissue. Advanced imaging, such as CT, is used to provide precise guidance to the tumor's location.

Image Guided Radiation Therapy (IGRT) takes advantage of sophisticated imaging technologies in order to best target radiation therapy. Prostate cancer is often treated with IGRT. To treat that disease, tiny metal markers are implanted in the prostate using an outpatient procedure. The IGRT equipment is then able to locate the position of the prostate exactly by determining the location of the markers in real time. Varian is a leading manufacturer of IGRT equipment. The technology is similar to IMRT, but better enables radiation technicians to use ultrasound, CT or X-ray images to line up the radiation beam with the intended target.

Brachytherapy is a method of internal radiation therapy whereby tiny containers of radioactive material, sometimes referred to as "seeds," are implanted directly in contact with tissue that is afflicted with cancerous tumors. It is a common method of treating prostate cancer and is sometimes used for the treatment of breast cancer. These seeds are never removed from the body. They typically have a radioactive half-life of six months. Eventually, the emit virtually no radiation at all.

The *Gamma Knife* is a unique type of radiation therapy with tissue-sparing properties. It involves focusing low-dose gamma radiation on a tumor, while exposing only a small amount of healthy, nearby tissue to radiation. It is often used to treat certain brain cancers.

Patient immobilization is an advancing technology. The point is to hold vital parts of the patient as still as possible so that the radiation beam affects only the desired targets. However, since patients must breathe during treatment, some movement of the body is always going to occur, and this can have an effect on radiation of areas such as the lungs. New technologies enable the radiation beam to allow for and synchronize with a patient's breathing rhythm.

Treating Cancer with Electricity: Another new high-tech tool for treating certain types of cancer is a short burst of electricity directed at the tumor. This process, called electroporation, involves treating the tumor with chemotherapy and then sending short electrical pulses into the tumor with a needle electrode. The electrical pulse allows the tumor to become more porous and thus more susceptible to the chemotherapeutic drugs.

Inovio Biomedical, www.inovio.com, is a leading company in the new field of electroporation therapy. The company's main device for the delivery of the therapy is the MedPulser Electroporation Therapy System, first introduced in 1998. Inovio has clinical trials ongoing for the use of its technology in the treatment of a wide variety of cancers, including breast, head and neck and melanoma.

Radio Frequency Ablation (RFA): RFA is the use of focused radiowaves to produce high levels of heat within tumors in order to kill cancer. It is typically applied via needles that have been placed in the tumor, using ultrasound or other imaging techniques to insure correct placement. It is often used in the treatment of cancer of the kidney.

Viruses: Yet another weapon for the war on cancer is a growing assortment of viruses that replicate in tumors and kill them, sparing the healthy tissue. Viruses are also being developed with the ability to carry a gene into the cancer, making the tumor more vulnerable to radiation and chemotherapy. This new method will also lessen the side effects associated with conventional treatments.

Onyx Pharmaceuticals and Calydon (now part of Cell Genesys) pioneered the modern application of viruses to cancer cells, using variants of the adenovirus (the cause of the common cold) to attack tumor cells. Research continues at various biotechnology companies and institutions such as Johns Hopkins. One of the most prevalent techniques is engineering the viruses to attack cells with certain active proteins or enzymes. For example, a virus that attacks cells with excessive amounts of melanin (the protein that makes cells darken) could be used for the destruction of melanoma cancer cells. Cell Genesys has two virus therapies in clinical trials as of mid-2007, one designed to treat bladder cancers and another to treat multiple types of malignancies.

Vaccines: Though not quite as amazing as the name suggests, cancer vaccines will certainly make an impression on the way cancer is treated. The vaccines cannot prevent cancer, but they can help fight it. The basic principal is to teach the immune system to identify tumors as an enemy and help fight them. For the most part, this is done by introducing an altered, harmless form of the cancer into the patient, much like a classic vaccine. As techniques have been refined, scientists have been able to find the specific proteins that have proven to be the most effective in educating the body to fight cancer.

Pharmaceutical companies and universities in the U.S., Canada and Europe are developing dozens of vaccines. These vaccines are targeted at the most common types of cancer including melanoma, kidney, lung and breast cancer. They have proven effective enough to send the cancers into remission or, at the very least, slow the spread of the cancer. One woman with late-stage melanoma experienced a remission of the cancer for 32 months after being treated with an early vaccine.

Although not all of the vaccines have proven so effective, the prospects are certainly remarkable; many have even reached late-stage human trials. Some of these are in the midst of clinical trials, including kidney, colorectal and metastatic melanoma vaccines being developed by Antigenics and prostate, breast, ovarian and colon cancer vaccines by Dendreon. In 2006, the FDA approved Gardasil, a vaccine developed to prevent cervical cancer in girls and women ages 9 to 26.

Biopharma companies have developed vaccines to carry specific proteins that can stimulate the human immune system to have a desired response to an infectious disease. For example, biotech vaccines that fight hepatitis B have been introduced. Vaccines are under development at various firms for such conditions as herpes and tuberculosis. Additional DNA therapies that are somewhat related to vaccines are being developed to fight specific cancers and immune system diseases such as AIDS.

Companies to Watch: Antigenics, New York, New York (www.antigenics.com); Micromet, Inc., Carlsbad, California and Munich, Germany (www.micromet-inc.com); Cell Genesys, South San Francisco, California (www.cellgenesys.com); Dendreon, Seattle, Washington (www.dendreon.com).

29) Proton Beams—The Ultimate Radiation Therapy

PBRT, or Proton Beam Radiation Therapy, is the use of a highly advanced technology to deliver external beam radiation therapy (EBRT) to a patient in order to kill cancerous cells and shrink tumors. While traditional radiation therapies rely on photons delivered by X-rays or gamma rays, Proton Beam Radiation Therapy relies on a particle accelerator to create and deliver protons. Protons are high-energy particles that carry a charge. By varying the velocity of the particles at the time that they enter the body, physicists are able to control the exact spot within the body where the radiation is released. The higher the velocity, the deeper within the body the radiation begins to take effect.

With traditional radiation (based on photons rather than protons), there is a significant entry dose of radiation that can be harmful to healthy tissues. Proton beam therapy has virtually no entry dose or exit dose, plus the ability to better focus the radiation on the exact place of the tumor, significantly cutting down on side effects and damage to surrounding tissues.

There are only a handful of proton beam centers in the world. In the U.S., centers are in place at locations including Loma Linda (California) University Medical Center, which is considered to a pioneer in applying this technology; Boston, Massachusetts; Jacksonville Florida; Indiana University; and the M.D. Anderson Cancer Center in Houston, Texas. The Houston facility was opened in 2006 at a cost of $125 million. PBRT is in wide use in Japan, and centers also are in use in nations such as Germany and Korea.

PBRT may be in very wide use worldwide over the long term. Its tissue sparing nature makes it ideal for eliminating side effects and for treating tumors in challenging locations, such as the eye and brain. It may be the best possible way to treat small children in order to spare healthy surrounding tissues that are not through growing. And, it has great potential for the treatment of non-cancerous conditions such as macular degeneration.

At least five additional treatment centers are under planning, construction or consideration in the United States. Major obstacles include the immense investment required, the complexity of the accelerator and other equipment, the need to acquire and train specialized staff, and the need to educate referring physicians about this revolutionary technology and its high success rate. Eventually, advances in design and technology may make it easier and less costly to establish proton centers. Today's proton units typically have four treatment rooms. One theory for advancement comes from Still River Systems based in Littleton, Massachusetts. This firm hopes to build smaller facilities containing only one treatment room that, intended to be much simpler to design and install. The first such installation is planned at Washington University in St. Louis, Missouri. Elsewhere, development of highly automated treatment rooms are planned that may greatly increase the number of patients that proton centers are able to handle each day.

The Loma Linda, California facility began operations in 1991. It was the only hospital-based proton radiation center in the U.S. until 2003. By 2007 it had treated more than 12,000 patients, including about 8,000 prostate cancer patients. Head and neck cancers and pediatric cancers are also treated there in large numbers. The center has treated nearly 50 different types of cancers.

For additional information, see The National Association for Proton Therapy, www.proton-therapy.org . Also, see the web site of Loma Linda University Medical Center's proton unit, www.protons.com.

30) Better Imaging, including MRI, PET and 64-Slice CT, Creates Advances in Detection

***Internet Research Tip*:**
For descriptions of advanced imaging procedures, see the web site of the Radiological Society of North America at www.rsna.org.

Today, improved diagnostic imaging, diagnostic catheterization and better monitoring procedures have made earlier detection of many diseases possible and reduced the need for exploratory surgery. Over the long-term, highly-advanced new imaging systems, eventually utilizing molecular diagnostics, will enable levels of early intervention undreamed of in the past.

Diagnostic imaging traces its roots to 1895 when a German physics professor, Conrad Roentgen, discovered x-rays by accident. Within a few short years, radiology was an accepted sector of medical practice. While x-ray technology is effective for observing a flat image of general anatomical features such as bones and organs, recent advances in imaging technology now provide medical professionals with a deeper understanding of the molecular structure of hard and soft tissues. These new technologies, which are now in common use throughout the industrialized world, include infrared imaging, ultrasound, CT, MRI and PET.

Magnetic resonance imaging (MRI) uses a combination of radio waves and a strong magnetic field to gauge the behavior of hydrogen atoms in water molecules. Improvements in hardware and software have made MRI scans faster and more thorough than before. Ultra-fast MRI has many important clinical applications. Recent studies show that MRI may be the best method for determining the extent of a patient's recovery after a heart attack. Rapid-imaging MRI machines also expedite the diagnosis and treatment of heart conditions and strokes, thus reducing the time and money needed to scan the patient.

However, this technology has been extremely expensive, with equipment costs alone running from $1 million to $2 million. Until recently, very heavy shielding was needed to encapsulate the imaging room, which necessitated special construction of new facilities or very costly reinforcement of older building space. Progress in shielding technology and facility design, combined with more cost-effective mid-field and low-field MRI, has dramatically lowered the cost of most new installations. Some of these lighter, less powerful devices can be used in mobile settings, which makes MRI available in rural areas that could never have justified the expense of permanent installations. Low-field MRI technology has also enabled the development of open-MRI devices, which do not require a patient to be completely surrounded by a tunnel-shaped magnet. Open MRIs reduce patient anxiety and claustrophobia. In addition, the lower intensity of the magnetic field allows technicians, physicians and even family members to be present in the room at the time of the test, if the patient prefers.

Whole-body MRI is a relatively new technology developed a decade ago that scans the entire body. This can be useful for checking the entire skeleton or multiple parts of the body for metastasis of cancer. Although not part of routine patient care in the U.S., many health manufacturers such as Siemens, General Electric and Philips, are making scanners with full-body capability. The technology utilizes a gliding table that moves the patient smoothly enough to keep images clear. Related software takes five to six sets of images and weaves them together for a complete picture. The process generally takes about 20 to 45 minutes, the same amount of time used in traditional MRI.

Magnetoencephalography (MEG) is a newer technology derived from both MRI and electroencephalography (EEG). Like EEG, MEG registers brain patterns, but whereas EEG measures electrical activity in the brain, MEG measures magnetic waves, primarily in the cerebral cortex of the brain. Computer enhancement of the generated data is improving EEG as a diagnostic tool. Recent refinements in EEG technology make it possible to use this device to help diagnose various forms of depression and schizophrenia. Computed tomography (also known as a CT scan or CAT scan) uses a circular pattern of x-rays to produce high-resolution, cross-sectional images, which can help precisely locate tumors, clots, narrowed arteries and aneurysms. Because CT essentially creates images of distinct slices of the body, it can be referred to as multislice or multi-row detector imaging. CT can produce three-dimensional images, which are beneficial in reconstructive surgery. However, CT machines cost $2.5 million or more for the latest 64-slice technology. The advanced electronics enabling 64-slice CT (compared to 8- and 16-slice CT in common use today) are an immense breakthrough in the evolution of imaging. For example, 64-slice CT can show a higher level of detail in arteries than angiography, which is the traditional method of looking for arterial blockage and plaque and checking cardiovascular health. In fact, 64-slice CT enables the user to see cross-sections of arteries, including the walls. And, this newest CT can provide vastly improved images of beating hearts, including the interior. (About 1.5 million U.S. patients undergo angiograms yearly, at a cost of $4,000 to $6,000 each. A CT scan costs in the neighborhood of $500 to $1,000 and does not bring the risk of arterial puncture associated with angiography's wire-guided probes.) This 64-slice CT is extremely useful for early detection of heart disease as a preventative measure, and for guiding surgeons during surgery.

There is some concern about the exposure of patients to radiation during CT scans. In response, General Electric Healthcare has developed a device that reduces radiation during cardiac CT scans by up to 70%. The systems is called "SnapShot Pulse" and it pulses with a patient's heartbeat, automatically turning the X-ray on and off at desired times during the heart rate cycle, which reduces the patient's radiation exposure time.

The next step over the mid-term will be 256-slice CT, which has the potential to provide astonishing levels of image resolution. Advanced 256-slice CTs will cost over $3 million, but they will be able to scan an entire heart in less than half a second. Extremely fast scans will mean that large numbers of patients can be processed daily with one of these expensive machines. The cost of scans may drop proportionately; eventually they could drop to as low as $300 in high volume imaging clinics.

As with MRIs, there has recently been some interest in whole-body CT scans. Many independent imaging centers have been offering such scans to the public at reasonable cost. However, there is concern among some physicians that whole-body CTs often lead to a large number of questionable findings, or false positives, and that such scans may be of little value.

Two other imaging machines, single photon emission computed tomography (SPECT) and positron emission tomography (PET), use forms of radioisotope imaging to detect and study conditions such as stroke, epilepsy, schizophrenia and Parkinson's and Alzheimer's diseases. PET is a major research tool for understanding the human brain, and has a substantial indirect impact on medical and surgical practices.

PET offers a unique advantage in that it can offer functional imaging. That is, it can show how an area of the body is functioning and responding. Because it is based on safe, short-lived radioactive substances that are injected into the body, PET enables physicians to see metabolic activity. For example, in addition to imaging of brain activity, PET can be used to determine how cancerous tumors react to certain drugs. The FDA is cooperating with the National Cancer Institute to determine whether PET should be used in clinical trials of new cancer treatments to determine whether tumors are responding to therapies.

Other improvements in x-ray technology include digital subtractive angiography (DSA) and mammography. DSA involves the use of enhanced x-ray pictures to see blood vessels and arteries. It can clearly image aneurysms and can be used in angioplasty, a procedure that reduces the need for heart bypass surgery. However, as advanced CT becomes more widely accepted, DSA may become irrelevant.

Mammography is another x-ray technology that has been refined over the years. While traditional mammography with film offers sufficient x-ray images of older women's breasts, the film lacks the versatility of gray values that radiologists need to interpret mammograms from younger women. A new digital x-ray sensitive camera produces digital images on a computer screen with a higher dynamic range of gray values. Modern mammography equipment gives detailed and precise images of breast tissue, resulting in high detection levels of very small malignant tumors. The sooner a malignancy is discovered, the better the prognosis is for excision and follow-up treatment success. Advanced mammography techniques reduce the chance for misdiagnoses, the amount of radiation needed to develop the image and the time spent in the exam room.

Another improved imaging technique, sonography, uses ultrasound to create images of internal body tissues and fetuses. Ultrasound is a cheaper alternative to many other imaging techniques, and results are available almost immediately. This scanning technique is recommended for pregnant women, since the sound waves apparently cause no harm to human tissue. Refinements in sonography have led to excellent prenatal images, which can be used to detect even small abnormalities in a fetus. Sonography is also being used in other imaging applications. For example, a recent ultrasound device is capable of displaying a three-dimensional image of organs such as the heart. Ultrasound in real time has even become sensitive enough to show blood flow. Ultrasound units are common in all but the very smallest hospitals.

New ultrasound diagnostic devices are now being that are small enough to carry and provide doctors with a comprehensive picture of a patient's major organs and possible problems. These devices, which resemble the handheld scanners used on *Star Trek*, use ultrasonic waves to map out the interior features of a patient and then enhance them to provide an accurate and easy-to-read picture. Not only can doctors spot heart murmurs and breathing abnormalities with a simple inspection, but they can also spot objects like kidney stones and gallstones, or the presence of an abnormal amount of fluid surrounding an organ. The machines could potentially save millions in radiology and other diagnostic bills. In addition, these devices will be carried on ambulances or even on a doctor's person, allowing diagnostics to be performed wherever they are needed. The popular SonoSite 180 portable ultrasound weighs only 5.4 pounds.

Another exciting monitoring technique involves measuring the levels of the chemical creatine in the heart, which indicate the extent of muscle damage caused by a heart attack. Using a combination of MRI and MRS (magnetic resonance spectroscopy), this noninvasive method allows doctors to pinpoint injured heart tissue by measuring depleted levels of creatine in areas of the heart that were difficult to view using older imaging techniques.

Some patients even carry monitoring equipment on or in their bodies for long-term diagnostic purposes relating to biochemical balances, brain and sleep disorders, heart and vascular diseases and metabolic problems. More accurate, easy-to-use equipment has been introduced. For example, Medtronic has released an implantable heart monitoring device the size of three sticks of gum. Called the Reveal Plus, the device can detect brief heart stoppages or other abnormalities and report them to a support network.

Light diagnostic devices have also been showing up to diagnose certain forms of cancer. Similar to spectroscopy, which has been used to analyze chemical compositions for decades, these small diagnostic devices detect cancer by finding abnormalities in the body's reaction to light. In one instance, doctors at the University of Texas at Austin found that cervical cancer could be detected using a small ultraviolet light shown on the cervix. Precancerous cells are distinctly more fluorescent than normal cells. A preliminary study showed that the technique was 50% more accurate than a PAP smear and microscope examination, reducing the need to perform further diagnostic biopsies on healthy women. In another instance of light diagnostics, researchers at the University of California, Irvine found that infrared light could assist in finding breast cancer.

31) Molecular Imaging will Lead to Early Detection and Early Cure of Cancerous Tumors

One of the most promising new fields in diagnostic medicine is molecular imaging. Molecular imaging allows doctors to inject a patient with imaging agents that cling to trace molecules that could be indicative of health problems such as cancer and diseases of the cardiovascular and nervous systems. This technique has the capability to spot these ailments with accuracy that ordinary x-rays and biopsies cannot match. Two of the most successful applications may be in the diagnosis of breast and colon cancer. Imaging molecules that are injected into the patient become active when they come into contact with enzymes found in cancerous cells, causing them to "light up" and expose the cancer cells. Molecular imaging also allows doctors to witness what is called apoptosis, or the dying of cells. Viewing this process is invaluable for observing the effectiveness of cancer treatment, actually providing a way to see cells in a malignant tumor die.

Eventually, molecular imaging will evolve into a synergy between biology, advanced databases, microelectronics and nanotechnology. Early detection and cure of a wide variety of cancers will be the result. Molecular imaging will search for the presence of genetic patterns associated with specific tumors. Each type of cancerous tumor will be known to express a specific protein. A specific antibody will be known to indicate the presence of an exact protein. In the laboratory, antibody microarrays will contain thousands of antibodies on one chips, connected to the chip via nanowires. When a specific protein (biomarker) is found to be present in a sample from a patient, the chip will provide a positive indication. At that point, target-specific drugs can be administered. Massive "patient outcome" databases will improve results, as records will show that patients who tested positive for specific biomarkers improved as a result of taking specific drugs.

32) Advances in Laboratory Testing

New rapid testing techniques, improved equipment and the growing list of conditions that can be detected through blood, tissue and fluid specimen tests have expanded the role of laboratory testing in routine hospital patient care. The growth in the variety of tests has caused an increase in the use of outside laboratories by hospitals, but rapid techniques are most effectively used in-house. Therefore, on-site laboratories remain necessary. New tests for AIDS, hepatitis, cancer and genetic diseases have been developed. There is now an at-home test for hepatitis C, which lurks in about 4.1 million Americans who are unaware that they have the virus. Hepatitis C is the leading cause of liver failure and kills up to 10,000 Americans each year.

Advances in the understanding of genetics have given rise to the ability to test for a predisposition towards inherited diseases with genetic testing. With a simple blood test that can be performed in a doctor's office, the genetic tests look for the hallmark genes that indicate whether someone is at risk for a variety of diseases. Tests for over 1,000 diseases now exist, including conditions such as colon and breast cancer, Alzheimer's and diabetes. These tests have also led many hospitals and medical centers to hire genetic counselors, not only to interpret the tests, but to help patients deal with the results, giving advice on the conceivably life-altering revelations as well as means of prevention if the patient is at high risk.

Early-Stage Testing: Many diseases can now be detected in their earliest stages. Such early detection often occurs before the patient has suffered significant harm, and it tends to lead to more effective treatment. Besides early cancer detection and genetic screening, an important focus is cardiovascular disease, the leading cause of death in the U.S. High blood pressure and high cholesterol levels are conditions that require testing to detect, yet control of cholesterol levels and blood pressure can lead to significant increases in longevity and general health levels. A new laboratory test detects levels of 15 blood cholesterol-containing particles called lipoproteins, which more accurately measures a person's risk of heart disease than standard lipid tests. The test uses NMR (proton nuclear magnetic resonance spectroscopy) to record radio signals emitted by fats in the blood. Although the equipment itself is expensive, the test can be done in minutes rather than hours, because it does not require the physical separation of blood components. Furthermore, the test is more accurate than traditional blood screening, resulting in fewer misdiagnoses and underestimates of cholesterol levels.

Another testing device has been developed that could detect disease from a patient's breath. As blood circulates through the body, gases in the lungs and blood equilibrate and are carried out through the lungs. Kidney problems may be diagnosed by a fishy smell produced by compounds called amines, and diabetes could be deduced from the sweet smell of acetone. Advances in breath-collection techniques and analysis have made it feasible to test for a variety of diseases, from asthma to schizophrenia, with a simple breath test. The technology is being developed to detect symptoms of a variety of cancers as well, the most prominent being lung and breast cancer. Preliminary studies have shown that breath tests can detect upwards of 85% of breast cancers, which is equivalent to mammography. Commercial versions of this new device could be available in 5-10 years.

A recently developed, noninvasive colonoscopy is also gaining popularity. In a virtual colonoscopy, doctors take a computed tomography (CT) scan of the patient's abdomen, which is rendered into a 3-D computer-generated model of the patient's colon. To date, the virtual colonoscopy has been able to detect polyps or abnormalities that are larger than six millimeters. Another noninvasive test for colorectal cancer on the horizon involves DNA testing of stool samples. DNA tests detect the cancer itself and not just blood as an indication of cancer. They have outperformed the traditional fecal occult blood test and could become standard procedure within a few years.

While the benefits of early testing are considerable, there has been criticism of the extent and cost of testing. Due to patient expectations and malpractice concerns, physicians may practice defensive medicine, which leads to greater use of diagnostic tests. Often the latest and most expensive testing procedures are used. Fortunately, the accuracy of most tests is increasing, and newer, more rapid procedures raise laboratory worker productivity, which helps hold down costs and staffing. Artificial intelligence research has produced expert systems that are beginning to help physicians gain accurate diagnosis without excessive testing. Computerized systems are being developed and implemented by third-party payors and hospital managers for review and monitoring of testing practices.

Cancer Testing: In testing for cancer, early detection leads to increased life expectancy and cure rates. Cancer cells can often be distinguished from healthy cells by microscopic inspection and biochemical tests. For decades, suspect tissue has been routinely gathered by minor exploratory surgery or biopsy. Such surgery is being augmented by fiberscopic and needle incisions. In direct cancer detection, the testing for chemical or biological markers has improved. The net impact on hospital labor is unclear, but cancer survival rates are slowly rising, in part due to early detection.

Cancer testing is often done rapidly enough to be integrated with a surgical procedure that is guided by the test results. Some procedures are very complex. An example is a new procedure that excises skin cancers layer by layer and maps the presence of cancer cells and their pattern in each layer of tissue. With this process, only 2% of patients have a recurrence of cancer at the site, as opposed to a 3% recurrence rate by simple excision, burning or freezing. In addition, there is slightly less scarring due to the removal of a smaller amount of healthy tissue. The tradeoff is the transformation of a simple procedure into a complex, costly and lengthy one.

A relatively new form of the PSA (prostate specific antigen) test for prostate cancer could spare up to 200,000 men each year in the U.S. the pain and anxiety associated with invasive surgical biopsies to detect cancer. The test, called Free PSA, measures the antigen levels in blood samples. Certain levels indicate the potential presence of cancer in the prostate and can help determine which men to biopsy. The test cuts the costs of prostate screening dramatically.

A new urine test may also allow doctors to check regularly and quickly for cancers in patients at risk for developing cancer due to genetic or environmental factors. The test temporarily slows DNA production in cancer cells, causing some elements of DNA to accumulate in the blood. When these materials are excreted in large amounts in urine, they indicate the presence of cancer. Clinical human trials have been promising, but the test still needs validation through additional research.

Ovarian cancer has typically been missed in its early stages due to symptoms that can be confused with other non-cancerous conditions. Recently, however, a new screening tool called OvaCheck has been developed that uses a method called low-molecular-weight serum protein pattern recognition. Ovarian cancer has a unique protein pattern, or signature, that makes its detection possible. The test, which was developed and patented by clinical proteomics firm Correlogic Systems, Inc. (www.correlogic.com), can be performed on a blood sample taken from a finger stick. The tool promises to be far more sensitive in detecting ovarian cancer than the current standard, the CA-125 test. It is still subject to the FDA review process and it will be a few years before it becomes available.

33) Advances in Surgery

The Hi-Tech Operating Room of the Future: Increasing technical skill, improved diagnostic imaging, better equipment and better laparoscopic techniques have made less-invasive surgery possible. Incisions are much smaller than in the past, and recovery from surgery is often more rapid. Lasers, computers, sonography, magnetic resonance imaging, stereo optiscopes, miniature precision tools, robotics, fiber optics, imaging chemicals and isotopes and better x-ray equipment are factors in these advances. In 1998, the National Science Foundation provided $12.9 billion in a grant to establish the Engineering Research Center in Computer-Integrated Surgical Systems Technology (ERC CISST), www.cisst.org . Today ERC CISST is a broad reaching organization that includes both schools and hospitals. Members include Johns Hopkins University and Institutions, Carnegie Mellon University and the Massachusetts Institute of Technology. Collaborating on the project are students, professors, doctors and engineers. Their communication is facilitated by a web-based Intranet that allows the transfer of ideas and technology. The ultimate goal of the project is a completely automated operating room, in which a surgeon uses a custom-tailored, computer-generated image of the patient to help diagnose the patient's condition, select the appropriate treatment option and practice the procedure before making an incision. This operating room of the future will allow surgeons to learn more from their own work, resulting in fewer mistakes and complications.

Minimally Invasive and Laparoscopic Surgery: Small-incision and micro-incision surgery may be the most cost-effective development in new technology. Surgery has evolved from large incisions at the site of entry to smaller and smaller incisions, to procedures that are performed with needles, catheters, lasers and ultrasound. Recovery periods are cut dramatically as the severity of the procedures is reduced. Because surgical procedures involve risk to the patient, surgeons are highly motivated to develop ever more efficient and rapid techniques to reduce the period of time a patient must be under anesthesia and exposed to potential infection or shock.

One example is the laparoscope (or endoscope). It is a device consisting of an extremely thin tube containing a video camera lighted by fiber optics, which allows a surgeon to view and operate on abdominal or pelvic organs through an incision between one and two centimeters long.

Over time, most surgical procedures have been greatly modified and simplified. In surgery for breast cancer, for example, radical and modified radical mastectomies have given way to less extensive surgeries. In some cases, simple lumpectomies are effective. Chemotherapy and radiation therapy reduce the severity of many surgical procedures for cancer. Angioplasty, a catheter procedure in which a balloon is used to open clogged arteries, is replacing some coronary bypass surgeries, or at least delaying the need for such surgeries.

Endovascular grafts are a new procedure for operating on abdominal aortic aneurysms (AAA). Where traditional AAA surgery involved an incision from the breastbone to the pubic bone, the endovascular graft only requires a small incision in the groin area. The graft is delivered to the aorta via the patient's blood vessels, where it attaches to the heart. So far, this procedure has exceeded expectations for safety and efficacy.

Using MRI and lasers or linear accelerators, stereoscopic surgery is being used to remove deep-seated brain tumors, and another operation, percutaneous automated dissectomy, is turning some herniated disk surgery into an outpatient procedure. MRI is partly replacing diagnostic knee surgery.

Breakthroughs in surgery will touch every type of operating room procedure. In one of the most exciting developments, a growing number of surgeons are now able to do revolutionary open-heart surgery, such as complicated bypass operations, by working through much smaller incisions and using the latest in minimally invasive techniques. This means that patients will have greatly reduced recovery times and will suffer fewer traumas during the operation. A technology known as MIDCAB (minimally invasive direct coronary artery bypass) is rapidly growing in popularity also.

Laser Surgery: Lasers have been used surgically for many years to reattach detached retinas, but there are several newer applications. Advanced videolaseroscopy, using an endoscope equipped with a laser, is being used in minimally-invasive surgery to excise and or cauterize damaged tissue in the abdomen and lungs. It has proven effective in treatment for appendicitis, bowel tumors and adhesions, gallstones, fibroid tumors, endometriosis, ectopic pregnancy and lung lesions.

The FDA has granted approval for the use of new lasers for a number of gynecological and other procedures. Lasers are being used to remove cancers of the vulva, destroy genital warts and remove infected toenails. They are also being used to vaporize deposits of fat in the blood vessels of the legs. Moreover, the vaporizing of fat deposits in the arteries of the heart, lungs and neck may prove feasible, reducing the need for bypass and carotid artery surgery.

New diode lasers that use quantum-well technology are expected to replace most of the current gas-based lasers. This situation is analogous to the replacement of vacuum tubes by transistors and integrated circuits. Quantum-well diode lasers' greater efficiency, speed and coolness of operation will multiply the potential medical applications of laser technology, and in the coming century, an even more advanced laser technology (called quantum wire) is expected to play an important role in medical research and patient care.

Microsurgery: The reattachment of limbs and digits, the implantation of middle ear prostheses and some eye surgeries are now routine microsurgery procedures. These successes required the development of precision instruments, magnifying systems, and microscopically fine sutures and other innovative closure systems. Microsurgery is also being used in fetal and infant treatments, and some applications make nerve, organ, vascular and trauma repair possible.

Surgeons have contributed to improvements in surgical tools and the development of equipment that makes possible very small incisions and repairs. However, nerve surgery advances are still highly dependent on new equipment and on progress in the use of steroids and other medications.

Robotics: Eventually, we may see widespread use of robotics in microsurgery as well as general surgery. Experts are now using advanced computer technology to enable surgeons to control tiny, robotic pincers that can perform surgical procedures through extremely small openings. This is laparoscopic surgery carried to its highest level. Using such systems, surgeons view the interior of the body using tiny cameras. They then work from remote consoles to manipulate the robotic arms that cut, cauterize or staple as needed. The use of robotics makes surgical procedures safer and more precise.

Intuitive Surgical, Inc. of Sunnyale, California (www.intuitivesurgical.com) is a leader in equipment for this field. At this time, Intuitive Surgical manufactures the first operative robotic system with FDA clearance. Its da Vinci system costs around $1 million. A surgeon sits at a control console and uses a joystick control to manipulate robotic arms that are equipped with surgical instruments. The surgeon observes the operation via a camera that projects 3-D images onto a computer screen. Fatigue may cause the surgeon's hands to shake after many hours at the operating table. The da Vinci system recognizes these minute tremors and ignores them, minimizing the chances of surgical error.

Wound and Incision Closures: Surgical staples are used as an alternative to suturing. Although several times more expensive than sutures, they require less skill to insert and speed surgical procedures. They also promote more rapid healing and recovery. This concept originated abroad many years ago but was of little interest in the U.S. until improvements were made in equipment, materials and methods. Stapling allows faster surgical procedures, which benefit both the patient and the surgical team, since the shorter the surgery is, the lower the chances are of complications from anesthesia, infection, blood loss and shock.

Some staples are made of surgical steel, while others are made of soluble materials that dissolve as healing takes place. One study indicated that the use of staples could reduce a hospital stay by three to five days compared to a similar operation with sutures. The current usage of staples largely depends on the nature of the procedure, which must be one handled close to the outer layer of skin in orthopedic procedures. Staples cannot be used in regions where tendons or nerves lie close to the surface; and they do often require a staple removal procedure, one which has been known to cause scarring and is generally taxing on nurses.

Some new systems use super adhesives or plastic coverings to close incisions and cuts instead of either sutures or staples. These are often called steri-strips, and when applied to the edges of an incision, they help a wound close. Though eminently practical, these products lack the precision of sutures and need to be removed after they have served their purpose. To remedy this shortcoming, some hospitals have recently begun using tissue glues. These glues act like steri-strips, but are designed to decompose into the body upon completion, making their use a good choice for facial surgeries and other procedures where scarring is an issue.

34) Other Treatment Technologies

Shock-Wave Treatment: The lithotripter is a high-intensity sound-generating device that pulverizes kidney stones with shock waves. It is widely used, mainly in larger hospitals. In most cases, it is no longer necessary to surgically remove kidney stones that cannot be passed naturally. The original version of this device required that the patient be partially immersed in water; however a newer version does not require immersion and allows a greater number of shocks to be administered in a single session, which usually lasts less than an hour. One session is generally all that is needed in either approach.

A lithotripsy facility costs about $2 million. The treatment is supervised by an M.D., usually an urologist or radiologist. Treatment is expensive, but the potential exists for cost reduction as equipment and staff costs are lowered and facility requirements are reduced due to more compact units. Reductions in average patient costs for diagnosis, treatment and follow-up appear feasible.

Lithotripsy also allows many people to avoid gallbladder surgery. Gallbladder surgery is typically followed by weeks of recuperation, although a new procedure cuts recovery periods in half. Lithotripsy treatment can be performed on an outpatient basis or, at most, requires an overnight stay in a hospital followed by a day or less of recuperation. Furthermore, the procedure costs significantly less than the surgical operation, and, as indicated above, there are good prospects that the costs of lithotripsy facilities will gradually decline.

Because it is expensive to construct a lithotripsy unit, permanent installations are found mainly in larger hospitals. Many metropolitan areas only require a single unit to meet all local demand for this service. Mobile units can be trucked to smaller communities on a regular schedule. HealthTronics, Inc. (www.healthtronics.com) is one of the leading providers of mobile lithotripsy services, serving hundreds of hospitals nationwide.

Implantable Pumps as Testing Devices: This category includes miniature pumps that administer medicines, hormones, insulin and chemotherapy agents. Miniatures pumps, about the size of a deck of cards or smaller, are used to infuse analgesics and other drugs into the body in a controlled, time-released fashion. Research in the use of such pumps to infuse insulin has been underway for some time.

Cancer patients and other victims of severe pain are already benefiting from new infusion technology. Implantable pumps and testing devices involve high levels of automation and computerized monitoring. Miniature electrocardiogram (EKG) systems, for example, are designed to be worn by patients with heart disease and to broadcast warnings of infarctions or other crises. These devices are used for long-term diagnosis and medical studies. (See also “Diabetes Treatment.”)

Advances in Transplantation and Immunology: Transplantation of organs and other body parts has grown very rapidly, due to improvements in immune system suppression that make it possible for the human body to tolerate foreign tissue instead of rejecting it. The most common implants are plastic lenses in the eyes of cataract patients. Over 1 million of these procedures are performed each year. Thousands of synthetic blood vessels, joints, bones, middle ears and teeth are also implanted. Transplantation of living tissues includes hearts, livers, lungs, kidneys, pancreases and corneas, as well as the transplantation of skin or bone from one part of a patient to another part. Advanced transgenics methods and genetic engineering will eventually provide transplantable tissues from laboratory-grown animals. Animals such as goats and mice are being developed that contain human DNA so that their milk or their cells made be used to make drugs that do everything from fighting blood clots to speeding the recovery of burn victims and heart surgery patients (see www.gtcbiotherapeutics.com, the web site for the company responsible for the technology that develops human therapeutic proteins in the milk of transgenic animals).

Transplantation of organs normally requires immunological treatment to prevent organ rejection. In recent years, a powerful immunosuppressive agent, cyclosporine, has dramatically reduced organ rejection rates. Steroids, cyclosporine and another suppressive agent called immuran have led the way toward the development and use of even more effective agents. Sometimes drug combinations prevent organ rejection, or even halt the rejection process after it has begun.

Internet Research Tip:
For more information on organ transplantation, visit www.transweb.org.

In the future, heart patients may be among the biggest beneficiaries of transgenics, the use of organs and tissues grown in laboratory animals for transplantation to humans. Over 30,000 patients per year already receive heart valve transplants from pigs. The next challenge is to use genetic engineering to produce pig hearts that contain the human immune system proteins that reduce the chance of rejection. The same techniques may eventually grow kidneys or other organs suitable for use in humans.

Lung and kidney transplants are now commonplace. Corneal eye transplants can often be performed on an outpatient basis, but the growth in other transplants is resulting in more hospitalization and surgery. The main constraint on the growth of transplant surgery is a shortage of replacement organs. On any given day, tens of thousands of patients are waiting for organs. Only 20% of the 25,000 Americans who die each year under circumstances conducive to organ use actually donate organs. It is hoped that the supply of transplantable organs and tissue will grow due to greater awareness and technological advances.

Dialysis: Dialysis is available to virtually all patients requiring it in the U.S. This government-funded system currently provides treatment to over 220,000 people. The sheer size of the program has created the proper environment for the improvement and refinement of methods and equipment. Important advances include more and better venous shunts (now usually internal), better and more compact machinery, more rapid treatment and more complete cleansing of the patient's body. Procedural simplification makes it easier for patients to be treated at home.

There are two basic types of dialysis for treating kidney failure. The older method, peritoneal dialysis, is used mainly to treat temporary kidney failure. This treatment involves a fluid exchange between an external reservoir and a patient's abdominal cavity. When introduced, this treatment required a one- or two-week period of immobility, but ambulatory peritoneal dialysis has now become common. Patients are mobile and provide much of their own care during treatment. This has reduced labor requirements related to treatment of acute kidney failure.

The second method of dialysis, hemodialysis, involves purging a patient's blood of waste products normally removed by functioning kidneys. Until long-lasting venous shunts were introduced, this treatment was impractical for more than a short period because catheters tended to destroy the patient's accessible arteries and veins. Over time, longer-lasting internal shunting systems were developed.

The federal government provides hemodialysis for any person with chronic kidney failure (end-stage renal disease). The number of patients in the program will probably correspond to the growth in the population over age 55. However, the patient population may remain close to its present level, assuming the number of kidney transplants grows as expected.

Most patients receive treatment in special centers, some of which are located in hospitals. The proportion of home dialysis patients can be expected to grow to one-third of the total, due to cost considerations and simpler self-care resulting from technical improvements. Annual cost of treatment in centers exceeds $20,000; the cost of home care is lower. Dialysis has many side effects, including depression and fatigue, however home treatment tends to improve a patient's feelings of control and self-worth and allows more time for work and other activities. Regardless, only a successful kidney transplant can return a patient to a nearly normal life.

Diabetes Treatment: Type I and Type II diabetes affect over 18 million Americans, and 246 million worldwide. Diabetes poses very serious health problems, as diabetics tend to suffer from many ailments that require hospitalization and intensive treatment. These include pregnancy complications, blindness, circulatory diseases, organ failure and diabetic coma. Under the new classification standard, a person is considered diabetic after the blood level reaches 115 milligrams (mg) of sugar per deciliter of blood. (The previous standard was 150 mg.) This reclassification will lead to an expansion in the number of patients defined as diabetic; however, though diabetes can lead to complications that require hospital treatment, most diabetic treatments do not require hospitalization.

Recent changes in routine treatment could improve the health of diabetics and lead to fewer hospitalizations. These new methods require diabetics to monitor blood sugar levels several times a day and to take more frequent dosages of insulin formulations that combine fast-acting insulin with intermediate forms. The diabetic must purchase a blood-glucose meter and incur other costs for testing materials.

Exciting new regimens are currently under testing. Generex Biotechnology Corp., Aradigm Corp. and Nektar Therapeutic are developing drug delivery via inhalation techniques that may eventually be used for the delivery of insulin. Several companies, including Bioject Medical Technologies and Antares Pharma, have needle-free injection systems for insulin and other drugs on the market. This is a particular asset for children with diabetes who may be afraid of needles.

The use of miniature insulin pumps, instead of insulin injection via needles, has been shown to raise the quality of life for many diabetics and increase their health levels. Traditional insulin injection methods are believed to exacerbate damage to the circulatory system and the retinas of the eyes. This can shorten the life span of diabetics and subject them to blindness, gangrene and other health problems. Medtronic MiniMed manufactures the Paradigm line of insulin pumps. However, the company's implantable pump that delivers a steady insulin dose, 24 hours a day, without syringes, may be the ultimate device. The device is implanted in the peritoneal cavity (the abdomen) and releases insulin in small, steady bursts into the body, actually mimicking the body's natural delivery system. With a reservoir that can last up to three months, along with a long-life battery, the device requires very little maintenance and can even be regulated externally.

Another needle-free alternative may be a recently discovered simple molecule that, when swallowed, mimics the action of insulin in diabetics. Insulin currently has no benefit when taken orally because the protein is broken down in the stomach. This new molecule has been shown to control blood glucose levels in mice bred to develop diabetes. The next step is to begin testing on humans.

Other Implantable and Replacement Devices and Therapies: New technology is rapidly creating a wealth of exciting devices that can be implanted in the body to increase health or to replace human parts or functions. For example, Cyberonics (based in Houston, Texas) received FDA approval in 1997 to market its pacemaker-sized implantable electric stimulator device, which can help deter epileptic seizures by sending carefully timed impulses to the vagus nerve. The same technology may eventually prove effective in treating many other conditions, such as Parkinson's disease and headaches. It was later approved by the FDA as an adjunctive treatment for treatment-resistant depression.

Medtronic has similarly developed the Activa Parkinson's Control Therapy. It utilizes an implanted device that sends impulses to the thalamus region of the brain to counteract the effects of Parkinson's disease tremors.

By the use of implanted chips, scientists can now make significant impacts on harmful neural conditions, and they have also begun to study how to interact with the brain on an electric level. One experiment implanted electrodes in monkeys' brains, and then began deciphering the impulses coming out. The monkeys were given joysticks which could move a cursor across a computer screen, and then the movements of the cursor were cross-referenced with the impulses coming from the brain. After the experimenters wrote programs for these thought intentions, the monkeys were able to move the cursor through the implants alone.

Another new technology called SIM (Surface Induced Mineralization) allows metal implants to be surface-coated with a water-based calcium phosphate material, which stimulates the growth of new bone. The material bonds with the natural bone surrounding the implant, offering a more secure scaffold for new bone to grow and thereby extending the life of the implant.

Rutgers University professor William Craelius has designed a prosthesis for the human hand which affords recipients independent control of each finger via a computer. Sensors detect signals from nerve pathways which go through the computer to orchestrate finger movement. The prosthesis is so effective that patients have enough control and mobility to manipulate keyboards.

Advances in Organ Replacements: An exciting piece of news in prosthetic organs is the Dobelle eye, the use of which resulted in a sightless study participant successfully driving a car through a closed test course. The Dobelle eye is a combination of two electrode arrays (called pedestals) embedded through the skull and onto the visual cortex, a miniature camera mounted on a pair of eyeglasses, and a three-pound microcomputer worn around the patient's waist. While vision is not fully restored, patients receive digital information taken from the camera and processed by the microcomputer. The data is translated into strings of electrical impulses that are fed through wires into the pedestals in the brain. Points of light similar to video pixels are formed, allowing the patient to see shapes and, in some cases, colors.

There are two similar projects underway. In one of these projects, electrodes will be implanted inside the visual cortex instead of on the surface, allowing for much finer stimulation and requiring much lower amperage. This means that the patient will not only have a higher image resolution, but will be at lower risk of experiencing seizures. The other project uses an implant placed atop the retina instead of inside the brain. The device is designed to assist functional rods and cones within an eye that is mostly non-functional. Though this approach is limited, it is a much less invasive implant.

Eyes are not the only big news in artificial organs. Artificial hearts are finally showing great promise. The Jarvik heart, which confines recipients to hospitals and requires a great deal of peripheral equipment, is quickly falling behind the AbioCor artificial heart. Weighing two pounds and roughly the size of a human heart, the AbioCor requires no additional equipment outside the body to function. The unit is designed to both extend a patient's life and to provide a reasonable quality of life. After implantation, the device does not require any tubes or wires to pass through the skin because power to drive the heart is transmitted across intact skin. Patients enjoy up to two hours of free movement at a time, after which they must connect to an external battery to recharge the device and its internal battery. Made by ABIOMED, Inc., it has received humanitarian use device (HUD) status from the FDA for use in patients with certain end-stage heart failure. In 2006, a special FDA panel approved the $250,000 device on a limited basis, allowing that sale of up to 4,000 devices per year (although the actual number estimated by the FDA is between 25 and 50 per year due to the high cost and the limited number of patients who are eligible for its use). Meanwhile, ABIOMED, Inc. is pursuing regulatory approval for the AbioCor in Europe.

A Houston, Texas firm developed the MicroMed DeBakey VAD (Ventricular Assist Device) heart assist device, a tiny turbine that pumps blood into the left ventricle. It was co-developed by NASA and famed heart surgeon Michael DeBakey. The pump is powered by an external battery pack and is designed to keep heart patients alive and active for several months while they await a transplant. Eventually, it may be useful for long-term needs. The device has now been used in over 330 patients, including a 14-year-old boy and an 11-year-old girl.

The Streamliner VAD is another exciting device, developed by a cardiologist at the University of Pittsburgh in Pennsylvania. Like the DeBakey device, it uses a turbine instead of the left ventricle to pump blood.

However, the device also features magnetic levitation and a motor that can be powered externally via induction, making it one of the most powerful ideas in heart-assist devices. The chief designer of the Streamliner, Brad Paden, has since gone on to design another device, the HeartQuest VAD, in partnership with MedQuest Products, Inc., a medical device manufacturer. Utilizing the same innovations found in the Streamliner, the HeartQuest also uses a circular flow design, which maximizes efficiency. MedQuest was acquired by the WorldHeart Corporation in 2005, which renamed the HeartQuest device the Levacor VAD. A surgical team in Greece implanted the first Levacor VAD in March 2006. In 2007, the company (as part of a consortium funded by the National Institutes of Health) completed an animal study of the PediaFlow device for use in children.

With regard to pulmonary advances, an implantable plastic lung has been successfully tested on sheep. The BioLung is powered by the patient's heart, requiring no additional pumps or power sources. The device and its patent are owned by MC3 Corp., and licensed to Novalung, GmbH in Germany. The first clinical application of the device is expected in 2007.

Advances in Treatments for Spinal Cord Injuries: As of 2005, researchers in the field of spinal cord injuries overturned the long-held belief that nerve cells in the spinal cord have no possibility of regeneration. New findings pinpoint a combination of proteins in the spinal cord that block nerve cell growth. Scientists and physicians are creating compounds that bind to and inactivate these proteins, which will hopefully free spinal nerve cells to naturally heal after an injury. Animal testing of these compounds have resulted in the restoration of partial walking ability for the partially paralyzed.

Several pharmaceutical companies have these compounds in clinical trials. Novartis, for example, had a monoclonal antibody to a protein called Nogo in early stage trial beginning in 2006. Bioaxone Therapeutic has a drug called Cethrin already in clinical trials, which promises to promote regeneration and protect nerves. Biogen Idec began trials involving stroke victims and spinal injury patients in 2007 for a protein that inactivates Nogo and other nerve growth inhibitors.

Physical therapy is also proving efficacious in many partially-paralyzed patients. In a study of 146 recent spinal cord patients, 90% with some sensation and movement recovered the ability to walk slowly after extensive therapy on a body-weight supported treadmill. The patient's weight is supported by a harness hanging over a treadmill while therapists help move both legs in a walking motion. There is also a robot called Lokomat, developed by Swiss biomechanics firm Hocoma AG, which manipulates a patient's legs while the patient exercises on the treadmill.

Chapter 2

HEALTH CARE STATISTICS

Including Medicare & Medicaid

Tables and Charts:

I. Health Care Industry Overview

Contents:

U.S. Health Care Industry Overview

	Amount	Units	Year	Source
National Health Care Expenditures	2,262.3	Bil. US$	2007*	CMS
In 2010	2,776.4	Bil. US$	2010*	CMS
National Health Care Expenditures per Capita	7,498	US$	2007*	CMS
National Health Care Expenditures by Type:				
Hospitals	651.8	Bil. US$	2007*	CMS
Physician & Clinical Services	447.0	Bil. US$	2007*	CMS
Dental	92.8	Bil. US$	2007*	CMS
Nursing Home and Home Health	179.4	Bil. US$	2007*	CMS
Prescription drugs	213.7	Bil. US$	2007*	CMS
Other	572.5	Bil. US$	2007*	CMS
U.S. Population Less Than 65 Years of Age	263.3	Million	2007*	WFB
In 2010	268.7	Million	2010*	Census
In 2020	281.2	Million	2020*	Census
U.S. Population Age 65 Years & Older	37.8	Million	2007*	WFB
In 2010	40.2	Million	2010*	Census
In 2020	54.6	Million	2020*	Census
Number of Medicare Beneficiaries	43.7	Million	2007*	CMS
Hospital Insurance (HI)	43.2	Million	2007*	CMS
Supplementary Medical Insurance (SMI)	40.6	Million	2007*	CMS
Number of Medicaid Beneficiaries	45.7	Million	30-Jun-06	CMS
U.S. Fertility Rate	2.09	Children Born/Woman	2007*	WFB
U.S. Birth Rate	14.16	Births /1,000 Pop.	2007*	WFB
U.S. Infant Mortality Rate	6.37	Deaths/1,000 Live Births	2007*	WFB
U.S. Life Expectancy at Birth	78	Years	2007*	WFB
U.S. Death Rate	8.26	Deaths/1,000 Pop.	2007*	WFB
Obesity, All Adults	32.1	%	2004	CDC
Overweight, All Adults	66.0	%	2004	CDC
Number of All U.S. Registered[1] Hospitals	5,756		2006	AHA
Staffed Beds in All U.S. Registered[1] Hospitals	946,997		2006	AHA
Admissions in All U.S. Registered[1] Hospitals	37,006,027		2006	AHA
Number of People Without Health Care for the Entire Year	46,995	Thousand	2006	Census
Percent of Population	15.8	%	2006	Census

*Estimate

CMS = U.S. Centers for Medicare & Medicaid Services; WFB = CIA World Fact Book 2007; Census = U.S. Census Bureau; CDC = U.S. Centers for Disease Control & Prevention; AHA = American Hospital Association.

[1] Registered hospitals are those hospitals that meet AHA's criteria for registration as a hospital facility. Registered hospitals include AHA member hospitals as well as nonmember hospitals. For a complete listing of the criteria used for registration, please see www.aha.org.

Plunkett's Health Care Industry Almanac 2008

Top 20 Global Health Insurance Companies by Revenues: 2006

(In Thousands of US$)

1	UnitedHealth Group Inc	71,542,000
2	Wellpoint Inc	56,953,000
3	Aetna Inc	25,145,700
4	Humana Inc	21,416,537
5	Cigna Corp	16,547,000
6	Health Care Service Corporation	12,971,600
7	Health Net Inc	12,908,350
8	Highmark Inc	11,083,800
9	Blue Cross and Blue Shield of Michigan	8,686,500
10	British United Provident Association (BUPA)	8,469,930
11	Assurant Inc	8,070,584
12	Blue Cross and Blue Shield of Minnesota	7,865,816
13	Coventry Health Care Inc	7,733,756
14	Blue Cross and Blue Shield of Florida	7,475,000
15	Horizon Healthcare Services Inc	6,730,317
16	Carefirst Inc	5,510,184
17	Blue Cross and Blue Shield of North Carolina	4,406,928
18	Premera Blue Cross	3,093,741
19	Amerigroup Corporation	2,835,089
20	Harvard Pilgrim Health Care Inc	2,488,095

Note: Because most industrialized countries have socialized medicine, each of the top twenty global health insurance companies (with the exception of British United Provident Association) are located in the United States.

Plunkett's Health Care Industry Almanac 2008

Employment in the Health Care Industry, U.S.: 2000-2006

(Annual Estimates in Thousands of Employed Workers)

NAICS Code[1]	Industry Sector	2000	2001	2002	2003	2004	2005	2006
62	**Total health care & social assistance**	**12,718.0**	**13,134.0**	**13,555.7**	**13,892.6**	**14,190.2**	**14,536.3**	**14,919.9**
621,2,3	**Health care**	**10,857.8**	**11,188.1**	**11,536.0**	**11,817.1**	**12,055.3**	**12,313.9**	**12,611.0**
621	**Ambulatory health care services**	**4,320.3**	**4,461.5**	**4,633.2**	**4,786.4**	**4,952.3**	**5,113.5**	**5,283.1**
6211	Offices of physicians	1,839.9	1,911.2	1,967.8	2,002.5	2,047.8	2,093.5	2,153.6
621111	Offices of physicians, except mental health	1,803.3	1,872.8	1,927.3	1,959.9	2,005.6	2,050.6	2,110.1
621112	Offices of mental health physicians	36.7	38.4	40.5	42.6	42.3	42.9	43.5
6212	Offices of dentists	687.7	704.9	724.5	744.4	760.2	773.7	784.0
6213	Offices of other health practitioners	438.1	456.5	485.9	503.3	527.4	548.8	570.8
62131	Offices of chiropractors	95.3	98.9	104.5	108.5	112.1	112.2	114.4
62132	Offices of optometrists	87.3	89.4	90.4	91.1	94.0	96.2	98.9
62133	Offices of mental health practitioners	51.3	53.1	54.1	53.7	53.1	53.0	55.0
62134	Offices of specialty therapists	149.0	157.5	174.3	184.2	197.7	211.4	222.1
62139	Offices of all other health practitioners	55.1	57.8	62.6	65.9	70.5	76.1	80.3
621391	Offices of podiatrists	29.5	30.3	31.9	32.2	32.3	33.3	32.9
621399	Offices of miscellaneous health practitioners	25.7	27.5	30.7	33.7	38.2	42.8	47.4
6214	Outpatient care centers	386.4	399.7	413.0	426.8	450.5	473.2	489.4
62142	Outpatient mental health centers	130.6	134.2	139.4	143.5	149.7	154.4	157.4
62141,9	Outpatient care centers, except mental health	255.8	265.5	273.6	283.3	300.8	318.8	332.0
621491	HMO medical centers	60.6	62.5	63.3	64.9	69.3	71.9	76.4
621492	Kidney dialysis centers	60.4	64.2	67.1	69.3	72.2	75.1	74.9
621493	Freestanding emergency medical centers	52.6	54.9	57.2	60.5	66.0	70.6	75.9
621441,98	Miscellaneous outpatient care centers	82.2	83.9	86.0	88.7	93.3	101.2	104.8
6215	Medical and diagnostic laboratories	161.9	170.2	175.4	181.7	190.0	197.6	202.3
621511	Medical laboratories	117.8	123.8	126.2	129.7	133.5	138.1	140.0
621512	Diagnostic imaging centers	44.0	46.5	49.2	51.9	56.5	59.5	62.3
6216	Home health care services	633.3	638.6	679.8	732.6	776.6	821.0	867.1
6219	Other ambulatory health care services	173.1	180.3	186.7	195.0	199.9	205.9	215.8
62191	Ambulance services	100.5	103.1	106.0	112.5	116.8	122.1	129.3
62199	All other ambulatory health care services	72.6	77.2	80.7	82.5	83.0	83.8	86.5
621991	Blood and organ banks	47.9	51.2	53.8	55.9	55.7	56.7	58.8
621999	Miscellaneous ambulatory health care svcs.	24.6	26.0	26.9	26.6	27.3	27.1	27.7

(Continued on next page)

Employment in the Health Care Industry, U.S.: 2000-2006 (cont.)

(Annual Estimates in Thousands of Employed Workers)

NAICS Code[1]	Industry Sector	2000	2001	2002	2003	2004	2005	2006
622	**Hospitals**	**3,954.3**	**4,050.9**	**4,159.6**	**4,244.6**	**4,284.7**	**4,345.4**	**4,427.1**
6221	General medical and surgical hospitals	3,745.3	3,832.9	3,929.8	4,005.0	4,042.4	4,096.3	4,166.5
6222	Psychiatric and substance abuse hospitals	85.7	86.5	90.2	91.8	91.8	93.2	98.4
6223	Other hospitals	123.3	131.5	139.6	147.9	150.5	156.0	162.2
623	**Nursing and residential care facilities**	**2,583.2**	**2,675.8**	**2,743.3**	**2,786.2**	**2,818.4**	**2,855.0**	**2,900.9**
6231	Nursing care facilities	1,513.6	1,546.8	1,573.2	1,579.8	1,576.9	1,577.4	1,584.2
6232	Residential mental health facilities	437.1	461.0	473.2	483.9	489.6	497.3	512.3
62321	Residential mental retardation facilities	301.5	317.9	326.2	331.4	334.2	337.8	346.4
62322	Residential mental and substance abuse care	135.6	143.1	147.0	152.5	155.4	159.6	165.9
6233	Community care facilities for the elderly	478.2	505.2	531.9	557.8	586.2	615.3	639.4
623311	Continuing care retirement communities	213.7	222.4	235.7	257.0	283.9	307.5	320.5
623212	Homes for the elderly	264.5	282.8	296.1	300.8	302.3	307.8	318.9
6239	Other residential care facilities	154.4	162.7	165.0	164.6	165.8	165.0	165.0
624	**Social assistance**	**1,860.2**	**1,949.9**	**2,019.7**	**2,075.4**	**2,134.8**	**2,222.3**	**2,308.9**
6241	Individual and family services	678.0	728.8	772.8	813.1	862.0	921.3	973.5
62411	Child and youth services	137.4	144.7	146.4	149.4	151.1	153.1	157.5
62412	Services for the elderly and disabled	286.4	310.8	340.1	367.1	406.6	452.4	493.4
62419	Other individual and family services	254.3	272.8	286.3	296.6	304.3	315.7	322.7

[1] For a full description of the NAICS codes used in this table, see www.census.gov/epcd/www/naics.html.

Source: U.S. Bureau of Labor Statistics

Plunkett's Health Care Industry Almanac 2008

Employment & Earnings in Health Care Practitioner & Technical Occupations, U.S.: May 2006

(Wage & Salary in US$; Latest Year Available)	Employ-ment[2]	Median Hourly Wage	Mean Hourly Wage	Mean Annual Salary[3]	Mean RSE[4] (%)
Healthcare Practitioner & Technical Occupations	6,713,780	24.99	29.82	62,030	0.2
Chiropractors	25,470	31.36	38.97	81,070	2.4
Dentists, General	86,110	63.53	67.76	140,950	1.7
Oral & Maxillofacial Surgeons	5,320	(5)	79.21	164,760	4.0
Orthodontists	5,200	(5)	85.05	176,900	3.1
Prosthodontists	480	(5)	76.42	158,940	6.8
Dentists, All Other Specialists	4,560	43.85	52.09	108,340	4.6
Dietitians & Nutritionists	51,230	22.59	23.02	47,890	0.5
Optometrists	24,220	43.77	47.38	98,550	1.4
Pharmacists	239,920	45.44	44.95	93,500	0.4
Anesthesiologists	29,890	(5)	88.63	184,340	1.8
Family & General Practitioners	109,400	(5)	72.04	149,850	1.0
Internists, General	48,700	(5)	77.34	160,860	1.2
Obstetricians & Gynecologists	22,520	(5)	85.60	178,040	1.6
Pediatricians, General	28,930	66.41	68.00	141,440	1.8
Psychiatrists	24,730	(5)	72.11	149,990	4.1
Surgeons	51,900	(5)	88.53	184,150	1.1
Physicians & Surgeons, All Other	208,960	(5)	68.38	142,220	1.1
Physician Assistants	62,960	36.05	35.71	74,270	0.7
Podiatrists	9,020	52.03	56.97	118,500	2.9
Registered Nurses	2,417,150	27.54	28.71	59,730	0.2
Audiologists	10,910	27.46	29.38	61,110	1.8
Occupational Therapists	88,570	29.07	30.05	62,510	0.5
Physical Therapists	156,100	31.83	32.72	68,050	0.3
Radiation Therapists	14,290	31.81	32.49	67,580	1.2
Recreational Therapists	24,130	16.82	17.55	36,510	0.5
Respiratory Therapists	99,330	22.80	23.37	48,610	0.3
Speech-Language Pathologists	98,690	27.74	29.25	60,840	0.7
Therapists, All Other	11,660	20.31	21.67	45,070	4.0
Veterinarians	49,750	34.61	39.18	81,490	1.1
Health Diagnosing & Treating Practitioners, All Other	53,270	29.60	39.96	83,110	2.6
Medical & Clinical Laboratory Technologists	160,760	23.90	24.30	50,550	0.3
Medical & Clinical Laboratory Technicians	144,710	15.79	16.65	34,620	0.4
Dental Hygienists	166,380	30.19	30.01	62,430	0.6
Cardiovascular Technologists & Technicians	43,870	20.34	21.15	43,990	0.6
Diagnostic Medical Sonographers	44,340	27.48	27.94	58,110	0.4
Nuclear Medicine Technologists	19,270	29.95	30.29	63,000	0.4
Radiologic Technologists & Technicians	190,180	23.16	23.71	49,320	0.4
Emergency Medical Technicians & Paramedics	196,190	13.01	14.13	29,390	0.7
Dietetic Technicians	24,450	11.56	12.55	26,090	0.8
Pharmacy Technicians	282,450	12.32	12.75	26,510	0.3
Psychiatric Technicians	58,940	13.36	14.64	30,450	0.9
Respiratory Therapy Technicians	18,710	18.81	19.17	39,860	0.6

(Continued on next page)

Employment & Earnings in Health Care Practitioner & Technical Occupations, U.S.: May 2006 (cont.)

(Wage & Salary in US$; Latest Year Available)	Employment[2]	Median Hourly Wage	Mean Hourly Wage	Mean Annual Salary[3]	Mean RSE[4] (%)
Surgical Technologists	84,330	17.35	17.97	37,370	0.4
Veterinary Technologists & Technicians	69,700	12.88	13.34	27,750	0.6
Licensed Practical & Licensed Vocational Nurses	720,380	17.57	18.05	37,530	0.2
Medical Records & Health Information Technicians	164,700	13.48	14.49	30,140	0.3
Opticians, Dispensing	65,190	14.57	15.49	32,220	0.8
Orthotists & Prosthetists	5,290	28.36	29.86	62,110	2.3
Health Technologists & Technicians, All Other	72,180	16.89	18.39	38,260	0.6
Occupational Health & Safety Specialists	42,220	27.90	28.50	59,270	0.6
Occupational Health & Safety Technicians	10,020	20.27	21.32	44,340	1.1
Athletic Trainers	15,440	(4)	(4)	38,860	1.3
Healthcare Practitioner & Technical Workers, All Other	50,690	17.89	21.68	45,090	1.4

[1] For a full description of the NAICS codes used in this table, see www.census.gov/epcd/www/naics.html.
[2] Estimates for detailed occupations do not sum to the totals because the totals include occupations not shown separately. Estimates do not include self-employed workers.
[3] Annual wages have been calculated by multiplying the hourly mean wage by a "year-round, full-time" hours figure of 2,080 hours; for those occupations where there is not an hourly mean wage published, the annual wage has been directly calculated from the reported survey data.
[4] The relative standard error (RSE) is a measure of the reliability of a survey statistic. The smaller the relative standard error, the more precise the estimate.
[5] This wage is equal to or greater than $70.00 per hour or $145,600 per year.

Source: U.S. Bureau of Labor Statistics

Plunkett's Health Care Industry Almanac 2008

Employment & Earnings in Health Care Support Occupations, U.S.: May 2006

(Wage & Salary in US$; Latest Year Available)	Employ-ment[2]	Median Hourly Wage	Mean Hourly Wage	Mean Annual Salary[3]	Mean RSE[4] (%)
Healthcare Support Occupations	3,483,270	11.00	11.83	24,610	0.2
Home Health Aides	751,480	9.34	9.66	20,100	0.3
Nursing Aides, Orderlies & Attendants	1,376,660	10.67	11.04	22,960	0.2
Psychiatric Aides	57,000	11.49	12.01	24,990	0.8
Occupational Therapist Assistants	23,700	20.22	20.25	42,110	0.6
Occupational Therapist Aides	7,780	12.03	13.35	27,760	1.5
Physical Therapist Assistants	59,350	19.88	19.91	41,410	0.4
Physical Therapist Aides	45,520	10.61	11.20	23,290	0.8
Massage Therapists	41,920	16.06	18.93	39,380	2.5
Dental Assistants	277,040	14.53	14.83	30,850	0.5
Medical Assistants	409,570	12.64	13.07	27,190	0.5
Medical Equipment Preparers	42,740	12.47	12.97	26,980	0.4
Medical Transcriptionists	86,790	14.40	14.74	30,660	0.3
Pharmacy Aides	47,810	9.35	10.07	20,950	1.0
Veterinary Assistants & Laboratory Animal Caretakers	70,310	9.60	10.13	21,060	0.6
Healthcare Support Workers, All Other	185,580	12.98	13.55	28,170	0.4

[1] For a full description of the NAICS codes used in this table, see www.census.gov/epcd/www/naics.html.
[2] Estimates for detailed occupations do not sum to the totals because the totals include occupations not shown separately. Estimates do not include self-employed workers.
[3] Annual wages have been calculated by multiplying the hourly mean wage by a "year-round, full-time" hours figure of 2,080 hours; for those occupations where there is not an hourly mean wage published, the annual wage has been directly calculated from the reported survey data.
[4] The relative standard error (RSE) is a measure of the reliability of a survey statistic. The smaller the relative standard error, the more precise the estimate.

Source: U.S. Bureau of Labor Statistics
Plunkett's Health Care Industry Almanac 2008

Federal R&D & R&D Plant Funding for National Institutes of Health, U.S.: Fiscal Years 2005-2007

(In Millions of US$)

Agency, by 2007 Funding Level	2005 Actual	2006 Prelim.	2007 Proposed	% Change (06-07)
Total	27,875	27,805	27,810	0.0
National Cancer Institute	4,758	4,724	4,685	-0.8
National Institute of Allergy and Infectious Diseases	4,341	4,322	4,337	0.4
National Heart, Lung, and Blood Institute	2,850	2,830	2,809	-0.7
National Institute of Diabetes and Digestive and Kidney Diseases	1,808	1,798	1,788	-0.5
National Institute of General Medical Sciences	1,754	1,746	1,734	-0.7
National Institute of Neurological Disorders and Stroke	1,505	1,501	1,491	-0.7
National Institute of Mental Health	1,351	1,343	1,335	-0.6
National Institute of Child Health and Human Development	1,232	1,227	1,220	-0.6
National Center for Research Resources	1,110	1,094	1,093	-0.1
National Institute on Aging	1,029	1,024	1,017	-0.7
National Institute on Drug Abuse	985	976	971	-0.5
National Institute of Environmental Health Sciences[1]	705	700	696	-0.6
Office of the Director	405	528	668	26.6
National Eye Institute	656	654	649	-0.8
National Institute of Arthritis and Musculoskeletal and Skin Diseases	496	493	490	-0.7
National Human Genome Research Institute	480	477	474	-0.7
National Institute on Alcohol Abuse and Alcoholism	428	425	422	-0.6
National Institute on Deafness and Other Communication Disorders	381	380	378	-0.5
National Institute of Dental and Craniofacial Research	375	373	370	-0.8
National Library of Medicine	315	315	313	-0.5
National Institute of Biomedical Imaging and Bioengineering	291	288	287	-0.7
National Center for Minority Health and Health Disparities	196	195	194	-0.6
National Institute of Nursing Research	128	127	126	-0.6
National Center for Complementary and Alternative Medicine	118	117	116	-0.8
Buildings and facilities	110	81	81	0.0
John E. Fogarty International Center	67	66	67	0.5

Notes: Detail may not add to total because of rounding. Percent change derived from unrounded data. Institute totals exclude non-R&D components of institute budgets. Data derived from departmental submissions to Office of Management and Budget per MAX Schedule C and supplemental data obtained from National Institutes of Health budget office.

[1] Includes funding from Superfund-related transfers and appropriations.

Source: U.S. National Science Foundation

Plunkett's Health Care Industry Almanac 2008

II. U.S. Health Care Expenditures & Costs

Contents:

The Nation's Health Dollar: 2007 Where It Came From (Estimated)

($2.26 Trillion)

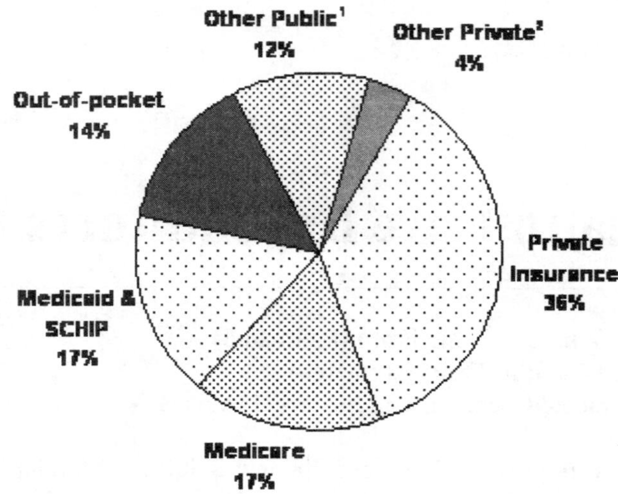

[1] "Other Public" includes programs such as workers' compensation, public health activity, Department of Defense, Department of Veterans Affairs, Indian Health Service, and State and local hospital subsidies and school health.
[2] "Other Private" includes industrial in-plant, privately funded construction, and non-patient revenues, including philanthropy.

Source: Plunkett Research, Ltd.

Plunkett's Health Care Industry Almanac 2008

The Nation's Health Dollar: 2007
Where It Went (Estimated)

($2.26 Trillion)

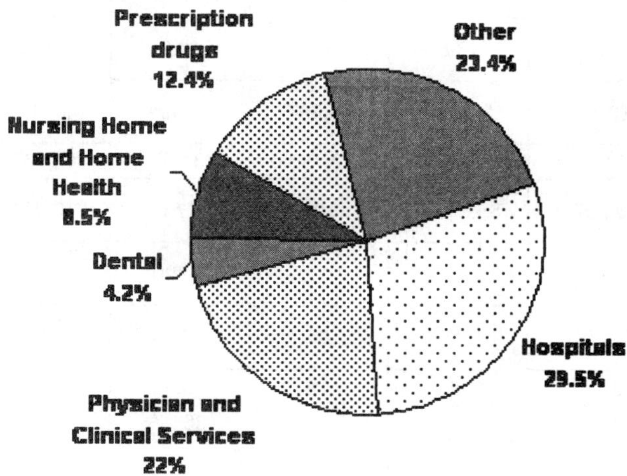

Source: Plunkett Research, Ltd.

Plunkett's Health Care Industry Almanac 2008

National Health Expenditures & Selected Economic Indicators, Levels & Average Annual Percent Change, U.S.: Selected Years, 1990-2016

(Based on the 2005 National Health Expenditures, Released January 2007)

Item	1990	2000	2005	2007	2008	2010	2016
National Health Expenditures (billions)	$696.0	$1,358.5	$1,987.7	$2,262.3	$2,420.0	$2,776.4	$4,136.9
National Health Expenditures (% of GDP)	12.0	13.8	16.0	16.2	16.5	17.2	19.6
National Health Expenditures Per Capita	$2,738	$4,729	$6,697	$7,498	$7,957	$8,985	$12,782
Gross Domestic Product (billions)	$5,803.3	$9,817.0	$12,455.8	$13,955.4	$14,667.1	$16,170.5	$21,138.7
Gross Domestic Product (billions of 2000 $)	$6,707.9	$9,817.0	$11,048.6	$11,744.1	$12,061.2	$12,696.9	$14,439.0
GDP Implicit Price Deflator (chain weighted 2000 base)	NA	1.000	1.127	1.190	1.219	1.278	1.474
Consumer Price Index (CPI-W) - 1982-1984 base	1.307	1.722	1.953	2.048	2.105	2.225	2.626
HCFA Implicit Medical Price Deflator[2]	0.774	1.000	1.205	1.289	1.339	1.448	1.836
U.S. Population[3] (millions)	254.2	287.3	296.8	301.7	304.1	309	323.6
Population age less than 65 years (millions)	222.7	251.9	260.4	264.5	266.2	269.8	277.0
Population age 65 years and older (millions)	31.5	35.4	36.4	37.2	37.9	39.2	46.6
Private Health Insurance - NHE (billions)	$233.5	$454.8	$694.4	$775.8	$829.9	$950.5	$1,371.1
Private Health Insurance - PHC (billions)	$203.6	$402.7	$596.7	$666.6	$712.0	$816.2	$1,188.9
Average Annual Percent Change from Previous Year Shown (in %)							
National Health Expenditures	--	6.9	6.9	6.6	7.0	6.9	6.8
National Health Expenditures (% of GDP)	--	1.0	0.5	1.2	1.8	1.9	2.2
National Health Expenditures Per Capita	--	5.7	5.9	5.7	6.1	6.1	6.0
Gross Domestic Product (GDP)	--	5.9	6.3	5.3	5.1	5.0	4.5
GDP (2000 $)	--	3.7	3.2	2.8	2.7	2.6	2.1
GDP Implicit Price Deflator (chain weighted 2000 base)	NA	NA	3.0	2.5	2.4	2.4	2.4
Consumer Price Index (CPI-W) - 1982-1984 base	--	3.4	3.4	2.4	2.8	2.8	2.8
HCFA Implicit Medical Price Deflator[2]	--	3.4	3.6	3.8	3.9	4.0	4.8
U.S. Population[2]	--	1.1	0.9	0.8	0.8	0.8	0.8
Population age less than 65 years	--	1.2	0.9	0.7	0.7	0.7	0.4
Population age 65 years and older	--	0.8	1.3	1.4	1.7	1.7	3.1
Private Health Insurance - NHE	--	8.9	6.6	6.7	7.0	6.7	5.8
Private Health Insurance - PHC	--	8.3	6.9	6.7	6.8	7.1	6.1

Note: Numbers and percents may not add to totals because of rounding. Figures for 2005-2015 are forecasts.
[1] 2000 base year. Calculated as the difference between nominal personal health care spending and real personal health care spending. Real personal health care spending is produced by deflating spending on each service type by the appropriate deflator (PPI, CPI, etc.) and adding real spending by service type.
[2] July 1 Census resident based population estimates.

Source: Centers for Medicare & Medicaid Services, Office of the Actuary
Plunkett's Health Care Industry Almanac 2008

National Health Expenditures & Average Annual Percent Change: Selected Calendar Years 1980-2016[1]

(By Source of Funds)

Year	Total	Out-of-Pocket Payments	Third-Party Payments			Public			Medicare[3]	Medicaid[4]
			Total	Private Health Insurance	Other Private Funds	Total	Federal[2]	State & Local[2]		
Amount in Billions of US$ (Historical Estimates)										
1980	$245.8	$58.2	$187.5	$68.2	$14.5	$104.8	$71.3	$33.5	$37.4	$26.0
1990	696.0	137.3	558.7	233.5	42.8	282.5	192.7	89.8	110.2	73.6
2001	1,469.6	200.0	1,269.6	498.7	109.7	661.1	464.3	196.9	247.7	225.3
2002	1,602.8	211.3	1,391.6	551.0	118.4	722.1	509.4	212.7	265.7	249.0
2003	1,733.4	224.5	1,508.9	603.8	127.4	777.7	553.1	224.6	283.5	271.6
2004	1,858.9	235.8	1,623.1	651.5	133.6	838.0	600.6	237.4	312.8	292.0
2005	1,987.7	249.4	1,738.2	694.4	141.2	902.7	643.7	259.0	342.0	313.1
(Projected)										
2006	2,122.5	250.6	1,871.9	727.4	151.5	992.9	725.4	267.6	417.6	313.5
2007	2,262.3	265.8	1,996.6	775.8	163.0	1,057.8	772.4	285.4	444.7	336.5
2008	2,420.0	281.3	2,138.7	829.9	175.4	1,133.4	829.1	304.3	478.6	362.0
2009	2,596.0	298.7	2,297.3	890.7	189.6	1,217.0	891.5	325.5	515.8	390.2
2010	2,776.4	316.6	2,459.8	950.5	204.2	1,305.1	956.8	348.2	553.6	421.0
2011	2,966.4	334.6	2,631.8	1,012.4	219.1	1,400.3	1,027.4	372.9	594.3	455.2
2012	3,173.4	353.3	2,820.1	1,078.3	235.2	1,506.6	1,107.0	399.6	641.2	492.4
2013	3,395.8	373.4	3,022.4	1,150.1	252.6	1,619.7	1,191.4	428.3	690.3	533.0
2014	3,628.6	395.0	3,233.6	1,222.8	270.7	1,740.0	1,281.1	458.9	742.1	577.1
2015	3,874.6	417.4	3,457.2	1,296.0	290.2	1,870.9	1,379.1	491.8	799.2	625.2
2016	4,136.9	440.8	3,696.1	1,371.1	311.4	2,013.6	1,486.5	527.1	862.7	677.0
Average Annual Percent Change from Previous Year Shown (Historical Estimates)										
2001	--	--	--	--	--	--	--	--	--	--
2002	9.1	5.7	9.6	10.5	7.9	9.2	9.7	8.1	7.3	10.5
2003	8.1	6.3	8.4	9.6	7.6	7.7	8.6	5.6	6.7	9.1
2004	7.2	5.0	7.6	7.9	4.9	7.8	8.6	5.7	10.3	7.5
2005	6.9	5.8	7.1	6.6	5.7	7.7	7.2	9.1	9.3	7.2
(Projected)										
2006	6.8	0.5	7.7	4.8	7.3	10.0	12.7	3.3	22.1	0.1
2007	6.6	6.1	6.7	6.7	7.6	6.5	6.5	6.7	6.5	7.3
2008	7.0	5.8	7.1	7.0	7.6	7.2	7.3	6.7	7.6	7.6
2009	7.3	6.2	7.4	7.3	8.1	7.4	7.5	6.9	7.8	7.8
2010	6.9	6.0	7.1	6.7	7.7	7.2	7.3	7.0	7.3	7.9
2011	6.8	5.7	7.0	6.5	7.3	7.3	7.4	7.1	7.4	8.1
2012	7.0	5.6	7.2	6.5	7.4	7.6	7.8	7.2	7.9	8.2
2013	7.0	5.7	7.2	6.7	7.4	7.5	7.6	7.2	7.7	8.3
2014	6.9	5.8	7.0	6.3	7.2	7.4	7.5	7.1	7.5	8.3
2015	6.8	5.7	6.9	6.0	7.2	7.5	7.6	7.2	7.7	8.3
2016	6.8	5.6	6.9	5.8	7.3	7.6	7.8	7.2	7.9	8.3

[1] The health spending projections were based on the 2005 version of the National Health Expenditures (NHE) released in January 2007.
[2] Includes Medicaid SCHIP Expansion and SCHIP.
[3] Subset of Federal funds.
[4] Subset of Federal and State and local funds. Includes Medicaid SCHIP Expansion.

Source: Centers for Medicare & Medicaid Services, Office of the Actuary
Plunkett's Health Care Industry Almanac 2008

National Health Expenditure Amounts by Type of Expenditure, U.S.: Selected Calendar Years 1980-2016[1]

(In Billions of US$)

Item	1980	1990	2000	2005	2006	2007	2008	2010	2016
National Health Expenditures	$245.8	$696.0	$1,358.5	$1,987.7	$2,122.5	$2,262.3	$2,420.0	$2,776.4	$4,136.9
Health Services & Supplies	233.5	669.6	1,264.5	1,860.9	1,987.7	2,118.9	2,267.3	2,600.8	3,869.9
Personal Health Care	214.6	609.4	1,139.9	1,661.4	1,769.2	1,885.3	2,016.6	2,312.9	3,449.4
Hospital Care	101.5	253.9	417.0	611.6	651.8	697.5	747.2	860.9	1,287.8
Professional Services	67.3	216.9	426.7	621.7	662.8	703.9	753.2	862.3	1,253.2
Physician & Clinical Services	47.1	157.5	288.6	421.2	447.0	474.2	506.2	577.1	819.9
Other Professional Services	3.6	18.2	39.1	56.7	60.9	64.9	69.1	78.0	111.0
Dental Services	13.3	31.5	62.0	86.6	92.8	98.6	104.9	118.4	163.4
Other Personal Health Care	3.3	9.6	37.1	57.2	62.0	66.2	73.0	88.8	159.0
Nursing Home & Home Health	20.1	65.3	125.8	169.3	179.4	190.0	201.5	226.1	322.0
Home Health Care	2.4	12.6	30.6	47.5	53.4	57.9	62.7	72.7	111.1
Nursing Home Care	17.7	52.7	95.3	121.9	126.1	132.1	138.8	153.4	210.9
Retail Outlet Sales of Medical Products	25.7	73.3	170.3	258.8	275.2	293.9	314.7	363.6	586.4
Prescription Drugs	12.0	40.3	120.8	200.7	213.7	229.5	247.6	291.5	497.5
Other Medical Products	13.7	33.1	49.5	58.1	61.5	64.3	67.1	72.2	88.9
Durable Medical Equipment	3.9	10.6	19.3	24.0	25.2	26.3	27.4	29.4	37.6
Other Non-Durable Medical Products	9.8	22.5	30.2	34.1	36.3	38.0	39.7	42.8	51.3
Program Administration & Net Cost of Private Health Insurance	12.1	40.0	81.2	143.0	156.8	167.4	179.8	206.2	295.7
Government Public Health Activities	6.7	20.2	43.4	56.6	61.7	66.2	70.9	81.7	124.8
Investment	12.3	26.4	94.0	126.8	134.8	143.4	152.8	175.6	267.0
Research[2]	5.5	12.7	25.6	40.0	41.7	43.9	46.3	52.1	75.0
Structures & Equipment	6.8	13.7	68.4	86.8	93.1	99.5	106.4	123.5	191.9

Note: Numbers may not add to totals because of rounding. Figures for 2006-2016 are forecasts.

[1] Health spending projections were based on the 2005 version of the National Health Expenditures (NHE) released in January 2007.

[2] Research and development expenditures of drug companies and other manufacturers and providers of medical equipment and supplies are excluded from research expenditures. These research expenditures are implicitly included in the expenditure class in which the product falls, in that they are covered by the payment received for that product.

Source: Centers for Medicare & Medicaid Services, Office of the Actuary

Plunkett's Health Care Industry Almanac 2008

Hospital Care Expenditures & Average Annual Percent Change, U.S.: Selected Calendar Years 1980-2016[1]

(By Source of Funds)

Year	Total	Out-of-Pocket Payments	Third-Party Payments						Medicare[3]	Medicaid[4]
			Total	Private Health Insurance	Other Private Funds	Public				
						Total	Federal[2]	State & Local[2]		
Amount in Billions of US$ (Historical Estimates)										
1980	$101.5	$5.3	$96.3	$36.1	$5.0	$55.2	$41.5	$13.7	$26.4	$10.6
1990	253.9	11.2	242.7	97.1	10.4	135.2	102.7	32.4	67.8	27.6
2001	451.4	14.2	437.2	157.0	20.9	259.3	210.4	48.9	137.1	76.9
2002	488.6	15.6	473.0	171.5	21.5	280.1	226.8	53.2	146.3	84.8
2003	525.4	17.0	508.4	186.2	24.4	297.8	241.8	56.0	153.8	90.9
2004	566.9	18.6	548.3	201.7	25.4	321.2	261.2	60.0	166.7	97.4
2005	611.6	20.1	591.5	217.0	27.4	347.1	279.4	67.7	180.3	106.3
(Projected)										
2006	651.8	22.0	629.7	232.9	29.9	366.9	295.9	71.0	193.5	110.0
2007	697.5	24.1	673.4	249.9	33.2	390.3	314.4	75.9	205.3	118.8
2008	747.2	26.2	721.0	269.3	36.5	415.2	334.9	80.3	219.2	126.9
2009	802.7	28.7	774.0	291.0	40.4	442.6	357.6	85.0	234.9	135.6
2010	860.9	31.1	829.8	314.1	44.4	471.3	381.4	90.0	251.3	144.9
2011	922.3	33.7	888.7	339.0	47.9	501.7	406.5	95.3	268.4	155.1
2012	988.2	36.2	952.0	365.1	51.9	535.1	434.2	100.9	287.6	166.1
2013	1058.0	38.7	1019.3	392.0	56.1	571.2	464.3	106.9	308.6	177.9
2014	1130.2	41.3	1088.8	419.5	60.4	608.9	495.7	113.2	330.4	190.6
2015	1206.7	44.0	1162.7	447.6	65.1	650.0	530.2	119.8	354.7	204.2
2016	1287.8	46.7	1241.1	475.8	69.9	695.3	568.6	126.8	382.3	218.7
Average Annual Percent Change from Previous Year Shown (Historical Estimates)										
2002	8.2	9.2	8.2	9.2	2.9	8.0	7.8	8.8	6.7	10.3
2003	7.5	9.3	7.5	8.6	13.5	6.3	6.6	5.2	5.1	7.2
2004	7.9	9.3	7.9	8.3	4.3	7.8	8.0	7.1	8.4	7.2
2005	7.9	8.2	7.9	7.6	7.6	8.1	6.9	12.9	8.1	9.2
(Projected)										
2006	6.6	9.6	6.5	7.3	9.4	5.7	5.9	4.8	7.3	3.5
2007	7.0	9.1	6.9	7.3	10.8	6.4	6.2	6.9	6.0	8.0
2008	7.1	9.1	7.1	7.8	9.9	6.4	6.5	5.8	6.8	6.8
2009	7.4	9.3	7.4	8.0	10.8	6.6	6.8	5.9	7.2	6.9
2010	7.2	8.4	7.2	7.9	9.9	6.5	6.6	5.8	7.0	6.8
2011	7.1	8.2	7.1	7.9	8.0	6.4	6.6	5.9	6.8	7.0
2012	7.1	7.4	7.1	7.7	8.2	6.7	6.8	5.9	7.2	7.1
2013	7.1	7.1	7.1	7.4	8.1	6.7	6.9	5.9	7.3	7.1
2014	6.8	6.8	6.8	7.0	7.8	6.6	6.8	5.9	7.1	7.1
2015	6.8	6.5	6.8	6.7	7.6	6.8	7.0	5.9	7.4	7.2
2016	6.7	6.1	6.7	6.3	7.5	7.0	7.2	5.8	7.8	7.1

[1] Health spending projections were based on the 2005 version of the National Health Expenditures (NHE) released in January 2007.
[2] Includes Medicaid SCHIP Expansion and SCHIP.
[3] Subset of Federal funds.
[4] Subset of Federal and State and local funds. Includes Medicaid SCHIP Expansion.

Source: Centers for Medicare & Medicaid Services, Office of the Actuary
Plunkett's Health Care Industry Almanac 2008

Hospital Care Expenditures, Percent Distribution & Per Capita Amount, U.S.: Selected Calendar Years 1980-2016[1]

(By Source of Funds)

Year	Total	Out-of-Pocket Payments	Third-Party Payments						Medicare[3]	Medicaid[4]
			Total	Private Health Insurance	Other Private Funds	Public				
						Total	Federal[2]	State & Local[2]		
Per Capita Amount in US$ (Historical Estimates)										
1980	$441	$23	$418	$157	$22	$239	$180	$59	(5)	(5)
1990	999	44	955	382	41	532	404	128	(5)	(5)
2001	1,581	50	1,532	550	73	908	737	171	(5)	(5)
2002	1,695	54	1,641	595	74	971	787	185	(5)	(5)
2003	1,804	58	1,746	639	84	1,023	830	192	(5)	(5)
2004	1,928	63	1,865	686	86	1,092	888	204	(5)	(5)
2005	2,061	68	1,993	731	92	1,169	941	228	(5)	(5)
(Projected)										
2006	2,178	74	2,104	778	100	1,226	989	237	(5)	(5)
2007	2,312	80	2,232	828	110	1,294	1,042	252	(5)	(5)
2008	2,457	86	2,370	886	120	1,365	1,101	264	(5)	(5)
2009	2,618	94	2,525	949	132	1,444	1,166	277	(5)	(5)
2010	2,786	101	2,685	1,016	144	1,525	1,234	291	(5)	(5)
2011	2,962	108	2,853	1,089	154	1,611	1,305	306	(5)	(5)
2012	3,148	115	3,033	1,163	165	1,705	1,383	322	(5)	(5)
2013	3,345	122	3,222	1,239	177	1,806	1,468	338	(5)	(5)
2014	3,545	130	3,416	1,316	190	1,910	1,555	355	(5)	(5)
2015	3,757	137	3,620	1,394	203	2,024	1,651	373	(5)	(5)
2016	3,979	144	3,835	1,470	216	2,148	1,757	392	(5)	(5)
Percent Distribution (Historical Estimates)										
1980	100.0	5.2	94.8	35.6	4.9	54.3	40.9	13.5	26.0	10.4
1990	100.0	4.4	95.6	38.3	4.1	53.2	40.5	12.8	26.7	10.9
2001	100.0	3.2	96.8	34.8	4.6	57.4	46.6	10.8	30.4	17.0
2002	100.0	3.2	96.8	35.1	4.4	57.3	46.4	10.9	29.9	17.4
2003	100.0	3.2	96.8	35.4	4.6	56.7	46.0	10.7	29.3	17.3
2004	100.0	3.3	96.7	35.6	4.5	56.7	46.1	10.6	29.4	17.2
2005	100.0	3.3	96.7	35.5	4.5	56.8	45.7	11.1	29.5	17.4
Percent Distribution (Projected)										
2006	100.0	3.4	96.6	35.7	4.6	56.3	45.4	10.9	29.7	16.9
2007	100.0	3.4	96.6	35.8	4.8	56.0	45.1	10.9	29.4	17.0
2008	100.0	3.5	96.5	36.0	4.9	55.6	44.8	10.7	29.3	17.0
2009	100.0	3.6	96.4	36.3	5.0	55.1	44.5	10.6	29.3	16.9
2010	100.0	3.6	96.4	36.5	5.2	54.7	44.3	10.4	29.2	16.8
2011	100.0	3.6	96.4	36.8	5.2	54.4	44.1	10.3	29.1	16.8
2012	100.0	3.7	96.3	36.9	5.2	54.2	43.9	10.2	29.1	16.8
2013	100.0	3.7	96.3	37.1	5.3	54.0	43.9	10.1	29.2	16.8
2014	100.0	3.7	96.3	37.1	5.3	53.9	43.9	10.0	29.2	16.9
2015	100.0	3.6	96.4	37.1	5.4	53.9	43.9	9.9	29.4	16.9
2016	100.0	3.6	96.4	37.0	5.4	54.0	44.1	9.8	29.7	17.0

[1] Health spending projections were based on the 2005 version of the National Health Expenditures (NHE) released in January 2007. 2 Includes Medicaid SCHIP Expansion and SCHIP. 3 Subset of Federal funds. 4 Subset of Federal and State and local funds. Includes Medicaid SCHIP Expansion. 5 Calculation of per capita estimates is inappropriate.

Notes: Per capita amounts based on July 1 Census resident based population estimates. Numbers and percents may not add to totals because of rounding.

Source: Centers for Medicare & Medicaid Services, Office of the Actuary

Plunkett's Health Care Industry Almanac 2008

Home Health Care Expenditures & Average Annual Percent Change, U.S.: Selected Calendar Years 1980-2016[1]

(By Source of Funds)

Year	Total	Out-of-Pocket Payments	Third-Party Payments						Medicare[3]	Medicaid[4]
			Total	Private Health Insurance	Other Private Funds	Public				
						Total	Federal2	State & Local[2]		
Amount in Billions of US$ (Historical Estimates)										
1980	$2.40	$0.40	$2.00	$0.30	$0.40	$1.30	$0.80	$0.50	$0.60	$0.30
1990	12.6	2.3	10.3	2.9	1.0	6.5	4.4	2.0	3.3	2.1
2001	32.2	5.4	26.8	5.8	1.0	20.0	14.5	5.5	9.9	8.4
2002	34.2	4.9	29.3	5.1	0.8	23.4	17.2	6.2	11.6	10.0
2003	38.0	4.8	33.2	5.2	0.9	27.1	20.4	6.7	13.7	11.8
2004	42.7	5.0	37.7	5.2	0.9	31.5	23.9	7.7	16.1	13.6
2005	47.5	5.1	42.3	5.8	1.1	35.5	26.5	9.0	17.9	15.5
(Projected)										
2006	53.4	5.4	48.0	6.2	1.2	40.6	30.0	10.6	19.8	18.6
2007	57.9	5.7	52.3	6.7	1.2	44.4	32.7	11.7	21.5	20.5
2008	62.7	6.0	56.7	7.1	1.3	48.4	35.6	12.8	23.2	22.7
2009	67.7	6.2	61.4	7.5	1.3	52.6	38.6	14.0	25.0	25.0
2010	72.7	6.5	66.2	7.9	1.4	56.9	41.6	15.3	26.7	27.4
2011	78.1	6.8	71.3	8.4	1.4	61.5	44.8	16.7	28.4	30.2
2012	83.7	7.1	76.7	8.8	1.5	66.4	48.2	18.2	30.2	33.1
2013	89.8	7.3	82.5	9.3	1.5	71.7	51.9	19.8	32.1	36.3
2014	96.3	7.6	88.7	9.7	1.6	77.3	55.8	21.6	34.1	39.7
2015	103.3	7.9	95.5	10.2	1.7	83.6	60.1	23.5	36.4	43.5
2016	111.1	8.2	102.9	10.8	1.7	90.4	64.9	25.6	39.0	47.5
Average Annual Percent Change from Previous Year Shown (Historical Estimates)										
2002	6.3	-9.4	9.5	-10.9	-16.7	16.7	18.3	12.5	16.9	20.0
2003	11.1	-2.0	13.3	1.0	8.3	16.2	18.9	8.8	18.4	16.9
2004	12.3	5.0	13.4	0.1	4.7	16.2	16.9	14.0	17.9	15.9
2005	11.1	2.1	12.3	11.2	15.7	12.4	10.8	17.3	10.7	14.0
(Projected)										
2006	12.5	5.5	13.3	7.9	4.9	14.5	13.2	18.2	10.8	19.8
2007	8.6	5.0	9.0	7.0	4.6	9.4	9.1	10.1	8.6	10.5
2008	8.2	4.9	8.6	6.6	4.5	9.0	8.8	9.6	7.9	10.4
2009	7.9	4.6	8.3	5.9	4.3	8.7	8.5	9.4	7.6	10.1
2010	7.5	4.4	7.8	5.5	4.2	8.2	7.9	9.1	6.8	9.8
2011	7.4	4.3	7.7	5.4	4.0	8.1	7.6	9.2	6.4	9.9
2012	7.3	4.0	7.6	5.1	3.9	8.0	7.6	9.0	6.4	9.7
2013	7.3	3.9	7.6	5.2	3.9	8.0	7.6	9.0	6.4	9.6
2014	7.2	3.8	7.5	5.2	3.9	7.9	7.5	8.8	6.3	9.5
2015	7.3	3.6	7.6	5.0	3.8	8.0	7.7	8.8	6.6	9.4
2016	7.5	3.7	7.8	5.0	3.9	8.2	8.0	8.8	7.2	9.3

[1] Health spending projections were based on the 2005 version of the National Health Expenditures (NHE) released in January 2007.
[2] Includes Medicaid SCHIP Expansion and SCHIP.
[3] Subset of Federal funds.
[4] Subset of Federal and State and local funds. Includes Medicaid SCHIP Expansion.

Source: Centers for Medicare & Medicaid Services, Office of the Actuary
Plunkett's Health Care Industry Almanac 2008

Home Health Care Expenditures, Percent Distribution & Per Capita Amounts, U.S.: Selected Calendar Years 1980-2016[1]

(By Source of Funds)

Year	Total	Out-of-Pocket Payments	Third-Party Payments						Medicare[3]	Medicaid[4]
			Total	Private Health Insurance	Other Private Funds	Public				
						Total	Federal[2]	State & Local[2]		
Percent Distribution (Historical Estimates)										
1980	100.0	15.3	84.7	14.7	15.5	54.5	33.6	21.0	26.8	11.7
1990	100.0	18.1	81.9	22.7	7.6	51.6	35.3	16.2	26.0	17.0
2001	100.0	16.7	83.3	17.9	3.1	62.2	45.1	17.1	30.7	26.0
2002	100.0	14.2	85.8	15.0	2.4	68.3	50.2	18.1	33.8	29.4
2003	100.0	12.6	87.4	13.7	2.4	71.4	53.7	17.7	36.0	30.9
2004	100.0	11.7	88.3	12.2	2.2	73.9	55.9	17.9	37.8	31.9
2005	100.0	10.8	89.2	12.2	2.3	74.7	55.8	18.9	37.7	32.7
(Projected)										
2006	100.0	10.1	89.9	11.7	2.2	76.0	56.1	19.9	37.1	34.8
2007	100.0	9.8	90.2	11.5	2.1	76.6	56.4	20.2	37.1	35.5
2008	100.0	9.5	90.5	11.3	2.0	77.2	56.7	20.4	37.0	36.2
2009	100.0	9.2	90.8	11.1	1.9	77.7	57.0	20.7	36.9	36.9
2010	100.0	8.9	91.1	10.9	1.9	78.2	57.2	21.0	36.7	37.7
2011	100.0	8.7	91.3	10.7	1.8	78.8	57.4	21.4	36.3	38.6
2012	100.0	8.4	91.6	10.5	1.8	79.3	57.6	21.7	36.0	39.5
2013	100.0	8.2	91.8	10.3	1.7	79.8	57.7	22.1	35.8	40.4
2014	100.0	7.9	92.1	10.1	1.7	80.3	57.9	22.4	35.5	41.2
2015	100.0	7.6	92.4	9.9	1.6	80.9	58.1	22.7	35.2	42.1
2016	100.0	7.3	92.7	9.7	1.5	81.4	58.4	23.0	35.1	42.8
Per Capita Amount in US$ (Historical Estimates)										
1980	$10	$2	$9	$2	$2	$6	$3	$2	(5)	(5)
1990	49	9	41	11	4	25	17	8	(5)	(5)
2001	113.0	19.0	94.0	20.0	4.0	70.0	51.0	19.0	(5)	(5)
2002	119.0	17.0	102.0	18.0	3.0	81.0	60.0	21.0	(5)	(5)
2003	131.0	16.0	114.0	18.0	3.0	93.0	70.0	23.0	(5)	(5)
2004	145.0	17.0	128.0	18.0	3.0	107.0	81.0	26.0	(5)	(5)
2005	160.0	17.0	143.0	19.0	4.0	119.0	89.0	30.0	(5)	(5)
(Projected)										
2006	178.0	18.0	160.0	21.0	4.0	136.0	100.0	36.0	(5)	(5)
2007	192.0	19.0	173.0	22.0	4.0	147.0	108.0	39.0	(5)	(5)
2008	206.0	20.0	187.0	23.0	4.0	159.0	117.0	42.0	(5)	(5)
2009	221.0	20.0	200.0	25.0	4.0	172.0	126.0	46.0	(5)	(5)
2010	235.0	21.0	214.0	26.0	4.0	184.0	135.0	49.0	(5)	(5)
2011	251.0	22.0	229.0	27.0	5.0	197.0	144.0	54.0	(5)	(5)
2012	267.0	22.0	244.0	28.0	5.0	212.0	154.0	58.0	(5)	(5)
2013	284.0	23.0	261.0	29.0	5.0	227.0	164.0	63.0	(5)	(5)
2014	302.0	24.0	278.0	31.0	5.0	243.0	175.0	68.0	(5)	(5)
2015	322.0	25.0	297.0	32.0	5.0	260.0	187.0	73.0	(5)	(5)
2016	343.0	25.0	318.0	33.0	5.0	279.0	200.0	79.0	(5)	(5)

[1] Health spending projections were based on the 2005 version of the National Health Expenditures (NHE) released in January 2007. 2 Includes Medicaid SCHIP Expansion and SCHIP. [3] Subset of Federal funds. [4] Subset of Federal and State and local funds. Includes Medicaid SCHIP Expansion. [5] Calculation of per capita estimates is inappropriate.

Notes: Per capita amounts based on July 1 Census resident based population estimates. Numbers and percents may not add to totals because of rounding.

Source: Centers for Medicare & Medicaid Services, Office of the Actuary

Plunkett's Health Care Industry Almanac 2008

Nursing Home Care Expenditures & Average Annual Percent Change, U.S.: Selected Calendar Years, 1980-2016[1]

(By Source of Funds)

Year	Total	Out-of-Pocket Payments	Third-Party Payments							
			Total	Private Health Insurance	Other Private Funds	Public			Medicare[3]	Medicaid[4]
						Total	Federal[2]	State & Local[2]		
Amount in Billions of US$ (Historical Estimates)										
1980	$17.7	$7.1	$10.6	$0.2	$0.8	$9.6	$5.7	$3.9	$0.3	$8.9
1990	52.7	19.8	32.9	3.1	3.9	25.9	15.8	10.2	1.7	23.2
2001	101.5	28.9	72.6	8.1	4.0	60.4	42.0	18.4	12.5	45.8
2002	105.7	29.6	76.1	8.7	4.0	63.4	44.5	18.9	13.9	47.1
2003	110.5	30.5	80.0	8.7	4.2	67.2	46.1	21.1	14.7	49.7
2004	115.0	30.6	84.4	8.6	4.2	71.5	49.3	22.2	17.1	51.5
2005	121.9	32.3	89.6	9.1	4.5	75.9	52.0	23.9	19.2	53.5
(Projected)										
2006	126.1	33.8	92.2	9.6	4.8	77.8	53.5	24.3	20.1	54.2
2007	132.1	35.1	97.0	10.0	5.0	82.0	56.5	25.5	21.7	56.5
2008	138.8	36.5	102.3	10.2	5.2	86.8	60.0	26.8	23.3	59.4
2009	146.1	38.1	107.9	10.5	5.4	92.0	63.7	28.3	24.8	62.8
2010	153.4	39.8	113.6	10.7	5.6	97.2	67.2	30.0	26.1	66.4
2011	161.2	41.5	119.7	11.0	5.8	102.9	71.1	31.8	27.4	70.4
2012	169.6	43.2	126.3	11.3	6.0	109.1	75.3	33.8	28.9	74.8
2013	178.7	45.1	133.6	11.6	6.3	115.7	79.8	35.9	30.3	79.6
2014	188.5	47.2	141.3	12.0	6.5	122.9	84.6	38.3	31.9	84.8
2015	199.2	49.3	149.9	12.4	6.7	130.8	90.0	40.9	33.7	90.5
2016	210.9	51.5	159.4	12.7	7.0	139.7	96.0	43.7	35.9	96.7
Average Annual Percent Change from Previous Year Shown (Historical Estimates)										
2002	4.1	2.4	4.8	7.0	0.3	4.9	5.8	2.7	11.6	3.0
2003	4.5	2.9	5.1	-0.2	3.2	6.0	3.7	11.4	5.7	5.5
2004	4.1	0.5	5.5	-0.6	1.4	6.5	7.0	5.4	16.2	3.6
2005	6.0	5.3	6.2	6.2	6.7	6.1	5.4	7.7	12.0	3.0
(Projected)										
2006	3.4	4.8	3.0	5.5	5.9	2.5	2.8	1.8	4.8	1.3
2007	4.8	3.8	5.1	3.6	4.7	5.3	5.6	4.7	7.9	4.3
2008	5.1	4.0	5.5	2.5	4.1	5.9	6.2	5.2	7.5	5.2
2009	5.2	4.4	5.5	2.6	4.0	6.0	6.1	5.6	6.5	5.6
2010	5.0	4.3	5.3	2.2	3.9	5.7	5.6	5.8	5.2	5.8
2011	5.1	4.2	5.4	2.2	3.7	5.8	5.7	6.0	5.1	6.0
2012	5.2	4.2	5.5	2.5	3.5	6.0	5.9	6.2	5.2	6.2
2013	5.4	4.5	5.7	2.9	3.8	6.1	6.0	6.4	5.1	6.4
2014	5.5	4.5	5.8	3.3	3.7	6.2	6.0	6.6	5.0	6.6
2015	5.7	4.5	6.1	3.3	3.6	6.5	6.4	6.8	5.6	6.8
2016	5.9	4.4	6.3	3.2	3.4	6.8	6.8	6.8	6.7	6.8

[1] Health spending projections are based on the 2005 version of the National Health Expenditures (NHE) released in January 2007.
[2] Includes Medicaid SCHIP Expansion and SCHIP.
[3] Subset of Federal funds.
[4] Subset of Federal and State and local funds.

Source: Centers for Medicare & Medicaid Services, Office of the Actuary
Plunkett's Healthcare Industry Almanac 2008

Nursing Home Care Expenditures, Percent Distribution & Per Capita Amount: Selected Calendar Years 1980-2016[1]

(By Source of Funds)

Year	Total	Out-of-Pocket Payments	Third-Party Payments						Medicare[3]	Medicaid[4]
			Total	Private Health Insurance	Other Private Funds	Public				
						Total	Federal[2]	State & Local[2]		
Per Capita Amount in US$ (Historical Estimates)										
1980	$77	$31	$46	$1	$3	$42	$25	$17	(5)	(5)
1990	207	78	130	12	16	102	62	40	(5)	(5)
2001	$356	$101	$254	$28	$14	$212	$147	$65	(5)	(5)
2002	367	103	264	30	14	220	154	66	(5)	(5)
2003	379	105	275	30	14	231	158	72	(5)	(5)
2004	391	104	287	29	14	243	168	76	(5)	(5)
2005	411	109	302	31	15	256	175	81	(5)	(5)
(Projected)										
2006	421	113	308	32	16	260	179	81	(5)	(5)
2007	438	116	321	33	17	272	187	85	(5)	(5)
2008	456	120	336	34	17	285	197	88	(5)	(5)
2009	476	124	352	34	18	300	208	92	(5)	(5)
2010	496	129	368	35	18	315	218	97	(5)	(5)
2011	517	133	384	35	19	330	228	102	(5)	(5)
2012	540	138	403	36	19	347	240	108	(5)	(5)
2013	565	143	422	37	20	366	252	114	(5)	(5)
2014	591	148	443	37	20	385	265	120	(5)	(5)
2015	620	154	467	38	21	407	280	127	(5)	(5)
2016	652	159	493	39	21	432	297	135	(5)	(5)
Percent Distribution (Historical Estimates)										
2001	100	28.5	71.5	8.0	4.0	59.5	41.4	18.1	12.3	45.1
2002	100	28.0	72.0	8.2	3.8	60.0	42.1	17.9	13.2	44.6
2003	100	27.6	72.4	7.8	3.8	60.8	41.7	19.1	13.3	45.0
2004	100	26.6	73.4	7.5	3.7	62.2	42.9	19.3	14.9	44.8
2005	100	26.5	73.5	7.5	3.7	62.3	42.7	19.6	15.7	43.9
(Projected)										
2006	100	26.8	73.2	7.7	3.8	61.7	42.4	19.3	15.9	43.0
2007	100	26.6	73.4	7.6	3.8	62.1	42.8	19.3	16.4	42.8
2008	100	26.3	73.7	7.4	3.7	62.6	43.2	19.3	16.8	42.8
2009	100	26.1	73.9	7.2	3.7	63.0	43.6	19.4	17.0	43.0
2010	100	25.9	74.1	7.0	3.7	63.4	43.8	19.6	17.0	43.3
2011	100	25.7	74.3	6.8	3.6	63.9	44.1	19.7	17.0	43.7
2012	100	25.5	74.5	6.6	3.6	64.3	44.4	19.9	17.0	44.1
2013	100	25.3	74.7	6.5	3.5	64.8	44.6	20.1	17.0	44.5
2014	100	25.0	75.0	6.3	3.4	65.2	44.9	20.3	16.9	45.0
2015	100	24.8	75.2	6.2	3.4	65.7	45.1	20.5	16.9	45.4
2016	100	24.4	75.6	6.0	3.3	66.2	45.5	20.7	17.0	45.0

[1] Health spending projections are based on the 2005 version of the National Health Expenditures (NHE) released in January 2007.

[2] Includes Medicaid SCHIP Expansion and SCHIP. [3] Subset of Federal funds. [4] Subset of Federal and State and local funds.

[5] Calculation of per capita estimates is inappropriate.

Note: Per capita amounts based on July 1 Census resident based population estimates. Numbers and percents may not add to totals because of rounding.

Source: Centers for Medicare & Medicaid Services, Office of the Actuary

Plunkett's Health Care Industry Almanac 2008

Prescription Drug Expenditures, U.S.: 1965-2016

(In Millions of US$)

Year	TOTAL	Private			Public							
						Federal				State & Local		
		Total Private	Out-of-Pocket	Insurance	Total Public	Total Fed	Medicare	Medicaid	Other	Total S&L	Medicaid	Other
1965	3,715	3,571	3,441	130	144	58	0	0	58	85	0	85
1966	3,985	3,776	3,594	182	210	95	0	50	45	115	53	62
1967	4,227	3,950	3,712	238	277	127	0	99	29	150	106	44
1968	4,742	4,437	4,120	317	306	141	0	114	27	165	106	59
1969	5,149	4,761	4,362	399	389	191	0	165	26	197	135	62
1970	5,497	5,015	4,531	484	483	237	0	224	13	245	193	53
1971	5,877	5,309	4,752	558	568	297	0	281	16	271	214	57
1972	6,325	5,678	5,035	644	646	328	0	308	20	318	255	63
1973	6,817	6,083	5,341	742	735	355	0	336	19	379	308	71
1974	7,422	6,567	5,714	854	855	443	0	419	24	412	321	91
1975	8,052	7,032	6,068	963	1,021	508	0	478	30	512	392	120
1976	8,723	7,566	6,476	1,089	1,157	610	0	576	35	547	394	153
1977	9,196	7,946	6,754	1,192	1,250	624	0	587	37	626	449	177
1978	9,891	8,531	7,115	1,416	1,361	655	0	613	41	706	493	213
1979	10,744	9,177	7,470	1,707	1,567	743	0	701	42	823	536	288
1980	12,049	10,249	8,466	1,783	1,800	857	0	813	44	943	595	348
1981	13,398	11,338	8,844	2,494	2,060	979	0	932	47	1,081	679	402
1982	15,029	12,840	10,272	2,568	2,189	990	0	934	56	1,199	735	464
1983	17,323	14,808	11,254	3,554	2,515	1,133	0	1,067	66	1,382	841	541
1984	19,618	16,670	12,503	4,168	2,948	1,311	2	1,238	71	1,637	982	655
1985	21,795	18,566	13,609	4,957	3,229	1,421	21	1,323	78	1,808	1,009	799
1986	24,290	20,197	15,451	4,746	4,093	1,834	44	1,707	84	2,259	1,279	980
1987	26,889	22,261	16,406	5,855	4,628	2,077	75	1,910	92	2,550	1,486	1,065
1988	30,646	25,325	18,335	6,990	5,321	2,398	102	2,184	111	2,923	1,630	1,293
1989	34,758	28,831	20,153	8,678	5,927	2,617	139	2,353	124	3,309	1,729	1,580
1990	40,291	33,002	22,376	10,627	7,288	3,247	185	2,915	147	4,041	2,162	1,879
1991	44,381	35,951	23,047	12,904	8,431	3,832	226	3,437	169	4,599	2,607	1,992
1992	47,573	38,071	23,417	14,654	9,502	4,463	281	3,990	193	5,038	2,894	2,145
1993	50,991	40,476	24,097	16,379	10,515	5,122	352	4,540	230	5,393	3,181	2,212
1994	54,302	42,653	23,384	19,269	11,649	5,739	468	4,990	282	5,910	3,638	2,272
1995	60,876	47,790	23,349	24,441	13,086	6,614	680	5,557	377	6,472	4,143	2,330
1996	68,536	53,873	24,180	29,694	14,662	7,832	967	6,308	558	6,830	4,517	2,314
1997	77,666	61,244	25,670	35,574	16,422	9,027	1,206	7,025	796	7,395	5,077	2,317
1998	88,595	69,589	27,477	42,112	19,006	10,672	1,499	8,108	1,065	8,334	5,976	2,358
1999	104,684	81,597	30,410	51,187	23,087	13,163	1,866	9,805	1,492	9,924	7,257	2,668
2000	120,803	93,166	33,444	59,722	27,638	15,847	2,055	11,727	2,066	11,790	8,575	3,215
2001	138,559	105,543	36,206	69,337	33,016	19,191	2,415	13,919	2,857	13,825	10,081	3,744
2002	157,941	118,605	40,389	78,217	39,336	23,071	2,417	16,366	4,288	16,265	11,645	4,620
2003	174,639	128,577	44,437	84,140	46,062	27,665	2,366	19,569	5,731	18,397	13,197	5,200
2004	189,651	137,826	47,864	89,962	51,825	31,413	3,340	21,470	6,602	20,412	15,082	5,330
2005	200,716	146,110	50,906	95,204	54,606	32,872	3,999	21,522	7,351	21,733	16,075	5,658
2006	213,714	129,653	40,376	89,278	84,060	67,976	46,058	13,829	8,089	16,084	10,064	6,020

(Continued on next page)

Prescription Drug Expenditures, U.S.: 1965-2016 (cont.)

(In Millions of US$)

Year	TOTAL	Private			Public							
		Total Private	Out-of-Pocket	Insurance	Total Public	Federal				State & Local		
						Total Fed	Medicare	Medicaid	Other	Total S&L	Medicaid	Other
2007	229,547	137,357	43,297	94,060	92,189	74,766	51,058	14,821	8,887	17,423	10,902	6,521
2008	247,612	144,278	46,119	98,158	103,334	84,726	59,222	15,600	9,904	18,609	11,466	7,143
2009	268,331	153,448	49,832	103,616	114,883	94,894	67,216	16,517	11,160	19,989	12,134	7,856
2010	291,492	163,299	53,967	109,332	128,193	106,510	76,199	17,770	12,541	21,682	13,050	8,633
2011	317,470	174,137	58,398	115,739	143,332	119,796	86,581	19,172	14,042	23,536	14,075	9,461
2012	346,496	185,564	63,253	122,311	160,931	135,357	98,873	20,708	15,775	25,575	15,198	10,376
2013	378,629	200,603	69,053	131,550	178,026	150,252	110,174	22,362	17,716	27,773	16,407	11,366
2014	414,162	217,271	75,548	141,723	196,890	166,738	122,687	24,147	19,904	30,153	17,712	12,441
2015	453,602	235,522	82,657	152,865	218,080	185,330	136,862	26,094	22,374	32,750	19,135	13,614
2016	497,526	255,547	90,454	165,093	241,978	206,420	153,054	28,174	25,191	35,559	20,655	14,903

Notes: Federal and State and Local Medicaid expenditures include Medicaid SCHIP Expansion. Federal and State and Local "Other" funds include SCHIP. The health spending projections were based on the 2005 version of the NHE released in January 2007. 2006-2016 are projections.

Source: Centers for Medicare & Medicaid Services (CMS), Office of the Actuary

Plunkett's Health Care Industry Almanac 2008

U.S. Prescription Drug Expenditures & Average Annual Percent Change: Selected Calendar Years 1990-2016[1]

(By Source of Funds)

Year	Total	Out-of-Pocket Payments	Third-Party Payments						Medicare[3]	Medicaid[4]
			Total	Private Health Insurance	Other Private Funds	Public				
						Total	Federal[2]	State & Local[2]		
Amount in Billions of US$ (Historical Estimates)										
1990	$40.30	$23.80	$16.50	$9.80	--	$6.70	$3.20	$3.40	$0.20	$5.10
2001	138.6	36.2	102.4	69.3	0	33.0	19.2	13.8	2.4	24.0
2002	157.9	40.4	117.6	78.2	0	39.3	23.1	16.3	2.4	28.0
2003	174.6	44.4	130.2	84.1	0	46.1	27.7	18.4	2.4	32.8
2004	189.7	47.9	141.8	90.0	0	51.8	31.4	20.4	3.3	36.6
2005	200.7	50.9	149.8	95.2	0	54.6	32.9	21.7	4.0	37.6
(Projected)										
2006	213.7	40.4	173.3	89.3	0	84.1	68.0	16.1	46.1	23.9
2007	229.5	43.3	186.2	94.1	0	92.2	74.8	17.4	51.1	25.7
2008	247.6	46.1	201.5	98.2	0	103.3	84.7	18.6	59.2	27.1
2009	268.3	49.8	218.5	103.6	0	114.9	94.9	20.0	67.2	28.7
2010	291.5	54.0	237.5	109.3	0	128.2	106.5	21.7	76.2	30.8
2011	317.5	58.4	259.1	115.7	0	143.3	119.8	23.5	86.6	33.2
2012	346.5	63.3	283.2	122.3	0	160.9	135.4	25.6	98.9	35.9
2013	378.6	69.1	309.6	131.6	0	178.0	150.3	27.8	110.2	38.8
2014	414.2	75.5	338.6	141.7	0	196.9	166.7	30.2	122.7	41.9
2015	453.6	82.7	370.9	152.9	0	218.1	185.3	32.7	136.9	45.2
2016	497.5	90.5	407.1	165.1	0	242.0	206.4	35.6	153.1	48.8
Average Annual Percent Change from Previous Year Shown (Historical Estimates)										
2002	14.0	11.6	14.8	12.8	--	19.1	20.2	17.6	0.1	16.7
2003	10.6	10.0	10.8	7.6	--	17.1	19.9	13.1	-2.1	17.0
2004	8.6	7.7	8.9	6.9	--	12.5	13.5	11.0	41.2	11.6
2005	5.8	6.4	5.7	5.8	--	5.4	4.6	6.5	19.7	2.9
(Projected)										
2006	6.5	-20.7	15.7	-6.2	--	53.9	106.8	-26.0	1,051.6	-36.5
2007	7.4	7.2	7.4	5.4	--	9.7	10.0	8.3	10.9	7.7
2008	7.9	6.5	8.2	4.4	--	12.1	13.3	6.8	16.0	5.2
2009	8.4	8.1	8.4	5.6	--	11.2	12.0	7.4	13.5	5.9
2010	8.6	8.3	8.7	5.5	--	11.6	12.2	8.5	13.4	7.6
2011	8.9	8.2	9.1	5.9	--	11.8	12.5	8.6	13.6	7.9
2012	9.1	8.3	9.3	5.7	--	12.3	13.0	8.7	14.2	8.0
2013	9.3	9.2	9.3	7.6	--	10.6	11.0	8.6	11.4	8.0
2014	9.4	9.4	9.4	7.7	--	10.6	11.0	8.6	11.4	8.0
2015	9.5	9.4	9.5	7.9	--	10.8	11.2	8.6	11.6	8.1
2016	9.7	9.4	9.7	8.0	--	11.0	11.4	8.6	11.8	8.0

[1] Health spending projections were based on the 2005 version of the National Health Expenditures (NHE) released in January 2007.
[2] Includes Medicaid SCHIP Expansion and SCHIP. [3] Subset of Federal funds. [4] Subset of Federal and State and local funds.

Source: Centers for Medicare & Medicaid Services, Office of the Actuary
Plunkett's Health Care Industry Almanac 2008

U.S. Prescription Drug Expenditures, Percent Distribution & Per Capita Amount: Selected Calendar Years, 1980-2016[1]

(By Source of Funds)

Year	Total	Out-of-Pocket Payments	Third-Party Payments						Medicare[3]	Medicaid[4]
			Total	Private Health Insurance	Other Private Funds	Public				
						Total	Federal[2]	State & Local[2]		
Per Capita Amount in US$ (Historical Estimates)										
1980	$52	$36	$16	$9	--	$7	$4	$4	(5)	(5)
1990	159	94	65	39	--	26	13	14	(5)	(5)
2001	$485	$127	$359	$243	$0	$116	$67	$48	(5)	(5)
2002	548	140	408	271	0	136	80	56	(5)	(5)
2003	600	153	447	289	0	158	95	63	(5)	(5)
2004	645	163	482	306	0	176	107	69	(5)	(5)
2005	676	172	505	321	0	184	111	73	(5)	(5)
(Projected)										
2006	714	135	579	298	0	281	227	54	(5)	(5)
2007	761	143	617	312	0	306	248	58	(5)	(5)
2008	814	152	663	323	0	340	279	61	(5)	(5)
2009	875	163	713	338	0	375	310	65	(5)	(5)
2010	943	175	769	354	0	415	345	70	(5)	(5)
2011	1,019	188	832	372	0	460	385	76	(5)	(5)
2012	1,104	202	902	390	0	513	431	81	(5)	(5)
2013	1,197	218	979	416	0	563	475	88	(5)	(5)
2014	1,299	237	1,062	445	0	618	523	95	(5)	(5)
2015	1,412	257	1,155	476	0	679	577	102	(5)	(5)
2016	1,537	279	1,258	510	0	748	638	110	(5)	(5)
Percent Distribution (Historical Estimates)										
1980	100.0	69.4	30.6	16.7	--	13.9	7.1	6.8	--	11.7
1990	100	59.1	40.9	24.4	--	16.6	8.0	8.5	0.5	12.6
2001	100	26.1	73.9	50.0	0	23.8	13.9	10.0	1.7	17.3
2002	100	25.6	74.4	49.5	0	24.9	14.6	10.3	1.5	17.7
2003	100	25.4	74.6	48.2	0	26.4	15.8	10.5	1.4	18.8
2004	100	25.2	74.8	47.4	0	27.3	16.6	10.8	1.8	19.3
2005	100	25.4	74.6	47.4	0	27.2	16.4	10.8	2.0	18.7
(Projected)										
2006	100	18.9	81.1	41.8	0	39.3	31.8	7.5	21.6	11.2
2007	100	18.9	81.1	41.0	0	40.2	32.6	7.6	22.2	11.2
2008	100	18.6	81.4	39.6	0	41.7	34.2	7.5	23.9	10.9
2009	100	18.6	81.4	38.6	0	42.8	35.4	7.4	25.0	10.7
2010	100	18.5	81.5	37.5	0	44.0	36.5	7.4	26.1	10.6
2011	100	18.4	81.6	36.5	0	45.1	37.7	7.4	27.3	10.5
2012	100	18.3	81.7	35.3	0	46.4	39.1	7.4	28.5	10.4
2013	100	18.2	81.8	34.7	0	47.0	39.7	7.3	29.1	10.2
2014	100	18.2	81.8	34.2	0	47.5	40.3	7.3	29.6	10.1
2015	100	18.2	81.8	33.7	0	48.1	40.9	7.2	30.2	10.0
2016	100	18.2	81.8	33.2	0	48.6	41.5	7.1	30.8	9.8

[1] Health spending projections were based on the 2005 version of the National Health Expenditures (NHE) released in January 2007. [2] Includes Medicaid SCHIP Expansion and SCHIP. [3] Subset of Federal funds. [4] Subset of Federal and State and local funds. Includes Medicaid SCHIP Expansion. [5] Calculation of per capita estimates is inappropriate.

Notes: Per capita amounts based on July 1 Census resident based population estimates. Numbers and percents may not add to totals because of rounding.

Source: Centers for Medicare & Medicaid Services, Office of the Actuary

Plunkett's Health Care Industry Almanac 2008

Index Levels of Medical Prices, U.S.: 2001-2006

(Latest Year Available)

	2001	2002	2003	2004	2005	2006
Consumer Price Indexes, All Urban Consumers*						
Medical Care Services[2]	278.8	292.9	306.0	321.3	336.7	350.6
Professional Services	246.5	253.9	261.2	271.5	281.7	289.3
Physicians' Services	253.6	260.6	267.7	278.3	287.5	291.9
Dental Services	269.0	281.0	292.5	306.9	324.0	340.9
Eyeglasses & Eye Care	154.5	155.5	155.9	159.3	163.2	168.1
Services by Other Medical Professionals	167.3	171.8	177.1	181.9	186.8	192.2
Hospital & Related Services	338.3	367.8	394.8	417.9	439.9	468.1
Hospital Services (12/96=100)	123.6	134.7	144.7	153.4	161.6	172.1
Inpatient Hospital Services (12/96=100)	121.0	131.2	140.1	148.1	156.6	167.5
Outpatient Hospital Services (12/86=100)	281.1	309.8	337.9	356.3	373.0	395.0
Nursing Homes & Adult Daycare (12/96=100)	121.8	127.9	135.2	140.4	145.0	151.0
Medical Care Commodities	247.6	256.4	262.8	269.3	276.0	285.9
Prescription Drugs	300.9	316.5	326.3	337.1	349.0	363.9
Non-prescription Drugs & Medical Supplies (1986=100)	150.6	150.4	152.0	152.3	151.7	154.6
Internal & Respiratory Over-the-Counter Drugs	178.9	178.8	181.2	180.9	179.7	183.4
Non-prescription Medical Equipment & Supplies	178.2	177.5	178.1	179.7	180.6	182.2
Producer Price Indexes: Industry Groupings						
Offices of Physicians, except Mental Health (12/93=100)	119.1	119.1	120.9	123.4	125.6	126.7
Medical & Diagnostic Laboratories (12/03=100)	NA	NA	NA	100.0	104.1	104.4
Medical Laboratories (12/03=100)	NA	NA	NA	99.9	105.5	106.0
Diagnostic Imaging Centers (12/03=100)	NA	NA	NA	100.1	101.6	101.6
Home Health Care Services (12/96=100)	114.0	116.6	117.0	119.8	121.1	121.8
Public Payors (12/03=100)	NA	NA	NA	100.6	101.9	103.5
Medicare Payors (12/96=100)	116.2	118.2	114.7	117.7	119.2	121.0
Private Payers (12/03=100)	NA	NA	NA	100.9	101.8	101.6
Primary Services (12/96=100)	111.0	113.6	113.4	115.9	117.2	118.1
Hospitals (12/92=100)	123.0	127.5	134.9	141.4	146.9	153.3
General Medical & Surgical Hospitals (12/92=100)	123.4	127.9	135.3	141.9	147.3	153.5
Medicare Patients (12/92=100)	113.0	116.1	122.1	126.5	131.2	137.1
Medicaid Patients (12/92=100)	117.3	121.0	125.5	128.4	130.3	133.0
All Other Patients (12/92=100)	129.4	136.1	147.0	157.4	164.1	171.2
Psychiatric & Substance Abuse Hospitals (12/92=100)	110.5	113.1	116.4	119.1	122.2	125.1
Other Specialty Hospitals (12/92=100)	126.5	134.3	146.4	155.7	164.3	184.1
Nursing Care Facilities (12/94=100)	139.3	144.6	149.4	155.6	161.4	166.2
Residential Mental Retardation Facilities (12/03=100)	NA	NA	NA	101.2	104.5	108.5
Pharmaceutical & Medicine Manufacturing (12/84=100)	220.5	226.3	235.4	244.2	255.2	266.3
Pharmaceutical Preparation Manufacturing (6/81=100)	314.5	326.7	343.3	360.1	378.7	397.9
In-Vitro Diagnostic Substance Mfg. (3/80=100)	192.0	196.2	200.9	202.6	206.4	209.6
Prescription Drugs (6/01=100)	NA	102.7	108.2	113.9	120.7	128.1
Non-Prescription (OTC) Drugs (6/01=100)	NA	99.5	99.5	99.7	100.0	101.7
Producer Price Indexes: Commodity Groupings						
Drugs & Pharmaceuticals (1982=100)	261.8	265.8	274.7	284.5	298.2	312.1
Pharmaceutical Preparations (6/01=100)	NA	102.7	107.3	112.0	117.9	124.4
Medical, Surgical & Personal Aid Devices (1982=100)	148.3	150.9	154.7	157.8	159.2	161.4
Personal Aid Equipment	155.2	161.4	162.3	165.5	167.6	172.1
Surgical & Medical Instruments & Equipment (6/82=100)	127.0	129.1	132.8	134.2	134.9	134.1
Surgical Appliances and Supplies (6/83=100)	170.4	173.9	178.2	184.3	186.0	188.9
Ophthalmic Goods (12/83=100)	118.5	119.3	120.0	120.8	121.8	124.9
Dental Equipment & Supplies (6/85=100)	170.4	172.0	179.1	182.3	187.0	206.0

NA = Not available. * Unless otherwise noted, base year is 1982-84 = 100.

Source: U.S. Bureau of Labor Statistics (BLS)
Plunkett's Health Care Industry Almanac 2008

III. Medicare & Medicaid

Contents:

Projected Federal Spending on Medicare & Medicaid: 2003-2012

(In Billions of US$)

Historical Data	2003	2004	2005	2006
Medicare (excluding premiums)	277.9	301.5	336.9	378.6
Medicare (including premiums)	249.5	269.4	298.7	329.9
Medicaid	160.7	176.2	181.7	180.6
Total*	410.2	445.6	480.4	510.5
Total Federal Government Outlays	2,160	2,293	2,472	2,655
Medicare/Medicaid % of All Federal Spending*	19.0%	19.4%	19.4%	19.2%

Projections	2007	2008	2009
Medicare (excluding premiums)	433.0	456.8	485.0
Medicare (including premiums)	372.3	391.6	414.4
Medicaid	191.9	201.9	216.4
Total*	564.2	593.5	630.8
	2010	**2011**	**2012**
Medicare (excluding premiums)	515.6	563.1	576.6
Medicare (including premiums)	439.3	480.7	487.0
Medicaid	232.7	250.4	270.2
Total*	672.0	731.1	757.2

* Medicare/Medicaid total = Medicare with Premiums + Medicaid.

Source: U.S. Office of Management and Budget

Plunkett's Health Care Industry Almanac 2008

U.S. Medicare Enrollment Estimates, Selected Years 2006-2080

(In Thousands)

	HI	SMI			
Year	Part A	Part B	Part D	Part C[1]	Total [2]
2006	42,506	39,870	39,129	6,654	42,917
2007	43,256	40,487	39,795	8,239	43,659
2008	44,102	41,201	40,546	9,293	44,496
2009	44,995	41,959	41,340	10,095	45,380
2010	45,952	42,754	42,193	10,956	46,328
2011	47,057	43,673	43,178	11,699	47,424
2012	48,373	44,807	44,354	12,536	48,731
2013	49,801	46,063	45,633	13,427	50,152
2014	51,257	47,337	46,936	14,288	51,600
2015	52,756	48,657	48,279	15,267	53,092
2020	61,027	55,966	55,778	(3)	61,339
2025	70,205	64,218	64,119	(3)	70,512
2030	78,015	71,363	71,225	(3)	78,327
2035	82,851	75,839	75,626	(3)	83,166
2040	85,735	78,546	78,252	(3)	86,054
2045	88,013	80,592	80,326	(3)	88,335
2050	90,465	82,853	82,562	(3)	90,794
2055	93,102	85,246	84,969	(3)	93,440
2060	96,193	88,106	87,794	(3)	96,547
2065	98,937	90,611	90,302	(3)	99,305
2070	101,987	93,442	93,094	(3)	102,376
2075	104,402	95,658	95,307	(3)	104,809
2080	106,849	97,908	97,552	(3)	107,278

[1]Number of beneficiaries enrolled in a Medicare Advantage plan. In order to enroll in a Medicare Advantage plan, a beneficiary must be enrolled in both Part A and Part B. Therefore, Part C enrollment is a subset of both Part A and Part B enrollment.
[2] Number of beneficiaries with HI and/or SMI coverage.
3 No estimates are available after 2015

Source: Centers for Medicare & Medicaid Services

Plunkett's Health Care Industry Almanac 2008

Medicare Aged & Disabled Enrollees: 1980-2007

(All Types of Medicare Coverage, as of July 1)

Year	All Persons	Aged Persons	Disabled Persons
1980	28,478,245	25,515,070	2,963,175
1981	29,009,034	26,010,978	2,998,956
1982	29,494,219	26,539,994	2,954,225
1983	30,026,082	27,108,500	2,917,582
1984	30,455,369	27,570,950	2,884,418
1985	31,082,801	28,175,916	2,906,885
1986	31,749,708	29,791,262	2,958,546
1987	32,411,204	29,380,480	3,030,724
1988	32,980,033	29,878,528	3,101,505
1989	33,579,449	30,408,525	3,170,924
1990	34,203,383	30,948,376	3,255,007
1991	34,870,240	31,484,779	3,385,461
1992	35,579,149	32,010,515	3,568,634
1993	36,305,903	32,461,719	3,844,184
1994	36,935,366	32,800,745	4,134,621
1995	37,535,024	33,141,730	4,394,294
1996	38,064,130	33,423,945	4,640,184
1997	38,444,739	33,629,955	4,814,784
1998	38,824,855	33,802,038	5,022,817
1999	39,140,386	33,928,752	5,211,634
2000	39,619,986	34,252,835	5,367,151
2001	40,025,724	34,462,465	5,563,259
2002	40,488,878	34,679,267	5,809,611
2003	41,086,981	35,007,557	6,079,424
2004	41,728,804	35,300,848	6,392,527
2005	42,394,926	35,633,683	6,708,551
2006*	43,000,000	36,100,000	6,800,000
2007*	43,700,000	36,700,000	7,000,000

* Projection. End of fiscal year.

Source: Centers for Medicare & Medicaid Services

Plunkett's Health Care Industry Almanac 2008

Medicare Enrollment by Type of Coverage: 1980-2007

(All Types of Enrollee, as of July 1)

Year	Part A: Hospital Insurance (HI)	Part B: Supplementary Medical Insurance (SMI)
1980	28,066,894	27,399,658
1981	28,589,504	27,941,227
1982	29,068,966	28,412,282
1983	29,587,295	28,974,535
1984	29,995,971	29,415,397
1985	30,589,468	29,988,763
1986	31,215,529	30,589,728
1987	31,852,860	31,169,960
1988	32,413,038	31,617,082
1989	33,039,977	32,098,770
1990	33,719,118	32,629,109
1991	34,428,810	33,237,474
1992	35,153,223	33,933,274
1993	35,904,436	34,612,360
1994	36,543,147	35,167,288
1995	37,134,949	35,684,584
1996	37,661,881	36,139,608
1997	38,052,242	39,460,143
1998	38,432,477	36,780,731
1999	38,727,108	37,039,848
2000	39,199,460	37,359,512
2001	39,606,975	37,685,281
2002	40,066,786	38,078,574
2003	40,656,995	38,589,685
2004	41,390,575	39,100,504
2005	42,033,263	39,694,772
2006*	42,500,000	40,000,000
2007*	43,200,000	40,600,000

* Projection. End of fiscal year.

Source: Centers for Medicare & Medicaid Services

Plunkett's Health Care Industry Almanac 2008

U.S. Medicare Enrollment Trends, Part A Hospital Insurance (HI)[1]: July 1970-2007

**Medicare Aged & Disabled, by Type of Coverage)*

Year	All Persons	Aged Persons	Disabled Persons
1970	20,361,152	20,361,152	NA
1971	20,742,250	20,742,250	NA
1972	21,115,261	21,115,261	NA
1973	23,301,082	21,570,544	1,730,538
1974	23,924,145	21,996,029	1,928,116
1975	24,640,497	22,472,104	2,168,393
1976	25,312,575	22,920,417	2,392,158
1977	26,093,919	23,474,546	2,619,373
1978	26,777,263	23,984,057	2,793,206
1979	27,459,157	24,548,391	2,910,766
1980	28,066,894	25,103,738	2,963,156
1981	28,589,504	25,590,555	2,998,949
1982	29,068,966	26,114,758	2,954,208
1983	29,587,295	26,669,745	2,917,550
1984	29,995,971	27,111,561	2,884,410
1985	30,589,468	27,682,592	2,906,876
1986	31,215,529	28,257,004	2,958,525
1987	31,852,860	28,822,152	3,030,708
1988	32,413,038	29,311,556	3,101,482
1989	33,039,977	29,869,060	3,170,917
1990	33,719,118	30,464,135	3,254,983
1991	34,428,810	31,043,371	3,385,439
1992	35,153,223	31,584,598	3,568,625
1993	35,904,436	32,060,258	3,844,178
1994	36,543,147	32,408,543	4,134,604
1995	37,134,949	32,741,662	4,393,287
1996	37,661,881	33,021,701	4,640,180
1997	38,052,242	33,237,460	4,814,782
1998	38,432,477	33,409,666	5,022,811
1999	38,432,477	33,409,666	5,022,811
2000	39,199,460	33,832,862	5,366,598
2001	39,606,975	34,044,115	5,562,860
2002	40,066,786	34,257,612	5,809,174
2003	40,656,995	34,580,961	6,076,034
2004	41,390,575	34,964,270	6,392,266
2005	42,033,263	35,272,766	6,708,358
2006*	42,500,000	35,700,000	6,800,000
2007*	43,200,000	36,200,000	7,000,000

* Projection. End of fiscal year.

[1] People enrolled in HI regardless if they are enrolled in SMI.

Source: Centers for Medicare and Medicaid Services

Plunkett's Health Care Industry Almanac 2008

U.S. Medicare Enrollment Trends, Part B Supplemental Medical Insurance (SMI)[1]: July 1970-2007

(Medicare Aged & Disabled, by Type of Coverage)

Year	All Persons	Aged Persons	Disabled Persons
1970	19,584,387	19,587,387	NA
1971	19,974,692	19,974,692	NA
1972	20,351,273	20,357,273	NA
1973	22,490,534	20,920,660	1,569,874
1974	23,166,570	21,421,545	1,745,025
1975	23,904,551	21,945,301	1,959,250
1976	24,614,402	22,445,911	2,168,491
1977	25,363,468	22,990,826	2,372,642
1978	26,074,085	23,530,893	2,543,192
1979	26,757,329	24,098,491	2,658,838
1980	27,399,658	24,680,432	2,719,226
1981	27,941,227	25,181,731	2,759,496
1982	28,412,282	25,706,792	2,705,490
1983	28,974,535	26,292,124	2,682,411
1984	29,415,397	26,764,150	2,651,247
1985	29,988,763	27,310,894	2,677,869
1986	30,589,728	27,862,737	2,726,991
1987	31,169,960	28,382,203	2,787,757
1988	31,617,082	28,780,154	2,836,928
1989	32,098,770	29,216,027	2,882,743
1990	32,629,109	29,685,629	2,943,480
1991	33,237,474	30,185,162	3,052,312
1992	33,933,274	30,712,791	3,220,483
1993	34,612,360	31,146,557	3,465,803
1994	35,167,288	31,447,255	3,720,033
1995	35,684,584	31,742,132	3,942,452
1996	36,139,608	31,984,257	4,155,351
1997	36,460,143	32,164,416	4,295,727
1998	36,780,731	32,308,268	4,472,463
1999	37,039,848	32,402,760	4,637,088
2000	37,359,512	32,589,708	4,769,804
2001	37,685,281	32,748,714	4,936,567
2002	38,078,574	32,934,153	5,144,421
2003	38,589,685	32,202,715	5,386,970
2004	39,100,504	33,408,368	5,661,315
2005	39,694,772	33,675,598	5,971,343
2006*	40,000,000	34,000,000	6,000,000
2007*	40,600,000	34,400,000	6,200,000

*Projection. End of fiscal year.

[1] People enrolled in SMI regardless their enrollment in Hospital Insurance.

Source: Centers for Medicare and Medicaid Services

Plunkett's Health Care Industry Almanac 2008

Total Medicare Beneficiaries with Drug Coverage

(Millions of People Receiving Benefits as of 6-11-2006; Latest Data Available)

Drug Coverage from Medicare or Former Employer	
Stand-Alone Prescription Drug Plan (PDP)	10.37
Medicare Advantage with Prescription Drugs (MA-PD)	6.04
Medicare-Medicaid (Automatically Enrolled)	6.07
Medicare Retiree Drug Subsidy (RDS)	6.90
FEHB Retiree Coverage	1.60
TRICARE Retiree Coverage	1.86
TOTAL	**32.84**

Additional Sources of Creditable Drug Coverage	
Veterans Affairs (VA) Coverage	2.01
Indian Health Service Coverage	0.11
Active Workers with Medicare Secondary Payer	2.57
Other Retiree Coverage, Not Enrolled in RDS	0.10
State Pharmaceutical Assistance Programs	0.59
TOTAL	**5.38**

Source: Centers for Medicare & Medicaid Services
Plunkett's Health Care Industry Almanac 2008

Medicare Deductible, Co-Payment & Premium Amounts: 2008

(Costs Paid by the Patient)

Hospital Insurance (Part A)[1]

$423 monthly premium (See Note 1, below).

Reduced Hospital Insurance Premium - $233

$1,024 deductible per each Benefit Period

Additional Costs

$256 a day for the 61st through the 90th day of hospitalization, per Benefit Period

$512 a day for days beyond the 90th day of hospitalization

Skilled Nursing Facility – $128 a day for the 21st through the 100th day per Benefit Period.

Medical Insurance (Part B)[2]

$96.40 monthly premium

$131 annual deductible

Medical Insurance (Part C)

Medicare Advantage (formerly Medicare + Choice) Plans is an alternative to Part B offered by private insurers which may include HMO's, PPOs, Private Fee for Services or other healthcare plans and a tax-free medical savings account. These plans offer different benefits, doctor choice, convenience, and quality. To join a Medicare Advantage Plan, enrollees must have Medicare Part A and Part B. Enrollees will have to pay the 2008 monthly Medicare Part B premium of $96.40 to Medicare. In addition, enrollees might have to pay a monthly premium to their Medicare Advantage Plan for the extra benefits that they offer.

Prescription Drug Plan (Part D)

Monthly premiums vary by plan and state

$275 Deductible

25% of the first $2,510 after the deductible

Enrollees pay 100% of cost between $2,510-$5726.25

$4,050 maximum out-of-pocket coverage

(Continued on next page)

Medicare Deductible, Co-Payment & Premium Amounts: 2008 (cont.)

Notes:

1. Approximately 99 percent of Medicare beneficiaries do not pay a premium for Part A services because they have at least 40 quarters of Medicare-covered employment. However, other seniors and certain people under age 65 with disabilities who have fewer than 30 quarters of coverage may obtain Part A coverage by paying a monthly premium set according to a statutory formula. This premium will be $423 per month for 2008, an increase of $13 from 2007. In addition, seniors with 30 to 39 quarters of coverage, and certain disabled persons with 30 or more quarters of coverage, will pay a premium of $233 in 2008, compared to $226 in 2007.

2. As required in the Medicare Modernization Act, beginning in 2007, the Part B premium a beneficiary pays each month is based on his or her annual income. Specifically, if a beneficiary's "modified adjusted gross income" is greater than the legislated threshold amounts ($82,000 in 2008 for a beneficiary filing an individual income tax return or married and filing a separate return, and $164,000 for a beneficiary filing a joint tax return) the beneficiary is responsible for a larger portion of the estimated total cost of Part B benefit coverage. In addition to the standard 25 percent premium, these beneficiaries will now have to pay an income-related monthly adjustment amount.

The 2008 Part B monthly premium rates to be paid by beneficiaries who file an individual tax return (including those who are single, head of household, qualifying widow(er) with dependent child, or married filing separately who lived apart from their spouse for the entire taxable year), or who file a joint tax return are:

Beneficiaries who file an individual tax return with income:	Beneficiaries who file a joint tax return with income:	Income-related monthly adjustment amount	Total monthly premium amount
≤ $82,000	≤ $164,000	$0.00	$96.40
> $82,000 and≤ $102,000	> $164,000 and≤ $204,000	$25.80	$122.20
> $102,000 and ≤ $153,000	> $204,000 and ≤ $306,000	$64.55	$160.90
> $153,000 and ≤ $205,000	> $306,000 and ≤ $410,000	$103.30	$199.70
> $205,000	> $410,000	$142.00	$238.40

In addition, the monthly premium rates to be paid by beneficiaries who are married, but file a separate return from their spouse and lived with their spouse at some time during the taxable year are:

Beneficiaries who are married but file a separate tax return from their spouse:	Income-related monthly adjustment amount	Total monthly premium amount
≤ $82,000	$0.00	$96.40
> $82,000 and ≤ $123,000	$103.30	$199.70
> $123,000	$142.00	$238.40

An estimated 5 percent of current Part B enrollees are expected to be subject to the higher premium amounts.

Source: Centers for Medicare & Medicaid Services

Plunkett's Health Care Industry Almanac 2008

IV. U.S. Health Insurance Coverage & the Uninsured

Contents:

Percent of Persons of All Ages without Health Insurance Coverage, U.S.: 1997-2006

(Latest Year Available)

Year	Percent	95% Confidence Interval
1997	15.4	15.0-15.8
1998	14.6	14.1-15.1
1999	14.2	13.8-14.6
2000	14.9	14.5-15.3
2001	14.3	13.8-14.8
2002	14.7	14.3-15.1
2003	15.2	14.8-15.7
2004	14.6	13.8-15.5
2005	14.2	13.8-14.6
2006	14.8	14.3-15.3

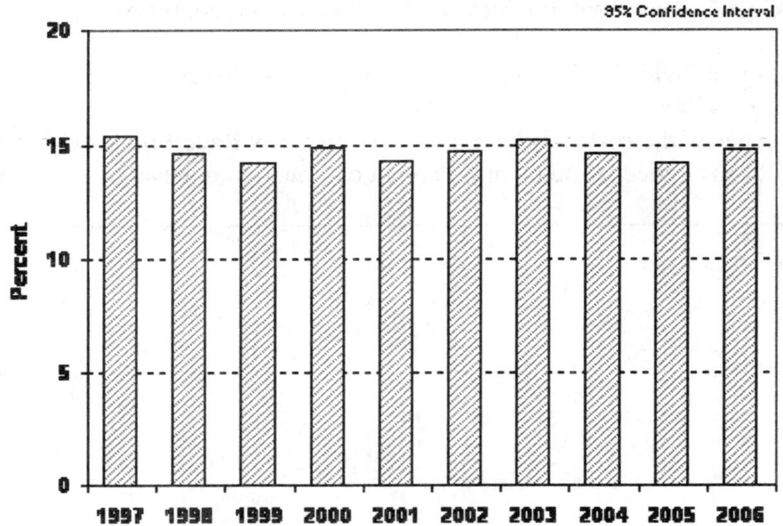

Data are based on household interviews of a sample of the civilian noninstitutionalized population.

Note: A person was defined as uninsured if he or she did not have any private health insurance, Medicare, Medicaid, State Children's Health Insurance Program (SCHIP), State-sponsored or other government-sponsored health plan, or military plan at the time of the interview. A person was also defined as uninsured if he or she had only Indian Health Service coverage or had only a private plan that paid for one type of service such as accidents or dental care. The analyses excluded persons with unknown health insurance status (about 1% of respondents each year). The data on health insurance status were edited using an automated system based on logic checks and keyword searches. For comparability, the estimates for all years were created using these same procedures. The resulting estimates of persons without health insurance coverage are generally 0.1-0.2 percentage points lower than those based on the editing procedures used for the final data files. CI is confidence interval. Beginning with the 2003 data, the National Health Interview Survey transitioned to weights derived from the 2000 census. In this Early Release, estimates for 2000-02 were recalculated using weights derived from the 2000 census.

Source: Centers for Disease Control & Prevention, Family Core component of the 1997-2006 National Health Interview Surveys

Plunkett's Health Care Industry Almanac 2008

Number & Percent of Persons without Health Insurance Coverage, by Age Group, U.S.: 1997-2006

(Latest Year Available)

Year	Number of Uninsured[1] in Millions				Percent Uninsured[1] (95% Confidence Interval)				
	All Ages	Under 65 Years	18-64 Years	Under 18 Years	All Ages	Under 65 Years: Crude	Under 65 Years: Age-Adjusted	18-64 Years	Under 18 Years
1997	41.0	40.7	30.8	9.9	15.4 (15.0-15.8)	17.4 (16.9-17.9)	17.2 (16.8-17.7)	18.9 (18.4-19.4)	13.9 (13.2-14.6)
1998	39.3	39.0	30.0	9.1	14.6 (14.1-15.1)	16.5 (16.0-17.0)	16.4 (15.9-16.9)	18.2 (17.7-18.7)	12.7 (12.0-13.4)
1999	38.7	38.3	29.8	8.5	14.2 (13.8-14.6)	16.0 (15.5-16.5)	16.0 (15.5-16.5)	17.8 (17.3-18.3)	11.8 (11.2-12.4)
2000	41.3	40.8	32.0	8.9	14.9 (14.5-15.3)	16.8 (16.3-17.2)	16.8 (16.3-17.3)	18.7 (18.1-19.2)	12.3 (11.7-12.9)
2001	40.2	39.8	31.9	7.9	14.3 (13.8-14.8)	16.2 (15.7-16.7)	16.2 (15.7-16.7)	18.3 (17.8-18.8)	11.0 (10.3-11.7)
2002	41.5	41.1	33.5	7.6	14.7 (14.3-15.1)	16.5 (16.0-16.9)	16.6 (16.1-17.1)	19.1 (18.6-19.6)	10.5 (9.9-11.1)
2003	43.6	43.2	35.9	7.3	15.2 (14.8-15.7)	17.2 (16.6-17.7)	17.3 (16.8-17.8)	20.1 (19.5-20.6)	10.1 (9.4-10.7)
2004 M1*	42.5	42.0	35.0	7.0	14.7 (14.3-15.2)	16.6 (16.1-17.0)	16.7 (16.3-17.2)	19.4 (18.9-19.9)	9.6 (9.0-10.2)
2004 M2*	42.1	41.7	34.9	6.8	14.6 (14.2-15.0)	16.4 (16.0-16.9)	16.6 (16.2-17.1)	19.3 (18.8-19.8)	9.4 (8.8-10.0)
2005	41.1	40.8	34.4	6.5	14.2 (13.45-14.58)	16.0 (15.53-16.46)	16.2 (15.72-16.65)	18.9 (18.34-19.38)	8.9 (8.34-9.49)
2006	43.6	43.3	36.5	6.8	14.8 (14.34-15.34)	16.8 (16.21-17.33)	17.0 (16.44-17.57)	19.8 (19.12-20.42)	9.3 (8.60-9.92)

Data are based on household interviews of a sample of the civilian noninstitutionalized population.

Notes: A person was defined as uninsured if he or she did not have any private health insurance, Medicare, Medicaid, State Children's Health Insurance Program (SCHIP), state-sponsored or other government-sponsored health plan, or military plan at the time of the interview. A person was also defined as uninsured if he or she had only Indian Health Service coverage or had only a private plan that paid for one type of service such as accidents or dental care. The analyses excluded persons with unknown health insurance status (about 1% of respondents each year). The data on health insurance status were edited using an automated system based on logic checks and keyword searches. For comparability, the estimates for all years were created using these same procedures. The resulting estimates of persons without health insurance coverage are generally 0.1–0.2 percentage points lower than those based on the editing procedures used for the final data files. The number of uninsured persons was calculated as the percentage of uninsured persons multiplied by the total weighted population, including persons with unknown coverage. The age-specific numbers of uninsured may not add to their respective totals due to rounding.

* In the third quarter of 2004, two additional questions were added to the National Health Interview Survey (NHIS) insurance section to reduce potential errors in reporting Medicare and Medicaid status. Persons aged 65 years and over not reporting Medicare coverage were asked explicitly about Medicare coverage, and persons under 65 years of age with no reported coverage were asked explicitly about Medicaid coverage. Depending on responses to these two questions, respondents may have been reclassified. Estimates of uninsurance for 2004 are calculated both without using the additional information from these new questions (noted as Method 1) and with using the responses to these new questions (noted as Method 2). Beginning in 2005, all estimates are reported using Method 2. See "About This Early Release" for additional information.

Source: Centers for Disease Control & Prevention, *Family Core component of the 1997-2006 National Health Interview Surveys*

Plunkett's Health Care Industry Almanac 2008

People without Health Insurance for the Entire Year, U.S.: 2004-2006

(In Thousands; Latest Year Available)

Characteristic	2004		2005*		2006	
	Without Insurance	Percent of Pop. (%)	Without Insurance	Percent of Pop. (%)	Without Insurance	Percent of Pop. (%)
Total	**45,306**	**15.6**	**44,815**	**15.3**	**46,995**	**15.8**
Region						
Northeast	6,782	12.6	6,353	11.7	6,648	12.3
Midwest	7,757	12.0	7,330	11.3	7,458	11.4
South	19,090	18.2	19,143	18.0	20,486	19.0
West	11,676	17.4	11,988	17.6	12,403	17.9
Age						
Under 18 years	7,949	10.8	8,050	10.9	8,661	11.7
18 to 24 years	8,590	30.7	8,201	29.3	8,323	29.3
25 to 34	10,023	25.5	10,161	25.7	10,713	26.9
35 to 44	8,093	18.7	7,901	18.3	8,018	18.8
45 to 64	10,157	14.2	10,053	13.6	10,738	14.2
65 years and over	493	1.4	449	1.3	541	1.5
Nativity						
Native	33,547	13.1	33,034	12.8	34,380	13.2
Foreign Born	11,759	33.4	11,781	33.0	12,615	33.8
Household Income						
Less than $25,000	15,130	24.3	14,452	24.2	13,933	24.9
$25,000 to $49,999	14,619	19.8	14,651	20.1	15,319	21.1
$50,000 to $74,999	7,688	13.0	7,826	13.3	8,459	14.4
$75,000 or more	7,869	8.2	7,886	7.7	9,283	8.5
Work Experience						
Worked during year	26,546	18.5	26,293	18.0	27,627	18.7
Did not work	10,378	26.9	10,022	26.1	10,165	26.1

* The 2005 data have been revised since originally published. See www.census.gov/hhes/www/hlthins/usernote/schedule.html.

Source: U.S. Census Bureau, Current Population Survey, 2006 and 2007 Annual Social and Economic Supplements

Plunkett's Health Care Industry Almanac 2008

Percent of Persons under Age 65 Years without Health Insurance Coverage, by Age Group & Sex: U.S.: 2006

(Latest Year Available)

Age & Sex	Percent	95% Confidence Interval
Total: Under 18 Years	9.3	8.60-9.92
Men	9.5	8.76-10.32
Women	9.0	8.20-9.74
Total: 18-24 Years	29.7	28.06-31.28
Men	34.1	21.99-36.27
Women	25.2	23.26-26.97
Total: 25-34 Years	26.9	25.62-28.25
Men	31.2	29.52-32.80
Women	22.7	21.26-24.21
Total: 35-44 Years	18.5	17.54-19.52
Men	20.8	19.25-22.20
Women	16.3	15.19-17.40
Total: 45-64 Years	13.0	12.29-13.61
Men	13.6	12.80-14.48
Women	12.3	11.57-13.04
Total: Under 65 Years[1]	17.0	16.44-17.57
Men	18.9	18.21-19.54
Women	15.2	14.57-15.74

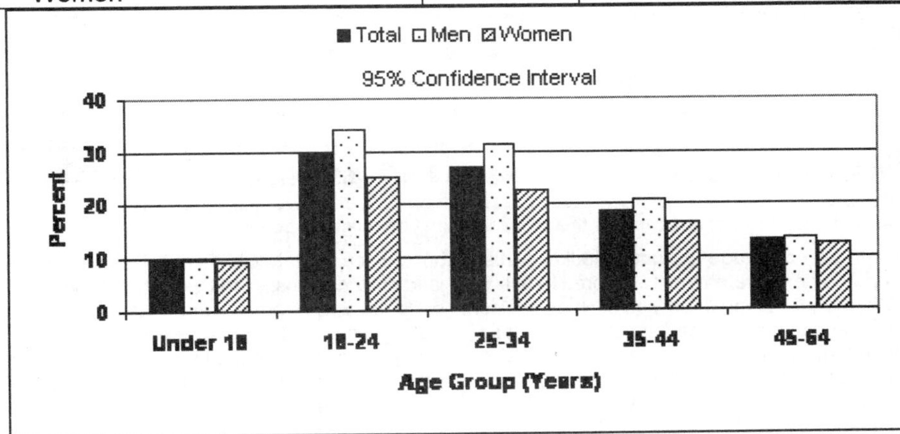

Data are based on household interviews of a sample of the civilian noninstitutionalized population.

[1] Estimates for this Healthy People 2010 Leading Health Indicator are for persons under 65 years and are age-adjusted to the 2000 projected U.S. standard population using three age groups: under 18 years, 18-44 years, and 45-64 years.

Notes: A person was defined as uninsured if he or she did not have any private health insurance, Medicare, Medicaid, State Children's Health Insurance Program (SCHIP), State-sponsored or other government-sponsored health plan, or military plan at the time of the interview. A person was also defined as uninsured if he or she had only Indian Health Service coverage or had only a private plan that paid for one type of service such as accidents or dental care. The analyses excluded 1065 persons (1.3%) with unknown health insurance status. The data on health insurance status were edited using an automated system based on logic checks and keyword searches. The resulting estimates of persons not having health insurance coverage are generally 0.1-0.2 percentage points lower than those based on the editing procedures used for the final data files. Early Release of Selected Estimates Based on Data From the 2003 National Health Interview Survey 6.

Source: Centers for Disease Control & Prevention, National Health Interview Survey 2006

Plunkett's Health Care Industry Almanac 2008

Percent of Persons under Age 65 with Public Health Plan Coverage & Private Health Insurance Coverage by Age Group, U.S.: 1997-2006

(Latest Year Available)

Percent (95% confidence interval)						
Year	Public[1]			Private[1]		
	Under 65 years	18-64 years	Under 18 years	Under 65 years	18-64 years	Under 18 years
1997	13.6 (13.1-14.1)	10.2 (9.8-10.6)	21.5 (20.5-22.4)	70.8 (70.1-71.5)	72.8 (72.2-73.4)	66.2 (65.1-67.3)
1998	12.7 (12.2-13.2)	9.5 (9.1-9.9)	20.0 (19.0-20.9)	72.0 (71.3-72.7)	73.5 (72.9-74.1)	68.5 (67.4-69.5)
1999	12.4 (12.0-12.9)	9.0 (8.6-9.3)	20.5 (19.5-21.4)	73.1 (72.3-73.8)	74.8 (74.1-75.4)	69.1 (68.0-70.2)
2000	12.9 (12.4-13.4)	9.1 (8.7-9.4)	22.0 (21.0-23.0)	71.8 (71.1-72.5)	73.8 (73.2-74.4)	67.1 (66.1-68.2)
2001	13.6 (13.1-14.1)	9.4 (9.0-9.8)	23.6 (22.6-24.5)	71.6 (70.9-72.3)	73.7 (73.1-74.4)	66.7 (66.4-68.6)
2002	15.2 (14.6-15.8)	10.3 (9.9-10.7)	27.1 (26.0-28.2)	69.8 (69.0-70.6)	72.3 (71.6-72.9)	63.9 (62.7-65.1)
2003	16.0 (15.4-16.6)	10.9 (10.4-11.4)	28.6 (27.4-29.7)	68.2 (67.5-69.0)	70.6 (69.9-71.3)	62.6 (61.4-63.8)
2004[2] M1	16.1 (15.6-16.7)	11.1 (10.6-11.5)	28.5 (27.5-29.6)	68.6 (67.9-69.4)	70.9 (70.2-71.6)	63.1 (61.9-64.3)
2004[2] M2	16.2 (15.7-16.8)	11.1 (10.7-11.6)	28.7 (27.7-29.8)	–	–	–
2005	16.8 (16.3-17.4)	11.5 (11.1-12.0)	29.9 (28.8-31.0)	68.4 (67.7-69.2)	70.9 (70.2-71.6)	62.4 (61.2-63.5)
2006	18.1 (17.4-18.8)	12.4 (11.9-12.9)	32.3 (30.9-33.6)	66.5 (65.5-67.4)	69.2 (68.3-70.0)	59.7 (58.3-61.1)

Data are based on household interviews of a sample of the civilian noninstitutionalized population.

[1]The category "public health plan coverage" includes Medicare (disability), Medicaid, State Children's Health Insurance Program (SCHIP), State-sponsored or other government-sponsored health plan, and military plans. The category "private health insurance" excludes plans that paid for only one type of service such as accidents or dental care. A small number of persons were covered by both public and private plans and were included in both categories. The analyses excluded persons with unknown health insurance status (about 1% of respondents each year). The data on type of coverage were edited using an automated system based on logic checks and keyword searches. For comparability, the estimates for all years were created using these same procedures. The resulting estimates of persons having public or private coverage are within 0.1-0.3 percentage points of those based on the editing procedures used for the final data files.

[2] In quarter 3 of 2004, two additional questions were added to the National Health Interview Survey (NHIS) insurance section to reduce potential errors in reporting Medicare and Medicaid status. Persons aged 65 years and over not reporting Medicare coverage were asked explicitly about Medicare coverage, and persons under 65 years of age with no reported coverage were asked explicitly about Medicaid coverage. Depending on responses to these two questions, respondents may have been reclassified. Estimates of uninsurance for 2004 are calculated both without using the additional information from these new questions (noted as Method 1, M1) and with using the responses to these new questions (noted as Method 2, M2). Estimates of private insurance are not affected by the two additional questions. Beginning in 2005, all estimates are reported using Method 2.

Note: Beginning with the 2003 data, the National Health Interview Survey transitioned to weights derived from the 2000 census. In this Early Release, estimates for 2000-02 were recalculated using weights derived from the 2000 census.

Source: Centers for Disease Control & Prevention, Family Core component of the 1997-2006 National Health Interview Surveys

Plunkett's Health Care Industry Almanac 2008

Percent of Persons of All Ages without Health Insurance Coverage, by Race/Ethnicity, U.S.: 2006

(Latest Year Available)

	Percent (95% Confidence Interval)	
Race/Ethnicity	Age-Sex-Adjusted[1]	Age-Adjusted[2]
Hispanic or Latino	32.1 (30.82-33.44)	31.4 (30.14-32.69)
White, Single Race	10.4 (9.90-10.90)	10.9 (10.34-11.38)
Black, Single Race	15.9 (14.85 - 16.86)	15.8 (14.78-16.77)

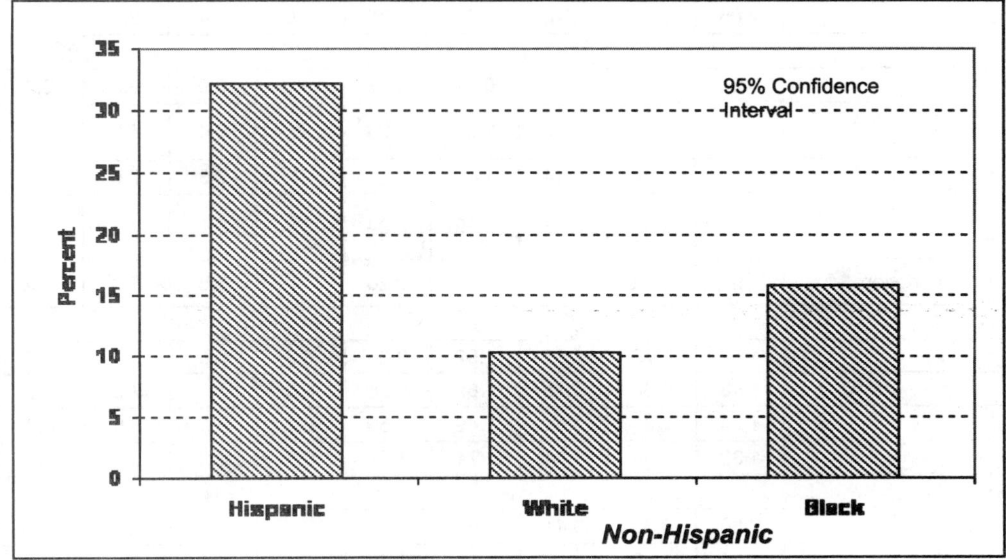

Data are based on household interviews of a sample of the civilian noninstitutionalized population.

[1] Age-sex-adjusted estimates are presented in the figure. Estimates are age-sex adjusted using the projected 2000 U.S. population as the standard population and using three age groups: under 18 years, 18–64 years, and 65 years and over.

2 Estimates for this Healthy People 2010 Leading Health Indicator are age adjusted using the projected 2000 U.S. population as the standard population and using four age groups: under 18 years, 18–44 years, 45–64 years, and 65 years and over.

Notes: A person was defined as uninsured if he or she did not have any private health insurance, Medicare, Medicaid, State Children's Health Insurance Program (SCHIP), State-sponsored or other government-sponsored health plan, or military plan at the time of the interview. A person was also defined as uninsured if he or she had only Indian Health Service coverage or had only a private plan that paid for one type of service such as accidents or dental care. The analyses excluded 1148 persons (1.3%) with unknown health insurance status. The data on health insurance status were edited using an automated system based on logic checks and keyword searches. The resulting estimates of persons not having health insurance coverage are generally 0.1-0.2 percentage points lower than those based on the editing procedures used for the final data files. Estimates are age-sex-adjusted to the 2000 projected U.S. standard population using three age groups: under 18 years, 18-64 years, and 65 years and over.

Source: Centers for Disease Control & Prevention, National Health Interview Survey, 2006

Plunkett's Health Care Industry Almanac 2008

Employers' Costs for Health Insurance, Amount and Percent of Total Compensation, U.S.: Selected Years 2002-2006

(Amount per Employee-Hour Worked in US$)

Characteristic	Health Insurance Cost per Employee-Hour Worked					Health Insurance as Percent of Total Compensation				
	2003	2004	2005	2006	2007	2003	2004	2005	2006	2007
	In US$					*In Percent (%)*				
State and local gov't	$2.99	$3.35	$3.63	$3.91	$4.21	9.2	9.8	10.2	10.6	10.9
Total private industry	$1.41	$1.43	$1.64	$1.72	$1.84	6.3	6.6	6.8	6.9	7.1
Industry:										
Goods-producing	1.98	2.11	2.28	2.47	2.54	7.5	7.8	8.0	8.4	8.4
Service-providing	1.25	1.39	1.48	1.54	2.12	5.9	6.2	6.4	6.4	7.7
Manufacturing	2.08	2.27	2.48	2.67	2.76	8.0	8.4	8.7	9.1	9.1
Occupation:										
Service	0.65	0.70	0.74	0.77	1.27	5.7	6.0	6.1	6.2	8.2
Management, Professional & Related	□	2.19	2.32	2.50	3.23	□	5.4	5.5	5.6	7.0
Sales & Office	□	1.34	1.44	1.49	1.78	□	7.3	7.5	7.5	8.5
Natural Resources, Construction & Maintenance	□	1.84	2.03	2.15	2.34	□	6.9	7.5	7.7	8.0
Production & Transportation	□	1.72	1.85	1.91	2.20	□	8.5	8.9	9.0	9.7
Census region:										
Northeast	1.63	1.72	1.83	1.92	2.04	6.3	6.5	6.8	6.7	6.9
Midwest	1.48	1.62	1.78	1.88	1.96	6.6	7.0	7.3	7.6	7.8
South	1.24	1.34	1.42	1.49	1.59	6.2	6.5	6.6	6.7	6.9
West	1.39	1.55	1.64	1.71	1.87	6.0	6.3	6.3	6.4	6.7
Union status*:										
Union	2.80	3.08	3.41	3.52	3.77	9.1	9.6	10.3	10.3	12.3
Nonunion	1.24	1.35	1.42	1.51	1.60	5.8	6.1	6.2	6.3	8.0
Establishment employment size:										
1–99 employees	1.05	1.13	1.19	1.23	1.29	5.5	5.8	5.9	6.0	6.1
100 or more	1.84	2.01	2.17	2.27	2.41	7.0	7.2	7.5	7.5	7.8
100–499	1.56	1.70	1.82	1.92	2.02	6.9	7.1	7.5	7.4	7.7
500 or more	2.17	2.37	2.62	2.72	2.88	7.0	7.3	7.6	7.6	7.9

Note: Costs are calculated from March survey data each year. Total compensation includes wages and salaries, and benefits.

* Union status numbers for 2007 are for all insurance, not just health insurance (which comprises the vast majority of insurance costs).

Source: U.S. Department of Labor, Bureau of Labor Statistics, National Compensation Survey, Employer Costs for Employee Compensation, March release

Plunkett's Health Care Industry Almanac 2008

V. U.S. Vital Statistics & Population Indicators

Contents:

Projected U.S. Population Distribution by Age Group: 2000-2050

	2000	2010	2020	2030	2040	2050
TOTAL	100.0	100.0	100.0	100.0	100.0	100.0
0-4	6.8	6.9	6.8	6.7	6.7	6.7
5-19	21.7	20.0	19.6	19.5	19.2	19.3
20-44	36.9	33.8	32.3	31.6	31.0	31.2
45-64	22.1	26.2	24.9	22.6	22.6	22.2
65-84	10.9	11.0	14.1	17.0	16.5	15.7
85+	1.5	2.0	2.2	2.6	3.9	5.0
MALE	100.0	100.0	100.0	100.0	100.0	100.0
0-4	7.1	7.2	7.1	6.9	7.0	6.9
5-19	22.7	20.8	20.4	20.3	20.0	20.1
20-44	37.8	34.7	33.3	32.5	31.9	32.0
45-64	21.9	26.0	24.8	22.7	22.8	22.4
65-84	9.5	9.9	12.9	15.7	15.3	14.8
85+	0.9	1.3	1.5	1.9	2.9	3.8
FEMALE	100.0	100.0	100.0	100.0	100.0	100.0
0-4	6.5	6.7	6.6	6.4	6.4	6.4
5-19	20.8	19.2	18.9	18.7	18.5	18.6
20-44	36.0	32.9	31.4	30.7	30.2	30.3
45-64	22.3	26.4	25.0	22.5	22.4	22.0
65-84	12.2	12.1	15.2	18.3	17.6	16.5
85+	2.1	2.7	2.9	3.4	4.9	6.1

Source: U.S. Census Bureau, 2004, "U.S. Interim Projections by Age, Sex, Race, and Hispanic Origin," ,http://www.census.gov/ipc/www/usinterimproj/>

Plunkett's Health Care Industry Almanac 2008

Life Expectancy at Age 65, U.S.

(Selected Years, 1965-2075

Year	Male	Female
1965	12.9	16.3
1980	14.0	18.4
1985	14.4	18.6
1990	15.0	19.0
1995	15.3	19.0
1996	15.4	19.0
1997	15.5	19.1
1998	15.6	19.0
1999	15.7	18.9
2000	15.7	18.9
2005	16.1	19.0
2010	16.4	19.3
2015	16.7	19.6
2020	17.1	19.7
2025	17.3	20.2
2030	17.7	20.5
2040	18.3	21.1
2050	18.8	21.7
2060	19.4	22.2
2070	19.9	22.7
2075	20.2	23.0

Note: Years 2000-2075 are estimated.

Source: Social Security Administration, Office of the Actuary

Plunkett's Health Care Industry Almanac 2008

Current Cigarette Smoking by Persons 18 Years of Age & Over According to Sex & Race, U.S.: Selected Years, 1965-2004

(Latest Year Available)

Sex & Race	1965[1]	1974[1]	1979[1]	1985[1]	1990[1]	1995[1]	1999	2000	2001	2002	2003	2004
18 years and over, age adjusted[2]												
All persons	41.9	37.0	33.3	24.6	24.6	24.0	23.3	23.1	22.6	22.3	21.5	20.8
Male	51.2	42.8	37.0	26.5	27.1	25.9	25.2	25.2	24.6	24.6	23.7	23.0
Female	33.7	32.2	30.1	22.7	22.2	22.1	21.6	21.1	20.7	20.0	19.4	18.7
White male[3]	50.4	41.7	36.4	26.2	26.8	26.0	25.0	25.4	24.8	24.9	23.8	23.0
Black or African American male[3]	58.8	53.6	43.9	29.4	32.4	29.0	28.4	25.7	27.5	26.6	25.3	23.5
White female[3]	33.9	32.0	30.3	23.4	22.8	23.0	22.5	22.0	22.0	21.0	20.1	19.5
Black or African American female[3]	31.8	35.6	30.5	23.5	22.5	21.1	20.5	20.7	18.0	18.3	17.9	16.9
18 years and over, not adjusted												
All persons	42.4	37.1	33.5	24.7	24.7	24.1	23.5	23.2	22.7	22.4	21.6	20.9
Male	51.9	43.1	37.5	27.0	27.6	26.4	25.7	25.6	25.1	25.1	24.1	23.4
Female	33.9	32.1	29.9	22.6	22.1	22.0	21.5	20.9	20.6	19.8	19.2	18.5
White male[3]	51.1	41.9	36.8	26.6	27.2	26.3	25.3	25.7	25.0	25.0	24.0	23.2
Black or African American male[3]	60.4	54.3	44.1	28.5	32.2	29.0	28.6	26.2	27.6	27.0	25.7	23.9
White female[3]	34.0	31.7	30.1	23.1	22.5	22.6	22.1	21.4	21.5	20.6	19.7	19.1
Black or African American female[3]	33.7	36.4	31.1	23.5	22.5	21.1	20.6	20.8	18.1	18.5	18.1	17.3

Note: Starting with 1993 data, current cigarette smokers were defined as ever smoking 100 cigarettes in their lifetime and smoking now on every day or some days.

[1] Data prior to 1997 are not strictly comparable with data for later years due to the 1997 questionnaire redesign.

[2] Estimates are age adjusted to the year 2000 standard population.

[3] The race groups, white and black, include persons of Hispanic and non-Hispanic origin. Starting with 1999 data, race-specific estimates are tabulated according to 1997 Revisions to the Standards for the Classification of Federal Data on Race and Ethnicity and are not strictly comparable with estimates for earlier years. The single race categories shown in the table conform to the 1997 Standards. Starting with 1999 data, race-specific estimates are for persons who reported only one racial group. Prior to 1999, data were tabulated according to the 1977 Standards. Estimates for single race categories prior to 1999 included persons who reported one race or, if they reported more than one race, identified one race as best representing their race. Starting with 2003 data, race responses of other race and unspecified multiple race were treated as missing, and then race was imputed if these were the only race responses. Almost all persons with a race response of other race were of Hispanic origin.

Source: National Center for Health Statistics, *Health, United States, 2006*

Plunkett's Health Care Industry Almanac 2008

Overweight & Obesity Among Persons 20 Years of Age & Over, According to Sex, Race & Hispanic Origin[1]: Selected Years, 1960-2004

(Percent of 20-74 Year Old Population; Age Adjusted[2]; Latest Year Available)

Overweight[3]	1960-1962	1971-1974	1976-1980[4]	1988-1994	2001-2004
Both sexes[5]	44.8	47.7	47.4	56.0	66.0
Male	49.5	54.7	52.9	61.0	70.7
Female	40.2	41.1	42.0	51.2	61.4
Not Hispanic or Latino:					
White only, male	---	---	53.8	61.6	71.1
White only, female	---	---	38.7	47.2	57.1
Black or African American only, male	---	---	51.3	58.2	66.8
Black or African American only, female	---	---	62.6	68.5	79.5
Mexican male	---	---	61.6	69.4	75.8
Mexican female	---	---	61.7	69.6	73.2
Obesity[6]	**1960-1962**	**1971-1974**	**1976-1980[3]**	**1988-1994**	**2001-2004**
Both sexes[5]	13.3	14.6	15.1	23.3	32.1
Male	10.7	12.2	12.8	20.6	30.2
Female	15.7	16.8	17.1	26.0	34.0
Not Hispanic or Latino:					
White only, male	---	---	12.4	20.7	31.0
White only, female	---	---	15.4	23.3	31.5
Black or African American only, male	---	---	16.5	21.3	31.2
Black or African American only, female	---	---	31.0	39.1	51.6
Mexican male	---	---	15.7	24.4	30.5
Mexican female	---	---	26.6	36.1	40.3

Note: Data are based on measured height and weight of a sample of the civilian noninstitutionalized population.

[1] Persons of Mexican origin may be of any race.
[2] Age adjusted to the 2000 standard population.
[3] Body mass index (BMI) greater than or equal to 25.
[4] Data for Mexicans are for 1982–1984.
[5] Includes persons of all races and Hispanic origins, not just those shown separately.
[6] Body mass index (BMI) greater than or equal to 30.

Source: National Center for Health Statistics, *Health, United States, 2006*
Plunkett's Health Care Industry Almanac 2008

Chapter 3

IMPORTANT HEALTH CARE INDUSTRY CONTACTS

Contents:

I. Aging

Administration on Aging (AOA)
1 Massachusetts Ave., Ste. 4100, 5100
Washington, DC 20201 US
Phone: 202-619-0724
Fax: 202-357-3555
E-mail Address: *aoainfo@aoa.gov*
Web Address: www.aoa.gov
The Administration on Aging (AOA) is the federal focal point and advocate agency for older persons and their concerns. In this role, AOA works to heighten awareness among other federal agencies, organizations, groups and the public.

Aging with Dignity
820 E. Park Ave., Ste. D100
Tallahassee, FL 32301-2600 US
Fax: 850-681-2481
Toll Free: 888-594-7437
E-mail Address: *fivewishes@agingwithdignity.org*
Web Address: www.agingwithdignity.org
Aging with Dignity is a nonprofit organization that offers information, advice and legal tools needed to ensure that the wishes of the elderly concerning health and death be respected.

American Association of Home Services for the Aging (AAHSA)
2519 Connecticut Ave. NW
Washington, DC 20008 US
Phone: 202-783-2242
Fax: 202-783-2255
E-mail Address: *info@aahsa.org*
Web Address: www2.aahsa.org
The American Association of Home Services for the Aging (AAHSA) is committed to advancing the vision of healthy, affordable, ethical long-term care for America.

American Society on Aging (ASA)
833 Market St., Ste. 511
San Francisco, CA 94103 US
Phone: 415-974-9600
Fax: 415-974-0300
Toll Free: 800-537-9728
E-mail Address: *info@asaging.org*
Web Address: www.asaging.org
The American Society on Aging (ASA) is a nonprofit organization committed to enhancing the knowledge and skills of those working with older adults and their families.

National Association of Area Agencies on Aging (N4A)
1730 Rhode Island Ave. NW, Ste. 1200
Washington, DC 20036 US
Phone: 202-872-0888
Fax: 202-872-0057
Web Address: www.n4a.org
The National Association of Area Agencies on Aging (N4A) is the umbrella organization for the 655 area agencies on aging and more than 230 Title VI Native American aging programs in the U.S.

National Citizen's Coalition for Nursing Home Reform (NCCNHR)
1828 L St. NW, Ste. 801
Washington, DC 20036 US
Phone: 202-332-2276
Fax: 202-332-2949
Web Address: www.nccnhr.org
The National Citizen's Coalition for Nursing Home Reform (NCCNHR) represents the grassroots membership of concerned advocates of quality long term care nationwide.

National Council on the Aging (NCOA)
1901 L St. NW, 4th Fl.
Washington, DC 20036 US
Phone: 202-479-1200
Fax: 202-479-0735
E-mail Address: *info@ncoa.org*
Web Address: www.ncoa.org
The National Council on the Aging (NCOA) is a group of organizations and professionals promoting the dignity, self-determination and well-being of older persons.

II. AIDS/HIV

AIDS Action
1730 M St. NW, Ste. 611
Washington, DC 20036 US
Phone: 202-530-8030
Fax: 202-530-8031
E-mail Address: *webmaster@aidsaction.org*
Web Address: www.aidsaction.org
AIDS Action is committed to the development, analysis, cultivation, encouragement and implementation of good programs and policies with regard to the HIV/AIDS virus.

CDC National Prevention Information Network (CDCNPIN)
P.O. Box 6003
Rockville, MD 20849-6003 US
Phone: 919-361-4892
Fax: 888-282-7681
Toll Free: 800-458-5231
E-mail Address: *info@cdcnpin.org*
Web Address: www.cdcnpin.org
The CDC National Prevention Information Network (CDCNPIN) is the U.S. reference, referral and distribution service for information on HIV/AIDS, sexually transmitted diseases and tuberculosis. It is operated by the Centers for Disease Control, a Federal Government agency.

HIV/AIDS Treatment Information Service
P.O. Box 6303
Rockville, MD 20849-6303 US
Fax: 301-519-6616
Toll Free: 800-448-0440
E-mail Address: *contactus@aidsinfo.nih.gov*
Web Address: www.aidsinfo.nih.gov
The HIV/AIDS Treatment Information Service is a central resource for federally approved treatment guidelines for HIV and AIDS.

III. Alzheimer's Disease

Alzheimer's Association
225 N. Michigan Ave., 17th Fl.
Chicago, IL 60601 US
Phone: 312-335-8700
Fax: 866-699-1246
E-mail Address: *info@alz.org*
Web Address: www.alz.org
The Alzheimer's Association is the largest national voluntary health organization committed to finding a cure for Alzheimer's and helping those affected by the disease.

Alzheimer's Disease Education and Referral Center (ADEAR)
P.O. Box 8250
Silver Spring, MD 20907 US
Fax: 301-495-3334
Toll Free: 800-438-4380
E-mail Address: *adear@nia.nih.gov*
Web Address: www.alzheimers.org
The Alzheimer's Disease Education and Referral Center (ADEAR) provides information about Alzheimer's disease, its impact on families and health professionals and research into possible causes and cures.

IV. Arthritis

Arthritis Central
P.O. Box 92344
Austin, TX 78709 US
Toll Free: 800-980-6255
E-mail Address: *info@arthritismall.com*
Web Address: www.arthritiscentral.com
Arthritis Central provides its members with information, referrals, articles and videos on arthritis.

Arthritis Foundation
P.O. Box 7669
Atlanta, GA 30357-0669 US
Toll Free: 800-568-4045
Web Address: www.arthritis.org
The Arthritis Foundation is a non-profit organization providing advocacy, programs, services and research for the treatment of more than 100 types of arthritis and related conditions.

Arthritis Insight
Web Address: www.arthritisinsight.com
Arthritis Insight provides information and education on arthritis, as well as news and referrals.

Arthritis National Research Foundation (ANRF)
200 Oceangate, Ste. 830
Long Beach, CA 90802 US
Fax: 562-983-1410
Toll Free: 800-588-2873
E-mail Address: *anrf@ix.netcom.com*
Web Address: www.curearthritis.org
The Arthritis National Research Foundation (ANRF) provides funding for researchers associated with major research institutes, universities and hospitals throughout the country seeking to discover new knowledge for the prevention, treatment and cure of arthritis and related rheumatic diseases.

Arthritis.com
Web Address: www.arthritis.com
Arthritis.com is an online resource for information on chronic joint symptoms.

V. Biotech Associations

BIOCOM
4510 Executive Dr., Plaza 1
San Diego, CA 92121 US
Phone: 858-455-0300
Fax: 858-455-0022
Web Address: www.biocom.org
BIOCOM is a trade association for the life science industry in San Diego and Southern California.

Biotechnology Industry Organization (BIO)
1201 Maryland Ave. SW, Ste. 900
Washington, DC 20024 US
Phone: 202-962-9200
E-mail Address: *info@bio.org*
Web Address: www.bio.org
The Biotechnology Industry Organization (BIO) is involved in the research and development of health care,

agricultural, industrial and environmental biotechnology products. BIO has both small and large member organizations.

International Society for Stem Cell Research (ISSCR)
60 Revere Dr., Ste. 500
Northbrook, IL 60062 US
Phone: 847-509-1944
Fax: 847-480-9282
E-mail Address: *isscr@isscr.org*
Web Address: www.isscr.org
The International Society for Stem Cell Research is an independent, nonprofit organization established to promote the exchange and dissemination of information and ideas relating to stem cells, to encourage the general field of research involving stem cells and to promote professional and public education in all areas of stem cell research and application.

Society for Biomaterials
15000 Commerce Pkwy., Ste. C
Mt. Laurel, NJ 08054 US
Phone: 856-439-0826
Fax: 856-439-0525
E-mail Address: *info@biomaterials.org*
Web Address: www.biomaterials.org
The Society for Biomaterials is a professional society that promotes advances in all phases of materials research and development by encouraging cooperative educational programs, clinical applications and professional standards in the biomaterials field.

VI. Biotech Investing

Medical Technology Stock Letter
P.O. Box 40460
Berkeley, CA 94704 US
Phone: 510-843-1857
Fax: 510-843-0901
E-mail Address: *mtsl@bioinvest.com*
Web Address: www.bioinvest.com
The Medical Technology Stock Letter is a newsletter that provides financial advice about investing in biotechnology. It is distributed by mail and electronically.

VII. Biotech Resources

Bio Online
1900 Powell St., Ste. 230
Emeryville, CA 94608 US
Phone: 510-601-7194
Fax: 510-601-1862
E-mail Address: *corp@bio.com*
Web Address: www.bio.com
Bio Online is an online community of scientists, professionals, businesses and organizations supporting life science for the purpose of an exchange of information.

Biospace.com
90 New Montgomery St., Ste. 414
San Francisco, CA 94104 US
Phone: 732-528-3688
Fax: 732-528-3668
Toll Free: 888-246-7722
E-mail Address:
Web Address: www.biospace.com
Biospace.com offers information, news and profiles on biotech companies. It also provides an outlet for business and scientific leaders in bioscience to communicate with each other.

BioTech
Austin, TX US
E-mail Address: *feedback@biotech.icmb.utexas.edu*
Web Address: biotech.icmb.utexas.edu
The BioTech web site offers a comprehensive dictionary of biotech terms, plus extensive research data regarding biotechnology.

Biotech Rumor Mill
E-mail Address: *info@biofind.com*
Web Address: www.biofind.com/rumor
The Biotech Rumor Mill is an online discussion forum that attracts participants from many biotech disciplines.

Burrill & Company
1 Embarcadero Ctr., Ste. 2700
San Francisco, CA 94111 US
Phone: 415-591-5400
Fax: 415-591-5401
E-mail Address: *burrill@b-c.com*
Web Address: www.burrillandco.com
Burrill & Company is a leading private merchant bank concentrated on companies in the life sciences industries: biotechnology, pharmaceuticals, medical technologies, agricultural technologies, animal health and nutraceuticals.

MedWeb: Biomedical Internet Resources
Web Address: www.medweb.emory.edu/medweb
MedWeb: Biomedical Internet Resources is a web site operated by Emory University, which lists resources by medical field, and allows users to search for articles by topic or date.

Tufts Center for the Study of Drug Development
75 Kneeland St., 11th Fl.
Boston, MA 02111 US
Phone: 617-636-2170
Fax: 617-636-2425
E-mail Address: *csdd@tufts.edu*
Web Address: csdd.tufts.edu
The Tufts Center for the Study of Drug Development, an affiliate of Tuft's University, provides analyses and commentary on pharmaceutical issues. Its mission is to improve the quality and efficiency of pharmaceutical development, research and utilization. It is famous, among

other things, for its analysis of the true total costs of developing and commercializing a new drug.

VIII. Blindness

American Council of the Blind (ACB)
1155 15th St. NW, Ste. 1004
Washington, DC 20005 US
Phone: 202-467-5081
Fax: 202-467-5085
Toll Free: 800-424-8666
E-mail Address: *info@acb.org*
Web Address: www.acb.org
The American Council of the Blind (ACB) is a leading membership organization of blind and visually impaired people.

Guide Dog Foundation for the Blind, Inc.
371 E. Jericho Tpke.
Smithtown, NY 11787-2976 US
Phone: 631-930-9000
Fax: 631-930-9009
Toll Free: 800-548-4337
E-mail Address: *info@guidedog.org*
Web Address: www.guidedog.org
The Guide Dog Foundation for the Blind, Inc. strives to be the leading resource and provider of premier services to facilitate the independence of people who are blind or visually impaired.

Helen Keller International Organization (HKI)
352 Park Ave. S, 12th Fl.
New York, NY 10010 US
Phone: 212-532-0544
Fax: 212-532-6014
Toll Free: 877-535-5374
E-mail Address: *info@hki.org*
Web Address: www.hki.org
The Helen Keller International Organization (HKI) directly addresses the causes of preventable blindness, provides rehabilitation services to blind people and helps reduce micronutrient malnutrition which can cause blindness and death in children.

Lighthouse International
111 E. 59th St.
New York, NY 10022-1202 US
Phone: 212-821-9200
Fax: 212-821-9707
Toll Free: 800-829-0500
E-mail Address: *visionrehab@lighthouse.org*
Web Address: www.lighthouse.org
Lighthouse International is a leading resource worldwide on vision impairment and vision rehabilitation.

National Association for the Visually Handicapped (NAVH)
22 W. 21st St., 6th Fl.
New York, NY 10010 US
Phone: 212-889-3141
Fax: 212-727-2931
E-mail Address: *navh@navh.org*
Web Address: www.navh.org
The National Association for the Visually Handicapped (NAVH) works with the visually impaired so that those affected can live with as little disruption as possible.

National Eye Institute (NEI)
31 Center Dr., MSC 2510
Bethesda, MD 20892-2510 US
Phone: 301-496-5248
E-mail Address: *2020@nei.nih.gov*
Web Address: www.nei.nih.gov
The National Eye Institute (NEI) conducts and supports research that helps prevent and treat eye diseases and other vision related disorders.

National Library Service for the Blind and Physically Handicapped (NLS)
1291 Taylor St. NW
Washington, DC 20011 US
Phone: 202-707-5100
Fax: 202-707-0712
Toll Free: 888-657-7323
E-mail Address: *nls@loc.gov*
Web Address: www.loc.gov/nls
National Library Service for the Blind and Physically Handicapped (NLS), part of the Library of Congress, administers a free library program of Braille and audio materials circulated to eligible borrowers in the United States by postage-free mail.

Prevent Blindness America (PBA)
211 W. Wacker Dr., Ste. 1700
Chicago, IL 60606 US
Toll Free: 800-331-2020
Web Address: www.preventblindness.org
Prevent Blindness America (PBA) is a leading volunteer eye health and safety organization dedicated to fighting blindness and saving sight.

Recording for the Blind and Dyslexic (RFB&D)
20 Roszel Rd.
Princeton, NJ 08540 US
Toll Free: 866-732-3585
Web Address: www.rfbd.org
Recording for the Blind and Dyslexic (RFB&D) is an educational library serving people who cannot effectively read standard print because of visual impairment, dyslexia or other disabilities.

VISIONS
500 Greenwich St., 3rd Fl.
New York, NY 10013-1354 US
Phone: 212-625-1616
Fax: 212-219-4078

E-mail Address: *info@visionsvcb.org*
Web Address: www.visionsvcb.org
VISIONS is a nonprofit agency that promotes the independence of people who are blind or visually impaired.

IX. Canadian Government Agencies

National Research Council (NRC)
1200 Montreal Rd., Bldg. M-58
Ottawa, ON K1A 0R6 Canada
Phone: 613-993-9101
Fax: 613-952-9907
Toll Free: 877-672-2672
E-mail Address: *info@nrc-cnrc.gc.ca*
Web Address: www.nrc-cnrc.gc.ca
Canada's National Research Council (NRC) is an government organization of 20 research institutes that carry out multidisciplinary research with partners in industries and sectors key to Canada's economic development.

X. Cancer

American Cancer Society (ACS)
1599 Clifton Rd. NE
Atlanta, GA 30345 US
Phone: 404-320-3333
Fax: 404-982-3677
Toll Free: 800-227-2345
E-mail Address: *encic@cancer.org*
Web Address: www.cancer.org
The American Cancer Society (ACS) is a nationwide community-based voluntary health organization dedicated to eliminating cancer as a major health problem by preventing the disease, saving lives and diminishing suffering from cancer.

Association of Community Cancer Centers (ACCC)
11600 Nebel St., Ste. 201
Rockville, MD 20852 US
Phone: 301-984-9496
Fax: 301-770-1949
Web Address: www.accc-cancer.org
The Association of Community Cancer Centers (ACCC) helps oncology professionals adapt to the complex challenges of program management, cuts in reimbursement, hospital consolidation and mergers, and legislation and regulations that threaten to compromise the delivery of quality cancer care.

Cancer Information Service (CIS)
Toll Free: 800-422-6237
E-mail Address: *cancer.gov_staff@mail.nih.gov*
Web Address: cis.nci.nih.gov
The Cancer Information Service (CIS) is a national information and education network provided by the National Cancer Institute.

Lance Armstrong Foundation (LAF)
P.O. Box 161150
Austin, TX 78716-1150 US
Phone: 512-236-8820
Toll Free: 866-235-7205
E-mail Address: *advocate@laf.org*
Web Address: www.livestrong.org
The Lance Armstrong Foundation (LAF) provides cancer patients, their families and caregivers with advocacy, education, public health and research programs relating to the treatment of and possible cures for all forms of cancer.

National Marrow Donor Program (NMDP)
3001 Broadway St. NE, Ste. 500
Minneapolis, MN 55413-1753 US
Toll Free: 800-627-7692
Web Address: www.marrow.org
The National Marrow Donor Program (NMDP) is an international leader in the facilitation of marrow and blood stem cell transplantation through non-family donors.

OncoLink
Abramson Cancer Center
3400 Spruce St., 2 Donner
Philadelphia, PA 19104-4283 US
Fax: 215-349-5445
Web Address: www.oncolink.upenn.edu
OncoLink strives to help cancer patients, families, health care professionals and the general public obtain accurate cancer-related information.

Susan G. Komen Breast Cancer Foundation
5005 LBJ Fwy., Ste. 250
Dallas, TX 75244 US
Phone: 972-855-1600
Fax: 972-855-1605
Toll Free: 800-462-9273
Web Address: www.komen.org
This Susan G. Komen Breast Cancer Foundation strives to eradicate breast cancer as a life-threatening disease by advancing research, education, screening and treatment.

Y-Me National Breast Cancer Organization
212 W. Van Buren, Ste. 1000
Chicago, IL 60607-3903 US
Phone: 312-986-8338
Fax: 312-294-8597
Toll Free: 800-221-2141
Web Address: www.y-me.org
The Y-Me National Breast Cancer Organization seeks to decrease the impact of breast cancer, create and increase breast cancer awareness and ensure that no one faces breast cancer alone.

XI. Careers-Biotech

Bio Online Career Center
1900 Powell St., Ste. 230

Emeryville, CA 94608 US
Phone: 510-601-7194
Fax: 510-601-1862
E-mail Address: *careers@bio.com*
Web Address: career.bio.com/careercenter/index.jhtml
The Bio Online Career Center enables the exchange of information within the life sciences, biotechnology and pharmaceutical industries. The center publishes daily news, information and research tools for professionals and students.

XII. Careers-First Time Jobs/New Grads

Black Collegian Home Page
140 Carondelet St.
New Orleans, LA 70130 US
Phone: 504-523-0154
Web Address: www.black-collegian.com
Black Collegian Home Page features listings for job and internship opportunities. The site includes a list of the top 100 minority corporate employers and an assessment of job opportunities.

Collegegrad.com
576 N. Washington Ave.
Cedarburg, WI 53012 US
Phone: 262-375-6700
Web Address: www.collegegrad.com
Collegegrad.com offers in-depth resources for college students and recent grads seeking entry-level jobs.

Job Web
62 Highland Ave.
Bethlehem, PA 18017-9085 US
Phone: 610-868-1421
Fax: 610-868-0208
Toll Free: 800-544-5272
Web Address: www.jobweb.com
Job Web, owned and sponsored by National Association of Colleges and Employers (NACE), displays job openings and employer descriptions. The site also offers a database of career fairs, searchable by state or keyword, with contact information.

MBAjobs.net
Fax: 413-556-8849
E-mail Address: *contact@mbajobs.net*
Web Address: www.mbajobs.net
MBAjobs.net is a unique international service for MBA students and graduates, employers, recruiters and business schools.

MonsterTrak
11845 W. Olympic Blvd., Ste. 500
Los Angeles, CA 90064 US
Toll Free: 800-999-8725
E-mail Address: *college.monstertrak@monster.com*
Web Address: www.monstertrak.monster.com
MonsterTrak features links to hundreds of university and college career centers across the U.S. with entry-level job listings categorized by industry. Major companies can also utilize MonsterTrak.

National Association of Colleges and Employers (NACE)
62 Highland Ave.
Bethlehem, PA 18017-9085 US
Phone: 610-868-1421
Fax: 610-868-0208
Toll Free: 800-544-5272
Web Address: www.naceweb.org
The National Association of Colleges and Employers (NACE) is a premier U.S. organization representing college placement offices and corporate recruiters who focus on hiring new grads.

XIII. Careers-General Job Listings

America's Job Bank
Toll Free: 877-348-0502
E-mail Address: *info@careeronestop.org*
Web Address: www.jobsearch.org
America's Job Bank was developed by the U.S. Department of Labor as part of an array of web-based job tools. It offers an extensive list of searchable employment vacancies as well as other job resources for employers and job seekers.

Career Exposure, Inc.
805 SW Broadway, Ste. 2250
Portland, OR 97205 US
Phone: 503-221-7779
Fax: 503-221-7780
E-mail Address: *feedback@CareerExposure.com*
Web Address: www.careerexposure.com
Career Exposure, Inc. is an online career center and job placement service, with resources for employers, recruiters and job seekers.

CareerBuilder
200 N. LaSalle St., Ste. 1100
Chicago, IL 60631 US
Phone: 773-527-3600
Fax: 773-399-6313
Toll Free: 800-638-4212
Web Address: www.careerbuilder.com
CareerBuilder focuses on the needs of companies and also provides a database of job openings, called the Mega Job Search. Hundreds of thousands of job openings are posted. Resumes are sent directly to the company, and applicants can set up a special e-mail account for job-seeking purposes. CareerBuilder, Inc. is a joint venture of three newspaper giants: Knight Ridder, Gannett and Tribune Company.

HotJobs
45 W. 18th St., 6th Fl.
New York, NY 10011 US
Phone: 646-351-5300
Fax: 212-944-8962
Web Address: hotjobs.yahoo.com
HotJobs, designed for experienced professionals, employers and job seekers, is a Yahoo-owned site that provides company profiles, a resume posting service and a resume workshop. The site allows posters to block resumes from being viewed by certain companies and provides a notification service of new jobs.

HRS Federal Job Search
Web Address: www.hrsjobs.com
HRS Federal Job Search features a database of federal jobs available across the U.S. Most jobs are within the public sector. The job seeker creates a profile with desired job type, salary and location to receive applicable postings by e-mail.

JobCentral
9002 N. Purdue Rd., Quad III, Ste. 100
Indianapolis, IN 46268 US
Phone: 317-874-9000
Fax: 317-874-9100
Toll Free: 866-268-6206
E-mail Address: *info@jobcentral.com*
Web Address: www.jobcentral.com
JobCentral, operated by the nonprofit DirectEmployers Association, links users directly to hundreds of thousands of job opportunities posted on the sites of participating employers, thus bypassing the usual job search sites. This saves employers money and allows job seekers to access many more job opportunities.

LaborMarketInfo
7000 Franklin Blvd., Ste. 1100
Sacramento, CA 95823 US
Phone: 916-262-2162
Fax: 916-262-2352
Web Address: www.labormarketinfo.edd.ca.gov
LaborMarketInfo, formerly the California Cooperative Occupational Information System, is sponsored by California's Economic Development Office. The web site is geared to providing job seekers and employers a wide range of resources, namely the ability to find, access and use labor market information and services. It provides demographical statistics for employment on both a local and regional level, as well as career searching tools for California residents.

Monster Worldwide, Inc.
622 3rd Ave., 39th Fl.
New York, NY 10017 US
Phone: 212-351-7000
Toll Free: 800-666-7837
Web Address: www.monster.com
Monster Worldwide, Inc. is an electronic career center that displays hundreds of thousands of job opportunities in 23 countries around the world. Job seekers can build and store a resume online and find job listings that match their profiles. Monster e-mails the results once per week.

Recruiters Online Network
Web Address: www.recruitersonline.com
The Recruiters Online Network provides job postings from thousands of recruiters, Careers Online Magazine, a resume database, as well as other career resources.

TrueCareers, Inc.
Web Address: www.truecareers.com
TrueCareers, Inc. offers job listings and provides an array of career resources. The company also offers a search of over 2 million scholarships.

Wall Street Journal - CareerJournal.com
P.O. Box 300
Princeton, NJ 08543-0300 US
Web Address: www.careers.wsj.com
The Wall Street Journal's executive career site, called CareerJournal.com, features a job database with more than 100,000 available positions. It provides a weekly career column and a range of articles about topics including diversity issues and promotion.

XIV. Careers-Health Care

Health Care Source
Web Address: www.healthcaresource.com
Health Care Source offers career-related information and job finding tools for health care professionals.

HMonster
Web Address: healthcare.monster.com
HMonster, managed by monster.com, provides job listings, job searches and search agents for the medical field.

Medicalworkers.com
191 University Blvd., Ste. 252
Denver, CO 80206 US
Phone: 720-227-9364
E-mail Address: *cs@medicalworkers.com*
Web Address: www.medicalworkers.com
Medicalworkers.com is an employment site for medical and health care professionals.

Medjump.com
7119 E. Shea Blvd., Ste. 109-535
Scottsdale, AZ 85254 US
E-mail Address: *info@medjump.net*
Web Address: www.medjump.com
Medjump.com is dedicated to empowering health care and medical-related professionals with the necessary tools to market their abilities and skills.

Medzilla.com
Web Address: www.medzilla.com
Medzilla.com offers job searches, salary surveys, a search agent and information on health care employment.

NationJob Network-Medical and Health Care Jobs Page
601 SW 9th St., Ste. J&K
Des Moines, IA 50309 US
Fax: 515-283-1223
Toll Free: 888-526-5967
E-mail Address: *customerservice@nationjob.com*
Web Address: www.nationjob.com/medical
The NationJob Network-Medical and Health Care Jobs Page offers information and listings for health care employment.

Nurse-Recruiter.com
36 Washington St., Ste. 170
Wellesley, MA 02481 US
Toll Free: 866-560-1034
E-mail Address: *info@nurse-recruiter.com*
Web Address: www.nurse-recruiter.com
Nurse-Recruiter.com is a nurse-owned, web-centric company devoted to bringing health care employers and the nursing community together.

PracticeLink
415 2nd Ave.
P.O. Box 100
Hinton, WV 25951 US
Fax: 877-847-0120
Toll Free: 800-776-8383
E-mail Address: *info@practicelink.com*
Web Address: www.practicelink.com
PracticeLink is one of the largest physician employment web sites. It is a free service used by more than 18,000 practice-seeking physicians annually to quickly search and locate potential physician practice opportunities. PracticeLink is financially supported by more than 700 hospitals, medical groups, private practices and health care systems that advertise more than 5,000 opportunities.

XV. Careers-Job Reference Tools

Newspaperlinks.com
E-mail Address: *sally.clarke@naa.org*
Web Address: www.newspaperlinks.com
Newspaperlinks.com, a service of the Newspaper Association of America, links individuals to local, national and international newspapers. Job seekers can search through thousands of classified sections.

Vault.com
150 W. 22nd St., 5th Fl.
New York, NY 10011 US
Phone: 212-366-4212
Web Address: www.vault.com
Vault.com is a comprehensive career web site for employers and employees, with job postings and valuable information on a wide variety of industries. Vault gears many of its features toward MBAs. The site has been recognized by Forbes and Fortune Magazines.

XVI. Careers-Science

Sciencejobs.com
Web Address: www.sciencejobs.com
Sciencejobs.com is a web site produced by the publishers of New Scientist Magazine, which helps jobseekers and employers in the bioscience fields find each other. The site includes a job search engine and a free-of-charge e-mail job alert service.

XVII. Child Abuse

Adult Survivors of Child Abuse (ASCA)
The Morris Center, P.O. Box 14477
San Francisco, CA 94114 US
Phone: 415-928-4576
E-mail Address: *tmc_asca@dnai.com*
Web Address: www.ascasupport.org
Adult Survivors of Child Abuse (ASCA) is a nonprofit support program for adult survivors of child neglect and abuse.

Child Welfare Information Gateway
1250 Maryland Ave. SW, 8th Fl.
Washington, DC 20024 US
Phone: 703-385-7565
Fax: 703-385-3206
Toll Free: 800-394-3366
E-mail Address: *info@childwelfare.gov*
Web Address: www.childwelfare.gov
The Child Welfare Information Gateway is a national resource for professionals and others seeking information on child abuse, neglect and child welfare.

National Center for Missing and Exploited Children (NCMEC)
699 Prince St.
Alexandria, VA 22314-3175 US
Phone: 703-274-3900
Fax: 703-274-2220
Toll Free: 800-843-5678
Web Address: www.ncmec.org
The National Center for Missing and Exploited Children (NCMEC) is an international resource for abducted, endangered and exploited children.

XVIII. Child Development

Human Growth Foundation
997 Glen Cove Ave., Ste. 5
Glen Head, NY 11545 US

Fax: 516-671-4055
Toll Free: 800-451-6434
E-mail Address: *hgfl@hgfound.org*
Web Address: www.hgfound.org
The Human Growth Foundation helps children and adults with disorders related to growth or growth hormone through research, education, support and advocacy.

XIX. Clinical Trials

Clinical Trials
8600 Rockville Pike
Bethesda, MD 20894 US
Phone: 301-594-5983
Fax: 301-402-1384
Toll Free: 888-346-3656
Web Address: www.clinicaltrials.gov
Clinical Trials offers up-to-date information for locating federally and privately supported clinical trials for a wide range of diseases and conditions. It is a service of the National Institutes of Health (NIH).

XX. Consulting Industry Associations

American Association of Healthcare Consultants (AAHC)
5938 N. Drake Ave.
Chicago, IL 60659 US
Fax: 773-463-3552
Toll Free: 888-350-2242
E-mail Address: *info@aahcmail.org*
Web Address: www.aahc.net
The American Association of Healthcare Consultants (AAHC) is a professional society for credentialed consultants practicing in health care organization and delivery.

American Association of Legal Nurse Consultants (AALNC)
401 N. Michigan Ave.
Chicago, IL 60611 US
Fax: 312-673-6655
Toll Free: 877-402-2562
E-mail Address: *info@aalnc.org*
Web Address: www.aalnc.org
The American Association of Legal Nurse Consultants (AALNC) is a nonprofit organization dedicated to the professional enhancement of registered nurses practicing in a consulting capacity in the legal field.

XXI. Corporate Information Resources

bizjournals.com
120 W. Morehead St., Ste. 400
Charlotte, NC 28202 US
Web Address: www.bizjournals.com
Bizjournals.com is the online media division of American City Business Journals, the publisher of dozens of leading city business journals nationwide. It provides access to research into the latest news regarding companies small and large.

Business Wire
44 Montgomery St., 39th Fl.
San Francisco, CA 94104 US
Phone: 415-986-4422
Fax: 415-788-5335
Toll Free: 888-381-9473
Web Address: www.businesswire.com
Business Wire offers news releases, industry- and company-specific news, top headlines, conference calls, IPOs on the Internet, media services and access to tradeshownews.com and BW Connect On-line through its informative and continuously updated web site.

Edgar Online
50 Washington St., 11th Fl.
Norwalk, CT 06854 US
Phone: 203-852-5666
Fax: 203-852-5667
Toll Free: 800-416-6651
Web Address: www.edgar-online.com
Edgar Online is a gateway and search tool for viewing corporate documents, such as annual reports on Form 10-K, filed with the U.S. Securities and Exchange Commission.

PRNewswire
810 7th Ave., 32nd Fl.
New York, NY 10019 US
Phone: 212-596-1500
Toll Free: 800-832-5522
E-mail Address: *information@prnewswire.com*
Web Address: www.prnewswire.com
PRNewswire provides comprehensive communications services for public relations and investor relations professionals ranging from information distribution and market intelligence to the creation of online multimedia content and investor relations web sites. Users can also view recent corporate press releases.

Silicon Investor
Web Address: www.siliconinvestor.com
Silicon Investor is focused on providing information about technology companies. The company's web site serves as a financial discussion forum and offers quotes, profiles and charts.

XXII. Diabetes

American Diabetes Association
1701 N. Beauregard St.
Alexandria, VA 22311 US
Toll Free: 800-342-2383

E-mail Address: *askada@diabetes.org*
Web Address: www.diabetes.org
The American Diabetes Association is a nonprofit health organization providing diabetes research, information and advocacy.

Juvenile Diabetes Research Foundation (JDRF)
120 Wall St.
New York, NY 10005-4001 US
Fax: 212-785-9595
Toll Free: 800-533-2873
E-mail Address: *info@jdrf.org*
Web Address: www.jdrf.org
The Juvenile Diabetes Research Foundation (JDRF) is a major nonprofit, nongovernmental sponsor of diabetes research.

XXIII. Disabling Conditions

Americans with Disabilities Act (ADA)
950 Pennsylvania Ave. NW, Civil Rights Div., Disability Rights Section-NYA
Washington, DC 20530 US
Phone: 202-307-0663
Fax: 202-307-1198
Toll Free: 800-514-0301
Web Address: www.ada.gov
The Americans with Disabilities Act (ADA) web site providing information and technical assistance on the Americans with Disabilities Act.

Job Accommodation Network (JAN)
P.O. Box 6080
Morgantown, WV 26506-6080 US
Phone: 304-293-7186
Fax: 304-293-5407
Toll Free: 800-526-7234
E-mail Address: *jan@jan.wvu.edu*
Web Address: janweb.icdi.wvu.edu
The Job Accommodation Network (JAN) is a free consulting service that provides information about job accommodations, the Americans with Disabilities Act and the employability of people with disabilities.

National Easter Seal Society
230 W. Monroe St., Ste. 1800
Chicago, IL 60606 US
Phone: 312-726-6200
Fax: 312-726-1494
Toll Free: 800-221-6827
E-mail Address: *info@easter-seals.org*
Web Address: www.easter-seals.org
The National Easter Seal Society provides services to children and adults with disabilities, as well as assistance to their families.

National Information Center for Children and Youth with Disabilities (NICHCY)
P.O. Box 1492
Washington, DC 20013 US
Fax: 202-884-8441
Toll Free: 800-695-0285
E-mail Address: *nichcy@aed.org*
Web Address: www.nichcy.org
National Information Center for Children and Youth with Disabilities (NICHCY) is a national information and referral center that provides information on disabilities and disability-related issues for families, educators and other professionals.

XXIV. Diseases, Rare & Other

American Association on Intellectual and Developmental Disabilities (AAIDD)
444 N. Capitol St. NW, Ste. 846
Washington, DC 20001-1512 US
Phone: 202-387-1968
Fax: 202-387-2193
Toll Free: 800-424-3688
E-mail Address: *bersanh@wou.edu*
Web Address: www.aamr.org
The American Association on Intellectual and Developmental Disabilities (AAIDD) promotes progressive policies, sound research, effective practices and universal human rights for people with mental challenges.

American SIDS Institute
509 Augusta Dr.
Marietta, GA 30067 US
Phone: 770-426-8746
Fax: 770-426-1369
Toll Free: 800-232-7437
Web Address: www.sids.org
The American SIDS Institute is dedicated to the prevention of sudden infant death and the promotion of infant health.

Amyotrophic Lateral Sclerosis Association (ALSA)
27001 Agoura Rd., Ste. 150
Calabasas Hills, CA 91301-5104 US
Phone: 818-880-9007
Fax: 818-880-9006
Web Address: www.alsa.org
The Amyotrophic Lateral Sclerosis Association (ALSA) seeks to be the primary resource for Lou Gehrig's Disease by providing information about the disease, products and services, physicians and other information.

Angelman Syndrome Foundation (ASF)
4255 Westbrook Dr., Ste. 216
Aurora, IL 60504 US
Phone: 630-978-4245
Fax: 630-978-7408
Toll Free: 800-432-6435

E-mail Address: *info@angelman.org*
Web Address: www.angelman.org
The mission of the Angelman Syndrome Foundation (ASF) is to advance the awareness and treatment of Angelman Syndrome through education, information exchange and research.

Autism Society of America (ASA)
7910 Woodmont Ave., Ste. 300
Bethesda, MD 20814-3067 US
Phone: 301-657-0881
Toll Free: 800-328-8476
E-mail Address: *media@autism-society.org*
Web Address: www.autism-society.org
The Autism Society of America (ASA) seeks to promote lifelong access and opportunity for all individuals affected by autism to be fully participating members of their communities.

Cleft Palate Foundation (CPF)
1504 E. Franklin St., Ste. 102
Chapel Hill, NC 27514-2820 US
Phone: 919-933-9044
Fax: 919-933-9604
Toll Free: 800-242-5338
E-mail Address: *info@cleftline.org*
Web Address: www.cleftline.org
The Cleft Palate Foundation (CPF) is a nonprofit organization dedicated to optimizing the quality of life for individuals affected by facial birth defects.

Cystic Fibrosis Foundation (CFF)
6931 Arlington Rd.
Bethesda, MD 20814 US
Phone: 301-951-4422
Fax: 301-951-6378
Toll Free: 800-344-4823
E-mail Address: *info@cff.org*
Web Address: www.cff.org
The Cystic Fibrosis Foundation (CFF) assures the development of the means to cure and control cystic fibrosis and to improve the quality of life for those with the disease.

Dystonia Medical Research Foundation
1 E. Wacker Dr., Ste. 2430
Chicago, IL 60601-1905 US
Phone: 312-755-0198
Fax: 312-803-0138
Toll Free: 800-377-3978
E-mail Address: *dystonia@dystonia-foundation.org*
Web Address: www.dystonia-foundation.org
The Dystonia Medical Research Foundation seeks to advance research for treatments and ultimately a cure for dystonia, to promote awareness and education of the disease and to support the needs and well-being of affected individuals and families.

Epilepsy Foundation of America
8301 Professional Pl.
Landover, MD 20785-7223 US
Toll Free: 800-332-1000
Web Address: www.epilepsyfoundation.org
The Epilepsy Foundation of America is the national voluntary agency devoted to the wellbeing of people with epilepsy in the U.S. and their families.

Hepatitis B Foundation
3805 Old Easton Rd.
Doylestown, PA 18901-2697 US
Phone: 215-489-4900
Fax: 215-489-4313
E-mail Address: *info@hepb.org*
Web Address: www.hepb.org
The Hepatitis B Foundation is a national nonprofit organization dedicated to finding a cure and improving the quality of life of those affected by hepatitis B worldwide through research, education and patient advocacy.

Huntington's Disease Society of America, Inc. (HDSA)
505 8th Ave., Ste. 902
New York, NY 10018 US
Phone: 212-242-1968
Fax: 212-239-3430
Toll Free: 800-345-4372
E-mail Address: *hdsainfo@hdsa.org*
Web Address: www.hdsa.org
The Huntington's Disease Society of America, Inc. (HDSA) is dedicated to finding a cure for Huntington's disease (HD) while providing support and services for those living with HD and their families.

International Myeloma Foundation (IMF)
12650 Riverside Dr., Ste. 206
North Hollywood, CA 91607-3421 US
Phone: 818-487-7455
Fax: 818-487-7454
Toll Free: 800-452-2873
E-mail Address: *theimf@myeloma.org*
Web Address: www.myeloma.org
The International Myeloma Foundation (IMF) is a network dedicated to the treatment of myeloma through its ties with more than 100 support groups from around the world.

Lupus Foundation of America
2000 L St. NW, Ste. 710
Washington, DC 20036 US
Phone: 202-349-1155
Fax: 202-349-1156
E-mail Address: *info@lupus.org*
Web Address: www.lupus.org
The Lupus Foundation of America is a nonprofit voluntary health organization dedicated to improving the diagnosis and treatment of lupus, supporting individuals and families affected by the disease, increasing awareness of lupus

among health professionals and the public, and finding the cure.

Muscular Dystrophy Association (MDA)
3300 E. Sunrise Dr.
Tucson, AZ 85718 US
Toll Free: 800-344-4863
E-mail Address: *mda@mdausa.org*
Web Address: www.mdausa.org
The Muscular Dystrophy Association (MDA) is a voluntary health agency aimed at conquering neuromuscular diseases that affect more than 1 million Americans.

Myasthenia Gravis Foundation of America (MGFA)
1821 University Ave. W, Ste. S256
St. Paul, MN 55104 US
Phone: 651-917-6256
Fax: 651-917-1835
Toll Free: 800-541-5454
E-mail Address: *mgfa@myasthenia.org*
Web Address: www.myasthenia.org
The Myasthenia Gravis Foundation of America (MGFA) is a national volunteer health agency dedicated solely to the fight against myasthenia gravis.

National Down Syndrome Congress (NDSC)
1370 Center Dr., Ste. 102
Atlanta, GA 30338 US
Phone: 770-604-9500
Fax: 770-604-9898
Toll Free: 800-232-6372
E-mail Address: *info@ndsccenter.org*
Web Address: www.ndsccenter.org
The National Down Syndrome Congress (NDSC) strives to be the national advocacy organization for Down syndrome and to provide leadership in all areas of concern related to persons with Down syndrome.

National Multiple Sclerosis Society (NMSS)
733 3rd Ave., 3rd Fl.
New York, NY 10017 US
Toll Free: 800-344-4867
Web Address: www.nmss.org
The National Multiple Sclerosis Society (NMSS) and its network of chapters nationwide promote research, educate and advocate on critical issues, as well as organize a wide range of programs for those living with multiple sclerosis.

National Organization for Rare Disorders (NORD)
55 Kenosia Ave.
PO Box 1968
Danbury, CT 06813-1968 US
Phone: 203-744-0100
Fax: 203-798-2291
Toll Free: 800-999-6673
E-mail Address: *orphan@rarediseases.org*
Web Address: www.rarediseases.org
The National Organization for Rare Disorders (NORD) is a unique federation of voluntary health organizations dedicated to helping people with rare diseases and assisting the organizations that serve them.

National Peticulosis Association (NPA)
P.O. Box 610189
Newton, MA 02461 US
Phone: 781-449-6487
Fax: 781-449-8129
E-mail Address: *npa@headlice.org*
Web Address: www.headlice.org
The National Peticulosis Association (NPA) is a nonprofit health and education agency dedicated to protecting children from the misuse and abuse of potentially harmful lice and scabies pesticidal treatments.

National Reye's Syndrome Foundation (NRSF)
Phone: 419-636-2679
Fax: 419-636-9897
Toll Free: 800-233-7393
E-mail Address: *nrsf@reyessyndrome.org*
Web Address: www.reyessyndrome.org
The National Reye's Syndrome Foundation (NRSF) attempts to generate a concerted, organized lay movement to eradicate Reye's syndrome.

Paget Foundation for Paget's Disease of Bone and Related Disorders
120 Wall St., Ste. 1602
New York, NY 10005-4001 US
Phone: 212-509-5335
Fax: 212-509-8492
Toll Free: 800-237-2438
E-mail Address: *pagetfdn@aol.com*
Web Address: www.paget.org
The Paget Foundation for Paget's Disease of Bone and Related Disorders is an informative web site dedicated to Paget's disease and other bone disorders for patients and health professionals.

Scleroderma Foundation
300 Rosewood Dr., Ste. 105
Danvers, MA 01923 US
Phone: 978-463-5843
Toll Free: 800-722-4673
E-mail Address: *sfinfo@scleroderma.org*
Web Address: www.scleroderma.org
The Scleroderma Foundation seeks to help patients and their families cope with scleroderma, as well as raise public awareness and stimulate research.

Sickle Cell Disease Association of America, Inc.
231 E. Baltimore St., Ste. 800
Baltimore, MD 21202 US
Phone: 410-528-1555
Fax: 410-528-1495
Toll Free: 800-421-8453

E-mail Address: *scdaa@sicklecelldisease.org*
Web Address: www.sicklecelldisease.org
The Sickle Cell Disease Association of America is devoted to the care and cure of individuals with sickle cell disease. The group also organizes conferences and prepares and distributes substantive educational materials about the sickle cell disease problem.

Spina Bifida Association of America (SBAA)
4590 MacArthur Blvd. NW
Washington, DC 20007 US
Phone: 202-944-3285
Fax: 202-944-3295
Toll Free: 800-621-3141
E-mail Address: *sbaa@sbaa.org*
Web Address: www.sbaa.org
The Spina Bifida Association of America (SBAA) is a national voluntary health agency that seeks to promote the prevention of spina bifida and to enhance the lives of all affected.

Tourette Syndrome Association, Inc. (TSA)
42-40 Bell Blvd., Ste. 205
Bayside, NY 11361-2820 US
Phone: 718-224-2999
Fax: 718-224-9596
Web Address: www.tsa-usa.org
The Tourette Syndrome Association, Inc. (TSA) is a voluntary, nonprofit membership organization that seeks to identify the cause, find the cure for and control the effects of Tourette syndrome.

United Cerebral Palsy (UCP)
1660 L St. NW, Ste. 700
Washington, DC 20036 US
Phone: 202-776-0406
Fax: 202-776-0414
Toll Free: 800-872-5827
E-mail Address: *info@ucp.org*
Web Address: www.ucp.org
United Cerebral Palsy (UCP) is a national organization that strives for change and progress for disabled persons within society.

XXV. Drug & Alcohol Abuse

Al-Anon/Alateen
1600 Corporate Landing Pkwy.
Virginia Beach, VA 23454-5617 US
Phone: 757-563-1600
Fax: 757-563-1655
Toll Free: 888-425-2666
E-mail Address: *wso@al-anon.org*
Web Address: www.al-anon.alateen.org
Al-Anon/Alateen strives to help families and friends of alcoholics recover from the effects of living with the problem drinking of a relative or friend.

Drug Information Association (DIA)
800 Enterprise Rd., Ste. 200
Horsham, PA 19044-3595 US
Phone: 215-442-6100
Fax: 215-442-6199
E-mail Address: *dia@diahome.org*
Web Address: www.diahome.org
The Drug Information Association (DIA) provides a neutral global forum for the exchange and dissemination of information on the discovery, development, evaluation and utilization of medicines and related health care technologies.

National Clearinghouse for Alcohol and Drug Information (NCADI)
P.O. Box 2345
Rockville, MD 20847-2345 US
Phone: 240-221-4019
Fax: 240-221-4292
Toll Free: 800-729-6686
Web Address: www.health.org
The National Clearinghouse for Alcohol and Drug Information (NCADI) is the information service of the Center for Substance Abuse Prevention of the Substance Abuse and Mental Health Services Administration in the U.S. Department of Health & Human Services.

Phoenix House Foundation (The)
Web Address: www.phoenixhouse.org
The Phoenix House Foundation is a drug awareness and rehabilitation group with operations in California, Florida, New England, New York and Texas.

XXVI. Economic Data & Research

STAT-USA
U.S. Department of Commerce, Rm. H-4885
Washington, DC 20230 US
Phone: 202-482-1986
Fax: 202-482-2164
Toll Free: 800-742-8872
E-mail Address: *statmail@doc.gov*
Web Address: www.stat-usa.gov
STAT-USA is an agency in the Economics and Statistics Administration of the U.S. Department of Commerce. The site offers daily economic news, statistical releases, and databases relating to export and trade, as well as the domestic economy.

XXVII. Electronic Health Records/Continuity of Care Records

Medical Records Institute (MRI)
425 Boylston St., 4th Fl.
Boston, MA 02116-3315 US
Phone: 617-964-3923
Fax: 617-964-3926
E-mail Address: *info@medrecinst.com*

Web Address: www.medrecinst.com
The Medical Records Institute (MRI) acts as an international forum for sharing knowledge, experience and solutions regarding electronic medical records, e-health and mobile health with the healthcare community.

XXVIII. Engineering, Research & Scientific Associations

American Association for the Advancement of Science (AAAS)
1200 New York Ave. NW
Washington, DC 20005 US
Phone: 202-326-6400
E-mail Address: *webmaster@aaas.org*
Web Address: www.aaas.org
The American Association for the Advancement of Science (AAAS) is the world's largest scientific society and the publisher of Science magazine. It is an international non-profit organization dedicating to advancing science.

American National Standards Institute (ANSI)
1819 L St. NW, 6th Fl.
Washington, DC 20036 US
Phone: 202-293-8020
Fax: 202-293-9287
E-mail Address: *info@ansi.org*
Web Address: www.ansi.org
The American National Standards Institute (ANSI) is a private, nonprofit organization that administers and coordinates the U.S. voluntary standardization and conformity assessment system. Its mission is to enhance both the global competitiveness of U.S. business and the quality of life by promoting and facilitating voluntary consensus standards and conformity assessment systems and safeguarding their integrity.

American Society for Healthcare Engineering (ASHE)
1 N. Franklin, 28th Fl.
Chicago, IL 60606 US
Phone: 312-422-3800
Fax: 312-422-4571
E-mail Address: *ashe@aha.org*
Web Address: www.ashe.org
The American Society for Healthcare Engineering (ASHE) is the advocate and resource for continuous improvement in the health care engineering and facilities management professions.

American Society of Safety Engineers (ASSE)
1800 E. Oakton St.
Des Plaines, IL 60018 US
Phone: 847-699-2929
Fax: 847-768-3434
E-mail Address: *customerservice@asse.org*
Web Address: www.asse.org
The American Society of Safety Engineers (ASSE) is the world's oldest and largest professional safety organization. It manages, supervises and consults on safety, health and environmental issues in industry, insurance, government and education.

Cryogenic Society of America (CSA)
218 Lake St.
Oak Park, IL 60302-2609 US
Phone: 708-383-6220
Fax: 708-383-9337
E-mail Address: *laurie@cryogenicsociety.org*
Web Address: www.cryogenicsociety.org
The Cryogenic Society of America (CSA) is a nonprofit organization that brings together those in all disciplines concerned with the applications of low-temperature technology. It also increases public awareness of the usefulness of cryogenic technology.

IEEE (Institute of Electrical and Electronics Engineers)
3 Park Ave., 17th Fl.
New York, NY 10016-5997 US
Phone: 212-419-7900
Fax: 212-752-4929
Toll Free: 800-701-4333
E-mail Address: *ieeeusa@ieee.org*
Web Address: www.ieee.org
The IEEE (Institute of Electrical and Electronics Engineers) is a nonprofit, technical professional association of more than 370,000 individual members in approximately 160 countries. The IEEE sets global technical standards and acts as an authority in technical areas ranging from computer engineering, biomedical technology and telecommunications, to electric power, aerospace and consumer electronics.

Industrial Research Institute (IRI)
2200 Clarendon Blvd., Ste. 1102
Arlington, VA 22201 US
Phone: 703-647-2580
Fax: 703-647-2581
Web Address: www.iriinc.org
The Industrial Research Institute (IRI) is a nonprofit organization of over 200 leading industrial companies, representing industries such as aerospace, automotive, chemical, computers and electronics, which carry out industrial research efforts in the U.S. manufacturing sector. IRI helps members improve research and development capabilities.

Institute of Biological Engineering (IBE)
P.O. Box 24267
Minneapolis, MN 55424-0267 US
Phone: 763-765-2388
Fax: 763-765-2329
E-mail Address: *director@ibeweb.org*
Web Address: www.ibeweb.org

The Institute of Biological Engineering (IBE) is a professional organization encouraging inquiry and interest in biological engineering and professional development for its members.

International Society of Pharmaceutical Engineers (ISPE)
3109 W. Dr. Martin Luther King, Jr. Blvd., Ste. 250
Tampa, FL 33607 US
Phone: 813-960-2105
Fax: 813-264-2816
E-mail Address: *customerservice@ispe.org*
Web Address: www.ispe.org
The International Society of Pharmaceutical Engineers (ISPE) is a worldwide nonprofit society dedicated to educating and advancing pharmaceutical manufacturing professionals and the pharmaceutical industry.

International Standards Organization (ISO)
1, ch de la Voie-Creuse, Case postale 56
Geneva, CH-1211 Switzerland
Phone: 41-22-749-01-11
Fax: 41-22-733-34-30
Web Address: www.iso.org
The International Standards Organization (ISO) is a global consortium national standards institutes from 157 countries. The established International Standards are designed to make products and services more efficient, safe and clean.

National Academy of Sciences (NAS)
500 5th St. NW
Washington, DC 20001 US
Phone: 202-334-2000
Web Address: www.nationalacademies.com
The National Academy of Sciences (NAS) is an honorific society of distinguished American scholars engaged in scientific and engineering research, dedicated to the furtherance of science and technology and to their use for the general welfare. The four units of the National Academies include the National Academy of Sciences, the National Academy of Engineering, the Institute of Medicine and the National Research Council.

Royal Society (The)
6-9 Carlton House Ter.
London, SW1Y 5AG UK
Phone: 44-20-7451-2500
Fax: 44-20-7930-2170
Web Address: www.royalsoc.ac.uk
The Royal Society is the UK's leading scientific organization. It operates as a national academy of science, supporting scientists, engineers, technologists and research. On its website, you will find a wealth of data about the research and development initiatives of its Fellows and Foreign Members.

XXIX. Fitness

Aerobics and Fitness Association of America (AFAA)
15250 Ventura Blvd., Ste. 200
Sherman Oaks, CA 91403 US
Toll Free: 877-968-7263
Web Address: www.afaa.com
The Aerobics and Fitness Association of America (AFAA) answers questions from the public regarding safe and effective exercise programs and practices.

American Fitness Professionals and Associates (AFPA)
P.O. Box 214
Ship Bottom, NJ 08008 US
Phone: 609-978-7583
Fax: 609-978-7582
E-mail Address: *afpa@afpafitness.com*
Web Address: www.afpafitness.com
American Fitness Professionals and Associates (AFPA) offers health and fitness professionals certification programs, continuing education courses, home correspondence courses and regional conventions.

YMCA of the USA
101 N. Wacker Dr.
Chicago, IL 60606 US
Toll Free: 800-872-9622
E-mail Address: *fulfillment@ymca.net*
Web Address: www.ymca.net
The YMCA of the USA is the largest nonprofit community service organization in America, and it strives to put Christian principles into practice through programs that build healthy spirit, mind and body.

XXX. Headache/Head Injury

American Council for Headache Education (ACHE)
19 Mantua Rd.
Mt. Royal, NJ 08061 US
Phone: 856-423-0258
Fax: 856-423-0082
E-mail Address: *achehq@talley.com*
Web Address: www.achenet.org
The American Council for Headache Education (ACHE) is a nonprofit patient-health professional partnership dedicated to advancing the treatment and management of headaches and to raising the public awareness of headaches as valid, biologically based illnesses.

Brain Injury Association, Inc.
8201 Greensboro Dr., Ste. 611
McLean, VA 22102 US
Phone: 703-761-0750
Fax: 703-761-0755
Toll Free: 800-444-6443
Web Address: www.biausa.org

The Brain Injury Association, Inc. works to create a better future through brain injury prevention, research, education and advocacy.

National Headache Foundation (NHF)
820 N. Orleans, Ste. 217
Chicago, IL 60610 US
Toll Free: 888-643-5552
E-mail Address: *info@headaches.org*
Web Address: www.headaches.org
The National Headache Foundation (NHF) is a nonprofit organization dedicated to educating headache sufferers and health care professionals about headache causes and treatments.

XXXI. Health & Nutrition Associations

Food Allergy and Anaphylaxis Network (FAAN)
11781 Lee Jackson Hwy., Ste. 160
Fairfax, VA 22033-3309 US
Fax: 703-691-2713
Toll Free: 800-929-4040
E-mail Address: *faan@foodallergy.org*
Web Address: www.foodallergy.org
The Food Allergy and Anaphylaxis Network (FAAN) is a leader in food allergy and anaphylaxis awareness and the issues surrounding these conditions.

XXXII. Health Associations-International

World Health Organization (WHO)
Ave. Appia 20, CH-1211
Geneva, 27 Switzerland
Phone: 41-22-791-2111
Fax: 41-22-791-3111
E-mail Address: *info@who.int*
Web Address: www.who.int
The World Health Organization (WHO), the United Nations' specialized agency for health, works for the attainment by all people of the highest possible level of health. Health is defined in WHO's constitution as a state of complete physical, mental and social well-being and not merely the absence of disease or infirmity. WHO is governed by 191 member states through the World Health Assembly, composed of representatives from the member states.

XXXIII. Health Care Business & Professional Associations

Academy of Laser Dentistry (ALD)
P.O. Box 8667
Coral Springs, FL 33075 US
Phone: 954-346-3776
Fax: 954-757-2598
Toll Free: 877-527-3776
E-mail Address: *memberservices@laserdentistry.org*
Web Address: www.laserdentistry.org
The Academy of Laser Dentistry (ALD) is an international professional membership association of dental practitioners and supporting organizations.

Academy of Medical-Surgical Nurses (AMSN)
E. Holly Ave., Box 56
Pitman, NJ 08071-0056 US
Toll Free: 866-877-2676
E-mail Address: *amsn@ajj.com*
Web Address: www.medsurgnurse.org
The Academy of Medical-Surgical Nurses (AMSN) is dedicated to fostering excellence in adult health and in the medical-surgical nursing practice.

Acute Long-Term Hospital Association (ALTHA)
625 Slaters Ln., Ste. 302
Alexandria, VA 22314 US
Phone: 703-518-9900
Fax: 703-518-9980
Web Address: www.altha.org
The Acute Long-Term Hospital Association (ALTHA) represents over 100 long-term care hospitals specializing in intensive care for critically ill patients.

Advanced Medical Technology Association (AdvaMed)
701 Pennsylvania Ave. NW, Ste. 800
Washington, DC 20004-2654 US
Phone: 202-783-8700
Fax: 202-783-8750
E-mail Address: *info@advamed.org*
Web Address: www.advamed.org
The Advanced Medical Technology Association (AdvaMed) strives to be the advocate for a legal, regulatory and economic climate that advances global health care by assuring worldwide access to the benefits of medical technology.

AFT Healthcare
555 New Jersey Ave. NW
Washington, DC 20001 US
Phone: 202-879-4400
Web Address: www.aft.org/healthcare
AFT Healthcare, a division of the American Federation of Teachers, represents its members in the health professions and seeks to enhance the professional norms and ethics of health care workers.

Air and Surface Transport Nurses Association (ASTNA)
7995 E. Prentice Ave., Ste 100
Greenwood Village, CO 80111 US
Fax: 303-770-1614
Toll Free: 800-897-6362
E-mail Address: *astna@gwami.com*
Web Address: www.astna.org
The Air and Surface Transport Nurses Association (ASTNA) is a nonprofit member organization whose

mission is to represent, promote and provide guidance to professional nurses who practice the unique and distinct specialty of transport nursing.

America's Health Insurance Plans (AHIP)
601 Pennsylvania Ave. NW, Ste. 500
Washington, DC 20004 US
Phone: 202-778-3200
Fax: 202-331-7487
E-mail Address: *ahip@ahip.org*
Web Address: www.ahip.org
America's Health Insurance Plans (AHIP) is a prominent trade association representing the private health care system.

American Academy of Ambulatory Care Nursing (AAACN)
E. Holly Ave., Box 56
Pitman, NJ 08071-0056 US
Phone: 856-256-2350
Toll Free: 800-262-6877
E-mail Address: *aaacn@ajj.com*
Web Address: www.aaacn.org
The American Academy of Ambulatory Care Nursing (AAACN) is the association of professional nurses who identify ambulatory care practice as essential to the continuum of high-quality, cost-effective health care.

American Academy of Facial Plastic and Reconstructive Surgery (AAFPRS)
310 S. Henry St.
Alexandria, VA 22314 US
Phone: 703-299-9291
Fax: 703-299-8898
E-mail Address: *info@aafprs.org*
Web Address: www.aafprs.org
The American Academy of Facial Plastic and Reconstructive Surgery (AAFPRS) is the world's largest association of facial plastic and reconstructive surgeons.

American Academy of Family Physicians (AAFP)
11400 Tomahawk Creek Pkwy.
Leawood, KS 66211-2672 US
Phone: 913-906-6000
Toll Free: 800-274-2237
E-mail Address: *fp@aafp.org*
Web Address: www.aafp.org
The American Academy of Family Physicians (AAFP) is a member association of family doctors, family medicine residents and medical students nationwide.

American Academy of Hospice and Palliative Medicine (AAHPM)
4700 W. Lake Ave.
Glenview, IL 60025-1485 US
Phone: 847-375-4712
Fax: 877-734-8671
E-mail Address: *info@aahpm.org*
Web Address: www.aahpm.org
The American Academy of Hospice and Palliative Medicine (AAHPM) is the only organization in the United States for physicians dedicated to the advancement of hospice and palliative medicine.

American Academy of Kinesiology and Physical Education (AAKPE)
c/o Human Kinetics
P.O. Box 5076
Champaign, IL 61820-2200 US
Phone: 217-351-5076
Fax: 217-351-2674
Toll Free: 800-747-4457
E-mail Address: *kims@aakpe.org*
Web Address: www.aakpe.org
The American Academy of Kinesiology and Physical Education (AAKPE) promotes research of human movement and physical activity. AAKPE's members transmit knowledge about human movement and physical activity through yearly meetings and publications.

American Academy of Medical Administrators (AAMA)
701 Lee St., Ste. 600
Des Plaines, IL 60016-4516 US
Phone: 847-759-8601
Fax: 847-759-8602
E-mail Address: *info@aameda.org*
Web Address: www.aameda.org
The American Academy of Medical Administrators (AAMA) is an association for health care leaders to enhance their profession and community health.

American Academy of Nurse Practitioners (AANP)
P.O. Box 12846
Austin, TX 78711 US
Phone: 512-442-4262
Fax: 512-442-6469
E-mail Address: *admin@aanp.org*
Web Address: www.aanp.org
The American Academy of Nurse Practitioners (AANP) is the only full-service organization for nurse practitioners of every specialty.

American Academy of Nursing
555 E. Wells St., Ste. 1100
Milwaukee, WI 53202-3823 US
Phone: 414-287-0289
Fax: 414-276-3349
E-mail Address: *info@aannet.org*
Web Address: www.aannet.org
The American Academy of Nursing works to help nursing leaders transform the health care system in order to optimize public well-being.

American Academy of Ophthalmology (AAO)
P.O. Box 7424

San Francisco, CA 94120-7424 US
Phone: 415-561-8500
Fax: 415-561-8533
E-mail Address: *comm@aao.org*
Web Address: www.aao.org
The American Academy of Ophthalmology (AAO) is dedicated to advancing the education and interests of ophthalmologists in order to ensure that the public can obtain the best possible eye care.

American Academy of Orthotics and Prosthetics (AAOP)
526 King St., Ste. 201
Alexandria, VA 22314 US
Phone: 703-836-0788
Fax: 703-836-0737
E-mail Address: *prosenstein@oandp.org*
Web Address: www.oandp.org
The American Academy of Orthotics and Prosthetics (AAOP) promotes high standards of patient care through advocacy, education, literature and research.

American Alliance for Health, Physical Education, Recreation & Dance (AAHPERD)
1900 Association Dr.
Reston, VA 20191-1598 US
Phone: 703-476-3400
Toll Free: 800-213-7193
Web Address: www.aahperd.org
The American Alliance for Health, Physical Education, Recreation & Dance (AAHPERD) is an organization of professionals who support and assist those involved in physical education, fitness, leisure, dance, health promotion and education. AAHPERD includes the National Association for Sport & Physical Education (NASPE) and the National Association for Girls and Women in Sport (NAGWS), as well as other national and district associations.

American Association of Blood Banks (AABB)
8101 Glenbrook Rd.
Bethesda, MD 20814-2749 US
Phone: 301-907-6977
Fax: 301-907-6895
E-mail Address: *aabb@aabb.org*
Web Address: www.aabb.org
The American Association of Blood Banks (AABB) promotes high standards of care for blood banking and transfusion medicine.

American Association of Colleges of Nursing (AACN)
1 Dupont Cir. NW, Ste. 530
Washington, DC 20036 US
Phone: 202-463-6930
Fax: 202-785-8320
Web Address: www.aacn.nche.edu
The American Association of Colleges of Nursing (AACN) is the national voice for U.S. nursing education programs.

American Association of Colleges of Pharmacy (AACP)
1426 Prince St.
Alexandria, VA 22314 US
Phone: 703-739-2330
Fax: 703-836-8982
E-mail Address: *mail@aacp.org*
Web Address: www.aacp.org
The American Association of Colleges of Pharmacy (AACP) is the national organization representing the interests of pharmaceutical education and educators.

American Association of Critical Care Nurses (AACN)
101 Columbia
Aliso Viejo, CA 92656-4109 US
Phone: 949-362-2000
Fax: 949-362-2020
Toll Free: 800-899-2226
E-mail Address: *info@aacn.org*
Web Address: www.aacn.org
The American Association of Critical Care Nurses (AACN) provides leadership to establish work/care environments that involve respect and healing.

American Association of Medical Assistants (AAMA)
20 N. Wacker Dr., Ste. 1575
Chicago, IL 60606-2903 US
Phone: 312-899-1500
Fax: 312-899-1259
Web Address: www.aama-ntl.org
The American Association of Medical Assistants (AAMA) seeks to promote the professional identity and stature of its members and the medical assisting profession through education and credentialing.

American Association of Neuroscience Nurses (AANN)
4700 W. Lake Ave.
Glenview, IL 60025 US
Phone: 847-375-4733
Fax: 877-734-8677
Toll Free: 888-557-2266
E-mail Address: *info@aann.org*
Web Address: www.aann.org
The American Association of Neuroscience Nurses (AANN) is a national organization of registered nurses and other health care professionals that work to improve the care of neuroscience patients and further the interests of health professionals in the neurosciences.

American Association of Nurse Anesthetists (AANA)
222 S. Prospect Ave.
Park Ridge, IL 60068 US
Phone: 847-692-7050
Fax: 847-692-6968
E-mail Address: *info@aana.com*
Web Address: www.aana.com
The American Association of Nurse Anesthetists (AANA) is a professional member organization that represents registered nurse anesthetists nationwide.

American Association of Occupational Health Nurses (AAOHN)
2920 Brandywine Rd., Ste. 100
Atlanta, GA 30341 US
Phone: 770-455-7757
Fax: 770-455-7271
Web Address: www.aaohn.org
The American Association of Occupational Health Nurses (AAOHN) seeks to advance the profession of occupational and environmental health nursing as the authority on health, safety, productivity and disability management for worker populations.

American Association of Preferred Provider Organizations (AAPPO)
222 S. First St., Ste. 303
Louisville, KY 40202 US
Phone: 502-403-1122
Fax: 502-403-1129
E-mail Address: *pcoffey@aappo.org*
Web Address: www.aappo.org
The American Association of Preferred Provider Organizations (AAPPO) is the leading national association of network-based preferred provider organizations and affiliate organizations.

American Association of Spinal Cord Injury Nurses (AASCIN)
75-20 Astoria Blvd.
Jackson Heights, NY 11370 US
Phone: 718-803-3782
Fax: 718-803-0414
E-mail Address: *aascin@unitedspinal.org*
Web Address: www.aascin.org
The American Association of Spinal Cord Injury Nurses (AASCIN) is dedicated to promoting quality care for individuals with spinal cord impairment.

American Board of Facial Plastic and Reconstructive Surgery (ABFPRS)
115C S. St. Asaph St.
Alexandria, VA 22314 US
Phone: 703-549-3223
Fax: 703-549-3357
E-mail Address: *lwirth@abfprs.org*
Web Address: www.abfprs.org
The American Board of Facial Plastic and Reconstructive Surgery (ABFPRS) is dedicated to improving the quality of facial plastic surgery available to the public by measuring the qualifications of candidate surgeons against rigorous standards.

American Board of Medical Specialties (ABMS)
1007 Church St., Ste. 404
Evanston, IL 60201-5913 US
Phone: 847-491-9091
Fax: 847-328-3596
Web Address: www.abms.org
The American Board of Medical Specialties (ABMS) is an organization that works with its 24 approved medical specialty boards in the evaluation and certification of physicians.

American Burn Association (ABA)
625 N. Michigan Ave., Ste. 2550
Chicago, IL 60611 US
Phone: 312-642-9260
Fax: 312-642-9130
E-mail Address: *info@ameriburn.org*
Web Address: www.ameriburn.org
The American Burn Association (ABA) dedicates its efforts to the problems of burn injuries and burn victims throughout the U.S., Canada and other countries.

American Chiropractic Association (ACA)
1701 Clarendon Blvd.
Arlington, VA 22209 US
Phone: 703-276-8800
Fax: 703-243-2593
E-mail Address: *memberinfo@acatoday.org*
Web Address: www.amerchiro.org
The American Chiropractic Association (ACA) exists to preserve, protect, improve and promote the chiropractic profession for the benefit of the patients it serves.

American College of Emergency Physicians (ACEP)
1125 Executive Cir.
Irving, TX 75038-2522 US
Phone: 972-550-0911
Fax: 972-580-2816
Toll Free: 800-798-1822
E-mail Address: *membership@acep.org*
Web Address: www.acep.org
The American College of Emergency Physicians (ACEP) exists to support quality emergency medical care and to promote the interests of emergency physicians.

American College of Health Care Administrators (ACHCA)
300 N. Lee St., Ste. 301
Alexandria, VA 22314 US
Phone: 703-739-7900
Fax: 703-739-7901
Web Address: www.achca.org
The American College of Health Care Administrators (ACHCA) offers educational programming and career development for health care administrators.

American College of Healthcare Executives (ACHE)
1 N. Franklin, Ste. 1700
Chicago, IL 60606-3424 US
Phone: 312-424-2800
Fax: 312-424-0023
E-mail Address: *geninfo@ache.org*
Web Address: www.ache.org

The American College of Healthcare Executives (ACHE) is an international professional society of health care executives that offers certification and educational programs.

American College of Legal Medicine (ACLM)
1100 E. Woodfield Rd., Ste. 520
Schaumburg, IL 60173 US
Phone: 847-969-0283
Fax: 847-517-7229
E-mail Address: *info@aclm.org*
Web Address: www.aclm.org
The American College of Legal Medicine (ACLM) is an organization for healthcare and legal professionals that works to promote interdisciplinary cooperation and an understanding of issues where law and medicine meet.

American College of Medical Quality (ACMQ)
4334 Montgomery Ave., Ste. B
Bethesda, MD 20814 US
Phone: 301-913-9149
Fax: 301-913-9142
Toll Free: 800-924-2149
Web Address: www.acmq.org
The American College of Medical Quality (ACMQ) strives to provide leadership and education for professionals in health care quality management.

American College of Nurse Practitioners (ACNP)
1501 Wilson Blvd., Ste. 509
Arlington, VA 22209 US
Phone: 703-740-2529
Fax: 703-740-2533
E-mail Address: *acnp@acnpweb.org*
Web Address: www.acnpweb.org
The American College of Nurse Practitioners (ACNP) is focused on advocacy and keeping nurse practitioners current on legislative, regulatory and clinical practice issues that effect them in the rapidly changing health care arena.

American College of Physician Executives (ACPE)
4890 W. Kennedy Blvd., Ste. 200
Tampa, FL 33609 US
Phone: 813-287-2000
Fax: 813-287-8993
Toll Free: 800-562-8088
E-mail Address: *acpe@acpe.org*
Web Address: www.acpe.org
The American College of Physician Executives (ACPE) represents physicians in health care leadership.

American College of Physicians (ACP)
190 N. Independence Mall W.
Philadelphia, PA 19106-1572 US
Phone: 215-351-2600
Toll Free: 800-523-1546
E-mail Address: *mle@acponline.org*
Web Address: www.acponline.org
The American College of Physicians (ACP) exists to enhance the quality and effectiveness of health care by fostering excellence and professionalism in the practice of medicine.

American College of Prosthodontists (ACP)
211 E. Chicago Ave., Ste. 1000
Chicago, IL 60611 US
Phone: 312-573-1260
Fax: 312-573-1257
E-mail Address: *acp@prosthodontics.org*
Web Address: www.prosthodontics.org
The American College of Prosthodontists (ACP) is the official sponsoring organization for dentists who specialize in dental implants, dentures, veneers, crowns and teeth whitening.

American College of Rheumatology (ACR)
1800 Century Pl., Ste. 250
Atlanta, GA 30345-4300 US
Phone: 404-633-3777
Fax: 404-633-1870
Web Address: www.rheumatology.org
The American College of Rheumatology (ACR) is the professional organization of rheumatologists and associated health professionals dedicated to healing, preventing disability and curing disorders of the joints, muscles and bones.

American College of Sports Medicine (ACSM)
P.O. Box 1440
Indianapolis, IN 46202-3233 US
Phone: 317-637-9200
Fax: 317-634-7817
Toll Free: 800-486-5643
Web Address: www.acsm.org
The American College of Sports Medicine (ACSM) promotes and integrates research, education and applications of sports medicine and exercise science to maintain and enhance quality of life. ACSM has more than 20,000 international, national and regional chapter members.

American Correctional Health Services Association (ACHSA)
250 Gatsby Pl.
Alpharetta, GA 30022-6161 US
Fax: 770-650-5789
Toll Free: 877-918-1842
E-mail Address: *admin@achsa.org*
Web Address: www.achsa.org
The American Correctional Health Services Association (ACHSA) serves as a forum for communications that address the current issues and needs confronting correctional healthcare.

American Dental Association (ADA)
211 E. Chicago Ave.
Chicago, IL 60611-2678 US
Phone: 312-440-2500
E-mail Address: *membership@ada.org*
Web Address: www.ada.org
The American Dental Association (ADA) is a professional association of dentists committed to the public's oral health, ethics, science and professional advancement.

American Dietetic Association (ADA)
120 S. Riverside Plz., Ste. 2000
Chicago, IL 60606-6995 US
Toll Free: 800-877-1600
E-mail Address: *foundation@eatright.org*
Web Address: www.eatright.org
The American Dietetic Association (ADA) is the world's largest organization of food and nutrition professionals, with nearly 65,000 members. In addition to services for its professional members, this organization's web site offers consumers a Nutrition Knowledge Center and a Healthy Lifestyle Center.

American Health Care Association (AHCA)
1201 L St. NW
Washington, DC 20005 US
Phone: 202-842-4444
Fax: 202-842-3860
E-mail Address: *webmaster@ahca.org*
Web Address: www.ahca.org
The American Health Care Association (AHCA) is a non-profit federation of affiliated state health organizations that represent assisted living, nursing facility, developmentally-disabled, and subacute care providers.

American Health Information Management Association (AHIMA)
233 N. Michigan Ave., 21st Fl.
Chicago, IL 60601-5800 US
Phone: 312-233-1100
Fax: 312-233-1090
E-mail Address: *info@ahima.org*
Web Address: www.ahima.org
The American Health Information Management Association (AHIMA) is a professional association that consists of specially educated health information management professionals who work throughout the health care industry.

American Health Lawyers Association (AHLA)
1025 Connecticut Ave. NW, Ste. 600
Washington, DC 20036-5405 US
Phone: 202-833-1100
Fax: 202-833-1105
Web Address: www.healthlawyers.org
American Health Lawyers Association (AHLA) is an educational organization devoted to legal issues in the healthcare field.

American Health Planning Association (AHPA)
7245 Arlington Blvd., Ste. 300
Falls Church, VA 22042 US
Phone: 703-573-3103
Fax: 703-573-3103
E-mail Address: *info@ahpanet.org*
Web Address: www.ahpanet.org
The American Health Planning Association (AHPA) is a nonprofit organization committed to the creation of health policies and systems that assure access for all people to quality care at a reasonable cost.

American Health Quality Association (AHQA)
1155 21st St. NW, Ste. 202
Washington, DC 20036 US
Phone: 202-331-5790
Fax: 202-331-9334
E-mail Address: *info@ahqa.org*
Web Address: www.ahqa.org
The American Health Quality Association (AHQA) is a nonprofit national association dedicated to community-based, quality evaluation of healthcare.

American Holistic Nurses Association (AHNA)
323 N San Francisco St., Ste. 201
Flagstaff, AZ 86001 US
Toll Free: 800-278-2462
E-mail Address: *info@ahna.org*
Web Address: www.ahna.org
The American Holistic Nurses Association (AHNA) embraces nursing as a lifestyle and a profession by acting as a bridge for nurses between traditional medical philosophy and alternative healing practices.

American Medical Association (AMA)
515 N. State St.
Chicago, IL 60610 US
Toll Free: 800-621-8335
E-mail Address:
Web Address: www.ama-assn.org
The American Medical Association (AMA) strives to promote the science and art of medicine and the betterment of public health.

American Medical Group Association (AMGA)
1422 Duke St.
Alexandria, VA 22314-3403 US
Phone: 703-838-0033
Fax: 703-548-1890
Web Address: www.amga.org
The American Medical Group Association (AMGA) represents medical groups by advancing high-quality, cost-effective, patient-centered and physician-directed health care.

American Medical Informatics Association (AMIA)
4915 St. Elmo Ave., Ste. 401
Bethesda, MD 20814 US

Phone: 301-657-1291
Fax: 301-657-1296
E-mail Address: *mail@amia.org*
Web Address: www.amia.org
The American Medical Informatics Association (AMIA) is a membership organization of individuals, institutions and corporations dedicated to developing and using information technologies to improve health care.

American Medical Society for Sports Medicine (AMSSM)
11639 Earnshaw
Overland Park, KS 66210 US
Phone: 913-327-1415
Fax: 913-327-1491
E-mail Address: *office@amssm.org*
Web Address: www.newamssm.org
The mission of the American Medical Society for Sports Medicine, Inc. (AMSSM) is to offer a forum that fosters a collegial relationship among dedicated, competent primary care sports medicine physicians as they seek to improve their individual expertise and raise the general level of the sports medicine practice.

American Medical Technologists (AMT)
10700 W. Higgins Rd., Ste. 150
Rosemont, IL 60018 US
Phone: 847-823-5169
Fax: 847-823-0458
Toll Free: 800-275-1268
Web Address: www.amt1.com
American Medical Technologists (AMT) is a nonprofit certification agency and professional membership association representing individuals in health care.

American Medical Women's Association (AMWA)
211 N. Union St., Ste. 100
Alexandria, VA 22314 US
Phone: 703-838-0500
Fax: 703-549-3864
Toll Free: 800-995-2692
Web Address: www.amwa-doc.org
The American Medical Women's Association (AMWA) is an organization of women physicians and medical students dedicated to serving as the unique voice for women's health and the advancement of women in medicine.

American Nephrology Nurses Association (ANNA)
E. Holly Ave., Box 56
Pitman, NJ 08071-0056 US
Phone: 856-256-2320
Fax: 856-589-7463
Toll Free: 888-600-2662
E-mail Address: *anna@ajj.com*
Web Address: www.annanurse.org
The American Nephrology Nurses Association (ANNA) is a member organization that seeks to advance the nephrology nursing practice and positively influence outcomes for patients with diseases that require replacement therapies.

American Occupational Therapy Association (AOTA)
4720 Montgomery Ln.
P.O. Box 31220
Bethesda, MD 20824 US
Phone: 301-652-2682
Fax: 301-652-7711
Toll Free: 800-377-8555
Web Address: www.aota.org
The American Occupational Therapy Association (AOTA) advances the quality, availability, use and support of occupational therapy through standard-setting, advocacy, education and research on behalf of its members and the public.

American Organization of Nurse Executives (AONE)
325 7th St. NW
Washington, DC 20004 US
Phone: 202-626-2240
Fax: 202-638-5499
E-mail Address: *aone@aha.org*
Web Address: www.aone.org
The American Organization of Nurse Executives (AONE) is a national organization of nurses who design, facilitate and manage health care.

American Orthopedic Society for Sports Medicine (AOSSM)
6300 N. River Rd., Ste. 500
Rosemont, IL 60018 US
Phone: 847-292-4900
Fax: 847-292-4905
E-mail Address: *aossm@aossm.org*
Web Address: www.sportsmed.org
American Orthopedic Society for Sports Medicine (AOSSM) is a trade association for orthopedic doctors and sports medicine practitioners. The AOSSM works to improve the identification, prevention, treatment and rehabilitation of sports injuries.

American Osteopathic Association (AOA)
142 E. Ontario St.
Chicago, IL 60611 US
Phone: 312-202-8000
Fax: 312-202-8200
Toll Free: 800-621-1773
E-mail Address: *info@osteotech.org*
Web Address: www.osteopathic.org
The American Osteopathic Association (AOA) is organized to advance the philosophy and practice of osteopathic medicine by promoting education, research and the delivery of cost-effective health care.

American Pediatric Surgical Association (APSA)
60 Revere Dr., Ste. 500
Northbrook, IL 60062 US

Phone: 847-480-9576
Fax: 847-480-9282
E-mail Address: *eapsa@eapsa.org*
Web Address: www.eapsa.org
The American Pediatric Surgical Association (APSA) is a surgical specialty organization composed of individuals who have dedicated themselves to the care of pediatric surgical patients.

American Psychiatric Association (APA)
1000 Wilson Blvd., Ste. 1825
Arlington, VA 22209-3901 US
Phone: 703-907-7300
Toll Free: 888-357-7924
E-mail Address: *apa@psych.org*
Web Address: www.psych.org
The American Psychiatric Association (APA) seeks to ensure humane care and effective treatment for all persons with mental disorders, including intellectual and developmental disabilities and substance-related disorders.

American Public Health Association (APHA)
800 I St. NW
Washington, DC 20001-3710 US
Phone: 202-777-2742
Fax: 202-777-2534
E-mail Address: *comments@apha.org*
Web Address: www.apha.org
The American Public Health Association (APHA) is an association of individuals and organizations working to improve the public's health and to achieve equity in health status for all.

American School Health Association (ASHA)
7263 State Rte. 43
P.O. Box 708
Kent, OH 44240 US
Phone: 330-678-1601
Fax: 330-678-4526
E-mail Address: *asha@ashaweb.org*
Web Address: www.ashaweb.org
The American School Health Association (ASHA) advocates high-quality school health instruction, health services and a healthy school environment.

American Society for Dermatologic Surgery, Inc. (ASDS)
5550 Meadowbrook Dr., Ste. 120
Rolling Meadows, IL 60008 US
Phone: 847-956-0900
Fax: 847-956-0999
E-mail Address: *info@asds.net*
Web Address: www.asds.net
The American Society for Dermatologic Surgery, Inc. (ASDS) is a member organization for dermasurgeons, which seeks to enhance dermatological surgery and foster the highest standards of patient care.

American Society for Healthcare Environmental Services (ASHES)
1 N. Franklin, Ste. 2800
Chicago, IL 60606 US
Phone: 312-422-3860
Fax: 312-422-4578
E-mail Address: *ashes@aha.org*
Web Address: www.ashes.org
The American Society for Healthcare Environmental Services (ASHES) is the premier health care association for environmental services, housekeeping and textile professionals.

American Society For Healthcare Food Service Administrators (ASHFSA)
304 W. Liberty St., Ste. 201
Louisville, KY 40202 US
Toll Free: 800-620-6422
E-mail Address: *khoward@hqtrs.com*
Web Address: www.ashfsa.org
The American Society For Healthcare Food Service Administrators (ASHFSA) is a member organization that is backed by the American Hospital Association. It seeks to provide its members with quality education, networking and opportunities for professional growth.

American Society for Healthcare Human Resources Administrators (ASHRM)
1 N. Franklin St.
Chicago, IL 60606 US
Phone: 312-422-3980
Fax: 312-422-4580
E-mail Address: *ashrm@aha.org*
Web Address: www.ashrm.org
The American Society for Healthcare Human Resources Administrators (ASHRM) is the professional society for healthcare risk management professionals and those responsible for decisions that will promote quality care, maintain a safe environment and preserve human and financial resources in health care organizations.

American Society of Addiction Medicine (ASAM)
4601 N. Park Ave., Ste. 101
Chevy Chase, MD 20815 US
Phone: 301-656-3920
Fax: 301-656-3815
Toll Free: E-mail Address: *email@asam.org*
Web Address: www.asam.org
The American Society of Addiction Medicine (ASAM) is dedicated to educating physicians and improving the treatment of individuals suffering from alcoholism and other addictions.

American Society of Clinical Oncology (ASCO)
1900 Duke St., Ste. 200
Alexandria, VA 22314 US
Phone: 703-299-0150
Fax: 703-299-1044

E-mail Address: *asco@asco.org*
Web Address: www.asco.org
The American Society of Clinical Oncology (ASCO) is a non-profit organization, founded in 1964, with overarching goals of improving cancer care and prevention and ensuring that all patients with cancer receive care of the highest quality. Nearly 25,000 oncology practitioners belong to ASCO, representing all oncology disciplines.

American Society of Directors of Volunteer Services (ASDVS)
1 N. Franklin, Ste. 2800
Chicago, IL 60606 US
Phone: 312-422-3936
Fax: 312-422-4579
E-mail Address: *asdvs@aha.org*
Web Address: www.asdvs.org
The American Society of Directors of Volunteer Services (ASDVS) exists to strengthen the profession of volunteer services administration, provide opportunities for professional development and promote volunteerism as a resource in serving the health care needs of the nation.

American Society of Pain Management Nurses (ASPMN)
P.O. Box 15473
Lenexa, KS 66285-5473 US
Phone: 913-895-4606
Fax: 913-895-4652
Toll Free: 888-342-7766
E-mail Address: *aspmn@goamp.com*
Web Address: www.aspmn.org
The American Society of Pain Management Nurses (ASPMN) is an organization of professional nurses dedicated to promoting and providing optimal care of patients with pain.

American Society of Peri-Anaesthesia Nurses (ASPAN)
10 Melrose Ave., Ste. 110
Cherry Hill, NJ 08003-3696 US
Phone: 856-616-9600
Fax: 856-616-9601
Toll Free: 877-737-9696
E-mail Address: *aspan@aspan.org*
Web Address: www.aspan.org
The American Society of Peri-Anaesthesia Nurses (ASPAN) advances perianesthesia nursing practice through education, research and standards.

American Society of Plastic Surgeons (ASPS)
444 E. Algonquin Rd.
Arlington Heights, IL 60005 US
Phone: 847-228-9900
Fax:
Toll Free: 888-475-2784
E-mail Address: *webmaster@plasticsurgery.org*
Web Address: www.plasticsurgery.org
The American Society of Plastic Surgeons (ASPS) seeks to support its members in their efforts to provide the highest-quality patient care and maintain professional and ethical standards through education, research and advocacy of socioeconomic and other professional activities.

American Society of Therapeutic Radiology and Oncology (ASTRO)
8280 Willow Oaks Corporate Dr., Ste. 500
Fairfax, VA 22031 US
Phone: 703-502-1550
Fax: 703-502-7852
Toll Free: 800-962-7876
Web Address: www.astro.org
The American Society of Therapeutic Radiology and Oncology (ASTRO) works to advance the practice of radiation oncology by promoting excellence in patient care, providing opportunities for educational and professional development, promoting research and disseminating research results and representing radiation oncology in a rapidly evolving healthcare environment.

American Telemedicine Association (ATA)
1100 Connecticut Ave. NW, Ste. 540
Washington, DC 20036 US
Phone: 202-223-3333
Fax: 202-223-2787
E-mail Address: *info@americantelemed.org*
Web Address: www.atmeda.org
The American Telemedicine Association (ATA) is the leading resource and advocate promoting access to medical care for consumers and health professionals via telecommunications technology.

America's Health Insurance Plans (AHIP)
601 Pennsylvania Ave. NW, Ste. 500
Washington, DC 20004 US
Phone: 202-778-3200
Fax: 202-331-7487
E-mail Address: *ahip@ahip.org*
Web Address: www.aahp.org
America's Health Insurance Plans (AHIP) represents more than 1,000 plans that provide coverage for approximately 150 million Americans nationwide.

Assisted Living Federation of America (ALFA)
1650 King St., Ste. 602
Alexandria, VA 22314-2747 US
Phone: 703-894-1805
Fax: 703-894-1831
E-mail Address: *info@alfa.org*
Web Address: www.alfa.org
The Assisted Living Federation of America (ALFA) represents for-profit and non-profit providers of assisted living, continuing care retirement communities, independent living and other forms of housing and services.

Association for the Advancement of Applied Sport Psychology (AAASP)
2810 Crossroads Dr., Ste. 3800
Madison, WI 53718 US
Phone: 608-443-2475
Fax: 608-443-2474, 608-443-2478
Web Address: www.aaasponline.org
The Association for the Advancement of Applied Sport Psychology (AAASP) provides information about applied sports psychology to coaches, athletes, students, parents, certified consultants and AAASP members.

Association of Behavioral Health and Wellness (ABHW)
1101 Pennsylvania Ave. NW, 6th Fl.
Washington, DC 20004 US
Phone: 202-756-7726
Fax: 202-756-7308
E-mail Address: *info@abhw.org*
Web Address: www.ambha.org
The Association of Behavioral Health and Wellness (ABHW), formerly the American Managed Behavioral Healthcare Association (AMBHA), is an organization of companies that provide services related to mental health, substance used, employee assistance, disease management, and other health and wellness programs.

Association of Camp Nurses (ACN)
8630 Thorsonveien NE
Bemidji, MN 56601 US
Phone: 218-586-2633
E-mail Address: *acn@campnurse.org*
Web Address: www.campnurse.org
The Association of Camp Nurses (ACN) promotes and develops the practice of camp nursing for a healthy camp community.

Association of Clinicians for the Underserved (ACU)
1420 Spring Hill Rd., Ste. 600
Tysons Corner, VA 22102 US
Phone: 703-442-5318
Fax: 703-749-5348
E-mail Address: *acu@clinicians.org*
Web Address: www.clinicians.org
The Association of Clinicians for the Underserved (ACU) is a nonprofit, interdisciplinary organization whose mission is to improve the health of underserved populations by enhancing the development and support of the health care clinicians serving these populations.

Association of Emergency Physicians (AEP)
911 Whitewater Dr.
Mars, PA 16046-4221 US
Fax: 866-422-7794
Toll Free: 866-772-1818
E-mail Address: *aep@aep.org*
Web Address: www.aep.org
The Association of Emergency Physicians (AEP) represents the emergency physicians who largely practice clinical emergency medicine.

Association of Nurses in AIDS Care (ANAC)
3538 Ridgewood Rd.
Akron, OH 44333-3122 US
Phone: 330-670-0101
Fax: 330-670-0109
Toll Free: 800-260-6780
E-mail Address: *anac@anacnet.org*
Web Address: www.anacnet.org
The Association of Nurses in AIDS Care (ANAC) addresses the specific needs of nurses working in HIV/AIDS. ANAC also publishes a peer-reviewed journal and runs an annual conference on the latest developments in HIV nursing.

Association of Operating Room Nurses (AORN)
2170 S. Parker Rd., Ste. 300
Denver, CO 80231-5711 US
Phone: 303-755-6304
Fax: 303-750-3212
Toll Free: 800-755-2676
E-mail Address: *custsvc@aorn.org*
Web Address: www.aorn.org
The Association of Operating Room Nurses (AORN) supports registered nurses in achieving optimal outcomes for patients undergoing operative and other invasive procedures.

Association of Rehabilitation Nurses (ARN)
4700 W. Lake Ave.
Glenview, IL 60025-1485 US
Phone: 847-375-4710
Fax: 877-734-9384
Toll Free: 800-229-7530
E-mail Address: *info@rehabnurse.org*
Web Address: www.rehabnurse.org
The Association of Rehabilitation Nurses (ARN) helps nurses stay on top of the skills and knowledge needed to provide quality rehabilitative and restorative care across settings, conditions and age spans.

Association of Telehealth Service Providers (ATSP)
4702 SW Scholls Ferry Rd., Ste. 400
Portland, OR 97225-2008 US
Phone: 503-922-0988
Fax: 315-222-2402
E-mail Address: *admin@atsp.org*
Web Address: www.atsp.org
The Association of Telehealth Service Providers (ATSP) is an international membership-based organization dedicated to improving health care through growth of the telehealth industry.

Association of Women's Health, Obstetric and Neonatal Nurses (AWHONN)
2000 L St. NW, Ste. 740
Washington, DC 20036 US
Phone: 202-261-2400
Fax: 202-728-0575
Toll Free: 800-673-8499
E-mail Address: *customerservice@awhonn.org*
Web Address: www.awhonn.org
The Association of Women's Health, Obstetric and Neonatal Nurses (AWHONN) serves and represents health care professionals in the U.S., Canada and abroad.

Blue Cross and Blue Shield Association
225 N. Michigan Ave.
Chicago, IL 60601-7680 US
Phone: 312-297-6000
Fax: 312-297-6609
Web Address: www.bcbs.com
Blue Cross and Blue Shield Association is a nonprofit professional association of health care insurance providers.

Chinese-American Medical Society (CAMS)
E-mail Address: *hw5@columbia.edu*
Web Address: www.camsociety.org
The Chinese-American Medical Society (CAMS) exists to promote the scientific association of medical professionals of Chinese descent, advance medical knowledge and scientific research with emphasis on aspects unique to the Chinese and establish scholarships for medical and dental students.

Clinical Immunology Society (CIS)
555 E. Wells St., Ste. 1100
Milwaukee, WI 53202-3823 US
Phone: 414-224-8095
Fax: 414-272-6070
E-mail Address: *info@clinimmsoc.org*
Web Address: www.clinimmsoc.org
The Clinical Immunology Society (CIS) is devoted to fostering developments in the science and practice of clinical immunology.

College of Healthcare Information Management Executives (CHIME)
3300 Washtenaw Ave., Ste. 225
Ann Arbor, MI 48104-4250 US
Phone: 734-665-0000
Fax: 734-665-4922
E-mail Address: *staff@cio-chime.org*
Web Address: www.cio-chime.org
College of Healthcare Information Management Executives (CHIME) was formed with the dual objective of serving the professional development needs of health care CIOs and advocating the more effective use of information management within health care.

Contact Lens Manufacturers Association (CLMA)
P.O. Box 29398
Lincoln, NE 68529 US
Phone: 402-465-4122
Fax: 402-465-4187
Toll Free: 800-344-9060
Web Address: www.clma.net
The Contact Lens Manufacturers Association (CLMA) seeks to increase awareness and utilization of custom-manufactured contact lenses.

Contact Lens Society of America (CLSA)
441 Carlisle Dr.
Herndon, VA 20170 US
Phone: 703-437-5100
Fax: 703-437-0727
Toll Free: 800-296-9776
E-mail Address: *clsa@clsa.info*
Web Address: www.clsa.info
The Contact Lens Society of America (CLSA) is a member organization that strives to educate and share knowledge among fitters of contact lenses.

Corporate Angel Network, Inc. (CAN)
Westchester County Airport, 1 Loop Rd.
White Plains, NY 10604-1215 US
Phone: 914-328-1313
Fax: 914-328-1313
Toll Free: 866-328-1313
E-mail Address: *info@corpangelnetwork.org*
Web Address: www.corpangelnetwork.org
The Corporate Angel Network (CAN) exists to ease the emotional stress, physical discomfort and financial burden of travel for cancer patients by arranging free flights to treatment centers, using the empty seats on corporate aircraft flying on routine business.

Delta Dental Plans Association (DDPA)
1515 W. 22nd St., Ste. 450
Oak Brook, IL 60523 US
Phone: 630-574-6001
Fax: 630-574-6999
E-mail Address: *cs@ddpa.org*
Web Address: www.deltadental.com
Delta Dental Plans Association (DDPA) is a dental benefits carrier for member companies throughout the United States.

Dental Trade Alliance (DTA)
2300 Clarendon Blvd., Ste. 1003
Arlington, VA 22201 US
Phone: 703-379-7755
Fax: 703-931-9429
E-mail Address: *info@dentaltradealliance.org*
Web Address: www.dmanews.org
The Dental Trade Alliance (DTA) represents dental manufacturers, dental dealers and dental laboratories.

Emergency Nurses Association (ENA)
915 Lee St.
Des Plaines, IL 60016-6569 US
Phone: 847-460-4095
Fax: 847-460-4006
Toll Free: 800-900-9659
E-mail Address: *execoffice@ena.org*
Web Address: www.ena.org
The Emergency Nurses Association (ENA) is the specialty nursing association serving the emergency nursing profession through research, publications, professional development and injury prevention.

Federation of American Hospitals (FAH)
801 Pennsylvania Ave. NW, Ste. 245
Washington, DC 20004-2604 US
Phone: 202-624-1500
Fax: 202-737-6462
E-mail Address: *info@fahs.com*
Web Address: www.americashospitals.com
The Federation of American Hospitals (FAH) is the national representative of privately owned and managed community hospitals and health systems in the U.S.

Health and Science Communications Association (H&SCA)
39 Wedgewood Dr., Ste. A
Jewett City, CT 06351 US
Phone: 860-376-5915
E-mail Address: *hesca@hesca.org*
Web Address: www.hesca.org
The Health and Science Communications Association (H&SCA) is an association of communications professionals committed to sharing knowledge and resources in the health sciences arena.

Health Industry Business Communications Council (HIBCC)
2525 E. Arizona Biltmore Cir., Ste. 127
Phoenix, AZ 85016 US
Phone: 602-381-1091
Fax: 602-381-1093
E-mail Address: *info@hibcc.org*
Web Address: www.hibcc.org
The Health Industry Business Communications Council (HIBCC) seeks to facilitate electronic communications by developing appropriate standards for information exchange among all health care trading partners.

Health Industry Distributors Association (HIDA)
310 Montgomery St.
Alexandria, VA 22314-1516 US
Phone: 703-549-4432
Fax: 703-549-6495
Web Address: www.hida.org
The Health Industry Distributors Association (HIDA) is the international trade association representing medical products distributors.

Healthcare Financial Management Association (HFMA)
2 Westbrook Corporate Ctr., Ste. 700
Westchester, IL 60154-5700 US
Phone: 708-531-9600
Fax: 708-531-0032
Toll Free: 800-252-4362
Web Address: www.hfma.org
The Healthcare Financial Management Association (HFMA) is one of the nation's leading personal membership organizations for health care financial management executives and leaders.

Healthcare Information and Management Systems Society (HIMSS)
230 E. Ohio St., Ste. 500
Chicago, IL 60611-3269 US
Phone: 312-664-4467
Fax: 312-664-6143
E-mail Address: *himss@himss.org*
Web Address: www.himss.org
The Healthcare Information and Management Systems Society (HIMSS) provides leadership in the optimal use of technology, information and management systems for the betterment of health care.

Hearing Industries Association (HIA)
515 King St., Ste. 420
Alexandria, VA 22314 US
Phone: 703-684-5744
Fax: 703-684-6048
E-mail Address: *ehawkins@clarionmr.com*
Web Address: www.hearing.org
The Hearing Industries Association (HIA) represents and unifies the many aspects of the hearing industry.

Home Healthcare Nurses Association (HHNA)
P.O. Box 91486
Washington, DC 20090 US
Phone: 202-547-7424
Fax: 202-547-3660
E-mail Address: *membership@nahc.org*
Web Address: www.hhna.org
The Home Healthcare Nurses Association (HHNA) is a national professional nursing organization of members involved in home health care practice, education, administration and research.

Independent Medical Distributors Association (IMDA)
5204 Fairmount Ave.
Downers Grove, IL 60515 US
Fax: 630-493-0798
Toll Free: 866-463-2937
E-mail Address: *imda@imda.org*
Web Address: www.imda.org
The Independent Medical Distributors Association (IMDA) is an association of medical product sales and marketing organizations.

Institute for Diversity in Health Management (IDHM)
Toll Free: 800-233-0996
Web Address: www.diversityconnection.org
The Institute for Diversity in Health Management (IDHM) is a nonprofit organization that collaborates with educators and health services organizations to expand leadership opportunities to ethnic minorities in health services management.

Institute for Health Care Improvement
20 University Rd., 7th Fl.
Cambridge, MA 02138 US
Phone: 617-301-4800
Fax: 617-301-4848
Toll Free: 866-787-0831
E-mail Address: *info@ihi.org*
Web Address: www.ihi.org
The Institute for Healthcare Improvement (IHI) is a nonprofit organization that strives for the improvement of health by advancing the quality and value of healthcare.

International Association of Flight Paramedics (IAFP)
4835 Riveredge Cove
Snellville, GA 30039 US
Phone: 770-979-6372
Fax: 770-979-6500
E-mail Address: *info@flightparamedic.org*
Web Address: www.flightparamedic.org
The International Association of Flight Paramedics (IAFP) promotes the global development and growth of the paramedic profession.

International Association of Forensic Nurses (IAFN)
1517 Ritchie Hwy., Ste. 208
Arnold, MD 21012-2461 US
Phone: 410-626-7805
Fax: 410-626-7804
E-mail Address: *info@iafn.org*
Web Address: www.forensicnurse.org
The International Association of Forensic Nurses (IAFN) is an international professional organization of registered nurses that develops, promotes and disseminates information about the science of forensic nursing.

International Association of Medical Equipment Remarketers & Servicers (IAMERS)
Phone: 201-833-2021
Fax: 201-833-2021
Toll Free: 877-304-2637
E-mail Address: *info@iamers.org*
Web Address: www.iamers.org
The International Association of Medical Equipment Remarketers & Servicers (IAMERS) works to improve the quality of pre-owned medical equipment, both domestically and internationally.

International Council of Nurses (ICN)
3, Place Jean Marteau
Geneva, 1201 Switzerland
Phone: 41-22-908-01-00
Fax: 41-22-908-01-01
Toll Free:
E-mail Address: *icn@icn.ch*
Web Address: www.icn.ch
The International Council of Nurses (ICN) is a federation of national nurses' associations representing nurses in more than 120 countries.

International Nurses Society on Addiction (IntNSA)
P.O. Box 163635
Columbus, OH 43216 US
Phone: 614-221-9989
Fax: 614-221-2335
Web Address: www.intnsa.org
The International Nurses Society on Addiction (IntNSA) is a global voice for nurses committed to addressing the impact of addictions on society.

International Pharmaceutical Excipients Council of the Americas (IPEC-Americas)
1655 N. Fort Myer Dr., Ste. 700
Arlington, VA 22209 US
Phone: 703-875-2127
Fax: 703-525-5157
E-mail Address: *info@ipecamericas.org*
Web Address: www.ipecamericas.org
International Pharmaceutical Excipients Council of the Americas (IPEC-Americas) is a trade organization that promotes standardized approval criteria for drug inert ingredients, or excipients, among different nations. The organization also works to promote safe and useful excipients in the U.S.

International Transplant Nurses Society (ITNS)
1739 E. Carson St., Box 351
Pittsburgh, PA 15203-1700 US
Phone: 412-343-4867
E-mail Address: *itns@msn.com*
Web Address: www.itns.org
The International Transplant Nurses Society (ITNS) is a member organization that promotes transplant clinical nursing through educational and professional growth opportunities, interdisciplinary networking, collaborative activities and transplant nursing research.

International Union of Microbiological Societies (IUMS)
PO Box 85167
Utrecht, 3508 AD The Netherlands
Phone: 31-30-212-2600
Fax: 31-30-251-2097
E-mail Address: *samson@cbs.knaw.nl*
Web Address: www.iums.org
The International Union of Microbiological Societies (IUMS) works to promote the study of microbiological sciences around the world through its three divisions:

Bacteriology & Applied Microbiology (BAM); Mycology; and Virology. The association is one of the 29 Scientific Unions of the International Council of Science (ICSU).

Joint Commission on Accreditation of Healthcare Organizations (JCAHO)
1 Renaissance Blvd.
Oakbrook Terrace, IL 60181 US
Phone: 630-792-5000
Fax: 630-792-5005
E-mail Address: *customerservice@jcaho.org*
Web Address: www.jcaho.org
The Joint Commission on Accreditation of Healthcare Organizations (JCAHO) evaluates and accredits health care organizations and programs in the United States.

Medical Device Manufacturers Association (MDMA)
1350 I St. NW, Ste. 540
Washington, DC 20005 US
Phone: 202-349-7171
Web Address: www.medicaldevices.org
The Medical Device Manufacturers Association (MDMA) is a national trade association that represents independent manufacturers of medical devices, diagnostic products and health care information systems.

Medical Group Management Association (MGMA)
104 Inverness Ter. E.
Englewood, CO 80112-5306 US
Phone: 303-799-1111
Fax: 303-643-4439
Toll Free: 877-275-6462
E-mail Address: *service@mgma.com*
Web Address: www.mgma.com
Medical Group Management Association (MGMA) is one of the nation's principal voices for medical group practice.

Michigan Medical Device Association (MMDA)
P.O. Box 170
Howell, MI 48844 US
Fax: 517-546-3356
Toll Free: 800-930-5698
E-mail Address: *info@mmda.org*
Web Address: www.mmda.org
The Michigan Medical Device Association (MMDA) sponsors educational seminars and informational programs; is active in the areas of government relations, networking and business development; and acts as a source for the dissemination of matters of interest to its members.

National Association for Healthcare Quality (NAHQ)
4700 W. Lake Ave.
Glenview, IL 60025 US
Phone: 847-375-4720
Toll Free: 800-966-9392
Web Address: www.nahq.org
The National Association for Healthcare Quality (NAHQ) is a member organization for quality healthcare professionals.

National Association for Home Care (NAHC)
228 7th St. SE
Washington, DC 20003 US
Phone: 202-547-7424
Fax: 202-547-3540
Web Address: www.nahc.org
The National Association for Home Care (NAHC) is committed to representing the interests of the home care and hospice community.

National Association for Proton Therapy (The)
1301 Highland Drive
Silver Spring, MD 20910 US
Phone: 301-587-6100
Web Address: www.proton-therapy.org
The National Association for Proton Therapy (NAPT) promotes the clinical benefits of proton beam radiation therapy for cancer patients and their families. Founded in 1990, NAPT is an independent, non-profit, public benefit corporation. It serves as a resource center for cancer patients and their families, physicians and health care providers, academic medical centers, cancer centers, the U.S. Centers for Medicare and Medicaid Services (CMS) and other federal health care agencies, members of Congress and staff, and the nation's news media.

National Association for the Support of Long-Term Care (NASL)
1321 Duke St., Ste. 304
Alexandria, VA 22314 US
Phone: 703-549-8500
Fax: 703-549-8342
Web Address: www.nasl.org
The National Association for the Support of Long-Term Care (NASL) provides a task-force-specific committee structure that focuses on payment reform, legislative policy, medical products and medical services for executives and their associated businesses.

National Association of Clinical Nurse Specialists (NACNS)
2090 Linglestown Rd., Ste. 107
Harrisburg, PA 17110 US
Phone: 717-234-6799
Fax: 717-234-6798
E-mail Address: *nacnsorg@nacns.org*
Web Address: www.nacns.org
The National Association of Clinical Nurse Specialists (NACNS) exists to enhance and promote the contributions of clinical nurse specialists to the health of individuals, families, groups and communities.

National Association of Health Data Organizations (NAHDO)
448 East 400 S, Ste. 301
Salt Lake City, UT 84111 US
Phone: 801-532-2299
Fax: 801-532-2228
E-mail Address: *nahdoinfo@nahdo.org*
Web Address: www.nahdo.org
The National Association of Health Data Organizations (NAHDO) is a nonprofit membership organization dedicated to strengthening the nation's health information system.

National Association of Health Services Executives (NAHSE)
8630 Fenton St., Ste. 126
Silver Spring, MD 20910 US
Phone: 202-628-3953
Fax: 301-588-0011
E-mail Address: *nahsehq@nahse.org*
Web Address: www.nahse.org
The National Association of Health Services Executives (NAHSE) is a nonprofit association of black health care executives who promote the advancement and development of black health care leaders and elevate the quality of health care services rendered to minority and underserved communities.

National Association of Hispanic Nurses (NAHN)
1501 16th St. NW
Washington, DC 20036 US
Phone: 202-387-2477
Fax: 202-483-7183
E-mail Address: *info@thehispanicnurses.org*
Web Address: www.thehispanicnurses.org
The National Association of Hispanic Nurses (NAHN) strives to serve the nursing and health care delivery needs of the Hispanic community and the professional needs of Hispanic nurses.

National Association of Neonatal Nurses (NANN)
4700 W. Lake Ave.
Glenview, IL 60025-1485 US
Phone: 847-375-3660
Fax: 888-477-6266
Toll Free: 800-451-3795
E-mail Address: *info@nann.org*
Web Address: www.nann.org
The National Association of Neonatal Nurses (NANN) represents the community of neonatal nurses that provide evidence-based care to high-risk neonatal patients.

National Association of Orthopedic Nurses (NAON)
401 N. Michigan Ave., Ste. 2200
Chicago, IL 60611 US
Fax: 312-527-6658
Toll Free: 800-289-6266
E-mail Address: *naon@smithbucklin.com*
Web Address: www.orthonurse.org
The National Association of Orthopedic Nurses (NAON) exists to promote education and research related to nursing care of persons with orthopedic conditions, as well as to advance the profession of nursing.

National Association of Pediatric Nurse Practitioners (NAPNAP)
20 Brace Rd., Ste. 200
Cherry Hill, NJ 08034-2634 US
Phone: 856-857-9700
Fax: 856-857-1600
E-mail Address: *info@napnap.org*
Web Address: www.napnap.org
The National Association of Pediatric Nurse Practitioners (NAPNAP) is the professional organization that advocates for children and provides leadership for pediatric nurse practitioners who deliver primary healthcare in a variety of settings.

National Association of Professional Geriatric Care Managers (GCM)
1604 N. Country Club Rd.
Tucson, AZ 85716-3102 US
Phone: 520-881-8008
Fax: 520-325-7925
Web Address: www.caremanager.org
The National Association of Professional Geriatric Care Managers (GCM) is a nonprofit, professional organization of practitioners whose goal is the advancement of dignified care for the elderly and their families.

National Association of School Nurses (NASN)
8484 Georgia Ave., Ste. 420
Silver Spring, MD 20910 US
Phone: 240-821-1130
Fax: 301-585-1791
Toll Free: 866-627-6767
E-mail Address: *nasn@nasn.org*
Web Address: www.nasn.org
The National Association of School Nurses (NASN) improves the health and educational success of children and youth by developing and providing leadership to advance school nursing practice.

National Association of State Mental Health Program Directors (NASMHPD)
66 Canal Ctr. Plz., Ste. 302
Alexandria, VA 22314 US
Phone: 703-739-9333
Fax: 703-548-9517
Web Address: www.nasmhpd.org
The National Association of State Mental Health Program Directors (NASMHPD) organizes to reflect and advocate for the collective interests of state mental health authorities and their directors at the national level.

National Black Nurses Association (NBNA)
8630 Fenton St., Ste. 330
Silver Spring, MD 20910-3803 US
Phone: 301-589-3200
Fax: 301-589-3223
Toll Free: 800-575-6298
E-mail Address: *nbna@erols.com*
Web Address: www.nbna.org
The National Black Nurses Association (NBNA) is a professional nursing organization representing African American nurses throughout the United States.

National Board of Medical Examiners (NBME)
3750 Market St.
Philadelphia, PA 19104-3102 US
Phone: 215-590-9500
Fax: 215-590-9457
E-mail Address: *webmail@nbme.org*
Web Address: www.nbme.org
The National Board of Medical Examiners (NBME) exists to protect the health of the public through state-of-the-art assessment of health professionals.

National Family Caregivers Association (NFCA)
10400 Connecticut Ave., Ste. 500
Kensington, MD 20895-3944 US
Phone: 301-942-6430
Fax: 301-942-2302
Toll Free: 800-896-3650
E-mail Address: *info@thefamilycaregiver.org*
Web Address: www.thefamilycaregiver.org
The National Family Caregivers Association (NFCA) is a grass-roots organization created to educate, support, empower and speak for the millions of Americans who care for loved ones that are chronically ill, aged or disabled.

National Hospice and Palliative Care Organization (NHPCO)
1700 Diagonal Rd., Ste. 625
Alexandria, VA 22314 US
Phone: 703-837-1500
Fax: 703-837-1233
Toll Free: 800-658-8898
E-mail Address: *nhpco_info@nhpco.org*
Web Address: www.nho.org
The National Hospice and Palliative Care Organization (NHPCO) is a nonprofit membership organization representing hospice and palliative care programs and professionals in the United States.

National Practitioner Data Bank (NPDB)
4094 Majestic Ln., PMB 332
Fairfax, VA 22033 US
Phone: 703-802-9380
Fax: 703-803-1964
Toll Free: 800-767-6732
Web Address: www.npdb-hipdb.com
The National Practitioner Data Bank (NPDB) is an alert or flagging system intended to facilitate a comprehensive review of health care practitioners' professional credentials.

National Student Nurses' Association (NSNA)
45 Main St., Ste. 606
Brooklyn, NY 11201 US
Phone: 728-210-0705
Fax: 728-210-0710
E-mail Address: *nsna@nsna.org*
Web Address: www.nsna.org
The National Student Nurses' Association (NSNA) is a membership organization representing those in programs preparing students for registered nurse licensure, as well as RNs in BSN completion programs.

North American Society for the Psychology of Sport and Physical Activity (NASPSPA)
E-mail Address: *asmiley@iastate.edu*
Web Address: www.naspspa.org
The North American Society for the Psychology of Sport and Physical Activity (NASPSPA) is an association of scholars from the behavioral sciences and related professions that seeks to advance the scientific study of human behavior in sport and physical activity.

Nurse Practitioner Associates for Continuing Education (NPACE)
209 W. Central St., Ste. 228
Natick, MA 01760 US
Phone: 508-907-6424
Fax: 508-907-6425
E-mail Address: *npace@npace.org*
Web Address: www.npace.org
Nurse Practitioner Associates for Continuing Education (NPACE) seeks to improve health care in the U.S. by providing continuing education and professional support to nurse practitioners and other clinicians in advanced practice.

Oncology Nursing Society (ONS)
125 Enterprise Dr.
Pittsburgh, PA 15275 US
Phone: 866-257-4667
Fax: 877-369-5497
E-mail Address: *customer.service@ons.org*
Web Address: www.ons.org
The Oncology Nursing Society (ONS) is a national organization of registered nurses and other health care professionals dedicated to excellence in patient care, teaching, research, administration and education in the field of oncology.

Regulatory Affairs Professionals Society (RAPS)
5635 Fishers Ln., Ste. 550
Rockville, MD 20852 US
Phone: 301-770-2920

Fax: 301-770-2924
E-mail Address: *raps@raps.org*
Web Address: www.raps.org
The Regulatory Affairs Professionals Society (RAPS) is an international professional society representing the health care regulatory affairs profession and individual professionals worldwide.

Shriners International Headquarters
2900 Rocky Point Dr.
Tampa, FL 33607-1460 US
Phone: 813-281-0300
Toll Free: 800-237-5055
Web Address: www.shrinershq.org
Shriners International Headquarters is an international fraternity of approximately 500,000 members throughout the United States, Mexico, Canada and Panama. The group offers philanthropy through Shriners Hospitals for Children.

Society for Vascular Nursing (SVN)
203 Washington St., PMB 311
Salem, MA 01970 US
Phone: 978-744-5005
Fax: 978-744-5029
Toll Free: 888-536-4786
E-mail Address: *svn@administrare.com*
Web Address: www.svnnet.org
The Society for Vascular Nursing (SVN) is a nonprofit international association dedicated to the compassionate and comprehensive care of persons with vascular disease. The group works to provide quality education, foster clinical expertise and support nursing research.

Society of Critical Care Medicine (SCCM)
701 Lee St., Ste. 200
Des Plaines, IL 60016 US
Phone: 847-827-6869
Fax: 847-827-6886
E-mail Address: *info@sccm.org*
Web Address: www.sccm.org
The Society of Critical Care Medicine (SCCM) is a multidisciplinary, multiprofessional organization dedicated to ensuring excellence and consistency in the practice of critical care medicine.

Society of Gastroenterology Nurses and Associates (SGNA)
401 N. Michigan Ave.
Chicago, IL 60611-4267 US
Phone: 312-321-5165
Fax: 312-673-6694
Toll Free: 800-245-7462
E-mail Address: *sgna@smithbucklin.com*
Web Address: www.sgna.org
The Society of Gastroenterology Nurses and Associates (SGNA) is a professional organization of nurses and associates dedicated to the safe and effective practice of gastroenterology and endoscopy nursing.

Society of Infectious Diseases Pharmacists (SIDP)
823 Congress Ave., Ste. 230
Austin, TX 78701 US
Phone: 512-479-0425
Fax: 512-495-9031
E-mail Address: *sidp@eami.com*
Web Address: www.sidp.org
The Society of Infectious Diseases Pharmacists (SIDP) is an association of health professionals dedicated to promoting the appropriate use of antimicrobials, providing its members with education, advocacy and leadership in all aspects of the treatment of infectious diseases.

Society of Nuclear Medicine (SNM)
1850 Samuel Morse Dr.
Reston, VA 20190-5316 US
Phone: 703-708-9000
Fax: 703-708-9015
Web Address: interactive.snm.org
The Society of Nuclear Medicine (SNM) is an international scientific and professional organization founded to promote the science, technology and practical application of nuclear medicine. The firm also works to advance molecular imaging and therapy.

Society of Pediatric Nurses (SPN)
7794 Grow Dr.
Pensacola, FL 32514 US
Phone: 850-494-9467
Fax: 850-484-8762
Toll Free: 800-723-2902
E-mail Address: *spn@puetzamc.com*
Web Address: www.pedsnurses.org
The Society of Pediatric Nurses (SPN) seeks to promote excellence in nursing care of children and their families through support of its members' clinical practice, education, research and advocacy.

Society of Trauma Nurses (STN)
1926 Waukegan Rd., Ste. 1
Glenview, IL 60025 US
Phone: 847-657-6745
Fax: 847-657-6819
E-mail Address: *info@traumanursesoc.org*
Web Address: www.traumanursesoc.org
The Society of Trauma Nurses (STN) is a membership-based, nonprofit organization whose members are trauma nurses from around the world.

Society of Urologic Nurses and Associates (SUNA)
E. Holly Ave., Box 56
Pitman, NJ 08071-0056 US
Toll Free: 888-827-7862
E-mail Address: *suna@ajj.com*
Web Address: www.suna.org

The Society of Urologic Nurses and Associates (SUNA) is a professional organization committed to excellence in patient care standards and a continuum of quality care, clinical practice and research through education of its members, patients, families and community.

Southern Nursing Research Society (SNRS)
10200 W. 44th Ave., Ste. 304
Wheat Ridge, CO 80033 US
Toll Free: 877-314-7677
E-mail Address: *snrs@resourcenter.com*
Web Address: www.snrs.org
The Southern Nursing Research Society (SNRS) exists to advance nursing research, promote the utilization of research finding and facilitate the career development of nurses as researchers.

Visiting Nurse Associations of America (VNAA)
99 Summer St., Ste. 1700
Boston, MA 02110 US
Phone: 617-737-3200
Fax: 617-737-1144
E-mail Address: *vnaa@vnaa.org*
Web Address: www.vnaa.org
Visiting Nurse Associations of America (VNAA) is the official, national association of freestanding, nonprofit, community-based visiting nurse agencies.

Wound, Ostomy and Continence Nurses Society (WOCN)
15000 Commerce Pkwy, Ste. C
Mt. Laurel, NJ 08054 US
Fax: 866-615-8560
Toll Free: 888-224-9626
E-mail Address: *wocn_info@wocn.org*
Web Address: www.wocn.org
The Wound, Ostomy and Continence Nurses Society (WOCN) is a professional, international nursing society of nurse professionals who are experts in the care of patients with wound, ostomy and continence problems.

XXXIV. Health Care Costs

Kaiser Family Foundation (The Henry J.)
2400 Sand Hill Rd.
Menlo Park, CA 94025 US
Phone: 650-854-9400
Fax: 650-854-4800
Web Address: www.kff.org
The Henry J. Kaiser Family Foundation publishes an annual study on employers' health care coverage costs and the amount of that coverage that is paid for by employees. The foundation also runs a large healthcare public opinion research program and publishes studies on a continuous basis.

XXXV. Health Facts-Global

Globalhealthfacts.org
Web Address: www.globalhealthfacts.org
Funded by the Kaiser Family Foundation, globalhealthfacts.org provides up-to-date data on HIV/AIDS, TB, Malaria and other diseases, on a country-by-country basis. It also provides data on programs and funding to combat global diseases.

GlobalHealthReporting.org
Web Address: www.globalhealthreporting.org
Globalhealthreporting.org, which is operated by the Kaiser Family Foundation with major support from the Bill & Melinda Gates Foundation, provides coverage of worldwide health care news and reporting on diseases and health programs.

Organisation for Economic Co-Operation and Development (OECD) - Health Statistics
2, rue André Pascal, F-75775
Paris, Cedex 16 France
Phone: 33-145-24-8200
Fax: 33-145-24-8500
E-mail Address: *health.contact@oecd.org*
Web Address: www.oecd.org
The Organisation for Economic Co-Operation and Development (OECD) offers extensive health statistics on a country-by-country basis. Data ranges from health expenditures per capita to health expenditures as percent of GDP for the 30 nations with the world's largest economies.

XXXVI. Health-General

MedicAlert Foundation
2323 Colorado Ave.
Turlock, CA 95382 US
Phone: 209-668-3333
Fax: 209-669-2450
Toll Free: 888-633-4298
Web Address: www.medicalert.org
The MedicAlert Foundation is a service that protects and saves the lives of its members by providing identification and critical personal health information in an emergency.

Society for Social Work Leadership in Health Care (SSWLHC)
100 N. 20th St., 4th Fl.
Philadelphia, PA 19103 US
Phone: 215-599-6134
Fax: 215-564-2175
Toll Free: 866-237-9542
E-mail Address: *lgroff@fernley.com*
Web Address: www.sswlhc.org
The Society for Social Work Leadership in Health Care (SSWLHC) is dedicated to promoting the universal availability, accessibility, coordination and effectiveness of

health care that addresses the psychosocial components of health and illness.

XXXVII. Hearing & Speech

Alexander Graham Bell Association for the Deaf and Hard of Hearing (AGBELL)
3417 Volta Pl. NW
Washington, DC 20007 US
Phone: 202-337-5220
Fax: 202-337-8314
E-mail Address: *info@agbell.org*
Web Address: www.agbell.org
The Alexander Graham Bell Association for the Deaf and Hard of Hearing (AGBELL) is an international membership organization and resource center on hearing loss and spoken language approaches and related issues.

American Speech-Language-Hearing Association (ASHA)
10801 Rockville Pike
Rockville, MD 20852 US
Fax: 240-333-4705
Toll Free: 800-638-8255
E-mail Address: *actioncenter@asha.org*
Web Address: www.asha.org
The American Speech-Language-Hearing Association (ASHA) is the professional, scientific and credentialing association for audiologists, speech-language pathologists and speech, language and hearing scientists.

Ear Foundation (The)
P.O. Box 330867
Nashville, TN 37203 US
Phone: 615-627-2724
Fax: 615-627-2728
Toll Free: 800-545-4327
E-mail Address: *info@earfoundation.org*
Web Address: www.earfoundation.org
The Ear Foundation is dedicated to the interests of the hearing impaired. The group funds programs to further medical education on the merits of the early detection of hearing loss.

National Family Association for Deaf-Blind (NFADB)
141 Middle Neck Rd.
Sands Point, NY 11050 US
Fax: 516-883-9060
Toll Free: 800-255-0411
E-mail Address: *nfadb@aol.com*
Web Address: www.nfadb.org
The National Family Association for Deaf-Blind (NFADB) is the largest national network of families focusing on issues surrounding deaf-blindness.

National Institute on Deafness and Other Communication Disorders (NIDCD)
31 Center Dr., MSC 2320
Bethesda, MD 20892-2320 US
Phone: 301-496-7243
Fax: 301-402-0018
Toll Free: 800-241-1044
E-mail Address: *nidcdinfo@nidcd.nih.gov*
Web Address: www.nidcd.nih.gov
The National Institute on Deafness and Other Communication Disorders (NIDCD) conducts and supports biomedical and behavioral research and research training in the normal and disordered processes of hearing, balance, smell, taste, voice, speech and language.

XXXVIII. Heart Disease

American Heart Association (AHA)
7272 Greenville Ave.
Dallas, TX 75231 US
Toll Free: 800-242-8721
Web Address: www.americanheart.org
The American Heart Association (AHA) is a national voluntary health agency that seeks to reduce disability and death from cardiovascular diseases and stroke.

XXXIX. Hormonal Disorders

Thyroid Foundation of America, Inc. (TFA)
1 Longfellow Pl., Ste. 1518
Boston, MA 02114 US
Fax: 617-534-1515
Toll Free: 800-832-8321
E-mail Address: *info@allthyroid.org*
Web Address: www.allthyroid.org
The Thyroid Foundation of America, Inc. (TFA) seeks to ensure timely, accurate diagnosis, appropriate treatment and ongoing support for all individuals with thyroid disease.

XL. Hospice Care

Children's Hospice International (CHI)
1101 King St., Ste. 360
Alexandria, VA 22314 US
Phone: 703-684-0330
Toll Free: 800-242-4453
E-mail Address: *info@chionline.org*
Web Address: www.chionline.org
The Children's Hospice International (CHI) is a nonprofit organization founded to promote hospice support through pediatric care facilities, to encourage the inclusion of children in existing and developing hospice and home-care programs and to include the hospice perspectives in all areas of pediatric care, education and the public arena.

Hospice Education Institute
3 Unity Sq.
P.O. Box 98
Machiasport, ME 04655 US

Phone: 207-255-8800
Fax: 207-255-8008
Toll Free: 800-331-1620
E-mail Address: *info@hospiceworld.org*
Web Address: www.hospiceworld.org
The Hospice Education Institute is an independent, not-for-profit organization serving members of the public and health care professions with information and education about the many facets of caring for the dying and the bereaved.

XLI. Hospital Care

American Hospital Association (AHA)
1 N. Franklin
Chicago, IL 60606-3421 US
Phone: 312-422-3000
Web Address: www.aha.org
The American Hospital Association (AHA) is a national organization that represents and serves all types of hospitals, health care networks, their patients and communities.

Council of Teaching Hospitals and Health Systems (COTH)
2450 N St. NW
Washington, DC 20037-1126 US
Phone: 202-828-0400
Fax: 202-828-1125
E-mail Address: *kgserrin@aamc.org*
Web Address: www.aamc.org/teachinghospitals.htm
The Council of Teaching Hospitals and Health Systems (COTH) provides representation and services related to the special needs, concerns and opportunities facing major teaching hospitals in the United States and Canada. The COTH web site offers a listing of member hospitals.

XLII. Human Resources Industry Associations

Society of Human Resource Management (SHRM)
1800 Duke St.
Alexandria, VA 22314 US
Phone: 703-548-3440
Fax: 703-535-6490
Toll Free: 800-283-7476
Web Address: www.shrm.org
The Society of Human Resource Management (SHRM) addresses the interests and needs of HR professionals through its resource materials.

XLIII. Human Resources Professionals Associations

American Society for Healthcare Central Service Professionals (ASHCSP)
1 N. Franklin, Ste. 2800
Chicago, IL 60606 US
Phone: 312-422-3701
Fax: 312-422-4577
E-mail Address: *vsylvestri@aha.org*
Web Address: www.ashcsp.org
The American Society for Healthcare Central Service Professionals (ASHCSP) exists to provide education, networking, recognition, membership advocacy and professional practices to promote innovative ideas toward the future of the industry.

XLIV. Immunization

CDC National Immunization Information Hotline (NIIH)
1600 Clifton Rd.
Atlanta, GA 30333
Toll Free: 800-232-4636
The CDC National Immunization Information Hotline (NIIH) offers up-to-date immunization information, including vaccine schedules, side effects, contraindications, recommendations and more.

XLV. Industry Research/Market Research

Forrester Research
400 Technology Sq.
Cambridge, MA 02139 US
Phone: 617-613-6000
Fax: 617-613-5200
Web Address: www.forrester.com
Forrester Research identifies and analyzes emerging trends in technology and their impact on business. Among the firm's specialties are the financial services, retail, health care, entertainment, automotive and information technology industries.

Marketresearch.com
11200 Rockville Pike, Ste. 504
Rockville, MD 20852 US
Phone: 240-747-3000
Fax: 240-747-3004
Toll Free: 800-298-5699
E-mail Address: *customerservice@marketresearch.com*
Web Address: www.marketresearch.com
Marketresearch.com is a leading broker for professional market research and industry analysis. Users are able to search the company's database of research publications including data on global industries, companies, products and trends.

Plunkett Research, Ltd.
P.O. Drawer 541737
Houston, TX 77254-1737 US
Phone: 713-932-0000
Fax: 713-932-7080
E-mail Address: *info@plunkettresearch.com*
Web Address: www.plunkettresearch.com
Plunkett Research, Ltd. is a leading provider of market research, industry trends analysis and business statistics.

Since 1985, it has served clients worldwide, including corporations, universities, libraries, consultants and government agencies. At the firm's web site, visitors can view product information and pricing and access a great deal of basic market information on industries such as financial services, InfoTech, e-commerce, health care and biotech.

Reuters Investor
Web Address: www.investor.reuters.com
Reuters Investor is an excellent source for industry and company reports written by professional stock and business analysts. It also offers news and advice on stocks, funds and personal finance, and allows users to screen a database of major corporations and view pertinent financial and business data on selected firms.

XLVI. Insurance Information

Center for Risk Management and Insurance Research
Georgia State University, 35 Broad St., 11th Fl.
Atlanta, GA 30303 US
Phone: 404-651-4031
E-mail Address: *rwklein@gsu.edu*
Web Address: rmictr.gsu.edu
The Center for Risk Management and Insurance Research in the Robinson College of Business at Georgia State University was established in 1969 through grants and general financial support from the insurance industry through the Educational Foundation, Inc. The Center is established as a leading information source on risk and insurance issues.

XLVII. Insurance, Agents & Brokers

National Association of Health Underwriters (NAHU)
2000 N. 14th St., Ste. 450
Arlington, VA 22201 US
Phone: 703-276-0220
Fax: 703-841-7797
E-mail Address: *info@nahu.org*
Web Address: www.nahu.org
The National Association of Health Underwriters (NAHU) is a professional association for healthcare insurance underwriters.

XLVIII. Learning Disorders

Children and Adults with Attention Deficit Disorder (CHADD)
8181 Professional Pl., Ste. 150
Landover, MD 20785 US
Phone: 301-306-7070
Fax: 301-306-7090
Toll Free: 800-233-4050
Web Address: www.chadd.org
Children and Adults with Attention Deficit Disorder (CHADD) is the nation's leading nonprofit organization serving individuals with AD/HD.

XLIX. Libraries

Library and Info Systems
Web Address: www.cellbio.wustl.edu/library.htm
Library and Info Systems provides information on libraries at various higher institutions of learning in the United States.

Library of the National Medical Society
Web Address: www.medical-library.org
The Library of the National Medical Society provides a free resource of medical information for both health care consumers and medical professionals.

Medical Library Association (MLA)
65 E. Wacker Pl., Ste. 1900
Chicago, IL 60601-7246 US
Phone: 312-419-9094
Fax: 312-419-8950
E-mail Address: *info@mlahq.org*
Web Address: www.mlanet.org
The Medical Library Association (MLA) is dedicated to improving the quality and leadership of health information professionals in order to foster the art and science of health information services.

National Library of Medicine (NLM)
8600 Rockville Pike
Bethesda, MD 20894 US
Phone: 301-594-5983
Fax: 301-402-1384
Toll Free: 888-346-3656
E-mail Address: *custserv@nlm.nih.gov*
Web Address: www.nlm.nih.gov
The National Library of Medicine (NLM) is the world's largest medical library. The web site offers links to several databases of medical research, as well as a variety of online health information.

Weill Cornell Medical Library
Weill Medical College, Cornell University, 1300 York Ave.
New York, NY 10021-4896 US
Phone: 212-746-6055
E-mail Address: *infodesk@med.cornell.edu*
Web Address: library.med.cornell.edu
The Weill Cornell Medical Library houses information on the biomedical sciences, as well as performing data retrieval, management and evaluation.

L. Liver Diseases

American Liver Foundation (ALF)
75 Maiden Ln., Ste. 603

New York, NY 10038 US
Phone: 212-668-1000
Fax: 212-483-8179
Toll Free: 800-223-0179
E-mail Address: *info@liverfoundation.org*
Web Address: www.liverfoundation.org
The American Liver Foundation (ALF) is a national, nonprofit organization dedicated to the prevention, treatment and cure of hepatitis and other liver diseases.

LI. Managed Care Information

Managed Care Information Center (MCIC)
1913 Atlantic Ave., Ste. F4
Manasquan, NJ 08736 US
Fax: 888-329-6242
Toll Free: 888-843-6242
E-mail Address: *webmaster@themcic.com*
Web Address: www.themcic.com
The Managed Care Information Center (MCIC) is a clearinghouse for health care executives' managed care information needs. MCIC publishes newsletters, advisories, guides, manuals, special reports and books.

Managed Care On-Line (MCOL)
1101 Standiford Ave., Ste. C-3
Modesto, CA 95350 US
Phone: 209-577-4888
Fax: 209-577-3557
E-mail Address: *mcare@mcol.com*
Web Address: www.mcol.com
Managed Care On-Line (MCOL) is an Internet-based health care company delivering business-to-business managed care resources. The web site includes a knowledge center and extensive resources.

LII. Maternal & Infant Health

Association of Maternal and Child Health Programs (AMCHP)
1220 19th St. NW, Ste. 801
Washington, DC 20036 US
Phone: 202-775-0436
Fax: 202-775-0061
Web Address: www.amchp.org
The Association of Maternal and Child Health Programs (AMCHP) is the national organization representing public health leaders and others working to improve the health and well-being of women, children and youth.

La Leche League International
957 N. Plum Grove Rd.
Schaumburg, IL 60173 US
Phone: 847-519-7730
Fax: 847-969-0460
Toll Free: 800-525-3243
Web Address: www.lalecheleague.org
The La Leche League International seeks to help mothers worldwide to breastfeed through mother-to-mother support, encouragement, information and education and to promote a better understanding of breastfeeding.

National Center for Education in Maternal and Child Health (NCEMCH)
2115 Wisconsin Ave. NW, Ste. 601
Washington, DC 20007-2292 US
Phone: 202-784-9770
Fax: 202-784-9777
E-mail Address: *mchlibrary@ncemch.org*
Web Address: www.ncemch.org
The National Center for Education in Maternal and Child Health (NCEMCH) provides national leadership to the maternal and child health community to improve the health and well-being of the nation's children and families.

LIII. MBA Resources

MBA Depot
1781 Spyglass Ln., Ste. 198
Austin, TX 78746 US
Phone: 512-499-8728
Fax: 847-556-0608
Toll Free: 888-858-8806
E-mail Address: *contact@mbadepot.com*
Web Address: www.mbadepot.com
MBA Depot is an online community for MBA professionals.

LIV. Medical & Health Indexes

Medical World Search
TLC Information Services, PO Box 944
Yorktown Heights, NY 10598 US
Phone: 914-248-6770
Fax: 914-248-6770
E-mail Address: *mwsearch@mwsearch.com*
Web Address: www.mwsearch.com
Medical World Search is a free medical search engine offered by TLC Information Services that helps patients to understand medical terms and acronyms.

LV. Medicare Information

Medicare Rights Center (MRC)
520 Eighth Ave., 3rd Fl.
New York, NY 10018 US
Phone: 212-869-3850
Fax: 212-869-3532
Web Address: www.medicarerights.org
The Medicare Rights Center (MRC) is a nonprofit organization that acts as a source for Medicare consumers and professionals. Its web site is a helpful, independent source of Medicare information.

Medicare.gov
7500 Security Blvd.
Baltimore, MD 21244-1850 US
Toll Free: 800-633-2273
Web Address: www.medicare.gov
Medicare.gov is the official U.S. Government web site for people with questions or problems relating to Medicare.

LVI. Mental Health

American Academy of Child and Adolescent Psychiatry (AACAP)
3615 Wisconsin Ave. NW
Washington, DC 20016-3007 US
Phone: 202-966-7300
Fax: 202-966-2891
E-mail Address: *communications@aacap.org*
Web Address: www.aacap.org
The American Academy of Child and Adolescent Psychiatry (AACAP) is the leading national professional medical association dedicated to treating and improving the quality of life for children, adolescents and families affected by these disorders.

Depression Awareness, Recognition and Treatment (D/ART)
6001 Executive Blvd., Rm. 8184, MSC 9663
Bethesda, MD 20892-9663 US
Phone: 301-443-4513
Fax: 301-443-4279
Toll Free: 866-615-6464
E-mail Address: *nimhinfo@nih.gov*
Web Address:
www.nimh.nih.gov/healthinformation/depressionmenu.cfm
Depression Awareness, Recognition and Treatment (D/ART), a web site supported by the National Institute of Mental Health, offers a wealth of information on depression.

International Society for Mental Health Online (ISMHO)
388 Chester St. SE
Marietta, GA 30060-2086 US
Phone: 603-222-6482
Toll Free: 888-875-3570
E-mail Address: *webmaster@ismho.org*
Web Address: www.ismho.org
The International Society for Mental Health Online (ISMHO) strives to promote online communication, information and technology for the mental health community.

National Mental Health Association (NMHA)
2000 N. Beauregard St., 6th Fl.
Alexandria, VA 22311 US
Phone: 703-684-7722
Fax: 703-684-5968
Toll Free: 800-969-6642
Web Address: www.nmha.org
The National Mental Health Association (NMHA) is a nonprofit organization addressing all aspects of mental health, mental wellness and mental illness.

The International Foundation for Research and Education on Depression (IFRED)
2017-D Renard Ct.
Annapolis, MD 21401 US
Phone: 410-268-0044
Fax: 443-782-0739
E-mail Address: *info@ifred.org*
Web Address: www.ifred.org
The International Foundation for Research and Education on Depression (IFRED) is an organization dedicated to researching causes of depression, to support those dealing with depression, and to combat the stigma associated with depression.

LVII. Nanotechnology Associations

Alliance for NanoHealth
1825 Herman Pressler St., Ste. 537A
Houston, TX 77030 US
Phone: 713-500-3288
E-mail Address: *Jason.Sakamoto@uth.tmc.edu*
Web Address: www.nanohealthalliance.org
The Alliance for NanoHealth is comprised of three medical research universities within the Texas Medical Center, located in Houston, and two highly-renowned scientific institutions, all within a five mile radius. Its purpose is to coordinate efforts to apply advanced research to the use of nanotechnology in health care.

NCI Alliance for Nanotechnology in Cancer
31 Center Dr., Bldg. 31, Rm. 10A49
Bethesda, MD 20892-2580 US
E-mail Address: *cancer.nano@mail.nih.gov*
Web Address: nano.cancer.gov
The NCI Alliance for Nanotechnology in Cancer's major goal is to catalyze targeted discovery and development efforts that offer the greatest opportunity for advances in the near and medium terms and to lower the barriers for those advances to be handed off to the private sector for commercial development. The Alliance focuses on translational research and development work in six major challenge areas, where nanotechnology can have the biggest and fastest impact on cancer treatment.

LVIII. Neurological Disease

American Neurological Association (ANA)
5841 Cedar Lake Rd., Ste. 204
Minneapolis, MN 55416 US
Phone: 952-545-6284
Fax: 952-545-6073
E-mail Address: *ana@llmsi.com*

Web Address: www.aneuroa.org
The American Neurological Association (ANA) is a professional society of academic neurologists and neuroscientists devoted to advancing the goals and science of neurology.

American Parkinson's Disease Association (APDA)
135 Parkinson Ave.
Staten Island, NY 10305 US
Phone: 718-981-8001
Fax: 718-981-4399
Toll Free: 800-223-2732
E-mail Address: *apda@apdaparkinson.org*
Web Address: www.apdaparkinson.org
The American Parkinson's Disease Association (APDA) seeks to promote a better quality of life for people in the Parkinson's community.

Christopher Reeve Paralysis Foundation (CRPF)
636 Morris Tpk., Ste. 3A
Short Hills, NJ 07078 US
Toll Free: 800-225-0292
Web Address: www.apacure.org
The Christopher Reeve Paralysis Foundation (CRPF) is committed to funding research that develops treatments and cures for paralysis caused by spinal cord injury and other central nervous system disorders.

National Rehabilitation Information Center (NARIC)
8201 Corporate Dr., Ste. 600
Landover, MD 20785 US
Phone: 301-459-5900
Toll Free: 800-346-2742
E-mail Address: *naricinfo@heitechservices.com*
Web Address: www.naric.com
The National Rehabilitation Information Center (NARIC) collects and disseminates the results of federally funded research projects.

LIX. Nutrition

Center for Science in the Public Interest (CSPI)
1875 Connecticut Ave. NW, Ste. 300
Washington, DC 20009 US
Phone: 202-332-9110
Fax: 202-265-4954
E-mail Address: *cspi@cspinet.org*
Web Address: www.cspinet.org
The Center for Science in the Public Interest (CSPI) is a nonprofit education and advocacy organization that focuses on improving the safety and nutritional quality of our food supply and on reducing the incidences of alcohol-related injuries.

LX. Online Health Data

Family Health Radio
9 S. College St.
Athens, OH 45701 US
Phone: 740-593-1771
Web Address: www.fhradio.org
Family Health Radio offers audio-files that provide practical answers to frequently asked questions about health.

Healthfinder
P.O. Box 1133
Washington, DC 20013-113 US
E-mail Address: *healthfinder@nhic.org.*
Web Address: www.healthfinder.gov
Healthfinder is a resource for finding government and nonprofit health and human services information on the Internet.

HealthLinks
University of Washington, Box 357155
Seattle, WA 98195-7155 US
Phone: 206-543-3390
Web Address: healthlinks.washington.edu
HealthLinks, based at the University of Washington Health Sciences Center, offers health-related information and articles from the center's HealthBeat publication.

HealthWeb
Web Address: www.healthweb.org
HealthWeb is a collaborative project of the health sciences libraries of the Greater Midwest Region of the National Network of Libraries of Medicine and those of the Committee for Institutional Cooperation.

HIV InSite
4150 Clement St., Box 111V
San Francisco, CA 94121 US
Fax: 415-379-5547
E-mail Address: *info@hivinsite.ucsf.edu*
Web Address: hivinsite.ucsf.edu
HIV InSite, which was developed by the Center for HIV Information at the University of California San Francisco, offers comprehensive, up-to-date information on HIV/AIDS treatment, prevention and policy.

Mayo Clinic
200 1st St. SW
Rochester, MN 55905 US
Phone: 507-284-2511
Fax: 507-284-0161
Web Address: www.mayoclinic.com
The Mayo Clinic is a nonprofit medical practice that is devoted to the diagnosis and treatment of complex diseases. Its web site seeks to empower people to manage their health using information and tools from the clinic's experts.

MEDEM
100 Pine St., 3rd Fl.
San Francisco, CA 94111 US

Phone: 415-644-3800
Fax: 415-644-3950
Toll Free: 877-926-3336
E-mail Address: *info@medem.com*
Web Address: medem.com
MEDEM provides tools and secure technologies for physicians to provide patients with access to trusted health information via the doctor's own web site.

MedlinePlus
8600 Rockville Pike
Bethesda, MD 20894 US
E-mail Address: *custserv@nlm.nih.gov*
Web Address: medlineplus.gov
MedlinePlus offers information from the National Library of Medicine, the world's largest medical library, as well as other governmental and health-related organizations.

Medscape
76 Ninth Ave., Ste. 719
New York, NY 10011 US
Phone: 212-624-3700
Toll Free: 888-506-6098
E-mail Address: *editor2@medscape.net*
Web Address: www.medscape.com
Medscape, an online resource for better patient care, provides links to journal articles, health care-related sites and health care information.

National Women's Health Information Center (NWHIC)
Toll Free: 800-994-9662
Web Address: www.4women.gov
The National Women's Health Information Center (NWHIC) provides a gateway to the vast array of federal and other women's health information resources.

New York Online Access to Health (NOAH)
Web Address: www.noah-health.org
New York Online Access to Health (NOAH) provides access to high-quality, full-text consumer health information in English and Spanish that is accurate, timely, relevant and unbiased.

PubMed
Web Address: www.ncbi.nlm.nih.gov/entrez/query
PubMed provides access to over 17 million MEDLINE citations dating back to the mid-1960s and additional life science journals. PubMed includes links to open access full text articles.

RevolutionHealth
1250 Connecticut Ave. NW, Ste. 600
Washington, DC 20036 US
Toll Free: 800-990-2892
E-mail Address: *customercare@revolutionhealth.com*
Web Address: www.revolutionhealth.com
RevolutionHealth.com is a free, comprehensive health and medical information site, specifically designed with the Family's Chief Medical Officer - women and other caregivers - in mind. RevolutionHealth.com offers the best health information, treatment advice and more than 125 online tools.

RxList
16092 San Dieguito Rd.
Rancho Sante Fe, CA 92067 US
Web Address: www.rxlist.com
RxList provides health and medical information to consumers and medical professionals.

The Paquin Group
1134 Celebration Blvd.
Celebration, FL 34747 US
Phone: 407-566-1010
E-mail Address: *info@thepaquingroup.com*
Web Address: www.thepaquingroup.com
The Paquin Group is an alliance of industry leading experts and resources created to assist hospitals in the implementation of healthcare retail strategies. The company's core mission is to increase revenue opportunities and minimize risks for healthcare organizations.

Virtual Hospital
Web Address: www.vh.org
The Virtual Hospital digital library provides medical reference and health promotion tools and information for health care providers and patients. Although the organization ceased operations in January 2006, the web site's content has remained available online.

WebMD
111 8th Ave, 7th Fl.
New York, NY 10011 US
Phone: 212-624-3700
Web Address: www.webmd.com
WebMD serves consumers, physicians, employers and health plans as a major provider of health information services through its broad selection of interrelated health topics, current medical news and its own medical search engine.

LXI. Online Health Information, Reliability & Ethics

Health Internet Ethics (Hi-Ethics)
7737 Southwest Fwy., Ste. 200
Houston, TX 77074 US
Phone: 713-448-5555
Web Address: www.memorialhermann.org/Policies/Hi-Ethics_Principles.htm
Health Internet Ethics (Hi-Ethics), a division of Memorial Hermann, is an organization devoted to ensuring that individual customers can fully utilize the Internet to improve the health of their families.

Health on the Net Foundation Code of Conduct
24, rue Micheli-du-Crest
Geneva 14, 1211 Switzerland
Phone: 41-22-372-62-50
Fax: 41-22-372-88-85
E-mail Address: *honsecretariat@healthonnet.org*
Web Address: www.hon.ch/HONcode
The Health on the Net Foundation Code of Conduct defines a set of rules to help standardize the reliability of medical and health information on the Internet.

LXII. Organ Donation

Living Bank (The)
4545 Post Oak Place Dr.
Houston, TX 77265-6725 US
Phone: 713-528-2971
Fax: 713-961-0979
Toll Free: 800-528-2971
E-mail Address: *info@livingbank.org*
Web Address: www.livingbank.org
The Living Bank is a national donor education organization that keeps computerized records of donor data for future retrieval in case of emergency.

LXIII. Osteoporosis

National Osteoporosis Foundation (NOF)
1232 22nd St. NW
Washington, DC 20037-1202 US
Phone: 202-223-2226
Toll Free: 800-231-4222
Web Address: www.nof.org
The National Osteoporosis Foundation (NOF) is a voluntary health organization that works to fight osteoporosis and promote bone health.

LXIV. Patent Resources

Patent Docs
E-mail Address: *patentdocs@gmail.com*
Web Address: http://patentdocs.typepad.com/patent_docs/
Patent Docs is an excellent blog about patent law and patent news in the fields of biotechnology and pharmaceuticals.

LXV. Patients Rights & Information

Electronic Privacy Information Center (EPIC) - Medical Record Privacy
1718 Connecticut Ave. NW, Ste. 200
Washington, DC 20009 US
Phone: 202-483-1140
Fax: 202-483-1248
Web Address: www.epic.org/privacy/medical
The Medical Record Privacy section of the Electronic Privacy Information Center (EPIC) tracks recent developments in medical privacy legislation.

FamiliesUSA
1201 New York Ave. NW, Ste. 1100
Washington, DC 20005 US
Phone: 202-628-3030
Fax: 202-347-2417
E-mail Address: *info@familiesusa.org*
Web Address: www.familiesusa.org
FamiliesUSA is a national nonprofit, non-partisan organization dedicated to the achievement of high-quality, affordable health and long-term care for all Americans.

National Committee for Quality Assurance (NCQA)
2000 L St. NW, Ste. 500
Washington, DC 20036 US
Phone: 202-955-3500
Fax: 202-955-3599
Toll Free: 888-275-7585
Web Address: www.ncqa.org
The National Committee for Quality Assurance (NCQA) is a private, nonprofit organization that seeks to drive improvement throughout the health care industry.

Society for Healthcare Consumer Advocacy (SHCA)
1 N. Franklin
Chicago, IL 60606 US
Phone: 312-422-3851
Fax: 312-422-4575
E-mail Address: *shca@aha.org*
Web Address: www.shca-aha.org
The Society for Healthcare Consumer Advocacy (SHCA) strives to advance health care consumer advocacy by supporting professionals that represent and advocate for consumers throughout the health care industry.

LXVI. Pharmaceutical Industry Associations

Academy of Pharmaceutical Physicians and Investigators (APPI)
500 Montgomery St., Ste. 800
Alexandria, VA 22314 US
Fax: 703-254-8101
Toll Free: 866-225-2779
E-mail Address: *andrea@acrpnet.org*
Web Address: www.aapp.org
The Academy of Pharmaceutical Physicians and Investigators (APPI) is an association that arose when the American Academy of Pharmaceutical Physicians and the Association of Clinical Research Professionals merged. It is a membership organization that provides scientific and educational activities on issues concerning pharmaceutical medicine.

Accreditation Council for Pharmacy Education (ACPE)
20 N. Clark St., Ste. 2500
Chicago, IL 60602-5109 US
Phone: 312-664-3575
Fax: 312-664-4652
E-mail Address: *info@acpe-accredit.org*
Web Address: www.acpe-accredit.org
The Accreditation Council for Pharmacy Education (ACPE) provides accreditation for pharmaceutical programs.

American Pharmaceutical Association (APhA)
1100 15th St. NW, Ste. 400
Washington, DC 20005-1707 US
Phone: 202-628-4410
Fax: 202-783-2351
Toll Free: 800-237-2742
Web Address: www.aphanet.org
American Pharmaceutical Association (APhA) is a national professional society that provides news and information to pharmacists.

Association of the British Pharmaceutical Industry (ABPI)
12 Whitehall
London, SW1A 2DY UK
Phone: 44-870-890-4333
Fax: 44-20-7747-1414
Web Address: www.abpi.org.uk
The Association of the British Pharmaceutical Industry (ABPI) is a trade association that provides research and information for the British pharmaceuticals industry.

Canadian Pharmacists Association (CPHA)
1785 Alta Vista Dr.
Ottawa, ON K1G 3Y6 Canada
Phone: 613-523-7877
Fax: 613-523-0445
Toll Free: 800-917-9489
E-mail Address: *info@pharmacists.ca*
Web Address: www.pharmacists.ca
The Canadian Pharmacists Association (CPHA) is a professional organization providing drug information, pharmacy practice support material, patient information and news about the pharmacy industry.

Canadian Research-Based Pharmaceutical Companies Association (CRBPCA)
55 Metcalfe St., Ste. 1220
Ottawa, ON K1P 6L5 Canada
Phone: 613-236-0455
Fax: 613-236-6756
E-mail Address: *info@canadapharma.org*
Web Address: www.canadapharma.org
The Canadian Research-Based Pharmaceutical Companies Association (CRBPCA) is a trade organization providing news and information to the Canadian biotech industry.

Institute of Clinical Research (ICR)
Thames House, Mere Park, Dedmere Rd.
Marlow, Buckinghamshire SL7 1PB UK
Phone: 44-0-1628-899755
Fax: 44-0-1628-899766
E-mail Address: *info@instituteofclinicalresearch.org*
Web Address: www.instituteofclinicalresearch.org
The Institute of Clinical Research (ICR) is a professional organization for clinical researchers in the pharmaceutical industry in the U.K.

International Federation of Pharmaceutical Manufacturers Associations (IFPMA)
15 Ch. Louis-Dunant
P.O. Box 195, 1211
Geneva, 20 Switzerland
Phone: 41-22-338-32-00
Fax: 41-22-338-32-99
E-mail Address: *admin@ifpma.org*
Web Address: www.ifpma.org
The International Federation of Pharmaceutical Manufacturers Associations (IFPMA) is a nonprofit organization that represents the world's research-based pharmaceutical and biotech companies.

Pharmaceutical Research and Manufacturers of America (PhRMA)
950 F St. NW, Ste. 300
Washington, DC 20004 US
Phone: 202-835-3400
Fax: 202-835-3414
Web Address: www.phrma.org
Pharmaceutical Research and Manufacturers of America (PhRMA) represents the nation's leading research-based pharmaceutical and biotechnology companies.

LXVII. Pharmaceutical Resources

Pharmaportal.com
Web Address: www.pharmaportal.com
Pharmaportal.com is a pharmaceutical portal containing information about the Pharmaceutical Magazine, as well as links for executives in the industry to meet each other.

LXVIII. Privacy & Consumer Matters

Federal Trade Commission-Privacy
600 Pennsylvania Ave. NW
Washington, DC 20580 US
Toll Free: 877-382-4357
Web Address: www.ftc.gov/privacy
Federal Trade Commission-Privacy is responsible for many aspects of business-to-consumer and business-to-business trade and regulation.

Privacy International
6-8, Amwell St., Clerkenwell
London, EC1R 1UQ UK

Phone: 44-208-123-7933
E-mail Address: *privacyint@privacy.org*
Web Address: www.privacyinternational.org
Privacy International is a government and business watchdog, alerting individuals to wiretapping and national security activities, medical privacy infringement, police information systems and the use of ID cards, video surveillance and data matching.

TRUSTe
685 Market St., Ste. 270
San Francisco, CA 94105 US
Phone: 415-520-3400
Fax: 415-520-3420
E-mail Address: *dotorg@truste.org*
Web Address: www.truste.org
TRUSTe, a nonprofit agency, formed an alliance with all major portal sites to launch the Privacy Partnership campaign, a consumer education program designed to raise the awareness of Internet privacy issues. The organization works to meet the needs of business web sites while protecting user privacy.

LXIX. Research & Development, Laboratories

Battelle Memorial Institute
505 King Ave.
Columbus, OH 43201 US
Phone: 614-424-6424
Toll Free: 800-201-2011
Web Address: www.battelle.org
Battelle Memorial Institute serve commercial and governmental customers in developing new technologies and products. The institute adds technology to systems and processes for manufacturers; pharmaceutical and agrochemical industries; trade associations; and government agencies supporting energy, the environment, health, national security and transportation.

Commonwealth Scientific and Industrial Research Organization (CSRIO)
Bag 10
Clayton South, VIC 3169 Australia
Phone: 61-3-9545-2176
Fax: 61-3-9545-2175
E-mail Address: *enquiries@csiro.au*
Web Address: www.csiro.au
The Commonwealth Scientific and Industrial Research Organization (CSRIO) is Australia's national science agency and a leading international research agency. CSRIO performs research in Australia over a broad range of areas including agriculture, minerals and energy, manufacturing, communications, construction, health and the environment.

Computational Neurobiology Laboratory
10010 N. Torrey Pines Rd.
La Jolla, CA 92037 US
Phone: 858-453-4100
Web Address: www.cnl.salk.edu
The Computational Neurobiology Laboratory strives to understand the computational resources of the brain from the biophysical to the systems levels.

SRI International
333 Ravenswood Ave.
Menlo Park, CA 94025-3493 US
Phone: 650-859-2000
E-mail Address: *webmaster@sri.com*
Web Address: www.sri.com
SRI International is a nonprofit organization offering a wide range of services, including engineering services, information technology, pure and applied physical sciences, product development, pharmaceutical discovery, biopharmaceutical discovery and policy issues. SRI conducts research for commercial and governmental customers.

LXX. Respiratory

American Academy of Allergy, Asthma & Immunology (AAAAI)
555 E. Wells St., Ste. 1100
Milwaukee, WI 53202-3823 US
Phone: 414-272-6071
Toll Free: 800-822-2762
E-mail Address: *info@aaaai.org*
Web Address: www.aaaai.org
The American Academy of Allergy, Asthma & Immunology (AAAAI) offers information and services to allergy and asthma sufferers and their families and friends.

American Lung Association (ALA)
61 Broadway, 6th Fl.
New York, NY 10006 US
Phone: 212-315-8700
Toll Free: 800-586-4872
Web Address: www.lungusa.org
The American Lung Association (ALA) fights lung disease in all its forms, with special emphasis on asthma, tobacco control and environmental health.

Asthma and Allergy Foundation of America (AAFA)
1233 20th St. NW, Ste. 402
Washington, DC 20036 US
Phone: 202-466-7643
Fax: 202-466-8940
Toll Free: 800-727-8462
E-mail Address: *info@aafa.org*
Web Address: www.aafa.org
The Asthma and Allergy Foundation of America (AAFA) is dedicated to improving the quality of life for people with asthma and allergies through education, advocacy and research.

Asthma in America Survey Project
Toll Free: 888-825-5249
Web Address: www.asthmainamerica.com
The Asthma in America Survey Project was conducted by Schulman, Ronca & Bucuvalas, a national research firm specializing in health issues.

LXXI. RFID Associations

EPCglobal
Rue Royale 29
Brussels, 1000 Belgium
Phone: 32-2-229-18-80
Fax: 32-2-217-43-47
E-mail Address: *info@gs1belu.org*
Web Address: www.epcglobalinc.org
EPCglobal is a global standards organization for the Electronic Product Code (EPC), which supports the use of RFID. The organization, a nonprofit joint venture between GS1, formerly known as EAN International, and GS1 US, formerly known as the Uniform Code Council, was initially developed by the Auto-ID Center, an academic research project at the Massachusetts Institute of Technology (MIT). Today, offices and affiliates of EPCglobal are based in nearly every nation of the world. (Also see GS1 US (UCC) under Logistics and Supply Chain Associations.)

LXXII. Sexually Transmitted Diseases

National Herpes Resource Center (HRC)
P.O. Box 13827
Research Triangle Park, NC 27709 US
Phone: 919-361-8400
Fax: 919-361-8425
Toll Free: 800-227-8922
Web Address:
www.ashastd.org/herpes/herpes_overview.cfm
The National Herpes Resource Center (HRC), as part of the American Social Health Association, focuses on increasing education, public awareness and support to anyone concerned about herpes.

LXXIII. Technology Transfer Associations

Association of University Technology Managers (AUTM)
60 Revere Dr., Ste. 500
Northbrook, IL 60062 US
Phone: 847-559-0846
Fax: 847-480-9282
E-mail Address: *info@autm.net*
Web Address: www.autm.net
The Association of University Technology Managers (AUTM) is a nonprofit professional association with membership of more than 3,000 intellectual property managers and business executives from 45 countries. The association's mission is to advance the field of technology transfer, and enhance our ability to bring academic and nonprofit research to people around the world.

LXXIV. Trade Associations

General Merchandise Distributors Council (GMDC)
1275 Lake Plaza Dr.
Colorado Springs, CO 80906 US
Phone: 719-576-4260
Fax: 719-576-2661
E-mail Address: *info@gmdc.org*
Web Address: www.gmdc.org
The General Merchandise Distributors Council (GMDC) is an international trade association serving the general merchandise, health and beauty care and pharmacy industries.

LXXV. Trade Associations-Global

World Trade Organization (WTO)
Rue de Lausanne 154, CH-1211
Geneva, 21 Switzerland
Phone: 41-22-739-51-11
Fax: 41-22-731-42-06
E-mail Address: *enquiries@wto.og*
Web Address: www.wto.org
The World Trade Organization (WTO) is a global organization dealing with the rules of trade between nations. To become a member, nations must agree to abide by certain guidelines. Membership increases a nation's ability to import and export efficiently.

LXXVI. U.S. Government Agencies

Agency for Health Care Research and Quality (AHCRQ)
540 Gaither Rd., Ste. 2000
Rockville, MD 20850 US
Phone: 301-427-1364
Web Address: www.ahcpr.gov
The Agency for Health Care Research and Quality (AHCRQ) provides evidence-based information on health care outcomes, quality, cost, use and access. Its research helps people make more informed decisions and improve the quality of health care services.

Bureau of Economic Analysis (BEA)
1441 L St. NW
Washington, DC 20230 US
Phone: 202-606-9900
E-mail Address: *customerservice@bea.gov*
Web Address: www.bea.gov/index.htm
The Bureau of Economic Analysis (BEA), an agency of the U.S. Department of Commerce, is the nation's economic accountant, preparing estimates that illuminate

key national, international and regional aspects of the U.S. economy.

Bureau of Labor Statistics (BLS)
2 Massachusetts Ave. NE
Washington, DC 20212-0001 US
Phone: 202-691-5200
Fax: 202-691-6325
Web Address: stats.bls.gov
The Bureau of Labor Statistics (BLS) is the principal fact-finding agency for the Federal Government in the field of labor economics and statistics. It is an independent national statistical agency that collects, processes, analyzes and disseminates statistical data to the American public, U.S. Congress, other federal agencies, state and local governments, business and labor. The BLS also serves as a statistical resource to the Department of Labor.

Centers for Disease Control and Prevention (CDC)
1600 Clifton Rd.
Atlanta, GA 30333 US
Phone: 404-639-3311
Toll Free: 800-311-3435
E-mail Address: *cdcinfo@cdc.gov*
Web Address: www.cdc.gov
The Centers for Disease Control and Prevention (CDC), headquartered in Atlanta and established as an operating health agency within the U.S. Public Health Service, is the federal agency charged with protecting the public health of the nation by providing leadership and direction in the prevention and control of diseases and other preventable conditions and responding to public health emergencies.

Centers for Medicare and Medicaid Services (CMMS)
7500 Security Blvd.
Baltimore, MD 21244-1850 US
Phone: 410-786-3000
Toll Free: 877-267-2323
Web Address: www.cms.hhs.gov
The Centers for Medicare and Medicaid Services (CMMS) runs the Medicare and Medicaid programs in the U.S., as well as State Children's Health Insurance Program.

Department of Health and Human Services (HHS)
200 Independence Ave. SW
Washington, DC 20201 US
Phone: 202-619-0257
Toll Free: 877-696-6775
Web Address: www.hhs.gov
The Department of Health and Human Services (HHS) is the principle agency in the United States for safeguarding the health of Americans and for providing necessary health care service programs. Some of the organization's 300 plus programs include Medicare, Medicaid, Head Start, food and drug safety, health information technology and health and social research.

Federal Emergency Management Agency (FEMA)
500 C St. SW
Washington, DC 20472 US
Phone: 202-646-1600
Toll Free: 800-621-3362
E-mail Address: *femawebmaster@dhs.gov*
Web Address: www.fema.gov
Federal Emergency Management Agency (FEMA) exists to reduce loss of life and property and protect the nation's infrastructure from all types of unexpected hazards. The site has information regarding floods, fires, storms, terrorism and other disaster information including assistance, recovery and preparation.

FedWorld
5285 Port Royal Rd.
Springfield, VA 22161 US
Phone: 703-605-6000
E-mail Address: *helpdesk@fedworld.gov*
Web Address: www.fedworld.gov/jobs/jobsearch.html
FedWorld, a program of the U.S. Department of Commerce, provides an annotated index of links to job-, labor- and management-related U.S. government web sites. Employment opportunities, labor statistics and links to other government information sites are also offered. The site is managed by the National Technical Information Service (NTIS).

Government Printing Office (GPO)
732 N. Capitol St. NW
Washington, DC 20401 US
Phone: 202-512-0000
Fax: 202-512-2104
E-mail Address: *contactcenter@gpo.gov*
Web Address: www.gpo.gov
The U.S. Government Printing Office (GPO) is the primary information source concerning the activities of Federal agencies. GPO gathers, catalogues, produces, provides, authenticates and preserves published information.

Health Resources and Services Administration (HRSA)
5600 Fishers Ln.
Rockville, MD 20857 US
Phone: 703-821-2098
Fax: 703-821-2098
E-mail Address: *ask@hrsa.gov*
Web Address: www.hrsa.gov
Health Resources and Services Administration (HRSA) is an agency within the U.S. Department of Health and Human Services. Its mission is to improve and expand access to quality health care to low income, uninsured, isolated, vulnerable and special needs populations.

Health.gov
E-mail Address: *odphpweb@osophs.dhhs.gov*
Web Address: www.health.gov

Health.gov is a portal to the web sites of a number of multi-agency health initiatives and activities of the U.S. Department of Health and Human Services (HHS) and other federal departments and agencies.

National Cancer Institute (NCI)
6116 Executive Blvd., Ste. 3036A
Bethesda, MD 20892-8322 US
Toll Free: 800-422-6237
Web Address: www.cancer.gov
The National Cancer Institute (NCI) is the Federal Government's principal agency for cancer research and training.

National Center for Chronic Disease Prevention and Health Promotion (NCCDPHP)
1600 Clifton Rd.
Atlanta, GA 30333 US
Phone: 404-639-3311
Toll Free: 800-311-3435
E-mail Address: *ccdinfo@cdc.gov*
Web Address: www.cdc.gov/nccdphp
The National Center for Chronic Disease Prevention and Health Promotion (NCCDPHP), a division of the Center for Disease Control (CDC), provides national leadership in areas of health promotion and chronic disease prevention largely through educational initiatives.

National Center for Complementary and Alternative Medicine (NCCAM)
9000 Rockville Pike
Rockville, MD 20892 US
Phone: 301-519-3153
Fax: 866-464-3616
Toll Free: 888-644-6226
E-mail Address: *info@nccam.nih.gov*
Web Address: nccam.nih.gov
The National Center for Complementary and Alternative Medicine (NCCAM) supports rigorous research on complementary and alternative medicine. It disseminates information to the public and professionals about which of these modalities work, which do not and why.

National Center for Health Statistics (NCHS)
3311 Toledo Rd.
Hyattsville, MD 20782 US
Toll Free: 800-232-4636
E-mail Address: *nchsquery@cdc.gov*
Web Address: www.cdc.gov/nchs/
The National Center for Health Statistics (NCHS), division of the Center for Disease Control and Prevention (CDC), is the federal government's principal vital and health statistics agency.

National Center for Research Resources (NCRR)
1 Democracy Plaza, 9th Fl.
6701 Democracy Blvd., MSC 4874
Bethesda, MD 20892-4874 US
Phone: 301-435-0888
Fax: 301-480-3558
E-mail Address: *info@ncrr.nih.gov*
Web Address: www.ncrr.nih.gov
The National Center for Research Resources (NCRR) supports primary health and life sciences research to create and develop critical resources, models and technologies.

National Heart, Lung, and Blood Institute (NHLBI)
P.O. Box 30105
Bethesda, MD 20824-0105 US
Phone: 301-592-8573
Fax: 240-629-3246
E-mail Address: *nhlbiinfo@nhlbi.nih.gov*
Web Address: www.nhlbi.nih.gov
The National Heart, Lung, and Blood Institute (NHLBI) provides leadership for a national program in diseases of the heart, blood vessels, lung and blood; blood resources; and sleep disorders.

National Institute of Allergy and Infectious Diseases (NIAID)
6610 Rockledge Dr., MSC 6612
Bethesda, MD 20892-6612 US
Phone: 301-496-5717
Fax: 301-402-3573
Web Address: www.niaid.nih.gov
The National Institute of Allergy and Infectious Diseases (NIAID) conducts and supports research that strives for understanding, treatment and prevention of the many infectious, immunologic and allergic diseases that threaten people worldwide.

National Institute of Child Health and Human Development (NICHD)
P.O. Box 3006
Rockville, MD 20847 US
Fax: 301-984-1473
Toll Free: 800-370-2943
E-mail Address:
NICHDInformationResourceCenter@mail.nih.gov
Web Address: www.nichd.nih.gov
The National Institute of Child Health and Human Development (NICHD) conducts and supports laboratory, clinical and epidemiological research on the reproductive, neurobiological, developmental and behavioral processes that determine and maintain the health of children, adults, families and populations.

National Institute of Diabetes and Digestive and Kidney Disorders (NIDDK)
31 Center Dr., MSC 2560, Bldg. 31, Rm. 9A06
Bethesda, MD 20892-2560 US
Phone: 301-496-3583
Web Address: www.niddk.nih.gov
The National Institute of Diabetes and Digestive and Kidney Disorders (NIDDK) conducts and supports basic

and clinical research on many of the most serious diseases affecting public health.

National Institute of Environmental Health Services (NIEHS)
111 T.W. Alexander Dr.
Research Triangle Park, NC 27709 US
Phone: 919-541-3345
Web Address: www.niehs.nih.gov
The National Institute of Environmental Health Services (NIEHS) is the segment of the National Institutes of Health that deals with the environmental effects on human health.

National Institute of General Medical Services (NIGMS)
45 Center Dr., MSC 6200
Bethesda, MD 20892-6200 US
Phone: 301-496-7301
E-mail Address: *info@nigms.nih.gov*
Web Address: www.nigms.nih.gov
The National Institute of General Medical Services (NIGMS) supports basic biomedical research that lays the foundation for advances in disease diagnosis, treatment and prevention.

National Institute of Mental Health (NIMH)
6001 Executive Blvd., Rm. 8184, MSC 9663
Bethesda, MD 20892-9663 US
Phone: 301-443-4513
Fax: 301-443-4279
Toll Free: 866-615-6464
E-mail Address: *nimhinfo@nih.gov*
Web Address: www.nimh.nih.gov
The National Institute of Mental Health (NIMH), a part of the U.S. Department of Health and Human Services, acts as the Federal governments principle biomedical and behavioral research agency. The organization strives to reduce the burden of mental illness and behavioral disorders through research on mind, brain, and behavior.

National Institute of Neurological Disorders and Stroke (NINDS)
6001 Executive Blvd., Ste. 3309
Bethesda, MD 20892 US
Phone: 301-496-5751
Toll Free: 800-352-9424
Web Address: www.ninds.nih.gov
The National Institute of Neurological Disorders and Stroke (NINDS) works to lead the neuroscience community in shaping the future of research and its relationship to brain diseases.

National Institute of Nursing Research (NINR)
31 Center Dr., Rm. 5B10
Bethesda, MD 20892-2178 US
Phone: 301-496-0207
Fax: 301-480-8845
Toll Free: 866-910-3804
Web Address: www.nih.gov/ninr
The National Institute of Nursing Research (NINR) supports clinical and basic research to establish a scientific basis for the care of individuals of all ages. From management of patients during illness and recovery to the reduction of risks for disease and disability, NINR promotes healthy lifestyles, quality of life for those with chronic illnesses and care for individuals at the end of life.

National Institute of Standards and Technology (NIST)
100 Bureau Dr., Stop 1070
Gaithersburg, MD 20899-1070 US
Phone: 301-975-6478
E-mail Address: *inquiries@nist.gov*
Web Address: www.nist.gov
The National Institute of Standards and Technology (NIST) is an agency of the U.S. Department of Commerce's Technology Administration. It works with various industries to develop and apply technology, measurements and standards.

National Institute on Aging (NIA)
31 Center Dr., MSC 2292, Bldg. 31, Rm. 5C27
Bethesda, MD 20892-2292 US
Phone: 301-496-1752
Fax: 301-496-1072
Web Address: www.nia.nih.gov
The National Institute on Aging (NIA) is one of the 27 institutes and centers of the National Institutes of Health and leads a broad scientific effort to understand the nature of aging and to extend the healthy, active years of life.

National Institute on Alcohol Abuse and Alcoholism (NIAAA)
5635 Fishers Ln., MSC 9304
Bethesda, MD 20892-9304 US
Phone: 301-443-3860
E-mail Address: *niaaaweb-r@exchange.nih.gov*
Web Address: www.niaaa.nih.gov
The National Institute on Alcohol Abuse and Alcoholism (NIAAA) provides information on alcohol abuse and the advancement of its treatment.

National Institute on Arthritis and Musculoskeletal and Skin Diseases (NIAMS)
1 AMS Cir.
Bethesda, MD 20892-3675 US
Phone: 301-495-4484
Fax: 301-718-6366
Toll Free: 877-226-4267
E-mail Address: *niamsinfo@mail.nih.gov*
Web Address: www.nih.gov/niams
The National Institute on Arthritis and Musculoskeletal and Skin Diseases (NIAMS) supports research into the causes, treatment and prevention of arthritis and musculoskeletal and skin diseases, the training of basic and clinical scientists to carry out this research and the

dissemination of information on research progress in these diseases.

National Institute on Drug Abuse (NIDA)
6001 Executive Blvd., Rm. 5213
Bethesda, MD 20892-9561 US
Phone: 301-443-1124
E-mail Address: *information@nida.nih.gov*
Web Address: www.nida.nih.gov
The National Institute on Drug Abuse (NIDA) seeks to lead the nation in bringing the power of science to the advantage of curbing drug abuse and addiction.

National Institutes of Health (NIH)
9000 Rockville Pike
Bethesda, MD 20892 US
Phone: 301-496-4000
E-mail Address: *nihinfo@od.nih.gov*
Web Address: www.nih.gov
The National Institutes of Health (NIH) is the leader of medical and behavioral research for the nation, with over 15 institutes ranging from the National Cancer Institute to the National Institute of Mental Health.

National Science Foundation (NSF)
4201 Wilson Blvd.
Arlington, VA 22230 US
Phone: 703-292-5111
Toll Free: 800-877-8339
E-mail Address: *info@nsf.gov*
Web Address: www.nsf.gov
The National Science Foundation (NSF) is an independent U.S. government agency responsible for promoting science and engineering. The foundation provides grants and funding for research.

Occupational Safety and Health Administration (OSHA)
200 Constitution Ave. NW
Washington, DC 20210 US
Toll Free: 800-321-6742
Web Address: www.osha.gov
The Occupational Safety and Health Administration (OSHA), regulates safety within the workplace. Its web site provides an abundance of information on laws and regulations, safety and health, statistics, compliance assistance and news. OSHA is a unit of the U.S. Department of Labor.

President's Council on Physical Fitness and Sports
200 Independence Ave. SW, Rm. 738-H
Washington, DC 20201-0004 US
Phone: 202-690-9000
Fax: 202-690-5211
Web Address: www.fitness.gov
The President's Council on Physical Fitness and Sports offers information about exercise for people of all ages and it works to promote physical activity and sports.

Social Security Administration (SSA)
6401 Security Blvd., Windsor Park Bldg.
Baltimore, MD 21235 US
Toll Free: 800-772-1213
Web Address: www.ssa.gov
The Social Security Administration (SSA) offers extensive information on social security and retirement through its web site, Social Security Online.

U.S. Business Advisor
Web Address: www.business.gov
U.S. Business Advisor offers a searchable directory of business-specific government information. Topics include taxes, regulations, international trade, financial assistance and business development. U.S. Business Advisor was created by the Small Business Administration in a partnership with 21 other federal agencies.

U.S. Census Bureau
4700 Silver Hill Rd.
Washington, DC 20233 US
E-mail Address: *pio@census.gov*
Web Address: www.census.gov
The U.S. Census Bureau is the official collector of data about the people and economy of the U.S. It provides official social, demographic and economic information.

U.S. Department of Commerce (DOC)
1401 Constitution Ave. NW
Washington, DC 20230 US
Phone: 202-482-2000
E-mail Address: *cgutierrez@doc.gov*
Web Address: www.doc.gov
The U.S. Department of Commerce (DOC) regulates trade and provides valuable economic analysis of the economy.

U.S. Department of Labor (DOL)
200 Constitution Ave. NW
Washington, DC 20210 US
Toll Free: 866-487-2365
Web Address: www.dol.gov
The U.S. Department of Labor (DOL) is the government agency responsible for labor regulations. This site provides tools to help citizens find out whether companies are complying with family and medical-leave requirements.

U.S. Environmental Protection Agency (EPA)
1200 Pennsylvania Ave. NW
Washington, DC 20460 US
Phone: 202-272-0167
Web Address: www.epa.gov
The U.S. Environmental Protection Agency (EPA) is a government organization that seeks to protect human health and to safeguard the natural environment by developing and enforcing regulations, performing environmental research, sponsoring voluntary programs and offering financial assistance to state environmental programs.

U.S. Food and Drug Administration (FDA)
5600 Fishers Ln.
Rockville, MD 20857 US
Toll Free: 888-463-6332
Web Address: www.fda.gov
The U.S. Food and Drug Administration (FDA) promotes and protects the public health by helping safe and effective products reach the market in a timely way and by monitoring products for continued safety after they are in use. It regulates both prescription and over-the-counter drugs as well as medical devices and food products.

U.S. Patent and Trademark Office (PTO)
Dulany St., 1st Fl.
Alexandria, VA 22314 US
Phone: 571-272-1000
Fax: 571-273-8300
Toll Free: 800-786-9199
Web Address: www.uspto.gov
The U.S. Patent and Trademark Office (PTO) administers patent and trademark laws for the U.S. and enables registration of patents and trademarks.

U.S. Securities and Exchange Commission (SEC)
Office of Investor Education and Assistance
100 F St. NE
Washington, DC 20549 US
Phone: 202-551-6551
Toll Free: 800-732-0330
E-mail Address: *help@sec.gov*
Web Address: www.sec.gov
The U.S. Securities and Exchange Commission (SEC) is a nonpartisan, quasi-judicial regulatory agency responsible for administering federal securities laws. These laws are designed to protect investors in securities markets and ensure that they have access to disclosure of all material information concerning publicly traded securities. Visitors to the web site can access the EDGAR database of corporate financial and business information.

U.S. Technology Administration
U.S. Department of Commerce
1401 Constitution Ave. NW
Washington, DC 20230 US
Phone: 202-482-1575
Fax: 202-482-5687
E-mail Address: *public_affairs@technology.gov*
Web Address: www.technology.gov
The U.S. Technology Administration seeks to maximize technology's contribution to economic growth, high-wage job creation and the social well-being of the United States. Its web site offers publications as well as information about events and services. Departments of this agency include the Office of Technology Policy, the National Institute of Standards & Technology and the National Technical Information Service.

LXXVII. Urological Disorders

American Urological Association Foundation (AUAF)
1000 Corporate Blvd.
Linthicum, MD 21090 US
Phone: 410-689-3700
Fax: 410-689-3800
Toll Free: 866-746-4282
E-mail Address: *auafoundation@auafoundation.org*
Web Address: www.auafoundation.org
The American Urological Association Foundation (AUAF) seeks the prevention and cure of urologic disease through the expansion of patient education, public awareness, research and advocacy.

National Association for Continence (NAFC)
P.O. Box 1019
Charleston, SC 29402 -1019 US
Phone: 843-377-0900
Fax: 843-377-0905
Toll Free: 800-252-3337
E-mail Address: *memberservices@nafc.org*
Web Address: www.nafc.org
The National Association for Continence (NAFC) is a national, private, nonprofit organization dedicated to improving the quality of life of people with incontinence.

National Kidney Foundation
30 E. 33rd St.
New York, NY 10016 US
Phone: 212-889-2210
Fax: 212-689-9261
Toll Free: 800-622-9010
Web Address: www.kidney.org
The National Kidney Foundation seeks to prevent kidney and urinary tract diseases, improve the health and well-being of individuals and families affected by these diseases and increase the availability of all organs for transplantation.

Chapter 4

THE HEALTH CARE 500: WHO THEY ARE AND HOW THEY WERE CHOSEN

Includes Indexes by Company Name, Industry & Location, And a Complete Table of Sales, Profits and Ranks

The companies chosen to be listed in PLUNKETT'S HEALTH CARE INDUSTRY ALMANAC comprise a unique list. THE HEALTH CARE 500 (the actual count is 494 companies) were chosen specifically for their dominance in the many facets of the health care industry in which they operate. Complete information about each firm can be found in the "Individual Profiles," beginning at the end of this chapter. These profiles are in alphabetical order by company name.

THE HEALTH CARE 500 includes leading companies from all parts of the United States as well as many other nations, and from all health care and related industry segments: insurance companies; manufacturers and distributors of health care supplies and products; pharmaceuticals manufacturers; health care providers of all types, including major firms owning clinics, physical rehabilitation centers, hospitals, outpatient surgery centers, nursing homes, home health care offices and other types of health care specialists; specialized service companies that are vital to the health care field, such as medical information management companies; health maintenance organizations and many others.

Simply stated, the list contains 494 of the largest, most successful, fastest growing firms in health care and related industries in the world. To be included in our list, the firms had to meet the following criteria:

1) Generally, these are corporations based in the U.S.; however, the headquarters of 56 firms are located in other nations.
2) Prominence, or a significant presence, in health care and supporting fields. (See the following Industry Codes section for a complete list of types of businesses that are covered).
3) The companies in THE HEALTH CARE 500 do not have to be exclusively in the health care field.
4) Financial data and vital statistics must have been available to the editors of this book, either directly from the company being written about or from outside sources deemed reliable and accurate by the editors. A small number of companies that we would like to have included

are not listed because of a lack of sufficient, objective data.

INDEXES TO THE HEALTH CARE 500, AS FOUND IN THIS CHAPTER AND IN THE BACK OF THE BOOK:

INDUSTRY LIST, WITH CODES

This book refers to the following list of unique industry codes, based on the 1997 NAIC code system (NAIC is used by many analysts as a replacement for older SIC codes because NAIC is more specific to today's industry sectors). Companies profiled in this book are given a primary NAIC code, reflecting the main line of business of each firm.

Financial Services

Banking, Credit & Finance

522320 Payment & Transaction Processing Services
522320A Payment & Transaction Processing--Benefits Management

Insurance

524113 Insurance-Life
524114 Insurance-Health, HMO's & PPO's
524114A Insurance--Health Supplemental & Specialty
524210 Insurance Brokerage, Agencies & Exchanges

Food & Restaurants

Food Service

722310 Food Service Contractors

Health Care

Health Products, Manufacturing

325412 Drugs (Pharmaceuticals), Discovery & Manufacturing
325412A Drug Delivery Systems
325413 Diagnostic Services and Substances Manufacturing
325414 Biological Products, Manufacturing
325416 Drugs (Pharmaceuticals), Generic Manufacturing
339113 Medical/Dental/Surgical Equipment & Supplies, Manufacturing

Health Products, Wholesale Distribution

421450 Medical/Dental/Surgical Equipment & Supplies, Distribution
422210 Drugs, Distribution

Equipment Rental

532400 Equipment Rental

Health Care-Clinics, Labs and Organizations

621111 Physician Practice Management
621340 Clinics--Physical Rehab Ctr.
621490 Clinics--Outpatient Clinics & Surgery
621511 Laboratories & Diagnostic Services--Medical
621610 Home Health Care
621991 Blood & Organ Banks
621999 Utilization Management, Health Care

Hospitals

622110 Hospitals/Clinics--General & Specialty Hospitals
622210 Hospitals/Clinics--Psychiatric Clinics

Nursing

623110 Long-Term Health Care & Assisted Living

Veterinary Care

541940 Veterinary Clinics

InfoTech

Computers & Electronics Manufacturing

334111 Computer Hardware, Manufacturing
334500 Instrument Manufacturing, including Measurement, Control, Test & Navigational

Software

511212 Computer Software, Healthcare & Biotechnology
511217 Computer Software, Supply Chain & Logistics

Information & Data Processing Services

514199 Online Publishing, Services & Niche Portals
514210 Data Processing Services

Information Services-Professional

541512 Consulting--Computer, Telecommunications & Internet

Manufacturing

Paper Products/Forest Products

322000 Forest Products/Paper, Manufacturing
322210 Packaging, Manufacturing

Chemicals

325000 Chemicals, Manufacturing

Machinery & Manufacturing Equipment

333000 Machinery, Manufacturing
333314 Optical Instrument & Lens, Manufacturing

Electrical Equipment, Appliances, Tools

335000 Electrical Equipment, Manufacturing

Retailing

Drug Stores, Beauty Supply & Health Items Stores

446110 Pharmacies & Drug Stores
446110A Pharmacies-Specialty
446130 Optical Goods Stores
446191 Health Supplement Stores

Personal Services & Salons

446190 Other Health & Personal Care Stores/Weight Management

Miscellaneous Retailers

453910 Pets/Pet Supplies Stores

Services

Consulting & Professional Services

541612 Consulting-Human Resources
541613 Consulting--Marketing
541710 Research & Development-Physical, Engineering & Life Sciences
541910 Market Research

Management

551110 Management of Companies & Enterprises

Personnel, Administrative & Support Services

561300 Staffing or Outsourcing
561400 Business Support Services

Waste Management

562000 Waste Disposal, Waste Management

Educational

611410 Business Training, Distance Learning

Telecommunications

Telecommunications Equipment

334210 Telecommunications Equipment Manufacturing

Telecommunications

513300D Telecommunications & Internet Services-Specialty

Transportation

Transportation-Manufacturing of Equipment

336300 Automobile Parts Manufacturing

INDEX OF RANKINGS WITHIN INDUSTRY GROUPS

Company	Industry Code	2006 Sales (U.S. $ thousands)	Sales Rank	2006 Profits (U.S. $ thousands)	Profits Rank
Automobile Parts Manufacturing					
TELEFLEX INC	336300	2,646,757	1	139,430	1
Biological Products, Manufacturing					
ALPHARMA INC	325414	653,828	2	82,544	2
CSL LIMITED	325414	2,146,111	1	88,406	1
GTC BIOTHERAPEUTICS INC	325414	6,128	4	-33,345	4
LIFECELL CORPORATION	325414	141,680	3	20,469	3
ORGANOGENESIS INC	325414				
Blood & Organ Banks					
HEMACARE CORPORATION	621991	36,484	1	1,851	1
Business Support Services					
NOVATION LLC (VHA INC)	561400				
PREMIER INC	561400				
Business Training, Distance Learning					
HEALTHSTREAM INC	611410	31,783	1	2,500	1
Chemicals, Manufacturing					
AKZO NOBEL NV	325000	19,659,800	2	1,566,190	2
BAYER AG	325000	38,710,400	1	2,249,950	1
BAYER CORP	325000	10,262,800	3		
SIGMA ALDRICH CORP	325000	1,797,500	4	276,800	3
Clinics--Outpatient Clinics & Surgery					
AMERICA SERVICE GROUP INC	621490	569,409	5	-3,380	14
AMSURG CORP	621490	464,592	6	37,739	5
CRITICAL CARE SYSTEMS	621490				
DAVITA INC	621490	4,880,662	2	289,691	2
DIALYSIS CORPORATION OF AMERICA	621490	62,460	15	3,049	12
DYNACQ HEALTHCARE INC	621490	35,989	16	-5,936	15
FRESENIUS AG	621490	14,218,100	1	435,400	1
FRESENIUS MEDICAL CARE AG	621490				
GAMBRO AB	621490				
HEALTHSOUTH CORP	621490	3,000,100	4	-647,200	16
HEALTHTRONICS INC	621490	142,891	11	8,683	9
HEALTHWAYS INC	621490	412,308	7	37,151	6
HEARUSA INC	621490	88,786	14	-3,174	13
HORIZON HEALTH CORP	621490	275,000	9	12,100	7
LCA-VISION INC	621490	256,927	10	38,296	4
MINUTECLINIC	621490				
NOVAMED INC	621490	108,434	13	5,737	11
OPTICARE HEALTH SYSTEMS	621490				
TAKE CARE HEALTH SYSTEMS	621490				
TLC VISION CORPORATION	621490	281,800	8	11,500	8
UNIVERSAL HEALTH SERVICES	621490	4,191,300	3	259,458	3
US PHYSICAL THERAPY INC	621490	135,194	12	6,296	10

Company	Industry Code	2006 Sales (U.S. $ thousands)	Sales Rank	2006 Profits (U.S. $ thousands)	Profits Rank
Clinics--Physical Rehab Ctr.					
HANGER ORTHOPEDIC GROUP	621340	598,766	2	3,434	2
REHABCARE GROUP INC	621340	614,793	1	7,280	1
Computer Hardware, Manufacturing					
TOSHIBA CORPORATION	334111	53,945,200	1	664,900	1
Computer Software, Healthcare & Biotechnology					
ALLSCRIPTS HEALTHCARE SOLUTIONS INC	511212	227,969	4	11,895	4
AMICAS INC	511212	49,437	7	-1,024	7
CEDARA SOFTWARE CORP	511212				
CERNER CORP	511212	1,378,038	1	109,891	1
ECLIPSYS CORPORATION	511212	427,542	2	4,093	5
EPIC SYSTEMS CORPORATION	511212				
HEALTHAXIS INC	511212	16,674	8	-526	6
MEDICAL INFORMATION TECHNOLOGY INC	511212	344,600	3	87,200	2
PER-SE TECHNOLOGIES INC	511212				
QUALITY SYSTEMS INC	511212	119,287	5	23,322	3
QUOVADX INC	511212	84,120	6	-13,115	8
SOLUCIENT LLC	511212				
Computer Software, Supply Chain & Logistics					
GLOBAL HEALTHCARE EXCHANGE	511217				
Consulting--Computer, Telecommunications & Internet					
FIRST CONSULTING GROUP INC	541512	277,842	1	20,860	1
Consulting-Human Resources					
MERCER INC	541612	3,021,000	1		
TOWERS PERRIN	541612	2,200,000	2		
Consulting--Marketing					
INVENTIV HEALTH INC	541613	766,245	1	51,235	1
PDI INC	541613	239,242	2	11,809	2
Data Processing Services					
TRANSCEND SERVICES INC	514210	32,912	1	2,047	1
Diagnostic Services and Substances Manufacturing					
BIOSITE INC	325413	308,592	2	39,994	3
DIGENE CORPORATION	325413	152,900	4	8,400	6
E-Z-EM INC	325413	137,083	5	9,766	5
IDEXX LABORATORIES INC	325413	739,117	1	93,678	1
MALLINCKRODT INC	325413				
MERIDIAN BIOSCIENCE INC	325413	108,413	6	18,325	4
SIEMENS MEDICAL SOLUTIONS DIAGNOSTICS	325413				
TECHNE CORP	325413	202,617	3	73,351	2
Drug Delivery Systems					
ARADIGM CORPORATION	325412A	4,814	3	-13,027	2
BIOVAIL CORPORATION	325412A	1,070,500	1	203,900	1
NANOBIO CORPORATION	325412A				
NEKTAR THERAPEUTICS	325412A	217,718	2	-154,761	3
Drugs (Pharmaceuticals), Discovery & Manufacturing					
3SBIO INC	325412	16,373	41	3,907	30
ABBOTT LABORATORIES	325412	22,476,322	9	1,716,755	14
ACTELION LTD	325412	776,912	29	198,066	23

Company	Industry Code	2006 Sales (U.S. $ thousands)	Sales Rank	2006 Profits (U.S. $ thousands)	Profits Rank
AETERNA ZENTARIS INC	325412	41,390	36	33,390	27
ALCON INC	325412	4,896,600	19	1,348,100	16
ALLERGAN INC	325412	3,010,100	21	-127,400	41
AMGEN INC	325412	14,268,000	13	2,950,000	10
ARQULE INC	325412	6,626	42	-31,440	34
ASTELLAS PHARMA INC	325412	7,758,480	17	1,106,390	19
ASTRAZENECA PLC	325412	26,475,000	7	4,392,000	8
BAYER SCHERING PHARMA AG	325412				
BIOGEN IDEC INC	325412	2,683,049	23	217,511	22
BRISTOL MYERS SQUIBB CO	325412	17,914,000	11	1,585,000	15
CAMBREX CORP	325412	452,255	32	-30,100	33
CELL GENESYS INC	325412	1,364	43	-82,929	38
CEPHALON INC	325412	1,764,069	25	144,816	25
CHIRON CORP	325412				
ELAN CORP PLC	325412	560,400	30	-267,300	43
ELI LILLY AND COMPANY	325412	15,691,000	12	2,662,700	12
ENDO PHARMACEUTICALS HOLDINGS INC	325412	909,659	27	137,839	26
FOREST LABORATORIES INC	325412	2,793,934	22	708,514	20
GENENTECH INC	325412	9,284,000	16	2,113,000	13
GENZYME CORP	325412	3,187,013	20	-16,797	32
GLAXOSMITHKLINE PLC	325412	45,595,800	3	10,793,000	3
HUMAN GENOME SCIENCES	325412	25,755	39	-210,327	42
INCYTE CORP	325412	27,643	38	-74,166	37
JOHNSON & JOHNSON	325412	53,324,000	1	11,053,000	2
KENDLE INTERNATIONAL INC	325412	373,936	33	8,530	29
MAXYGEN INC	325412	25,021	40	-16,482	31
MERCK & CO INC	325412	22,636,000	8	4,433,800	7
MERCK SERONO SA	325412				
MILLENNIUM PHARMACEUTICALS INC	325412	486,830	31	-43,953	35
NEUROCRINE BIOSCIENCES	325412	39,234	37	-107,205	40
NOVARTIS AG	325412	36,031,000	5	7,202,000	4
NOVO-NORDISK AS	325412	6,913,700	18	1,126,020	18
PFIZER INC	325412	48,371,000	2	19,337,000	1
REGENERON PHARMACEUTICALS INC	325412	63,447	35	-102,337	39
ROCHE HOLDING LTD	325412	34,851,500	6	7,116,030	5
SANOFI-AVENTIS	325412	38,722,100	4	6,003,540	6
SCHERING-PLOUGH CORP	325412	10,594,000	14	1,143,000	17
SEPRACOR INC	325412	1,196,534	26	184,562	24
SHIRE PLC	325412	1,796,500	24	278,200	21
SIMCERE PHARMACEUTICAL GROUP	325412	121,800	34	22,100	28
TAKEDA PHARMACEUTICAL COMPANY LTD	325412	10,360,744	15	2,677,342	11
VALEANT PHARMACEUTICALS INTERNATIONAL	325412	907,238	28	-56,565	36
WARNER CHILCOTT PLC	325412				
WYETH	325412	20,350,655	10	4,196,706	9
Drugs (Pharmaceuticals), Distribution					
AMERISOURCEBERGEN CORP	422210	61,203,145	3	467,714	3
CARDINAL HEALTH INC	422210	79,664,200	2	1,000,100	1

Company	Industry Code	2006 Sales (U.S. $ thousands)	Sales Rank	2006 Profits (U.S. $ thousands)	Profits Rank
FAMILYMEDS GROUP INC	422210	230,500	4	-7,200	4
MCKESSON CORPORATION	422210	86,983,000	1	751,000	2
Drugs (Pharmaceuticals), Generic Manufacturing					
BARR PHARMACEUTICALS INC	325416	1,314,465	3	336,477	2
MYLAN LABORATORIES INC	325416	1,257,164	4	184,542	3
PAR PHARMACEUTICAL COMPANIES INC	325416	725,168	5	6,741	4
TEVA PHARMACEUTICAL INDUSTRIES	325416	8,408,000	1	546,000	1
WATSON PHARMACEUTICALS	325416	1,979,244	2	-445,005	5
Electrical Equipment, Manufacturing					
DANAHER CORP	335000	9,596,404	1	1,122,029	1
Equipment Rental					
UNIVERSAL HOSPITAL SERVICES INC	532400	225,100	1	100	1
Food Service Contractors					
MORRISON MANAGEMENT SPECIALISTS INC	722310				
Forest Products/Paper, Manufacturing					
KIMBERLY CLARK CORP	322000	16,746,900	1	1,499,500	1
Health Supplement Stores					
GNC CORPORATION	446191				
Home Health Care					
ALLIED HEALTHCARE INTERNATIONAL INC	621610	294,607	9	-123,771	13
AMEDISYS INC	621610	541,148	5	38,255	4
AMERICAN HOMEPATIENT INC	621610	328,080	8	-2,587	11
APRIA HEALTHCARE GROUP	621610	1,517,307	1	74,980	1
CHEMED CORPORATION	621610	1,018,587	3	50,651	3
CONTINUCARE CORP	621610	132,991	10	5,338	9
GENTIVA HEALTH SERVICES	621610	1,106,588	2	20,776	7
MATRIA HEALTHCARE INC	621610	336,139	7	52,690	2
NATIONAL HOME HEALTH CARE	621610	102,365	12	3,655	10
NEW YORK HEALTH CARE INC	621610	45,558	13	-3,756	12
ODYSSEY HEALTHCARE INC	621610	409,831	6	19,729	8
OPTION CARE INC	621610	659,412	4	21,685	6
PEDIATRIC SERVICES OF AMERICA INC	621610	119,360	11	24,126	5
Hospitals/Clinics--General & Specialty Hospitals					
ADVENTIST HEALTH SYSTEM	622110	4,968,700	11	325,400	6
ADVOCATE HEALTH CARE	622110				
ALLINA HOSPITALS AND CLINICS	622110	2,350,000	23		
ASCENSION HEALTH	622110	11,405,552	3	802,965	2
AVERA HEALTH	622110				
BANNER HEALTH	622110	3,119,375	18	144,028	13
BJC HEALTHCARE	622110	2,800,000	20		
BON SECOURS HEALTH SYSTEM INC	622110				
CATHOLIC HEALTH INITIATIVES	622110	7,636,233	5	693,701	3
CATHOLIC HEALTHCARE PARTNERS	622110	3,505,081	15	143,093	14
CATHOLIC HEALTHCARE WEST	622110	6,730,138	7	437,917	5
CHRISTUS HEALTH	622110	2,688,300	21	231,904	9
CLARIAN HEALTH PARTNERS	622110				
COMMUNITY HEALTH SYSTEMS	622110	4,365,576	12	168,263	12
DETROIT MEDICAL CENTER	622110				

Company	Industry Code	2006 Sales (U.S. $ thousands)	Sales Rank	2006 Profits (U.S. $ thousands)	Profits Rank
FAIRVIEW HEALTH SERVICES	622110	2,114,710	24	35,415	19
HCA INC	622110	25,477,000	2	1,036,000	1
HEALTH MANAGEMENT ASSOCIATES INC	622110	4,056,599	13	182,749	11
HENRY FORD HEALTH SYSTEMS	622110				
INTERMOUNTAIN HEALTH CARE	622110				
JEFFERSON HEALTH SYSTEM	622110	3,202,500	16	237,700	8
JOHNS HOPKINS MEDICINE	622110				
KAISER PERMANENTE	622110	34,600,000	1		
LIFEPOINT HOSPITALS INC	622110	2,439,700	22	142,200	15
MARIAN HEALTH SYSTEMS	622110	3,144,406	17	84,095	16
MAYO FOUNDATION FOR MEDICAL EDUCATION AND RESEARCH	622110	5,234,100	10	279,000	7
MEDCATH CORPORATION	622110	706,374	26	12,576	20
MEDSTAR HEALTH	622110	2,950,000	19		
MEMORIAL HERMANN HEALTHCARE SYSTEM	622110				
MEMORIAL SLOAN KETTERING CANCER CENTER	622110	1,837,899	25	78,741	17
NEW YORK CITY HEALTH AND HOSPITALS CORPORATION	622110	5,731,620	8	-1,638,815	22
NEW YORK-PRESBYTERIAN HEALTHCARE SYSTEM	622110				
OHIOHEALTH CORPORATION	622110				
PARTNERS HEALTHCARE SYSTEM	622110				
PROVIDENCE HEALTH & SERVICES	622110				
SENTARA HEALTHCARE	622110				
SISTERS OF MERCY HEALTH SYSTEMS	622110	3,579,454	14	45,708	18
SPECTRUM HEALTH	622110				
SSM HEALTH CARE SYSTEM	622110				
ST JUDE CHILDRENS RESEARCH HOSPITAL	622110				
SUTTER HEALTH	622110	7,258,000	6	587,000	4
TENET HEALTHCARE CORP	622110	8,701,000	4	-803,000	21
TEXAS HEALTH RESOURCES	622110				
TRIAD HOSPITALS INC	622110	5,537,900	9	207,900	10
TRINITY HEALTH COMPANY	622110				
Hospitals/Clinics--Psychiatric Clinics					
MAGELLAN HEALTH SERVICES	622210	1,690,270	1	86,871	1
PSYCHIATRIC SOLUTIONS INC	622210	1,026,490	3	60,632	2
RES CARE INC	622210	1,302,118	2	36,243	3
Instrument Manufacturing, including Measurement, Control, Test & Navigational					
ART ADVANCED RESEARCH TECHNOLOGIES	334500	3,080	3	-8,750	3
METTLER-TOLEDO INTERNATIONAL	334500	1,594,912	1	157,532	1
PERKINELMER INC	334500	1,546,358	2	119,583	2
Insurance Brokerages, Agencies & Exchanges					
AON CORPORATION	524210	8,954,000	2	720,000	2
MARSH & MCLENNAN COMPANIES INC	524210	11,921,000	1	990,000	1
Insurance--Health Supplemental & Specialty					
AFLAC INC	524114A	14,616,000	1	1,483,000	1
ASSURANT EMPLOYEE BENEFITS	524114A				
ASSURANT HEALTH	524114A				

Company	Industry Code	2006 Sales (U.S. $ thousands)	Sales Rank	2006 Profits (U.S. $ thousands)	Profits Rank
CIGNA BEHAVIORAL HEALTH	524114A				
DELTA DENTAL PLANS ASSOCIATION	524114A				
DENTAL BENEFITS PROVIDERS	524114A				
EYEMED VISION CARE LLC	524114A				
SAFEGUARD HEALTH ENTERPRISES INC	524114A				
VISION SERVICE PLAN	524114A				
Insurance--Health, HMO's & PPO's					
AETNA INC	524114	25,145,700	3	1,701,700	3
AMERICHOICE CORPORATION	524114				
AMERIGROUP CORPORATION	524114	2,835,089	21	107,106	20
ARKANSAS BLUE CROSS AND BLUE SHIELD	524114				
ASSURANT INC	524114	8,070,584	11	717,418	6
AVMED HEALTH PLAN	524114				
AXA PPP HEALTHCARE	524114				
BLUE CARE NETWORK OF MICHIGAN	524114				
BLUE CROSS AND BLUE SHIELD ASSOCIATION	524114				
BLUE CROSS AND BLUE SHIELD OF FLORIDA	524114	7,475,000	14	311,000	12
BLUE CROSS AND BLUE SHIELD OF GEORGIA INC	524114				
BLUE CROSS AND BLUE SHIELD OF KANSAS	524114				
BLUE CROSS AND BLUE SHIELD OF LOUISIANA	524114				
BLUE CROSS AND BLUE SHIELD OF MASSACHUSETTS	524114	2,097,457	25	157,250	16
BLUE CROSS AND BLUE SHIELD OF MICHIGAN	524114	8,686,500	9	-14,100	26
BLUE CROSS AND BLUE SHIELD OF MINNESOTA	524114	7,865,816	12	4,921	24
BLUE CROSS AND BLUE SHIELD OF MONTANA	524114				
BLUE CROSS AND BLUE SHIELD OF NEBRASKA	524114				
BLUE CROSS AND BLUE SHIELD OF NORTH CAROLINA	524114	4,406,928	18	189,412	13
BLUE CROSS AND BLUE SHIELD OF OKLAHOMA	524114				
BLUE CROSS AND BLUE SHIELD OF TENNESSEE INC	524114				
BLUE CROSS AND BLUE SHIELD OF TEXAS	524114				
BLUE CROSS AND BLUE SHIELD OF VERMONT	524114				
BLUE CROSS AND BLUE SHIELD OF WYOMING	524114				
BLUE CROSS OF CALIFORNIA	524114				
BLUE CROSS OF IDAHO	524114				
BLUE SHIELD OF CALIFORNIA	524114				
BRITISH UNITED PROVIDENT ASSOCIATION (BUPA)	524114	8,469,930	10	473,210	9
CAPITAL BLUECROSS	524114				
CAREFIRST INC	524114	5,510,184	16	164,256	15
CENTENE CORPORATION	524114	2,279,020	24	-43,629	27
CIGNA CORP	524114	16,547,000	5	1,155,000	4
COVENTRY HEALTH CARE INC	524114	7,733,756	13	560,045	7
FIRST CHOICE HEALTH NETWORK INC	524114				
FIRST HEALTH GROUP CORP	524114				

Company	Industry Code	2006 Sales (U.S. $ thousands)	Sales Rank	2006 Profits (U.S. $ thousands)	Profits Rank
GROUP HEALTH COOPERATIVE OF PUGET SOUND	524114				
GROUP HEALTH INCORPORATED	524114	2,741,540	22	33,754	23
HARVARD PILGRIM HEALTH CARE INC	524114	2,488,095	23	70,536	21
HEALTH CARE SERVICE CORPORATION	524114	12,971,600	6	1,115,400	5
HEALTH INSURANCE PLAN OF GREATER NEW YORK	524114				
HEALTH NET INC	524114	12,908,350	7	329,313	11
HEALTHNOW NEW YORK	524114				
HIGHMARK INC	524114	11,083,800	8	398,300	10
HORIZON HEALTHCARE SERVICES INC	524114	6,730,317	15	180,066	14
HUMANA INC	524114	21,416,537	4	487,423	8
LIFETIME HEALTHCARE COMPANIES	524114	4,814,077	17	151,722	17
MEDICAL MUTUAL OF OHIO	524114				
METROPOLITAN HEALTH NETWORKS	524114	228,216	28	473	25
MID ATLANTIC MEDICAL SERVICES INC	524114				
MOLINA HEALTHCARE INC	524114	2,004,995	26	45,727	22
PACIFICARE HEALTH SYSTEMS	524114				
PREMERA BLUE CROSS	524114	3,093,741	20	121,360	19
REGENCE GROUP (THE)	524114				
SIERRA HEALTH SERVICES INC	524114	1,718,892	27	140,471	18
TUFTS ASSOCIATED HEALTH PLANS	524114				
UNITEDHEALTH GROUP INC	524114	71,542,000	1	4,159,000	1
WELLCARE GROUP OF COMPANIES	524114	3,762,926	19		
WELLPOINT INC	524114	56,953,000	2	3,094,900	2
Insurance--Life					
INDEPENDENCE HOLDING CO	524113	364,688	1	14,061	1
Laboratories & Diagnostic Services--Medical					
ALLIANCE IMAGING INC	621511	455,775	4	19,288	4
BIO REFERENCE LABORATORIES INC	621511	193,134	6	11,291	5
CRYOLIFE INC	621511	81,311	8	365	6
HOOPER HOLMES INC	621511	293,862	5	-85,181	8
LABORATORY CORP OF AMERICA HOLDINGS	621511	3,590,800	2	431,600	2
MDS INC	621511	1,017,200	3	123,100	3
QUEST DIAGNOSTICS INC	621511	6,268,659	1	586,421	1
RADNET INC	621511	161,005	7	-6,894	7
SPECIALTY LABORATORIES INC	621511				
Long-Term Health Care & Assisted Living					
ADVOCAT INC	623110	216,763	7	12,944	5
AMERICAN RETIREMENT CORP	623110				
ATRIA SENIOR LIVING GROUP	623110				
BROOKDALE SENIOR LIVING	623110				
CAPITAL SENIOR LIVING CORP	623110	159,070	8	-2,600	6
EMERITUS CORP	623110	421,865	6	-14,618	7
EXTENDICARE REAL ESTATE INVESTMENT TRUST	623110	1,650,696	3		
HARBORSIDE HEALTHCARE	623110				
KINDRED HEALTHCARE INC	623110	4,266,661	1	78,711	2
LIFE CARE CENTERS OF AMERICA	623110				

Company	Industry Code	2006 Sales (U.S. $ thousands)	Sales Rank	2006 Profits (U.S. $ thousands)	Profits Rank
MANOR CARE INC	623110	3,613,185	2	169,560	1
NATIONAL HEALTHCARE CORP	623110	562,958	5	36,740	3
OUTLOOK POINTE CORP	623110				
SKILLED HEALTHCARE GROUP	623110				
SUN HEALTHCARE GROUP	623110	1,045,637	4	27,118	4
SUNRISE SENIOR LIVING	623110				
Machinery, Manufacturing					
ATS AUTOMATION TOOLING SYSTEMS INC	333000	725,775	2	-69,293	2
SMITHS GROUP PLC	333000	6,564,200	1	45,100	1
Management of Companies & Enterprises					
AVIDYN	551110				
Market Research					
IMS HEALTH INC	541910	1,958,588	1	315,511	1
Medical/Dental/Surgical Equipment & Supplies, Distribution					
CHINDEX INTERNATIONAL INC	421450	90,836	6	167	7
HENRY SCHEIN INC	421450	5,153,097	2	163,759	3
MOORE MEDICAL CORP	421450				
NYER MEDICAL GROUP INC	421450	63,597	7	858	6
OWENS & MINOR INC	421450	5,533,736	1	48,752	4
PATTERSON COMPANIES INC	421450	2,615,123	4	198,425	1
PSS WORLD MEDICAL INC	421450	1,619,417	5	44,257	5
THERMO FISHER SCIENTIFIC	421450	3,791,617	3	168,935	2
Medical/Dental/Surgical Equipment & Supplies, Manufacturing					
3M COMPANY	339113	22,923,000	1	3,851,000	1
ABIOMED INC	339113	43,670	93	-29,449	93
ADVANCED BIONICS CORP	339113				
ADVANCED MEDICAL OPTICS	339113	997,496	29	79,471	26
ADVANCED NEUROMODULATION SYSTEMS	339113				
ALIGN TECHNOLOGY INC	339113	206,354	60	-34,963	94
AMERICAN MEDICAL SYSTEMS HOLDINGS INC	339113	358,318	51	-49,317	95
ANALOGIC CORP	339113	351,445	52	25,066	48
ANSELL LIMITED COMPANY	339113	859,600	31	88,700	24
APPLERA CORPORATION	339113	1,949,400	19	212,500	17
ARROW INTERNATIONAL INC	339113	481,587	40	56,009	34
ARTHROCARE CORP	339113	253,376	56	31,675	40
ASPECT MEDICAL SYSTEMS	339113	91,334	82	37,089	39
ATRION CORPORATION	339113	81,020	84	10,765	63
ATS MEDICAL INC	339113	40,449	94	-27,674	92
BAUSCH & LOMB INC	339113	2,293,400	15		
BAXTER INTERNATIONAL INC	339113	10,378,000	4	1,397,000	3
BECKMAN COULTER INC	339113	2,528,500	14	186,900	19
BECTON DICKINSON & CO	339113	5,834,800	7	752,300	7
BESPAK PLC	339113	186,790	66	20,810	52
BIO RAD LABORATORIES INC	339113	1,273,930	25	103,263	22
BIOMET INC	339113	2,025,739	16	405,908	11
BIOPHAN TECHNOLOGIES INC	339113	1,044	102	-14,315	89
BOSTON SCIENTIFIC CORP	339113	7,821,000	6	-3,577,000	99
CANDELA CORP	339113	149,466	72	14,934	54

Company	Industry Code	2006 Sales (U.S. $ thousands)	Sales Rank	2006 Profits (U.S. $ thousands)	Profits Rank
CANTEL MEDICAL CORP	339113	192,179	64	23,697	50
CARDIOGENESIS CORP	339113	17,117	101	-1,979	82
CHOLESTECH CORP	339113	64,093	86	5,634	72
CIVCO MEDICAL SOLUTIONS	339113				
COHERENT INC	339113	584,600	36		
CONMED CORP	339113	646,812	34	-12,507	88
CONVATEC	339113				
COOPER COMPANIES INC	339113	858,960	32	66,234	30
CORDIS CORP	339113				
COVIDIEN LTD	339113	9,647,000	5	1,155,000	4
CR BARD INC	339113	1,985,500	17	272,100	12
CRITICARE SYSTEMS INC	339113	31,351	97	212	76
CYBERONICS INC	339113	123,441	75	-59,069	96
DADE BEHRING HOLDINGS INC	339113	1,739,200	21	120,000	21
DATASCOPE CORP	339113	373,000	48	25,843	45
DENTSPLY INTERNATIONAL	339113	1,810,496	20	223,718	15
DEPUY INC	339113				
DJO INC	339113	413,058	46	12,641	59
EDWARDS LIFESCIENCES	339113	1,037,000	28	130,500	20
EMERGENCY FILTRATION PRODUCTS INC	339113				
EMPI INC	339113				
ENVIRONMENTAL TECTONICS	339113	25,069	100	-6,714	85
ESSILOR INTERNATIONAL SA	339113	3,548,900	9	436,900	10
ETHICON INC	339113				
EXACTECH INC	339113	102,430	77	7,752	66
EXCEL TECHNOLOGY INC	339113	154,496	68	14,019	57
GE HEALTHCARE	339113				
GISH BIOMEDICAL INC	339113				
GSI GROUP INC	339113	428,616	42	16,254	53
GYRUS GROUP PLC	339113	417,800	45	25,800	46
HAEMONETICS CORPORATION	339113	419,733	43	69,076	29
HILLENBRAND INDUSTRIES	339113	1,962,900	18	221,200	16
HILL-ROM COMPANY INC	339113				
HITACHI MEDICAL CORP	339113				
HITACHI MEDICAL SYSTEMS AMERICA	339113				
HOLOGIC INC	339113	462,680	41	27,423	44
HOSPIRA INC	339113	2,688,505	13	237,679	14
I FLOW CORPORATION	339113	93,582	81	13,674	58
ICU MEDICAL INC	339113	201,613	62	25,660	47
IMMUCOR INC	339113	183,506	67	39,843	37
INAMED CORP	339113				
INSTITUT STRAUMANN AG	339113				
INTEGRA LIFESCIENCES HOLDINGS CORP	339113	419,297	44	29,407	43
INTUITIVE SURGICAL INC	339113	372,682	49	72,044	27
INVACARE CORP	339113	1,498,035	23	-317,774	97
INVERNESS MEDICAL INNOVATIONS INC	339113	569,454	37	-16,842	91
IRIDEX CORP	339113	35,904	96	-5,753	84
IRIS INTERNATIONAL INC	339113	70,494	85	-175	77

Company	Industry Code	2006 Sales (U.S. $ thousands)	Sales Rank	2006 Profits (U.S. $ thousands)	Profits Rank
KINETIC CONCEPTS INC	339113	1,371,636	24	195,468	18
KYPHON INC	339113	407,790	47	39,732	38
LAKELAND INDUSTRIES INC	339113	98,740	80	6,329	69
LASERSCOPE	339113				
LIFECORE BIOMEDICAL INC	339113	63,097	88	7,040	67
LIFESCAN INC	339113				
LUMENIS LTD	339113				
MEDICAL ACTION INDUSTRIES	339113	150,942	69	11,461	61
MEDTRONIC CARDIOVASCULAR	339113				
MEDTRONIC INC	339113	11,292,000	2	2,546,700	2
MEDTRONIC MINIMED INC	339113				
MEDTRONIC SOFAMOR DANEK	339113				
MEDTRONIC XOMED SURGICAL PRODUCTS INC	339113				
MENTOR CORP	339113	268,272	54	62,357	32
MERIDIAN MEDICAL TECHNOLOGIES INC	339113				
MERIT MEDICAL SYSTEMS INC	339113	190,674	65	12,301	60
MICROTEK MEDICAL HOLDINGS	339113	141,577	73	7,915	65
MINDRAY MEDICAL INTERNATIONAL LIMITED	339113	194,126	63	46,358	36
MINE SAFETY APPLIANCES	339113	913,714	30	63,918	31
MINNTECH CORP	339113				
MISONIX INC	339113	39,067	95	-3,759	83
MIV THERAPEUTICS INC	339113	0		-9,094	87
MOLNLYCKE HEALTH CARE GROUP AB	339113				
NATIONAL DENTEX CORP	339113	150,107	71	5,763	71
NMT MEDICAL INC	339113	28,151	99	5,883	70
ORTHOFIX INTERNATIONAL NV	339113	365,359	50	-7,042	86
OSTEOTECH INC	339113	99,241	78	1,907	75
PALOMAR MEDICAL TECHNOLOGIES INC	339113	126,544	74	52,977	35
PHILIPS MEDICAL SYSTEMS	339113				
POLYMEDICA CORPORATION	339113	491,515	39	60,398	33
QUIDEL CORP	339113	106,015	76	21,718	51
REABLE THERAPEUTICS INC	339113				
RESMED INC	339113	606,996	35	88,211	25
RESPIRONICS INC	339113	1,046,141	27	99,893	23
ROTECH HEALTHCARE INC	339113	498,751	38	-534,099	98
SCHICK TECHNOLOGIES INC	339113				
SIEMENS MEDICAL SOLUTIONS	339113	11,121,700	3		
SMITH & NEPHEW PLC	339113	2,779,000	12	745,000	8
SONIC INNOVATIONS INC	339113	150,492	70	-1,580	80
SPAN AMERICA MEDICAL SYSTEMS INC	339113	51,557	92	3,055	74
SPECTRANETICS CORP	339113	63,490	87	-1,447	78
SRI/SURGICAL EXPRESS INC	339113	98,831	79	-1,953	81
SSL INTERNATIONAL PLC	339113	783,800	33		
ST JUDE MEDICAL INC	339113	3,302,447	11	548,251	9
STAAR SURGICAL CO	339113	56,282	89	-15,044	90
STERIS CORP	339113	1,160,285	26	70,289	28
STRYKER CORP	339113	5,405,600	8	777,700	6

Company	Industry Code	2006 Sales (U.S. $ thousands)	Sales Rank	2006 Profits (U.S. $ thousands)	Profits Rank
SUNRISE MEDICAL INC	339113				
SYBRON DENTAL SPECIALTIES	339113				
SYMMETRY MEDICAL INC	339113	253,569	55	24,149	49
SYNOVIS LIFE TECHNOLOGIES	339113	55,835	90	-1,481	79
THERAGENICS CORP	339113	54,096	91	6,865	68
THORATEC CORPORATION	339113	214,133	59	3,973	73
UTAH MEDICAL PRODUCTS INC	339113	28,753	98	8,168	64
VARIAN MEDICAL SYSTEMS	339113	1,597,800	22	245,100	13
VENTANA MEDICAL SYSTEMS	339113	238,223	58	31,578	41
VITAL SIGNS INC	339113	204,058	61	30,117	42
WELCH ALLYN INC	339113				
WRIGHT MEDICAL GROUP INC	339113	338,938	53	14,411	56
YOUNG INNOVATIONS INC	339113	90,805	83	14,799	55
ZIMMER HOLDINGS INC	339113	3,495,400	10	834,500	5
ZLB BEHRING LLC	339113				
ZOLL MEDICAL CORP	339113	248,849	57	11,140	62
Online Publishing, Services & Niche Portals					
HEALTH GRADES INC	514199	27,770	2	3,181	2
REVOLUTION HEALTH GROUP	514199				
WEBMD HEALTH CORP	514199	253,881	1	4,546	1
Optical Goods Stores					
EMERGING VISION INC	446130	21,712	1	1,860	1
Optical Instrument & Lens, Manufacturing					
LUXOTTICA GROUP SPA	333314	5,175,835	1	405,345	1
SIGNATURE EYEWEAR INC	333314	23,162	2	683	2
Other Health & Personal Care Stores/Weight Management					
JENNY CRAIG INC	446190				
WEIGHT WATCHERS INTERNATIONAL INC	446190	1,233,300	1	209,800	1
Packaging, Manufacturing					
WEST PHARMACEUTICAL SERVICES INC	322210	913,300	1	67,100	1
Payment & Transaction Processing Services					
ATHENAHEALTH INC	522320	80,000	4		
FISERV INC	522320	4,544,151	1	449,914	2
HEALTH MANAGEMENT SYSTEMS INC	522320	87,940	3	5,325	3
HLTH CORP	522320	1,098,608	2	767,739	1
MEDAVANT HEALTHCARE SOLUTIONS	522320	65,462	5	-6,610	4
Payment & Transaction Processing--Benefits Management					
BIOSCRIP INC	522320A	1,152,459	4	-38,289	5
CAREMARK RX INC	522320A	36,750,203	2	1,074,015	1
EXPRESS SCRIPTS INC	522320A	17,660,000	3	474,400	3
MEDCO HEALTH SOLUTIONS	522320A	42,543,700	1	630,200	2
NATIONAL MEDICAL HEALTH CARD SYSTEMS INC	522320A	862,853	5	9,657	4
TRUSTMARK COMPANIES	522320A	100,900	6		
UNIPRISE INCORPORATED	522320A				
Pets/Pet Supplies Stores					
PETMED EXPRESS INC	453910	137,583	1	12,063	1

Company	Industry Code	2006 Sales (U.S. $ thousands)	Sales Rank	2006 Profits (U.S. $ thousands)	Profits Rank
Pharmacies & Drug Stores					
BROOKS ECKERD	446110				
CVS CAREMARK CORPORATION	446110	43,813,800	2	1,368,900	2
DUANE READE INC	446110	1,584,778	6	-80,103	6
JEAN COUTU GROUP INC	446110	11,143,100	4	103,800	4
LONGS DRUG STORES CORP	446110	4,670,303	5	73,884	5
RITE AID CORPORATION	446110	17,270,968	3	1,273,006	3
WALGREEN CO	446110	47,409,000	1	1,750,600	1
Pharmacies-Specialty					
ACCREDO HEALTH GROUP INC	446110A				
CURASCRIPT INC	446110A				
OMNICARE INC	446110A	6,492,993	1	183,572	1
PHARMERICA CORP	446110A	1,119,964	2	16,757	2
Physician Practice Management					
AMERIPATH INC	621111	752,300	3	10,500	4
BRIGHT NOW! DENTAL INC	621111				
CASTLE DENTAL CENTERS INC	621111				
COAST DENTAL SERVICES INC	621111				
INTEGRAMED AMERICA INC	621111	126,438	6	3,224	5
LOGISTICARE INC	621111	252,000	5		
PEDIATRIX MEDICAL GROUP	621111	818,554	2	124,465	1
PROXYMED INC	621111	65,462	7	-3,370	6
TEAM HEALTH	621111				
UNITED SURGICAL PARTNERS	621111	578,825	4	34,246	2
US ONCOLOGY INC	621111	2,811,400	1	26,200	3
Research & Development--Physical, Engineering & Life Sciences					
CELERA GENOMICS GROUP	541710	44,200	3	-62,700	4
COVANCE INC	541710	1,406,058	1	144,998	2
PHARMACEUTICAL PRODUCT DEVELOPMENT INC	541710	1,247,682	2	156,652	1
PHARMACOPEIA DRUG DISCOVERY	541710	16,936	4	-27,764	3
QUINTILES TRANSNATIONAL	541710				
Staffing or Outsourcing					
ATC HEALTHCARE INC	561300	71,528	1	-2,332	1
Telecommunications & Internet Services-Specialty					
SHL TELEMEDICINE LTD	513300D				
Telecommunications Equipment Manufacturing					
SIEMENS AG	334210	113,740,000	1	3,950,360	1
Utilization Management, Health Care					
CONCENTRA INC	621999	1,298,829	1	32,737	1
CORVEL CORP	621999	266,504	2	9,753	2
Veterinary Clinics					
VCA ANTECH INC	541940	983,313	1	105,529	1
Waste Disposal, Waste Management					
STERICYCLE INC	562000	789,637	1	105,270	1

ALPHABETICAL INDEX

MINNTECH CORP
MINUTECLINIC
MISONIX INC
MIV THERAPEUTICS INC
MOLINA HEALTHCARE INC
MOLNLYCKE HEALTH CARE GROUP AB
MOORE MEDICAL CORP
MORRISON MANAGEMENT SPECIALISTS INC
MYLAN LABORATORIES INC
NANOBIO CORPORATION
NATIONAL DENTEX CORP
NATIONAL HEALTHCARE CORP
NATIONAL HOME HEALTH CARE CORP
NATIONAL MEDICAL HEALTH CARD SYSTEMS INC
NEKTAR THERAPEUTICS
NEUROCRINE BIOSCIENCES INC
NEW YORK CITY HEALTH AND HOSPITALS CORPORATION
NEW YORK HEALTH CARE INC
NEW YORK-PRESBYTERIAN HEALTHCARE SYSTEM
NMT MEDICAL INC
NOVAMED INC
NOVARTIS AG
NOVATION LLC (VHA INC)
NOVO-NORDISK AS
NYER MEDICAL GROUP INC
ODYSSEY HEALTHCARE INC
OHIOHEALTH CORPORATION
OMNICARE INC
OPTICARE HEALTH SYSTEMS
OPTION CARE INC
ORGANOGENESIS INC
ORTHOFIX INTERNATIONAL NV
OSTEOTECH INC
OUTLOOK POINTE CORP
OWENS & MINOR INC
PACIFICARE HEALTH SYSTEMS INC
PALOMAR MEDICAL TECHNOLOGIES
PAR PHARMACEUTICAL COMPANIES
PARTNERS HEALTHCARE SYSTEM
PATTERSON COMPANIES INC
PDI INC
PEDIATRIC SERVICES OF AMERICA INC
PEDIATRIX MEDICAL GROUP INC
PERKINELMER INC
PER-SE TECHNOLOGIES INC
PETMED EXPRESS INC
PFIZER INC
PHARMACEUTICAL PRODUCT DEVELOPMENT INC
PHARMACOPEIA DRUG DISCOVERY
PHARMERICA CORP
PHILIPS MEDICAL SYSTEMS
POLYMEDICA CORPORATION
PREMERA BLUE CROSS
PREMIER INC
PROVIDENCE HEALTH & SERVICES
PROXYMED INC
PSS WORLD MEDICAL INC
PSYCHIATRIC SOLUTIONS INC
QUALITY SYSTEMS INC
QUEST DIAGNOSTICS INC
QUIDEL CORP
QUINTILES TRANSNATIONAL CORP
QUOVADX INC
RADNET INC
REABLE THERAPEUTICS INC
REGENCE GROUP (THE)
REGENERON PHARMACEUTICALS INC
REHABCARE GROUP INC
RES CARE INC
RESMED INC
RESPIRONICS INC
REVOLUTION HEALTH GROUP LLC
RITE AID CORPORATION
ROCHE HOLDING LTD
ROTECH HEALTHCARE INC
SAFEGUARD HEALTH ENTERPRISES INC
SANOFI-AVENTIS
SCHERING-PLOUGH CORP
SCHICK TECHNOLOGIES INC
SENTARA HEALTHCARE
SEPRACOR INC
SHIRE PLC
SHL TELEMEDICINE LTD
SIEMENS AG
SIEMENS MEDICAL SOLUTIONS
SIEMENS MEDICAL SOLUTIONS DIAGNOSTICS
SIERRA HEALTH SERVICES INC
SIGMA ALDRICH CORP
SIGNATURE EYEWEAR INC
SIMCERE PHARMACEUTICAL GROUP
SISTERS OF MERCY HEALTH SYSTEMS
SKILLED HEALTHCARE GROUP INC
SMITH & NEPHEW PLC
SMITHS GROUP PLC
SOLUCIENT LLC
SONIC INNOVATIONS INC
SPAN AMERICA MEDICAL SYSTEMS INC
SPECIALTY LABORATORIES INC
SPECTRANETICS CORP
SPECTRUM HEALTH
SRI/SURGICAL EXPRESS INC
SSL INTERNATIONAL PLC
SSM HEALTH CARE SYSTEM INC
ST JUDE CHILDRENS RESEARCH HOSPITAL
ST JUDE MEDICAL INC
STAAR SURGICAL CO
STERICYCLE INC
STERIS CORP
STRYKER CORP
SUN HEALTHCARE GROUP
SUNRISE MEDICAL INC
SUNRISE SENIOR LIVING
SUTTER HEALTH
SYBRON DENTAL SPECIALTIES INC
SYMMETRY MEDICAL INC
SYNOVIS LIFE TECHNOLOGIES INC
TAKE CARE HEALTH SYSTEMS LLC
TAKEDA PHARMACEUTICAL COMPANY LTD
TEAM HEALTH
TECHNE CORP
TELEFLEX INC
TENET HEALTHCARE CORPORATION
TEVA PHARMACEUTICAL INDUSTRIES
TEXAS HEALTH RESOURCES
THERAGENICS CORP
THERMO FISHER SCIENTIFIC INC
THORATEC CORPORATION
TLC VISION CORPORATION
TOSHIBA CORPORATION
TOWERS PERRIN
TRANSCEND SERVICES INC
TRIAD HOSPITALS INC
TRINITY HEALTH COMPANY
TRUSTMARK COMPANIES
TUFTS ASSOCIATED HEALTH PLANS
UNIPRISE INCORPORATED
UNITED SURGICAL PARTNERS
UNITEDHEALTH GROUP INC
UNIVERSAL HEALTH SERVICES INC
UNIVERSAL HOSPITAL SERVICES INC
US ONCOLOGY INC
US PHYSICAL THERAPY INC
UTAH MEDICAL PRODUCTS INC
VALEANT PHARMACEUTICALS INTERNATIONAL
VARIAN MEDICAL SYSTEMS INC
VCA ANTECH INC
VENTANA MEDICAL SYSTEMS INC
VISION SERVICE PLAN
VITAL SIGNS INC
WALGREEN CO
WARNER CHILCOTT PLC
WATSON PHARMACEUTICALS INC
WEBMD HEALTH CORP
WEIGHT WATCHERS INTERNATIONAL INC
WELCH ALLYN INC
WELLCARE GROUP OF COMPANIES
WELLPOINT INC
WEST PHARMACEUTICAL SERVICES INC
WRIGHT MEDICAL GROUP INC
WYETH
YOUNG INNOVATIONS INC
ZIMMER HOLDINGS INC
ZLB BEHRING LLC
ZOLL MEDICAL CORP

INDEX OF HEADQUARTERS LOCATION BY U.S. STATE

To help you locate members of THE HEALTH CARE 500 geographically, the city and state of the headquarters of each company are in the following index.

ALABAMA
HEALTHSOUTH CORP; Birmingham

ARIZONA
BANNER HEALTH; Phoenix
VENTANA MEDICAL SYSTEMS INC; Tucson

ARKANSAS
ARKANSAS BLUE CROSS AND BLUE SHIELD; Little Rock

CALIFORNIA
ADVANCED BIONICS CORPORATION; Sylmar
ADVANCED MEDICAL OPTICS INC; Santa Ana
ALIGN TECHNOLOGY INC; Santa Clara
ALLERGAN INC; Irvine
ALLIANCE IMAGING INC; Anaheim
AMGEN INC; Thousand Oaks
APRIA HEALTHCARE GROUP INC; Lake Forest
ARADIGM CORPORATION; Hayward
BECKMAN COULTER INC; Fullerton
BIO RAD LABORATORIES INC; Hercules
BIOSITE INC; San Diego
BLUE CROSS OF CALIFORNIA; Thousand Oaks
BLUE SHIELD OF CALIFORNIA; San Francisco
BRIGHT NOW! DENTAL INC; Santa Ana
CARDIOGENESIS CORP; Foothill Ranch
CATHOLIC HEALTHCARE WEST; San Francisco
CELL GENESYS INC; South San Francisco
CHIRON CORP; Emeryville
CHOLESTECH CORP; Hayward
COHERENT INC; Santa Clara
COOPER COMPANIES INC; Lake Forest
CORVEL CORP; Irvine
DAVITA INC; El Segundo
DJO INC; Vista
EDWARDS LIFESCIENCES CORP; Irvine
FIRST CONSULTING GROUP INC ; Long Beach
GENENTECH INC; South San Francisco
GISH BIOMEDICAL INC; Rancho Santa Margarita
HARBORSIDE HEALTHCARE CORP; Irvine
HEALTH NET INC; Woodland Hills
HEMACARE CORPORATION; Van Nuys
I FLOW CORPORATION; Lake Forest
ICU MEDICAL INC; San Clemente
INAMED CORP; Santa Barbara
INTUITIVE SURGICAL INC; Sunnyvale
IRIDEX CORP; Mountain View
IRIS INTERNATIONAL INC; Chatsworth
JENNY CRAIG INC; Carlsbad
KAISER PERMANENTE; Oakland
KYPHON INC; Sunnyvale
LASERSCOPE; San Jose
LIFESCAN INC; Milpitas
LONGS DRUG STORES CORPORATION; Walnut Creek
MAXYGEN INC; Redwood City
MCKESSON CORPORATION; San Francisco
MEDTRONIC CARDIOVASCULAR; Santa Rosa
MEDTRONIC MINIMED INC; Northridge
MENTOR CORP; Santa Barbara
MOLINA HEALTHCARE INC; Long Beach
NEKTAR THERAPEUTICS; San Carlos
NEUROCRINE BIOSCIENCES INC; San Diego
PACIFICARE HEALTH SYSTEMS INC; Cypress
PREMIER INC; San Diego
QUALITY SYSTEMS INC; Irvine
QUIDEL CORP; San Diego
RADNET INC; Los Angeles
RESMED INC; Poway
SAFEGUARD HEALTH ENTERPRISES INC; Aliso Viejo
SIEMENS MEDICAL SOLUTIONS DIAGNOSTICS; Los Angeles
SIGNATURE EYEWEAR INC; Inglewood
SKILLED HEALTHCARE GROUP INC; Foothill Ranch
SPECIALTY LABORATORIES INC; Valencia
STAAR SURGICAL CO; Monrovia
SUNRISE MEDICAL INC; Carlsbad
SUTTER HEALTH; Sacramento
SYBRON DENTAL SPECIALTIES INC; Orange
THORATEC CORPORATION; Pleasanton
VALEANT PHARMACEUTICALS INTERNATIONAL; Aliso Viejo
VARIAN MEDICAL SYSTEMS INC; Palo Alto
VCA ANTECH INC; Los Angeles
VISION SERVICE PLAN; Rancho Cordova
WATSON PHARMACEUTICALS INC; Corona

COLORADO
CATHOLIC HEALTH INITIATIVES; Denver
GLOBAL HEALTHCARE EXCHANGE; Westminster
HEALTH GRADES INC; Golden
SPECTRANETICS CORP; Colorado Springs

CONNECTICUT
AETNA INC; Hartford
APPLERA CORPORATION; Norwalk
FAMILYMEDS GROUP INC; Farmington
IMS HEALTH INC; Fairfield
INDEPENDENCE HOLDING CO; Stamford
MAGELLAN HEALTH SERVICES INC; Avon
MOORE MEDICAL CORP; New Britain
TOWERS PERRIN; Stamford
UNIPRISE INCORPORATED; Hartford

DELAWARE
INCYTE CORP; Wilmington

DISTRICT OF COLUMBIA
DANAHER CORP; Washington
REVOLUTION HEALTH GROUP LLC; Washington

FLORIDA
ADVENTIST HEALTH SYSTEM; Winter Park
AMERIPATH INC; Riviera Beach
AVMED HEALTH PLAN; Gainesville
BLUE CROSS AND BLUE SHIELD OF FLORIDA; Jacksonville
COAST DENTAL SERVICES INC; Tampa
CONTINUCARE CORP; Miami
CORDIS CORP; Miami Lakes
CURASCRIPT INC; Orlando
ECLIPSYS CORPORATION; Boca Raton
EXACTECH INC; Gainesville
HEALTH MANAGEMENT ASSOCIATES INC; Naples
HEARUSA INC; West Palm Beach
MEDTRONIC XOMED SURGICAL PRODUCTS INC; Jacksonville
METROPOLITAN HEALTH NETWORKS; West Palm Beach
PEDIATRIX MEDICAL GROUP INC; Sunrise
PETMED EXPRESS INC; Pompano Beach
PSS WORLD MEDICAL INC; Jacksonville
ROTECH HEALTHCARE INC; Orlando
SRI/SURGICAL EXPRESS INC; Tampa
WELLCARE GROUP OF COMPANIES; Tampa

GEORGIA
AFLAC INC; Columbus
BLUE CROSS AND BLUE SHIELD OF GEORGIA INC; Atlanta
CRYOLIFE INC; Kennesaw
IMMUCOR INC; Norcross
LOGISTICARE INC; Atlanta
MATRIA HEALTHCARE INC; Marietta
MEDAVANT HEALTHCARE SOLUTIONS; Norcross
MICROTEK MEDICAL HOLDINGS INC; Alpharetta
MORRISON MANAGEMENT SPECIALISTS INC; Atlanta
PEDIATRIC SERVICES OF AMERICA INC; Norcross
PER-SE TECHNOLOGIES INC; Alpharetta
PROXYMED INC; Norcross
THERAGENICS CORP; Buford
TRANSCEND SERVICES INC; Atlanta

IDAHO
BLUE CROSS OF IDAHO; Meridian

ILLINOIS
ABBOTT LABORATORIES; Abbott Park
ADVOCATE HEALTH CARE; Oak Brook
ALLSCRIPTS HEALTHCARE SOLUTIONS INC; Chicago
AON CORPORATION; Chicago
BAXTER INTERNATIONAL INC; Deerfield
BLUE CROSS AND BLUE SHIELD ASSOCIATION; Chicago
BROOKDALE SENIOR LIVING INC; Chicago
DADE BEHRING HOLDINGS INC; Deerfield
DELTA DENTAL PLANS ASSOCIATION; Oak Brook
FIRST HEALTH GROUP CORP; Downers Grove
HEALTH CARE SERVICE CORPORATION; Chicago
HOSPIRA INC; Lake Forest
NOVAMED INC; Chicago
OPTION CARE INC; Buffalo Grove
SOLUCIENT LLC; Evanston
STERICYCLE INC; Lake Forest
TRUSTMARK COMPANIES; Lake Forest
WALGREEN CO; Deerfield

INDIANA
BIOMET INC; Warsaw
CLARIAN HEALTH PARTNERS INC; Indianapolis
DEPUY INC; Warsaw
ELI LILLY AND COMPANY; Indianapolis
HILLENBRAND INDUSTRIES; Batesville
HILL-ROM COMPANY INC; Batesville
SYMMETRY MEDICAL INC; Warsaw
WELLPOINT INC; Indianapolis
ZIMMER HOLDINGS INC; Warsaw

IOWA
CIVCO MEDICAL SOLUTIONS; Kalona

KANSAS
BLUE CROSS AND BLUE SHIELD OF KANSAS; Topeka

KENTUCKY
ATRIA SENIOR LIVING GROUP; Louisville
HUMANA INC; Louisville
KINDRED HEALTHCARE INC; Louisville
OMNICARE INC; Covington
PHARMERICA CORP; Louisville
RES CARE INC; Louisville

LOUISIANA
AMEDISYS INC; Baton Rouge
BLUE CROSS AND BLUE SHIELD OF LOUISIANA; Baton Rouge

MAINE
IDEXX LABORATORIES INC; Westbrook
NYER MEDICAL GROUP INC; Bangor

MARYLAND
BON SECOURS HEALTH SYSTEM INC; Marriottsville
CAREFIRST INC; Owings Mills
CELERA GENOMICS GROUP; Rockville
CHINDEX INTERNATIONAL INC; Bethesda
COVENTRY HEALTH CARE INC; Bethesda
DENTAL BENEFITS PROVIDERS; Bethesda
DIALYSIS CORPORATION OF AMERICA; Linthicum
DIGENE CORPORATION; Gaithersburg
HANGER ORTHOPEDIC GROUP INC; Bethesda
HUMAN GENOME SCIENCES INC; Rockville
JOHNS HOPKINS MEDICINE; Baltimore
MEDSTAR HEALTH; Columbia
MERIDIAN MEDICAL TECHNOLOGIES INC; Columbia
MID ATLANTIC MEDICAL SERVICES INC; Rockville

MASSACHUSETTS
ABIOMED INC; Danvers
AMICAS INC; Boston
ANALOGIC CORP; Peabody
ARQULE INC; Woburn
ASPECT MEDICAL SYSTEMS INC; Newton
ATHENAHEALTH INC; Watertown
BIOGEN IDEC INC; Cambridge
BLUE CROSS AND BLUE SHIELD OF MASSACHUSETTS; Boston
BOSTON SCIENTIFIC CORP; Natick
CANDELA CORP; Wayland
GENZYME CORP; Cambridge
GSI GROUP INC; Billerica
GTC BIOTHERAPEUTICS INC; Framingham
HAEMONETICS CORPORATION; Braintree
HARVARD PILGRIM HEALTH CARE INC; Wellesley
HOLOGIC INC; Bedford
INVERNESS MEDICAL INNOVATIONS INC; Waltham
MEDICAL INFORMATION TECHNOLOGY INC; Westwood
MILLENNIUM PHARMACEUTICALS INC; Cambridge
NATIONAL DENTEX CORP; Wayland
NMT MEDICAL INC; Boston
ORGANOGENESIS INC; Canton
PALOMAR MEDICAL TECHNOLOGIES INC; Burlington
PARTNERS HEALTHCARE SYSTEM; Boston
PERKINELMER INC; Waltham
POLYMEDICA CORPORATION; Wakefield
SEPRACOR INC; Marlborough
THERMO FISHER SCIENTIFIC INC; Waltham
TUFTS ASSOCIATED HEALTH PLANS; Watertown
ZOLL MEDICAL CORP; Chelmsford

MICHIGAN
BLUE CARE NETWORK OF MICHIGAN; Southfield
BLUE CROSS AND BLUE SHIELD OF MICHIGAN; Detroit
DETROIT MEDICAL CENTER; Detroit
HENRY FORD HEALTH SYSTEMS; Detroit
NANOBIO CORPORATION; Ann Arbor
SPECTRUM HEALTH; Grand Rapids
STRYKER CORP; Kalamazoo
TRINITY HEALTH COMPANY; Novi

MINNESOTA
3M COMPANY; St. Paul
ALLINA HOSPITALS AND CLINICS; Minneapolis
AMERICAN MEDICAL SYSTEMS HOLDINGS INC; Minnetonka
ATS MEDICAL INC; Minneapolis
BLUE CROSS AND BLUE SHIELD OF MINNESOTA; Eagan
CIGNA BEHAVIORAL HEALTH; Eden Prairie
EMPI INC; St. Paul

FAIRVIEW HEALTH SERVICES; Minneapolis
LIFECORE BIOMEDICAL INC; Chaska
MAYO FOUNDATION FOR MEDICAL EDUCATION AND RESEARCH; Rochester
MEDTRONIC INC; Minneapolis
MINNTECH CORP; Minneapolis
MINUTECLINIC; Minneapolis
PATTERSON COMPANIES INC; St. Paul
ST JUDE MEDICAL INC; St. Paul
SYNOVIS LIFE TECHNOLOGIES INC; St. Paul
TECHNE CORP; Minneapolis
UNITEDHEALTH GROUP INC; Minnetonka
UNIVERSAL HOSPITAL SERVICES INC; Edina

MISSOURI

ASCENSION HEALTH; St. Louis
ASSURANT EMPLOYEE BENEFITS; Kansas City
BJC HEALTHCARE; St. Louis
CENTENE CORPORATION; St. Louis
CERNER CORP; Kansas City
EXPRESS SCRIPTS INC; Maryland Heights
MALLINCKRODT INC; Hazelwood
REHABCARE GROUP INC; St. Louis
SIGMA ALDRICH CORP; St. Louis
SISTERS OF MERCY HEALTH SYSTEMS; Chesterfield
SSM HEALTH CARE SYSTEM INC; St. Louis
YOUNG INNOVATIONS INC; Earth City

MONTANA

BLUE CROSS AND BLUE SHIELD OF MONTANA; Helena

NEBRASKA

BLUE CROSS AND BLUE SHIELD OF NEBRASKA; Omaha

NEVADA

EMERGENCY FILTRATION PRODUCTS INC; Las Vegas
SIERRA HEALTH SERVICES INC; Las Vegas

NEW HAMPSHIRE

CRITICAL CARE SYSTEMS; Nashua

NEW JERSEY

ALPHARMA INC; Bridgewater
BECTON DICKINSON & CO; Franklin Lakes
BIO REFERENCE LABORATORIES INC; Elmwood Park
CAMBREX CORP; E. Rutherford
CANTEL MEDICAL CORP; Little Falls
CONVATEC; Skillman
COVANCE INC; Princeton
CR BARD INC; Murray Hill
DATASCOPE CORP; Montvale
ETHICON INC; Somerville
HLTH CORP; Elmwood Park
HOOPER HOLMES INC; Basking Ridge
HORIZON HEALTHCARE SERVICES INC; Newark
INTEGRA LIFESCIENCES HOLDINGS CORP; Plainsboro
INVENTIV HEALTH INC; Somerset
JOHNSON & JOHNSON; New Brunswick
LIFECELL CORPORATION; Branchburg
MEDCO HEALTH SOLUTIONS; Franklin Lakes
MERCK & CO INC; Whitehouse Station
OSTEOTECH INC; Eatontown
PAR PHARMACEUTICAL COMPANIES INC; Woodcliff Lake
PDI INC; Saddle River
PHARMACOPEIA DRUG DISCOVERY; Cranbury
QUEST DIAGNOSTICS INC; Lyndhurst
SCHERING-PLOUGH CORP; Kenilworth
VITAL SIGNS INC; Totowa
WARNER CHILCOTT PLC; Rockaway
WYETH; Madison

NEW MEXICO

SUN HEALTHCARE GROUP; Albuquerque

NEW YORK

ALLIED HEALTHCARE INTERNATIONAL INC; New York
ASSURANT INC; New York
ATC HEALTHCARE INC; Lake Success
BARR PHARMACEUTICALS INC; Pomona
BAUSCH & LOMB INC; Rochester
BIOPHAN TECHNOLOGIES INC; Pittsford
BIOSCRIP INC; Elmsford
BRISTOL MYERS SQUIBB CO; New York
CONMED CORP; Utica
DUANE READE INC; New York
EMERGING VISION INC; Garden City
EXCEL TECHNOLOGY INC; East Setauket
E-Z-EM INC; Lake Success
FOREST LABORATORIES INC; New York
GENTIVA HEALTH SERVICES INC; Melville
GROUP HEALTH INCORPORATED; New York
HEALTH INSURANCE PLAN OF GREATER NEW YORK; New York
HEALTH MANAGEMENT SYSTEMS INC; New York
HEALTHNOW NEW YORK; Buffalo
HENRY SCHEIN INC; Melville
INTEGRAMED AMERICA INC; Purchase
LAKELAND INDUSTRIES INC; Ronkonkoma
LIFETIME HEALTHCARE COMPANIES (THE); Rochester
MARSH & MCLENNAN COMPANIES INC; New York
MEDICAL ACTION INDUSTRIES INC; Hauppauge
MEMORIAL SLOAN KETTERING CANCER CENTER; New York
MERCER INC; New York
MISONIX INC; Farmingdale
NATIONAL HOME HEALTH CARE CORP; Scarsdale
NATIONAL MEDICAL HEALTH CARD SYSTEMS INC; Port Washington
NEW YORK CITY HEALTH AND HOSPITALS CORPORATION; New York
NEW YORK HEALTH CARE INC; Brooklyn
NEW YORK-PRESBYTERIAN HEALTHCARE SYSTEM; New York
PFIZER INC; New York
REGENERON PHARMACEUTICALS INC; Tarrytown
SCHICK TECHNOLOGIES INC; Long Island City
WEBMD HEALTH CORP; New York
WEIGHT WATCHERS INTERNATIONAL INC; New York
WELCH ALLYN INC; Skaneateles Falls

NORTH CAROLINA

BLUE CROSS AND BLUE SHIELD OF NORTH CAROLINA; Durham
LABORATORY CORP OF AMERICA HOLDINGS; Burlington
MEDCATH CORPORATION; Charlotte
OPTICARE HEALTH SYSTEMS; Rocky Mount
PHARMACEUTICAL PRODUCT DEVELOPMENT INC; Wilmington
QUINTILES TRANSNATIONAL CORP; Durham

OHIO

CARDINAL HEALTH INC; Dublin
CATHOLIC HEALTHCARE PARTNERS; Cincinnati
CHEMED CORPORATION; Cincinnati
EYEMED VISION CARE LLC; Mason
HITACHI MEDICAL SYSTEMS AMERICA; Twinsburg
INVACARE CORP; Elyria
KENDLE INTERNATIONAL INC; Cincinnati
LCA-VISION INC; Cincinnati
MANOR CARE INC; Toledo
MEDICAL MUTUAL OF OHIO; Cleveland
MERIDIAN BIOSCIENCE INC; Cincinnati
OHIOHEALTH CORPORATION; Columbus

STERIS CORP; Mentor

OKLAHOMA

BLUE CROSS AND BLUE SHIELD OF OKLAHOMA; Tulsa
MARIAN HEALTH SYSTEMS; Tulsa

OREGON

REGENCE GROUP (THE); Portland

PENNSYLVANIA

AMERISOURCEBERGEN CORP; Chesterbrook
ARROW INTERNATIONAL INC; Reading
BAYER CORP; Pittsburgh
BROOKS ECKERD; Warwick
CAPITAL BLUECROSS; Harrisburg
CEPHALON INC; Frazer
CIGNA CORP; Philadelphia
DENTSPLY INTERNATIONAL INC; York
ENDO PHARMACEUTICALS HOLDINGS INC; Chadds Ford
ENVIRONMENTAL TECTONICS CORP; Southampton
GNC CORPORATION; Pittsburgh
HIGHMARK INC; Pittsburgh
JEFFERSON HEALTH SYSTEM INC; Radnor
MINE SAFETY APPLIANCES CO; Pittsburgh
MYLAN LABORATORIES INC; Canonsburg
OUTLOOK POINTE CORP; Mechanicsburg
RESPIRONICS INC; Murrysville
RITE AID CORPORATION; Camp Hill
TAKE CARE HEALTH SYSTEMS LLC; Conshohocken
TELEFLEX INC; Limerick
UNIVERSAL HEALTH SERVICES INC; King of Prussia
WEST PHARMACEUTICAL SERVICES INC; Lionville
ZLB BEHRING LLC; King of Prussia

RHODE ISLAND

CVS CAREMARK CORPORATION; Woonsocket

SOUTH CAROLINA

SPAN AMERICA MEDICAL SYSTEMS INC; Greenville

SOUTH DAKOTA

AVERA HEALTH; Sioux Falls

TENNESSEE

ACCREDO HEALTH GROUP INC; Memphis
ADVOCAT INC; Brentwood
AMERICA SERVICE GROUP INC; Brentwood
AMERICAN HOMEPATIENT INC; Brentwood
AMERICAN RETIREMENT CORP; Brentwood
AMSURG CORP; Nashville
BLUE CROSS AND BLUE SHIELD OF TENNESSEE INC; Chattanooga
CAREMARK RX INC; Nashville
COMMUNITY HEALTH SYSTEMS INC; Brentwood
HCA INC; Nashville
HEALTHSTREAM INC; Nashville
HEALTHWAYS INC; Nashville
LIFE CARE CENTERS OF AMERICA; Cleveland
LIFEPOINT HOSPITALS INC; Brentwood
MEDTRONIC SOFAMOR DANEK; Memphis
NATIONAL HEALTHCARE CORP; Murfreesboro
PSYCHIATRIC SOLUTIONS INC; Franklin
ST JUDE CHILDRENS RESEARCH HOSPITAL; Memphis
TEAM HEALTH; Knoxville
WRIGHT MEDICAL GROUP INC; Arlington

TEXAS

ADVANCED NEUROMODULATION SYSTEMS; Plano
ARTHROCARE CORP; Austin
ATRION CORPORATION; Allen
AVIDYN; Dallas
BLUE CROSS AND BLUE SHIELD OF TEXAS; Richardson
CAPITAL SENIOR LIVING CORP; Dallas
CASTLE DENTAL CENTERS INC; Houston
CHRISTUS HEALTH; Irving
CONCENTRA INC; Addison
CYBERONICS INC; Houston
DYNACQ HEALTHCARE INC; Houston
HEALTHAXIS INC; Irving
HEALTHTRONICS INC; Austin
HORIZON HEALTH CORPORATION; Lewisville
KIMBERLY CLARK CORP; Irving
KINETIC CONCEPTS INC; San Antonio
MEMORIAL HERMANN HEALTHCARE SYSTEM; Houston
NOVATION LLC (VHA INC); Irving
ODYSSEY HEALTHCARE INC; Dallas
QUOVADX INC; Dallas
REABLE THERAPEUTICS INC; Austin
TENET HEALTHCARE CORPORATION; Dallas
TEXAS HEALTH RESOURCES; Arlington
TRIAD HOSPITALS INC; Plano
UNITED SURGICAL PARTNERS; Addison
US ONCOLOGY INC; Houston
US PHYSICAL THERAPY INC; Houston

UTAH

INTERMOUNTAIN HEALTH CARE; Salt Lake City
MERIT MEDICAL SYSTEMS INC; South Jordan
SONIC INNOVATIONS INC; Salt Lake City
UTAH MEDICAL PRODUCTS INC; Midvale

VIRGINIA

AMERICHOICE CORPORATION; Vienna
AMERIGROUP CORPORATION; Virginia Beach
OWENS & MINOR INC; Mechanicsville
SENTARA HEALTHCARE; Norfolk
SUNRISE SENIOR LIVING; McLean

VERMONT

BLUE CROSS AND BLUE SHIELD OF VERMONT; Berlin

WASHINGTON

EMERITUS CORP; Seattle
FIRST CHOICE HEALTH NETWORK INC; Seattle
GROUP HEALTH COOPERATIVE OF PUGET SOUND; Seattle
PHILIPS MEDICAL SYSTEMS; Bothell
PREMERA BLUE CROSS; Mountlake Terrace
PROVIDENCE HEALTH & SERVICES; Seattle

WISCONSIN

ASSURANT HEALTH; Milwaukee
CRITICARE SYSTEMS INC; Waukesha
EPIC SYSTEMS CORPORATION; Verona
FISERV INC; Brookfield

WYOMING

BLUE CROSS AND BLUE SHIELD OF WYOMING; Cheyenne

INDEX OF NON-U.S. HEADQUARTERS LOCATION BY COUNTRY

AUSTRALIA
ANSELL LIMITED COMPANY; Richmond
CSL LIMITED; Parkville

BERMUDA
COVIDIEN LTD; Pembroke

CANADA
AETERNA ZENTARIS INC; Quebec
ART ADVANCED RESEARCH TECHNOLOGIES; Saint-Laurent
ATS AUTOMATION TOOLING SYSTEMS INC; Cambridge
BIOVAIL CORPORATION; Mississauga
CEDARA SOFTWARE CORP; Mississauga
EXTENDICARE REAL ESTATE INVESTMENT TRUST; Markham
JEAN COUTU GROUP INC (THE); Longueil
MDS INC; Mississauga
MIV THERAPEUTICS INC; Vancouver
TLC VISION CORPORATION; Mississauga

CHINA
3SBIO INC; Shenyang
MINDRAY MEDICAL INTERNATIONAL LIMITED; Nanshan
SIMCERE PHARMACEUTICAL GROUP; Nanjing

DENMARK
NOVO-NORDISK AS; Basgvaerd

FRANCE
ESSILOR INTERNATIONAL SA; Charenton-le-Pont
SANOFI-AVENTIS; Paris

GERMANY
BAYER AG; Leverkusen
BAYER SCHERING PHARMA AG; Berlin
FRESENIUS AG; Bas Homburg
FRESENIUS MEDICAL CARE AG; Bad Homburg
SIEMENS AG; Munich
SIEMENS MEDICAL SOLUTIONS; Erlangen

IRELAND
ELAN CORP PLC; Dublin

ISRAEL
LUMENIS LTD; Yokneam
SHL TELEMEDICINE LTD; Tel Aviv
TEVA PHARMACEUTICAL INDUSTRIES; Petach Tikva

ITALY
LUXOTTICA GROUP SPA; Milan
ORTHOFIX INTERNATIONAL NV; Bussolengo

JAPAN
ASTELLAS PHARMA INC; Tokyo
HITACHI MEDICAL CORPORATION; Tokyo
TAKEDA PHARMACEUTICAL COMPANY LTD; Osaka
TOSHIBA CORPORATION; Tokyo

SWEDEN
GAMBRO AB; Stockholm
MOLNLYCKE HEALTH CARE GROUP AB; Goteborg

SWITZERLAND
ACTELION LTD; Allschwil
ALCON INC; Hunenberg
INSTITUT STRAUMANN AG; Basel
MERCK SERONO SA; Geneva
METTLER-TOLEDO INTERNATIONAL; Greifensee
NOVARTIS AG; Basel
ROCHE HOLDING LTD; Basel

THE NETHERLANDS
AKZO NOBEL NV; Arnhem

UNITED KINGDOM
ASTRAZENECA PLC; London
AXA PPP HEALTHCARE; Tunbridge Wells
BESPAK PLC; Wolverton Mill South
BRITISH UNITED PROVIDENT ASSOCIATION (BUPA); London
GE HEALTHCARE; Chalfont St. Giles
GLAXOSMITHKLINE PLC; Middlesex
GYRUS GROUP PLC; Cardiff
SHIRE PLC; Basingstoke
SMITH & NEPHEW PLC; London
SMITHS GROUP PLC; London
SSL INTERNATIONAL PLC; London

INDEX BY REGIONS OF THE U.S. WHERE THE HEALTH CARE 500 FIRMS HAVE LOCATIONS

WEST
3M COMPANY
ABBOTT LABORATORIES
ADVANCED BIONICS CORPORATION
ADVANCED MEDICAL OPTICS INC
ADVENTIST HEALTH SYSTEM
AETNA INC
AFLAC INC
ALCON INC
ALIGN TECHNOLOGY INC
ALLERGAN INC
ALLIANCE IMAGING INC
ALLSCRIPTS HEALTHCARE SOLUTIONS INC
ALPHARMA INC
AMERICAN HOMEPATIENT INC
AMERICAN MEDICAL SYSTEMS HOLDINGS INC
AMERICAN RETIREMENT CORP
AMERICHOICE CORPORATION
AMERIPATH INC
AMERISOURCEBERGEN CORP
AMGEN INC
AMICAS INC
AMSURG CORP
AON CORPORATION
APPLERA CORPORATION
APRIA HEALTHCARE GROUP INC
ARADIGM CORPORATION
ARTHROCARE CORP
ASCENSION HEALTH
ASSURANT EMPLOYEE BENEFITS
ASTRAZENECA PLC
ATC HEALTHCARE INC
ATRIA SENIOR LIVING GROUP
ATS AUTOMATION TOOLING SYSTEMS INC
ATS MEDICAL INC
BANNER HEALTH
BAUSCH & LOMB INC
BAXTER INTERNATIONAL INC
BAYER AG
BAYER CORP
BAYER SCHERING PHARMA AG
BECKMAN COULTER INC
BECTON DICKINSON & CO
BIO RAD LABORATORIES INC
BIOGEN IDEC INC
BIOMET INC
BIOSCRIP INC
BIOSITE INC
BLUE CROSS AND BLUE SHIELD ASSOCIATION
BLUE CROSS AND BLUE SHIELD OF MONTANA
BLUE CROSS AND BLUE SHIELD OF WYOMING
BLUE CROSS OF CALIFORNIA

BLUE CROSS OF IDAHO
BLUE SHIELD OF CALIFORNIA
BOSTON SCIENTIFIC CORP
BRIGHT NOW! DENTAL INC
BRISTOL MYERS SQUIBB CO
BROOKDALE SENIOR LIVING INC
CANTEL MEDICAL CORP
CAPITAL SENIOR LIVING CORP
CARDINAL HEALTH INC
CARDIOGENESIS CORP
CAREMARK RX INC
CASTLE DENTAL CENTERS INC
CATHOLIC HEALTH INITIATIVES
CATHOLIC HEALTHCARE WEST
CELERA GENOMICS GROUP
CELL GENESYS INC
CENTENE CORPORATION
CEPHALON INC
CERNER CORP
CHEMED CORPORATION
CHIRON CORP
CHOLESTECH CORP
CHRISTUS HEALTH
CIGNA CORP
CIVCO MEDICAL SOLUTIONS
COHERENT INC
COMMUNITY HEALTH SYSTEMS INC
CONCENTRA INC
CONMED CORP
COOPER COMPANIES INC
CORDIS CORP
CORVEL CORP
COVANCE INC
CR BARD INC
CRITICAL CARE SYSTEMS
CURASCRIPT INC
CVS CAREMARK CORPORATION
DADE BEHRING HOLDINGS INC
DANAHER CORP
DAVITA INC
DELTA DENTAL PLANS ASSOCIATION
DENTAL BENEFITS PROVIDERS
DENTSPLY INTERNATIONAL INC
DEPUY INC
DJO INC
ECLIPSYS CORPORATION
EDWARDS LIFESCIENCES CORP
ELAN CORP PLC
ELI LILLY AND COMPANY
EMERGENCY FILTRATION PRODUCTS INC
EMERGING VISION INC
EMERITUS CORP
ESSILOR INTERNATIONAL SA
EXCEL TECHNOLOGY INC
EXPRESS SCRIPTS INC
EXTENDICARE REAL ESTATE INVESTMENT TRUST
FIRST CHOICE HEALTH NETWORK INC
FIRST CONSULTING GROUP INC
FIRST HEALTH GROUP CORP
FISERV INC
FRESENIUS AG
FRESENIUS MEDICAL CARE AG
GAMBRO AB
GENENTECH INC
GENTIVA HEALTH SERVICES INC
GENZYME CORP
GISH BIOMEDICAL INC
GLAXOSMITHKLINE PLC
GLOBAL HEALTHCARE EXCHANGE
GNC CORPORATION
GROUP HEALTH COOPERATIVE OF PUGET SOUND
GSI GROUP INC
HANGER ORTHOPEDIC GROUP INC
HARBORSIDE HEALTHCARE CORP
HARVARD PILGRIM HEALTH CARE INC
HCA INC
HEALTH CARE SERVICE CORPORATION
HEALTH GRADES INC
HEALTH MANAGEMENT ASSOCIATES INC
HEALTH MANAGEMENT SYSTEMS INC
HEALTH NET INC
HEALTHSOUTH CORP
HEALTHSTREAM INC
HEALTHWAYS INC
HEARUSA INC
HEMACARE CORPORATION
HENRY SCHEIN INC
HILL-ROM COMPANY INC
HOLOGIC INC
HOOPER HOLMES INC
HORIZON HEALTH CORPORATION
HOSPIRA INC
HUMANA INC
I FLOW CORPORATION
ICU MEDICAL INC
IDEXX LABORATORIES INC
IMS HEALTH INC
INAMED CORP
INCYTE CORP
INTEGRA LIFESCIENCES HOLDINGS CORP
INTEGRAMED AMERICA INC
INTERMOUNTAIN HEALTH CARE
INTUITIVE SURGICAL INC
INVACARE CORP
INVENTIV HEALTH INC
INVERNESS MEDICAL INNOVATIONS INC
IRIDEX CORP
IRIS INTERNATIONAL INC
JENNY CRAIG INC
JOHNSON & JOHNSON
KAISER PERMANENTE
KIMBERLY CLARK CORP
KINDRED HEALTHCARE INC
KYPHON INC
LABORATORY CORP OF AMERICA HOLDINGS
LASERSCOPE
LCA-VISION INC
LIFE CARE CENTERS OF AMERICA
LIFEPOINT HOSPITALS INC
LIFESCAN INC
LOGISTICARE INC
LONGS DRUG STORES CORPORATION
LUMENIS LTD
LUXOTTICA GROUP SPA
MAGELLAN HEALTH SERVICES INC
MALLINCKRODT INC
MANOR CARE INC
MARSH & MCLENNAN COMPANIES INC
MATRIA HEALTHCARE INC
MAXYGEN INC
MCKESSON CORPORATION
MDS INC
MEDAVANT HEALTHCARE SOLUTIONS
MEDCATH CORPORATION
MEDCO HEALTH SOLUTIONS
MEDICAL ACTION INDUSTRIES INC
MEDTRONIC CARDIOVASCULAR
MEDTRONIC INC
MEDTRONIC MINIMED INC
MEDTRONIC XOMED SURGICAL PRODUCTS INC
MENTOR CORP
MERCER INC
MERCK & CO INC
MERIT MEDICAL SYSTEMS INC
METTLER-TOLEDO INTERNATIONAL
MILLENNIUM PHARMACEUTICALS INC
MINE SAFETY APPLIANCES CO
MINNTECH CORP
MINUTECLINIC
MISONIX INC
MOLINA HEALTHCARE INC
MOORE MEDICAL CORP
NATIONAL DENTEX CORP
NATIONAL MEDICAL HEALTH CARD SYSTEMS INC
NEKTAR THERAPEUTICS
NEUROCRINE BIOSCIENCES INC
NOVAMED INC
NOVARTIS AG
NOVATION LLC (VHA INC)
NOVO-NORDISK AS
NYER MEDICAL GROUP INC
ODYSSEY HEALTHCARE INC
OMNICARE INC
OPTION CARE INC
ORTHOFIX INTERNATIONAL NV
OWENS & MINOR INC
PACIFICARE HEALTH SYSTEMS INC
PATTERSON COMPANIES INC
PEDIATRIC SERVICES OF AMERICA INC
PEDIATRIX MEDICAL GROUP INC
PERKINELMER INC
PFIZER INC
PHARMACEUTICAL PRODUCT DEVELOPMENT INC
PHARMERICA CORP
PHILIPS MEDICAL SYSTEMS

PREMERA BLUE CROSS
PREMIER INC
PROVIDENCE HEALTH & SERVICES
PROXYMED INC
PSS WORLD MEDICAL INC
PSYCHIATRIC SOLUTIONS INC
QUALITY SYSTEMS INC
QUEST DIAGNOSTICS INC
QUIDEL CORP
QUINTILES TRANSNATIONAL CORP
QUOVADX INC
RADNET INC
REGENCE GROUP (THE)
REHABCARE GROUP INC
RES CARE INC
RESMED INC
RESPIRONICS INC
RITE AID CORPORATION
ROCHE HOLDING LTD
ROTECH HEALTHCARE INC
SAFEGUARD HEALTH ENTERPRISES INC
SANOFI-AVENTIS
SCHERING-PLOUGH CORP
SIEMENS AG
SIEMENS MEDICAL SOLUTIONS DIAGNOSTICS
SIERRA HEALTH SERVICES INC
SIGNATURE EYEWEAR INC
SKILLED HEALTHCARE GROUP INC
SMITHS GROUP PLC
SOLUCIENT LLC
SONIC INNOVATIONS INC
SPAN AMERICA MEDICAL SYSTEMS INC
SPECIALTY LABORATORIES INC
SPECTRANETICS CORP
SRI/SURGICAL EXPRESS INC
ST JUDE MEDICAL INC
STAAR SURGICAL CO
STERICYCLE INC
STERIS CORP
STRYKER CORP
SUN HEALTHCARE GROUP
SUNRISE MEDICAL INC
SUNRISE SENIOR LIVING
SUTTER HEALTH
SYBRON DENTAL SPECIALTIES INC
TAKE CARE HEALTH SYSTEMS LLC
TAKEDA PHARMACEUTICAL COMPANY LTD
TEAM HEALTH
TELEFLEX INC
TENET HEALTHCARE CORPORATION
TEVA PHARMACEUTICAL INDUSTRIES
THERAGENICS CORP
THERMO FISHER SCIENTIFIC INC
THORATEC CORPORATION
TLC VISION CORPORATION
TOSHIBA CORPORATION
TOWERS PERRIN
TRANSCEND SERVICES INC
TRIAD HOSPITALS INC
TRINITY HEALTH COMPANY
TRUSTMARK COMPANIES
UNITED SURGICAL PARTNERS
UNITEDHEALTH GROUP INC
UNIVERSAL HEALTH SERVICES INC
UNIVERSAL HOSPITAL SERVICES INC
US ONCOLOGY INC
US PHYSICAL THERAPY INC
UTAH MEDICAL PRODUCTS INC
VALEANT PHARMACEUTICALS INTERNATIONAL
VARIAN MEDICAL SYSTEMS INC
VCA ANTECH INC
VISION SERVICE PLAN
WALGREEN CO
WATSON PHARMACEUTICALS INC
WEIGHT WATCHERS INTERNATIONAL INC
WELCH ALLYN INC
WELLPOINT INC
WYETH
YOUNG INNOVATIONS INC
ZIMMER HOLDINGS INC
ZOLL MEDICAL CORP

SOUTHWEST

3M COMPANY
ABBOTT LABORATORIES
ADVANCED NEUROMODULATION SYSTEMS
ADVENTIST HEALTH SYSTEM
ADVOCAT INC
AETNA INC
AFLAC INC
ALCON INC
ALLERGAN INC
ALLIANCE IMAGING INC
ALLSCRIPTS HEALTHCARE SOLUTIONS INC
ALPHARMA INC
AMEDISYS INC
AMERICAN HOMEPATIENT INC
AMERICAN MEDICAL SYSTEMS HOLDINGS INC
AMERICAN RETIREMENT CORP
AMERICHOICE CORPORATION
AMERIGROUP CORPORATION
AMERIPATH INC
AMERISOURCEBERGEN CORP
AMSURG CORP
AON CORPORATION
APRIA HEALTHCARE GROUP INC
ARKANSAS BLUE CROSS AND BLUE SHIELD
ARTHROCARE CORP
ASCENSION HEALTH
ASSURANT EMPLOYEE BENEFITS
ASTELLAS PHARMA INC
ASTRAZENECA PLC
ATC HEALTHCARE INC
ATRIA SENIOR LIVING GROUP
ATRION CORPORATION
ATS AUTOMATION TOOLING SYSTEMS INC
AVIDYN
BANNER HEALTH
BAXTER INTERNATIONAL INC
BAYER AG
BAYER CORP
BECKMAN COULTER INC
BECTON DICKINSON & CO
BIO RAD LABORATORIES INC
BIOMET INC
BIOSCRIP INC
BLUE CROSS AND BLUE SHIELD ASSOCIATION
BLUE CROSS AND BLUE SHIELD OF OKLAHOMA
BLUE CROSS AND BLUE SHIELD OF TEXAS
BOSTON SCIENTIFIC CORP
BRIGHT NOW! DENTAL INC
BRISTOL MYERS SQUIBB CO
BROOKDALE SENIOR LIVING INC
CAPITAL SENIOR LIVING CORP
CARDINAL HEALTH INC
CAREMARK RX INC
CASTLE DENTAL CENTERS INC
CATHOLIC HEALTH INITIATIVES
CATHOLIC HEALTHCARE WEST
CENTENE CORPORATION
CERNER CORP
CHEMED CORPORATION
CHRISTUS HEALTH
CIGNA CORP
COMMUNITY HEALTH SYSTEMS INC
CONCENTRA INC
CONMED CORP
CORVEL CORP
COVANCE INC
CR BARD INC
CRITICAL CARE SYSTEMS
CURASCRIPT INC
CVS CAREMARK CORPORATION
CYBERONICS INC
DANAHER CORP
DELTA DENTAL PLANS ASSOCIATION
DENTAL BENEFITS PROVIDERS
DENTSPLY INTERNATIONAL INC
DEPUY INC
DYNACQ HEALTHCARE INC
ECLIPSYS CORPORATION
ELI LILLY AND COMPANY
EMERITUS CORP
ESSILOR INTERNATIONAL SA
ETHICON INC
EXPRESS SCRIPTS INC
EXTENDICARE REAL ESTATE INVESTMENT TRUST
FIRST CONSULTING GROUP INC
FIRST HEALTH GROUP CORP
FISERV INC
FRESENIUS MEDICAL CARE AG
GENTIVA HEALTH SERVICES INC
GENZYME CORP
GLAXOSMITHKLINE PLC
GLOBAL HEALTHCARE EXCHANGE
GNC CORPORATION

HANGER ORTHOPEDIC GROUP INC
HCA INC
HEALTH CARE SERVICE CORPORATION
HEALTH MANAGEMENT ASSOCIATES INC
HEALTH MANAGEMENT SYSTEMS INC
HEALTH NET INC
HEALTHAXIS INC
HEALTHSOUTH CORP
HEALTHTRONICS INC
HEALTHWAYS INC
HENRY SCHEIN INC
HLTH CORP
HOOPER HOLMES INC
HORIZON HEALTH CORPORATION
HOSPIRA INC
HUMANA INC
IDEXX LABORATORIES INC
INTEGRAMED AMERICA INC
INVACARE CORP
INVENTIV HEALTH INC
IRIDEX CORP
IRIS INTERNATIONAL INC
JENNY CRAIG INC
JOHNSON & JOHNSON
KIMBERLY CLARK CORP
KINDRED HEALTHCARE INC
KINETIC CONCEPTS INC
LABORATORY CORP OF AMERICA HOLDINGS
LASERSCOPE
LCA-VISION INC
LIFE CARE CENTERS OF AMERICA
LIFEPOINT HOSPITALS INC
LOGISTICARE INC
LUXOTTICA GROUP SPA
MAGELLAN HEALTH SERVICES INC
MANOR CARE INC
MARIAN HEALTH SYSTEMS
MARSH & MCLENNAN COMPANIES INC
MATRIA HEALTHCARE INC
MAYO FOUNDATION FOR MEDICAL EDUCATION AND RESEARCH
MCKESSON CORPORATION
MDS INC
MEDCATH CORPORATION
MEDCO HEALTH SOLUTIONS
MEDTRONIC INC
MEDTRONIC MINIMED INC
MEDTRONIC XOMED SURGICAL PRODUCTS INC
MEMORIAL HERMANN HEALTHCARE SYSTEM
MENTOR CORP
MERCER INC
MERCK & CO INC
MICROTEK MEDICAL HOLDINGS INC
MINNTECH CORP
MINUTECLINIC
MOLINA HEALTHCARE INC
MOORE MEDICAL CORP
MYLAN LABORATORIES INC
NATIONAL DENTEX CORP
NATIONAL MEDICAL HEALTH CARD SYSTEMS INC
NOVAMED INC
NOVATION LLC (VHA INC)
NOVO-NORDISK AS
ODYSSEY HEALTHCARE INC
OMNICARE INC
OPTION CARE INC
OWENS & MINOR INC
PACIFICARE HEALTH SYSTEMS INC
PATTERSON COMPANIES INC
PEDIATRIC SERVICES OF AMERICA INC
PEDIATRIX MEDICAL GROUP INC
PFIZER INC
PHARMERICA CORP
POLYMEDICA CORPORATION
PROXYMED INC
PSS WORLD MEDICAL INC
PSYCHIATRIC SOLUTIONS INC
QUEST DIAGNOSTICS INC
QUINTILES TRANSNATIONAL CORP
QUOVADX INC
RADNET INC
REABLE THERAPEUTICS INC
REHABCARE GROUP INC
RES CARE INC
RESPIRONICS INC
RITE AID CORPORATION
ROCHE HOLDING LTD
ROTECH HEALTHCARE INC
SAFEGUARD HEALTH ENTERPRISES INC
SANOFI-AVENTIS
SCHERING-PLOUGH CORP
SIEMENS AG
SIERRA HEALTH SERVICES INC
SISTERS OF MERCY HEALTH SYSTEMS
SKILLED HEALTHCARE GROUP INC
SMITHS GROUP PLC
SRI/SURGICAL EXPRESS INC
ST JUDE MEDICAL INC
STERICYCLE INC
STERIS CORP
STRYKER CORP
SUN HEALTHCARE GROUP
SUNRISE MEDICAL INC
SUNRISE SENIOR LIVING
TEAM HEALTH
TELEFLEX INC
TENET HEALTHCARE CORPORATION
TEVA PHARMACEUTICAL INDUSTRIES
TEXAS HEALTH RESOURCES
THERAGENICS CORP
TLC VISION CORPORATION
TOSHIBA CORPORATION
TOWERS PERRIN
TRANSCEND SERVICES INC
TRIAD HOSPITALS INC
TRUSTMARK COMPANIES
UNITED SURGICAL PARTNERS
UNITEDHEALTH GROUP INC
UNIVERSAL HEALTH SERVICES INC
UNIVERSAL HOSPITAL SERVICES INC
US ONCOLOGY INC
US PHYSICAL THERAPY INC
VCA ANTECH INC
VENTANA MEDICAL SYSTEMS INC
VISION SERVICE PLAN
WALGREEN CO
WEIGHT WATCHERS INTERNATIONAL INC
WELLPOINT INC
WEST PHARMACEUTICAL SERVICES INC
WYETH
YOUNG INNOVATIONS INC

MIDWEST

3M COMPANY
ABBOTT LABORATORIES
ACCREDO HEALTH GROUP INC
ADVENTIST HEALTH SYSTEM
ADVOCAT INC
ADVOCATE HEALTH CARE
AETNA INC
AFLAC INC
AKZO NOBEL NV
ALCON INC
ALLIANCE IMAGING INC
ALLINA HOSPITALS AND CLINICS
ALLSCRIPTS HEALTHCARE SOLUTIONS INC
ALPHARMA INC
AMEDISYS INC
AMERICAN HOMEPATIENT INC
AMERICAN MEDICAL SYSTEMS HOLDINGS INC
AMERICAN RETIREMENT CORP
AMERICHOICE CORPORATION
AMERIGROUP CORPORATION
AMERIPATH INC
AMERISOURCEBERGEN CORP
AMSURG CORP
ANALOGIC CORP
AON CORPORATION
APRIA HEALTHCARE GROUP INC
ARKANSAS BLUE CROSS AND BLUE SHIELD
ASCENSION HEALTH
ASSURANT EMPLOYEE BENEFITS
ASSURANT HEALTH
ASSURANT INC
ASTELLAS PHARMA INC
ASTRAZENECA PLC
ATC HEALTHCARE INC
ATRIA SENIOR LIVING GROUP
ATS AUTOMATION TOOLING SYSTEMS INC
ATS MEDICAL INC
AVERA HEALTH
AVIDYN
BANNER HEALTH
BARR PHARMACEUTICALS INC
BAUSCH & LOMB INC

BAXTER INTERNATIONAL INC
BAYER AG
BAYER CORP
BECKMAN COULTER INC
BECTON DICKINSON & CO
BIOMET INC
BIOSCRIP INC
BJC HEALTHCARE
BLUE CARE NETWORK OF MICHIGAN
BLUE CROSS AND BLUE SHIELD ASSOCIATION
BLUE CROSS AND BLUE SHIELD OF KANSAS
BLUE CROSS AND BLUE SHIELD OF MICHIGAN
BLUE CROSS AND BLUE SHIELD OF MINNESOTA
BLUE CROSS AND BLUE SHIELD OF NEBRASKA
BON SECOURS HEALTH SYSTEM INC
BOSTON SCIENTIFIC CORP
BRIGHT NOW! DENTAL INC
BRISTOL MYERS SQUIBB CO
BROOKDALE SENIOR LIVING INC
CAMBREX CORP
CANTEL MEDICAL CORP
CAPITAL SENIOR LIVING CORP
CARDINAL HEALTH INC
CAREMARK RX INC
CATHOLIC HEALTH INITIATIVES
CATHOLIC HEALTHCARE PARTNERS
CENTENE CORPORATION
CEPHALON INC
CERNER CORP
CHEMED CORPORATION
CHIRON CORP
CIGNA BEHAVIORAL HEALTH
CIGNA CORP
CIVCO MEDICAL SOLUTIONS
CLARIAN HEALTH PARTNERS INC
COMMUNITY HEALTH SYSTEMS INC
CONCENTRA INC
CORVEL CORP
COVANCE INC
CR BARD INC
CRITICAL CARE SYSTEMS
CRITICARE SYSTEMS INC
CSL LIMITED
CURASCRIPT INC
CVS CAREMARK CORPORATION
DADE BEHRING HOLDINGS INC
DANAHER CORP
DELTA DENTAL PLANS ASSOCIATION
DENTAL BENEFITS PROVIDERS
DENTSPLY INTERNATIONAL INC
DEPUY INC
DETROIT MEDICAL CENTER
DJO INC
ELI LILLY AND COMPANY
EMERGING VISION INC
EMERITUS CORP
EMPI INC
EPIC SYSTEMS CORPORATION
ESSILOR INTERNATIONAL SA
EXPRESS SCRIPTS INC
EXTENDICARE REAL ESTATE INVESTMENT TRUST
EYEMED VISION CARE LLC
FAIRVIEW HEALTH SERVICES
FAMILYMEDS GROUP INC
FIRST CONSULTING GROUP INC
FIRST HEALTH GROUP CORP
FISERV INC
FOREST LABORATORIES INC
FRESENIUS MEDICAL CARE AG
GAMBRO AB
GE HEALTHCARE
GENTIVA HEALTH SERVICES INC
GENZYME CORP
GLAXOSMITHKLINE PLC
GLOBAL HEALTHCARE EXCHANGE
GNC CORPORATION
GSI GROUP INC
GYRUS GROUP PLC
HANGER ORTHOPEDIC GROUP INC
HARBORSIDE HEALTHCARE CORP
HCA INC
HEALTH CARE SERVICE CORPORATION
HEALTH MANAGEMENT ASSOCIATES INC
HEALTH MANAGEMENT SYSTEMS INC
HEALTHSOUTH CORP
HEALTHWAYS INC
HEARUSA INC
HENRY FORD HEALTH SYSTEMS
HENRY SCHEIN INC
HILLENBRAND INDUSTRIES
HILL-ROM COMPANY INC
HITACHI MEDICAL CORPORATION
HITACHI MEDICAL SYSTEMS AMERICA
HLTH CORP
HOLOGIC INC
HOOPER HOLMES INC
HORIZON HEALTH CORPORATION
HOSPIRA INC
HUMANA INC
I FLOW CORPORATION
IDEXX LABORATORIES INC
INTEGRA LIFESCIENCES HOLDINGS CORP
INTEGRAMED AMERICA INC
INVACARE CORP
INVENTIV HEALTH INC
IRIDEX CORP
JENNY CRAIG INC
JOHNSON & JOHNSON
KAISER PERMANENTE
KENDLE INTERNATIONAL INC
KIMBERLY CLARK CORP
KINDRED HEALTHCARE INC
LABORATORY CORP OF AMERICA HOLDINGS
LAKELAND INDUSTRIES INC
LASERSCOPE
LCA-VISION INC
LIFE CARE CENTERS OF AMERICA
LIFECORE BIOMEDICAL INC
LIFEPOINT HOSPITALS INC
LOGISTICARE INC
LUXOTTICA GROUP SPA
MAGELLAN HEALTH SERVICES INC
MALLINCKRODT INC
MANOR CARE INC
MARIAN HEALTH SYSTEMS
MARSH & MCLENNAN COMPANIES INC
MATRIA HEALTHCARE INC
MAYO FOUNDATION FOR MEDICAL EDUCATION AND RESEARCH
MCKESSON CORPORATION
MDS INC
MEDAVANT HEALTHCARE SOLUTIONS
MEDCATH CORPORATION
MEDCO HEALTH SOLUTIONS
MEDICAL MUTUAL OF OHIO
MEDTRONIC INC
MEDTRONIC MINIMED INC
MEDTRONIC XOMED SURGICAL PRODUCTS INC
MENTOR CORP
MERCER INC
MERCK & CO INC
MERIDIAN MEDICAL TECHNOLOGIES INC
METTLER-TOLEDO INTERNATIONAL
MINE SAFETY APPLIANCES CO
MINNTECH CORP
MINUTECLINIC
MOLINA HEALTHCARE INC
MYLAN LABORATORIES INC
NANOBIO CORPORATION
NATIONAL DENTEX CORP
NATIONAL HEALTHCARE CORP
NOVAMED INC
NOVARTIS AG
NOVATION LLC (VHA INC)
NOVO-NORDISK AS
ODYSSEY HEALTHCARE INC
OHIOHEALTH CORPORATION
OMNICARE INC
OPTION CARE INC
OUTLOOK POINTE CORP
OWENS & MINOR INC
PATTERSON COMPANIES INC
PDI INC
PEDIATRIC SERVICES OF AMERICA INC
PEDIATRIX MEDICAL GROUP INC
PERKINELMER INC
PFIZER INC
PHARMACEUTICAL PRODUCT DEVELOPMENT INC
PHARMERICA CORP
POLYMEDICA CORPORATION
PREMIER INC
PROXYMED INC
PSS WORLD MEDICAL INC
PSYCHIATRIC SOLUTIONS INC
QUEST DIAGNOSTICS INC

QUINTILES TRANSNATIONAL CORP
RADNET INC
REHABCARE GROUP INC
RES CARE INC
RITE AID CORPORATION
ROCHE HOLDING LTD
ROTECH HEALTHCARE INC
SANOFI-AVENTIS
SCHERING-PLOUGH CORP
SHL TELEMEDICINE LTD
SIEMENS AG
SIGMA ALDRICH CORP
SISTERS OF MERCY HEALTH SYSTEMS
SKILLED HEALTHCARE GROUP INC
SMITHS GROUP PLC
SOLUCIENT LLC
SPECTRUM HEALTH
SRI/SURGICAL EXPRESS INC
SSM HEALTH CARE SYSTEM INC
ST JUDE MEDICAL INC
STERICYCLE INC
STERIS CORP
STRYKER CORP
SUN HEALTHCARE GROUP
SUNRISE MEDICAL INC
SUNRISE SENIOR LIVING
SYBRON DENTAL SPECIALTIES INC
SYMMETRY MEDICAL INC
SYNOVIS LIFE TECHNOLOGIES INC
TAKE CARE HEALTH SYSTEMS LLC
TAKEDA PHARMACEUTICAL COMPANY LTD
TEAM HEALTH
TECHNE CORP
TELEFLEX INC
TENET HEALTHCARE CORPORATION
TEVA PHARMACEUTICAL INDUSTRIES
THERMO FISHER SCIENTIFIC INC
THORATEC CORPORATION
TLC VISION CORPORATION
TOWERS PERRIN
TRIAD HOSPITALS INC
TRINITY HEALTH COMPANY
TRUSTMARK COMPANIES
UNITED SURGICAL PARTNERS
UNITEDHEALTH GROUP INC
UNIVERSAL HOSPITAL SERVICES INC
US ONCOLOGY INC
US PHYSICAL THERAPY INC
VCA ANTECH INC
VISION SERVICE PLAN
VITAL SIGNS INC
WALGREEN CO
WATSON PHARMACEUTICALS INC
WEIGHT WATCHERS INTERNATIONAL INC
WELCH ALLYN INC
WELLCARE GROUP OF COMPANIES
WELLPOINT INC
WEST PHARMACEUTICAL SERVICES INC
WYETH
YOUNG INNOVATIONS INC
ZIMMER HOLDINGS INC
ZLB BEHRING LLC

SOUTHEAST

3M COMPANY
ACCREDO HEALTH GROUP INC
ADVENTIST HEALTH SYSTEM
ADVOCAT INC
AETNA INC
AFLAC INC
AKZO NOBEL NV
ALCON INC
ALLIANCE IMAGING INC
ALPHARMA INC
AMEDISYS INC
AMERICA SERVICE GROUP INC
AMERICAN HOMEPATIENT INC
AMERICAN RETIREMENT CORP
AMERICHOICE CORPORATION
AMERIGROUP CORPORATION
AMERIPATH INC
AMERISOURCEBERGEN CORP
AMGEN INC
AMSURG CORP
AON CORPORATION
APRIA HEALTHCARE GROUP INC
ARKANSAS BLUE CROSS AND BLUE SHIELD
ASCENSION HEALTH
ASSURANT EMPLOYEE BENEFITS
ASSURANT HEALTH
ASSURANT INC
ASTRAZENECA PLC
ATC HEALTHCARE INC
ATRIA SENIOR LIVING GROUP
ATRION CORPORATION
AVMED HEALTH PLAN
BAUSCH & LOMB INC
BAXTER INTERNATIONAL INC
BAYER CORP
BECKMAN COULTER INC
BECTON DICKINSON & CO
BIOMET INC
BIOSCRIP INC
BLUE CROSS AND BLUE SHIELD ASSOCIATION
BLUE CROSS AND BLUE SHIELD OF FLORIDA
BLUE CROSS AND BLUE SHIELD OF GEORGIA INC
BLUE CROSS AND BLUE SHIELD OF LOUISIANA
BLUE CROSS AND BLUE SHIELD OF TENNESSEE INC
BON SECOURS HEALTH SYSTEM INC
BOSTON SCIENTIFIC CORP
BRIGHT NOW! DENTAL INC
BRISTOL MYERS SQUIBB CO
BROOKDALE SENIOR LIVING INC
BROOKS ECKERD
CANTEL MEDICAL CORP
CAPITAL SENIOR LIVING CORP
CARDINAL HEALTH INC
CAREFIRST INC
CAREMARK RX INC
CASTLE DENTAL CENTERS INC
CATHOLIC HEALTH INITIATIVES
CATHOLIC HEALTHCARE PARTNERS
CERNER CORP
CHEMED CORPORATION
CHRISTUS HEALTH
CIGNA CORP
CIVCO MEDICAL SOLUTIONS
COAST DENTAL SERVICES INC
COMMUNITY HEALTH SYSTEMS INC
CONCENTRA INC
CONMED CORP
CONTINUCARE CORP
CORDIS CORP
CORVEL CORP
COVANCE INC
CR BARD INC
CRITICAL CARE SYSTEMS
CRYOLIFE INC
CSL LIMITED
CURASCRIPT INC
CVS CAREMARK CORPORATION
DADE BEHRING HOLDINGS INC
DANAHER CORP
DAVITA INC
DELTA DENTAL PLANS ASSOCIATION
DENTAL BENEFITS PROVIDERS
DENTSPLY INTERNATIONAL INC
DEPUY INC
DIALYSIS CORPORATION OF AMERICA
DYNACQ HEALTHCARE INC
ECLIPSYS CORPORATION
ELAN CORP PLC
ELI LILLY AND COMPANY
EMERGING VISION INC
EMERITUS CORP
ESSILOR INTERNATIONAL SA
ETHICON INC
EXACTECH INC
EXCEL TECHNOLOGY INC
EXPRESS SCRIPTS INC
EXTENDICARE REAL ESTATE INVESTMENT TRUST
FAMILYMEDS GROUP INC
FIRST CONSULTING GROUP INC
FIRST HEALTH GROUP CORP
FISERV INC
FRESENIUS MEDICAL CARE AG
GAMBRO AB
GENTIVA HEALTH SERVICES INC
GENZYME CORP
GLAXOSMITHKLINE PLC
GLOBAL HEALTHCARE EXCHANGE
GNC CORPORATION
GYRUS GROUP PLC
HAEMONETICS CORPORATION
HANGER ORTHOPEDIC GROUP INC
HCA INC
HEALTH MANAGEMENT ASSOCIATES INC

HEALTH MANAGEMENT SYSTEMS INC
HEALTHSOUTH CORP
HEALTHSTREAM INC
HEALTHTRONICS INC
HEALTHWAYS INC
HEARUSA INC
HEMACARE CORPORATION
HENRY SCHEIN INC
HILLENBRAND INDUSTRIES
HLTH CORP
HOOPER HOLMES INC
HORIZON HEALTH CORPORATION
HOSPIRA INC
HUMANA INC
IDEXX LABORATORIES INC
IMMUCOR INC
INTEGRAMED AMERICA INC
INVACARE CORP
INVENTIV HEALTH INC
IRIDEX CORP
JENNY CRAIG INC
JOHNSON & JOHNSON
KAISER PERMANENTE
KIMBERLY CLARK CORP
KINDRED HEALTHCARE INC
LABORATORY CORP OF AMERICA HOLDINGS
LAKELAND INDUSTRIES INC
LASERSCOPE
LCA-VISION INC
LIFE CARE CENTERS OF AMERICA
LIFEPOINT HOSPITALS INC
LOGISTICARE INC
LUXOTTICA GROUP SPA
MAGELLAN HEALTH SERVICES INC
MANOR CARE INC
MATRIA HEALTHCARE INC
MAYO FOUNDATION FOR MEDICAL EDUCATION AND RESEARCH
MCKESSON CORPORATION
MDS INC
MEDAVANT HEALTHCARE SOLUTIONS
MEDCATH CORPORATION
MEDCO HEALTH SOLUTIONS
MEDTRONIC INC
MEDTRONIC MINIMED INC
MEDTRONIC SOFAMOR DANEK
MEDTRONIC XOMED SURGICAL PRODUCTS INC
MERCER INC
MERCK & CO INC
METROPOLITAN HEALTH NETWORKS
METTLER-TOLEDO INTERNATIONAL
MICROTEK MEDICAL HOLDINGS INC
MID ATLANTIC MEDICAL SERVICES INC
MINNTECH CORP
MINUTECLINIC
MIV THERAPEUTICS INC
MOLNLYCKE HEALTH CARE GROUP AB
MOORE MEDICAL CORP
MORRISON MANAGEMENT SPECIALISTS INC
NATIONAL DENTEX CORP
NATIONAL HEALTHCARE CORP
NATIONAL MEDICAL HEALTH CARD SYSTEMS INC
NEKTAR THERAPEUTICS
NOVAMED INC
NOVARTIS AG
NOVATION LLC (VHA INC)
NOVO-NORDISK AS
NYER MEDICAL GROUP INC
ODYSSEY HEALTHCARE INC
OMNICARE INC
OPTION CARE INC
ORTHOFIX INTERNATIONAL NV
OUTLOOK POINTE CORP
OWENS & MINOR INC
PATTERSON COMPANIES INC
PEDIATRIC SERVICES OF AMERICA INC
PEDIATRIX MEDICAL GROUP INC
PER-SE TECHNOLOGIES INC
PETMED EXPRESS INC
PFIZER INC
PHARMACEUTICAL PRODUCT DEVELOPMENT INC
PHARMERICA CORP
PHILIPS MEDICAL SYSTEMS
POLYMEDICA CORPORATION
PROXYMED INC
PSS WORLD MEDICAL INC
PSYCHIATRIC SOLUTIONS INC
QUALITY SYSTEMS INC
QUEST DIAGNOSTICS INC
QUINTILES TRANSNATIONAL CORP
RADNET INC
REHABCARE GROUP INC
RES CARE INC
RESPIRONICS INC
RITE AID CORPORATION
ROCHE HOLDING LTD
ROTECH HEALTHCARE INC
SAFEGUARD HEALTH ENTERPRISES INC
SANOFI-AVENTIS
SCHERING-PLOUGH CORP
SIEMENS AG
SISTERS OF MERCY HEALTH SYSTEMS
SMITH & NEPHEW PLC
SMITHS GROUP PLC
SPAN AMERICA MEDICAL SYSTEMS INC
SRI/SURGICAL EXPRESS INC
SSL INTERNATIONAL PLC
SSM HEALTH CARE SYSTEM INC
ST JUDE CHILDRENS RESEARCH HOSPITAL
ST JUDE MEDICAL INC
STERICYCLE INC
STERIS CORP
SUN HEALTHCARE GROUP
SUNRISE MEDICAL INC
SUNRISE SENIOR LIVING
TEAM HEALTH
TELEFLEX INC
TENET HEALTHCARE CORPORATION
TEVA PHARMACEUTICAL INDUSTRIES
THERAGENICS CORP
THERMO FISHER SCIENTIFIC INC
TLC VISION CORPORATION
TOWERS PERRIN
TRANSCEND SERVICES INC
TRIAD HOSPITALS INC
TRUSTMARK COMPANIES
UNITED SURGICAL PARTNERS
UNITEDHEALTH GROUP INC
UNIVERSAL HEALTH SERVICES INC
UNIVERSAL HOSPITAL SERVICES INC
US ONCOLOGY INC
US PHYSICAL THERAPY INC
VCA ANTECH INC
VISION SERVICE PLAN
WALGREEN CO
WATSON PHARMACEUTICALS INC
WEIGHT WATCHERS INTERNATIONAL INC
WELCH ALLYN INC
WELLCARE GROUP OF COMPANIES
WELLPOINT INC
WEST PHARMACEUTICAL SERVICES INC
WRIGHT MEDICAL GROUP INC
WYETH
ZIMMER HOLDINGS INC

NORTHEAST

3M COMPANY
ABBOTT LABORATORIES
ABIOMED INC
ADVENTIST HEALTH SYSTEM
ADVOCAT INC
AETNA INC
AFLAC INC
AKZO NOBEL NV
ALCON INC
ALLIANCE IMAGING INC
ALLIED HEALTHCARE INTERNATIONAL INC
ALLSCRIPTS HEALTHCARE SOLUTIONS INC
ALPHARMA INC
AMEDISYS INC
AMERICAN HOMEPATIENT INC
AMERICAN RETIREMENT CORP
AMERICHOICE CORPORATION
AMERIGROUP CORPORATION
AMERIPATH INC
AMERISOURCEBERGEN CORP
AMGEN INC
AMICAS INC
AMSURG CORP
ANALOGIC CORP
ANSELL LIMITED COMPANY
AON CORPORATION
APPLERA CORPORATION

APRIA HEALTHCARE GROUP INC
ARKANSAS BLUE CROSS AND BLUE SHIELD
ARQULE INC
ARROW INTERNATIONAL INC
ASCENSION HEALTH
ASPECT MEDICAL SYSTEMS INC
ASSURANT EMPLOYEE BENEFITS
ASSURANT INC
ASTELLAS PHARMA INC
ASTRAZENECA PLC
ATC HEALTHCARE INC
ATHENAHEALTH INC
ATRIA SENIOR LIVING GROUP
ATS AUTOMATION TOOLING SYSTEMS INC
BARR PHARMACEUTICALS INC
BAUSCH & LOMB INC
BAXTER INTERNATIONAL INC
BAYER AG
BAYER CORP
BAYER SCHERING PHARMA AG
BECKMAN COULTER INC
BECTON DICKINSON & CO
BESPAK PLC
BIO RAD LABORATORIES INC
BIO REFERENCE LABORATORIES INC
BIOGEN IDEC INC
BIOMET INC
BIOPHAN TECHNOLOGIES INC
BIOSCRIP INC
BIOVAIL CORPORATION
BLUE CROSS AND BLUE SHIELD ASSOCIATION
BLUE CROSS AND BLUE SHIELD OF MASSACHUSETTS
BLUE CROSS AND BLUE SHIELD OF NORTH CAROLINA
BLUE CROSS AND BLUE SHIELD OF VERMONT
BON SECOURS HEALTH SYSTEM INC
BOSTON SCIENTIFIC CORP
BRISTOL MYERS SQUIBB CO
BROOKDALE SENIOR LIVING INC
BROOKS ECKERD
CAMBREX CORP
CANDELA CORP
CANTEL MEDICAL CORP
CAPITAL BLUECROSS
CAPITAL SENIOR LIVING CORP
CARDINAL HEALTH INC
CAREFIRST INC
CAREMARK RX INC
CATHOLIC HEALTH INITIATIVES
CATHOLIC HEALTHCARE PARTNERS
CELERA GENOMICS GROUP
CENTENE CORPORATION
CEPHALON INC
CERNER CORP
CHEMED CORPORATION
CHINDEX INTERNATIONAL INC
CHIRON CORP
CIGNA CORP
COAST DENTAL SERVICES INC
COHERENT INC
COMMUNITY HEALTH SYSTEMS INC
CONCENTRA INC
CONMED CORP
CONVATEC
COOPER COMPANIES INC
CORVEL CORP
COVANCE INC
COVENTRY HEALTH CARE INC
CR BARD INC
CRITICAL CARE SYSTEMS
CSL LIMITED
CURASCRIPT INC
CVS CAREMARK CORPORATION
DADE BEHRING HOLDINGS INC
DANAHER CORP
DATASCOPE CORP
DAVITA INC
DELTA DENTAL PLANS ASSOCIATION
DENTAL BENEFITS PROVIDERS
DENTSPLY INTERNATIONAL INC
DEPUY INC
DIALYSIS CORPORATION OF AMERICA
DIGENE CORPORATION
DUANE READE INC
ECLIPSYS CORPORATION
ELAN CORP PLC
ELI LILLY AND COMPANY
EMERGING VISION INC
EMERITUS CORP
ENDO PHARMACEUTICALS HOLDINGS INC
ENVIRONMENTAL TECTONICS CORP
ESSILOR INTERNATIONAL SA
ETHICON INC
EXACTECH INC
EXCEL TECHNOLOGY INC
EXPRESS SCRIPTS INC
EXTENDICARE REAL ESTATE INVESTMENT TRUST
E-Z-EM INC
FAMILYMEDS GROUP INC
FIRST CONSULTING GROUP INC
FIRST HEALTH GROUP CORP
FISERV INC
FOREST LABORATORIES INC
FRESENIUS AG
FRESENIUS MEDICAL CARE AG
GAMBRO AB
GENTIVA HEALTH SERVICES INC
GENZYME CORP
GLAXOSMITHKLINE PLC
GLOBAL HEALTHCARE EXCHANGE
GNC CORPORATION
GROUP HEALTH INCORPORATED
GSI GROUP INC
GTC BIOTHERAPEUTICS INC
GYRUS GROUP PLC
HAEMONETICS CORPORATION
HANGER ORTHOPEDIC GROUP INC
HARBORSIDE HEALTHCARE CORP
HARVARD PILGRIM HEALTH CARE INC
HCA INC
HEALTH CARE SERVICE CORPORATION
HEALTH INSURANCE PLAN OF GREATER NEW YORK
HEALTH MANAGEMENT ASSOCIATES INC
HEALTH MANAGEMENT SYSTEMS INC
HEALTH NET INC
HEALTHNOW NEW YORK
HEALTHSOUTH CORP
HEALTHSTREAM INC
HEALTHWAYS INC
HEARUSA INC
HEMACARE CORPORATION
HENRY SCHEIN INC
HIGHMARK INC
HILLENBRAND INDUSTRIES
HILL-ROM COMPANY INC
HLTH CORP
HOLOGIC INC
HOOPER HOLMES INC
HORIZON HEALTH CORPORATION
HORIZON HEALTHCARE SERVICES INC
HOSPIRA INC
HUMAN GENOME SCIENCES INC
HUMANA INC
ICU MEDICAL INC
IDEXX LABORATORIES INC
IMS HEALTH INC
INCYTE CORP
INDEPENDENCE HOLDING CO
INSTITUT STRAUMANN AG
INTEGRA LIFESCIENCES HOLDINGS CORP
INTEGRAMED AMERICA INC
INVACARE CORP
INVENTIV HEALTH INC
INVERNESS MEDICAL INNOVATIONS INC
IRIDEX CORP
IRIS INTERNATIONAL INC
JEFFERSON HEALTH SYSTEM INC
JENNY CRAIG INC
JOHNS HOPKINS MEDICINE
JOHNSON & JOHNSON
KAISER PERMANENTE
KENDLE INTERNATIONAL INC
KIMBERLY CLARK CORP
KINDRED HEALTHCARE INC
LABORATORY CORP OF AMERICA HOLDINGS
LAKELAND INDUSTRIES INC
LASERSCOPE
LCA-VISION INC
LIFE CARE CENTERS OF AMERICA
LIFECELL CORPORATION
LIFEPOINT HOSPITALS INC
LIFETIME HEALTHCARE COMPANIES (THE)
LOGISTICARE INC
LUXOTTICA GROUP SPA
MAGELLAN HEALTH SERVICES INC
MALLINCKRODT INC

MANOR CARE INC
MARIAN HEALTH SYSTEMS
MARSH & MCLENNAN COMPANIES INC
MATRIA HEALTHCARE INC
MCKESSON CORPORATION
MDS INC
MEDAVANT HEALTHCARE SOLUTIONS
MEDCO HEALTH SOLUTIONS
MEDICAL ACTION INDUSTRIES INC
MEDICAL INFORMATION TECHNOLOGY INC
MEDSTAR HEALTH
MEDTRONIC INC
MEDTRONIC MINIMED INC
MEDTRONIC SOFAMOR DANEK
MEDTRONIC XOMED SURGICAL PRODUCTS INC
MEMORIAL SLOAN KETTERING CANCER CENTER
MERCER INC
MERCK & CO INC
MERCK SERONO SA
MERIDIAN BIOSCIENCE INC
MERIDIAN MEDICAL TECHNOLOGIES INC
METTLER-TOLEDO INTERNATIONAL
MID ATLANTIC MEDICAL SERVICES INC
MILLENNIUM PHARMACEUTICALS INC
MINDRAY MEDICAL INTERNATIONAL LIMITED
MINE SAFETY APPLIANCES CO
MINNTECH CORP
MINUTECLINIC
MISONIX INC
MOLNLYCKE HEALTH CARE GROUP AB
MOORE MEDICAL CORP
MYLAN LABORATORIES INC
NATIONAL DENTEX CORP
NATIONAL HEALTHCARE CORP
NATIONAL HOME HEALTH CARE CORP
NATIONAL MEDICAL HEALTH CARD SYSTEMS INC
NEW YORK CITY HEALTH AND HOSPITALS CORPORATION
NEW YORK HEALTH CARE INC
NEW YORK-PRESBYTERIAN HEALTHCARE SYSTEM
NMT MEDICAL INC
NOVAMED INC
NOVARTIS AG
NOVATION LLC (VHA INC)
NOVO-NORDISK AS
NYER MEDICAL GROUP INC
ODYSSEY HEALTHCARE INC
OMNICARE INC
OPTICARE HEALTH SYSTEMS
OPTION CARE INC
ORGANOGENESIS INC
ORTHOFIX INTERNATIONAL NV
OSTEOTECH INC
OUTLOOK POINTE CORP
OWENS & MINOR INC
PALOMAR MEDICAL TECHNOLOGIES INC
PAR PHARMACEUTICAL COMPANIES INC
PARTNERS HEALTHCARE SYSTEM
PATTERSON COMPANIES INC
PDI INC
PEDIATRIC SERVICES OF AMERICA INC
PEDIATRIX MEDICAL GROUP INC
PERKINELMER INC
PFIZER INC
PHARMACEUTICAL PRODUCT DEVELOPMENT INC
PHARMACOPEIA DRUG DISCOVERY
PHARMERICA CORP
POLYMEDICA CORPORATION
PREMIER INC
PROXYMED INC
PSS WORLD MEDICAL INC
PSYCHIATRIC SOLUTIONS INC
QUALITY SYSTEMS INC
QUEST DIAGNOSTICS INC
QUINTILES TRANSNATIONAL CORP
RADNET INC
REGENERON PHARMACEUTICALS INC
REHABCARE GROUP INC
RES CARE INC
RESPIRONICS INC
REVOLUTION HEALTH GROUP LLC
RITE AID CORPORATION
ROCHE HOLDING LTD
ROTECH HEALTHCARE INC
SANOFI-AVENTIS
SCHERING-PLOUGH CORP
SCHICK TECHNOLOGIES INC
SENTARA HEALTHCARE
SEPRACOR INC
SHIRE PLC
SHL TELEMEDICINE LTD
SIEMENS AG
SIEMENS MEDICAL SOLUTIONS
SIEMENS MEDICAL SOLUTIONS DIAGNOSTICS
SMITH & NEPHEW PLC
SMITHS GROUP PLC
SOLUCIENT LLC
SPAN AMERICA MEDICAL SYSTEMS INC
SRI/SURGICAL EXPRESS INC
ST JUDE MEDICAL INC
STERICYCLE INC
STERIS CORP
STRYKER CORP
SUN HEALTHCARE GROUP
SUNRISE MEDICAL INC
SUNRISE SENIOR LIVING
SYBRON DENTAL SPECIALTIES INC
SYMMETRY MEDICAL INC
TAKE CARE HEALTH SYSTEMS LLC
TEAM HEALTH
TELEFLEX INC
TENET HEALTHCARE CORPORATION
TEVA PHARMACEUTICAL INDUSTRIES
THERMO FISHER SCIENTIFIC INC
THORATEC CORPORATION
TLC VISION CORPORATION
TOSHIBA CORPORATION
TOWERS PERRIN
TRIAD HOSPITALS INC
TRINITY HEALTH COMPANY
TRUSTMARK COMPANIES
TUFTS ASSOCIATED HEALTH PLANS
UNIPRISE INCORPORATED
UNITED SURGICAL PARTNERS
UNITEDHEALTH GROUP INC
UNIVERSAL HEALTH SERVICES INC
UNIVERSAL HOSPITAL SERVICES INC
US ONCOLOGY INC
US PHYSICAL THERAPY INC
VCA ANTECH INC
VISION SERVICE PLAN
VITAL SIGNS INC
WALGREEN CO
WARNER CHILCOTT PLC
WATSON PHARMACEUTICALS INC
WEBMD HEALTH CORP
WEIGHT WATCHERS INTERNATIONAL INC
WELCH ALLYN INC
WELLCARE GROUP OF COMPANIES
WELLPOINT INC
WEST PHARMACEUTICAL SERVICES INC
WYETH
ZIMMER HOLDINGS INC
ZLB BEHRING LLC
ZOLL MEDICAL CORP

INDEX OF FIRMS WITH OPERATIONS OUTSIDE THE U.S.

MIV THERAPEUTICS INC
MOLNLYCKE HEALTH CARE GROUP AB
MYLAN LABORATORIES INC
NATIONAL DENTEX CORP
NEKTAR THERAPEUTICS
NOVARTIS AG
NOVO-NORDISK AS
OMNICARE INC
ORGANOGENESIS INC
ORTHOFIX INTERNATIONAL NV
OSTEOTECH INC
PATTERSON COMPANIES INC
PEDIATRIX MEDICAL GROUP INC
PERKINELMER INC
PER-SE TECHNOLOGIES INC
PFIZER INC
PHARMACEUTICAL PRODUCT DEVELOPMENT INC
PHILIPS MEDICAL SYSTEMS
QUEST DIAGNOSTICS INC
QUINTILES TRANSNATIONAL CORP
QUOVADX INC
RES CARE INC
RESMED INC
RESPIRONICS INC
ROCHE HOLDING LTD
SANOFI-AVENTIS
SCHERING-PLOUGH CORP
SHIRE PLC
SHL TELEMEDICINE LTD
SIEMENS AG
SIEMENS MEDICAL SOLUTIONS
SIEMENS MEDICAL SOLUTIONS DIAGNOSTICS
SIGMA ALDRICH CORP
SIGNATURE EYEWEAR INC
SIMCERE PHARMACEUTICAL GROUP
SISTERS OF MERCY HEALTH SYSTEMS
SMITH & NEPHEW PLC
SMITHS GROUP PLC
SOLUCIENT LLC
SONIC INNOVATIONS INC
SPECTRANETICS CORP
SSL INTERNATIONAL PLC
ST JUDE MEDICAL INC
STAAR SURGICAL CO
STERICYCLE INC
STERIS CORP
STRYKER CORP
SUNRISE MEDICAL INC
SUNRISE SENIOR LIVING
SYBRON DENTAL SPECIALTIES INC
SYMMETRY MEDICAL INC
TAKEDA PHARMACEUTICAL COMPANY LTD
TEAM HEALTH
TECHNE CORP
TELEFLEX INC
TEVA PHARMACEUTICAL INDUSTRIES
THERMO FISHER SCIENTIFIC INC
THORATEC CORPORATION
TLC VISION CORPORATION
TOSHIBA CORPORATION
TOWERS PERRIN
TRINITY HEALTH COMPANY
UNITED SURGICAL PARTNERS
UTAH MEDICAL PRODUCTS INC
VALEANT PHARMACEUTICALS INTERNATIONAL
VENTANA MEDICAL SYSTEMS INC
VITAL SIGNS INC
WALGREEN CO
WARNER CHILCOTT PLC
WATSON PHARMACEUTICALS INC
WEIGHT WATCHERS INTERNATIONAL INC
WELCH ALLYN INC
WEST PHARMACEUTICAL SERVICES INC
WRIGHT MEDICAL GROUP INC
WYETH
YOUNG INNOVATIONS INC
ZIMMER HOLDINGS INC
ZLB BEHRING LLC
ZOLL MEDICAL CORP

Individual Profiles On Each Of THE HEALTH CARE 500

3M COMPANY

www.mmm.com

Industry Group Code: 339113 **Ranks within this company's industry group:** Sales: 1 Profits: 1

Insurance/HMO/PPO:		Drugs:		Equipment/Supplies:		Hospitals/Clinics:		Services:		Health Care:	
Insurance:		Manufacturer:	Y	Manufacturer:	Y	Acute Care:		Diagnostics:		Home Health:	
Managed Care:		Distributor:		Distributor:		Sub-Acute:		Labs/Testing:		Long-Term Care:	
Utilization Management:		Specialty Pharmacy:		Leasing/Finance:		Outpatient Surgery:		Staffing:		Physical Therapy:	
Payment Processing:		Vitamins/Nutritionals:		Information Systems:	Y	Physical Rehab. Ctr.:		Waste Disposal:		Physician Prac. Mgmt.:	
		Clinical Trials:				Psychiatric Clinics:		Specialty Svcs.:			

TYPES OF BUSINESS:

Health Care Products
Specialty Materials & Textiles
Industrial Products
Safety, Security & Protection Products
Display & Graphics Products
Consumer & Office Products
Electronics & Communications Products
Fuel-Cell Technology

BRANDS/DIVISIONS/AFFILIATES:

Security Printing and Systems, Ltd.
Brontes Technologies, Inc.
Scotch
Post-It

CONTACTS:

Note: Officers with more than one job title may be intentionally listed here more than once.

George W. Buckley, CEO
George W. Buckley, Pres.
Patrick D. Campbell, CFO/Sr. VP
Robert D. MacDonald, Sr. VP-Mktg. & Sales
Angela S. Lalor, Sr. VP-Human Resources
Frederick J. Palensky, Sr. VP-R&D
Richard F. Ziegler, General Counsel/Sr. VP
William J. Schmoll, Treas.
Brad T. Sauer, Exec. VP-Health Care Bus.
H. C. Shin, Exec. VP-Industrial Bus.
James B. Stake, Exec. VP-Enterprise Svcs.
Moe S. Nozari, Exec. VP-Consumer & Office Bus.
George W. Buckley, Chmn.
Inge Thulin, Exec. VP-Int'l Oper.
John K. Woodworth, Sr. VP-Corp. Supply Chain Oper.

Phone: 651-733-1110	**Fax:** 651-733-9973
Toll-Free: 800-364-3577	
Address: 3M Center, Bldg. 220-11W-02, St. Paul, MN 55144-1000 US	

GROWTH PLANS/SPECIAL FEATURES:

3M Company is involved in the research, manufacturing and marketing of a variety of products. The firm is organized into six segments: health care; consumer and office; display and graphics; electronics and communications; industrial and transportation; and safety, security and protection. The health care segment's products include medical and surgical supplies, skin infection prevention products, pharmaceuticals, drug delivery systems, orthodontic products, health information systems and microbiology products. The consumer and office segment includes office supply, stationery, construction and home improvement, protective material and visual systems products. The display and graphics segment's products include optical film and lens for electronic displays; touch screens and monitors; screen filters; reflective sheeting; and commercial graphics systems. The electronics and communications segment's products include packaging and interconnection devices (used in circuits); fluids used in computer chips; high-temperature and display tapes; pressure-sensitive tapes and resins; and products for telecommunications systems. The industrial and transportation segment's products include vinyl, polyester, tapes, a variety of non-woven abrasives, adhesives, specialty materials, supply chain execution software, filtration systems, paint finishing products, engineering fluids, components for catalytic converters and many others. The safety, security and protection services segment provides products for personal protection, safety and security, energy control, commercial cleaning and protection, passports and secure cards. 3M has recently completed the sale of its global branded pharmaceuticals business, different portions of which were acquired by Graceway Pharmaceuticals, Inc., Ironbridge Capital, Archer Capital and Meda AB. In 2006, 3M closed on 19 acquisitions. The two largest acquisitions were Security Printing and Systems, Ltd. and Brontes Technologies, Inc.

3M offers its employees benefits including on-site fitness centers, tuition reimbursement, adoption and employee assistance programs, a 401(k) savings plan and retirement benefits. Additionally, the company provides resources including dry cleaning, notary services, banking and ATMs, photo processing, license tabs and rideshare services.

FINANCIALS:

Sales and profits are in thousands of dollars—add 000 to get the full amount. 2007 Note: Financial information for 2007 was not available for all companies at press time.

2007 Sales: $	2007 Profits: $	**U.S. Stock Ticker: MMM**
2006 Sales: $22,923,000	2006 Profits: $3,851,000	**Int'l Ticker:** Int'l Exchange:
2005 Sales: $21,167,000	2005 Profits: $3,111,000	Employees: 75,333
2004 Sales: $20,011,000	2004 Profits: $2,841,000	Fiscal Year Ends: 12/31
2003 Sales: $18,232,000	2003 Profits: $2,403,000	Parent Company:

SALARIES/BENEFITS:

Pension Plan: Y	ESOP Stock Plan: Y	Profit Sharing:	Top Exec. Salary: $1,600,000	Bonus: $4,117,500
Savings Plan: Y	Stock Purch. Plan:		Second Exec. Salary: $714,595	Bonus: $

OTHER THOUGHTS:

Apparent Women Officers or Directors: 5
Hot Spot for Advancement for Women/Minorities: Y

LOCATIONS: ("Y" = Yes)

West:	Southwest:	Midwest:	Southeast:	Northeast:	International:
Y	Y	Y	Y	Y	Y

3SBIO INC

www.3sbio.com

Industry Group Code: 325412 **Ranks within this company's industry group:** Sales: 41 Profits: 30

Insurance/HMO/PPO:		Drugs:		Equipment/Supplies:		Hospitals/Clinics:		Services:		Health Care:	
Insurance:		Manufacturer:	Y	Manufacturer:		Acute Care:		Diagnostics:		Home Health:	
Managed Care:		Distributor:		Distributor:		Sub-Acute:		Labs/Testing:		Long-Term Care:	
Utilization Management:		Specialty Pharmacy:		Leasing/Finance:		Outpatient Surgery:		Staffing:		Physical Therapy:	
Payment Processing:		Vitamins/Nutritionals:		Information Systems:		Physical Rehab. Ctr.:		Waste Disposal:		Physician Prac. Mgmt.:	
		Clinical Trials:				Psychiatric Clinics:		Specialty Svcs.:			

TYPES OF BUSINESS:

Biopharmaceutical Manufacturing & Design
Anemia Treatments
Cancer Treatments
Exporting Biopharmaceuticals

BRANDS/DIVISIONS/AFFILIATES:

EPIAO
TPIAO
Intefen
Inleusin
Tietai Iron Sucrose Supplement
Baolijin
NuPIAO

CONTACTS:

Note: Officers with more than one job title may be intentionally listed here more than once.

Jing Lou, CEO
Clara Mak, CFO
Yingfei Wei, Chief Scientific Officer
Dongmei Su, CTO
Ke Li, Corp. Sec.
Yingfei Wei, VP-Bus. Dev.
Yongfu Chen, Controller
Dan Lou, Chmn.

Phone: 86-24-2581-1820 **Fax:**
Toll-Free:
Address: No. 3 A1, Rd. 10, Shenyang Development Zone, Shenyang, Liaoning 110027 China

GROWTH PLANS/SPECIAL FEATURES:

3SBio, Inc., is a leading biotechnology company that researches, develops, manufactures and markets biopharmaceutical products, primarily in China. The company currently markets six drugs. EPIAO is an injectable drug used to stimulate the production of red blood cells for anemic patients, thereby reducing their need for transfusions. Launched in January 2006, TPIAO is a protein-based treatment for chemotherapy-induced thrombocytopenia, a deficiency of platelets. Intefen is a treatment for lymphatic or hematopoietic system carcinomas, such as lymphoma and leukemia, as well as for viral infections such as hepatitis C. Inleusin is a treatment for the most common type of kidney cancer, renal cell carcinoma; the skin cancer, metastatic melanoma; and thoratic fluid build-up caused by cancer or tuberculosis. Tietai Iron Sucrose Supplement is an intravenously administered anemia treatment, indicated for patients with end-stage renal disease requiring iron replacement therapy. Baolijin is a treatment for neutopenia, a condition characterized by low levels of a specific type of white blood cell. It is currently developing six products. NuPIAO is a second generation EPIAO product. NuLeusin is a next generation Inleusin product. The company is adapting TPIAO for the treatment of idiopathic thrombocytopenic purpura (ITP), an immune disorder that causes the body to destroy its own platelets. A human papilloma virus (HPV) vaccine is being developed; HPV has been tied to 70% of cervical cancers and 90% of genital warts. Finally, an anti-TNF (Tumor necrosis factor alpha) antibody is underway; TNF is responsible for regulating the inflammatory process and plays an underlying role in rheumatoid arthritis, psoriasis and other inflammatory disorders. Its products are exported to Egypt, Pakistan, Thailand, Brazil, Mexico, Trinidad and Tobago, Guatemala and Columbia. Approximately 77.4% of its 2006 income came from EPIAO, 12.6% from TPIAO, 3.9% from Intefen, 0.9% from Inleusin, 4.6% from exports and 0.7% from others.

FINANCIALS:

Sales and profits are in thousands of dollars—add 000 to get the full amount. 2007 Note: Financial information for 2007 was not available for all companies at press time.

2007 Sales: $
2006 Sales: $16,373
2005 Sales: $
2004 Sales: $
2003 Sales: $

2007 Profits: $
2006 Profits: $3,907
2005 Profits: $
2004 Profits: $
2003 Profits: $

U.S. Stock Ticker: SSRX
Int'l Ticker: Int'l Exchange:
Employees: 313
Fiscal Year Ends: 12/31
Parent Company:

SALARIES/BENEFITS:

Pension Plan: ESOP Stock Plan: Profit Sharing: Top Exec. Salary: $ Bonus: $
Savings Plan: Stock Purch. Plan: Second Exec. Salary: $ Bonus: $

OTHER THOUGHTS:

Apparent Women Officers or Directors: 2
Hot Spot for Advancement for Women/Minorities:

LOCATIONS: ("Y" = Yes)

West:	Southwest:	Midwest:	Southeast:	Northeast:	International:
					Y

Note: Financial information, benefits and other data can change quickly and may vary from those stated here.

ABBOTT LABORATORIES

www.abbott.com

Industry Group Code: 325412 **Ranks within this company's industry group:** Sales: 9 Profits: 14

Insurance/HMO/PPO:		Drugs:		Equipment/Supplies:		Hospitals/Clinics:		Services:		Health Care:	
Insurance:		Manufacturer:	Y	Manufacturer:	Y	Acute Care:		Diagnostics:		Home Health:	
Managed Care:		Distributor:		Distributor:		Sub-Acute:		Labs/Testing:		Long-Term Care:	
Utilization Management:		Specialty Pharmacy:		Leasing/Finance:		Outpatient Surgery:		Staffing:		Physical Therapy:	
Payment Processing:		Vitamins/Nutritionals:	Y	Information Systems:		Physical Rehab. Ctr.:		Waste Disposal:		Physician Prac. Mgmt.:	
		Clinical Trials:				Psychiatric Clinics:		Specialty Svcs.:			

TYPES OF BUSINESS:

Pharmaceuticals Manufacturing
Nutritional Products
Diagnostics
Consumer Health Products
Medical & Surgical Devices
Pharmaceutical Products
Animal Health

BRANDS/DIVISIONS/AFFILIATES:

GLYCO-FLEX
HUMIRA
FreeStyle Flash
AdvantEdge
PathVysion
SevoFlo
Similac
Ensure

CONTACTS: *Note: Officers with more than one job title may be intentionally listed here more than once.*

Miles D. White, CEO
Thomas C. Freyman, CFO
Stephen R. Fussell, Sr. VP-Human Resources
John C. Landgraf, Sr. VP Global Pharmaceutical Mgmt. & Supply
Laura J. Schumacher, General Counsel/Exec. VP/Corp. Sec.
William G. Dempsey, Sr. VP-Pharm. Oper.
Richard Ashley, Exec. VP-Corp. Dev.
Catherine V. Babington, VP-Public Affairs
Thomas C. Freyman, Exec. VP-Finance
Jefrey M. Leiden, Pres./COO-Pharmaceutical Prod./Dir.
William G. Dempsey, Exec. VP-Pharmaceutical Group
Holger Liepmann, Exec. VP-Global Nutrition
Olivier Bohuon, Sr. VP-Int'l Oper.
Miles D. White, Chmn.
Olivier Bohuon, Sr. VP-Int'l Oper.

Phone: 847-937-6100	**Fax:** 847-937-1511
Toll-Free:	
Address: 100 Abbott Park Rd., Abbott Park, IL 60064-3500 US	

GROWTH PLANS/SPECIAL FEATURES:

Abbott Laboratories' principal business is to discover, develop, manufacture and sell health care products and technologies ranging from pharmaceuticals, animal health products and medical devices. The pharmaceutical segment deals with adult and pediatric conditions such as rheumatoid arthritis, HIV, epilepsy and manic depression. The diagnostics segment deals with molecular diagnostics and diabetes care through glucose monitoring, while vascular devices target vessel closure using StarClose. Spinal implants for back problems include PathFinder. The company operates in and outside the U.S., in Europe, Asia, Africa, Latin and South America and the Middle East, marketing its products worldwide. Abbott's 50% shares in TAP Pharmaceutical Products, which makes the prostate cancer drug, Lupron, and Prevacid (Ogastro), a proton pump inhibitor for the short-term treatment of gastroesophageal reflux disease, gives it an edge. Abbott initiated the first complete blood glucose monitoring system designed for diabetic cats and dogs. In agreement with Boston Scientific, it acquired Guidant's vascular intervention and endovascular businesses. The company further acquired Kos Pharmaceuticals in 2006 through which it develops and commercializes hepatitis C virus protease inhibitors. It further received worldwide rights to market and distribute the Verax Platelet Test, used to detect the presence of a broad range of bacterial contaminants in platelets just prior to transfusion. In 2007, Abbott announced its intention to sell its core laboratory diagnostics business included in the Abbott Diagnostics Division and Abbott Point of Call to GE for $8.13 billion.

Abbott promotes employee diversity and supports working mothers. It offers internships and professional development programs for employees at all levels. Forms of compensation extend to savings and pension plans and profit sharing. Other benefits include child and elder care, wellness programs, health and dental insurance and tuition reimbursement.

FINANCIALS: Sales and profits are in thousands of dollars—add 000 to get the full amount. 2007 Note: Financial information for 2007 was not available for all companies at press time.

2007 Sales: $	2007 Profits: $	**U.S. Stock Ticker: ABT**
2006 Sales: $22,476,322	2006 Profits: $1,716,755	**Int'l Ticker:** Int'l Exchange:
2005 Sales: $22,337,808	2005 Profits: $3,372,065	Employees: 66,663
2004 Sales: $19,680,016	2004 Profits: $3,235,851	Fiscal Year Ends: 12/31
2003 Sales: $19,680,600	2003 Profits: $2,753,200	Parent Company:

SALARIES/BENEFITS:

Pension Plan: Y	ESOP Stock Plan:	Profit Sharing: Y	Top Exec. Salary: $1,605,990	Bonus: $2,650,000
Savings Plan: Y	Stock Purch. Plan:		Second Exec. Salary: $905,943	Bonus: $1,050,000

OTHER THOUGHTS:

Apparent Women Officers or Directors: 2
Hot Spot for Advancement for Women/Minorities: Y

LOCATIONS: ("Y" = Yes)

West:	Southwest:	Midwest:	Southeast:	Northeast:	International:
Y	Y	Y		Y	Y

ABIOMED INC

www.abiomed.com

Industry Group Code: 339113 **Ranks within this company's industry group:** Sales: 93 Profits: 93

Insurance/HMO/PPO:		Drugs:		Equipment/Supplies:		Hospitals/Clinics:		Services:		Health Care:	
Insurance:		Manufacturer:		Manufacturer:	Y	Acute Care:		Diagnostics:		Home Health:	
Managed Care:		Distributor:		Distributor:		Sub-Acute:		Labs/Testing:		Long-Term Care:	
Utilization Management:		Specialty Pharmacy:		Leasing/Finance:		Outpatient Surgery:		Staffing:		Physical Therapy:	
Payment Processing:		Vitamins/Nutritionals:		Information Systems:		Physical Rehab. Ctr.:		Waste Disposal:		Physician Prac. Mgmt.:	
		Clinical Trials:				Psychiatric Clinics:		Specialty Svcs.:			

TYPES OF BUSINESS:

Equipment-Cardiac Assistance
Heart Replacement Technology

BRANDS/DIVISIONS/AFFILIATES:

AB5000
AbioCor
BVS-5000

CONTACTS:

Note: Officers with more than one job title may be intentionally listed here more than once.

Michael R. Minogue, CEO
David Weber, COO
Michael R. Minogue, Pres.
Daniel J. Sutherby, CFO
Christopher Macdonald, Sr. VP-Global Sales & Clinical Applications
Robert T. V. Kung, Chief Scientific Officer/Sr. VP
Thorsten Siess, CTO
William J. Bolt, Sr. VP-Global Quality & Service
Andrew J. Greenfield, VP-Healthcare Solutions
Karim Benali, Chief Medical Officer
Michael R. Minogue, Chmn.
Paul Krell, Gen. Mgr.-Abiomed Europe

Phone: 978-777-5410	**Fax:** 978-777-8411
Toll-Free:	
Address: 22 Cherry Hill Dr., Danvers, MA 01923 US	

GROWTH PLANS/SPECIAL FEATURES:

ABIOMED, Inc. is a provider of medical devices in circulatory support. The firm offers a continuum of care in heart recovery to acute heart failure patients. The company's products are designed to enable the heart to rest, heal and recover by improving blood flow and/or performing the pumping function of the heart. Products can be used in a broad range of clinical settings, including by heart surgeons for patients in profound shock and by interventional cardiologists for patients who are in pre-shock or in need of prophylactic support in the cardiac catheterization lab. The AB5000 and BV 5000 products are capable of assuming the pumping function of the heart and are designed for the recovery of the heart. The AB5000 provides up to six liters of pulsatile flow, can provide support from days to months, provides patient mobility and has supported more than 500 patients globally. Subsidiary Impella CarioSystems AG, located in Germany, offers a product portfolio that include devices that address the larger population of heart attack and high-risk angioplastry patients. The Impella 2.5 and 5.0 catheter are micro heart pumps that can be utilized in the cath lab by cardiologists and quickly inserted percutaneously through the femoral artery over a guide wire to reach the left ventricle of the heart. In September 2006, ABIOMED received Humanitarian Device Exemption approval from the FDA for its AbioCor Implantable Replacement Heart, the first completely self-contained artificial heart.

FINANCIALS:

Sales and profits are in thousands of dollars—add 000 to get the full amount. 2007 Note: Financial information for 2007 was not available for all companies at press time.

2007 Sales: $50,649	2007 Profits: $-27,881	**U.S. Stock Ticker: ABMD**
2006 Sales: $43,670	2006 Profits: $-29,449	**Int'l Ticker:** Int'l Exchange:
2005 Sales: $38,216	2005 Profits: $-2,342	Employees: 324
2004 Sales: $25,739	2004 Profits: $-9,446	Fiscal Year Ends: 3/31
2003 Sales: $23,300	2003 Profits: $-18,200	Parent Company:

SALARIES/BENEFITS:

Pension Plan:	ESOP Stock Plan:	Profit Sharing:	Top Exec. Salary: $341,667	Bonus: $278,000
Savings Plan:	Stock Purch. Plan:		Second Exec. Salary: $225,000	Bonus: $40,000

OTHER THOUGHTS:

Apparent Women Officers or Directors: 1
Hot Spot for Advancement for Women/Minorities: Y

LOCATIONS: ("Y" = Yes)

West:	Southwest:	Midwest:	Southeast:	Northeast:	International:
				Y	Y

ACCREDO HEALTH GROUP INC www.accredohealthgroup.com

Industry Group Code: 446110A **Ranks within this company's industry group:** Sales: Profits:

Insurance/HMO/PPO:		Drugs:		Equipment/Supplies:		Hospitals/Clinics:		Services:		Health Care:	
Insurance:		Manufacturer:		Manufacturer:		Acute Care:		Diagnostics:		Home Health:	
Managed Care:		Distributor:	Y	Distributor:		Sub-Acute:		Labs/Testing:		Long-Term Care:	
Utilization Management:		Specialty Pharmacy:	Y	Leasing/Finance:		Outpatient Surgery:		Staffing:		Physical Therapy:	
Payment Processing:		Vitamins/Nutritionals:		Information Systems:		Physical Rehab. Ctr.:		Waste Disposal:		Physician Prac. Mgmt.:	
		Clinical Trials:				Psychiatric Clinics:		Specialty Svcs.:	Y		

TYPES OF BUSINESS:

Drug Distribution-Specialty Pharmacy
Reimbursement Assistance Services

BRANDS/DIVISIONS/AFFILIATES:

Medco Health Solutions
Accredo Nova Factor
Accredo Therapeutics
Hemophilia Health Services
Clinical Business Solutions

CONTACTS: *Note: Officers with more than one job title may be intentionally listed here more than once.*

Tim C. Wentworth, CEO
Steven R. Fitzpatrick, COO
Tim C. Wentworth, Pres.
Kenneth J. Bodmer, CFO
Jon B. Peters, Sr. VP-Tech. & Reimbursement
Michael R. Hess, Chief Legal Officer
Kenneth J. Bodmer, Sr. VP-Finance
Kyle J. Callahan, Pres., Hemophilia Health Svcs.
Michael A. James, Pres., Accredo Therapeutics
Sumit Dutta, Pres., Accredo Nova Factor

Phone: 901-385-3688	**Fax:** 901-385-3689
Toll-Free: 866-591-9075	
Address: 1640 Century Center Pkwy., Memphis, TN 38134 US	

GROWTH PLANS/SPECIAL FEATURES:

Accredo Health Group, Inc., recently acquired by Medco Health Solutions for $2.2 billion, provides specialized pharmacy and related services to treat certain chronic diseases. The chronic diseases the company treats include growth hormone deficiency, cystic fibrosis, Gaucher's, hemophilia, cancer, multiple sclerosis, Crohn's disease, Parkinson's, respiratory syncytial virus, infertility, rheumatoid arthritis, psoriasis, immune deficiencies and pulmonary arterial hypertension. Additionally, the company provides services including the collection of medication use and patient compliance information; patient education and monitoring; reimbursement expertise; and overnight, temperature-controlled drug delivery. Some of its reimbursement services include managing complex paperwork associated with medication payment through insurance companies or other payors. The group has three main divisions: Accredo Nova Factor, Accredo Therapeutics and Hemophilia Health Services (HHS). Nova Factor primarily dispenses injectable, infusible and oral biopharmaceuticals that treat chronic diseases, but it also offers clinical management and reimbursement assistance. The therapeutics division specifically targets patients who need intravenous immunoglobulin (IVIG) therapy. These patients lack immunoglobulin, a protein that normally helps fight off viruses, bacteria and other microbiological parasites; and hence need injections of the protein which is derived from blood plasma donations. IVIG treatments are used for those with autoimmune neuromuscular disorders such as myasthenia gravis and multiple sclerosis patients; and other immunological disorders such as Wiskott-Aldrich Syndrome patients. The therapeutics division provides pharmacy, nursing and reimbursement support. The HHS division provides patients with bleeding disorders blood clotting proteins, also called factors, as well as information to help patients and their families live with the disorder. Clinical Business Solutions, an affiliate of the company, customizes outsourcing plans for clinical call centers, research support, benefits investigation and other needs.

Accredo Health offers employees paid time off and some health and other welfare benefits.

FINANCIALS: **Sales and profits are in thousands of dollars—add 000 to get the full amount. 2007 Note: Financial information for 2007 was not available for all companies at press time.**

2007 Sales: $	2007 Profits: $	**U.S. Stock Ticker: Subsidiary**
2006 Sales: $	2006 Profits: $	**Int'l Ticker:** Int'l Exchange:
2005 Sales: $	2005 Profits: $	Employees: 2,491
2004 Sales: $1,516,868	2004 Profits: $78,313	Fiscal Year Ends: 12/31
2003 Sales: $1,337,400	2003 Profits: $29,500	Parent Company: MEDCO HEALTH SOLUTIONS

SALARIES/BENEFITS:

Pension Plan:	ESOP Stock Plan:	Profit Sharing:	Top Exec. Salary: $378,239	Bonus: $123,070
Savings Plan: Y	Stock Purch. Plan: Y		Second Exec. Salary: $244,281	Bonus: $58,753

OTHER THOUGHTS:

Apparent Women Officers or Directors:
Hot Spot for Advancement for Women/Minorities:

LOCATIONS: ("Y" = Yes)

West:	Southwest:	Midwest:	Southeast:	Northeast:	International:
		Y	Y		

ACTELION LTD

www.actelion.com

Industry Group Code: 325412 **Ranks within this company's industry group:** Sales: 29 Profits: 23

Insurance/HMO/PPO:		Drugs:		Equipment/Supplies:		Hospitals/Clinics:		Services:		Health Care:	
Insurance:		Manufacturer:		Manufacturer:	Y	Acute Care:		Diagnostics:		Home Health:	
Managed Care:		Distributor:		Distributor:		Sub-Acute:		Labs/Testing:		Long-Term Care:	
Utilization Management:		Specialty Pharmacy:		Leasing/Finance:		Outpatient Surgery:		Staffing:		Physical Therapy:	
Payment Processing:		Vitamins/Nutritionals:		Information Systems:		Physical Rehab. Ctr.:		Waste Disposal:		Physician Prac. Mgmt.:	
		Clinical Trials:				Psychiatric Clinics:		Specialty Svcs.:			

TYPES OF BUSINESS:

Drugs, Discovery & Development
Pharmaceutical Research
Cardiovascular Treatment
Genetic Disorder Treatment

BRANDS/DIVISIONS/AFFILIATES:

Curl Acquisition Subsidiary, Inc.
Zavesca
Tracleer
Clazosentan
Actelion Pharmaceuticals U.S., Inc.
Palosuran
Orexon RA
Actelion-1

CONTACTS: *Note: Officers with more than one job title may be intentionally listed here more than once.*

Jean-Paul Clozel, CEO
Andrew J. Oakley, CFO/VP
Frederic Bodin, Sr. VP-Head Global Medical Mktg.
Marian Borovsky, General Counsel/VP
Christian Chavy, Pres., Bus. Oper.
Simon Buckingham, Pres., Corp. & Bus. Dev.
Roland Haefeli, VP-Public Affairs
Roland Haefeli, VP-Investor Rel.
Louis de Lassence, VP-Corp. Svcs.
Isaac Kobrin, Sr. VP-Clinical Dev.
Martine Cozel, Sr. VP-Drug Discovery & Pharmacology
Walter Fischli, Sr. VP-Drug Discovery & Molecular Biology
Robert Cawthorn, Chmn.

Phone: 41-61-565-65-65	**Fax:** 41-61-565-65-00
Toll-Free:	
Address: Gewerbestrasse 16, Allschwil, Baselland 4123 Switzerland	

GROWTH PLANS/SPECIAL FEATURES:

Actelion, Ltd. is a biopharmaceutical company that focuses on the discovery, development and marketing of drugs for unaddressed medical needs. The firm typically focuses its treatments on diseases within limited patient populations and then expands and commercializes additional products to address a wider spectrum of ailments within the general practice market. The majority of Actelion's drug discovery products address medical needs in cardiovascular, central nervous system, oncology and immunology areas. The firm's research division uses a technology known as high-throughput screening, which is used to identify targeted compounds using molecular modeling and crystallography. Actelion's most recognized product is Tracleer, a dual entothelin receptor antagonist used for pulmonary arterial hypertension. Another popular Acetelion drug, Zavesca, is one of the first approved oral drug therapy treatments for a genetic lipid metabolic disorder called Gaucher disease. Additional drugs that are currently in the developmental stage include Clazosentan, Palosuran, Actelion-1 and Orexon RA. Clazosentan is intended for the prevention and treatment of vasospasms, a life threatening condition that leads to neurological deficits after a patient suffers an aneurysm. Palosuran is an oral form of Urotensin-II, one of the most potent vasoconstrictor substances, and is used in the treatment of cardiovascular and metabolic diseases. Actelion-1 is one of the first tissue targeting endothelin receptor antagonists. Orexon RA treats sleeping disorders. Actelion is based in Switzerland and has subsidiaries in 22 countries. Actelion and Roche recently entered into an autoimmune disorder collaboration in 2006 to jointly develop and commercialize Actelion's selective S1P1 receptor agonist. In 2007, a subsidiary of Actelion, Curl Acquisition Subsidiary, Inc., acquired CoTherix, Inc.

FINANCIALS: **Sales and profits are in thousands of dollars—add 000 to get the full amount. 2007 Note: Financial information for 2007 was not available for all companies at press time.**

2007 Sales: $	2007 Profits: $	**U.S. Stock Ticker: ALIOF**
2006 Sales: $776,912	2006 Profits: $198,066	**Int'l Ticker: ATLN** Int'l Exchange: Zurich-SWX
2005 Sales: $545,168	2005 Profits: $103,135	Employees: 400
2004 Sales: $471,880	2004 Profits: $87,219	Fiscal Year Ends: 12/31
2003 Sales: $247,600	2003 Profits: $-8,000	Parent Company:

SALARIES/BENEFITS:

Pension Plan:	ESOP Stock Plan:	Profit Sharing:	Top Exec. Salary: $	Bonus: $
Savings Plan:	Stock Purch. Plan:		Second Exec. Salary: $	Bonus: $

OTHER THOUGHTS:

Apparent Women Officers or Directors: 1
Hot Spot for Advancement for Women/Minorities:

LOCATIONS: ("Y" = Yes)

West:	Southwest:	Midwest:	Southeast:	Northeast:	International:
					Y

ADVANCED BIONICS CORPORATION

www.advancedbionics.com

Industry Group Code: 339113 **Ranks within this company's industry group:** Sales: Profits:

Insurance/HMO/PPO:		Drugs:		Equipment/Supplies:		Hospitals/Clinics:		Services:		Health Care:	
Insurance:		Manufacturer:		Manufacturer:	Y	Acute Care:		Diagnostics:		Home Health:	
Managed Care:		Distributor:		Distributor:		Sub-Acute:		Labs/Testing:		Long-Term Care:	
Utilization Management:		Specialty Pharmacy:		Leasing/Finance:		Outpatient Surgery:		Staffing:		Physical Therapy:	
Payment Processing:		Vitamins/Nutritionals:		Information Systems:		Physical Rehab. Ctr.:		Waste Disposal:		Physician Prac. Mgmt.:	
		Clinical Trials:				Psychiatric Clinics:		Specialty Svcs.:			

TYPES OF BUSINESS:

Medical Equipment-Manufacturing
Bionic Devices
Cochlear Implant Technology
Spinal Cord Stimulation Systems
Software
Chronic Pain Treatment

BRANDS/DIVISIONS/AFFILIATES:

HiResolution Bionic Ear System
Harmony
HiRes
Auria
Platinum
PrecisionPlus
Boston Scientific
Nihon Bionics Co., Ltd.

CONTACTS: *Note: Officers with more than one job title may be intentionally listed here more than once.*

Al Mann, Co-CEO
Jeff Greiner, Pres./Co-CEO
Jim Surek, VP-Sales
Tom Santogrossi, VP-Mfg.
Al Mann, Chmn.

Phone: 661-362-1400 **Fax:** 661-362-1500
Toll-Free: 800-678-2575
Address: 12740 San Fernando Rd., Sylmar, CA 91342 US

GROWTH PLANS/SPECIAL FEATURES:

Advanced Bionics Corporation, a subsidiary of Boston Scientific, develops and markets bionic technologies that employ implantable neutrostimulation devices to treat neurological conditions such as deafness and chronic pain. Advanced Bionics is currently the only company in the U.S. that develops cochlear implant technology, which restores hearing to deaf individuals. Products in the company's HiResolution Bionic Ear System include Harmony, a behind-the-ear processor that produces high-quality sound resolution; Auria, a line of sound processing products which include headpieces, earhooks, battery chargers, moisturizing kits and carrying cases; Platinum, a sound processor that is worn around a belt instead of behind the ears, and a 90K implant that uses integrated circuit computer technology with an internal memory and Hifocus electrodes for neutral targeting. Chronic Pain sufferers are offered Precision Plus, a spinal Cord stimulation therapy that masks pain signals by sending out doses of electricity which the brain interprets as pleasant sensations. PrecisionPlus is typically offered to patients with failed back surgeries, phantom limb pain, sciatica, reflex sympathetic dystrophy (RSD) and/or complex regional pain syndrome (CRPS). Advanced Bionics currently has operations in California, France, Asia-Pacific and Latin America. The firm additionally maintains a Japanese subsidiary company, Nihon Bionics Co., Ltd.

Advanced Bionics offers employees health, disability and life insurance; flexible and dependent care spending accounts; and employee appreciation events such as picnics and volleyball tournaments.

FINANCIALS: Sales and profits are in thousands of dollars—add 000 to get the full amount. 2007 Note: Financial information for 2007 was not available for all companies at press time.

2007 Sales: $	2007 Profits: $	**U.S. Stock Ticker: Subsidiary**
2006 Sales: $	2006 Profits: $	**Int'l Ticker:** Int'l Exchange:
2005 Sales: $	2005 Profits: $	Employees: 500
2004 Sales: $	2004 Profits: $	Fiscal Year Ends: 12/31
2003 Sales: $56,400	2003 Profits: $	Parent Company: BOSTON SCIENTIFIC CORP

SALARIES/BENEFITS:

Pension Plan:	ESOP Stock Plan: Y	Profit Sharing:	Top Exec. Salary: $	Bonus: $
Savings Plan: Y	Stock Purch. Plan:		Second Exec. Salary: $	Bonus: $

OTHER THOUGHTS:

Apparent Women Officers or Directors:
Hot Spot for Advancement for Women/Minorities:

LOCATIONS: ("Y" = Yes)

West:	Southwest:	Midwest:	Southeast:	Northeast:	International:
Y					Y

ADVANCED MEDICAL OPTICS INC www.amo-inc.com

Industry Group Code: 339113 **Ranks within this company's industry group:** Sales: 29 Profits: 26

Insurance/HMO/PPO:		Drugs:		Equipment/Supplies:		Hospitals/Clinics:		Services:		Health Care:	
Insurance:		Manufacturer:		Manufacturer:	Y	Acute Care:		Diagnostics:		Home Health:	
Managed Care:		Distributor:		Distributor:		Sub-Acute:		Labs/Testing:		Long-Term Care:	
Utilization Management:		Specialty Pharmacy:		Leasing/Finance:		Outpatient Surgery:		Staffing:		Physical Therapy:	
Payment Processing:		Vitamins/Nutritionals:		Information Systems:		Physical Rehab. Ctr.:		Waste Disposal:		Physician Prac. Mgmt.:	
		Clinical Trials:				Psychiatric Clinics:		Specialty Svcs.:			

TYPES OF BUSINESS:

Equipment/Supplies-Ophthalmic
Ophthalmic Surgical Supplies
Contact Lens Care Products
Laser Eye Surgical Products
Glaucoma Surgical Products

BRANDS/DIVISIONS/AFFILIATES:

Phacoflex II
Tecnis
Baerveldt
blink Contacts
Ultrazyme
WaveScan Wavefront
WaveFront Sciences, Inc.
IntraLase Corp.

CONTACTS: *Note: Officers with more than one job title may be intentionally listed here more than once.*

James V. Mazzo, CEO
Richard A. Meier,, COO
James V. Mazzo, Pres.
Richard A. Meier, CFO
C. Russell Trenary III, Chief Mktg. Officer/Corp. VP
Francine D. Meza, Sr. VP-Human Resources
Peter P. Nolan, Sr. VP-Mfg.
Aimee S. Weisner, General Counsel/Corp. Sec./Corp. VP
Richard A. Meier, Exec. VP-Oper.
Jane E. Rady, Exec. VP-Strategy
Sheree L. Aronson, VP-Corp. Comm.
Sheree L. Aronson, VP-Investor Rel.
Douglas H. Post, Corp. VP/Pres., Laser Vision Correction Group
Holger Heidrich, Corp. VP/Pres., EAM Region & Int'l Gov. Affairs
C. Russell Trenary III, Exec. VP/Pres., Cataract Refractive Group
James Mazzo, Chmn.

Phone: 714-247-8200	**Fax:** 714.247.8672
Toll-Free:	
Address: 1700 E. St. Andrew Pl., Santa Ana, CA 92705 US	

GROWTH PLANS/SPECIAL FEATURES:

Advanced Medical Optics, Inc. (AMO) develops, manufactures and markets medical devices for the eye and eye care markets. The company has three major product lines, which it sells in over 60 countries: cataract/implant, laser vision correction and eye care. The cataract/implant line includes foldable intraocular lenses implanted in the lens capsule to restore sight; phacoemulsification machines used to break up the cloudy human lens prior to its replacement with an intraocular lens; and related surgical accessories such as implantation systems, viscoelastics and disposables. The firm's surgical products customers include surgeons who perform cataract surgeries, hospitals and ambulatory surgical centers. In the laser vision correction market, AMO markets laser systems, diagnostic devices, treatment cards and microkeratomes for use in laser eye surgery. The AMO eye care product line provides a full range of contact lens care products for use with most types of contact lenses. These products include single-bottle, multi-purpose cleaning and disinfecting solutions, hydrogen peroxide-based disinfecting solutions, daily cleaners, enzymatic cleaners and contact lens rewetting drops. Eye care product customers include optometrists, opticians, ophthalmologists, retailers and clinics that sell directly to consumers. These retailers include mass merchandisers such as Wal-Mart and Walgreens as well as commercial optical chains and food stores. In January 2007, the company acquired WaveFront Sciences, Inc., a leading provider of the proprietary wavefront diagnostic systems for refractive surgery and medical research. Also, in March 2007, the AMO completed the acquisition of IntraLase Corp., a leader in the femtosecond lasers used in LASIK surgery.

AMO offers employees benefits including paid vacation and paid holidays; a medical, vision and dental plan; employee stock purchase plan; education assistance program; and domestic partner benefits.

FINANCIALS: **Sales and profits are in thousands of dollars—add 000 to get the full amount. 2007 Note: Financial information for 2007 was not available for all companies at press time.**

2007 Sales: $	2007 Profits: $	**U.S. Stock Ticker: EYE**
2006 Sales: $997,496	2006 Profits: $79,471	**Int'l Ticker:** Int'l Exchange:
2005 Sales: $920,673	2005 Profits: $-453,197	Employees: 3,800
2004 Sales: $742,099	2004 Profits: $-129,370	Fiscal Year Ends: 12/31
2003 Sales: $601,453	2003 Profits: $10,357	Parent Company:

SALARIES/BENEFITS:

Pension Plan:	ESOP Stock Plan:	Profit Sharing:	Top Exec. Salary: $684,865	Bonus: $357,500
Savings Plan: Y	Stock Purch. Plan: Y		Second Exec. Salary: $466,173	Bonus: $171,375

OTHER THOUGHTS:

Apparent Women Officers or Directors: 4
Hot Spot for Advancement for Women/Minorities: Y

LOCATIONS: ("Y" = Yes)

West:	Southwest:	Midwest:	Southeast:	Northeast:	International:
Y					Y

ADVANCED NEUROMODULATION SYSTEMS www.ans-medical.com

Industry Group Code: 339113 **Ranks within this company's industry group:** Sales: Profits:

Insurance/HMO/PPO:		Drugs:		Equipment/Supplies:		Hospitals/Clinics:		Services:		Health Care:	
Insurance:		Manufacturer:		Manufacturer:	Y	Acute Care:		Diagnostics:		Home Health:	
Managed Care:		Distributor:		Distributor:		Sub-Acute:		Labs/Testing:		Long-Term Care:	
Utilization Management:		Specialty Pharmacy:		Leasing/Finance:		Outpatient Surgery:		Staffing:		Physical Therapy:	
Payment Processing:		Vitamins/Nutritionals:		Information Systems:		Physical Rehab. Ctr.:		Waste Disposal:		Physician Prac. Mgmt.:	
		Clinical Trials:				Psychiatric Clinics:		Specialty Svcs.:			

TYPES OF BUSINESS:

Medical Equipment Manufacturing
Implantable Devices
Drug Delivery Devices

BRANDS/DIVISIONS/AFFILIATES:

St. Jude Medical, Inc.
Renew
Genesis
GenesisXP
Eon
Rapid Programmer 3.0
ANS Germany GmbH
ANS Asia Pacific

CONTACTS: *Note: Officers with more than one job title may be intentionally listed here more than once.*

Christopher G. Chavez, CEO
Christopher G. Chavez, Pres.
F. Robert Merrill, III, CFO
Scott F. Drees, Exec. VP-Sales & Mktg.
James P. Calhoun, VP-Human Resources
John H. Erickson, VP-R&D
Stuart B. Johnson, VP-Mfg.
Kenneth G. Hawari, General Counsel/Corp. Sec.
Kenneth G. Hawari, Exec. VP-Corp. Dev.
F. Robert Merrill, III, Exec. VP-Finance/Treas.

Phone: 972-309-8000	**Fax:** 972-309-8150
Toll-Free: 800-727-7846	
Address: 6901 Preston Rd., Plano, TX 75024 US	

GROWTH PLANS/SPECIAL FEATURES:

Advanced Neuromodulation Systems (ANS), which was recently acquired by St. Jude Medical, Inc., designs, develops, manufactures and markets advanced implantable neuromodulation devices used to ease the symptoms of patients suffering from chronic pain and related nervous system disorders. These devices include implantable neurostimulation units, which deliver low levels of electric current to targeted nerve fibers or tissue, interrupting pain signals before they reach the brain; and related technology, mainly leads. The company's products are marketed to physicians who specialize in the treatment of chronic pain. Neurostimulation implants include Renew radio frequency systems, which have an external power source and are generally needed by patients that require complex treatment solutions; and Genesis, GenesisXP and Eon implantable pulse generator systems, which are needed by patients with simpler complex solutions that draw less power since surgery is required to replace the internal, limited-life, battery power source. The company's leads provide the actual targeting for its implant's pulses, offering up to 16 closely spaced electrodes that can target specific spinal column nerves. ANS produces the Rapid Programmer 3.0, which uses a Windows graphics interface to allow clinicians to test implants intra-operatively and program postoperatively. Subsidiary Hi-tronics Designs, Inc. designs and manufactures medical devices for the company as well as for other companies on an original equipment manufacturer basis. ANS has grown significantly through the acquisition of three U.S. distributors: Sun Medical, Inc.; Comedical, Inc. and State of the Art Medical Products. International operations are conducted through subsidiaries ANS Germany GmbH; ANS Suisse AG; ANS Sanitarios; ANS, UK Ltd; ANS France; ANS Asia Pacific; and ANS Australia Pty Ltd.

ANS offers employees insurance for medical, dental, life, disability, long term care and legal coverage; a flexible spending account; and a discount on vision as well as home and auto insurance. Benefits cover children and spouses.

FINANCIALS: **Sales and profits are in thousands of dollars—add 000 to get the full amount. 2007 Note: Financial information for 2007 was not available for all companies at press time.**

2007 Sales: $	2007 Profits: $	**U.S. Stock Ticker: Subsidiary**
2006 Sales: $	2006 Profits: $	**Int'l Ticker:** Int'l Exchange:
2005 Sales: $	2005 Profits: $	Employees: 700
2004 Sales: $120,744	2004 Profits: $18,167	Fiscal Year Ends: 12/31
2003 Sales: $91,082	2003 Profits: $13,217	Parent Company: ST JUDE MEDICAL INC

SALARIES/BENEFITS:

Pension Plan:	ESOP Stock Plan:	Profit Sharing:	Top Exec. Salary: $333,692	Bonus: $155,520
Savings Plan:	Stock Purch. Plan:		Second Exec. Salary: $240,277	Bonus: $116,650

OTHER THOUGHTS:

Apparent Women Officers or Directors:
Hot Spot for Advancement for Women/Minorities:

LOCATIONS: ("Y" = Yes)

West:	Southwest:	Midwest:	Southeast:	Northeast:	International:
	Y				Y

ADVENTIST HEALTH SYSTEM

www.ahss.org

Industry Group Code: 622110 **Ranks within this company's industry group:** Sales: 11 Profits: 6

Insurance/HMO/PPO:		Drugs:		Equipment/Supplies:		Hospitals/Clinics:		Services:		Health Care:	
Insurance:		Manufacturer:		Manufacturer:		Acute Care:	Y	Diagnostics:		Home Health:	Y
Managed Care:		Distributor:		Distributor:		Sub-Acute:	Y	Labs/Testing:		Long-Term Care:	Y
Utilization Management:		Specialty Pharmacy:		Leasing/Finance:		Outpatient Surgery:	Y	Staffing:		Physical Therapy:	
Payment Processing:		Vitamins/Nutritionals:		Information Systems:		Physical Rehab. Ctr.:	Y	Waste Disposal:		Physician Prac. Mgmt.:	
		Clinical Trials:				Psychiatric Clinics:		Specialty Svcs.:	Y		

TYPES OF BUSINESS:

Hospitals
Nursing Homes
Home Health Care Services
Information Management
Artificial Intelligence Research

BRANDS/DIVISIONS/AFFILIATES:

Florida Hospital
Sunbelt Systems Concepts
MEDai

CONTACTS:

Note: Officers with more than one job title may be intentionally listed here more than once.

Donald L. Jernigan, CEO
Donald L. Jernigan, Pres.
Terry D. Shaw, CFO
Donald G. Jones, VP-Human Resources
Brent G. Snyder, CIO
Robert R. Henderschedt, Sr. VP-Admin.
T. L. Trimble, VP-Legal Svcs.
Sandra K. Johnson, VP-Bus. Dev., Risk Mgmt. & Compliance
Lewis A. Seifert, Sr. VP-Finance
Richard K. Reiner, Pres./CEO-Multi-State Division
John R. Brownlow, Sr. VP-Managed Care
Gary Skilton, Sr. VP/Treas.
Timothy L. Thompson, Sr. VP-Info. Svcs.

Phone: 407-647-4400	**Fax:** 407-975-1469
Toll-Free:	
Address: 111 N. Orlando Ave., Winter Park, FL 32789 US	

GROWTH PLANS/SPECIAL FEATURES:

Adventist Health System, sponsored by the Seventh-day Adventist Church, is the largest not-for-profit Protestant health care organizations in the U.S. The firm operates 36 hospitals in ten states, totaling over 6,300 beds; 17 affiliated extended care centers within the long-term care division with over 2,200 beds; and over 20 home health care agencies. The company serves about 4 million patients annually. The firm's flagship organization, Florida Hospital, is the largest health care provider in central Florida and a national leader in cardiac care. The hospital offers over 1,800 beds on seven campuses and provides care in the areas of cancer, neurosciences, orthopedics, kidney disease, limb replantation, sports medicine, rehabilitation and women's medicine programs. Adventist Health is a world leader in the use of tissue-sparing radiation based on proton beams, rather than traditional photon-based radiation. The company also manages Sunbelt Systems Concepts, an information management company, and MEDai, an artificial intelligence and outcome research company. The firm is guided by its Christian mission to extend the healing ministry of Christ through a combination of disease treatment, preventative medicine education and advocacy of a wholesome lifestyle. The hospitals in the Adventist group provide a wide range of free or reduced-price services in their communities, including free medical vans and community clinics, free screening and education programs, debt forgiveness, abuse shelters and programs for the homeless and jobless.

FINANCIALS:

Sales and profits are in thousands of dollars—add 000 to get the full amount. 2007 Note: Financial information for 2007 was not available for all companies at press time.

2007 Sales: $	2007 Profits: $	**U.S. Stock Ticker: Nonprofit**
2006 Sales: $4,968,700	2006 Profits: $325,400	**Int'l Ticker:** Int'l Exchange:
2005 Sales: $4,668,100	2005 Profits: $251,400	Employees: 43,000
2004 Sales: $4,379,200	2004 Profits: $236,200	Fiscal Year Ends:
2003 Sales: $4,085,900	2003 Profits: $203,100	Parent Company:

SALARIES/BENEFITS:

Pension Plan:	ESOP Stock Plan:	Profit Sharing:	Top Exec. Salary: $	Bonus: $
Savings Plan:	Stock Purch. Plan:		Second Exec. Salary: $	Bonus: $

OTHER THOUGHTS:

Apparent Women Officers or Directors: 3
Hot Spot for Advancement for Women/Minorities: Y

LOCATIONS: ("Y" = Yes)

West:	Southwest:	Midwest:	Southeast:	Northeast:	International:
Y	Y	Y	Y	Y	

ADVOCAT INC

www.irinfo.com/avc

Industry Group Code: 623110 **Ranks within this company's industry group:** Sales: 7 Profits: 5

Insurance/HMO/PPO:		**Drugs:**		**Equipment/Supplies:**		**Hospitals/Clinics:**		**Services:**		**Health Care:**	
Insurance:		Manufacturer:		Manufacturer:		Acute Care:		Diagnostics:		Home Health:	
Managed Care:		Distributor:		Distributor:		Sub-Acute:		Labs/Testing:		Long-Term Care:	Y
Utilization Management:		Specialty Pharmacy:		Leasing/Finance:		Outpatient Surgery:		Staffing:		Physical Therapy:	
Payment Processing:		Vitamins/Nutritionals:		Information Systems:		Physical Rehab. Ctr.:		Waste Disposal:		Physician Prac. Mgmt.:	
		Clinical Trials:				Psychiatric Clinics:		Specialty Svcs.:			

TYPES OF BUSINESS:

Nursing Homes
Assisted Living Facilities

BRANDS/DIVISIONS/AFFILIATES:

CONTACTS:

Note: Officers with more than one job title may be intentionally listed here more than once.

William R. Council, III, CEO
Raymond L. Tyler, COO/Exec. VP
William R. Council, III, Pres.
L. Glynn Riddle, CFO
Wallace E. Olson, Chmn.

Phone: 615-771-7575	**Fax:** 615-771-7409
Toll-Free:	
Address: 1621 Galleria Blvd., Brentwood, TN 37027 US	

GROWTH PLANS/SPECIAL FEATURES:

Advocat, Inc. provides long-term care services to nursing home patients and residents of assisted living facilities in eight states, primarily in the Southeast. The company's total operations are composed of 43 nursing homes containing over 4,500 licensed nursing beds and 66 assisted living facilities units. Facilities are located in the states of Alabama, Arkansas, Florida, Kentucky, Ohio, Tennessee, Texas and West Virginia. The company's leased and managed homes provide a range of health care services to its residents. In addition to the nursing and social services usually provided in long-term care facilities, Advocat offers a variety of rehabilitative, nutritional, respiratory and other specialized ancillary services. The firm's nursing centers provide skilled nursing health care services, including room and board; nutrition services; recreational therapy; social services; and housekeeping and laundry services. In addition, nursing centers dispense medications prescribed by the patients' physicians, and a plan of care is developed by professional nursing staff for each resident as well as providing for the delivery of ancillary medical services. These specialty services include rehabilitation therapy services, such as audiology, speech, occupational and physical therapies, which are provided through licensed therapists and registered nurses, and the provision of medical supplies, nutritional support, infusion therapies, and related clinical services. The significant majority of these services are provided using internal resources and clinicians. In 2006, the company sold 11 of its assisted living facilities in North Carolina for approximately $11 million.

FINANCIALS:

Sales and profits are in thousands of dollars—add 000 to get the full amount. 2007 Note: Financial information for 2007 was not available for all companies at press time.

2007 Sales: $	2007 Profits: $	**U.S. Stock Ticker: AVCA**
2006 Sales: $216,763	2006 Profits: $12,944	**Int'l Ticker:** Int'l Exchange:
2005 Sales: $203,653	2005 Profits: $25,302	Employees: 4,716
2004 Sales: $191,224	2004 Profits: $2,781	Fiscal Year Ends: 12/31
2003 Sales: $172,226	2003 Profits: $-11,221	Parent Company:

SALARIES/BENEFITS:

Pension Plan:	ESOP Stock Plan:	Profit Sharing:	Top Exec. Salary: $375,000	Bonus: $188,112
Savings Plan: Y	Stock Purch. Plan:		Second Exec. Salary: $275,000	Bonus: $83,112

OTHER THOUGHTS:

Apparent Women Officers or Directors:
Hot Spot for Advancement for Women/Minorities:

LOCATIONS: ("Y" = Yes)

West:	Southwest:	Midwest:	Southeast:	Northeast:	International:
	Y	Y	Y	Y	

ADVOCATE HEALTH CARE www.advocatehealth.com

ndustry Group Code: 622110 **Ranks within this company's industry group:** Sales: Profits:

ısurance/HMO/PPO:		Drugs:		Equipment/Supplies:		Hospitals/Clinics:		Services:		Health Care:	
ısurance:		Manufacturer:		Manufacturer:		Acute Care:	Y	Diagnostics:		Home Health:	Y
lanaged Care:		Distributor:		Distributor:		Sub-Acute:	Y	Labs/Testing:		Long-Term Care:	Y
tilization Management:		Specialty Pharmacy:		Leasing/Finance:		Outpatient Surgery:	Y	Staffing:		Physical Therapy:	
ayment Processing:		Vitamins/Nutritionals:		Information Systems:		Physical Rehab. Ctr.:		Waste Disposal:		Physician Prac. Mgmt.:	
		Clinical Trials:				Psychiatric Clinics:		Specialty Svcs.:	Y		

TYPES OF BUSINESS:

Iospitals
Clinics & Outpatient Centers
Iome Health Care
Physician Groups

BRANDS/DIVISIONS/AFFILIATES:

Advocate Hope Children's Hospital
Advocate Trinity Hospital
Advocate Christ Medical Center
Advocate Illinois Masonic Medical Center
Advocate Lutheran General Hospital
Advocate Medical Campus Southwest
Center for Complementary Medicine
Iealthy Steps for Young Children

CONTACTS: *Note: Officers with more than one job title may be ıtentionally listed here more than once.*

ames H. Skogsbergh, CEO
Villiam P. Santulli, COO/Exec. VP
ames H. Skogsbergh, Pres.
ominic J. Nakis, CFO/Sr. VP
en Grigaliunas, Sr. VP-Human Resources
ruce Smith, CIO/Sr. VP
ail D. Hasbrouck, General Counsel/Corp. Sec./Sr. VP
usan J. Ell, Chief Dev. Officer/Pres., Charitable Foundation
nthony A. Mitchell, Sr. VP-Comm.
ee B. Sacks, Chief Medical Officer/Exec. VP
usan N. Lopez, Pres., Advocate Illinois Masonic Medical Center
enneth W. Lukhard, Pres., Advocate Christ Medical Center
ruce C. Campbell, Pres., Advocate Lutheran General Hospital
ohn F. Timmer, Chmn.
on Bruss, VP-Supply Chain Mgmt.

Phone: 630-572-9393	**Fax:** 630-990-4752
Toll-Free:	
Address: 2025 Windsor Dr., Oak Brook, IL 60523-1586 US	

GROWTH PLANS/SPECIAL FEATURES:

Advocate Health Care is a not-for-profit health care network that provides acute care and outpatient services at more than 200 sites in the Chicago area. The company's operations include eight hospitals with approximately 3,500 beds; two children's hospitals, Advocate Hope Children's Hospital and Advocate Lutheran General Children's Hospital; and Advocate Home Health Services, one of the state's largest full-service home health care companies. The firm's hospitals include Advocate Bethany Hospital, Advocate Good Samaritan Hospital, Advocate Good Shepherd Hospital, Advocate South Suburban General Hospital and Advocate Trinity Hospital. U.S. News & World Report, on its list of America's Best Hospitals 2006, recognized the excellence in specialty areas of three Advocate hospitals: Advocate Christ Medical Center, for respiratory disorders; Advocate Illinois Masonic Medical Center, for heart surgery and heart care; and Advocate Lutheran General Hospital, for neurology, neurosurgery, oncology, cancer care, digestive disorders, orthopedics and ENT (ear, nose and throat) disorders. The company has more than 4,600 affiliated physicians and 7,000 nurses. Advocate's outpatient facilities include the sites run by its physician groups, as well as Advocate Medical Campus Southwest, Advocate Occupational Health, High Tech Medical Park, Midwest Center for Day Surgery, Naperville Surgical Center, Tinley Woods Surgery Center and the Center for Complementary Medicine. Advocate has an Electronic Intensive Care program (eICU) that links real time audio and video monitoring from all adult ICU beds in Advocate's eight hospitals to a central command center. Advocate sponsors several community outreach programs such as school-based health centers, free and reduced cost clinics, nutritional services and educational programs such as Healthy Steps for Young Children and Baby Advocate, programs that remind parents of children's immunization dates.

Advocate offers its employees including flexible spending accounts; medical, dental and vision plans; an education assistance program; life, accident and disability insurance programs; and adoption assistance.

FINANCIALS: **Sales and profits are in thousands of dollars—add 000 to get the full amount. 2007 Note: Financial information for 2007 was not available for all companies at press time.**

007 Sales: $	2007 Profits: $	**U.S. Stock Ticker: Nonprofit**
006 Sales: $	2006 Profits: $	**Int'l Ticker:** Int'l Exchange:
005 Sales: $	2005 Profits: $	Employees: 24,500
004 Sales: $2,779,675	2004 Profits: $143,611	Fiscal Year Ends: 12/31
003 Sales: $2,715,900	2003 Profits: $123,600	Parent Company:

SALARIES/BENEFITS:

ension Plan: Y	ESOP Stock Plan:	Profit Sharing:	Top Exec. Salary: $	Bonus: $
avings Plan: Y	Stock Purch. Plan:		Second Exec. Salary: $	Bonus: $

OTHER THOUGHTS:

pparent Women Officers or Directors: 7
ot Spot for Advancement for Women/Minorities: Y

LOCATIONS: ("Y" = Yes)

West:	Southwest:	Midwest:	Southeast:	Northeast:	International:
		Y			

AETERNA ZENTARIS INC www.aeternazentaris.com

Industry Group Code: 325412 **Ranks within this company's industry group:** Sales: 36 Profits: 27

Insurance/HMO/PPO:		Drugs:		Equipment/Supplies:		Hospitals/Clinics:		Services:		Health Care:	
Insurance:		Manufacturer:	Y	Manufacturer:		Acute Care:		Diagnostics:		Home Health:	
Managed Care:		Distributor:		Distributor:		Sub-Acute:		Labs/Testing:		Long-Term Care:	
Utilization Management:		Specialty Pharmacy:		Leasing/Finance:		Outpatient Surgery:		Staffing:		Physical Therapy:	
Payment Processing:		Vitamins/Nutritionals:		Information Systems:		Physical Rehab. Ctr.:		Waste Disposal:		Physician Prac. Mgmt.:	
		Clinical Trials:				Psychiatric Clinics:		Specialty Svcs.:			

TYPES OF BUSINESS:

Drug Development
Oncology Products
Endocrine Therapy Products

BRANDS/DIVISIONS/AFFILIATES:

Cetrotide
Impavido
Merck Serono
Shionogi
Nippon Kayaku
Ozarelix
Perifosine
Cetrorelix

GROWTH PLANS/SPECIAL FEATURES:

AEterna Zentaris, Inc. is a Canadian biopharmaceutical company focused on endocrine therapy and oncology. The company is devoted to discovering and developing drugs for the treatment of certain forms of cancer, endocrine disorders and infectious diseases. The firm has two products on the market: Cetrotide and Impavido. Cetrotride was the first hormone antagonist treatment approved for in vitro fertilization. The drug is administered to women in order to prevent premature ovulation in order to increase the fertility success rate. Cetrotide is approved in over 80 countries. The drug is marketed worldwide by Merck Serono, except in Japan where it is marketed by Shionogi and Nippon Kayaku. Impavido is an oral drug used for the treatment of visceral and cutaneous leishmaniasis. Currently, the company has three drugs in Phase I of clinical trial, two in Phase II and one in Phase III. The drug in Phase III clinical trials is Cetrorelix for benign prostatic hyperplasia and endometriosis. The firm's Phase II drugs are Ozarelix for prostate cancer and Perifosine for multiple cancers. In addition, the firm has two products in preclinical in vitro testing and three in preclinical development. In May 2006, AEterna began research with the University of Montreal to investigate the role of ghrelin, a hormone with effects on appetite and fat tissue, on trends in obesity. The company owns 100% of Zentaris GmbH, an integrated clinical research company. In January 2007 AEterna Zentaris became a pure play biopharmaceutical company, having completed the spin-off of Atrium Biotechnologies, Inc., the company's former subsidiary.

CONTACTS: *Note: Officers with more than one job title may be intentionally listed here more than once.*

David G. Mazzo, CEO
Jurgen Engel, COO
David G. Mazzo, Pres.
Dennis Turpin, CFO/Sr. VP
Jurgen Engel, Exec. VP-Global R&D
Mario Paradis, Sr. VP-Admin. Affairs
Mario Paradis, Sr. VP-Legal Affairs/Sec.
Ellen McDonald, Sr. VP-Bus. Oper./Chief Bus. Officer
Jenene Thomas, Sr. Dir.-Corp. Comm.
Jenene Thomas, Sr. Dir.-Investor Rel.
Nicholas J. Pelliccione, Sr. VP-Regulatory Affairs & Quality Assurance
Eric Dupont, Chmn.

Phone: 418-652-8525 **Fax:** 418-652-0881
Toll-Free:
Address: 1405 du Parc-Technologique Blvd., Quebec City, Quebec G1P 4P5 Canada

FINANCIALS: **Sales and profits are in thousands of dollars—add 000 to get the full amount. 2007 Note: Financial information for 2007 was not available for all companies at press time.**

2007 Sales: $	2007 Profits: $
2006 Sales: $41,390	2006 Profits: $33,390
2005 Sales: $247,389	2005 Profits: $10,571
2004 Sales: $179,212	2004 Profits: $-4,425
2003 Sales: $128,587	2003 Profits: $-32,426

U.S. Stock Ticker: AEZS
Int'l Ticker: AEZ Int'l Exchange: Toronto-TSX
Employees: 500
Fiscal Year Ends: 12/31
Parent Company:

SALARIES/BENEFITS:

Pension Plan:	ESOP Stock Plan:	Profit Sharing:	Top Exec. Salary: $	Bonus: $
Savings Plan:	Stock Purch. Plan:		Second Exec. Salary: $	Bonus: $

OTHER THOUGHTS:

Apparent Women Officers or Directors: 1
Hot Spot for Advancement for Women/Minorities:

LOCATIONS: ("Y" = Yes)

West:	Southwest:	Midwest:	Southeast:	Northeast:	International:
					Y

AETNA INC

www.aetna.com

Industry Group Code: 524114 **Ranks within this company's industry group:** Sales: 3 Profits: 3

Insurance/HMO/PPO:		Drugs:		Equipment/Supplies:		Hospitals/Clinics:		Services:		Health Care:	
Insurance:	Y	Manufacturer:		Manufacturer:		Acute Care:		Diagnostics:		Home Health:	
Managed Care:	Y	Distributor:		Distributor:		Sub-Acute:		Labs/Testing:		Long-Term Care:	
Utilization Management:		Specialty Pharmacy:		Leasing/Finance:		Outpatient Surgery:		Staffing:		Physical Therapy:	
Payment Processing:		Vitamins/Nutritionals:		Information Systems:		Physical Rehab. Ctr.:		Waste Disposal:		Physician Prac. Mgmt.:	
		Clinical Trials:				Psychiatric Clinics:		Specialty Svcs.:			

TYPES OF BUSINESS:

Insurance-Medical & Health
Long-Term Care Insurance
Group Insurance
Pension Products
Dental Insurance
Disability Insurance
Life Insurance

BRANDS/DIVISIONS/AFFILIATES:

Schaller Anderson, Inc.

CONTACTS: *Note: Officers with more than one job title may be intentionally listed here more than once.*

Ronald A. Williams, CEO
Mark T. Bertolini, Pres.
Joseph M. Zubretsky, CFO/Exec. VP
Robert M. Mead, Sr. VP-Strategic Mktg.
Elease E. Wright, Head-Human Resources
Troyen A. Brennan, Chief Medical Officer/Sr. VP
Meg McCarthy, CIO/Sr. VP-Performance Improvement
William J. Casazza, General Counsel/Sr. VP
Craig R. Callen, Sr. VP/Head-Strategic Planning & Bus. Dev.
Robert M. Mead, Sr. VP-Comm.
Timothy A. Holt, Sr. VP/Chief Investment Officer
Joseph Zubretsky, Chief Enterprise Risk Officer
Ronald A. Williams, Chmn.

Phone: 860-273-0123	**Fax:** 860-273-3971
Toll-Free: 800-872-3862	
Address: 151 Farmington Ave., Hartford, CT 06156 US	

GROWTH PLANS/SPECIAL FEATURES:

Aetna, Inc. is a diversified healthcare benefits companies, serving about 36 million people with information and resources to help them make informed decision about their health care. The company offers a broad range of traditional and consumer-directed health insurance products and related services, including medical, pharmacy, dental, behavioral health, group life, long-term care and disability plans and medical management capabilities. The firm operates in three segments: health care, group insurance and large case pensions. The health care segment's products consist of medical, pharmacy, benefits management, dental and vision plans offered on both a risk basis and an employee-funded basis. Medical products also include point of service, health maintenance organization, preferred provider organization and indemnity benefit plans. The group insurance segment's products consist primarily of life insurance products, including renewable life insurance; disability insurance products, which provide employee income replacement benefits for both short- and long-term disability; and long-term care insurance products, which provide befits to cover the cost of care in private home settings, adult day care, assisted living or nursing facilities. The large case pensions segment manages retirement products primarily for tax qualified pension plans. Customers include employer groups; individuals; college students; part-time and hourly workers; health plans; and government-sponsored plans. In August 2007, Aetna acquired Schaller Anderson, Inc., a provider of healthcare management services, for roughly $535 million. In September 2007, the company agreed to acquire Goodhealth Worldwide, a managing general underwriter for international private medical insurance.

The company offers its employees medical, dental and vision insurance; flexible spending accounts; life insurance; short- and long-term disability insurance; a 401(k) plan; a retirement plan; an employee stock purchase plan; and tuition assistance.

FINANCIALS: **Sales and profits are in thousands of dollars—add 000 to get the full amount. 2007 Note: Financial information for 2007 was not available for all companies at press time.**

2007 Sales: $	2007 Profits: $	**U.S. Stock Ticker: AET**
2006 Sales: $25,145,700	2006 Profits: $1,701,700	**Int'l Ticker:** Int'l Exchange:
2005 Sales: $22,491,900	2005 Profits: $1,634,500	Employees: 30,000
2004 Sales: $19,904,100	2004 Profits: $2,245,100	Fiscal Year Ends: 12/31
2003 Sales: $17,976,400	2003 Profits: $933,800	Parent Company:

SALARIES/BENEFITS:

Pension Plan: Y	ESOP Stock Plan:	Profit Sharing:	Top Exec. Salary: $1,073,077	Bonus: $7,732,500
Savings Plan: Y	Stock Purch. Plan: Y		Second Exec. Salary: $825,000	Bonus: $7,437,015

OTHER THOUGHTS:

Apparent Women Officers or Directors:
Hot Spot for Advancement for Women/Minorities: Y

LOCATIONS: ("Y" = Yes)

West:	Southwest:	Midwest:	Southeast:	Northeast:	International:
Y	Y	Y	Y	Y	

Note: Financial information, benefits and other data can change quickly and may vary from those stated here.

AFLAC INC

www.aflac.com

Industry Group Code: 524114A **Ranks within this company's industry group:** Sales: 1 Profits: 1

Insurance/HMO/PPO:		Drugs:		Equipment/Supplies:		Hospitals/Clinics:		Services:		Health Care:	
Insurance:	Y	Manufacturer:		Manufacturer:		Acute Care:		Diagnostics:		Home Health:	
Managed Care:		Distributor:		Distributor:		Sub-Acute:		Labs/Testing:		Long-Term Care:	
Utilization Management:		Specialty Pharmacy:		Leasing/Finance:		Outpatient Surgery:		Staffing:		Physical Therapy:	
Payment Processing:		Vitamins/Nutritionals:		Information Systems:		Physical Rehab. Ctr.:		Waste Disposal:		Physician Prac. Mgmt.:	
		Clinical Trials:				Psychiatric Clinics:		Specialty Svcs.:			

TYPES OF BUSINESS:

Insurance-Supplemental & Specialty Health
Life Insurance
Cancer Insurance
Medicare Supplement Insurance
Accident & Disability Insurance
Long-Term Care Insurance
Dental Plans

BRANDS/DIVISIONS/AFFILIATES:

AFLAC Japan
AFLAC U.S.
American Family Life Assurance Company of Columbus
Ever

CONTACTS:

Note: Officers with more than one job title may be intentionally listed here more than once.

Daniel P. Amos, CEO
Paul Amos, II, COO
Kriss Cloninger, III, Pres.
Kriss Cloninger, III, CFO
Jeffrey M. Herbert, Sr. VP/Chief Mktg. Officer
Audrey Boone Tillman, Sr. VP/Dir.-Human Resources, Facilities & Health
Gerald Shields, CIO/Sr. VP-IT
James D. Lester III, Sr. VP-Global Tech. Strategy
Rebecca C. Davis, Chief Admin. Officer/Exec. VP
Joey M. Loudermilk, General Counsel/Exec. VP/Corp. Sec.
Angela S. Hart, Sr. VP-Community Rel.
Kenneth S. Janke, Jr., Sr. VP-Investor Rel.
Ralph A. Rogers, Chief Acct. Officer/Sr. VP-Financial Svcs.
Janet Baker, Sr. VP-Client Svcs.
Paul Amos, II, Pres./COO-Aflac U.S.
Kermitt L. Cox, Sr. VP/Corp. Actuary
Phillip J. Friou, Sr. VP-Gov't Relations
Daniel P. Amos, Chmn.
Akitoshi Kan, Chmn., Aflac Int'l

Phone: 706-323-3431	**Fax:** 706-324-6330
Toll-Free: 800-992-3522	
Address: 1932 Wynnton Rd., Columbus, GA 31999 US	

GROWTH PLANS/SPECIAL FEATURES:

AFLAC, Inc. is a holding company whose principle subsidiary, AFLAC (American Family Life Assurance Company of Columbus), insures more than 40 million people worldwide. The subsidiary is a leading writer of supplemental insurance marketed to employers in the U.S. offering policies for 370,000 payroll accounts. AFLAC U.S. sells cancer plans and various types of health insurance including accident and disability, fixed-benefit dental personal sickness and hospital indemnity, hospital intensive care, long-term care, ordinary life and short-term disability plans. In addition, AFLAC offers specified health event coverage for major medical crises such as heart attack and stroke, among others. U.S. insurance products are designed to provide supplemental coverage to individuals who already have major medical or primary insurance coverage. Another subsidiary, AFLAC Japan, is the largest foreign-based insurer in that country, insuring one in four households. AFLAC Japan's insurance products are designed to help consumers pay for medical and non-medical costs that are not reimbursed under Japan's national health insurance system. Ever, a whole life medical insurance policy sold in Japan, hit the 500,000 policy sales mark the year it was introduced. AFLAC Japan accounted for about 72% of AFLAC's pretax insurance earnings in 2006. AFLAC Japan sells cancer plans, care plans, general medical expense plans, medical/sickness riders to our cancer plan, a living benefit life plan, ordinary life insurance plans and annuities. In June 2007, the company opened the first phase of a new $100 million headquarters facility in Columbus, Georgia. Two subsequent phases, planned for completion by 2009 and 2012 respectively, will expand the facility to a total of more then 300,000 square feet.

AFLAC offers employees on-site childcare and fitness centers; extensive training; a health clinic; employee discount programs; continuing education programs; and up to $20,000 in college tuition reimbursement for employee dependents with at least a 2.5 GPA.

FINANCIALS:

Sales and profits are in thousands of dollars—add 000 to get the full amount. 2007 Note: Financial information for 2007 was not available for all companies at press time.

2007 Sales: $	2007 Profits: $	**U.S. Stock Ticker: AFL**
2006 Sales: $14,616,000	2006 Profits: $1,483,000	**Int'l Ticker:** Int'l Exchange:
2005 Sales: $14,363,000	2005 Profits: $1,483,000	Employees: 7,411
2004 Sales: $13,281,000	2004 Profits: $1,266,000	Fiscal Year Ends: 12/31
2003 Sales: $11,447,000	2003 Profits: $795,000	Parent Company:

SALARIES/BENEFITS:

Pension Plan:	ESOP Stock Plan:	Profit Sharing: Y	Top Exec. Salary: $1,242,000	Bonus: $2,208,897
Savings Plan: Y	Stock Purch. Plan: Y		Second Exec. Salary: $796,000	Bonus: $1,109,027

OTHER THOUGHTS:

Apparent Women Officers or Directors: 5
Hot Spot for Advancement for Women/Minorities: Y

LOCATIONS: ("Y" = Yes)

West:	Southwest:	Midwest:	Southeast:	Northeast:	International:
Y	Y	Y	Y	Y	Y

Note: Financial information, benefits and other data can change quickly and may vary from those stated here.

AKZO NOBEL NV

www.akzonobel.com

Industry Group Code: 325000 **Ranks within this company's industry group:** Sales: 2 Profits: 2

Insurance/HMO/PPO:		Drugs:		Equipment/Supplies:		Hospitals/Clinics:		Services:		Health Care:	
Insurance:		Manufacturer:	Y	Manufacturer:		Acute Care:		Diagnostics:		Home Health:	
Managed Care:		Distributor:	Y	Distributor:		Sub-Acute:		Labs/Testing:		Long-Term Care:	
Utilization Management:		Specialty Pharmacy:		Leasing/Finance:		Outpatient Surgery:		Staffing:		Physical Therapy:	
Payment Processing:		Vitamins/Nutritionals:		Information Systems:		Physical Rehab. Ctr.:		Waste Disposal:		Physician Prac. Mgmt.:	
		Clinical Trials:				Psychiatric Clinics:		Specialty Svcs.:			

TYPES OF BUSINESS:

Specialty Chemicals-Coatings
Pharmaceuticals
Veterinary Pharmaceuticals
Over-the-Counter Drugs
Nanotechnology Research

BRANDS/DIVISIONS/AFFILIATES:

Organon International
Intervet, Inc.
Eka Chemicals
Sico, Inc.
The Flood Company

CONTACTS:

Note: Officers with more than one job title may be intentionally listed here more than once.

G. J. Wijers, CEO
Rob Frohn, CFO
Leif Darner, Mgr.
Maarten van den Bergh, Chmn.

Phone: 31-26-366-4433	**Fax:** 31-26-366-3250
Toll-Free:	
Address: Velperweg 76, Arnhem, 6800 SB The Netherlands	

GROWTH PLANS/SPECIAL FEATURES:

Akzo Nobel N.V. produces health care products, coatings and chemicals, and operates in over 80 countries. The pharmaceuticals division provides products for the human health care market through Organon International, whose products include medicine for gynecology, including contraceptive NuvaRing, fertility, neuroscience, anesthesia and urology. Additionally, this division produces products for the animal health care market through Intervet, Inc., which is the third-largest animal health care company in the world. Its products include vaccines, antiparasitics, anti-infectives, endocrine products, feed additives and productivity enhancers. Akzo Nobel's coatings division makes a variety of chemical products including powder, wood, coil, and marine coatings; tile and wood adhesives; and a line of car refinishes. The company's chemical products division produces pulp and paper chemicals; polymer chemicals such as metal alkyls and suspending agents; surfactants used in hair and skincare products; base chemicals such as salt and chlor-alkali products used in the manufacture of glass and plastics; and functional chemicals used in toothpaste, ice cream and flame retardants. In early 2006, the company began a program to divest itself of its chemical production interests, including the sale of its oleochemicals joint ventures in Malaysia to the Lam Soon Group and its Electro Magnetic Compatibility business to ETL Semko KK. In 2006, the firm divested its Polymerization Catalysts and Components business to Basell Polyolefins (February), and sold the Technical Services Department of Akzo Nobel Base Chemichals to Stork NV (May). In June 2006, Akzo acquired Sico, Inc., and sold its Ink and Adhesives resins business to Hexion Specialty Chemicals. Also in 2006, Akzo Nobel acquired The Flood Company, a US woodcare business. In 2007, Schering-Plough Corp. agreed to acquire Akzo Nobel's Organon BioSciences unit $14.4 billion; the company sold its PVC additives business to GIL Investments; and the firm agreed to acquire Imperial Chemical Industries PLC for $16.18 billion.

FINANCIALS:

Sales and profits are in thousands of dollars—add 000 to get the full amount. 2007 Note: Financial information for 2007 was not available for all companies at press time.

2007 Sales: $	2007 Profits: $	**U.S. Stock Ticker: AKZOY**
2006 Sales: $19,659,800	2006 Profits: $1,566,190	**Int'l Ticker: AKZA** Int'l Exchange: Amsterdam-Euronext
2005 Sales: $15,386,000	2005 Profits: $1,137,000	Employees: 61,340
2004 Sales: $17,187,000	2004 Profits: $1,159,000	Fiscal Year Ends: 12/31
2003 Sales: $16,408,000	2003 Profits: $757,000	Parent Company:

SALARIES/BENEFITS:

Pension Plan:	ESOP Stock Plan:	Profit Sharing:	Top Exec. Salary: $	Bonus: $
Savings Plan:	Stock Purch. Plan:		Second Exec. Salary: $	Bonus: $

OTHER THOUGHTS:

Apparent Women Officers or Directors: 1
Hot Spot for Advancement for Women/Minorities:

LOCATIONS: ("Y" = Yes)

West:	Southwest:	Midwest:	Southeast:	Northeast:	International:
		Y	Y	Y	Y

Note: Financial information, benefits and other data can change quickly and may vary from those stated here.

ALCON INC

www.alconlabs.com

Industry Group Code: 325412 **Ranks within this company's industry group:** Sales: 19 Profits: 16

Insurance/HMO/PPO:		Drugs:		Equipment/Supplies:		Hospitals/Clinics:		Services:		Health Care:	
Insurance:		Manufacturer:	Y	Manufacturer:	Y	Acute Care:		Diagnostics:		Home Health:	
Managed Care:		Distributor:		Distributor:		Sub-Acute:		Labs/Testing:		Long-Term Care:	
Utilization Management:		Specialty Pharmacy:		Leasing/Finance:		Outpatient Surgery:		Staffing:		Physical Therapy:	
Payment Processing:		Vitamins/Nutritionals:		Information Systems:	Y	Physical Rehab. Ctr.:		Waste Disposal:		Physician Prac. Mgmt.:	
		Clinical Trials:				Psychiatric Clinics:		Specialty Svcs.:			

TYPES OF BUSINESS:

Eye Care Products
Ophthalmic Products & Equipment
Contact Lens Care Products
Surgical Instruments

BRANDS/DIVISIONS/AFFILIATES:

Opti-Free
Patanol
AcrySof
Betoptic
Falcon Pharmaceuticals
Alcon Surgical
William C. Conner Research Center
Nestle Corporation

CONTACTS: *Note: Officers with more than one job title may be intentionally listed here more than once.*

Cary Rayment, CEO
Allen Baker, COO/Exec. VP
Cary Rayment, Pres.
Jacqualyn Fouse, CFO
Kevin J. Buehler, Chief Mktg. Officer
Gerald D. Cagle, Sr. VP-R&D
Andre Bens, Sr. VP-Global Mfg. & Tech. Support
Elaine E. Whitbeck, General Counsel/Chief Legal Officer
Cary Rayment, Sr. VP-U.S. Oper.
Doug MacHatton, Strategic Corp. Comm.
Doug MacHatton, VP-Investor Rel.
Jacqualyn Fouse, Sr. VP-Finance
Kevin Buehler, Sr. VP-Alcon U.S.
Cary Rayment, Chmn.
Fred Pettinato, Sr. VP-Intl. Oper.

Phone: 41-41-785-8888	**Fax:**
Toll-Free:	
Address: Bosch 69, Hunenberg, 6331 Switzerland	

GROWTH PLANS/SPECIAL FEATURES:

Alcon, Inc. is one of the world's largest eye care produc companies. The company's three divisions (surgical pharmaceutical and consumer vision care) develop manufacture and market ophthalmic pharmaceuticals surgical equipment and devices, contact lens care products and other consumer eye care products that treat diseases and conditions of the eye. Alcon maintains manufacturing plants, laboratories and offices in 50 countries and offers its products and services in over 75 countries. The company makes more than 10,000 unique products, including prescription and over-the-counter drugs, contact lens solutions, surgical instruments, intraocular lenses and office systems for ophthalmologists. Its brand names include Patanol solution for eye allergies, AcrySof intraocular lenses Betoptic for glaucoma and the Opti-Free system for contact lens care. Alcon's research and development headquarters houses the 400,000-square-foot William C. Conner Research Center. Subsidiary Falcon Pharmaceuticals manufactures and markets generic ophthalmic and otic (ear-related) pharmaceuticals in the U.S. Falcon's main product is Timolo GFS, a patented gel forming solution used to treat glaucoma Alcon Surgical creates implantable lenses, viscoelastics and medical tools specifically made for ocular surgeons, including phacoemulsification instruments for cataract removal and absorbable sutures. Alcon's global sales represent 22% of the ophthalmic pharmaceutical market, 51% of the ophthalmic surgical market and 21% of the ophthalmic consumer market. The FDA recently approved Alcon's AcrySof ReSTOR intraocular lens for us in the visual correction of aphakia following cataract surgery. In 2006, the firm signed a marketing agreement with Eli Lilly and Co. to co-promote ruboxistaurin mesylate (proposed brand name Arxxant) in the U.S. and Puerto Rico. Nestle Corporation owns approximately 75% of the firm.

Alcon matches 240% of employee contributions to a 401(k), up to 5% of total compensation. Alcon has been named to FORTUNE magazine's list of the 100 Best Companies to Work for in the U.S. for eight consecutive years.

FINANCIALS: **Sales and profits are in thousands of dollars—add 000 to get the full amount. 2007 Note: Financial information for 2007 was not available for all companies at press time.**

2007 Sales: $	2007 Profits: $	**U.S. Stock Ticker: ACL**
2006 Sales: $4,896,600	2006 Profits: $1,348,100	**Int'l Ticker:** Int'l Exchange:
2005 Sales: $4,368,500	2005 Profits: $931,000	Employees: 13,500
2004 Sales: $3,913,600	2004 Profits: $871,800	Fiscal Year Ends: 12/31
2003 Sales: $3,406,900	2003 Profits: $595,400	Parent Company:

SALARIES/BENEFITS:

Pension Plan: Y	ESOP Stock Plan:	Profit Sharing:	Top Exec. Salary: $	Bonus: $
Savings Plan: Y	Stock Purch. Plan:		Second Exec. Salary: $	Bonus: $

OTHER THOUGHTS:

Apparent Women Officers or Directors: 2
Hot Spot for Advancement for Women/Minorities: Y

LOCATIONS: ("Y" = Yes)

West:	Southwest:	Midwest:	Southeast:	Northeast:	International:
Y	Y	Y	Y	Y	Y

ALIGN TECHNOLOGY INC www.aligntech.com

Industry Group Code: 339113 **Ranks within this company's industry group:** Sales: 60 Profits: 94

Insurance/HMO/PPO:		Drugs:		Equipment/Supplies:		Hospitals/Clinics:		Services:		Health Care:	
Insurance:		Manufacturer:		Manufacturer:	Y	Acute Care:		Diagnostics:		Home Health:	
Managed Care:		Distributor:		Distributor:		Sub-Acute:		Labs/Testing:		Long-Term Care:	
Utilization Management:		Specialty Pharmacy:		Leasing/Finance:		Outpatient Surgery:		Staffing:		Physical Therapy:	
Payment Processing:		Vitamins/Nutritionals:		Information Systems:	Y	Physical Rehab. Ctr.:		Waste Disposal:		Physician Prac. Mgmt.:	
		Clinical Trials:				Psychiatric Clinics:		Specialty Svcs.:			

TYPES OF BUSINESS:

Orthodontic Equipment

BRANDS/DIVISIONS/AFFILIATES:

Invisalign
ClinCheck
Invisalign Express
ClinAdvisor
Invisalign Pty. Ltd.
Invisalign Hong Kong Pty. Ltd.

CONTACTS: *Note: Officers with more than one job title may be intentionally listed here more than once.*

Thomas M. Prescott, CEO
Thomas M. Prescott, Pres.
Eldon M. Bullington, CFO
Darrell Zoromski, VP-Global Mktg./Chief Mktg. Officer
Sonia Clark, VP-Human Resources
Hossein Arjomand, VP-R&D
Michael Henry, CIO/VP-IT
Roger E. George, General Counsel/VP-Legal Affairs/Sec.
Len Hedge, VP-Oper.
Eldon M. Bullington, VP-Finance
Dan S. Ellis, VP-North American Sales
C. Raymond Larkin, Chmn.
Gil Laks, VP-Int'l

Phone: 408-470-1000 **Fax:**
Toll-Free:
Address: 881 Martin Ave., Santa Clara, CA 95050 US

GROWTH PLANS/SPECIAL FEATURES:

Align Technology, Inc. (ATI), founded in 1997, is engaged in the design, manufacture and marketing of Invisalign, a proprietary system for treating malocclusion, or the misalignment of teeth. The Invisalign system has two components: ClinCheck and Aligners. ClinCheck is an Internet-based application that allows dental professionals to simulate treatment, in three dimensions, by modeling two-week stages of tooth movement. Aligners are thin, clear plastic, removable dental appliances that are manufactured in a series to correspond to each two-week stage of the ClinCheck simulation. Aligners are customized to perform the treatment prescribed for an individual patient by dental professionals using ClinCheck. ATI offers two products: the Full Invisalign Treatment, which provides as many Aligners as needed and accounts for 81% of company sales, and Invisalign Express, which provides up to ten Aligners and accounts for 13% of company sales. Two of the company's key production steps are performed outside the U.S. At ATI's facility in Costa Rica, technicians use a sophisticated, internally developed computer modeling program to prepare electronic treatment plans, which are transmitted electronically back to the U.S. These files form the basis of ClinCheck and are used in conjunction with stereo lithography technology to manufacture Aligner molds. A third-party manufacturer in Mexico fabricates Aligners from the molds and ships the completed products to ATI's customers. In recent news, ATI signed an agreement with Insivalign Australia Pty. Ltd. and Invisalign Hong Kong Pty. Ltd. granting sole distribution rights in Australia and Hong Kong respectively. In October 2006 the company launched ClinAdvisor, software providing more efficient treatment options.

FINANCIALS: Sales and profits are in thousands of dollars—add 000 to get the full amount. 2007 Note: Financial information for 2007 was not available for all companies at press time.

2007 Sales: $	2007 Profits: $	**U.S. Stock Ticker: ALGN**
2006 Sales: $206,354	2006 Profits: $-34,963	**Int'l Ticker:** Int'l Exchange:
2005 Sales: $207,125	2005 Profits: $1,413	Employees: 1,253
2004 Sales: $172,800	2004 Profits: $8,768	Fiscal Year Ends: 12/31
2003 Sales: $122,725	2003 Profits: $-20,122	Parent Company:

SALARIES/BENEFITS:

Pension Plan:	ESOP Stock Plan:	Profit Sharing:	Top Exec. Salary: $445,000	Bonus: $376,000
Savings Plan: Y	Stock Purch. Plan: Y		Second Exec. Salary: $284,000	Bonus: $153,360

OTHER THOUGHTS:

Apparent Women Officers or Directors: 1
Hot Spot for Advancement for Women/Minorities:

LOCATIONS: ("Y" = Yes)

West:	Southwest:	Midwest:	Southeast:	Northeast:	International:
Y					Y

ALLERGAN INC

www.allergan.com

Industry Group Code: 325412 **Ranks within this company's industry group:** Sales: 21 Profits: 41

Insurance/HMO/PPO:		Drugs:		Equipment/Supplies:		Hospitals/Clinics:		Services:		Health Care:	
Insurance:		Manufacturer:	Y	Manufacturer:	Y	Acute Care:		Diagnostics:		Home Health:	
Managed Care:		Distributor:		Distributor:		Sub-Acute:		Labs/Testing:		Long-Term Care:	
Utilization Management:		Specialty Pharmacy:		Leasing/Finance:		Outpatient Surgery:		Staffing:		Physical Therapy:	
Payment Processing:		Vitamins/Nutritionals:		Information Systems:		Physical Rehab. Ctr.:		Waste Disposal:		Physician Prac. Mgmt.:	
		Clinical Trials:				Psychiatric Clinics:		Specialty Svcs.:			

TYPES OF BUSINESS:

Pharmaceutical Development
Eye Care Supplies
Dermatological Products
Neuromodulator Products

BRANDS/DIVISIONS/AFFILIATES:

Alphagan
Lumigan
Azelex
Ocuflux
Botox
Restasis
Inamed Corp.
EndoArt S.A.

CONTACTS: *Note: Officers with more than one job title may be intentionally listed here more than once.*

David E. I. Pyott, CEO
F. Michael Ball, Pres.
Jeffrey L. Edwards, CFO
Scott M. Whitcup, Exec. VP-R&D
Raymond H. Diradoorian, Exec. VP-Global Tech. Oper.
Douglas S. Ingram, General Counsel/Exec. VP/Corp. Sec.
Jeffrey L. Edwards, Exec. VP-Bus. Dev.
Jeffrey L. Edwards, Exec. VP-Finance
David E. I. Pyott, Chmn.

Phone: 714-246-4500	**Fax:** 714-246-4971
Toll-Free:	
Address: 2525 Dupont Dr., Irvine, CA 92612 US	

GROWTH PLANS/SPECIAL FEATURES:

Allergan, Inc. is a technology-driven global health care company that develops and commercializes specialty pharmaceutical products for the ophthalmic, neuromodulator, dermatological and other specialty markets. The company focuses on treatments for glaucoma and retinal disease, cataracts, dry eye, psoriasis, acne and neuromuscular disorders. Current research and development efforts are focused on gastroenterology, neuropathic pain and genitourinary diseases. Allergan's eye care pharmaceutical products include Alphagan, Alphagan P and Lumigan ophthalmic solutions, which are used for the treatment of open-angle glaucoma and ocular hypertension; Acular LS, which reduces ocular pain; and Ocuflux, Oflox and Exocin ophthalmic anti-infective solutions. The firm's neuromodulator products include Botox, which is used for the treatment of neuromuscular disorders, and Botox Cosmetic for the temporary improvement of wrinkles. Allergan's skin care product line is comprised of tazarotene products in cream and gel formulations for the treatment of acne, facial wrinkles and psoriasis, marketed under the names Tazorac and Avage; Azelex, an acne product; and M.D. Forte, a line of glycolic and alpha-hydroxy-acid-based products. The firm's fastest growing product is its Restasis dry-eye treatment. In March 2006, Allergan acquired Inamed Corp., maker of the Lap-Band gastric-banding system, for $3 billion dollars. In early 2007, Allergan acquired EndoArt S.A., a Swiss company with technology to remotely tighten or loosen a gastric band, for $97 million.

Allergan offers its employees benefits including a 401(k) plan, a defined benefit retirement contribution, adoption assistance, education assistance, before-tax flex dollars and flexible spending accounts, backup child care, company store, on-site gym and athletic fields, computer training facilities, an employee credit union, an employee assistance program, dependent scholarship awards and U.S. savings bond deductions.

FINANCIALS: **Sales and profits are in thousands of dollars—add 000 to get the full amount. 2007 Note: Financial information for 2007 was not available for all companies at press time.**

2007 Sales: $	2007 Profits: $	**U.S. Stock Ticker: AGN**
2006 Sales: $3,010,100	2006 Profits: $-127,400	**Int'l Ticker:** Int'l Exchange:
2005 Sales: $2,319,200	2005 Profits: $403,900	Employees: 6,772
2004 Sales: $2,045,600	2004 Profits: $377,100	Fiscal Year Ends: 12/31
2003 Sales: $1,171,400	2003 Profits: $-52,500	Parent Company:

SALARIES/BENEFITS:

Pension Plan: Y	ESOP Stock Plan:	Profit Sharing: Y	Top Exec. Salary: $1,125,769	Bonus: $1,243,000
Savings Plan: Y	Stock Purch. Plan: Y		Second Exec. Salary: $507,754	Bonus: $338,500

OTHER THOUGHTS:

Apparent Women Officers or Directors:
Hot Spot for Advancement for Women/Minorities:

LOCATIONS: ("Y" = Yes)

West:	Southwest:	Midwest:	Southeast:	Northeast:	International:
Y	Y				Y

ALLIANCE IMAGING INC

www.allianceimaging.com

Industry Group Code: 621511 **Ranks within this company's industry group:** Sales: 4 Profits: 4

Insurance/HMO/PPO:		Drugs:		Equipment/Supplies:		Hospitals/Clinics:		Services:		Health Care:	
Insurance:		Manufacturer:		Manufacturer:		Acute Care:		Diagnostics:	Y	Home Health:	
Managed Care:		Distributor:		Distributor:		Sub-Acute:		Labs/Testing:		Long-Term Care:	
Utilization Management:		Specialty Pharmacy:		Leasing/Finance:		Outpatient Surgery:		Staffing:		Physical Therapy:	
Payment Processing:		Vitamins/Nutritionals:		Information Systems:		Physical Rehab. Ctr.:		Waste Disposal:		Physician Prac. Mgmt.:	
		Clinical Trials:				Psychiatric Clinics:		Specialty Svcs.:	Y		

TYPES OF BUSINESS:

Diagnostic Imaging
Outsourcing & Support Services

BRANDS/DIVISIONS/AFFILIATES:

CONTACTS:

Note: Officers with more than one job title may be intentionally listed here more than once.

Paul S. Viviano, CEO
Michael F. Frisch, COO
Andrew P. Hayek, Pres.
Howard K. Aihara, CFO/Exec. VP
Eli H. Glovinsky, General Counsel
Paul S. Viviano, Chmn.

Phone: 714-688-7100 **Fax:** 714-688-3333
Toll-Free: 800-544-3215
Address: 1900 S. State College Blvd., Ste. 600, Anaheim, CA 92806 US

GROWTH PLANS/SPECIAL FEATURES:

Alliance Imaging, Inc. (AII) provides shared-service and fixed-site diagnostic imaging services to small and mid-sized hospitals, helping its clients to avoid capital investment and financial risk associated with the purchase of equipment. It serves 1,000 clients in 44 states. The company generates 68% of its revenue from magnetic resonance imaging, or MRI; 23% was derived from positron emission tomography and positron emission tomography/computed tomography, or PET and PET/CT. The company provides imaging services primarily to hospitals and other healthcare providers on a shared and full-time service basis, in addition to operating a growing number of fixed-site imaging centers primarily in partnerships with hospitals or health systems. AII's services normally include the use of its imaging systems, technicians to operate the systems, equipment maintenance and upgrades and management of day-to-day operations. AII has 507 diagnostic imaging systems, including 351 MRI systems and 68 PET or PET/CT systems. Of these systems, 73 were located in fixed-sites, which constitute systems installed in hospitals or other buildings on hospital campuses. Of these fixed sites, 58 were MRI fixed-sites, three were PET or PET/CT fixed-sites and 12 were other modality fixed-sites.

Alliance Imaging offers its employees a benefits package, which includes education assistance and a 401(k) plan.

FINANCIALS:

Sales and profits are in thousands of dollars—add 000 to get the full amount. 2007 Note: Financial information for 2007 was not available for all companies at press time.

2007 Sales: $	2007 Profits: $	**U.S. Stock Ticker: AIQ**
2006 Sales: $455,775	2006 Profits: $19,288	**Int'l Ticker:** Int'l Exchange:
2005 Sales: $430,788	2005 Profits: $19,849	Employees: 1,955
2004 Sales: $432,080	2004 Profits: $- 486	Fiscal Year Ends: 12/31
2003 Sales: $415,283	2003 Profits: $-31,610	Parent Company:

SALARIES/BENEFITS:

Pension Plan:	ESOP Stock Plan:	Profit Sharing:	Top Exec. Salary: $465,000	Bonus: $520,554
Savings Plan: Y	Stock Purch. Plan:		Second Exec. Salary: $325,000	Bonus: $386,280

OTHER THOUGHTS:

Apparent Women Officers or Directors:
Hot Spot for Advancement for Women/Minorities:

LOCATIONS: ("Y" = Yes)

West:	Southwest:	Midwest:	Southeast:	Northeast:	International:
Y	Y	Y	Y	Y	

ALLIED HEALTHCARE INTERNATIONAL INC
www.alliedhealthcare.com

Industry Group Code: 621610 **Ranks within this company's industry group:** Sales: 9 Profits: 13

Insurance/HMO/PPO:		Drugs:		Equipment/Supplies:		Hospitals/Clinics:		Services:		Health Care:	
Insurance:		Manufacturer:		Manufacturer:		Acute Care:		Diagnostics:		Home Health:	Y
Managed Care:		Distributor:		Distributor:		Sub-Acute:		Labs/Testing:		Long-Term Care:	
Utilization Management:		Specialty Pharmacy:		Leasing/Finance:		Outpatient Surgery:		Staffing:	Y	Physical Therapy:	
Payment Processing:		Vitamins/Nutritionals:		Information Systems:		Physical Rehab. Ctr.:		Waste Disposal:		Physician Prac. Mgmt.:	
		Clinical Trials:				Psychiatric Clinics:		Specialty Svcs.:	Y		

TYPES OF BUSINESS:
Home Health Care
Nursing & Para-Professional Services
Home Medical Equipment & Oxygen
Respiration Therapy
Medical Staffing

BRANDS/DIVISIONS/AFFILIATES:
Allied Staffing Professionals, Ltd.
Medigas
Nightingale Nursing Bureau, Ltd.
Allied Healthcare Group, Ltd.

CONTACTS: *Note: Officers with more than one job title may be intentionally listed here more than once.*
Timothy M. Aitken, CEO
David Moffatt, CFO
Leslie J. Levinson, Corp. Sec.
Sarah L. Eames, Exec. VP
Timothy M. Aitken, Chmn.

Phone: 212-750-0064	Fax:
Toll-Free:	
Address: 245 Park Ave., New York, NY 10167 US	

GROWTH PLANS/SPECIAL FEATURES:
Allied Healthcare International Inc. (AHI) is a leading provide of flexible healthcare staffing to the U.K. healthcare industry The company operates a network of 100 branche throughout the U.K., providing staff including nurses, nurs aides and home health aides. AHI places its staff wit hospitals, nursing homes, care homes, private companies the prison service, the police service, armed service hospitals and private homes on a per diem basis from a poc of over 22,000 employees. The firm's staffing business provided under the names Allied Healthcare Group, Allie Staffing Professionals and Nightingale Nursing Bureau makes up 95% of AHI's revenues, while the remaining 5% comes from the company's medical-grade oxygen suppl business, which provides oxygen for use in respirato therapy under the names Allied Respiratory and Medigas AHI generally focuses on the per diem staffing market rathe than the long-term staffing market, as the per diem marke has favorable pricing structure and commands higher servic fees. In addition, the company provides staffing services fo the National Health Service through Allied Staffin Professionals Ltd. and Allied Healthcare Group Ltd.

Allied offers its employees ongoing training and a pensio plan.

FINANCIALS: **Sales and profits are in thousands of dollars—add 000 to get the full amount. 2007 Note: Financial information for 2007 was not available for all companies at press time.**

2007 Sales: $	2007 Profits: $	**U.S. Stock Ticker: AHCI**
2006 Sales: $294,607	2006 Profits: $-123,771	**Int'l Ticker:** Int'l Exchange:
2005 Sales: $351,189	2005 Profits: $18,736	Employees: 960
2004 Sales: $325,298	2004 Profits: $9,869	Fiscal Year Ends: 9/30
2003 Sales: $294,400	2003 Profits: $8,000	Parent Company:

SALARIES/BENEFITS:

Pension Plan: Y	ESOP Stock Plan:	Profit Sharing:	Top Exec. Salary: $537,617	Bonus: $
Savings Plan:	Stock Purch. Plan:		Second Exec. Salary: $336,337	Bonus: $

OTHER THOUGHTS:
Apparent Women Officers or Directors: 3
Hot Spot for Advancement for Women/Minorities: Y

LOCATIONS: ("Y" = Yes)

West:	Southwest:	Midwest:	Southeast:	Northeast:	International:
				Y	Y

ALLINA HOSPITALS AND CLINICS

www.allina.com

Industry Group Code: 622110 **Ranks within this company's industry group:** Sales: 23 Profits:

Insurance/HMO/PPO:		Drugs:		Equipment/Supplies:		Hospitals/Clinics:		Services:		Health Care:	
Insurance:		Manufacturer:		Manufacturer:		Acute Care:	Y	Diagnostics:		Home Health:	Y
Managed Care:		Distributor:		Distributor:	Y	Sub-Acute:	Y	Labs/Testing:		Long-Term Care:	
Utilization Management:		Specialty Pharmacy:		Leasing/Finance:	Y	Outpatient Surgery:	Y	Staffing:		Physical Therapy:	
Payment Processing:		Vitamins/Nutritionals:		Information Systems:		Physical Rehab. Ctr.:	Y	Waste Disposal:		Physician Prac. Mgmt.:	
		Clinical Trials:				Psychiatric Clinics:		Specialty Svcs.:	Y		

TYPES OF BUSINESS:

Hospitals
Clinics & Ambulatory Care Centers
Medical Equipment Rental
Emergency Medical Transportation Services
Hospice Care
Pharmacies
Rehabilitation Services

BRANDS/DIVISIONS/AFFILIATES:

Allina Medical Clinic
Phillips Eye Institute
Sister Kenny Rehabilitation Insitute
Allina Home Oxygen & Medical Equipment
Allina Medical Transportation
medformation.com
Abbot Northwestern Hospital
Buffalo Hospital

CONTACTS: *Note: Officers with more than one job title may be intentionally listed here more than once.*

Richard R. Pettingill, CEO
Kenneth Paulus, COO
Richard R. Pettingill, Pres.
Michael McAnder, CFO
Patricia Jones, Exec. VP-Human Resources
Laurel A. Krause, VP-Allina Medical Laboratories
Robert Plaszcz, CIO
Gary Strong, Chief Admin. Officer
Mary P. Foarde, General Counsel/Corp. Sec.
David B. Orbuch, Exec. VP-Public Policy & Compliance
Brian Anderson, Chief Medical Officer
Barbara Balik, Exec. VP-Safety & Quality Systems
Dan Foley, VP-Medical Affairs/Medical Dir.-United Hospital
Penny Ann Wheeler, Chief Clinical Officer
Rollin Crawford, Chmn.

Phone: 612-262-5000	**Fax:** 612-863-5667
Toll-Free:	
Address: 2925 Chicago Ave., Minneapolis, MN 55407 US	

GROWTH PLANS/SPECIAL FEATURES:

Allina Hospitals and Clinics (AHC) is a nonprofit network of hospitals, clinics and other health care services located throughout Minnesota and western Wisconsin. The company owns and operates 11 hospitals, 39 Allina Medical Clinic sites, 22 hospital-based clinics, 15 community pharmacy sites and four ambulatory care centers. The firm's hospitals include Abbot Northwestern Hospital, Buffalo Hospital, Cambridge Medical Center, Mercy and Unity Hospitals, New Ulm Medical Center, Owatonna Hospital, River Falls Area Hospital, St. Francis Regional Medical Center, United Hospital and Phillips Eye Institute, the third-largest specialty hospital in the U.S. dedicated to eye diseases and disorders. Another specialized health care facility, Allina Hospice and Palliative Care, provides advanced illness or end-of-life care, while the Sister Kenny Rehabilitation Institute treats more than 60,000 patients each year for a variety of conditions, such as stroke and back pain, as well as sports-related, spinal cord and brain injuries. In addition, AHC operates Allina Home Oxygen and Medical Equipment, which supplies oxygen, respiratory and other medical equipment and supplies to a patient's home; and Allina Medical Transportation, which provides pre-hospital emergency medical services, including advanced and basic life support, and scheduled transport in more than 75 Minnesota communities. The company also provides general medical information through its medformation.com web site, offering health classes and other community events.

Allina offers employee benefits including flexible spending accounts, same-sex partner benefits, an employee assistance program, tuition reimbursement, Sallie Mae education program, a legal plan, 529 college savings, adoption assistance, employee discounts, banking services, fitness center memberships, bonuses for quitting smoking and on-site Weight Watchers groups.

FINANCIALS: **Sales and profits are in thousands of dollars—add 000 to get the full amount. 2007 Note: Financial information for 2007 was not available for all companies at press time.**

2007 Sales: $	2007 Profits: $	**U.S. Stock Ticker: Nonprofit**
2006 Sales: $2,350,000	2006 Profits: $	**Int'l Ticker:** Int'l Exchange:
2005 Sales: $	2005 Profits: $	Employees: 22,018
2004 Sales: $2,080,000	2004 Profits: $	Fiscal Year Ends: 12/31
2003 Sales: $1,940,000	2003 Profits: $23,000	Parent Company:

SALARIES/BENEFITS:

Pension Plan: Y	ESOP Stock Plan:	Profit Sharing:	Top Exec. Salary: $	Bonus: $
Savings Plan: Y	Stock Purch. Plan:		Second Exec. Salary: $	Bonus: $

OTHER THOUGHTS:

Apparent Women Officers or Directors: 6
Hot Spot for Advancement for Women/Minorities: Y

LOCATIONS: ("Y" = Yes)

West:	Southwest:	Midwest:	Southeast:	Northeast:	International:
		Y			

ALLSCRIPTS HEALTHCARE SOLUTIONS INC

www.allscripts.com

Industry Group Code: 511212 **Ranks within this company's industry group:** Sales: 4 Profits: 4

Insurance/HMO/PPO:		Drugs:		Equipment/Supplies:		Hospitals/Clinics:		Services:		Health Care:	
Insurance:		Manufacturer:		Manufacturer:		Acute Care:		Diagnostics:		Home Health:	
Managed Care:		Distributor:		Distributor:		Sub-Acute:		Labs/Testing:		Long-Term Care:	
Utilization Management:		Specialty Pharmacy:		Leasing/Finance:		Outpatient Surgery:		Staffing:		Physical Therapy:	
Payment Processing:		Vitamins/Nutritionals:		Information Systems:	Y	Physical Rehab. Ctr.:		Waste Disposal:		Physician Prac. Mgmt.:	
		Clinical Trials:				Psychiatric Clinics:		Specialty Svcs.:	Y		

TYPES OF BUSINESS:

Prescription Management Software
Point-of-Care Decision Support Solutions
Interactive Education Services

BRANDS/DIVISIONS/AFFILIATES:

TouchWorks Professional
TouchWorks Enterprise
Allscripts Direct
Medem, Inc.
A4 Health Systems, Inc.

CONTACTS: *Note: Officers with more than one job title may be intentionally listed here more than once.*

Glen E. Tullman, CEO
Benjamin Bulkley, COO
Lee Shapiro, Pres.
William J. Davis, CFO
Dan Michelson, Chief Mktg. Officer
Brian Vandenberg, General Counsel/VP
Steven P. Schwartz, Sr. VP-Bus. Dev.
Laurie McGraw, Pres., Clinical Solutions
Douglas A. Gentile, Chief Medical Officer
Troy Moritz, Chief Security Officer
David Bond, Pres., HealthMatics
Glen E. Tullman, Chmn.

Phone: 312-506-1200 **Fax:** 312-506-1201
Toll-Free: 800-654-0889
Address: 222 Merchandise Mart Plaza, Ste. 2024, Chicago, IL 60654 US

GROWTH PLANS/SPECIAL FEATURES:

Allscripts Healthcare Solutions, Inc. provides clinica software, connectivity and information solutions tha physicians use to improve healthcare. Its business groups are designed to deliver timely information connecting physicians to each other and to the entire community of care, and to transform healthcare by improving both the quality and efficiency of care. The software and related services segment of the company's business provides clinical software solutions, including electronic health record, electronic prescribing and document imaging solutions. The information services segment, through the physicians interactive business unit, provides clinical education and information solutions for physicians and patients, along with physician-patient connectivity solutions through a partnership with Medem, Inc. The prepackaged medications segment provides prepackaged medication fulfillment solutions, which includes both medications and software for dispensing and inventory control. TouchWorks Professional is a point-of-care clinical solution for small to mid-size physician practices that provides e-prescribing. The TouchWorks Professional solution is delivered online via the physician's PDA (personal digital assistant) to a nearby pharmacy. TouchWorks Enterprise is a similar product used for large physician groups, academic medical centers and integrated delivery networks. Allscripts also owns a pre-packaged medications segment with its Allscripts Direct business, which provides point-of-care medication and medical supply management solutions for physicians. Companies employing Allscripts products include Integris Health, NEA Clinic, The University of Colorado Hospital, Cooper Clinic and Summit Medical Group. In March 2006, Allscripts acquired A4 Health Systems, Inc., a privately held company and a provider of clinical and practice management solutions to physician practice groups.

FINANCIALS: **Sales and profits are in thousands of dollars—add 000 to get the full amount. 2007 Note: Financial information for 2007 was not available for all companies at press time.**

2007 Sales: $
2006 Sales: $227,969
2005 Sales: $120,564
2004 Sales: $100,770
2003 Sales: $85,841

2007 Profits: $
2006 Profits: $11,895
2005 Profits: $9,710
2004 Profits: $3,108
2003 Profits: $-4,989

U.S. Stock Ticker: MDRX
Int'l Ticker: Int'l Exchange:
Employees: 914
Fiscal Year Ends: 12/31
Parent Company:

SALARIES/BENEFITS:

Pension Plan: ESOP Stock Plan: Profit Sharing: Top Exec. Salary: $375,000 Bonus: $226,144
Savings Plan: Stock Purch. Plan: Second Exec. Salary: $315,000 Bonus: $191,117

OTHER THOUGHTS:

Apparent Women Officers or Directors: 1
Hot Spot for Advancement for Women/Minorities:

LOCATIONS: ("Y" = Yes)

West:	Southwest:	Midwest:	Southeast:	Northeast:	International:
Y	Y	Y		Y	

ALPHARMA INC

www.alpharma.com

Industry Group Code: 325414 **Ranks within this company's industry group:** Sales: 2 Profits: 2

Insurance/HMO/PPO:		Drugs:		Equipment/Supplies:		Hospitals/Clinics:		Services:		Health Care:	
Insurance:		Manufacturer:	Y	Manufacturer:		Acute Care:		Diagnostics:		Home Health:	
Managed Care:		Distributor:		Distributor:		Sub-Acute:		Labs/Testing:		Long-Term Care:	
Utilization Management:		Specialty Pharmacy:		Leasing/Finance:		Outpatient Surgery:		Staffing:		Physical Therapy:	
Payment Processing:		Vitamins/Nutritionals:		Information Systems:		Physical Rehab. Ctr.:		Waste Disposal:		Physician Prac. Mgmt.:	
		Clinical Trials:				Psychiatric Clinics:		Specialty Svcs.:			

TYPES OF BUSINESS:

Drugs-Animal Health
Human Pharmaceuticals
Animal Feed Additives
Active Pharmaceutical Ingredients

BRANDS/DIVISIONS/AFFILIATES:

Kadian
Bacitracin
BMD
Albac
3-Nitro
Histostat
Zoamix
Nystatin

CONTACTS: *Note: Officers with more than one job title may be intentionally listed here more than once.*

Dean J. Mitchell, CEO
Dean J. Mitchell, Pres.
Jeffrey S. Campbell, CFO
Peter Watts, Exec. VP-Human Resources
Thomas J. Spellman III, Chief Legal Officer/Exec. VP/Corp. Sec.
Stefan Aigner, Exec. VP-Corp. Dev.
Peter Watts, Exec. VP-Comm.
Carl-Ake Carlsson, Pres., API Active Pharmaceutical Ingredients
Carol A. Wrenn, Pres., Animal Health Div.
Ronald N. Warner, Pres., Pharmaceuticals
Peter G. Tombros, Chmn.

Phone: 908-566-3800 **Fax:** 908-566-4137
Toll-Free: 866-322-2525
Address: 440 U.S. Highway 22 East, 3rd Fl., Bridgewater, NJ 08807 US

GROWTH PLANS/SPECIAL FEATURES:

Alpharma, Inc. is a multinational pharmaceutical company that manufactures specialty and proprietary human pharmaceutical and animal health products. The company operates in three business segments: pharmaceuticals, active pharmaceutical ingredients (API) and animal health. The pharmaceuticals unit manufactures one branded product, Kadian, which is a morphine sulfate sustained release capsule. The medication accounted for 21% of the company's total revenues in 2006. Alpharma is also a leading producer of APIs, marketing and selling 14 APIs, specializing in fermented antibiotics in including Bacitracin, Polymyxin B, Vancomycin, Amphotericin B and Colistin. Alpharma's animal health segment is a leading provider of animal feed additives and water soluable therapeutics for poultry and livestock. It provides over 100 medicated feed-additive products in over 80 countries. Key products include BMD, a feed additive that promotes growth and feed efficiency, as well as prevents or treats diseases in poultry and swine; Albac, a feed additive for poultry, swine and calves; and 3-Nitro, Histostat, Zoamix and CTC feed grade antibiotics, all of which are used in combination or sequentially with BMD. In March 2006, Alpharma sold ParMed, its generics pharmaceutical telemarketing business, to Cardinal Health for $40 million. In October 2006, the FDA approved the Kaidian 80 mg dose, and in February 2007, it approved the 200mg dose strength. In June 2007, the company announced that it has acquired certain assets of Yantai JinHai Pharmaceutical Co. Ltd. in China and plans to use it to expand the animal health division.

Alpharma offers employees benefits including medical, dental, prescription and vision coverage; life and disability insurance; paid time off; and tuition reimbursement.

FINANCIALS: **Sales and profits are in thousands of dollars—add 000 to get the full amount. 2007 Note: Financial information for 2007 was not available for all companies at press time.**

2007 Sales: $
2006 Sales: $653,828
2005 Sales: $553,617
2004 Sales: $513,329
2003 Sales: $1,297,285

2007 Profits: $
2006 Profits: $82,544
2005 Profits: $133,769
2004 Profits: $-314,737
2003 Profits: $16,936

U.S. Stock Ticker: ALO
Int'l Ticker: Int'l Exchange:
Employees: 1,400
Fiscal Year Ends: 12/31
Parent Company:

SALARIES/BENEFITS:

Pension Plan:	ESOP Stock Plan:	Profit Sharing:	Top Exec. Salary: $410,000	Bonus: $429,067
Savings Plan: Y	Stock Purch. Plan: Y		Second Exec. Salary: $400,000	Bonus: $619,067

OTHER THOUGHTS:

Apparent Women Officers or Directors: 1
Hot Spot for Advancement for Women/Minorities:

LOCATIONS: ("Y" = Yes)

West:	Southwest:	Midwest:	Southeast:	Northeast:	International:
Y	Y	Y	Y	Y	Y

AMEDISYS INC

www.amedisys.com

Industry Group Code: 621610 **Ranks within this company's industry group:** Sales: 5 Profits: 4

Insurance/HMO/PPO:		Drugs:		Equipment/Supplies:		Hospitals/Clinics:		Services:		Health Care:	
Insurance:		Manufacturer:		Manufacturer:		Acute Care:		Diagnostics:		Home Health:	Y
Managed Care:		Distributor:		Distributor:		Sub-Acute:		Labs/Testing:		Long-Term Care:	
Utilization Management:		Specialty Pharmacy:		Leasing/Finance:		Outpatient Surgery:		Staffing:		Physical Therapy:	Y
Payment Processing:		Vitamins/Nutritionals:		Information Systems:	Y	Physical Rehab. Ctr.:		Waste Disposal:		Physician Prac. Mgmt.:	
		Clinical Trials:				Psychiatric Clinics:		Specialty Svcs.:			

TYPES OF BUSINESS:

Home Health Care
Medical Software

BRANDS/DIVISIONS/AFFILIATES:

Partners in Wound Care Program
River Region Home Health
Freedom Home Health
SpectraCare Home Health Services, Inc.
NCARE Inc.
Housecall Medical Resources, Inc.
West Virginia Home Health Services, Inc.

CONTACTS: *Note: Officers with more than one job title may be intentionally listed here more than once.*

William F. Borne, CEO
Larry R. Graham, COO
Larry R. Graham, Pres.
Dale E. Redman, Interim CFO
Patty Graham, Sr. VP-Mktg.
Cindy Phillips, Sr. VP-Human Resources
Alice Ann Schwartz, CIO
Jeffrey D. Jeter, Corporate Counsel/Chief Compliance Officer
Jill Cannon, Sr. VP-Oper.
John R. Nugent, Chief Dev. Officer
Dorrie Rambo, Sr. VP-Finance
Beth Boulet, VP-Audit
Deborah Hackman, Sr. VP-Oper.
Pete Hartley, Sr. VP-MIS
William Mayes, Sr. VP-Bus. Dev.
William F. Borne, Chmn.
Francis Mayer, Sr. VP-Contracting

Phone: 225-292-2031	**Fax:** 225-295-9624
Toll-Free: 800-467-2662	
Address: 11100 Mead Rd., Ste. 300, Baton Rouge, LA 70816 US	

GROWTH PLANS/SPECIAL FEATURES:

Amedisys, Inc. is a leading multi-regional provider of home health care nursing services. The company operates over 200 home care nursing offices and three corporate offices in the southern and southeastern U.S. Home health care, in addition to providing patient comfort and convenience, can usually provide lower costs as an alternative to traditional institutional settings. Amedisys's services include skilled nursing; physical, occupational and speech therapy; infusion therapy; oncology and psychiatric services; diabetes assistance; pain management; and hospice care. The company has successfully consolidated its assets in the usually fragmented industry through various measures, including the implementation of internally developed clinical management software now licensed to CareSouth Home Health Services, Inc. In addition, the Medicare Prospective Payment System (PPS) places a greater emphasis upon wound care and stasis ulcers in the clinical scoring process, which validates Amedisys's Partners in Wound Care Program. The program integrates the firm's expert clinical and support services with ConvaTec, a Bristol-Myers Squibb company, MeadJohnson Nutritionals and Hill-Rom, a leader in specialty medical beds and other therapeutic support surfaces. In July 2005, Amedisys acquired Housecall Medical Resources, a Tennessee-based provider of home care services. Two more acquisitions followed in August: NCARE, Inc. and Spectracare Home Health Services. Additionally, in May 2006, the company acquired West Virginia Home Health Services, Inc., a home health agency in Charleston, West Virginia.

FINANCIALS: **Sales and profits are in thousands of dollars—add 000 to get the full amount. 2007 Note: Financial information for 2007 was not available for all companies at press time.**

2007 Sales: $	2007 Profits: $	**U.S. Stock Ticker: AMED**
2006 Sales: $541,148	2006 Profits: $38,255	**Int'l Ticker:** Int'l Exchange:
2005 Sales: $381,558	2005 Profits: $30,102	Employees: 6,892
2004 Sales: $227,100	2004 Profits: $20,500	Fiscal Year Ends: 12/31
2003 Sales: $142,500	2003 Profits: $84,800	Parent Company:

SALARIES/BENEFITS:

Pension Plan:	ESOP Stock Plan:	Profit Sharing:	Top Exec. Salary: $396,153	Bonus: $
Savings Plan: Y	Stock Purch. Plan: Y		Second Exec. Salary: $315,230	Bonus: $

OTHER THOUGHTS:

Apparent Women Officers or Directors: 8
Hot Spot for Advancement for Women/Minorities: Y

LOCATIONS: ("Y" = Yes)

West:	Southwest:	Midwest:	Southeast:	Northeast:	International:
	Y	Y	Y	Y	

AMERICA SERVICE GROUP INC

www.asgr.com

Industry Group Code: 621490 Ranks within this company's industry group: Sales: 5 Profits: 14

Insurance/HMO/PPO:		Drugs:		Equipment/Supplies:		Hospitals/Clinics:		Services:		Health Care:	
Insurance:		Manufacturer:		Manufacturer:		Acute Care:	Y	Diagnostics:	Y	Home Health:	
Managed Care:		Distributor:		Distributor:		Sub-Acute:	Y	Labs/Testing:		Long-Term Care:	
Utilization Management:		Specialty Pharmacy:		Leasing/Finance:		Outpatient Surgery:		Staffing:		Physical Therapy:	
Payment Processing:		Vitamins/Nutritionals:		Information Systems:		Physical Rehab. Ctr.:		Waste Disposal:		Physician Prac. Mgmt.:	
		Clinical Trials:				Psychiatric Clinics:		Specialty Svcs.:	Y		

TYPES OF BUSINESS:

Diversified Health Care Services-Prisons
Military Health Care
Administrative Support Services

BRANDS/DIVISIONS/AFFILIATES:

EMSA Limited Partnership
Correctional Health Services, LLC
SEcure Pharmacy Plus, LLC
Prison Health Services, Inc.

CONTACTS: *Note: Officers with more than one job title may be intentionally listed here more than once.*

Michael Catalano, CEO
Richard Hallworth, COO
Michael Catalano, Pres.
Michael W. Taylor, CFO/Sr. VP
Eric W. Thrailkill, CIO/Sr. VP
T. Scott Hoffman, Chief Admin. Officer/Sr. VP
Lawrence H. Pomeroy, Chief Dev. Officer/Sr. VP
Carl J. Keldie, Chief Medical Officer-Prison Health Svcs.
Richard Hallworth, Pres./CEO-Prison Health Svcs.
Michael Catalano, Chmn.

Phone: 615-373-3100 **Fax:** 615-376-1350
Toll-Free: 800-729-0069
Address: 105 Westpark Dr., Ste. 200, Brentwood, TN 37027 US

GROWTH PLANS/SPECIAL FEATURES:

America Service Group, Inc. (ASG), through its subsidiaries Prison Health Services, Inc., EMSA Limited Partnership, Correctional Health Services, LLC and Secure Pharmacy Plus, LLC, contracts to provide and/or administer managed healthcare services, including the distribution of pharmaceuticals, to over 280 correctional facilities throughout the U.S. The company contracts with state, county and local government agencies to provide a wide range of on-site health care programs as well as off-site hospitalization and specialty outpatient care. The firm's clinics emphasize inmate treatment during the initial stages of incarceration in order to identify illness. Medical services provided on-site include physical and mental health screening upon intake. After initial screening, the company may provide regular physical and dental screening and care; psychiatric care; OB-GYN screening; and care and diagnostic testing. ASG holds sick call on a regular basis and provides infirmary bed care in some facilities. Medical services provided off-site include specialty outpatient diagnostic testing and care, emergency room care, surgery and hospitalization. In addition, the company provides administrative support services both on-site and at its headquarters and regional offices. Administrative programs include on-site medical records and management and employee education and licensing. Central and regional offices provide quality assurance, medical audits, credentialing, continuing education and clinical program development activities. Aside from correctional facility-based health care, ASG provides emergency medicine and primary health care services to active and retired military personnel.

The company offers its employees health and dental insurance; a 401(k) plan; group life insurance; long-term disability insurance; and an employee stock purchase program.

FINANCIALS: **Sales and profits are in thousands of dollars—add 000 to get the full amount. 2007 Note: Financial information for 2007 was not available for all companies at press time.**

2007 Sales: $	2007 Profits: $	**U.S. Stock Ticker: ASGR**
2006 Sales: $569,409	2006 Profits: $-3,380	**Int'l Ticker:** Int'l Exchange:
2005 Sales: $539,470	2005 Profits: $4,365	Employees: 5,030
2004 Sales: $495,465	2004 Profits: $9,010	Fiscal Year Ends: 12/31
2003 Sales: $549,257	2003 Profits: $11,875	Parent Company:

SALARIES/BENEFITS:

Pension Plan:	ESOP Stock Plan:	Profit Sharing:	Top Exec. Salary: $539,810	Bonus: $
Savings Plan: Y	Stock Purch. Plan: Y		Second Exec. Salary: $311,622	Bonus: $

OTHER THOUGHTS:

Apparent Women Officers or Directors:
Hot Spot for Advancement for Women/Minorities:

LOCATIONS: ("Y" = Yes)

West:	Southwest:	Midwest:	Southeast:	Northeast:	International:
			Y		

AMERICAN HOMEPATIENT INC www.ahom.com

Industry Group Code: 621610 **Ranks within this company's industry group:** Sales: 8 Profits: 11

Insurance/HMO/PPO:		Drugs:		Equipment/Supplies:		Hospitals/Clinics:		Services:		Health Care:	
Insurance:		Manufacturer:		Manufacturer:		Acute Care:		Diagnostics:		Home Health:	Y
Managed Care:		Distributor:		Distributor:	Y	Sub-Acute:		Labs/Testing:		Long-Term Care:	
Utilization Management:		Specialty Pharmacy:		Leasing/Finance:	Y	Outpatient Surgery:		Staffing:		Physical Therapy:	
Payment Processing:		Vitamins/Nutritionals:		Information Systems:		Physical Rehab. Ctr.:		Waste Disposal:		Physician Prac. Mgmt.:	
		Clinical Trials:				Psychiatric Clinics:		Specialty Svcs.:	Y		

TYPES OF BUSINESS:

Health Care-Home Health
Respiratory Therapy Services
Infusion Therapy Services
Equipment Leasing
Home Health Supplies

BRANDS/DIVISIONS/AFFILIATES:

CONTACTS:

Note: Officers with more than one job title may be intentionally listed here more than once.

Joseph F. Furlong III, CEO
Frank Powers, COO/Exec. VP
Joseph F. Furlong III, Pres.
Stephen L. Clanton, CFO/Exec. VP

Phone: 615-221-8884 **Fax:** 615-373-9932
Toll-Free: 800-890-7271
Address: 5200 Maryland Way, Ste. 400, Brentwood, TN 37027-5018 US

GROWTH PLANS/SPECIAL FEATURES:

American HomePatient, Inc. (AHP) provides respiratory and infusion therapies and rents and sells home medical equipment and home health care supplies. The company runs approximately 249 centers in 34 states. Revenues come primarily from Medicare, Medicaid and other third parties. AHP generates approximately 75% of its revenues from respiratory services including oxygen systems to assist in breathing, nebulizers, home ventilators, non-invasive positive-pressure ventilation masks, continuous and bi-level positive airway pressure therapies, apnea monitors and home sleep screenings and studies. The company's infusion therapy business generates approximately 12% of revenues and primarily consists of the delivery of necessary equipment, medication and supplies to the patient's home. These patients are generally people who need nutrition through a feeding tube or IV or need pain management or anti-infective therapy. The company's home medical equipment and medical supply provides a comprehensive line of equipment and supplies to serve the needs of home care patients. Revenues from home equipment and supplies are derived principally from the rental and sale of wheelchairs, hospital beds, ambulatory aids, bathroom aids and safety equipment, and rehabilitation equipment. Sales of home medical equipment and medical supplies account for approximately 13% of the company's revenues. In April 2007, the company sold its skilled nursing home health services business to Amedisys, Inc.

AHP offers its employees a 401(k) plan, credit union membership, a dependent care assistance program and medical and dental insurance.

FINANCIALS:

Sales and profits are in thousands of dollars—add 000 to get the full amount. 2007 Note: Financial information for 2007 was not available for all companies at press time.

2007 Sales: $
2006 Sales: $328,080
2005 Sales: $328,418
2004 Sales: $335,823
2003 Sales: $336,181

2007 Profits: $
2006 Profits: $-2,587
2005 Profits: $7,744
2004 Profits: $13,231
2003 Profits: $14,025

U.S. Stock Ticker: AHOM
Int'l Ticker: Int'l Exchange:
Employees: 2,454
Fiscal Year Ends: 12/31
Parent Company:

SALARIES/BENEFITS:

Pension Plan: ESOP Stock Plan: Profit Sharing: Top Exec. Salary: $550,000 Bonus: $495,000
Savings Plan: Y Stock Purch. Plan: Second Exec. Salary: $300,000 Bonus: $216,000

OTHER THOUGHTS:

Apparent Women Officers or Directors:
Hot Spot for Advancement for Women/Minorities:

LOCATIONS: ("Y" = Yes)

West:	Southwest:	Midwest:	Southeast:	Northeast:	International:
Y	Y	Y	Y	Y	

Note: Financial information, benefits and other data can change quickly and may vary from those stated here.

AMERICAN MEDICAL SYSTEMS HOLDINGS INC

www.visitams.com

dustry Group Code: 339113 **Ranks within this company's industry group:** Sales: 51 Profits: 95

surance/HMO/PPO:		Drugs:		Equipment/Supplies:		Hospitals/Clinics:		Services:		Health Care:	
surance:		Manufacturer:		Manufacturer:	Y	Acute Care:		Diagnostics:		Home Health:	
anaged Care:		Distributor:		Distributor:		Sub-Acute:		Labs/Testing:		Long-Term Care:	
ilization Management:		Specialty Pharmacy:		Leasing/Finance:		Outpatient Surgery:		Staffing:		Physical Therapy:	
ayment Processing:		Vitamins/Nutritionals:		Information Systems:		Physical Rehab. Ctr.:		Waste Disposal:		Physician Prac. Mgmt.:	
		Clinical Trials:				Psychiatric Clinics:		Specialty Svcs.:			

YPES OF BUSINESS:

rological Devices Manufacturing
rectile Dysfunction Products
continence Products
rostate Disease Products

BRANDS/DIVISIONS/AFFILIATES:

herMatrx, Inc.
olarant Medical, Inc.
aserscope

CONTACTS: *Note: Officers with more than one job title may be ntentionally listed here more than once.*

Aartin J. Emerson, CEO
Ross A. Longhini, COO/Exec. VP
Aartin J. Emerson, Pres.
Aark A. Heggestad, CFO/Exec. VP
Stephen J. McGill, Sr. VP-Global Sales
anet L. Dick, Sr. VP-Human Resources
awrence W. Getlin, Sr. VP-Legal, Compliance & Quality Systems
R. Scott Etlinger, Sr. VP-Global Oper.
ohn F. Nealon, Sr. VP-Bus. Dev.
Andrew E. Joiner, VP/General Mgr.-Women's Health
Whitney D. Erickson, VP/General Mgr.-Men's Health
Thomas A. Letscher, Sec.
Douglas W. Kohrs, Chmn.

Phone: 952-930-6000	Fax: 952-930-6373
Toll-Free: 800-328-3881	
Address: 10700 Bren Rd. W., Minnetonka, MN 55343 US	

GROWTH PLANS/SPECIAL FEATURES:

American Medical Systems, Inc. (AMS) supplies medical devices for treating urological and gynecological disorders. The company manufactures and markets a broad and well-established line of proprietary products, focusing on three major urological disorders: incontinence, erectile dysfunction and prostate disease. AMS offers a broad line of products designed to treat men and women suffering from urinary and fecal incontinence. Products include artificial sphincters, male and female sling systems, a vaginal vault prolapse system and graft materials. Men's health products contribute to 64.4% of the company's sales, while women's health products contribute to 35.6% of sales. In late 2006, the AdVance sling system was introduced for the improved treatment of mild to moderate stress urinary incontinence in men, while the company offers the AMS 800 Urinary Control System, as well as the In-Fast, SPARC, Monarc, and Bioarc systems for women. AMS provides products for the diagnosis and treatment of erectile dysfunction such as inflatable and malleable penile prostheses and accessories, including its AMS 700 inflatable prostheses. The company sells its products through 72 independent international distributors. In April 2006, the company acquired exclusive rights to use certain proprietary technologies of BioControl Medical, Ltd., pertaining to pelvic health applications. In May 2006, the company acquired Solarant Medical, Inc., a private company focused on developing minimally invasive solutions for women suffering from stress-induced urinary incontinence. AMS acquired Laserscope, a company which provides minimally invasive medical products, in July 2006.

AMS offers its employees a benefits package which includes an educational assistance plan, an on-site fitness center, wellness programs, an on-site cafeteria, profit sharing, a 401(k) savings plan and an employee stock purchase plan.

FINANCIALS: **Sales and profits are in thousands of dollars—add 000 to get the full amount. 2007 Note: Financial information for 2007 was not available for all companies at press time.**

2007 Sales: $	2007 Profits: $	**U.S. Stock Ticker: AMMD**
2006 Sales: $358,318	2006 Profits: $-49,317	**Int'l Ticker:** Int'l Exchange:
2005 Sales: $262,591	2005 Profits: $39,275	Employees: 1,095
2004 Sales: $208,772	2004 Profits: $-3,120	Fiscal Year Ends: 12/29
2003 Sales: $168,283	2003 Profits: $29,050	Parent Company:

SALARIES/BENEFITS:

Pension Plan:	ESOP Stock Plan:	Profit Sharing: Y	Top Exec. Salary: $327,692	Bonus: $215,624
Savings Plan: Y	Stock Purch. Plan: Y		Second Exec. Salary: $268,462	Bonus: $138,515

OTHER THOUGHTS:

Apparent Women Officers or Directors: 2
Hot Spot for Advancement for Women/Minorities:

LOCATIONS: ("Y" = Yes)

West:	Southwest:	Midwest:	Southeast:	Northeast:	International:
Y	Y	Y			Y

AMERICAN RETIREMENT CORP

www.arclp.com

Industry Group Code: 623110 **Ranks within this company's industry group:** Sales: Profits:

Insurance/HMO/PPO:		Drugs:		Equipment/Supplies:		Hospitals/Clinics:		Services:		Health Care:	
Insurance:		Manufacturer:		Manufacturer:		Acute Care:		Diagnostics:		Home Health:	Y
Managed Care:		Distributor:		Distributor:		Sub-Acute:		Labs/Testing:		Long-Term Care:	Y
Utilization Management:		Specialty Pharmacy:		Leasing/Finance:		Outpatient Surgery:		Staffing:		Physical Therapy:	Y
Payment Processing:		Vitamins/Nutritionals:		Information Systems:		Physical Rehab. Ctr.:		Waste Disposal:		Physician Prac. Mgmt.:	
		Clinical Trials:				Psychiatric Clinics:		Specialty Svcs.:			

TYPES OF BUSINESS:

Retirement Communities
Assisted Living Services
Long-Term Health Care
Home Health Care

BRANDS/DIVISIONS/AFFILIATES:

Brookdale Senior Living Incorporated
Freedom Village

CONTACTS:

Note: Officers with more than one job title may be intentionally listed here more than once.

William E. Sheriff, CEO
Gregory B. Richard, COO/Exec. VP
William E. Sheriff, Pres.
Bryan Richardson, CFO/Exec. VP
James T. Money, Exec. VP-Sales & Mktg.
Terry Frisby, Sr. VP-Human Resources, Corp. Compliance & Culture
Jack Leebron, Sr. VP-Legal Svcs.
Gary Anderson, Regional VP-Oper.
H. Todd Kaestner, Exec. VP-Corp. Dev.
Matt Fontana, VP-Public Rel.
Ross Roadman, Sr. VP-Investor Rel. & Strategic Planning
George T. Hicks, Exec. VP-Finance & Audit/Treas./Corp. Sec.
Ron Aylor, Sr. VP-Sales
Lee Anne Fein, Sr. VP-Innovative Sr. Care
Fred Ewing, Regional VP-Oper.
Eddie Fenoglio, Regional VP-Oper.
William E. Sheriff, Chmn.
Richard Raessler, VP-Asset Mgmt. & Purchasing

Phone: 615-221-2250 **Fax:** 615-221-2269
Toll-Free:
Address: 111 Westwood Pl., Ste. 305, Brentwood, TN 37027 US

GROWTH PLANS/SPECIAL FEATURES:

American Retirement Corp. (ACR) is a senior living and health care provider that offers services for independent living, assisted living, skilled nursing and therapy. The company currently manages 83 senior living communities in 19 states with an aggregate capacity of close to 15,950 residents. ACR operates within three business sectors: retirement centers, free-standing assisted living communities and management services. In ACR retirement centers, the company's main objective is to develop and operate senior living networks within populous metropolitan areas. Retirement centers offer services such as skilled nursing and therapy in campus-style surroundings for residents in independent living communities. These centers form the largest segment of the ACR business since approximately 68% of the total resident capacity is within its retirement communities. Free-standing assisted living residencies are generally stand-alone communities that aim to provide a home-like setting instead of a clinical and institutional setting. Skilled nursing care is provided for residents with Alzheimer's and other forms of dementia. The management services segment of ACR consists of six retirement centers which are operated by independent parties under multi-year management agreements with ACR. Communities are owned by retirement cooperatives, non-profit organizations and third-party affiliates. In the middle of 2006, the company acquired Freedom Village, a continuing care retirement community in Bradenton, Florida, two communities in Shawnee, Kansas and four senior living communities from Cypress Senior Living, Inc. Brookdale Senior Living Incorporated is currently in the process of merging with ACR to constitute a company that will become one of the largest operators of senior living facilities within the U.S.

FINANCIALS:

Sales and profits are in thousands of dollars—add 000 to get the full amount. 2007 Note: Financial information for 2007 was not available for all companies at press time.

2007 Sales: $
2006 Sales: $
2005 Sales: $495,000
2004 Sales: $447,609
2003 Sales: $368,096

2007 Profits: $
2006 Profits: $
2005 Profits: $69,698
2004 Profits: $-11,317
2003 Profits: $-17,314

U.S. Stock Ticker: ACR
Int'l Ticker: Int'l Exchange:
Employees:
Fiscal Year Ends: 12/31
Parent Company:

SALARIES/BENEFITS:

Pension Plan: ESOP Stock Plan: Profit Sharing: Y Top Exec. Salary: $395,955 Bonus: $166,944
Savings Plan: Y Stock Purch. Plan: Second Exec. Salary: $233,788 Bonus: $

OTHER THOUGHTS:

Apparent Women Officers or Directors: 5
Hot Spot for Advancement for Women/Minorities: Y

LOCATIONS: ("Y" = Yes)

West:	Southwest:	Midwest:	Southeast:	Northeast:	International:
Y	Y	Y	Y	Y	

AMERICHOICE CORPORATION www.americhoice.com

Industry Group Code: 524114 **Ranks within this company's industry group:** Sales: Profits:

Insurance/HMO/PPO:		Drugs:		Equipment/Supplies:		Hospitals/Clinics:		Services:		Health Care:	
Insurance:	Y	Manufacturer:		Manufacturer:		Acute Care:		Diagnostics:		Home Health:	
Managed Care:		Distributor:		Distributor:		Sub-Acute:		Labs/Testing:		Long-Term Care:	
Utilization Management:		Specialty Pharmacy:		Leasing/Finance:		Outpatient Surgery:		Staffing:		Physical Therapy:	
Payment Processing:		Vitamins/Nutritionals:		Information Systems:		Physical Rehab. Ctr.:		Waste Disposal:		Physician Prac. Mgmt.:	
		Clinical Trials:				Psychiatric Clinics:		Specialty Svcs.:	Y		

TYPES OF BUSINESS:

Insurance-Medical & Health, HMOs & PPOs

BRANDS/DIVISIONS/AFFILIATES:

AmeriChoice Personal Care Model
Telemedicine
Healthy First Steps
UnitedHealth Group Inc

CONTACTS: *Note: Officers with more than one job title may be intentionally listed here more than once.*

Rick Jelenik, CEO
Steve Swift, CFO

Phone: 703-506-3555 **Fax:** 703-506-3556
Toll-Free:
Address: 8045 Leesburg Pike, 6th Fl., Vienna, VA 22182 US

GROWTH PLANS/SPECIAL FEATURES:

AmeriChoice Corporation, a UnitedHealth Group company, serves recipients of government health care programs. The company operates its own government program health insurance plans and provides management and information technology services to other managed care organizations, serving over 1.3 million members in 16 states. AmeriChoice features community-based networks, a focus on preventative services, outreach and intensive case management. AmeriChoice tries to promote prevention through health education and programs. It targets the most frequent causes of severe illness in its service areas, addressing conditions such as asthma, diabetes, sickle cell disease and high-risk pregnancies. The AmeriChoice Personal Care Model assigns members to nurses and social workers who build a support network involving family, physicians, ancillary providers and government and community-based organizations and resources. Its Telemedicine program uses video units in members' homes, allowing case managers to monitor certain vital signs and check medications over the phone. The company's Healthy First Steps maternal and obstetrical care program helps women schedule prenatal doctor visits, select a pediatrician and get health services for the baby. The company sends reminders to members encouraging them to get annual physicals and routine diagnostic and screening tests, and often makes special arrangements, including door-to-door transportation, child care and private appointments, for groups of women to receive mammograms and for children to be immunized.

FINANCIALS: Sales and profits are in thousands of dollars—add 000 to get the full amount. 2007 Note: Financial information for 2007 was not available for all companies at press time.

2007 Sales: $	2007 Profits: $	**U.S. Stock Ticker: Subsidiary**
2006 Sales: $	2006 Profits: $	**Int'l Ticker:** Int'l Exchange:
2005 Sales: $3,387,000	2005 Profits: $	Employees: 2,000
2004 Sales: $3,121,000	2004 Profits: $	Fiscal Year Ends:
2003 Sales: $2,674,000	2003 Profits: $	Parent Company: UNITEDHEALTH GROUP INC

SALARIES/BENEFITS:

Pension Plan:	ESOP Stock Plan:	Profit Sharing:	Top Exec. Salary: $	Bonus: $
Savings Plan:	Stock Purch. Plan:		Second Exec. Salary: $	Bonus: $

OTHER THOUGHTS:

Apparent Women Officers or Directors:
Hot Spot for Advancement for Women/Minorities:

LOCATIONS: ("Y" = Yes)

West:	Southwest:	Midwest:	Southeast:	Northeast:	International:
Y	Y	Y	Y	Y	

AMERIGROUP CORPORATION www.amerigroupcorp.com

Industry Group Code: 524114 **Ranks within this company's industry group:** Sales: 21 Profits: 20

Insurance/HMO/PPO:		Drugs:		Equipment/Supplies:		Hospitals/Clinics:		Services:		Health Care:	
Insurance:		Manufacturer:		Manufacturer:		Acute Care:		Diagnostics:		Home Health:	
Managed Care:	Y	Distributor:		Distributor:		Sub-Acute:		Labs/Testing:		Long-Term Care:	
Utilization Management:		Specialty Pharmacy:		Leasing/Finance:		Outpatient Surgery:		Staffing:		Physical Therapy:	
Payment Processing:		Vitamins/Nutritionals:		Information Systems:		Physical Rehab. Ctr.:		Waste Disposal:		Physician Prac. Mgmt.:	
		Clinical Trials:				Psychiatric Clinics:		Specialty Svcs.:			

TYPES OF BUSINESS:

Managed Health Care

BRANDS/DIVISIONS/AFFILIATES:

AMERICAID
AMERIKIDS
AMERIPLUS
AMERIFAM
AMERIADVANTAGE

CONTACTS: *Note: Officers with more than one job title may be intentionally listed here more than once.*

James G. Carlson, CEO
Richard C. Zoretic, COO
James G. Carlson, Pres.
James W. Truess, CFO/Exec. VP
Nancy L. Groden, Chief Mktg. Officer/Exec. VP
Leon A. Root, Jr., CIO/Exec. VP
Stanley F. Baldwin, General Counsel/Exec. VP/Corp. Sec.
Kent Jenkins, Jr., Sr. VP-Comm.
Catherine S. Callahan, Exec. VP-Associate Svcs.
William T. Keena, Exec. VP-Support Oper.
John E. Littel, Exec. VP-External Affairs
Mary McCluskev, Chief Medical Officer
Jeffrey L. McWaters, Chmn.

Phone: 757-490-6900	**Fax:** 757-222-2330
Toll-Free:	
Address: 4425 Corporation Ln., Virginia Beach, VA 23462 US	

GROWTH PLANS/SPECIAL FEATURES:

AMERIGROUP Corp. is a managed health care company focused on serving people who receive health care benefits through publicly sponsored programs, including Medicaid, State Children's Health Insurance Program (S CHIP), FamilyCare and Special Needs Plans (SNP). Since the company does not offer Medicare or commercial products, people served by AMERIGROUP are generally younger, tend to access health care in an inefficient manner and have a greater percentage of medical expenses related to obstetrics, diabetes and circulatory and respiratory conditions. In addition, because new members typically use the emergency room as a primary care provider, the firm reduces costs for families and state governments by combining social and behavioral health services to help members obtain health care. The company currently enrolls members in Texas, Florida, Georgia, Ohio, New Jersey, New York, Maryland, Washington, D.C. and Virginia, serving over 1.3 million members. The firm offers a variety of insurance products, including AMERICAID, a Medicaid product designed for low-income children and pregnant women; AMERIKIDS, an S CHIP product for uninsured children not eligible for Medicaid; AMERIPLUS, a product for the low-income aged, blind and disabled who receive Social Security; AMERIFAM, designed for uninsured parents of S CHIP and Medicaid children; and AMERIADVANTAGE, one of the company's SNP managed care product for dual eligibles. The plans all include some combination of primary and specialty physician care; inpatient and outpatient hospital care; emergency care; prenatal care; laboratory and x-ray services; home health and medical equipment; behavioral health services; substance abuse; long-term and nursing home care; vision care; dental care; chiropractic care; and prescription coverage. In September 2007, AMERIGROUP agreed to acquire Memphis Managed Care Corp.

The company offers its employees medical, dental and vision insurance; life insurance; a 401(k) plan; an employee stock purchase plan; flexible spending accounts; short- and long-term disability insurance; and an employee assistance program.

FINANCIALS: **Sales and profits are in thousands of dollars—add 000 to get the full amount. 2007 Note: Financial information for 2007 was not available for all companies at press time.**

2007 Sales: $	2007 Profits: $	**U.S. Stock Ticker: AGP**
2006 Sales: $2,835,089	2006 Profits: $107,106	**Int'l Ticker:** Int'l Exchange:
2005 Sales: $2,329,909	2005 Profits: $53,651	Employees: 3,500
2004 Sales: $1,823,731	2004 Profits: $86,014	Fiscal Year Ends: 12/31
2003 Sales: $1,622,234	2003 Profits: $67,324	Parent Company:

SALARIES/BENEFITS:

Pension Plan:	ESOP Stock Plan:	Profit Sharing:	Top Exec. Salary: $655,636	Bonus: $1,681,725
Savings Plan: Y	Stock Purch. Plan: Y		Second Exec. Salary: $518,605	Bonus: $1,203,877

OTHER THOUGHTS:

Apparent Women Officers or Directors: 2
Hot Spot for Advancement for Women/Minorities: Y

LOCATIONS: ("Y" = Yes)

West:	Southwest:	Midwest:	Southeast:	Northeast:	International:
	Y	Y	Y	Y	

Note: Financial information, benefits and other data can change quickly and may vary from those stated here.

AMERIPATH INC

www.ameripath.com

Industry Group Code: 621111 **Ranks within this company's industry group:** Sales: 3 Profits: 4

Insurance/HMO/PPO:		Drugs:		Equipment/Supplies:		Hospitals/Clinics:		Services:		Health Care:	
Insurance:		Manufacturer:		Manufacturer:		Acute Care:		Diagnostics:	Y	Home Health:	
Managed Care:		Distributor:		Distributor:		Sub-Acute:		Labs/Testing:	Y	Long-Term Care:	
Utilization Management:		Specialty Pharmacy:		Leasing/Finance:		Outpatient Surgery:		Staffing:	Y	Physical Therapy:	
Payment Processing:		Vitamins/Nutritionals:		Information Systems:		Physical Rehab. Ctr.:		Waste Disposal:		Physician Prac. Mgmt.:	Y
		Clinical Trials:				Psychiatric Clinics:		Specialty Svcs.:	Y		

TYPES OF BUSINESS:

Anatomic Pathology Practice Management
Cancer Diagnostic Services
Staffing Services
Operations Management
Health Care Information Services

BRANDS/DIVISIONS/AFFILIATES:

Ameripath Esoteric Institute
AmeriPath Institute of Gastrointestinal Pathology
AmeriPathInstitute for Podiatric Pathology
Specialty Laboratories Inc
Center for Advanced Diagnostics (The)
Dermpath Diagnostics
Institute for Immunofluorescence (The)
Rose Pathology Associates, P.C.

CONTACTS: *Note: Officers with more than one job title may be intentionally listed here more than once.*

David L. Redmond, Pres.
Stephen V. Fuller, Sr. VP-Human Resources
Bob J. Copeland, VP/CIO
Jeffrey A. Mossler, VP/Chief Anatomic Pathology Officer
Steven E. Casper, Pres., Dermatopathology Svcs.
Philip A. Spencer, Pres., Anatomic Pathology Svcs.
Russell L. Maiese, Dir.-Hematopathology
Donald E. Steen, Chmn.

Phone: 561-712-6200	**Fax:** 561-845-0129
Toll-Free: 800-330-6565	
Address: 7289 Garden Rd., Ste. 200, Riviera Beach, FL 33404 US	

GROWTH PLANS/SPECIAL FEATURES:

AmeriPath, which is owned by Welsh, Carson, Anderson & Stowe, is one of the nation's leading providers of anatomic pathology, cancer diagnostic and health care information services to physicians, hospitals, national clinical laboratories and managed care organizations. The company provides services at 200 hospitals and more than 50 outpatient laboratories, with over 400 working pathologists. AmirPath directly offers comprehensive diagnostic, prognostic and therapeutic services in the field of oncology. The company's primary business, though, is developing, staffing and operating clinical pathology laboratories, which it does through long-term service management agreements. Currently, the company operates seven major centers through this management model: Ameripath Esoteric Institute, AmeriPath Institute of Gastrointestinal Pathology and Digestive Disease, AmeriPathInstitute for Podiatric Pathology, AmeriPath Institute of Urologic Pathology and Renal Disease, The Center for Advanced Diagnostics, Dermpath Diagnostics and The Institute for Immunofluorescence. These state-of-the-art centers cover such diverse fields of medical research and analysis as hematopathology and genetics examination; podiatric skin, soft tissue and bone pathology; diagnoses of biopsy specimens for urologic pathology and renal diseases; diagnostic tests and diseases management for leukemia, lymphoma and cancers of the breast, prostate and colon; immunofluorescence testing for autoimmune and inflammatory skin diseases; and dermatopathology services. The Ameripath Esoteric Institute, located in Shelton, Connecticut and the Institute for Immunofluoresces in Pompano Beach, FL recently opened its doors to patients. In April 2006, the company underwent a major expansion and remodel at its Cleveland, Ohio facility, going from 9,000 to 15,000 square feet. The additional space includes a new conference room and a separate multiheaded microscope room, specifically dedicated to physician education and training. Also in April, AmeriPath acquired Rose Pathology Associates, P.C., a Colorado-based provider of physician-based anatomic pathology, dermatopathology and molecular diagnostic services.

AmeriPath offers its employees tuition reimbursement and child and dependant care.

FINANCIALS: **Sales and profits are in thousands of dollars—add 000 to get the full amount. 2007 Note: Financial information for 2007 was not available for all companies at press time.**

2007 Sales: $	2007 Profits: $	**U.S. Stock Ticker: Private**
2006 Sales: $752,300	2006 Profits: $10,500	**Int'l Ticker:** Int'l Exchange:
2005 Sales: $563,600	2005 Profits: $9,200	Employees: 3,979
2004 Sales: $507,300	2004 Profits: $1,500	Fiscal Year Ends: 12/31
2003 Sales: $485,000	2003 Profits: $23,400	Parent Company:

SALARIES/BENEFITS:

Pension Plan:	ESOP Stock Plan:	Profit Sharing:	Top Exec. Salary: $425,000	Bonus: $255,000
Savings Plan: Y	Stock Purch. Plan:		Second Exec. Salary: $348,769	Bonus: $100,000

OTHER THOUGHTS:

Apparent Women Officers or Directors:
Hot Spot for Advancement for Women/Minorities:

LOCATIONS: ("Y" = Yes)

West:	Southwest:	Midwest:	Southeast:	Northeast:	International:
Y	Y	Y	Y	Y	

AMERISOURCEBERGEN CORP www.amerisourcebergen.com

Industry Group Code: 422210 **Ranks within this company's industry group:** Sales: 3 Profits: 3

Insurance/HMO/PPO:		Drugs:		Equipment/Supplies:		Hospitals/Clinics:		Services:		Health Care:	
Insurance:		Manufacturer:		Manufacturer:		Acute Care:		Diagnostics:		Home Health:	
Managed Care:		Distributor:	Y	Distributor:	Y	Sub-Acute:		Labs/Testing:		Long-Term Care:	
Utilization Management:		Specialty Pharmacy:	Y	Leasing/Finance:		Outpatient Surgery:		Staffing:		Physical Therapy:	
Payment Processing:		Vitamins/Nutritionals:		Information Systems:	Y	Physical Rehab. Ctr.:		Waste Disposal:		Physician Prac. Mgmt.:	
		Clinical Trials:				Psychiatric Clinics:		Specialty Svcs.:	Y		

TYPES OF BUSINESS:

Drug Distribution
Pharmacy Management & Consulting Services
Packaging Solutions
Information Technology
Healthcare Equipment

BRANDS/DIVISIONS/AFFILIATES:

AmerisourceBergen Drug Corp.
AmerisourceBergen Specialty Group
AmerisourceBergen Packaging Group
American Health Packaging
Anderson Packaging
Brecon Pharmaceutical, Ltd.
Kindred Healthcare, Inc.
PharMerica Corp.

CONTACTS: *Note: Officers with more than one job title may be intentionally listed here more than once.*

R. David Yost, CEO
R. David Yost, Pres.
Michael D. DiCandilo, CFO/Exec. VP
David W. Neu, Sr. VP-Retail Sales & Mktg.
Jeanne Fisher, Sr. VP-Human Resources
Thomas H. Murphy, CIO/Sr. VP
John G. Chou, General Counsel/Sr. VP/Sec.
David M. Senior, Sr. VP-Strategy & Corp. Dev.
J.F. Quinn, Treas./VP
Steven H. Collis, Exec. VP/Pres., AmerisourceBergen Specialty Group
Terrance P. Hass, Exec. VP/Chief Integration Officer
John Palumbo, Sr. VP-Health Systems Solutions
Tim G. Guttman, Corp. Controller/VP
Richard C. Gozon, Chmn.
Len DeCandia, Sr. VP-Supply Chain Mgmt.

Phone: 610-727-7000	**Fax:** 610-727-3600
Toll-Free: 800-829-3132	
Address: 1300 Morris Dr., Ste. 100, Chesterbrook, PA 19087 US	

GROWTH PLANS/SPECIAL FEATURES:

AmerisourceBergen Corp. is a pharmaceutical services company, with operations in the U.S., Canada and the U.K. The company provides drug distribution and related services to both pharmaceutical manufacturers and healthcare providers in the pharmaceutical supply channel. The firm operates in two business segments: pharmaceutical distribution and PharMerica. The pharmaceutical distribution segment includes the operations of AmerisourceBergen Drug Corp. (ABDC), AmerisourceBergen Specialty Group (ABSG) and AmerisourceBergen Packaging Group (ABPG). ABDC distributes brand name and generic pharmaceuticals; over-the-counter healthcare products; and home healthcare supplies and equipment. ABDC also provides pharmacy management and consulting services; and scalable automated pharmacy dispensing equipment, medical and supply dispending cabinets and supply management software. ABSG distributes vaccines, other injectibles, plasma and other blood products. In addition, ABSG provides a number of commercialization, third party logistics, group purchasing services and other services for biotech and other pharmaceutical manufacturers. ABPG consists of American Health Packaging, which delivers unit dose, punch card, unit-of-use and other packaging solutions; Anderson Packaging, which provides contract packaging services; and Brecon Pharmaceutical, Ltd., a provider of contract packaging and clinical trial materials services. The PharMerica segment includes the operation of the long-term care business, a dispenser of pharmaceutical products and services to patients in long-term care and alternate site settings; and workers' compensation-related business, a provider of proprietary information technology for workers' compensation solutions. In addition, AmerisourceBergen offers several specialty programs, including Good Neighbor Pharmacy, which enables independent community pharmacies to compete more effectively. In July 2007, the company and Kindred Healthcare, Inc. combined their respective institutional pharmacy businesses to create PharMerica Corp., a new independent and publicly-traded company.

The company offers its employees medical, dental and vision insurance; a 401(k) plan; short- and long-term disability insurance; an employee stock purchase plan; tuition reimbursement; and an employee assistance program.

FINANCIALS: **Sales and profits are in thousands of dollars—add 000 to get the full amount. 2007 Note: Financial information for 2007 was not available for all companies at press time.**

2007 Sales: $	2007 Profits: $	**U.S. Stock Ticker: ABC**
2006 Sales: $61,203,145	2006 Profits: $467,714	**Int'l Ticker:** Int'l Exchange:
2005 Sales: $54,577,300	2005 Profits: $264,645	Employees: 14,700
2004 Sales: $53,178,954	2004 Profits: $468,390	Fiscal Year Ends: 9/30
2003 Sales: $49,657,300	2003 Profits: $441,200	Parent Company:

SALARIES/BENEFITS:

Pension Plan:	ESOP Stock Plan:	Profit Sharing:	Top Exec. Salary: $1,081,718	Bonus: $1,585,479
Savings Plan: Y	Stock Purch. Plan: Y		Second Exec. Salary: $647,116	Bonus: $869,440

OTHER THOUGHTS:

Apparent Women Officers or Directors: 2
Hot Spot for Advancement for Women/Minorities:

LOCATIONS: ("Y" = Yes)

West:	Southwest:	Midwest:	Southeast:	Northeast:	International:
Y	Y	Y	Y	Y	

AMGEN INC

www.amgen.com

Industry Group Code: 325412 **Ranks within this company's industry group:** Sales: 13 Profits: 10

Insurance/HMO/PPO:		Drugs:		Equipment/Supplies:		Hospitals/Clinics:		Services:		Health Care:	
Insurance:		Manufacturer:	Y	Manufacturer:		Acute Care:		Diagnostics:		Home Health:	
Managed Care:		Distributor:		Distributor:		Sub-Acute:		Labs/Testing:		Long-Term Care:	
Utilization Management:		Specialty Pharmacy:		Leasing/Finance:		Outpatient Surgery:		Staffing:		Physical Therapy:	
Payment Processing:		Vitamins/Nutritionals:		Information Systems:		Physical Rehab. Ctr.:		Waste Disposal:		Physician Prac. Mgmt.:	
		Clinical Trials:				Psychiatric Clinics:		Specialty Svcs.:			

TYPES OF BUSINESS:

Drugs-Diversified
Oncology Drugs
Nephrology Drugs
Inflammation Drugs
Neurology Drugs
Metabolic Drugs

BRANDS/DIVISIONS/AFFILIATES:

Neupogen
Epogen
Aranesp
Enbrel
Kineret
Sensipar
Neulasta
Avidia

CONTACTS: *Note: Officers with more than one job title may be intentionally listed here more than once.*

Kevin W. Sharer, CEO
Kevin W. Sharer, Pres.
Richard D. Nanula, CFO/Exec. VP
Craig Brooks, VP-Global Mktg.
Brian McNamee, Sr. VP-Human Resources
Roger Perlmutter, Exec. VP-R&D
Tom Flanagan, CIO/Sr. VP
Fabrizio Bonanni, Sr. VP-Mfg.
David J. Scott, General Counsel/Sr. VP/Corp. Sec.
Dennis M. Fenton, Exec. VP-Oper.
Sean Harper, Sr. VP-Global Dev./Chief Medical Officer
Phyllis Piano, VP-Corp. Comm./Philanthropy
Steve Schoch, VP-Finance
Nahed Ahmed, VP-Project Mgmt. R&D
Jim Daly, Sr. VP-Commercial Oper., N. America
David Beier, Sr. VP-Global Government Affairs
George Morrow, Exec. VP-Global Commercial Oper.
Kevin W. Sharer, Chmn.
Rollf Hoffmann, Sr. VP-Amgen Int'l Oper.
Laurel Junk, VP-Supply Chain

Phone: 805-447-1000 **Fax:** 805-447-1010
Toll-Free:
Address: 1 Amgen Center Dr., Thousand Oaks, CA 91320-1799 US

GROWTH PLANS/SPECIAL FEATURES:

Amgen, Inc. is a global biotechnology company that develops, manufactures and markets human therapeutics based on advanced cellular and molecular biology. Its products are used for treatment in the fields of nephrology, oncology, inflammation, neurology and metabolic disorders. The company manufactures and markets a line of human therapeutic products including Neupogen, Epogen, Aranesp, Enbrel, Kineret, Neulasta and Sensipar. Neupogen and Neulasta selectively stimulate the growth of infection-fighting white blood cells. Kineret and Enbrel reduce the signs and symptoms of moderately to severely active rheumatoid arthritis. Epogen and Aranesp stimulate the production of red blood cells. Amgen's research and development efforts are focused on human therapeutics delivered in the form of proteins, monoclonal antibodies and small molecules in the areas of hematology; oncology; inflammation; metabolic and bone disorders; and neuroscience. Sensipar is the firm's first small-molecule drug. It is used to treat forms of hyperparathyroidism and is licensed from NPS Pharmaceuticals, Inc. Amgen plans to complete an additional large-scale cell culture commercial manufacturing facility adjacent to the current Rhode Island facility. In February 2006, the firm announced that its plans to invest more than $1 billion over the next four years to expand its manufacturing capacity in Puerto Rico. In 2006, Amgen acquired Avidia, a privately held biopharmaceutical company, and Abgenix, a manufacturer of human therapeutic antibodies. In August 2007, the firm announced a restructuring plan that will slash staff by 14% and capital expenses by $1.9 billion.

Amgen offers an employee benefits package that includes an education reimbursement plan, a company pension, a voluntary retirement savings plan, employee stock purchase plan, deferred compensation plan, and, in some locations, on-site health clubs, yoga and pilates classes, massages, hair salons, gift shops, discount ski lift tickets, day care centers, dry cleaners, cafeterias and shoe repair services.

FINANCIALS: **Sales and profits are in thousands of dollars—add 000 to get the full amount. 2007 Note: Financial information for 2007 was not available for all companies at press time.**

2007 Sales: $	2007 Profits: $	**U.S. Stock Ticker: AMGN**
2006 Sales: $14,268,000	2006 Profits: $2,950,000	**Int'l Ticker:** Int'l Exchange:
2005 Sales: $12,430,000	2005 Profits: $3,674,000	Employees: 20,100
2004 Sales: $10,550,000	2004 Profits: $2,363,000	Fiscal Year Ends: 12/31
2003 Sales: $8,356,000	2003 Profits: $2,259,500	Parent Company:

SALARIES/BENEFITS:

Pension Plan: Y	ESOP Stock Plan:	Profit Sharing:	Top Exec. Salary: $1,390,385	Bonus: $4,500,000
Savings Plan: Y	Stock Purch. Plan: Y		Second Exec. Salary: $887,385	Bonus: $1,800,000

OTHER THOUGHTS:

Apparent Women Officers or Directors: 3
Hot Spot for Advancement for Women/Minorities: Y

LOCATIONS: ("Y" = Yes)

West:	Southwest:	Midwest:	Southeast:	Northeast:	International:
Y			Y	Y	Y

AMICAS INC

www.amicas.com

Industry Group Code: 511212 **Ranks within this company's industry group:** Sales: 7 Profits: 7

Insurance/HMO/PPO:		Drugs:		Equipment/Supplies:		Hospitals/Clinics:		Services:		Health Care:	
Insurance:		Manufacturer:		Manufacturer:		Acute Care:		Diagnostics:		Home Health:	
Managed Care:		Distributor:		Distributor:		Sub-Acute:		Labs/Testing:		Long-Term Care:	
Utilization Management:		Specialty Pharmacy:		Leasing/Finance:		Outpatient Surgery:		Staffing:		Physical Therapy:	
Payment Processing:		Vitamins/Nutritionals:		Information Systems:	Y	Physical Rehab. Ctr.:		Waste Disposal:		Physician Prac. Mgmt.:	
		Clinical Trials:				Psychiatric Clinics:		Specialty Svcs.:	Y		

TYPES OF BUSINESS:

Radiology Software Solutions
Image & Information Management Solutions
Software & Hardware Support

BRANDS/DIVISIONS/AFFILIATES:

AMICAS Insight Solutions
AMICAS Vision Series
RadStream

CONTACTS: *Note: Officers with more than one job title may be intentionally listed here more than once.*

Stephen N. Kahane, CEO
Peter McClennen, COO
Peter McClennen, Pres.
Joseph Hill, CFO/Sr. VP
Paul Merrild, VP-Mktg.
Denise Mitchell, VP-Human Resources
Kang Wang, Sr. VP-R&D
Kevin Burns, VP-Corp. Dev.
Kevin Burns, VP-Finance
Rodney Hawkins, VP-Prod. Mgmt.
John Esposito, VP-Sales & Hospital Strategy
Kurt Hammond, VP-Sales & Outpatient Strategy
Barry Gutwillig, VP-Strategic Partnerships & Initiatives
Stephen N. Kahane, Chmn.

Phone: 617-779-7878 **Fax:** 617-779-7879
Toll-Free: 800-490-8465
Address: 20 Guest St., Boston, MA 02135 US

GROWTH PLANS/SPECIAL FEATURES:

AMICAS, Inc., formerly VitalWorks, Inc, is a provider of radiology and medical image and information management solutions. The company offers a suite of radiology information system, picture archiving and communication system, document management and revenue cycle management software solutions to radiology and other specialty healthcare providers in the ambulatory setting. The firm provides a set of products called the AMICAS Vision Series, which provides end-to-end information technology solutions for imaging centers, ambulatory care facilities, radiology practices and billing services. Solutions include automation support for workflow, imaging, revenue cycle management and document management. Hospital customers are provided a picture archiving and communication system, featuring advanced enterprise workflow support and a scalable design that can fully integrate with any hospital information system, radiology information system or electronic medical record. The AMICAS Insight Solutions is a set of client-centered professional and consulting services that assist customers with transition to a digital enterprise. In addition, the company provides customers with ongoing software and hardware support, implementation, training and electronic data interchange. Products and services are marketed in the U.S. primarily through a direct sales force located in Daytona Beach, Florida and Boston, Massachusetts. AMICAS purchased exclusive licensing and worldwide distribution rights to the RadStream software, a product designed to accelerate radiology workflow, improve radiologist soft copy reading productivity and both improve and fully document communication of positive results of radiology studies.

The company offers its employees health, dental and vision insurance; life and AD&D insurance; short- and long-term disability insurance; a 401(k) plan; tuition assistance; and an employee assistance program.

FINANCIALS: **Sales and profits are in thousands of dollars—add 000 to get the full amount. 2007 Note: Financial information for 2007 was not available for all companies at press time.**

2007 Sales: $	2007 Profits: $	**U.S. Stock Ticker: AMCS**
2006 Sales: $49,437	2006 Profits: $-1,024	**Int'l Ticker:** Int'l Exchange:
2005 Sales: $52,811	2005 Profits: $44,215	Employees: 247
2004 Sales: $42,319	2004 Profits: $-12,457	Fiscal Year Ends: 12/31
2003 Sales: $111,519	2003 Profits: $7,963	Parent Company:

SALARIES/BENEFITS:

Pension Plan:	ESOP Stock Plan:	Profit Sharing:	Top Exec. Salary: $350,000	Bonus: $
Savings Plan: Y	Stock Purch. Plan:		Second Exec. Salary: $300,000	Bonus: $

OTHER THOUGHTS:

Apparent Women Officers or Directors: 2
Hot Spot for Advancement for Women/Minorities:

LOCATIONS: ("Y" = Yes)

West:	Southwest:	Midwest:	Southeast:	Northeast:	International:
Y				Y	

AMSURG CORP

www.amsurg.com

Industry Group Code: 621490 **Ranks within this company's industry group:** Sales: 6 Profits: 5

Insurance/HMO/PPO:		Drugs:		Equipment/Supplies:		Hospitals/Clinics:		Services:		Health Care:	
Insurance:		Manufacturer:		Manufacturer:		Acute Care:		Diagnostics:		Home Health:	
Managed Care:		Distributor:		Distributor:		Sub-Acute:		Labs/Testing:		Long-Term Care:	
Utilization Management:		Specialty Pharmacy:		Leasing/Finance:		Outpatient Surgery:	Y	Staffing:		Physical Therapy:	
Payment Processing:		Vitamins/Nutritionals:		Information Systems:		Physical Rehab. Ctr.:		Waste Disposal:		Physician Prac. Mgmt.:	Y
		Clinical Trials:				Psychiatric Clinics:		Specialty Svcs.:			

TYPES OF BUSINESS:

Practice-Based Ambulatory Surgery Centers
Outpatient Surgery Facilities Management

BRANDS/DIVISIONS/AFFILIATES:

CONTACTS:

Note: Officers with more than one job title may be intentionally listed here more than once.

Ken P. McDonald, CEO
Ken P. McDonald, Pres.
Claire M. Gulmi, CFO/Exec. VP
David L. Manning, Exec. VP/Chief Dev. Officer
Claire M. Gulmi, Corp. Sec.
Frank J. Coll, Sr. VP-Oper.
Royce D. Harrell, Chief Compliance Officer/Sr. VP-Corp. Svcs.
Thomas G. Cigarran, Chmn.

Phone: 615-665-1283 **Fax:** 615-665-0755
Toll-Free: 800-945-2301
Address: 20 Burton Hills Blvd., Ste. 350, Nashville, TN 37215 US

GROWTH PLANS/SPECIAL FEATURES:

AmSurg Corp. is a leader in the development, acquisition and management of practice-based ambulatory surgery centers and specialty physician networks with a majority interest in 156 surgery centers in 32 states and Washington, D.C. The ambulatory surgery centers are licensed outpatient facilities equipped and staffed for a single medical specialty. The centers are usually located in or near a physician group practice, as the firm's objective is to form partnerships with physicians. The company has targeted ownership in centers that perform gastrointestinal endoscopy, ophthalmology, urology, orthopedics or otolaryngology procedures. These centers perform many high-volume, lower-risk procedures that are appropriate for the practice-based setting. The focus at each center on procedures in a single specialty results in these centers generally having significantly lower capital and operating costs than hospitals, which are designed to provide more intensive services in a broader array of surgical specialties. The types of procedures performed at each center depend on the specialty of the resident physicians. Those most often performed include laser eye surgery, carpal tunnel repair, colonoscopy and knee surgery. AmSurg provides services to its business partners that include financial feasibility pro forma analysis; assistance in the state CON approval process; site selection; assistance in space planning and schematic floor plan design; analysis of local, state and federal building codes; financing for equipment and buildout; equipment budgeting, specification, bidding and purchasing; construction financing; architectural oversight; contractor bidding; construction management; and assistance with licensing, Medicare certification and contracting with third-party payers.

FINANCIALS:

Sales and profits are in thousands of dollars—add 000 to get the full amount. 2007 Note: Financial information for 2007 was not available for all companies at press time.

2007 Sales: $	2007 Profits: $	**U.S. Stock Ticker: AMSG**
2006 Sales: $464,592	2006 Profits: $37,739	**Int'l Ticker:** Int'l Exchange:
2005 Sales: $387,798	2005 Profits: $35,151	Employees: 2,000
2004 Sales: $326,679	2004 Profits: $39,706	Fiscal Year Ends: 12/31
2003 Sales: $301,408	2003 Profits: $30,126	Parent Company:

SALARIES/BENEFITS:

Pension Plan:	ESOP Stock Plan:	Profit Sharing:	Top Exec. Salary: $485,000	Bonus: $269,878
Savings Plan: Y	Stock Purch. Plan:		Second Exec. Salary: $325,000	Bonus: $167,314

OTHER THOUGHTS:

Apparent Women Officers or Directors: 1
Hot Spot for Advancement for Women/Minorities:

LOCATIONS: ("Y" = Yes)

West:	Southwest:	Midwest:	Southeast:	Northeast:	International:
Y	Y	Y	Y	Y	

ANALOGIC CORP

www.analogic.com

Industry Group Code: 339113 **Ranks within this company's industry group:** Sales: 52 Profits: 48

Insurance/HMO/PPO:		Drugs:		Equipment/Supplies:		Hospitals/Clinics:		Services:		Health Care:	
Insurance:		Manufacturer:		Manufacturer:	Y	Acute Care:		Diagnostics:		Home Health:	
Managed Care:		Distributor:		Distributor:		Sub-Acute:		Labs/Testing:		Long-Term Care:	
Utilization Management:		Specialty Pharmacy:		Leasing/Finance:		Outpatient Surgery:		Staffing:		Physical Therapy:	
Payment Processing:		Vitamins/Nutritionals:		Information Systems:	Y	Physical Rehab. Ctr.:		Waste Disposal:		Physician Prac. Mgmt.:	
		Clinical Trials:				Psychiatric Clinics:		Specialty Svcs.:			

TYPES OF BUSINESS:

Equipment-Medical Image Processing
Signal Processing Equipment
Patient Monitoring Equipment
Computed Tomography Imaging Systems
Financing
Explosive Detection Security Systems

BRANDS/DIVISIONS/AFFILIATES:

Anexa
Anrad
Sound Technology, Inc.
B-K Medical Systems ApS
LIFEGARD
FETALGARD
EXACT (EXplosive Assessment Computed Tomography)

CONTACTS: *Note: Officers with more than one job title may be intentionally listed here more than once.*

James W. Green, CEO
Edmund F. Becker, Jr., COO
James W. Green, Pres.
John J. Millerick, CFO
Alex A. Van Adzin, General Counsel/Corp. Sec./VP
John J. Millerick, Treas./Sr. VP
John A. Tarello, Chmn.

Phone: 978-326-4000 **Fax:** 978-977-6809
Toll-Free:
Address: 8 Centennial Dr., Peabody, MA 01960 US

GROWTH PLANS/SPECIAL FEATURES:

Analogic Corporation designs, manufactures and sells high-precision health and security systems and subsystems to be utilized in medical, industrial and scientific applications. The company operates primarily within two major markets within the electronics industry: Medical Technology Products and Security Technology Products. Medical Technology Products consists of two reporting segments: Medical Imaging Products and B-K Medical Systems ApS for ultrasound systems and probes in the urology, surgery and radiology markets. A number of Analogic's medical imaging data acquisition systems and related computing equipment are incorporated by manufacturers in North America, Europe and Asia into CT scanners. The company also designs and manufactures other advanced subsystems such as Radio Frequency amplifiers and Gradient Coil amplifiers for use in MRI scanners. Direct Digital Radiography (DDR) systems are also designed, developed and manufactured by Analogic. DDR systems convert X-rays into electrical signals, digitize these signals and create an image, and are developed and manufactured for direct sale to select markets by the company's subsidiary, Anexa Corporation. Anrad Corporation, another subsidiary, designs and manufactures direct conversion amorphous Selenium-based X-ray detectors, while Analogic's Sound Technology, Inc. subsidiary develops and manufactures ultrasound transducers and probes. Analogic also manufactures a variety of multi-functional, custom patient monitoring instruments and a family of non-invasive patient monitors for direct sale under the LIFEGARD brand. The company manufactures fetal monitoring products for acquisition, conversion and display of biomedical signals under the FETALGARD brand. Security Technology Products consists of advanced explosives detection systems for checked luggage and weapons detection systems for checkpoints. Analogic designs and manufactures the EXplosive Assessment Computed Tomography scanner (EXACT), the only certified security detection system capable of generating data for full three-dimensional images of every object contained within a piece of luggage. The company also owns a hotel, managed under a contract with Marriott Corporation.

FINANCIALS: **Sales and profits are in thousands of dollars—add 000 to get the full amount. 2007 Note: Financial information for 2007 was not available for all companies at press time.**

2007 Sales: $
2006 Sales: $351,445
2005 Sales: $326,479
2004 Sales: $304,205
2003 Sales: $471,500

2007 Profits: $
2006 Profits: $25,066
2005 Profits: $28,862
2004 Profits: $8,354
2003 Profits: $49,500

U.S. Stock Ticker: ALOG
Int'l Ticker: Int'l Exchange:
Employees: 1,500
Fiscal Year Ends: 7/31
Parent Company:

SALARIES/BENEFITS:

Pension Plan:
Savings Plan: Y
ESOP Stock Plan:
Stock Purch. Plan: Y
Profit Sharing:
Top Exec. Salary: $406,000 Bonus: $
Second Exec. Salary: $301,323 Bonus: $15,000

OTHER THOUGHTS:

Apparent Women Officers or Directors:
Hot Spot for Advancement for Women/Minorities:

LOCATIONS: ("Y" = Yes)

West:	Southwest:	Midwest:	Southeast:	Northeast:	International:
		Y		Y	Y

ANSELL LIMITED COMPANY

www.ansell.com

Industry Group Code: 339113 **Ranks within this company's industry group:** Sales: 31 Profits: 24

Insurance/HMO/PPO:		Drugs:		Equipment/Supplies:		Hospitals/Clinics:		Services:		Health Care:	
Insurance:		Manufacturer:		Manufacturer:	Y	Acute Care:		Diagnostics:		Home Health:	
Managed Care:		Distributor:		Distributor:	Y	Sub-Acute:		Labs/Testing:		Long-Term Care:	
Utilization Management:		Specialty Pharmacy:		Leasing/Finance:		Outpatient Surgery:		Staffing:		Physical Therapy:	
Payment Processing:		Vitamins/Nutritionals:		Information Systems:		Physical Rehab. Ctr.:		Waste Disposal:		Physician Prac. Mgmt.:	
		Clinical Trials:				Psychiatric Clinics:		Specialty Svcs.:			

TYPES OF BUSINESS:

Protective Wear Manufacture
Latex Gloves
Condoms
Protective Clothing

BRANDS/DIVISIONS/AFFILIATES:

Pacific Dunlop Limited
Ansell
Ansell Perry
Gammex
NuTex
LifeStyles
Synsation
AnsellCares

CONTACTS: *Note: Officers with more than one job title may be intentionally listed here more than once.*

Douglas D. Tough, CEO/Managing Dir.
Rustom Jilla, CFO
Phil Corke, Sr. VP-Human Resources
Mike Zedalis, Sr. VP-Science
Shawn Knox, CIO/Sr. VP
Mike Zedalis, Sr. VP-Tech.
Rainer Wolf, Head-Global Mfg.
Bill Reilly, General Counsel/Sr. VP
Scott Corriveau, Head-Global Bus. Dev.
David Graham, General Manager-Finance & Acct.
Rob Bartlett, General Manager/Corp. Sec.
Bill Reed, Sr. VP/Regional Dir.-Americas
Peter L. Barnes, Chmn.
Werner Heintz, Regional Dir.-Europe/Sr. VP
Scott Papier, VP-Global Supply & Logistics

Phone: 61-3-9270-7270	**Fax:** 61-3-9270-7300
Toll-Free:	
Address: 678 Victoria St., Level 3, Richmond, Victoria 3121 Australia	

GROWTH PLANS/SPECIAL FEATURES:

Ansell Ltd. Co., formerly Pacific Dunlop Ltd., is a provider of barrier protection products against injury, infection and contamination in the healthcare market. The company operates in three segments: professional healthcare, consumer healthcare and occupational healthcare. The professional healthcare segment manufactures and markets synthetic and natural latex surgical and medical examination gloves worldwide under the brand names Ansell and Ansell Perry. It also manufactures other latex products, such as tubing and wall brackets, under product-specific brand names, including Gammex, Conform, Encore, NuTex, MicrOptic, X-AM, Synsation, Dermaclean and Nitratouch. The consumer healthcare division manufactures and distributes a variety of condom lines worldwide under the LifeStyles, Mates, Manix, Contempo and Kama Sutra brand names, including condoms with flavors, colors, spermicide, studded and ribbed features. It also makes and distributes Medi-Touch gloves and personal lubricants. The occupational healthcare segment manufactures and markets a wide range of industrial and consumer gloves, as well as protective clothing (rainwear, aprons, sleeves and vests). Its products include critical environment gloves, which are used by companies in the semiconductor, electronics and other high-technology markets to protect workers from the manufacturing process, as well as protect the manufactured product from contamination. The division also offers a full line of gloves developed for the food-processing and foodservice industry. However, its core market is the automotive and durable-goods industry, which uses chemical-resistant, cut-resistant and special-purpose gloves. The company's AnsellCares program is a global, multifaceted research and education program directed by an independent scientific advisory board that addresses latex allergies and barrier protection issues. In 2006, Ansell acquired 75% of Chinese firm Wuhan Jissbon Sanitary Products Company Ltd., which manufactures and markets condoms. In May 2007, the company acquired Fabrica de Artefatos de Latex Blowtex of Brazil.

FINANCIALS: Sales and profits are in thousands of dollars—add 000 to get the full amount. 2007 Note: Financial information for 2007 was not available for all companies at press time.

2007 Sales: $	2007 Profits: $	**U.S. Stock Ticker:**
2006 Sales: $859,600	2006 Profits: $88,700	**Int'l Ticker: ANN** Int'l Exchange: Sydney-ASX
2005 Sales: $821,400	2005 Profits: $41,500	Employees: 11,530
2004 Sales: $792,000	2004 Profits: $49,100	Fiscal Year Ends:
2003 Sales: $862,961	2003 Profits: $37,291	Parent Company:

SALARIES/BENEFITS:

Pension Plan:	ESOP Stock Plan:	Profit Sharing:	Top Exec. Salary: $742,352	Bonus: $322,085
Savings Plan:	Stock Purch. Plan:		Second Exec. Salary: $306,295	Bonus: $145,870

OTHER THOUGHTS:

Apparent Women Officers or Directors: 1
Hot Spot for Advancement for Women/Minorities:

LOCATIONS: ("Y" = Yes)

West:	Southwest:	Midwest:	Southeast:	Northeast:	International:
				Y	Y

AON CORPORATION

www.aon.com

Industry Group Code: 524210 **Ranks within this company's industry group:** Sales: 2 Profits: 2

Insurance/HMO/PPO:		Drugs:		Equipment/Supplies:		Hospitals/Clinics:		Services:		Health Care:	
Insurance:	Y	Manufacturer:		Manufacturer:		Acute Care:		Diagnostics:		Home Health:	
Managed Care:		Distributor:		Distributor:		Sub-Acute:		Labs/Testing:		Long-Term Care:	
Utilization Management:		Specialty Pharmacy:		Leasing/Finance:		Outpatient Surgery:		Staffing:		Physical Therapy:	
Payment Processing:		Vitamins/Nutritionals:		Information Systems:		Physical Rehab. Ctr.:		Waste Disposal:		Physician Prac. Mgmt.:	
		Clinical Trials:				Psychiatric Clinics:		Specialty Svcs.:	Y		

TYPES OF BUSINESS:

Insurance Brokerage & Management
Consumer Insurance Underwriting
Risk Management
Online Business Services
Outsourcing

BRANDS/DIVISIONS/AFFILIATES:

Aon Risk Services Companies, Inc.
Aon Limited
Cananwill, Inc.
Combined Insurance Company of America
Combined Life Insurance Company of New York
Sterling Life Insurance
AonLine
Aon Market Exchange

CONTACTS:

Note: Officers with more than one job title may be intentionally listed here more than once.

Gregory C. Case, CEO
Gregory C. Case, Pres.
David P. Bolger, CFO/Exec. VP-Finance
Philip B. Clement, Global Chief Mktg. Officer
Jeremy G. O. Farmer, Sr. VP/Head-Human Resources
Baljit Dail, Global CIO
David P. Bolger, Chief Admin. Officer
D. Cameron Findlay, General Counsel/Chief Legal Officer/Exec. VP
Ted T. Devine, Exec. VP/Head-Corp. Strategy
Philip B. Clement, Global Chief Comm. Officer
Scott Malchow, VP/Head-Investor Rel.
Diane M. Aigotti, Sr. VP/Treas./Chief Risk Officer
Michael D. O'Halleran, Chmn./CEO-Aon Global Re & Wholesale/Sr. Exec. VP
Andrew M. Appel, CEO-Aon Consulting Worldwide Inc.
Dennis L. Mahoney, Chmn./CEO-Aon Ltd.
Stephen P. McGill, CEO-Aon Risk Svcs. Americas/Global Large Corp. Bus
Patrick G. Ryan, Exec. Chmn.
Dirk P. M. Verbeek, Chmn./CEO-Aon Risk Svcs. Int'l

Phone: 312-381-1000	**Fax:** 312-381-6032
Toll-Free:	
Address: 200 E. Randolph St., Chicago, IL 60601 US	

GROWTH PLANS/SPECIAL FEATURES:

Aon Corporation, one of the world's largest insuranc brokerages, is a holding company engaged in three majo business segments: Risk and Insurance Brokerage Services Consulting; and Insurance Underwriting. Risk and Insuranc Brokerage Services, which generated 63% of the company' 2006 revenue, operates subsidiaries Aon Risk Service Companies, Inc.; Aon Holdings International bv; Aon R Global, Inc.; Aon Limited; and Cananwill, Inc. Service include risk identification and assessment; safet engineering; claims and loss cost management; and progran administration. The Consulting segment, which generate 14% of Aon's 2006 revenue, operates Aon Consultin Worldwide, Inc., and works through two sub-segments Consulting Services and Outsourcing. It is active in seve areas: employee benefits; compensation; managemen consulting; communications; strategic human resourc consulting; financial advisory and litigation consulting; an human resource outsourcing. Some of its services includ designing salary structures, human capital developmen assistance, securities litigation consulting and employmen processing. Insurance Underwriting, which generated 23% of Aon's 2006 revenue, operates through two sub-segments Accident & Health and life; and Property and Casualty. Th Accident & Health and Life sub-segment operates Combine Insurance Company of America and Combined Lif Insurance Company of New York, which offer acciden disability, health and life insurance targeting middle incom consumers; and it offers Medicare Advantage coverage fo seniors through subsidiary Sterling Life Insurance. The fir offers many of its services online, including AonLine, Ao Market Exchange and Aon Risk Monitor. The firm operate in more than 120 countries and sovereignties around th world through more than 500 offices. Approximately 68% o its 2006 revenue came from the U.S., 10% from th Americas other than the U.S., 10 from the U.K., 7% fro EMEA and 5% from Asia Pacific.

Aon provides an employee assistance program, tuitio reimbursement and matching gifts for charitabl contributions.

FINANCIALS:

Sales and profits are in thousands of dollars—add 000 to get the full amount. 2007 Note: Financial information for 2007 was not available for all companies at press time.

2007 Sales: $	2007 Profits: $	**U.S. Stock Ticker: AOC**
2006 Sales: $8,954,000	2006 Profits: $720,000	**Int'l Ticker:** Int'l Exchange:
2005 Sales: $8,496,000	2005 Profits: $733,000	Employees: 43,100
2004 Sales: $8,607,000	2004 Profits: $543,000	Fiscal Year Ends: 12/31
2003 Sales: $9,718,000	2003 Profits: $625,000	Parent Company:

SALARIES/BENEFITS:

Pension Plan:	ESOP Stock Plan:	Profit Sharing:	Top Exec. Salary: $1,500,000	Bonus: $2,400,000
Savings Plan: Y	Stock Purch. Plan: Y		Second Exec. Salary: $1,125,000	Bonus: $1,600,000

OTHER THOUGHTS:

Apparent Women Officers or Directors: 3
Hot Spot for Advancement for Women/Minorities: Y

LOCATIONS: ("Y" = Yes)

West:	Southwest:	Midwest:	Southeast:	Northeast:	International:
Y	Y	Y	Y	Y	Y

Note: Financial information, benefits and other data can change quickly and may vary from those stated here.

APPLERA CORPORATION

www.applera.com

Industry Group Code: 339113 **Ranks within this company's industry group:** Sales: 19 Profits: 17

Insurance/HMO/PPO:		Drugs:		Equipment/Supplies:		Hospitals/Clinics:		Services:		Health Care:	
Insurance:		Manufacturer:		Manufacturer:	Y	Acute Care:		Diagnostics:		Home Health:	
Managed Care:		Distributor:		Distributor:		Sub-Acute:		Labs/Testing:		Long-Term Care:	
Utilization Management:		Specialty Pharmacy:		Leasing/Finance:		Outpatient Surgery:		Staffing:		Physical Therapy:	
Payment Processing:		Vitamins/Nutritionals:		Information Systems:	Y	Physical Rehab. Ctr.:		Waste Disposal:		Physician Prac. Mgmt.:	
		Clinical Trials:				Psychiatric Clinics:		Specialty Svcs.:	Y		

TYPES OF BUSINESS:

Equipment-Life Sciences & Genomics
Genetic Database Management
Proteomics
Medical Software
DNA Sequencing
Drug Discovery & Development
Diagnostics

BRANDS/DIVISIONS/AFFILIATES:

Applied Biosystems
Celera Genomics
Celera Discovery System
Celera Diagnostics
Abbott Molecular

CONTACTS: *Note: Officers with more than one job title may be intentionally listed here more than once.*

Tony L. White, CEO
Tony L. White, Pres.
Dennis L. Winger, CFO/Sr. VP
Barbara J. Kerr, VP-Human Resources
Tama Olver, CIO/VP
William B. Sawch, General Counsel/Sr. VP
Peter Dworkin, VP-Corp. Comm.
Peter Dworkin, VP-Investor Rel.
Ugo D. DeBlasi, Controller/VP
Dennis Gilbert, Chief Scientific Officer-Applied Biosystem
Kathy P. Ordonez, Sr. VP/Pres., Celera Genomics & Celera Diagnostics
Robert F. G. Booth, Chief Scientific Officer, Celera Genomics
Tony L. White, Chmn.

Phone: 203-840-2000 **Fax:** 203-840-2312
Toll-Free: 800-761-5381
Address: 301 Merritt 7, Norwalk, CT 06851-1070 US

GROWTH PLANS/SPECIAL FEATURES:

Applera Corporation provides technology and information solutions for genomics research. The company operates as an administrative parent for two publicly traded subsidiaries: Applied Biosystems and Celera Genomics. Applied Biosystems develops, manufactures, sells and services instrument systems, consumables and informatics products for life science research and related applications. The division has installed approximately 180,000 instrument systems in nearly 100 countries. Its products are used for synthesis, amplification, purification, isolation, analysis and sequencing of DNA, RNA, proteins and other biological molecules. Customers use these products for applications including research, pharmaceutical discovery and development, biosecurity, food and environmental testing, analysis of infectious diseases, human identification and forensic DNA analysis. Celera Genomics works internally and through collaborations to discover and develop new small molecule and antibody-based therapies and diagnostics for cancer, autoimmune and inflammatory diseases, with a focus on tumor surface cell proteins as potential antibody targets. The Celera Discovery System, an online service through which users can access the firm's database of genomic and medical information, is now marketed by Applied Biosciences. Celera's collaborators include Abbott Laboratories, General Electric Company, Merck and Bristol-Myers Squibb. Celera Diagnostics, a full subsidiary of Celera since early 2006, focuses on discovering, developing and commercializing diagnostic tests. Its products, mostly marketed by Abbott Molecular, include tests relating to HIV, cystic fibrosis, tissue transplant rejection and hepatitis C. Its research activities are also focused on heart disease, breast cancer, Alzheimer's and rheumatoid arthritis. In March 2006, Applied Biosystems acquired the research products division of Ambion, Inc., an RNA technology company. In May 2007, Celera and Abbott announced the FDA has approved Abbott's RealTime HIV-1 viral load test, which uses Celera's m2000 automated instrument system.

Applera offers its employees health coverage, an educational assistance plan, employee assistance programs, gift matching programs and adoption assistance.

FINANCIALS: **Sales and profits are in thousands of dollars—add 000 to get the full amount. 2007 Note: Financial information for 2007 was not available for all companies at press time.**

2007 Sales: $ | 2007 Profits: $
2006 Sales: $1,949,400 | 2006 Profits: $212,500
2005 Sales: $1,845,140 | 2005 Profits: $159,795
2004 Sales: $1,825,200 | 2004 Profits: $114,953
2003 Sales: $1,777,232 | 2003 Profits: $118,480

U.S. Stock Ticker: Private
Int'l Ticker: Int'l Exchange:
Employees: 220
Fiscal Year Ends: 6/30
Parent Company:

SALARIES/BENEFITS:

Pension Plan: | ESOP Stock Plan: | Profit Sharing: | Top Exec. Salary: $1,096,154 | Bonus: $2,107,432
Savings Plan: Y | Stock Purch. Plan: Y | | Second Exec. Salary: $571,154 | Bonus: $717,978

OTHER THOUGHTS:

Apparent Women Officers or Directors: 4
Hot Spot for Advancement for Women/Minorities: Y

LOCATIONS: ("Y" = Yes)

West:	Southwest:	Midwest:	Southeast:	Northeast:	International:
Y				Y	Y

Note: Financial information, benefits and other data can change quickly and may vary from those stated here.

APRIA HEALTHCARE GROUP INC www.apria.com

Industry Group Code: 621610 **Ranks within this company's industry group:** Sales: 1 Profits: 1

Insurance/HMO/PPO:		Drugs:		Equipment/Supplies:		Hospitals/Clinics:		Services:		Health Care:	
Insurance:		Manufacturer:		Manufacturer:		Acute Care:		Diagnostics:		Home Health:	Y
Managed Care:		Distributor:		Distributor:	Y	Sub-Acute:		Labs/Testing:		Long-Term Care:	
Utilization Management:		Specialty Pharmacy:		Leasing/Finance:		Outpatient Surgery:		Staffing:		Physical Therapy:	
Payment Processing:		Vitamins/Nutritionals:		Information Systems:		Physical Rehab. Ctr.:		Waste Disposal:		Physician Prac. Mgmt.:	
		Clinical Trials:				Psychiatric Clinics:		Specialty Svcs.:	Y		

TYPES OF BUSINESS:

Home Health Care
Home Medical Equipment Distribution
Respiratory Therapy
Infusion Therapy
Patient Travel Programs

BRANDS/DIVISIONS/AFFILIATES:

Great Escapes Travel Program

CONTACTS: *Note: Officers with more than one job title may be intentionally listed here more than once.*

Lawrence M. Higby, CEO
Lawrence A. Mastrovich, COO
Lawrence A. Mastrovich, Pres.
Chris A. Karkenny, CFO/Exec. VP
Jeff Ingram, Exec. VP-Sales
Frank C. Bianchi, Sr. VP-Human Resources
Jeri L. Lose, CIO/Exec. VP
Robert S. Holcombe, General Counsel/Exec. VP/Corp. Sec.
Lisa M. Getson, Exec. VP-Investor Svcs. & Gov't Rel.
Peter A. Reynolds, Chief Acct. Officer/Controller
Kimberlie Rogers-Bowers, Sr. VP-Regulatory Affairs & Acquisitions
Robert G. Abood, Sr. VP-Acquisitions & Infusion Services
Daniel J. Starck, Exec. VP-Bus. Oper.
Ralph V. Whitworth, Chmn.
Cameron Thompson, Exec. VP-Logistics

Phone: 949-639-2000 **Fax:** 949-587-9363
Toll-Free: 800-647-5404
Address: 26220 Enterprise Ct., Lake Forest, CA 92630-8405 US

GROWTH PLANS/SPECIAL FEATURES:

Apria Healthcare Group, Inc. is one of the largest providers of home healthcare services in the U.S., offering home respiratory therapy, home infusion and home medical equipment through 504 branches serving patients across all 50 states. The home respiratory division provides oxygen systems, stationary and portable ventilators, obstructive sleep apnea equipment, nebulizers and respiratory medications. Home infusion therapy consists of the intravenous administration of anti-infectives, pain management, chemotherapy, nutrients, immune globulin and other medications. The company's home medical equipment unit provides patients with safety items, ambulatory aids and in-home equipment such as wheelchairs and hospital beds. In each of its service lines, Apria provides patients with a variety of clinical and ancillary services in addition to products and supplies, most of which are prescribed by a physician as part of a care plan. These services include in home care, pharmacy management, patient and caregiver education and training, monitoring of patients' treatment plans, reporting patient progress and status to the physician, maintaining and repairing equipment and processing claims to third-party payors. Through its field sales force, Apria markets its services primarily to managed care organizations, physicians, hospitals, medical groups, home health agencies and case managers. Apria also offers its Great Escapes Travel Program for patients who wish to travel but have special needs such as oxygen, infusion or other therapy. The firm markets its services through both referrals and managed care contracts with companies including United HealthCare Group, Aetna, and Kaiser Permanente.

FINANCIALS: **Sales and profits are in thousands of dollars—add 000 to get the full amount. 2007 Note: Financial information for 2007 was not available for all companies at press time.**

2007 Sales: $
2006 Sales: $1,517,307
2005 Sales: $1,474,101
2004 Sales: $1,451,449
2003 Sales: $1,380,900

2007 Profits: $
2006 Profits: $74,980
2005 Profits: $66,941
2004 Profits: $114,008
2003 Profits: $116,000

U.S. Stock Ticker: AHG
Int'l Ticker: Int'l Exchange:
Employees: 11,258
Fiscal Year Ends: 12/31
Parent Company:

SALARIES/BENEFITS:

Pension Plan: ESOP Stock Plan: Profit Sharing: Top Exec. Salary: $746,918 Bonus: $686,817
Savings Plan: Y Stock Purch. Plan: Second Exec. Salary: $507,376 Bonus: $467,859

OTHER THOUGHTS:

Apparent Women Officers or Directors: 3
Hot Spot for Advancement for Women/Minorities: Y

LOCATIONS: ("Y" = Yes)

West:	Southwest:	Midwest:	Southeast:	Northeast:	International:
Y	Y	Y	Y	Y	

ARADIGM CORPORATION

www.aradigm.com

Industry Group Code: 325412A **Ranks within this company's industry group:** Sales: 3 Profits: 2

Insurance/HMO/PPO:		Drugs:		Equipment/Supplies:		Hospitals/Clinics:		Services:		Health Care:	
Insurance:		Manufacturer:		Manufacturer:	Y	Acute Care:		Diagnostics:		Home Health:	
Managed Care:		Distributor:		Distributor:		Sub-Acute:		Labs/Testing:		Long-Term Care:	
Utilization Management:		Specialty Pharmacy:		Leasing/Finance:		Outpatient Surgery:		Staffing:		Physical Therapy:	
Payment Processing:		Vitamins/Nutritionals:		Information Systems:		Physical Rehab. Ctr.:		Waste Disposal:		Physician Prac. Mgmt.:	
		Clinical Trials:				Psychiatric Clinics:		Specialty Svcs.:			

TYPES OF BUSINESS:

Drug Delivery Systems
Pulmonary Drug Delivery Systems

BRANDS/DIVISIONS/AFFILIATES:

Intraject
AERx
AERx Insulin Diabetes Management System

CONTACTS:

Note: Officers with more than one job title may be intentionally listed here more than once.

Igor Gonda, CEO
Igor Gonda, Pres.
Norman Halleen, Interim CFO
Babatunde A. Otulana, Sr. VP-Dev.
Jeffery Grimes, General Counsel
Babatunde A. Otulana, Chief Medical Officer
Virgil D. Thompson, Chmn.

Phone: 510-265-9000	**Fax:** 510-265-0277
Toll-Free:	
Address: 3929 Point Eden Way, Hayward, CA 94545 US	

GROWTH PLANS/SPECIAL FEATURES:

Aradigm Corporation develops advanced pulmonary drug delivery systems for the treatment of systemic conditions and lung diseases. The company is focused on improving the quality and cost-effectiveness of medical treatment by enabling patients to self-administer drugs without needles or lengthy nebulizer treatments. Aradigm's operations are centered on its AERx pulmonary drug delivery system, which creates aerosols from liquid drug formulations. This system is marketed as a replacement for medical devices, such as nebulizers, metered-dose inhalers and dry powder inhalers. AERx also has a wide array of possible applications, including cardiovascular health, oncology, respiratory issues, endocrinology, infection and neurology. AERx's current product pipeline consists of AERx for Asthma and other respiratory uses, which are undergoing clinical trials, and AERx applications of liposomal ciprofloxacin and liposomal treprostinil, as well as treatments for nicotine addiction. In August 2006, Aradigm sold its Intraject subcutaneous delivery technology to Zogenix for $4 million, plus royalties from future products based on the technology. The technology exploits the lungs' natural ability to absorb and rapidly transfer molecules into the bloodstream, for delivery of medication. Zogenix plans to complete development of the Intraject technology and commercialize the Intraject Sumatriptan product for migraine, and other uses. In January 2007, Aradigm received orphan drug designation from the FDA for an inhaled liposomal formulation of ciprofloxacin for the management of bronchiectasis (BE). Aradigm previously received orphan drug designation for the same formulation of ciprofloxacin for the management of cystic fibrosis in April 2006.

Aradigm offers employees medical and dental coverage; life and disability insurance; company-wide bonus programs; a company matching 401(K) savings plan; stock options; a 529 college saving plan; tuition reimbursement; and an educational rewards program.

FINANCIALS:

Sales and profits are in thousands of dollars—add 000 to get the full amount. 2007 Note: Financial information for 2007 was not available for all companies at press time.

2007 Sales: $	2007 Profits: $	**U.S. Stock Ticker: ARDM**
2006 Sales: $4,814	2006 Profits: $-13,027	**Int'l Ticker:** Int'l Exchange:
2005 Sales: $10,507	2005 Profits: $-29,215	Employees: 54
2004 Sales: $28,045	2004 Profits: $-30,189	Fiscal Year Ends: 12/31
2003 Sales: $33,857	2003 Profits: $-25,970	Parent Company:

SALARIES/BENEFITS:

Pension Plan:	ESOP Stock Plan:	Profit Sharing:	Top Exec. Salary: $287,038	Bonus: $45,352
Savings Plan: Y	Stock Purch. Plan: Y		Second Exec. Salary: $274,139	Bonus: $

OTHER THOUGHTS:

Apparent Women Officers or Directors:
Hot Spot for Advancement for Women/Minorities:

LOCATIONS: ("Y" = Yes)

West:	Southwest:	Midwest:	Southeast:	Northeast:	International:
Y					

ARKANSAS BLUE CROSS AND BLUE SHIELD

www.arkbluecross.com

Industry Group Code: 524114 **Ranks within this company's industry group:** Sales: Profits:

Insurance/HMO/PPO:		Drugs:		Equipment/Supplies:		Hospitals/Clinics:		Services:		Health Care:	
Insurance:	Y	Manufacturer:		Manufacturer:		Acute Care:		Diagnostics:		Home Health:	
Managed Care:	Y	Distributor:		Distributor:		Sub-Acute:		Labs/Testing:		Long-Term Care:	
Utilization Management:		Specialty Pharmacy:		Leasing/Finance:		Outpatient Surgery:		Staffing:		Physical Therapy:	
Payment Processing:		Vitamins/Nutritionals:		Information Systems:		Physical Rehab. Ctr.:		Waste Disposal:		Physician Prac. Mgmt.:	
		Clinical Trials:				Psychiatric Clinics:		Specialty Svcs.:			

TYPES OF BUSINESS:

Insurance-Medical & Health, HMOs & PPOs
Charitable Foundation

BRANDS/DIVISIONS/AFFILIATES:

Medi-Pak
Blue Solution
BlueChoice
BlueAdvantage
Blue-by-Design
DentalBlue
Group BasicBlue
National Institute for Health Care Management

CONTACTS: *Note: Officers with more than one job title may be intentionally listed here more than once.*

Robert L. Shoptaw, CEO
Sharon Allen, COO
Sharon Allen, Pres.
Mark White, CFO/Exec. VP/Treas.
Richard Cooper, VP-Human Resources
Bob Heard, VP-IT Infrastructure
Karen Raley, VP-Prod. Dev.
Lee Douglass, Chief Legal Officer/Sr. VP-Law & Gov't Rel.
David Bridges, Exec. VP-Internal Oper.
Ron DeBerry, Sr. VP-Statewide Bus.
Karen Raley, VP-Comm.
Steve Short, VP-Financial Svcs.
James Adamson, VP/Chief Medical Officer
Mike Brown, Exec. VP-External Oper.
Steve Abell, VP-Enterprise Networks
Cal Kellogg, VP-Enterprise Dev. Svcs.
Hays C. McClerkin, Chmn.

Phone: 501-378-2000	**Fax:** 501-378-3258
Toll-Free:	
Address: 601 S. Gaines St., Little Rock, AR 72201 US	

GROWTH PLANS/SPECIAL FEATURES:

Arkansas Blue Cross and Blue Shield is a nonprofit mutua insurance company providing comprehensive healt insurance and related services to a membership c approximately 425,000 spread throughout Arkansas. Th company provides its Medi-Pak plans for Medicare eligible Arkansans, Blue Solution and BlueChoice plans fo individuals and families and employee group plans includin BlueAdvantage, Blue-by-Design, DentalBlue and Grou BasicBlue. As an independent licensee of the Blue Cros and Blue Shield name and service mark, the company' board of directors must contain a majority of public member from the community who are not employed in the healthcar industry, maintaining the company's commitment to loca communities. Arkansas Blue Cross is one of the 11 healt care companies nationwide which have formed the Nationa Institute for Health Care Management (NIHCM), a non-prof organization based in Washington, D.C. which sponsors non partisan research of health care issues. Arkansas Blu Cross provides health insurance through subsidiar BlueAdvantage Administrators of Arkansas, along with ove 12 affiliates. These affiliates include AHIN, Ideal Medica Services, HMO Partners, Inc., Pinnacle Business Solution and USAble Life. Additionally, the company operates charitable foundation known as Blue & You Foundation for Healthier Arkansas.

Employee benefits include free parking, business casua dress, Casual Day, an on-site cafeteria, credit unio membership, an employee wellness program, employe assistance, tuition reimbursement and health, dental an vision insurance.

FINANCIALS: **Sales and profits are in thousands of dollars—add 000 to get the full amount. 2007 Note: Financial information for 2007 was not available for all companies at press time.**

2007 Sales: $	2007 Profits: $	**U.S. Stock Ticker: Nonprofit**
2006 Sales: $	2006 Profits: $	**Int'l Ticker:** Int'l Exchange:
2005 Sales: $	2005 Profits: $	Employees: 2,700
2004 Sales: $916,620	2004 Profits: $61,856	Fiscal Year Ends: 12/31
2003 Sales: $907,130	2003 Profits: $52,363	Parent Company:

SALARIES/BENEFITS:

Pension Plan:	ESOP Stock Plan:	Profit Sharing:	Top Exec. Salary: $	Bonus: $
Savings Plan: Y	Stock Purch. Plan:		Second Exec. Salary: $	Bonus: $

OTHER THOUGHTS:

Apparent Women Officers or Directors: 2
Hot Spot for Advancement for Women/Minorities:

LOCATIONS: ("Y" = Yes)

West:	Southwest:	Midwest:	Southeast:	Northeast:	International:
	Y	Y	Y	Y	

ARQULE INC

www.arqule.com

Industry Group Code: 325412 **Ranks within this company's industry group:** Sales: 42 Profits: 34

Insurance/HMO/PPO:		Drugs:		Equipment/Supplies:		Hospitals/Clinics:		Services:		Health Care:	
Insurance:		Manufacturer:		Manufacturer:		Acute Care:		Diagnostics:		Home Health:	
Managed Care:		Distributor:		Distributor:		Sub-Acute:		Labs/Testing:	Y	Long-Term Care:	
Utilization Management:		Specialty Pharmacy:		Leasing/Finance:		Outpatient Surgery:		Staffing:		Physical Therapy:	
Payment Processing:		Vitamins/Nutritionals:		Information Systems:	Y	Physical Rehab. Ctr.:		Waste Disposal:		Physician Prac. Mgmt.:	
		Clinical Trials:				Psychiatric Clinics:		Specialty Svcs.:	Y		

TYPES OF BUSINESS:

Research-Drug Discovery
Small-Molecule Compounds
Systems & Software
Predictive Modeling

BRANDS/DIVISIONS/AFFILIATES:

AMAP Chemistry Operating System
Optimal Chemical Entities
Activated Checkpoint Therapy
ARQ 501
ARQ 101
ARQ-650RP
ARQ 197
ARQ-550RP

CONTACTS:

Note: Officers with more than one job title may be intentionally listed here more than once.

Stephen Hill, CEO
Stephen Hill, Pres.
Richard H. Woodrich, CFO
Peter S. Lawrence, General Counsel/Exec. VP
Peter S. Lawrence, Chief Bus. Officer
Nigel J. Rulewski, Chief Medical Officer
Patrick Zenner, Chmn.

Phone: 781-994-0300	**Fax:** 781-376-6019
Toll-Free:	
Address: 19 Presidential Way, Woburn, MA 01801-5140 US	

GROWTH PLANS/SPECIAL FEATURES:

ArQule, Inc. seeks to bring together genomics and clinical development by applying its proprietary technology platform and world-class chemistry capabilities to drug discovery. It is committed to developing cancer medicine that is less toxic than chemotherapy and effective on more cancer types. ArQule provides library design and compound production to pharmaceutical collaborators (such as Pfizer) and uses the gains from these endeavors to fund its internal cancer drug discovery. The firm designs small-molecule compounds called Optimal Chemical Entities (OCEs), which have a greater chance of success in clinical trials. ArQule uses a multi-disciplinary approach consisting of intelligent design of molecules, high-throughput automated chemistry and experimental/prognostic analysis of absorption, distribution, metabolism and elimination (ADME) properties. The company researches and develops small-molecule cancer therapeutics based on its Activated Checkpoint Therapy (ACT). ACT compounds selectively kill cancer cells by restoring and activating defective cellular checkpoints. The firm's chief compounds under investigation are ARQ 501 for solid tumors and ARQ 101 for rheumatoid arthritis. ArQule's Automated Molecular Assembly Plant (AMAP) Chemistry Operating System allows it to perform high-throughput, automated production of new compounds. AMAP consists of an integrated series of automated workstations that perform tasks including weighing and dissolution, chemical synthesis, thermally controlled agitation and reaction process development.

ArQule offers its employees counseling; legal services; tuition reimbursement; performance based stock option and cash bonus plans; college savings plans; aid in seeking permanent resident status for foreign nationals; dry cleaning services; mortgage services; discounted ski vouchers; yoga classes; a subsidized cafeteria; an onsite fitness center; ping pong and pool tables; discounted Six Flags Tickets; and movie passes.

FINANCIALS:

Sales and profits are in thousands of dollars—add 000 to get the full amount. 2007 Note: Financial information for 2007 was not available for all companies at press time.

2007 Sales: $	2007 Profits: $	**U.S. Stock Ticker: ARQL**
2006 Sales: $6,626	2006 Profits: $-31,440	**Int'l Ticker:** Int'l Exchange:
2005 Sales: $6,628	2005 Profits: $-7,520	Employees: 98
2004 Sales: $5,012	2004 Profits: $-4,921	Fiscal Year Ends: 12/31
2003 Sales: $65,500	2003 Profits: $-34,800	Parent Company:

SALARIES/BENEFITS:

Pension Plan:	ESOP Stock Plan:	Profit Sharing:	Top Exec. Salary: $427,212	Bonus: $203,528
Savings Plan: Y	Stock Purch. Plan: Y		Second Exec. Salary: $304,640	Bonus: $107,015

OTHER THOUGHTS:

Apparent Women Officers or Directors:
Hot Spot for Advancement for Women/Minorities:

LOCATIONS: ("Y" = Yes)

West:	Southwest:	Midwest:	Southeast:	Northeast:	International:
				Y	

Note: Financial information, benefits and other data can change quickly and may vary from those stated here.

ARROW INTERNATIONAL INC www.arrowintl.com

Industry Group Code: 339113 **Ranks within this company's industry group:** Sales: 40 Profits: 34

Insurance/HMO/PPO:		Drugs:		Equipment/Supplies:		Hospitals/Clinics:		Services:		Health Care:	
Insurance:		Manufacturer:		Manufacturer:	Y	Acute Care:		Diagnostics:		Home Health:	
Managed Care:		Distributor:		Distributor:		Sub-Acute:		Labs/Testing:		Long-Term Care:	
Utilization Management:		Specialty Pharmacy:		Leasing/Finance:		Outpatient Surgery:		Staffing:		Physical Therapy:	
Payment Processing:		Vitamins/Nutritionals:		Information Systems:		Physical Rehab. Ctr.:		Waste Disposal:		Physician Prac. Mgmt.:	
		Clinical Trials:				Psychiatric Clinics:		Specialty Svcs.:			

TYPES OF BUSINESS:

Equipment-Catheters & Related Products
Cardiac Assistance Devices

BRANDS/DIVISIONS/AFFILIATES:

Arrow-Howes
ARROWguard
FlexTip Plus
AutoCAT
Berman
Edge
Super Arrow-Flex
CorAide

CONTACTS:

Note: Officers with more than one job title may be intentionally listed here more than once.

Philip B. Fleck, Interim CEO
Philip B. Fleck, Interim Pres.
Frederick J. Hirt, CFO
Carl W. Staples, Sr. VP-Human Resources
James T. Hatlan, Sr. VP-Mfg.
John C. Long, Corp. Sec.
Frederick J. Hirt, Sr. VP-Finance
Phillip M. Croxford, Group VP-Critical Care & Cardiac Assist
John C. Long, VP/Treas.
Paul L. Frankhouser, Exec. VP
Kenneth E. Imler, Sr. VP-Regulatory Affairs & Quality Assurance
Philip B. Fleck, Chmn.

Phone: 610-378-0131	**Fax:** 610-374-5360
Toll-Free: 800-233-3187	
Address: 2400 Bernville Rd., Reading, PA 19612 US	

GROWTH PLANS/SPECIAL FEATURES:

Arrow International, Inc. develops, manufactures an markets a broad range of clinically advanced disposabl catheters and related products for critical care medicine an interventional cardiology and radiology. The company critical care catheterization products are used to access th central vascular system for administration of fluids, drug and blood products. Arrow's cardiac care products are use for the diagnosis and treatment of patients with heart an vascular disease. Anesthesiologists, critical care specialist surgeons, cardiologists, nephrologists, emergency an trauma physicians and other health care providers use th company's products. Arrow's critical care products includ the Arrow-Howes multi-lumen catheter, a catheter equippe with three or four channels that enables the simultaneou administration of multiple critical care therapies through single puncture site; FlexTip Plus epidural catheters, whic are designed to minimize in-dwelling complication associated with conventional epidural catheters; an percutaneous thrombolytic devices, which are designed f clearance of thrombosed hemodialysis grafts in chron hemodialysis patients. Cardiac care products include intr aortic balloon (IAB) pumps and catheters, used t temporarily augment the pumping capability of the hea following cardiac surgery, serious heart attack or balloo angioplasty; AutoCAT, an advanced automatic IAB pum that continuously monitors and selects the best signal fro multiple electrocardiogram and arterial pressure sources t automatically adjust balloon inflation; the Berma angiographic catheter, used for pediatric cardi angiographic procedures; and the Super Arrow-Flex, sheath that provides a kink-resistant passageway for th introduction of catheters into the vascular system. The fir is also currently developing the CorAide Left Ventricul Assist System (LVAS), a small non-pulsatile, centrifugal flo ventricular assist device. In July 2007, the firm agreed to b acquired by Teleflex, Inc. for roughly $2 billion.

The firm offers its employees a continuing educatio program, an incentive commission program, matching gi donations and a fitness center (at the corporat headquarters only).

FINANCIALS:

Sales and profits are in thousands of dollars—add 000 to get the full amount. 2007 Note: Financial information for 2007 was not available for all companies at press time.

2007 Sales: $	2007 Profits: $	**U.S. Stock Ticker: ARRO**
2006 Sales: $481,587	2006 Profits: $56,009	**Int'l Ticker:** Int'l Exchange:
2005 Sales: $454,296	2005 Profits: $39,513	Employees: 4,000
2004 Sales: $433,134	2004 Profits: $55,942	Fiscal Year Ends: 10/31
2003 Sales: $380,400	2003 Profits: $45,700	Parent Company:

SALARIES/BENEFITS:

Pension Plan: Y	ESOP Stock Plan:	Profit Sharing:	Top Exec. Salary: $364,587	Bonus: $300,003
Savings Plan: Y	Stock Purch. Plan:		Second Exec. Salary: $306,576	Bonus: $220,735

OTHER THOUGHTS:

Apparent Women Officers or Directors:
Hot Spot for Advancement for Women/Minorities:

LOCATIONS: ("Y" = Yes)

West:	Southwest:	Midwest:	Southeast:	Northeast:	International:
				Y	Y

ART ADVANCED RESEARCH TECHNOLOGIES www.art.ca

Industry Group Code: 334500 **Ranks within this company's industry group:** Sales: 3 Profits: 3

Insurance/HMO/PPO:		Drugs:		Equipment/Supplies:		Hospitals/Clinics:		Services:		Health Care:	
Insurance:		Manufacturer:		Manufacturer:	Y	Acute Care:		Diagnostics:		Home Health:	
Managed Care:		Distributor:		Distributor:		Sub-Acute:		Labs/Testing:		Long-Term Care:	
Utilization Management:		Specialty Pharmacy:		Leasing/Finance:		Outpatient Surgery:		Staffing:		Physical Therapy:	
Payment Processing:		Vitamins/Nutritionals:		Information Systems:		Physical Rehab. Ctr.:		Waste Disposal:		Physician Prac. Mgmt.:	
		Clinical Trials:				Psychiatric Clinics:		Specialty Svcs.:			

TYPES OF BUSINESS:

Equipment-Optical Imaging Technology
Diagnostic Equipment

BRANDS/DIVISIONS/AFFILIATES:

eXplore Optix
SoftScan
Fenestra

CONTACTS: *Note: Officers with more than one job title may be intentionally listed here more than once.*

Sebastien Gignac, CEO
Warren Baker, COO
Sebastien Gignac, Pres.
Jacques Bedard, CFO
Pierre Couture, VP-Sales & Mktg.
Mario Khayat, VP-Optical Products
Jacques Raymond, VP-Bus. Dev.
Joseph Kozikowski, Chief Medical Officer
Benoit La Salle, Chmn.

Phone: 514-832-0777	**Fax:** 514-832-0778
Toll-Free:	
Address: 2300 Alfred-Nobel Blvd., Saint-Laurent, QC H4S 2A4 Canada	

GROWTH PLANS/SPECIAL FEATURES:

ART Advanced Research Technologies, Inc., researches, designs, develops and markets optical imaging technologies used to detect biological anomalies and visualize processes in living systems. The company's products are based on its time domain (TD) optical imaging. TD measures light absorption and scatter characteristics in the visible and near-infrared region of the spectrum to provide detailed profiles of biological tissues. These profiles allow the characterization of diseases like cancer. They also allow the user to analyze the molecular pathways leading to disease. ART's eXplore Optix, a pre-clinical optical molecular imager, provides in vivo pharmacokinetics and biodistribution. The company also offers SoftScan, a digital imagining device developed to detect and diagnose breast cancer. SoftScan will be introduced as a diagnostic technology, able to complement standard diagnostic technologies like x-ray, and was launched in 2006.

FINANCIALS: Sales and profits are in thousands of dollars—add 000 to get the full amount. 2007 Note: Financial information for 2007 was not available for all companies at press time.

2007 Sales: $	2007 Profits: $	**U.S. Stock Ticker:**
2006 Sales: $3,080	2006 Profits: $-8,750	**Int'l Ticker: ARA** Int'l Exchange: Toronto-TSX
2005 Sales: $1,240	2005 Profits: $-3,313	Employees: 49
2004 Sales: $1,935	2004 Profits: $-9,929	Fiscal Year Ends: 12/31
2003 Sales: $681,875	2003 Profits: $-5,832	Parent Company:

SALARIES/BENEFITS:

Pension Plan:	ESOP Stock Plan:	Profit Sharing:	Top Exec. Salary: $275,423	Bonus: $72,430
Savings Plan:	Stock Purch. Plan:		Second Exec. Salary: $163,135	Bonus: $43,435

OTHER THOUGHTS:

Apparent Women Officers or Directors: 1
Hot Spot for Advancement for Women/Minorities:

LOCATIONS: ("Y" = Yes)

West:	Southwest:	Midwest:	Southeast:	Northeast:	International:
					Y

ARTHROCARE CORP www.arthrocare.com

Industry Group Code: 339113 **Ranks within this company's industry group:** Sales: 56 Profits: 40

Insurance/HMO/PPO:		Drugs:		Equipment/Supplies:		Hospitals/Clinics:		Services:		Health Care:	
Insurance:		Manufacturer:		Manufacturer:	Y	Acute Care:		Diagnostics:		Home Health:	
Managed Care:		Distributor:		Distributor:		Sub-Acute:		Labs/Testing:		Long-Term Care:	
Utilization Management:		Specialty Pharmacy:		Leasing/Finance:		Outpatient Surgery:		Staffing:		Physical Therapy:	
Payment Processing:		Vitamins/Nutritionals:		Information Systems:		Physical Rehab. Ctr.:		Waste Disposal:		Physician Prac. Mgmt.:	
		Clinical Trials:				Psychiatric Clinics:		Specialty Svcs.:			

TYPES OF BUSINESS:

Equipment-Tissue Removal Systems
Cosmetic & Dermatologic Surgery Products
Advanced Radiofrequency Devices

BRANDS/DIVISIONS/AFFILIATES:

Coblation
Opus Medical, Inc.
Medical Device Alliance, Inc.
Atlantech Medical Devices, Ltd.
Atlantech AG
Parallax Medical

CONTACTS: *Note: Officers with more than one job title may be intentionally listed here more than once.*

Michael A. Baker, CEO
Michael A. Baker, Pres.
Michael Gluk, CFO/Sr. VP
Ross Beam, VP-Sales
Jean Woloszko, Chief Science Officer
Jean Woloszko, CTO
Richard A. Christensen, Sr. VP-Oper.
John T. Raffle, Esq., Sr. VP-Strategic Bus. Units
Bruce Prothro, VP/Mgr.-Coblation Tech. & Regulatory Affairs
John (Jack) H. Giroux, Sr. VP/Pres., Sports Medicine
David Applegate, VP/Mgr.-ArthroCare Spine
Sten I. Dahlborg, VP/Mgr.-ArthroCare Europe

Phone: 512-391-3900	**Fax:** 512-391-3901
Toll-Free: 800-348-8929	
Address: 7500 Rialto Blvd., Bldg. 2, Ste. 100, Austin, TX 78735 US	

GROWTH PLANS/SPECIAL FEATURES:

ArthroCare Corp. is a medical device company tha develops, manufactures and markets minimally invasiv surgical products, many of which are based on its patente Coblation technology. Coblation employs radio frequenc energy for soft tissue removal with minimal damage t surrounding tissue. The firm's products operate at lowe temperatures than traditional electrosurgical or laser surger tools and enable surgeons to ablate, shrink, sculpt, cu aspirate and suction soft tissue and to seal small bleedin vessels. The firm's strategy includes applying its patente technology to a wide range of soft tissue surgical markets including arthroscopic surgery, spinal surgery, neurosurgery cosmetic surgery, urologic surgery, various cardiolog applications, gynecological surgery and laparoscopic/genera surgical procedures and ear, nose and throat procedures The company has recently received FDA approval t specifically label its Coblation-based systems for use i neurosurgery; arthroscopic surgery of the knee, shoulde ankle, elbow, wrist and hip; and for general dermatologi procedures. In addition, ArthroCare manufactures othe disposable devices for spinal surgery, which are designed t improve the ease of use and functionality of the company' Coblation-based spinal surgery system. The company' technology is also applied in its sports medicine market i particular to the performance of arthroscopic surgery o selected joints. ArthroCare markets its surgery product both domestically and internationally through a combinatio of distributors supported by regional sales managers, a direc sales force and corporate partners. Subsidiaries c ArthroCare include Opus Medical, Inc., a manufacturer c arthroscopic repair products; Atlantech Medical Devices Ltd., a U.K. based ArthroCare distributor; Atlantech AG, a German ArthroCare distributor; Medical Device Alliance, Inc. a supplier of vertebral compression fracture treatmen products; and Parallax Medical, a majority-owned subsidiar of Medical Device Alliance.

ArthroCare offers its employees flexible spending accounts performance-based bonuses, tuition reimbursement, ar employee stock purchase plan and a 401(k) plan.

FINANCIALS: Sales and profits are in thousands of dollars—add 000 to get the full amount. 2007 Note: Financial information for 2007 was not available for all companies at press time.

2007 Sales: $	2007 Profits: $	**U.S. Stock Ticker: ARTC**
2006 Sales: $253,376	2006 Profits: $31,675	**Int'l Ticker:** Int'l Exchange:
2005 Sales: $206,533	2005 Profits: $23,530	Employees: 746
2004 Sales: $147,830	2004 Profits: $-26,189	Fiscal Year Ends: 12/31
2003 Sales: $118,900	2003 Profits: $7,500	Parent Company:

SALARIES/BENEFITS:

Pension Plan:	ESOP Stock Plan:	Profit Sharing:	Top Exec. Salary: $442,504	Bonus: $283,500
Savings Plan: Y	Stock Purch. Plan: Y		Second Exec. Salary: $238,243	Bonus: $120,120

OTHER THOUGHTS:

Apparent Women Officers or Directors: 1
Hot Spot for Advancement for Women/Minorities:

LOCATIONS: ("Y" = Yes)

West:	Southwest:	Midwest:	Southeast:	Northeast:	International:
Y	Y				Y

Note: Financial information, benefits and other data can change quickly and may vary from those stated here.

ASCENSION HEALTH

www.ascensionhealth.org

Industry Group Code: 622110 **Ranks within this company's industry group:** Sales: 3 Profits: 2

Insurance/HMO/PPO:		Drugs:		Equipment/Supplies:		Hospitals/Clinics:		Services:		Health Care:	
Insurance:		Manufacturer:		Manufacturer:		Acute Care:	Y	Diagnostics:		Home Health:	
Managed Care:		Distributor:		Distributor:		Sub-Acute:	Y	Labs/Testing:		Long-Term Care:	Y
Utilization Management:		Specialty Pharmacy:		Leasing/Finance:		Outpatient Surgery:		Staffing:		Physical Therapy:	
Payment Processing:		Vitamins/Nutritionals:		Information Systems:		Physical Rehab. Ctr.:	Y	Waste Disposal:		Physician Prac. Mgmt.:	
		Clinical Trials:				Psychiatric Clinics:	Y	Specialty Svcs.:			

TYPES OF BUSINESS:

Hospitals
Acute Care Hospitals
Rehabilitation Hospitals
Psychiatric Hospitals

BRANDS/DIVISIONS/AFFILIATES:

Daughters of Charity National Health System
Sisters of St. Joseph Health System
Sisters of St. Joseph of Carondelet
Ascension Health Ventures
Impulse Monitoring
Interventional Spine
Isto Technologies
Millennium Pharmacy Systems

CONTACTS: *Note: Officers with more than one job title may be intentionally listed here more than once.*

Anthony R. Tersigni, CEO
Robert J. Henkel, COO
Anthony R. Tersigni, Pres.
Anthony J. Speranzo, CFO
Marvin Russell, Chief Human Resources Officer
Hyung T. Kim, VP-R&D
Sherry L. Browne, Pres., Ascension Health Info. Svcs.
Joseph R. Impicciche, General Counsel/Sr. VP-Legal Svcs.
John D. Doyle, Chief Strategy Officer
Stephen D. LeResche, VP-Comm.
Elizabeth Foshage, VP-Finance
James K. Beckmann, Jr., Sr. VP/Chief Risk Officer
Andrew W. Allen, Sr. VP-Leadership Dev. & Succession Planning
Bernice Coreil, Sr. Exec. Advisor
Sally Jeffcoat, CEO/Pres., Carondelet Health
John O. Mudd, Chmn.
Michael T. Langlois, Chief Supply Chain Officer/Sr. VP

Phone: 314-733-8000 **Fax:** 314-733-8013
Toll-Free:
Address: 4600 Edmundson Rd., St. Louis, MO 63134 US

GROWTH PLANS/SPECIAL FEATURES:

Ascension Health is one of the leading not-for-profit health systems in the U.S., with 27 general acute care hospitals in 20 states, two long-term acute care hospitals and five clinics. The Catholic organization was formed in 1999 through the union of the Daughters of Charity National Health System based in St. Louis, Missouri and the Sisters of St. Joseph Health System based in Ann Arbor, Michigan. In 2002, Ascension Health added the hospitals and health facilities of the Sisters of St. Joseph of Carondelet, also based in St. Louis, Missouri. Ascension Health Ventures (AHV), the organization's investment subsidiary, identifies and supports companies that offer potential breakthroughs in health-care-related products, services and technologies. AHV invested in five companies in 2007, making it the most prolific year since the company's formation. The five companies are Impulse Monitoring, which provides intraoperative neurophysiological monitoring; Interventional Spine, which is an early stage developer of a spinal device platform enabling percutaneous approaches for spinal fusion; Isto Technologies, which is an early stage developer of orthobiologic products for sports medicine and spinal therapy applications; Millennium Pharmacy Systems, which provides pharmaceutical management services to the long-term care industry; and United Surgical Partners, which operates ambulatory and short-stay surgical facilities in the U.S. and owns private hospitals in Europe. Ascension Health is committed to assisting uninsured and underinsured patients as part of its hope to move U.S. health care toward a more compassionate system. Ascension Health offers an online resource center that provides information about programs for the uninsured. In recent news, Via Christi Health Systems became formally affiliated with Ascension Health.

FINANCIALS: **Sales and profits are in thousands of dollars—add 000 to get the full amount. 2007 Note: Financial information for 2007 was not available for all companies at press time.**

2007 Sales: $	2007 Profits: $	**U.S. Stock Ticker: Nonprofit**
2006 Sales: $11,405,552	2006 Profits: $802,965	**Int'l Ticker:** Int'l Exchange:
2005 Sales: $10,770,887	2005 Profits: $651,245	Employees: 100,000
2004 Sales: $10,046,370	2004 Profits: $469,694	Fiscal Year Ends: 6/30
2003 Sales: $	2003 Profits: $	Parent Company:

SALARIES/BENEFITS:

Pension Plan:	ESOP Stock Plan:	Profit Sharing:	Top Exec. Salary: $	Bonus: $
Savings Plan:	Stock Purch. Plan:		Second Exec. Salary: $	Bonus: $

OTHER THOUGHTS:

Apparent Women Officers or Directors: 7
Hot Spot for Advancement for Women/Minorities: Y

LOCATIONS: ("Y" = Yes)

West:	Southwest:	Midwest:	Southeast:	Northeast:	International:
Y	Y	Y	Y	Y	

Note: Financial information, benefits and other data can change quickly and may vary from those stated here.

ASPECT MEDICAL SYSTEMS INC www.aspectms.com

Industry Group Code: 339113 **Ranks within this company's industry group:** Sales: 82 Profits: 39

Insurance/HMO/PPO:		Drugs:		Equipment/Supplies:		Hospitals/Clinics:		Services:		Health Care:	
Insurance:		Manufacturer:		Manufacturer:	Y	Acute Care:		Diagnostics:		Home Health:	
Managed Care:		Distributor:		Distributor:		Sub-Acute:		Labs/Testing:		Long-Term Care:	
Utilization Management:		Specialty Pharmacy:		Leasing/Finance:		Outpatient Surgery:		Staffing:		Physical Therapy:	
Payment Processing:		Vitamins/Nutritionals:		Information Systems:		Physical Rehab. Ctr.:		Waste Disposal:		Physician Prac. Mgmt.:	
		Clinical Trials:				Psychiatric Clinics:		Specialty Svcs.:			

TYPES OF BUSINESS:

Equipment-Anesthesia Monitoring Systems
Patient Monitoring Systems

BRANDS/DIVISIONS/AFFILIATES:

Bispectral Index
BIS System
BIS Module Kit
BIS Sensors
BIS Sensor Plus
BIS Pediatric Sensor

CONTACTS: *Note: Officers with more than one job title may be intentionally listed here more than once.*

Nassib G. Chamoun, CEO
Nassib G. Chamoun, Pres.
Michael Falvey, CFO/VP
William Floyd, VP-Sales & Mktg.
Margery Ahearn, VP-Human Resources
Marc Davidson, VP-Eng.
John Coolidge, VP-Mfg. Oper.
Michael Falvey, Corp. Sec.
Paul J. Manberg, VP-Clinical, Regulatory & Quality Assurance
Scott D. Kelley, VP/Dir.-Medical
Philip H. Devlin, VP/General Mgr.-Neuroscience
J. Breckenridge Eagle, Chmn.
Boudewijn L.P.M. Bollen, Pres., International Oper.

Phone: 617-559-7000	**Fax:** 619-559-7400
Toll-Free:	
Address: 141 Needham St., Newton, MA 02464-1505 US	

GROWTH PLANS/SPECIAL FEATURES:

Aspect Medical Systems, Inc. develops, manufactures and markets the BIS System, an anesthesia monitoring system. The BIS System enables anesthesia providers to assess and manage a patient's level of consciousness during surgery. Patient monitoring with the BIS System provides several benefits, such as reducing the amount of anesthetics used and lessening the risk of surgical awareness, which is the unintentional regaining of consciousness during surgery. The BIS System is based on the firm's patented core technology, the Bispectral Index, commonly known as the BIS Index. The BIS Index is a numerical index that correlates with levels of consciousness and is displayed as a number between 0 and 100. The BIS System includes the BIS Monitor or BIS Module Kit and single-use, disposable BIS Sensors. The BIS Sensor is applied to a patient's forehead to measure the electrical activity of the brain, which is then analyzed by the BIS Monitor or BIS Module Kit to produce the BIS Index. The firm's product line includes the BIS Pediatric Sensor, a smaller sensor designed to visually appeal to children. More than 19,000 BIS monitors and modules have been installed worldwide. Aspect markets its products in the U.S. through direct sales organizations and specialty distributors. Internationally, the firm sells the BIS System through distributors and several marketing partners including Nihon Kohden and Instrumentarium's Datex Ohmeda division. Aspect also has original equipment manufacturer (OEM) relationships with several patient monitoring and anesthesia equipment companies.

In 2006, Aspect was selected by Boston Business Journal as being one of the Best Places to Work, an honor that recognizes Aspect's efforts to create a positive work environment.

FINANCIALS: **Sales and profits are in thousands of dollars—add 000 to get the full amount. 2007 Note: Financial information for 2007 was not available for all companies at press time.**

2007 Sales: $	2007 Profits: $	**U.S. Stock Ticker: ASPM**
2006 Sales: $91,334	2006 Profits: $37,089	**Int'l Ticker:** Int'l Exchange:
2005 Sales: $76,995	2005 Profits: $8,475	Employees: 288
2004 Sales: $55,564	2004 Profits: $ 303	Fiscal Year Ends: 12/31
2003 Sales: $44,091	2003 Profits: $-6,523	Parent Company:

SALARIES/BENEFITS:

Pension Plan:	ESOP Stock Plan:	Profit Sharing:	Top Exec. Salary: $345,079	Bonus: $104,780
Savings Plan: Y	Stock Purch. Plan: Y		Second Exec. Salary: $272,416	Bonus: $131,820

OTHER THOUGHTS:

Apparent Women Officers or Directors:
Hot Spot for Advancement for Women/Minorities:

LOCATIONS: ("Y" = Yes)

West:	Southwest:	Midwest:	Southeast:	Northeast:	International:
				Y	Y

ASSURANT EMPLOYEE BENEFITS

www.assurantemployeebenefits.com

Industry Group Code: 524114A **Ranks within this company's industry group:** Sales: Profits:

Insurance/HMO/PPO:		Drugs:		Equipment/Supplies:		Hospitals/Clinics:		Services:		Health Care:	
Insurance:	Y	Manufacturer:		Manufacturer:		Acute Care:		Diagnostics:		Home Health:	
Managed Care:		Distributor:		Distributor:		Sub-Acute:		Labs/Testing:		Long-Term Care:	
Utilization Management:		Specialty Pharmacy:		Leasing/Finance:		Outpatient Surgery:		Staffing:		Physical Therapy:	
Payment Processing:		Vitamins/Nutritionals:		Information Systems:		Physical Rehab. Ctr.:		Waste Disposal:		Physician Prac. Mgmt.:	
		Clinical Trials:				Psychiatric Clinics:		Specialty Svcs.:			

TYPES OF BUSINESS:

Insurance-Supplemental & Specialty Health
Group Disability Insurance
Group Term Life Insurance
Group Dental Insurance

BRANDS/DIVISIONS/AFFILIATES:

Assurant Inc
Fortis Benefits Insurance Co

CONTACTS: *Note: Officers with more than one job title may be intentionally listed here more than once.*

John S. Roberts, Interim CEO
John S. Roberts, Interim Pres.
Stacia N. Almquist, CFO
Mark J. Bohen, Sr. VP-Mktg.
Sylvia R. Wagner, Sr. VP-Human Resources & Dev.
Karla J. Schacht, CIO/Sr. VP
R. Scott Martin, CTO/VP
Katherine L. Greenzang, Sec.
Mark A. Andruss, VP-Corp. Dev.
Stacia N. Almquist, Treas.
Dianna D. Duvall, Sr. VP-Risk
Clifford S. Korte, Sr. VP-Claims, Clinical & Dental Network
J. Marc Warrington, Sr. VP-Sales
Peter J. Post, VP-IT Finance

Phone: 816-474-2345	**Fax:** 816-881-8996
Toll-Free:	
Address: 2323 Grand Blvd., Kansas City, MO 64108 US	

GROWTH PLANS/SPECIAL FEATURES:

Assurant Employee Benefits, a subsidiary of Assurant, Inc. formerly known as Fortis Benefits Insurance Co., provides non-medical insurance and investment products to businesses, with a focus on group dental, disability and group term life insurance. The company is licensed nationwide, serving mainly companies with fewer than 1,000 employees. Assurant offers long- and short-term disability insurance; accidental death and dismemberment insurance; term life; and dental insurance. The firm also provides a series of employee-paid benefits, the premiums of which are paid 100% by employees, as well as an Employee Assistance Program. Voluntary benefits are also offered, including additional long- and short-term disability, life and dental plans. Parent company Assurant, Inc., formerly Fortis, Inc., has divisions across the U.S. as well as in Belgium and the Netherlands. Assurant recently acquired American Bankers Insurance Group, Inc. and merged it with its own subsidiaries to create Assurant Group. The company also owns the dental PPO, Dental Health Alliance, which formed an alliance with Aetna Dental Access network in August 2006.

The company offers its employees medical and dental insurance; life, AD&D and long-term disability insurance; a 401(k) plan; pension plans; tuition reimbursement; and employee stock purchase programs.

FINANCIALS: **Sales and profits are in thousands of dollars—add 000 to get the full amount. 2007 Note: Financial information for 2007 was not available for all companies at press time.**

2007 Sales: $	2007 Profits: $	**U.S. Stock Ticker: Subsidiary**
2006 Sales: $	2006 Profits: $	**Int'l Ticker:** Int'l Exchange:
2005 Sales: $1,300,000	2005 Profits: $68,400	Employees: 630
2004 Sales: $1,456,000	2004 Profits: $62,200	Fiscal Year Ends:
2003 Sales: $1,450,000	2003 Profits: $	Parent Company: ASSURANT INC

SALARIES/BENEFITS:

Pension Plan:	ESOP Stock Plan:	Profit Sharing:	Top Exec. Salary: $375,000	Bonus: $155,025
Savings Plan:	Stock Purch. Plan:		Second Exec. Salary: $282,500	Bonus: $101,264

OTHER THOUGHTS:

Apparent Women Officers or Directors: 30
Hot Spot for Advancement for Women/Minorities: Y

LOCATIONS: ("Y" = Yes)

West:	Southwest:	Midwest:	Southeast:	Northeast:	International:
Y	Y	Y	Y	Y	

Note: Financial information, benefits and other data can change quickly and may vary from those stated here.

ASSURANT HEALTH

www.assuranthealth.com

Industry Group Code: 524114A **Ranks within this company's industry group:** Sales: Profits:

Insurance/HMO/PPO:		Drugs:		Equipment/Supplies:		Hospitals/Clinics:		Services:		Health Care:	
Insurance:	Y	Manufacturer:		Manufacturer:		Acute Care:		Diagnostics:		Home Health:	
Managed Care:		Distributor:		Distributor:		Sub-Acute:		Labs/Testing:		Long-Term Care:	
Utilization Management:		Specialty Pharmacy:		Leasing/Finance:		Outpatient Surgery:		Staffing:		Physical Therapy:	
Payment Processing:		Vitamins/Nutritionals:		Information Systems:		Physical Rehab. Ctr.:		Waste Disposal:		Physician Prac. Mgmt.:	
		Clinical Trials:				Psychiatric Clinics:		Specialty Svcs.:			

TYPES OF BUSINESS:

Insurance-Medical & Health, HMOs & PPOs
Student Health Insurance
Short-Term Medical Insurance
Health Savings Accounts
Small-Group Insurance
Temporary Medical Insurance

BRANDS/DIVISIONS/AFFILIATES:

Fortis Health
Time Insurance Co.
John Alden Life Insurance Co.
Union Security Insurance Co.
Assurant Inc

CONTACTS: *Note: Officers with more than one job title may be intentionally listed here more than once.*

Don Hamm, CEO
Raj Bal, COO
Don Hamm, Pres.
Howard Miller, CFO/Sr. VP
Laura Hohing, Chief Sales Officer

Phone: 414-271-3011	**Fax:** 414-224-0472
Toll-Free: 800-800-1212	
Address: 501 W. Michigan St., Milwaukee, WI 53201 US	

GROWTH PLANS/SPECIAL FEATURES:

Assurant Health, formerly Fortis Health, is a national provide of health insurance, focusing on individual, small-group short-term, student and specialty insurance products. The company provides coverage to over 1 million people and is one of the top sellers of temporary health insurance in the U.S. Its individual major medical product is targeted to individuals that are not offered health insurance by thei workplace; small-group insurance is designed for smal businesses that are looking for a flexible, appropriate health plan for their employees; short-term medical is a plan made for people between jobs that still want coverage during interim periods; and student select is designed fo undergraduate and graduate college students. Assurant's insurance plans are issued and underwritten by Time Insurance Co.; John Alden Life Insurance Co.; and Union Security Insurance Co. In addition to these lines o insurance, Assurant Health offers health savings accounts accounts set up specifically for individuals to plan for future medical expenses and to pay for health care expenses no covered by insurance, using pre-taxed dollars. It also provides health reimbursement arrangements, which are employer-sponsored accounts used for employee reimbursement.

The company offers its employees medical, dental and vision insurance; flexible spending accounts; life and AD&D insurance; a pension plan; a 401(k) plan; an employee assistance program; and wellness programs.

FINANCIALS: **Sales and profits are in thousands of dollars—add 000 to get the full amount. 2007 Note: Financial information for 2007 was not available for all companies at press time.**

2007 Sales: $	2007 Profits: $	**U.S. Stock Ticker: Subsidiary**
2006 Sales: $	2006 Profits: $	**Int'l Ticker:** Int'l Exchange:
2005 Sales: $2,200,000	2005 Profits: $178,100	Employees: 3,000
2004 Sales: $2,200,000	2004 Profits: $158,300	Fiscal Year Ends:
2003 Sales: $2,000,000	2003 Profits: $121,000	Parent Company: ASSURANT INC

SALARIES/BENEFITS:

Pension Plan: Y	ESOP Stock Plan:	Profit Sharing:	Top Exec. Salary: $	Bonus: $
Savings Plan: Y	Stock Purch. Plan:		Second Exec. Salary: $	Bonus: $

OTHER THOUGHTS:

Apparent Women Officers or Directors: 1
Hot Spot for Advancement for Women/Minorities:

LOCATIONS: ("Y" = Yes)

West:	Southwest:	Midwest:	Southeast:	Northeast:	International:
		Y	Y		

ASSURANT INC

www.assurant.com

Industry Group Code: 524114 **Ranks within this company's industry group:** Sales: 11 Profits: 6

Insurance/HMO/PPO:		Drugs:		Equipment/Supplies:		Hospitals/Clinics:		Services:		Health Care:	
Insurance:	Y	Manufacturer:		Manufacturer:		Acute Care:		Diagnostics:		Home Health:	
Managed Care:	Y	Distributor:		Distributor:		Sub-Acute:		Labs/Testing:		Long-Term Care:	
Utilization Management:		Specialty Pharmacy:		Leasing/Finance:		Outpatient Surgery:		Staffing:		Physical Therapy:	
Payment Processing:		Vitamins/Nutritionals:		Information Systems:		Physical Rehab. Ctr.:		Waste Disposal:		Physician Prac. Mgmt.:	
		Clinical Trials:				Psychiatric Clinics:		Specialty Svcs.:			

TYPES OF BUSINESS:

Insurance-Medical & Health, HMOs & PPOs
Property & Casualty Insurance
Life Insurance
Funeral Insurance
Homeowners' Insurance
Credit Insurance
Warranties
Debt Protection Administration

BRANDS/DIVISIONS/AFFILIATES:

Assurant Employee Benefits
Assurant Health
Assurant PreNeed
Assurant Solutions
Fortis, Inc.
Safeco Financial Institution Solutions, Inc.

CONTACTS: *Note: Officers with more than one job title may be intentionally listed here more than once.*

J. Kerry Clayton, Interim CEO
J. Kerry Clayton, Interim Pres.
Michael J. Peninger, Interim CFO
Mark J. Bohen, Sr. VP-Mktg.
Melissa Kivett, Sr. VP-Investor Rel.
Lesley Silvester, Exec. VP
Michael J. Peninger, Exec. VP/CEO-Assurant Employee Benefits
Donald Hamm, Exec. VP/CEO-Assurant Health
John Michael Palms, Chmn.

Phone: 212-859-7000 **Fax:** 212-859-7010
Toll-Free:
Address: 1 Chase Manhattan Plaza, 41st Fl., New York, NY 10005 US

GROWTH PLANS/SPECIAL FEATURES:

Assurant, Inc. provides insurance products and services around the world for its customers. The firm provides creditor-placed homeowners' insurance, manufactured housing homeowners' insurance, debt protection administration, credit insurance, warranties and extended service contracts, individual health and small employer group health insurance, group dental insurance, group disability insurance, group life insurance and pre-funded funeral insurance. The company is divided into the following businesses: Assurant Solutions, Assurant Health, Assurant Employee Benefits and Assurant PreNeed. Each business has its own management team and a certain autonomy in making operating decisions. Through its Assurant Solutions business, clients can apply for homeowners' insurance through the company's main distribution channel, mortgage lenders. This segment also provides credit insurance and warranties for products including appliances, automobiles and recreational vehicles, consumer electronics and wireless devices. Assurant Health operates largely through independent agents, national accounts, the Internet and offers both individual and small employer group health plans. Through the Assurant Employee Benefits business, Assurant writes group dental, group disability and group term life plans sponsored by employers. Lastly, through its Assurant PreNeed business, the firm offers its clients pre-funded funeral insurance. In June 2007, the company acquired Swansure Group, a distributor of its mortgage payment protection products in the UK. Additionally, Assurant purchased Mayflower National Life Insurance Company from Service Corporation International for $67.5 million.

FINANCIALS: **Sales and profits are in thousands of dollars—add 000 to get the full amount. 2007 Note: Financial information for 2007 was not available for all companies at press time.**

2007 Sales: $	2007 Profits: $	**U.S. Stock Ticker: AIZ**
2006 Sales: $8,070,584	2006 Profits: $717,418	**Int'l Ticker:** Int'l Exchange:
2005 Sales: $7,497,675	2005 Profits: $479,355	Employees: 13,400
2004 Sales: $7,410,714	2004 Profits: $350,560	Fiscal Year Ends: 12/31
2003 Sales: $7,066,213	2003 Profits: $185,652	Parent Company:

SALARIES/BENEFITS:

Pension Plan: Y	ESOP Stock Plan:	Profit Sharing:	Top Exec. Salary: $873,500	Bonus: $1,415,070
Savings Plan: Y	Stock Purch. Plan: Y		Second Exec. Salary: $721,000	Bonus: $1,168,020

OTHER THOUGHTS:

Apparent Women Officers or Directors: 2
Hot Spot for Advancement for Women/Minorities:

LOCATIONS: ("Y" = Yes)

West:	Southwest:	Midwest:	Southeast:	Northeast:	International:
		Y	Y	Y	

ASTELLAS PHARMA INC www.astellas.com

Industry Group Code: 325412 **Ranks within this company's industry group:** Sales: 17 Profits: 19

Insurance/HMO/PPO:		Drugs:		Equipment/Supplies:		Hospitals/Clinics:		Services:		Health Care:	
Insurance:		Manufacturer:	Y	Manufacturer:		Acute Care:		Diagnostics:		Home Health:	
Managed Care:		Distributor:		Distributor:		Sub-Acute:		Labs/Testing:		Long-Term Care:	
Utilization Management:		Specialty Pharmacy:		Leasing/Finance:		Outpatient Surgery:		Staffing:		Physical Therapy:	
Payment Processing:		Vitamins/Nutritionals:		Information Systems:		Physical Rehab. Ctr.:		Waste Disposal:		Physician Prac. Mgmt.:	
		Clinical Trials:				Psychiatric Clinics:		Specialty Svcs.:	Y		

TYPES OF BUSINESS:

Drugs, Manufacturing
Immunological Pharmaceuticals
Over-the-Counter Products
Reagents
Genomic Research
Venture Capital
Drug Licensing

BRANDS/DIVISIONS/AFFILIATES:

Yamanouchi Pharmaceutical Co., Ltd.
Fujisawa Pharmaceutical Co., Ltd.
Prograf
Protopic
Lipitor
Flomax
Pepcid
Astellas Venture Capital, LLC

CONTACTS: *Note: Officers with more than one job title may be intentionally listed here more than once.*

Masafumi Nogimori, CEO
Masafumi Nogimori, Pres.
Kunihide Ichikawa, Sr. VP-Sales & Mktg.
Toshinari Tamura, Exec. VP/Chief Science Officer
Isao Kishi, Sr. VP-Info. Sys.
Hitoshi Ohta, Sr. VP-Tech.
Masao Shimizu, Sr. VP-Dev.
Toshio Ohsawa, Sr. VP-Corp. Admin.
Hirofumi Onosaka, Sr. VP-Corp. Strategy
Osamu Nagai, Sr. VP-Corp. Finance & Acct.
Toshinari Tamura, Exec. VP
Makoto Nishimura, CEO/Chmn., Astellas Pharma U.S. Inc.
Iwaki Miyazaki, Sr. VP-QA, RA & Pharmacovigilance
Toichi Takenaka, Co-Chmn.
Yasuo Ishii, CEO/Chmn., Astellas Pharma Europe Ltd.

Phone: 81-3-3244-3000 **Fax:** 80-3-3244-3272
Toll-Free:
Address: 2-3-11 Nihonbashi-Honcho, Chuo-ku, Tokyo, 103-8411 Japan

GROWTH PLANS/SPECIAL FEATURES:

Astellas Pharma, Inc., the result of a 2005 merger of Yamanouchi Pharmaceutical Co., Ltd. and Fujisawa Pharmaceutical Co., Ltd., is one of the top 20 pharmaceuticals manufacturers in the world and the second-largest in Japan (behind Takeda Chemical Industries, Ltd.) The company has operations in Europe and North America, as well as in Taiwan, Hong Kong, China, the Philippines, Thailand, Indonesia and South Korea. Roughly 90% of Astellas's revenue relates to sales of pharmaceuticals, led by Prograf, which is used as an immunosuppressant in conjunction with organ transplantation. Other products target needs in dermatology, urology, immunology and cardiology, including Protopic for the treatment of atopic dermatitis; Mycamine for the treatment of fungal infections; VESIcare for treating overactive bladders; Lipitor for high cholesterol; Flomax for symptoms caused by enlarged prostates; and Pepcid for heartburn. The firm's research and development budget is over $1.3 billion (exceeding 17% of sales). In addition to developing its own pharmaceuticals, Astellas pursues in-licensing and co-promotion agreements with biotechnology firms and a host of other pharmaceutical companies such as Bristol-Meyers Squibb and GlaxoSmithKline. Moreover, subsidiary Astellas Venture Capital, LLC is engaged in investing in biotechnology companies, starting with $30 million in initial capitalization. In December 2006, Astellas Pharma dissolved its insurance subsidiary, Astellas Insurance Service Co., Ltd, and transferred the business to Ginsen Co., Ltd. In February 2007, the company began construction of new research laboratory buildings at the Miyukigaoka Research Center in Ibaraki, Japan.

FINANCIALS: Sales and profits are in thousands of dollars—add 000 to get the full amount. 2007 Note: Financial information for 2007 was not available for all companies at press time.

2007 Sales: $	2007 Profits: $	**U.S. Stock Ticker: ALPMF.PK**
2006 Sales: $7,758,480	2006 Profits: $1,106,390	**Int'l Ticker: 4503** Int'l Exchange: Tokyo-TSE
2005 Sales: $7,410,740	2005 Profits: $873,569	Employees: 9,500
2004 Sales: $4,839,100	2004 Profits: $568,500	Fiscal Year Ends: 3/31
2003 Sales: $	2003 Profits: $	Parent Company:

SALARIES/BENEFITS:

Pension Plan:	ESOP Stock Plan:	Profit Sharing:	Top Exec. Salary: $	Bonus: $
Savings Plan:	Stock Purch. Plan:		Second Exec. Salary: $	Bonus: $

OTHER THOUGHTS:

Apparent Women Officers or Directors:
Hot Spot for Advancement for Women/Minorities:

LOCATIONS: ("Y" = Yes)

West:	Southwest:	Midwest:	Southeast:	Northeast:	International:
	Y	Y		Y	Y

ASTRAZENECA PLC

www.astrazeneca.com

Industry Group Code: 325412 **Ranks within this company's industry group:** Sales: 7 Profits: 8

Insurance/HMO/PPO:		Drugs:		Equipment/Supplies:		Hospitals/Clinics:		Services:		Health Care:	
Insurance:		Manufacturer:	Y	Manufacturer:		Acute Care:		Diagnostics:		Home Health:	
Managed Care:		Distributor:	Y	Distributor:		Sub-Acute:		Labs/Testing:		Long-Term Care:	
Utilization Management:		Specialty Pharmacy:		Leasing/Finance:		Outpatient Surgery:		Staffing:		Physical Therapy:	
Payment Processing:		Vitamins/Nutritionals:		Information Systems:		Physical Rehab. Ctr.:		Waste Disposal:		Physician Prac. Mgmt.:	
		Clinical Trials:	Y			Psychiatric Clinics:		Specialty Svcs.:			

TYPES OF BUSINESS:

Drugs-Diversified
Pharmaceutical Research & Development

BRANDS/DIVISIONS/AFFILIATES:

Rhinocort
Zomig
Nolvadex
Prilosec
Nexium
Pulmicort
Cambridge Antibody Technology Group
Arrow Therapeutics Ltd.

CONTACTS:

Note: Officers with more than one job title may be intentionally listed here more than once.

David Brennan, CEO
Martin Nicklasson, Exec. VP-Global Mktg.
Tony Bloxham, Exec. VP-Human Resources
Jan Lundberg, Exec. VP-Discovery Research
David Smith, Exec. VP-Oper.
John Patterson, Exec. Dir.-Dev.
Edel McCaffrey, Media
Mina Blair, Investor Rel.
John Patterson, VP-Prod. Strategy & Licensing
Tony Zook, Exec. VP-North America
Louis Schweitzer, Chmn.
Bruno Angelici, VP-Europe, Japan & Asia

Phone: 44-20-7304-5000 **Fax:** 44-20-7304-5151
Toll-Free:
Address: 15 Stanhope Gate, London, W1K 1LN UK

GROWTH PLANS/SPECIAL FEATURES:

AstraZeneca plc is a leading global pharmaceutical company that provides products to fight disease in areas of medical necessity. The company is the result of the merger of the Zeneca Group with Astra. The firm invests approximately $3.9 billion in annual research and development and enjoys sales in over 100 countries. It operates 27 manufacturing sites in 19 countries and 16 major research centers in 8 countries. The company focuses on therapeutic interventions in six therapy areas: cancer, respitory and inflammation, cardiovascular, gastrointestinal, infection and neuroscience. AstraZeneca's cardiovascular products include Seloken ZOK, Crestor, Atacand, Plendil, Zestril and Tenormin. The firm's gastrointestinal products include Nexium, Entocort and Prilosec. Merrem, its primary infection product, is an antibiotic for serious hospital-acquired infections. The company's primary neuroscience offering is Zomig, an anti-migraine drug. AstraZeneca's cancer treatments include Casodex for prostate cancer, Zoladex, Armidex for breast cancer, Iressa for lung cancer, Faslodex and Nolvadex. The firm's respiratory and inflammation brands include Pulmicort, Symbicort, Rhinocort, Accolate and Oxis. Seloken, Seroquel, Nexium, Prilosec, Casodex and Pulmicort all have sales in excess of $1 billion. In 2006, AstraZeneca acquired Cambridge Antibody Technology Group. In 2007, the company acquired Arrow Therapeutics Ltd., a developer of anti-viral therapies. The May 2007, the firm agreed to acquire MedImmune for $15.6 billion. MedImmune is a biotech company, and the deal would push AstraZeneca into vaccines with MedImmune's FluMist.

FINANCIALS:

Sales and profits are in thousands of dollars—add 000 to get the full amount. 2007 Note: Financial information for 2007 was not available for all companies at press time.

2007 Sales: $	2007 Profits: $	**U.S. Stock Ticker: AZN**
2006 Sales: $26,475,000	2006 Profits: $4,392,000	**Int'l Ticker: AZN** Int'l Exchange: London-LSE
2005 Sales: $23,950,000	2005 Profits: $3,881,000	Employees: 66,000
2004 Sales: $21,426,000	2004 Profits: $3,813,000	Fiscal Year Ends: 12/31
2003 Sales: $18,849,000	2003 Profits: $3,036,000	Parent Company:

SALARIES/BENEFITS:

Pension Plan:	ESOP Stock Plan:	Profit Sharing:	Top Exec. Salary: $1,191,000	Bonus: $588,000
Savings Plan:	Stock Purch. Plan:		Second Exec. Salary: $732,000	Bonus: $347,000

OTHER THOUGHTS:

Apparent Women Officers or Directors: 5
Hot Spot for Advancement for Women/Minorities: Y

LOCATIONS: ("Y" = Yes)

West:	Southwest:	Midwest:	Southeast:	Northeast:	International:
Y	Y	Y	Y	Y	Y

ATC HEALTHCARE INC

www.atchealthcare.com

Industry Group Code: 561300 **Ranks within this company's industry group:** Sales: 1 Profits: 1

Insurance/HMO/PPO:		Drugs:		Equipment/Supplies:		Hospitals/Clinics:		Services:		Health Care:	
Insurance:		Manufacturer:		Manufacturer:		Acute Care:		Diagnostics:		Home Health:	
Managed Care:		Distributor:		Distributor:		Sub-Acute:		Labs/Testing:		Long-Term Care:	
Utilization Management:		Specialty Pharmacy:		Leasing/Finance:		Outpatient Surgery:		Staffing:	Y	Physical Therapy:	
Payment Processing:		Vitamins/Nutritionals:		Information Systems:		Physical Rehab. Ctr.:		Waste Disposal:		Physician Prac. Mgmt.:	
		Clinical Trials:				Psychiatric Clinics:		Specialty Svcs.:	Y		

TYPES OF BUSINESS:

Health Care Staffing
Management Consulting Services

BRANDS/DIVISIONS/AFFILIATES:

Travel Nurse Program

CONTACTS:

Note: Officers with more than one job title may be intentionally listed here more than once.

David Savitsky, CEO
Stephen Savitsky, Pres.
Daniel M. Press, CFO/Sr. VP
Stephen Savitsky, Chmn.

Phone: 516-750-1600	**Fax:** 516-750-1755
Toll-Free:	
Address: 1983 Marcus Ave., Ste. E122, Lake Success, NY 11042 US	

GROWTH PLANS/SPECIAL FEATURES:

ATC Healthcare, Inc. is a national provider of supplemental staffing and management consulting services to health care institutions through its network of 54 owned and franchised offices in 31 states. The company's supplemental staffing operations provide clients with registered nurses, licensed practical nurses and certified nursing assistants in over 60 job categories, including critical care, neonatal, labor and delivery, as well as administrative assistants, collection personnel and medical records clerks. It also offers allied health staffing, which includes mental health technicians, radiology technicians, phlebotomists and speech, occupational and physical therapists. Health care institutions use supplemental staffing to cover permanent positions for which they have openings, for peak periods, vacations and emergencies and to accommodate periodic increases in the number of patients. ATC Healthcare takes care of the payment of wages, benefits, payroll taxes, workers' compensation and unemployment insurance for supplemental staff. The company also operates a travel nurse program whereby nurses and physical and occupational therapists are recruited from the U.S. and other countries to perform services on a long-term basis in the U.S. ATC has recently expanded its client base to include nursing homes, physician practice management groups, managed care facilities, insurance companies, surgery centers, community health centers and schools. In February 2007, the company launched its new Business Staffing Division, which will provide temporary staffing and permanent placement in the areas of Accounting, IT, Human Resources, Legal, and General/Clerical/Administrative positions.

ATC Healthcare offers a benefits package including tuition reimbursement, flexible spending accounts, flexible work schedules, health care work apparel discounts and a 401(k) savings plan.

FINANCIALS:

Sales and profits are in thousands of dollars—add 000 to get the full amount. 2007 Note: Financial information for 2007 was not available for all companies at press time.

2007 Sales: $89,401	2007 Profits: $-2,159	**U.S. Stock Ticker: AHN**
2006 Sales: $71,528	2006 Profits: $-2,332	**Int'l Ticker:** Int'l Exchange:
2005 Sales: $67,937	2005 Profits: $-10,404	Employees: 7,074
2004 Sales: $130,401	2004 Profits: $-6,180	Fiscal Year Ends: 2/28
2003 Sales: $148,700	2003 Profits: $-2,800	Parent Company:

SALARIES/BENEFITS:

Pension Plan:	ESOP Stock Plan:	Profit Sharing:	Top Exec. Salary: $363,000	Bonus: $
Savings Plan: Y	Stock Purch. Plan: Y		Second Exec. Salary: $272,244	Bonus: $

OTHER THOUGHTS:

Apparent Women Officers or Directors:
Hot Spot for Advancement for Women/Minorities:

LOCATIONS: ("Y" = Yes)

West:	Southwest:	Midwest:	Southeast:	Northeast:	International:
Y	Y	Y	Y	Y	

ATHENAHEALTH INC

www.athenahealth.com

Industry Group Code: 522320 **Ranks within this company's industry group:** Sales: 4 Profits:

Insurance/HMO/PPO:		Drugs:		Equipment/Supplies:		Hospitals/Clinics:		Services:		Health Care:	
Insurance:		Manufacturer:		Manufacturer:		Acute Care:		Diagnostics:		Home Health:	
Managed Care:		Distributor:		Distributor:		Sub-Acute:		Labs/Testing:		Long-Term Care:	
Utilization Management:		Specialty Pharmacy:		Leasing/Finance:		Outpatient Surgery:		Staffing:		Physical Therapy:	
Payment Processing:		Vitamins/Nutritionals:		Information Systems:		Physical Rehab. Ctr.:		Waste Disposal:		Physician Prac. Mgmt.:	
		Clinical Trials:				Psychiatric Clinics:		Specialty Svcs.:	Y		

TYPES OF BUSINESS:

Outsourced Health Reimbursement Services
Patient Information Management
Billing & Collection Services for Health Care Providers

BRANDS/DIVISIONS/AFFILIATES:

athenaCollector
athenaEnterprise
athenaClinicals

CONTACTS: *Note: Officers with more than one job title may be intentionally listed here more than once.*

Jonathan Bush, CEO
James M. MacDonald, COO/Sr. VP
Jonathan Bush, Pres.
Carl B. Byers, CFO/Sr. VP
Robert M. Hueber, Sr. VP-Sales
Amy Pooser, VP-People & Process
Ed Y. Park, CTO
Christopher E. Nolin, General Counsel/Sr. VP/Sec.
Todd Y. Park, Chief Dev. Officer/Exec. VP
Carl B. Byers, Treas.
Nancy G. Brown, Sr. VP-Bus. Dev. & Gov't Rel.
Jonathan Bush, Chmn.

Phone: 617-402-1000	**Fax:** 617-402-1099
Toll-Free: 888-652-8200	
Address: 311 Arsenal St., Watertown, MA 02472 US	

GROWTH PLANS/SPECIAL FEATURES:

athenahealth, Inc. is a provider of Internet-based business services to physician practices and one of the largest firms in the health reimbursement field. The company offers its integrated business services over the Internet on a subscription basis. The firm offers several medical group office automation subscription services, as well as related services. athenahealth's flagship product, athenaCollector, is a revenue cycle management service that includes a management platform and automates and manages billing-related functions for physicians practices. athenaCollector tracks, controls and executes claims and billing processes. athenaClinicals, aimed at providing a solution for the EMRs, provides a wholly integrated solution for managing the processes of providing the receiving pay for care. athenaEnterprise is an optional add-on overlay designed specifically for provider networks, integrated delivery systems and other physician enterprises. athenahealth is one of the largest firms in the health reimbursement field. It has clients in more than 30 states in the U.S., and its offices include operations in India. The company has over 775 clients. Over 10,000 providers are served nationwide, and about 54 medical specialties are covered. The firm manages over $2 billion in client revenues annually. Customers include The Methodist Hospital System, Ohio Health Practice Management Services, Centra Health, Professionals for Women's Health, TriHealth Physician Services, Columbus Regional Healthcare System and Rockford Health Physicians. In September 2007, the company went public.

FINANCIALS: **Sales and profits are in thousands of dollars—add 000 to get the full amount. 2007 Note: Financial information for 2007 was not available for all companies at press time.**

2007 Sales: $	2007 Profits: $	**U.S. Stock Ticker: ATHN**
2006 Sales: $80,000	2006 Profits: $	**Int'l Ticker:** Int'l Exchange:
2005 Sales: $55,000	2005 Profits: $	Employees:
2004 Sales: $39,500	2004 Profits: $	Fiscal Year Ends:
2003 Sales: $23,000	2003 Profits: $	Parent Company:

SALARIES/BENEFITS:

Pension Plan:	ESOP Stock Plan:	Profit Sharing:	Top Exec. Salary: $	Bonus: $
Savings Plan:	Stock Purch. Plan:		Second Exec. Salary: $	Bonus: $

OTHER THOUGHTS:

Apparent Women Officers or Directors: 2
Hot Spot for Advancement for Women/Minorities:

LOCATIONS: ("Y" = Yes)

West:	Southwest:	Midwest:	Southeast:	Northeast:	International:
				Y	Y

Note: Financial information, benefits and other data can change quickly and may vary from those stated here.

ATRIA SENIOR LIVING GROUP

www.arvi.com

Industry Group Code: 623110 **Ranks within this company's industry group:** Sales: Profits:

Insurance/HMO/PPO:		Drugs:		Equipment/Supplies:		Hospitals/Clinics:		Services:		Health Care:	
Insurance:		Manufacturer:		Manufacturer:		Acute Care:		Diagnostics:		Home Health:	
Managed Care:		Distributor:		Distributor:		Sub-Acute:		Labs/Testing:		Long-Term Care:	Y
Utilization Management:		Specialty Pharmacy:		Leasing/Finance:		Outpatient Surgery:		Staffing:		Physical Therapy:	
Payment Processing:		Vitamins/Nutritionals:		Information Systems:		Physical Rehab. Ctr.:		Waste Disposal:		Physician Prac. Mgmt.:	
		Clinical Trials:				Psychiatric Clinics:		Specialty Svcs.:			

TYPES OF BUSINESS:

Long-Term Health Care
Assisted Living Centers
Alzheimer Care

BRANDS/DIVISIONS/AFFILIATES:

Prometheus Assisted Living, LLC
Atria Author Series

CONTACTS:

Note: Officers with more than one job title may be intentionally listed here more than once.

John A. Moore, CEO
Mark Jesse, CFO
Doug Owens, VP-Info. Systems

Phone: 502-719-1600	**Fax:** 502-719-1699
Toll-Free: 888-287-4201	
Address: Brown & Williamson Tower, Louisville, KY 40202 US	

GROWTH PLANS/SPECIAL FEATURES:

Atria Senior Living Group is one of the nation's largest operators of facilities providing assisted living services for the country's burgeoning senior population. The company currently operates 123 communities across 27 states, which provide support for seniors' day-to-day activities and chores, such as shopping and cleaning, but exclude any sort of acute care that would be found in a nursing home. Each program that Atria offers is tailored to the individual, with residents free to bring their own furnishings and even pets. Atria provides seniors with the following programs: the Independent Living program, which is a retirement lifestyle that frees seniors from the worries of home maintenance, encourages them to engage in activities and hobbies and allows them to choose their own degree of privacy or sociability; the Assisted Living program, which is available to help seniors with daily activities such as bathing, eating, dressing and medication management; the Life Guidance program, which is available at some communities to provide a separate and secure environment for seniors with Alzheimer's disease and other forms of memory impairment; and respite stay programs, which are tailored for seniors on a temporary basis for seasonal stays, hospital recovery or trail-period stays. In addition the company works to engage seniors through extra programs such as the Atria Author Series, which allows residents to write for publications that are available to families, organizations, schools and churches. Also, Atria's Engage Life program strives to provide residents with other interesting and meaningful activities, which are coordinated by Engage Life Directors.

FINANCIALS:

Sales and profits are in thousands of dollars—add 000 to get the full amount. 2007 Note: Financial information for 2007 was not available for all companies at press time.

2007 Sales: $	2007 Profits: $	**U.S. Stock Ticker: Private**
2006 Sales: $	2006 Profits: $	**Int'l Ticker:** Int'l Exchange:
2005 Sales: $	2005 Profits: $	Employees: 3,070
2004 Sales: $	2004 Profits: $	Fiscal Year Ends: 12/31
2003 Sales: $	2003 Profits: $	Parent Company:

SALARIES/BENEFITS:

Pension Plan:	ESOP Stock Plan:	Profit Sharing:	Top Exec. Salary: $350,000	Bonus: $210,000
Savings Plan:	Stock Purch. Plan:		Second Exec. Salary: $225,000	Bonus: $110,000

OTHER THOUGHTS:

Apparent Women Officers or Directors:
Hot Spot for Advancement for Women/Minorities:

LOCATIONS: ("Y" = Yes)

West:	Southwest:	Midwest:	Southeast:	Northeast:	International:
Y	Y	Y	Y	Y	

ATRION CORPORATION

www.atrioncorp.com

ndustry Group Code: 339113 **Ranks within this company's industry group:** Sales: 84 Profits: 63

nsurance/HMO/PPO:		Drugs:		Equipment/Supplies:		Hospitals/Clinics:		Services:		Health Care:	
nsurance:		Manufacturer:		Manufacturer:	Y	Acute Care:		Diagnostics:		Home Health:	
Managed Care:		Distributor:		Distributor:		Sub-Acute:		Labs/Testing:		Long-Term Care:	
Jtilization Management:		Specialty Pharmacy:		Leasing/Finance:		Outpatient Surgery:		Staffing:		Physical Therapy:	
Payment Processing:		Vitamins/Nutritionals:		Information Systems:		Physical Rehab. Ctr.:		Waste Disposal:		Physician Prac. Mgmt.:	
		Clinical Trials:				Psychiatric Clinics:		Specialty Svcs.:			

TYPES OF BUSINESS:

Equipment-Ophthalmic, Diagnostic & Cardiovascular
Fluid Delivery Devices
Medical Device Components
Contract Manufacturing

BRANDS/DIVISIONS/AFFILIATES:

Quest Medical, Inc.
MPS2 Myocardial Protection System
Halkey-Roberts Corp.
LacriCATH
Atrion Medical Products, Inc.
ACTester

CONTACTS: *Note: Officers with more than one job title may be intentionally listed here more than once.*

Emile A. Battat, CEO
David A. Battat, COO
David A. Battat, Pres.
Jeffery Strickland, CFO
Jeffery Strickland, Sec./VP
Jeffery Strickland, Treas.
Emile A. Battat, Chmn.

Phone: 972-390-9800	**Fax:** 972-396-7581
Toll-Free:	
Address: 1 Allentown Pkwy., Allen, TX 75002-4211 US	

GROWTH PLANS/SPECIAL FEATURES:

Atrion Corporation designs, develops, manufactures, markets, sells and distributes products and components for the medical and health care industries. It sells components to other equipment manufacturers and finished products to physicians, hospitals, clinics and other treatment centers. Its cardiovascular products, which accounted for 29% of its 2006 revenues, manufactured by subsidiary Quest Medical, Inc., include cardiac surgery vacuum relief valves and other tools used in cardiac surgery, such as the MPS2 Myocardial Protection System, a proprietary system used for the delivery of solutions to the heart during open-heart surgery, mixing drugs into the bloodstream without diluting the blood. Subsidiary Halkey-Roberts Corporation is responsible for designing, developing, manufacturing and selling Atrion's fluid delivery products, 32% of 2006 revenue, such as intravenous fluid delivery lines, medical tubing clamps and various valves. Atrion's ophthalmic products, 17% of 2006 revenue, include soft contact lens storage and disinfection cases and the LacriCATH line of balloon catheters; and it also provides custom packaging, warehousing and inventory management as part of its pharmaceutical reselling business. Its other medical and non-medical products, 22% of 2006 revenue, many of which are manufactured by subsidiary Atrion Medical Products, Inc., include the manufacturing of inflation devices, right angle connectors and closures for life rafts and other inflatable structures. Some of its non-medical valves include those for use on electronics or munitions cases; pressure vessels; and transportation container cases. Its other medical devices include the ACTester line of tests, measuring blood clotting time; and safe needle and scalpel blade containment products. It also owns a 22 mile pipeline in north Alabama that is leased to an industrial gas producer supplying one of its customers with gaseous oxygen.

Atrion provides medical, dental and life insurance; prescription drug plans; retirement plans; paid holidays and vacations; and short and long-term disability benefits.

FINANCIALS: **Sales and profits are in thousands of dollars—add 000 to get the full amount. 2007 Note: Financial information for 2007 was not available for all companies at press time.**

2007 Sales: $	2007 Profits: $	**U.S. Stock Ticker: ATRI**
2006 Sales: $81,020	2006 Profits: $10,765	**Int'l Ticker:** Int'l Exchange:
2005 Sales: $72,089	2005 Profits: $8,958	Employees: 486
2004 Sales: $66,081	2004 Profits: $6,470	Fiscal Year Ends: 12/31
2003 Sales: $62,800	2003 Profits: $5,100	Parent Company:

SALARIES/BENEFITS:

Pension Plan: Y	ESOP Stock Plan:	Profit Sharing:	Top Exec. Salary: $500,000	Bonus: $100,000
Savings Plan:	Stock Purch. Plan:		Second Exec. Salary: $195,000	Bonus: $59,603

OTHER THOUGHTS:

Apparent Women Officers or Directors:
Hot Spot for Advancement for Women/Minorities:

LOCATIONS: ("Y" = Yes)

West:	Southwest:	Midwest:	Southeast:	Northeast:	International:
	Y		Y		

Note: Financial information, benefits and other data can change quickly and may vary from those stated here.

ATS AUTOMATION TOOLING SYSTEMS INC

www.atsautomation.com

Industry Group Code: 333000 **Ranks within this company's industry group:** Sales: 2 Profits: 2

Insurance/HMO/PPO:		Drugs:		Equipment/Supplies:		Hospitals/Clinics:		Services:		Health Care:	
Insurance:		Manufacturer:		Manufacturer:	Y	Acute Care:		Diagnostics:		Home Health:	
Managed Care:		Distributor:		Distributor:		Sub-Acute:		Labs/Testing:		Long-Term Care:	
Utilization Management:		Specialty Pharmacy:		Leasing/Finance:		Outpatient Surgery:		Staffing:		Physical Therapy:	
Payment Processing:		Vitamins/Nutritionals:		Information Systems:		Physical Rehab. Ctr.:		Waste Disposal:		Physician Prac. Mgmt.:	
		Clinical Trials:				Psychiatric Clinics:		Specialty Svcs.:			

TYPES OF BUSINESS:

Automated Systems Manufacturing
Precision Systems Manufacturing
Photovoltaic Cells
Repetitive Equipment Manufacturing
Manufacturing Consulting

BRANDS/DIVISIONS/AFFILIATES:

Photowatt Technologies, Inc.

CONTACTS: *Note: Officers with more than one job title may be intentionally listed here more than once.*

Ronald J. Jutras, CEO
Bruce E. Seeley, Interim COO
Ronald J. Jutras, Pres.
Gerry R. Beard, CFO/VP
Lynne Brenegan, VP-Human Resources
Ron Keyser, CIO
Mike Cybulski, Exec. VP-Automation Sys. Oper.
Lynne Brenegan, VP-Strategy
Lalitha Mony, Investor Rel. Coordinator
Carl Galloway, Treas./VP
James Rowan, COO/Pres., Automation Systems Group
Tom Hayes, General Mgr.-Compliant Solutions
Eric Kiisel, VP-Project Mgmt.
Gary Seiter, COO-Photowatt Tech.
Lawrence G. Tapp, Chmn.
Bruce E. Seeley, Pres., Automation Systems Group Europe & Asia

Phone: 519-653-6500	**Fax:** 519-650-6520
Toll-Free:	
Address: 250 Royal Oak Rd., Cambridge, ON A6 N3H 4R6 Canada	

GROWTH PLANS/SPECIAL FEATURES:

ATS Automation Tooling Systems, Inc., based in Ontario, Canada, is a leading designer and producer of turn-key automated manufacturing and test systems. These systems are used primarily by multinational corporations operating in industries including automotive, computer/electronics, healthcare, telecommunications and consumer products. The company also makes precision components and sub-assemblies using its own custom-built manufacturing systems, process knowledge and automation technology. ATS operates a segment under the subsidiary Photowatt Technologies, Inc. that manufactures energy cells and modules The firm has operations in North America, Europe, Southeast Asia and China, with 24 manufacturing facilities. Photowatt Technologies has been growing rapidly and is now the company's second-largest operating segment after its primary automated systems group (ASG), surpassing the precision components group (PCG). Photowatt recently filed for an initial public offering in the U.S and will control ATS's solar business once the offering is completed. ATS plans to focus solely on automation systems by exiting from the solar business and from its PCG. The firm has made a number of divestures, including PCG facilities in the U.S. and Canada; and its Berlin, Germany coal winding subsidiary in June 2006. The company plans to seek alternatives for its PCG, which it considers to be non-strategic to its automation business. ATS is expanding in Asia, and in 2006 launched a 60,000-square-foot ASG facility in Penang, Malaysia and a 17,000-square-foot PCG facility in Shanghai, China. In 2007, the firm announced plans to broaden its PCG base in the healthcare and electronics industries; and to expand its current facilities in China, working with a private Chinese precision machining company.

ATS offers its employees a computer purchase plan, on-the-job training, an educational program and scholarships.

FINANCIALS: **Sales and profits are in thousands of dollars—add 000 to get the full amount. 2007 Note: Financial information for 2007 was not available for all companies at press time.**

2007 Sales: $700,075	2007 Profits: $-85,015	**U.S. Stock Ticker: ATA**
2006 Sales: $725,775	2006 Profits: $-69,293	**Int'l Ticker: ATA** Int'l Exchange: Toronto-TSX
2005 Sales: $681,857	2005 Profits: $8,223	Employees: 3,900
2004 Sales: $545,628	2004 Profits: $-1,993	Fiscal Year Ends: 3/31
2003 Sales: $	2003 Profits: $	Parent Company:

SALARIES/BENEFITS:

Pension Plan:	ESOP Stock Plan:	Profit Sharing: Y	Top Exec. Salary: $439,403	Bonus: $193,338
Savings Plan:	Stock Purch. Plan: Y		Second Exec. Salary: $316,361	Bonus: $61,567

OTHER THOUGHTS:

Apparent Women Officers or Directors: 1
Hot Spot for Advancement for Women/Minorities:

LOCATIONS: ("Y" = Yes)

West:	Southwest:	Midwest:	Southeast:	Northeast:	International:
Y	Y	Y		Y	Y

ATS MEDICAL INC

www.atsmedical.com

Industry Group Code: 339113 **Ranks within this company's industry group:** Sales: 94 Profits: 92

Insurance/HMO/PPO:		Drugs:		Equipment/Supplies:		Hospitals/Clinics:		Services:		Health Care:	
Insurance:		Manufacturer:		Manufacturer:	Y	Acute Care:		Diagnostics:		Home Health:	
Managed Care:		Distributor:		Distributor:	Y	Sub-Acute:		Labs/Testing:		Long-Term Care:	
Utilization Management:		Specialty Pharmacy:		Leasing/Finance:		Outpatient Surgery:		Staffing:		Physical Therapy:	
Payment Processing:		Vitamins/Nutritionals:		Information Systems:		Physical Rehab. Ctr.:		Waste Disposal:		Physician Prac. Mgmt.:	
		Clinical Trials:				Psychiatric Clinics:		Specialty Svcs.:			

TYPES OF BUSINESS:

Equipment-Mechanical Heart Valves
Grafts & Prostheses
Cardiovascular Accessories
Surgical Cryotherapy Products

BRANDS/DIVISIONS/AFFILIATES:

ATS Open Pivot
3F Therapeutics

CONTACTS: *Note: Officers with more than one job title may be intentionally listed here more than once.*

Michael D. Dale, CEO
Michael D. Dale, Pres.
Michael Kramer, CFO
Jeremy J. Curtis, VP-Mktg.
David R. Elizondo, VP-R&D
Richard A. Curtis, VP-Bus. Dev.
Marc R. Sportsman, VP-Sales
Michael D. Dale, Chmn.

Phone: 763-553-7736 **Fax:** 763-557-2244
Toll-Free: 800-399-1381
Address: 3905 Annapolis Ln., Ste. 105, Minneapolis, MN 55447 US

GROWTH PLANS/SPECIAL FEATURES:

ATS Medical, Inc. develops, manufactures and markets medical devices primarily for use by cardiovascular or cardiothoracic surgeons during cardiac surgery. These devices include mechanical heart valves, aortic valve graft prostheses and related cardiovascular accessories. The company has FDA approval to sell the ATS Open Pivot bileaflet heart valve for the treatment of heart valve failure caused by the natural aging process, rheumatic heart disease, prosthetic valve failure and congenital defects. The Open Pivot valve has been designed to eliminate the cavity associated with the pivot of other bileaflet valves and to improve the ability of the blood to flow through the valve without forming clots. The company markets the ATS Open Pivot valve in the U.S. through a sales organization divided into four regions and 28 sales territories. It focuses its sales and marketing efforts on developing awareness of the pivot valve in approximately 970 U.S. open heart centers. ATS Medical currently works with cardiac surgeons in approximately 170 of these centers. The firm sells its products through an independent distribution network in all of its international markets except France, where it has a direct sales organization. In 2007, the company acquired the surgical cryoablation business of CryoCath Technologies.

The company offers its employees health coverage, flexible spending accounts, educational assistance and health club reimbursement.

FINANCIALS: **Sales and profits are in thousands of dollars—add 000 to get the full amount. 2007 Note: Financial information for 2007 was not available for all companies at press time.**

2007 Sales: $	2007 Profits: $	**U.S. Stock Ticker: ATSI**
2006 Sales: $40,449	2006 Profits: $-27,674	**Int'l Ticker:** Int'l Exchange:
2005 Sales: $34,636	2005 Profits: $-14,394	Employees: 254
2004 Sales: $28,015	2004 Profits: $-16,643	Fiscal Year Ends: 12/31
2003 Sales: $18,484	2003 Profits: $-13,292	Parent Company:

SALARIES/BENEFITS:

Pension Plan:	ESOP Stock Plan:	Profit Sharing:	Top Exec. Salary: $350,000	Bonus: $178,400
Savings Plan: Y	Stock Purch. Plan: Y		Second Exec. Salary: $248,062	Bonus: $53,058

OTHER THOUGHTS:

Apparent Women Officers or Directors: 1
Hot Spot for Advancement for Women/Minorities:

LOCATIONS: ("Y" = Yes)

West:	Southwest:	Midwest:	Southeast:	Northeast:	International:
Y		Y			Y

AVERA HEALTH

www.avera.org

Industry Group Code: 622110 **Ranks within this company's industry group:** Sales: Profits:

Insurance/HMO/PPO:		Drugs:		Equipment/Supplies:		Hospitals/Clinics:		Services:		Health Care:	
Insurance:	Y	Manufacturer:		Manufacturer:		Acute Care:	Y	Diagnostics:	Y	Home Health:	Y
Managed Care:	Y	Distributor:		Distributor:		Sub-Acute:	Y	Labs/Testing:	Y	Long-Term Care:	Y
Utilization Management:		Specialty Pharmacy:		Leasing/Finance:		Outpatient Surgery:	Y	Staffing:		Physical Therapy:	Y
Payment Processing:		Vitamins/Nutritionals:		Information Systems:		Physical Rehab. Ctr.:	Y	Waste Disposal:		Physician Prac. Mgmt.:	
		Clinical Trials:				Psychiatric Clinics:	Y	Specialty Svcs.:	Y		

TYPES OF BUSINESS:

Hospitals
Nursing Homes
HMO
Health Insurance Consultation

BRANDS/DIVISIONS/AFFILIATES:

Avera McKennan
Avera Sacred Heart
Avera Queen of Peace
Avera St. Luke's
Avera Marshall
Avera Health Plans Benefit Administrators
Avera Health Plans

CONTACTS: *Note: Officers with more than one job title may be intentionally listed here more than once.*

John T. Porter, CEO
John T. Porter, Pres.
Jim Breckenridge, Sr. VP-Finance
Jerry Soholt, Pres., Avera Health Foundation
Dan Cook, Associate Dir.-Avera Health Foundation
Mildred Busch, Chairperson

Phone: 605-322-4700 **Fax:** 605-322-4799
Toll-Free:
Address: 3900 W. Avera Dr., Sioux Falls, SD 57108 US

GROWTH PLANS/SPECIAL FEATURES:

Avera Health was created by, and is currently sponsored through an agreement between the Benedictine Sisters of Yankton, South Dakota and the Presentation Sisters of Aberdeen, South Dakota. The partnership combined independent hospitals, nursing homes, clinics and other health services at over 229 locations in South Dakota, Minnesota, Iowa and Nebraska. The organization is divided into five regions: Avera McKennan, Avera Sacred Heart, Avera Queen of Peace, Avera St. Luke's and Avera Marshall. Avera Health operates through its subsidiaries, one of which includes Avera Health Plans (AHP), a health maintenance organization (HMO). The subsidiary offers an array of employer-sponsored health plans from its central office in Sioux Falls, South Dakota, utilizing more than 60 hospitals and over 3,100 providers in its regional network. A division of AHP, Avera Health Plans Benefit Administrators, has the task of providing benefit consultation to employer groups with over 75 eligible employees. Avera Health recently opened the Avera McKennan Imaging Center that features a women-only breast care center. The Avera Health Foundation distributes donations to people living throughout eastern South Dakota and neighboring states to help them meet their health care needs. Donor's gifts go towards purchasing meals, assisting burn victims, establishing wellness programs, remodeling emergency rooms, testing infants' hearing, developing hospice services, providing lodging for out-of-town patients, purchasing pianos for retirement centers and supplying jackets and shoes for patients.

FINANCIALS: **Sales and profits are in thousands of dollars—add 000 to get the full amount. 2007 Note: Financial information for 2007 was not available for all companies at press time.**

2007 Sales: $	2007 Profits: $	**U.S. Stock Ticker: Nonprofit**
2006 Sales: $	2006 Profits: $	**Int'l Ticker:** Int'l Exchange:
2005 Sales: $	2005 Profits: $	Employees:
2004 Sales: $	2004 Profits: $	Fiscal Year Ends: 6/30
2003 Sales: $	2003 Profits: $	Parent Company:

SALARIES/BENEFITS:

Pension Plan:	ESOP Stock Plan:	Profit Sharing:	Top Exec. Salary: $	Bonus: $
Savings Plan:	Stock Purch. Plan:		Second Exec. Salary: $	Bonus: $

OTHER THOUGHTS:

Apparent Women Officers or Directors: 1
Hot Spot for Advancement for Women/Minorities:

LOCATIONS: ("Y" = Yes)

West:	Southwest:	Midwest:	Southeast:	Northeast:	International:
		Y			

AVIDYN

www.avidyn.com

Industry Group Code: 551110 **Ranks within this company's industry group:** Sales: Profits:

Insurance/HMO/PPO:		Drugs:		Equipment/Supplies:		Hospitals/Clinics:		Services:		Health Care:	
Insurance:		Manufacturer:		Manufacturer:		Acute Care:		Diagnostics:		Home Health:	
Managed Care:		Distributor:		Distributor:		Sub-Acute:		Labs/Testing:		Long-Term Care:	
Utilization Management:	Y	Specialty Pharmacy:		Leasing/Finance:		Outpatient Surgery:		Staffing:		Physical Therapy:	
Payment Processing:	Y	Vitamins/Nutritionals:		Information Systems:		Physical Rehab. Ctr.:		Waste Disposal:		Physician Prac. Mgmt.:	
		Clinical Trials:				Psychiatric Clinics:		Specialty Svcs.:	Y		

TYPES OF BUSINESS:

Business Management Services
Application Service Provider
Claims Management
Software
Utilization Review
Case Management Services

BRANDS/DIVISIONS/AFFILIATES:

Fiserv, Inc.
ppoONE
ValueCHECK, Inc.
Avidyn Health

CONTACTS: *Note: Officers with more than one job title may be intentionally listed here more than once.*

Jeff Mills, CEO
Chris Thomas, COO/Sr. VP
Jeff Mills, Pres.
Patricia Michalik, CFO/Sr. VP
Gary Spurrier, Exec. VP/CIO
John D. Weymer, Pres./CEO-ValueCHECK
Joseph Hensley, Pres./CEO-ppoONE
Fred Volkman, M.D., Sr. VP/Chief Medical Officer

Phone: 214-920-9076	**Fax:** 214-920-9370
Toll-Free:	
Address: 8625 King George Dr., Ste.400, Dallas, TX 75235 US	

GROWTH PLANS/SPECIAL FEATURES:

Avidyn, Inc., a subsidiary of Fiserv, Inc., provides care management services ranging from traditional services, such as utilization management and case management to newer disease management, population health and prevention programs targeted to the self-funded health care market. All of the company's programs focus on improving the health of plan members, lowering plan sponsor costs and creating a positive return on investment. Avidyn delivers products from its headquarters in Dallas, Texas and regional offices in San Antonio, Texas and Wasau, Wisconsin, for niche health care segments through wholly-owned subsidiaries, ppoONE and ValueCHECK. As an application service provider (ASP), ppoONE offers claims repricing and data management services for preferred provider organizations (PPOs), third-party administrators (TPAs), health care plans and insurance carriers nationwide. The company facilitates communication between payer and health care organizations, helps to exchange information and to perform transactions via a scalable Internet, EDI or XML platform. ValueCHECK provides Internet-accessible utilization review and case management services for PPOs, TPAs, health care plans and insurance carriers. Its business objective is to help customers reduce costs while improving review response time and patient satisfaction. Avidyn also offers integrated medical management (IMM) services to the self-funded health care market. IMM gives Avidyn Health the ability to provide centralized reporting and to form a centralized source of clinical information for utilization management, case management, disease management and health and wellness programs. The company's model is based on the fact that less than 20% of the nation's population incurs over 80% of its health costs. By addressing the specific needs of that 20%, Avidyn aims to reduce the costs for companies providing group health care to their employees. Its customers consist of employers, insurance carriers, third-party administrators, unions, state and municipal governments and managed care organizations.

FINANCIALS: **Sales and profits are in thousands of dollars—add 000 to get the full amount. 2007 Note: Financial information for 2007 was not available for all companies at press time.**

2007 Sales: $	2007 Profits: $	**U.S. Stock Ticker: Subsidiary**
2006 Sales: $	2006 Profits: $	**Int'l Ticker:** Int'l Exchange:
2005 Sales: $	2005 Profits: $	Employees: 74
2004 Sales: $	2004 Profits: $	Fiscal Year Ends: 12/31
2003 Sales: $	2003 Profits: $	Parent Company: FISERV INC

SALARIES/BENEFITS:

Pension Plan:	ESOP Stock Plan:	Profit Sharing:	Top Exec. Salary: $201,800	Bonus: $
Savings Plan: Y	Stock Purch. Plan:		Second Exec. Salary: $201,800	Bonus: $

OTHER THOUGHTS:

Apparent Women Officers or Directors: 3
Hot Spot for Advancement for Women/Minorities: Y

LOCATIONS: ("Y" = Yes)

West:	Southwest:	Midwest:	Southeast:	Northeast:	International:
	Y	Y			

Note: Financial information, benefits and other data can change quickly and may vary from those stated here.

AVMED HEALTH PLAN

www.avmed.com

Industry Group Code: 524114 **Ranks within this company's industry group:** Sales: Profits:

Insurance/HMO/PPO:		Drugs:		Equipment/Supplies:		Hospitals/Clinics:		Services:		Health Care:	
Insurance:	Y	Manufacturer:		Manufacturer:		Acute Care:		Diagnostics:		Home Health:	
Managed Care:	Y	Distributor:		Distributor:		Sub-Acute:		Labs/Testing:		Long-Term Care:	
Utilization Management:		Specialty Pharmacy:		Leasing/Finance:		Outpatient Surgery:		Staffing:		Physical Therapy:	
Payment Processing:		Vitamins/Nutritionals:		Information Systems:		Physical Rehab. Ctr.:		Waste Disposal:		Physician Prac. Mgmt.:	
		Clinical Trials:				Psychiatric Clinics:		Specialty Svcs.:	Y		

TYPES OF BUSINESS:

Insurance-Medical & Health, HMOs & PPOs
HMO & POS Plans
Health Education Services
Disease Management

BRANDS/DIVISIONS/AFFILIATES:

Nurse On-Call

CONTACTS: *Note: Officers with more than one job title may be intentionally listed here more than once.*

Douglas G. Cueny, CEO
Douglas G. Cueny, Pres.
Mike Gallagher, CFO/Exec. VP
Mike Gallagher, CEO/Pres., SantaFe Healthcare
Joe G. Dunlop, Chmn.

Phone: 352-372-8400 **Fax:** 352-337-8521
Toll-Free: 800-346-0231
Address: 4300 NW 89th Blvd., Gainesville, FL 32606 US

GROWTH PLANS/SPECIAL FEATURES:

AvMed Health Plan is a statewide not-for-profit and one of Florida's leading HMO providers, serving nearly 300,000 members. The firm's policies include employer group HMO, Medicare HMO, POS and self-funded plans. In addition, the company offers health promotion opportunities, smoking cessation programs and a number of on-site health-related seminars. For members with chronic conditions, AvMed's 11 Care Management Programs, Asthma Program, Diabetes Care, High Risk Obstetrics, Neonatal Management, Congestive Heart Failure, Chronic Obstructive Pulmonary Disease, Oncology Care, Wound Care, Catastrophic Cases, End-Stage Renal Disease and Organ/Bone Marrow Transplant, focus on education and individualized attention. These programs help patients navigate the healthcare systems to actively manage their health. In addition, it provides Nurse On-Call, a free, 24-hour phone service staffed by Florida based registered nurses, who help members make informed healthcare decisions. In addition to standard health care, AvMed offers a range of alternative health and wellness programs in fields such as massage therapy, acupuncture, nutrition, relaxation/meditation training, Yoga, Myotherapy, Tai Chi, Qi Gong, reflexology, Reiki, biofeedback, holistic medicine, Chinese herbal medicine, homeopathy, fitness and spa services.

AvMed offers its employees tuition reimbursement, credit union membership, an employee assistance program, an employer contribution toward Weight Watchers programs and health and dental insurance.

FINANCIALS: **Sales and profits are in thousands of dollars—add 000 to get the full amount. 2007 Note: Financial information for 2007 was not available for all companies at press time.**

2007 Sales: $	2007 Profits: $	**U.S. Stock Ticker: Nonprofit**
2006 Sales: $	2006 Profits: $	**Int'l Ticker:** Int'l Exchange:
2005 Sales: $	2005 Profits: $	Employees:
2004 Sales: $	2004 Profits: $	Fiscal Year Ends: 12/31
2003 Sales: $	2003 Profits: $	Parent Company: SANTAFE HEALTHCARE

SALARIES/BENEFITS:

Pension Plan:	ESOP Stock Plan:	Profit Sharing:	Top Exec. Salary: $	Bonus: $
Savings Plan: Y	Stock Purch. Plan:		Second Exec. Salary: $	Bonus: $

OTHER THOUGHTS:

Apparent Women Officers or Directors:
Hot Spot for Advancement for Women/Minorities:

LOCATIONS: ("Y" = Yes)

West:	Southwest:	Midwest:	Southeast:	Northeast:	International:
			Y		

AXA PPP HEALTHCARE www.axappphealthcare.co.uk

Industry Group Code: 524114 **Ranks within this company's industry group:** Sales: Profits:

Insurance/HMO/PPO:		Drugs:		Equipment/Supplies:		Hospitals/Clinics:		Services:		Health Care:	
Insurance:	Y	Manufacturer:		Manufacturer:		Acute Care:		Diagnostics:		Home Health:	
Managed Care:	Y	Distributor:		Distributor:		Sub-Acute:		Labs/Testing:		Long-Term Care:	
Utilization Management:		Specialty Pharmacy:		Leasing/Finance:		Outpatient Surgery:		Staffing:		Physical Therapy:	
Payment Processing:		Vitamins/Nutritionals:		Information Systems:		Physical Rehab. Ctr.:		Waste Disposal:		Physician Prac. Mgmt.:	
		Clinical Trials:				Psychiatric Clinics:		Specialty Svcs.:			

TYPES OF BUSINESS:

Insurance-Medical & Health, HMOs & PPOs
Health Information Services
Dental & Travel Insurance
Employee Assistance

BRANDS/DIVISIONS/AFFILIATES:

AXA Group
CashBack

CONTACTS:

Note: Officers with more than one job title may be intentionally listed here more than once.

Keith Gibbs, CEO
Mark Moorton, Dir.-Human Resources
Dudley Lusted, Head-Corp. Healthcare Dev.
Candy Ravenscroft, Dir.-Finance
Martin Steed, Head-Provider Mgmt.
Sue Newman, Manager-Corp. Svcs.
Mark Winwood, Clinical Dir.-Employee Support
Eugene Farrell, Bus. Manager-Employee Support

Phone: 44-870-608-0850 **Fax:** 44-189-251-5143
Toll-Free:
Address: Phillips House, Crescent Rd., Tunbridge Wells, Kent TN1 2PL UK

GROWTH PLANS/SPECIAL FEATURES:

AXA PPP Healthcare, a subsidiary of the AXA Group, is one of the U.K.'s largest managed care companies, controlling 25% of the private health insurance market in the U.K. The company's U.K. health care products include employer medical insurance for different sizes of businesses, voluntary employee-paid medical insurance and an employee support program, which offers professional counseling and stress management to employees. Its occupational health insurance services include a fixed-cost package of occupational health and safety services, on-call expert support, executive care health assessment for key employees, safety services that manage the risk of work-related accidents or illnesses, a free health information service, a tailored package of health and fitness services for employees, an independent referral review service for patients with long-term health problems, attendance management and pre-employment medical clearance services. AXA provides dental and travel insurance, as well as its CashBack program, which provides money back on the cost of everyday health care, such as optical and dental bills. In addition, the company provides international health insurance plans to expatriates that live or work outside of their own country for more than six months a year; and in some cases, to individuals living in their home country. The firm provides three international health insurance plans, standard, comprehensive and prestige, for three geographical areas: worldwide coverage, worldwide coverage except the U.S. and Canada, and European coverage. In addition, it provides tailor-made health plans in Malta, Cyprus, United Arab Emirates, Saudi Arabia and Bahrain, as well as health insurance plans for people living in the Channel Islands. In October 2007, the company announced it would no longer cover injuries incurred by clients participating in professional sports.

AXA offers its employees ongoing training opportunities; staff discounts; subsidized gym membership; a sports and social club; and an occupational health nursing service.

FINANCIALS:

Sales and profits are in thousands of dollars—add 000 to get the full amount. 2007 Note: Financial information for 2007 was not available for all companies at press time.

2007 Sales: $ | 2007 Profits: $
2006 Sales: $ | 2006 Profits: $
2005 Sales: $ | 2005 Profits: $
2004 Sales: $ | 2004 Profits: $
2003 Sales: $1,200,100 | 2003 Profits: $

U.S. Stock Ticker: Subsidiary
Int'l Ticker: Int'l Exchange:
Employees:
Fiscal Year Ends: 12/31
Parent Company: AXA GROUP

SALARIES/BENEFITS:

Pension Plan: | ESOP Stock Plan: | Profit Sharing: | Top Exec. Salary: $ | Bonus: $
Savings Plan: Y | Stock Purch. Plan: | | Second Exec. Salary: $ | Bonus: $

OTHER THOUGHTS:

Apparent Women Officers or Directors: 2
Hot Spot for Advancement for Women/Minorities:

LOCATIONS: ("Y" = Yes)

West:	Southwest:	Midwest:	Southeast:	Northeast:	International:
					Y

Note: Financial information, benefits and other data can change quickly and may vary from those stated here.

BANNER HEALTH www.bannerhealth.com

Industry Group Code: 622110 **Ranks within this company's industry group:** Sales: 18 Profits: 13

Insurance/HMO/PPO:		Drugs:		Equipment/Supplies:		Hospitals/Clinics:		Services:		Health Care:	
Insurance:		Manufacturer:		Manufacturer:		Acute Care:	Y	Diagnostics:	Y	Home Health:	Y
Managed Care:		Distributor:		Distributor:		Sub-Acute:	Y	Labs/Testing:	Y	Long-Term Care:	Y
Utilization Management:		Specialty Pharmacy:		Leasing/Finance:		Outpatient Surgery:	Y	Staffing:		Physical Therapy:	Y
Payment Processing:		Vitamins/Nutritionals:		Information Systems:		Physical Rehab. Ctr.:	Y	Waste Disposal:		Physician Prac. Mgmt.:	
		Clinical Trials:				Psychiatric Clinics:	Y	Specialty Svcs.:	Y		

TYPES OF BUSINESS:

Hospitals
Long-Term Care Centers
Home Care Services
Home Medical Equipment Services
Family Clinics
Nursing Registry
Medical Research

BRANDS/DIVISIONS/AFFILIATES:

Banner Gateway Medical

CONTACTS: *Note: Officers with more than one job title may be intentionally listed here more than once.*

Peter S. Fine, CEO
Peter S. Fine, Pres.
Ron Bunnell, CFO/Sr. VP
Gerri Twomey, VP-Human Resources
Mike Warden, CIO
Ron Bunnell, Chief Admin. Officer/Exec. VP
David Bixby, General Counsel
Dennis Dahlen, VP-Finance
Daniel J. Snyder, Pres., Western Region
Susan Edwards, Pres., Arizona Region
Andy Kramer, CEO/Pres., Banner Health Foundation
Mike Powers, CEO-Fairbanks Memorial Hospital & Denali Center
Thomas F. Madison, Chmn.

Phone: 602-495-4000	**Fax:** 602-495-4559
Toll-Free:	
Address: 1441 N. 12th St., Phoenix, AZ 85006 US	

GROWTH PLANS/SPECIAL FEATURES:

Banner Health, based in Phoenix, Arizona, is one of the nation's largest non-profit health care systems, with 20 hospitals encompassing about 3,000 beds and six long-term care centers located in Alaska, Arizona, California, Colorado, Nebraska, Nevada and Wyoming. Banner Health offers an array of services including home care, home medical equipment services, family clinics and a nursing registry. In addition to basic medical and emergency services, the firm's hospitals provide specialized services including heart care, organ transplants, cancer treatment, multiple-birth deliveries, rehabilitation services and behavioral health services. Banner Health's major programs include cancer, critical care, emergency medicine, heart care, medical education, medical imaging, neurosciences, obstetrics, pediatrics, rehabilitation and surgery. Specialized services include Alzheimer's research and treatment, behavioral health, blood conservation medicine, high-risk obstetrics, home care, hospice, level I trauma and organ and bone marrow transplant. Annually, the company offers about $37 million in charity care, facilitates about 30,000 births, performs about 130,000 surgeries and administers to about 77,000 intensive care patients. The company is also involved in research in areas including Alzheimer's disease and spinal cord injuries. Banner supports school-based clinics in 16 school districts serving 96 elementary schools in poorer neighborhoods. In September 2007, Banner Health's new $207 million hospital, Banner Gateway Medical, opened its doors to patients for the first time. With 176 private rooms and seven operating suites, the new hospital, located in Gilbert, Arizona, will focus on obstetrics, pediatrics, general surgery, orthopedics and emergency services.

Banner Health offers its employees flexible spending accounts, an employee assistance program, tuition reimbursement, savings plans, legal plans and medical, pharmacy, dental and vision insurance.

FINANCIALS: **Sales and profits are in thousands of dollars—add 000 to get the full amount. 2007 Note: Financial information for 2007 was not available for all companies at press time.**

2007 Sales: $	2007 Profits: $	**U.S. Stock Ticker: Nonprofit**
2006 Sales: $3,119,375	2006 Profits: $144,028	**Int'l Ticker:** Int'l Exchange:
2005 Sales: $2,870,947	2005 Profits: $36,548	Employees: 25,000
2004 Sales: $2,593,794	2004 Profits: $186,136	Fiscal Year Ends: 12/31
2003 Sales: $2,325,594	2003 Profits: $138,932	Parent Company:

SALARIES/BENEFITS:

Pension Plan:	ESOP Stock Plan:	Profit Sharing:	Top Exec. Salary: $	Bonus: $
Savings Plan: Y	Stock Purch. Plan:		Second Exec. Salary: $	Bonus: $

OTHER THOUGHTS:

Apparent Women Officers or Directors: 2
Hot Spot for Advancement for Women/Minorities:

LOCATIONS: ("Y" = Yes)

West:	Southwest:	Midwest:	Southeast:	Northeast:	International:
Y	Y	Y			

BARR PHARMACEUTICALS INC www.barrlabs.com

Industry Group Code: 325416 **Ranks within this company's industry group:** Sales: 3 Profits: 2

Insurance/HMO/PPO:		Drugs:		Equipment/Supplies:		Hospitals/Clinics:		Services:		Health Care:	
Insurance:		Manufacturer:	Y	Manufacturer:		Acute Care:		Diagnostics:		Home Health:	
Managed Care:		Distributor:		Distributor:		Sub-Acute:		Labs/Testing:		Long-Term Care:	
Utilization Management:		Specialty Pharmacy:		Leasing/Finance:		Outpatient Surgery:		Staffing:		Physical Therapy:	
Payment Processing:		Vitamins/Nutritionals:		Information Systems:		Physical Rehab. Ctr.:		Waste Disposal:		Physician Prac. Mgmt.:	
		Clinical Trials:				Psychiatric Clinics:		Specialty Svcs.:			

TYPES OF BUSINESS:

Drugs-Generic Pharmaceuticals
Contraceptives
Hormone Therapy Drugs
Female Healthcare Pharmaceuticals

BRANDS/DIVISIONS/AFFILIATES:

Barr Laboratories
Duramed Pharmaceuticals, Inc.
Seasonale
Sesonique
Mircette
Cenestin
Enjuvia
Plan B

CONTACTS: *Note: Officers with more than one job title may be intentionally listed here more than once.*

Bruce L. Downey, CEO
Paul M. Bisaro, COO
Paul M. Bisaro, Pres.
William T. McKee, CFO/Treas./Sr. VP
Timothy P. Catlett, Sr. VP-Generic Mktg. & Sales
Catherine F. Higgins, Sr. VP-Human Resources
Salah U. Ahmed, Sr. VP-R&D
Michael J. Bogda, Sr. VP-Eng.
Michael J. Bogda, Sr. VP-Mfg.
Fredrick J. Killion, General Counsel/Sr. VP
Christopher Mengler, Sr. VP-Corp. Dev.
Carol A. Cox, Sr. VP-Corp. Comm.
Carol A. Cox, Sr. VP-Global Investor Rel.
Sigurd C. Kirk, Controller/VP
Christine A. Mundkur, Sr. VP-Quality & Regulatory Counsel
Emad M. Alkhawan, VP-Analytical R&D
Charles E. Diliberti, VP-Scientific Affairs
G. Frederick Wilkinson, COO/Pres., Duramed Pharmaceuticals, Inc.
Bruce L. Downey, Chmn.
Timothy B. Sawyer, Sr. VP/Head-European Comm. Dev.

Phone: 845-362-1100	**Fax:** 845-362-2774
Toll-Free: 800-222-0190	
Address: 223 Quaker Rd., Pomona, NY 10970 US	

GROWTH PLANS/SPECIAL FEATURES:

Barr Pharmaceuticals, Inc. engages in the development, manufacture and marketing of generic and proprietary prescription pharmaceuticals. The company manufactures generic products under the Barr label through its Barr Laboratories subsidiary, and it produces proprietary products under the Duramed label through subsidiary Duramed Pharmaceuticals, Inc. Part of the firm's business strategy is to develop generic versions of other companies' drugs and then challenge the patents that protect them under the claim that such patents are invalid, unenforceable or not infringed by the company's product. The company's generic business segment manufactures and distributes over 100 dosage forms and strengths of over 75 different generic pharmaceutical products, including 22 oral contraceptive products, which represent the largest category of the generic portfolio, and an anticoagulant, Warfarin Sodium, for heart disease patients and those at high risk of stroke. The company currently has 19 proprietary products, which include the Seasonale, Seasonique and Mircette oral contraceptive product lines; the Cenestin and Enjuvia lines of hormone therapy products; and the Plan B emergency contraceptive product, approved by the FDA in August 2006 for non-prescription sale to people 18 years or older. In July 2007, the company received FDA approval to manufacture and market a generic version of Dostinex, currently supplied by Pharmacia and Upjohn Company, which it will supply through an agreement it has with Teva Pharmaceuticals Industries Ltd. The drug treats hyperprolactinemic disorders, a condition caused by an excess of the hormone prolactin in the blood often due to a tumor and sometimes by some other cause. In July 2007, the firm received FDA approval to market a generic form of the antifungal drug, Lamisil, currently supplied by Novartis Pharmaceutical Corp., which will be manufactured by Gedeon Richter Plc. Barr will only market the product in the U.S.

Barr Laboratories provides employees with tuition reimbursement programs.

FINANCIALS: Sales and profits are in thousands of dollars—add 000 to get the full amount. 2007 Note: Financial information for 2007 was not available for all companies at press time.

2007 Sales: $	2007 Profits: $	**U.S. Stock Ticker: BRL**
2006 Sales: $1,314,465	2006 Profits: $336,477	**Int'l Ticker:** Int'l Exchange:
2005 Sales: $1,047,399	2005 Profits: $214,988	Employees: 2,040
2004 Sales: $1,309,088	2004 Profits: $123,103	Fiscal Year Ends: 6/30
2003 Sales: $902,900	2003 Profits: $167,600	Parent Company:

SALARIES/BENEFITS:

Pension Plan:	ESOP Stock Plan:	Profit Sharing:	Top Exec. Salary: $548,077	Bonus: $300,000
Savings Plan: Y	Stock Purch. Plan:		Second Exec. Salary: $422,115	Bonus: $250,000

OTHER THOUGHTS:

Apparent Women Officers or Directors: 3
Hot Spot for Advancement for Women/Minorities: Y

LOCATIONS: ("Y" = Yes)

West:	Southwest:	Midwest:	Southeast:	Northeast:	International:
		Y		Y	

Note: Financial information, benefits and other data can change quickly and may vary from those stated here.

BAUSCH & LOMB INC

www.bausch.com

Industry Group Code: 339113 **Ranks within this company's industry group:** Sales: 15 Profits:

Insurance/HMO/PPO:		Drugs:		Equipment/Supplies:		Hospitals/Clinics:		Services:		Health Care:	
Insurance:		Manufacturer:	Y	Manufacturer:	Y	Acute Care:		Diagnostics:		Home Health:	
Managed Care:		Distributor:	Y	Distributor:		Sub-Acute:		Labs/Testing:		Long-Term Care:	
Utilization Management:		Specialty Pharmacy:		Leasing/Finance:		Outpatient Surgery:		Staffing:		Physical Therapy:	
Payment Processing:		Vitamins/Nutritionals:		Information Systems:		Physical Rehab. Ctr.:		Waste Disposal:		Physician Prac. Mgmt.:	
		Clinical Trials:				Psychiatric Clinics:		Specialty Svcs.:			

TYPES OF BUSINESS:

Supplies-Eye Care
Contact Lens Products
Ophthalmic Pharmaceuticals
Surgical Products

BRANDS/DIVISIONS/AFFILIATES:

Bausch & Lomb
ReNu
Alrex
SofLens
Lotemax
Ocuvite
ReNu with MoistureLoc
ReNu MultiPlus

CONTACTS: *Note: Officers with more than one job title may be intentionally listed here more than once.*

Ronald L. Zarrella, CEO
Efrain Rivera, CFO/Sr. VP
David R. Nachbar, Sr. VP-Human Resources
Praveen Tyle, Chief Scientific Officer/Sr. VP-R&D
Evon L. Jones, CIO/VP
Gerhard Bauer, Sr. VP-Eng.
Robert B. Stiles, General Counsel/Sr. VP
Gehard Bauer, Sr. VP-Global Oper.
Stephen McCluski, Sr. VP-Corp. Strategy
Barbara M. Kelley, Corp. VP-Comm.
Barbara M. Kelley, Corp. VP-Investor Rel.
Efrain Riviera, Treas./VP
Brian Levy, Chief Medical Officer/VP
Jurij Z. Kushner, Controller/VP
Angela J. Panzarella, VP-Global Vision Care
Henry Tung, VP-Global Surgical
Ronald L. Zarrella, Chmn.
Alan H. Farnsworth, Sr. VP/Pres., EMEA

Phone: 585-338-6000	**Fax:** 585-338-6007
Toll-Free: 800-344-8815	
Address: One Bausch & Lomb Pl., Rochester, NY 14604-2701 US	

GROWTH PLANS/SPECIAL FEATURES:

Bausch & Lomb, Inc. (B&L) is a world leader in the development, marketing and manufacturing of eye care products. The firm's products are marketed in over 100 countries and in five categories: contact lenses; lens care products; ophthalmic pharmaceuticals; cataract and vitreoretinal surgery; and refractive surgery. In its contact lens category, which generates the largest percentage of revenues, B&L's product portfolio includes traditional, planned replacement disposable, daily disposable, multifocal, continuous wear, toric soft contact lenses and rigid gas-permeable materials. The firm's lens care products include multi-purpose solutions, enzyme cleaners and saline solutions. These products are marketed to licensed eye care professionals, health product retailers, independent pharmacies, drug stores, food stores and mass merchandisers. The firm's pharmaceuticals include generic and branded prescription ophthalmic pharmaceuticals, ocular vitamins, over-the-counter medications and vision accessories. Key pharmaceutical trademarks of the firm are Bausch & Lomb, Alrex, Liposic, Lotemax, Ocuvite, PreserVision and Zylet. B&L's cataract and vitreoretinal division offers a broad line of intraocular lenses as well as the Millennium line of phacoemulsification equipment used in the extraction of the patient's natural lens during cataract surgery. The company's refractive surgery products include lasers and diagnostic equipment used in the LASIK surgical procedure. B&L's global operations include research and development units across the world, all of which are dedicated to product research across all five segments of the firm. In 2006, the firm announced a number of new technologies in the lens, lens care and surgical products segments of the firm. The firm also announced an equity investment and an exclusive option to acquire AcuFocus, a privately held company. Lastly, the firm issued a worldwide recall of its ReNu with MoistureLoc contact lens solution in 2006, and also recalled over one million bottles of its ReNu MultiPlus contact lens solution in early 2007. In May 2007, the firm agreed to be acquired by private equity group Warburg Pincus for $4.5 billion.

FINANCIALS: **Sales and profits are in thousands of dollars—add 000 to get the full amount. 2007 Note: Financial information for 2007 was not available for all companies at press time.**

2007 Sales: $	2007 Profits: $	**U.S. Stock Ticker: BOL**
2006 Sales: $2,293,400	2006 Profits: $	**Int'l Ticker:** Int'l Exchange:
2005 Sales: $2,353,800	2005 Profits: $19,200	Employees: 13,700
2004 Sales: $2,233,500	2004 Profits: $153,900	Fiscal Year Ends: 12/26
2003 Sales: $2,019,500	2003 Profits: $125,500	Parent Company:

SALARIES/BENEFITS:

Pension Plan: Y	ESOP Stock Plan:	Profit Sharing:	Top Exec. Salary: $1,100,000	Bonus: $
Savings Plan: Y	Stock Purch. Plan:		Second Exec. Salary: $410,001	Bonus: $295,000

OTHER THOUGHTS:

Apparent Women Officers or Directors: 3
Hot Spot for Advancement for Women/Minorities: Y

LOCATIONS: ("Y" = Yes)

West:	Southwest:	Midwest:	Southeast:	Northeast:	International:
Y		Y	Y	Y	Y

BAXTER INTERNATIONAL INC

www.baxter.com

Industry Group Code: 339113 **Ranks within this company's industry group:** Sales: 4 Profits: 3

Insurance/HMO/PPO:		Drugs:		Equipment/Supplies:		Hospitals/Clinics:		Services:		Health Care:	
Insurance:		Manufacturer:	Y	Manufacturer:	Y	Acute Care:		Diagnostics:		Home Health:	
Managed Care:		Distributor:		Distributor:		Sub-Acute:		Labs/Testing:		Long-Term Care:	
Utilization Management:		Specialty Pharmacy:		Leasing/Finance:		Outpatient Surgery:		Staffing:		Physical Therapy:	
Payment Processing:		Vitamins/Nutritionals:		Information Systems:		Physical Rehab. Ctr.:		Waste Disposal:		Physician Prac. Mgmt.:	
		Clinical Trials:				Psychiatric Clinics:		Specialty Svcs.:			

TYPES OF BUSINESS:

Medical Equipment Manufacturing
Supplies-Intravenous & Renal Dialysis Systems
Medication Delivery Products & IV Fluids
Biopharmaceutical Products
Plasma Collection & Processing
Vaccines
Software
Contract Research

BRANDS/DIVISIONS/AFFILIATES:

Colleague CX
BioPharma Solutions
Advate
RenalSoft HD
Global Technical Services
BioLife Plasma Services
Fenwal, Inc.
Guangzhou Baiyunshan Pharmaceutical Co. Ltd.

CONTACTS: *Note: Officers with more than one job title may be intentionally listed here more than once.*

Robert L. Parkinson, CEO
Robert L. Parkinson, Pres.
Robert M. Davis, CFO/VP
Karen J. May, VP-Human Resources
Norbert G. Riedel, Chief Scientific Officer
Karenann Terrell, CIO/VP
J. Michael Gatling, VP-Mfg.
Susan R. Lichtenstein, General Counsel/VP
Joy A. Amundson, Pres., Bioscience
Bruce McGillivray, Pres., Renal
Peter J. Arduini, Pres., Medication Delivery
Carlos Alonso, Pres., Latin American Region
Robert L. Parkinson, Chmn.
John J. Greisch, Pres., Int'l

Phone: 847-948-2000	**Fax:** 847-948-3642
Toll-Free: 800-422-9837	
Address: 1 Baxter Pkwy., Deerfield, IL 60015-4625 US	

GROWTH PLANS/SPECIAL FEATURES:

Baxter International, Inc. is a global medical products, software and services company with expertise in medical devices, pharmaceuticals and biotechnology. Baxter markets its offerings to hospitals; clinical and medical research labs; blood and blood dialysis centers; rehab facilities; nursing homes; doctor's offices; and patients undergoing supervised home care. The firm has manufacturing facilities in 28 countries and offers products and services in 100 countries. Baxter operates in three segments: Medication Delivery, its largest sector, which provides a range of intravenous solutions and specialty products that are used in combination for fluid replenishment, nutrition therapy, pain management, antibiotic therapy and chemotherapy; Bioscience, which develops biopharmaceuticals, biosurgery products, vaccines, blood collection, processing and storage products and technologies; and Renal, which develops products and provides services to treat end-stage kidney disease. Products include the Colleague CX infusion pump; the Enlightened bar-coding system for flexible IV containers; Advate, a coagulant for hemophilia patients; and RenalSoft HD, a software module for the management of prescription, therapy and monitoring information relating to patients suffering from kidney failure. In addition, the company provides the following services: BioLife Plasma Services, a plasma collection and processing business; BioPharma Solutions, biotechnology; Global Technical Services, providing instrument service and support for devices manufactured and marketed by Baxter; Renal Clinical Helpline; Renal Services, an education and research operation; and Training and Education, a portfolio of interactive clinical web sites. In November 2006, Baxter entered a joint venture with Guangzhou Baiyunshan Pharmaceutical Co. Ltd. to produce and sell parenteral nutrition products in China. Also in 2006, Baxter expanded its agreement with Halozyme Therapeutics, Inc. to include the use of the HYLENEX recombinant with Baxter small molecule drugs. In March 2007, the firm sold its Transfusion Therapies business (now called Fenwal, Inc.) to Texas Pacific Group and Maverick Capital, Ltd. for $540 million.

FINANCIALS: **Sales and profits are in thousands of dollars—add 000 to get the full amount. 2007 Note: Financial information for 2007 was not available for all companies at press time.**

2007 Sales: $	2007 Profits: $	**U.S. Stock Ticker: BAX**
2006 Sales: $10,378,000	2006 Profits: $1,397,000	**Int'l Ticker:** Int'l Exchange:
2005 Sales: $9,849,000	2005 Profits: $956,000	Employees: 48,000
2004 Sales: $9,509,000	2004 Profits: $388,000	Fiscal Year Ends: 12/31
2003 Sales: $8,916,000	2003 Profits: $881,000	Parent Company:

SALARIES/BENEFITS:

Pension Plan: Y	ESOP Stock Plan:	Profit Sharing:	Top Exec. Salary: $1,133,651	Bonus: $1,941,420
Savings Plan: Y	Stock Purch. Plan: Y		Second Exec. Salary: $810,600	Bonus: $418,700

OTHER THOUGHTS:

Apparent Women Officers or Directors: 5
Hot Spot for Advancement for Women/Minorities: Y

LOCATIONS: ("Y" = Yes)

West:	Southwest:	Midwest:	Southeast:	Northeast:	International:
Y	Y	Y	Y	Y	Y

BAYER AG

www.bayer.com

Industry Group Code: 325000 **Ranks within this company's industry group:** Sales: 1 Profits: 1

Insurance/HMO/PPO:		Drugs:		Equipment/Supplies:		Hospitals/Clinics:		Services:		Health Care:	
Insurance:		Manufacturer:	Y	Manufacturer:		Acute Care:		Diagnostics:		Home Health:	
Managed Care:		Distributor:		Distributor:		Sub-Acute:		Labs/Testing:		Long-Term Care:	
Utilization Management:		Specialty Pharmacy:		Leasing/Finance:		Outpatient Surgery:		Staffing:		Physical Therapy:	
Payment Processing:		Vitamins/Nutritionals:	Y	Information Systems:		Physical Rehab. Ctr.:		Waste Disposal:		Physician Prac. Mgmt.:	
		Clinical Trials:				Psychiatric Clinics:		Specialty Svcs.:			

TYPES OF BUSINESS:

Chemicals Manufacturing
Pharmaceuticals
Animal Health Products
Synthetic Materials
Crop Science
Plant Biotechnology
Health Care Products

BRANDS/DIVISIONS/AFFILIATES:

Lanxess
Bayer CropScience
Bayer HealthCare
Bayer MaterialScience
Cipro
Levitra
Aleve
Schering AG

CONTACTS:

Note: Officers with more than one job title may be intentionally listed here more than once.

Werner Wenning, Chmn.-Mgmt. Board
Klaus Kuhn, Dir.-Finance
Richard Pott, Dir.-Human Resources & Labor
Wolfgang Plischke, Dir.-Innovation
Wolfgang Plischke, Dir.-Tech.
Richard Pott, Dir.-Strategy
Wolfgang Plischke, Dir.-Environment
Richard Pott, Dir.-North, Central & South America
Manfred Schneider, Chmn.-Supervisory Board
Klaus Kuhn, Dir.-EMEA

Phone: 49-214-30-1 **Fax:** 49-214-30-66328
Toll-Free: 800-269-2377
Address: Bayerwerk Gebaeude W11, Leverkusen, D-51368 Germany

GROWTH PLANS/SPECIAL FEATURES:

The Bayer Group is a German holding company encompassing some 280 consolidated subsidiaries on five continents. The company has three business segments: Bayer HealthCare, Bayer CropScience and Bayer MaterialScience. The health care segment develops, produces and markets products for the prevention, diagnosis and treatment of human and animal diseases. Within the health care segment, the pharmaceutical and biological products division manufactures prescription drugs and treatments including: Cipro, a wide-spectrum antibiotic; Kogenate, a biological treatment for hemophilia; and Levitra, a treatment for impotence. The consumer care and diagnostic division provides professional and home diagnostic testing equipment and over-the-counter medications. Its products include Bayer Aspirin, Aleve, Midol, Alka-Seltzer and One-a-Day Vitamins. The animal health segment manufactures livestock and companion animal medicines, nutritional supplements and pesticides. The Bayer HealthCare segment accounts for approximately 47% of the company's total revenue. Bayer CropScience is active in the areas of chemical crop protection and seed treatment, non-agricultural pest and weed control and plant biotechnology. The segment accounts for approximately 33% of total revenue. Bayer MaterialScience develops, manufactures and markets polyurethane, polycarbonate, cellulose derivatives and special metals products. The segment accounts for approximately 18% of total revenue. The company has an annual research and development budget of approximately $2.1 billion. In 2006, Bayer purchased Schering AG for roughly $22.4 billion. In February 2007, Bayer completed the sale of its chemical unit, H.C. Starck, to a consortium formed by the Carlyle Group and Advent International for $899 million and the assumption of $588.8 million of debt. In March 2007, Bayer announced that it planned to cut 6,100 jobs pursuant to its acquisition of Schering. Over half of the jobs will be cut from its Europe operations.

Bayer offers its employees deferred compensation, a defined benefit pension fund, sports amenities, flexible work schedules and a varied program of cultural events.

FINANCIALS:

Sales and profits are in thousands of dollars—add 000 to get the full amount. 2007 Note: Financial information for 2007 was not available for all companies at press time.

2007 Sales: $
2006 Sales: $38,710,400
2005 Sales: $32,662,374
2004 Sales: $27,731,937
2003 Sales: $35,914,000

2007 Profits: $
2006 Profits: $2,249,950
2005 Profits: $1,902,517
2004 Profits: $816,045
2003 Profits: $-1,585,000

U.S. Stock Ticker: BAY
Int'l Ticker: BAY GR Int'l Exchange: Frankfurt-Euronext
Employees: 93,300
Fiscal Year Ends: 12/31
Parent Company:

SALARIES/BENEFITS:

Pension Plan: Y
Savings Plan: Y
ESOP Stock Plan:
Stock Purch. Plan: Y
Profit Sharing:
Top Exec. Salary: $862,878 Bonus: $1,640,607
Second Exec. Salary: $499,286 Bonus: $935,368

OTHER THOUGHTS:

Apparent Women Officers or Directors: 1
Hot Spot for Advancement for Women/Minorities:

LOCATIONS: ("Y" = Yes)

West:	Southwest:	Midwest:	Southeast:	Northeast:	International:
Y	Y	Y		Y	Y

Note: Financial information, benefits and other data can change quickly and may vary from those stated here.

BAYER CORP

www.bayerus.com

Industry Group Code: 325000 **Ranks within this company's industry group:** Sales: 3 Profits:

Insurance/HMO/PPO:		Drugs:		Equipment/Supplies:		Hospitals/Clinics:		Services:		Health Care:	
Insurance:		Manufacturer:	Y	Manufacturer:		Acute Care:		Diagnostics:	Y	Home Health:	
Managed Care:		Distributor:		Distributor:		Sub-Acute:		Labs/Testing:	Y	Long-Term Care:	
Utilization Management:		Specialty Pharmacy:		Leasing/Finance:		Outpatient Surgery:		Staffing:		Physical Therapy:	
Payment Processing:		Vitamins/Nutritionals:		Information Systems:		Physical Rehab. Ctr.:		Waste Disposal:		Physician Prac. Mgmt.:	
		Clinical Trials:				Psychiatric Clinics:		Specialty Svcs.:			

TYPES OF BUSINESS:

Chemicals Manufacturing
Animal Health Products
Over-the-Counter Drugs
Diagnostic Products
Coatings, Adhesives & Sealants
Polyurethanes & Plastics
Herbicides, Fungicides & Insecticides

BRANDS/DIVISIONS/AFFILIATES:

Bayer AG
Bayer HealthCare AG
Bayer MaterialSciences, LLC
Bayer CropScience, LP
Schering AG
California Planting Cotton Seed Distributors
Reliance Genetics LLC
Ure-Tech Group

CONTACTS: *Note: Officers with more than one job title may be intentionally listed here more than once.*

Attila Molnar, CEO
Attila Molnar, Pres.
Joyce Burgess, Dir.-Human Resources
Claudio Abreu, CIO
George J. Lykos, Chief Legal Officer
Mark Ryan, Chief Comm. Officer
Andreas Beier, Chief Acct. Officer
Willy Scherf, CEO/Pres., Bayer Corp. & Bus. Svcs.
Arthur Higgins, Chmn.-Bayer HealthCare AG
William Buckner, CEO/Pres., Bayer CropScience, LP
Gregory Babe, CEO/Pres., Bayer MaterialScience, LLC
Timothy Roseberry, Chief Procurement Officer/VP-Corp. Materials Mgmt.

Phone: 412-777-2000 **Fax:** 412-777-2034
Toll-Free:
Address: 100 Bayer Rd., Pittsburgh, PA 15205-9741 US

GROWTH PLANS/SPECIAL FEATURES:

Bayer Corporation is the U.S. subsidiary of chemical and pharmaceutical giant Bayer AG. The company operates through four subsidiaries: Bayer HealthCare; Bayer MaterialScience; Bayer Corporate and Business Services; and Bayer CropScience. Bayer HealthCare operates through five divisions: pharmaceuticals, consumer care, diagnostics, diabetes care and animal health. Its animal health products include vaccines and other preventative measures for farm and domestic animals. Its consumer care products include analgesics (Aleve and Bayer); cold and cough treatments (Alka-Seltzer Plus and Talcio); digestive relief products (Alka-Mints and Phillips' Milk of Magnesia); topical skin preparations (Domeboro and Bactine); and vitamins (One-A-Day and Flintstones). The diabetes care division is a leader in self-test blood glucose diagnostic systems, and has recently released the BREEZE product family that offers alternate site testing and automatic coding and requires smaller blood samples. Bayer HealthCare's diagnostics division, now called Siemens Medical Solutions Diagnostics, produces diagnostic systems for critical and intensive care, hematology, urinalysis, immunology, clinical chemistry and molecular testing. The Advia Centaur system is used for the diagnosis of diseases like cancer, cardiovascular diseases, allergies and infections; the Versant and Trugent brands of assays are used for the detection of HIV and hepatitis virus. Bayer's MaterialScience segment produces coatings, adhesives and sealant raw materials; polyurethanes; and plastics. Bayer CropScience makes products directed toward crop protection, environmental science and bioscience, which include herbicides, fungicides and insecticides. Bayer Corporate and Business Services provides business services to the aforementioned Bayer subsidiaries, such as administration, technology services, mergers/acquisitions and internal auditing. In 2006, the firm strengthened its pharmaceuticals segment with the acquisition of Schering AG, previously based in Berlin; the CropScience segment acquired California Planting Cotton Seed Distributors and Reliance Genetics LLC; and the firm announced plans to acquire Taiwan's Ure-Tech Group, the largest thermoplastic polyurethane producer in the Asia Pacific, in 2007.

FINANCIALS: **Sales and profits are in thousands of dollars—add 000 to get the full amount. 2007 Note: Financial information for 2007 was not available for all companies at press time.**

2007 Sales: $	2007 Profits: $	**U.S. Stock Ticker: Subsidiary**
2006 Sales: $10,262,800	2006 Profits: $	**Int'l Ticker:** Int'l Exchange:
2005 Sales: $8,747,200	2005 Profits: $	Employees: 17,200
2004 Sales: $11,504,000	2004 Profits: $	Fiscal Year Ends: 12/31
2003 Sales: $10,999,300	2003 Profits: $	Parent Company: BAYER AG

SALARIES/BENEFITS:

Pension Plan:	ESOP Stock Plan:	Profit Sharing:	Top Exec. Salary: $	Bonus: $
Savings Plan: Y	Stock Purch. Plan: Y		Second Exec. Salary: $	Bonus: $

OTHER THOUGHTS:

Apparent Women Officers or Directors: 1
Hot Spot for Advancement for Women/Minorities:

LOCATIONS: ("Y" = Yes)

West:	Southwest:	Midwest:	Southeast:	Northeast:	International:
Y	Y	Y	Y	Y	

Note: Financial information, benefits and other data can change quickly and may vary from those stated here.

BAYER SCHERING PHARMA AG www.schering.de

Industry Group Code: 325412 **Ranks within this company's industry group:** Sales: Profits:

Insurance/HMO/PPO:		Drugs:		Equipment/Supplies:		Hospitals/Clinics:		Services:		Health Care:	
Insurance:		Manufacturer:	Y	Manufacturer:		Acute Care:		Diagnostics:		Home Health:	
Managed Care:		Distributor:		Distributor:		Sub-Acute:		Labs/Testing:		Long-Term Care:	
Utilization Management:		Specialty Pharmacy:		Leasing/Finance:		Outpatient Surgery:		Staffing:		Physical Therapy:	
Payment Processing:		Vitamins/Nutritionals:		Information Systems:		Physical Rehab. Ctr.:		Waste Disposal:		Physician Prac. Mgmt.:	
		Clinical Trials:				Psychiatric Clinics:		Specialty Svcs.:			

TYPES OF BUSINESS:

Pharmaceuticals Discovery, Development & Manufacturing
Gynecology & Andrology Treatments
Contraceptives
Cancer Treatments
Multiple Sclerosis Treatments
Circulatory Disorder Treatments
Diagnostic & Radiopharmaceutical Agents
Proteomics

BRANDS/DIVISIONS/AFFILIATES:

Yasmin
Angeliq
Testogel
Androcur
Betaseron
Fludara
Illomedin
Bayer AG

CONTACTS: *Note: Officers with more than one job title may be intentionally listed here more than once.*

Arthur J. Higgins, Chmn.-Exec. Board
Werner Baumann, Member-Exec. Board, Human Resources
Werner Baumann, Member-Exec. Board, Production
Werner Baumann, Member-Exec. Board, Admin. & Organization
Andreas Busch, Member-Exec. Board
Ulrich Kostlin, Member-Exec. Board
Kemal Malik, Member-Exec. Board
Gunnar Riemann, Member-Exec. Board
Werner Wenning, Chmn.-Supervisory Board

Phone: 49-30-468-1111	**Fax:** 49-30-468-15305
Toll-Free:	
Address: Mullerstrasse 178, Berlin, 13353 Germany	

GROWTH PLANS/SPECIAL FEATURES:

Bayer Schering Pharma AG, formerly Schering AG and a subsidiary of Bayer, is a major global research-based pharmaceutical company that operates through more than 140 subsidiaries. The firm concentrates its activities on four business areas: gynecology and andrology, oncology, specialized therapeutics, and diagnostics and radiopharmaceuticals. Schering's gynecology and andrology products include birth control pills (Yasmin), hormone therapy (Angeliq and Menostar) and other contraceptives for women (Mirena); products for the treatment of testosterone deficiency in men (Testoviron, Testogel and Nebido); and prostate cancer (Androcur). The firm's oncology unit has introduced the drug Fludara, to provide treatment for chronic lymphocytic leukemia, a variety of leukemia. Another product, Leukine, is a drug administered to treat the immune system weakened by chemotherapy. Zevalin is a readioimmunotherapy for follicular B-cell non-Hodgkin's lymphoma in E.U. countries, and MabCampath/Campath is a chemotherapy drug often used on those patients who do not respond to traditional chemotherapy. Schering's specialized therapeutic products focus on treating multiple sclerosis (MS). The firm has contributed to the body of research on MS through its Beyond and Benefit studies. Its Betaferon drug reduces the frequency of MS episodes significantly. In addition, the division produces Ilomedin to improve blood flow for those suffering with peripheral arterial occlusive disease; and Ventavis, to increase physical capability of patients suffering from primary pulmonary hypertension. Schering's diagnostics imaging products include a range of contrast media, such as Magnevist, a general MRI contrast agent; Resovist, a liver-specific MRI contrast agent; and Gadovist, a central nervous system MRI contrast agent. The company recently transferred its dermatology business to an independent company, Intendis GmbH. In June 2006, Bayer AG acquired sufficient stock in Schering to give Bayer effective control of the firm. In March 2007, Bayer announced that it would cut 6,100 jobs as a result of its purchase of Schering.

FINANCIALS: Sales and profits are in thousands of dollars—add 000 to get the full amount. 2007 Note: Financial information for 2007 was not available for all companies at press time.

2007 Sales: $	2007 Profits: $	**U.S. Stock Ticker: Subsidiary**
2006 Sales: $	2006 Profits: $	**Int'l Ticker: SCH** Int'l Exchange: Berlin-BBB
2005 Sales: $6,393,216	2005 Profits: $745,554	Employees: 24,658
2004 Sales: $6,647,000	2004 Profits: $677,000	Fiscal Year Ends: 12/31
2003 Sales: $6,070,000	2003 Profits: $557,000	Parent Company: BAYER AG

SALARIES/BENEFITS:

Pension Plan:	ESOP Stock Plan:	Profit Sharing:	Top Exec. Salary: $	Bonus: $
Savings Plan:	Stock Purch. Plan:		Second Exec. Salary: $	Bonus: $

OTHER THOUGHTS:

Apparent Women Officers or Directors:
Hot Spot for Advancement for Women/Minorities:

LOCATIONS: ("Y" = Yes)

West:	Southwest:	Midwest:	Southeast:	Northeast:	International:
Y				Y	Y

Note: Financial information, benefits and other data can change quickly and may vary from those stated here.

BECKMAN COULTER INC www.beckmancoulter.com

Industry Group Code: 339113 **Ranks within this company's industry group:** Sales: 14 Profits: 19

Insurance/HMO/PPO:		Drugs:		Equipment/Supplies:		Hospitals/Clinics:		Services:		Health Care:	
Insurance:		Manufacturer:		Manufacturer:	Y	Acute Care:		Diagnostics:		Home Health:	
Managed Care:		Distributor:		Distributor:		Sub-Acute:		Labs/Testing:		Long-Term Care:	
Utilization Management:		Specialty Pharmacy:		Leasing/Finance:		Outpatient Surgery:		Staffing:		Physical Therapy:	
Payment Processing:		Vitamins/Nutritionals:		Information Systems:		Physical Rehab. Ctr.:		Waste Disposal:		Physician Prac. Mgmt.:	
		Clinical Trials:				Psychiatric Clinics:		Specialty Svcs.:			

TYPES OF BUSINESS:

Equipment-Laboratory Instruments
Laboratory Test Kits
Tests & Reagents
Biomedical Research Supplies

BRANDS/DIVISIONS/AFFILIATES:

Lumigen, Inc.
Biosite, Inc.
Industrial Robotics Solutions
Motoman HP3JC Robots
Yaskawa Electric Company
Advanced SAMI Workstation EX Software

CONTACTS: *Note: Officers with more than one job title may be intentionally listed here more than once.*

Scott Garrett, CEO
Scott Garrett, Pres.
Charles (Charlie) Slacik, CFO
Bob Hurley, Sr. VP-Human Resources
Russ Bell, Chief Scientific Officer/Sr. VP
Charlie Slacik, Sr. VP-IT
Arnold (Arnie) Pinkston, General Counsel/Sr. VP/Corp. Sec.
Paul Glyer, Sr. VP-Bus. Dev. & Strategy
Bob Hurley, Sr. VP-Comm.
Paul Glyer, Sr. VP-Investor Rel.
Carolyn D. Beaver, Chief Acct. Officer/Controller/VP
Bob Boghosian, Sr. VP-Quality & Regulatory Affairs
Robert (Bob) Kleinert, Exec. VP-Worldwide Commercial Oper.
Mike Whelan, Group VP-High Sensitivity Testing Group
Betty Woods, Chmn.
Pam Miller, Sr. VP-Supply Chain Mgmt.

Phone: 714-871-4848 **Fax:** 714-773-8283
Toll-Free: 800-233-4685
Address: 4300 N. Harbor Blvd., Fullerton, CA 92834-3100 US

GROWTH PLANS/SPECIAL FEATURES:

Beckman Coulter, Inc. designs, manufactures and markets systems that consist of instruments, chemistries, software and supplies that simplify and automate a variety of laboratory processes. Its main product areas are chemistry, immunoassay, cellular and discovery and automation systems. Chemistry systems cover everything from simple blood-sugar testing to electrophoresis systems that utilize electric charges to separate samples into constituent elements. Immunoassay systems include tests for cancer or cardiac risk, as well as providing vital information for reproductive testing. Cellular systems primarily analyze blood cell information, such as performing a white blood cell count, as well as analyzing tumors and other cells. Discovery and automation systems include bar code sorting technology and DNA sequencers. The organization has approximately 200,000 installed systems operating in laboratories around the world, with 75% of its annual revenues coming from sales of test kits, supplies, services and operating-type lease payments. Beckman markets its products in approximately 130 countries, with approximately half of its revenues coming from outside the U.S. The firm's customers include hospital clinical laboratories, physicians' offices, group practices, commercial reference laboratories, universities, medical research laboratories, pharmaceutical companies and biotechnology firms. In November 2006, the company acquired Lumigen, Inc., augmenting the company's immunoassay system capabilities, for $187 million. In August 2007, the company began offering Industrial Robotics Solutions, featuring customizable capabilities for each clients needs. The systems are powered by Motoman HP3JC Robots produced by Yaskawa Electric Company, and controlled by the company's own Advanced SAMI Workstation EX Software.

The company offers tuition assistance, paid vacations, holidays and some medical benefits.

FINANCIALS: **Sales and profits are in thousands of dollars—add 000 to get the full amount. 2007 Note: Financial information for 2007 was not available for all companies at press time.**

2007 Sales: $ | 2007 Profits: $ | **U.S. Stock Ticker: BEC**
2006 Sales: $2,528,500 | 2006 Profits: $186,900 | **Int'l Ticker:** Int'l Exchange:
2005 Sales: $2,443,800 | 2005 Profits: $150,600 | Employees: 10,340
2004 Sales: $2,408,300 | 2004 Profits: $210,900 | Fiscal Year Ends: 12/31
2003 Sales: $2,192,500 | 2003 Profits: $207,200 | Parent Company:

SALARIES/BENEFITS:

Pension Plan: Y | ESOP Stock Plan: | Profit Sharing: | Top Exec. Salary: $730,366 | Bonus: $655,000
Savings Plan: Y | Stock Purch. Plan: | | Second Exec. Salary: $380,000 | Bonus: $177,600

OTHER THOUGHTS:

Apparent Women Officers or Directors: 3
Hot Spot for Advancement for Women/Minorities: Y

LOCATIONS: ("Y" = Yes)

West:	Southwest:	Midwest:	Southeast:	Northeast:	International:
Y	Y	Y	Y	Y	Y

Note: Financial information, benefits and other data can change quickly and may vary from those stated here.

BECTON DICKINSON & CO

www.bd.com

Industry Group Code: 339113 **Ranks within this company's industry group:** Sales: 7 Profits: 7

Insurance/HMO/PPO:		Drugs:		Equipment/Supplies:		Hospitals/Clinics:		Services:		Health Care:	
Insurance:		Manufacturer:		Manufacturer:	Y	Acute Care:		Diagnostics:		Home Health:	
Managed Care:		Distributor:		Distributor:		Sub-Acute:		Labs/Testing:		Long-Term Care:	
Utilization Management:		Specialty Pharmacy:		Leasing/Finance:		Outpatient Surgery:		Staffing:		Physical Therapy:	
Payment Processing:		Vitamins/Nutritionals:		Information Systems:		Physical Rehab. Ctr.:		Waste Disposal:		Physician Prac. Mgmt.:	
		Clinical Trials:				Psychiatric Clinics:		Specialty Svcs.:			

TYPES OF BUSINESS:

Medical Equipment-Injection/Infusion
Drug Delivery Systems
Infusion Therapy Products
Diabetes Care Products
Surgical Products
Microbiology Products
Diagnostic Products
Consulting Services

BRANDS/DIVISIONS/AFFILIATES:

Becton Dickinson Medical
Becton Dickinson Biosciences
Becton Dickinson Diagnostics
Vacutainer
Hypak
GeneOhm Sciences
TriPath Imaging

CONTACTS: *Note: Officers with more than one job title may be intentionally listed here more than once.*

Edward J. Ludwig, CEO
Edward J. Ludwig, Pres.
John R. Considine, CFO/Sr. VP
Donna M. Boles, Sr. VP-Human Resources
Jeffrey S. Sherman, General Counsel/Sr. VP
Vincent A. Forlenza, Exec. VP
Gary M. Cohen, Exec. VP
William A. Kozy, Exec. VP
A. John Hanson, Exec. VP
Edward J. Ludwig, Chmn.

Phone: 201-847-6800	**Fax:** 201-847-6475
Toll-Free: 800-284-6845	
Address: 1 Becton Dr., Franklin Lakes, NJ 07417-1880 US	

GROWTH PLANS/SPECIAL FEATURES:

Becton, Dickinson & Company (BD) manufactures and sell a broad line of medical supplies, devices and diagnosti systems used by health care professionals, medical researc institutions and the general public. The company operates i three segments, medical, biosciences and diagnostics. Th medical segment offers hypodermic products, speciall designed devices for diabetes care; prefillable drug deliver systems; and infusion therapy products. It also offer anesthesia and surgical products; ophthalmic surger devices; critical care systems; elastic support products; an thermometers. The biosciences segment offers industria microbiology products; cellular analysis systems; research and clinical reagents for cellular and nucleic acid analysis cell culture lab ware and growth media; hematolog instruments; and other diagnostic systems, includin immunodiagnostic test kits. The diagnostics segment offer specimen collection products and services, consultin services and customized, automated barcode systems fo patient identification and point-of-care data capture. Two c BD's most popular products are Hypak prefillable syringe and Vacutainer blood-collection products. Outside of th U.S., BD's products are manufactured and sold in Europe Japan, Mexico, Asia Pacific, Canada and Brazil. In Februar 2006, the company acquired GeneOhm Sciences, developer of molecular diagnostic testing for the rapi detection of bacterial organisms. In December 2006, BD acquired TriPath Imaging, a developer of solutions t improve the clinical management of cancer. BD als furthered its global position: in Canada through a majo expansion of its BD Diagnostics manufacturing operation i Québec; and through establishing BD Rapid Diagnostic (Suzhou) Co., Ltd., in China, which will produce diagnosti products for flu and viral infections.

The firm offers its employees fitness centers, an employe assistance program and adoption assistance, as well a stock options and scholarship programs. Larger facilitie have heath centers offering preventive health screenings an routine examinations.

FINANCIALS: **Sales and profits are in thousands of dollars—add 000 to get the full amount. 2007 Note: Financial information for 2007 was not available for all companies at press time.**

2007 Sales: $	2007 Profits: $	**U.S. Stock Ticker: BDX**
2006 Sales: $5,834,800	2006 Profits: $752,300	**Int'l Ticker:** Int'l Exchange:
2005 Sales: $5,414,700	2005 Profits: $722,300	Employees: 27,000
2004 Sales: $4,934,745	2004 Profits: $467,402	Fiscal Year Ends: 9/30
2003 Sales: $4,527,940	2003 Profits: $547,056	Parent Company:

SALARIES/BENEFITS:

Pension Plan: Y	ESOP Stock Plan:	Profit Sharing:	Top Exec. Salary: $1,020,915	Bonus: $1,150,000
Savings Plan: Y	Stock Purch. Plan:		Second Exec. Salary: $620,693	Bonus: $500,000

OTHER THOUGHTS:

Apparent Women Officers or Directors: 1
Hot Spot for Advancement for Women/Minorities:

LOCATIONS: ("Y" = Yes)

West:	Southwest:	Midwest:	Southeast:	Northeast:	International:
Y	Y	Y	Y	Y	Y

BESPAK PLC

www.bespak.com

Industry Group Code: 339113 **Ranks within this company's industry group:** Sales: 66 Profits: 52

Insurance/HMO/PPO:		**Drugs:**		**Equipment/Supplies:**		**Hospitals/Clinics:**		**Services:**		**Health Care:**	
Insurance:		Manufacturer:		Manufacturer:	Y	Acute Care:		Diagnostics:		Home Health:	
Managed Care:		Distributor:		Distributor:		Sub-Acute:		Labs/Testing:		Long-Term Care:	
Utilization Management:		Specialty Pharmacy:		Leasing/Finance:		Outpatient Surgery:		Staffing:		Physical Therapy:	
Payment Processing:		Vitamins/Nutritionals:		Information Systems:		Physical Rehab. Ctr.:		Waste Disposal:		Physician Prac. Mgmt.:	
		Clinical Trials:				Psychiatric Clinics:		Specialty Svcs.:	Y		

TYPES OF BUSINESS:

Drug Delivery Technologies
Drug Delivery Devices
Development & Manufacturing Services

BRANDS/DIVISIONS/AFFILIATES:

Exubera
Bang & Olufsen Medicom
Emergent Respiratory Products, Inc.

CONTACTS: *Note: Officers with more than one job title may be intentionally listed here more than once.*

Mark C. Throdahl, CEO
Martin P. Hopcroft, Group Finance Dir.
Theresa Hobson-Frohock, Dir.-Human Resources
Paul Boughton, Dir.-Corp. Dev.
John Robinson, Chmn.

Phone: 44-1908-552-600 **Fax:** 44-1908-552-613
Toll-Free:
Address: Blackhill Dr., Featherstone Rd., Wolverton Mill South, Milton Keynes MK12 5TS UK

GROWTH PLANS/SPECIAL FEATURES:

Bespak plc is a leading developer, manufacturer and supplier of drug delivery technologies, medical devices and associated services to pharmaceutical, drug delivery and biotechnology companies. The firm's proprietary drug delivery devices and technologies include pressurized metered-dose inhalers and actuators, dose counters, breath-coordinated and breath-activated devices, dry powder inhalers and electrostatic atomization, as well as a range of unit and multi-dose, liquid and dry powder nasal devices. The company's devices enable patients to take their medications without using needle injections or having to swallow a pill. In addition, Bespak provides complete medical device development services to other companies, from prototyping and testing to clinical trials and regulatory compliance to industrialization and full-scale manufacture. The firm also offers access to its range of proprietary drug delivery devices. In April 2007, the company acquired a 51% interest in Emergent Respiratory Products, Inc.

Bespak's employees receive individualized training programs.

FINANCIALS: **Sales and profits are in thousands of dollars—add 000 to get the full amount. 2007 Note: Financial information for 2007 was not available for all companies at press time.**

2007 Sales: $255,020 | 2007 Profits: $19,770
2006 Sales: $186,790 | 2006 Profits: $20,810
2005 Sales: $94,628 | 2005 Profits: $-2,844
2004 Sales: $147,500 | 2004 Profits: $11,700
2003 Sales: $140,800 | 2003 Profits: $4,400

U.S. Stock Ticker: BPAKY.PK
Int'l Ticker: BPK Int'l Exchange: London-LSE
Employees: 667
Fiscal Year Ends: 4/30
Parent Company:

SALARIES/BENEFITS:

Pension Plan: ESOP Stock Plan: Profit Sharing: Top Exec. Salary: $ Bonus: $
Savings Plan: Stock Purch. Plan: Second Exec. Salary: $ Bonus: $

OTHER THOUGHTS:

Apparent Women Officers or Directors:
Hot Spot for Advancement for Women/Minorities:

LOCATIONS: ("Y" = Yes)

West:	Southwest:	Midwest:	Southeast:	Northeast:	International:
				Y	Y

BIO RAD LABORATORIES INC www.bio-rad.com

Industry Group Code: 339113 **Ranks within this company's industry group:** Sales: 25 Profits: 22

Insurance/HMO/PPO:		Drugs:		Equipment/Supplies:		Hospitals/Clinics:		Services:		Health Care:	
Insurance:		Manufacturer:		Manufacturer:	Y	Acute Care:		Diagnostics:	Y	Home Health:	
Managed Care:		Distributor:		Distributor:		Sub-Acute:		Labs/Testing:	Y	Long-Term Care:	
Utilization Management:		Specialty Pharmacy:		Leasing/Finance:		Outpatient Surgery:		Staffing:		Physical Therapy:	
Payment Processing:		Vitamins/Nutritionals:		Information Systems:	Y	Physical Rehab. Ctr.:		Waste Disposal:		Physician Prac. Mgmt.:	
		Clinical Trials:				Psychiatric Clinics:		Specialty Svcs.:			

TYPES OF BUSINESS:

Equipment-Life Sciences Research
Clinical Diagnostics Products
Analytical Instruments
Laboratory Devices
Biomaterials
Imaging Products
Assays
Software

BRANDS/DIVISIONS/AFFILIATES:

KnowItAll
HaveItAll
PhD Workstation
VersArray
SmartSpec Plus
Variant II Turbo Hemoglobin Testing System
MiniOpticon
Blackhawk BioSystems

CONTACTS: *Note: Officers with more than one job title may be intentionally listed here more than once.*

Norman Schwartz, CEO
Norman Schwartz, Pres.
Christine Tsingos, CFO/VP
Sanford S. Wadler, General Counsel/VP
Tina Cuccia, Mgr.-Corp. Comm.
John Goetz, VP
David Schwartz, Chmn.

Phone: 510-724-7000 **Fax:** 510-741-5817
Toll-Free: 800-424-6723
Address: 1000 Alfred Nobel Dr., Hercules, CA 94547 US

GROWTH PLANS/SPECIAL FEATURES:

Bio-Rad Laboratories supplies the life science research, health care and analytical chemistry markets with a broad range of products and systems used to separate complex chemical and biological materials and to identify, analyze and purify components. The company operates through two industry segments: Life Sciences and Clinical Diagnostics. The firm's Life Sciences division develops laboratory devices, biomaterials, imaging products and microscopy systems. The division uses electrophoresis, image analysis, microplate readers, chromatography, gene transfer and sample preparation and amplification as its primary technological applications. Bio-Rad Life Sciences provides its services to universities and medical schools, industrial research organizations, government agencies and biotechnology researchers. The company's Clinical Diagnostics division encompasses a broad array of technologies incorporated into a variety of tests used to detect, identify and quantify substances in blood or other body fluids and tissues. The test results are used as aids for medical diagnosis, detection, evaluation, monitoring and treatment of diseases and other medical conditions. In addition, Bio-Rad is a leading provider of bovine spongiform encephalopathy (mad cow disease) tests throughout the world. Some of Bio-Rad's numerous brand name systems include: KnowItAll and HaveItAll, which are informatics systems integrating software and database management for a variety of biological information; the PhD System, for autoimmune detection; the VersArray hybridization chamber; the SmartSpec Plus spectrophotometer; the MiniOpticon PCR (polymerase chain reaction) detection system; and the Variant II Turbo hemoglobin testing system. In October 2006, Bio-Rad acquired Blackhawk BioSystems, a producer of quality control products for laboratories that work with infectious diseases. In November 2006, the company purchased a life sciences research business from Ciphergen Biosystems, Inc. for $20 million. In May 2007, Bio-Rad announced that it agreed to acquire DiaMed Holding AG, which develops, manufactures and markets products used in blood typing and screening, for approximately $397.5 million.

FINANCIALS: **Sales and profits are in thousands of dollars—add 000 to get the full amount. 2007 Note: Financial information for 2007 was not available for all companies at press time.**

2007 Sales: $	2007 Profits: $	**U.S. Stock Ticker: BIO**
2006 Sales: $1,273,930	2006 Profits: $103,263	**Int'l Ticker:** Int'l Exchange:
2005 Sales: $1,180,985	2005 Profits: $81,553	Employees: 5,400
2004 Sales: $1,090,012	2004 Profits: $68,242	Fiscal Year Ends: 12/31
2003 Sales: $1,003,382	2003 Profits: $76,171	Parent Company:

SALARIES/BENEFITS:

Pension Plan:	ESOP Stock Plan:	Profit Sharing:	Top Exec. Salary: $526,065	Bonus: $266,938
Savings Plan:	Stock Purch. Plan:		Second Exec. Salary: $515,760	Bonus: $261,709

OTHER THOUGHTS:

Apparent Women Officers or Directors: 2
Hot Spot for Advancement for Women/Minorities: Y

LOCATIONS: ("Y" = Yes)

West:	Southwest:	Midwest:	Southeast:	Northeast:	International:
Y	Y			Y	Y

BIO REFERENCE LABORATORIES INC www.bio-referencelabs.com

Industry Group Code: 621511 **Ranks within this company's industry group:** Sales: 6 Profits: 5

Insurance/HMO/PPO:		Drugs:		Equipment/Supplies:		Hospitals/Clinics:		Services:		Health Care:	
Insurance:		Manufacturer:		Manufacturer:		Acute Care:		Diagnostics:		Home Health:	
Managed Care:		Distributor:		Distributor:		Sub-Acute:		Labs/Testing:	Y	Long-Term Care:	
Utilization Management:		Specialty Pharmacy:		Leasing/Finance:		Outpatient Surgery:		Staffing:		Physical Therapy:	
Payment Processing:		Vitamins/Nutritionals:		Information Systems:	Y	Physical Rehab. Ctr.:		Waste Disposal:		Physician Prac. Mgmt.:	
		Clinical Trials:				Psychiatric Clinics:		Specialty Svcs.:	Y		

TYPES OF BUSINESS:

Medical Laboratories & Testing
Clinical Laboratory Services
Clinical Knowledge Database
Online Practice Management Services
Drug Testing

BRANDS/DIVISIONS/AFFILIATES:

PSIMedica
CareEvolve
GenFlow
Cancer Genetics, Inc.
GeneDx

CONTACTS: *Note: Officers with more than one job title may be intentionally listed here more than once.*

Marc D. Grodman, CEO
Howard Dubinett, COO/Exec. VP
Marc D. Grodman, Pres.
Sam Singer, CFO/Sr. VP
Charles T. Todd, Sr. VP-Sales & Mktg.
James Weisberger, Chief Medical Officer/VP/Laboratory Dir.
Richard L. Faherty, CIO
Cory Fishkin, Pres., CareEvolve
Kara Sheffel, Coordinator-Investor Rel.
Nicholas Papazicos, VP-Financial Oper.
Azmy Awad, Sr. VP
John W. Littleton, VP/Dir.-Sale
Nick Cetani, VP/Lab Mgr.
Sally Howlett, VP-Billing
Marc D. Grodman, Chmn.

Phone: 201-791-2600	**Fax:**
Toll-Free:	
Address: 481 Edward H. Ross Dr., Elmwood Park, NJ 07407-3118 US	

GROWTH PLANS/SPECIAL FEATURES:

Bio-Reference Laboratories, Inc. (BRLI) is a regional clinical laboratory offering services to clients in the greater New York metropolitan area and New Jersey. Serving health care providers in these areas, the firm offers testing services utilized in detection, diagnosis, evaluation, monitoring and treatment of diseases. The company processes nearly 3.1 million requisitions annually for customers including doctors, employers, clinics and governmental units. BRLI operates a network of over 50 patient service centers for the collection of patient specimens. Routine tests, which account for approximately 62% of the company's clinical business, include blood cell counts, cholesterol level testing, HIV-related tests, pap smears, pregnancy tests, urinalysis and drug testing. The company also performs specialized esoteric tests, which account for approximately 38% of its net revenues, in medical fields such as endocrinology, genetics, immunology, microbiology, oncology, serology and toxicology. BRLI's PSIMedica division is based on a Clinical Knowledge Management (ACKM) System that analyzes enrollment, claims, pharmacy, laboratory results and other data, providing administrative and clinical analysis of a population. In addition, the company hosts CareEvolve (careevolve.com), a physician-based Internet health portal that seeks to provide physicians with secure messaging to patients, payers, vendors and other health care facilities. These communications include secure laboratory, pathology and radiology ordering and result delivery. In early 2006, the firm introduced a new lab procedure that can identify and detect the early onset of prostate cancer in some high-risk patients. Recently, BRLI acquired the gene-based testing facilities of GeneDx, located in Gaithersburg, MD.

FINANCIALS: Sales and profits are in thousands of dollars—add 000 to get the full amount. 2007 Note: Financial information for 2007 was not available for all companies at press time.

2007 Sales: $	2007 Profits: $	**U.S. Stock Ticker: BRLI**
2006 Sales: $193,134	2006 Profits: $11,291	**Int'l Ticker:** Int'l Exchange:
2005 Sales: $163,896	2005 Profits: $7,621	Employees: 1,551
2004 Sales: $136,184	2004 Profits: $8,516	Fiscal Year Ends: 10/31
2003 Sales: $109,033	2003 Profits: $6,539	Parent Company:

SALARIES/BENEFITS:

Pension Plan:	ESOP Stock Plan:	Profit Sharing:	Top Exec. Salary: $806,000	Bonus: $
Savings Plan:	Stock Purch. Plan:		Second Exec. Salary: $306,000	Bonus: $

OTHER THOUGHTS:

Apparent Women Officers or Directors: 2
Hot Spot for Advancement for Women/Minorities:

LOCATIONS: ("Y" = Yes)

West:	Southwest:	Midwest:	Southeast:	Northeast:	International:
				Y	

BIOGEN IDEC INC www.biogenidec.com

Industry Group Code: 325412 **Ranks within this company's industry group:** Sales: 23 Profits: 22

Insurance/HMO/PPO:		Drugs:		Equipment/Supplies:		Hospitals/Clinics:		Services:		Health Care:	
Insurance:		Manufacturer:	Y	Manufacturer:		Acute Care:		Diagnostics:		Home Health:	
Managed Care:		Distributor:		Distributor:		Sub-Acute:		Labs/Testing:		Long-Term Care:	
Utilization Management:		Specialty Pharmacy:		Leasing/Finance:		Outpatient Surgery:		Staffing:		Physical Therapy:	
Payment Processing:		Vitamins/Nutritionals:		Information Systems:		Physical Rehab. Ctr.:		Waste Disposal:		Physician Prac. Mgmt.:	
		Clinical Trials:				Psychiatric Clinics:		Specialty Svcs.:			

TYPES OF BUSINESS:

Drugs-Immunology, Neurology & Oncology
Autoimmune & Inflammatory Disease Treatments
Drugs-Multiple Sclerosis
Drugs-Cancer
Genetic Engineering
Vaccines
Cell Cultures
Bulk Manufacturing

BRANDS/DIVISIONS/AFFILIATES:

AVONEX
AMEVIVE
TYSABRI
ANTEGREN
RITUXAN
Fumapharm AG
Fumarderm

CONTACTS: *Note: Officers with more than one job title may be intentionally listed here more than once.*

James C. Mullen, CEO
William R. Rohn, COO
James C. Mullen, Pres.
Craig E. Schneier, Exec. VP-Human Resources & Public Affairs
Cecil B. Pickett, Pres., R&D
Michael D. Kowolenko, Sr. VP-Pharmaceutical Oper. & Tech.
Susan H. Alexander, General Counsel/Exec. VP/Corp. Sec.
Mark Wiggins, Exec. VP-Corp. & Bus. Dev.
Craig E. Schneier, Exec. VP-Corp. Comm.
Michael F. MacLean, Chief Acct. Officer/Sr. VP/Controller
John M. Dunn, Exec. VP-New Ventures
Burt A. Adelman, Exec. VP-Portfolio Strategy
Robert A. Hamm, Sr. VP-Neurology Strategic Bus.
Faheem Hasnain, Sr. VP-Oncology Rheumatology Strategic Bus.
Bruce R. Ross, Chmn.
Hans Peter Hasler, Sr. VP-Int'l Strategic Business

Phone: 617-679-2000	**Fax:** 617-679-2617
Toll-Free:	
Address: 14 Cambridge Ctr., Cambridge, MA 02142-1481 US	

GROWTH PLANS/SPECIAL FEATURES:

Biogen IDEC, Inc. (Biogen), a leading biotech firm forme through the merger of IDEC Pharmaceuticals and Bioger develops, manufactures and markets therapeuti pharmaceuticals for immunology, neurology and oncolog Biogen currently has five products: AVONEX is used t decrease the frequency of neurological attacks in patient with relapsing forms of multiple sclerosis (MS) and is used b 135,000 patients globally; TYSABRI is approved for th treatment of relapsing forms of MS; RITUXAN is globall approved for the treatment of relapsed or refractory low grade or follicular, CD20-positive, B-cell non-Hodgkin' lymphomas (NHLs), or B-cell NHLs; ZEVALIN is radioimmuno therapy approved for the treatment of patient with relapsed or refractory low-grade, follicular, c transformed B-cell NHL; and FUMADERM, acquired with th purchase of Fumapharm AG in June 2006, acts as a immunomodulator and is approved in Germany for th treatment of severe psoriasis. In February 2006, the FD approved the RITUXAN supplemental Biologics Licens Application for use of RITUXAN in combination wit methotrexate, for reducing signs and symptoms in adu patients with moderately-to-severely active rheumatoi arthritis who have had an inadequate response to one c more tumor necrosis factor antagonist therapies. Biogen i working with Genentech and Roche on the development c RITUXAN in additional oncology and other indications Biogen also generates revenue by licensing drugs it ha developed to other companies, including Schering-Plough Merck and GlaxoSmithKline. In January 2007, Bioge agreed to acquire Syntonix Pharmaceuticals, a privately hel biopharmaceutical company focused on discovering an developing long-acting therapeutic products to improv treatment regimens for chronic diseases.

Biogen offers its employees dental insurance, tuitio reimbursement, commuter benefits, fitness benefits, a employee assistance program and concierge services.

FINANCIALS: **Sales and profits are in thousands of dollars—add 000 to get the full amount. 2007 Note: Financial information for 2007 was not available for all companies at press time.**

2007 Sales: $	2007 Profits: $	**U.S. Stock Ticker: BIIB**
2006 Sales: $2,683,049	2006 Profits: $217,511	**Int'l Ticker:** Int'l Exchange:
2005 Sales: $2,422,500	2005 Profits: $160,711	Employees: 3,750
2004 Sales: $2,211,562	2004 Profits: $25,086	Fiscal Year Ends: 12/31
2003 Sales: $679,183	2003 Profits: $-875,097	Parent Company:

SALARIES/BENEFITS:

Pension Plan:	ESOP Stock Plan:	Profit Sharing:	Top Exec. Salary: $1,084,616	Bonus: $2,000,000
Savings Plan: Y	Stock Purch. Plan: Y		Second Exec. Salary: $568,387	Bonus: $271,256

OTHER THOUGHTS:

Apparent Women Officers or Directors: 1
Hot Spot for Advancement for Women/Minorities:

LOCATIONS: ("Y" = Yes)

West:	Southwest:	Midwest:	Southeast:	Northeast:	International:
Y				Y	Y

Note: Financial information, benefits and other data can change quickly and may vary from those stated here.

BIOMET INC

www.biomet.com

Industry Group Code: 339113 **Ranks within this company's industry group:** Sales: 16 Profits: 11

Insurance/HMO/PPO:		Drugs:		Equipment/Supplies:		Hospitals/Clinics:		Services:		Health Care:	
Insurance:		Manufacturer:		Manufacturer:	Y	Acute Care:		Diagnostics:		Home Health:	
Managed Care:		Distributor:		Distributor:		Sub-Acute:		Labs/Testing:		Long-Term Care:	
Utilization Management:		Specialty Pharmacy:		Leasing/Finance:		Outpatient Surgery:		Staffing:		Physical Therapy:	
Payment Processing:		Vitamins/Nutritionals:		Information Systems:		Physical Rehab. Ctr.:		Waste Disposal:		Physician Prac. Mgmt.:	
		Clinical Trials:				Psychiatric Clinics:		Specialty Svcs.:			

TYPES OF BUSINESS:

Orthopedic Supplies
Electrical Bone Growth Stimulators
Orthopedic Support Devices
Operating Room Supplies
Powered Surgical Instruments
Arthroscopy Products
Imaging Equipment
Human Bone Joint Replacement Systems

BRANDS/DIVISIONS/AFFILIATES:

Anthrotek, Inc.
Walter Lorenz Surgical, Inc.
EBI, LP
Implant Innovations, Inc.
Regenerex
Biomet Orthopedics, Inc.
Maxim Total Knee System
Vanguard System

CONTACTS: *Note: Officers with more than one job title may be intentionally listed here more than once.*

Jeffrey R. Binder, CEO
Jeffrey R. Binder, Pres.
Daniel P. Florin, CFO/Sr. VP
Wilber C. Boren, Corp. VP-Contract Sales Admin.
Darlene Whaley, Sr. VP-Human Resources
Richard J. Borror, CIO
Lance Perry, Corp. VP-Global Prod. Dev. Reconstructive Devices
Richard J. Borror, Sr. VP-Mfg. Oper.
Daniel P. Hann, Exec. VP-Admin.
Bradley J. Tandy, General Counsel/Sr. VP/Sec.
Greg W. Sasso, Sr. VP-Corp. Dev.
Greg W. Sasso, Sr. VP-Corp. Comm.
J. Pat Richardson, VP-Finance/Treas.
Glen A. Kashuba, Sr. VP/Pres., Biomet Trauma & Biomet Spine
Steven F. Schiess, VP/Pres., Biomet 3i
Thomas R. Allen, Pres., Int'l Oper.-Americas & Asia Pacific
William C. Kolter, Pres., Biomet Orthopedics
Niles L. Noblitt, Chmn.
Roger P. van Broek, VP/Pres., Int'l Oper.

Phone: 574-267-6639	**Fax:** 574-267-8137
Toll-Free:	
Address: 56 E. Bell Dr., Warsaw, IN 46582 US	

GROWTH PLANS/SPECIAL FEATURES:

Biomet, Inc., founded in 1977, designs, manufactures and markets products that are used primarily by musculoskeletal medical specialists in both surgical and non-surgical therapy. The company's product portfolio encompasses reconstructive products, fixation devices, spinal products and other products. Biomet has four major market segments: reconstructive products, which accounted for 68% of the company's net revenues in 2006; fixation devices, which accounted for 12%; spinal products, which accounted for 11%, and other products, which account for 9%. Reconstructive products include knee, hip and extremity joint replacement systems, as well as dental reconstructive implants, bone cements and accessories. Fixation devices include electrical stimulation systems, internal and external fixation devices, craniomaxillofacial fixation systems and bone substitution materials. Spinal products include spinal fusion stimulation systems, spinal fixation systems, spinal bone substitution materials, precision machine allograft and motion preservation products. The other product market segment includes arthroscopy products, orthopedic support products, operating room supplies, casting materials, general surgical instruments and wound care products. Biomet manufactures numerous knee systems, including the Vanguard System, the Oxford Unicompartmental Knee, the Alpina Unicompartmental Knee, the Vanguard M System, the Repicci II Unicondylar Knee System and the Biomet OSS Orthopaedic Salvage System. Biomet's Arthrotek, Inc. subsidiary manufactures arthroscopy products in five product categories: power instruments, manual instruments, visualization products, soft tissue anchors and procedure-specific instruments and implants. In December 2006, Biomet agreed to be acquired for $10.9 billion by a private-equity group that includes affiliates of Blackstone Group, Goldman Sachs Capital Partners, Kohlberg Kravis Roberts & Co. and Texas Pacific Group. The private equity consortium increased its offer to $11.4 billion in June 2007. In May 2007, Biomet introduced the first vitamin E stabilized acetabular hip liners, which are expected to improve the longevity of the implant bearings used in total joint replacements.

FINANCIALS: **Sales and profits are in thousands of dollars—add 000 to get the full amount. 2007 Note: Financial information for 2007 was not available for all companies at press time.**

2007 Sales: $2,107,428	2007 Profits: $335,892	**U.S. Stock Ticker: BMET**
2006 Sales: $2,025,739	2006 Profits: $405,908	**Int'l Ticker:** Int'l Exchange:
2005 Sales: $1,879,950	2005 Profits: $349,373	Employees: 4,254
2004 Sales: $1,615,751	2004 Profits: $320,324	Fiscal Year Ends: 5/31
2003 Sales: $1,390,300	2003 Profits: $286,700	Parent Company:

SALARIES/BENEFITS:

Pension Plan:	ESOP Stock Plan:	Profit Sharing:	Top Exec. Salary: $358,800	Bonus: $250,000
Savings Plan:	Stock Purch. Plan:		Second Exec. Salary: $341,300	Bonus: $289,200

OTHER THOUGHTS:

Apparent Women Officers or Directors: 1
Hot Spot for Advancement for Women/Minorities:

LOCATIONS: ("Y" = Yes)

West:	Southwest:	Midwest:	Southeast:	Northeast:	International:
Y	Y	Y	Y	Y	Y

Note: Financial information, benefits and other data can change quickly and may vary from those stated here.

BIOPHAN TECHNOLOGIES INC www.biophan.com

Industry Group Code: 339113 **Ranks within this company's industry group:** Sales: 102 Profits: 89

Insurance/HMO/PPO:		Drugs:		Equipment/Supplies:		Hospitals/Clinics:		Services:		Health Care:	
Insurance:		Manufacturer:		Manufacturer:	Y	Acute Care:		Diagnostics:		Home Health:	
Managed Care:		Distributor:		Distributor:		Sub-Acute:		Labs/Testing:		Long-Term Care:	
Utilization Management:		Specialty Pharmacy:		Leasing/Finance:		Outpatient Surgery:		Staffing:		Physical Therapy:	
Payment Processing:		Vitamins/Nutritionals:		Information Systems:		Physical Rehab. Ctr.:		Waste Disposal:		Physician Prac. Mgmt.:	
		Clinical Trials:				Psychiatric Clinics:		Specialty Svcs.:			

TYPES OF BUSINESS:

Medical Equipment-Manufacturing
MRI Products & Contrast Agents
Nanomagnetic Coatings
Polymer Composites
Photonics
Drug Delivery Systems
Cardiovascular Devices

BRANDS/DIVISIONS/AFFILIATES:

NanoView
AMRIS
Nanolution
MYO-VAD
PR Financial Marketing LLC
Myotech LLC

CONTACTS: *Note: Officers with more than one job title may be intentionally listed here more than once.*

Michael L. Weiner, CEO
John F. Lanzafame, COO
Darryl Canfield, CFO
Stuart G. MacDonald, VP-R&D
Jeffrey L. Helfer, VP-Eng.
John F. Lanzafame, VP-Bus. Dev.
Darryl Canfield, Treas./VP/Corp. Sec.
Jeffrey L. Helfer, Pres., Cardiovascular Div.
Stephen H. Curry, Pres., Nanolution LLC
Guenter Jaensch, Chmn.

Phone: 585-267-4800	**Fax:** 585-267-4819
Toll-Free:	
Address: 15 Schoen Place, Pittsford, NY 14534 US	

GROWTH PLANS/SPECIAL FEATURES:

Biophan Technologies, Inc. develops MRI-compatible products and technologies for biomedical devices within markets in the medical technology sector. Products that are currently under development include pacemakers, neurostimulators, vena cava filters, heart valves, drug pumps, drug delivery systems and powersystems. The company's ultimate goal is to manufacture devices that are safe and image-compatible with MRI technology. In 2006 the company entered into a cooperative research and development agreement with the FDA's science and engineering laboratories to develop guidelines and standards for assessing cardiac pacemaker and neurostimulation leads used in the MRI environment. Technologies developed by the firm include thin film nanomagnetic particle coatings which allow for better visualizations and easier tracking of devices utilized during MRI scans. Nanomagnetic coatings shield any strong electromagnetic (EM) radio waves that are generated when the EM fields interact with any implanted medical devices within a patient. Without such shielding, the EM fields would prove to by fatal if any waves heated the metal implants and consequently damaged any surrounding tissues. In addition to nanomagnetic coating capabilities nanomaterials can also be employed as MRI contrasting agents that highlight specific infected or malfunctioning tissues. Through subsidiary Nanolution, the firm is also developing a proprietary nanotube drug delivery system which utilizes halloysite nanotubes to effectively deliver and releases pharmaceuticals at specific times to precise targeted locations. The company has a minority interest in MYOTECH, LLC and has collaborated in the development of MYO-VAD, an MRI-compatible ventricular assistance device used for the treatment of heart disease. Additionally Biophan owns AMRIS GmbH, a German maker of MRI compatible stents and medical devices. In June 2006 Biophan reviewed $1 million in government grants to further the development of its MYO-VAD cardiac support system.

FINANCIALS: Sales and profits are in thousands of dollars—add 000 to get the full amount. 2007 Note: Financial information for 2007 was not available for all companies at press time.

2007 Sales: $ 989	2007 Profits: $-17,722	**U.S. Stock Ticker: BIPH**
2006 Sales: $1,044	2006 Profits: $-14,315	**Int'l Ticker:** Int'l Exchange:
2005 Sales: $	2005 Profits: $-5,793	Employees: 22
2004 Sales: $ 75	2004 Profits: $-3,718	Fiscal Year Ends: 2/28
2003 Sales: $	2003 Profits: $-3,438	Parent Company:

SALARIES/BENEFITS:

Pension Plan:	ESOP Stock Plan:	Profit Sharing:	Top Exec. Salary: $237,115	Bonus: $
Savings Plan:	Stock Purch. Plan:		Second Exec. Salary: $176,153	Bonus: $

OTHER THOUGHTS:

Apparent Women Officers or Directors:
Hot Spot for Advancement for Women/Minorities:

LOCATIONS: ("Y" = Yes)

West:	Southwest:	Midwest:	Southeast:	Northeast:	International:
				Y	

BIOSCRIP INC

www.bioscrip.com

Industry Group Code: 522320A **Ranks within this company's industry group:** Sales: 4 Profits: 5

Insurance/HMO/PPO:		Drugs:		Equipment/Supplies:		Hospitals/Clinics:		Services:		Health Care:	
Insurance:		Manufacturer:		Manufacturer:		Acute Care:		Diagnostics:		Home Health:	
Managed Care:		Distributor:		Distributor:		Sub-Acute:		Labs/Testing:		Long-Term Care:	
Utilization Management:	Y	Specialty Pharmacy:	Y	Leasing/Finance:		Outpatient Surgery:		Staffing:		Physical Therapy:	
Payment Processing:	Y	Vitamins/Nutritionals:		Information Systems:		Physical Rehab. Ctr.:		Waste Disposal:		Physician Prac. Mgmt.:	
		Clinical Trials:				Psychiatric Clinics:		Specialty Svcs.:	Y		

TYPES OF BUSINESS:

Pharmacy Benefits Management
Retail, Online & Mail-Order Pharmacies
Disease Management
Home Infusion Services
Specialty Pharmacy Services

BRANDS/DIVISIONS/AFFILIATES:

MIM Corporation
Chronimed
BioScrip
ADIMA Infusion Therapy
ScripPharmacy
ScripPBM
StatScript Pharmacies
Fair Pharmacy

CONTACTS: *Note: Officers with more than one job title may be intentionally listed here more than once.*

Richard H. Friedman, CEO
Stanley Rosenbaum, CFO
Kristin Johnson, VP-Mktg.
Douglas Lee, CIO
Tom Staloch, CTO
Barry A. Posner, General Counsel/Exec. VP
Russel J. Corvese, VP-Oper.
Gregory H. Keane, Exec. VP/Treas.
Alfred Carfora, Exec. VP-Mail Service & PBM
Brian J. Reagan, Exec. VP-Infusion Division
John Brewer, Exec. VP-Community Pharmacy Division
Scott W. Friedman, VP-Pharmaceutical Rel.
Richard H. Friedman, Chmn.

Phone: 914-460-1600	**Fax:** 914-460-1660
Toll-Free: 888-818-3939	
Address: 100 Clearbrook Rd., Elmsford, NY 10523 US	

GROWTH PLANS/SPECIAL FEATURES:

BioScrip, Inc., formed in a 2005 merger between MIM Corporation and Chronimed, Inc., is a pharmaceutical health care organization that provides pharmacy benefits management (PBM), specialty pharmaceutical management, distribution and other pharmacy-related health care solutions to individual patients or enrollees receiving health benefits through HMOs, indemnity plans, PPOs, managed care organizations and other plan sponsors. It operates throughout the U.S., with offices and mail centers in New York, California, Rhode Island, Ohio, New Jersey and Tennessee. The company's specialty management and delivery services segment distributes biotech and other high-cost pharmaceuticals and provides clinically focused case and therapy management programs to members that are chronically ill or genetically impaired. Its BioScrip specialty pharmacy and disease programs provide pharmacy case management, prior authorizations, in-clinic and in-home infusion therapy, therapy assessment, patient enrollment, risk assessment, education, medication delivery, pharmacy data services and disease management for Crohn's disease, Gaucher's disease, growth hormone deficiency, HIV/AIDS, hemophilia, hepatitis C, immune deficiency, infertility, multiple sclerosis, oncology, psoriasis, rheumatoid arthritis, transplants and other diseases. BioScrip's PBM services group offers plan sponsors, employers and third-party administrators services that ensure cost-effective drug delivery. Its services include formulary and benefit design, clinical services, drug use evaluation, pharmacy data services, disease management, behavioral health pharmacy services, capitated billing arrangements and a mail-order pharmacy. The company's community pharmacy division administers 37 retail pharmacies across the U.S. In March 2006, the company acquired Intravenous Therapy Services, a specialty infusion company.

BioScrip offers its employees a complete benefits package that includes flexible spending accounts.

FINANCIALS: **Sales and profits are in thousands of dollars—add 000 to get the full amount. 2007 Note: Financial information for 2007 was not available for all companies at press time.**

2007 Sales: $	2007 Profits: $	**U.S. Stock Ticker: BIOS**
2006 Sales: $1,152,459	2006 Profits: $-38,289	**Int'l Ticker:** Int'l Exchange:
2005 Sales: $1,073,235	2005 Profits: $-23,847	Employees: 1,092
2004 Sales: $630,516	2004 Profits: $7,033	Fiscal Year Ends: 12/31
2003 Sales: $588,770	2003 Profits: $9,130	Parent Company:

SALARIES/BENEFITS:

Pension Plan:	ESOP Stock Plan:	Profit Sharing:	Top Exec. Salary: $698,259	Bonus: $
Savings Plan: Y	Stock Purch. Plan:		Second Exec. Salary: $517,969	Bonus: $83,333

OTHER THOUGHTS:

Apparent Women Officers or Directors: 1
Hot Spot for Advancement for Women/Minorities:

LOCATIONS: ("Y" = Yes)

West:	Southwest:	Midwest:	Southeast:	Northeast:	International:
Y	Y	Y	Y	Y	

BIOSITE INC www.biosite.com

Industry Group Code: 325413 **Ranks within this company's industry group:** Sales: 2 Profits: 3

Insurance/HMO/PPO:		Drugs:		Equipment/Supplies:		Hospitals/Clinics:		Services:		Health Care:	
Insurance:		Manufacturer:	Y	Manufacturer:	Y	Acute Care:		Diagnostics:		Home Health:	
Managed Care:		Distributor:		Distributor:		Sub-Acute:		Labs/Testing:		Long-Term Care:	
Utilization Management:		Specialty Pharmacy:		Leasing/Finance:		Outpatient Surgery:		Staffing:		Physical Therapy:	
Payment Processing:		Vitamins/Nutritionals:		Information Systems:		Physical Rehab. Ctr.:		Waste Disposal:		Physician Prac. Mgmt.:	
		Clinical Trials:				Psychiatric Clinics:		Specialty Svcs.:			

TYPES OF BUSINESS:

Medical Diagnostics Products
Rapid Immunoassays
Antibody Development Services

BRANDS/DIVISIONS/AFFILIATES:

Biosite Discovery
Triage Drugs of Abuse Panel
Triage Cardiac Panel
Triage TOX Drug Screen
Triage BNP Test
Triage Profiler Panels
Triage Parasite Panel
Triage D-Dimer Test

CONTACTS: *Note: Officers with more than one job title may be intentionally listed here more than once.*

Kim D. Blickenstaff, CEO
Kenneth F. Buechler, Pres./Chief Scientific Officer
Christopher J. Twomey, CFO
Robert Anacone, Sr. VP-Worldwide Mktg. & Sales
Paul H. McPherson, VP-R&D
Stephen Lesefko, VP-Eng.
David Berger, VP-Legal Affairs
Christopher R. Hibberd, Sr. VP-Corp. Dev.
Nadine E. Padilla, VP-Corp. Rel.
Nadine E. Padilla, VP-Corp. & Investor Rel.
Christopher J. Twomey, Sr. VP-Finance/Sec.
Robin G. Weiner, VP-Quality Assurance & Govt. Affairs
Gunars E. Valkirs, Sr. VP-Biosite Discovery
Thomas G. Blassey, VP-U.S. Sales
S. Elaine Walton, VP-Quality Assurance & Program Mgt.
Kim D. Blickenstaff, Chmn.
Gary A. King, VP-Int'l Oper.

Phone: 858-805-4808	**Fax:**
Toll-Free: 888-246-7483	
Address: 9975 Summers Ridge Rd., San Diego, CA 92121 US	

GROWTH PLANS/SPECIAL FEATURES:

Biosite, Inc. is a global diagnostics company dedicated t utilizing biotechnology in the development of diagnosti products. The firm validates and patents novel protei biomarkers and panels of biomarkers, develops and market products, conducts strategic research on its products an educates healthcare providers about its products. Biosit markets immunoassay diagnostics in the areas c cardiovascular disease, drug overdose and infectiou disease. Cardiovascular products account for 83% c product sales and include the Triage BNP Test, Triag Cardiac Panel, Triage Profiler Panels, Triage D-Dimer Tes and Triage Stroke Panel. The Triage Drugs of Abuse Pane and Triage TOX Drug Screen are rapid, qualitative urin screens that test for up to nine different illicit and prescriptio drugs or drug classes and provide results in less than 1 minutes. The Triage C. Difficile Panel and Triage Parasit Panel aid in the diagnosis of infectious diseases. The firm' Biosite Discovery research business seeks to identify nev protein markers of diseases that lack effective diagnosti tests. Additionally, with Biosite Discovery, the company ha the capacity to offer antibody development services t companies seeking high-affinity antibodies for use in dru research. In return, Biosite seeks diagnostic licenses. I May 2006, the company withdrew its pre-market approva submission to the FDA for the Triage Stroke Panel. Th withdrawal will allow the company time for an additiona clinical study of the product, which the firm hopes will suppo a new U.S. regulatory submission. In May 2007, Biosit agreed to be acquired by Inverness Medical Innovations Inc., a diagnostics developing company, for $92.50 pe share.

Biosite offers employees a benefits package includin flexible spending accounts, an employee assistanc program, bereavement leave, education reimbursement, a 401(k) plan and an employee stock purchase plan.

FINANCIALS: **Sales and profits are in thousands of dollars—add 000 to get the full amount. 2007 Note: Financial information for 2007 was not available for all companies at press time.**

2007 Sales: $	2007 Profits: $	**U.S. Stock Ticker: BSTE**
2006 Sales: $308,592	2006 Profits: $39,994	**Int'l Ticker:** Int'l Exchange:
2005 Sales: $287,699	2005 Profits: $54,029	Employees: 1,036
2004 Sales: $244,900	2004 Profits: $41,400	Fiscal Year Ends: 12/31
2003 Sales: $173,364	2003 Profits: $24,763	Parent Company:

SALARIES/BENEFITS:

Pension Plan:	ESOP Stock Plan:	Profit Sharing:	Top Exec. Salary: $553,500	Bonus: $264,424
Savings Plan: Y	Stock Purch. Plan: Y		Second Exec. Salary: $430,961	Bonus: $203,944

OTHER THOUGHTS:

Apparent Women Officers or Directors: 3
Hot Spot for Advancement for Women/Minorities: Y

LOCATIONS: ("Y" = Yes)

West:	Southwest:	Midwest:	Southeast:	Northeast:	International:
Y					Y

Note: Financial information, benefits and other data can change quickly and may vary from those stated here.

BIOVAIL CORPORATION

www.biovail.com

Industry Group Code: 325412A **Ranks within this company's industry group:** Sales: 1 Profits: 1

Insurance/HMO/PPO:		Drugs:		Equipment/Supplies:		Hospitals/Clinics:		Services:		Health Care:	
Insurance:		Manufacturer:	Y	Manufacturer:		Acute Care:		Diagnostics:		Home Health:	
Managed Care:		Distributor:		Distributor:		Sub-Acute:		Labs/Testing:		Long-Term Care:	
Utilization Management:		Specialty Pharmacy:		Leasing/Finance:		Outpatient Surgery:		Staffing:		Physical Therapy:	
Payment Processing:		Vitamins/Nutritionals:		Information Systems:		Physical Rehab. Ctr.:		Waste Disposal:		Physician Prac. Mgmt.:	
		Clinical Trials:				Psychiatric Clinics:		Specialty Svcs.:			

TYPES OF BUSINESS:

Drug Delivery Systems Technologies
Generic Drugs
Drugs-Hypertension
Drugs-Antidepressants
Nutraceuticals
Contract Research Services

BRANDS/DIVISIONS/AFFILIATES:

Biovail Pharmaceuticals, Inc.
Biovail Pharmaceuticals Canada
Shearform
Zero Order Release System
Wellbutrin XL
FlashDose
Cardizem LA
Zovirax

CONTACTS: *Note: Officers with more than one job title may be intentionally listed here more than once.*

Douglas J. P. Squires, CEO
Gilbert Godin, COO/Exec. VP
Kenneth G. Howling, CFO/Sr. VP
Mark Durham, Sr. VP-Human Resources
Peter Silverstone, Sr. VP-Scientific & Medical Affairs
Mark Durham, Sr. VP-IT
John Sebben, VP-Mfg.
Wendy Kelley, General Counsel/Sr. VP/Corp. Sec.
Gregory Gubitz, Sr. VP-Corp. Dev.
Nelson F. Isabel, VP-Corp. Comm.
Nelson F. Isabel, VP-Investor Rel.
Christopher Bovaird, VP-Corp. Finance
John Miszuk, VP/Controller
Adrian de Saldanha, VP-Finance/Treas.
David Keefer, Sr. VP-Commercial Oper.
Christine Mayer, Sr. VP-Bus. Dev., Biovail Pharmaceuticals, Inc.
Douglas J.P. Squires, Interim Chmn.
Michel Chouinard, COO-Biovail Laboratories Int'l SRL

Phone: 905-286-3000 **Fax:** 905-286-3050
Toll-Free:
Address: 7150 Mississauga Rd., Mississauga, ON L5N 8M5 Canada

GROWTH PLANS/SPECIAL FEATURES:

Biovail Corporation is a full-service pharmaceutical company that develops, tests and commercializes its proprietary drug delivery technologies to improve the clinical effectiveness of medications. The firm's primary areas of focus include cardiovascular disease, Type II diabetes, central nervous system disorders and pain management. Biovail markets its products through its marketing divisions, Biovail Pharmaceuticals, Inc. and Biovail Pharmaceuticals Canada, and through other strategic partners to health care professionals. The company primarily employs its drug delivery technologies to develop enhanced formulations and controlled-release generic versions of existing and pre-market oral medications. These delivery technologies include controlled release, graded release, enhanced absorption, rapid absorption, taste masking and oral disintegration processes. Trademarks for these technologies include FlashDose, CEFORM, Shearform, Consurf and Zero Order Release System (ZORS). Biovail's products include Wellbutrin XL, which is marketed worldwide through GlaxoSmithKline to treat depression through a once-daily formulation. Other noteworthy products produced by the firm include Cardizem LA, a hypertension medication, and Zovirax, an antiviral ointment. Biovail currently maintains fully integrated pharmaceutical manufacturing facilities in Canada, Ireland, North Carolina, Barbados and Puerto Rico. In addition, the company operates a contract research division that provides Biovail and other pharmaceutical companies with a broad range of Phase I/II clinical research services in pharmacokinetic studies and bioanalytical laboratory testing. Biovail also owns Nutravail Technologies, Inc., which specializes in the development of over 80 patented nutraceuticals, nutritional products and functional foods. In May 2006, Biovail Pharmaceuticals Canada entered into an agreement with Novartis Pharmaceuticals Canada, Inc. to market and promote Lescol fluvastatin sodium capsules and once-daily Lescol XL to Canadian physicians. Biovail's subsidiary, Biovail Pharmaceuticals, Inc. entered into an exclusive promotional services agreement in late 2006 with Sciele Pharma, Inc. to promote the company's Zovirax Ointment and Zovirax Cream to the U.S.

FINANCIALS: **Sales and profits are in thousands of dollars—add 000 to get the full amount. 2007 Note: Financial information for 2007 was not available for all companies at press time.**

2007 Sales: $	2007 Profits: $	**U.S. Stock Ticker: BVF**
2006 Sales: $1,070,500	2006 Profits: $203,900	**Int'l Ticker: BVF** Int'l Exchange: Toronto-TSX
2005 Sales: $935,500	2005 Profits: $89,000	Employees: 1,734
2004 Sales: $886,500	2004 Profits: $161,000	Fiscal Year Ends: 10/31
2003 Sales: $823,700	2003 Profits: $-27,300	Parent Company:

SALARIES/BENEFITS:

Pension Plan:	ESOP Stock Plan:	Profit Sharing:	Top Exec. Salary: $750,607	Bonus: $
Savings Plan:	Stock Purch. Plan:		Second Exec. Salary: $700,000	Bonus: $525,000

OTHER THOUGHTS:

Apparent Women Officers or Directors: 3
Hot Spot for Advancement for Women/Minorities: Y

LOCATIONS: ("Y" = Yes)

West:	Southwest:	Midwest:	Southeast:	Northeast:	International:
				Y	Y

BJC HEALTHCARE

www.bjc.org

Industry Group Code: 622110 **Ranks within this company's industry group:** Sales: 20 Profits:

Insurance/HMO/PPO:		**Drugs:**		**Equipment/Supplies:**		**Hospitals/Clinics:**		**Services:**		**Health Care:**	
Insurance:		Manufacturer:		Manufacturer:		Acute Care:	Y	Diagnostics:	Y	Home Health:	Y
Managed Care:		Distributor:		Distributor:		Sub-Acute:	Y	Labs/Testing:	Y	Long-Term Care:	Y
Utilization Management:		Specialty Pharmacy:		Leasing/Finance:		Outpatient Surgery:	Y	Staffing:		Physical Therapy:	Y
Payment Processing:		Vitamins/Nutritionals:		Information Systems:		Physical Rehab. Ctr.:	Y	Waste Disposal:		Physician Prac. Mgmt.:	Y
		Clinical Trials:				Psychiatric Clinics:	Y	Specialty Svcs.:	Y		

TYPES OF BUSINESS:

Hospitals
Home Health Services
Physical Rehab Center
Physician Groups
Long-Term Health Care
Occupational Health Services
Hospice Services
Teaching Hospitals

BRANDS/DIVISIONS/AFFILIATES:

Barnes-Jewish Hospital
St. Louis Children's Hospital
Rehabilitation Institute of St. Louis (The)
BJC Home Care Services
BJC Corporate Health Services
BarnesCare
OccuMed
BJC Medical Group

CONTACTS: *Note: Officers with more than one job title may be intentionally listed here more than once.*

Steven H. Lipstein, CEO
Steven H. Lipstein, Pres.
Patrick Dupuis, CFO/VP
Carlos Perea, Chief Human Resource Officer/VP
David A. Weiss, CIO/VP
Michael A. DeHaven, General Counsel/Sr. VP
June M. Fowler, VP-Corp. & Public Comm.
Robert W. Cannon, VP-Capital Asset Management
JoAnn M. Shaw, VP/Chief Learning Officer
W. Claiborne Dunagan, VP-Center for Healthcare Quality & Effectiveness
Sandra A. Van Trease, Group Pres.
Paul McKee, Jr., Chmn.

Phone: 314-747-9322 **Fax:** 314-286-2060
Toll-Free:
Address: 4444 Forest Park Ave., St. Louis, MO 63108 US

GROWTH PLANS/SPECIAL FEATURES:

BJC Healthcare is one of the largest nonprofit health care organizations in the U.S. The firm operates 13 hospitals and several other health care organizations. Two of the company's hospitals, Barnes-Jewish Hospital and St. Louis Children's Hospital, are ranked highly among America's elite medical centers and teaching hospitals. Both are affiliated with Washington University School of Medicine, which is considered one of the best medical schools in the nation. The company's services include inpatient and outpatient care, primary care, community health, workplace health, home health, mental health, rehabilitation, long-term care and hospice. The BJC Home Care Services division offers patients in over 25 Missouri and Illinois counties a wide range of in-home services, including skilled nursing, adult and pediatric supportive care, rehabilitation therapy, respiratory care, infusion therapy and hospice services. Through the BJC Corporate Health Services segment, the company provides occupational health services through five locations run by BarnesCare; access to OccuMed, a comprehensive occupational medicine network that helps companies control workers' compensation costs; the mammography van, which offers screenings at worksites; Travelers' Health Service, which provides immunizations and information on international health risks to patients prior to flying; and BJC Employee Assistance Program, which assists in identification and resolution of health, behavioral and productivity problems. One of BarnesCare's newest services is the Corporate Health Nurse Program, which allows local employers to contract for workplace nursing services on a full- or part-time basis. Recently, BJC opened its new hospital, Progressive West HealthCare Center, in southern St. Charles County, Missouri.

FINANCIALS: **Sales and profits are in thousands of dollars—add 000 to get the full amount. 2007 Note: Financial information for 2007 was not available for all companies at press time.**

2007 Sales: $	2007 Profits: $	**U.S. Stock Ticker: Nonprofit**
2006 Sales: $2,800,000	2006 Profits: $	**Int'l Ticker:** Int'l Exchange:
2005 Sales: $	2005 Profits: $	Employees: 25,819
2004 Sales: $2,600,000	2004 Profits: $	Fiscal Year Ends: 12/31
2003 Sales: $2,500,000	2003 Profits: $	Parent Company:

SALARIES/BENEFITS:

Pension Plan:	ESOP Stock Plan:	Profit Sharing:	Top Exec. Salary: $	Bonus: $
Savings Plan:	Stock Purch. Plan:		Second Exec. Salary: $	Bonus: $

OTHER THOUGHTS:

Apparent Women Officers or Directors: 5
Hot Spot for Advancement for Women/Minorities: Y

LOCATIONS: ("Y" = Yes)

West:	Southwest:	Midwest:	Southeast:	Northeast:	International:
		Y			

BLUE CARE NETWORK OF MICHIGAN www.mibcn.com

Industry Group Code: 524114 **Ranks within this company's industry group:** Sales: Profits:

Insurance/HMO/PPO:		Drugs:		Equipment/Supplies:		Hospitals/Clinics:		Services:		Health Care:	
Insurance:	Y	Manufacturer:		Manufacturer:		Acute Care:		Diagnostics:		Home Health:	
Managed Care:	Y	Distributor:		Distributor:		Sub-Acute:		Labs/Testing:		Long-Term Care:	
Utilization Management:		Specialty Pharmacy:		Leasing/Finance:		Outpatient Surgery:		Staffing:		Physical Therapy:	
Payment Processing:		Vitamins/Nutritionals:		Information Systems:		Physical Rehab. Ctr.:		Waste Disposal:		Physician Prac. Mgmt.:	
		Clinical Trials:				Psychiatric Clinics:		Specialty Svcs.:	Y		

TYPES OF BUSINESS:

Insurance-Medical & Health, HMOs & PPOs
Online Resources & Information
Disease Management

BRANDS/DIVISIONS/AFFILIATES:

Blue Cross Blue Shield of Michigan
Health e-Blue
BlueHealthConnection
Subimo
Blue Elect Self-Referral Option
Healthy Blue Living

CONTACTS: *Note: Officers with more than one job title may be intentionally listed here more than once.*

Jeanne Carlson, CEO
Laurie Westfall, COO
Jeanne Carlson, Pres.
Susan A. Kluge, CFO/Sr. VP
Kevin Klobucar, VP-Mktg.
Joan Morehead, VP-Human Resources
David R. Nelson, Sr. VP/Chief Actuarial Officer
Douglas R. Woll, Sr. VP/Chief Medical Officer
Frank Garrison, Chmn.

Phone: 248-354-7450 **Fax:** 248-799-6327
Toll-Free: 800-662-6667
Address: 20500 Civic Center Drive, Southfield, MI 48076 US

GROWTH PLANS/SPECIAL FEATURES:

Blue Care Network of Michigan (BCN), a subsidiary of Blue Cross Blue Shield of Michigan (BCBSM), is the largest HMO network in the state with over 500,000 members. The company works together with BCBSM by sharing resources to identify and fight fraud, protect member privacy and to support each others technology infrastructure. The BCN offers its members traditional indemnity and Medicare, as well as supplementary management and care services. BCN works closely with its physician network and provides services and tools, such as its Health e-Blue software, to support its partners. Its BlueHealthConnection service, in collaboration with Blue Cross Blue Shield of Michigan, combines diverse programs to assist members with chronic or complex illnesses. The company's products include coverage options for individuals, groups and for extending coverage after having left a group. Its individual coverage options consist of OneBlue, which is available to individuals that are impacted by automotive or large group buyouts; Personal Plus, which is designed for individuals under the age of 65; BCN Advantage for the individual, which replaces Medicare coverage with comprehensive HMO coverage; and BCN 65, which works with Medicare to cover more health care costs. The company's group coverage options include the Blue Care Network standard HMO; the Blue Elect Self-Referral Option for employer groups of two or more in size; Healthy Blue Living, which has decreased co-payment and deductibles for members who live a healthy lifestyle; the Self-funded Option, which lets the employer assume the claims cost risk; BCN Advantage for groups; and BCN 65 for groups. Also, under the federal Consolidated Omnibus Budget Reconciliation Act (COBRA), BCN allows members to extend coverage after having left a group by paying their own premiums. In March 2007, the five month old Healthy Blue Living service reached an enrollment of 18,000 members.

FINANCIALS: **Sales and profits are in thousands of dollars—add 000 to get the full amount. 2007 Note: Financial information for 2007 was not available for all companies at press time.**

2007 Sales: $
2006 Sales: $
2005 Sales: $1,439,429
2004 Sales: $1,395,438
2003 Sales: $1,352,667

2007 Profits: $
2006 Profits: $
2005 Profits: $78,396
2004 Profits: $80,999
2003 Profits: $53,130

U.S. Stock Ticker: Subsidiary
Int'l Ticker: Int'l Exchange:
Employees: 1,000
Fiscal Year Ends: 12/31
Parent Company: BLUE CROSS AND BLUE SHIELD OF MICHIGAN

SALARIES/BENEFITS:

Pension Plan:	ESOP Stock Plan:	Profit Sharing:	Top Exec. Salary: $	Bonus: $
Savings Plan:	Stock Purch. Plan:		Second Exec. Salary: $	Bonus: $

OTHER THOUGHTS:

Apparent Women Officers or Directors: 4
Hot Spot for Advancement for Women/Minorities: Y

LOCATIONS: ("Y" = Yes)

West:	Southwest:	Midwest:	Southeast:	Northeast:	International:
		Y			

Note: Financial information, benefits and other data can change quickly and may vary from those stated here.

BLUE CROSS AND BLUE SHIELD ASSOCIATION

www.bcbs.com

Industry Group Code: 524114 **Ranks within this company's industry group:** Sales: Profits:

Insurance/HMO/PPO:		Drugs:		Equipment/Supplies:		Hospitals/Clinics:		Services:		Health Care:	
Insurance:	Y	Manufacturer:		Manufacturer:		Acute Care:		Diagnostics:		Home Health:	
Managed Care:	Y	Distributor:		Distributor:		Sub-Acute:		Labs/Testing:		Long-Term Care:	
Utilization Management:	Y	Specialty Pharmacy:		Leasing/Finance:		Outpatient Surgery:		Staffing:		Physical Therapy:	
Payment Processing:	Y	Vitamins/Nutritionals:		Information Systems:		Physical Rehab. Ctr.:		Waste Disposal:		Physician Prac. Mgmt.:	
		Clinical Trials:				Psychiatric Clinics:		Specialty Svcs.:			

TYPES OF BUSINESS:

Insurance-Medical & Health, HMOs & PPOs

BRANDS/DIVISIONS/AFFILIATES:

Blue Cross and Blue Shield System
Blue Cross Association
National Association of Blue Shield Plans
BlueCard
BlueWorks
WalkingWorks
Your Choices Count
BeneFits

CONTACTS: *Note: Officers with more than one job title may be intentionally listed here more than once.*

Scott P. Serota, CEO
Scott P. Serota, Pres.
Kathryn M. Sullivan, CFO/Sr. VP
William J. Colbourne, Sr. VP-Human Resources
Doug Porter, CIO/Sr. VP
William B. O'Loughlin, CTO
William J. Colbourne, Sr. VP-Admin. Svcs.
Roger G. Wilson, General Counsel/Sr. VP/Corp. Sec.
Maureen E. Sullivan, Sr. VP-Strategic Svcs.
Mary Nell Lehnhard, Sr. VP-Policy & Representation
Jack Ericksen, VP-Federal Rel.
Frank E. Coyne, VP-Inter-Plan Programs
Stephen W. Gammarino, Sr. VP-National Programs

Phone: 312-297-6000 **Fax:** 312-297-6609
Toll-Free:
Address: 225 N. Michigan Ave., Chicago, IL 60601-7680 US

GROWTH PLANS/SPECIAL FEATURES:

Blue Cross and Blue Shield Association (BCBSA coordinates 39 independent and locally operated Blue Cros and Blue Shield Plans across America. Together thes health insurance and care providers constitute the Blu Cross and Blue Shield System, the oldest and largest grou of health care companies in the country. BCBSA Plan provide health care for over 93 million people, nearly one third of all Americans, in every state, Washington, D.C. an Puerto Rico. Currently, more than 90% of hospitals an nearly 80% of physicians contract with BCBSA plans. Blu Cross and Blue Shield's Federal Employee Program is th largest privately underwritten health insurance contract in th world. The firm's BlueCard program electronically link independent Blue Plans nationwide through a singl electronic network for claims processing and reimbursement allowing employees of nationwide corporations to participat and allowing individuals with local plans to file claims whil traveling outside their region. In an effort to keep healthcar affordable in the face of expected cost increases, BCBS implemented the Healthcare Cost Campaign, which consist of signature programs BlueWorks, WalkingWorks, You Choices Count and a comprehensive research agenda BCBSA recently introduced BeneFits, a program designe for Colorado's Uninsured Small Businesses, which offers five targeted plans priced for cost-sensitive groups, lowe employment contribution levels and lower employee participation requirements than traditional plans. In 2007 the company received federal approval to open Blu Healthcare Bank, which will provide healthcare-relate banking services in all 50 states.

The company's BluePrint program gives employees credi dollars, allowing them to choose the combination of benefits that best meet their individual needs. Other perks include annual bonuses.

FINANCIALS: Sales and profits are in thousands of dollars—add 000 to get the full amount. 2007 Note: Financial information for 2007 was not available for all companies at press time.

2007 Sales: $	2007 Profits: $	**U.S. Stock Ticker: Nonprofit**
2006 Sales: $	2006 Profits: $	**Int'l Ticker:** Int'l Exchange:
2005 Sales: $256,800,000	2005 Profits: $	Employees: 850
2004 Sales: $238,900,000	2004 Profits: $	Fiscal Year Ends: 12/31
2003 Sales: $216,800,000	2003 Profits: $	Parent Company:

SALARIES/BENEFITS:

Pension Plan:	ESOP Stock Plan:	Profit Sharing:	Top Exec. Salary: $	Bonus: $
Savings Plan: Y	Stock Purch. Plan:		Second Exec. Salary: $	Bonus: $

OTHER THOUGHTS:

Apparent Women Officers or Directors: 5
Hot Spot for Advancement for Women/Minorities: Y

LOCATIONS: ("Y" = Yes)

West:	Southwest:	Midwest:	Southeast:	Northeast:	International:
Y	Y	Y	Y	Y	

BLUE CROSS AND BLUE SHIELD OF FLORIDA www.bcbsfl.com

Industry Group Code: 524114 **Ranks within this company's industry group:** Sales: 14 Profits: 12

Insurance/HMO/PPO:		Drugs:		Equipment/Supplies:		Hospitals/Clinics:		Services:		Health Care:	
Insurance:	Y	Manufacturer:		Manufacturer:		Acute Care:		Diagnostics:		Home Health:	
Managed Care:	Y	Distributor:		Distributor:		Sub-Acute:		Labs/Testing:		Long-Term Care:	
Utilization Management:	Y	Specialty Pharmacy:		Leasing/Finance:		Outpatient Surgery:		Staffing:	Y	Physical Therapy:	
Payment Processing:	Y	Vitamins/Nutritionals:		Information Systems:		Physical Rehab. Ctr.:		Waste Disposal:		Physician Prac. Mgmt.:	
		Clinical Trials:				Psychiatric Clinics:		Specialty Svcs.:	Y		

TYPES OF BUSINESS:

Insurance-Medical & Health, HMOs & PPOs
Life Insurance
Dental Insurance
Medicare & Medicaid Services
Staffing
Administrative Services
Information Technology Services

BRANDS/DIVISIONS/AFFILIATES:

RelayHealth
Availity, Inc.
TriCenturion, Inc.
Navigy, Inc
Incepture, Inc.
Florida Combined Life Insurance Company, Inc.
First Coast Service Options, Inc.
Health Options, Inc.

CONTACTS: *Note: Officers with more than one job title may be intentionally listed here more than once.*

Robert I. Lufrano, CEO
R. Chris Doerr, CFO/Sr. VP
Alan Guzzino, VP-Sales
Robert E. Wall, Sr. VP-Human Services
Duke Livermore, CIO/Sr. VP
Jonathan B. Gavras, VP-Medical Oper.
L. Joseph Grantham, Chief Strategy Officer/Sr. VP
Sharon Wamble-King, VP-Corp. Comm.
Cyrus M. Jollivette, Group VP-Public Affairs
Maureen West, Exec. Dir.-Central Florida
Steve Snell, VP-Florida Combined Life/Insurance Agency
Barbara Benevento, Pres., Comp Options
Robert I. Lufrano, Chmn.

Phone: 904-791-6111 **Fax:** 904-905-4486
Toll-Free: 800-477-3736
Address: 4800 Deerwood Campus Pkwy., DC 1-6, Jacksonville, FL 32246 US

GROWTH PLANS/SPECIAL FEATURES:

Blue Cross Blue Shield of Florida (BCBSF) is a nonprofit mutual health insurance company providing comprehensive health insurance and related services to a membership of approximately 8.6 million. BlueChoice and BlueCare are the company's PPO and HMO group health care plans for both small and large companies. For individuals under 65, the company provides the BlueOptions and BlueChoice PPOs. Individuals over 65 have several plans to choose from involving a combination of Medicare supplements, HMOs and other services. The company also provides multiple options for pharmacy coverage, dental coverage (DentalBlue), life insurance (LifeEssentials), accidental death and dismemberment, disability, long-term care and workers' compensation. The Health Dialog program provides resources for health information and support to help members make educated health care choices. Hospital Advisor, a web-based utility, gives members access to detailed information about hospitals, such as success rates in medical procedures, complication and infection rates and technological capabilities. BCBSF operates through various subsidiaries, including Health Options, Inc., a combination individual practice association and network model HMO; Florida Combined Life Insurance Company, Inc.; First Coast Service Options, Inc., a Medicare administrator for over 3 million people in Florida and Connecticut; Navigy, Inc., which focuses on increasing the efficiency of health care administration; TriCenturion, Inc., a contractor for Medicare and Medicaid services; and Availity, Inc., which addresses administrative efficiency primarily through information technology solutions. In January 2006, the firm partnered with Subimo, a provider of Web-based health care decision-support resources, to provide members with new online resources to review options relating to health care. In February 2007, the company introduced its new concept retail store, Florida Blue, which will sell health related products including dental and life insurance.

BCBSF offers its employees flexible spending accounts, an on-site fitness center, scholarship, training, mentoring and development programs, employee assistance and tuition reimbursement.

FINANCIALS: Sales and profits are in thousands of dollars—add 000 to get the full amount. 2007 Note: Financial information for 2007 was not available for all companies at press time.

2007 Sales: $	2007 Profits: $	**U.S. Stock Ticker: Nonprofit**
2006 Sales: $7,475,000	2006 Profits: $311,000	**Int'l Ticker:** Int'l Exchange:
2005 Sales: $6,975,000	2005 Profits: $340,000	Employees: 9,500
2004 Sales: $6,490,000	2004 Profits: $297,300	Fiscal Year Ends: 12/31
2003 Sales: $5,991,000	2003 Profits: $281,000	Parent Company:

SALARIES/BENEFITS:

Pension Plan: Y	ESOP Stock Plan:	Profit Sharing:	Top Exec. Salary: $	Bonus: $
Savings Plan: Y	Stock Purch. Plan:		Second Exec. Salary: $	Bonus: $

OTHER THOUGHTS:

Apparent Women Officers or Directors: 3
Hot Spot for Advancement for Women/Minorities: Y

LOCATIONS: ("Y" = Yes)

West:	Southwest:	Midwest:	Southeast:	Northeast:	International:
			Y		

Note: Financial information, benefits and other data can change quickly and may vary from those stated here.

BLUE CROSS AND BLUE SHIELD OF GEORGIA INC

www.bcbsga.com

Industry Group Code: 524114 **Ranks within this company's industry group:** Sales: Profits:

Insurance/HMO/PPO:		Drugs:		Equipment/Supplies:		Hospitals/Clinics:		Services:		Health Care:	
Insurance:	Y	Manufacturer:		Manufacturer:		Acute Care:		Diagnostics:		Home Health:	
Managed Care:	Y	Distributor:		Distributor:		Sub-Acute:		Labs/Testing:		Long-Term Care:	
Utilization Management:	Y	Specialty Pharmacy:		Leasing/Finance:		Outpatient Surgery:		Staffing:		Physical Therapy:	
Payment Processing:	Y	Vitamins/Nutritionals:		Information Systems:		Physical Rehab. Ctr.:		Waste Disposal:		Physician Prac. Mgmt.:	
		Clinical Trials:				Psychiatric Clinics:		Specialty Svcs.:	Y		

TYPES OF BUSINESS:

Insurance-Medical & Health, HMOs & PPOs
Dental & Vision Plans
Pharmacy Programs
POS
Life Insurance

BRANDS/DIVISIONS/AFFILIATES:

Cerulean Companies Inc
Group Benefits of Georgia Inc
Greater Georgia Life Insurance Company Inc
WellPoint Health Networks Inc
Blue Value
FlexPlus
BlueChoice Vision
Healthy Extensions

CONTACTS: *Note: Officers with more than one job title may be intentionally listed here more than once.*

Monye Connolly, Gen. Mgr.
Monye Connolly, Pres.
Lynn Welborn, Dir.-Sales
Darlene Andrews, Dir.-Human Resources
Carter Beck, VP-Legal
Doris Anderson, Staff VP-Oper.
Merri Rivers, VP-Network Management
Louise Cherry, Dir.-eBusiness
Cindy Sanders, Dir.-Corp. Comm.

Phone: 404-842-8000 **Fax:** 404-842-8100
Toll-Free:
Address: 3350 Peachtree Rd. NE, Atlanta, GA 30326 US

GROWTH PLANS/SPECIAL FEATURES:

Blue Cross Blue Shield of Georgia provides comprehensive health insurance and related services to a membership of more than 2.2 million, making it one of the largest heath care coverage providers in the state. The company is a subsidiary of Well Point, Inc., a holding company created in 1996 for the Blue Cross Blue Shield branded affiliates, which include Blue Cross and Blue Shield Healthcare Plan of Georgia, Inc., a health maintenance organization; Group Benefits of Georgia, Inc., a general insurance agency; and Greater Georgia Life Insurance Company, a life insurer. Blue Cross Blue Shield of Georgia offers a range of plans for individuals, seniors and small and large groups to choose from. Its individual plans are offered under the names Blue Value, a range of PPO offerings, and FlexPlus, an array of traditional plans. For seniors, Blue Cross Blue Shield of Georgia offers Medicare supplements, dental plans, BlueChoice Vision (which provides discounts on eye exams, glasses, contact lenses and LASIK eye surgery) and Healthy Extensions, a program for discounts in vitamins, wellness books, videos and yoga, among other things. For small and large groups, the company offers HMO, POS, PPO, dental plans, pharmacy programs and a range of life insurance options.

FINANCIALS: **Sales and profits are in thousands of dollars—add 000 to get the full amount. 2007 Note: Financial information for 2007 was not available for all companies at press time.**

2007 Sales: $
2006 Sales: $
2005 Sales: $
2004 Sales: $
2003 Sales: $

2007 Profits: $
2006 Profits: $
2005 Profits: $
2004 Profits: $
2003 Profits: $

U.S. Stock Ticker: Subsidiary
Int'l Ticker: Int'l Exchange:
Employees: 3,000
Fiscal Year Ends: 12/31
Parent Company: WELLPOINT INC

SALARIES/BENEFITS:

Pension Plan: ESOP Stock Plan: Profit Sharing: Top Exec. Salary: $ Bonus: $
Savings Plan: Y Stock Purch. Plan: Y Second Exec. Salary: $ Bonus: $

OTHER THOUGHTS:

Apparent Women Officers or Directors: 7
Hot Spot for Advancement for Women/Minorities: Y

LOCATIONS: ("Y" = Yes)

West:	Southwest:	Midwest:	Southeast:	Northeast:	International:
			Y		

BLUE CROSS AND BLUE SHIELD OF KANSAS

www.bcbsks.com

Industry Group Code: 524114 **Ranks within this company's industry group:** Sales: Profits:

Insurance/HMO/PPO:		Drugs:		Equipment/Supplies:		Hospitals/Clinics:		Services:		Health Care:	
Insurance:	Y	Manufacturer:		Manufacturer:		Acute Care:		Diagnostics:		Home Health:	
Managed Care:	Y	Distributor:		Distributor:		Sub-Acute:		Labs/Testing:		Long-Term Care:	
Utilization Management:		Specialty Pharmacy:		Leasing/Finance:		Outpatient Surgery:		Staffing:		Physical Therapy:	
Payment Processing:	Y	Vitamins/Nutritionals:		Information Systems:		Physical Rehab. Ctr.:		Waste Disposal:		Physician Prac. Mgmt.:	
		Clinical Trials:				Psychiatric Clinics:		Specialty Svcs.:			

TYPES OF BUSINESS:

Insurance-Medical & Health, HMOs & PPOs
Life, Disability & Accidental Death Insurance
Medicare Claims Processing
Electronic Claims Clearinghouse

BRANDS/DIVISIONS/AFFILIATES:

Premier Health, Inc.
Premier Blue
Advance Insurance Company of Kansas
Administrative Services of Kansas, Inc.

CONTACTS: *Note: Officers with more than one job title may be intentionally listed here more than once.*

Andy Corbin, CEO
Andy Corbin, Pres.
Andrew C. Corbin, VP-External Sales & Provider Affairs
Matthew D. All, General Counsel
Beryl Lowery-Born, VP-Finance
William H. Pitsenberger, Sr. VP
Shelley Pittman, VP-Internal Sales & Member Rel.
Ralph H. Weber, VP-Medical Affairs
James M. Alley III, Chmn.

Phone: 785-291-7000 **Fax:** 785-290-0711
Toll-Free: 800-432-3990
Address: 1133 SW Topeka Blvd., Topeka, KS 66629-0001 US

GROWTH PLANS/SPECIAL FEATURES:

Blue Cross and Blue Shield of Kansas, Inc. (BCBSK), an independent member of the Blue Cross and Blue Shield Association, is one of Kansas's largest health insurance providers, serving close to 890,000 members. As a mutual insurance company, the firm is owned by its policyholders. The company also provides Medicare claims processing services to Kansas, Missouri and Nebraska. In addition, the company is a subcontractor in Kansas for TRICARE, the U.S. military health system. BCBSK operates four subsidiaries: Wheatlands Administrative Services, Inc.; Premier Health, Inc. (d.b.a. Premier Blue); Advance Insurance Company of Kansas (AICK); and Administrative Services of Kansas, Inc. (ASK). Wheatlands Administrative Services handles all current and future Medicare business. Premier Blue is a for-profit HMO with more than 40,000 members in Kansas. AICK underwrites ancillary coverage, such as group term life, disability and accidental death, in the firm's service area. ASK leases and sells computer hardware and software for the company's paperless claims network. A subsidiary of ASK, EDI Midwest, is an electronic claims clearinghouse used by more than 800 insurance carriers.

The firm provides its employees with flexible spending accounts, cancer insurance, tuition reimbursement, health/wellness programs, free parking, adoption assistance, a 401(k) savings plan, retirement benefits and discounts on various retail stores, day care centers, fitness centers, restaurants and movie theaters. In addition, the company's main campus boasts an on-site credit union and cafeteria.

FINANCIALS: **Sales and profits are in thousands of dollars—add 000 to get the full amount. 2007 Note: Financial information for 2007 was not available for all companies at press time.**

2007 Sales: $ | 2007 Profits: $
2006 Sales: $ | 2006 Profits: $
2005 Sales: $ | 2005 Profits: $
2004 Sales: $1,100,000 | 2004 Profits: $
2003 Sales: $1,125,400 | 2003 Profits: $100,600

U.S. Stock Ticker: Nonprofit
Int'l Ticker: Int'l Exchange:
Employees: 1,940
Fiscal Year Ends: 12/31
Parent Company:

SALARIES/BENEFITS:

Pension Plan: Y | ESOP Stock Plan: | Profit Sharing: | Top Exec. Salary: $ | Bonus: $
Savings Plan: Y | Stock Purch. Plan: | | Second Exec. Salary: $ | Bonus: $

OTHER THOUGHTS:

Apparent Women Officers or Directors: 2
Hot Spot for Advancement for Women/Minorities: Y

LOCATIONS: ("Y" = Yes)

West:	Southwest:	Midwest:	Southeast:	Northeast:	International:
		Y			

Note: Financial information, benefits and other data can change quickly and may vary from those stated here.

BLUE CROSS AND BLUE SHIELD OF LOUISIANA

www.bcbsla.com

Industry Group Code: 524114 **Ranks within this company's industry group:** Sales: Profits:

Insurance/HMO/PPO:		Drugs:		Equipment/Supplies:		Hospitals/Clinics:		Services:		Health Care:	
Insurance:	Y	Manufacturer:		Manufacturer:		Acute Care:		Diagnostics:		Home Health:	
Managed Care:	Y	Distributor:		Distributor:		Sub-Acute:		Labs/Testing:		Long-Term Care:	
Utilization Management:		Specialty Pharmacy:		Leasing/Finance:		Outpatient Surgery:		Staffing:		Physical Therapy:	
Payment Processing:		Vitamins/Nutritionals:		Information Systems:		Physical Rehab. Ctr.:		Waste Disposal:		Physician Prac. Mgmt.:	
		Clinical Trials:				Psychiatric Clinics:		Specialty Svcs.:	Y		

TYPES OF BUSINESS:

Insurance-Medical & Health, HMOs & PPOs
Life Insurance

BRANDS/DIVISIONS/AFFILIATES:

Louisiana, Inc.
Southern National Life Insurance Company, Inc.
BlueSelect
RxBLUE
Pennington Biomedical Research Center
Louisiana 2 Step
Healthcare Facts

CONTACTS:

Note: Officers with more than one job title may be intentionally listed here more than once.

Gery J. Barry, CEO
Gery J. Barry, Pres.
Peggy Scott, CFO/Exec. VP
Mike Reitz, Chief Mktg. Officer/Sr. VP
Todd Schexnayder, Sr. VP-Human Resources
James J. Carney, Chief Medical Officer/Sr. VP
Ob Soonthornsima, CIO/Sr. VP
Michele Calandro, General Counsel/Sr. VP
John Maginnis, VP-Corp. Comm.
Adam Short, Controller
Sabrina Heltz, Sr. VP-Medical Economics
Allison Young, VP-Benefits Admin.
J. Richard Williams, Sr. VP-Provider & Customer Relations
Brian Small, VP/Chief Actuary
Virgil Robinson, Jr., Chmn.

Phone: 225-295-3307 **Fax:** 225-295-2054
Toll-Free: 800-599-2583
Address: 5525 Reitz Ave., Baton Rouge, LA 70809-3802 US

GROWTH PLANS/SPECIAL FEATURES:

Blue Cross and Blue Shield of Louisiana (BCBSLA) and its subsidiary, HMO Louisiana, Inc., provide health insurance and services to more than 1 million members in Louisiana. The company also provides life insurance through Southern National Life Insurance Company, Inc. BCBSLA offers a diverse range of coverage options, including HMO, point-of service (POS) and small group coverage. BlueSelect features basic catastrophic coverage as well as inpatient and outpatient rehabilitation benefits, with a wide variety of deductibles. RxBLUE is the company's Medicare Part D program, which enrolls approximately 8,400 senior members. BCBSLA, with the Pennington Biomedical Research Center recently launched the Louisiana 2 Step program focused on providing information related to obesity, metabolic syndrome nutrition, chronic diseases and preventive medicine. Using research conducted by the Pennington Biomedical Research Center, BCBSLA has created a website as part of its Louisiana 2 Step program, www.louisiana2step.com, focused on providing information and assistance for managing health. The Louisiana 2 Step campaign has approximately 3,200 members. In 2006, the company launched its Healthcare Facts website, www.HealthcareFacts.org, a free resource for comparing cost, quality, safety and other information provided by Louisiana hospitals. BCBSLA also launched its e-prescribing pilot program in 2006, which enables physicians to write prescriptions through a handheld PDA and electronically transmit prescriptions to pharmacies. In April 2007, BCBSLA announced that it had obtained funding for its plans, developed in 2003, for the construction of a new Operations building and parking garage at its headquarters in Baton Rouge. The new operations building is scheduled for completion by the end of 2008.

FINANCIALS:

Sales and profits are in thousands of dollars—add 000 to get the full amount. 2007 Note: Financial information for 2007 was not available for all companies at press time.

2007 Sales: $
2006 Sales: $
2005 Sales: $
2004 Sales: $1,497,000
2003 Sales: $1,351,000

2007 Profits: $
2006 Profits: $
2005 Profits: $
2004 Profits: $
2003 Profits: $

U.S. Stock Ticker: Nonprofit
Int'l Ticker: Int'l Exchange:
Employees:
Fiscal Year Ends: 12/31
Parent Company:

SALARIES/BENEFITS:

Pension Plan: ESOP Stock Plan: Profit Sharing: Top Exec. Salary: $ Bonus: $
Savings Plan: Stock Purch. Plan: Second Exec. Salary: $ Bonus: $

OTHER THOUGHTS:

Apparent Women Officers or Directors: 5
Hot Spot for Advancement for Women/Minorities: Y

LOCATIONS: ("Y" = Yes)

West:	Southwest:	Midwest:	Southeast:	Northeast:	International:
			Y		

Note: Financial information, benefits and other data can change quickly and may vary from those stated here.

BLUE CROSS AND BLUE SHIELD OF MASSACHUSETTS

www.bcbsma.com

Industry Group Code: 524114 **Ranks within this company's industry group:** Sales: 25 Profits: 16

Insurance/HMO/PPO:		Drugs:		Equipment/Supplies:		Hospitals/Clinics:		Services:		Health Care:	
Insurance:	Y	Manufacturer:		Manufacturer:		Acute Care:		Diagnostics:		Home Health:	
Managed Care:	Y	Distributor:		Distributor:		Sub-Acute:		Labs/Testing:		Long-Term Care:	
Utilization Management:		Specialty Pharmacy:		Leasing/Finance:		Outpatient Surgery:		Staffing:		Physical Therapy:	
Payment Processing:		Vitamins/Nutritionals:		Information Systems:		Physical Rehab. Ctr.:		Waste Disposal:		Physician Prac. Mgmt.:	
		Clinical Trials:				Psychiatric Clinics:		Specialty Svcs.:			

TYPES OF BUSINESS:

Insurance-Medical & Health, HMOs & PPOs
Indemnity Insurance
Insurance-Dental
Medicare Extension Programs

BRANDS/DIVISIONS/AFFILIATES:

Associated Hospital Service Corp. of Massachusetts
HMO Blue
HMO Blue New England
Blue Choice New England
Medex
MedsInfo-ED

CONTACTS: *Note: Officers with more than one job title may be intentionally listed here more than once.*

Cleve L. Killingsworth, CEO
Cleve L. Killingsworth, Pres.
Allen P. Maltz, CFO/Exec. VP
Stephen R. Booma, Exec. VP-Sales & Mktg.
Stephen R. Booma, Exec. VP-IT & Service
Sandra L. Jesse, Chief Legal Officer/Exec. VP
Vinod K. Sahney, Chief Strategy Officer/Sr. VP
Peter Meade, Exec. VP-Corp. Affairs
John A. Fallon, Chief Physician Exec.
Andrew Dreyfus, Exec. VP-Health Care Services
John Schoenbaum, Chief-Staff Exec. Office
Cleve L. Killingsworth, Chmn.

Phone: 617-246-5000 **Fax:** 617-246-4832
Toll-Free: 800-262-2583
Address: Landmark Center, 401 Park Dr., Boston, MA 00215-3326 US

GROWTH PLANS/SPECIAL FEATURES:

Blue Cross and Blue Shield of Massachusetts (BCBSMA) is an independent, not-for-profit health care company that provides health services and insurance in Massachusetts. The firm began as the Associated Hospital Service Corporation of Massachusetts in 1937 and is now New England's largest health plan provider, with approximately 3 million members, approximately 1.3 million HMO members, approximately 18,000 participating HMO physicians and 69 participating HMO acute care hospitals, providing a wide range of health care programs, educational services and insurance plans. Insurance plans include indemnity insurance, dental plans, HMOs, PPOs and Medicare extension programs under the names HMO Blue, HMO Blue New England, Blue Choice New England and Medex. Customers receive health care coverage through a range of employer-sponsored group plans, non-group and senior citizen programs and individual and family plans. The company has joined with other regional Blue Cross and Blue Shield companies to offer additional plans through HMO Blue New England and Blue Choice New England, which include discounts for healthy living and some health clubs. The firm uses new patient safety tool called MedsInfo-ED, an electronic health information exchange project with hospitals and emergency medical teams, for patient information.

Employee benefits include a 401(k) savings plan, tuition reimbursement, child and elder care, health and eyewear discounts, an employee assistance program, a 529 education savings plan, a health management program, fitness center reimbursement and health, dental and vision coverage.

FINANCIALS: Sales and profits are in thousands of dollars—add 000 to get the full amount. 2007 Note: Financial information for 2007 was not available for all companies at press time.

2007 Sales: $	2007 Profits: $	**U.S. Stock Ticker: Nonprofit**
2006 Sales: $2,097,457	2006 Profits: $157,250	**Int'l Ticker:** Int'l Exchange:
2005 Sales: $1,976,829	2005 Profits: $123,723	Employees: 3,850
2004 Sales: $4,927,604	2004 Profits: $242,762	Fiscal Year Ends: 12/31
2003 Sales: $4,298,194	2003 Profits: $232,309	Parent Company:

SALARIES/BENEFITS:

Pension Plan: Y	ESOP Stock Plan:	Profit Sharing:	Top Exec. Salary: $	Bonus: $
Savings Plan: Y	Stock Purch. Plan:		Second Exec. Salary: $	Bonus: $

OTHER THOUGHTS:

Apparent Women Officers or Directors: 2
Hot Spot for Advancement for Women/Minorities:

LOCATIONS: ("Y" = Yes)

West:	Southwest:	Midwest:	Southeast:	Northeast:	International:
				Y	

BLUE CROSS AND BLUE SHIELD OF MICHIGAN

www.bcbsm.com

Industry Group Code: 524114 **Ranks within this company's industry group:** Sales: 9 Profits: 26

Insurance/HMO/PPO:		Drugs:		Equipment/Supplies:		Hospitals/Clinics:		Services:		Health Care:	
Insurance:	Y	Manufacturer:		Manufacturer:		Acute Care:		Diagnostics:		Home Health:	
Managed Care:	Y	Distributor:		Distributor:		Sub-Acute:		Labs/Testing:		Long-Term Care:	
Utilization Management:	Y	Specialty Pharmacy:		Leasing/Finance:		Outpatient Surgery:		Staffing:		Physical Therapy:	
Payment Processing:		Vitamins/Nutritionals:		Information Systems:		Physical Rehab. Ctr.:		Waste Disposal:		Physician Prac. Mgmt.:	
		Clinical Trials:				Psychiatric Clinics:		Specialty Svcs.:			

TYPES OF BUSINESS:

Insurance-Medical & Health, HMOs & PPOs
Workers Compensation
Dental & Vision Insurance
Health Care Management Services
Prescription Drug Plans

BRANDS/DIVISIONS/AFFILIATES:

Blue Care Network of Michigan
Blue Elect
Blue Care Network HMO
Blue Traditional
Blue Prefferred PPO
Blue Choice POS
Blue Vision PPO

CONTACTS: *Note: Officers with more than one job title may be intentionally listed here more than once.*

Daniel J. Loepp, CEO
Daniel J. Loepp, Pres.
Mark R. Bartlett, CFO/Exec. VP
Kenneth R. Dallafior, Sr. VP-Group Sales & Corp. Mktg.
Darrell E. Middleton, Sr. VP-Human Resources
Lisa S. DeMoss, General Counsel/Sr. VP
Carolynn Walton, Treas./VP
Mark R. Bartlett, Pres., Emerging Markets
Leslie A. Viegas, Exec. VP-Auto, Federal Programs &Bus. Intelligence
Tricia Keith, Corp. Sec./VP-Svcs.
J. Paul Austin, Sr. VP/Chief Actuarial Officer

Phone: 313-225-9000	**Fax:** 313-225-5629
Toll-Free:	
Address: 600 E. Lafayette Blvd., Detroit, MI 48226 US	

GROWTH PLANS/SPECIAL FEATURES:

Blue Cross Blue Shield of Michigan (BCBSM) is a not-for profit organization and one of the nation's top Blue Cross Blue Shield health insurance associations, serving nearly 4.7 million members. The firm's insurance plans include Blue Traditional, Blue Preferred and Community Blue PPOs, Blue Choice POS and BCN HMO. Blue Care Network of Michigan (BCNM) is one of the largest statewide HMO networks in Michigan. It operates the company's BCN (Blue Care Network) HMO, which encompasses more than 3,100 primary care physicians, 7,600 specialists and 110 hospitals, serving more than 500,000 members. BCNM also provides traditional indemnity and supplemental Medicare, as well as wellness and disease management services to its members. In addition, BCBSM offers Community, Traditional and Exclusive Dental; Blue Vision PPO; Preferred Rx, Traditional Rx and Blue MedSave; and Medicare supplement coverage, as well as workers' compensation insurance, health assessment and health care management services.

FINANCIALS: Sales and profits are in thousands of dollars—add 000 to get the full amount. 2007 Note: Financial information for 2007 was not available for all companies at press time.

2007 Sales: $	2007 Profits: $	**U.S. Stock Ticker: Nonprofit**
2006 Sales: $8,686,500	2006 Profits: $-14,100	**Int'l Ticker:** Int'l Exchange:
2005 Sales: $8,150,600	2005 Profits: $189,100	Employees: 8,500
2004 Sales: $8,044,200	2004 Profits: $411,000	Fiscal Year Ends:
2003 Sales: $7,909,100	2003 Profits: $174,000	Parent Company:

SALARIES/BENEFITS:

Pension Plan:	ESOP Stock Plan:	Profit Sharing:	Top Exec. Salary: $	Bonus: $
Savings Plan:	Stock Purch. Plan:		Second Exec. Salary: $	Bonus: $

OTHER THOUGHTS:

Apparent Women Officers or Directors: 14
Hot Spot for Advancement for Women/Minorities: Y

LOCATIONS: ("Y" = Yes)

West:	Southwest:	Midwest:	Southeast:	Northeast:	International:
		Y			

Note: Financial information, benefits and other data can change quickly and may vary from those stated here.

BLUE CROSS AND BLUE SHIELD OF MINNESOTA

www.bluecrossmn.com

Industry Group Code: 524114 **Ranks within this company's industry group:** Sales: 12 Profits: 24

Insurance/HMO/PPO:		Drugs:		Equipment/Supplies:		Hospitals/Clinics:		Services:		Health Care:	
Insurance:	Y	Manufacturer:		Manufacturer:		Acute Care:		Diagnostics:		Home Health:	
Managed Care:	Y	Distributor:		Distributor:		Sub-Acute:		Labs/Testing:		Long-Term Care:	
Utilization Management:		Specialty Pharmacy:		Leasing/Finance:		Outpatient Surgery:		Staffing:		Physical Therapy:	
Payment Processing:		Vitamins/Nutritionals:		Information Systems:		Physical Rehab. Ctr.:		Waste Disposal:		Physician Prac. Mgmt.:	
		Clinical Trials:				Psychiatric Clinics:		Specialty Svcs.:	Y		

TYPES OF BUSINESS:

Insurance-Medical & Health, HMOs & PPOs
Managed Care
Insurance-Life
Investment Management
Pharmacy Benefit Management
Behavioral Health Services
Workers' Compensation

BRANDS/DIVISIONS/AFFILIATES:

Blue Cross Blue Shield Association
Blue Plus
Cross and Blue Shield Associati
BCBSM Foundation
First Plan of Minnesota
Consumer Aware
Healthcare Facts
MII Life, Inc.
Prevention Minnesota

CONTACTS: *Note: Officers with more than one job title may be intentionally listed here more than once.*

Mark W. Banks, CEO
Colleen Reitan, COO
Colleen Reitan, Pres.
Timothy M. Peterson, CFO/Sr. VP
Richard Neuner, Chief Mktg. Officer/Sr. VP
Roger Kleppe, Sr. VP-Human Resources & Facilities Svcs.
David W. Plocher, Chief Medical Officer
David W. Plocher, Sr. VP-Health Mgmt. & Informatics
Scott Lynch, Chief Legal Officer/Sr. VP
Denise McKenna, Sr. VP-Oper.
Michael Morrow, Sr. VP-Bus. Dev. & Network Mgmt.
Kathleen Mock, VP-Public Affairs
Patricia Riley, Sr. VP-Gov't Programs
Marsha Shotley, VP-Board & Community Rel.
MaryAnn Stump, Sr. VP/Chief Innovation Officer

Phone: 615-662-8000	**Fax:** 615-622-2777
Toll-Free: 800-382-2000	
Address: 3535 Blue Cross Rd., Eagan, MN 55122-1154 US	

GROWTH PLANS/SPECIAL FEATURES:

Blue Cross Blue Shield of Minnesota (BCBSM), founded in 1933, operates health insurance plans for Minnesota and has more than 2.7 million members. The firm is a member of the Blue Cross Blue Shield Association and offers medical, dental, life, indemnity and short-term insurance. Insurance plans include HMOs, such as Blue Plus; PPOs; and Medicare supplementals for corporations, groups and individuals. BCBSM has over 125,000 government-sponsored program members and approximately 184,000 Medicare program members. The Blue Cross and Blue Shield of Minnesota Foundation is the largest grant-making foundation in Minnesota, focused on early childhood development, housing, social connectedness and the environment. First Plan of Minnesota is BCBSM's affiliated regional HMO based in northeastern Minnesota. BCBSM's Consumer Aware program offers Healthcare Facts, which provides information on hospitals and clinics. MII Life, Inc. is an affiliated Minnesota stock insurance corporation authorized to write life insurance in Minnesota. SupportSource, Inc. is a not-for-profit affiliate of BCBSM that provides employee assistance programs. The company also has a number of affiliates not licensed by the Blue Cross and Blue Shield Association that cover behavioral health services, fixed-income investment management, health insurance, life insurance/long-term care, pharmacy benefits management and workers' compensation. In January 2006, BCBSM launched Prevention Minnesota, a long-term health improvement initiative focused on addressing the problems of tobacco use, physical inactivity and poor nutrition. In August 2007, the company introduced a new health plan, Simply Blue, tailored for young adults.

Employee benefits include free on-site fitness centers, an on-site daycare, an on-site cafeteria, free parking, casual dress code, flexible work schedules, fitness center discounts, a stop-smoking program, eyewear discounts, Weight Watchers meetings, flexible spending accounts, credit union membership, tuition reimbursement, employee workshops, seminar allowances and medical and dental insurance.

FINANCIALS: **Sales and profits are in thousands of dollars—add 000 to get the full amount. 2007 Note: Financial information for 2007 was not available for all companies at press time.**

2007 Sales: $	2007 Profits: $	**U.S. Stock Ticker: Nonprofit**
2006 Sales: $7,865,816	2006 Profits: $4,921	**Int'l Ticker:** Int'l Exchange:
2005 Sales: $7,115,307	2005 Profits: $55,577	Employees: 4,000
2004 Sales: $6,568,289	2004 Profits: $65,839	Fiscal Year Ends: 12/31
2003 Sales: $5,983,900	2003 Profits: $149,886	Parent Company:

SALARIES/BENEFITS:

Pension Plan:	ESOP Stock Plan:	Profit Sharing:	Top Exec. Salary: $	Bonus: $
Savings Plan: Y	Stock Purch. Plan:		Second Exec. Salary: $	Bonus: $

OTHER THOUGHTS:

Apparent Women Officers or Directors: 9
Hot Spot for Advancement for Women/Minorities: Y

LOCATIONS: ("Y" = Yes)

West:	Southwest:	Midwest:	Southeast:	Northeast:	International:
		Y			

Note: Financial information, benefits and other data can change quickly and may vary from those stated here.

BLUE CROSS AND BLUE SHIELD OF MONTANA

www.bcbsmt.com

Industry Group Code: 524114 **Ranks within this company's industry group:** Sales: Profits:

Insurance/HMO/PPO:		Drugs:		Equipment/Supplies:		Hospitals/Clinics:		Services:		Health Care:	
Insurance:	Y	Manufacturer:		Manufacturer:		Acute Care:		Diagnostics:		Home Health:	
Managed Care:	Y	Distributor:		Distributor:		Sub-Acute:		Labs/Testing:		Long-Term Care:	
Utilization Management:		Specialty Pharmacy:		Leasing/Finance:		Outpatient Surgery:		Staffing:		Physical Therapy:	
Payment Processing:		Vitamins/Nutritionals:		Information Systems:		Physical Rehab. Ctr.:		Waste Disposal:		Physician Prac. Mgmt.:	
		Clinical Trials:				Psychiatric Clinics:		Specialty Svcs.:			

TYPES OF BUSINESS:

Insurance-Medical & Health, HMOs & PPOs

BRANDS/DIVISIONS/AFFILIATES:

Caring Foundation of Montana, Inc.
Combined Benefits Management, Inc.

CONTACTS: *Note: Officers with more than one job title may be intentionally listed here more than once.*

Sherry L. Cladouhos, CEO
Sheila Shapiro, COO/Exec. VP
Sherry L. Cladouhos, Pres.
Eric L. Schindler, CFO
Randal C. Cline, VP/Chief Mktg. Exec.
Sheldon C. Boe, VP-Info. Svcs.
Richard S. Miltenberger, Sr. Dir.-Underwriting & Prod. Dev.
Terry Cosgrove, General Counsel
Jane M. Delong, VP-Strategic Planning & Corp. Resources
Linda McGillen, Dir.-Corp. Comm.
Kirk A. Smith, VP/Chief Actuary
Mark A. Burzynski, VP-Health Affairs
Michael E. Frank, VP-Compliance & Corp. Integrity
Jerry Lusk, Chmn.

Phone: 406-444-8200	**Fax:** 406-447-3454
Toll-Free: 800-447-7828	
Address: 560 N. Park Ave., Helena, MT 59604 US	

GROWTH PLANS/SPECIAL FEATURES:

Blue Cross Blue Shield of Montana, Inc. (BCBSMT), provides over 240,000 members with a full spectrum of health care coverage, including prepaid health plans that cover hospital expenses and plans to cover physician services. More than 1,800 licensed physicians, approximately 93% of Montana's physicians, are BCBSMT providers. In addition, all of Montana's 59 hospitals, 2,300 allied health care professionals and 250 other facilities are associated with the firm. Subsidiaries include the Caring Foundation of Montana, which offers health coverage for children and mammograms and prostate screening for adults in low-income families, and Combined Benefits Management. Through partnerships with community-based health care providers in western, north-central and southwestern Montana, BCBSMT members can choose their own primary care doctor. MontanaHealth and MontanaCare are partnerships the company has established with doctors and hospitals, which give its members a choice of physicians that offer personalized health care. Other programs the firm is involved in include being one of Montana's lead carriers of the Montana Comprehensive Health Association aimed at the state's high-risk customers; and the Caring Foundation of Montana, Inc., which provides preventative health medicine for lower-income families.

BCBSMT offers its employees earned personal time, tuition reimbursement, an employee assistance program, a defined contribution retirement plan and a 401(k) savings plan.

FINANCIALS: **Sales and profits are in thousands of dollars—add 000 to get the full amount. 2007 Note: Financial information for 2007 was not available for all companies at press time.**

2007 Sales: $	2007 Profits: $	**U.S. Stock Ticker: Nonprofit**
2006 Sales: $	2006 Profits: $	**Int'l Ticker:** Int'l Exchange:
2005 Sales: $536,426	2005 Profits: $10,767	Employees: 1,000
2004 Sales: $511,921	2004 Profits: $3,706	Fiscal Year Ends: 12/31
2003 Sales: $478,310	2003 Profits: $17,798	Parent Company:

SALARIES/BENEFITS:

Pension Plan: Y	ESOP Stock Plan:	Profit Sharing:	Top Exec. Salary: $	Bonus: $
Savings Plan: Y	Stock Purch. Plan:		Second Exec. Salary: $	Bonus: $

OTHER THOUGHTS:

Apparent Women Officers or Directors: 4
Hot Spot for Advancement for Women/Minorities: Y

LOCATIONS: ("Y" = Yes)

West:	Southwest:	Midwest:	Southeast:	Northeast:	International:
Y					

BLUE CROSS AND BLUE SHIELD OF NEBRASKA
www.bcbsne.com

Industry Group Code: 524114 **Ranks within this company's industry group:** Sales: Profits:

Insurance/HMO/PPO:		Drugs:		Equipment/Supplies:		Hospitals/Clinics:		Services:		Health Care:	
Insurance:	Y	Manufacturer:		Manufacturer:		Acute Care:		Diagnostics:		Home Health:	
Managed Care:	Y	Distributor:		Distributor:		Sub-Acute:		Labs/Testing:		Long-Term Care:	
Utilization Management:		Specialty Pharmacy:		Leasing/Finance:		Outpatient Surgery:		Staffing:		Physical Therapy:	
Payment Processing:		Vitamins/Nutritionals:		Information Systems:		Physical Rehab. Ctr.:		Waste Disposal:		Physician Prac. Mgmt.:	
		Clinical Trials:				Psychiatric Clinics:		Specialty Svcs.:			

TYPES OF BUSINESS:
Insurance-Medical & Health, HMOs & PPOs
POS
Dental Insurance
Medicare Supplemental Insurance
Alternative Healing Benefits

BRANDS/DIVISIONS/AFFILIATES:
BluePreferred
Rx Nebraska
BluePrime
BlueClassic
BlueChoice
NaturalBlue
MedicareBlue Solutions
Primary Care+

CONTACTS: *Note: Officers with more than one job title may be intentionally listed here more than once.*
Steven S. Martin, CEO
Steven S. Martin, Pres.
Dwayne Wilson, CFO
Sarah Waldman, VP-Human Resources & Ethical Practices
Steve Grandfield, CIO
Russ Collins, Associate General Cousel/VP-Provider Contracts
Bobby Buls, VP-Special Project Implementation
Jerry Feilmeier, VP-Government Programs
Lee Handke, VP-Health Network & Wellness Svcs.
William (Bill) Minier, VP-Medical Policy/Medical Dir.

Phone: 402-390-1820 **Fax:** 402-398-3736
Toll-Free: 800-642-8980
Address: 7261 Mercy Rd., Omaha, NE 68180 US

GROWTH PLANS/SPECIAL FEATURES:
BlueCross BlueShield of Nebraska (BCBSN) provides health services to about 550,000 Nebraskans, representing over one-third of the state's population. Its network of BluePreferred hospitals, physicians and other health care professionals is the state's largest, encompassing every non-governmental acute care hospital in the state and 93% of physicians. The company's Rx Nebraska network includes 448 pharmacies statewide and 55,468 pharmacies nationwide. BCBSN offers a number of health plans, including its BluePrime HMO, BlueClassic traditional major medical, BlueChoice POS plans, dental, MedicareBlue Solutions and Primary Care+ plan for low and moderate income families. It also provides plans designed specifically for Nebraska Farm Bureau members and Comprehensive Health Insurance Pool plans for individuals who have difficulty purchasing a policy because of medical problems. The company also provides the Coverage Advisor, a free online tool for comparing insurance plans. BCBSN's BlueCard Program processes health care claims members incur while traveling outside of Nebraska. In addition, its NaturalBlue discount program provides reduced-rate massages, acupuncture, wellness products and fitness club memberships and its BlueCard program provides medical services to members traveling outside Nebraska. In June 2006, BCBSN and the Greater Omaha Chamber of Commerce launched ChamberBlue, a small group product offering 13 coverage plans designed exclusively for members of the Greater Omaha Chamber of Commerce with two to 50 employees.

FINANCIALS: **Sales and profits are in thousands of dollars—add 000 to get the full amount. 2007 Note: Financial information for 2007 was not available for all companies at press time.**

2007 Sales: $	2007 Profits: $	**U.S. Stock Ticker: Nonprofit**
2006 Sales: $	2006 Profits: $	**Int'l Ticker:** Int'l Exchange:
2005 Sales: $	2005 Profits: $	Employees: 985
2004 Sales: $	2004 Profits: $	Fiscal Year Ends: 12/31
2003 Sales: $705,600	2003 Profits: $45,800	Parent Company:

SALARIES/BENEFITS:

Pension Plan:	ESOP Stock Plan:	Profit Sharing:	Top Exec. Salary: $	Bonus: $
Savings Plan:	Stock Purch. Plan:		Second Exec. Salary: $	Bonus: $

OTHER THOUGHTS:
Apparent Women Officers or Directors:
Hot Spot for Advancement for Women/Minorities:

LOCATIONS: ("Y" = Yes)

West:	Southwest:	Midwest:	Southeast:	Northeast:	International:
		Y			

BLUE CROSS AND BLUE SHIELD OF NORTH CAROLINA

www.bcbsnc.com

Industry Group Code: 524114 **Ranks within this company's industry group:** Sales: 18 Profits: 13

Insurance/HMO/PPO:		Drugs:		Equipment/Supplies:		Hospitals/Clinics:		Services:		Health Care:	
Insurance:	Y	Manufacturer:		Manufacturer:		Acute Care:		Diagnostics:		Home Health:	
Managed Care:	Y	Distributor:		Distributor:		Sub-Acute:		Labs/Testing:		Long-Term Care:	
Utilization Management:		Specialty Pharmacy:		Leasing/Finance:		Outpatient Surgery:		Staffing:		Physical Therapy:	
Payment Processing:		Vitamins/Nutritionals:		Information Systems:		Physical Rehab. Ctr.:		Waste Disposal:		Physician Prac. Mgmt.:	
		Clinical Trials:				Psychiatric Clinics:		Specialty Svcs.:			

TYPES OF BUSINESS:

Insurance-Medical & Health, HMOs & PPOs
Dental Insurance
Life Insurance

BRANDS/DIVISIONS/AFFILIATES:

BlueAdvantage
DentalBlue
BlueCare
BlueOptions
ClassicBlue
Partners National Health Plans of North Carolina
Group Insurance Services, Inc.
Behavioral Health Resources, Inc.

CONTACTS: *Note: Officers with more than one job title may be intentionally listed here more than once.*

Robert Greczyn, Jr., CEO
J. Bradley Wilson, COO
Robert Greczyn, Jr., Pres.
Daniel E. Glaser, CFO
John T. Roos, Chief Sales & Mktg. Officer
Maureen K. O'Connor, Chief Admin. Officer
Maureen K. O'Connor, General Counsel/Corp. Sec.

Phone: 919-489-7431 **Fax:** 919-765-7818
Toll-Free: 800-250-3630
Address: 5901 Chapel Hill Rd., Durham, NC 27707 US

GROWTH PLANS/SPECIAL FEATURES:

Blue Cross Blue Shield of North Carolina is a nonprofit mutual insurance company providing comprehensive health insurance and related services to a membership of more than 3.4 million members throughout North Carolina. The company offers short- and long-term care; Medicare supplement; BlueAdvantage, for individuals interested in low co-payments for doctor visits with the freedom to choose between doctors; DentalBlue, allowing the freedom to choose any North Carolina dentist; BlueCare, an HMO with flexible benefit plan design; BlueOptions, a PPO; ClassicBlue, a major medical plan; small group coverage; and life insurance and other ancillary plans. The BlueExtras program provides members with a variety of services at no added cost, including discounts on medicine services, hearing aids and vitamin supplements; cash back on online shopping; discounts on corrective laser eye surgery, nutrition and fitness information resources; and discounts and information on cosmetic surgery. The BlueCard Program allows members to submit claims while traveling outside of their plan's area, including a network of participating hospitals around the world. Blue Cross Blue Shield of North Carolina also operates two subsidiaries that sell their own health insurance: Partners National Health Plans of North Carolina, Inc. and Group Insurance Services, Inc.

FINANCIALS: **Sales and profits are in thousands of dollars—add 000 to get the full amount. 2007 Note: Financial information for 2007 was not available for all companies at press time.**

2007 Sales: $	2007 Profits: $	**U.S. Stock Ticker: Nonprofit**
2006 Sales: $4,406,928	2006 Profits: $189,412	**Int'l Ticker:** Int'l Exchange:
2005 Sales: $3,848,309	2005 Profits: $167,552	Employees: 4,000
2004 Sales: $3,443,812	2004 Profits: $155,937	Fiscal Year Ends:
2003 Sales: $3,156,011	2003 Profits: $196,284	Parent Company:

SALARIES/BENEFITS:

Pension Plan:	ESOP Stock Plan:	Profit Sharing:	Top Exec. Salary: $	Bonus: $
Savings Plan:	Stock Purch. Plan:		Second Exec. Salary: $	Bonus: $

OTHER THOUGHTS:

Apparent Women Officers or Directors: 1
Hot Spot for Advancement for Women/Minorities:

LOCATIONS: ("Y" = Yes)

West:	Southwest:	Midwest:	Southeast:	Northeast:	International:
				Y	

BLUE CROSS AND BLUE SHIELD OF OKLAHOMA

www.bcbsok.com

Industry Group Code: 524114 **Ranks within this company's industry group:** Sales: Profits:

Insurance/HMO/PPO:		Drugs:		Equipment/Supplies:		Hospitals/Clinics:		Services:		Health Care:	
Insurance:	Y	Manufacturer:		Manufacturer:		Acute Care:		Diagnostics:		Home Health:	
Managed Care:	Y	Distributor:		Distributor:		Sub-Acute:		Labs/Testing:		Long-Term Care:	
Utilization Management:		Specialty Pharmacy:		Leasing/Finance:		Outpatient Surgery:		Staffing:		Physical Therapy:	
Payment Processing:		Vitamins/Nutritionals:		Information Systems:		Physical Rehab. Ctr.:		Waste Disposal:		Physician Prac. Mgmt.:	
		Clinical Trials:				Psychiatric Clinics:		Specialty Svcs.:			

TYPES OF BUSINESS:

Insurance-Medical & Health, HMOs & PPOs
Managed Care
Life Insurance
Property & Casualty Insurance
Prescription & Dental Insurance

BRANDS/DIVISIONS/AFFILIATES:

GHS Holding Company, Inc.
Member Service Life Insurance Company
Group Health Service of Oklahoma, Inc.
GHS Property and Casualty Insurance Company
GHS General Insurance Agency
Health Care Service Corporation
BlueLincs HMO
O-EPIC

CONTACTS: *Note: Officers with more than one job title may be intentionally listed here more than once.*

Rodney L. Huey, Pres.
Greg Burn, VP-Mktg. & Sales
Jerry D. Scherer, CIO
Jon Polcha, VP-Planning
Gary Trennepohl, Chmn.
Jon Polcha, VP-Bus/ Process Improvements

Phone: 918-560-3500	**Fax:** 918-560-3060
Toll-Free:	
Address: 1215 S. Boulder Ave., Tulsa, OK 74102-3283 US	

GROWTH PLANS/SPECIAL FEATURES:

Blue Cross and Blue Shield of Oklahoma (BCBSO), also known as Group Health Service of Oklahoma, is a subsidiary of Chicago-based Health Care Service Corporation (HCSC). The company is Oklahoma's oldest and largest private health insurer with 835,000 customers. The firm has been operating for 65 years as a nonprofit insurance company and a member of the Blue Cross and Blue Shield Association. BCBSO offers health, life, prescription and dental insurances, as well as Medicare supplemental insurance for corporations, groups and individuals. The firm also offers hearing aid, laser vision correction and child proofing discounts with membership. BCBSO runs all subsidiary operations through GHS Holding Company, Inc. Subsidiaries include Member Service Life Insurance Company, BlueLincs HMO, GHS Property and Casualty Insurance Company, GHS General Insurance Agency and The Oklahoma Caring Foundation. BCBSO offers the Oklahoma Employer/Employee Partnership for Insurance Coverage (O-EPIC), a premium assistance program for small business employees. O-EPIC is funded by a tobacco products tax and is available to businesses with 25 or fewer employees.

FINANCIALS: **Sales and profits are in thousands of dollars—add 000 to get the full amount. 2007 Note: Financial information for 2007 was not available for all companies at press time.**

2007 Sales: $	2007 Profits: $	**U.S. Stock Ticker: Subsidiary**
2006 Sales: $	2006 Profits: $	**Int'l Ticker:** Int'l Exchange:
2005 Sales: $	2005 Profits: $	Employees: 1,300
2004 Sales: $1,067,154	2004 Profits: $52,548	Fiscal Year Ends: 12/31
2003 Sales: $1,063,873	2003 Profits: $156,010	Parent Company: HEALTH CARE SERVICE CORPORATION

SALARIES/BENEFITS:

Pension Plan:	ESOP Stock Plan:	Profit Sharing:	Top Exec. Salary: $	Bonus: $
Savings Plan: Y	Stock Purch. Plan:		Second Exec. Salary: $	Bonus: $

OTHER THOUGHTS:

Apparent Women Officers or Directors:
Hot Spot for Advancement for Women/Minorities:

LOCATIONS: ("Y" = Yes)

West:	Southwest:	Midwest:	Southeast:	Northeast:	International:
	Y				

Note: Financial information, benefits and other data can change quickly and may vary from those stated here.

BLUE CROSS AND BLUE SHIELD OF TENNESSEE INC

www.bcbst.com

Industry Group Code: 524114 **Ranks within this company's industry group:** Sales: Profits:

Insurance/HMO/PPO:		Drugs:		Equipment/Supplies:		Hospitals/Clinics:		Services:		Health Care:	
Insurance:	Y	Manufacturer:		Manufacturer:		Acute Care:		Diagnostics:		Home Health:	
Managed Care:	Y	Distributor:		Distributor:		Sub-Acute:		Labs/Testing:		Long-Term Care:	
Utilization Management:	Y	Specialty Pharmacy:		Leasing/Finance:		Outpatient Surgery:		Staffing:		Physical Therapy:	
Payment Processing:		Vitamins/Nutritionals:		Information Systems:		Physical Rehab. Ctr.:		Waste Disposal:		Physician Prac. Mgmt.:	
		Clinical Trials:				Psychiatric Clinics:		Specialty Svcs.:			

TYPES OF BUSINESS:

Insurance-Medical & Health, HMOs & PPOs
Health & Disease Management

BRANDS/DIVISIONS/AFFILIATES:

Blue Perks
Blue Network P
Demand Generics
SimplyBlue
Volunteer State Health Plan, Inc.
Group Insurance Services, Inc.
Southern Diversified Business Services, Inc.
Gordian Health Solutions, Inc.

CONTACTS: *Note: Officers with more than one job title may be intentionally listed here more than once.*

Vicky Gregg, CEO
Vicky Gregg, Pres.
John Giblin, CFO
Jim Gray, Chief Mktg. Officer/VP
Vicki Cansler, Sr. VP-People Svcs.
Chris Levan, VP-Info. Systems
Linda Andreae, VP-Underwriting & Prod. Dev.
John Blake, VP-Bus. Eng.
Bill Young, General Counsel/Chief Compliance Officer/Sr. VP
Bob Worthington, Sr. VP-Bus. Oper.
John Shull, VP-Strategic Services
Calvin Anderson, VP-Federal & Community Rel.
Harold Cantrell, VP-Finance
Steven Coulter, Pres., Gov't Bus. & Emerging Markets
Ron Harr, Sr. VP-Gov't Programs
Joan Harp, Pres., Commercial Bus. & Established Markets
Sonya Nelson, VP-Medicaid Admin.
DeWitt Ezell, Jr., Chmn.

Phone: 423-755-5600 **Fax:** 423-755-5792
Toll-Free: 800-565-9140
Address: 801 Pine St., Chattanooga, TN 37402-2555 US

GROWTH PLANS/SPECIAL FEATURES:

BlueCross BlueShield of Tennessee, Inc. (BCBST) is one of the largest health benefits companies in its home state. As part of the nationwide BlueCross BlueShield Association, i offers customers the full range of Blue Cross and Blue Shield insurance products. The firm serves over 5 million people nationwide and provides benefits to more than 15,000 companies, paying over 65 million claims. Its Blue Network Plan includes more than 17,000 physicians, hospitals and pharmacies. The firm owns and operates three subsidiaries Volunteer State Health Plan, Inc., a licensed large affiliate for BlueCare HMO business; Group Insurance Services, Inc., an agency that facilitates ancillary and flexible benefit programs; and Southern Diversified Business Services, Inc. Its Demand Generics cost-cutting program promotes use of generic drugs among BCBST's customers and offers periodic incentives for customers who choose generic over name-brand drugs. The company also offers Blue Perks, a program featuring discounts for members on massages, alternative medicine, fitness centers, LASIK and PRK vision surgery and other services. Recently, the company announced that the Tennessee Blues plan will acquire Gordian Health Solutions, a health and disease management services company and BCBST also launched SimplyBlue, a low-cost traditional deductible and coinsurance benefit plan.

BCBST provides employees with bonus and advancement opportunities, tuition reimbursement and flexible work hours.

FINANCIALS: **Sales and profits are in thousands of dollars—add 000 to get the full amount. 2007 Note: Financial information for 2007 was not available for all companies at press time.**

2007 Sales: $	2007 Profits: $	**U.S. Stock Ticker: Nonprofit**
2006 Sales: $	2006 Profits: $	**Int'l Ticker:** Int'l Exchange:
2005 Sales: $	2005 Profits: $	Employees: 4,200
2004 Sales: $	2004 Profits: $	Fiscal Year Ends: 12/31
2003 Sales: $1,965,300	2003 Profits: $101,000	Parent Company:

SALARIES/BENEFITS:

Pension Plan:	ESOP Stock Plan:	Profit Sharing:	Top Exec. Salary: $	Bonus: $
Savings Plan:	Stock Purch. Plan:		Second Exec. Salary: $	Bonus: $

OTHER THOUGHTS:

Apparent Women Officers or Directors: 4
Hot Spot for Advancement for Women/Minorities: Y

LOCATIONS: ("Y" = Yes)

West:	Southwest:	Midwest:	Southeast:	Northeast:	International:
			Y		

Note: Financial information, benefits and other data can change quickly and may vary from those stated here.

BLUE CROSS AND BLUE SHIELD OF TEXAS www.bcbstx.com

Industry Group Code: 524114 **Ranks within this company's industry group:** Sales: Profits:

Insurance/HMO/PPO:		Drugs:		Equipment/Supplies:		Hospitals/Clinics:		Services:		Health Care:	
Insurance:	Y	Manufacturer:		Manufacturer:		Acute Care:		Diagnostics:		Home Health:	
Managed Care:	Y	Distributor:		Distributor:		Sub-Acute:		Labs/Testing:		Long-Term Care:	
Utilization Management:		Specialty Pharmacy:		Leasing/Finance:		Outpatient Surgery:		Staffing:		Physical Therapy:	
Payment Processing:		Vitamins/Nutritionals:		Information Systems:		Physical Rehab. Ctr.:		Waste Disposal:		Physician Prac. Mgmt.:	
		Clinical Trials:				Psychiatric Clinics:		Specialty Svcs.:			

TYPES OF BUSINESS:

Insurance-Medical & Health, HMOs & PPOs
POS
Behavioral Health & Dental Insurance
Medicare Supplement Plan

BRANDS/DIVISIONS/AFFILIATES:

Health Care Service Corporation
HMO Blue Texas
Magellan Behavioral Health
BlueEdge PPO
Select Blue Advantage PPO
SelecTEMP
Select Saver
Dental Indemnity USA

CONTACTS: *Note: Officers with more than one job title may be intentionally listed here more than once.*

Martin G. Foster, Pres.
Margaret Jarvis, Media Contact

Phone: 972-766-6900	**Fax:** 972-766-6234
Toll-Free:	
Address: 901 S. Central Expy., Richardson, TX 75080 US	

GROWTH PLANS/SPECIAL FEATURES:

Blue Cross and Blue Shield of Texas (BCBSTX), a division of Health Care Service Corporation, is a not-for-profit insurer serving more than 4 million members throughout all 254 Texas counties. The company's health care provider network consists of more than 36,000 physicians and 400 hospitals across Texas. The firm places great emphasis on preventive medicine in order to control operating costs. Its group health insurance products include HMO Blue Texas, a PPO plan, a POS plan, Magellan Behavioral Health plan, consumer choice plans and BlueEdge PPO, while its individual health insurance products include Select Blue Advantage PPO, Select Choice PPO, Select Saver, SelecTEMP, Medicare Supplement Plan and Dental Indemnity USA. BCBSTX serves Texas companies, including Brinker International, Brookshire Grocery, the City of Houston, Continental Airlines, the Employees Retirement System of Texas, Halliburton, H.E.B. Grocery, Pilgrim's Pride, the Teacher Retirement System of Texas, the Texas A&M System, Texas Instruments, TXU and The University of Texas System.

FINANCIALS: Sales and profits are in thousands of dollars—add 000 to get the full amount. 2007 Note: Financial information for 2007 was not available for all companies at press time.

2007 Sales: $	2007 Profits: $	**U.S. Stock Ticker: Subsidiary**
2006 Sales: $	2006 Profits: $	**Int'l Ticker:** Int'l Exchange:
2005 Sales: $	2005 Profits: $	Employees: 5,700
2004 Sales: $	2004 Profits: $	Fiscal Year Ends: 12/31
2003 Sales: $2,549,000	2003 Profits: $	Parent Company: HEALTH CARE SERVICE CORPORATION

SALARIES/BENEFITS:

Pension Plan:	ESOP Stock Plan:	Profit Sharing:	Top Exec. Salary: $	Bonus: $
Savings Plan:	Stock Purch. Plan:		Second Exec. Salary: $	Bonus: $

OTHER THOUGHTS:

Apparent Women Officers or Directors:
Hot Spot for Advancement for Women/Minorities:

LOCATIONS: ("Y" = Yes)

West:	Southwest:	Midwest:	Southeast:	Northeast:	International:
	Y				

Note: Financial information, benefits and other data can change quickly and may vary from those stated here.

BLUE CROSS AND BLUE SHIELD OF VERMONT

www.bcbsvt.com

Industry Group Code: 524114 **Ranks within this company's industry group:** Sales: Profits:

Insurance/HMO/PPO:		Drugs:		Equipment/Supplies:		Hospitals/Clinics:		Services:		Health Care:	
Insurance:	Y	Manufacturer:		Manufacturer:		Acute Care:		Diagnostics:		Home Health:	
Managed Care:	Y	Distributor:		Distributor:		Sub-Acute:		Labs/Testing:		Long-Term Care:	
Utilization Management:	Y	Specialty Pharmacy:		Leasing/Finance:		Outpatient Surgery:		Staffing:		Physical Therapy:	
Payment Processing:	Y	Vitamins/Nutritionals:		Information Systems:		Physical Rehab. Ctr.:		Waste Disposal:		Physician Prac. Mgmt.:	
		Clinical Trials:				Psychiatric Clinics:		Specialty Svcs.:			

TYPES OF BUSINESS:

Insurance-Medical & Health, HMOs & PPOs
POS
Administrative Services
Case Management

BRANDS/DIVISIONS/AFFILIATES:

Vermont Freedom Plan
Vermont Health Partnership Plan
Vermont Health Plan
Comprehensive Benefits Administrators
Blue HealthSolutions
Heathwise Knowledgebase

CONTACTS: *Note: Officers with more than one job title may be intentionally listed here more than once.*

William R. Milnes, Jr., CEO
Walter Merrow, COO
William R. Milnes, Jr., Pres.
David Krupa, VP-Mktg.
Guy Boyer, Chmn.

Phone: 802-223-6131	**Fax:** 802-223-4229
Toll-Free: 800-255-4550	
Address: 445 Industrial Ln., Berlin, VT 05601 US	

GROWTH PLANS/SPECIAL FEATURES:

Blue Cross and Blue Shield of Vermont, a nonprofit organization, is the largest health insurance provider in Vermont and the only health insurance provider based in the state, serving more than 200,000 members. In addition to offering Medicare supplement, vision and dental plans, Blue Cross and Blue Shield of Vermont offers the Vermont Freedom Plan, a PPO; the Vermont Health Partnership Plan, a POS; and the Vermont Health Plan, an HMO. Subsidiary Comprehensive Benefits Administrators offers third-party administrative services. The company's Blue HealthSolutions division focuses on reducing health care costs through specialty case management, focused inpatient review, tiered and incentive programs for purchasing pharmacy drugs and decision support, among other things. The Healthwise Knowledgebase is an online resource center for members only, offering up-to-date medical information.

Along with a comprehensive suite of health, vision, life and dental insurance, BCBSVT also offers employees tuition reimbursement, fitness club membership, the STRIVE! employee encouragement program, as well as other surplus benefits.

FINANCIALS: **Sales and profits are in thousands of dollars—add 000 to get the full amount. 2007 Note: Financial information for 2007 was not available for all companies at press time.**

2007 Sales: $	2007 Profits: $	**U.S. Stock Ticker: Nonprofit**
2006 Sales: $	2006 Profits: $	**Int'l Ticker:** Int'l Exchange:
2005 Sales: $	2005 Profits: $	Employees: 300
2004 Sales: $547,016	2004 Profits: $17,251	Fiscal Year Ends: 12/31
2003 Sales: $492,947	2003 Profits: $14,295	Parent Company:

SALARIES/BENEFITS:

Pension Plan: Y	ESOP Stock Plan:	Profit Sharing:	Top Exec. Salary: $	Bonus: $
Savings Plan: Y	Stock Purch. Plan:		Second Exec. Salary: $	Bonus: $

OTHER THOUGHTS:

Apparent Women Officers or Directors: 1
Hot Spot for Advancement for Women/Minorities:

LOCATIONS: ("Y" = Yes)

West:	Southwest:	Midwest:	Southeast:	Northeast:	International:
				Y	

Note: Financial information, benefits and other data can change quickly and may vary from those stated here.

BLUE CROSS AND BLUE SHIELD OF WYOMING

www.bcbswy.com

Industry Group Code: 524114 **Ranks within this company's industry group:** Sales: Profits:

Insurance/HMO/PPO:		Drugs:		Equipment/Supplies:		Hospitals/Clinics:		Services:		Health Care:	
Insurance:	Y	Manufacturer:		Manufacturer:		Acute Care:		Diagnostics:		Home Health:	
Managed Care:	Y	Distributor:		Distributor:		Sub-Acute:		Labs/Testing:		Long-Term Care:	
Utilization Management:		Specialty Pharmacy:		Leasing/Finance:		Outpatient Surgery:		Staffing:		Physical Therapy:	
Payment Processing:		Vitamins/Nutritionals:		Information Systems:		Physical Rehab. Ctr.:		Waste Disposal:		Physician Prac. Mgmt.:	
		Clinical Trials:				Psychiatric Clinics:		Specialty Svcs.:			

TYPES OF BUSINESS:

Insurance-Medical & Health, HMOs & PPOs
Life Insurance
Annuities

BRANDS/DIVISIONS/AFFILIATES:

Employer Plan Services
Caring Foundation of Wyoming

CONTACTS:

Note: Officers with more than one job title may be intentionally listed here more than once.

Tim J. Crilly, CEO
Tim J. Crilly, Pres.
Diane Gore, CFO
Tim Crilly, Corp. Sec.
Cliff Kirk, Vice Chmn.
Dave Bonner Powell, Chmn.

Phone: 307-634-1393 **Fax:** 307-634-5742
Toll-Free: 800-442-2376
Address: 4000 House Ave., Cheyenne, WY 82001 US

GROWTH PLANS/SPECIAL FEATURES:

Blue Cross Blue Shield of Wyoming (BCBSWY) is a nonprofit insurance company and a Blue Cross Blue Shield Association member serving over a quarter of the population of Wyoming. The firm provides medical, vision and dental insurance to groups and individuals as well as Medicare supplemental coverage, group life insurance, cancer and dread disease coverage, annuities, flexible benefits administration, worksite benefits and a prescription drug program. Employer Plan Services, a subsidiary of the company, offers allied health and accident coverage. The company is the TriCare Provider for Wyoming, which covers military retirees and dependents of active duty personnel. BCBSWY covers all administrative costs for the Caring Foundation of Wyoming, which provides basic health care services to uninsured children, meets the health care needs of uninsured women and aids in the prevention of domestic violence.

Employees at BCBSWY are offered an extended illness time bank, a wellness program and educational assistance.

FINANCIALS:

Sales and profits are in thousands of dollars—add 000 to get the full amount. 2007 Note: Financial information for 2007 was not available for all companies at press time.

2007 Sales: $	2007 Profits: $	**U.S. Stock Ticker: Nonprofit**
2006 Sales: $	2006 Profits: $	**Int'l Ticker:** Int'l Exchange:
2005 Sales: $	2005 Profits: $	Employees: 200
2004 Sales: $	2004 Profits: $	Fiscal Year Ends: 12/31
2003 Sales: $	2003 Profits: $	Parent Company:

SALARIES/BENEFITS:

Pension Plan: Y	ESOP Stock Plan:	Profit Sharing:	Top Exec. Salary: $	Bonus: $
Savings Plan: Y	Stock Purch. Plan:		Second Exec. Salary: $	Bonus: $

OTHER THOUGHTS:

Apparent Women Officers or Directors: 2
Hot Spot for Advancement for Women/Minorities:

LOCATIONS: ("Y" = Yes)

West:	Southwest:	Midwest:	Southeast:	Northeast:	International:
Y					

BLUE CROSS OF CALIFORNIA www.bluecrossca.com

Industry Group Code: 524114 **Ranks within this company's industry group:** Sales: Profits:

Insurance/HMO/PPO:		Drugs:		Equipment/Supplies:		Hospitals/Clinics:		Services:		Health Care:	
Insurance:	Y	Manufacturer:		Manufacturer:		Acute Care:		Diagnostics:		Home Health:	
Managed Care:	Y	Distributor:		Distributor:		Sub-Acute:		Labs/Testing:		Long-Term Care:	
Utilization Management:		Specialty Pharmacy:		Leasing/Finance:		Outpatient Surgery:		Staffing:		Physical Therapy:	
Payment Processing:		Vitamins/Nutritionals:		Information Systems:		Physical Rehab. Ctr.:		Waste Disposal:		Physician Prac. Mgmt.:	
		Clinical Trials:				Psychiatric Clinics:		Specialty Svcs.:			

TYPES OF BUSINESS:

Insurance-Medical & Health, HMOs & PPOs
POS

BRANDS/DIVISIONS/AFFILIATES:

Medi-Cal
WellPoint Health Networks
Healthy Families Program

CONTACTS:

Note: Officers with more than one job title may be intentionally listed here more than once.

Brian Sassi, CEO
Brian Sassi, Pres.
Ron Ragland, VP-Group Sales
Josh Valdez, Sr. VP-Network Dev.
Gregory B. Baird, Sr. VP-Large Group Sales.
Ivan J. Kamil, VP/Dir.-Medical, Medical Policy & Quality
Stephen Synott, Sr. VP-Sales, Individual & Small Group Div.

Phone: 805-557-6655 **Fax:** 805-557-6872
Toll-Free: 800-333-0912
Address: 1 WellPoint Way, Thousand Oaks, CA 91362 US

GROWTH PLANS/SPECIAL FEATURES:

Blue Cross of California, a subsidiary of WellPoint Health Networks, provides health insurance and related care services to more than 7.4 million members in California. The company provides HMO, PPO and point-of-service plans, as well as Medicare and Medicaid. Blue Cross of California is the largest health plan provider of state-managed programs in California, with more than 1 million Medi-Cal (Medicaid) members in 12 counties, as well as children in all 58 California counties through the Healthy Families Program. The company's large business segment serves groups with 51 to 500,000 employees and accounts for 3.8 million medical members. The large business group also includes the state and federal employees division. The individual and small group division serves 1.6 million individuals and businesses with 50 employees or less. The seniors division, which offers various Medicare supplemental plans and Medicare risk plans, has been expanded to address needs of the aging baby-boomer population, offering prescription discount and dental programs. In addition to the Healthy Families Program, Blue Cross of California offers other state sponsored programs including, Access for Infants and Mothers (AIM) and the Major Risk Medical Insurance Program (MRMIP). The company also offers specialty products including pharmacy benefit management, long term care insurance, dental, life and disability insurance, behavioral health, utilization management, vision, flexible spending accounts and COBRA administration.

Employees of Blue Cross of California receive a full benefits package that includes tuition assistance. Company offices have a business-casual dress policy.

FINANCIALS:

Sales and profits are in thousands of dollars—add 000 to get the full amount. 2007 Note: Financial information for 2007 was not available for all companies at press time.

2007 Sales: $
2006 Sales: $
2005 Sales: $
2004 Sales: $
2003 Sales: $11,808,600

2007 Profits: $
2006 Profits: $
2005 Profits: $
2004 Profits: $
2003 Profits: $

U.S. Stock Ticker: Subsidiary
Int'l Ticker: Int'l Exchange:
Employees: 7,000
Fiscal Year Ends: 12/31
Parent Company: WELLPOINT INC

SALARIES/BENEFITS:

Pension Plan: Y
Savings Plan: Y
ESOP Stock Plan:
Stock Purch. Plan:
Profit Sharing:
Top Exec. Salary: $ Bonus: $
Second Exec. Salary: $ Bonus: $

OTHER THOUGHTS:

Apparent Women Officers or Directors: 3
Hot Spot for Advancement for Women/Minorities: Y

LOCATIONS: ("Y" = Yes)

West:	Southwest:	Midwest:	Southeast:	Northeast:	International:
Y					

BLUE CROSS OF IDAHO

www.bcidaho.com

Industry Group Code: 524114 **Ranks within this company's industry group:** Sales: Profits:

Insurance/HMO/PPO:		Drugs:		Equipment/Supplies:		Hospitals/Clinics:		Services:		Health Care:	
Insurance:	Y	Manufacturer:		Manufacturer:		Acute Care:		Diagnostics:		Home Health:	
Managed Care:	Y	Distributor:		Distributor:		Sub-Acute:		Labs/Testing:		Long-Term Care:	
Utilization Management:		Specialty Pharmacy:		Leasing/Finance:		Outpatient Surgery:		Staffing:		Physical Therapy:	
Payment Processing:		Vitamins/Nutritionals:		Information Systems:		Physical Rehab. Ctr.:		Waste Disposal:		Physician Prac. Mgmt.:	
		Clinical Trials:				Psychiatric Clinics:		Specialty Svcs.:			

TYPES OF BUSINESS:

Insurance-Medical & Health, HMOs & PPOs
Dental & Vision Insurance
Life Insurance
Health Savings Accounts

BRANDS/DIVISIONS/AFFILIATES:

BlueCare
HMOBlue
AccessBlue
PersonalBlue
DentalBlue
ClassicBlue
True Blue
ChamberBlue

CONTACTS:

Note: Officers with more than one job title may be intentionally listed here more than once.

Ray Flachbart, CEO
Ray Flachbart, Pres.
Jack A. Myers, CFO
Jerry Dworak, Sr. VP/Chief Mktg. Officer
Debra M. Henry, VP-Human Resources
Michael D. Cannon, VP-Info. Svcs.
Debra M. Henry, VP-Admin. Svcs.
Thomas B. Bassler, General Counsel/Sr. VP-Gov't Affairs
Jack A. Myers, Sr. VP-Finance
Richard M. Armstrong, Sr. VP-Sales & Mktg.
Douglas W. Dammrose, Sr. VP/Medical Dir.
Drew S. Forney, VP-Benefits Mgmt. & Member Svcs.
David J. Hutchins, VP-Actuarial Services
Jack Gustavel, Chmn.

Phone: 208-345-4550 **Fax:** 208-331-7311
Toll-Free: 800-274-4018
Address: 3000 E. Pine Ave., Meridian, ID 83642 US

GROWTH PLANS/SPECIAL FEATURES:

Blue Cross of Idaho (BCI) is Idaho's oldest health insurer, with over 408,000 members, nearly one-third of the state's population, enrolled in its traditional, PPO and managed care programs. Every hospital in Idaho and 97% of the state's physicians participate in its traditional network, while 98% of hospitals and 90% of physicians contract in its BlueCare PPO network. The company's HMOBlue managed care product is the largest in the state. BCI's other plans include AccessBlue, a lower-cost plan for small businesses; BusinessBlue, a traditional employer-sponsored plan; PersonalBlue for individuals; a DentalBlue PPO; ClassicBlue and True Blue Medicare Advantage plans; HSA Blue, a high-deductible plan designed to be compatible with health savings accounts; and health savings accounts, as well as other group products including dental, vision, life, accidental death and disability coverage. Through My Health Plan, customers can obtain personalized health insurance information via the company's web site.

BCI offers its employees medical, dental and vision care; tuition reimbursement; employee assistance; personal paid leave; flexible spending accounts; incentive programs; disability and life insurance; business casual dress code; flextime; credit union membership; company sponsored events; and on-site cafeterias and fitness centers.

FINANCIALS:

Sales and profits are in thousands of dollars—add 000 to get the full amount. 2007 Note: Financial information for 2007 was not available for all companies at press time.

2007 Sales: $	2007 Profits: $	**U.S. Stock Ticker: Nonprofit**
2006 Sales: $	2006 Profits: $	**Int'l Ticker:** Int'l Exchange:
2005 Sales: $	2005 Profits: $	Employees: 750
2004 Sales: $	2004 Profits: $	Fiscal Year Ends: 12/31
2003 Sales: $660,300	2003 Profits: $	Parent Company:

SALARIES/BENEFITS:

Pension Plan: Y	ESOP Stock Plan:	Profit Sharing:	Top Exec. Salary: $	Bonus: $
Savings Plan: Y	Stock Purch. Plan:		Second Exec. Salary: $	Bonus: $

OTHER THOUGHTS:

Apparent Women Officers or Directors: 4
Hot Spot for Advancement for Women/Minorities: Y

LOCATIONS: ("Y" = Yes)

West:	Southwest:	Midwest:	Southeast:	Northeast:	International:
Y					

Note: Financial information, benefits and other data can change quickly and may vary from those stated here.

BLUE SHIELD OF CALIFORNIA www.mylifepath.com

Industry Group Code: 524114 **Ranks within this company's industry group:** Sales: Profits:

Insurance/HMO/PPO:		Drugs:		Equipment/Supplies:		Hospitals/Clinics:		Services:		Health Care:	
Insurance:	Y	Manufacturer:		Manufacturer:		Acute Care:		Diagnostics:		Home Health:	
Managed Care:	Y	Distributor:		Distributor:		Sub-Acute:		Labs/Testing:		Long-Term Care:	
Utilization Management:		Specialty Pharmacy:		Leasing/Finance:		Outpatient Surgery:		Staffing:		Physical Therapy:	
Payment Processing:		Vitamins/Nutritionals:		Information Systems:		Physical Rehab. Ctr.:		Waste Disposal:		Physician Prac. Mgmt.:	
		Clinical Trials:				Psychiatric Clinics:		Specialty Svcs.:			

TYPES OF BUSINESS:

Insurance-Medical & Health, HMOs & PPOs
Managed Care
Life Insurance
Dental Insurance

BRANDS/DIVISIONS/AFFILIATES:

California Physician's Service
TriWest
Blue Shield of California Life & Health Insurance
Blue Shield of California Foundation
Mylifepath.com
Essential Plans 3000/4500

CONTACTS: *Note: Officers with more than one job title may be intentionally listed here more than once.*

Bruce G. Bodaken, CEO
Kenneth F. Wood, COO/Exec. VP
Bruce G. Bodaken, Pres.
Heidi Kunz, CFO/Exec. VP
Marianne Jackson, Sr. VP-Human Resources
Elinor MacKinnon, CIO
Bob Wadsworth, VP-Prod. Dev.
Charles Sweeris, VP-General Counsel
Bob Novelli, Exec. VP-Customer Services & Corporate Mktg.
Jan Vorfeld, VP-Bus. Transformation & eBusiness
Tom Epstein, VP-Public Affairs
Karman Chan, VP-Finance & Treasury Services
Eric Book, Chief Medical Officer
Peter G. Duncan, VP-Group Sales
Charles Sweeris, Chief Compliance Officer
Edward Cymerys, Sr. VP/Chief Actuary
Bruce G. Bodaken, Chmn.

Phone: 415-229-5000	**Fax:** 415-229-5744
Toll-Free:	
Address: 50 Beale St., San Francisco, CA 94105-1808 US	

GROWTH PLANS/SPECIAL FEATURES:

Blue Shield of California (BSC), the operating subsidiary o California Physician's Service, is a not-for-profit Blue Cross Blue Shield Association member with more than 3 million customers. The firm offers insurance packages including HMOs, PPOs, dental, Medicare supplemental and TriWest through 20 offices in California. BSC also offers executive medical reimbursement, life and vision insurance and short term health plans through Blue Shield of California Life and Health Insurance Company (Blue Shield Life). The Blue Shield of California Foundation provides charitable contributions, conducts research and supports programs with an emphasis on domestic violence prevention and medical technology assessments. Mylifepath.com is Blue Shield o California's online resource for its members, employers producers and providers. BSC recently introduced the Essential plans 3000 and 4500 for self-employed California workers not covered by employer-sponsored health plans Additionally, the company began an enhanced small group dental benefit for pregnant women to reduce risks o periodontal disease and pregnancy gingivitis, and is expanding dental coverage options with four new dental PPC plans for small groups.

BSC offers its employees tuition reimbursement, the Blue Shield Scholarship Program for dependants, employee assistance plans, pre-tax commuter benefits and flexible spending accounts.

FINANCIALS: Sales and profits are in thousands of dollars—add 000 to get the full amount. 2007 Note: Financial information for 2007 was not available for all companies at press time.

2007 Sales: $	2007 Profits: $	**U.S. Stock Ticker: Nonprofit**
2006 Sales: $	2006 Profits: $	**Int'l Ticker:** Int'l Exchange:
2005 Sales: $7,518,900	2005 Profits: $329,500	Employees: 4,300
2004 Sales: $6,956,035	2004 Profits: $334,222	Fiscal Year Ends: 12/31
2003 Sales: $6,000,000	2003 Profits: $314,300	Parent Company:

SALARIES/BENEFITS:

Pension Plan: Y	ESOP Stock Plan:	Profit Sharing:	Top Exec. Salary: $	Bonus: $
Savings Plan: Y	Stock Purch. Plan:		Second Exec. Salary: $	Bonus: $

OTHER THOUGHTS:

Apparent Women Officers or Directors: 9
Hot Spot for Advancement for Women/Minorities: Y

LOCATIONS: ("Y" = Yes)

West:	Southwest:	Midwest:	Southeast:	Northeast:	International:
Y					

BON SECOURS HEALTH SYSTEM INC

www.bshsi.com

Industry Group Code: 622110 **Ranks within this company's industry group:** Sales: Profits:

Insurance/HMO/PPO:		Drugs:		Equipment/Supplies:		Hospitals/Clinics:		Services:		Health Care:	
Insurance:		Manufacturer:		Manufacturer:		Acute Care:	Y	Diagnostics:		Home Health:	Y
Managed Care:		Distributor:		Distributor:		Sub-Acute:	Y	Labs/Testing:		Long-Term Care:	Y
Utilization Management:		Specialty Pharmacy:		Leasing/Finance:		Outpatient Surgery:	Y	Staffing:		Physical Therapy:	
Payment Processing:		Vitamins/Nutritionals:		Information Systems:		Physical Rehab. Ctr.:	Y	Waste Disposal:		Physician Prac. Mgmt.:	
		Clinical Trials:				Psychiatric Clinics:	Y	Specialty Svcs.:			

TYPES OF BUSINESS:

Hospitals
Assisted Living Facilities
Psychiatric Facilities
Hospice Care

BRANDS/DIVISIONS/AFFILIATES:

Sisters of Bon Secours
St. Francis Medical Center
Bon Secours Cottage Health Services
Bon Secours Kentucky Health System
Bon Secours Baltimore Health System
Bon Secours St. Petersburg Health System

CONTACTS:

Note: Officers with more than one job title may be intentionally listed here more than once.

Richard J. Statuto, CEO
Richard J. Statuto, Pres.
Patricia A. Eck, Chmn.

Phone: 410-442-5511	**Fax:** 410-442-1082
Toll-Free:	
Address: 1505 Marriottsville Rd., Marriottsville, MD 21104 US	

GROWTH PLANS/SPECIAL FEATURES:

Bon Secours Health System, Inc. (BSHSI) is a Catholic health care ministry operated by the Sisters of Bon Secours. The BSHSI system includes 20 acute-care hospitals, six assisted living facilities, six long-term care facilities and seven home health service and hospice care facilities, with a total of nearly 6,000 beds and 551 assisted living units. Its facilities comprise 12 regional health systems in Michigan, New York, Pennsylvania, Maryland, Virginia, Kentucky, South Carolina and Florida. These systems include Bon Secours Cottage Health Services in Michigan, Bon Secours Baltimore Health System, Bon Secours Kentucky Health System and the Bon Secours St. Petersburg Health System in Florida. BSHSI also has strategic relationships with the Henry Ford Health System, Conemaugh Health System, Health Corporation of Virginia, Medical Society of South Carolina, Carolinas Health Care System, Life Care Services and Manor House. The company recently sold two of its Florida hospitals, Bon Secours Venice Hospital and Bon Secours St. Joseph Hospital, to Health Management Associates, Inc.

BSHSI offers its employees flexible spending accounts, tuition assistance, a variety of insurance options and an employee assistance program.

FINANCIALS:

Sales and profits are in thousands of dollars—add 000 to get the full amount. 2007 Note: Financial information for 2007 was not available for all companies at press time.

2007 Sales: $	2007 Profits: $	**U.S. Stock Ticker: Nonprofit**
2006 Sales: $	2006 Profits: $	**Int'l Ticker:** Int'l Exchange:
2005 Sales: $	2005 Profits: $	Employees: 16,900
2004 Sales: $	2004 Profits: $	Fiscal Year Ends: 8/31
2003 Sales: $2,523,400	2003 Profits: $	Parent Company:

SALARIES/BENEFITS:

Pension Plan:	ESOP Stock Plan:	Profit Sharing:	Top Exec. Salary: $	Bonus: $
Savings Plan:	Stock Purch. Plan:		Second Exec. Salary: $	Bonus: $

OTHER THOUGHTS:

Apparent Women Officers or Directors: 1
Hot Spot for Advancement for Women/Minorities:

LOCATIONS: ("Y" = Yes)

West:	Southwest:	Midwest:	Southeast:	Northeast:	International:
		Y	Y	Y	

BOSTON SCIENTIFIC CORP www.bostonscientific.com

Industry Group Code: 339113 **Ranks within this company's industry group:** Sales: 6 Profits: 99

Insurance/HMO/PPO:		Drugs:		Equipment/Supplies:		Hospitals/Clinics:		Services:		Health Care:	
Insurance:		Manufacturer:		Manufacturer:	Y	Acute Care:		Diagnostics:		Home Health:	
Managed Care:		Distributor:		Distributor:		Sub-Acute:		Labs/Testing:		Long-Term Care:	
Utilization Management:		Specialty Pharmacy:		Leasing/Finance:		Outpatient Surgery:		Staffing:		Physical Therapy:	
Payment Processing:		Vitamins/Nutritionals:		Information Systems:		Physical Rehab. Ctr.:		Waste Disposal:		Physician Prac. Mgmt.:	
		Clinical Trials:				Psychiatric Clinics:		Specialty Svcs.:			

TYPES OF BUSINESS:

Supplies-Surgery
Interventional Medical Products
Catheters
Guide wires
Stents
Oncology & Electrophysiology Research

BRANDS/DIVISIONS/AFFILIATES:

Advanced Bionics Corp.
IQ Guide Wire
Taxus
Advanced Stent Technologies
TriVascular
Radial Jaw
Guidant
iLab

CONTACTS: *Note: Officers with more than one job title may be intentionally listed here more than once.*

James R. Tobin, CEO
Paul A. LaViolette, COO
James R. Tobin, Pres.
Sam Leno, CFO/Exec. VP
Jim Gilbert, Sr. VP-Corp. Sales, Mktg. Science & E-Mktg.
Lucia Luce Quinn, Exec. VP-Human Resources
Donald S. Baim, Chief Medical & Scientific Officer/Exec. VP
Sam Leno, Exec. VP-Info. Sys.
Fredericus A. Colen, CTO/Exec. VP-Oper./Tech./Cardiac Rhythm Mngt.
Paul W. Sandman, General Counsel/Exec. VP/Corp. Sec.
Kenneth J. Pucel, Exec. VP-Oper
Jim Gilbert, Sr. VP-Strategic Support & Outcomes Planning
Paul Donovan, Sr. VP-Corp. Comm.
Sam Leno, Exec. VP-Finance
Stephen F. Moreci, Sr. VP/Group Pres., Endosurgery
Jim Gilbert, Pres., Cardiovascular
William H. (Hank) Kucheman, Sr. VP/Pres., Interventional Cardiology Group
Brian R. Burns, Sr. VP-Quality
Peter M. Nicholas, Chmn.
Jeff H. Goodman, Exec VP-Int'l

Phone: 508-650-8000 **Fax:** 508-647-2393
Toll-Free: 888-272-1001
Address: 1 Boston Scientific Pl., Natick, MA 01760-1537 US

GROWTH PLANS/SPECIAL FEATURES:

Boston Scientific Corp. (BSC), with offices in over 30 countries, manufactures minimally invasive medical devices intended as an alternative to major surgical procedures that reduces risk, trauma, cost, procedure time and the need for aftercare. The company's products are used in a wide range of interventional medical applications, including cardiology, electrophysiology, gastroenterology, neuro-endovascular therapy, pulmonary medicine, radiology, urology and vascular surgery. Products include steerable catheters, micro-guidewires, polypectomy snares and stents. Stents, flexible metal tubes used to open arteries, account for 20% of sales. Currently, BSC is developing drug-eluting stents, which have been proven more effective than bare metal stents. The company sells its products to over 10,000 hospitals, clinics, outpatient facilities and medical offices. Boston Scientific's electrophysiology division is currently investigating advanced modalities for arrhythmia diagnosis and treatment of atrial flutter and atrial fibrillation. The firm's electrophysiology products are used to map the electrical structure of a patient's heart, the map is then used as a guide for minimally invasive surgery. Additionally, the firm's oncology division is studying technologies intended to treat kidney disease and symptomatic uterine fibroids. TriVascular, a recently acquired subsidiary, makes devices and treatments for abdominal aortic aneurysms. Boston Scientific recently launched Radial Jaw 4, its newest version of single-use biopsy forceps, designed to extract larger tissue specimens in endoscopic biopsies; the TAXUS Liberte coronary stent system is currently undergoing trials; and the iLab Ultrasound Imaging System allows physicians to use intravascular ultrasounds in everyday procedures. Boston Scientific recently completed a merger with Guidant, a developer of cardiovascular medical products. In 2006, the FDA approved the Harmony HiResolution Bionic Ear System, a cochlear implant that delivers 120 spectral bands. The firm is currently exploring an IPO of a minority stake in its endosurgery group.

Boston Scientific offers its employees a complete benefits package including tuition reimbursement and adoption assistance.

FINANCIALS: **Sales and profits are in thousands of dollars—add 000 to get the full amount. 2007 Note: Financial information for 2007 was not available for all companies at press time.**

2007 Sales: $
2006 Sales: $7,821,000
2005 Sales: $6,283,000
2004 Sales: $5,624,000
2003 Sales: $3,476,000

2007 Profits: $
2006 Profits: $-3,577,000
2005 Profits: $628,000
2004 Profits: $1,062,000
2003 Profits: $472,000

U.S. Stock Ticker: BSX
Int'l Ticker: Int'l Exchange:
Employees: 28,600
Fiscal Year Ends: 12/31
Parent Company:

SALARIES/BENEFITS:

Pension Plan: ESOP Stock Plan: Y Profit Sharing: Top Exec. Salary: $922,576 Bonus: $324,100
Savings Plan: Y Stock Purch. Plan: Second Exec. Salary: $660,000 Bonus: $616,400

OTHER THOUGHTS:

Apparent Women Officers or Directors: 5
Hot Spot for Advancement for Women/Minorities: Y

LOCATIONS: ("Y" = Yes)

West:	Southwest:	Midwest:	Southeast:	Northeast:	International:
Y	Y	Y	Y	Y	Y

Note: Financial information, benefits and other data can change quickly and may vary from those stated here.

BRIGHT NOW! DENTAL INC www.brightnow.com

Industry Group Code: 621111 **Ranks within this company's industry group:** Sales: Profits:

Insurance/HMO/PPO:		Drugs:		Equipment/Supplies:		Hospitals/Clinics:		Services:		Health Care:	
Insurance:		Manufacturer:		Manufacturer:		Acute Care:		Diagnostics:		Home Health:	
Managed Care:		Distributor:		Distributor:		Sub-Acute:		Labs/Testing:		Long-Term Care:	
Utilization Management:		Specialty Pharmacy:		Leasing/Finance:		Outpatient Surgery:		Staffing:		Physical Therapy:	
Payment Processing:		Vitamins/Nutritionals:		Information Systems:		Physical Rehab. Ctr.:		Waste Disposal:		Physician Prac. Mgmt.:	Y
		Clinical Trials:				Psychiatric Clinics:		Specialty Svcs.:			

TYPES OF BUSINESS:

Dental Practice Management

BRANDS/DIVISIONS/AFFILIATES:

Monarch Dental Inc.
Freeman Spofli and Co.

CONTACTS: *Note: Officers with more than one job title may be intentionally listed here more than once.*

Steven C. Bilt, CEO
Roy Smith, COO
Steven C. Bilt, Pres.
Bradley E. Schmidt, CFO
Richard Brown, VP-Mktg.
Karen Lieber, General Counsel/VP
Steven Tumbarello, VP-Finance
Alan Sechrest, VP-Credit Svcs.
Dennis Fratt, Sr. VP-Oper. Service Group
William McCarthy, VP-Real Estate & Facility Dev.
Mark Merriweather, Area VP-Southwest

Phone: 714-668-1300 **Fax:** 714-428-1300
Toll-Free: 800-347-6453
Address: 201 E. Sandpointe, Ste. 800, Santa Ana, CA 92707 US

GROWTH PLANS/SPECIAL FEATURES:

Bright Now! Dental, Inc. (BN!D) and its wholly owned subsidiaries provide business support services to approximately 300 dental offices in 18 states nationwide. The group, which is funded primarily by Freeman Spofli and Co., supports the practices of independent dentists by managing the all of the time-consuming business functions of the practice, such as the dentist's finances, sales and marketing, information technology, human resources, purchasing and real estate development. This provides dentists with the ability to devote the majority of their time to caring for patients and to keeping up their dental knowledge and skills. Affiliated dentists deliver general dentistry, cosmetic dentistry, and specialty services such as orthodontics to more than 2.5 million patients each year. Every office in the network provides care to a wide range of patients by having extended evening and weekend office hours, convenient locations, affordable prices, and flexible payment plans. Within the last few years the company began expanding outward from its base in Santa Ana, California through a series of acquisitions and by opening new offices. Its service area now includes locations in California, Colorado, Arizona, New Mexico, Florida, New Jersey, Ohio, Oregon, Pennsylvania, Tennessee, Texas, Virginia and Washington. In November 2006, the company opened a new dental office in Beaverton, Oregon and in Philadelphia, Pennsylvania.

BrightNow! Dental offers its employees benefits that include health and group life insurance; dental and vision care; health and dependent care flexible spending plans; a 401(k) plan; and time-off benefits.

FINANCIALS: **Sales and profits are in thousands of dollars—add 000 to get the full amount. 2007 Note: Financial information for 2007 was not available for all companies at press time.**

2007 Sales: $	2007 Profits: $	**U.S. Stock Ticker: Private**
2006 Sales: $	2006 Profits: $	**Int'l Ticker:** Int'l Exchange:
2005 Sales: $	2005 Profits: $	Employees: 1,500
2004 Sales: $	2004 Profits: $	Fiscal Year Ends: 12/31
2003 Sales: $	2003 Profits: $	Parent Company:

SALARIES/BENEFITS:

Pension Plan:	ESOP Stock Plan:	Profit Sharing:	Top Exec. Salary: $450,000	Bonus: $83,262
Savings Plan: Y	Stock Purch. Plan:		Second Exec. Salary: $208,154	Bonus: $33,566

OTHER THOUGHTS:

Apparent Women Officers or Directors: 1
Hot Spot for Advancement for Women/Minorities:

LOCATIONS: ("Y" = Yes)

West:	Southwest:	Midwest:	Southeast:	Northeast:	International:
Y	Y	Y	Y		

BRISTOL MYERS SQUIBB CO

www.bms.com

Industry Group Code: 325412 **Ranks within this company's industry group:** Sales: 11 Profits: 15

Insurance/HMO/PPO:		Drugs:		Equipment/Supplies:		Hospitals/Clinics:		Services:		Health Care:	
Insurance:		Manufacturer:	Y	Manufacturer:	Y	Acute Care:		Diagnostics:		Home Health:	
Managed Care:		Distributor:		Distributor:		Sub-Acute:		Labs/Testing:		Long-Term Care:	
Utilization Management:		Specialty Pharmacy:		Leasing/Finance:		Outpatient Surgery:		Staffing:		Physical Therapy:	
Payment Processing:		Vitamins/Nutritionals:		Information Systems:		Physical Rehab. Ctr.:		Waste Disposal:		Physician Prac. Mgmt.:	
		Clinical Trials:				Psychiatric Clinics:		Specialty Svcs.:			

TYPES OF BUSINESS:

Drugs-Diversified
Medical Imaging Products
Nutritional Products
Wound Care Products
Over-the-Counter Medicines

BRANDS/DIVISIONS/AFFILIATES:

Mead Johnson Nutritionals
ConvaTec
Enfamil
Cardiolite
Excedrin
TAXOL
Pravachol
Glucophage

CONTACTS: *Note: Officers with more than one job title may be intentionally listed here more than once.*

James M. Cornelius, CEO
Andrew R. J. Bonfield, CFO/Exec. VP
Wendy L. Dixon, Chief Mktg. Officer/Pres., Global Mktg.
Stephen E. Bear, Sr. VP-Human Resources
Elliott Sigal, Chief Scientific Officer
Susan O'Day, CIO
Carlo de Notaristefani, Pres., Tech. Oper.
Sandra Leung, Sr. VP/General Counsel
Robert T. Zito, Sr. VP-Corp. & Bus. Comm.
Anthony C. Hooper, Pres., U.S. Pharmaceuticals
Elliott Sigal, Pres., Pharmaceutical Research Institute
Jonathan K. Sprole, VP/Chief Compliance Officer
Pete Paradossi, Health Care Group
James D. Robinson, III, Chmn.
Lamberto Andreotti, Exec. VP/Pres., Worldwide Pharmaceuticals

Phone: 212-546-4000	**Fax:** 212-546-4020
Toll-Free:	
Address: 345 Park Ave., New York, NY 10154-0037 US	

GROWTH PLANS/SPECIAL FEATURES:

Bristol-Myers Squibb is one of the largest pharmaceutical and health care products companies in the world. The company operates through three segments: pharmaceuticals, nutritionals and other health care. The pharmaceutical segment, which accounts for 77% of total sales, discovers, develops, licenses, manufactures, markets, distributes and sells branded pharmaceuticals worldwide. It is a leading provider of drugs for anti-cancer therapies (TAXOL, Paraplatin and Erbitux) and treatments for high blood pressure (Avapro and Monopril), high cholesterol (Pravachol), stroke (Plavix), deep venous thrombosis/pulmonary embolism (Coumadin), type-2 diabetes (Glucophage), HIV/AIDS (Sustiva, Reyataz and Zerit), infectious diseases (Cefzil and Tequin) and schizophrenia (Abilify). The nutritionals segment, through Mead Johnson Nutritionals, manufactures and markets infant formulas, including the Enfamil line of products and children's nutritionals. The other health care segment consists of the ConvaTec, Medical Imaging and Consumer Medicines businesses. ConvaTec provides ostomy care and modern wound care products under the Natura, Sur-Fit, Esteem, Aquacel and DuoDerm brands. Medical Imaging manufactures, distributes and sells imaging products under the Cardiolite and Definity brands. Consumer Medicines manufactures, distributes and sells over-the-counter products including Excedrin, Bufferin, the Keri line of moisturizers and Comtrex for cold, cough and flu. Recently, the company partnered with AstraZeneca to develop Type 2 diabetes compounds; with Gilead Sciences to commercialize Atripla (the first once-daily single tablet HIV-1 treatment) in Canada; and with Adnexus to develop adnectin-based therapeutics for oncology-related patients. In addition, the company partnered with Onmark in 2007 to develop anti-cancer products. In recent news, the firm sold its inventory, trademark, patent and intellectual property rights related to DOVONEX, a treatment for psoriasis, to Warner Chilcott Company for $200 million in cash. In 2007, the company bought 89 acres of land for a new biologics facility that will be complete in 2010.

Bristol-Myers Squibb offers its employees medical plans and dependent life insurance.

FINANCIALS: **Sales and profits are in thousands of dollars—add 000 to get the full amount. 2007 Note: Financial information for 2007 was not available for all companies at press time.**

2007 Sales: $	2007 Profits: $	**U.S. Stock Ticker: BMY**
2006 Sales: $17,914,000	2006 Profits: $1,585,000	**Int'l Ticker:** Int'l Exchange:
2005 Sales: $19,207,000	2005 Profits: $3,000,000	Employees: 43,000
2004 Sales: $19,380,000	2004 Profits: $2,388,000	Fiscal Year Ends: 12/31
2003 Sales: $20,671,000	2003 Profits: $2,952,000	Parent Company:

SALARIES/BENEFITS:

Pension Plan: Y	ESOP Stock Plan:	Profit Sharing:	Top Exec. Salary: $1,250,000	Bonus: $2,224,875
Savings Plan: Y	Stock Purch. Plan:		Second Exec. Salary: $829,806	Bonus: $723,701

OTHER THOUGHTS:

Apparent Women Officers or Directors: 3
Hot Spot for Advancement for Women/Minorities: Y

LOCATIONS: ("Y" = Yes)

West:	Southwest:	Midwest:	Southeast:	Northeast:	International:
Y	Y	Y	Y	Y	Y

Note: Financial information, benefits and other data can change quickly and may vary from those stated here.

BRITISH UNITED PROVIDENT ASSOCIATION (BUPA)

www.bupa.co.uk

Industry Group Code: 524114 **Ranks within this company's industry group:** Sales: 10 Profits: 9

Insurance/HMO/PPO:		Drugs:		Equipment/Supplies:		Hospitals/Clinics:		Services:		Health Care:	
Insurance:	Y	Manufacturer:		Manufacturer:		Acute Care:	Y	Diagnostics:		Home Health:	
Managed Care:	Y	Distributor:		Distributor:		Sub-Acute:	Y	Labs/Testing:		Long-Term Care:	Y
Utilization Management:		Specialty Pharmacy:		Leasing/Finance:		Outpatient Surgery:	Y	Staffing:	Y	Physical Therapy:	Y
Payment Processing:		Vitamins/Nutritionals:		Information Systems:		Physical Rehab. Ctr.:		Waste Disposal:		Physician Prac. Mgmt.:	
		Clinical Trials:				Psychiatric Clinics:	Y	Specialty Svcs.:	Y		

TYPES OF BUSINESS:

Insurance-Medical & Health, HMOs & PPOs
Life & Disability Insurance
Long-Term Health Care
Hospitals, Clinics & Health Screening Centers
Travel Insurance
Child Care Services
Cosmetic Surgery

BRANDS/DIVISIONS/AFFILIATES:

BUPA
BUPA Health Insurance
BUPA International
BUPA Heartbeat
BUPA TravelCover
BUPA Care Homes
BUPA Childcare
Teddies Nurseries

CONTACTS: *Note: Officers with more than one job title may be intentionally listed here more than once.*

Valerie Gooding, CEO
Ray King, Dir.-Finance
Natalie Macdonald, Dir.-Medical
Alexander P. Leitch, Chmn.

Phone: 44-20-7656-2000	**Fax:** 44-20-7656-2700
Toll-Free: 0800-600-500	
Address: 15-19 Bloomsbury Way, BUPA House, London, WC1A 2BA UK	

GROWTH PLANS/SPECIAL FEATURES:

British United Provident Association (BUPA) is a leading international health care company with locations on three continents and well over 7 million customers. BUPA is the largest health insurance company in the U.K., both for individuals and corporations. BUPA Health Insurance provides medical insurance in the U.K., while BUPA International covers U.K. expatriates and other customers in Australia, Hong Kong, Ireland, Thailand, Saudi Arabia and over 180 other countries. The company's primary health insurance plan is BUPA Heartbeat, with the BUPA Cash Plan available for everyday health expenses. In addition, the company provides critical illness and other long-term financial protection products, including Life Cover, Critical Illness Cover and Lifestyle and Income Protection, while BUPA TravelCover offers travel insurance, which covers both health care expenses and baggage insurance. BUPA also offers a wide range of cosmetic surgeries for men and women, including facial surgeries, body re-shaping and skin treatments. BUPA offers cosmetic surgery services from over 130 consultants who carry out cosmetic treatments in its 34 hospitals. In the U.K., BUPA operates more than 250 retirement and aged-care homes. The company also features child care homes under the corporate heading of Children@work, which is a service that provides day care to employers and nanny placement to private individuals. Sanitas, the BUPA business in Spain, has 1 million insured customers who have access to a network of 18,000 medical professionals and 450 medical centers. In April 2007, BUPA's Sanitas Group acquired Spanish care home and day center Euroresidencias, and in August 2007, BUPA acquired care home business Avalon Care Homes Limited.

FINANCIALS: **Sales and profits are in thousands of dollars—add 000 to get the full amount. 2007 Note: Financial information for 2007 was not available for all companies at press time.**

2007 Sales: $	2007 Profits: $	**U.S. Stock Ticker: Mutual Company**
2006 Sales: $8,469,930	2006 Profits: $473,210	**Int'l Ticker:** Int'l Exchange:
2005 Sales: $7,737,970	2005 Profits: $506,130	Employees: 44,000
2004 Sales: $6,986,300	2004 Profits: $	Fiscal Year Ends: 12/31
2003 Sales: $	2003 Profits: $	Parent Company:

SALARIES/BENEFITS:

Pension Plan:	ESOP Stock Plan:	Profit Sharing:	Top Exec. Salary: $	Bonus: $
Savings Plan:	Stock Purch. Plan:		Second Exec. Salary: $	Bonus: $

OTHER THOUGHTS:

Apparent Women Officers or Directors: 2
Hot Spot for Advancement for Women/Minorities:

LOCATIONS: ("Y" = Yes)

West:	Southwest:	Midwest:	Southeast:	Northeast:	International:
					Y

BROOKDALE SENIOR LIVING INC www.brookdaleliving.com

Industry Group Code: 623110 **Ranks within this company's industry group:** Sales: Profits:

Insurance/HMO/PPO:		Drugs:		Equipment/Supplies:		Hospitals/Clinics:		Services:		Health Care:	
Insurance:		Manufacturer:		Manufacturer:		Acute Care:		Diagnostics:		Home Health:	
Managed Care:		Distributor:		Distributor:		Sub-Acute:		Labs/Testing:		Long-Term Care:	Y
Utilization Management:		Specialty Pharmacy:		Leasing/Finance:		Outpatient Surgery:		Staffing:		Physical Therapy:	
Payment Processing:		Vitamins/Nutritionals:		Information Systems:		Physical Rehab. Ctr.:		Waste Disposal:		Physician Prac. Mgmt.:	
		Clinical Trials:				Psychiatric Clinics:		Specialty Svcs.:			

TYPES OF BUSINESS:

Long-Term Health Care & Assisted Living

BRANDS/DIVISIONS/AFFILIATES:

Brookdale Living Communities, Inc.
Alterra Healthcare Corporation
American Retirement Corp.
Innovative Senior Care Program

CONTACTS: *Note: Officers with more than one job title may be intentionally listed here more than once.*

Mark J. Schulte, Co-CEO
John P. Rijos, Co-Pres.
Mark W. Ohlendorf, CFO/Co-Pres.
T. Andrew Smith, General Counsel/Exec. VP/Sec.
Gregory B. Richard, Exec. VP-Oper.
H. Todd Kaestner, Exec. VP-Corp. Dev.
Kristin A. Ferge, Treas./Exec. VP
W.E. Sheriff, Co-CEO
Bryan D. Richardson, Exec. VP/Chief Accounting Officer
Paul A. Froning, Exec. VP/Chief Investment Officer
Wesley R. Edens, Chmn.

Phone: 312-977-3700	**Fax:** 312-977-3701
Toll-Free: 877-977-3800	
Address: 330 N. Wabash Ave., Ste. 1400, Chicago, IL 60611 US	

GROWTH PLANS/SPECIAL FEATURES:

Brookdale Senior Living, Inc. is one of the largest senic living facilities in the United States, with 546 facilities in 3 states and the ability to serve over 51,000 residents. Th company formed through the recent merger betwee Brookdale Living Communities, Inc. and Alterra Healthcar Corporation, two of the country's leading senior livin operating companies. Brookdale offers its residents a home like setting that includes assistance with activities of dail living and licensed nursing services. The company operate through four segments: assisted living, through which th company operates 408 facilities; independent living,which i made up of 66 facilities; retirement centers/CCRCs, of whic there are 48 centers; and management services, throug which the company maintains the business operations of it many facilities. The assisted living facilities offer housin and 24-hour basic care, which includes ongoing healt assessments, three meals per day and snacks, coordinatio of special diets planned by a registered dietitian, assistanc with coordination of physician care, social and recreationa activities and housekeeping and personal laundry services The company also operates memory care facilities fc residents with Alzheimer's disease and other dementias The independent living facilities are designed for middle t upper income seniors over the age of 70 who desire a upscale residential environment. The majority of th company's independent living facilities also contain assiste living units on premises, in order to avoid difficult and ofte stressful moves when a resident's health begins to declin Brookdale's retirement centers/CCRCs, are larg communities that offer a variety of living arrangements an services to accommodate all levels of physical ability an health. Also, through the Innovative Senior Care Progran residents receive therapy, home health and other ancillar services. In July 2006, the company completed its $1. billion acquisition of American Retirement Corp., increase Brookdale's resident capacity by nearly 50% through th addition of 83 retirement centers.

FINANCIALS: **Sales and profits are in thousands of dollars—add 000 to get the full amount. 2007 Note: Financial information for 2007 was not available for all companies at press time.**

2007 Sales: $	2007 Profits: $	**U.S. Stock Ticker: BKD**
2006 Sales: $	2006 Profits: $	**Int'l Ticker:** Int'l Exchange:
2005 Sales: $	2005 Profits: $	Employees:
2004 Sales: $	2004 Profits: $	Fiscal Year Ends:
2003 Sales: $	2003 Profits: $	Parent Company:

SALARIES/BENEFITS:

Pension Plan:	ESOP Stock Plan:	Profit Sharing:	Top Exec. Salary: $200,000	Bonus: $100,000
Savings Plan: Y	Stock Purch. Plan:		Second Exec. Salary: $196,154	Bonus: $50,000

OTHER THOUGHTS:

Apparent Women Officers or Directors: 1
Hot Spot for Advancement for Women/Minorities:

LOCATIONS: ("Y" = Yes)

West:	Southwest:	Midwest:	Southeast:	Northeast:	International:
Y	Y	Y	Y	Y	

BROOKS ECKERD

www.brooks-rx.com

Industry Group Code: 446110 **Ranks within this company's industry group:** Sales: Profits:

Insurance/HMO/PPO:		**Drugs:**		**Equipment/Supplies:**		**Hospitals/Clinics:**		**Services:**		**Health Care:**	
nsurance:		Manufacturer:		Manufacturer:		Acute Care:		Diagnostics:		Home Health:	
Managed Care:		Distributor:	Y	Distributor:		Sub-Acute:		Labs/Testing:		Long-Term Care:	
Utilization Management:		Specialty Pharmacy:		Leasing/Finance:		Outpatient Surgery:		Staffing:		Physical Therapy:	
Payment Processing:		Vitamins/Nutritionals:		Information Systems:		Physical Rehab. Ctr.:		Waste Disposal:		Physician Prac. Mgmt.:	
		Clinical Trials:				Psychiatric Clinics:		Specialty Svcs.:			

TYPES OF BUSINESS:

Drug Stores-Retail
Pharmacies

BRANDS/DIVISIONS/AFFILIATES:

The Jean Coutu Group Inc
Eckerd
Brooks Pharmacy

CONTACTS: *Note: Officers with more than one job title may be intentionally listed here more than once.*

Michel Coutu, CEO
William Z. Welsh Jr., COO
Michel Coutu, Pres.
Randy Wyrofsky, CFO

Phone: 401-825-3900	**Fax:** 401-825-3587
Toll-Free: 800-276-6573	
Address: 50 Service Ave., Warwick, PA 02886 US	

GROWTH PLANS/SPECIAL FEATURES:

Brooks Eckerd, a wholly-owned subsidiary of The Jean Coutu Group, Inc., operates about 1,900 drug stores in the New England region. More than 1,500 of these stores are former Eckerd outlets, which the company acquired in 2004, and added to about 330 of its existing Brooks Pharmacies. The deal was contracted with J.C. Penny and worth about $2.3 billion. The company's stores offer pharmaceuticals, general merchandise and vitamins and laundry products under its own proprietary brand. Many of the Brooks Eckerd stores offer drive-through pharmacies, 24-hour service, one-hour photo centers and ATM machines. The firm is planning a large expansion throughout New England to be accomplished through pharmacy acquisitions and the opening of new stores. The company's real estate development plan is searching for land containing at least 50,000 square feet of space. New prototype stores are planned to feature patient counseling space and further pharmacy services. The firm maintains distribution centers in Dayville, Connecticut; Charlotte, North Carolina; Bohemia and Liverpool, New York; Langhorn, Pennsylvania; and Newnan, Georgia, to service its locations up and down the coast. In June 2007, the Brooks Eckerd chain was acquired by Rite Aid Corp. for roughly $2.36 billion. All the stores will be re-branded Rite Aid, which is expected to be completed by March 2008.

FINANCIALS: **Sales and profits are in thousands of dollars—add 000 to get the full amount. 2007 Note: Financial information for 2007 was not available for all companies at press time.**

2007 Sales: $	2007 Profits: $	**U.S. Stock Ticker: Subsidiary**
2006 Sales: $	2006 Profits: $	**Int'l Ticker:** Int'l Exchange:
2005 Sales: $	2005 Profits: $	Employees:
2004 Sales: $	2004 Profits: $	Fiscal Year Ends: 5/31
2003 Sales: $	2003 Profits: $	Parent Company: JEAN COUTU GROUP INC (THE)

SALARIES/BENEFITS:

Pension Plan:	ESOP Stock Plan:	Profit Sharing:	Top Exec. Salary: $	Bonus: $
Savings Plan: Y	Stock Purch. Plan:		Second Exec. Salary: $	Bonus: $

OTHER THOUGHTS:

Apparent Women Officers or Directors:
Hot Spot for Advancement for Women/Minorities:

LOCATIONS: ("Y" = Yes)

West:	Southwest:	Midwest:	Southeast:	Northeast:	International:
			Y	Y	

CAMBREX CORP

www.cambrex.com

Industry Group Code: 325412 **Ranks within this company's industry group:** Sales: 32 Profits: 33

Insurance/HMO/PPO:		Drugs:		Equipment/Supplies:		Hospitals/Clinics:		Services:		Health Care:	
Insurance:		Manufacturer:	Y	Manufacturer:		Acute Care:		Diagnostics:		Home Health:	
Managed Care:		Distributor:		Distributor:		Sub-Acute:		Labs/Testing:		Long-Term Care:	
Utilization Management:		Specialty Pharmacy:		Leasing/Finance:		Outpatient Surgery:		Staffing:		Physical Therapy:	
Payment Processing:		Vitamins/Nutritionals:		Information Systems:		Physical Rehab. Ctr.:		Waste Disposal:		Physician Prac. Mgmt.:	
		Clinical Trials:				Psychiatric Clinics:		Specialty Svcs.:	Y		

TYPES OF BUSINESS:

Contract Pharmaceutical Manufacturing
Contract Research
Pharmaceutical Ingredients
Testing Products & Services
Technical Support

BRANDS/DIVISIONS/AFFILIATES:

Cambrex Bio Science Walkersville, Inc.
FlashGel
Platimun UltraPAK

CONTACTS: *Note: Officers with more than one job title may be intentionally listed here more than once.*

James A. Mack, CEO
Gary L. Mossman, COO/Exec. VP
James A. Mack, Pres.
Greg Sargen, CFO/Exec. VP
Melissa M. Lesko, VP-Human Resources
Robert J. Conguisti, VP-IT
Peter E. Thauer, General Counsel/Sr. VP/Corp. Sec.
Luke M. Beshar, VP-Corp. Dev.
Anup Gupta, VP-Finance
Steven M. Klosk, Exec. VP/COO-Biopharma Business Unit
Paolo Russolo, Pres., Cambrex Profarmaco Milano
Charles W. Silvey, VP-Internal Audit
James A. Mack, Chmn.

Phone: 201-804-3000	**Fax:** 201-804-9852
Toll-Free:	
Address: 1 Meadowlands Plaza, E. Rutherford, NJ 07073 US	

GROWTH PLANS/SPECIAL FEATURES:

Cambrex Corporation provides products and services to aid and enhance the discovery and commercialization of therapeutics. The company offers a variety of outsourcing products and services for drug discovery research and therapeutic testing. The firm manufactures more than 1,800 products, which are sold to more than 14,000 customers worldwide, including research organizations, pharmaceutical, biopharmaceutical and generic drug companies. Outsourcing options include bulk biologics manufacturing; development, manufacturing and commercialization services for cell-based therapeutics and pharmaceutical products; and testing services including assays for microbiology, sterility and veterinary services. Products offered for drug discovery research include bioassays; cell model systems; cell analysis stains; electrophoresis products, including the FlashGel Rapid Electrophoresis System; and protein analysis products. Cambrex offers technical support for all its research products. In addition, Cambrex offers Platinum UltraPAK, a line of flexible packaging systems that can be modified to fit specific customer needs. Therapeutic testing products include a range of endotoxin services and products, including endotoxin detection assays, removal products, testing services accessory products, instrumentation and software. The company also offers testing products using a wide range of assays. Recently, Cambrex Bio Science Walkersville, Inc., a subsidiary of the company, announced its intent to purchase Cutanogen Corporation, a company specializing in the treatment of severe burns. In February 2007, Camrex announced that the sale of Bioproducts and Biopharma subsidiaries to Lonza Group AG was completed.

Cambrex provides its employees with complete health coverage, flexible spending plans, tuition reimbursement, a 401(k) and an employee assistance program.

FINANCIALS: **Sales and profits are in thousands of dollars—add 000 to get the full amount. 2007 Note: Financial information for 2007 was not available for all companies at press time.**

2007 Sales: $	2007 Profits: $	**U.S. Stock Ticker: CBM**
2006 Sales: $452,255	2006 Profits: $-30,100	**Int'l Ticker:** Int'l Exchange:
2005 Sales: $414,761	2005 Profits: $-110,458	Employees: 1,916
2004 Sales: $395,906	2004 Profits: $-26,870	Fiscal Year Ends: 12/31
2003 Sales: $405,600	2003 Profits: $-54,100	Parent Company:

SALARIES/BENEFITS:

Pension Plan:	ESOP Stock Plan:	Profit Sharing:	Top Exec. Salary: $458,333	Bonus: $
Savings Plan: Y	Stock Purch. Plan:		Second Exec. Salary: $382,000	Bonus: $100,000

OTHER THOUGHTS:

Apparent Women Officers or Directors: 2
Hot Spot for Advancement for Women/Minorities: Y

LOCATIONS: ("Y" = Yes)

West:	Southwest:	Midwest:	Southeast:	Northeast:	International:
		Y		Y	Y

CANDELA CORP

www.candelalaser.com

Industry Group Code: 339113 **Ranks within this company's industry group:** Sales: 72 Profits: 54

Insurance/HMO/PPO:		Drugs:		Equipment/Supplies:		Hospitals/Clinics:		Services:		Health Care:	
Insurance:		Manufacturer:		Manufacturer:	Y	Acute Care:		Diagnostics:		Home Health:	
Managed Care:		Distributor:		Distributor:	Y	Sub-Acute:		Labs/Testing:		Long-Term Care:	
Utilization Management:		Specialty Pharmacy:		Leasing/Finance:		Outpatient Surgery:		Staffing:		Physical Therapy:	
Payment Processing:		Vitamins/Nutritionals:		Information Systems:		Physical Rehab. Ctr.:		Waste Disposal:		Physician Prac. Mgmt.:	
		Clinical Trials:				Psychiatric Clinics:		Specialty Svcs.:			

TYPES OF BUSINESS:

Equipment-Laser Systems
Cosmetic Clinical Products

BRANDS/DIVISIONS/AFFILIATES:

GentleMax
AlexTriVantage
SmoothPeel
Serenity
GentleLASE
GentleYAG
Vbeam
Smoothbeam

CONTACTS: *Note: Officers with more than one job title may be intentionally listed here more than once.*

Gerard E. Puorro, CEO
Gerard E. Puorro, Pres.
F. Paul Broyer, CFO/Sr. VP
Nancy L. Compton, VP-Human Resources
Kathleen McMillan, VP-Research
James C. Hsia, CTO
Charles A. Johnson, VP-Dev. Eng.
Paul R. Luchese, General Counsel/Corp. Sec./VP
William H. McGrail, Sr. VP-Oper.
Catherine Kniker, VP-Corp. Strategic Dev.
Robert E. Quinn, Treas./Corp. Controller
Dennis S. Herman, Sr. VP-North American Sales, Mktg. & Service
L. Bryant Helton, VP-Eastern Regional Sales
Toshio Mori, VP/Pres., Candela K.K.
Robert J. Wilber, Sr. VP-European Sales, Mktg. & Service
Kenneth D. Roberts, Chmn.
Michael R. Lemarier, VP-Worldwide Service

Phone: 508-358-7400 **Fax:** 508-358-5602
Toll-Free: 800-733-8550
Address: 530 Boston Post Rd., Wayland, MA 01778 US

GROWTH PLANS/SPECIAL FEATURES:

Candela Corporation develops, manufactures and distributes aesthetic laser systems that enable physicians, surgeons and personal care practitioners to treat various cosmetic and medical conditions. The company markets and services its products in over 70 countries from offices in the United States, Europe, Japan and other Asian locations. The firm has shipped approximately 12,000 systems worldwide. Candela's products include GentleMax, AlexTriVantage, SmoothPeel, Serenity, GentleLASE, GentleYAG, Vbeam and Smoothbeam. GentleMax is an integrated aesthetic treatment workstation with multiple wavelength capability, offering chilled air cooling and the patented Dynamic Cooling Device which utilizes bursts of cryogen before and after the laser pulse. AlexTriVantage is a tattoo and pigmented lesion removal device using multi-wavelength technology and a laser-pumped-laser hand piece. SmoothPeel is an Erbium: YAG laser for skin resurfacing. Serenity is a pneumatic skin flattening technology designed for reduced pain and improved efficacy and safety. The GentleLASE family of lasers is used for permanent hair reduction, vascular lesion removal, wrinkle reduction and pigmented lesion treatment. The GentleYAG family of lasers is used for hair reduction on tanned and dark skin, treatment of pseudofolliculitis barbae, removal of leg and facial veins and skin tightening. The Vbeam Perfecta, Platinum and Aesthetica family of lasers use a pulsed dye technology to eliminate pigmentation and vascular lesions including port wine stain birthmarks, rosacea and leg and facial veins as well as to reduce wrinkles, scars, warts, psoriasis and hemangiomas. The Smoothbeam diode laser is used for the treatment of acne, acne scars and sebaceous hyperplasia and non-ablative dermal remodeling of wrinkles. In March 2007, Candela acquired Inolase, LTD. of Netanya, Israel for approximately $16.5 million. In August Candela received FDA clearance for its Serenity device enabling its use for pain reduction during all laser and intense pulse light treatments.

FINANCIALS: **Sales and profits are in thousands of dollars—add 000 to get the full amount. 2007 Note: Financial information for 2007 was not available for all companies at press time.**

2007 Sales: $148,557	2007 Profits: $6,256	**U.S. Stock Ticker: CLZR**
2006 Sales: $149,466	2006 Profits: $14,934	**Int'l Ticker:** Int'l Exchange:
2005 Sales: $123,901	2005 Profits: $7,323	Employees: 386
2004 Sales: $104,438	2004 Profits: $8,119	Fiscal Year Ends: 6/30
2003 Sales: $80,800	2003 Profits: $6,800	Parent Company:

SALARIES/BENEFITS:

Pension Plan:	ESOP Stock Plan:	Profit Sharing:	Top Exec. Salary: $477,662	Bonus: $303,750
Savings Plan: Y	Stock Purch. Plan: Y		Second Exec. Salary: $241,316	Bonus: $96,484

OTHER THOUGHTS:

Apparent Women Officers or Directors: 3
Hot Spot for Advancement for Women/Minorities: Y

LOCATIONS: ("Y" = Yes)

West:	Southwest:	Midwest:	Southeast:	Northeast:	International:
				Y	Y

CANTEL MEDICAL CORP www.cantelmedical.com

Industry Group Code: 339113 **Ranks within this company's industry group:** Sales: 64 Profits: 50

Insurance/HMO/PPO:		Drugs:		Equipment/Supplies:		Hospitals/Clinics:		Services:		Health Care:	
Insurance:		Manufacturer:		Manufacturer:	Y	Acute Care:		Diagnostics:		Home Health:	
Managed Care:		Distributor:		Distributor:	Y	Sub-Acute:		Labs/Testing:		Long-Term Care:	
Utilization Management:		Specialty Pharmacy:		Leasing/Finance:		Outpatient Surgery:		Staffing:		Physical Therapy:	
Payment Processing:		Vitamins/Nutritionals:		Information Systems:		Physical Rehab. Ctr.:		Waste Disposal:		Physician Prac. Mgmt.:	
		Clinical Trials:				Psychiatric Clinics:		Specialty Svcs.:	Y		

TYPES OF BUSINESS:

Equipment-Disinfection & Disposable Equipment
Infection Control Products
Diagnostic Medical Equipment
Precision Instruments
Industrial Equipment
Water Treatment Equipment & Services
Maintenance Services
Dental Care Products

BRANDS/DIVISIONS/AFFILIATES:

Fluid Solutions, Inc.
Minntech Corporation
Endoscope Reprocessing System
Mar Cor Services
Biolab Group (The)
Saf-T-Pak
Crosstex

CONTACTS: *Note: Officers with more than one job title may be intentionally listed here more than once.*

R. Scott Jones, CEO
Andrew A. Krakauer, COO/Exec. VP
R. Scott Jones, Pres.
Craig A. Sheldon, CFO/Sr. VP
Eric W. Nodiff, General Counsel/Sr. VP
Seth R. Segel, Sr. VP-Corp. Dev.
Steven C. Anaya, VP/Controller
Charles M. Diker, Chmn.

Phone: 973-890-7220 **Fax:** 973-890-7270
Toll-Free:
Address: 150 Clove Rd., 9th Fl., Little Falls, NJ 07424-2139 US

GROWTH PLANS/SPECIAL FEATURES:

Cantel Medical Corp. provides products and services for th control and prevention of infection. It operates through diverse circle of subsidiaries. Minntech Corporatio develops, manufactures and markets disinfection an reprocessing systems for renal dialysis, as well as filtratio and separation products for medical and non-medic applications. Minntech recently acquired the state-of-the-a Endoscope Reprocessing System and accessory infectio control technologies of Netherlands-based Dyped Medic BV. Cantel also owns water treatment companies Mar Co Services, the Biolab Group and Saf-T-Pak. Mar Co provides design, project management, installation an maintenance services for water treatment equipment, as we as deionization and mixing systems to the medic community. Biolab produces water purification systems fo the medical, pharmaceutical, biotechnology an semiconductor industries. Saf-T-Pak, based in Albert produces specialty packaging and compliance trainin services for the transport of infectious and biologic material. Cantel's subsidiaries provide technic maintenance services for their own products as well as fo selected competitors' products. Cantel's newest divisio Crosstex, focuses on single-use infection control product primarily for the dental care market. Crosstex runs faciliti in the U.S., the Netherlands, Japan and Argentina. In Ma 2006, subsidiary Mar Cor purchased Fluid Solutions, Inc., water purity systems development and implementatio specialist operating throughout New England. Cantel' subsidiary, Carsen Group, Inc., was acquired in July 2006 b Olympus America, Inc. In April 2007, Cantel acquired G Water & Process Technologies' water dialysis business.

FINANCIALS: **Sales and profits are in thousands of dollars—add 000 to get the full amount. 2007 Note: Financial information for 2007 was not available for all companies at press time.**

2007 Sales: $	2007 Profits: $	**U.S. Stock Ticker: CMN**
2006 Sales: $192,179	2006 Profits: $23,697	**Int'l Ticker:** Int'l Exchange:
2005 Sales: $137,157	2005 Profits: $15,505	Employees: 794
2004 Sales: $123,041	2004 Profits: $10,654	Fiscal Year Ends: 7/31
2003 Sales: $129,300	2003 Profits: $7,900	Parent Company:

SALARIES/BENEFITS:

Pension Plan:	ESOP Stock Plan:	Profit Sharing:	Top Exec. Salary: $450,000	Bonus: $197,438
Savings Plan: Y	Stock Purch. Plan: Y		Second Exec. Salary: $353,208	Bonus: $

OTHER THOUGHTS:

Apparent Women Officers or Directors:
Hot Spot for Advancement for Women/Minorities:

LOCATIONS: ("Y" = Yes)

West:	Southwest:	Midwest:	Southeast:	Northeast:	International:
Y		Y	Y	Y	Y

CAPITAL BLUECROSS www.capbluecross.com

Industry Group Code: 524114 **Ranks within this company's industry group:** Sales: Profits:

Insurance/HMO/PPO:		Drugs:		Equipment/Supplies:		Hospitals/Clinics:		Services:		Health Care:	
Insurance:	Y	Manufacturer:		Manufacturer:		Acute Care:		Diagnostics:		Home Health:	
Managed Care:	Y	Distributor:		Distributor:		Sub-Acute:		Labs/Testing:		Long-Term Care:	
Utilization Management:		Specialty Pharmacy:		Leasing/Finance:		Outpatient Surgery:		Staffing:		Physical Therapy:	
Payment Processing:		Vitamins/Nutritionals:		Information Systems:		Physical Rehab. Ctr.:		Waste Disposal:		Physician Prac. Mgmt.:	
		Clinical Trials:				Psychiatric Clinics:		Specialty Svcs.:			

TYPES OF BUSINESS:

Insurance-Medical & Health, HMOs & PPOs
Administrative Services
Life Insurance

BRANDS/DIVISIONS/AFFILIATES:

Keystone Health Plan Central
Consolidated Benefits, Inc.
Capital Administrative Services
Capital Advantage Insurance Company

CONTACTS: *Note: Officers with more than one job title may be intentionally listed here more than once.*

Anita M. Smith, CEO
Anita M. Smith, Pres.
Debra B. Cohen, Sr. VP-Human Resources
Debra B. Cohen, Sr. VP-Oper.
Mike Cleary, VP-Finance
William Lehr, Jr., Chmn.

Phone: 717-541-7000	**Fax:** 717-541-6915
Toll-Free: 800-962-2242	
Address: 2500 Elmerton Ave., Harrisburg, PA 17177 US	

GROWTH PLANS/SPECIAL FEATURES:

Capital BlueCross provides health insurance and related services to nearly 1 million members spread through 21 counties in central Pennsylvania and the Lehigh Valley. The company has a physician network of more than 8,300 and works with 37 hospitals in the region. Capital BlueCross offers a comprehensive range of products for groups and individuals, including a choice of several PPOs and dental, vision and pharmacy benefit programs. Capital BlueCross also offers the Children's Health Insurance Program (CHIP), a low-cost or free health insurance program for uninsured children and adolescents who do not qualify for medical assistance through the Department of Public Welfare and who meet certain guidelines with respect to family size and income. Capital Administrative Services, a wholly-owned subsidiary, operates as a third-party administrator for employers, members and visitors needing information on services, physicians, clinical management and wellness. Capital Advantage Insurance Company, a wholly-owned subsidiary, offers comprehensive health coverage alone or in combination with Capital BlueCross. Keystone Health Plan Central administers Capital BlueCross' family health plans under the brand KHP Central. Consolidated Benefits, Inc., the only subsidiary not licensed under the Blue Cross name, offers life, short-term disability and accidental death and dismemberment (AD&D) coverage.

Capital BlueCross provides its employees with a benefits package that includes tuition reimbursement, employee assistance, wellness activities, flexible spending accounts and health education.

FINANCIALS: **Sales and profits are in thousands of dollars—add 000 to get the full amount. 2007 Note: Financial information for 2007 was not available for all companies at press time.**

2007 Sales: $	2007 Profits: $	**U.S. Stock Ticker: Nonprofit**
2006 Sales: $	2006 Profits: $	**Int'l Ticker:** Int'l Exchange:
2005 Sales: $	2005 Profits: $	Employees: 2,300
2004 Sales: $1,801,270	2004 Profits: $53,562	Fiscal Year Ends: 12/31
2003 Sales: $1,675,000	2003 Profits: $-46,274	Parent Company:

SALARIES/BENEFITS:

Pension Plan: Y	ESOP Stock Plan:	Profit Sharing:	Top Exec. Salary: $	Bonus: $
Savings Plan: Y	Stock Purch. Plan:		Second Exec. Salary: $	Bonus: $

OTHER THOUGHTS:

Apparent Women Officers or Directors: 2
Hot Spot for Advancement for Women/Minorities: Y

LOCATIONS: ("Y" = Yes)

West:	Southwest:	Midwest:	Southeast:	Northeast:	International:
				Y	

Note: Financial information, benefits and other data can change quickly and may vary from those stated here.

CAPITAL SENIOR LIVING CORP www.capitalsenior.com

Industry Group Code: 623110 **Ranks within this company's industry group:** Sales: 8 Profits: 6

Insurance/HMO/PPO:		Drugs:		Equipment/Supplies:		Hospitals/Clinics:		Services:		Health Care:	
Insurance:		Manufacturer:		Manufacturer:		Acute Care:		Diagnostics:		Home Health:	Y
Managed Care:		Distributor:		Distributor:		Sub-Acute:		Labs/Testing:		Long-Term Care:	Y
Utilization Management:		Specialty Pharmacy:		Leasing/Finance:		Outpatient Surgery:		Staffing:		Physical Therapy:	
Payment Processing:		Vitamins/Nutritionals:		Information Systems:		Physical Rehab. Ctr.:		Waste Disposal:		Physician Prac. Mgmt.:	
		Clinical Trials:				Psychiatric Clinics:		Specialty Svcs.:			

TYPES OF BUSINESS:

Long-Term Health Care
Nursing Homes
Assisted Living Services
Home Care Services

BRANDS/DIVISIONS/AFFILIATES:

CONTACTS:

Note: Officers with more than one job title may be intentionally listed here more than once.

Lawrence A. Cohen, CEO
Keith N. Johannessen, COO
Keith N. Johannessen, Pres.
Ralph A. Beattie, CFO/Exec. VP
James A. Stroud, Chmn.

Phone: 972-770-5600	**Fax:** 972-770-5666
Toll-Free:	
Address: 14160 Dallas Pkwy., Ste. 300, Dallas, TX 75254 US	

GROWTH PLANS/SPECIAL FEATURES:

Capital Senior Living Corporation (CSL) is one of the nation' largest operators and developers of residential communitie for seniors. The firm operates 64 communities in 23 state with an aggregate capacity of 9,500 residents, including 3 communities that it owns or in which it has an ownershi interest and 4 communities which it manages for thir parties. 95% of the company's revenue is generated throug private pay parties at these communities. The firm provide senior living services to the elderly, including independen living, assisted living, skilled nursing and home car services. Many of CSL's communities offer a continuum o care to meet its residents' needs as they change over time This continuum of care, which integrates independent livin and assisted living and is bridged by home care throug independent home care agencies or the company's hom care agency, sustains residents' autonomy an independence based on their physical and mental abilities Each Capital community features social and recreationa programs, maid service, restaurant-quality meals an complimentary laundry rooms. In May 2006, Capita announced its entering into a joint-venture, in which it has a 15% stake, to acquire three senior housing communities fo approximately $38.2 million. The acquisition comprises o 300 units of senior housing, including 198 units of assiste living and 102 units of memory care.

FINANCIALS:

Sales and profits are in thousands of dollars—add 000 to get the full amount. 2007 Note: Financial information for 2007 was not available for all companies at press time.

2007 Sales: $	2007 Profits: $	**U.S. Stock Ticker: CSU**
2006 Sales: $159,070	2006 Profits: $-2,600	**Int'l Ticker:** Int'l Exchange:
2005 Sales: $126,404	2005 Profits: $-5,354	Employees: 3,681
2004 Sales: $108,935	2004 Profits: $-6,758	Fiscal Year Ends: 12/31
2003 Sales: $66,325	2003 Profits: $4,990	Parent Company:

SALARIES/BENEFITS:

Pension Plan:	ESOP Stock Plan:	Profit Sharing:	Top Exec. Salary: $381,423	Bonus: $228,366
Savings Plan: Y	Stock Purch. Plan:		Second Exec. Salary: $317,852	Bonus: $126,851

OTHER THOUGHTS:

Apparent Women Officers or Directors:
Hot Spot for Advancement for Women/Minorities:

LOCATIONS: ("Y" = Yes)

West:	Southwest:	Midwest:	Southeast:	Northeast:	International:
Y	Y	Y	Y	Y	

CARDINAL HEALTH INC

www.cardinal.com

Industry Group Code: 422210 **Ranks within this company's industry group:** Sales: 2 Profits: 1

Insurance/HMO/PPO:		Drugs:		Equipment/Supplies:		Hospitals/Clinics:		Services:		Health Care:	
Insurance:		Manufacturer:		Manufacturer:		Acute Care:		Diagnostics:		Home Health:	
Managed Care:		Distributor:	Y	Distributor:	Y	Sub-Acute:		Labs/Testing:		Long-Term Care:	
Utilization Management:		Specialty Pharmacy:	Y	Leasing/Finance:		Outpatient Surgery:		Staffing:		Physical Therapy:	
Payment Processing:		Vitamins/Nutritionals:		Information Systems:	Y	Physical Rehab. Ctr.:		Waste Disposal:		Physician Prac. Mgmt.:	
		Clinical Trials:				Psychiatric Clinics:		Specialty Svcs.:	Y		

TYPES OF BUSINESS:

Healthcare Products & Services

BRANDS/DIVISIONS/AFFILIATES:

Alaris
Pyxis
MedMined, Inc.
Viasys Healthcare, Inc.

CONTACTS:

Note: Officers with more than one job title may be intentionally listed here more than once.

R. Kerry Clark, CEO
Jeff Henderson, CFO
Carole Watkins, Chief Human Resources Officer
Jody Davids, CIO/Exec. VP-Global Shares Svcs.
Ivan Fong, Chief Legal Officer/Sec.
Vivek Jain, Exec. VP-Strategy & Corp. Dev.
Shelley Bird, Exec. VP-Global Comm.
Gary Dolch, Exec. VP-Quality & Regulatory Affairs
Frank Segrave, Pres., Generics
Mike Lynch, Group Pres., Medical Prod. Mfg.
Mark Parrish, CEO-Healthcare Supply Chain Svcs.
R. Kerry Clark, Chmn.
Rudy Mareel, Pres., Int'l

Phone: 614-757-5000	**Fax:** 614-757-8871
Toll-Free: 800-234-8701	
Address: 7000 Cardinal Pl., Dublin, OH 43017 US	

GROWTH PLANS/SPECIAL FEATURES:

Cardinal Health, Inc. is a provider of products and services in the healthcare industry. The company operates in four segments. The healthcare supply chain services-pharmaceutical segment distributes branded and generic pharmaceutical products, over-the-counter healthcare products and consumer products. In addition, the division offers support services, including online procurement, fulfillment and information provided through the company's web site; computerized order entry and order confirmation systems; generic sourcing programs; and consultation on store operations and merchandising. The healthcare supply chain services-medical segment distributes branded and private-label medical and laboratory products, as well as the firm's own line of surgical and respiratory therapy products to hospitals, laboratories and ambulatory care customers. The clinical technologies and services segment develops, manufactures, leases and sells dispensing systems for medical supplies and medical technology products, including Alaris intravenous medication safety and infusion therapy delivery systems; software applications; needle-free disposables and related patient monitoring equipment; and Pyxis dispensing systems that automate the distribution and management of medications in hospitals and other healthcare facilities. The medical products manufacturing segment develops and manufactures medical and surgical products such as infection prevention products, including single-use surgical drapes, gowns and apparel, exam and surgical gloves and fluid suction and collection systems; and medical specialties products, including respiratory therapy products, surgical instruments and special procedure products. In July 2006, Cardinal acquired MedMined, Inc., a leader in technology and services that identify and prevent hospital-acquired infections. In May 2007, Cardinal sold its pharmaceutical technologies and services segment to the Blackstone Group for $3.3 billion. In June 2007, the company purchased Viasys Healthcare, Inc. for about $1.5 billion.

The company offers its employees medical, dental, vision and life insurance; a 401(k) plan; an employee assistance program; an employee stock purchase plan; business travel insurance; and tuition reimbursement.

FINANCIALS:

Sales and profits are in thousands of dollars—add 000 to get the full amount. 2007 Note: Financial information for 2007 was not available for all companies at press time.

2007 Sales: $86,852,000	2007 Profits: $1,931,100	**U.S. Stock Ticker: CAH**
2006 Sales: $79,664,200	2006 Profits: $1,000,100	**Int'l Ticker:** Int'l Exchange:
2005 Sales: $72,666,000	2005 Profits: $1,050,700	Employees: 43,500
2004 Sales: $63,043,100	2004 Profits: $1,474,500	Fiscal Year Ends: 6/30
2003 Sales: $56,737,000	2003 Profits: $1,405,800	Parent Company:

SALARIES/BENEFITS:

Pension Plan:	ESOP Stock Plan:	Profit Sharing:	Top Exec. Salary: $1,065,116	Bonus: $2,911,527
Savings Plan: Y	Stock Purch. Plan: Y		Second Exec. Salary: $701,885	Bonus: $400,000

OTHER THOUGHTS:

Apparent Women Officers or Directors: 5
Hot Spot for Advancement for Women/Minorities: Y

LOCATIONS: ("Y" = Yes)

West:	Southwest:	Midwest:	Southeast:	Northeast:	International:
Y	Y	Y	Y	Y	Y

CARDIOGENESIS CORP

www.cardiogenesis.com

Industry Group Code: 339113 **Ranks within this company's industry group:** Sales: 101 Profits: 82

Insurance/HMO/PPO:		Drugs:		Equipment/Supplies:		Hospitals/Clinics:		Services:		Health Care:	
Insurance:		Manufacturer:		Manufacturer:	Y	Acute Care:		Diagnostics:		Home Health:	
Managed Care:		Distributor:		Distributor:	Y	Sub-Acute:		Labs/Testing:		Long-Term Care:	
Utilization Management:		Specialty Pharmacy:		Leasing/Finance:		Outpatient Surgery:		Staffing:		Physical Therapy:	
Payment Processing:		Vitamins/Nutritionals:		Information Systems:		Physical Rehab. Ctr.:		Waste Disposal:		Physician Prac. Mgmt.:	
		Clinical Trials:				Psychiatric Clinics:		Specialty Svcs.:			

TYPES OF BUSINESS:

Equipment-Laser & Fiber-Optic Systems
Laser-Based Surgical Products
Disposable Fiber-Optic Accessories
Cardiovascular Surgical Products

BRANDS/DIVISIONS/AFFILIATES:

TMR 2000
New Star PMR
Axcis
Sologrip III

CONTACTS: *Note: Officers with more than one job title may be intentionally listed here more than once.*

Richard P. Lanigan, Pres.
William R. Abbot, CFO/Sr. VP
Charles J. Scarano, Sr. VP-Mktg.
Marvin J. Slepian, Chief Scientific Officer
Gerard A. Arthur, Sr. VP-Oper.
William R. Abbot, Treas.
Paul J. McCormick, Chmn.

Phone: 714-649-5000 **Fax:** 714-649-5103
Toll-Free: 800-238-2205
Address: 26632 Towne Centre Dr., Ste. 320, Foothill Ranch, CA 92610 US

GROWTH PLANS/SPECIAL FEATURES:

CardioGenesis is a medical device company specializing i the treatment of cardiovascular disease, and is a leader i the manufacturing of devices that stimulate cardia angiogenesis, the growth of new blood vessels. Th company's main products, the YAG laser system and it disposable fiber-optic accessories, are used to perfor transmyocardial revascularization (TMR) to treat patient suffering from angina. The firm's newest procedure percutaneous transluminal myocardial revascularizatio (PMR), is currently being marketed in Europe and othe international markets, but is still under review by the U.S FDA. TMR and PMR are recent laser-based hea treatments in which channels are made in the heart muscle In the TMR procedure, the surgeon inserts a laser devic through the myocardium to create a new pathway into th heart. This procedure can be done through open che surgery or less invasive methods. The PMR procedure i less invasive than TMR, in that a catheter is inserted in th femoral artery in the leg. CardioGenesis' products includ the TMR 2000 laser system and Sologrip III laser deliver system for TMR, which are sold in the U.S., as well as th New Star PMR laser system and Axcis laser catheter fo PMR, which are sold internationally and are awaiting FD approval. Cardiogenesis, formerly known as Eclips Surgical Technologies, markets its products for sale primaril in the United States, Europe and Asia.

FINANCIALS: Sales and profits are in thousands of dollars—add 000 to get the full amount. 2007 Note: Financial information for 2007 was not available for all companies at press time.

2007 Sales: $	2007 Profits: $	**U.S. Stock Ticker: CGCP**
2006 Sales: $17,117	2006 Profits: $-1,979	**Int'l Ticker:** Int'l Exchange:
2005 Sales: $16,341	2005 Profits: $-1,857	Employees: 30
2004 Sales: $15,454	2004 Profits: $-1,319	Fiscal Year Ends: 12/31
2003 Sales: $13,518	2003 Profits: $- 348	Parent Company:

SALARIES/BENEFITS:

Pension Plan:	ESOP Stock Plan:	Profit Sharing:	Top Exec. Salary: $301,745	Bonus: $
Savings Plan: Y	Stock Purch. Plan:		Second Exec. Salary: $264,688	Bonus: $

OTHER THOUGHTS:

Apparent Women Officers or Directors: 1
Hot Spot for Advancement for Women/Minorities:

LOCATIONS: ("Y" = Yes)

West:	Southwest:	Midwest:	Southeast:	Northeast:	International:
Y					

CAREFIRST INC

www.carefirst.com

ndustry Group Code: 524114 **Ranks within this company's industry group:** Sales: 16 Profits: 15

nsurance/HMO/PPO:		Drugs:		Equipment/Supplies:		Hospitals/Clinics:		Services:		Health Care:	
nsurance:	Y	Manufacturer:		Manufacturer:		Acute Care:		Diagnostics:		Home Health:	
Managed Care:	Y	Distributor:		Distributor:		Sub-Acute:		Labs/Testing:		Long-Term Care:	
Utilization Management:		Specialty Pharmacy:		Leasing/Finance:		Outpatient Surgery:		Staffing:		Physical Therapy:	
Payment Processing:		Vitamins/Nutritionals:		Information Systems:		Physical Rehab. Ctr.:		Waste Disposal:		Physician Prac. Mgmt.:	
		Clinical Trials:				Psychiatric Clinics:		Specialty Svcs.:	Y		

TYPES OF BUSINESS:

nsurance-Medical & Health, HMOs & PPOs
HMO
Claims Processing
Administrative Services

BRANDS/DIVISIONS/AFFILIATES:

CareFirst BlueCross BlueShield
CareFirst of Maryland, Inc.
Group Hospitalization & Medical Services, Inc.
BlueCross BlueShield of Delaware
CareFirst BlueChoice
BlueFund
BlueVision
CASCI

CONTACTS: *Note: Officers with more than one job title may be intentionally listed here more than once.*

David D. Wolf, Interim CEO
David D. Wolf, Interim Pres.
G. Mark Chaney, CFO/Exec. VP
Gregory A. Devou, Chief Mktg. Officer/Exec. VP
Sharon J. Vecchioni, Exec. VP-Human Resources/Chief of Staff
John A. Picciotto, General Counsel/Corp. Sec./Exec. VP
Leon Kaplan, Exec. VP-Oper.
Maynard G. McAlpin, VP-Strategic Planning
Gregory A. Devou, Pres., National Capital Admin. Svcs., Inc.
Gregory A. Devou, Pres., National Capital Insurance Agency, Inc.
Sharon J. Vecchioni, Exec. VP-Bus. Planning
Michael R. Merson, Chmn.

Phone: 410-528-7000 **Fax:** 410-998-5351
Toll-Free: 800-914-6397
Address: 10455 Mill Run Cir., Owings Mills, MD 21117 US

GROWTH PLANS/SPECIAL FEATURES:

CareFirst, Inc. is one of the largest health care insurers in the Mid-Atlantic, with approximately 3.1 million members. The company includes 165 hospitals across Maryland, Delaware, northern Virginia and Washington, D.C. in its provider network. CareFirst, Inc. is the nonprofit parent company of Group Hospitalization and Medical Services, Inc. (GHMSI) and CareFirst of Maryland, Inc., which collectively do business as CareFirst BlueCross BlueShield. GHMSI's subsidiary, Service Benefit Plan Administrative Services Corporation, was created to operate the Federal Employee Program (FEP) Operations Center, which GHMSI has previously operated. CareFirst serves approximately 515,000 members in FEP. CareFirst also operates West Virginia-based subsidiary CASI, which annually processes over 5 million claims from federal government subscribers and dependents as part of FEP. The company offers client businesses health plans for their employees such as the following: BlueFund Consumer Directed Health Plans, BlueVision, BlueChoice Options and Regional Dental. The company's expansive reach is shown by the fact that over 80% of health care providers in the company's operating region participate in one or more of its provider networks. Through a third-party administrator, NCAS, the company also offers administrative services to self-insured employers. In addition, CareFirst operates a for-profit regional HMO subsidiary, CareFirst BlueChoice, with more than 3,500 primary care physicians. In September 2006, CareFirst ceased to be the sole member of BlueCross BlueShield of Delaware.

CareFirst's offers its employees a college savings plan, flexible spending accounts, tuition reimbursement, a pension plan, a 401(k) savings plan and medical, dental, vision and prescription coverage.

FINANCIALS: Sales and profits are in thousands of dollars—add 000 to get the full amount. 2007 Note: Financial information for 2007 was not available for all companies at press time.

2007 Sales: $
2006 Sales: $5,510,184
2005 Sales: $5,168,942
2004 Sales: $4,983,145
2003 Sales: $4,642,999

2007 Profits: $
2006 Profits: $164,256
2005 Profits: $118,503
2004 Profits: $140,483
2003 Profits: $171,300

U.S. Stock Ticker: Nonprofit
Int'l Ticker: Int'l Exchange:
Employees: 4,800
Fiscal Year Ends: 12/31
Parent Company:

SALARIES/BENEFITS:

Pension Plan: Y | ESOP Stock Plan: | Profit Sharing: | Top Exec. Salary: $ | Bonus: $
Savings Plan: Y | Stock Purch. Plan: | | Second Exec. Salary: $ | Bonus: $

OTHER THOUGHTS:

Apparent Women Officers or Directors: 2
Hot Spot for Advancement for Women/Minorities: Y

LOCATIONS: ("Y" = Yes)

West:	Southwest:	Midwest:	Southeast:	Northeast:	International:
			Y	Y	

CAREMARK RX INC

www.caremark.com

Industry Group Code: 522320A **Ranks within this company's industry group:** Sales: 2 Profits: 1

Insurance/HMO/PPO:		Drugs:		Equipment/Supplies:		Hospitals/Clinics:		Services:		Health Care:	
Insurance:		Manufacturer:		Manufacturer:		Acute Care:		Diagnostics:		Home Health:	
Managed Care:		Distributor:	Y	Distributor:		Sub-Acute:		Labs/Testing:		Long-Term Care:	
Utilization Management:		Specialty Pharmacy:		Leasing/Finance:		Outpatient Surgery:		Staffing:		Physical Therapy:	
Payment Processing:	Y	Vitamins/Nutritionals:		Information Systems:		Physical Rehab. Ctr.:		Waste Disposal:		Physician Prac. Mgmt.:	
		Clinical Trials:				Psychiatric Clinics:		Specialty Svcs.:	Y		

TYPES OF BUSINESS:

Prescription Benefit Management
Disease Management Programs

BRANDS/DIVISIONS/AFFILIATES:

Caremark, Inc.
CaremarkPCS
AdvancePCS
CarePatterns
Accordant

CONTACTS: *Note: Officers with more than one job title may be intentionally listed here more than once.*

Mac Crawford, CEO
Howard McLure, COO/Exec. VP
Mac Crawford, Pres.
Peter Clemens, CFO/Exec. VP
David Joyner, Exec. VP-Sales & Acct. Mgmt.
Dennis Zeleny, Exec. VP-Human Resources
Edward L. Hardin, Jr., General Counsel/Exec. VP
James C. Luthin, Exec. VP-Oper.
Brad Karro, Exec. VP-Corp. Dev.
Mark Weeks, Sr. VP/Controller
Rudy Mladenovic, Exec. VP-Industry Rel.
Diane Nobles, Exec. VP-Compliance & Integrity
William R. Spalding, Exec. VP-Strategic Dev.
Sara J. Finley, Sr. VP/Corp. Sec.
Mac Crawford, Chmn.

Phone: 615-743-6600	**Fax:** 615-743-6599
Toll-Free:	
Address: 211 Commerce St., Ste. 800, Nashville, TN 37201 US	

GROWTH PLANS/SPECIAL FEATURES:

Caremark Rx is one of the largest pharmaceutical services companies in the U.S., operating primarily through its Caremark Inc. and CaremarkPCS (formerly AdvancePCS) subsidiaries. The company's primary line of business is the dispensation of pharmaceuticals to eligible participants in benefit plans maintained by Caremark Rx customers and the performance of safety checks, drug interaction screening and generic substitution. Caremark Rx manages over 484 million prescriptions for individuals from over 2,000 organizations. While the firm does not operate or own pharmacies, it maintains contracts with retail pharmacy chains and independents to form a network of more than 60,000 retail pharmacies at which plan participants may fill prescriptions. Caremark operates a mail order pharmacy service that fills more than 43 million prescriptions annually. This service conducts its operations through seven automated pharmacies in the U.S., as well as 21 smaller specialty mail service pharmacies which provide medication to patients with chronic or genetic diseases and disorders. Caremark also operates the industry's only FDA-regulated repackaging plant. Company disease management programs such as CarePatterns and Accordant cover over 20 diseases, including asthma, coronary artery disease, congestive heart failure, diabetes, hemophilia, rheumatoid arthritis and multiple sclerosis. The CaremarkPCS subsidiary provides services and pharmaceuticals-by-mail to managed care organizations. Caremark clients include corporate health plans, managed care organizations, insurance companies, unions, government agencies and other funded benefit plans. In March 2007, Caremark shareholders approved a merger of equals with CVS Corp., a leading national drug store chain. The merged company will be called CVS/Caremark Corporation, with a total of about $75 billion in annual revenues.

Caremark offers its employees education reimbursement, credit union membership, flexible spending accounts, employee assistance, adoption assistance, an incentive salary program and professional development programs.

FINANCIALS: **Sales and profits are in thousands of dollars—add 000 to get the full amount. 2007 Note: Financial information for 2007 was not available for all companies at press time.**

2007 Sales: $	2007 Profits: $	**U.S. Stock Ticker: CMX**
2006 Sales: $36,750,203	2006 Profits: $1,074,015	**Int'l Ticker:** Int'l Exchange:
2005 Sales: $32,991,251	2005 Profits: $932,371	Employees: 13,360
2004 Sales: $25,801,121	2004 Profits: $600,309	Fiscal Year Ends: 12/31
2003 Sales: $9,067,291	2003 Profits: $290,838	Parent Company:

SALARIES/BENEFITS:

Pension Plan:	ESOP Stock Plan:	Profit Sharing:	Top Exec. Salary: $1,615,384	Bonus: $4,000,000
Savings Plan: Y	Stock Purch. Plan: Y		Second Exec. Salary: $556,640	Bonus: $675,000

OTHER THOUGHTS:

Apparent Women Officers or Directors: 3
Hot Spot for Advancement for Women/Minorities: Y

LOCATIONS: ("Y" = Yes)

West:	Southwest:	Midwest:	Southeast:	Northeast:	International:
Y	Y	Y	Y	Y	Y

CASTLE DENTAL CENTERS INC www.castledental.com

Industry Group Code: 621111 **Ranks within this company's industry group:** Sales: Profits:

Insurance/HMO/PPO:		Drugs:		Equipment/Supplies:		Hospitals/Clinics:		Services:		Health Care:	
Insurance:		Manufacturer:		Manufacturer:		Acute Care:		Diagnostics:		Home Health:	
Managed Care:		Distributor:		Distributor:		Sub-Acute:		Labs/Testing:		Long-Term Care:	
Utilization Management:		Specialty Pharmacy:		Leasing/Finance:		Outpatient Surgery:		Staffing:		Physical Therapy:	
Payment Processing:		Vitamins/Nutritionals:		Information Systems:		Physical Rehab. Ctr.:		Waste Disposal:		Physician Prac. Mgmt.:	Y
		Clinical Trials:				Psychiatric Clinics:		Specialty Svcs.:			

TYPES OF BUSINESS:

Dental Practice Management

BRANDS/DIVISIONS/AFFILIATES:

Bright Now! Dental Inc

CONTACTS:
Note: Officers with more than one job title may be intentionally listed here more than once.

Steven C. Bilt, Pres./CEO, Bright Now! Dental, Inc.

Phone: 281-999-9999	**Fax:** 713-490-8415
Toll-Free: 800-867-6453	
Address: 3701 Kirby Dr., Ste. 550, Houston, TX 77098 US	

GROWTH PLANS/SPECIAL FEATURES:

Castle Dental Centers, Inc., a subsidiary of Bright Now! Dental, Inc., develops, manages and operates integrated dental networks through contracts with general, orthodontic and multi-specialty dental practices in the U.S. The company manages over 100 dental centers with over 200 affiliated dentists, orthodontists and specialists in Texas, Florida, Tennessee and California. The typical Castle Dental Center provides general dentistry as well as a full range of dental specialties including orthodontics, pedodontics, periodontics, endodontics, oral surgery and implantology. Bringing together multi-specialty dental services within a single practice allows Castle to operate more efficiently, use facilities more completely and share dental specialists among multiple locations. Its operating model also incorporates quality assurance and quality control programs, such as peer review and continuing education. Castle establishes regional dental care networks in order to centralize its advertising, billing and collections, payroll and accounting systems.

FINANCIALS:
Sales and profits are in thousands of dollars—add 000 to get the full amount. 2007 Note: Financial information for 2007 was not available for all companies at press time.

2007 Sales: $	2007 Profits: $	**U.S. Stock Ticker: Subsidiary**
2006 Sales: $	2006 Profits: $	**Int'l Ticker:** Int'l Exchange:
2005 Sales: $	2005 Profits: $	Employees: 1,025
2004 Sales: $	2004 Profits: $	Fiscal Year Ends: 12/31
2003 Sales: $93,889	2003 Profits: $26,104	Parent Company: BRIGHT NOW! DENTAL INC

SALARIES/BENEFITS:

Pension Plan:	ESOP Stock Plan:	Profit Sharing:	Top Exec. Salary: $249,722	Bonus: $63,334
Savings Plan:	Stock Purch. Plan:		Second Exec. Salary: $237,138	Bonus: $61,584

OTHER THOUGHTS:

Apparent Women Officers or Directors:

Hot Spot for Advancement for Women/Minorities:

LOCATIONS: ("Y" = Yes)

West:	Southwest:	Midwest:	Southeast:	Northeast:	International:
Y	Y		Y		

CATHOLIC HEALTH INITIATIVES www.catholichealthinit.org

Industry Group Code: 622110 **Ranks within this company's industry group:** Sales: 5 Profits: 3

Insurance/HMO/PPO:		Drugs:		Equipment/Supplies:		Hospitals/Clinics:		Services:		Health Care:	
Insurance:		Manufacturer:		Manufacturer:		Acute Care:	Y	Diagnostics:		Home Health:	Y
Managed Care:		Distributor:		Distributor:		Sub-Acute:	Y	Labs/Testing:		Long-Term Care:	Y
Utilization Management:		Specialty Pharmacy:		Leasing/Finance:		Outpatient Surgery:		Staffing:		Physical Therapy:	
Payment Processing:		Vitamins/Nutritionals:		Information Systems:		Physical Rehab. Ctr.:		Waste Disposal:		Physician Prac. Mgmt.:	
		Clinical Trials:				Psychiatric Clinics:		Specialty Svcs.:	Y		

TYPES OF BUSINESS:

Hospitals
Long-Term Care
Assisted & Independent Living Facilities
Community Health Organizations
Home Care Services
Occupational Health Clinic
Cancer Prevention Institute

BRANDS/DIVISIONS/AFFILIATES:

Centura Health
CARITAS Health Services
Alegant Health
Good Samaritan Health Systems
Premier Health Partners
Franciscan Health System

CONTACTS: *Note: Officers with more than one job title may be intentionally listed here more than once.*

Kevin E. Lofton, CEO
Michael T. Rowan, COO/Exec. VP
Kevin E. Lofton, Pres.
Colleen M. Blye, CFO
Herbert J. Vallier, Chief Human Resource Officer/Sr. VP
Michael O'Rourke, Interim CIO
Michael L. Fordyce, Chief Admin. Officer
Paul G. Neumann, General Counsel/Sr. VP-Legal Svcs.
Larry A. Schulz, Sr. VP-Oper.
John F. DiCola, Sr. VP-Strategy & Bus. Dev.
Joyce M. Ross, Sr. VP-Comm.
Colleen M. Blye, Sr. VP-Finance & Treasury
A. Michelle Cooper, VP-Corp. Responsibility
Mitch H. Merlfi, Chief Risk Officer/Sr. VP
Susan E. Peach, Sr. VP-Performance Mgmt.
John F. Anderson, Chief Medical Officer/Sr. VP
Phillip W. Mears, Sr. VP-Supply Chain

Phone: 303-298-9100	**Fax:** 303-298-9690
Toll-Free:	
Address: 1999 Broadway, Ste. 2600, Denver, CO 80202 US	

GROWTH PLANS/SPECIAL FEATURES:

Catholic Health Initiatives is a national nonprofit health care organization focused on strengthening and advancing the Catholic health ministry. The organization encompasses approximately 73 hospitals; more than 40 long-term care assisted and independent living residential facilities; and two community health organizations, across 19 states. The group's major affiliates include Centura Health, CARITAS Health Services, Alegent Health, Good Samaritan Health Systems, Premier Health Partners and Franciscan Health System, located in Colorado, Kentucky, Nebraska, Ohio, and Washington. Altogether, CHI has over 10,000 beds Catholic Health is the second largest Catholic health system in the US. Centura Health, jointly operated between CHI and PorterCare Adventist Health Care, has 12 hospitals and eight senior residences and home care and hospice services. CARITAS Health Services operates through the CARITAS Medical Center, a primary care hospital offering cancer treatment, surgery and emergency services. Alegent Health, jointly operated with Immanuel Healthcare System, is made up of seven acute care hospitals with 1,400 beds, two long-term care facilities and a primary care physician network. Good Samaritan Health Systems is a network of hospitals and services serving more than 350,000 customers in its region. Premier Health Partners, jointly operated with MedAmerica Health Systems, includes three hospitals, one assisted living community, a home health care service and a cancer prevention institute. The Franciscan Health System includes three full-service hospitals, a long-term care facility, a women's health center and midwife service and an occupational health clinic, among other services.

FINANCIALS: Sales and profits are in thousands of dollars—add 000 to get the full amount. 2007 Note: Financial information for 2007 was not available for all companies at press time.

2007 Sales: $	2007 Profits: $	**U.S. Stock Ticker: Nonprofit**
2006 Sales: $7,636,233	2006 Profits: $693,701	**Int'l Ticker:** Int'l Exchange:
2005 Sales: $7,091,448	2005 Profits: $498,374	Employees: 65,070
2004 Sales: $6,659,711	2004 Profits: $538,295	Fiscal Year Ends:
2003 Sales: $6,071,600	2003 Profits: $202,900	Parent Company:

SALARIES/BENEFITS:

Pension Plan:	ESOP Stock Plan:	Profit Sharing:	Top Exec. Salary: $	Bonus: $
Savings Plan:	Stock Purch. Plan:		Second Exec. Salary: $	Bonus: $

OTHER THOUGHTS:

Apparent Women Officers or Directors: 8
Hot Spot for Advancement for Women/Minorities: Y

LOCATIONS: ("Y" = Yes)

West:	Southwest:	Midwest:	Southeast:	Northeast:	International:
Y	Y	Y	Y	Y	

CATHOLIC HEALTHCARE PARTNERS www.health-partners.org

Industry Group Code: 622110 **Ranks within this company's industry group:** Sales: 15 Profits: 14

Insurance/HMO/PPO:		Drugs:		Equipment/Supplies:		Hospitals/Clinics:		Services:		Health Care:	
Insurance:		Manufacturer:		Manufacturer:		Acute Care:	Y	Diagnostics:		Home Health:	Y
Managed Care:		Distributor:		Distributor:		Sub-Acute:	Y	Labs/Testing:		Long-Term Care:	Y
Utilization Management:		Specialty Pharmacy:		Leasing/Finance:		Outpatient Surgery:		Staffing:		Physical Therapy:	
Payment Processing:		Vitamins/Nutritionals:		Information Systems:		Physical Rehab. Ctr.:		Waste Disposal:		Physician Prac. Mgmt.:	
		Clinical Trials:				Psychiatric Clinics:		Specialty Svcs.:	Y		

TYPES OF BUSINESS:

Hospitals
Long-Term Care
Hospice Programs
Home Health Services
Low-Income Housing

BRANDS/DIVISIONS/AFFILIATES:

Mercy Health Partners
Community Health Partners
West Central Ohio Health Partners
Humility of Mary Health Partners
Community Mercy Health Partners
St. Mary's Health Partners
Health Fellowship
Sisters of Mercy

CONTACTS: *Note: Officers with more than one job title may be intentionally listed here more than once.*

Michael D. Connelly, CEO
David Jimenez, COO
Michael D. Connelly, Pres.
James R. Gravell, Jr., CFO/Sr. VP
John Starcher, Sr. VP-Human Resources
Rebecca Sykes, CIO/Sr. VP
Jane Durney Crowley, Chief Admin. Officer/Exec. VP
Michael A. Bezney, General Counsel/Sr. VP
Doris Gottenmoeller, Sr. VP-Mission & Values Integration
R. Jeffrey Copeland, Sr. VP-Insurance & Physician Services

Phone: 513-639-2800 **Fax:** 513-639-2700
Toll-Free:
Address: 615 Elsinore Pl., Cincinnati, OH 45202 US

GROWTH PLANS/SPECIAL FEATURES:

Catholic Healthcare Partners (CHP) is a not-for-profit health system consisting of more than 100 organizations in Ohio, Indiana, Kentucky, Pennsylvania and Tennessee. The organization has a total of 29 hospitals, 17 of which have long-term care beds, 14 long-term care facilities, 848 HUD housing units, 168 low-income tax credit housing units, nine hospice programs, nine home health agencies and 7,438 affiliated physicians. CHP was originally founded in 1986 by the Sisters of Mercy, Regional Community of Cincinnati and has since grown to include sponsorship by four other Catholic Organizations: the Sisters of Mercy, Regional Community of Dallas, PA; the Sisters of the Humility of Mary; the Franciscan Sisters of the Poor; and Covenant Health Systems. It is separated into nine main divisions, each exercising considerable autonomy, yet still profiting from improved strategic, operational and organizational benefits as a result of its partnership in CHP: Mercy Health Partners (with northern, southwest Ohio and Kentucky/Indiana regions), Community Health Partners, West Central Ohio Health Partners, Humility of Mary Health Partners, Community Mercy Health Partners and St. Mary's Health Partners. Together these divisions have as their mission the extension of a healing ministry with emphasis on the poor and under-served. The group offers a highly competitive fellowship, the Health Fellowship, which provides an intensive, customized two years of study and mentorship customized to professionals with graduate degrees in health care administration, business administration, ethics or other related fields.

CHP offers its employees a comprehensive benefits package, including flexible spending accounts, tuition reimbursement and numerous educational opportunities such as seminars, retreats and conferences.

FINANCIALS: **Sales and profits are in thousands of dollars—add 000 to get the full amount. 2007 Note: Financial information for 2007 was not available for all companies at press time.**

2007 Sales: $	2007 Profits: $	**U.S. Stock Ticker: Nonprofit**
2006 Sales: $3,505,081	2006 Profits: $143,093	**Int'l Ticker:** Int'l Exchange:
2005 Sales: $3,360,573	2005 Profits: $154,172	Employees:
2004 Sales: $3,239,837	2004 Profits: $98,412	Fiscal Year Ends: 12/31
2003 Sales: $8,989,522	2003 Profits: $89,588	Parent Company:

SALARIES/BENEFITS:

Pension Plan:	ESOP Stock Plan:	Profit Sharing:	Top Exec. Salary: $	Bonus: $
Savings Plan:	Stock Purch. Plan:		Second Exec. Salary: $	Bonus: $

OTHER THOUGHTS:

Apparent Women Officers or Directors: 4
Hot Spot for Advancement for Women/Minorities: Y

LOCATIONS: ("Y" = Yes)

West:	Southwest:	Midwest:	Southeast:	Northeast:	International:
		Y	Y	Y	

CATHOLIC HEALTHCARE WEST www.chwhealth.com

Industry Group Code: 622110 **Ranks within this company's industry group:** Sales: 7 Profits: 5

Insurance/HMO/PPO:		Drugs:		Equipment/Supplies:		Hospitals/Clinics:		Services:		Health Care:	
Insurance:		Manufacturer:		Manufacturer:		Acute Care:	Y	Diagnostics:		Home Health:	
Managed Care:		Distributor:		Distributor:		Sub-Acute:		Labs/Testing:		Long-Term Care:	
Utilization Management:		Specialty Pharmacy:		Leasing/Finance:		Outpatient Surgery:		Staffing:		Physical Therapy:	
Payment Processing:		Vitamins/Nutritionals:		Information Systems:		Physical Rehab. Ctr.:		Waste Disposal:		Physician Prac. Mgmt.:	
		Clinical Trials:				Psychiatric Clinics:		Specialty Svcs.:			

TYPES OF BUSINESS:

Acute-Care Hospitals
Skilled Nursing Facilities
Medical Centers

BRANDS/DIVISIONS/AFFILIATES:

St. Mary's Regional Medical Center

CONTACTS:
Note: Officers with more than one job title may be intentionally listed here more than once.

Lloyd H. Dean, CEO
Michael Erne, COO/Exec. VP
Lloyd H. Dean, Pres.
Michael D. Blaszyk, CFO/Exec. VP
Ernest H. Urquhart, Sr. VP-Human Resources
Elizabeth Shih, Chief Admin. Officer/Sr. VP
Derek F. Covert, General Counsel/Sr. VP
Charles P. Francis, Chief Strategy Officer/Sr. VP
George Bo-Linn, Sr. VP/Chief Medical Officer
Bernita McTernan, Sr. VP-Sponsorship & Mission Integration
John Wray, Sr. VP-Managed Care
Adrienne Crowe, Chairperson

Phone: 415-438-5500	**Fax:** 415-438-5724
Toll-Free:	
Address: 185 Berry St., Ste. 300, San Francisco, CA 94107 US	

GROWTH PLANS/SPECIAL FEATURES:

Catholic Healthcare West, a nonprofit healthcare provider based in San Francisco, was founded when the Sisters of Mercy Burlingame Regional Community and the Sisters of Mercy Auburn Regional Community Catholic Healthcare merged their respective health care ministries into one. The group comprises 43 acute-care hospitals, skilled nursing facilities and medical centers, totaling approximately 8,000 beds, located in California, Arizona and Nevada. The organization is the eighth largest hospital system in the country and the largest nonprofit hospital provider in California. Catholic Healthcare is committed to offering health care services to all, without regard to financial resources, providing roughly $465 million in community benefit and free care for the poor. The Catholic Healthcare network includes nearly 8,500 physicians and provides health care services during more than 4 million patient visits annually. In January 2007, St. Mary's Regional Medical Center in Nevada became a member of the organization's network.

The company offers its employees medical, dental and vision insurance; life and AD&D insurance; short- and long-term disability insurance; flexible spending accounts; an employee assistance program; a retirement plan; access to a credit union; fitness program discounts; and cafeteria discounts. The firm was recognized as one of the Best Places to Work in the San Francisco Bay area among companies with 3,000 or more employees.

FINANCIALS:
Sales and profits are in thousands of dollars—add 000 to get the full amount. 2007 Note: Financial information for 2007 was not available for all companies at press time.

2007 Sales: $	2007 Profits: $	**U.S. Stock Ticker: Nonprofit**
2006 Sales: $6,730,138	2006 Profits: $437,917	**Int'l Ticker:** Int'l Exchange:
2005 Sales: $6,002,092	2005 Profits: $348,156	Employees: 40,000
2004 Sales: $5,392,198	2004 Profits: $248,771	Fiscal Year Ends:
2003 Sales: $4,758,858	2003 Profits: $70,222	Parent Company:

SALARIES/BENEFITS:

Pension Plan: Y	ESOP Stock Plan:	Profit Sharing:	Top Exec. Salary: $	Bonus: $
Savings Plan:	Stock Purch. Plan:		Second Exec. Salary: $	Bonus: $

OTHER THOUGHTS:

Apparent Women Officers or Directors: 12
Hot Spot for Advancement for Women/Minorities: Y

LOCATIONS: ("Y" = Yes)

West:	Southwest:	Midwest:	Southeast:	Northeast:	International:
Y	Y				

CEDARA SOFTWARE CORP

www.cedara.com

Industry Group Code: 511212 **Ranks within this company's industry group:** Sales: Profits:

Insurance/HMO/PPO:		Drugs:		Equipment/Supplies:		Hospitals/Clinics:		Services:		Health Care:	
Insurance:		Manufacturer:		Manufacturer:	Y	Acute Care:		Diagnostics:		Home Health:	
Managed Care:		Distributor:		Distributor:		Sub-Acute:		Labs/Testing:		Long-Term Care:	
Utilization Management:		Specialty Pharmacy:		Leasing/Finance:		Outpatient Surgery:		Staffing:		Physical Therapy:	
Payment Processing:		Vitamins/Nutritionals:		Information Systems:	Y	Physical Rehab. Ctr.:		Waste Disposal:		Physician Prac. Mgmt.:	
		Clinical Trials:				Psychiatric Clinics:		Specialty Svcs.:	Y		

TYPES OF BUSINESS:

Software-Medical Imaging
Custom-Designed Medical Products
Engineering Services

BRANDS/DIVISIONS/AFFILIATES:

Merge Technologies Inc
Cedara I-ReadMammo
Cedara B-CAD
Molecular Therapeutics, Inc.
Axicare
aXigate
C4

CONTACTS: *Note: Officers with more than one job title may be intentionally listed here more than once.*

Loris Sartor, Pres.
Vernon Colaco, VP-Sales
Peter Bascom, VP-Eng.
Antonia Wells, VP-Customer Oper.

Phone: 905-672-2100 **Fax:** 905-672-2307
Toll-Free: 800-724-5970
Address: 6509 Airport Rd., Mississauga, ON L4V 1S7 Canada

GROWTH PLANS/SPECIAL FEATURES:

Cedara Software Corp., a subsidiary of Merge Technologies, Inc. (which does business as Merge Healthcare), is a leading independent provider of medical imaging software. It develops and manufactures custom engineered software applications and development tools for the medical imaging OEM and international markets. Its software is deployed in hospitals and clinics worldwide. Cedara's technologies include nearly all of the major digital imaging modalities including computed tomography (CT), magnetic resonance imaging (MRI), digital X-ray, mammography, ultrasound, echo-cardiology, angiography, nuclear medicine, positron emission tomography (PET) and fluoroscopy. Cedara's software spans DICOM-compliant teleradiology Picture Archiving and Communication Systems (PACS) for clinic and departmental use, high-performance radiology workstations, clinical applications, acquisition consoles, security-conscious archives and hospital connectivity solutions. Cedara also offers two specialty products aimed at diagnosing breast cancer: Cedara I-ReadMammo, a multi-modality breast imaging workstation; and Cedara B-CAD, the world's first CAD solution designed to assist radiologists in the analysis of breast lesions using ultrasound images. Recently, Cedara announced an agreement with Molecular Therapeutics, Inc. of Ann Arbor, Michigan, to market and sell products based on functional diffusion mapping, a groundbreaking technique in cancer assessment. The new technique should allow radiologists to study tumor activity at both the molecular and anatomical level. In February 2006, Cedara acquired the assets of Paris-based medical software company, Axicare, granting it exclusive ownership of aXigate, a comprehensive solution for healthcare data and workflow management. In September 2007, the company announced an adaptation for its I-ReadMammo platform that will allow it to be plugged into its C4 (Cedara Clinical Control Center) equipped workstations that feature PACS or some other operating software and an appropriate clinical application program. This upgrade allows for simple installation and integration.

The firm offers its employees three weeks vacation, an in-house massage therapist, vision insurance, departmental events, flex hours and discounted tickets to recreation sites.

FINANCIALS: **Sales and profits are in thousands of dollars—add 000 to get the full amount. 2007 Note: Financial information for 2007 was not available for all companies at press time.**

2007 Sales: $27,800	2007 Profits: $	**U.S. Stock Ticker: Subsidiary**
2006 Sales: $	2006 Profits: $	**Int'l Ticker:** Int'l Exchange:
2005 Sales: $	2005 Profits: $	Employees: 270
2004 Sales: $48,001	2004 Profits: $14,829	Fiscal Year Ends: 6/30
2003 Sales: $28,721	2003 Profits: $-12,682	Parent Company: MERGE TECHNOLOGIES INC

SALARIES/BENEFITS:

Pension Plan:	ESOP Stock Plan:	Profit Sharing:	Top Exec. Salary: $	Bonus: $
Savings Plan:	Stock Purch. Plan:		Second Exec. Salary: $	Bonus: $

OTHER THOUGHTS:

Apparent Women Officers or Directors: 2
Hot Spot for Advancement for Women/Minorities:

LOCATIONS: ("Y" = Yes)

West:	Southwest:	Midwest:	Southeast:	Northeast:	International:
					Y

Note: Financial information, benefits and other data can change quickly and may vary from those stated here.

CELERA GENOMICS GROUP

www.celera.com

Industry Group Code: 541710 **Ranks within this company's industry group:** Sales: 3 Profits: 4

Insurance/HMO/PPO:		Drugs:		Equipment/Supplies:		Hospitals/Clinics:		Services:		Health Care:	
Insurance:		Manufacturer:		Manufacturer:		Acute Care:		Diagnostics:		Home Health:	
Managed Care:		Distributor:		Distributor:		Sub-Acute:		Labs/Testing:	Y	Long-Term Care:	
Utilization Management:		Specialty Pharmacy:		Leasing/Finance:		Outpatient Surgery:		Staffing:		Physical Therapy:	
Payment Processing:		Vitamins/Nutritionals:		Information Systems:	Y	Physical Rehab. Ctr.:		Waste Disposal:		Physician Prac. Mgmt.:	
		Clinical Trials:				Psychiatric Clinics:		Specialty Svcs.:	Y		

TYPES OF BUSINESS:

Research-Human Genome Mapping
Information Management & Analysis Software
Consulting, Research & Development Services

BRANDS/DIVISIONS/AFFILIATES:

Celera Discovery System
Applera Corp.
Celera Diagnostics
Applied Biosystems
Paracel

CONTACTS: *Note: Officers with more than one job title may be intentionally listed here more than once.*

Kathy Ordonez, Pres./Pres., Celera Diagnostics
Tom White, Chief Scientific Officer/VP-R&D
Victor K. Lee, Chief Group Counsel/VP
James Yee, VP-Dev.
David P. Speechly, Sr. Dir.-Corp. Comm.
David P. Speechly, Sr. Dir.-Investor Rel.
Joel Jung, VP-Finance
Samuel Broder, Chief Medical Officer
Stacey Sias, Chief Bus. Officer
Victoria Mackinnon, VP-Regulatory Affairs
Steven M. Ruben, VP-Protein Therapeutics

Phone: 240-453-3000	**Fax:** 240-453-4000
Toll-Free: 877-235-3721	
Address: 45 W. Gude Dr., Rockville, MD 20850 US	

GROWTH PLANS/SPECIAL FEATURES:

Celera Genomics Group, a division of Applera Corporation is engaged in the discovery and development of targeted therapeutics for cancer, autoimmune and inflammatory diseases. The company utilizes genomics, proteomics and bioinformatics platforms to identify gene markers linked to disease. Celera divides its research into two sectors Genomics R&D and Proteomics R&D. In the Genomics R&D sector, Celera houses an industrial-scale facility that can perform high volume genotyping and gene expression analyses through it ABI PRISM 7900 HT Sequence Detection System. Discovery efforts are focused on the identification of genetic variations associated with diseases, which are useful in predicting the predisposition or severity of a disease, the progression of a disease, and any predictable monitoring responses that can be achieved through drug therapy. In Proteomics R&D, Celera has developed proprietary techniques for capturing cell surface proteins in order to identify and quantify the proteins using mass spectrometry and informatics platforms. Areas that this sector is currently investigating include cancer stem cells and tumor angiogenesis (the growth of new blood vessels). In recent news, the company identified novel genes that were associated with late-onset Alzheimer's disease and two genetic variations that put individuals at a higher risk for psoriasis. In 2006, Celera received a NIH Grant to develop and commercialize Avian Flu diagnostic tests. The company sold its Cathepsin S Inhibitor Program to Schering AG and also sold its therapeutic program to Pharmacyclics.

Celera provides its employees a comprehensive benefits package that includes educational assistance, a survivor support program, adoption and employee assistance programs and a corporate matching gift program.

FINANCIALS: **Sales and profits are in thousands of dollars—add 000 to get the full amount. 2007 Note: Financial information for 2007 was not available for all companies at press time.**

2007 Sales: $	2007 Profits: $	**U.S. Stock Ticker: Subsidiary**
2006 Sales: $44,200	2006 Profits: $-62,700	**Int'l Ticker:** Int'l Exchange:
2005 Sales: $31,000	2005 Profits: $-77,100	Employees: 300
2004 Sales: $60,100	2004 Profits: $-57,500	Fiscal Year Ends: 6/30
2003 Sales: $88,300	2003 Profits: $-81,900	Parent Company: APPLERA CORPORATION

SALARIES/BENEFITS:

Pension Plan:	ESOP Stock Plan: Y	Profit Sharing:	Top Exec. Salary: $468,077	Bonus: $451,250
Savings Plan: Y	Stock Purch. Plan:		Second Exec. Salary: $484,069	Bonus: $258,851

OTHER THOUGHTS:

Apparent Women Officers or Directors: 5
Hot Spot for Advancement for Women/Minorities: Y

LOCATIONS: ("Y" = Yes)

West:	Southwest:	Midwest:	Southeast:	Northeast:	International:
Y				Y	

CELL GENESYS INC

www.cellgenesys.com

Industry Group Code: 325412 **Ranks within this company's industry group:** Sales: 43 Profits: 38

Insurance/HMO/PPO:		Drugs:		Equipment/Supplies:		Hospitals/Clinics:		Services:		Health Care:	
Insurance:		Manufacturer:	Y	Manufacturer:	Y	Acute Care:		Diagnostics:		Home Health:	
Managed Care:		Distributor:		Distributor:		Sub-Acute:		Labs/Testing:		Long-Term Care:	
Utilization Management:		Specialty Pharmacy:		Leasing/Finance:		Outpatient Surgery:		Staffing:		Physical Therapy:	
Payment Processing:		Vitamins/Nutritionals:		Information Systems:		Physical Rehab. Ctr.:		Waste Disposal:		Physician Prac. Mgmt.:	
		Clinical Trials:				Psychiatric Clinics:		Specialty Svcs.:			

TYPES OF BUSINESS:

Cancer Immunotherapies
Oncolytic Virus Therapy Drugs

BRANDS/DIVISIONS/AFFILIATES:

GVAX
CG0070
CG5757

CONTACTS: *Note: Officers with more than one job title may be intentionally listed here more than once.*

Stephen A. Sherwin, CEO
Sharon E. Tetlow, CFO/Sr. VP
Christine McKinley, Sr. VP-Human Resources
Peter K. Working, Sr. VP-R&D
Michael W. Ramsay, Sr. VP-Oper.
Robert H. Tidwell, Sr. VP-Corp. Dev.
Robert J. Dow, Sr. VP-Medical Affairs
Carol C. Grundfest, Sr. VP-Regulatory Affairs & Portfolio Mgmt.
Kristen M. Hege, VP-Clinical Research
Stephen A. Sherwin, Chmn.

Phone: 650-266-3000 **Fax:** 650-266-3010
Toll-Free:
Address: 500 Forbes Blvd., South San Francisco, CA 94080 US

GROWTH PLANS/SPECIAL FEATURES:

Cell Genesys, Inc. is a biotechnology company that focuses on the development and commercialization of biological therapies for patients with cancer. The company currently develops cell-based immunoherapies and oncolytic virus therapies to threat different types of cancer. The firm's clinical stage cancer programs involve cell- or viral-based products that have been genetically modified to impart disease-fighting characteristics. Cell Genesys' lead program is the GVAX cell-based immunotherapy for cancer. The company is conducting Phase III clinical trials in prostrate cancer and Phase II trials in each of pancreatic cancer and leukemia. Ongoing clinical programs evaluating the company's oncolytic virus therapies focus on CG0070, a therapy for bladder cancer, which could be evaluated in multiple types of cancer in the future. In addition, Cell Genesys has preclinical oncolytic virus therapy programs, including CG5757, which the company is evaluating as potential therapies for multiple types of cancer. The company owns roughly 4122 U.S. and foreign patents issued or granted to it or available based on licensing arrangements and roughly 305 U.S. and foreign applications pending in its name or available based on licensing agreements. In May 2006, the company was granted Fast Track designation for GVAX immunotherapy for prostrate cancer by the FDA.

The company offers its employees medical, dental and vision insurance; short- and long-term disability; a 401(k) plan; an employee stock purchase plan; life, AD&D and travel accident insurance; and an employee assistance program. Additional perks include an alternative commute program, annual company events, same sex partner health insurance benefits, Friday raves, a fitness center and lunchtime seminars.

FINANCIALS: **Sales and profits are in thousands of dollars—add 000 to get the full amount. 2007 Note: Financial information for 2007 was not available for all companies at press time.**

2007 Sales: $	2007 Profits: $	**U.S. Stock Ticker: CEGE**
2006 Sales: $1,364	2006 Profits: $-82,929	**Int'l Ticker:** Int'l Exchange:
2005 Sales: $4,584	2005 Profits: $-64,939	Employees: 296
2004 Sales: $11,458	2004 Profits: $-97,411	Fiscal Year Ends: 12/31
2003 Sales: $18,128	2003 Profits: $-56,406	Parent Company:

SALARIES/BENEFITS:

Pension Plan:	ESOP Stock Plan:	Profit Sharing:	Top Exec. Salary: $555,000	Bonus: $237,500
Savings Plan: Y	Stock Purch. Plan: Y		Second Exec. Salary: $330,000	Bonus: $155,757

OTHER THOUGHTS:

Apparent Women Officers or Directors: 5
Hot Spot for Advancement for Women/Minorities: Y

LOCATIONS: ("Y" = Yes)

West:	Southwest:	Midwest:	Southeast:	Northeast:	International:
Y					

CENTENE CORPORATION www.centene.com

Industry Group Code: 524114 **Ranks within this company's industry group:** Sales: 24 Profits: 27

Insurance/HMO/PPO:		Drugs:		Equipment/Supplies:		Hospitals/Clinics:		Services:		Health Care:	
Insurance:	Y	Manufacturer:		Manufacturer:		Acute Care:		Diagnostics:		Home Health:	
Managed Care:	Y	Distributor:		Distributor:		Sub-Acute:		Labs/Testing:		Long-Term Care:	
Utilization Management:		Specialty Pharmacy:		Leasing/Finance:		Outpatient Surgery:		Staffing:		Physical Therapy:	
Payment Processing:		Vitamins/Nutritionals:		Information Systems:		Physical Rehab. Ctr.:		Waste Disposal:		Physician Prac. Mgmt.:	
		Clinical Trials:				Psychiatric Clinics:		Specialty Svcs.:	Y		

TYPES OF BUSINESS:

Insurance-Medical & Health, HMOs & PPOs
Life Insurance
Health Insurance
Medicare HMO
Medicaid HMO
Specialty Services

BRANDS/DIVISIONS/AFFILIATES:

State Children's Health Insurance Program (SCHIP)
Supplemental Security Income (SSI)
Cenpatico Behavioral Health
AirLogix
Cardium
Bridgeway Health Solutions
OptiCare
ScriptAssist

CONTACTS: *Note: Officers with more than one job title may be intentionally listed here more than once.*

Michael F. Neidorff, CEO
Michael F. Neidorff, Pres.
Eric R. Slusser, CFO/Exec. VP
Mary V. Mason, Chief Medical Officer/Sr. VP
Glendon A. Schuster, CIO/Sr. VP
Carol E. Goldman, Chief Admin. Officer/Exec. VP
Keith H. Williamson, General Counsel/Corp. Sec./Sr. VP
Patricia J. Darnley, Sr. VP-Oper.
Cary D. Hobbs, Sr. VP-Strategy & Bus. Implementation
Edmund E. Kroll, Sr. VP-Finance & Investor Rel.
J. Per Brodin, Chief Acct. Officer/Sr. VP
Marie J. Glancy, Sr. VP-Operational Services & Regulatory Affairs
Jesse N. Hunter, Sr. VP-Corp. Dev.
Christopher D. Bowers, Acting Head-Health Plan Bus. Unit
Robert C. Packman, Sr. VP-Medical Affairs
Michael F. Neidorff, Chmn.

Phone: 314-725-4477 **Fax:** 314-725-2065
Toll-Free: 800-225-2573
Address: 7711 Carondelet Ave., Ste. 800, St. Louis, MO 63105 US

GROWTH PLANS/SPECIAL FEATURES:

CENTENE Corporation is a multi-line healthcare enterprise operating in primarily two segments: Medicaid Managed Care and Specialty Services. The Medicaid Managed Care segment provides Medicaid and Medicaid-related health plan coverage to individuals through government subsidized programs, including Medicaid, the State Children's Health Insurance Program (SCHIP) and Supplemental Security Income (SSI). The company's Medicaid Managed Care membership totals approximately 1.3 million, with six health plan subsidiaries offering healthcare services in Georgia, Indiana, New Jersey, Ohio, Texas and Wisconsin. CENTENE also provides education and outreach programs to inform and assist members in accessing quality, appropriate healthcare services. CENTENE's Specialty Services segment provides behavioral health, disease management, long-term care programs, managed vision, nurse triage, pharmacy benefits management and treatment compliance through its subsidiaries. Subsidiary Cenpatico Behavioral Health manages behavioral healthcare for members via a contracted network of providers. The company's disease management providers, AirLogix and Cardium, specialize in respiratory disease management and cardiac disease management. Bridgeway Health Solutions, another subsidiary, provides long-term care services to the elderly and people with disabilities on SSI that meet income and resources requirements who are at risk of being institutionalized. Subsidiary OptiCare manages vision benefits for members and NurseWise provides a toll-free nurse triage line. U.S. Script is the company's pharmacy benefits manager and ScriptAssist is the company's treatment compliance program that uses psychological-based tools to predict which patients are likely to be non-compliant regarding taking their medications. In December 2006, CENTENE agreed to sell its subsidiary FirstGuard Health Plan Missouri, Inc. to HealthCare USA of Missouri, LLC, a subsidiary of Coventry Health Care, Inc.

CENTENE offers its employees tuition reimbursement; a savings bond purchase program; flexible spending accounts; paid parking; an employee assistance plan; a free on-site fitness center; company sponsored daycare; and medical, dental and vision insurance.

FINANCIALS: **Sales and profits are in thousands of dollars—add 000 to get the full amount. 2007 Note: Financial information for 2007 was not available for all companies at press time.**

2007 Sales: $
2006 Sales: $2,279,020
2005 Sales: $1,505,864
2004 Sales: $1,007,400
2003 Sales: $769,730

2007 Profits: $
2006 Profits: $-43,629
2005 Profits: $55,632
2004 Profits: $44,300
2003 Profits: $33,270

U.S. Stock Ticker: CNC
Int'l Ticker: Int'l Exchange:
Employees: 2,600
Fiscal Year Ends: 12/31
Parent Company:

SALARIES/BENEFITS:

Pension Plan: ESOP Stock Plan: Profit Sharing: Top Exec. Salary: $950,000 Bonus: $
Savings Plan: Y Stock Purch. Plan: Y Second Exec. Salary: $434,615 Bonus: $11,947

OTHER THOUGHTS:

Apparent Women Officers or Directors: 5
Hot Spot for Advancement for Women/Minorities: Y

LOCATIONS: ("Y" = Yes)

West:	Southwest:	Midwest:	Southeast:	Northeast:	International:
Y	Y	Y		Y	

CEPHALON INC

www.cephalon.com

ndustry Group Code: 325412 **Ranks within this company's industry group:** Sales: 25 Profits: 25

nsurance/HMO/PPO:		Drugs:		Equipment/Supplies:		Hospitals/Clinics:		Services:		Health Care:	
nsurance:		Manufacturer:	Y	Manufacturer:		Acute Care:		Diagnostics:		Home Health:	
Managed Care:		Distributor:		Distributor:		Sub-Acute:		Labs/Testing:		Long-Term Care:	
Utilization Management:		Specialty Pharmacy:		Leasing/Finance:		Outpatient Surgery:		Staffing:		Physical Therapy:	
Payment Processing:		Vitamins/Nutritionals:		Information Systems:		Physical Rehab. Ctr.:		Waste Disposal:		Physician Prac. Mgmt.:	
		Clinical Trials:				Psychiatric Clinics:		Specialty Svcs.:			

TYPES OF BUSINESS:

Pharmaceutical Discovery & Development
Neurological Disorder Treatments
Cancer Treatments
Pain Medications
Addiction Treatment

BRANDS/DIVISIONS/AFFILIATES:

Provigil
Actiq
Spasfon
Myocet
Abelcet
Vivitrol
Fentora
Nuvigil

CONTACTS: *Note: Officers with more than one job title may be intentionally listed here more than once.*

Frank Baldino, Jr., CEO
J. Kevin Buchi, CFO/Exec. VP
Jeffry L. Vaught, Exec. VP-R&D
Peter E. Grebow, Sr. VP-Worldwide Tech. Oper.
Carl Savini, Chief Admin. Officer/Exec. VP
John E. Osborn, General Counsel/Exec. VP/Sec.
Lesley Russell, Exec. VP-Worldwide Medical & Regulatory Affairs
Frank Baldino, Jr., Chmn.
Robert P. Roche, Jr., Sr. VP-Worldwide Pharmaceutical Oper.

Phone: 610-344-0200	**Fax:** 610-738-6590
Toll-Free:	
Address: 41 Moores Rd., Frazer, PA 19355 US	

GROWTH PLANS/SPECIAL FEATURES:

Cephalon, Inc. is a biopharmaceutical company focused on the discovery, development and marketing of products in four core areas: central nervous system (CNS) disorders, pain, cancer and addiction. In addition to actively conducting research and development, the company markets six products in the U.S., as well as numerous other products throughout Europe. Cephalon's technology principally focuses on an understanding of kinases and the role they play in cellular survival and proliferation. The company's most significant products include Provigil tablets, which generated 43% of total revenue in 2006, and Actiq (oral transmucosal fentanyl citrate), which comprised roughly 34% of net sales in 2006. The firm discontinued studying Gabitril for the treatment of generalized anxiety disorders due to unsatisfactory Phase III clinical studies results. Cephalon markets and sells over 25 products in nearly 25 European countries. The five largest products in terms of sales in Europe are Spasfon, Provigil, Myocet, Actiq and Abelcet. Together, these products accounted for 64% of European revenue. During 2006, two products were approved by the FDA: Fentora, a pain product indicated for the management of pain in patients with cancer who are already receiving and are tolerant to opioid therapy for underlying persistent cancer pain; and Vivitrol, indicated for the treatment of alcohol dependant patients who are able to abstain from alcohol in an outpatient setting and are not actively drinking when initiating treatment. In March 2006, FDA did not approve Sparlon for the treatment of ADHD in children and adolescents. In June 2007, Cephalon received FDA approval to market Nuvigil tablets for the treatment of excessive sleepiness.

The company offers its employees a 401(k) plan; health, life and disability coverage; educational reimbursement; and an employee assistance program.

FINANCIALS: Sales and profits are in thousands of dollars—add 000 to get the full amount. 2007 Note: Financial information for 2007 was not available for all companies at press time.

2007 Sales: $	2007 Profits: $	**U.S. Stock Ticker: CEPH**
2006 Sales: $1,764,069	2006 Profits: $144,816	**Int'l Ticker:** Int'l Exchange:
2005 Sales: $1,211,892	2005 Profits: $-174,954	Employees: 2,895
2004 Sales: $1,015,400	2004 Profits: $-73,800	Fiscal Year Ends: 12/31
2003 Sales: $714,800	2003 Profits: $83,900	Parent Company:

SALARIES/BENEFITS:

Pension Plan:	ESOP Stock Plan:	Profit Sharing:	Top Exec. Salary: $1,129,000	Bonus: $1,772,500
Savings Plan: Y	Stock Purch. Plan:		Second Exec. Salary: $525,000	Bonus: $404,300

OTHER THOUGHTS:

Apparent Women Officers or Directors: 1
Hot Spot for Advancement for Women/Minorities:

LOCATIONS: ("Y" = Yes)

West:	Southwest:	Midwest:	Southeast:	Northeast:	International:
Y		Y		Y	Y

Note: Financial information, benefits and other data can change quickly and may vary from those stated here.

CERNER CORP

www.cerner.com

Industry Group Code: 511212 **Ranks within this company's industry group:** Sales: 1 Profits: 1

Insurance/HMO/PPO:		Drugs:		Equipment/Supplies:		Hospitals/Clinics:		Services:		Health Care:	
Insurance:		Manufacturer:		Manufacturer:		Acute Care:		Diagnostics:		Home Health:	
Managed Care:		Distributor:		Distributor:		Sub-Acute:		Labs/Testing:		Long-Term Care:	
Utilization Management:		Specialty Pharmacy:		Leasing/Finance:		Outpatient Surgery:		Staffing:		Physical Therapy:	
Payment Processing:		Vitamins/Nutritionals:		Information Systems:	Y	Physical Rehab. Ctr.:		Waste Disposal:		Physician Prac. Mgmt.:	
		Clinical Trials:				Psychiatric Clinics:		Specialty Svcs.:	Y		

TYPES OF BUSINESS:

Software-Clinical
Medical Information Systems
Application Hosting
Integrated Delivery Networks
Access Management
Consulting Services
Safety & Risk Management

BRANDS/DIVISIONS/AFFILIATES:

Cerner Millennium
CareAware
CernerWorks
Lights On Network
Millennium Lighthouse
Galt Associates, Inc.
Etreby Computer Company, Inc.

CONTACTS: *Note: Officers with more than one job title may be intentionally listed here more than once.*

Neal L. Patterson, CEO
Paul M. Black, COO/Exec. VP
Earl H. (Trace) Devanny III, Pres.
Marc G. Naughton, CFO/Sr. VP
Donald D. Trigg, Chief Mktg. Officer/Sr. VP
Julia M. Wilson, Chief People Officer/Sr. VP
Kevin S. Smyth, CIO/VP
Randy D. Sims, Chief Legal Officer/Corp. Sec./VP
Clifford W. Illig, Vice Chmn.
Paul N. Gorup, Sr. VP/Chief-Innovation
Jeffrey A. Townsend, Exec. VP
Shellee K. Spring, VP-Power Works
Neal L. Patterson, Chmn.
Douglas M. Krebs, Sr. VP/Gen. Manager-Global

Phone: 816-221-1024 **Fax:** 816-474-1742
Toll-Free:
Address: 2800 Rockcreek Pkwy., Ste. 601, Kansas City, MO 64117 US

GROWTH PLANS/SPECIAL FEATURES:

Cerner Corporation, designs, develops, installs and supports information technology and content solutions for health care organizations, consumers and physicians. It boasts 5,578 worldwide clients. Cerner's solutions are designed to help eliminate error, variance and waste in the care process, as well as provide appropriate health information and knowledge to care givers, clinicians and consumers and appropriate management information to health care administrations. The company's solutions have been designed and developed on the unified Cerner Millennium architecture. The framework combines clinical, financial and management information systems and provides secure access to an individual's electronic medical record at the point of care and organizes and proactively delivers information to meet the specific needs of the physician, nurse, laboratory technician, pharmacist or other care provider, front- and back-office professionals as well as consumers. Cerner's CareAware device architecture is designed to bridge the gap between medical devices and patient information by connecting information from various devices to the clinician workflow and electronic medical record. Cerner also offers a broad range of services including implementation and training, remote hosting, support and maintenance, healthcare data analysis and clinical process optimization. CernerWorks is the company's remote-hosting business. Introduced in 2006, Lights On Network monitors client-hosted and Cerner-hosted systems in near real-time. In 2007, the company began focusing on Millennium Lighthouse, a consulting practice that works with clients to determine previously unidentified and unconnected relationships among healthcare processes and outcomes. In June 2006, Cerner acquired Galt Associates, Inc., a leading provider of safety and risk management solutions for pharmaceutical, medical device and biotechnical companies. In February 2007, Cerner agreed to acquire Etreby Computer Company, Inc., a leading software provider of retail pharmacy management systems.

Cerner offers its employees an on-site athletic club, eatery, health clinic and day care, as well as health, dental and vision coverage.

FINANCIALS:
Sales and profits are in thousands of dollars—add 000 to get the full amount. 2007 Note: Financial information for 2007 was not available for all companies at press time.

2007 Sales: $	2007 Profits: $	**U.S. Stock Ticker: CERN**
2006 Sales: $1,378,038	2006 Profits: $109,891	**Int'l Ticker:** Int'l Exchange:
2005 Sales: $1,160,785	2005 Profits: $86,251	Employees: 7,419
2004 Sales: $926,356	2004 Profits: $64,648	Fiscal Year Ends: 12/31
2003 Sales: $839,587	2003 Profits: $42,791	Parent Company:

SALARIES/BENEFITS:

Pension Plan:	ESOP Stock Plan:	Profit Sharing:	Top Exec. Salary: $848,750	Bonus: $1,017,384
Savings Plan: Y	Stock Purch. Plan: Y		Second Exec. Salary: $442,500	Bonus: $442,033

OTHER THOUGHTS:

Apparent Women Officers or Directors: 3
Hot Spot for Advancement for Women/Minorities: Y

LOCATIONS: ("Y" = Yes)

West:	Southwest:	Midwest:	Southeast:	Northeast:	International:
Y	Y	Y	Y	Y	Y

CHEMED CORPORATION

www.chemed.com

Industry Group Code: 621610 **Ranks within this company's industry group:** Sales: 3 Profits: 3

Insurance/HMO/PPO:		Drugs:		Equipment/Supplies:		Hospitals/Clinics:		Services:		Health Care:	
Insurance:		Manufacturer:		Manufacturer:		Acute Care:		Diagnostics:		Home Health:	Y
Managed Care:		Distributor:		Distributor:		Sub-Acute:		Labs/Testing:		Long-Term Care:	Y
Utilization Management:		Specialty Pharmacy:		Leasing/Finance:		Outpatient Surgery:		Staffing:		Physical Therapy:	
Payment Processing:		Vitamins/Nutritionals:		Information Systems:		Physical Rehab. Ctr.:		Waste Disposal:		Physician Prac. Mgmt.:	
		Clinical Trials:				Psychiatric Clinics:		Specialty Svcs.:	Y		

TYPES OF BUSINESS:

Hospice & Home Health Care Services
Drain Cleaning Services
Outpatient Care
In-Home Care
Continuous Care
End-of-Life Care

BRANDS/DIVISIONS/AFFILIATES:

Roto-Rooter Group, Inc.
Vitas Healthcare Corporation

CONTACTS: *Note: Officers with more than one job title may be intentionally listed here more than once.*

Kevin McNamara, CEO
Kevin McNamara, Pres.
David P. Williams, CFO/Exec. VP
Lisa A. Reinhard, Chief Admin. Officer
Naomi C. Dallob, Sec./VP
Arthur V. Tucker, Controller/VP
Tim S. O'Toole, CEO-VITAS Healthcare Corp./Exec. VP
Spencer S. Lee, Exec. VP/Chmn./CEO-Roto-Rooter Mgmt. Co.
Thomas C. Hutton, VP
Thomas J. Reilly, VP
Edward L. Hutton, Chmn.

Phone: 513-726-6900 **Fax:** 513-762-6919
Toll-Free:
Address: 2600 Chemed Ctr., 255 E. 5th St., Cincinnati, OH 45202-4726 US

GROWTH PLANS/SPECIAL FEATURES:

Chemed Corporation, formerly Roto-Rooter, Inc., does business through two segments: Roto-Rooter Group, Inc., and VITAS Healthcare Corporation. Founded in 1935, Roto-Rooter provides plumbing, sewer, drain and pipe cleaning, pipe rehabilitation, drain cleaning equipment and drain cleaning products, supporting the maintenance needs of the residential, industrial, commercial and municipal markets. One of the largest businesses of its type in North America, Roto-Rooter has approximately 68 office and service facilities in 27 states, with 110 branches and independent contractors as well as 500 franchisees. It is equipped to service 90% of the population of the U.S., and has additional operations in Indonesia, the Philippines, Hong Kong, Singapore, China, Japan, Mexico, Canada and the U.K. Roto-Rooter provided approximately 31% of the company's 2006 revenue. VITAS Healthcare is one of the largest providers of end-of-life hospice care in the U.S. Through its 42 hospice programs in California, Texas, Kansas, Missouri, Illinois, Wisconsin, Michigan, Ohio, Pennsylvania, Connecticut, New Jersey, Delaware, Washington, D.C., Virginia, Georgia, and Florida, Vitas provides end-of-life care to approximately 63,000 patients per year as well as assisting family members through the grieving process. It provides in-home care as well as operating inpatient units such as in hospitals, assisted living facilities and nursing homes. Its team consists of nurses, doctors, home health aids, clergy, social workers and volunteers. Vitas provided approximately 68% of the firm's 2006 revenue. The company recently discontinued the Service America segment, which provided services for appliances and heating/air-conditioning systems. In November 2006, Vitas sold its hospice center located in Phoenix, Arizona, which had been providing care for approximately 200 patients, for an undisclosed amount.

VITAS Healthcare offers its employees benefits including tuition reimbursement, an employee assistance program; and medical, disability and life insurance programs.

FINANCIALS: **Sales and profits are in thousands of dollars—add 000 to get the full amount. 2007 Note: Financial information for 2007 was not available for all companies at press time.**

2007 Sales: $	2007 Profits: $	**U.S. Stock Ticker: CHE**
2006 Sales: $1,018,587	2006 Profits: $50,651	**Int'l Ticker:** Int'l Exchange:
2005 Sales: $915,970	2005 Profits: $35,817	Employees: 11,621
2004 Sales: $734,877	2004 Profits: $27,512	Fiscal Year Ends: 12/31
2003 Sales: $260,776	2003 Profits: $-3,435	Parent Company:

SALARIES/BENEFITS:

Pension Plan: Y	ESOP Stock Plan: Y	Profit Sharing:	Top Exec. Salary: $625,000	Bonus: $900,000
Savings Plan: Y	Stock Purch. Plan:		Second Exec. Salary: $435,750	Bonus: $225,000

OTHER THOUGHTS:

Apparent Women Officers or Directors: 2
Hot Spot for Advancement for Women/Minorities: Y

LOCATIONS: ("Y" = Yes)

West:	Southwest:	Midwest:	Southeast:	Northeast:	International:
Y	Y	Y	Y	Y	Y

CHINDEX INTERNATIONAL INC

www.chindex.com

Industry Group Code: 421450 **Ranks within this company's industry group:** Sales: 6 Profits: 7

Insurance/HMO/PPO:		Drugs:		Equipment/Supplies:		Hospitals/Clinics:		Services:		Health Care:	
Insurance:		Manufacturer:		Manufacturer:		Acute Care:	Y	Diagnostics:		Home Health:	
Managed Care:		Distributor:		Distributor:	Y	Sub-Acute:		Labs/Testing:		Long-Term Care:	
Utilization Management:		Specialty Pharmacy:		Leasing/Finance:		Outpatient Surgery:		Staffing:		Physical Therapy:	
Payment Processing:		Vitamins/Nutritionals:		Information Systems:		Physical Rehab. Ctr.:		Waste Disposal:		Physician Prac. Mgmt.:	
		Clinical Trials:				Psychiatric Clinics:		Specialty Svcs.:	Y		

TYPES OF BUSINESS:

Health Care Products Distribution
Technical Services

BRANDS/DIVISIONS/AFFILIATES:

United Family Healthcare
Beijing United Family Hospital
Shanghai United Family Hospital
Wuxi United Family International Healthcare Center

CONTACTS:

Note: Officers with more than one job title may be intentionally listed here more than once.

Roberta Lipson, CEO
Lawrence Pemble, CFO/Exec. VP
Daniel Fulton, VP-IT Svcs.
Elyse B. Siverberg, Exec. VP
Judy Zakreski, VP-US Oper.
Walter Xue, VP/Controller-China
Zhang Pin Qing, VP-Tech. Service
A. Kenneth Nilsson, Chmn.
Walter Stryker, Sr. VP-China Admin.

Phone: 301-215-7777 **Fax:** 301-215-7719
Toll-Free:
Address: 4340 E. W. Highway, Ste. 1100, Bethesda, MD 20814 US

GROWTH PLANS/SPECIAL FEATURES:

Chindex International, Inc., an American company operating in several healthcare markets in China, including Hong Kong provides healthcare services and sells medical equipment instruments and products. The firm operates in two segments: healthcare services and medical products. The healthcare services division, which generated 45% of revenue in 2007, operates the United Family Healthcare network of private hospitals and clinics. The segment operates the Beijing United Family Hospital and the Shanghai United Family Hospital. The United Family Healthcare facilities offer a wide range of family healthcare services, including 24/7 emergency rooms, intensive care units, neonatal intensive care units, operating rooms, clinical laboratory, radiology and blood baking services for men, women and children. The medical products division markets, formerly known as medical capital equipment division, which generated 55% of revenue in 2007, distributes and sells select medical capital equipment, instrumentation and other medical products for use in hospitals in China and Hong Kong on the basis of both exclusive and non-exclusive agreements with the manufacturers of these products. Products sold include diagnostic color ultrasound imaging devices; robotic surgical systems and instrumentation; chemistry analyzers; sterilization systems; bone densitometers; mammography; and breast biopsy devices and lasers for cosmetic surgery. The division includes a technical service department, which is responsible for the technical support of virtually all the medical equipment that the company sells. In May 2007, Chindex signed an agreement with International Travel Healthcare Association Wuxi Centre for the operations of the Wuxi United Family International Healthcare Center.

FINANCIALS:

Sales and profits are in thousands of dollars—add 000 to get the full amount. 2007 Note: Financial information for 2007 was not available for all companies at press time.

2007 Sales: $105,921	2007 Profits: $2,982	**U.S. Stock Ticker: CHDX**
2006 Sales: $90,836	2006 Profits: $ 167	**Int'l Ticker:** Int'l Exchange:
2005 Sales: $83,159	2005 Profits: $-3,924	Employees: 1,007
2004 Sales: $75,419	2004 Profits: $- 854	Fiscal Year Ends: 3/31
2003 Sales: $21,849	2003 Profits: $ 76	Parent Company:

SALARIES/BENEFITS:

Pension Plan:	ESOP Stock Plan:	Profit Sharing:	Top Exec. Salary: $238,930	Bonus: $67,500
Savings Plan:	Stock Purch. Plan:		Second Exec. Salary: $236,500	Bonus: $75,000

OTHER THOUGHTS:

Apparent Women Officers or Directors: 6
Hot Spot for Advancement for Women/Minorities: Y

LOCATIONS: ("Y" = Yes)

West:	Southwest:	Midwest:	Southeast:	Northeast:	International:
				Y	Y

Note: Financial information, benefits and other data can change quickly and may vary from those stated here.

CHIRON CORP

www.chiron.com

Industry Group Code: 325412 **Ranks within this company's industry group:** Sales: Profits:

Insurance/HMO/PPO:		Drugs:		Equipment/Supplies:		Hospitals/Clinics:		Services:		Health Care:	
Insurance:		Manufacturer:	Y	Manufacturer:		Acute Care:		Diagnostics:	Y	Home Health:	
Managed Care:		Distributor:		Distributor:		Sub-Acute:		Labs/Testing:	Y	Long-Term Care:	
Utilization Management:		Specialty Pharmacy:		Leasing/Finance:		Outpatient Surgery:		Staffing:		Physical Therapy:	
Payment Processing:		Vitamins/Nutritionals:		Information Systems:		Physical Rehab. Ctr.:		Waste Disposal:		Physician Prac. Mgmt.:	
		Clinical Trials:				Psychiatric Clinics:		Specialty Svcs.:	Y		

TYPES OF BUSINESS:

Pharmaceuticals Discovery & Development
Biopharmaceuticals
Vaccines
Blood Screening Assays

BRANDS/DIVISIONS/AFFILIATES:

Novartis AG
TOBI
Betaseron
Fluad
RabAvert
Chiron Blood Testing
Chiron Biopharmaceuticals
Chiron Vaccines

CONTACTS: *Note: Officers with more than one job title may be intentionally listed here more than once.*

Gene Walther, Pres.

Phone: 510-655-8730	**Fax:** 510-655-9910
Toll-Free:	
Address: 4560 Horton St., Emeryville, CA 94608-2916 US	

GROWTH PLANS/SPECIAL FEATURES:

Chiron, a subsidiary of Novatis AG, is a biotechnology company that participates in three global health care businesses: biopharmaceuticals, vaccines and blood testing. The company develops innovative products for preventing and treating cancer, infectious diseases and cardiovascular disease. Chiron BioPharmaceuticals discovers, develops, manufactures and markets a range of therapeutic products, including TOBI for lung infections in cystic fibrosis patients, Betaseron for multiple sclerosis and Proleukin for cancer. Chiron Vaccines, the fifth-largest vaccines business in the world, currently offers more than 30 vaccines. They include Menjugate for meningococcal meningitis, Fluad for influenza, Encepur for tick-borne encephalitis and RabAvert for exposure to rabies. Menjugate has not been approved for use in the U.S. Chiron Blood Testing provides screening products used by the blood bank industry. Its nucleic acid testing blood screening assays include the Procleix HIV-1/HCV and Procleix West Nile Virus assays. In addition, the firm produces the Ultrio assay, designed to detect HIV and hepatitis C and B viruses. Chiron maintains partnerships with several major pharmaceutical companies, including Schering AG/Berlex Laboratories, Gen-Probe, Nektar Therapeutics and Ortho-Clinical Diagnostics to expand its portfolio of intellectual properties, develop new products and license those products in key markets. In April 2006, Novartis AG, a major pharmaceutical company, purchased Chiron.

Chiron offers its employees educational assistance, credit union membership and access to prepaid legal services, as well as discounted auto and home insurance. The company also has a LifeCare service that provides information and support on topics such as adoption, prenatal planning and child care.

FINANCIALS: **Sales and profits are in thousands of dollars—add 000 to get the full amount. 2007 Note: Financial information for 2007 was not available for all companies at press time.**

2007 Sales: $	2007 Profits: $	**U.S. Stock Ticker: Subsidiary**
2006 Sales: $	2006 Profits: $	**Int'l Ticker:** Int'l Exchange:
2005 Sales: $1,921,000	2005 Profits: $187,000	Employees: 5,500
2004 Sales: $1,723,355	2004 Profits: $78,917	Fiscal Year Ends: 12/31
2003 Sales: $1,776,361	2003 Profits: $227,313	Parent Company: NOVARTIS AG

SALARIES/BENEFITS:

Pension Plan:	ESOP Stock Plan: Y	Profit Sharing:	Top Exec. Salary: $800,000	Bonus: $897,293
Savings Plan: Y	Stock Purch. Plan: Y		Second Exec. Salary: $552,461	Bonus: $1,500,000

OTHER THOUGHTS:

Apparent Women Officers or Directors:
Hot Spot for Advancement for Women/Minorities:

LOCATIONS: ("Y" = Yes)

West:	Southwest:	Midwest:	Southeast:	Northeast:	International:
Y		Y		Y	Y

Note: Financial information, benefits and other data can change quickly and may vary from those stated here.

CHOLESTECH CORP

www.cholestech.com

Industry Group Code: 339113 **Ranks within this company's industry group:** Sales: 86 Profits: 72

Insurance/HMO/PPO:		Drugs:		Equipment/Supplies:		Hospitals/Clinics:		Services:		Health Care:	
Insurance:		Manufacturer:		Manufacturer:	Y	Acute Care:		Diagnostics:		Home Health:	
Managed Care:		Distributor:		Distributor:	Y	Sub-Acute:		Labs/Testing:		Long-Term Care:	
Utilization Management:		Specialty Pharmacy:		Leasing/Finance:		Outpatient Surgery:		Staffing:		Physical Therapy:	
Payment Processing:		Vitamins/Nutritionals:		Information Systems:		Physical Rehab. Ctr.:		Waste Disposal:		Physician Prac. Mgmt.:	
		Clinical Trials:				Psychiatric Clinics:		Specialty Svcs.:			

TYPES OF BUSINESS:

Equipment-Blood Diagnostic Test Systems
Cholesterol Tests

BRANDS/DIVISIONS/AFFILIATES:

LDX System
GDX System
LDX Analyzer
Itamar Medical Limited
Aspartate Aminotransferase (AST) Test
Boule Diagnostic International
Inverness Medical Innovations, Inc.

CONTACTS:

Note: Officers with more than one job title may be intentionally listed here more than once.

Warren E. Pinckert, II, CEO
Warren E. Pinckert, II, Pres.
John F. Glenn, CFO
Kenneth F. Miller, VP-Mktg. & Sales
Terry Wassmann, VP-Human Resources
Gregory L. Bennett, VP-R&D
John F. Glenn, Corp. Sec.
Donald P. Wood, VP-Oper.
John F. Glenn, VP-Finance/Treas.
Barbara McAleer, VP-Quality Assurance & Regulatory Affairs
John H. Landon, Chmn.

Phone: 510-732-7200 **Fax:** 510-732-7227
Toll-Free: 800-733-0404
Address: 3347 Investment Blvd., Hayward, CA 94545-3808 US

GROWTH PLANS/SPECIAL FEATURES:

Cholestech Corporation, a subsidiary of Inverness Medical Innovations, Inc., provides diagnostic tools for immediate risk assessment and monitoring of heart disease, inflammatory disorders and diabetes. The company manufactures the LDX System, which includes the LDX Analyzer and a variety of single-use test cassettes. Cholestech markets the LDX System in the United States, Europe, Asia, Australia and South America. The LDX System allows health care providers to perform individual tests or combinations of tests for blood cholesterol, related lipids, glucose and liver function using a single drop of blood within five minutes. Cholestech also markets and distributes the GDX System, which measures hemoglobin A1C, an indicator of a patient's long-term glycemic control. Cholestech distributes the GDX under a multi-year global agreement with Provalis Diagnostics, Ltd. Unlike daily glucose monitoring, which only measures a patient's glucose level at the time of testing, A1C provides an average glucose level over the previous 90 days which indicates the long-term progress of a patient's diabetes and therapy management. Cholestech specifically targets its products for markets outside of traditional hospital or clinical laboratories. The firm's primary market is the physician office laboratory market. Cholestech has a development and product distribution agreement with Itamar Medical Limited, involving a system for assessing vascular endothelial dysfunction, which is recognized as an early stage in the development of atherosclerosis. The company also provides an Aspartate Aminotransferase (AST) Test for monitoring the effects of various drugs on the liver. Cholestech is also collaborating with Boule Diagnostic International to develop and distribute a Complete Blood Count test system. In September 2007, Cholestech was acquired by Inverness Medical Innovations, Inc. and went private.

Cholestech offers its employees a flexible spending account, an employee assistance program, credit union membership, membership to a fitness club and medical and dental coverage.

FINANCIALS:

Sales and profits are in thousands of dollars—add 000 to get the full amount. 2007 Note: Financial information for 2007 was not available for all companies at press time.

2007 Sales: $69,500
2006 Sales: $64,093
2005 Sales: $52,877
2004 Sales: $52,376
2003 Sales: $48,500

2007 Profits: $9,400
2006 Profits: $5,634
2005 Profits: $4,148
2004 Profits: $8,707
2003 Profits: $4,900

U.S. Stock Ticker: Subsidiary
Int'l Ticker: Int'l Exchange:
Employees: 216
Fiscal Year Ends: 3/26
Parent Company: INVERNESS MEDICAL INNOVATIONS INC

SALARIES/BENEFITS:

Pension Plan:
Savings Plan: Y
ESOP Stock Plan:
Stock Purch. Plan: Y
Profit Sharing:
Top Exec. Salary: $437,077 Bonus: $218,790
Second Exec. Salary: $262,163 Bonus: $111,038

OTHER THOUGHTS:

Apparent Women Officers or Directors: 2
Hot Spot for Advancement for Women/Minorities:

LOCATIONS: ("Y" = Yes)

West:	Southwest:	Midwest:	Southeast:	Northeast:	International:
Y					

CHRISTUS HEALTH

www.christushealth.org

Industry Group Code: 622110 **Ranks within this company's industry group:** Sales: 21 Profits: 9

Insurance/HMO/PPO:		Drugs:		Equipment/Supplies:		Hospitals/Clinics:		Services:		Health Care:	
Insurance:		Manufacturer:		Manufacturer:		Acute Care:	Y	Diagnostics:		Home Health:	
Managed Care:		Distributor:		Distributor:		Sub-Acute:	Y	Labs/Testing:		Long-Term Care:	Y
Utilization Management:		Specialty Pharmacy:		Leasing/Finance:		Outpatient Surgery:	Y	Staffing:		Physical Therapy:	
Payment Processing:		Vitamins/Nutritionals:		Information Systems:		Physical Rehab. Ctr.:	Y	Waste Disposal:		Physician Prac. Mgmt.:	
		Clinical Trials:				Psychiatric Clinics:	Y	Specialty Svcs.:			

TYPES OF BUSINESS:

Hospitals
Long-Term & Hospice Care
Behavioral Health
Orthopedic Medicine
Online Health Information

BRANDS/DIVISIONS/AFFILIATES:

Sisters of Charity of the Incarnate Word
CHRISTUS Fund
St. Joseph Village, Inc.

CONTACTS: *Note: Officers with more than one job title may be intentionally listed here more than once.*

Thomas C. Royer, CEO
Thomas C. Royer, Pres.
Linda McClung, Sr. VP-Comm. & Public Affairs
Ernie W. Sadau, Sr. VP-Patient & Resident Care Oper.
John Gillean, Sr. VP-Physician Integration Svcs.
Benton Baker III, Chief Medical Officer/VP
Catherine Dulle, Chmn.

Phone: 214-492-8500 **Fax:** 214-492-8540
Toll-Free: 877-980-0100
Address: 6363 N. Hwy. 161, Las Colinas Corp. Ctr., Ste. 450, Irving, TX 75038 US

GROWTH PLANS/SPECIAL FEATURES:

CHRISTUS Health is a faith-based, not-for-profit organization formed from the combination of two Catholic charities, Sisters of Charity of the Incarnate Word in Houston and Sisters of Charity of the Incarnate Word in San Antonio. Today, CHRISTUS is one of the top 10 Catholic health systems in the U.S. as ranked by size, with more than 40 hospitals, inpatient and long-term care facilities; dozens of clinics and physician offices; and roughly 9,000 physicians on staff. In all, CHRISTUS operates in more than 60 communities in Texas, Arkansas, Louisiana, Georgia, Missouri, Oklahoma and Utah as well as six Mexican states. Some of the services provided by CHRISTUS's facilities include hospice; long-term and assisted care; emergency and outpatient treatment; surgical; behavioral health; cardiology; emergency; rehabilitation; orthopedics; and women's and children's health. The group's web site provides a support and resource site for physicians, information on healthy recipes, health news and information and a section of miracles and success stories connected with the organization. The group also operates an advocacy program on both the state and federal levels in the health care field with the hope of providing its patients with a health care system that can better serve them. Community outreach, especially focusing on the underserved, is a priority for CHRISTUS. The group partners with members and organizations in the communities it serves to create programs for the betterment of the community. In addition, the group operates CHRISTUS Fund, a foundation that makes grants to non-profits or community programs whose aims are compatible with those of the group. In May 2006, CHRISTUS acquired St. Joseph Village, Inc., a Catholic continuing care retirement community located in Coppell, Texas; and it is now called CHRISTUS St. Joseph Village.

CHRISTUS provides its employees with benefits including day care, tuition reimbursement and various career development programs.

FINANCIALS: **Sales and profits are in thousands of dollars—add 000 to get the full amount. 2007 Note: Financial information for 2007 was not available for all companies at press time.**

2007 Sales: $	2007 Profits: $	**U.S. Stock Ticker: Nonprofit**
2006 Sales: $2,688,300	2006 Profits: $231,904	**Int'l Ticker:** Int'l Exchange:
2005 Sales: $2,479,774	2005 Profits: $135,757	Employees: 8,000
2004 Sales: $2,272,792	2004 Profits: $108,949	Fiscal Year Ends: 6/30
2003 Sales: $2,302,400	2003 Profits: $20,000	Parent Company:

SALARIES/BENEFITS:

Pension Plan:	ESOP Stock Plan:	Profit Sharing:	Top Exec. Salary: $	Bonus: $
Savings Plan:	Stock Purch. Plan:		Second Exec. Salary: $	Bonus: $

OTHER THOUGHTS:

Apparent Women Officers or Directors: 2
Hot Spot for Advancement for Women/Minorities:

LOCATIONS: ("Y" = Yes)

West:	Southwest:	Midwest:	Southeast:	Northeast:	International:
Y	Y		Y		Y

Note: Financial information, benefits and other data can change quickly and may vary from those stated here.

CIGNA BEHAVIORAL HEALTH apps.cignabehavioral.com

Industry Group Code: 524114A **Ranks within this company's industry group:** Sales: Profits:

Insurance/HMO/PPO:		Drugs:		Equipment/Supplies:		Hospitals/Clinics:		Services:		Health Care:	
Insurance:		Manufacturer:		Manufacturer:		Acute Care:		Diagnostics:		Home Health:	
Managed Care:	Y	Distributor:		Distributor:		Sub-Acute:		Labs/Testing:		Long-Term Care:	
Utilization Management:		Specialty Pharmacy:		Leasing/Finance:		Outpatient Surgery:		Staffing:		Physical Therapy:	
Payment Processing:		Vitamins/Nutritionals:		Information Systems:		Physical Rehab. Ctr.:		Waste Disposal:		Physician Prac. Mgmt.:	
		Clinical Trials:				Psychiatric Clinics:	Y	Specialty Svcs.:			

TYPES OF BUSINESS:

Insurance-Supplemental & Specialty Health
Employee Assistance Programs
Behavioral Healthcare

BRANDS/DIVISIONS/AFFILIATES:

Cigna Corp
Taft-Hartley Trust

CONTACTS:

Note: Officers with more than one job title may be intentionally listed here more than once.

Keith Dixon, CEO
Keith Dixon, Pres.
Kay Hall, VP-Sales
Julie Vayer, VP-Professional Rel. & Network Svcs.

Phone: 952-996-2000	**Fax:** 952-996-2579
Toll-Free: 800-433-5768	
Address: 11095 Viking Dr., Ste. 350, Eden Prairie, MN 55344 US	

GROWTH PLANS/SPECIAL FEATURES:

CIGNA Behavioral Health, Inc. (CBH), a subsidiary of CIGNA Corp., provides managed behavioral health care services and employee assistance programs (EAPs). Its more than 14 million customers in the U.S. receive their benefits through health plans offered by large U.S. employers; unions; national and regional health maintenance organizations (HMOs); Taft-Hartley trusts; and disability insurers. The company provides services that include employee assistance, life events, behavioral care and productivity solutions. The firm's services address problems such as stress; personal crisis; family conflict; bereavement; mental illness; alcohol and drug abuse; and disability and disease management. In addition, CBH offers assistance programs for students and for employees deployed internationally. The company's large employer and HMO plans provide behavioral health management, utilization review, EAP services, life event programs and disability management programs. Taft-Hartley trusts specialize in services for stress, substance abuse and other treatable behavioral problems. The firm operates five care management centers around the U.S. in support of a national network of more than 60,000 independent psychiatrists, psychologists and clinical social workers, with more than 4,000 facilities and clinics.

FINANCIALS:

Sales and profits are in thousands of dollars—add 000 to get the full amount. 2007 Note: Financial information for 2007 was not available for all companies at press time.

2007 Sales: $	2007 Profits: $	**U.S. Stock Ticker: Subsidiary**
2006 Sales: $	2006 Profits: $	**Int'l Ticker:** Int'l Exchange:
2005 Sales: $	2005 Profits: $	Employees:
2004 Sales: $	2004 Profits: $	Fiscal Year Ends:
2003 Sales: $	2003 Profits: $	Parent Company: CIGNA CORP

SALARIES/BENEFITS:

Pension Plan:	ESOP Stock Plan:	Profit Sharing:	Top Exec. Salary: $	Bonus: $
Savings Plan:	Stock Purch. Plan:		Second Exec. Salary: $	Bonus: $

OTHER THOUGHTS:

Apparent Women Officers or Directors: 1
Hot Spot for Advancement for Women/Minorities: Y

LOCATIONS: ("Y" = Yes)

West:	Southwest:	Midwest:	Southeast:	Northeast:	International:
		Y			

CIGNA CORP

www.cigna.com

Industry Group Code: 524114 **Ranks within this company's industry group:** Sales: 5 Profits: 4

Insurance/HMO/PPO:		Drugs:		Equipment/Supplies:		Hospitals/Clinics:		Services:		Health Care:	
Insurance:	Y	Manufacturer:		Manufacturer:		Acute Care:		Diagnostics:		Home Health:	
Managed Care:	Y	Distributor:		Distributor:		Sub-Acute:		Labs/Testing:		Long-Term Care:	
Utilization Management:		Specialty Pharmacy:		Leasing/Finance:		Outpatient Surgery:		Staffing:		Physical Therapy:	
Payment Processing:		Vitamins/Nutritionals:		Information Systems:		Physical Rehab. Ctr.:		Waste Disposal:		Physician Prac. Mgmt.:	
		Clinical Trials:				Psychiatric Clinics:		Specialty Svcs.:	Y		

TYPES OF BUSINESS:

Insurance-Medical & Health, HMOs & PPOs
Indemnity Insurance
Investment Management Services
Group Life, Accident & Disability

BRANDS/DIVISIONS/AFFILIATES:

CIGNA International
CIGNA Group Insurance
CIGNA HealthCare
CIGNATURE
CareAllies
Star HRG
vielife
Sagamore Health Network, Inc.

CONTACTS: *Note: Officers with more than one job title may be intentionally listed here more than once.*

H. Edward Hanway, CEO
Paul E. Hartley, Pres.
Michael W. Bell, CFO/Exec. VP
David M. Cordani, Sr. VP-Customer Segments & Mktg.
John M. Murabito, Exec. VP-Human Resources & Services
Scott A. Storrer, Exec. VP-IT
Carol Ann Petren, General Counsel/Exec. VP
Scott A. Storrer, Exec. VP-Service Oper.
John Cannon, III, Sr. VP-Public Affairs
David M. Cordani, Pres., CIGNA Health Care
Karen S. Rohan, Pres., CIGNA Dental & Vision Care
Karen S. Rohan, Pres., CIGNA Group Insurance
Keith Dixon, Pres./CEO-CIGNA Behavioral Health
H. Edward Hanway, Chmn.
Paul E. Hartley, Pres., CIGNA Int'l

Phone: 215-761-1000 **Fax:** 215-761-5515
Toll-Free:
Address: 1 Liberty Pl., 1650 Chestnut St., Philadelphia, PA 19192-1550 US

GROWTH PLANS/SPECIAL FEATURES:

CIGNA Corporation and its subsidiaries constitute one of the largest investor-owned employee benefits organizations in the U.S. The group is a major provider of employee benefits, including health care products and services, group life, accident and disability insurance, retirement products and services and investment management. CIGNA HealthCare offers a wide range of medical insurance plans, including consumer-directed health plans, health maintenance organizations (HMOs), network only and point-of-services (POS) medical plans, preferred provider plans (PPOs) and traditional medical indemnity coverage. CIGNA offers a modular product portfolio, including CIGNATURE, CareAllies and CIGNA Choice Fund solutions, which offer a choice of benefit, participating provider network, funding, medical management, consumerism and health advocacy options for employers and consumers. CIGNA's networks include approximately 518,600 physicians and 5,000 hospitals. CIGNA Group Insurance markets benefits packages to employers that include life insurance, accident insurance, disability insurance and specialty programs. CIGNA International services clients in Asia, Europe and the Americas. In July 2006, CIGNA announced it had acquired Star HRG, an operating division of HealthMarkets, Inc., a leading provider of voluntary, limited benefit, low-cost health plans. In December 2006, CIGNA acquired vielife, a private U.K.-based provider of integrated online health management and coaching programs. In August 2007, the company acquired Sagamore Health Network, Inc., the largest health care provider Network in Indiana.

CIGNA offers its employees flexible work arrangements; child and dependent care discounts; adoption assistance; tuition reimbursement; on-site health centers; wellness and fitness programs; an employee retail discount program; lactation centers for working mothers; a health focused work environment; and medical, dental, disability, life and mental-health coverage.

FINANCIALS: **Sales and profits are in thousands of dollars—add 000 to get the full amount. 2007 Note: Financial information for 2007 was not available for all companies at press time.**

2007 Sales: $
2006 Sales: $16,547,000
2005 Sales: $16,684,000
2004 Sales: $18,176,000
2003 Sales: $18,808,000

2007 Profits: $
2006 Profits: $1,155,000
2005 Profits: $1,625,000
2004 Profits: $1,438,000
2003 Profits: $668,000

U.S. Stock Ticker: CI
Int'l Ticker: Int'l Exchange:
Employees: 27,100
Fiscal Year Ends: 12/31
Parent Company:

SALARIES/BENEFITS:

Pension Plan: ESOP Stock Plan: Profit Sharing: Top Exec. Salary: $1,101,923 Bonus: $11,249,400
Savings Plan: Y Stock Purch. Plan: Second Exec. Salary: $569,615 Bonus: $3,729,800

OTHER THOUGHTS:

Apparent Women Officers or Directors: 2
Hot Spot for Advancement for Women/Minorities: Y

LOCATIONS: ("Y" = Yes)

West:	Southwest:	Midwest:	Southeast:	Northeast:	International:
Y	Y	Y	Y	Y	Y

CIVCO MEDICAL SOLUTIONS www.civco.com

Industry Group Code: 339113 **Ranks within this company's industry group:** Sales: Profits:

Insurance/HMO/PPO:		Drugs:		Equipment/Supplies:		Hospitals/Clinics:		Services:		Health Care:	
Insurance:		Manufacturer:		Manufacturer:	Y	Acute Care:		Diagnostics:		Home Health:	
Managed Care:		Distributor:		Distributor:	Y	Sub-Acute:		Labs/Testing:		Long-Term Care:	
Utilization Management:		Specialty Pharmacy:		Leasing/Finance:		Outpatient Surgery:		Staffing:		Physical Therapy:	
Payment Processing:		Vitamins/Nutritionals:		Information Systems:		Physical Rehab. Ctr.:		Waste Disposal:		Physician Prac. Mgmt.:	
		Clinical Trials:				Psychiatric Clinics:		Specialty Svcs.:	Y		

TYPES OF BUSINESS:

Diagnostic & Therapeutic Medical Equipment
Ultrasound Products
Minimally Invasive Surgical Products
Medical Monitors
Needle & Biopsy Instruments
Disinfectants
Medical Printers & Print Supplies
Custom Design Services

BRANDS/DIVISIONS/AFFILIATES:

Roper Industries Inc
Sinmed BV

CONTACTS: *Note: Officers with more than one job title may be intentionally listed here more than once.*

Charles Klasson, Pres.
Geoffrey Dalbow, CTO
Leo de Mooy, Managing Dir.-Prod. Dev.
Tom Doughty, General Manager-Radiation Oncology
Patrick Dammekens, Dir.-Asia-Pacific Sales
Pieter-Jan Wegman, Managing Dir.-European Sales

Phone: 319-656-4447	**Fax:** 319-656-4451
Toll-Free: 800-445-6741	
Address: 102 First St. S., Kalona, IA 52247 US	

GROWTH PLANS/SPECIAL FEATURES:

CIVCO Medical Solutions, formerly CIVCO Medica Instruments, is a designer, manufacturer and distributor c ultrasound and minimally invasive surgical products. Th company is a subsidiary of Roper Industries, a manufacture of products and solutions for global niche markets, includin water, energy, radio frequency, and research and medica applications. CIVCO manufactures cardiology products disinfectants, needle guidance systems, biopsy instruments laparoscopic surgery products, urology products, oncolog products, medical monitors, imaging equipment, transduce covers, positioners and stabilizers. Cardiology product include disposable electrodes, bite blocks and instrumer accessories. The company also produces a respiratio monitor that is compatible with ECGs and ultrasoun systems. In addition, CIVCO produces medical printers, prir media and associated supplies. The firm's engineering tea custom designs ultrasound devices for both future an existing imaging systems and procedures. The company' biopsy supplies are mostly a variety of disposable an reusable needles. These products are sold worldwid through CIVCO's partners in Europe, Asia, Australia, th Middle East and Central and South America. The compan supplies original equipment manufacturers (OEMs) includin Philips Medical Systems, GE Healthcare, Siemens Medica Solutions, Toshiba Medical Systems, Aloka Ltd., B-K Medica and SonoSite. In addition to OEMs, CIVCO's products ar sold to over 6,500 hospitals and clinics in the U.S. an through distributors worldwide. In May 2006, the compan acquired the assets of Netherlands-based Sinmed BV another provider of cancer treatment products.

FINANCIALS: **Sales and profits are in thousands of dollars—add 000 to get the full amount. 2007 Note: Financial information for 2007 was not available for all companies at press time.**

2007 Sales: $	2007 Profits: $	**U.S. Stock Ticker: Subsidiary**
2006 Sales: $	2006 Profits: $	**Int'l Ticker:** Int'l Exchange:
2005 Sales: $	2005 Profits: $	Employees: 360
2004 Sales: $	2004 Profits: $	Fiscal Year Ends:
2003 Sales: $	2003 Profits: $	Parent Company: ROPER INDUSTRIES INC

SALARIES/BENEFITS:

Pension Plan:	ESOP Stock Plan:	Profit Sharing:	Top Exec. Salary: $205,891	Bonus: $142,439
Savings Plan:	Stock Purch. Plan:		Second Exec. Salary: $162,293	Bonus: $107,043

OTHER THOUGHTS:

Apparent Women Officers or Directors:
Hot Spot for Advancement for Women/Minorities:

LOCATIONS: ("Y" = Yes)

West:	Southwest:	Midwest:	Southeast:	Northeast:	International:
Y		Y	Y		Y

CLARIAN HEALTH PARTNERS INC

www.clarian.org

Industry Group Code: 622110 **Ranks within this company's industry group:** Sales: Profits:

Insurance/HMO/PPO:		Drugs:		Equipment/Supplies:		Hospitals/Clinics:		Services:		Health Care:	
Insurance:		Manufacturer:		Manufacturer:		Acute Care:	Y	Diagnostics:		Home Health:	Y
Managed Care:		Distributor:		Distributor:		Sub-Acute:	Y	Labs/Testing:		Long-Term Care:	
Utilization Management:		Specialty Pharmacy:		Leasing/Finance:		Outpatient Surgery:	Y	Staffing:		Physical Therapy:	
Payment Processing:		Vitamins/Nutritionals:		Information Systems:		Physical Rehab. Ctr.:	Y	Waste Disposal:		Physician Prac. Mgmt.:	Y
		Clinical Trials:				Psychiatric Clinics:	Y	Specialty Svcs.:	Y		

TYPES OF BUSINESS:

Hospitals
Children's Services

BRANDS/DIVISIONS/AFFILIATES:

Methodist Hospital
Indiana University Hospital
Riley Hospital for Children
Riley Children's Foundaton
Methodist Health Foundation
Camp Riley
Clarian Noth Medical Center
Clarian West Medical Center

CONTACTS: *Note: Officers with more than one job title may be intentionally listed here more than once.*

Daniel F. Evans, Jr., CEO
Daniel F. Evans, Jr., Pres.
Marvin Pember, CFO/Exec. VP
David Hesson, VP-Oper.
Jonathan Goble, Pres./CEO-Clarian North Medical Center
Randall Yust, COO/CFO-Clarian North Medical Center
Kathy Mathena, Chief Nurse Executive-Clarian North Medical Center
Lynda Smirz, Chief Medical Officer-Clarian North Medical Center

Phone: 317-962-2000 **Fax:** 317-962-4533
Toll-Free:
Address: 1701 N. Senate Blvd., Indianapolis, IN 46206 US

GROWTH PLANS/SPECIAL FEATURES:

Clarian Health Partners was formed in 1997 from the union of Methodist Hospital, Indiana University Hospital and Riley Hospital for Children, all located in Indianapolis. In addition to these three hospitals, the group recently opened Clarian West Medical Center, a full service, community based hospital in Avon, Indiana and Clarian North Medical Center, an independent, for-profit medical center with 170 beds and an attached medical office building. The three original hospitals have approximately 1,400 beds in total, with over 56,500 total inpatient admissions and over 920,600 total outpatient visits, 95% of which came from Indiana. The group employs over 1,400 physicians and serves approximately 300,000 people through various community outreach programs. Two foundations raise funds for Clarian, Riley Children's Foundation and Methodist Health Foundation. Riley Children's Foundation provides support and philanthropic leadership for Riley Hospital for Children; Camp Riley, an outdoor recreation camp for children with physical disabilities; and the James Whitcomb Riley Museum Home, the Victorian house of poet James Whitcomb Riley, for whom the foundation, hospital and camp are named. The Methodist Health Foundation supports Methodist Hospital's research and education initiatives as well as various clinical services and programs.

Clarian offers its employees tuition reimbursement and a variety of educational and certification programs including a nursing scholarship. Employees are eligible for discounts at local businesses, including discounts on child care; apartment rent; auto and banking services; and clothing. Clarian also offers flexible spending accounts, adoption assistance and an employee assistance program.

FINANCIALS: **Sales and profits are in thousands of dollars—add 000 to get the full amount. 2007 Note: Financial information for 2007 was not available for all companies at press time.**

2007 Sales: $
2006 Sales: $
2005 Sales: $
2004 Sales: $
2003 Sales: $2,102,200

2007 Profits: $
2006 Profits: $
2005 Profits: $
2004 Profits: $
2003 Profits: $89,000

U.S. Stock Ticker: Nonprofit
Int'l Ticker: Int'l Exchange:
Employees: 11,088
Fiscal Year Ends: 12/31
Parent Company:

SALARIES/BENEFITS:

Pension Plan: Y	ESOP Stock Plan:	Profit Sharing:	Top Exec. Salary: $	Bonus: $
Savings Plan: Y	Stock Purch. Plan:		Second Exec. Salary: $	Bonus: $

OTHER THOUGHTS:

Apparent Women Officers or Directors: 3
Hot Spot for Advancement for Women/Minorities: Y

LOCATIONS: ("Y" = Yes)

West:	Southwest:	Midwest:	Southeast:	Northeast:	International:
		Y			

COAST DENTAL SERVICES INC www.coastdental.com

Industry Group Code: 621111 **Ranks within this company's industry group:** Sales: Profits:

Insurance/HMO/PPO:		Drugs:		Equipment/Supplies:		Hospitals/Clinics:		Services:		Health Care:	
Insurance:		Manufacturer:		Manufacturer:		Acute Care:		Diagnostics:		Home Health:	
Managed Care:		Distributor:		Distributor:		Sub-Acute:		Labs/Testing:		Long-Term Care:	
Utilization Management:		Specialty Pharmacy:		Leasing/Finance:		Outpatient Surgery:		Staffing:		Physical Therapy:	
Payment Processing:		Vitamins/Nutritionals:		Information Systems:		Physical Rehab. Ctr.:		Waste Disposal:		Physician Prac. Mgmt.:	Y
		Clinical Trials:				Psychiatric Clinics:		Specialty Svcs.:	Y		

TYPES OF BUSINESS:

Dental Practice Management

BRANDS/DIVISIONS/AFFILIATES:

Coast Comprehensive Care
VizLite
Kodak Digital Radiography
Coast Dental Advantage
Smile Plus

CONTACTS: *Note: Officers with more than one job title may be intentionally listed here more than once.*

Thomas J. Marler, CEO
Donald T. Kelly, CFO
Lauren K. Key, VP-Mktg.
Tarla Butler, Dir.-Human Resources
Michael T. Smith, CIO
Patricia A. Huie, General Counsel
Adam Diasti, Dir.-Dental/Pres., Coast P.A.
Dawn Vanderlinden, Regional VP-Central Florida Region
Kathy Marin, Regional VP-East Florida Region
Tim Hill, Regional VP-West Florida Region
Terek Diasti, Chmn.

Phone: 813-288-1999	**Fax:** 813-281-9284
Toll-Free:	
Address: 2502 N. Rocky Point Dr., Ste. 1000, Tampa, FL 33607 US	

GROWTH PLANS/SPECIAL FEATURES:

Coast Dental Services, Inc. is a provider of dental practice management services to affiliated general dentists and support staffs in the southeastern U.S. The company serves over 115 dental centers in Florida, Georgia, Tennessee and Virginia. The affiliated group of dental practices, known as Coast P.A., is comprised of, among others, Coast Florida P.A.; Coast Dental, P.A.; Coast Dental of Georgia, P.A. Coast Dental Services of Tennessee, P.C.; and Adam Diasti D.D.S. & Associates, P.C. The firm's operating model allows dentists to focus on providing high quality dentistry, while the company's system takes care of aspects of office administration, including human resources, training insurance processing and marketing. Coast Dental has a revolving credit program for its patients, which has the backing of a financial institution. The company fabricates its own dentures in an in-house laboratory. Programs offered by the company include the Coast Comprehensive Care program, which diagnoses and manages periodontal disease; VizLite, a non-invasive oral cancer screening exam Kodak Digital Radiography, a replacement of traditional X rays with digital imaging; Smile Plus, a discounted dental service for patients with no insurance; and Coast Dental Advantage, a payment plan with monthly payments starting at $25 and no annual fee. In April 2006, Coast Dental signed a multi-million-dollar agreement with Eastman Kodak Co that would put the Kodak RVG 6000 Digital Radiography System in the company's practice firms.

The company offers its employees medical insurance; life and AD&D insurance; disability insurance; a 401(k) plan; an employee assistance program; a dental discount program and access to a credit union.

FINANCIALS: **Sales and profits are in thousands of dollars—add 000 to get the full amount. 2007 Note: Financial information for 2007 was not available for all companies at press time.**

2007 Sales: $	2007 Profits: $	**U.S. Stock Ticker: Private**
2006 Sales: $	2006 Profits: $	**Int'l Ticker:** Int'l Exchange:
2005 Sales: $	2005 Profits: $	Employees: 677
2004 Sales: $	2004 Profits: $	Fiscal Year Ends:
2003 Sales: $56,416	2003 Profits: $-2,986	Parent Company:

SALARIES/BENEFITS:

Pension Plan:	ESOP Stock Plan:	Profit Sharing:	Top Exec. Salary: $273,077	Bonus: $
Savings Plan: Y	Stock Purch. Plan:		Second Exec. Salary: $219,231	Bonus: $

OTHER THOUGHTS:

Apparent Women Officers or Directors: 7
Hot Spot for Advancement for Women/Minorities: Y

LOCATIONS: ("Y" = Yes)

West:	Southwest:	Midwest:	Southeast:	Northeast:	International:
			Y	Y	

COHERENT INC

www.cohr.com

ndustry Group Code: 339113 **Ranks within this company's industry group:** Sales: 36 Profits:

nsurance/HMO/PPO:		Drugs:		Equipment/Supplies:		Hospitals/Clinics:		Services:		Health Care:	
nsurance:		Manufacturer:		Manufacturer:	Y	Acute Care:		Diagnostics:		Home Health:	
Managed Care:		Distributor:		Distributor:		Sub-Acute:		Labs/Testing:		Long-Term Care:	
Jtilization Management:		Specialty Pharmacy:		Leasing/Finance:		Outpatient Surgery:		Staffing:		Physical Therapy:	
Payment Processing:		Vitamins/Nutritionals:		Information Systems:		Physical Rehab. Ctr.:		Waste Disposal:		Physician Prac. Mgmt.:	
		Clinical Trials:				Psychiatric Clinics:		Specialty Svcs.:			

TYPES OF BUSINESS:

Equipment-Lasers & Laser Systems
Precision Optics
Research Services

BRANDS/DIVISIONS/AFFILIATES:

Lambda Physik
Electro-Optics
Azure
Paladin
Vitesse
Verdi
AVIA
DIAMOND

CONTACTS: *Note: Officers with more than one job title may be intentionally listed here more than once.*

John R. Ambroseo, CEO
John R. Ambroseo, Pres.
Helene Simonet, CFO/Exec. VP
Ron A. Victor, Exec. VP-Human Resources
Luis Spinelli, CTO/Exec. VP
Bret DiMarco, General Counsel/Exec. VP
Paul L. Meissner, Exec. VP-Laser Systems
Bernard J. Couillaud, Chmn.

Phone: 408-764-4000	**Fax:** 408-764-4800
Toll-Free:	
Address: 5100 Patrick Henry Dr., Santa Clara, CA 95054 US	

GROWTH PLANS/SPECIAL FEATURES:

Coherent, Inc. designs, manufactures and markets photonics-based solutions for a broad range of commercial and scientific research applications. The company specializes in lasers, precision optics and related accessories, and it currently sells its products in over 80 countries. Coherent is active in the microelectronics industry in four areas: semiconductor front-end manufacturing, back-end fabrication using PCB (printed circuit board) technologies, flat panel displays and emerging technologies. Front-end manufacturing uses microlithography, which relies on a high resolution photomask of quartz and chrome, to produce semiconductor wafers with a large number of circuits. Since semiconductor devices are prone to exhibit small defects after the manufacturing process, the company's Azure, Paladin, Vitesse and Verdi lasers are made for the sole purpose of detecting defects as small as 0.1 microns within semiconductor chips and printed circuit boards. Back-end fabrication then packages the resulting semiconductor wafer into an encapsulated silicon chip for future assembly into circuits. In its flat panel display sector, Coherent utilizes its AVIA and DIAMOND lasers to perform excimer-based processes to produce polysilicon layers for high-quality displays. Coherent's emerging technologies sector focuses on solar cell technology and the hydrogen cell as a clean alternative power source for automobiles. Coherent's two main operating subsidiaries are Electro-Optics and Lambda Physik. Electro-Optics specializes in semiconductors and engages in materials processing, OEM laser components, scientific research, government programs and graphic arts. Lambda Physik is based in Gottingden, Germany and manufactures lasers for thin-film transistors in flat-panel displays, microlithography applications, ink-jet printers, automotive, environmental research, scientific research, medical equipment manufacturing and micro-machining applications. In April 2007, Coherent acquired Nuvonyx, Inc., a company that specializes in high-power laser diode components, arrays and industrial laser systems for materials processing and defense applications.

Coherent offers employees educational assistance; Co-Rec, an employee volunteer program; a productivity incentive plan and reimbursement accounts.

FINANCIALS: **Sales and profits are in thousands of dollars—add 000 to get the full amount. 2007 Note: Financial information for 2007 was not available for all companies at press time.**

2007 Sales: $	2007 Profits: $	**U.S. Stock Ticker: COHR**
2006 Sales: $584,600	2006 Profits: $	**Int'l Ticker:** Int'l Exchange:
2005 Sales: $516,252	2005 Profits: $39,861	Employees: 2,189
2004 Sales: $494,954	2004 Profits: $17,360	Fiscal Year Ends: 9/30
2003 Sales: $406,235	2003 Profits: $-45,891	Parent Company:

SALARIES/BENEFITS:

Pension Plan:	ESOP Stock Plan:	Profit Sharing: Y	Top Exec. Salary: $506,629	Bonus: $622,477
Savings Plan: Y	Stock Purch. Plan: Y		Second Exec. Salary: $329,000	Bonus: $287,876

OTHER THOUGHTS:

Apparent Women Officers or Directors: 1
Hot Spot for Advancement for Women/Minorities:

LOCATIONS: ("Y" = Yes)

West:	Southwest:	Midwest:	Southeast:	Northeast:	International:
Y				Y	Y

Note: Financial information, benefits and other data can change quickly and may vary from those stated here.

COMMUNITY HEALTH SYSTEMS INC www.chs.net

Industry Group Code: 622110 **Ranks within this company's industry group:** Sales: 12 Profits: 12

Insurance/HMO/PPO:		Drugs:		Equipment/Supplies:		Hospitals/Clinics:		Services:		Health Care:	
Insurance:		Manufacturer:		Manufacturer:		Acute Care:	Y	Diagnostics:		Home Health:	Y
Managed Care:		Distributor:		Distributor:		Sub-Acute:		Labs/Testing:		Long-Term Care:	Y
Utilization Management:		Specialty Pharmacy:		Leasing/Finance:		Outpatient Surgery:		Staffing:		Physical Therapy:	
Payment Processing:		Vitamins/Nutritionals:		Information Systems:		Physical Rehab. Ctr.:		Waste Disposal:		Physician Prac. Mgmt.:	
		Clinical Trials:				Psychiatric Clinics:		Specialty Svcs.:			

TYPES OF BUSINESS:

Hospitals
Surgical & Emergency Services
Acute Care Facilities
Home Health & Nursing

BRANDS/DIVISIONS/AFFILIATES:

Pottstown Memorial Medical Center
Brandywine Hospital
Easton Hospital
Gateway Regional Medical Center
Dyersburg Regional Medical Center
Springs Memorial Hospital
Phoenixville Hospital
Galesburg Cottage Hospital

CONTACTS: *Note: Officers with more than one job title may be intentionally listed here more than once.*

Wayne T. Smith, CEO
Wayne T. Smith, Pres.
W. Larry Cash, CFO/Exec. VP
Linda K. Parsons, VP-Human Resources
J. Gary Seay, CIO/VP
Robert A. Horrar, VP-Admin.
Rachel A. Seifert, General Counsel/Sr. VP/Corp. Sec.
Martin G. Schweinhart, Sr. VP-Oper.
Robert O. Horrar, VP-Bus. Dev.
T. Mark Buford, Chief Acct. Officer/VP/Corp. Controller
David L. Miller, Sr. VP-Group Oper.
Gary D. Newsome, Sr. VP-Group Oper.
Michael T. Portacci, Sr. VP-Group Oper.
William S. Hussey, Sr. VP-Group Oper.
Wayne T. Smith, Chmn.
Carolyn S. Lipp, Sr. VP-Quality & Resource Mgmt.

Phone: 615-373-9600 **Fax:** 615-371-1068
Toll-Free:
Address: 155 Franklin Rd., Ste. 400, Brentwood, TN 37027-4600 US

GROWTH PLANS/SPECIAL FEATURES:

Community Health Systems, Inc. is the largest non-urba provider of general hospital healthcare services in the U.S The company owns, leases and operates 70 hospitals acros 21 states with 7,974 registered beds. In approximately 85% of the markets in which Community Health System operates, it is the sole provider of general healthcar services. The company continues to expand based on selective acquisition strategy of primarily targetin municipally owned or not-for-profit hospitals. However, it primary method of adding or expanding medical services i the recruitment of new physicians into the communit Community Health focuses its operations on rural areas tha usually have a small but growing population base and tha generally have a lack of community health services. Som of the company's hospitals offer personalized home an nursing care, and they all offer a full range of services tha include surgical and emergency provision. Communit Health's hospitals gain a competitive advantage by benefitin through their large corporate structure. These advantage which include greater purchasing efficiencies, optimize resource allocation and inter-hospital collaboration, lead t more efficient, standardized operations. Since 1996 Community Health Systems has added 48 hospitals to it portfolio, mostly municipal or other non-profit hospitals. I July 2006, Community Health acquired Union Count Hospital, a 25-bed facility in Anna, IL; that month it als acquired Vista Health and St. Therese Medical Center, bot of which are located in Waukegan, IL, totaling 407 beds. I March 2007, the firm agreed to acquire Triad Hospitals, Inc one of the nation's largest hospital companies, for $6. billion.

FINANCIALS: **Sales and profits are in thousands of dollars—add 000 to get the full amount. 2007 Note: Financial information for 2007 was not available for all companies at press time.**

2007 Sales: $	2007 Profits: $	**U.S. Stock Ticker: CYH**
2006 Sales: $4,365,576	2006 Profits: $168,263	**Int'l Ticker:** Int'l Exchange:
2005 Sales: $3,738,320	2005 Profits: $167,544	Employees: 39,000
2004 Sales: $3,203,507	2004 Profits: $151,433	Fiscal Year Ends: 12/31
2003 Sales: $2,834,624	2003 Profits: $131,472	Parent Company:

SALARIES/BENEFITS:

Pension Plan:	ESOP Stock Plan:	Profit Sharing:	Top Exec. Salary: $990,000	Bonus: $712,800
Savings Plan: Y	Stock Purch. Plan:		Second Exec. Salary: $625,000	Bonus: $337,500

OTHER THOUGHTS:

Apparent Women Officers or Directors: 4
Hot Spot for Advancement for Women/Minorities: Y

LOCATIONS: ("Y" = Yes)

West:	Southwest:	Midwest:	Southeast:	Northeast:	International:
Y	Y	Y	Y	Y	

CONCENTRA INC

www.concentra.com

Industry Group Code: 621999 **Ranks within this company's industry group:** Sales: 1 Profits: 1

Insurance/HMO/PPO:		Drugs:		Equipment/Supplies:		Hospitals/Clinics:		Services:		Health Care:	
Insurance:	Y	Manufacturer:		Manufacturer:		Acute Care:		Diagnostics:		Home Health:	
Managed Care:		Distributor:		Distributor:		Sub-Acute:		Labs/Testing:	Y	Long-Term Care:	
Utilization Management:	Y	Specialty Pharmacy:		Leasing/Finance:		Outpatient Surgery:		Staffing:		Physical Therapy:	Y
Payment Processing:	Y	Vitamins/Nutritionals:		Information Systems:		Physical Rehab. Ctr.:		Waste Disposal:		Physician Prac. Mgmt.:	
		Clinical Trials:				Psychiatric Clinics:		Specialty Svcs.:	Y		

TYPES OF BUSINESS:

Utilization Management, Health Care
Workplace Injury Treatment & Management
Group Health & Automobile Claims Management
Claims Cost Control
Case Management

BRANDS/DIVISIONS/AFFILIATES:

Concentra Health Services
Concentra Medical Centers
Concentra Auto Injury Solutions
Viant Holdings, Inc.
Welsh, Carson, Anderson & Stowe

CONTACTS: *Note: Officers with more than one job title may be intentionally listed here more than once.*

James M. Greenwood, CEO
W. Keith Newton, COO
W. Keith Newton, Pres.
Thomas E. Kiraly, CFO/Exec. VP
Jay B. Blakey, Sr. VP-Sales
Tammy S. Steele, Sr. VP-Human Resources & Compliance
Suzanne C. Siemik, CIO/Sr. VP
Mark A. Solls, General Counsel/Exec. VP
James M. Greenwood, Exec. VP-Corp. Dev.
John A. deLorimier, Sr. VP-Comm.
Su Zan Nelson, VP-Acct. & Finance
W. Tom Fogarty, Exec. VP/Chief Medical Officer
Ted Bucknam, Sr. VP-Medical Center Oper.
A. Michael McCollum, Sr. VP-Health Solutions
Gregory M. Gilbert, Sr. VP-Reimbursement & Gov't Affairs.
Paul Queally, Chmn.

Phone: 972-364-8000 **Fax:** 972-381-1938
Toll-Free: 800-232-3550
Address: 5080 Spectrum Dr., Ste. 1200W, Addison, TX 75001 US

GROWTH PLANS/SPECIAL FEATURES:

Concentra, Inc. is a leading national provider of workers' compensation and occupational health care services, as well as group health and auto liability. Following a major restructure of the company's primary operating subsidiary in June 2007, Concentra has merged with two of its primary businesses, Diversified Services and Care Management Services, as the newly renamed Concentra Health Services. These businesses were previously managed by Concentra Operations, a subsidiary that has been subsumed by Concentra, Inc. Through Health Services, the company monitors workers' compensation claims by facilitating the return to work of injured employees who have been out of work for an extended period of time, due primarily to work-related illness or injury. It also treats workplace injuries and illnesses, provides physical therapy, pre-placement physicals and drug and alcohol screening. All of this is accomplished through more than 300 owned and managed centers around the country and over 500 affiliated primary care physicians, as well as through affiliated physical therapists, nurses and other health care providers. The company's other two divisions, Medical Centers and Auto Injury Solutions (AIS), are now also being operated directly by Concentra. AIS is run through technology centers, claims processing centers and professional service centers that are dedicated to providing services to the property and casualty insurance industry. The clinics operated by Concentra's Medical Center offer injury care, wellness and preventative services to over 30,000 patients per day. As a major part of the recent restructure, Concentra formed its Network Services division into a wholly-owned subsidiary called Viant Holdings, Inc. This subsidiary assists insurance companies and other payors in reviewing, repricing and reducing the out-of-network bills they receive from medical providers. It attempts to increase customer savings through fee negotiations, bill repricing and access to provider networks. Concentra is majority owned by the private equity firm, Welsh, Carson, Anderson & Stowe.

FINANCIALS: **Sales and profits are in thousands of dollars—add 000 to get the full amount. 2007 Note: Financial information for 2007 was not available for all companies at press time.**

2007 Sales: $	2007 Profits: $
2006 Sales: $1,298,829	2006 Profits: $32,737
2005 Sales: $1,133,347	2005 Profits: $53,801
2004 Sales: $1,074,181	2004 Profits: $-9,975
2003 Sales: $1,050,700	2003 Profits: $43,300

U.S. Stock Ticker: Private
Int'l Ticker: Int'l Exchange:
Employees: 11,585
Fiscal Year Ends: 12/31
Parent Company: WELSH CARSON ANDERSON & STOWE

SALARIES/BENEFITS:

Pension Plan:	ESOP Stock Plan:	Profit Sharing:	Top Exec. Salary: $	Bonus: $
Savings Plan:	Stock Purch. Plan:		Second Exec. Salary: $	Bonus: $

OTHER THOUGHTS:

Apparent Women Officers or Directors: 3
Hot Spot for Advancement for Women/Minorities: Y

LOCATIONS: ("Y" = Yes)

West:	Southwest:	Midwest:	Southeast:	Northeast:	International:
Y	Y	Y	Y	Y	

CONMED CORP

www.conmed.com

Industry Group Code: 339113 **Ranks within this company's industry group:** Sales: 34 Profits: 88

Insurance/HMO/PPO:		Drugs:		Equipment/Supplies:		Hospitals/Clinics:		Services:		Health Care:	
Insurance:		Manufacturer:		Manufacturer:	Y	Acute Care:		Diagnostics:		Home Health:	
Managed Care:		Distributor:		Distributor:	Y	Sub-Acute:		Labs/Testing:		Long-Term Care:	
Utilization Management:		Specialty Pharmacy:		Leasing/Finance:		Outpatient Surgery:		Staffing:		Physical Therapy:	
Payment Processing:		Vitamins/Nutritionals:		Information Systems:		Physical Rehab. Ctr.:		Waste Disposal:		Physician Prac. Mgmt.:	
		Clinical Trials:				Psychiatric Clinics:		Specialty Svcs.:			

TYPES OF BUSINESS:

Equipment-Surgical & Medical Procedure
Patient Care Products
Sports Medicine Equipment

BRANDS/DIVISIONS/AFFILIATES:

Hall Surgical
Linvatec Corporation
Reflex
Universal
Trogard Finesse
CONMED Electrosurgery
CONMED Endoscopic Technologies
CONMED Integrated Systems

CONTACTS: *Note: Officers with more than one job title may be intentionally listed here more than once.*

Joseph J. Corasanti, CEO
Joseph J. Corasanti, Pres.
Robert D. Shallish, Jr., CFO
Alexander R. Jones, VP-Corp. Sales
Dennis M. Werger, VP/Gen. Manager-Endoscopic Tech.
Daniel S. Jonas, VP-Legal Affairs
Thomas M. Acey, Treas./Corp. Sec.
William W. Abraham, Sr. VP
Luke A. Pomilio, VP
David R. Murray, Pres., Electrosurgery
Jane E. Metcalf, VP-Corp. Regulatory Affairs
Eugene R. Corasanti, Chmn.

Phone: 315-797-8375	**Fax:** 315-797-0321
Toll-Free:	
Address: 525 French Rd., Utica, NY 13502 US	

GROWTH PLANS/SPECIAL FEATURES:

Conmed Corporation is a leading developer, manufacture and supplier of a broad range of medical instruments an systems used in surgical and other procedures. The firr specializes in instruments and implants for arthroscopi sports medicine and powered surgical instruments fc orthopedic surgery and neurosurgery. In addition, Conmed' product offerings include arthroscopic surgery devices an imaging products for minimally invasive surgery. Conmed' arthroscopy products include powered resection instrument arthroscopes, reconstructive systems, tissue repair sets metal and bioabsorbable implants and related disposabl products and fluid management systems. Conmed' powered surgical instruments division sells tools for cutting drilling and reaming, primarily under the Hall Surgical brand Its Linvatec subsidiary is developing a technology base fc large-bone, small-bone, arthroscopic, neurosurgical an spine instruments that can be adapted and modified for nev procedures. The firm's radio frequency electrosurger products are used in a wide variety of procedures an include electrosurgical pencils and blades, ground pads generators, the argon-beam coagulation system and relate disposable products. Its endoscopy products include th Reflex clip applier; Universal laparoscopic instruments surgical staplers; and the Trogard Finesse, whicl incorporates a blunt-tipped trocar, resulting in smalle wounds and less bleeding. The company also produce patient care products for monitoring cardiac rhythms, woun care management and intravenous therapy, including ECC electrodes and cables, wound dressings, cathete stabilization dressings, disposable surgical suctio instruments and connecting tubing. Conmed's produc breadth has enhanced its ability to market to hospitals surgery centers, group purchasing organizations and othe customers, particularly as institutions seek to reduce cost and minimize the number of suppliers.

Conmed offers its employees a 401(k) plan, a pension plan an employee assistance plan, educational assistance, a vision care plan, a cancer protection plan, a healthcare plan and a dental plan.

FINANCIALS: **Sales and profits are in thousands of dollars—add 000 to get the full amount. 2007 Note: Financial information for 2007 was not available for all companies at press time.**

2007 Sales: $	2007 Profits: $	**U.S. Stock Ticker: CNMD**
2006 Sales: $646,812	2006 Profits: $-12,507	**Int'l Ticker:** Int'l Exchange:
2005 Sales: $617,305	2005 Profits: $31,994	Employees: 3,200
2004 Sales: $558,388	2004 Profits: $33,465	Fiscal Year Ends: 12/31
2003 Sales: $497,100	2003 Profits: $32,100	Parent Company:

SALARIES/BENEFITS:

Pension Plan: Y	ESOP Stock Plan:	Profit Sharing:	Top Exec. Salary: $461,750	Bonus: $304,538
Savings Plan: Y	Stock Purch. Plan:		Second Exec. Salary: $408,332	Bonus: $268,710

OTHER THOUGHTS:

Apparent Women Officers or Directors: 1
Hot Spot for Advancement for Women/Minorities:

LOCATIONS: ("Y" = Yes)

West:	Southwest:	Midwest:	Southeast:	Northeast:	International:
Y	Y		Y	Y	Y

CONTINUCARE CORP

www.mycontinucare.com

Industry Group Code: 621610 **Ranks within this company's industry group:** Sales: 10 Profits: 9

Insurance/HMO/PPO:		Drugs:		Equipment/Supplies:		Hospitals/Clinics:		Services:		Health Care:	
Insurance:		Manufacturer:		Manufacturer:		Acute Care:		Diagnostics:		Home Health:	
Managed Care:		Distributor:		Distributor:		Sub-Acute:	Y	Labs/Testing:		Long-Term Care:	
Utilization Management:	Y	Specialty Pharmacy:		Leasing/Finance:		Outpatient Surgery:	Y	Staffing:		Physical Therapy:	
Payment Processing:		Vitamins/Nutritionals:		Information Systems:		Physical Rehab. Ctr.:		Waste Disposal:		Physician Prac. Mgmt.:	Y
		Clinical Trials:				Psychiatric Clinics:		Specialty Svcs.:	Y		

TYPES OF BUSINESS:

Outpatient Health Care
Managed Health Care
Practice Management Services

BRANDS/DIVISIONS/AFFILIATES:

Humana
Vista
MDHC Companies

CONTACTS:

Note: Officers with more than one job title may be intentionally listed here more than once.

Richard C. Pfenniger, Jr., CEO
Richard C. Pfenniger, Jr., Pres.
Fernando Fernandez, CFO
Luis H. Izquierdo, Sr. VP-Mktg.
Gemma Rosello, Exec. VP-Oper.
Luis H. Izquierdo, Sr. VP-Bus. Dev.
Fernando L. Fernandez, Sr. VP-Finance/Treas./Sec.
Luis Cruz, Vice Chmn.
Jose M. Garcia, Exec. VP
Holly Lopez, VP-IPA Oper./Special Projects
Sadita Bustamante, Sr. VP-Center Oper.
Richard C. Pfenniger, Jr., Chmn.

Phone: 305-500-2000 **Fax:**
Toll-Free:
Address: 7200 Corporate Center Dr., Ste. 600, Miami, FL 33126 US

GROWTH PLANS/SPECIAL FEATURES:

Continucare Corporation is a provider of primary care physician services. Through a network of 15 medical centers the company provides primary health care services on an outpatient basis. The company also provides practice management services to 15 independent physician associates (IPAs). All of Continucare's medical centers and IPAs are located in Miami-Dade, Broward and Hillsborough Counties, Florida. The facilities operated by the firm provide services for approximately 15,400 patients on a risk basis and 9,300 patients on a limited or non-risk basis, with a majority of its patients participating in the Medicare Advantage program. Medicare eligible patients under risk arrangements with Continucare accounted for approximately 96% of its revenue for 2006. Continucare's medical centers provide facilities for physicians practicing in the area of general, family and internal medicine, and most are staffed by two to three physicians. Services provided to independent physician associate clinics enrolled in Humana health plans include assistance with medical utilization management, pharmacy management, specialist network development and financial reports. The company's affiliated IPAs provide services to approximately 2,200 patients on a full risk basis and to nearly 3,300 on a limited or non-risk basis. In January 2006, Continucare entered into a Risk IPA Agreement, replacing its Humana PGP Agreement, with Humana under which it agreed to assume certain management responsibilities on a risk basis for Humana's Medicare and Medicaid members assigned to 14 IPAs practicing in Miami-Dade and Broward Counties, Florida. In May 2006, Continucare acquired the MDHC Companies, which provide medical services at five clinical locations throughout Miami-Dade County, Florida. In addition to its risk agreement with Humana, which accounts for approximately 80% of its net medical services, Continucare is currently in managed care agreement with Vista, also a risk agreement, which accounts for approximately 20% of its net medical services.

FINANCIALS:

Sales and profits are in thousands of dollars—add 000 to get the full amount. 2007 Note: Financial information for 2007 was not available for all companies at press time.

2007 Sales: $217,146 | 2007 Profits: $6,303
2006 Sales: $132,991 | 2006 Profits: $5,338
2005 Sales: $112,231 | 2005 Profits: $15,891
2004 Sales: $101,824 | 2004 Profits: $4,652
2003 Sales: $101,400 | 2003 Profits: $ 100

U.S. Stock Ticker: CNU
Int'l Ticker: Int'l Exchange:
Employees: 563
Fiscal Year Ends: 6/30
Parent Company:

SALARIES/BENEFITS:

Pension Plan: | ESOP Stock Plan: | Profit Sharing: | Top Exec. Salary: $328,327 | Bonus: $150,000
Savings Plan: | Stock Purch. Plan: Y | | Second Exec. Salary: $214,062 | Bonus: $50,000

OTHER THOUGHTS:

Apparent Women Officers or Directors: 3
Hot Spot for Advancement for Women/Minorities: Y

LOCATIONS: ("Y" = Yes)

West:	Southwest:	Midwest:	Southeast:	Northeast:	International:
			Y		

Note: Financial information, benefits and other data can change quickly and may vary from those stated here.

CONVATEC

www.convatec.com

Industry Group Code: 339113 **Ranks within this company's industry group:** Sales: Profits:

Insurance/HMO/PPO:		Drugs:		Equipment/Supplies:		Hospitals/Clinics:		Services:		Health Care:	
Insurance:		Manufacturer:		Manufacturer:	Y	Acute Care:		Diagnostics:		Home Health:	
Managed Care:		Distributor:		Distributor:		Sub-Acute:		Labs/Testing:		Long-Term Care:	
Utilization Management:		Specialty Pharmacy:		Leasing/Finance:		Outpatient Surgery:		Staffing:		Physical Therapy:	
Payment Processing:		Vitamins/Nutritionals:		Information Systems:		Physical Rehab. Ctr.:		Waste Disposal:		Physician Prac. Mgmt.:	
		Clinical Trials:				Psychiatric Clinics:		Specialty Svcs.:			

TYPES OF BUSINESS:

Wound Care Products
Skin Care Products
Ostomy Products

BRANDS/DIVISIONS/AFFILIATES:

Bristol Myers Squibb Co
AQUACEL
DuoDerm
SAF-Clens
ActiveLife
Little Ones
Aloe Vesta
Septi-Soft

CONTACTS: *Note: Officers with more than one job title may be intentionally listed here more than once.*

David I. Johnson, Pres.

Phone: 908-904-2500	**Fax:** 908-904-2780
Toll-Free: 800-422-8811	
Address: 200 Headquarters Park Dr., Skillman, NJ 08558 US	

GROWTH PLANS/SPECIAL FEATURES:

ConvaTec, a subsidiary of Bristol-Myers Squib manufactures, distributes and sells wound care, ostomy ca and skin care products for the health care industry. Th company's wound care products include wound cleanser dressings, bandages and hydration products sold under th AQUACEL, CarboFlex, DuoDerm, Hyalofill, KALTOSTA LYOFOAM, OPTIPORE, SurePress, SAF-Clens, SAF-GE Shur-Clens, Tubifast, Tubigrip, Tubipad and UNNA-FLE brand names. ConvaTec's ostomy products includ pouching systems, which allow patients with artifici openings (or stomas) to dispose of bodily waste in attachable pouches. These ostomy products are markete under various names: Esteem Synergy, SUR-FIT Natura an SUR-FIT AutoLock two-piece pouching systems; ActiveLi one-piece pouching systems; and Little Ones pediatr pouching systems. ConvaTec's newest ostomy product include Durahesive and Moldable Convex Skin Barrier wi flange, a customizable skin barrier for difficult-to-manag stomas. In addition, the company offers a range of skin car products, including skin cleansers, moisturizers, barrier bathing and antifungal products, under the Aloe Vest Sensi-Care and Septi-Soft brand names. Aloe Vesta bathin cloths are its newest skin care product. ConvaTec products are marketed worldwide, primarily to hospitals, th medical profession and medical suppliers. The compan relies mainly on an internal sales force, and sales are mad through various distributors around the world. The fir manufactures its products in the U.S., the U.K. and th Dominican Republic. ConvaTec's website features a ostomy retailer search feature that allows customers to find ConvaTec authorized ostomy retailers throughout the U.S.

FINANCIALS: **Sales and profits are in thousands of dollars—add 000 to get the full amount. 2007 Note: Financial information for 2007 was not available for all companies at press time.**

2007 Sales: $	2007 Profits: $	**U.S. Stock Ticker: Subsidiary**
2006 Sales: $	2006 Profits: $	**Int'l Ticker:** Int'l Exchange:
2005 Sales: $	2005 Profits: $	Employees:
2004 Sales: $	2004 Profits: $	Fiscal Year Ends:
2003 Sales: $	2003 Profits: $	Parent Company: BRISTOL MYERS SQUIBB CO

SALARIES/BENEFITS:

Pension Plan:	ESOP Stock Plan:	Profit Sharing:	Top Exec. Salary: $	Bonus: $
Savings Plan:	Stock Purch. Plan:		Second Exec. Salary: $	Bonus: $

OTHER THOUGHTS:

Apparent Women Officers or Directors:
Hot Spot for Advancement for Women/Minorities:

LOCATIONS: ("Y" = Yes)

West:	Southwest:	Midwest:	Southeast:	Northeast:	International:
				Y	

COOPER COMPANIES INC

www.coopercos.com

Industry Group Code: 339113 **Ranks within this company's industry group:** Sales: 32 Profits: 30

Insurance/HMO/PPO:		Drugs:		Equipment/Supplies:		Hospitals/Clinics:		Services:		Health Care:	
Insurance:		Manufacturer:		Manufacturer:	Y	Acute Care:		Diagnostics:		Home Health:	
Managed Care:		Distributor:		Distributor:		Sub-Acute:		Labs/Testing:		Long-Term Care:	
Utilization Management:		Specialty Pharmacy:		Leasing/Finance:		Outpatient Surgery:		Staffing:		Physical Therapy:	
Payment Processing:		Vitamins/Nutritionals:		Information Systems:		Physical Rehab. Ctr.:		Waste Disposal:		Physician Prac. Mgmt.:	
		Clinical Trials:				Psychiatric Clinics:		Specialty Svcs.:			

TYPES OF BUSINESS:

Medical Devices
Contact Lenses
Gynecological Instruments
Diagnostic Products

BRANDS/DIVISIONS/AFFILIATES:

CooperVision, Inc.
CooperSurgical, Inc.
Cerveillance Scope
Lone Star Medical Products, Inc.

CONTACTS: *Note: Officers with more than one job title may be intentionally listed here more than once.*

A. Thomas Bender, CEP
Robert S. Weiss, COO/Exec. VP/Pres., CooperVision
A. Thomas Bender, Pres.
Steven M. Neil, CFO/Exec. VP
Carol R. Kaufman, Chief Admin. Officer
Carol R. Kaufman, Sr. VP-Legal Affairs/Sec.
B. Norris Battin, VP-Comm.
B. Norris Battin, VP-Investor Rel.
Albert G. White, III, Treas./VP
John C. Calcagno, CFO/VP-Bus. Dev., CooperVision, Inc.
Daniel G. McBride, VP/Sr. Corp. Counsel
Nicholas J. Pichotta, CEO-CooperSurgical, Inc.
Rodney E. Folden, Corp. Controller
A. Thomas Bender, Chmn.
Andrew Sedgwick, Pres., European Oper.-CooperVision, Inc.

Phone: 949-597-4700	**Fax:** 949-768-3688
Toll-Free:	
Address: 21062 Bake Pkwy., Ste. 200, Lake Forest, CA 92630 US	

GROWTH PLANS/SPECIAL FEATURES:

Cooper Companies, Inc. develops, manufactures and markets healthcare products, primarily medical devices. The company operates through two business units: CooperVision, Inc. and CooperSurgical, Inc. CooperVision manufactures and markets a broad range of contact lenses for the worldwide vision correction market. The subsidiary particularly focuses on specialty contact lenses, such as toric lenses, cosmetic lenses, multifocal lenses, lenses for patients with dry eye symptoms and long-term extended wear lenses. Leading products are disposable spherical and specialty contact lenses. The Proclear line of spherical, multifocal and toric lenses are manufactured with omafilcon A, a material that incorporates a proprietary phosphorylcholine technology that helps enhance tissue-device compatibility. CooperVision's products are primarily manufactured at its facilities located in the U.K., Puerto Rico and Norfolk, Virginia. CooperSurgical develops, manufactures and markets medical devices, diagnostic products and surgical instruments and accessories for the women's healthcare market used primarily by gynecologists and obstetricians. The subsidiary has produced a number of innovative products for in-office practices where physicians screen, diagnose and treat commonly occurring gynecological conditions. One such product is the innovative digital colposcopy system, Cerveillance Scope. Using Cerveillance Scope, physicians can examine the cervix and then document, store and recall digital images of their findings. CooperSurgical's products are primarily manufactured and distributed at its facility in Connecticut. In November 2006, CooperSurgical acquired Lone Star Medical Products, Inc., advancing its expansion into the hospital segment of women's healthcare.

FINANCIALS: **Sales and profits are in thousands of dollars—add 000 to get the full amount. 2007 Note: Financial information for 2007 was not available for all companies at press time.**

2007 Sales: $	2007 Profits: $	**U.S. Stock Ticker: COO**
2006 Sales: $858,960	2006 Profits: $66,234	**Int'l Ticker:** Int'l Exchange:
2005 Sales: $806,617	2005 Profits: $91,722	Employees: 7,500
2004 Sales: $490,176	2004 Profits: $92,825	Fiscal Year Ends: 10/31
2003 Sales: $411,790	2003 Profits: $68,770	Parent Company:

SALARIES/BENEFITS:

Pension Plan:	ESOP Stock Plan:	Profit Sharing:	Top Exec. Salary: $725,000	Bonus: $95,156
Savings Plan:	Stock Purch. Plan:		Second Exec. Salary: $462,500	Bonus: $52,609

OTHER THOUGHTS:

Apparent Women Officers or Directors: 1
Hot Spot for Advancement for Women/Minorities:

LOCATIONS: ("Y" = Yes)

West:	Southwest:	Midwest:	Southeast:	Northeast:	International:
Y				Y	Y

Note: Financial information, benefits and other data can change quickly and may vary from those stated here.

CORDIS CORP www.cordis.com

Industry Group Code: 339113 **Ranks within this company's industry group:** Sales: Profits:

Insurance/HMO/PPO:		Drugs:		Equipment/Supplies:		Hospitals/Clinics:		Services:		Health Care:	
Insurance:		Manufacturer:		Manufacturer:	Y	Acute Care:		Diagnostics:		Home Health:	
Managed Care:		Distributor:		Distributor:	Y	Sub-Acute:		Labs/Testing:		Long-Term Care:	
Utilization Management:		Specialty Pharmacy:		Leasing/Finance:		Outpatient Surgery:		Staffing:		Physical Therapy:	
Payment Processing:		Vitamins/Nutritionals:		Information Systems:		Physical Rehab. Ctr.:		Waste Disposal:		Physician Prac. Mgmt.:	
		Clinical Trials:				Psychiatric Clinics:		Specialty Svcs.:			

TYPES OF BUSINESS:

Vascular Treatment Products
Guidewires & Balloons
Stents & Catheters

BRANDS/DIVISIONS/AFFILIATES:

Johnson & Johnson
Cordis Cardiology
Cordis Endovascular
Cordis Neurovascular, Inc.
Biosense Webster, Inc.
CYPHER Sirolimus-eluting Coronary Stent
Ensure Medical, Inc.
REGATTA

CONTACTS: *Note: Officers with more than one job title may be intentionally listed here more than once.*

Todd M. Pope, Pres.
Joseph M. Smith, VP-Microelectronic Tech.
Campbell Rogers, CTO
Jan Keltjens, Gen. Manager-Cordis Neurovascular, Inc.
Roy Tanaka, Pres., Biosense Webster, Inc.
David E. Kandzari, Chief Medical Officer, Cordis Cardiology Div.
Rick Anderson, Chmn.

Phone: 786-313-2000	**Fax:** 786-313-2080
Toll-Free: 800-327-7714	
Address: 14201 NW 60th Ave., Miami Lakes, FL 33014 US	

GROWTH PLANS/SPECIAL FEATURES:

Cordis Corp., a subsidiary of Johnson & Johnson, develop minimally invasive treatments for circulatory syster diseases. The company is a leading developer an manufacturer of products for interventional medicine minimally-invasive computer-based imaging an electrophysiology. The company has four primary busines units: Cordis Cardiology, which handles cardiovascula disease management; Cordis Endovascular for the treatmer of peripheral vascular and obstructive diseases; Cordi Neurovascular, Inc. for the neurovascular management c stroke; and Biosense Webster, Inc. for electrophysiology an medical sensor technology in cardiovascular procedures Cordis products include regular and balloon expandabl stents and accessories; dilation, guiding and diagnosti catheters including percutaneous transluminal coronar angioplasty (PTCA) and Vista Brite Tip catheters as well a catheter sheath introducers and accessories includin extensions; STEER-IT Deflecting Tip and Emerald diagnosti guidewires; biopsy forceps; Easy Twist torquing devices Unistasis and hemostasis valves; and transradial systems The company's most recent product is the CYPHEF Sirolimus-eluting Coronary Stent, designed as an alternativ for patients who would otherwise require bypass surgery. I July 2006, Cordis announced the acquisition of Ensur Medical, Inc., a privately held healthcare company based i Sunnyvale, California. In September 2006, the compan signed an agreement with Brivant Ltd., wherein Cordis wi become the worldwide distributor of the REGATTA line c guidewires. Also in September 2006, Cordis Endovascula received FDA approval for its PRECISE Nitinol Stent an ANGIOGUARD Emboli Capture Guidewire, designed to trea clogged neck arteries.

FINANCIALS: Sales and profits are in thousands of dollars—add 000 to get the full amount. 2007 Note: Financial information for 2007 was not available for all companies at press time.

2007 Sales: $	2007 Profits: $	**U.S. Stock Ticker: Subsidiary**
2006 Sales: $	2006 Profits: $	**Int'l Ticker:** Int'l Exchange:
2005 Sales: $	2005 Profits: $	Employees: 7,000
2004 Sales: $3,213,000	2004 Profits: $	Fiscal Year Ends: 12/31
2003 Sales: $	2003 Profits: $	Parent Company: JOHNSON & JOHNSON

SALARIES/BENEFITS:

Pension Plan: Y	ESOP Stock Plan:	Profit Sharing:	Top Exec. Salary: $	Bonus: $
Savings Plan: Y	Stock Purch. Plan:		Second Exec. Salary: $	Bonus: $

OTHER THOUGHTS:

Apparent Women Officers or Directors:
Hot Spot for Advancement for Women/Minorities:

LOCATIONS: ("Y" = Yes)

West:	Southwest:	Midwest:	Southeast:	Northeast:	International:
Y			Y		Y

CORVEL CORP

www.corvel.com

Industry Group Code: 621999 **Ranks within this company's industry group:** Sales: 2 Profits: 2

Insurance/HMO/PPO:		Drugs:		Equipment/Supplies:		Hospitals/Clinics:		Services:		Health Care:	
Insurance:		Manufacturer:		Manufacturer:		Acute Care:		Diagnostics:		Home Health:	
Managed Care:		Distributor:		Distributor:		Sub-Acute:		Labs/Testing:		Long-Term Care:	
Utilization Management:	Y	Specialty Pharmacy:		Leasing/Finance:		Outpatient Surgery:		Staffing:		Physical Therapy:	
Payment Processing:	Y	Vitamins/Nutritionals:		Information Systems:	Y	Physical Rehab. Ctr.:		Waste Disposal:		Physician Prac. Mgmt.:	
		Clinical Trials:				Psychiatric Clinics:		Specialty Svcs.:	Y		

TYPES OF BUSINESS:

Utilization Management
Managed Care Services
Preferred Provider Networks
Payment Processing
Workers' Compensation Services

BRANDS/DIVISIONS/AFFILIATES:

CorCase
CareIQ
Advocacy
MedCheck
CorCare
CorCareRX

CONTACTS: *Note: Officers with more than one job title may be intentionally listed here more than once.*

Gordon Clemons, CEO
Daniel J. Starck, COO
Daniel J. Starck, Pres.
Scott McCloud, CFO
Sharon O'Connor, Dir.-Human Resources
Don McFarlane, CIO
Sharon O'Connor, Dir.-Legal
Richard Schweppe, Sec.
Gordon Clemons, Chmn.

Phone: 949-851-1473 **Fax:** 949-851-1469
Toll-Free: 888-726-7835
Address: 2010 Main St., Ste. 600, Irvine, CA 92614 US

GROWTH PLANS/SPECIAL FEATURES:

CorVel Corp. is an independent nationwide provider of medical cost containment and managed care services designed to manage the medical costs of workers' compensation and other healthcare benefits, primarily for coverage under group health and auto insurance policies. The company's services are sold as separate services directed toward managing claims, care, networks, reimbursements and settlements and include automated medical fee auditing; preferred provider networks; out-of-network/line-item bill negotiation and re-pricing; utilization review and management; medical case management; vocational rehabilitation services; early interventions; Medicare set-asides and life-care planning; and a variety of directed care services including independent medical examinations, diagnosis imaging, transportation, translation and durable medical equipment. CorVel's products include MedCheck and MedCheck Select, which are automated medical bill review services; the CorCare network for Preferred Provider Organization services; CorCareRX for workers' compensation pharmacy management; and CareIQ, a directed care service line. The patient management services category, otherwise known as CorCase, which provide a suite of services including first notice of loss, early intervention, utilization management, telephonic case management, vocational rehabilitation and life care planning. CorCase uses CorVel's proprietary advocacy software to determine available indemnity payments from the employer and coordinate case management information and issues. The firm offers its services to insurance companies, third-party administrators and self-administered employers to assist them in managing the medical costs and monitoring the quality of care associated with healthcare claims. In January 2007, CorVel's wholly-owned subsidiary CorVel Enterprise Comp, Inc. purchased certain assets and liabilities of Hazelrigg Risk Management Services, Inc., a workers compensation claims administrator in California, for roughly $12 million.

CorVel offers its employees a stock purchase plan and a 401(k) plan.

FINANCIALS: **Sales and profits are in thousands of dollars—add 000 to get the full amount. 2007 Note: Financial information for 2007 was not available for all companies at press time.**

2007 Sales: $274,581	2007 Profits: $18,576	**U.S. Stock Ticker: CRVL**
2006 Sales: $266,504	2006 Profits: $9,753	**Int'l Ticker:** Int'l Exchange:
2005 Sales: $291,000	2005 Profits: $10,157	Employees: 2,631
2004 Sales: $305,279	2004 Profits: $16,013	Fiscal Year Ends: 3/31
2003 Sales: $282,800	2003 Profits: $16,600	Parent Company:

SALARIES/BENEFITS:

Pension Plan:	ESOP Stock Plan:	Profit Sharing:	Top Exec. Salary: $350,000	Bonus: $
Savings Plan:	Stock Purch. Plan:		Second Exec. Salary: $137,964	Bonus: $

OTHER THOUGHTS:

Apparent Women Officers or Directors: 1
Hot Spot for Advancement for Women/Minorities:

LOCATIONS: ("Y" = Yes)

West:	Southwest:	Midwest:	Southeast:	Northeast:	International:
Y	Y	Y	Y	Y	

Note: Financial information, benefits and other data can change quickly and may vary from those stated here.

COVANCE INC

www.covance.com

Industry Group Code: 541710 **Ranks within this company's industry group:** Sales: 1 Profits: 2

Insurance/HMO/PPO:		Drugs:		Equipment/Supplies:		Hospitals/Clinics:		Services:		Health Care:	
Insurance:		Manufacturer:		Manufacturer:		Acute Care:		Diagnostics:	Y	Home Health:	
Managed Care:		Distributor:		Distributor:		Sub-Acute:		Labs/Testing:	Y	Long-Term Care:	
Utilization Management:		Specialty Pharmacy:		Leasing/Finance:		Outpatient Surgery:		Staffing:		Physical Therapy:	
Payment Processing:		Vitamins/Nutritionals:		Information Systems:		Physical Rehab. Ctr.:		Waste Disposal:		Physician Prac. Mgmt.:	
		Clinical Trials:	Y			Psychiatric Clinics:		Specialty Svcs.:	Y		

TYPES OF BUSINESS:

Pharmaceutical Research & Development
Drug Preclinical/Clinical Trials
Laboratory Testing & Analysis
Approval Assistance
Health Economics & Outcomes Services
Online Tools

BRANDS/DIVISIONS/AFFILIATES:

LabLink
Study Tracker
Trial Tracker
Digitography
Signet Laboratories, Inc.

CONTACTS:

Note: Officers with more than one job title may be intentionally listed here more than once.

Joseph L. Herring, CEO
William Klitgaard, CFO/Sr. VP
Donald Kraft, Sr. VP-Human Resources
James W. Lovett, General Counsel/Sr. VP
Joseph L. Herring, Chmn.

Phone: 609-452-4440	**Fax:** 609-452-9375
Toll-Free: 888-268-2623	
Address: 210 Carnegie Ctr., Princeton, NJ 08540 US	

GROWTH PLANS/SPECIAL FEATURES:

Covance, Inc. is a leading drug development service company and contract research organization. It provides wide range of product development services t pharmaceutical, biotechnology and medical device industrie across the globe. The company also provides laborator testing services for clients in the chemical, agrochemical an food businesses. Covance's early development service include preclinical services (such as toxicolog pharmaceutical development, research products an BioLink, a bioanalytical testing service) and Phase I clinica services. Its late-stage development services cover clinica development and support; clinical trials; periapproval an market access; central laboratory operations; and centra ECG diagnostics. Covance has also introduced severa Internet-based products: Study Tracker is an Internet-base client access product, which permits customers of toxicolog services to review study data and schedules on a near real time basis; LabLink is a client access program that allow customers of central laboratory services to review and quer lab data on a near real-time basis; and Trial Tracker is web-enabled clinical trial project management and trackin tool intended to allow both employees and customers of it late-stage clinical business to review and manage all aspect of clinical-trial projects. Digitography, another electroni system, allows on-screen digital ECG waveforn measurement. In 2006 Covance acquired two companies Signet Laboratories, Inc., which is a leading provider c monoclonal antibodies used in the research of cance infectious disease and neurodegenerative disease; and th Early Phase Clinical Research Business Unit (Phase I/IIA) c Radiant Research Inc., which includes eight sites located i Texas, Idaho, Florida, Hawaii, Oregon and California. T complete its plans for the acquired sites, the compan relocated and expanded the Austin- and Daytona Beach based clinical research units.

Covance offers its employees benefits such as medica dental and vision plans; a range of insurance benefits employee assistance; financial planning services; and tuitio reimbursement.

FINANCIALS:

Sales and profits are in thousands of dollars—add 000 to get the full amount. 2007 Note: Financial information for 2007 was not available for all companies at press time.

2007 Sales: $	2007 Profits: $	**U.S. Stock Ticker: CVD**
2006 Sales: $1,406,058	2006 Profits: $144,998	**Int'l Ticker:** Int'l Exchange:
2005 Sales: $1,250,400	2005 Profits: $119,600	Employees: 8,100
2004 Sales: $1,056,397	2004 Profits: $97,947	Fiscal Year Ends: 12/31
2003 Sales: $974,210	2003 Profits: $76,136	Parent Company:

SALARIES/BENEFITS:

Pension Plan:	ESOP Stock Plan:	Profit Sharing:	Top Exec. Salary: $600,000	Bonus: $
Savings Plan: Y	Stock Purch. Plan: Y		Second Exec. Salary: $525,000	Bonus: $900,000

OTHER THOUGHTS:

Apparent Women Officers or Directors:
Hot Spot for Advancement for Women/Minorities:

LOCATIONS: ("Y" = Yes)

West:	Southwest:	Midwest:	Southeast:	Northeast:	International:
Y	Y	Y	Y	Y	Y

COVENTRY HEALTH CARE INC www.coventryhealth.com

Industry Group Code: 524114 **Ranks within this company's industry group:** Sales: 13 Profits: 7

Insurance/HMO/PPO:		Drugs:		Equipment/Supplies:		Hospitals/Clinics:		Services:		Health Care:	
Insurance:		Manufacturer:		Manufacturer:		Acute Care:		Diagnostics:		Home Health:	
Managed Care:	Y	Distributor:		Distributor:		Sub-Acute:		Labs/Testing:		Long-Term Care:	
Utilization Management:	Y	Specialty Pharmacy:		Leasing/Finance:		Outpatient Surgery:		Staffing:		Physical Therapy:	
Payment Processing:	Y	Vitamins/Nutritionals:		Information Systems:		Physical Rehab. Ctr.:		Waste Disposal:		Physician Prac. Mgmt.:	
		Clinical Trials:				Psychiatric Clinics:		Specialty Svcs.:			

TYPES OF BUSINESS:

Health Plans
Insurance
Managed Care Products

BRANDS/DIVISIONS/AFFILIATES:

Altius
Carelink
HealthAmerica
HealthAssurance
OmniCare
PersonalCare
WellPath
Southern Health

CONTACTS: *Note: Officers with more than one job title may be intentionally listed here more than once.*

Dale B. Wolf, CEO
Thomas P. McDonough, Pres.
Shawn M. Guertin, CFO/Exec. VP
Harvey C. DeMovick, Jr., Exec. VP
Francis S. Soistman, Jr., Exec. VP-Health Plan Oper.
John H. Austin, Chmn.

Phone: 301-581-0600	**Fax:** 301-493-0731
Toll-Free:	
Address: 6705 Rockledge Dr., Ste. 900, Bethesda, MD 20817 US	

GROWTH PLANS/SPECIAL FEATURES:

Coventry Health Care, Inc., formerly Coventry Corp., is a managed healthcare company operating health plans, insurance companies, network rental/managed care services companies and workers' compensation services companies. The firm provides risk and fee-based managed care products and services, including health maintenance organization, preferred provider organizations, point of service, Medicare Advantage, Medicare Prescription Drug Plans, Medicaid, Worker's Compensation and Network Rental to a broad cross section of individuals, employer and government-funded groups, government agencies and other insurance carriers and administrators in all 50 states, as well as Washington, D.C. and Puerto Rico. Coventry operates in two segments: health plans and first health. The health plans segment serves 17 markets, primarily in the mid-Atlantic, Midwest and southeast U.S. The company's health plans operate under the names Altius Health Plans, Carelink Health Plans, Coventry Health Care, Coventry Health and Life, Group Health Plan, HealthAmerica, HealthAssurance, HealthCare USA, OmniCare, PersonalCare, Southern Health and WellPath. The first health segment serves the group health, workers' compensation and state public program markets and assists a broad range of payor clients through a portfolio of both integrated and stand-alone managed care and administrative products. The components of this segment's offerings include national preferred provider organization of directly contracted healthcare providers; clinical programs, including case management, disease management and return to work programs; administrative products, including group health claims administration and workers compensation business process outsourcing; pharmacy benefit management; fiscal agent services; and group health insurance products. In April 2007, Coventry acquired Concentra's Workers' Compensation Managed Care Services business. In July 2007, the firm agreed to buy Florida Health Plan Administrators, LLC for $685 million.

The company offers its employees medical, dental and vision insurance; flexible spending accounts; life and AD&D insurance; a 401(k) plan; tuition assistance; short- and long-term disability insurance; and an employee assistance plan.

FINANCIALS: **Sales and profits are in thousands of dollars—add 000 to get the full amount. 2007 Note: Financial information for 2007 was not available for all companies at press time.**

2007 Sales: $	2007 Profits: $	**U.S. Stock Ticker: CVH**
2006 Sales: $7,733,756	2006 Profits: $560,045	**Int'l Ticker:** Int'l Exchange:
2005 Sales: $6,611,246	2005 Profits: $501,639	Employees: 10,250
2004 Sales: $5,311,969	2004 Profits: $337,117	Fiscal Year Ends: 12/31
2003 Sales: $4,535,143	2003 Profits: $250,145	Parent Company:

SALARIES/BENEFITS:

Pension Plan:	ESOP Stock Plan:	Profit Sharing:	Top Exec. Salary: $850,000	Bonus: $3,532,047
Savings Plan: Y	Stock Purch. Plan:		Second Exec. Salary: $850,000	Bonus: $3,076,985

OTHER THOUGHTS:

Apparent Women Officers or Directors: 1
Hot Spot for Advancement for Women/Minorities:

LOCATIONS: ("Y" = Yes)

West:	Southwest:	Midwest:	Southeast:	Northeast:	International:
				Y	

COVIDIEN LTD

www.covidien.com

Industry Group Code: 339113 **Ranks within this company's industry group:** Sales: 5 Profits: 4

Insurance/HMO/PPO:		Drugs:		Equipment/Supplies:		Hospitals/Clinics:		Services:		Health Care:	
Insurance:		Manufacturer:		Manufacturer:	Y	Acute Care:		Diagnostics:		Home Health:	
Managed Care:		Distributor:		Distributor:		Sub-Acute:		Labs/Testing:		Long-Term Care:	
Utilization Management:		Specialty Pharmacy:		Leasing/Finance:		Outpatient Surgery:		Staffing:		Physical Therapy:	
Payment Processing:		Vitamins/Nutritionals:		Information Systems:		Physical Rehab. Ctr.:		Waste Disposal:		Physician Prac. Mgmt.:	
		Clinical Trials:				Psychiatric Clinics:		Specialty Svcs.:			

TYPES OF BUSINESS:

Medical Equipment & Supplies, Manufacturing
Imaging Agents
Pharmaceutical Products
Retail Products

BRANDS/DIVISIONS/AFFILIATES:

Kendall
Autosuture
Syneture
Valleylab
Mallinckrodt Pharmaceuticals
Nellcor
Puritan Bennett
Tyco Healthcare

CONTACTS: *Note: Officers with more than one job title may be intentionally listed here more than once.*

Richard J. Meelia, CEO
Richard J. Meelia, Pres.
Charles J. Dockendorff, CFO/Exec. VP
Karen A. Quinn-Quintin, Sr. VP-Human Resources
Steven M. McManama, CIO
Brian D. King, Sr. VP-Oper.
Amy A. Wendell, Sr. VP-Bus. Dev. & Strategy
Eric Kraus, Sr. VP-Corp. Comm.
Coleman Lannum, VP-Investor Rel.
Richard G. Brown, Jr., Chief Acct. Officer/Controller
Jose E. Almeida, Pres., Medical Devices
Timothy R. Wright, Pres., Pharmaceutical Products & Imaging Solutions
James C. Clemmer, Pres., Medical Supplies
Richard G. Brown, Jr., Pres., Retail Products

Phone: 441-292-8674	**Fax:**
Toll-Free:	
Address: 90 Pitts Bay Rd., 2nd Fl., Pembroke, HM 08 Bermuda	

GROWTH PLANS/SPECIAL FEATURES:

Covidien Ltd., formerly Tyco Healthcare, is a global healthcare products company that provides medical solutions. Covidien manufactures, distributes and services a diverse range of industry-leading brands such as Kendall, Autosuture, Syneture, Valleylab, Mallinckrodt Pharmaceuticals, Nellcor and Puritan Bennett. The company's business consists of five segments: medical devices, imaging solutions, pharmaceutical products, medical supplies and retail products. The medical devices segment includes surgical devices, energy-based devices, respiratory and monitoring solutions, patient care and safety products, in addition to laparoscopic instruments, surgical staplers, sutures, energy-based instruments, pulse oximeters, ventilators, vascular compression devices, needles and syringes and sharps collection systems. The imaging solutions segment includes contrast agents, contrast delivery systems and radiopharmaceuticals. The pharmaceutical products segment produces active pharmaceutical ingredients, dosage pharmaceuticals and specialty chemicals. The medical supplies segment provides traditional wound care products, absorbent hygiene products, operating room kits and OEM products. The retail products segment includes private label adult incontinence, feminine hygiene and infant care products. Covidien operates in approximately 57 countries, and its products are sold in over 130 countries. The company was formed from Tyco International's healthcare division, Tyco Healthcare, in July 2007.

FINANCIALS: Sales and profits are in thousands of dollars—add 000 to get the full amount. 2007 Note: Financial information for 2007 was not available for all companies at press time.

2007 Sales: $	2007 Profits: $	**U.S. Stock Ticker: COV**
2006 Sales: $9,647,000	2006 Profits: $1,155,000	**Int'l Ticker:** Int'l Exchange:
2005 Sales: $	2005 Profits: $	Employees: 43,000
2004 Sales: $	2004 Profits: $	Fiscal Year Ends: 9/30
2003 Sales: $	2003 Profits: $	Parent Company:

SALARIES/BENEFITS:

Pension Plan:	ESOP Stock Plan:	Profit Sharing:	Top Exec. Salary: $	Bonus: $
Savings Plan:	Stock Purch. Plan:		Second Exec. Salary: $	Bonus: $

OTHER THOUGHTS:

Apparent Women Officers or Directors: 2
Hot Spot for Advancement for Women/Minorities: Y

LOCATIONS: ("Y" = Yes)

West:	Southwest:	Midwest:	Southeast:	Northeast:	International:
					Y

CR BARD INC

www.crbard.com

Industry Group Code: 339113 **Ranks within this company's industry group:** Sales: 17 Profits: 12

Insurance/HMO/PPO:		Drugs:		Equipment/Supplies:		Hospitals/Clinics:		Services:		Health Care:	
Insurance:		Manufacturer:		Manufacturer:	Y	Acute Care:		Diagnostics:		Home Health:	
Managed Care:		Distributor:		Distributor:		Sub-Acute:		Labs/Testing:		Long-Term Care:	
Utilization Management:		Specialty Pharmacy:		Leasing/Finance:		Outpatient Surgery:		Staffing:		Physical Therapy:	
Payment Processing:		Vitamins/Nutritionals:		Information Systems:		Physical Rehab. Ctr.:		Waste Disposal:		Physician Prac. Mgmt.:	
		Clinical Trials:				Psychiatric Clinics:		Specialty Svcs.:	Y		

TYPES OF BUSINESS:

Equipment-Urological Catheters
Diagnostic and Interventional Products
Minimally Invasive Vascular Products
Surgical Specialty Products
Supply Chain and Business Services

BRANDS/DIVISIONS/AFFILIATES:

Bard Access Systems
Bard Electrophysiology Division
Bard Medical Systems
Bard Peripheral Vascular-Biopsy
Bard Peripheral Vascular-Interventional
Genyx Medical, Inc.
Salute Fixation
Davol, Inc.

CONTACTS: *Note: Officers with more than one job title may be intentionally listed here more than once.*

Timothy M. Ring, CEO
John H. Weiland, COO
John H. Weiland, Pres.
Todd C. Schermerhorn, CFO/Sr. VP
Bronwen K. Kelly, VP-Human Resources
John A. DeFord, VP-Science & Technology
Vincent J. Gurnari, Jr., VP-IT
Stephen J. Long, General Counsel/Sec.
Joseph A. Cherry, VP-Oper.
Robert L. Mellen, VP-Strategic Planning & Bus. Dev.
Holly Glass, VP-Investor Rel.
Scott T. Lowry, VP/Treas.
Amy S. Paul, Group VP
Brian P. Kelly, Group VP
James M. Howard, VP-Regulatory Sciences
Christopher D. Ganser, VP-Quality, Environmental Sciences & Safety
Timothy M. Ring, Chmn.

Phone: 908-277-8000	**Fax:** 908-277-8240
Toll-Free: 800-367-2273	
Address: 730 Central Ave., Murray Hill, NJ 07974 US	

GROWTH PLANS/SPECIAL FEATURES:

C.R. Bard, Inc. designs, manufactures, packages, distributes and sells medical, surgical and diagnostic devices. The company commands a strong market share in vascular, urological, oncological and surgical diagnostic and interventional products. C.R. Bard's line of minimally invasive vascular products includes peripheral angioplasty stents, catheters, guidewires, introducers and accessories, vena cava filters and biopsy devices; electrophysiology products including cardiac mapping and electrophysiology laboratory systems and diagnostic and temporary pacing electrode catheters; fabrics and meshes; and implantable blood vessel replacements. Its surgical specialty products include meshes for vessel and hernia repair; irrigation devices for orthopedic, laparoscopic and gynecological procedures; and products for topical hemostasis. These products include the PerFix plug, Kugel patch, Composix sheet, HydroFlex Multi-Application Irrigation Pump System, Avitene and Avifoam. Hernia operations using these products can be done in an outpatient setting in a mere 20 minutes. The company's products are distributed in the United States directly to hospitals and other health care institutions as well as through numerous hospital/surgical supply and other medical specialty distributors with whom the company has distributor agreements. Internationally, C.R. Bard markets its products through 20 subsidiaries and a joint venture in over 90 countries outside the U.S. About 62% of C.R. Bard's internationals sales are of products manufactured in the U.S., Puerto Rico or Mexico.

FINANCIALS: **Sales and profits are in thousands of dollars—add 000 to get the full amount. 2007 Note: Financial information for 2007 was not available for all companies at press time.**

2007 Sales: $	2007 Profits: $	**U.S. Stock Ticker: BCR**
2006 Sales: $1,985,500	2006 Profits: $272,100	**Int'l Ticker:** Int'l Exchange:
2005 Sales: $1,771,300	2005 Profits: $337,100	Employees: 9,400
2004 Sales: $1,656,100	2004 Profits: $302,800	Fiscal Year Ends: 12/31
2003 Sales: $1,433,100	2003 Profits: $233,000	Parent Company:

SALARIES/BENEFITS:

Pension Plan: Y	ESOP Stock Plan:	Profit Sharing:	Top Exec. Salary: $900,000	Bonus: $1,389,420
Savings Plan: Y	Stock Purch. Plan:		Second Exec. Salary: $726,500	Bonus: $905,502

OTHER THOUGHTS:

Apparent Women Officers or Directors: 2
Hot Spot for Advancement for Women/Minorities: Y

LOCATIONS: ("Y" = Yes)

West:	Southwest:	Midwest:	Southeast:	Northeast:	International:
Y	Y	Y	Y	Y	Y

CRITICAL CARE SYSTEMS www.criticalcaresystems.com

Industry Group Code: 621490 **Ranks within this company's industry group:** Sales: Profits:

Insurance/HMO/PPO:		Drugs:		Equipment/Supplies:		Hospitals/Clinics:		Services:		Health Care:	
Insurance:		Manufacturer:		Manufacturer:		Acute Care:	Y	Diagnostics:		Home Health:	
Managed Care:		Distributor:	Y	Distributor:	Y	Sub-Acute:		Labs/Testing:		Long-Term Care:	
Utilization Management:		Specialty Pharmacy:	Y	Leasing/Finance:		Outpatient Surgery:		Staffing:		Physical Therapy:	
Payment Processing:		Vitamins/Nutritionals:		Information Systems:		Physical Rehab. Ctr.:		Waste Disposal:		Physician Prac. Mgmt.:	
		Clinical Trials:				Psychiatric Clinics:		Specialty Svcs.:	Y		

TYPES OF BUSINESS:

Clinics-Chronic Wound Care
Pharmacy Management

BRANDS/DIVISIONS/AFFILIATES:

Curative Health Services

CONTACTS: *Note: Officers with more than one job title may be intentionally listed here more than once.*

Paul F. McConnell, CEO
John C. Prior, COO
Paul F. McConnell, Pres.
John C. Prior, CFO
Craig J. Vollmer, Sr. VP-Sales & Mktg.
Andrew C. Walk, Sr. VP-Oper.
Sean Mahoney, Investor Rel. Contact

Phone: 603-888-1500	**Fax:** 603-888-0990
Toll-Free:	
Address: 61 Spit Brook Rd., Ste. 505, Nashua, NH 03060 US	

GROWTH PLANS/SPECIAL FEATURES:

Critical Care Systems, formerly Curative Health Services Inc., provides health care products, services and support to patients with chronic medical conditions. It operates both a specialty infusion business unit and a wound care management business. The specialty infusion unit provides intravenous and injectable biopharmaceutical and compounded pharmaceutical products and comprehensive infusion services to patients with chronic and critical disease states. All such patient care services are delivered through a national footprint of community-based branches, each including a multidisciplinary team of pharmacists, nurses reimbursement specialists and patient service representatives. The wound care management business provides wound care services specializing in chronic wound care management. It manages, on behalf of hospital clients a nationwide network of Wound Care Center programs that offer a range of services across a continuum of care for treatment of chronic wounds. These programs consist of diagnostic and therapeutic treatment procedures designed to meet each patient's specific wound care needs. The company has approximately 485 payor contracts and provides products or services in approximately 45 states nationwide. Critical Care Systems also operates eBioCare, a specialty online pharmacy, and Apex, a company that caters to the needs of hemophiliacs. In March 2006, the predecessor company, Curative Health, and all its subsidiaries filed voluntary Chapter 11 bankruptcy petitions. This was in order to implement and affect its prepackaged reorganization plan of February 2006. Later, it acquired Critical Care Systems and subsequently changed the company name.

Critical Care Systems offers its employees a benefits plan that includes flexible spending accounts; educational assistance; in-house training; car allowances; stock options; life insurance; and medical and dental coverage.

FINANCIALS: **Sales and profits are in thousands of dollars—add 000 to get the full amount. 2007 Note: Financial information for 2007 was not available for all companies at press time.**

2007 Sales: $	2007 Profits: $	**U.S. Stock Ticker: Private**
2006 Sales: $	2006 Profits: $	**Int'l Ticker:** Int'l Exchange:
2005 Sales: $261,059	2005 Profits: $-101,592	Employees: 1,292
2004 Sales: $224,980	2004 Profits: $-141,405	Fiscal Year Ends: 12/31
2003 Sales: $163,494	2003 Profits: $13,075	Parent Company:

SALARIES/BENEFITS:

Pension Plan:	ESOP Stock Plan:	Profit Sharing:	Top Exec. Salary: $353,077	Bonus: $
Savings Plan: Y	Stock Purch. Plan:		Second Exec. Salary: $291,509	Bonus: $100,000

OTHER THOUGHTS:

Apparent Women Officers or Directors:
Hot Spot for Advancement for Women/Minorities:

LOCATIONS: ("Y" = Yes)

West:	Southwest:	Midwest:	Southeast:	Northeast:	International:
Y	Y	Y	Y	Y	

CRITICARE SYSTEMS INC

www.csiusa.com

Industry Group Code: 339113 **Ranks within this company's industry group:** Sales: 97 Profits: 76

Insurance/HMO/PPO:		**Drugs:**		**Equipment/Supplies:**		**Hospitals/Clinics:**		**Services:**		**Health Care:**	
Insurance:		Manufacturer:		Manufacturer:	Y	Acute Care:		Diagnostics:		Home Health:	
Managed Care:		Distributor:		Distributor:		Sub-Acute:		Labs/Testing:		Long-Term Care:	
Utilization Management:		Specialty Pharmacy:		Leasing/Finance:		Outpatient Surgery:		Staffing:		Physical Therapy:	
Payment Processing:		Vitamins/Nutritionals:		Information Systems:	Y	Physical Rehab. Ctr.:		Waste Disposal:		Physician Prac. Mgmt.:	
		Clinical Trials:				Psychiatric Clinics:		Specialty Svcs.:			

TYPES OF BUSINESS:

Equipment-Vital Sign Monitors
Patient Monitoring Systems
Noninvasive Sensors

BRANDS/DIVISIONS/AFFILIATES:

VitalCare 506N3
ComfortCuff
nGenuity 8100E
DOX Interface
Poet Plus 8100
VitalView
WaterChek
UltraSync

CONTACTS: *Note: Officers with more than one job title may be intentionally listed here more than once.*

Emil H. Soika, CEO
Emil H. Soika, Pres.
Drew M. Diaz, VP-Worldwide Sales
Reinhart Boerner Van Deuren, Corp. General Counsel
Deborah A. Zane, VP-Bus. Dev.
Joel Knudson, VP-Finance/Sec.
Michael T. Larsen, VP-Quality & Regulatory Affairs
Deborah A. Zane, VP-Mktg.
Higgins D. Bailey, Chmn.

Phone: 262-798-8282	**Fax:** 262-798-8290
Toll-Free:	
Address: 20925 Crossroads Cir., Ste. 100, Waukesha, WI 53186-4054 US	

GROWTH PLANS/SPECIAL FEATURES:

Criticare Systems, Inc. designs, manufactures and markets vital signs and gas monitoring instruments and related noninvasive sensors used to monitor patients in many healthcare environments. Its products include the VitalCare 506N3 portable cardiac monitors, which are available in multiple configurations, offering combinations of oximetry (blood oxygen content measurement) systems, ComfortCuff noninvasive blood pressure monitors and temperature sensors. Criticare's nGenuity 8100E multi-parameter vital signs monitors combine an ECG (Electro-Cardio-Gram, a heart activity monitor), ComfortCuff and the DOX digital oximetry, heart rate, temperature, respiration rate and nurse call interface with optional arrhythmia and ST analysis features as well as an integrated printer option. The Poet Plus 8100 vital signs monitors combine numerous systems, such as the DOX interface, ComfortCuff and ECG, as well as having optional oxygen and carbon dioxide monitors, invasive blood pressure monitors or integrated printers. The Poet IQ 8500 and Poet IQ2 8500Q anesthetic gas monitors, used in conjunction with the Poet Plus, are driven by a proprietary infrared technology, and automatically monitor up to five anesthetic agents plus nitrous oxide, oxygen and carbon dioxide. The Model 503DX and 504DX pulse oximeters work with adult, pediatric, neonatal intensive care unit, operating room, emergency room, nursing home, physician's office and ambulance environments. The VitalView central monitoring system allows one nurse or technician to monitor up to sixteen patients simultaneously, receiving, displaying and storing data from vital sign monitors. Its reusable pulse oximetry sensors help hospitals contain costs by substituting in for disposable sensors, and are available in finger or multisite sensors. Finally, its WaterChek and Chek-Mate disposable filter systems remove respiratory secretions and moisture, respectively, from breath samples. Additionally, its UltraSync signal processing software was the first ECG synchronization tool to monitor oxygen saturation in highly active and poorly perfused patients.

FINANCIALS: **Sales and profits are in thousands of dollars—add 000 to get the full amount. 2007 Note: Financial information for 2007 was not available for all companies at press time.**

2007 Sales: $	2007 Profits: $	**U.S. Stock Ticker: CMD**
2006 Sales: $31,351	2006 Profits: $ 212	**Int'l Ticker:** Int'l Exchange:
2005 Sales: $26,782	2005 Profits: $- 422	Employees: 93
2004 Sales: $28,591	2004 Profits: $-2,100	Fiscal Year Ends: 6/30
2003 Sales: $28,600	2003 Profits: $- 900	Parent Company:

SALARIES/BENEFITS:

Pension Plan:	ESOP Stock Plan:	Profit Sharing:	Top Exec. Salary: $308,579	Bonus: $
Savings Plan: Y	Stock Purch. Plan:		Second Exec. Salary: $248,833	Bonus: $

OTHER THOUGHTS:

Apparent Women Officers or Directors: 1
Hot Spot for Advancement for Women/Minorities:

LOCATIONS: ("Y" = Yes)

West:	Southwest:	Midwest:	Southeast:	Northeast:	International:
		Y			Y

Note: Financial information, benefits and other data can change quickly and may vary from those stated here.

CRYOLIFE INC

www.cryolife.com

Industry Group Code: 621511 **Ranks within this company's industry group:** Sales: 8 Profits: 6

Insurance/HMO/PPO:		Drugs:		Equipment/Supplies:		Hospitals/Clinics:		Services:		Health Care:	
Insurance:		Manufacturer:		Manufacturer:	Y	Acute Care:		Diagnostics:		Home Health:	
Managed Care:		Distributor:		Distributor:	Y	Sub-Acute:		Labs/Testing:		Long-Term Care:	
Utilization Management:		Specialty Pharmacy:		Leasing/Finance:		Outpatient Surgery:		Staffing:		Physical Therapy:	
Payment Processing:		Vitamins/Nutritionals:		Information Systems:		Physical Rehab. Ctr.:		Waste Disposal:		Physician Prac. Mgmt.:	
		Clinical Trials:				Psychiatric Clinics:		Specialty Svcs.:	Y		

TYPES OF BUSINESS:

Transplant Tissue Preservation & Distribution
Surgical Adhesives
Heart Valves
Medical Implants
Biomedical Research

BRANDS/DIVISIONS/AFFILIATES:

BioGlue
SynerGraft
BioFoam
BioDisc
AuraZyme Pharmaceuticals, Inc.
CryoLife O'Brien Porcine Aortic Heart Valve
ProPatch Soft Tissue Repair Matrix
CardioWrap

CONTACTS: *Note: Officers with more than one job title may be intentionally listed here more than once.*

Steven G. Anderson, CEO
D. Ashley Lee, COO/Exec. VP
Steven G. Anderson, Pres.
D. Ashley Lee, CFO
Gerald B. Seery, Sr. VP-Mktg. & Sales
Albert E. Heacox, Sr. VP-R&D
Philip A. Theodore, General Counsel/VP
Amy D. Horton, Chief Acct. Officer
David M. Fronk, VP-Regulatory Affairs & Quality Assurance
Scott B. Capps, Pres., CryoLife Europa
Suzanne K. Gabbert, Corp. Sec.
Steven G. Anderson, Chmn.

Phone: 770-419-3355	**Fax:** 770-426-0031
Toll-Free: 800-438-8285	
Address: 1655 Roberts Blvd. NW, Kennesaw, GA 30144 US	

GROWTH PLANS/SPECIAL FEATURES:

CryoLife, Inc. develops and commercializes implantable medical devices and preserves and distributes human tissues for cardiovascular and vascular transplant applications. The firm's implantable medical devices include BioGlue surgical adhesive, porcine heart valves and vascular grafts of bovine tissue processed using the company's SynerGraft technology. BioGlue, designed for cardiovascular, vascular, pulmonary and general surgical applications, is a polymer based on bovine blood protein and an agent for cross-linking proteins. SynerGraft technology involves the removal of cells from the structure of animal tissue, leaving a collagen matrix that has the potential to repopulate in vivo with the recipient's own cells. CryoLife distributes the CryoLife O'Brien porcine aortic heart valve and the SynerGraft bovine vascular graft in Europe, the Middle East and Africa. The company maintains two separate facilities: one in Atlanta, Georgia, which consists of laboratories, warehouse space and offices; and another facility in Fareham in the United Kingdom. Subsidiary AuraZyme Pharmaceuticals, Inc. is dedicated to the commercial development of Activation Control Technology (ACT), allowing CryoLife to focus on its core business practices. ACT has potential uses in the areas of cancer therapy, blood clot dissolving and other drug delivery applications. In 2007, the company began the exclusive distribution of CardioWrap, a bioresorbable thin film sheet used to replace the pericardium in cardiac reconstruction and other cardiac surgeries where the patient may face re-operation within six months. The company was recently awarded a patent for BioFoam, a self-expanding adhesive designed to rapidly arrest bleeding of large vessel injuries and seal wounds. Other products in pre-clinical development are BioDisc, a replacement for vertebral discs, and ProPatch Soft Tissue Repair Matrix for rotator cuff repair.

CryoLife offers its employees a 401(k) plan, an employee stock purchase plan, tuition reimbursement and medical, prescription drug and dental coverage.

FINANCIALS: **Sales and profits are in thousands of dollars—add 000 to get the full amount. 2007 Note: Financial information for 2007 was not available for all companies at press time.**

2007 Sales: $	2007 Profits: $	**U.S. Stock Ticker: CRY**
2006 Sales: $81,311	2006 Profits: $ 365	**Int'l Ticker:** Int'l Exchange:
2005 Sales: $69,282	2005 Profits: $-19,535	Employees: 388
2004 Sales: $62,384	2004 Profits: $-18,749	Fiscal Year Ends: 12/31
2003 Sales: $59,532	2003 Profits: $-32,294	Parent Company:

SALARIES/BENEFITS:

Pension Plan:	ESOP Stock Plan:	Profit Sharing:	Top Exec. Salary: $600,000	Bonus: $353,786
Savings Plan: Y	Stock Purch. Plan: Y		Second Exec. Salary: $340,000	Bonus: $200,479

OTHER THOUGHTS:

Apparent Women Officers or Directors: 2
Hot Spot for Advancement for Women/Minorities:

LOCATIONS: ("Y" = Yes)

West:	Southwest:	Midwest:	Southeast:	Northeast:	International:
			Y		Y

Note: Financial information, benefits and other data can change quickly and may vary from those stated here.

CSL LIMITED

www.csl.com.au

Industry Group Code: 325414 **Ranks within this company's industry group:** Sales: 1 Profits: 1

Insurance/HMO/PPO:		Drugs:		Equipment/Supplies:		Hospitals/Clinics:		Services:		Health Care:	
Insurance:		Manufacturer:	Y	Manufacturer:		Acute Care:		Diagnostics:		Home Health:	
Managed Care:		Distributor:	Y	Distributor:		Sub-Acute:		Labs/Testing:		Long-Term Care:	
Utilization Management:		Specialty Pharmacy:		Leasing/Finance:		Outpatient Surgery:		Staffing:		Physical Therapy:	
Payment Processing:		Vitamins/Nutritionals:		Information Systems:		Physical Rehab. Ctr.:		Waste Disposal:		Physician Prac. Mgmt.:	
		Clinical Trials:				Psychiatric Clinics:		Specialty Svcs.:			

TYPES OF BUSINESS:

Human Blood-Plasma Collection
Plasma Products
Immunohematology Products
Vaccines
Pharmaceutical Marketing
Antivenom
Drugs-Cancer

BRANDS/DIVISIONS/AFFILIATES:

ZLB Behring
CSL Bioplasma
CSL Behring
CSL Pharmaceutical
CSL Biotherapies
Zenyth Therapeutics
CytoGam
ZLB Plasma Services

CONTACTS: *Note: Officers with more than one job title may be intentionally listed here more than once.*

Brian McNamee, CEO
Kevin Milroy, Gen. Mgr.-Human Resources
Andrew Cuthbertson, Chief Scientific Officer
Peter R. Turvey, General Counsel/Corp. Sec.
Peter Turner, Pres., ZLB Behring
Colin Armit, Pres., CSL Pharmaceutical
Paul Bordonaro, Pres., CSL Bioplasma
Peter H. Wade, Chmn.
T. Giarla, Pres., Bioplasma Asia Pacific

Phone: 61-3-9389-1911 **Fax:** 61-3-9389-1434
Toll-Free:
Address: 45 Poplar Rd., Parkville, Victoria 3052 Australia

GROWTH PLANS/SPECIAL FEATURES:

CSL Limited develops, manufactures and markets pharmaceutical products of biological origin in 27 countries worldwide. The company operates through several subsidiaries that manufacture and distribute pharmaceuticals, vaccines and diagnostics derived from human plasma. Subsidiary CSL Behring is a world leader in the manufacture of plasma products such as hemophilia treatments, immunoglobulins and wound healing agents. CSL Limites operates one of the largest plasma collection networks in the world, named ZLB Plasma Services, which includes 65 collection centers in the U.S. and eight in Germany. CSL Bioplasma is one of the largest manufacturers of plasma products in the southern hemisphere and works with the Red Cross and government entities to supply such products in Australia, New Zealand, Singapore, Malaysia and Hong Kong. It also provides contract plasma fractionation services. CSL Biotherapies, formerly CSL Pharmaceutical, manufactures and markets vaccines for human use, including children's vaccines, travel vaccines, respiratory vaccines and antivenom. Currently, its primary focus is the manufacturing of flu vaccines. The company's research and development portfolio includes treatments for stroke, acute coronary syndromes, cervical cancer, melanoma, genital warts, papilloma viruses and hepatitis C, in addition to a method of topical delivery of drugs to the eye. In November 2006, Zenyth Therapeutics became a wholly-owned subsidiary of CSL when it was acquired for nearly $96 million. Also in November 2006, subsidiary ZLB Behring acquired CytoGam, an intravenous drug for the prevention of antibodies against cytomegalovirus in transplant patients, from MedImmune for $70 million.

FINANCIALS: **Sales and profits are in thousands of dollars—add 000 to get the full amount. 2007 Note: Financial information for 2007 was not available for all companies at press time.**

2007 Sales: $	2007 Profits: $	**U.S. Stock Ticker: CSLX.PK**
2006 Sales: $2,146,111	2006 Profits: $88,406	**Int'l Ticker: CSL** Int'l Exchange: Sydney-ASX
2005 Sales: $1,965,359	2005 Profits: $176,824	Employees: 7,000
2004 Sales: $1,650,196	2004 Profits: $219,625	Fiscal Year Ends: 6/30
2003 Sales: $1,313,000	2003 Profits: $47,000	Parent Company:

SALARIES/BENEFITS:

Pension Plan:	ESOP Stock Plan:	Profit Sharing:	Top Exec. Salary: $782,154	Bonus: $782,735
Savings Plan:	Stock Purch. Plan: Y		Second Exec. Salary: $409,753	Bonus: $273,292

OTHER THOUGHTS:

Apparent Women Officers or Directors: 1
Hot Spot for Advancement for Women/Minorities:

LOCATIONS: ("Y" = Yes)

West:	Southwest:	Midwest:	Southeast:	Northeast:	International:
		Y	Y	Y	Y

Note: Financial information, benefits and other data can change quickly and may vary from those stated here.

CURASCRIPT INC

www.curascript.com

Industry Group Code: 446110A **Ranks within this company's industry group:** Sales: Profits:

Insurance/HMO/PPO:		Drugs:		Equipment/Supplies:		Hospitals/Clinics:		Services:		Health Care:	
Insurance:		Manufacturer:		Manufacturer:		Acute Care:		Diagnostics:		Home Health:	
Managed Care:		Distributor:	Y	Distributor:		Sub-Acute:		Labs/Testing:		Long-Term Care:	
Utilization Management:		Specialty Pharmacy:	Y	Leasing/Finance:		Outpatient Surgery:		Staffing:		Physical Therapy:	
Payment Processing:		Vitamins/Nutritionals:		Information Systems:		Physical Rehab. Ctr.:		Waste Disposal:		Physician Prac. Mgmt.:	
		Clinical Trials:				Psychiatric Clinics:		Specialty Svcs.:			

TYPES OF BUSINESS:

Drug Distribution-Specialty Pharmacy
Alternative-Site Drug Distribution
Disease Treatment Programs
Specialty Biopharmaceuticals

BRANDS/DIVISIONS/AFFILIATES:

Priority Healthcare Pharmacy
Integrity Healthcare Services
Priority Healthcare Corp

CONTACTS: *Note: Officers with more than one job title may be intentionally listed here more than once.*

David A. Lowenberg, CEO
David A. Lowenberg, Pres.
Steve Jenson, CFO/Sr. VP

Phone: 407-852-4903	**Fax:** 888-773-7386
Toll-Free: 888-773-7376	
Address: 6272 Lee Vista Blvd., Orlando, FL 32822 US	

GROWTH PLANS/SPECIAL FEATURES:

CuraScript Inc., formerly Priority Healthcare Corp., is a leading national distributor of specialty pharmaceuticals and related medical supplies. It derives revenues primarily from the alternative-site health care market. The firm also provides patient-specific, self-administered biopharmaceuticals and disease treatment programs to its customers with chronic diseases. CuraScript sells specialty pharmaceuticals and medical supplies to outpatient renal care centers and office-based physicians in oncology and other specialty markets. The firm also offers value-added services to meet the specific needs of these markets, including shipping refrigerated pharmaceuticals overnight in special packaging and offering automated order entry services and customized distribution for group accounts. CuraScript sells over 5,000 stock keeping units of its specialty pharmaceuticals and medical supplies to outpatient renal care centers and office-based physicians in oncology and other physician specialty markets. In doing so, it services over 7,000 customers in all 50 states. The company ships from distribution centers in Nevada and Ohio. It fills individual patient prescriptions, primarily for self-administered biopharmaceuticals, at licensed pharmacies in Florida, Massachusetts, Pennsylvania, Delaware, New York and Tennessee. The company also provides disease treatment programs for hepatitis, cancer, hemophilia, human growth deficiency, rheumatoid arthritis, Crohn's disease, infertility, pulmonary hypertension, pain management, multiple sclerosis and others.

CuraScript offers its employees tuition reimbursement, stock options and discount programs, such as a Costco corporate membership.

FINANCIALS: **Sales and profits are in thousands of dollars—add 000 to get the full amount. 2007 Note: Financial information for 2007 was not available for all companies at press time.**

2007 Sales: $	2007 Profits: $	**U.S. Stock Ticker: Subsidiary**
2006 Sales: $	2006 Profits: $	**Int'l Ticker:** Int'l Exchange:
2005 Sales: $	2005 Profits: $	Employees: 1,380
2004 Sales: $1,739,618	2004 Profits: $44,626	Fiscal Year Ends: 12/31
2003 Sales: $1,461,811	2003 Profits: $50,600	Parent Company: EXPRESS SCRIPTS INC

SALARIES/BENEFITS:

Pension Plan:	ESOP Stock Plan:	Profit Sharing: Y	Top Exec. Salary: $544,598	Bonus: $282,792
Savings Plan: Y	Stock Purch. Plan: Y		Second Exec. Salary: $330,850	Bonus: $81,616

OTHER THOUGHTS:

Apparent Women Officers or Directors: 2
Hot Spot for Advancement for Women/Minorities:

LOCATIONS: ("Y" = Yes)

West:	Southwest:	Midwest:	Southeast:	Northeast:	International:
Y	Y	Y	Y	Y	

CVS CAREMARK CORPORATION www.cvs.com

ndustry Group Code: 446110 **Ranks within this company's industry group:** Sales: 2 Profits: 2

nsurance/HMO/PPO:		Drugs:		Equipment/Supplies:		Hospitals/Clinics:		Services:		Health Care:	
nsurance:		Manufacturer:		Manufacturer:		Acute Care:		Diagnostics:		Home Health:	
Managed Care:		Distributor:	Y	Distributor:		Sub-Acute:		Labs/Testing:		Long-Term Care:	
Utilization Management:	Y	Specialty Pharmacy:	Y	Leasing/Finance:		Outpatient Surgery:		Staffing:		Physical Therapy:	
Payment Processing:	Y	Vitamins/Nutritionals:		Information Systems:		Physical Rehab. Ctr.:		Waste Disposal:		Physician Prac. Mgmt.:	
		Clinical Trials:				Psychiatric Clinics:		Specialty Svcs.:			

TYPES OF BUSINESS:

Drug Stores
Pharmacy Benefits Management
Online Pharmacy Services

BRANDS/DIVISIONS/AFFILIATES:

PharmaCare Pharmacy
PharmaCare Management Services
MinuteClinic
Caremark Rx., Inc.

CONTACTS: *Note: Officers with more than one job title may be intentionally listed here more than once.*

Thomas M. Ryan, CEO
Thomas M. Ryan, Pres.
David B. Rickard, CFO/Exec. VP
V. Michael Ferdinandi, Sr. VP-Human Resources
David B. Rickard, Chief Admin. Officer
Douglas A. Sgarro, Chief Legal Officer/Exec. VP/Pres., CVS Realty Co.
William R. Spalding, Exec. VP-Strategy & Managed Care
V. Michael Ferdinandi, Sr. VP-Corp. Comm.
Paula A. Price, Controller/Chief Acct. Officer/Sr. VP
Larry J. Merlo, Exec. VP/Pres., CVS Caremark-Retail
Chris W. Bodine, Exec. VP/Pres., CVS Caremark Health Svcs.
Howard A. McLure, Exec. VP/Pres., Caremark Pharmacy Svcs.
Jonathan C. Roberts, Sr. VP/CIO-CVS Pharmacy, Inc.
Thomas M. Ryan, Chmn.

Phone: 401-765-1500	**Fax:** 401-766-9227
Toll-Free:	
Address: 1 CVS Dr., Woonsocket, RI 02895 US	

GROWTH PLANS/SPECIAL FEATURES:

CVS Caremark Corp. is a drugstore industry retailer that operates roughly 6,200 stores in 43 states and Washington, DC. The company operates in two segments: retail pharmacy and pharmacy benefit management. The retail pharmacy segment included 6,150 retail drugstores located in 40 states and Washington, D.C. operating under the DVS or CVS/pharmacy name. CVS/pharmacy stores sell prescription drugs and an assortment of general merchandise, including over-the-counter drugs; beauty products and cosmetics; film and photo finishing services; seasonal merchandise; greeting cards; and convenience foods. The firm operated 146 retail healthcare clinics in 18 states under the MinuteClinic name, of which 129 are located within CVS retail drugstores. The pharmacy benefit management segment provides prescription benefit management services to managed care and other organizations. These services include mail order pharmacy; specialty pharmacy; plan design and administration; formulary management; and claims processing, as well as providing reinsurance services in conjunction with prescription drug benefit policies. The firm operates about 52 specialty pharmacies under the PharmaCare Management Services and PharmaCare Pharmacy name, located in 22 states and Washington, D.C., and four mail order facilities. In June 2006, the firm acquired 700 standalone Sav-On and Osco drug stores from Albertson's, along with a major distribution center. In July 2006, CVS announced it acquired MinuteClinic, a provider of retail-based health clinics. In March 2007, CVS Corp. merged with Caremark Rx, Inc., a pharmaceutical services company, to form CVS/Caremark Corp., with a total of $75 billion in annual revenues.

The company offers its employees a 401(k) plan; a stock ownership plan; an employee stock purchase plan; short- and long-term disability insurance; medical insurance; prescription coverage; domestic partner benefits; life insurance; dental and vision insurance; business travel insurance; auto and home insurance discount plans; education assistance; and merchandise discounts.

FINANCIALS: **Sales and profits are in thousands of dollars—add 000 to get the full amount. 2007 Note: Financial information for 2007 was not available for all companies at press time.**

2007 Sales: $	2007 Profits: $	**U.S. Stock Ticker: CVS**
2006 Sales: $43,813,800	2006 Profits: $1,368,900	**Int'l Ticker:** Int'l Exchange:
2005 Sales: $37,006,200	2005 Profits: $1,224,700	Employees: 176,000
2004 Sales: $30,594,300	2004 Profits: $918,800	Fiscal Year Ends: 12/31
2003 Sales: $26,588,000	2003 Profits: $847,300	Parent Company:

SALARIES/BENEFITS:

Pension Plan:	ESOP Stock Plan: Y	Profit Sharing:	Top Exec. Salary: $1,150,000	Bonus: $8,172,600
Savings Plan: Y	Stock Purch. Plan: Y		Second Exec. Salary: $713,750	Bonus: $2,413,200

OTHER THOUGHTS:

Apparent Women Officers or Directors: 4
Hot Spot for Advancement for Women/Minorities: Y

LOCATIONS: ("Y" = Yes)

West:	Southwest:	Midwest:	Southeast:	Northeast:	International:
Y	Y	Y	Y	Y	

CYBERONICS INC

www.cyberonics.com

Industry Group Code: 339113 **Ranks within this company's industry group:** Sales: 75 Profits: 96

Insurance/HMO/PPO:		Drugs:		Equipment/Supplies:		Hospitals/Clinics:		Services:		Health Care:	
Insurance:		Manufacturer:		Manufacturer:	Y	Acute Care:		Diagnostics:		Home Health:	
Managed Care:		Distributor:		Distributor:		Sub-Acute:		Labs/Testing:		Long-Term Care:	
Utilization Management:		Specialty Pharmacy:		Leasing/Finance:		Outpatient Surgery:		Staffing:		Physical Therapy:	
Payment Processing:		Vitamins/Nutritionals:		Information Systems:		Physical Rehab. Ctr.:		Waste Disposal:		Physician Prac. Mgmt.:	
		Clinical Trials:				Psychiatric Clinics:		Specialty Svcs.:			

TYPES OF BUSINESS:

Equipment-Epilepsy Therapy
Vagus Nerve Stimulation Devices

BRANDS/DIVISIONS/AFFILIATES:

Vagus Nerve Stimulation Therapy System

CONTACTS: *Note: Officers with more than one job title may be intentionally listed here more than once.*

Daniel J. Moore, CEO
George E. Parker, III, Interim COO
Daniel J. Moore, Pres.
Gregory H. Browne, CFO
Michael A. Cheney, VP-Mktg.
Shawn P. Lunney, VP-Eng.
David S. Wise, General Counsel/VP/Sec.
Randal L. Simpson, VP-Oper.
Shawn P. Lunney, VP-Market Dev.
Pamela B. Westbrook, VP-Finance
Richard L. Rudolph, Chief Medical Officer/VP-Clinical Affairs
Tony Coelho, Chmn.

Phone: 281-228-7200 **Fax:** 281-218-9332
Toll-Free: 888-867-7846
Address: 100 Cyberonics Blvd., Ste. 600, Houston, TX 77058 US

GROWTH PLANS/SPECIAL FEATURES:

Cyberonics, Inc. is the designer, developer, manufacturer and marketer of the Vagus Nerve Stimulation (VNS) Therapy System, an implantable medical device for the treatment of epilepsy, depression and other debilitating chronic disorders. The VNS system is the first FDA-approved medical device for the treatment of epilepsy, departing from traditional drug and surgery methods. The product delivers an electrical signal through an implantable lead to the left cervical vagus nerve in the patient's neck on a chronic, intermittent basis. The patient or caregiver may also initiate stimulation with a hand-held magnet. In the company's studies, treatment groups using the VNS system reported a mean seizure reduction of 24% to 28%. Many patients, including some reporting no change or increases in seizure frequency, reported a reduction in seizure severity. Other studies suggest that efficacy is maintained or improves over time when the VNS Therapy System is used with drugs as part of a patient's optimized long-term treatment regimen. To date, more than 32,000 epilepsy patients in 24 countries have accumulated over 100,000 patient years of experience using VNS Therapy. Cyberonics is also studying this system for treatment of depression in patients who have not responded to other treatments and has pilot studies underway for the treatment of Alzheimer's, anxiety, bulimia and chronic headache/migraine. The FDA has approved the VNS Therapy system for treatment-resistant depression. Cyberonics markets VNS as a safe and effective alternative to prescription drugs or surgery for chronic neurological disorders. In July 2006, Cyberonics received FDA approval for a harmonized/modularized VNS Therapy System labeling format and FDA approval to market the VNS Therapy Model 250 Version 7.1.4 Programming Software in the United States.

Employee benefits at Cyberonics include education assistance and employee assistance. Employees can receive sales incentives and stock options based on the company's long term success.

FINANCIALS: **Sales and profits are in thousands of dollars—add 000 to get the full amount. 2007 Note: Financial information for 2007 was not available for all companies at press time.**

2007 Sales: $130,968	2007 Profits: $-51,180	**U.S. Stock Ticker: CYBX**
2006 Sales: $123,441	2006 Profits: $-59,069	**Int'l Ticker:** Int'l Exchange:
2005 Sales: $103,443	2005 Profits: $-12,218	Employees: 547
2004 Sales: $110,721	2004 Profits: $6,759	Fiscal Year Ends: 4/30
2003 Sales: $104,500	2003 Profits: $5,200	Parent Company:

SALARIES/BENEFITS:

Pension Plan:	ESOP Stock Plan:	Profit Sharing:	Top Exec. Salary: $542,788	Bonus: $5,507
Savings Plan: Y	Stock Purch. Plan: Y		Second Exec. Salary: $308,385	Bonus: $45,507

OTHER THOUGHTS:

Apparent Women Officers or Directors: 1
Hot Spot for Advancement for Women/Minorities:

LOCATIONS: ("Y" = Yes)

West:	Southwest:	Midwest:	Southeast:	Northeast:	International:
	Y				Y

DADE BEHRING HOLDINGS INC www.dadebehring.com

Industry Group Code: 339113 **Ranks within this company's industry group:** Sales: 21 Profits: 21

Insurance/HMO/PPO:		Drugs:		Equipment/Supplies:		Hospitals/Clinics:		Services:		Health Care:	
Insurance:		Manufacturer:		Manufacturer:	Y	Acute Care:		Diagnostics:		Home Health:	
Managed Care:		Distributor:		Distributor:		Sub-Acute:		Labs/Testing:		Long-Term Care:	
Utilization Management:		Specialty Pharmacy:		Leasing/Finance:		Outpatient Surgery:		Staffing:		Physical Therapy:	
Payment Processing:		Vitamins/Nutritionals:		Information Systems:		Physical Rehab. Ctr.:		Waste Disposal:		Physician Prac. Mgmt.:	
		Clinical Trials:				Psychiatric Clinics:		Specialty Svcs.:	Y		

TYPES OF BUSINESS:

Equipment/Supplies-Diagnostic & Testing Instruments
Clinical Chemistry Instrument Systems
Immunochemistry Instrument Systems
Automated Microbiology Instrument Systems
Hemostasis Instrument Systems
Cardiac Diagnostic Systems

BRANDS/DIVISIONS/AFFILIATES:

Dimension
Syva
MicroScan

CONTACTS:

Note: Officers with more than one job title may be intentionally listed here more than once.

James Reid-Anderson, CEO
Donal M. Quinn, COO
James Reid-Anderson, Pres.
John M. Duffey, CFO/Sr. VP
Kathy Kennedy, Sr. VP-Human Resources
David G. Edelstein, CIO/Sr. VP
Mark Wolsey-Paige, CTO
Lance C. Balk, General Counsel/Sr. VP
Mark Wolsey-Paige, Chief Strategy Officer
Nancy A. Krejsas, VP-Corp. Comm.
Nancy A. Krejsas, VP-Investor Rel.
Randy Daniel, Pres., Global Customer Management
Louise S. Pearson, VP/Corp. Sec.
James Reid-Anderson, Chmn.

Phone: 847-267-5300 **Fax:** 847-267-1066
Toll-Free:
Address: 1717 Deerfield Rd., Deerfield, IL 60015-0778 US

GROWTH PLANS/SPECIAL FEATURES:

Dade Behring Holdings, Inc. is one of the world's largest companies dedicated solely to clinical diagnostics. Serving approximately $13 billion of the $29 billion annual worldwide market for clinical diagnostic products, the company focuses primarily on the central lab segment of the market, manufacturing and marketing a broad offering of diagnostic products and services, which include medical diagnostic instruments, maintenance services and reagents and consumables. In 2006, Dade Behring boasted a worldwide installed base of approximately 40,600 diagnostic instruments. Dade Behring has a strong position in each of its core product markets: Chemistry, hemostasis, microbiology and infectious disease diagnostics. Its chemistry products, which accounted for 66% of the company's 2006 revenue, include routine chemistry tests such as glucose, iron or cholesterol tests. Other chemistry tests include cardiac tests: the company was the first to introduce a widely adopted testing system for the cardiac proteins Troponin I, CK-MB and Myoglobin. The company also supplies this market with drug abuse testing products for its Dimension systems under the Syva brand name. Hemostasis products test a patient's ability to dissolve blood clots, a factor in cardiovascular health. The microbiology market is served with the company's MicroScan products, which identifies a microbe as well as testing its antibiotic susceptibility. Finally, the company supplies the infectious disease diagnostics market with test equipment for bacteriology, parasitology and virology testing, including HIV and hepatitis testing, as well as providing screening tests to help insure a safe blood supply. The company's research and development activities primarily occur in the U.S. and Germany. In July 2007, the firm agreed to be acquired by Siemens AG for approximately $3 billion.

Dade Behring offers employees flexible hours, educational assistance, adoption assistance, day care and health reimbursement accounts.

FINANCIALS:

Sales and profits are in thousands of dollars—add 000 to get the full amount. 2007 Note: Financial information for 2007 was not available for all companies at press time.

2007 Sales: $	2007 Profits: $	**U.S. Stock Ticker: DADE**
2006 Sales: $1,739,200	2006 Profits: $120,000	**Int'l Ticker:** Int'l Exchange:
2005 Sales: $1,658,100	2005 Profits: $124,900	Employees: 6,400
2004 Sales: $1,559,800	2004 Profits: $79,900	Fiscal Year Ends: 12/31
2003 Sales: $1,436,400	2003 Profits: $48,100	Parent Company:

SALARIES/BENEFITS:

Pension Plan: Y	ESOP Stock Plan:	Profit Sharing:	Top Exec. Salary: $913,846	Bonus: $1,872,720
Savings Plan: Y	Stock Purch. Plan:		Second Exec. Salary: $613,570	Bonus: $722,657

OTHER THOUGHTS:

Apparent Women Officers or Directors: 3
Hot Spot for Advancement for Women/Minorities: Y

LOCATIONS: ("Y" = Yes)

West:	Southwest:	Midwest:	Southeast:	Northeast:	International:
Y		Y	Y	Y	Y

DANAHER CORP

www.danaher.com

Industry Group Code: 335000 **Ranks within this company's industry group:** Sales: 1 Profits: 1

Insurance/HMO/PPO:		Drugs:		Equipment/Supplies:		Hospitals/Clinics:		Services:		Health Care:	
Insurance:		Manufacturer:		Manufacturer:	Y	Acute Care:		Diagnostics:		Home Health:	
Managed Care:		Distributor:		Distributor:		Sub-Acute:		Labs/Testing:		Long-Term Care:	
Utilization Management:		Specialty Pharmacy:		Leasing/Finance:		Outpatient Surgery:		Staffing:		Physical Therapy:	
Payment Processing:		Vitamins/Nutritionals:		Information Systems:		Physical Rehab. Ctr.:		Waste Disposal:		Physician Prac. Mgmt.:	
		Clinical Trials:				Psychiatric Clinics:		Specialty Svcs.:			

TYPES OF BUSINESS:

Power Tools Manufacturing
Test & Calibration Equipment
Controls
Bar Code Equipment

BRANDS/DIVISIONS/AFFILIATES:

VIDEOJET
ACCU-SORT
Delta Consolidated Industries
Hennessy Industries
Jacobs Chuck Manufacturing Company
Jacobs Vehicle Systems
Craftsman
ChemTreat, Inc.

CONTACTS: *Note: Officers with more than one job title may be intentionally listed here more than once.*

H. Lawrence Culp, Jr., CEO
H. Lawrence Culp, Jr., Pres.
Daniel L. Comas, CFO/Exec. VP
Jonathan P. Graham, General Counsel/Sr. VP
Daniel A. Raskas, VP-Corp. Dev.
Andy Wilson, VP-Investor Rel.
Robert S. Lutz, Chief Acct. Officer/VP
James H. Ditkoff, Sr. VP-Finance & Tax
Mitchell P. Rales, Chmn.-Exec. Committee
Phillip W. Knisely, Exec. VP
Thomas P. Joyce, Exec. VP
Steven M. Rales, Chmn.

Phone: 202-828-0850	**Fax:** 202-828-0860
Toll-Free:	
Address: 2099 Pennsylvania Ave., Washington, DC 20006-1813 US	

GROWTH PLANS/SPECIAL FEATURES:

Danaher Corp. derives its sales from the design, manufacture and marketing of industrial and consumer products, which are typically characterized by strong brand names, proprietary technology and major market positions, in four business segments: Professional Instrumentation; Medical Technologies; Industrial Technologies; and Tools & Components. Businesses in the Professional Instrumentation segment offer professional and technical customers various products and services that are used in connection with the performance of their work. Danaher's Medical Technologies segment offers dentists, other doctors and hospital, research and scientific professionals various products and services that are used in connection with the performance of their work. The Industrial Technologies segment manufactures products and sub-systems that are typically incorporated by customers and systems integrators into production and packaging lines and by original equipment manufacturers into various end-products and systems. Industries served include motion, with products including standard and custom motors; product identification, with products marketed under such brands as VIDEOJET and ACCU-SORT; aerospace and defense, with products including smoke detection systems and submarine periscopes; sensors and controls; and power quality. The Tools & Components segment produces mechanic's hand tools, and contains four niche businesses: Delta Consolidated Industries, Hennessy Industries, Jacobs Chuck Manufacturing Company and Jacobs Vehicle Systems. The mechanics' hand tools platform is the principal manufacturer of Sears' Craftsman line of hand tools and the primary supplier of automotive service tools to the National Automotive Parts Association (NAPA). In July 2007 Danaher sold its Power Quality business to Thomas & Betts Corp. for approximately $280 million and acquired ChemTreat, Inc., a leading provider of industrial water treatment solutions. Danaher has a goal of growing to $25 billion in revenues by 2012. Much of that growth will come through continued acquisitions. As of 2007, the firm owned about 600 subsidiaries.

FINANCIALS: **Sales and profits are in thousands of dollars—add 000 to get the full amount. 2007 Note: Financial information for 2007 was not available for all companies at press time.**

2007 Sales: $	2007 Profits: $	**U.S. Stock Ticker: DHR**
2006 Sales: $9,596,404	2006 Profits: $1,122,029	**Int'l Ticker:** Int'l Exchange:
2005 Sales: $7,984,704	2005 Profits: $897,800	Employees: 45,000
2004 Sales: $6,889,301	2004 Profits: $746,000	Fiscal Year Ends: 12/31
2003 Sales: $5,293,900	2003 Profits: $536,800	Parent Company:

SALARIES/BENEFITS:

Pension Plan:	ESOP Stock Plan:	Profit Sharing:	Top Exec. Salary: $1,100,000	Bonus: $3,525,000
Savings Plan:	Stock Purch. Plan:		Second Exec. Salary: $610,000	Bonus: $1,000,000

OTHER THOUGHTS:

Apparent Women Officers or Directors:
Hot Spot for Advancement for Women/Minorities:

LOCATIONS: ("Y" = Yes)

West:	Southwest:	Midwest:	Southeast:	Northeast:	International:
Y	Y	Y	Y	Y	Y

DATASCOPE CORP

www.datascope.com

Industry Group Code: 339113 **Ranks within this company's industry group:** Sales: 48 Profits: 45

Insurance/HMO/PPO:		Drugs:		Equipment/Supplies:		Hospitals/Clinics:		Services:		Health Care:	
Insurance:		Manufacturer:		Manufacturer:	Y	Acute Care:		Diagnostics:		Home Health:	
Managed Care:		Distributor:		Distributor:		Sub-Acute:		Labs/Testing:		Long-Term Care:	
Utilization Management:		Specialty Pharmacy:		Leasing/Finance:		Outpatient Surgery:		Staffing:		Physical Therapy:	
Payment Processing:		Vitamins/Nutritionals:		Information Systems:	Y	Physical Rehab. Ctr.:		Waste Disposal:		Physician Prac. Mgmt.:	
		Clinical Trials:				Psychiatric Clinics:		Specialty Svcs.:			

TYPES OF BUSINESS:

Equipment-Intra-Aortic Pumps & Catheters
Cardiac Assist Products
Patient Monitoring Systems
Collagen Products
Vascular Products

BRANDS/DIVISIONS/AFFILIATES:

Clearglide
InterVascular, Inc.
Panorama Patient Monitoring Network
Anestar Plus Anesthesia Delivery System
Artema Medical AB

CONTACTS: *Note: Officers with more than one job title may be intentionally listed here more than once.*

Lawrence Saper, CEO
Henry M. Scaramelli, CFO/VP-Finance
James L. Cooper, VP-Human Resources
Boris Leschinsky, VP-Tech.
Fred Adelman, Chief Acct. Officer/VP
Nicholas E. Barker, VP-Corp. Design
Robert O. Cathcart, VP/Pres., Interventional Prod. Div.
David A. Gibson, VP/Pres., Patient Monitoring & Tech. Svcs. Div.
Timothy J. Krauskopf, VP-Regulatory & Clinical Affairs
Lawrence Saper, Chmn.

Phone: 201-391-8100	**Fax:** 201-307-5400
Toll-Free:	
Address: 14 Phillips Pkwy., Montvale, NJ 07645-9998 US	

GROWTH PLANS/SPECIAL FEATURES:

Datascope Corp. is a medical device company that develops, manufactures and markets proprietary products for clinical health care markets in interventional cardiology and radiology, cardiovascular and vascular surgery, anesthesiology, emergency medicine and critical care. Cardiac assist, patient monitoring, interventional and InterVascular products constitute the company's four main product lines. Cardiac assist products include intra-aortic balloon pump and catheter technologies as well as endoscopic vessel harvesting. The intra-aortic balloon system is used principally to treat cardiac shock, acute heart failure and irregular heart rhythms. In January 2006, Datascope acquired the Clearglide endoscopic vessel harvesting product line from Ethicon, Inc. Endoscopic vessel harvesting devices enable less-invasive techniques for the harvesting of suitable vessels for use in conjunction with coronary artery bypass grafting. Datascope manufactures and markets a broad line of physiological monitors designed to provide for patient safety and management of patient care, including the Panorama Patient Monitoring Network as well as the Anestar Plus Anesthesia Delivery System. Datascope's InterVascular, Inc. subsidiary markets and sells a proprietary line of knitted and woven polyester vascular grafts, patches and interventional products for reconstructive vascular and cardiovascular surgery. Datascope is planning to exit the vascular closure market and phase out its interventional products business. All of the company's products are sold through direct sales representatives in the U.S. and a combination of direct sales representatives and independent distributors in international markets. In February 2007, Datascope announced the sale of its ProGuide Chronic Dialysis Catheter to Merit Medical Systems, Inc. for $3 million. In June 2007, the company acquired Artema Medical AB, a Swedish manufacturer of proprietary gas analyzers.

Datascope offers its employees flexible spending accounts, an assistance program, tuition assistance, a referral program, in-house training, work life referral services, a matching gift program, a credit union membership, casual attire and medical and dental insurance.

FINANCIALS: **Sales and profits are in thousands of dollars—add 000 to get the full amount. 2007 Note: Financial information for 2007 was not available for all companies at press time.**

2007 Sales: $378,800	2007 Profits: $17,465	**U.S. Stock Ticker: DSCP**
2006 Sales: $373,000	2006 Profits: $25,843	**Int'l Ticker:** Int'l Exchange:
2005 Sales: $352,700	2005 Profits: $14,646	Employees: 1,200
2004 Sales: $343,300	2004 Profits: $23,908	Fiscal Year Ends: 6/30
2003 Sales: $328,300	2003 Profits: $23,300	Parent Company:

SALARIES/BENEFITS:

Pension Plan:	ESOP Stock Plan:	Profit Sharing:	Top Exec. Salary: $1,000,000	Bonus: $
Savings Plan: Y	Stock Purch. Plan: Y		Second Exec. Salary: $337,254	Bonus: $150,730

OTHER THOUGHTS:

Apparent Women Officers or Directors:
Hot Spot for Advancement for Women/Minorities:

LOCATIONS: ("Y" = Yes)

West:	Southwest:	Midwest:	Southeast:	Northeast:	International:
				Y	Y

Note: Financial information, benefits and other data can change quickly and may vary from those stated here.

DAVITA INC

www.davita.com

Industry Group Code: 621490 **Ranks within this company's industry group:** Sales: 2 Profits: 2

Insurance/HMO/PPO:		Drugs:		Equipment/Supplies:		Hospitals/Clinics:		Services:		Health Care:	
Insurance:		Manufacturer:		Manufacturer:		Acute Care:		Diagnostics:		Home Health:	
Managed Care:		Distributor:		Distributor:		Sub-Acute:	Y	Labs/Testing:	Y	Long-Term Care:	
Utilization Management:		Specialty Pharmacy:		Leasing/Finance:		Outpatient Surgery:		Staffing:		Physical Therapy:	
Payment Processing:		Vitamins/Nutritionals:		Information Systems:		Physical Rehab. Ctr.:		Waste Disposal:		Physician Prac. Mgmt.:	
		Clinical Trials:				Psychiatric Clinics:		Specialty Svcs.:	Y		

TYPES OF BUSINESS:

Renal Care Services
Clinical Research

BRANDS/DIVISIONS/AFFILIATES:

DaVita Rx
DaVita Clinical Research

CONTACTS:

Note: Officers with more than one job title may be intentionally listed here more than once.

Kent J. Thiry, CEO
Joseph C. Mello, COO
Mark G. Harrison, CFO
Joseph Schohl, General Counsel/VP/Sec.
Mary R. Kowenhoven, VP-Strategy
James Hilger, Controller/VP
Christopher J. Riopelle, Chief Compliance Officer
Charlie McAllister, Chief Medical Officer
Georgina Randolph, Sr. VP
Thomas O. Usilton, Sr. VP
Kent J. Thiry, Chmn.

Phone: 310-536-2400	**Fax:** 310-536-2675
Toll-Free: 800-310-4872	
Address: 601 Hawaii St., El Segundo, CA 90245 US	

GROWTH PLANS/SPECIAL FEATURES:

DaVita, Inc. is a provider of dialysis services in the United States for patients suffering from chronic kidney failure, also known as end stage renal disease, or ESRD. The company operates or provides administrative services to roughly 1,300 outpatient dialysis centers located in 42 states and Washington, D.C., serving about 103,000 patients. The firm also provides acute inpatient dialysis services in approximately 770 hospitals and related laboratory services. The firm's dialysis services include hemodialysis, peritoneal dialysis, acute dialysis and pre-ESRD education. DaVita also provides training, supplies and on-call support services to peritoneal dialysis patients. In addition, the company provides certain patients the option of home-based hemodialysis. The firm owns two licensed clinical laboratories, located in Florida, specialized in ERSD patient testing. These specialized laboratories provide routine laboratory tests covered by the Medicare composite payment rate for dialysis and other physician-prescribed laboratory tests for ESRD patients. DaVita Rx is a wholly-owned pharmacy that provides oral medications to DaVita's patients with chronic kidney disease and ERSD. DaVita Clinical Research conducts research trials with dialysis patients and provides administrative support for research conducted by DaVita-affiliated nephrology practices. Other ancillary services provided by DaVita include management and administrative services to physician-owned vascular access clinics; and advanced care management services to employers, health plans and government agencies for employees/members diagnosed with chronic kidney disease.

The company provides its employees medical, dental and vision insurance; short- and long-term disability insurance; flexible spending accounts; life insurance; a 401(k) plan; a stock purchase program; and tuition reimbursement.

FINANCIALS:

Sales and profits are in thousands of dollars—add 000 to get the full amount. 2007 Note: Financial information for 2007 was not available for all companies at press time.

2007 Sales: $	2007 Profits: $
2006 Sales: $4,880,662	2006 Profits: $289,691
2005 Sales: $2,973,918	2005 Profits: $228,643
2004 Sales: $2,177,330	2004 Profits: $222,254
2003 Sales: $2,016,418	2003 Profits: $175,791

U.S. Stock Ticker: DVA
Int'l Ticker: Int'l Exchange:
Employees: 28,900
Fiscal Year Ends: 12/31
Parent Company:

SALARIES/BENEFITS:

Pension Plan:	ESOP Stock Plan:	Profit Sharing:	Top Exec. Salary: $885,079	Bonus: $1,800,000
Savings Plan: Y	Stock Purch. Plan: Y		Second Exec. Salary: $630,768	Bonus: $1,200,000

OTHER THOUGHTS:

Apparent Women Officers or Directors: 3
Hot Spot for Advancement for Women/Minorities: Y

LOCATIONS: ("Y" = Yes)

West:	Southwest:	Midwest:	Southeast:	Northeast:	International:
Y			Y	Y	

DELTA DENTAL PLANS ASSOCIATION www.deltadental.com

Industry Group Code: 524114A **Ranks within this company's industry group:** Sales: Profits:

Insurance/HMO/PPO:		Drugs:		Equipment/Supplies:		Hospitals/Clinics:		Services:		Health Care:	
Insurance:	Y	Manufacturer:		Manufacturer:		Acute Care:		Diagnostics:		Home Health:	
Managed Care:	Y	Distributor:		Distributor:		Sub-Acute:		Labs/Testing:		Long-Term Care:	
Utilization Management:		Specialty Pharmacy:		Leasing/Finance:		Outpatient Surgery:		Staffing:		Physical Therapy:	
Payment Processing:		Vitamins/Nutritionals:		Information Systems:		Physical Rehab. Ctr.:		Waste Disposal:		Physician Prac. Mgmt.:	
		Clinical Trials:				Psychiatric Clinics:		Specialty Svcs.:			

TYPES OF BUSINESS:

Dental Insurance & Dental Care
Dental PPO & HMO

BRANDS/DIVISIONS/AFFILIATES:

Delta Dental Premier
Delta Dental PPO
TRICARE
DeltaCare USA
Delta Dental Select

CONTACTS: *Note: Officers with more than one job title may be intentionally listed here more than once.*

Kim Volk, CEO
Kim Volk, Pres.
Tom Dolatowski, VP-Mktg.
Karron Callaghan, VP-Tech.

Phone: 630-574-6001 **Fax:** 630-574-6999
Toll-Free:
Address: 1515 W. 22nd St., Ste. 1200, Oak Brook, IL 60523 US

GROWTH PLANS/SPECIAL FEATURES:

Delta Dental Plans Association, a nonprofit organization, is one of the nation's largest dental benefits systems and dental service corporations. The firm serves more than one-quarter of the U.S. population with dental insurance, over 50 million people, enrolled in 81,000 employer groups. Its nationwide network of independent affiliates operates in all 50 states, Washington, D.C. and Puerto Rico. In 2006, the company processed over 73 million dental claims, or approximately 1.3 million every week, with an accuracy rate of 99%. Delta Dental Premier, formerly DeltaPremier USA, Delta's traditional fee-for-service program, offers a provider network that encompasses more than 121,000 providers and 174,000 office locations. Delta Dental PPO, formerly DeltaPreferred Option USA, the firm's preferred provider option, has a national network of more than 60,000 dentists practicing in over 97,000 locations. DeltaCare USA, formerly DHMO, the company's dental health maintenance organization, consists of a network of more than 9,000 contracted dentists practicing in over 21,000 office locations. Delta Dental Select, formerly DeltaSelect USA/TRICARE is the firm's national program for group-voluntary customers, including the TRICARE program, which covers the nation's non-active military personnel and their dependents.

FINANCIALS: **Sales and profits are in thousands of dollars—add 000 to get the full amount. 2007 Note: Financial information for 2007 was not available for all companies at press time.**

2007 Sales: $	2007 Profits: $	**U.S. Stock Ticker: Nonprofit**
2006 Sales: $	2006 Profits: $	**Int'l Ticker:** Int'l Exchange:
2005 Sales: $	2005 Profits: $	Employees:
2004 Sales: $	2004 Profits: $	Fiscal Year Ends: 12/31
2003 Sales: $	2003 Profits: $	Parent Company:

SALARIES/BENEFITS:

Pension Plan:	ESOP Stock Plan:	Profit Sharing:	Top Exec. Salary: $	Bonus: $
Savings Plan:	Stock Purch. Plan:		Second Exec. Salary: $	Bonus: $

OTHER THOUGHTS:

Apparent Women Officers or Directors: 2
Hot Spot for Advancement for Women/Minorities: Y

LOCATIONS: ("Y" = Yes)

West:	Southwest:	Midwest:	Southeast:	Northeast:	International:
Y	Y	Y	Y	Y	

Note: Financial information, benefits and other data can change quickly and may vary from those stated here.

DENTAL BENEFITS PROVIDERS www.dbp.com

Industry Group Code: 524114A **Ranks within this company's industry group:** Sales: Profits:

Insurance/HMO/PPO:		Drugs:		Equipment/Supplies:		Hospitals/Clinics:		Services:		Health Care:	
Insurance:	Y	Manufacturer:		Manufacturer:		Acute Care:		Diagnostics:		Home Health:	
Managed Care:	Y	Distributor:		Distributor:		Sub-Acute:		Labs/Testing:		Long-Term Care:	
Utilization Management:		Specialty Pharmacy:		Leasing/Finance:		Outpatient Surgery:		Staffing:		Physical Therapy:	
Payment Processing:	Y	Vitamins/Nutritionals:		Information Systems:		Physical Rehab. Ctr.:		Waste Disposal:		Physician Prac. Mgmt.:	
		Clinical Trials:				Psychiatric Clinics:		Specialty Svcs.:			

TYPES OF BUSINESS:

Insurance-Supplemental & Specialty Health
Dental Benefits
Dental HMOs, PPOs & POS
Administrative Services

BRANDS/DIVISIONS/AFFILIATES:

UnitedHealth Group

CONTACTS:

Note: Officers with more than one job title may be intentionally listed here more than once.

David Hall, CEO
Karen Schievelbein, COO
Karen Schievelbein, Pres.
Mete Sahin, CFO

Phone: 240-632-8000 **Fax:** 240-632-8100
Toll-Free: 800-445-9090
Address: 3 Irvington Center, 800 King Farm Blvd., Ste. 600, Bethesda, MD 20850 US

GROWTH PLANS/SPECIAL FEATURES:

Dental Benefits Providers, Inc. (DBP), a subsidiary of UnitedHealth Group Incorporated, is a U.S.-leading private-label dental benefit company. It has more than 5 million members and dentist networks in 48 states, the District of Columbia, Puerto Rico and the Virgin Islands. DBP serves its members through more than 20 distributor clients and 67,000 participating dentists. The company subcontracts dental health maintenance organization plans (DHMOs), PPOs, POS plans, indemnity plans, preventive plans, Medicaid/Child Health Plus Plans and Medicare plans, as well as claims and administrative services to HMOs, unions, insurance companies, municipalities and large corporations. Such plans can be customized depending on clients' needs: DBP offers full benefits plans and limited benefits plans; net rate plans that have the ability to offer a risk- or profit-sharing arrangement; lock-in, gatekeeper networks and open access, point-of-service networks; commercial, government or federal employee plans; and either interlocking dental and medical plans or freestanding dental plans. DBP members, dentists and clients have access to online tools such as a dentist directory, fee schedules, eligibility verification and claims information. The company's website also offers voluminous dental education resources.

FINANCIALS:

Sales and profits are in thousands of dollars—add 000 to get the full amount. 2007 Note: Financial information for 2007 was not available for all companies at press time.

2007 Sales: $	2007 Profits: $
2006 Sales: $	2006 Profits: $
2005 Sales: $	2005 Profits: $
2004 Sales: $	2004 Profits: $
2003 Sales: $	2003 Profits: $

U.S. Stock Ticker: Subsidiary
Int'l Ticker: Int'l Exchange:
Employees:
Fiscal Year Ends: 12/31
Parent Company: UNITEDHEALTH GROUP INC

SALARIES/BENEFITS:

Pension Plan:	ESOP Stock Plan:	Profit Sharing:	Top Exec. Salary: $	Bonus: $
Savings Plan:	Stock Purch. Plan:		Second Exec. Salary: $	Bonus: $

OTHER THOUGHTS:

Apparent Women Officers or Directors: 2
Hot Spot for Advancement for Women/Minorities:

LOCATIONS: ("Y" = Yes)

West:	Southwest:	Midwest:	Southeast:	Northeast:	International:
Y	Y	Y	Y	Y	Y

DENTSPLY INTERNATIONAL INC

www.dentsply.com

Industry Group Code: 339113 **Ranks within this company's industry group:** Sales: 20 Profits: 15

Insurance/HMO/PPO:		Drugs:		Equipment/Supplies:		Hospitals/Clinics:		Services:		Health Care:	
Insurance:		Manufacturer:		Manufacturer:	Y	Acute Care:		Diagnostics:		Home Health:	
Managed Care:		Distributor:		Distributor:	Y	Sub-Acute:		Labs/Testing:		Long-Term Care:	
Utilization Management:		Specialty Pharmacy:		Leasing/Finance:		Outpatient Surgery:		Staffing:		Physical Therapy:	
Payment Processing:		Vitamins/Nutritionals:		Information Systems:		Physical Rehab. Ctr.:		Waste Disposal:		Physician Prac. Mgmt.:	
		Clinical Trials:				Psychiatric Clinics:		Specialty Svcs.:			

TYPES OF BUSINESS:

Dental Consumable Products
Dental Specialty Products
Dental Laboratory products

BRANDS/DIVISIONS/AFFILIATES:

Rinn
Golden Gate
Xylocaine
Aquasil
Delton
Elephant
Frialit
Ankylos

CONTACTS: *Note: Officers with more than one job title may be intentionally listed here more than once.*

Bret W. Wise, CEO
Christopher T. Clark, COO/Exec. VP
Bret W. Wise, Pres.
William R. Jellison, CFO/Sr. VP
Brian M. Addison, General Counsel/VP/Sec.
William E. Reardon, Treas./VP
Timothy S. Warady, Corp. Controller/VP
Linda C. Niessen, VP/Chief Clinical Officer
James G. Mosch, Sr. VP
Bob Size, Sr. VP
Bret W. Wise, Chmn.

Phone: 717-845-7511 **Fax:** 717-849-4762
Toll-Free: 800-877-0020
Address: 221 W. Philadelphia St., Susquehanna Commerce Cts., York, PA 17405 US

GROWTH PLANS/SPECIAL FEATURES:

DENTSPLY International, Inc. is a global designer, manufacturer and marketer of a broad range of products for the dental market. The company's operating segments are engaged in the design, manufacture and distribution of dental products in three principal categories: dental consumables, dental laboratory products and specialty dental products. Dental consumable products, which accounted for about 40% of revenue in 2006, consist of dental sundries and small equipment used in dental offices. The dental sundry products in this category include dental anesthetics, prophylaxis paste, dental sealants, impression materials, restorative materials, bone grafting materials, tooth whiteners and topical fluoride. Small equipment products include high and low speed handpieces, intraoral curing light systems and ultrasonic scalers and polishers. The dental laboratory products, which accounted for roughly 19% of revenue in 2006, are used in preparation of dental appliances by dental laboratories and include dental prosthetics, including artificial teeth; precious metal dental alloys; dental ceramics; and crown and bridge materials. Equipment in this category includes computer aided machining ceramic systems and porcelain furnaces. Dental specialty products, which accounted for about 38% of net sales in 2006, are specialized treatment products used within dental offices and laboratory settings. Products in this category include endodontic (root canal) instruments and materials; implants and related products; and orthodontic appliances and accessories. Sales of dental products accounted for about 97% of net sales in 2006. Brand names of DENTSPLY's products include Ankylos, Aquasil, Delton, Elephant, Frialit, Midwest, Rinn, Golden Gate and Xylocaine. The company has operations in over 120 countries.

FINANCIALS: **Sales and profits are in thousands of dollars—add 000 to get the full amount. 2007 Note: Financial information for 2007 was not available for all companies at press time.**

2007 Sales: $	2007 Profits: $	**U.S. Stock Ticker: XRAY**
2006 Sales: $1,810,496	2006 Profits: $223,718	**Int'l Ticker:** Int'l Exchange:
2005 Sales: $1,715,135	2005 Profits: $45,413	Employees: 8,500
2004 Sales: $1,694,232	2004 Profits: $253,165	Fiscal Year Ends: 12/31
2003 Sales: $1,570,925	2003 Profits: $174,183	Parent Company:

SALARIES/BENEFITS:

Pension Plan:	ESOP Stock Plan:	Profit Sharing:	Top Exec. Salary: $800,000	Bonus: $748,800
Savings Plan:	Stock Purch. Plan:		Second Exec. Salary: $477,000	Bonus: $334,900

OTHER THOUGHTS:

Apparent Women Officers or Directors: 2
Hot Spot for Advancement for Women/Minorities: Y

LOCATIONS: ("Y" = Yes)

West:	Southwest:	Midwest:	Southeast:	Northeast:	International:
Y	Y	Y	Y	Y	Y

DEPUY INC

www.depuy.com

Industry Group Code: 339113 **Ranks within this company's industry group:** Sales: Profits:

Insurance/HMO/PPO:		Drugs:		Equipment/Supplies:		Hospitals/Clinics:		Services:		Health Care:	
Insurance:		Manufacturer:		Manufacturer:	Y	Acute Care:		Diagnostics:		Home Health:	
Managed Care:		Distributor:		Distributor:	Y	Sub-Acute:		Labs/Testing:		Long-Term Care:	
Utilization Management:		Specialty Pharmacy:		Leasing/Finance:		Outpatient Surgery:		Staffing:		Physical Therapy:	
Payment Processing:		Vitamins/Nutritionals:		Information Systems:		Physical Rehab. Ctr.:		Waste Disposal:		Physician Prac. Mgmt.:	
		Clinical Trials:				Psychiatric Clinics:		Specialty Svcs.:			

TYPES OF BUSINESS:

Orthopedic Devices
Fixative Products
Implants

BRANDS/DIVISIONS/AFFILIATES:

Johnson & Johnson
DePuy Mitek
DePuy Spine, Inc.
DePuy Orthopaedics
Codman & Shurtleff, Inc.

CONTACTS: *Note: Officers with more than one job title may be intentionally listed here more than once.*

Kevin Dwyer, CFO
Eric Dremel, VP-Sales
Kevin Dwyer, VP-Finance
Gordon Van Ummersen, VP-Mktg.

Phone: 574-267-8143	**Fax:** 574-267-7196
Toll-Free: 800-473-3789	
Address: 700 Orthopaedic Dr., Warsaw, IN 46581 US	

GROWTH PLANS/SPECIAL FEATURES:

DePuy, Inc., a subsidiary of Johnson & Johnson, is a designer, manufacturer and distributor of orthopedic devices and supplies. Its products are used primarily by orthopedic medical specialists and, in the case of the company's spinal implants, by spinal specialists and neurosurgeons. The products are used in both surgical and non-surgical therapies to treat patients with musculoskeletal conditions resulting from degenerative diseases, deformities, trauma and sports related injuries. The company operates through four subsidiaries. DePuy Orthopaedics develops products for hip and extremity implants, knee implants, environmental protection products and other surgical equipment. Codman & Shurtleff, Inc. enables treatment of central nervous system disorders through its hydrocephalic shunt valve systems, neuro endoscopes and spinal fixation implant products. DePuy Mitek produces orthopedic trauma products and joint reconstructive products for shoulder, ankle, elbow, wrist and finger joints. Subsidiary DePuy Spine, Inc. develops, manufactures and markets implants and technologies for the treatment of cervical, thoracic, lumbar and sacral spinal pathologies. Its many products include artificial discs, various spinal systems, bone graft replacements and a bone growth stimulator. DePuy also operates several web sites providing educational information on joint replacement, hydrocephalus, back and neck pain, arthritis and other medical conditions.

FINANCIALS: **Sales and profits are in thousands of dollars—add 000 to get the full amount. 2007 Note: Financial information for 2007 was not available for all companies at press time.**

2007 Sales: $	2007 Profits: $	**U.S. Stock Ticker: Subsidiary**
2006 Sales: $	2006 Profits: $	**Int'l Ticker:** Int'l Exchange:
2005 Sales: $	2005 Profits: $	Employees:
2004 Sales: $	2004 Profits: $	Fiscal Year Ends: 12/31
2003 Sales: $	2003 Profits: $	Parent Company: JOHNSON & JOHNSON

SALARIES/BENEFITS:

Pension Plan:	ESOP Stock Plan:	Profit Sharing:	Top Exec. Salary: $	Bonus: $
Savings Plan:	Stock Purch. Plan:		Second Exec. Salary: $	Bonus: $

OTHER THOUGHTS:

Apparent Women Officers or Directors:
Hot Spot for Advancement for Women/Minorities:

LOCATIONS: ("Y" = Yes)

West:	Southwest:	Midwest:	Southeast:	Northeast:	International:
Y	Y	Y	Y	Y	

DETROIT MEDICAL CENTER

www.dmc.org

Industry Group Code: 622110 **Ranks within this company's industry group:** Sales: Profits:

Insurance/HMO/PPO:		Drugs:		Equipment/Supplies:		Hospitals/Clinics:		Services:		Health Care:	
Insurance:		Manufacturer:		Manufacturer:		Acute Care:	Y	Diagnostics:		Home Health:	
Managed Care:		Distributor:		Distributor:		Sub-Acute:	Y	Labs/Testing:		Long-Term Care:	Y
Utilization Management:		Specialty Pharmacy:		Leasing/Finance:		Outpatient Surgery:	Y	Staffing:		Physical Therapy:	Y
Payment Processing:		Vitamins/Nutritionals:		Information Systems:		Physical Rehab. Ctr.:	Y	Waste Disposal:		Physician Prac. Mgmt.:	
		Clinical Trials:				Psychiatric Clinics:	Y	Specialty Svcs.:	Y		

TYPES OF BUSINESS:

Hospitals
Children's Hospital
Emergency Care
Cancer Care
Women's Health
Orthopaedic Services
Teaching Facilities
Clinical Research

BRANDS/DIVISIONS/AFFILIATES:

Children's Hospital of Michigan
Detroit Receiving Hospital
Harper University Hospital
Huron Valley-Sinal Hospital
Hutzel Women's Hospital
Rehabilitation Institute of Michigan (The)
Sinai-Grace Hospital
Michigan Orthopedic Specialty Hospital

CONTACTS: *Note: Officers with more than one job title may be intentionally listed here more than once.*

Michael E. Duggan, CEO
Benjamin R. Carter, COO/Exec. VP
Michael E. Duggan, Pres.
Jay B. Rising, CFO/Exec. VP
Floyd Allen, General Counsel
Mary Zuckerman, Chief Bus. Oper./Exec. VP
William R. Alvin, Exec. VP-Strategy Dev.
Thomas A. Malone, Chief Medical Officer/Exec. VP
Herman B. Gray, Pres., Children's Hospital of Michigan
Frank P. Iacobell, Pres., Michigan Orthopedic Specialty Hospital
Conrad L. Mallett Jr., Pres., Sinai-Grace Hospital
Donald Groth, Corp. VP-Materials Resource Mgmt.

Phone: 313-578-2000 **Fax:** 313-578-3225
Toll-Free: 888-362-2500
Address: 3990 John R. St., Detroit, MI 48201 US

GROWTH PLANS/SPECIAL FEATURES:

Detroit Medical Center (DMC), established as a non-profit organization in 1985, is one of the largest health care providers in southeast Michigan, with two nursing centers, more than 100 outpatient facilities and nine hospitals. The organization's hospitals are as follows. The Children's Hospital of Michigan, founded in 1886, is an international leader in pediatric neurology, neurosurgery, cardiology and pediatric critical care with a staff of over 300 physicians and 500 nurses. Detroit Receiving Hospital trains almost 60% of Michigan's emergency physicians and its emergency department annually treats over 85,000 patients. It has a number of unique achievements, such as being Michigan's first Level 1 Trauma Center, being the first certified primary stroke center in metro Detroit, and having the first hospital-based hyperbaric oxygen therapy program open 24-hours a day, seven days a week. Harper University Hospital, established in 1863, is a premier teaching institution; and it offers neurological, hypertension and heart failure treatments as well as vascular and organ transplants. Huron Valley-Sinai Hospital offers covers every stage of life from birthing to senior services including a bone and joint program, rehabilitation services, surgery and the Charach Cancer treatment Center. Hutzel Women's Hospital's offerings include high-risk obstetrics, infertility treatment and reproductive genetics. The Rehabilitation Institute of Michigan's patients include people with spinal cord and brain injuries; musculoskeletal disorders; amputations; sports injuries; and it also does research on rehabilitation medicine. Sinai-Grace Hospital's general medical services include family medicine, neurology, surgery, psychiatry and a pharmacy, to name just a few. Michigan Orthopedic Specialty Hospital focuses on orthopedic surgery and its web site features an orthopedic medical library to answer physical therapy questions. Finally, the Kresge Eye Institute offers a variety of ophthalmic services including surgery and diabetic eye care. DMC's network has a total of 2,000 licensed beds and approximately 3,000 affiliated physicians.

FINANCIALS: **Sales and profits are in thousands of dollars—add 000 to get the full amount. 2007 Note: Financial information for 2007 was not available for all companies at press time.**

2007 Sales: $ | 2007 Profits: $
2006 Sales: $ | 2006 Profits: $
2005 Sales: $ | 2005 Profits: $
2004 Sales: $ | 2004 Profits: $
2003 Sales: $1,600,000 | 2003 Profits: $

U.S. Stock Ticker: Nonprofit
Int'l Ticker: Int'l Exchange:
Employees: 14,311
Fiscal Year Ends: 12/31
Parent Company:

SALARIES/BENEFITS:

Pension Plan: ESOP Stock Plan: Profit Sharing: Top Exec. Salary: $ Bonus: $
Savings Plan: Stock Purch. Plan: Second Exec. Salary: $ Bonus: $

OTHER THOUGHTS:

Apparent Women Officers or Directors: 3
Hot Spot for Advancement for Women/Minorities: Y

LOCATIONS: ("Y" = Yes)

West:	Southwest:	Midwest:	Southeast:	Northeast:	International:
		Y			

DIALYSIS CORPORATION OF AMERICA

www.dialysiscorporation.com

Industry Group Code: 621490 **Ranks within this company's industry group:** Sales: 15 Profits: 12

Insurance/HMO/PPO:		Drugs:		Equipment/Supplies:		Hospitals/Clinics:		Services:		Health Care:	
Insurance:		Manufacturer:		Manufacturer:	Y	Acute Care:		Diagnostics:	Y	Home Health:	
Managed Care:		Distributor:		Distributor:		Sub-Acute:	Y	Labs/Testing:	Y	Long-Term Care:	
Utilization Management:		Specialty Pharmacy:		Leasing/Finance:		Outpatient Surgery:	Y	Staffing:		Physical Therapy:	
Payment Processing:		Vitamins/Nutritionals:		Information Systems:		Physical Rehab. Ctr.:		Waste Disposal:		Physician Prac. Mgmt.:	
		Clinical Trials:				Psychiatric Clinics:		Specialty Svcs.:			

TYPES OF BUSINESS:

Dialysis Facilities and Services

BRANDS/DIVISIONS/AFFILIATES:

Medicore, Inc.

CONTACTS:

Note: Officers with more than one job title may be intentionally listed here more than once.

Stephen Everett, CEO
Stephen Everett, Pres.
Daniel Ouzts, CFO
Thomas P. Carey, VP-Oper.
Daniel R. Ouzts, VP-Finance
Joanne Zimmerman, VP-Clinical Svcs.
Thomas Langbein, Chmn.

Phone: 410-694-0500 **Fax:** 410-694-0596
Toll-Free: 800-694-6945
Address: 1302 Concourse Dr., Ste. 204, Linthicum, MD 21090 US

GROWTH PLANS/SPECIAL FEATURES:

Dialysis Corporation of America (DCA) provides a variety c services to patients suffering from kidney failure. It operate 34 outpatient dialysis facilities, in Pennsylvania, New Jersey Georgia, Ohio, Maryland, Virginia and South Carolina. 19 c these locations are wholly-owned and 13 are majority-owne through company subsidiaries. The remaining facilities ar leased from local medical practices. The locations provid patients, many of whom are Medicare patients, conventiona hemodialysis service in a comfortable environmen Facilities are equipped with space for dialysis treatments, nurses' station, a patient weigh-in area, a supply room, wate treatment areas, a dialyszer reprocessing room and sta offices. Furthermore, most of its dialysis facilities have th capacity to provide training, monitoring, equipment an supplies, follow-up assistance and on-call support service for home care peritoneal patients. In addition to it outpatient services, the company also provides acute car inpatient dialysis services to ten hospitals in areas service by its dialysis facilities. All these services are geare generally to the treatment of end stage renal diseas (ESRD), a chronic kidney failure which causes a build-up c toxins in the bloodstream, treated with options ranging fror hemodialysis to peritoneal dialysis to kidney transplant, fo which the company provided approximately 219,00 hemodialysis treatments in 2006 alone. The company ha recently been undergoing a great deal of expansion including: the acquisition of a dialysis center in Columbus Ohio with 21 treatment stations in February 2007; th acquisition of a dialysis center in Selinsgrove, PA with 2 treatment stations in March 2007; the addition of a three yea contract for dialysis services to patients admitted to Marylan General Hospital in July 2007; and the expansion int Indiana through the development of a 12 station new cente in September 2007.

FINANCIALS:

Sales and profits are in thousands of dollars—add 000 to get the full amount. 2007 Note: Financial information for 2007 was not available for all companies at press time.

2007 Sales: $	2007 Profits: $	**U.S. Stock Ticker: DCAI**
2006 Sales: $62,460	2006 Profits: $3,049	**Int'l Ticker:** Int'l Exchange:
2005 Sales: $45,392	2005 Profits: $1,900	Employees: 429
2004 Sales: $40,986	2004 Profits: $2,214	Fiscal Year Ends: 12/31
2003 Sales: $29,997	2003 Profits: $1,150	Parent Company:

SALARIES/BENEFITS:

Pension Plan:	ESOP Stock Plan:	Profit Sharing:	Top Exec. Salary: $274,039	Bonus: $100,000
Savings Plan: Y	Stock Purch. Plan:		Second Exec. Salary: $165,770	Bonus: $

OTHER THOUGHTS:

Apparent Women Officers or Directors: 1
Hot Spot for Advancement for Women/Minorities:

LOCATIONS: ("Y" = Yes)

West:	Southwest:	Midwest:	Southeast:	Northeast:	International:
			Y	Y	

Note: Financial information, benefits and other data can change quickly and may vary from those stated here.

DIGENE CORPORATION

www.digene.com

Industry Group Code: 325413 **Ranks within this company's industry group:** Sales: 4 Profits: 6

Insurance/HMO/PPO:		Drugs:		Equipment/Supplies:		Hospitals/Clinics:		Services:		Health Care:	
Insurance:		Manufacturer:		Manufacturer:	Y	Acute Care:		Diagnostics:		Home Health:	
Managed Care:		Distributor:		Distributor:	Y	Sub-Acute:		Labs/Testing:		Long-Term Care:	
Utilization Management:		Specialty Pharmacy:		Leasing/Finance:		Outpatient Surgery:		Staffing:		Physical Therapy:	
Payment Processing:		Vitamins/Nutritionals:		Information Systems:		Physical Rehab. Ctr.:		Waste Disposal:		Physician Prac. Mgmt.:	
		Clinical Trials:				Psychiatric Clinics:		Specialty Svcs.:			

TYPES OF BUSINESS:

Gene-Based Diagnostic Tests
Diagnostics Test Kits

BRANDS/DIVISIONS/AFFILIATES:

Hybrid Capture

CONTACTS:

Note: Officers with more than one job title may be intentionally listed here more than once.

Daryl J. Faulkner, CEO
Daryl J. Faulkner, Pres.
Joseph P. Slattery, CFO/Sr. VP
Robert McG. Lilley, Sr. VP-Global Sales & Mktg.
James H. Godsey, Sr. VP-R&D
Belinda O. Patrick, Sr. VP-Mfg. Oper.
Donna Marie Seyfried, VP-Bus. Dev.
Attila T. Lorincz, Chief Scientific Officer
C. Douglas White, Sr. VP-Sales & Mktg.-Americas & Asia Pacific

Phone: 301-944-7000 **Fax:** 240-632-7121
Toll-Free: 800-344-3631
Address: 1201 Clopper Rd., Gaithersburg, MD 20878 US

GROWTH PLANS/SPECIAL FEATURES:

Digene Corp. develops, manufactures and markets its proprietary gene-based diagnostic tests for the screening, monitoring and diagnosis of human diseases. The company's primary focus is women's cancers and infectious diseases. The firm applies its proprietary Hybrid Capture technology to develop successful diagnostic test for human papillomavirus (HPV), which is the primary cause of cervical cancer. The Hybrid Capture platform is a signal amplification technology that combines the convenience of a direct probe test with the sensitivity of an amplification test, requires minimal sample preparation and provides objective test results. Digene also developed its Hybrid Capture technology in the form of diagnostic test kits to include tests for the detection of chlamydia, gonorrhea and other sexually transmitted infections. Products in development include hc4, a fully automated screening and genotyping platform; HPV genotyping products, whose potential uses include HPV genotyping in connection with HPV vaccines and revised patient care management; and Signature cystic fibrosis tests, which are molecular diagnosis tests for cystic fibrosis. The firm's core research efforts include research program for improved molecular diagnosis assay systems for detection of HPV and other targets in the area of women's cancers and infectious diseases; and research on nucleic acid detection technology.

The company offers its employees medical, dental and vision insurance; a 401(k) plan; an employee assistance program; life, AD&D, short- and long-term disability coverage; tuition reimbursement; a college savings plan; flexible spending accounts; and access to credit unions.

FINANCIALS:

Sales and profits are in thousands of dollars—add 000 to get the full amount. 2007 Note: Financial information for 2007 was not available for all companies at press time.

2007 Sales: $
2006 Sales: $152,900
2005 Sales: $115,142
2004 Sales: $90,160
2003 Sales: $63,100

2007 Profits: $
2006 Profits: $8,400
2005 Profits: $-8,167
2004 Profits: $21,542
2003 Profits: $-4,300

U.S. Stock Ticker: DIGE
Int'l Ticker: Int'l Exchange:
Employees: 490
Fiscal Year Ends: 6/30
Parent Company:

SALARIES/BENEFITS:

Pension Plan: ESOP Stock Plan: Profit Sharing: Top Exec. Salary: $449,533 Bonus: $505,300
Savings Plan: Y Stock Purch. Plan: Second Exec. Salary: $392,463 Bonus: $357,300

OTHER THOUGHTS:

Apparent Women Officers or Directors: 3
Hot Spot for Advancement for Women/Minorities: Y

LOCATIONS: ("Y" = Yes)

West:	Southwest:	Midwest:	Southeast:	Northeast:	International:
				Y	Y

DJO INC

www.djortho.com

Industry Group Code: 339113 **Ranks within this company's industry group:** Sales: 46 Profits: 59

Insurance/HMO/PPO:		Drugs:		Equipment/Supplies:		Hospitals/Clinics:		Services:		Health Care:	
Insurance:		Manufacturer:		Manufacturer:	Y	Acute Care:		Diagnostics:		Home Health:	
Managed Care:		Distributor:		Distributor:	Y	Sub-Acute:		Labs/Testing:		Long-Term Care:	
Utilization Management:		Specialty Pharmacy:		Leasing/Finance:		Outpatient Surgery:		Staffing:		Physical Therapy:	
Payment Processing:		Vitamins/Nutritionals:		Information Systems:		Physical Rehab. Ctr.:		Waste Disposal:		Physician Prac. Mgmt.:	
		Clinical Trials:				Psychiatric Clinics:		Specialty Svcs.:			

TYPES OF BUSINESS:

Orthopedic Device Manufacturing
Bone Growth Stimulators
Rehabilitation Products
Pain Management Products
Soft Goods-Braces & Fracture Boots
Regeneration Products

BRANDS/DIVISIONS/AFFILIATES:

DonJoy
Regentek
KD Innovation
ProCare
OfficeCare
SpinaLogic
Orthologic
Aircast, Inc.

CONTACTS: *Note: Officers with more than one job title may be intentionally listed here more than once.*

Leslie H. Cross, CEO
Luke T. Faulstick, COO
Leslie H. Cross, Pres.
Vickie L. Capps, CFO
Louis T. Ruggiero, Sr. VP-Mktg. & Sales
Donald M. Roberts, General Counsel/Sr. VP/Sec.
Luke T. Faulstick, Sr. VP-Oper.
Vickie L. Capps, Sr. VP-Finance/Treas.
Jack R. Blair, Chmn.

Phone: 760-727-1280 **Fax:** 760-734-3595
Toll-Free: 800-321-9549
Address: 2985 Scott St., Vista, CA 92081 US

GROWTH PLANS/SPECIAL FEATURES:

DJO, Inc. (formerly DJ Orthopedics, Inc.) is a global medica device company specializing in rehabilitation and regeneration products for the non-operative orthopedic and spine markets. The company changed its name to DJO in 2006 to reflect the diversification of its business beyond the original DonJoy brand. Its broad portfolio of over 600 products is marketed under the DonJoy and ProCare brands. Products include rigid knee braces, soft goods and pain management products, which are used to prevent injury, to treat chronic conditions and to aid in recovery after surger or injury. Sales of rigid knee braces represented approximately 23% of DJO's revenues during 2006. DJO's soft goods product line consists of over 500 soft goods products that offer immobilization and support from head to toe. DJO's portfolio of pain management products primarily includes cold therapy products to assist in the reduction of pain and swelling. It also offers a system that employs ambulatory infusion pumps for the delivery of local anestheti to a surgical site. Its pain management products accounted for approximately 8% of its revenues for 2006. DJO sells its products in the U.S. and over 70 other countries through a network of agents, distributors and the company's direc sales force. Customers are primarily orthopedic and spine surgeons, podiatrists, orthopedic and prosthetic centers third-party distributors, hospitals, surgery centers, physica therapists, athletic trainers and other healthcare professionals. The company's major registered trademarks include Defiance, dj Ortho, FourcePoint, IceMan, OfficeCare SpinaLogic, Velocity, Knee Guarantee and others. In 2006 the company acquired Aircast, Inc., a leading designer and manufacturer of orthopedic devices, including ankle bracing products and vascular systems. In July 2007, the firm agreed to be acquired by ReAble Therapeutics, Inc. for $1.1 billion. ReAble is owned by the Blackstone Group, which is financing the acquisition.

DJO offers its employees a fitness room, income protection flexible spending accounts, tuition reimbursement and credi union membership.

FINANCIALS: Sales and profits are in thousands of dollars—add 000 to get the full amount. 2007 Note: Financial information for 2007 was not available for all companies at press time.

2007 Sales: $	2007 Profits: $	**U.S. Stock Ticker: DJO**
2006 Sales: $413,058	2006 Profits: $12,641	**Int'l Ticker:** Int'l Exchange:
2005 Sales: $286,167	2005 Profits: $29,198	Employees: 3,000
2004 Sales: $255,999	2004 Profits: $14,015	Fiscal Year Ends: 12/31
2003 Sales: $197,939	2003 Profits: $12,071	Parent Company:

SALARIES/BENEFITS:

Pension Plan:	ESOP Stock Plan:	Profit Sharing:	Top Exec. Salary: $499,167	Bonus: $236,554
Savings Plan: Y	Stock Purch. Plan: Y		Second Exec. Salary: $301,667	Bonus: $111,639

OTHER THOUGHTS:

Apparent Women Officers or Directors: 2
Hot Spot for Advancement for Women/Minorities:

LOCATIONS: ("Y" = Yes)

West:	Southwest:	Midwest:	Southeast:	Northeast:	International:
Y		Y			Y

DUANE READE INC

www.duanereade.com

ndustry Group Code: 446110 **Ranks within this company's industry group:** Sales: 6 Profits: 6

nsurance/HMO/PPO:		**Drugs:**		**Equipment/Supplies:**		**Hospitals/Clinics:**		**Services:**		**Health Care:**	
nsurance:		Manufacturer:		Manufacturer:		Acute Care:		Diagnostics:		Home Health:	
‹anaged Care:		Distributor:	Y	Distributor:		Sub-Acute:		Labs/Testing:		Long-Term Care:	
Jtilization Management:		Specialty Pharmacy:	Y	Leasing/Finance:		Outpatient Surgery:		Staffing:		Physical Therapy:	
ᵓayment Processing:		Vitamins/Nutritionals:	Y	Information Systems:		Physical Rehab. Ctr.:		Waste Disposal:		Physician Prac. Mgmt.:	
		Clinical Trials:				Psychiatric Clinics:		Specialty Svcs.:			

TYPES OF BUSINESS:

Drug Stores
Retail Pharmacies
Nutraceuticals & Cosmetics
Photo Processing

BRANDS/DIVISIONS/AFFILIATES:

Rock Bottom
Value Drug
Oak Hill Capital Partners

CONTACTS: *Note: Officers with more than one job title may be intentionally listed here more than once.*

Richard W. Dreiling, CEO
Richard W. Dreiling, Pres.
John K. Henry, CFO/Sr. VP
David D'Arezzo, Sr. VP/Chief Mktg. Officer
Vincent A. Scarfone, Sr. VP-Human Resources
Vincent A. Scarfone, Sr. VP-Admin.
Michelle D. Bergman, General Counsel/VP
Charles Newsom, Sr. VP-Store Oper.
Anthony M. Goldrick, VP-Finance
Jerry M. Ray, Sr. VP-Pharmacy Oper.
Robert Storch, VP-Pharmacy Mktg. & Benefits Mgmt. Services
Mark Bander, VP-Real Estate
Jeffrey Thompson, VP-Mktg.
Richard W. Dreiling, Chmn.

Phone: 212-273-5700	**Fax:** 212-244-6527
Toll-Free:	
Address: 440 9th Ave., New York, NY 10001 US	

GROWTH PLANS/SPECIAL FEATURES:

Duane Reade, owned by the private equity firm Oak Hill Capital Partners, is one of the largest retail drug store chains in New York City. The drugstore chain operates approximately 250 stores in Manhattan's business and residential districts, 82 stores in New York's outer boroughs and 33 stores in the surrounding New York and New Jersey suburbs, including the Hudson River communities of northeastern New Jersey. The company's stores are small and tightly packed. Products and services offered include prescription and over-the-counter medications, vitamins, food and beverages, health aids, beauty products, greeting cards and photo processing. Duane Reade's extensive network of conveniently located pharmacies, strong local market position, pricing policies and reputation for high-quality health care products and services provide it with a competitive advantage in attracting pharmacy business from individual customers as well as managed care organizations, insurance companies and employers. The company's pharmacies employ computer systems that link all Duane Reade stores and enable them to provide customers with a broad range of services. The firm's pharmacy computer network profiles customer medical and other relevant information, supplies customers with information concerning their drug purchases for income tax and insurance purposes and prepares prescription labels and receipts. Duane Reade also has an interactive Website, www.duanereade.com, which customers may use to access company information, refill prescriptions and purchase over-the-counter medications as well as health and beauty care products and other non-pharmacy items. The firm has consolidated its distribution infrastructure into one mammoth 500,000-square-foot center in Queens, New York.

FINANCIALS: **Sales and profits are in thousands of dollars—add 000 to get the full amount. 2007 Note: Financial information for 2007 was not available for all companies at press time.**

2007 Sales: $	2007 Profits: $	**U.S. Stock Ticker: Private**
2006 Sales: $1,584,778	2006 Profits: $-80,103	**Int'l Ticker:** Int'l Exchange:
2005 Sales: $1,589,451	2005 Profits: $-100,388	Employees: 6,100
2004 Sales: $1,600,000	2004 Profits: $	Fiscal Year Ends: 12/31
2003 Sales: $1,383,828	2003 Profits: $5,074	Parent Company:

SALARIES/BENEFITS:

Pension Plan:	ESOP Stock Plan:	Profit Sharing:	Top Exec. Salary: $750,000	Bonus: $1,500,000
Savings Plan: Y	Stock Purch. Plan:		Second Exec. Salary: $330,000	Bonus: $396,000

OTHER THOUGHTS:

Apparent Women Officers or Directors: 1
Hot Spot for Advancement for Women/Minorities:

LOCATIONS: ("Y" = Yes)

West:	Southwest:	Midwest:	Southeast:	Northeast:	International:
				Y	

DYNACQ HEALTHCARE INC www.dynacq.com

Industry Group Code: 621490 **Ranks within this company's industry group:** Sales: 16 Profits: 15

Insurance/HMO/PPO:		Drugs:		Equipment/Supplies:		Hospitals/Clinics:		Services:		Health Care:	
Insurance:		Manufacturer:		Manufacturer:		Acute Care:	Y	Diagnostics:		Home Health:	
Managed Care:		Distributor:		Distributor:		Sub-Acute:	Y	Labs/Testing:		Long-Term Care:	
Utilization Management:		Specialty Pharmacy:		Leasing/Finance:		Outpatient Surgery:	Y	Staffing:		Physical Therapy:	
Payment Processing:		Vitamins/Nutritionals:		Information Systems:		Physical Rehab. Ctr.:		Waste Disposal:		Physician Prac. Mgmt.:	Y
		Clinical Trials:				Psychiatric Clinics:		Specialty Svcs.:	Y		

TYPES OF BUSINESS:

Emergency & Inpatient Surgery Facilities
Outpatient Surgery Facilities
Acute Care Hospital
Fertility Treatments

BRANDS/DIVISIONS/AFFILIATES:

Dynacq International, Inc.
Vista Medical Center Hospital
Vista Hospital of Dallas
Vista Surgical Hospital
Vista Surgical Center West
Vista Fertility Institute
Shanghai DeAn Hospital

CONTACTS: *Note: Officers with more than one job title may be intentionally listed here more than once.*

Chiu Moon Chan, CEO
Alan A. Beauchamp, COO/Exec. VP
Philip S. Chan, CFO/VP
Ringo Cheng, Dir.-IT
Hermant Khemka, Controller
Chiu Moon Chan, Chmn.

Phone: 713-673-6639	**Fax:** 713-673-6432
Toll-Free:	
Address: 10304 Interstate 10 E., Ste. 369, Houston, TX 77029 US	

GROWTH PLANS/SPECIAL FEATURES:

Dynacq Healthcare, Inc. is a holding company that develop and manages general acute care hospitals that provid specialized general surgeries. The company develops an operates hospitals designed to handle surgeries such a bariatric, orthopedic and neuro-spine surgeries. Dynac hospitals also provide facilities for fertility, sleep laborator and pain management services, as well as minor emergenc treatment services and ear, nose and throat services. Th firm's facilities include Vista Medical Center Hospital i Pasadena, Texas (near Houston); Vista Hospital of Dalla Vista Surgical Hospital of Baton Rouge; and Vista Surgic Center West in Houston, Texas. Vista Medical Center c Pasadena's primary areas of practice include orthopedic an general surgery, especially focused on spinal and bariatri surgeries. Vista Hospital of Dallas is the largest of Dynacq' hospitals at 90,000 square feet, and specializes in orthopedi surgery, bariatric surgery, general surgery and pai management. Vista Surgical Hospital of Baton Roug focuses on bariatric surgery, orthopedic surgery, gener surgery, pain management and cosmetic surgery. Vist Surgical Center West is primarily a satellite ambulator surgical center for the Pasadena, Texas facility, whic houses two operating rooms and focuses primarily o orthopedic surgery, general surgery and pain managemen Vista Surgical Center West also houses the Vista Fertilit Institute that provides invitro fertilization to couples unable t conceive by other means. Dynacq is currently attempting t locate a buyer for Vista Surgical Center West. The compan owns a 70% interest in Shanghai DeAn Hospital, a joir venture formed under the laws of China. Dynacq Healthcar began participation in certain managed care contracts i 2006, though they have not resulted in any meaningfu patient revenues; the firm's procedures are primarily funde through worker's compensation insurance plans or throug commercial insurers on an out-of-network health plan basis.

FINANCIALS: **Sales and profits are in thousands of dollars—add 000 to get the full amount. 2007 Note: Financial information for 2007 was not available for all companies at press time.**

2007 Sales: $	2007 Profits: $	**U.S. Stock Ticker: DYII**
2006 Sales: $35,989	2006 Profits: $-5,936	**Int'l Ticker:** Int'l Exchange:
2005 Sales: $41,618	2005 Profits: $-5,137	Employees: 332
2004 Sales: $39,234	2004 Profits: $-1,600	Fiscal Year Ends: 8/31
2003 Sales: $90,000	2003 Profits: $21,000	Parent Company:

SALARIES/BENEFITS:

Pension Plan:	ESOP Stock Plan:	Profit Sharing:	Top Exec. Salary: $180,000	Bonus: $
Savings Plan:	Stock Purch. Plan:		Second Exec. Salary: $180,000	Bonus: $

OTHER THOUGHTS:

Apparent Women Officers or Directors:
Hot Spot for Advancement for Women/Minorities: Y

LOCATIONS: ("Y" = Yes)

West:	Southwest:	Midwest:	Southeast:	Northeast:	International:
	Y		Y		Y

ECLIPSYS CORPORATION www.eclipsys.com

ndustry Group Code: 511212 Ranks within this company's industry group: Sales: 2 Profits: 5

nsurance/HMO/PPO:		Drugs:		Equipment/Supplies:		Hospitals/Clinics:		Services:		Health Care:	
nsurance:		Manufacturer:		Manufacturer:		Acute Care:		Diagnostics:		Home Health:	
/lanaged Care:		Distributor:		Distributor:		Sub-Acute:		Labs/Testing:		Long-Term Care:	
Jtilization Management:		Specialty Pharmacy:		Leasing/Finance:		Outpatient Surgery:		Staffing:		Physical Therapy:	
?ayment Processing:		Vitamins/Nutritionals:		Information Systems:	Y	Physical Rehab. Ctr.:		Waste Disposal:		Physician Prac. Mgmt.:	
		Clinical Trials:				Psychiatric Clinics:		Specialty Svcs.:	Y		

TYPES OF BUSINESS:

Computer Software
Health Care IT Products & Services

BRANDS/DIVISIONS/AFFILIATES:

SunriseXA
Sunrise Clinical Manager
Sunrise Access Manager
Sunrise Patient Financial Manager
Sunrise Decision Support Manager
Remote Access Services
Pocket Sunrise
eSys Medical Systems, Inc.

CONTACTS: *Note: Officers with more than one job title may be intentionally listed here more than once.*

R. Andrew Eckert, CEO
R. Andrew Eckert, Pres.
Robert J. Colletti, CFO/Sr. VP
Jan Smith, Sr. VP-Human Resources
John Gomez, Exec. VP/CTO
Joe Petro, Sr. VP-Prod. Dev.
Brian W. Copple, Chief Legal Officer/General Counsel/Corp. Sec.
Frank Stearns, Exec. VP-Client Oper.
Jay Deady, Exec. VP-Client Solutions
John McAuley, Exec. VP-Outsourcing
Frank Stearns, Exec. VP-Client Oper.
Eugene V. Fife, Chmn.

Phone: 561-322-4321	Fax: 561-322-4320
Toll-Free:	
Address: 1750 Clint Moore Rd., Boca Raton, FL 33487 US	

GROWTH PLANS/SPECIAL FEATURES:

Eclipsys Corporation is a health care information technology company and a leading provider of advanced clinical, financial and management information software and service solutions. The company develops and licenses proprietary software and content that is designed for use in connection with many of the key clinical, administrative and financial functions that hospitals and other healthcare organizations require. The company's flagship offering is the SunriseXA line of products, which includes Sunrise Clinical Manager, Sunrise Access Manager, Sunrise Patient Financial Manager, Sunrise Decision Support Manager, Sunrise Record Manager, Sunrise Enterprise Person Identifier, Eclipsys Diagnostic Imaging Solutions and eLink. This software allows hospitals to automate many of the key clinical, administrative and financial functions that they require, letting them admit patients, maintain patient records, create invoices for billing, control inventories, effect cost accounting, schedule doctor's visits and understand the profitability of specific medical procedures. It also enables physicians and nurses to check on a patient's condition, order tests, review test results, monitor a patient's medications and provide alerts to changes in a patient's condition. The company's applications, which are installed in approximately 1,500 hospitals, are available for implementation on-site or through its remote hosting service. In addition, Eclipsys offers support services to its customers, including implementation, integration, support, maintenance and training. In recent news, the company acquired Sysware Healthcare Systems, Inc., including Sysware's related software-development organization in India.

The company's employee benefits include flexible spending accounts and an employee assistance program.

FINANCIALS: Sales and profits are in thousands of dollars—add 000 to get the full amount. 2007 Note: Financial information for 2007 was not available for all companies at press time.

2007 Sales: $	2007 Profits: $	U.S. Stock Ticker: ECLP
2006 Sales: $427,542	2006 Profits: $4,093	Int'l Ticker: Int'l Exchange:
2005 Sales: $383,342	2005 Profits: $ 269	Employees: 2,200
2004 Sales: $309,075	2004 Profits: $-34,029	Fiscal Year Ends: 12/31
2003 Sales: $254,679	2003 Profits: $-55,964	Parent Company:

SALARIES/BENEFITS:

Pension Plan:	ESOP Stock Plan:	Profit Sharing:	Top Exec. Salary: $453,606	Bonus: $
Savings Plan: Y	Stock Purch. Plan:		Second Exec. Salary: $450,000	Bonus: $225,000

OTHER THOUGHTS:

Apparent Women Officers or Directors: 1
Hot Spot for Advancement for Women/Minorities:

LOCATIONS: ("Y" = Yes)

West:	Southwest:	Midwest:	Southeast:	Northeast:	International:
Y	Y		Y	Y	Y

Note: Financial information, benefits and other data can change quickly and may vary from those stated here.

EDWARDS LIFESCIENCES CORP www.edwards.com

Industry Group Code: 339113 **Ranks within this company's industry group:** Sales: 28 Profits: 20

Insurance/HMO/PPO:		Drugs:		Equipment/Supplies:		Hospitals/Clinics:		Services:		Health Care:	
Insurance:		Manufacturer:		Manufacturer:	Y	Acute Care:		Diagnostics:		Home Health:	
Managed Care:		Distributor:		Distributor:	Y	Sub-Acute:		Labs/Testing:		Long-Term Care:	
Utilization Management:		Specialty Pharmacy:		Leasing/Finance:		Outpatient Surgery:		Staffing:		Physical Therapy:	
Payment Processing:		Vitamins/Nutritionals:		Information Systems:		Physical Rehab. Ctr.:		Waste Disposal:		Physician Prac. Mgmt.:	
		Clinical Trials:				Psychiatric Clinics:		Specialty Svcs.:			

TYPES OF BUSINESS:

Supplies-Cardiovascular Disease Related
Cardiac Surgery Products
Critical Care Products
Vascular Products
Heart Valve Implants

BRANDS/DIVISIONS/AFFILIATES:

PERIMOUNT
GeoForm
Myxo ETlogix
Swan-Ganz
FloTrac

CONTACTS: *Note: Officers with more than one job title may be intentionally listed here more than once.*

Michael A. Mussallem, CEO
Thomas M. Abate, CFO/Treas./Corp. VP
Robert C. Reindl, Corp. VP-Human Resources & Comm.
Stanton Rowe, Corp. VP-Advanced Tech.
Bruce P. Garren, General Counsel/Corp. VP-Gov't Affairs
Corinne H. Lyle, Corp. VP/Pres., Global Oper.
John H. Kehl, Jr., Corp. VP-Strategy & Bus. Dev.
Grant Johnson, VP-Global Comm.
David K. Erikson, VP-Investor Rel.
Thomas M. Abate, VP-Financial Control
John (Alex) Martin, Corp. VP-North America
Donald E. Bobo, Jr., Corp. VP-Heart Valve Therapy
Stuart L. Foster, Corp. VP-Critical Care & Vascular
Anita B. Bessler, Corp. VP-Heart Valve & Cardiac Surgery Systems
Michael A. Mussallem, Chmn.
Huimin Wang, M.D., Corp. VP-Japan & Intercontinental

Phone: 949-250-2500	**Fax:** 949-250-2525
Toll-Free: 800-424-3278	
Address: 1 Edwards Way, Irvine, CA 92614 US	

GROWTH PLANS/SPECIAL FEATURES:

Edwards Lifesciences Corp. is an international leader i providing products and services for patients wit cardiovascular disease. The firm designs products fo cardiovascular diseases, such as heart valve diseas coronary artery disease, peripheral vascular disease (PVD and congestive heart failure. Its products and technologie are categorized into five main areas: Heart valve therap which generated 47% of the firm's 2006 sales; critical car 34%; cardiac surgery systems, 9%; vascular, 7%; and othe distributed products, 3%. Heart valve therapy product include PERIMOUNT line of pericardial heart valves mad from biologically inert porcine tissue, often sewn onto a wire form stent. It also develops valve repair therapies such a the GeoForm and Myxo ETlogix annuloplasty rings whic help a valve maintain proper shape. The company's critic care products include the Swan-Ganz brand hemodynami monitoring devices used for measuring heart pressure an output during surgery. Its newest hemodynamic monitor i the minimally invasive continuous cardiac output monitorin system called FloTrac. Cardiac surgery products includ disposable products used in heart surgery procedure especially cannula (small tubes used to extract fluid), as we as products designed to reduce vascular trauma durin cannula placement, usage and removal. This category als produces carbon dioxide lasers and associated hand-piece used in some heart surgeries. Vascular products includ balloon-tipped, catheter-based products; surgical clips an inserts; angioscopy equipment; and implantable graft These products most often treat PVD in the arms, legs c abdomen. The other distributed products category include intra-aortic balloon pumps and other products main distributed in Japan and Europe. Edwards' sells its product and services in approximately 100 countries worldwide Approximately 46% of its 2006 sales came from the U.S 26% from Europe, 16% from Japan and 12% from othe countries.

Edwards' employee benefits include medical, dental, visio and group life insurance; and adoption, tuition and employe assistance programs.

FINANCIALS: Sales and profits are in thousands of dollars—add 000 to get the full amount. 2007 Note: Financial information for 2007 was not available for all companies at press time.

2007 Sales: $	2007 Profits: $	**U.S. Stock Ticker: EW**
2006 Sales: $1,037,000	2006 Profits: $130,500	**Int'l Ticker:** Int'l Exchange:
2005 Sales: $997,900	2005 Profits: $79,300	Employees: 5,550
2004 Sales: $931,500	2004 Profits: $1,700	Fiscal Year Ends: 12/31
2003 Sales: $860,500	2003 Profits: $79,000	Parent Company:

SALARIES/BENEFITS:

Pension Plan:	ESOP Stock Plan:	Profit Sharing:	Top Exec. Salary: $747,308	Bonus: $459,940
Savings Plan: Y	Stock Purch. Plan: Y		Second Exec. Salary: $410,385	Bonus: $152,500

OTHER THOUGHTS:

Apparent Women Officers or Directors: 2
Hot Spot for Advancement for Women/Minorities: Y

LOCATIONS: ("Y" = Yes)

West:	Southwest:	Midwest:	Southeast:	Northeast:	International:
Y					Y

Note: Financial information, benefits and other data can change quickly and may vary from those stated here.

ELAN CORP PLC

www.elan.com

ndustry Group Code: 325412 **Ranks within this company's industry group:** Sales: 30 Profits: 43

nsurance/HMO/PPO:		Drugs:		Equipment/Supplies:		Hospitals/Clinics:		Services:		Health Care:	
nsurance:		Manufacturer:	Y	Manufacturer:		Acute Care:		Diagnostics:		Home Health:	
ʼlanaged Care:		Distributor:		Distributor:		Sub-Acute:		Labs/Testing:		Long-Term Care:	
Jtilization Management:		Specialty Pharmacy:		Leasing/Finance:		Outpatient Surgery:		Staffing:		Physical Therapy:	
ʼayment Processing:		Vitamins/Nutritionals:		Information Systems:		Physical Rehab. Ctr.:		Waste Disposal:		Physician Prac. Mgmt.:	
		Clinical Trials:				Psychiatric Clinics:		Specialty Svcs.:			

TYPES OF BUSINESS:

Drugs-Neurology
Acute Care Drugs
Pain Management Drugs
Autoimmune Disease Drugs
Drug Delivery Technologies

BRANDS/DIVISIONS/AFFILIATES:

NanoCrystal
Maxipime
Prialt
Tysabri
Azactam
Elan Drug Technologies (EDT)

CONTACTS:

Note: Officers with more than one job title may be intentionally listed here more than once.

Kelly Martin, CEO
Kelly Martin, Pres.
Shane Cooke, CFO/Exec. VP
Lars Ekman, Exec. VP/Pres., Global R&D/Head-Neurodegeneration
Richard T. Collier, General Counsel/Exec. VP
Karen Kim, Exec. VP-Strategy, Bus. Dev. & Brand Mgmt.
Chris Burns, Sr. VP-Investor Rel.
Nigel Clerkin, Sr. VP-Finance/Controller
Paul Breen, Exec. VP-Elan Drug Tech.
Dale Schenk, Sr. VP/Chief Scientific Officer
Lars Ekman, Head-Neurodegeneration Franchise
Allison Hulme, Exec. VP-Autoimmune & Tysabri Franchise
Kyran McLaughlin, Chmn.

Phone: 353-1-709-4444	**Fax:** 353-1-709-4108
Toll-Free:	
Address: Treasury Bldg., Lower Grand Canal St., Dublin, 2 Ireland	

GROWTH PLANS/SPECIAL FEATURES:

Elan Corporation, a leading global specialty pharmaceutical company, focuses on the discovery, development and marketing of therapeutic products and services in neurology, acute care and pain management. Elan is divided into two segments: Biopharmaceuticals and Elan Drug Technologies (EDT). The Irish company conducts its worldwide business through subsidiaries in Ireland, the U.S., the U.K. and other countries. Nearly half of its revenue is generated from EDT, which controls its four marketed products. The biopharmaceuticals division focuses its research and development on Alzheimer's disease, Parkinson's disease, multiple sclerosis, pain management and Crohn's. The company uses proprietary technologies to develop, market and license drug delivery products to its pharmaceutical clients. It does not manufacture any of its products. It has developed three novel therapeutic approaches in its breakthrough research program in Alzheimer's disease: immunotherapy, beta secretase inhibitors and gamma secretase inhibitors. The company's four products are: Tysabri, an alpha four integrin antagonist for the treatment of recurring multiple sclerosis; Prialt, used for the management of severe chronic pain; Azactam, which is used to treat gram-negative organism induced disorders such as urinary and lower respiratory tract infections and intra-abdominal infections (this product lost patent protection in 2005, and Elan expects a generic to appear on the market sometime in 2007); and Maxipime, which treats a number of disorders including urinary tract infections and pneumonia. Elan also owns proprietary rights to NanoCrystal technology, which it licenses to Roche and Johnson & Johnson. In the European Union, the firm's primary product is Prialt. In 2006, Elan and its partner Biogen Idec, Inc. received approval to reintroduce Tysabri as a treatment for MS to the U.S. and European markets. The firm is currently trying to have Tysabri approved for treatment of Crohn's Disease.

Employee benefits include an educational assistance program.

FINANCIALS:

Sales and profits are in thousands of dollars—add 000 to get the full amount. 2007 Note: Financial information for 2007 was not available for all companies at press time.

2007 Sales: $	2007 Profits: $	**U.S. Stock Ticker: ELN**
2006 Sales: $560,400	2006 Profits: $-267,300	**Int'l Ticker: DRX** Int'l Exchange: Dublin-ISE
2005 Sales: $490,300	2005 Profits: $-383,600	Employees: 1,734
2004 Sales: $481,700	2004 Profits: $-394,700	Fiscal Year Ends: 12/31
2003 Sales: $746,000	2003 Profits: $-529,400	Parent Company:

SALARIES/BENEFITS:

Pension Plan: Y	ESOP Stock Plan:	Profit Sharing:	Top Exec. Salary: $702,854	Bonus: $800,000
Savings Plan: Y	Stock Purch. Plan: Y		Second Exec. Salary: $266,666	Bonus: $150,000

OTHER THOUGHTS:

Apparent Women Officers or Directors: 2
Hot Spot for Advancement for Women/Minorities: Y

LOCATIONS: ("Y" = Yes)

West:	Southwest:	Midwest:	Southeast:	Northeast:	International:
Y			Y	Y	Y

Note: Financial information, benefits and other data can change quickly and may vary from those stated here.

ELI LILLY AND COMPANY www.lilly.com

Industry Group Code: 325412 **Ranks within this company's industry group:** Sales: 12 Profits: 12

Insurance/HMO/PPO:		Drugs:		Equipment/Supplies:		Hospitals/Clinics:		Services:		Health Care:	
Insurance:		Manufacturer:	Y	Manufacturer:	Y	Acute Care:		Diagnostics:		Home Health:	
Managed Care:		Distributor:		Distributor:		Sub-Acute:		Labs/Testing:		Long-Term Care:	
Utilization Management:	Y	Specialty Pharmacy:		Leasing/Finance:		Outpatient Surgery:		Staffing:		Physical Therapy:	
Payment Processing:	Y	Vitamins/Nutritionals:	Y	Information Systems:	Y	Physical Rehab. Ctr.:		Waste Disposal:		Physician Prac. Mgmt.:	
		Clinical Trials:	Y			Psychiatric Clinics:		Specialty Svcs.:	Y		

TYPES OF BUSINESS:

Pharmaceuticals Discovery & Development
Veterinary Products

BRANDS/DIVISIONS/AFFILIATES:

Zyprexa
Prozac
Humalog
Gemzar
Coban
Cialis
Icos Corp.
Xigris

CONTACTS: *Note: Officers with more than one job title may be intentionally listed here more than once.*

Sidney Taurel, CEO
John Lechleiter, COO
John Lechleiter, Pres.
Derica Rice, CFO/Sr. VP
Richard Pilnik, Chief Mktg. Officer/VP
Anthony Murphy, Sr. VP-Human Resources
Thomas Verhoeven, VP-R&D
Michael Heim, CIO/VP-IT
Steven M. Paul, Exec. VP-Science & Tech.
Thomas Verhoeven, VP-Prod. R&D
Robert A. Cole, VP-Eng./Environmental Health & Safety
Scott Canute, Pres., Mfg. Oper.
Robert A. Armitage, General Counsel/Sr. VP
Peter Johnson, Exec. Dir.-Corp. Strategic Dev.
Alex M. Azar II, Sr. VP-Corp. Affairs & Comm.
Thomas W. Grein, Treas./VP
Alan Brier, Chief Medical Officer/VP-Medical
Bryce Carmine, Pres., Global Brand Dev.
Jacques Tapiero, Pres., Intercontinental Oper.
Abbas Hussain, Pres., European Oper.
Sidney Taurel, Chmn.
Lorenzo Tallarigo, Pres., Int'l Oper.

Phone: 317-276-2000 **Fax:** 317-277-6579
Toll-Free:
Address: Lilly Corporate Center, Drop Code 1112, Indianapolis, IN 46285-0001 US

GROWTH PLANS/SPECIAL FEATURES:

Eli Lilly and Company researches, develops, manufacture and sells pharmaceuticals designed to treat a variety conditions. The company manufactures and distributes i products through facilities in the U.S., Puerto Rico and 2 other countries, which are then sold to markets in 14 countries throughout the world. Most of Eli Lilly's product are developed by its in-house research staff, which primari directs its research efforts towards the search for products prevent and treat cancer and diseases of the centr nervous, endocrine and cardiovascular systems. The firm other research lies in anti-infectives and products to tre animal diseases. In 2006, research and developme expenditures exceeded $3.1 billion. Major brands includ neuroscience products Zyprexa, Strattera, Prozac, Cymbal and Permax; endocrine products Humalog, Humulin an Actos; oncology products Gemzar and Alimta; animal heal products Tylan, Rumensin and Coban; cardiovascul products ReoPro and Xigris; anti-infectives Ceclor an Vancocin; and Cialis, for erectile dysfunction. In the U.S the company distributes pharmaceuticals primarily throug independent wholesale distributors. Marketing is through a in-house sales force who call upon physicians, hospitals an managed care providers directly. Outside of the U.S., E Lilly products are primarily marketed either through this dire sales force or by way of standing partnerships with sever companies, including Takeda Chemical Industries, ICO Corporation, Quintiles Transnational and Boehringe Ingelheim. In January 2007 the company acquired Ico Corp., maker of the drug Cialis, for $2.3 billion. In Marc 2007, Eli Lily agreed to acquire Hypnion, Inc., neuroscience drug company focused on sleep disorders.

Eli Lilly offers its employees domestic partner benefits an an employee assistance program, as well as up to 10 week of paid maternity leave. The firm also offers an on-sit fitness center, flexible hours or telecommuting, parenting an dependant care leaves, adoption assistance and tuitio reimbursement, among many other things.

FINANCIALS: **Sales and profits are in thousands of dollars—add 000 to get the full amount. 2007 Note: Financial information for 2007 was not available for all companies at press time.**

2007 Sales: $
2006 Sales: $15,691,000
2005 Sales: $14,645,300
2004 Sales: $13,857,900
2003 Sales: $12,582,500

2007 Profits: $
2006 Profits: $2,662,700
2005 Profits: $1,979,600
2004 Profits: $1,810,100
2003 Profits: $2,560,800

U.S. Stock Ticker: LLY
Int'l Ticker: Int'l Exchange:
Employees: 41,500
Fiscal Year Ends: 12/31
Parent Company:

SALARIES/BENEFITS:

Pension Plan: Y	ESOP Stock Plan:	Profit Sharing:	Top Exec. Salary: $1,650,333	Bonus: $2,764,308
Savings Plan: Y	Stock Purch. Plan:		Second Exec. Salary: $1,112,000	Bonus: $1,490,080

OTHER THOUGHTS:

Apparent Women Officers or Directors: 10
Hot Spot for Advancement for Women/Minorities: Y

LOCATIONS: ("Y" = Yes)

West:	Southwest:	Midwest:	Southeast:	Northeast:	International:
Y	Y	Y	Y	Y	Y

EMERGENCY FILTRATION PRODUCTS INC

www.emergencyfiltration.com

Industry Group Code: 339113 **Ranks within this company's industry group:** Sales: Profits:

Insurance/HMO/PPO:		**Drugs:**		**Equipment/Supplies:**		**Hospitals/Clinics:**		**Services:**		**Health Care:**	
Insurance:		Manufacturer:		Manufacturer:	Y	Acute Care:		Diagnostics:		Home Health:	
Managed Care:		Distributor:		Distributor:		Sub-Acute:		Labs/Testing:		Long-Term Care:	
Utilization Management:		Specialty Pharmacy:		Leasing/Finance:		Outpatient Surgery:		Staffing:		Physical Therapy:	
Payment Processing:		Vitamins/Nutritionals:		Information Systems:		Physical Rehab. Ctr.:		Waste Disposal:		Physician Prac. Mgmt.:	
		Clinical Trials:				Psychiatric Clinics:		Specialty Svcs.:			

TYPES OF BUSINESS:

Medical Equipment-Anti-Contamination
Filtration Products
Blood Clotting Agents
CPR Masks
Personal Environmental Protection Devices

BRANDS/DIVISIONS/AFFILIATES:

RespAide
Superstat
NanoMask
ELVIS BVM
NanoMask Filters
2M technology

CONTACTS: *Note: Officers with more than one job title may be intentionally listed here more than once.*

Philip Dascher, CEO
Douglas K. Beplate, Pres.
Steve M. Hanni, CFO
John Masenheimer, VP-Mfg.
Steve M. Hanni, Treas./Corp. Sec.
Raymond Yuan, Dir.
Sherman Lazrus, Chmn.

Phone: 702-307-4102	**Fax:** 702-307-4103
Toll-Free:	
Address: 1111 Grier Dr., Ste. B, Las Vegas, NV 89119 US	

GROWTH PLANS/SPECIAL FEATURES:

Emergency Filtration Products, Inc. (EFPI) is a producer and distributor of specialty filter products. The firm is recognized for its state-of-the-art air filtration technology which removes infectious bacteria and viruses in air flow systems. With EFPI's patented 2H technology, a combination of micro-particle air filters can be effectively utilized in medical filtration and a variety of applications outside of the medical products industry. The company's main product lines includes the Nano-Enhanced Environmental Mark (NanoMask) and NanoMask Filters. NanoMasks are personal environmental masks that have been enhanced with nanoparticles within its combination of hydrophobic and hydrophilic filters. NanoMasks have the capacity to capture and isolate 99.9% of bacterial and viral microorganisms in biohazardous workplaces and environments. An additional mask, the RespAide CPR Isolation Mask, uses dual-filtered vapor isolation valve (VIV) technology to protect emergency response personnel against infectious diseases during mouth-to-mouth resuscitation. The same filters in RespAide product line are also utilized in bag valve mask (BVM) resuscitation devices in order to keep equipment contaminant-free. In addition to mask filters, the company also markets Superstat, a product that provides safe and rapid surgical clotting of the blood for surgery, trauma and burn wound management. Products that are currently under development include breathing circuit filters and the ELVIS BVM, a self-contained device that delivers medicine in aerosol form in a bag with built-in CO(2) monitoring capabilities.

FINANCIALS: **Sales and profits are in thousands of dollars—add 000 to get the full amount. 2007 Note: Financial information for 2007 was not available for all companies at press time.**

2007 Sales: $	2007 Profits: $	**U.S. Stock Ticker: EMFP.PK**
2006 Sales: $	2006 Profits: $	**Int'l Ticker:** Int'l Exchange:
2005 Sales: $ 655	2005 Profits: $-1,613	Employees: 25
2004 Sales: $ 406	2004 Profits: $-1,605	Fiscal Year Ends: 12/31
2003 Sales: $ 764	2003 Profits: $- 706	Parent Company:

SALARIES/BENEFITS:

Pension Plan:	ESOP Stock Plan:	Profit Sharing:	Top Exec. Salary: $96,000	Bonus: $
Savings Plan:	Stock Purch. Plan:		Second Exec. Salary: $96,000	Bonus: $34,300

OTHER THOUGHTS:

Apparent Women Officers or Directors:
Hot Spot for Advancement for Women/Minorities:

LOCATIONS: ("Y" = Yes)

West:	Southwest:	Midwest:	Southeast:	Northeast:	International:
Y					Y

EMERGING VISION INC www.emergingvision.com

Industry Group Code: 446130 **Ranks within this company's industry group:** Sales: 1 Profits: 1

Insurance/HMO/PPO:		Drugs:		Equipment/Supplies:		Hospitals/Clinics:		Services:		Health Care:	
Insurance:		Manufacturer:		Manufacturer:	Y	Acute Care:		Diagnostics:		Home Health:	
Managed Care:	Y	Distributor:		Distributor:	Y	Sub-Acute:		Labs/Testing:		Long-Term Care:	
Utilization Management:		Specialty Pharmacy:		Leasing/Finance:		Outpatient Surgery:		Staffing:		Physical Therapy:	
Payment Processing:		Vitamins/Nutritionals:		Information Systems:		Physical Rehab. Ctr.:		Waste Disposal:		Physician Prac. Mgmt.:	
		Clinical Trials:				Psychiatric Clinics:		Specialty Svcs.:	Y		

TYPES OF BUSINESS:

Eyeglasses & Related Products, Retail
Franchise Operations
Group Vision Plan

BRANDS/DIVISIONS/AFFILIATES:

Sterling Vision
Sterling Optical
Site For Sore Eyes
Duling Optical
Singer Specs
VisionCare of California, Inc.
Insight Managed Vision Care
Combine Optical Management Corp.

CONTACTS: *Note: Officers with more than one job title may be intentionally listed here more than once.*

Christopher G. Payan, CEO
Myles S. Lewis, COO
Brian P. Alessi, CFO
Samuel Z. Herskowitz, Chief Mktg. Officer
Nicholas Shashati, Pres., VisionCare of California, Inc.

Phone: 516-390-2106	**Fax:**
Toll-Free:	
Address: 100 Quentin Roosevelt Blvd., Ste. 508, Garden City, NY 11530 US	

GROWTH PLANS/SPECIAL FEATURES:

Emerging Vision, Inc., formerly Sterling Vision, operates chain of retail optical stores and a franchise optical chain i the U.S. The company and its franchises develop an operate retail optical stores principally under such trad names as Sterling Optical, Site for Sore Eyes, Duling Optica and Singer Specs. The firm also operates VisionCare c California, Inc. (VCC), a specialized health care maintenanc organization. VCC employs licensed optometrists wh render services in offices located immediately adjacent to, c within, most Sterling stores located in California. There ar approximately 154 Emerging Vision stores in operation in 1 states, Washington D.C., Canada and the U.S. Virgi Islands. Most stores offer eye care products and service such as prescription and non-prescription eyeglasses eyeglass frames; ophthalmic lenses; contact lenses sunglasses; and a broad range of ancillary items. Emergin Vision also fills prescriptions from its own or affiliate optometrists, as well as from unaffiliated optometrists an ophthalmologists. Most stores have an inventory c ophthalmic and contact lenses, as well as on-site la equipment for cutting and edging ophthalmic lenses to fit int eyeglass frames. In many cases, the stores offer same-da service. Emerging Vision also owns and manages a exclusive group vision plan, Insight Managed Vision Care Under the plan, the company contracts with payors that offe eye care benefits to their covered participants and offer discounted prices to members of the plan. In October 2006 Emerging Vision acquired Combine Optical Managemen Corp. for roughly $2.5 million. In May 2007, the compan agreed to acquire The Optical Group, an optical grou purchasing organizations in Canada.

FINANCIALS: **Sales and profits are in thousands of dollars—add 000 to get the full amount. 2007 Note: Financial information for 2007 was not available for all companies at press time.**

2007 Sales: $	2007 Profits: $	**U.S. Stock Ticker: ISEE**
2006 Sales: $21,712	2006 Profits: $1,860	**Int'l Ticker:** Int'l Exchange:
2005 Sales: $13,979	2005 Profits: $ 266	Employees: 146
2004 Sales: $14,484	2004 Profits: $ 884	Fiscal Year Ends: 12/31
2003 Sales: $14,546	2003 Profits: $-2,967	Parent Company:

SALARIES/BENEFITS:

Pension Plan:	ESOP Stock Plan:	Profit Sharing:	Top Exec. Salary: $275,000	Bonus: $
Savings Plan:	Stock Purch. Plan:		Second Exec. Salary: $190,000	Bonus: $

OTHER THOUGHTS:

Apparent Women Officers or Directors:
Hot Spot for Advancement for Women/Minorities:

LOCATIONS: ("Y" = Yes)

West:	Southwest:	Midwest:	Southeast:	Northeast:	International:
Y		Y	Y	Y	

EMERITUS CORP

www.emeritus.com

Industry Group Code: 623110 **Ranks within this company's industry group:** Sales: 6 Profits: 7

Insurance/HMO/PPO:		Drugs:		Equipment/Supplies:		Hospitals/Clinics:		Services:		Health Care:	
Insurance:		Manufacturer:		Manufacturer:		Acute Care:		Diagnostics:		Home Health:	
Managed Care:		Distributor:		Distributor:		Sub-Acute:		Labs/Testing:		Long-Term Care:	Y
Utilization Management:		Specialty Pharmacy:		Leasing/Finance:		Outpatient Surgery:		Staffing:		Physical Therapy:	
Payment Processing:		Vitamins/Nutritionals:		Information Systems:		Physical Rehab. Ctr.:		Waste Disposal:		Physician Prac. Mgmt.:	
		Clinical Trials:				Psychiatric Clinics:		Specialty Svcs.:			

TYPES OF BUSINESS:

Long-Term Health Care
Assisted Living Communities

BRANDS/DIVISIONS/AFFILIATES:

Arbor Place at Silverlake

CONTACTS: *Note: Officers with more than one job title may be intentionally listed here more than once.*

Daniel R. Baty, CEO
Raymond R. Brandstrom, CFO
Frank A. Ruffo, VP-Admin.
Gary S. Becker, Sr. VP-Oper.
Martin D. Roffe, VP-Financial Planning
Raymond R. Brandstorm, VP-Finance
Christopher M. Belford, VP-Oper., Central Div.
Suzette McCanless, VP-Oper., Eastern Div.
P. Kacy Kang, VP-Oper., Western Div.
Daniel R. Baty, Chmn.

Phone: 206-298-2909	**Fax:** 206-301-4500
Toll-Free: 800-429-4828	
Address: 3131 Elliott Ave., Ste. 500, Seattle, WA 98121 US	

GROWTH PLANS/SPECIAL FEATURES:

Emeritus Corp. operates assisted living residential communities in the U.S. It operates or has an interest in 203 communities across 35 states, totaling approximately 16,500 units with a capacity for 20,149 residents. These communities cater to senior citizens who need help with daily living, but do not require the intensive care provided in skilled nursing facilities. Assisted living generally provides housing and 24-hour personal support services. Seniors reside in a private or semi-private residential unit for a monthly fee based on each resident's individual service needs. Emeritus's specialty is in Alzheimer's and dementia related care, for which the company has developed a program that links memory training, familiar environments and personalized care services. Accessing the market for Alzheimer's care is one of the firm's key business strategies. In its other assisted living programs, Emeritus business strategy calls for customer service that addresses both physical and social health. The firm's target customers are middle to upper-middle income seniors living in smaller cities (50,000 to 150,000 persons). Emeritus attempts to generate growth through increases in residential occupancy rates and revenue per occupied unit as well as through investments in information technology infrastructure and through the selective acquisition of assisted living communities. In recent years, the company has sought to increase the number of communities it owns and decrease the number it merely manages. In July 2006, Emeritus acquired Arbor Place at Silverlake, an assisted living community in Everett, Washington. In March 2007, the firm purchased three communities that it had previously leased for roughly $28.7 million. In the past year, it has purchased 45 of its leased communities.

Emeritus offers its employees a benefit package that includes medical, dental, prescription, vision, life and AD&D insurance options; bereavement leave; a 401(k); and an employee stock purchase plan.

FINANCIALS: **Sales and profits are in thousands of dollars—add 000 to get the full amount. 2007 Note: Financial information for 2007 was not available for all companies at press time.**

2007 Sales: $	2007 Profits: $	**U.S. Stock Ticker: ESC**
2006 Sales: $421,865	2006 Profits: $-14,618	**Int'l Ticker:** Int'l Exchange:
2005 Sales: $387,732	2005 Profits: $12,302	Employees: 10,100
2004 Sales: $316,866	2004 Profits: $-40,540	Fiscal Year Ends: 12/31
2003 Sales: $206,657	2003 Profits: $-8,081	Parent Company:

SALARIES/BENEFITS:

Pension Plan:	ESOP Stock Plan:	Profit Sharing:	Top Exec. Salary: $300,000	Bonus: $
Savings Plan: Y	Stock Purch. Plan: Y		Second Exec. Salary: $207,083	Bonus: $

OTHER THOUGHTS:

Apparent Women Officers or Directors: 1
Hot Spot for Advancement for Women/Minorities:

LOCATIONS: ("Y" = Yes)

West:	Southwest:	Midwest:	Southeast:	Northeast:	International:
Y	Y	Y	Y	Y	

EMPI INC

www.empi.com

Industry Group Code: 339113 **Ranks within this company's industry group:** Sales: Profits:

Insurance/HMO/PPO:		Drugs:		Equipment/Supplies:		Hospitals/Clinics:		Services:		Health Care:	
Insurance:		Manufacturer:		Manufacturer:	Y	Acute Care:		Diagnostics:		Home Health:	
Managed Care:		Distributor:		Distributor:	Y	Sub-Acute:		Labs/Testing:		Long-Term Care:	
Utilization Management:		Specialty Pharmacy:		Leasing/Finance:		Outpatient Surgery:		Staffing:		Physical Therapy:	
Payment Processing:		Vitamins/Nutritionals:		Information Systems:		Physical Rehab. Ctr.:		Waste Disposal:		Physician Prac. Mgmt.:	
		Clinical Trials:				Psychiatric Clinics:		Specialty Svcs.:			

TYPES OF BUSINESS:

Medical Device Manufacturing
Pain Management Products
Tissue Rehabilitation Products
Incontinence Products
Clinic Supplies

BRANDS/DIVISIONS/AFFILIATES:

Encore Medical Corporation
Epix VT
Dupel Iontophoresis System
Saunders/Pronex Traction Devices
300 PV
Advance Dynamic ROM
Innosense Minnova
Infinity Plus

CONTACTS: *Note: Officers with more than one job title may be intentionally listed here more than once.*

Barbara Hutto, COO
Brian T. Ennis, Pres.
Anna Skar, Dir.-Human Resources
Rudiger Hausherr, Pres., Ormed

Phone: 651-415-9000	**Fax:** 651-415-7447
Toll-Free: 888-328-3536	
Address: 599 Cardigan Rd., St. Paul, MN 55126-4099 US	

GROWTH PLANS/SPECIAL FEATURES:

Empi, Inc., a wholly-owned subsidiary of ReAbl Therapeutics, Inc., is a leading medical device company tha develops, manufactures, markets and distributes a range o products for pain management, tissue rehabilitation an incontinence, as well as clinic supplies. The firm's pai management products include Epix VT, a non-invasive pai control system that works through transcutaneous electrica nerve stimulation; Infinity Plus, a four channel multifunctio electrotherapy device that allows patients to us interferential, pre-modulated interferential, high volt an NMES treatments; the Dupel Iontophoresis System, a non invasive drug delivery system that uses electricity t administer medicine through the skin; VitalStim Therapy which is the first proven treatment for dysphagia, using sma electrical currents to stimulate the muscles responsible fo swallowing; and Saunders Traction Devices, providin cervical and lumbar traction for effective spine pai management. The company's tissue rehabilitation product include 300 PV, a neuromuscular electrical stimulatio portable multifunction device that helps slow or preven disuse atrophy, re-educate muscles and control pain. I addition, Empi markets clinic supplies, such as electrodes lead wires, batteries and electrotherapy skin care products The firm sells its products to more than 13,000 clinic nationwide and markets its products throughout Asia Canada and Europe. Recently, the company has release the Select TENS Pain Management System, which is a portable device that relives chronic, arthritic and post surgical pain by controlling and patterning electrical nerve stimulation. In 2006, Empi acquired Compex Technologies Inc. In May 2007, ReAble Therapeutics agreed to acquire IOMED, Inc., a leading manufacturer of drug-delivery device used for pain relief. With the successful completion of th acquisition, IOMED will be made into an operating divisio under Empi, Inc.

Empi, Inc. offers its employees a range of benefits includin medical, dental and life insurance; an employee assistance program; tuition reimbursement; flexible spending accounts career development benefits; and a 401(k) savings plan.

FINANCIALS: **Sales and profits are in thousands of dollars—add 000 to get the full amount. 2007 Note: Financial information for 2007 was not available for all companies at press time.**

2007 Sales: $	2007 Profits: $	**U.S. Stock Ticker: Subsidiary**
2006 Sales: $	2006 Profits: $	**Int'l Ticker:** Int'l Exchange:
2005 Sales: $	2005 Profits: $	Employees: 780
2004 Sales: $	2004 Profits: $	Fiscal Year Ends: 12/31
2003 Sales: $150,300	2003 Profits: $13,300	Parent Company: REABLE THERAPEUTICS INC

SALARIES/BENEFITS:

Pension Plan:	ESOP Stock Plan:	Profit Sharing:	Top Exec. Salary: $	Bonus: $
Savings Plan: Y	Stock Purch. Plan:		Second Exec. Salary: $	Bonus: $

OTHER THOUGHTS:

Apparent Women Officers or Directors: 2
Hot Spot for Advancement for Women/Minorities:

LOCATIONS: ("Y" = Yes)

West:	Southwest:	Midwest:	Southeast:	Northeast:	International:
		Y			

ENDO PHARMACEUTICALS HOLDINGS INC www.endo.com

Industry Group Code: 325412 **Ranks within this company's industry group:** Sales: 27 Profits: 26

Insurance/HMO/PPO:		Drugs:		Equipment/Supplies:		Hospitals/Clinics:		Services:		Health Care:	
Insurance:		Manufacturer:	Y	Manufacturer:		Acute Care:		Diagnostics:		Home Health:	
Managed Care:		Distributor:		Distributor:		Sub-Acute:		Labs/Testing:		Long-Term Care:	
Utilization Management:		Specialty Pharmacy:		Leasing/Finance:		Outpatient Surgery:		Staffing:		Physical Therapy:	
Payment Processing:		Vitamins/Nutritionals:		Information Systems:		Physical Rehab. Ctr.:		Waste Disposal:		Physician Prac. Mgmt.:	
		Clinical Trials:				Psychiatric Clinics:		Specialty Svcs.:			

TYPES OF BUSINESS:

Drugs-Pain Management
Pharmaceutical Preparations

BRANDS/DIVISIONS/AFFILIATES:

Endo Pharmaceuticals, Inc.
Lidoderm
Percocet
Zydone
Percodan
Ketoprofen
Frova
Synera

CONTACTS: *Note: Officers with more than one job title may be intentionally listed here more than once.*

Peter A. Lankau, CEO
Peter A. Lankau, Pres.
Charles A. Rowland Jr., CFO/Exec. VP
David A. H. Lee, Exec. VP-R&D/Chief Scientific Officer
Caroline B. Manogue, Chief Legal Officer/Corp. Sec./Exec. VP
Charles A. Rowland Jr., Treas.
Nancy J. Wysenski, COO-Endo Pharmaceuticals, Inc.
Roger H. Kimmel, Chmn.

Phone: 610-558-9800 | **Fax:** 610-558-8979
Toll-Free:
Address: 100 Endo Blvd., Chadds Ford, PA 19317 US

GROWTH PLANS/SPECIAL FEATURES:

Endo Pharmaceuticals Holdings, Inc., through subsidiary Endo Pharmaceuticals, Inc., is a specialty pharmaceutical company with market leadership in pain management. Under both generic and brand names, the company discovers, produces and markets pharmaceutical products, principally for the treatment of pain. The branded products, Percodan, Zydone, Lidoderm, Frova and Percocet, are sold to health care professionals by a dedicated force of approximately 590 sales representatives in the U.S. Percocet and Zydone are used to treat moderate to severe pain; Lidoderm is used to treat postherpetic neuralgia; and Percodan is used to treat severe pain. Endo focuses on generic products that are challenging to bring to market due to complex formulation, regulatory or legal problems or barriers in raw material sourcing. Endo has a licensing agreement with Vernalis to market Frova, an acute migraine treatment for adults. In addition, the company has come to an agreement with the FDA over its design of clinical trials for oxymorphone extended-release tablets. The company has exclusive rights to develop and market Orexo AB's patented sublingual muco-adhesive fentanyl product, Rapinyl, in North America. Endo has licensed a topical Ketoprofen patch with ProEthic Pharmaceuticals for treating inflammation and pain, currently in Phase III trials. Endo launched three products in 2006: Opana ER, Opana and Synera. In late 2006, the company purchased RxKinetix, Inc., a privately held company headquartered in Boulder, Colorado, that develops new formulations of approved products for oral mucositis and other supportive care oncology conditions.

The firm offers employees dependent care and medical spending accounts, an enhanced vacation package and an educational assistance program.

FINANCIALS: **Sales and profits are in thousands of dollars—add 000 to get the full amount. 2007 Note: Financial information for 2007 was not available for all companies at press time.**

2007 Sales: $	2007 Profits: $	**U.S. Stock Ticker: ENDP**
2006 Sales: $909,659	2006 Profits: $137,839	**Int'l Ticker:** Int'l Exchange:
2005 Sales: $820,164	2005 Profits: $202,295	Employees: 1,024
2004 Sales: $615,100	2004 Profits: $143,300	Fiscal Year Ends: 12/31
2003 Sales: $595,608	2003 Profits: $69,790	Parent Company:

SALARIES/BENEFITS:

Pension Plan:	ESOP Stock Plan:	Profit Sharing:	Top Exec. Salary: $519,500	Bonus: $
Savings Plan: Y	Stock Purch. Plan: Y		Second Exec. Salary: $404,431	Bonus: $

OTHER THOUGHTS:

Apparent Women Officers or Directors: 2
Hot Spot for Advancement for Women/Minorities:

LOCATIONS: ("Y" = Yes)

West:	Southwest:	Midwest:	Southeast:	Northeast:	International:
				Y	

Note: Financial information, benefits and other data can change quickly and may vary from those stated here.

ENVIRONMENTAL TECTONICS CORP www.etcusa.com

Industry Group Code: 339113 **Ranks within this company's industry group:** Sales: 100 Profits: 85

Insurance/HMO/PPO:		Drugs:		Equipment/Supplies:		Hospitals/Clinics:		Services:		Health Care:	
Insurance:		Manufacturer:		Manufacturer:	Y	Acute Care:		Diagnostics:		Home Health:	
Managed Care:		Distributor:		Distributor:		Sub-Acute:		Labs/Testing:		Long-Term Care:	
Utilization Management:		Specialty Pharmacy:		Leasing/Finance:		Outpatient Surgery:		Staffing:		Physical Therapy:	
Payment Processing:		Vitamins/Nutritionals:		Information Systems:		Physical Rehab. Ctr.:		Waste Disposal:		Physician Prac. Mgmt.:	
		Clinical Trials:				Psychiatric Clinics:		Specialty Svcs.:	Y		

TYPES OF BUSINESS:

Medical Equipment & Supplies Manufacturing
Flight Simulators
Decompression Chambers
Hyperbaric Chambers
Human Centrifuges
Motion-Based Simulation Amusement Rides
Steam & Gas Sterilizers
Environmental Simulation Systems

BRANDS/DIVISIONS/AFFILIATES:

National AeroSpace Training & Research Center, LLC
Advanced Disaster Management Simulator
Entertainment Technology Corporation
Wild Earth
Monster Truck
eMotion Theaters
ETC-PZL Aerospace Industries
ETC-Europe

CONTACTS: *Note: Officers with more than one job title may be intentionally listed here more than once.*

William F. Mitchell, CEO
William F. Mitchell, Pres.
Duane D. Deaner, CFO
Husnu Onus, VP-Int'l Mktg. & Sales
Dick Leland, VP-Aircrew Training Systems
Mark Compo, Sales Dir.-Sterilization Systems
Robert B. Henstenburg, Chief Eng.-High-Performance Composites
William F. Mitchell, Chmn.

Phone: 215-355-9100	**Fax:** 215-357-4000
Toll-Free:	
Address: 125 James Way, Southampton, PA 18966-3877 US	

GROWTH PLANS/SPECIAL FEATURES:

Environmental Tectonics Corp. (ETC) designs, manufactures and sells software driven products mainly used to create and monitor the physiological effects of motion on humans. ETC operates two primary business segments: Training Services Group (TSG) and Control Systems Group (CSG). TSG has three product groups. Aircrew Training is performed through its National AeroSpace Training and Research (NASTAR) Center LLC, subsidiary, established in January 2007. It offers both training and research opportunities for military jet pilots and civil aviation as well as space travel and tourism. This product group also designs, develops and manufactures pilot training devices used for medical research; advanced tactical and physiological flight training; and to indoctrinate and test military and commercial pilots. TSG's Disaster Management product group produces real-time interactive simulators to provide instruction on various disaster situations. The Advanced Disaster Management Simulator (ADMS) trains response teams and simulates emergency incidents including terrorist acts, weapons of mass destruction, hazardous material spills, road accidents and natural disasters. Entertainment Products offer motion-based simulation rides and other products through wholly-owned subsidiary Entertainment Technology Corporation (EnTCo), including the Wild Earth and Monster Truck eMotion Theaters, mainly to educational and entertainment facilities, such as zoos and amusement parks. CSG also has three product lines. CSG manufactures large, custom-designed steam and gas sterilizers, mainly for the pharmaceutical and medical device industries. Environmental Control Systems include sampling and analysis systems; and test equipment and systems. This product line is used by the automotive industry and for heating, ventilation and air conditioning (HVAC) products. Hyperbarics include single person, or monoplace, and multiple person, or multiplace, chambers with high altitude training, decompression and wound care applications. Additional subsidiaries include 95% owned ETC-PZL Aerospace Industries, manufacturing simulators; and 99% owned ETC-Europe, focusing on generating international sales. TSG provided 53% of the firm's 2007 revenue, and CSG 47%.

FINANCIALS: **Sales and profits are in thousands of dollars—add 000 to get the full amount. 2007 Note: Financial information for 2007 was not available for all companies at press time.**

2007 Sales: $17,419	2007 Profits: $-8,940	**U.S. Stock Ticker: ETC**
2006 Sales: $25,069	2006 Profits: $-6,714	**Int'l Ticker:** Int'l Exchange:
2005 Sales: $27,814	2005 Profits: $-8,113	Employees: 257
2004 Sales: $25,995	2004 Profits: $- 793	Fiscal Year Ends: 2/28
2003 Sales: $43,100	2003 Profits: $2,500	Parent Company:

SALARIES/BENEFITS:

Pension Plan:	ESOP Stock Plan:	Profit Sharing:	Top Exec. Salary: $225,000	Bonus: $
Savings Plan: Y	Stock Purch. Plan:		Second Exec. Salary: $98,000	Bonus: $6,000

OTHER THOUGHTS:

Apparent Women Officers or Directors:
Hot Spot for Advancement for Women/Minorities:

LOCATIONS: ("Y" = Yes)

West:	Southwest:	Midwest:	Southeast:	Northeast:	International:
				Y	Y

EPIC SYSTEMS CORPORATION www.epicsystems.com

Industry Group Code: 511212 **Ranks within this company's industry group:** Sales: Profits:

Insurance/HMO/PPO:		Drugs:		Equipment/Supplies:		Hospitals/Clinics:		Services:		Health Care:	
Insurance:		Manufacturer:		Manufacturer:		Acute Care:		Diagnostics:		Home Health:	
Managed Care:		Distributor:		Distributor:		Sub-Acute:		Labs/Testing:		Long-Term Care:	
Utilization Management:		Specialty Pharmacy:		Leasing/Finance:		Outpatient Surgery:		Staffing:		Physical Therapy:	
Payment Processing:		Vitamins/Nutritionals:		Information Systems:	Y	Physical Rehab. Ctr.:		Waste Disposal:		Physician Prac. Mgmt.:	
		Clinical Trials:				Psychiatric Clinics:		Specialty Svcs.:	Y		

TYPES OF BUSINESS:

Health Industry Computer Software
Information Networks
Support Services

BRANDS/DIVISIONS/AFFILIATES:

Epicenter
MyChart
MyEpic
EpicWeb
AffiliateLink
EpicCare Inpatient
Community Library Exchange

CONTACTS: *Note: Officers with more than one job title may be intentionally listed here more than once.*

Judith R. Faulkner, CEO
Terri Leigh Rhody, Dir.-Press Rel.

Phone: 608-271-9000 **Fax:** 608-271-7237
Toll-Free:
Address: 1979 Milky Way, Verona, WI 53593 US

GROWTH PLANS/SPECIAL FEATURES:

Epic Systems Corp. is a developer of health industry software, including integrated inpatient, ambulatory and payment systems. All Epic software applications are designed to share a single database, called Epicenter, so that each viewer can access all available patient data through a single interface from anywhere in the organization. The firm's products include programs for sharing medical records between affiliates, hospital and professional billing, data repository management, nursing documentation, ambulatory clinical systems, inpatient pharmacy systems, operating room management, ICU/acute care support and radiology information systems. Epic can deploy its systems with full-client workstations, thin-client devices, wireless laptops, handheld devices, the Internet, remote access servers and virtual private networks. The firm's shared medical records programs, including MyChart, MyEpic, EpicWeb and AffiliateLink, help organizations, providers, and patients improve their ability to access information and communicate with one another. The firm's inpatient clinical information system, EpicCare Inpatient, connects each member of a care team to a single record, ensuring that treatment decisions are based on the most up–to-date information and that care is well coordinated when patients are treated by multiple providers. In conjunction with its software applications, the company provides extensive client services, including training, tailoring of applications to the client's situation and access to network specialists who plan and implement the client's system. In addition, Epic hosts Community Library Exchange, an online collection of application tools and pre-made content that allows clients to share report and registration templates, custom forms, enterprise report formats and documentation shortcuts. The company has 140 clients.

The firm offers its employees health insurance; life and disability insurance; a 401(k) plan; stock appreciation rights; and flexible spending accounts.

FINANCIALS: **Sales and profits are in thousands of dollars—add 000 to get the full amount. 2007 Note: Financial information for 2007 was not available for all companies at press time.**

2007 Sales: $	2007 Profits: $	**U.S. Stock Ticker: Private**
2006 Sales: $	2006 Profits: $	**Int'l Ticker:** Int'l Exchange:
2005 Sales: $	2005 Profits: $	Employees: 36
2004 Sales: $	2004 Profits: $	Fiscal Year Ends:
2003 Sales: $15,300	2003 Profits: $	Parent Company:

SALARIES/BENEFITS:

Pension Plan:	ESOP Stock Plan:	Profit Sharing:	Top Exec. Salary: $	Bonus: $
Savings Plan: Y	Stock Purch. Plan:		Second Exec. Salary: $	Bonus: $

OTHER THOUGHTS:

Apparent Women Officers or Directors: 2
Hot Spot for Advancement for Women/Minorities:

LOCATIONS: ("Y" = Yes)

West:	Southwest:	Midwest:	Southeast:	Northeast:	International:
		Y			

ESSILOR INTERNATIONAL SA www.essilor.com

Industry Group Code: 339113 **Ranks within this company's industry group:** Sales: 9 Profits: 10

Insurance/HMO/PPO:		Drugs:		Equipment/Supplies:		Hospitals/Clinics:		Services:		Health Care:	
Insurance:		Manufacturer:		Manufacturer:	Y	Acute Care:		Diagnostics:		Home Health:	
Managed Care:		Distributor:		Distributor:	Y	Sub-Acute:		Labs/Testing:		Long-Term Care:	
Utilization Management:		Specialty Pharmacy:		Leasing/Finance:		Outpatient Surgery:		Staffing:		Physical Therapy:	
Payment Processing:		Vitamins/Nutritionals:		Information Systems:		Physical Rehab. Ctr.:		Waste Disposal:		Physician Prac. Mgmt.:	
		Clinical Trials:				Psychiatric Clinics:		Specialty Svcs.:			

TYPES OF BUSINESS:

Supplies-Ophthalmic Products
Corrective Lenses
Lens Treatments
Ophthalmic Instruments
Technical Consulting

BRANDS/DIVISIONS/AFFILIATES:

Varilux
Airwear
Essilor Anti-Fatigue
Crizal
Essilor of America, Inc.
The Spectacle Lens Group
OOGP, Inc.
Integrated Lens Technology Pte Ltd

CONTACTS: *Note: Officers with more than one job title may be intentionally listed here more than once.*

Xavier Fontanet, CEO
Philippe Alfroid, COO
Laurent Vacherot, CFO
Bertrand Roy, Corp. Sr. VP-Strategic Mktg.
Henri Vidal, Corp. Sr. VP-Human Resources
Jean-Luc Schuppiser, Corp. Sr. VP-R&D
Didier Lambert, Corp. Sr. VP-Info. Sys.
Patrick Poncin, Corp. Sr. VP-Global Eng.
Carol Xueref, Corp. Sr. VP-Legal Affairs
Claude Brignon, Corp. Sr. VP-Oper.
Carol Xueref, Corp. Sr. VP-Group Dev.
Thierry Robin, Pres., Essilor Canada
Jean Carrier-Guillomet, Pres., Essilor of America
Thomas Bayer, Pres., Essilor European Network
Bertrand de Lime, Pres., Latin America & Instruments
Xavier Fontanet, Chmn.
Hubert Sagnieres, Pres., North America & Europe

Phone: 33-1-49-77-42-24 **Fax:** 33-1-49-77-44-20
Toll-Free:
Address: 147 rue de Paris, Charenton-le-Pont, Cedex 94227 France

GROWTH PLANS/SPECIAL FEATURES:

Essilor International S.A. is a leading global designer manufacturer and distributor of ophthalmic and optica products and supplies, especially corrective lenses. The firm focuses on lens manufacturing and lens finishing in prescription laboratories. Its products treat common sigh problems, including myopia (nearsightedness), hyperopia (farsightedness), astigmatism and presbyopia (an aging related process affecting the crystalline lens). Essilor's brands include three Varilux progressive lenses (lenses tha gradually change in magnification from weak at the top, fo distance, to great at the bottom, for near object viewing) Eclipse, specially designed for small eyeglasses; Ipseo personalized to adapt to the specific head and eye movements of individual wearers; the basic Panamic fifth-generation progressive lens; and Physio, which offers strong contrast in distant vision and a wide area of clear vision a mid distances. The company also offers Airwea polycarbonate lenses that block UVA and UVB rays, Essilor Anti-Fatigue ergonomic lenses and the Crizal anti-reflective treatment. Through partnerships, Essilor also offers high-tech lenses made by Nikon, famous for its photographic equipment, and Transitions variable-tint lenses. The firm supplies its products through a global network of 244 prescription laboratories and 15 production plants, which manufactured 215 million lenses in 2006. It has 200,000 points-of-sale worldwide. Wholly-owned U.S. subsidiary Essilor of America, Inc., holds majority interests in two prescription laboratories: Jorgenson Optical Supply Company, based in Washington; and Optical One, based in Ohio. Essilor recently acquired the ophthalmic lens business of The Spectacle Lens Group, a division of Johnson and Johnson Vision Care, Inc., which developed Definity progressive lenses. In May 2007, Essilor of America acquired a majority stake in OOGP, Inc., one of the largest contact lens distributors in the U.S. In May 2007, Essilor acquired 51% of Integrated Lens Technology Pte Ltd, a distributor of ophthalmic lenses in Asia, the Middle East, Europe and Latin America.

FINANCIALS: **Sales and profits are in thousands of dollars—add 000 to get the full amount. 2007 Note: Financial information for 2007 was not available for all companies at press time.**

2007 Sales: $	2007 Profits: $	**U.S. Stock Ticker: ESLOY**
2006 Sales: $3,548,900	2006 Profits: $436,900	**Int'l Ticker: EF** Int'l Exchange: Paris-Euronext
2005 Sales: $2,886,653	2005 Profits: $	Employees: 25,900
2004 Sales: $2,623,401	2004 Profits: $309,800	Fiscal Year Ends: 12/31
2003 Sales: $2,656,500	2003 Profits: $251,500	Parent Company:

SALARIES/BENEFITS:

Pension Plan:	ESOP Stock Plan:	Profit Sharing:	Top Exec. Salary: $	Bonus: $
Savings Plan:	Stock Purch. Plan:		Second Exec. Salary: $	Bonus: $

OTHER THOUGHTS:

Apparent Women Officers or Directors:
Hot Spot for Advancement for Women/Minorities: Y

LOCATIONS: ("Y" = Yes)

West:	Southwest:	Midwest:	Southeast:	Northeast:	International:
Y	Y	Y	Y	Y	Y

ETHICON INC

www.ethiconinc.com

Industry Group Code: 339113 **Ranks within this company's industry group:** Sales: Profits:

Insurance/HMO/PPO:		Drugs:		Equipment/Supplies:		Hospitals/Clinics:		Services:		Health Care:	
Insurance:		Manufacturer:		Manufacturer:	Y	Acute Care:		Diagnostics:		Home Health:	
Managed Care:		Distributor:		Distributor:	Y	Sub-Acute:		Labs/Testing:		Long-Term Care:	
Utilization Management:		Specialty Pharmacy:		Leasing/Finance:		Outpatient Surgery:		Staffing:		Physical Therapy:	
Payment Processing:		Vitamins/Nutritionals:		Information Systems:		Physical Rehab. Ctr.:		Waste Disposal:		Physician Prac. Mgmt.:	
		Clinical Trials:				Psychiatric Clinics:		Specialty Svcs.:			

TYPES OF BUSINESS:

Medical Equipment & Supplies
Sutures, Surgical Mesh, Needles & Skin Adhesives
Wound Management Products
Burn & Skin Care Products
Women's Health Surgical Products
Cardiovascular Surgery Products

BRANDS/DIVISIONS/AFFILIATES:

Johnson & Johnson
ETHICON Women's Health & Urology
CARDIOVATIONS
Johnson & Johnson Wound Management
ETHICON Products
Advanced Wound Care
Surgical Wound Care
PORT ACCESS

CONTACTS: *Note: Officers with more than one job title may be intentionally listed here more than once.*

Gary Pruden, Worldwide Pres., ETHICON Products
Rene Selman, Worldwide Pres., ETHICON Women's Health & Urology
Dan Wildman, Worldwide Pres., Johnson & Johnson Wound Mgmt.
Dennis Longstreet, Company Group Chmn.

Phone: 908-218-0707 **Fax:** 908-218-2471
Toll-Free: 800-255-2500
Address: Rte. 22, Box 151, Somerville, NJ 08876 US

GROWTH PLANS/SPECIAL FEATURES:

ETHICON, Inc., a Johnson & Johnson subsidiary, markets women's health, wound management and cardiovascular surgery products in 52 countries around the world. The company has four business units: ETHICON Women's Health and Urology, selling products under the GYNECARE brand; CARDIOVATIONS, which manufactures surgical devices for the treatment of cardiovascular diseases; Johnson & Johnson Wound Management (WM), which sells burn and skin care products; and ETHICON Products (EP), a manufacturer of wound closure and cardiovascular surgery products. The ETHICON Women's Health and Urology unit offers a variety of products for enlarged prostate, female stress urinary incontinence, pelvic floor repair, post-surgical adhesions, heavy periods and benign uterine conditions, such as fibroids and polyps. CARDIOVATIONS products include the PORT ACCESS valve repair surgery line, which assists mitral valve repair surgery by creating small incisions in the chest to cause faster recovery and to lessen cosmetic damage; and the EMBRACE Beating Heart Stabilization System, which eliminates the need for a cardiopulmonary bypass during bypass surgery. The Wound Management division is divided into two sections: Advanced Wound Care, which produces REGRANEX Gel, a substance that helps in the complete healing of diabetic ulcers; and Surgical Wound Care, which produces a variety of products, including the Endoscopic Applicator, the Surgical NU-KNIT and SURGIFOAM Absorbable Gelatin Powder. In addition, it sells traditional wound care products, such as sponges, bandages, dressings, transparent films and tapes, as well as hemostasis products, which are used by surgeons to control mild to moderate bleeding. The ETHICON Products division manufactures and sells products for wound closure and cardiovascular surgery, including sutures, topical adhesives, surgical meshes and wound drains.

ETHICON offers its employees benefits that include medical and dental healthcare coverage, life and accident insurance, a 401(k) plan, a retirement plan and tuition assistance.

FINANCIALS: **Sales and profits are in thousands of dollars—add 000 to get the full amount. 2007 Note: Financial information for 2007 was not available for all companies at press time.**

2007 Sales: $	2007 Profits: $	**U.S. Stock Ticker: Subsidiary**
2006 Sales: $	2006 Profits: $	**Int'l Ticker:** Int'l Exchange:
2005 Sales: $	2005 Profits: $	Employees: 11,000
2004 Sales: $	2004 Profits: $	Fiscal Year Ends: 12/31
2003 Sales: $	2003 Profits: $	Parent Company: JOHNSON & JOHNSON

SALARIES/BENEFITS:

Pension Plan: Y	ESOP Stock Plan:	Profit Sharing:	Top Exec. Salary: $	Bonus: $
Savings Plan: Y	Stock Purch. Plan:		Second Exec. Salary: $	Bonus: $

OTHER THOUGHTS:

Apparent Women Officers or Directors: 1
Hot Spot for Advancement for Women/Minorities:

LOCATIONS: ("Y" = Yes)

West:	Southwest:	Midwest:	Southeast:	Northeast:	International:
	Y		Y	Y	

Note: Financial information, benefits and other data can change quickly and may vary from those stated here.

EXACTECH INC

www.exac.com

Industry Group Code: 339113 **Ranks within this company's industry group:** Sales: 77 Profits: 66

Insurance/HMO/PPO:		Drugs:		Equipment/Supplies:		Hospitals/Clinics:		Services:		Health Care:	
Insurance:		Manufacturer:		Manufacturer:	Y	Acute Care:		Diagnostics:		Home Health:	
Managed Care:		Distributor:		Distributor:	Y	Sub-Acute:		Labs/Testing:		Long-Term Care:	
Utilization Management:		Specialty Pharmacy:		Leasing/Finance:		Outpatient Surgery:		Staffing:		Physical Therapy:	
Payment Processing:		Vitamins/Nutritionals:		Information Systems:		Physical Rehab. Ctr.:		Waste Disposal:		Physician Prac. Mgmt.:	
		Clinical Trials:				Psychiatric Clinics:		Specialty Svcs.:			

TYPES OF BUSINESS:

Equipment-Joint Replacement
Orthopedic Implant Devices
Surgical Instruments
Biologic Products
Bone Fusion Materials

BRANDS/DIVISIONS/AFFILIATES:

Optetrak
AcuMatch
Link Saddle Prosthesis
Opteform
Optefil
Cemex
AcuDriver Automated Osteotome System
Saddle

CONTACTS: *Note: Officers with more than one job title may be intentionally listed here more than once.*

William Petty, CEO
William Petty, Pres.
Joel C. Phillips, CFO
David W. Petty, Exec. VP-Mktg. & Sales
Betty B. Petty, VP-Human Resources
Gary J. Miller, Exec. VP-R&D
Betty B. Petty, VP-Admin.
Betty B. Petty, Corp. Sec.
Joel C. Phillips, Treas.
William Petty, Chmn.

Phone: 352-377-1140	**Fax:** 352-378-2617
Toll-Free: 800-392-2832	
Address: 4613 NW 6th St., Gainesville, FL 32609 US	

GROWTH PLANS/SPECIAL FEATURES:

Exactech, Inc. develops, manufactures, distributes and sells orthopedic implant devices, related surgical instrumentation and materials and biologic materials to hospitals and physicians in the U.S. and internationally. The company's orthopedic implant products are used to repair or replace joints that have deteriorated as a result of injury or disease. These products include Optetrak, a knee replacement system, and the AcuMatch integrated hip system with the C-Series cemented femoral stem, the A-series acetabular components for the hip socket, the P-series press-fit femoral stem, the M-Series modular femoral stem, the L-Series femoral stem system, bipolar and unipolar partial hip replacement components, a variety of femoral heads and a cemented acetabular component. Other hip implant products include the Link Saddle Prosthesis, which supports unreconstructable pelvic regions, the Link SPII hip stem and the Link Partial Pelvis. Biologic allograft materials, such as Exactech's Opteform and Optefil, are used by surgeons to repair bone defects and provide an interface to stimulate new bone growth. The company also offers Cemex, a bone cement system, and the AcuDriver Automated Osteotome System, an air-driven impact hand piece used by surgeons during joint implant revision procedures to remove failed prostheses and bone cement. Exactech's oncology products include the Link MP, Partial Pelvis, Saddle Prosthesis, Total Femur and the M-series Modular Femoral Stem for hip implant devices; along with the Link Endo-Model Modular Rotating Hinge and the Total Femor joint knee systems. In late 2006 the company completed a clinical evaluation of the Accelerate Platelet Concentration System, and it plans to introduce Accelerate in early 2007 as a means of extracting autologous growth factors and fibronigen from patients' own blood to improve the healing quality of joints and tissue following orthopedic procedures.

FINANCIALS: **Sales and profits are in thousands of dollars—add 000 to get the full amount. 2007 Note: Financial information for 2007 was not available for all companies at press time.**

2007 Sales: $	2007 Profits: $	**U.S. Stock Ticker: EXAC**
2006 Sales: $102,430	2006 Profits: $7,752	**Int'l Ticker:** Int'l Exchange:
2005 Sales: $91,016	2005 Profits: $6,604	Employees: 215
2004 Sales: $81,815	2004 Profits: $7,304	Fiscal Year Ends: 12/31
2003 Sales: $71,255	2003 Profits: $6,501	Parent Company:

SALARIES/BENEFITS:

Pension Plan:	ESOP Stock Plan:	Profit Sharing:	Top Exec. Salary: $364,816	Bonus: $221,503
Savings Plan: Y	Stock Purch. Plan: Y		Second Exec. Salary: $293,805	Bonus: $44,785

OTHER THOUGHTS:

Apparent Women Officers or Directors: 1
Hot Spot for Advancement for Women/Minorities:

LOCATIONS: ("Y" = Yes)

West:	Southwest:	Midwest:	Southeast:	Northeast:	International:
			Y	Y	Y

EXCEL TECHNOLOGY INC www.exceltechinc.com

Industry Group Code: 339113 **Ranks within this company's industry group:** Sales: 68 Profits: 57

Insurance/HMO/PPO:		Drugs:		Equipment/Supplies:		Hospitals/Clinics:		Services:		Health Care:	
Insurance:		Manufacturer:		Manufacturer:	Y	Acute Care:		Diagnostics:		Home Health:	
Managed Care:		Distributor:		Distributor:		Sub-Acute:		Labs/Testing:		Long-Term Care:	
Utilization Management:		Specialty Pharmacy:		Leasing/Finance:		Outpatient Surgery:		Staffing:		Physical Therapy:	
Payment Processing:		Vitamins/Nutritionals:		Information Systems:		Physical Rehab. Ctr.:		Waste Disposal:		Physician Prac. Mgmt.:	
		Clinical Trials:				Psychiatric Clinics:		Specialty Svcs.:			

TYPES OF BUSINESS:

Equipment-Electro-Optical Components & Laser Systems
Optical Scanning Equipment
Photomask Repair Systems
Scientific & Industrial Lasers
Medical Lasers-Skin & Eye Treatment

BRANDS/DIVISIONS/AFFILIATES:

Control Systemation, Inc.
Baublys
Control Laser
Synrad
Cambridge Technology
Quantronix
Photo Research

CONTACTS: *Note: Officers with more than one job title may be intentionally listed here more than once.*

Antoine Dominic, CEO
Antoine Dominic, COO
Antoine Dominic, Pres.
Alice Varisano, CFO/Sec.
Greg Anderson, Pres., Control Systemation, Inc.
Redmond P. Aylward, Pres., Cambridge Tech., Inc.
Laurence E. Cramer, Pres., Continuum Electro-Optics, Inc.
Dave Clarke, Pres., Synrad, Inc.
J. Donald Hill, Chmn.
Reinhard Baumert, Pres., Excel Tech. Europe GmbH

Phone: 631-784-6175 **Fax:** 631-784-6195
Toll-Free:
Address: 41 Research Way, East Setauket, NY 11733 US

GROWTH PLANS/SPECIAL FEATURES:

Excel Technology, Inc. designs, develops, manufactures and markets laser systems and electro-optical components for industry, science and medicine. The company's many subsidiaries include Control Systemation, Inc., which focuses on turnkey laser based micro-machining systems and part-handling workstations for factory automation. In recent years, Excel consolidated the product lines and development efforts of subsidiaries Baublys and Control Laser to eliminate duplicative products and efforts, to increase efficiency and to create a unified market presence for the firm's laser marking and engraving operations. Current products and applications include Baublys-Control Laser marking and engraving systems; Synrad carbon dioxide lasers; Cambridge scanners; Quantronix photomask repair systems and scientific and industrial solid-state lasers; TOC optical products; and Photo Research light and color measurement products. Excel's Cambridge Technology subsidiary provides beam steering scanner-based applications, servicing a growing number of laser-based medical applications. These include digital radiography, skin resurfacing and eye treatment. Through its subsidiary Continuum, Excel develops, manufactures and markets pulsed lasers and related accessories for the scientific and commercial marketplaces. Excel Europe, the company's European subsidiary, buys laser systems, spare parts and related consumable materials from Quantronix, Baublys-Control Laser and Synrad for resale to European and other foreign customers, as well as providing field repair services. Excel Japan, the firm's Japanese subsidiary, focuses on marketing, selling, distributing, integrating and servicing Quantronix and Continuum products in Japan.

FINANCIALS: Sales and profits are in thousands of dollars—add 000 to get the full amount. 2007 Note: Financial information for 2007 was not available for all companies at press time.

2007 Sales: $ | 2007 Profits: $
2006 Sales: $154,496 | 2006 Profits: $14,019
2005 Sales: $137,717 | 2005 Profits: $15,208
2004 Sales: $136,631 | 2004 Profits: $14,762
2003 Sales: $122,681 | 2003 Profits: $11,318

U.S. Stock Ticker: XLTC
Int'l Ticker: Int'l Exchange:
Employees: 704
Fiscal Year Ends: 12/31
Parent Company:

SALARIES/BENEFITS:

Pension Plan: | ESOP Stock Plan: | Profit Sharing: | Top Exec. Salary: $542,000 | Bonus: $1,153,764
Savings Plan: Y | Stock Purch. Plan: Y | | Second Exec. Salary: $275,000 | Bonus: $65,200

OTHER THOUGHTS:

Apparent Women Officers or Directors: 1
Hot Spot for Advancement for Women/Minorities:

LOCATIONS: ("Y" = Yes)

West:	Southwest:	Midwest:	Southeast:	Northeast:	International:
Y			Y	Y	Y

EXPRESS SCRIPTS INC www.express-scripts.com

Industry Group Code: 522320A **Ranks within this company's industry group:** Sales: 3 Profits: 3

Insurance/HMO/PPO:		Drugs:		Equipment/Supplies:		Hospitals/Clinics:		Services:		Health Care:	
Insurance:		Manufacturer:		Manufacturer:		Acute Care:		Diagnostics:		Home Health:	
Managed Care:		Distributor:		Distributor:		Sub-Acute:		Labs/Testing:		Long-Term Care:	
Utilization Management:	Y	Specialty Pharmacy:	Y	Leasing/Finance:		Outpatient Surgery:		Staffing:		Physical Therapy:	
Payment Processing:	Y	Vitamins/Nutritionals:		Information Systems:		Physical Rehab. Ctr.:		Waste Disposal:		Physician Prac. Mgmt.:	
		Clinical Trials:				Psychiatric Clinics:		Specialty Svcs.:	Y		

TYPES OF BUSINESS:

Pharmacy Benefits Management
Mail & Internet Pharmacies
Formulary Management
Integrated Drug & Medical Data Analysis
Market Research Programs
Medical Information Management
Workers' Compensation Programs
Informed-Decision Counseling

BRANDS/DIVISIONS/AFFILIATES:

CuraScript
Priority Healthcare Corporation

CONTACTS: *Note: Officers with more than one job title may be intentionally listed here more than once.*

George Paz, CEO
David A. Lowenberg, COO
George Paz, Pres.
Edward J. Stiften, CFO/Sr. VP
George Paz, Chmn.

Phone: 314-770-1666 **Fax:** 314-702-7037
Toll-Free:
Address: 13900 Riverport Dr., Maryland Heights, MO 63043 US

GROWTH PLANS/SPECIAL FEATURES:

Express Scripts, Inc. is one of the nation's larges independent pharmacy benefit managers, providin pharmacy service and pharmacy benefit plan desig consultation for clients including HMOs, unions an government health care plans. The company's core service include pharmacy network management, mail and Intern pharmacies, formulary management, targeted clinica programs, integrated drug and medical data analysis, marke research programs, medical information management workers' compensation programs and informed-decisio counseling. Express Scripts provides progressive healt care management by leveraging expertise in pharmac benefit management (PBM) in order to positively impac clients' total health care benefits. The firm combine pharmacy and medical claims data to develop new strategie for decreasing total health care spending and improvin health outcomes. The PBM business provides manage prescription drug services to members in the U.S. an Canada. Health Management Services, a subsidiary provides comprehensive demand and disease managemen support services through a 24-hour call center staffed b registered nurses and pharmacists. Through pharmac network management, Express Scripts contracts with retai pharmacies to provide prescription drugs to members of th pharmacy benefit plans it manages. Express Scripts als provides a number of Internet-based services, includin disease tracking, consumer prescription drug information an electronic claims processing. The company has over 59,20 participating pharmacies nationwide, and fills over 43 million prescriptions a year.

FINANCIALS: **Sales and profits are in thousands of dollars—add 000 to get the full amount. 2007 Note: Financial information for 2007 was not available for all companies at press time.**

2007 Sales: $	2007 Profits: $	**U.S. Stock Ticker: ESRX**
2006 Sales: $17,660,000	2006 Profits: $474,400	**Int'l Ticker:** Int'l Exchange:
2005 Sales: $16,212,000	2005 Profits: $400,100	Employees: 11,300
2004 Sales: $15,114,700	2004 Profits: $278,200	Fiscal Year Ends: 12/31
2003 Sales: $13,294,517	2003 Profits: $249,600	Parent Company:

SALARIES/BENEFITS:

Pension Plan:	ESOP Stock Plan:	Profit Sharing:	Top Exec. Salary: $625,000	Bonus: $1,200,500
Savings Plan: Y	Stock Purch. Plan: Y		Second Exec. Salary: $456,750	Bonus: $649,600

OTHER THOUGHTS:

Apparent Women Officers or Directors:
Hot Spot for Advancement for Women/Minorities:

LOCATIONS: ("Y" = Yes)

West:	Southwest:	Midwest:	Southeast:	Northeast:	International:
Y	Y	Y	Y	Y	Y

EXTENDICARE REAL ESTATE INVESTMENT TRUST

www.extendicare.com

Industry Group Code: 623110 **Ranks within this company's industry group:** Sales: 3 Profits:

Insurance/HMO/PPO:		Drugs:		Equipment/Supplies:		Hospitals/Clinics:		Services:		Health Care:	
Insurance:		Manufacturer:		Manufacturer:		Acute Care:		Diagnostics:		Home Health:	Y
Managed Care:		Distributor:		Distributor:		Sub-Acute:	Y	Labs/Testing:		Long-Term Care:	Y
Utilization Management:		Specialty Pharmacy:		Leasing/Finance:		Outpatient Surgery:		Staffing:		Physical Therapy:	
Payment Processing:		Vitamins/Nutritionals:		Information Systems:		Physical Rehab. Ctr.:	Y	Waste Disposal:		Physician Prac. Mgmt.:	
		Clinical Trials:				Psychiatric Clinics:		Specialty Svcs.:			

TYPES OF BUSINESS:

Long-Term Care
Assisted Living Facilities
Sub-Acute Care
Rehabilitative Services

BRANDS/DIVISIONS/AFFILIATES:

Extendicare Health Services, Inc.
Assisted Living Concepts, Inc.
Extendicare REIT

CONTACTS: *Note: Officers with more than one job title may be intentionally listed here more than once.*

Philip W. Small, CEO
Philip W. Small, Pres.
Douglas J. Harris, Interim CFO
Jillian E. Fountain, Corp. Sec.
Frederick B. Ladly, Chmn.

Phone: 905-470-4000	**Fax:** 905-470-4003
Toll-Free:	
Address: 3000 Steeles Ave. E., Markham, ON L3R 9W2 Canada	

GROWTH PLANS/SPECIAL FEATURES:

Extendicare Real Estate Investment Trust, formerly Extendicare Inc., is a Canadian real estate investment trust (REIT) operating long-term care facilities and related services. Through its subsidiaries it operates 235 long-term care and assisted living facilities across North America, with capacity for over 26,800 residents. Through its operations in the U.S., Extendicare offers medical specialty services such as sub-acute care and rehabilitative therapy services, while home health care services are provided in Canada. All of these facilities are operated through two operating subsidiaries: Extendicare Health Services, Inc. (EHSI), based in the U.S., and Extendicare Canada Inc., based in Canada. EHSI offers, in addition to standard nursing and assistance, specialty care services such as subacute care and rehabilitative therapy services through ProStep, the company's progressive step rehabilitation service. The company also offers information technology services to small long-term care providers through Virtual Care Provider, Inc. in order to help care providers reduce their in-house technology costs. In Canada, EI offers ParaMed, which provides home health care services to subscribers. In addition to these subsidiaries and products, the firm offers management and consulting services and group supply purchasing services for third-party customers. The company has recently concluded a corporate restructuring which included separating its U.S.-based assisted living business Assisted Living Concepts, Inc. that subsequently went public. In 2007, the company sold its interest in Crown Life Insurance Company to Canada Life Insurance Company.

FINANCIALS: **Sales and profits are in thousands of dollars—add 000 to get the full amount. 2007 Note: Financial information for 2007 was not available for all companies at press time.**

2007 Sales: $	2007 Profits: $	**U.S. Stock Ticker:**
2006 Sales: $1,650,696	2006 Profits: $	**Int'l Ticker: EXE** Int'l Exchange: Toronto-TSX
2005 Sales: $1,698,634	2005 Profits: $81,930	Employees: 37,600
2004 Sales: $1,471,505	2004 Profits: $107,857	Fiscal Year Ends: 12/31
2003 Sales: $1,338,800	2003 Profits: $47,100	Parent Company:

SALARIES/BENEFITS:

Pension Plan:	ESOP Stock Plan:	Profit Sharing:	Top Exec. Salary: $	Bonus: $
Savings Plan:	Stock Purch. Plan:		Second Exec. Salary: $	Bonus: $

OTHER THOUGHTS:

Apparent Women Officers or Directors: 1
Hot Spot for Advancement for Women/Minorities:

LOCATIONS: ("Y" = Yes)

West:	Southwest:	Midwest:	Southeast:	Northeast:	International:
Y	Y	Y	Y	Y	Y

EYEMED VISION CARE LLC www.eyemedvisioncare.com

Industry Group Code: 524114A **Ranks within this company's industry group:** Sales: Profits:

Insurance/HMO/PPO:		Drugs:		Equipment/Supplies:		Hospitals/Clinics:		Services:		Health Care:	
Insurance:	Y	Manufacturer:		Manufacturer:		Acute Care:		Diagnostics:		Home Health:	
Managed Care:		Distributor:		Distributor:		Sub-Acute:		Labs/Testing:		Long-Term Care:	
Utilization Management:		Specialty Pharmacy:		Leasing/Finance:		Outpatient Surgery:		Staffing:		Physical Therapy:	
Payment Processing:		Vitamins/Nutritionals:		Information Systems:		Physical Rehab. Ctr.:		Waste Disposal:		Physician Prac. Mgmt.:	
		Clinical Trials:				Psychiatric Clinics:		Specialty Svcs.:	Y		

TYPES OF BUSINESS:

Vision Plans

BRANDS/DIVISIONS/AFFILIATES:

Luxottica Group SPA
LensCrafters
WiseEyes
Pearle Vision
Private Practitioners
EyeMed Access
Sears Optical
Target Optical

CONTACTS: *Note: Officers with more than one job title may be intentionally listed here more than once.*

Kerry Bradley, COO
Jack Dennis, CFO
Jack Dennis, Chief Admin. Officer

Phone: 513-765-6000	**Fax:** 513-765-6388
Toll-Free:	
Address: 4000 Luxottica Pl., Mason, OH 45040 US	

GROWTH PLANS/SPECIAL FEATURES:

EyeMed Vision Care, LLC, a subsidiary of Italian eyewear designer Luxottica Group S.p.A., administers vision care plans that serve over 120 million unique members in the U.S. The firm's nationwide network of providers is composed of private optometrists, ophthalmologists and opticians. In addition, EyeMed's sister company, LensCrafters, is a nationwide optical retailer. The company's optical network also includes Private Practitioners, JC Penney Optical, Target Optical, Pearle Vision and Sears Optical. The company has a myriad of vision care plans. EyeMed Access E is a materials only plan. EyeMed Access D is a discount-only plan for exams, frames, lenses, lens options, contact lenses, laser surgery and accessories at an unlimited frequency. The EyeMed Access C plan provides for a fully funded exam benefit at a designated frequency and scheduled discounts for materials such as frames, lenses and contact lenses at an unlimited frequency. The EyeMed Access B plan offers fully funded exams and materials. EyeMed Access A provides for a fully funded exam, contact lens fit and follow-up and materials. The company also provides access to LCA-Vision, a laser vision correction network in the U.S. Most EyeMed plans offer a discount on LASIK or PRK procedures at LCA-Vision providers. EyeMed is able to offer customers affordable pricing because of its corporate ties to Luxottica Group, a worldwide frame manufacturer, and its company-owned optical retailers such as LensCrafters and Pearle Vision. EyeMed's website allows customers to access providers and benefit information online, while its automated WiseEyes interactive voice response system offers customer service. In addition, EyeMed offers customer service hours that extend to the weekend and into evenings.

FINANCIALS: **Sales and profits are in thousands of dollars—add 000 to get the full amount. 2007 Note: Financial information for 2007 was not available for all companies at press time.**

2007 Sales: $	2007 Profits: $	**U.S. Stock Ticker: Subsidiary**
2006 Sales: $	2006 Profits: $	**Int'l Ticker:** Int'l Exchange:
2005 Sales: $	2005 Profits: $	Employees:
2004 Sales: $	2004 Profits: $	Fiscal Year Ends: 12/31
2003 Sales: $	2003 Profits: $	Parent Company: LUXOTTICA GROUP SPA

SALARIES/BENEFITS:

Pension Plan:	ESOP Stock Plan:	Profit Sharing:	Top Exec. Salary: $	Bonus: $
Savings Plan:	Stock Purch. Plan:		Second Exec. Salary: $	Bonus: $

OTHER THOUGHTS:

Apparent Women Officers or Directors:
Hot Spot for Advancement for Women/Minorities:

LOCATIONS: ("Y" = Yes)

West:	Southwest:	Midwest:	Southeast:	Northeast:	International:
		Y			

E-Z-EM INC

www.ezem.com

Industry Group Code: 325413 **Ranks within this company's industry group:** Sales: 5 Profits: 5

Insurance/HMO/PPO:		Drugs:		Equipment/Supplies:		Hospitals/Clinics:		Services:		Health Care:	
Insurance:		Manufacturer:	Y	Manufacturer:	Y	Acute Care:		Diagnostics:		Home Health:	
Managed Care:		Distributor:		Distributor:		Sub-Acute:		Labs/Testing:		Long-Term Care:	
Utilization Management:		Specialty Pharmacy:		Leasing/Finance:		Outpatient Surgery:		Staffing:		Physical Therapy:	
Payment Processing:		Vitamins/Nutritionals:		Information Systems:		Physical Rehab. Ctr.:		Waste Disposal:		Physician Prac. Mgmt.:	
		Clinical Trials:				Psychiatric Clinics:		Specialty Svcs.:			

TYPES OF BUSINESS:

Medical Diagnostics Products
Virtual Colonoscopy Products
Diagnostic Contrast Media
Diagnostic Radiology Devices
Custom Pharmaceuticals
Gastrointestinal Diagnostic Products
Decontaminant Lotions

BRANDS/DIVISIONS/AFFILIATES:

NutraPrep
CT Smoothies
Readi-CAT
Varibar
innerviewGI
Reactive Skin Decontaminant Lotion (RSDL)
EmpowerSync

CONTACTS: *Note: Officers with more than one job title may be intentionally listed here more than once.*

Anthony A. Lombardo, CEO
Anthony A. Lombardo, Pres.
Joseph Cacchioli, Acting CFO
Peter J. Graham, Head-Human Resources
Jeffrey S. Peacock, Sr. VP-Global Scientific
Jeffrey S. Peacock, Sr. VP-Tech. Oper.
Peter J. Graham, General Counsel/VP/Sec.
Joseph J. Palma, Sr. VP-Corp. Rel.
Brad S. Schreck, Sr. VP-Global Mktg. Eng.
Paul S. Echenberg, Chmn.

Phone: 516-333-8230 **Fax:** 516-333-8278
Toll-Free: 800-544-4624
Address: 1111 Marcus Ave., Ste. LL26, Lake Success, NY 11042 US

GROWTH PLANS/SPECIAL FEATURES:

E-Z-EM, Inc. develops, manufactures and markets diagnostic products used by physicians during image-assisted procedures to detect anatomic abnormalities and diseases. Its products and services are designed for use in the radiology, gastroenterology, speech pathology and virtual colonoscopy industries for colorectal cancer screening and testing for other gastrointestinal disorders. E-Z-EM's products coat portions of the throat or digestive tract to help targeted systems appear under imaging systems such as X-ray fluoroscopy and CT imaging. The company's lead products include CT Smoothies, Readi-CAT contrast products, NutraPrep low residue pre-procedural foods, the Varibar line of swallowing evaluation agents, CT injector systems and the innerviewGI hardware and software system for conducting virtual colonoscopy. E-Z-EM provides contract manufacturing in the areas of diagnostic contrast media, pharmaceuticals and cosmetics. In November 2006, the Food and Drug Administration approved E-Z-EM's EmpowerSync system—a product based on the CAN-CiA (Controller Area Network-CAN in Automation) DSP 425 protocol. EmpowerSync permits synchronized operation of EmpowerCT and EmpowerCTA injector systems and CT scanners from all of the manufacturers who also adopt the DSP 425 standard. The company is currently working with O'Dell Engineering Ltd. to commercialize a product line of Reactive Skin Decontaminant Lotions (RSDL) for neutralizing chemical warfare agents. These RSDL products are in use in the armed forces of Canada, Australia, Ireland and the Netherlands. In April 2007, the U.S. Army Space & Missile Defense Command (USASMD) placed a $5 million procurement order for E-Z-EM's RSDL personal skin decontamination product. Recently, RSDL received Milestone C approval from the Joint Program Executive Office for Chemical Biological Defense (JPEO-CBD), clearing the way for procurement by the individual service branches of the DoD.

E-Z-EM offers its employees medical, dental, life and travel insurance; long term disability; a 401(k); a stock purchase plan; employee training and development programs; tuition reimbursement; and flexible spending accounts.

FINANCIALS: **Sales and profits are in thousands of dollars—add 000 to get the full amount. 2007 Note: Financial information for 2007 was not available for all companies at press time.**

2007 Sales: $137,840	2007 Profits: $8,543	**U.S. Stock Ticker: EZEM**
2006 Sales: $137,083	2006 Profits: $9,766	**Int'l Ticker:** Int'l Exchange:
2005 Sales: $111,700	2005 Profits: $6,936	Employees: 590
2004 Sales: $148,771	2004 Profits: $6,726	Fiscal Year Ends: 5/31
2003 Sales: $133,200	2003 Profits: $2,700	Parent Company:

SALARIES/BENEFITS:

Pension Plan:	ESOP Stock Plan:	Profit Sharing: Y	Top Exec. Salary: $350,784	Bonus: $249,769
Savings Plan: Y	Stock Purch. Plan: Y		Second Exec. Salary: $224,591	Bonus: $101,610

OTHER THOUGHTS:

Apparent Women Officers or Directors:
Hot Spot for Advancement for Women/Minorities:

LOCATIONS: ("Y" = Yes)

West:	Southwest:	Midwest:	Southeast:	Northeast:	International:
				Y	Y

Note: Financial information, benefits and other data can change quickly and may vary from those stated here.

FAIRVIEW HEALTH SERVICES www.fairview.org

Industry Group Code: 622110 **Ranks within this company's industry group:** Sales: 24 Profits: 19

Insurance/HMO/PPO:		Drugs:		Equipment/Supplies:		Hospitals/Clinics:		Services:		Health Care:	
Insurance:		Manufacturer:		Manufacturer:		Acute Care:	Y	Diagnostics:	Y	Home Health:	Y
Managed Care:		Distributor:		Distributor:		Sub-Acute:	Y	Labs/Testing:	Y	Long-Term Care:	Y
Utilization Management:		Specialty Pharmacy:		Leasing/Finance:		Outpatient Surgery:	Y	Staffing:		Physical Therapy:	Y
Payment Processing:		Vitamins/Nutritionals:		Information Systems:		Physical Rehab. Ctr.:	Y	Waste Disposal:		Physician Prac. Mgmt.:	
		Clinical Trials:				Psychiatric Clinics:	Y	Specialty Svcs.:	Y		

TYPES OF BUSINESS:

Hospitals
Specialty Clinics
Home Care
Hospice Services
Children's Services
Cancer Care
Senior Care
Academic Teaching Hospital

BRANDS/DIVISIONS/AFFILIATES:

Ebenezer
Minnesota Heart & Vascular Center
Southdale Heart, Stroke and Vascular Center
Minnesota Cystic Fibrosis Center
National Institute on Media and the Family
Robert Wood Johnson Foundation
Palliative Care Leadership Center

CONTACTS: *Note: Officers with more than one job title may be intentionally listed here more than once.*

Mark A. Eustis, CEO
Gary J. Strong, COO
Mark A. Eustis, Pres.
James M. Fox, CFO/Sr. VP
Diane Iorfida, Sr. VP-Human Resources
George Chresand, General Counsel/Sr. VP
Lois A. Lenarz, Sr. VP/Chief Clinical Officer
Alison Page, Chief Safety Officer
Mary C. Edwards, VP-Public Policy
Kent Eklund, Pres., Fairview Foundation
Rodney Burwell, Chmn.

Phone: 612-672-6000	**Fax:** 612-672-7186
Toll-Free: 866-871-5627	
Address: 2450 Riverside Ave., Minneapolis, MN 55454 US	

GROWTH PLANS/SPECIAL FEATURES:

Fairview Health Services, founded in 1906, is one of the top integrated health networks in the Midwest, serving the Twin Cities area and suburbs, the Minnesota Valley and the Red Wing, Northland, Lakes and Range areas of Minnesota. The system contains seven hospitals with over 2,500 beds, including six community hospitals, 36 primary care facilities, 55 specialty clinics, the region's most comprehensive children's hospital, home care and hospice services, rehabilitation services and inpatient and retail pharmacies. Through its subsidiary Ebenezer, Fairview provides senior housing facilities including apartments, assisted living complexes, cooperatives, condominiums, a memory care facility for patients living with Alzheimer's or other early-stage dementias and adult and intergenerational daycare programs. The company is home to Fairview Southdale Heart, Stroke and Vascular Center, the Minnesota Cystic Fibrosis Center, Fairview's National Institute on Media and the Family and a Robert Wood Johnson Foundation-designated Palliative Care Leadership Center. The Fairview Foundation is the group's funding entity for operations, special projects, programs, allocations and endowments. Fairview has entered into a partnership with several other health care groups to build a new full service hospital and health care campus in Maple Grove, Minnesota. The 120-bed hospital is expected to open in 2007 and will offer a wide variety of services, including obstetrics, senior care, cancer care and mental health services.

Fairview offers its employees an employee assistance program, an employee NurseLine, employee wellness services, health coaches, disease management services, spiritual health services, smoking cessation services, weight management services, health club discounts, a 529 college savings plan, adoption assistance, day care assistance, onsite continuing education programs, transfer opportunities, tuition reimbursement, educational initiatives, over 100 annual scholarship opportunities, Sallie Mae partnership and medical mission grants.

FINANCIALS: **Sales and profits are in thousands of dollars—add 000 to get the full amount. 2007 Note: Financial information for 2007 was not available for all companies at press time.**

2007 Sales: $
2006 Sales: $2,114,710
2005 Sales: $1,982,778
2004 Sales: $1,793,733
2003 Sales: $1,681,760

2007 Profits: $
2006 Profits: $35,415
2005 Profits: $66,323
2004 Profits: $50,641
2003 Profits: $

U.S. Stock Ticker: Nonprofit
Int'l Ticker: Int'l Exchange:
Employees: 20,233
Fiscal Year Ends: 12/31
Parent Company:

SALARIES/BENEFITS:

Pension Plan: Y	ESOP Stock Plan:	Profit Sharing:	Top Exec. Salary: $	Bonus: $
Savings Plan: Y	Stock Purch. Plan:		Second Exec. Salary: $	Bonus: $

OTHER THOUGHTS:

Apparent Women Officers or Directors: 4
Hot Spot for Advancement for Women/Minorities: Y

LOCATIONS: ("Y" = Yes)

West:	Southwest:	Midwest:	Southeast:	Northeast:	International:
		Y			

Note: Financial information, benefits and other data can change quickly and may vary from those stated here.

FAMILYMEDS GROUP INC www.familymedsgroup.com

ndustry Group Code: 422210 **Ranks within this company's industry group:** Sales: 4 Profits: 4

nsurance/HMO/PPO:		Drugs:		Equipment/Supplies:		Hospitals/Clinics:		Services:		Health Care:	
nsurance:		Manufacturer:		Manufacturer:		Acute Care:		Diagnostics:		Home Health:	
Managed Care:		Distributor:	Y	Distributor:		Sub-Acute:		Labs/Testing:		Long-Term Care:	
Jtilization Management:		Specialty Pharmacy:	Y	Leasing/Finance:		Outpatient Surgery:		Staffing:		Physical Therapy:	
Payment Processing:		Vitamins/Nutritionals:	Y	Information Systems:		Physical Rehab. Ctr.:		Waste Disposal:		Physician Prac. Mgmt.:	
		Clinical Trials:				Psychiatric Clinics:		Specialty Svcs.:			

TYPES OF BUSINESS:

Pharmacies
Online Pharmacy
Nutraceuticals & Cosmetics
Worksite Pharmacies

BRANDS/DIVISIONS/AFFILIATES:

Familymeds Group, Inc.
Arrow Pharmacy & Nutrition Center
Familymeds Pharmacy
Worksite Pharmacy

CONTACTS: *Note: Officers with more than one job title may be intentionally listed here more than once.*

Edgardo A. Mercadante, CEO
Jim Searson, COO/Sr. VP
Edgardo A. Mercadante, Pres.
Jim Bologna, CFO/Sr. VP
Thomas Ferranti, VP-IT
Kent Clark, Asst. VP-Merch.
Allison D. Kiene, General Counsel/Sr. VP
Edgardo A. Mercadante, Chmn.

Phone: 860-676-1222 **Fax:** 860-679-9337
Toll-Free: 800-203-2776
Address: 312 Farmington Ave., Farmington, CT 06032-1968 US

GROWTH PLANS/SPECIAL FEATURES:

Familymeds Group, Inc. is a pharmacy and drug distribution provider. The company operates 77 locations including 74 pharmacies; one health and beauty location; one non-pharmacy mail order center; and a drug distribution business primarily focused on the direct distribution of specialty pharmaceuticals to physicians, medical clinics and other health care providers. The firm's pharmacies are located in 13 states and operate under the brands: Familymeds Pharmacy; Arrow Pharmacy & Nutrition Center; and Worksite Pharmacy. Familymeds has 43 pharmacies that are located at the point of care between physicians and patients, oftentimes inside medical office buildings or on a medical campus. The majority of the company's revenue from the pharmacy operations come from the sale of prescription pharmaceuticals, which represented roughly 94% of the net sales in 2006. The firm's corporate pharmacies provide service to roughly 400,000 acute or chronically ill patients. In January 2007, the company's third Worksite Pharmacy opened to provide exclusive service to Toyota team members, participating on-site suppliers and their dependants in San Antonio, Texas. In February 2007, Familymeds together with its wholly owned subsidiaries Familymeds, Inc. and Arrow Prescription Corp., entered into an asset purchase agreement with Walgreen Co. and Walgreen Eastern Co., Inc. pursuant to which Familymeds will sell up to 53 of its locations and certain assets to Walgreens for a total estimated price of $60 million. In March 2007, the company's shareholders approved the proposed plan of complete liquidation and dissolution of the company.

FINANCIALS: **Sales and profits are in thousands of dollars—add 000 to get the full amount. 2007 Note: Financial information for 2007 was not available for all companies at press time.**

2007 Sales: $	2007 Profits: $	**U.S. Stock Ticker: FMRX**
2006 Sales: $230,500	2006 Profits: $-7,200	**Int'l Ticker:** Int'l Exchange:
2005 Sales: $239,231	2005 Profits: $-39,844	Employees: 835
2004 Sales: $213,789	2004 Profits: $-7,039	Fiscal Year Ends: 12/30
2003 Sales: $291,800	2003 Profits: $-13,200	Parent Company:

SALARIES/BENEFITS:

Pension Plan:	ESOP Stock Plan:	Profit Sharing:	Top Exec. Salary: $346,000	Bonus: $
Savings Plan: Y	Stock Purch. Plan:		Second Exec. Salary: $275,000	Bonus: $

OTHER THOUGHTS:

Apparent Women Officers or Directors: 1
Hot Spot for Advancement for Women/Minorities:

LOCATIONS: ("Y" = Yes)

West:	Southwest:	Midwest:	Southeast:	Northeast:	International:
		Y	Y	Y	

Note: Financial information, benefits and other data can change quickly and may vary from those stated here.

FIRST CHOICE HEALTH NETWORK INC www.fchn.com

Industry Group Code: 524114 **Ranks within this company's industry group:** Sales: Profits:

Insurance/HMO/PPO:		Drugs:		Equipment/Supplies:		Hospitals/Clinics:		Services:		Health Care:	
Insurance:		Manufacturer:		Manufacturer:		Acute Care:		Diagnostics:		Home Health:	
Managed Care:	Y	Distributor:		Distributor:		Sub-Acute:		Labs/Testing:		Long-Term Care:	
Utilization Management:	Y	Specialty Pharmacy:		Leasing/Finance:		Outpatient Surgery:		Staffing:		Physical Therapy:	
Payment Processing:		Vitamins/Nutritionals:		Information Systems:		Physical Rehab. Ctr.:		Waste Disposal:		Physician Prac. Mgmt.:	
		Clinical Trials:				Psychiatric Clinics:		Specialty Svcs.:	Y		

TYPES OF BUSINESS:

Insurance-Medical & Health, HMOs & PPOs
Medical Management Services
Third Party Administration
Employee Assistance Program
Physician Assistance Program

BRANDS/DIVISIONS/AFFILIATES:

Healthcare Direct

CONTACTS:

Note: Officers with more than one job title may be intentionally listed here more than once.

Kenneth A. Hamm, CEO
Kenneth A. Hamm, Pres.
Bela M. Biro, CFO/VP
Curtis Taylor, Chief Mktg. Officer

Phone: 206-292-8255	**Fax:** 206-667-8062
Toll-Free: 800-467-5281	
Address: 1 Union Square, Ste. 1400, Seattle, WA 98101 US	

GROWTH PLANS/SPECIAL FEATURES:

First Choice Health Network, Inc. (FCHN) is owned by approximately 450 physicians and 11 hospital systems that offer preferred provider organization (PPO) and health benefits management services to large self-funded plan sponsors. The company's principal business is the development and operation of a preferred provider network of hospitals, physicians and ancillary service providers, which currently consists of approximately 220 hospitals. The network serves approximately one million people through contracts with 107 payors including insurers, third-party administrators, union trusts and employers. The company boasts well over 27,000 directly contracted and credentialed providers. FCHN's network is primarily in Washington, with additional health care providers in Alaska, Idaho and Montana. The firm also contracts with self-insured employers, indemnity insurers, health maintenance organizations, union trusts and third-party administrators to provide subscribers with access to the PPO, for which it receives a fee. Additionally, hospitals participating in the PPO pay the network an administrative fee. FCHN's health benefits management business segment offers benefits management and administration services to self-funded employers and insurance carriers. In addition to the PPO network, the company provides medical management services, an employee assistance program, a physician assistance program and third party administration. In June 2006, FCHN acquired Healthcare Direct, an Oregon-based PPO.

FINANCIALS:

Sales and profits are in thousands of dollars—add 000 to get the full amount. 2007 Note: Financial information for 2007 was not available for all companies at press time.

2007 Sales: $	2007 Profits: $	**U.S. Stock Ticker: Private**
2006 Sales: $	2006 Profits: $	**Int'l Ticker:** Int'l Exchange:
2005 Sales: $	2005 Profits: $	Employees: 156
2004 Sales: $23,860	2004 Profits: $5,948	Fiscal Year Ends:
2003 Sales: $21,412	2003 Profits: $4,690	Parent Company:

SALARIES/BENEFITS:

Pension Plan:	ESOP Stock Plan:	Profit Sharing:	Top Exec. Salary: $308,766	Bonus: $183,645
Savings Plan:	Stock Purch. Plan:		Second Exec. Salary: $243,462	Bonus: $94,842

OTHER THOUGHTS:

Apparent Women Officers or Directors:
Hot Spot for Advancement for Women/Minorities:

LOCATIONS: ("Y" = Yes)

West:	Southwest:	Midwest:	Southeast:	Northeast:	International:
Y					

FIRST CONSULTING GROUP INC www.fcg.com

Industry Group Code: 541512 **Ranks within this company's industry group:** Sales: 1 Profits: 1

Insurance/HMO/PPO:		Drugs:		Equipment/Supplies:		Hospitals/Clinics:		Services:		Health Care:	
Insurance:		Manufacturer:		Manufacturer:		Acute Care:		Diagnostics:		Home Health:	
Managed Care:		Distributor:		Distributor:		Sub-Acute:		Labs/Testing:		Long-Term Care:	
Utilization Management:		Specialty Pharmacy:		Leasing/Finance:		Outpatient Surgery:		Staffing:		Physical Therapy:	
Payment Processing:		Vitamins/Nutritionals:		Information Systems:	Y	Physical Rehab. Ctr.:		Waste Disposal:		Physician Prac. Mgmt.:	
		Clinical Trials:				Psychiatric Clinics:		Specialty Svcs.:	Y		

TYPES OF BUSINESS:

Consulting & Outsourcing Services
Drug Development Consulting
Data Warehousing
Life Sciences Organization Consulting
Application Integration
Information Technology Consulting
Systems Development & Implementation
Health Providers Consulting

BRANDS/DIVISIONS/AFFILIATES:

FCG Management Services, LLC
FirstGateways Health View
FirstDoc
FirstGateways Vlink
Enterprise Content Management
Zorch, Inc.

CONTACTS: *Note: Officers with more than one job title may be intentionally listed here more than once.*

Larry R. Ferguson, CEO
Thomas A. Watford, COO
Thomas A. Watford, CFO
Jan L. Blue, VP-Human Resources
Joseph M. Casper, Sr., CTO
Michael A. Zuercher, General Counsel/VP/Corp. Sec.
Philip H. Ockelmann, Chief Acct. Officer/VP-Finance/Controller
Joseph M. Casper, Sr. VP/Pres., Software Prod. Bus. Unit
Donald L. Driscoll, Sr. VP/Pres., Health Delivery Svcs. Bus. Unit
Robert J. Smith, Sr. VP/Pres., Health Delivery Outsourcing Bus. Uni
Scot McConkey, Sr. VP/Pres., Health Plan Bus. Unit
Thomas D. Underwood, Sr. VP/Pres., Global Shared Svcs. Bus. Unit

Phone: 562-624-5200 **Fax:** 678-229-1110
Toll-Free: 800-345-0957
Address: 111 W. Ocean Blvd., 4th Fl., Long Beach, CA 90802 US

GROWTH PLANS/SPECIAL FEATURES:

First Consulting Group, Inc. (FCG) is a healthcare and technology focused consulting firm. FCG provides outsourcing, systems implementation and integration, consulting, software development, staff augmentation and research services to integrated delivery networks (IDNs), health plans, acute care centers, academic medical centers, physician organizations, government healthcare agencies, pharmaceutical companies, biotech companies and independent software vendors (ISVs). Services are designed to increase efficiency of clients' operations through reduced cost, enhanced quality of patient care and more rapid introduction of new pharmaceutical compounds in North America, Europe, India and Vietnam. The company applies industry knowledge and skills combined with advanced information technologies to make improvements in health care delivery, financing and administration, maintenance and research and development, by assembling multi-disciplinary teams that provide comprehensive services. The company's Life Sciences services include licensing and support of FirstDoc, an enterprise content management (ECM) solution for life sciences organizations. FCG's software products consist of FirstGateways HealthView, a web-based viewer providing access to patient clinical data, and FirstGateways VLink, an integration engine that enables the collection, integration, aggregation and distribution of clinical data. The company sold its software product CyberView and phased out its Full Contact software product in late 2006. In June 2007, FCG acquired Zorch, Inc., a provider of software solutions for the life sciences industry.

FCG offers its employees discretionary performance rewards, publishing bonuses, recruiting referral fees, an employee assistance program, commuter reimbursement accounts, a prepaid group legal plan, a matching gift program and tuition reimbursement.

FINANCIALS: **Sales and profits are in thousands of dollars—add 000 to get the full amount. 2007 Note: Financial information for 2007 was not available for all companies at press time.**

2007 Sales: $ | 2007 Profits: $
2006 Sales: $277,842 | 2006 Profits: $20,860
2005 Sales: $293,152 | 2005 Profits: $-18,609
2004 Sales: $287,289 | 2004 Profits: $4,118
2003 Sales: $287,739 | 2003 Profits: $-16,953

U.S. Stock Ticker: FCGI
Int'l Ticker: Int'l Exchange:
Employees: 2,716
Fiscal Year Ends: 12/31
Parent Company:

SALARIES/BENEFITS:

Pension Plan: | ESOP Stock Plan: | Profit Sharing: | Top Exec. Salary: $401,860 | Bonus: $128,656
Savings Plan: Y | Stock Purch. Plan: Y | | Second Exec. Salary: $372,500 | Bonus: $83,766

OTHER THOUGHTS:

Apparent Women Officers or Directors: 1
Hot Spot for Advancement for Women/Minorities: Y

LOCATIONS: ("Y" = Yes)

West:	Southwest:	Midwest:	Southeast:	Northeast:	International:
Y	Y	Y	Y	Y	Y

FIRST HEALTH GROUP CORP www.firsthealth.com

Industry Group Code: 524114 **Ranks within this company's industry group:** Sales: Profits:

Insurance/HMO/PPO:		Drugs:		Equipment/Supplies:		Hospitals/Clinics:		Services:		Health Care:	
Insurance:	Y	Manufacturer:		Manufacturer:		Acute Care:		Diagnostics:		Home Health:	
Managed Care:	Y	Distributor:		Distributor:		Sub-Acute:		Labs/Testing:		Long-Term Care:	
Utilization Management:	Y	Specialty Pharmacy:		Leasing/Finance:		Outpatient Surgery:		Staffing:		Physical Therapy:	
Payment Processing:	Y	Vitamins/Nutritionals:		Information Systems:	Y	Physical Rehab. Ctr.:		Waste Disposal:		Physician Prac. Mgmt.:	
		Clinical Trials:				Psychiatric Clinics:		Specialty Svcs.:	Y		

TYPES OF BUSINESS:

Insurance-Medical & Health, HMOs & PPOs
Insurance Underwriting
Claims Administration
Pharmacy Benefit Management
Utilization Review Services
Workers' Compensation Services
Managed Care Services
IT Services

BRANDS/DIVISIONS/AFFILIATES:

First Health Network
Coventry Health Care Inc

CONTACTS: *Note: Officers with more than one job title may be intentionally listed here more than once.*

Thomas P. McDonough, CEO
Thomas P. McDonough, Pres.
Dennis Meulemans, CFO
Karyn R. Glogowski, Sr. VP-Group Health & Acct. Mgmt.

Phone: 630-737-7900	**Fax:**
Toll-Free:	
Address: 3200 Highland Ave., Downers Grove, IL 60515 US	

GROWTH PLANS/SPECIAL FEATURES:

First Health Group Corp., a wholly-owned subsidiary of Coventry Health Care, Inc., is one of the nation's premier full-service preferred provider organizations (PPO). Its First Health Network has approximately 4,300 participating hospitals and 450,000 outpatient care providers in all 50 states, Washington, D.C. and Puerto Rico. Doctors and hospital administrators are given the ability to apply for membership in First Health's network by filing an application on-line. The company specializes in providing large, national employers with a fully integrated single source for their group health programs. Its offerings include clinical programs such as case management, disease management and return-to-work programs; administrative products such as bill review, first report of injury and front end processing; pharmacy benefit management; fiscal agent services; and group health insurance products. These are supported by an IT infrastructure that includes proprietary integrated applications; centralized data; 24-hour customer service; and member, provider, client and consultant web sites. First Health serves federal employees, self-insured corporations, third-party administrators, worker's compensation payors, small and mid-sized group health insurers and state Medicaid programs.

First Health offers its employees medical, dental and vision insurance; flexible spending accounts; life and AD&D insurance; a 401(k) plan; short- and long-term disability insurance; tuition assistance; and an employee assistance plan.

FINANCIALS: Sales and profits are in thousands of dollars—add 000 to get the full amount. 2007 Note: Financial information for 2007 was not available for all companies at press time.

2007 Sales: $	2007 Profits: $	**U.S. Stock Ticker: Subsidiary**
2006 Sales: $	2006 Profits: $	**Int'l Ticker:** Int'l Exchange:
2005 Sales: $812,314	2005 Profits: $	Employees: 6,000
2004 Sales: $	2004 Profits: $	Fiscal Year Ends: 12/31
2003 Sales: $890,926	2003 Profits: $152,734	Parent Company: COVENTRY HEALTH CARE INC

SALARIES/BENEFITS:

Pension Plan:	ESOP Stock Plan:	Profit Sharing:	Top Exec. Salary: $798,663	Bonus: $440,005
Savings Plan: Y	Stock Purch. Plan:		Second Exec. Salary: $705,388	Bonus: $114,412

OTHER THOUGHTS:

Apparent Women Officers or Directors: 1
Hot Spot for Advancement for Women/Minorities:

LOCATIONS: ("Y" = Yes)

West:	Southwest:	Midwest:	Southeast:	Northeast:	International:
Y	Y	Y	Y	Y	

FISERV INC

www.fiserv.com

Industry Group Code: 522320 **Ranks within this company's industry group:** Sales: 1 Profits: 2

Insurance/HMO/PPO:		Drugs:		Equipment/Supplies:		Hospitals/Clinics:		Services:		Health Care:	
Insurance:		Manufacturer:		Manufacturer:		Acute Care:		Diagnostics:		Home Health:	
Managed Care:		Distributor:		Distributor:		Sub-Acute:		Labs/Testing:		Long-Term Care:	
Utilization Management:		Specialty Pharmacy:		Leasing/Finance:		Outpatient Surgery:		Staffing:		Physical Therapy:	
Payment Processing:	Y	Vitamins/Nutritionals:		Information Systems:		Physical Rehab. Ctr.:		Waste Disposal:		Physician Prac. Mgmt.:	
		Clinical Trials:				Psychiatric Clinics:		Specialty Svcs.:			

TYPES OF BUSINESS:

Data & Transaction Processing
Software System Development
Virtual Banking
Information Management Services
Electronic Funds Transfer
Backroom Automation
Systems Integration
Disaster Recovery Services

BRANDS/DIVISIONS/AFFILIATES:

Benefit Planners
Benesight
Fiserv Health
Harrington Benefit Services
CheckAGAIN, LLC
Results International Systems, Inc.
Pharmacy Fulfillment, Inc.
Xcipio, Inc.

CONTACTS:

Note: Officers with more than one job title may be intentionally listed here more than once.

Jeffery W. Yabuki, CEO
Norman J. Balthasar, COO/Sr. Exec. VP
Jeffery W. Yabuki, Pres.
Thomas Hirsch, CFO
Dean C. Schmelzer, Group Pres., Mktg. & Sales
Charles W. Sprague, Chief Admin. Officer/Exec. VP
Charles W. Sprague, General Counsel
Patrick C. Foy, Group Pres., Bank Servicing Group
Terry R. Wade, Group Pres., Insurance Solutions Group
Thomas A. Neill, Group Pres., Depository Institution Processing
Robert H. Beriault, Group Pres., Investment Support Svcs.
Donald F. Dillon, Chmn.

Phone: 262-879-5000 **Fax:** 262-879-5013
Toll-Free: 800-425-3478
Address: 255 Fiserv Dr., Brookfield, WI 53045 US

GROWTH PLANS/SPECIAL FEATURES:

Fiserv, Inc. provides integrated data processing and information management systems to more than 18,000 financial services providers, including banks, credit unions, financial planners, investment advisers and insurance companies. The company operates centers nationwide for full-service data processing, software development, item processing and check imaging, technology support and related product businesses, and additionally has support centers in Argentina, Australia, Canada, Colombia, Indonesia, the Philippines, Puerto Rico, Poland, Singapore and the U.K. Fiserv operates through three primary business segments. The financial institution outsourcing, systems and services segment provides account and transaction processing systems and services to more than 10,000 financial institutions. The insurance services segment provides services and solutions to more than 2,400 insurance companies, more than 1,200 employer-sponsored health plans and more than 5,000 agencies and brokerages. Its services include handling payments to health care providers, assisting with cost controls, plan design services, medical provider administration, prescription benefit management and other related services. The investment support services segment provides a variety of administrative, custodial and processing services to individual investors; third-party retirement plan and pension administrators; investment advisors; financial planners; and financial intermediaries. Its products include self-directed retirement plan administration services, mutual fund custody trading services, back-office services and trust and asset custodial services. The company has a history of aggressive acquisitions, including the July 2006 purchase of The Jerome Group LLC, a provider of communications to industries such as financial services, healthcare, telecommunications services and retail. Other recent acquisitions include Insurance Wholesalers, Inc.; CareGain, Inc.; Xcipio, Inc.; InsureWorx; Urban Settlement Services LLC; and Innovative Cost Solutions.

FINANCIALS:

Sales and profits are in thousands of dollars—add 000 to get the full amount. 2007 Note: Financial information for 2007 was not available for all companies at press time.

2007 Sales: $
2006 Sales: $4,544,151
2005 Sales: $4,059,478
2004 Sales: $3,729,746
2003 Sales: $3,033,700

2007 Profits: $
2006 Profits: $449,914
2005 Profits: $516,438
2004 Profits: $377,642
2003 Profits: $315,000

U.S. Stock Ticker: FISV
Int'l Ticker: Int'l Exchange:
Employees: 23,000
Fiscal Year Ends: 12/31
Parent Company:

SALARIES/BENEFITS:

Pension Plan: ESOP Stock Plan: Profit Sharing: Top Exec. Salary: $840,000 Bonus: $810,457
Savings Plan: Y Stock Purch. Plan: Y Second Exec. Salary: $730,000 Bonus: $610,032

OTHER THOUGHTS:

Apparent Women Officers or Directors: 1
Hot Spot for Advancement for Women/Minorities:

LOCATIONS: ("Y" = Yes)

West:	Southwest:	Midwest:	Southeast:	Northeast:	International:
Y	Y	Y	Y	Y	Y

Note: Financial information, benefits and other data can change quickly and may vary from those stated here.

FOREST LABORATORIES INC

www.frx.com

Industry Group Code: 325412 **Ranks within this company's industry group:** Sales: 22 Profits: 20

Insurance/HMO/PPO:		Drugs:		Equipment/Supplies:		Hospitals/Clinics:		Services:		Health Care:	
Insurance:		Manufacturer:	Y	Manufacturer:		Acute Care:		Diagnostics:		Home Health:	
Managed Care:		Distributor:	Y	Distributor:		Sub-Acute:		Labs/Testing:		Long-Term Care:	
Utilization Management:		Specialty Pharmacy:		Leasing/Finance:		Outpatient Surgery:		Staffing:		Physical Therapy:	
Payment Processing:		Vitamins/Nutritionals:		Information Systems:		Physical Rehab. Ctr.:		Waste Disposal:		Physician Prac. Mgmt.:	
		Clinical Trials:				Psychiatric Clinics:		Specialty Svcs.:			

TYPES OF BUSINESS:

Drugs, Manufacturing
Over-the-Counter Pharmaceuticals
Generic Pharmaceuticals
Antidepressants
Asthma Medications
Cardiovascular Products
OB/Gyn-Pediatrics
Endocrinology

BRANDS/DIVISIONS/AFFILIATES:

Lexapro
Namenda
Celexa
Benicar
Tiazac
AeroChamber Plus
Armour Thyroid
Aerobid

CONTACTS: *Note: Officers with more than one job title may be intentionally listed here more than once.*

Howard Solomon, CEO
Kenneth E. Goodman, COO
Kenneth E. Goodman, Pres.
Francis I. Perier, Jr., CFO
Elaine Hochberg, Sr. VP-Mktg.
Ivan Gergel, VP-Scientific Affairs
Charles E. Triano, VP-Investor Rel.
Francis I. Perier, Jr., Sr. VP-Finance
Ivan Gergel, Sr. VP/Pres., Forest Research Institute
Howard Solomon, Chmn.

Phone: 212-421-7850	**Fax:** 212-750-9152
Toll-Free: 800-947-5227	
Address: 909 3rd Ave., New York, NY 10022 US	

GROWTH PLANS/SPECIAL FEATURES:

Forest Laboratories, Inc., based in New York, identifies develops and delivers pharmaceutical products that are used to treat a wide range of illnesses. Through its therapeutic franchises such as respiratory, pain management, ob/gyn pediatrics, endocrinology, central nervous system and cardiovascular, the firm has come up with brands such a Lexapro, an antidepressant, Benicar for the treatment of hypertension, Namenda, a therapy for moderate or severe Alzheimer's disease and Tiazac for cardiovascular disease The company has developed medications to treat asthma and an inhalant delivery system called AeroChamber Plus. It markets directly to physicians who have the most potential for growth and are agreeable to the introduction of new products. Forest has operations on Long Island, in New Jersey, Missouri, Ohio, Ireland and the United Kingdom Forest Laboratories Europe is the company's European subsidiary, with offices in Dublin, Ireland and Bexley Kent England. In the U.S., Forest Laboratories maintains eight separate labs in New York and one in New Jersey. Forest Pharmaceuticals, Inc., a wholly-owned subsidiary headquartered in St. Louis, Missouri, also manufactures and distributes branded and generic prescription and over-the counter drugs. The firm acquired Cerexa, Inc., a privately held biopharmaceutical company based in Alameda California, in a cash-for-stock transaction in January 2007 In February 2007, Forest began collaborating with Aurigene a Bangalore-based discovery services company to discover small molecule drug candidates for a novel obesity and metabolic disorders target. That same month, Forest and Replidyne, Inc. terminated their collaboration agreement for the development of faropenem medoxomil, a novel oral community antibiotic.

Employees at Forest receive financial assistance for adoption and fertility treatments, in addition to flexible spending accounts, child-care resource and referral and a commuter benefit program. The company also offers medical, dental and life insurance.

FINANCIALS: **Sales and profits are in thousands of dollars—add 000 to get the full amount. 2007 Note: Financial information for 2007 was not available for all companies at press time.**

2007 Sales: $3,183,324	2007 Profits: $454,103	**U.S. Stock Ticker: FRX**
2006 Sales: $2,793,934	2006 Profits: $708,514	**Int'l Ticker:** Int'l Exchange:
2005 Sales: $3,052,408	2005 Profits: $838,805	Employees: 5,126
2004 Sales: $2,650,432	2004 Profits: $735,874	Fiscal Year Ends: 3/31
2003 Sales: $2,206,700	2003 Profits: $622,000	Parent Company:

SALARIES/BENEFITS:

Pension Plan:	ESOP Stock Plan: Y	Profit Sharing: Y	Top Exec. Salary: $1,067,500	Bonus: $525,000
Savings Plan: Y	Stock Purch. Plan: Y		Second Exec. Salary: $725,500	Bonus: $330,000

OTHER THOUGHTS:

Apparent Women Officers or Directors: 3
Hot Spot for Advancement for Women/Minorities: Y

LOCATIONS: ("Y" = Yes)

West:	Southwest:	Midwest:	Southeast:	Northeast:	International:
		Y		Y	Y

FRESENIUS AG

www.fresenius-ag.com

Industry Group Code: 621490 **Ranks within this company's industry group:** Sales: 1 Profits: 1

Insurance/HMO/PPO:		Drugs:		Equipment/Supplies:		Hospitals/Clinics:		Services:		Health Care:	
Insurance:		Manufacturer:	Y	Manufacturer:	Y	Acute Care:	Y	Diagnostics:		Home Health:	Y
Managed Care:		Distributor:		Distributor:	Y	Sub-Acute:	Y	Labs/Testing:		Long-Term Care:	
Utilization Management:		Specialty Pharmacy:		Leasing/Finance:		Outpatient Surgery:		Staffing:		Physical Therapy:	
Payment Processing:		Vitamins/Nutritionals:		Information Systems:		Physical Rehab. Ctr.:		Waste Disposal:		Physician Prac. Mgmt.:	
		Clinical Trials:				Psychiatric Clinics:		Specialty Svcs.:	Y		

TYPES OF BUSINESS:

Medical Equipment Manufacturing
Dialysis Products & Services
Nutrition, Infusion Therapy & Transfusion Products
Hospital Management & Engineering
Management & Consulting Services
Pharmaceutical Plant Engineering
Information Technology Services

BRANDS/DIVISIONS/AFFILIATES:

Fresenius Medical Care AG
Fresenius Kabi
Fresenius ProServe
Fujitsu Laboratories Ltd
Fresenius Netcare
Helios Kliniken GmbH
Wittgensteiner Kliniken
Renal Care Group Inc.

CONTACTS: *Note: Officers with more than one job title may be intentionally listed here more than once.*

Ulf M. Schneider, Chmn.-Mgmt. Board
Stephan Sturm, CFO
Stephan Sturm, Dir.-Labor Rel.
Dieter Schenk, Lawyer/Tax Consultant
Joachim Weith, Sr. VP-Corp. Comm. & Gov't Affairs
Brigit Grund, Sr. VP-Investor Rel.
Rainer Baule, CEO-Fresenius Kabi
Rainer Hohmann, CEO-Fresenius ProServe
Ben Lipps, CEO-Fresenius Medical Care
Gerd Krick, Chmn.

Phone: 49-6172-608-0 **Fax:** 49-6172-608-2488
Toll-Free:
Address: Else-Kroner-Strasse 1, Bas Homburg, 61346 Germany

GROWTH PLANS/SPECIAL FEATURES:

Fresenius SE is an international health care group offering products and services primarily for dialysis. The firm has operations in 100 countries. The company operates the Fresenius Health Care Group (FHCG), which has five segments: Fresenius Medical Care AG (FMC), Fresenius Kabi, Fresenius ProServe, Fresenius Biotech and Fresenius Netcare. FMC is a leading manufacturer of chronic kidney failure products, such as hemodialysis machines, dialyzers and related disposable products. It owns and operates approximately 2,210 dialysis clinics in Asia Pacific, Latin America, North America, Europe and Africa. Kabi provides parenteral nutrition products that supply nutrients to patients while bypassing the gastro-intestinal tract; enteral nutrition products that artificially feed a patient via the intestinal tract; infusion therapy products, including electrolyte, glucose solutions, blood replacement and rinsing solutions as well as carrier solutions for drugs; transfusion technology products such as cell separators, blood bag systems, blood filters and blood bank products; and ambulatory care outpatient services that allow patients return to home while still receiving care. ProServe operates through several subsidiaries: HELIOS Kliniken GmbH, operating and managing German acute care hospitals; Wittgensteiner Kliniken, operating and managing German post acute care hospitals; and Vamed, providing many services worldwide, including feasibility studies, architectural planning, facility management and medical-technical maintenance. The Biotech segment develops and markets biopharmaceuticals in the fields of oncology, immunology and regenerative medicine; and Netcare offers services in the field of information technology both inside and outside of the company. In March 2006, subsidiary Fresenius Medical Care Holdings, Inc. acquired Renal Care Group Inc. In September 2006, Helios Kliniken acquired Humaine Kliniken GmbH, a company that operates six acute and post acute care hospitals in the fields of neurology, oncology and traumatolgy. In March 2007, NNE A/S acquired ProServe's former subsidiary, Pharmaplan GmbH.

FINANCIALS: **Sales and profits are in thousands of dollars—add 000 to get the full amount. 2007 Note: Financial information for 2007 was not available for all companies at press time.**

2007 Sales: $	2007 Profits: $	**U.S. Stock Ticker: FSNPF.PK**
2006 Sales: $14,218,100	2006 Profits: $435,400	**Int'l Ticker: FRE** Int'l Exchange: Frankfurt-Euronext
2005 Sales: $6,772,000	2005 Profits: $455,000	Employees: 99,687
2004 Sales: $9,917,600	2004 Profits: $229,200	Fiscal Year Ends: 12/31
2003 Sales: $8,866,700	2003 Profits: $144,300	Parent Company:

SALARIES/BENEFITS:

Pension Plan:	ESOP Stock Plan:	Profit Sharing:	Top Exec. Salary: $	Bonus: $
Savings Plan:	Stock Purch. Plan:		Second Exec. Salary: $	Bonus: $

OTHER THOUGHTS:

Apparent Women Officers or Directors: 1
Hot Spot for Advancement for Women/Minorities:

LOCATIONS: ("Y" = Yes)

West:	Southwest:	Midwest:	Southeast:	Northeast:	International:
Y				Y	Y

FRESENIUS MEDICAL CARE AG

www.fmc-ag.com

Industry Group Code: 621490 **Ranks within this company's industry group:** Sales: Profits:

Insurance/HMO/PPO:		Drugs:		Equipment/Supplies:		Hospitals/Clinics:		Services:		Health Care:	
Insurance:		Manufacturer:		Manufacturer:	Y	Acute Care:		Diagnostics:		Home Health:	
Managed Care:		Distributor:		Distributor:		Sub-Acute:		Labs/Testing:		Long-Term Care:	
Utilization Management:		Specialty Pharmacy:		Leasing/Finance:		Outpatient Surgery:		Staffing:		Physical Therapy:	
Payment Processing:		Vitamins/Nutritionals:		Information Systems:		Physical Rehab. Ctr.:		Waste Disposal:		Physician Prac. Mgmt.:	
		Clinical Trials:				Psychiatric Clinics:		Specialty Svcs.:	Y		

TYPES OF BUSINESS:

Dialysis Products & Services

BRANDS/DIVISIONS/AFFILIATES:

Fresenius AG

CONTACTS:

Note: Officers with more than one job title may be intentionally listed here more than once.

Ben Lipps, CEO
Lawrence A. Rosen, Dir.-Finance
Rainer Runte, Dir.-Law & Compliance
Mats Wahlstrom, Dir.-Svcs. Div. North America
Emanuele Gatti, Dir.-Europe, Latin America, Middle East & Africa
Rice Powell, Dir.-Dialysis Products & Lab Group North America
Ben Lipps, Chmn.
Roberto Fuste, Dir.-Asia-Pacific Region

Phone: 49-6172-609-0	**Fax:** 49-6172-608-2488
Toll-Free:	
Address: Else-Kroner Strasse 1, Bad Homburg, 61352 Germany	

GROWTH PLANS/SPECIAL FEATURES:

Fresenius Medical Care AG & Co. KGaA, formerly known a Fresenius Medical Care AG, is a kidney dialysis compan operating in both the field of dialysis products and field dialysis services. The company operates in two segment North America, which generated about 71% of revenue 2006; and international, which was responsible for 29% net sales in 2006. Fresenius Medical develops an manufactures a full range of equipment, systems an disposable products for chronic hemodialysis, acute therap home therapies, liver support and therapeutic apheresis (which blood is treated and cleansed of undesirable an pathogenic substances outside the patient's body and the transfused back to the patient), which it sells to customers over 100 countries. Products include chronic kidney failu products, such as hemodialysis machines, dialyzers an related disposable products. The company provided over 2 million dialysis treatments to roughly 163,500 patients in ov 2,100 clinics worldwide located in more than 25 countries 2006. The company owns rights to about 1,800 patents an patent applications. In March 2006, the firm completed th acquisition of Renal Care Group, Inc., a Nashvill Tennessee-based provider of dialysis services through th U.S. As a result of the transaction, Fresenius Medic gained approximately 456 dialysis clinics in the U.S. addition to providing acute dialysis services to more than 20 hospitals. The acquisition also afforded the management the dialysis programs at Vanderbilt University Medical Cent and the ownership or managing partner status at vario other programs, including St. Louis University Hospita Northwestern Memorial Hospital of Chicago and th Cleveland Clinic Foundation. In November 2006, th company acquired the phosphate binder business from Na Pharmaceuticals, Inc.

FINANCIALS:

Sales and profits are in thousands of dollars—add 000 to get the full amount. 2007 Note: Financial information for 2007 was not available for all companies at press time.

2007 Sales: $	2007 Profits: $	**U.S. Stock Ticker: FMS**
2006 Sales: $	2006 Profits: $	**Int'l Ticker: FWB** Int'l Exchange: Frankfurt-Euronext
2005 Sales: $	2005 Profits: $	Employees: 47,521
2004 Sales: $	2004 Profits: $	Fiscal Year Ends: 12/31
2003 Sales: $	2003 Profits: $	Parent Company: FRESENIUS AG

SALARIES/BENEFITS:

Pension Plan:	ESOP Stock Plan:	Profit Sharing:	Top Exec. Salary: $501,000	Bonus: $461,250
Savings Plan:	Stock Purch. Plan:		Second Exec. Salary: $389,231	Bonus: $433,000

OTHER THOUGHTS:

Apparent Women Officers or Directors:
Hot Spot for Advancement for Women/Minorities: Y

LOCATIONS: ("Y" = Yes)

West:	Southwest:	Midwest:	Southeast:	Northeast:	International:
Y	Y	Y	Y	Y	Y

GAMBRO AB

www.gambro.com

Industry Group Code: 621490 **Ranks within this company's industry group:** Sales: Profits:

Insurance/HMO/PPO:		**Drugs:**		**Equipment/Supplies:**		**Hospitals/Clinics:**		**Services:**		**Health Care:**	
Insurance:		Manufacturer:		Manufacturer:	Y	Acute Care:	Y	Diagnostics:		Home Health:	
Managed Care:		Distributor:		Distributor:	Y	Sub-Acute:		Labs/Testing:		Long-Term Care:	
Utilization Management:		Specialty Pharmacy:		Leasing/Finance:		Outpatient Surgery:		Staffing:		Physical Therapy:	
Payment Processing:		Vitamins/Nutritionals:		Information Systems:		Physical Rehab. Ctr.:		Waste Disposal:		Physician Prac. Mgmt.:	
		Clinical Trials:				Psychiatric Clinics:		Specialty Svcs.:	Y		

TYPES OF BUSINESS:

Medical Equipment Manufacturing
Dialysis Products & Services
Dialysis Clinics
Cell Therapy & Apheresis Technologies
Blood Component Collection & Purification Technologies
Liver Failure Products & Services

BRANDS/DIVISIONS/AFFILIATES:

Gambro, Inc.
Gambro Healthcare, Inc.
Gambro Healthcare Laboratory Services, Inc.
Gambro BCT
Gambro Renal Products
Hospal
Teraklin AG
Hemapure

CONTACTS: *Note: Officers with more than one job title may be intentionally listed here more than once.*

Thomas H. Glanzmann, CEO
Thomas H. Glanzmann, Pres.
Lars Granlof, CFO/Sr. VP
Maris Hartmanis, Sr. VP/Head-Corp. Research/Chief Science Officer
Asa Hedin, Head-Strategic Dev.
Peter Sjostrand, Chmn.

Phone: 46-8-613-65-00	**Fax:** 46-8-611-28-30
Toll-Free:	
Address: Jakobsgatan 6, Stockholm, SE-103 91 Sweden	

GROWTH PLANS/SPECIAL FEATURES:

Gambro AB, a subsidiary of Indap AB, is a global medical technology and health care company that manufactures dialysis products, operates kidney dialysis clinics and develops and supplies blood bank technology worldwide. The firm operates through Gambro, Inc. and Gambro BCT (blood component technology). Gambro, Inc. provides products, therapies and services for in-center care dialysis, home care dialysis and blood purification in intensive care units, including dialysis machines and disposables. Gambro BCT provides technology, products and systems to blood centers and hospital blood banks worldwide. It is a global leader in cell therapy and apheresis (the separation of blood into its components, i.e. red blood cells, white blood cells, blood platelets and plasma), as well as in the development of blood component collection and purification technologies. In May 2007, the company sold its subsidiary Gambro Healthcare, along with its two organizational segments Gambro Healthcare U.S. and Gambro Healthcare International, to the private equity firm Bridgepoint Capital Limited.

FINANCIALS: **Sales and profits are in thousands of dollars—add 000 to get the full amount. 2007 Note: Financial information for 2007 was not available for all companies at press time.**

2007 Sales: $	2007 Profits: $	**U.S. Stock Ticker: Subsidiary**
2006 Sales: $	2006 Profits: $	**Int'l Ticker:** Int'l Exchange:
2005 Sales: $1,862,987	2005 Profits: $1,208,372	Employees: 19,143
2004 Sales: $1,700,475	2004 Profits: $-76,371	Fiscal Year Ends: 12/31
2003 Sales: $3,606,400	2003 Profits: $196,200	Parent Company: INDAP AB

SALARIES/BENEFITS:

Pension Plan:	ESOP Stock Plan:	Profit Sharing:	Top Exec. Salary: $	Bonus: $
Savings Plan:	Stock Purch. Plan:		Second Exec. Salary: $	Bonus: $

OTHER THOUGHTS:

Apparent Women Officers or Directors:
Hot Spot for Advancement for Women/Minorities: Y

LOCATIONS: ("Y" = Yes)

West:	Southwest:	Midwest:	Southeast:	Northeast:	International:
Y		Y	Y	Y	Y

GE HEALTHCARE

www.gehealthcare.com

Industry Group Code: 339113 **Ranks within this company's industry group:** Sales: Profits:

Insurance/HMO/PPO:		Drugs:		Equipment/Supplies:		Hospitals/Clinics:		Services:		Health Care:	
Insurance:		Manufacturer:		Manufacturer:	Y	Acute Care:		Diagnostics:		Home Health:	
Managed Care:		Distributor:		Distributor:		Sub-Acute:		Labs/Testing:		Long-Term Care:	
Utilization Management:		Specialty Pharmacy:		Leasing/Finance:		Outpatient Surgery:		Staffing:		Physical Therapy:	
Payment Processing:		Vitamins/Nutritionals:		Information Systems:	Y	Physical Rehab. Ctr.:		Waste Disposal:		Physician Prac. Mgmt.:	
		Clinical Trials:				Psychiatric Clinics:		Specialty Svcs.:	Y		

TYPES OF BUSINESS:

Medical Imaging & Information Technology
Magnetic Resonance Imaging Systems
Patient Monitoring Systems
Clinical Information Systems
Nuclear Medicine
Surgery & Vascular Imaging
X-Ray & Ultrasound Bone Densitometers
Clinical & Business Services

BRANDS/DIVISIONS/AFFILIATES:

GE Electric Co.
GE Healthcare Bio-Sciences
GE Healthcare Technologies
GE Healthcare Information Technologies
Centricity
Giraffe OmniBed
Innova
InstaTrak

CONTACTS: *Note: Officers with more than one job title may be intentionally listed here more than once.*

Joseph M. Hogan, CEO/Sr. VP
William Castell, Pres.
Kathryn McCarthy, CFO/Exec. VP
Jean-Michel Cossery, Chief Mktg. Officer
Mike Hanley, VP-Human Resources
James Rothman, Chief Scientific Advisor
Russel P. Meyer, CIO
William R. Clarke, CTO/Chief Medical Officer/Exec. VP
Peter Y. Solmssen, General Counsel/Exec. VP
Ralph Strosin, General Mgr.-Oper.
Michael A. Jones, Exec. VP-Bus. Dev.
Lynne Gailey, Dir.-Global Comm.
Dan Peters, CEO/Pres., Medical Diagnostics
Omar Ishrak, CEO/Pres., Clinical Systems
Peter Ehrenheim, CEO/Pres., Life Sciences
Mark Vachon, CEO/Pres., Global Diagnostic Imaging

Phone: 44-1494-544-000 **Fax:**
Toll-Free:
Address: Pollards Wood, Nightingales Ln., Chalfont St. Giles, Buckinghamshire HP8 4SP UK

GROWTH PLANS/SPECIAL FEATURES:

GE Healthcare, a subsidiary of GE, is a global leader in medical imaging and information technologies, patient monitoring systems and health care services. The company operates through seven divisions, including diagnostic imaging; global services; clinical systems; life systems; medical diagnostics; integrated information technology solutions; and interventional, cardiology and surgery. The diagnostic imaging business provides X-ray, digital mammography, computed tomography, magnetic resonance and molecular imaging technologies. GE Healthcare's global services business provides maintenance of a wide range of medical systems and devices. The clinical systems business provides technologies and services for clinicians and healthcare administrators, including ultrasound, ECG, bone densitometry, patient monitoring, incubators, infant warmers, respiratory care and anesthesia management. GE Healthcare's life sciences segment offers drug discovery, biopharmaceutical manufacturing and cellular technologies, enabling scientists and specialists around the world to discover new ways to predict, diagnose and treat disease earlier. The segment also makes systems and equipment for the purification of biopharmaceuticals. The firm's medical diagnostics business researches, manufactures and markets agents used during medical scanning procedures to highlight organs, tissue and functions inside the human body. The integrated information technology (IT) solutions business provides clinical and financial information technology solutions including enterprise and departmental IT products, revenue cycle management and practice applications, to help customers streamline healthcare costs and improve the quality of care. GE Healthcare's interventional, cardiology and surgery (ICS) business provides tools and technologies for fully integrated cardiac, surgical and interventional care. The company's major products include Centricity, a suite of applications designed to provide real-time patient information at the point of care; Giraffe OmniBed and Incubators for critically ill and premature infants; Innova 3100, a digital imaging system for visualizing the heart and fine vessels; and InstaTrak, which creates an anatomical roadmap and real-time visualization of surgical instrumentation to guide surgeons during life-critical procedures.

FINANCIALS: **Sales and profits are in thousands of dollars—add 000 to get the full amount. 2007 Note: Financial information for 2007 was not available for all companies at press time.**

2007 Sales: $
2006 Sales: $
2005 Sales: $15,153,000
2004 Sales: $13,456,000
2003 Sales: $10,200,000

2007 Profits: $
2006 Profits: $
2005 Profits: $2,665,000
2004 Profits: $2,286,000
2003 Profits: $1,701,000

U.S. Stock Ticker: Subsidiary
Int'l Ticker: Int'l Exchange:
Employees: 43,000
Fiscal Year Ends: 12/31
Parent Company: GENERAL ELECTRIC CO (GE)

SALARIES/BENEFITS:

Pension Plan: Y ESOP Stock Plan: Profit Sharing: Top Exec. Salary: $ Bonus: $
Savings Plan: Y Stock Purch. Plan: Second Exec. Salary: $ Bonus: $

OTHER THOUGHTS:

Apparent Women Officers or Directors: 1
Hot Spot for Advancement for Women/Minorities:

LOCATIONS: ("Y" = Yes)

West:	Southwest:	Midwest:	Southeast:	Northeast:	International:
		Y			Y

GENENTECH INC

www.gene.com

ndustry Group Code: 325412 **Ranks within this company's industry group:** Sales: 16 Profits: 13

nsurance/HMO/PPO:		Drugs:		Equipment/Supplies:		Hospitals/Clinics:		Services:		Health Care:	
nsurance:		Manufacturer:	Y	Manufacturer:		Acute Care:		Diagnostics:		Home Health:	
lanaged Care:		Distributor:		Distributor:		Sub-Acute:		Labs/Testing:		Long-Term Care:	
tilization Management:		Specialty Pharmacy:		Leasing/Finance:		Outpatient Surgery:		Staffing:		Physical Therapy:	
ayment Processing:		Vitamins/Nutritionals:		Information Systems:		Physical Rehab. Ctr.:		Waste Disposal:		Physician Prac. Mgmt.:	
		Clinical Trials:				Psychiatric Clinics:		Specialty Svcs.:			

TYPES OF BUSINESS:

)rug Development & Manufacturing
ienetically Engineered Drugs

BRANDS/DIVISIONS/AFFILIATES:

vastin
NKase
lerceptin
ituxan
ctivase
ulmozyme
lutropin

CONTACTS: *Note: Officers with more than one job title may be ntentionally listed here more than once.*

rthur D. Levinson, CEO
lyrtle S. Potter, COO
rthur D. Levinson, Pres.
)avid A. Ebersman, CFO/Exec. VP
ichard H. Scheller, Exec. VP-Research
iusan Desmond-Hellmann, Pres., Prod. Dev.
itephen G. Juelsgaard, Exec. VP/General Counsel
an T. Clark, Exec. VP-Comm. Oper.
itephen G. Juelsgaard, Corp. Sec.
atrick Y. Yang, Exec. VP-Product Oper.
rthur D. Levinson, Chmn.

hone: 650-225-1000	**Fax:** 650-225-6000
oll-Free:	
ddress: 1 DNA Way, South San Francisco, CA 94080 US	

GROWTH PLANS/SPECIAL FEATURES:

Genentech, Inc. makes medicines by splicing genes into fast-growing bacteria that then produce therapeutic proteins and combat diseases on a molecular level. Genentech uses cutting-edge technologies such as computer visualization of molecules, micro arrays and sensitive assaying techniques to develop, manufacture and market pharmaceuticals for unmet medical needs. Genentech's research is directed toward the oncology, immunology and vascular biology fields. The company's products consist of a variety of cardio-centric medications, as well as cancer, growth hormone deficiency (GHD) and cystic fibrosis treatments. Biotechnology products offered by Genentech include Herceptin, used to treat metastatic breast cancers; Avastin, used to inhibit angiogenesis of solid-tumor cancers Nutropin, a growth hormone for the treatment of GHD in children and adults; TNKase, for the treatment of acute myocardial infarction; and Pulmozyme, for the treatment of cystic fibrosis. The company also produces the Rituxan antibody, used for the treatment of patients with non-Hodgkin's lymphoma. Through its long-standing Genentech Access to Care Foundation, Genentech assists those without sufficient health insurance to receive its medicines. The company's scientists publish around 250 scientific papers per year and are regarded as among the most prolific in the industry. In 2006, 18% of operating revenues (roughly $1.6 billion) was dedicated to research and development. In November 2006, the FDA approved Herceptin for treatment of a specific kind of breast cancer. The firm recently agreed to acquire Tanox, a firm that focuses on monoclonal antibody technology. Roche Holdings, Ltd. owns 55.8% of Genentech.

For the last nine years, the company has been named to Fortune Magazine's 100 Best Companies to Work For. Every Friday evening, Genentech hosts socials called Ho-Hos, providing free food, beverages and a chance to socialize with co-workers.

FINANCIALS: **Sales and profits are in thousands of dollars—add 000 to get the full amount. 2007 Note: Financial information for 2007 was not available for all companies at press time.**

007 Sales: $	2007 Profits: $	**U.S. Stock Ticker: DNA**
006 Sales: $9,284,000	2006 Profits: $2,113,000	**Int'l Ticker:** Int'l Exchange:
005 Sales: $6,633,372	2005 Profits: $1,278,991	Employees: 10,533
004 Sales: $4,621,157	2004 Profits: $784,816	Fiscal Year Ends: 12/31
003 Sales: $2,799,400	2003 Profits: $562,527	Parent Company:

SALARIES/BENEFITS:

ension Plan:	ESOP Stock Plan:	Profit Sharing:	Top Exec. Salary: $995,000	Bonus: $2,725,000
avings Plan: Y	Stock Purch. Plan: Y		Second Exec. Salary: $625,000	Bonus: $870,000

OTHER THOUGHTS:

pparent Women Officers or Directors: 2
lot Spot for Advancement for Women/Minorities: Y

LOCATIONS: ("Y" = Yes)

West:	Southwest:	Midwest:	Southeast:	Northeast:	International:
Y					Y

GENTIVA HEALTH SERVICES INC www.gentiva.com

Industry Group Code: 621610 **Ranks within this company's industry group:** Sales: 2 Profits: 7

Insurance/HMO/PPO:		Drugs:		Equipment/Supplies:		Hospitals/Clinics:		Services:		Health Care:	
Insurance:		Manufacturer:		Manufacturer:		Acute Care:		Diagnostics:		Home Health:	Y
Managed Care:		Distributor:		Distributor:		Sub-Acute:		Labs/Testing:		Long-Term Care:	
Utilization Management:		Specialty Pharmacy:		Leasing/Finance:		Outpatient Surgery:		Staffing:		Physical Therapy:	
Payment Processing:		Vitamins/Nutritionals:		Information Systems:		Physical Rehab. Ctr.:	Y	Waste Disposal:		Physician Prac. Mgmt.:	
		Clinical Trials:				Psychiatric Clinics:		Specialty Svcs.:	Y		

TYPES OF BUSINESS:

Home Health Care Services
Administrative Services

BRANDS/DIVISIONS/AFFILIATES:

CareCentrix
Gentiva Safe Strides
Gentiva Orthopedics
Gentiva Cardiopulmonary
Gentive Rehab Without Walls
Lazarus House Hospice, Inc.
Carolina Vital Care

CONTACTS: *Note: Officers with more than one job title may be intentionally listed here more than once.*

Ron Malone, CEO
John Potapchuk, CFO/Exec. VP
Brian Silva, Sr. VP-Human Resources
Brian Jones, CIO/VP
Steve Paige, General Counsel/Sr. VP/Sec.
John Potapchuk, Treas.
Tony Strange, Exec. VP/Pres., Gentiva Home Health
Thomas Boelsen, VP-CareCentrix
John Camperlengo, VP/Chief Compliance Officer
David Gieringer, Controller/VP
Ron Malone, Chmn.

Phone: 631-501-7000	Fax: 631-501-7148
Toll-Free:	
Address: 3 Huntington Quadrangle, 200S, Melville, NY 11747 US	

GROWTH PLANS/SPECIAL FEATURES:

Gentiva Health Services, Inc. is a provider of home health care services. The company operates in three segments: home health, CareCentrix and other related services. The home health segment is comprised of direct home nursing and therapy services operations, conducting its business through over 300 locations in 35 states. The segment's operations are conducted through licensed and Medicare-certified agencies from which the company provides various combinations of nursing and therapy services; paraprofessional nursing services; and homemaker services to pediatric, adult and elderly patients. The division also delivers services to customers through focused specialty programs, including: Gentiva Orthopedics, which provides individualized home orthopedic rehabilitation services to patients recovering from joint replacement or other major orthopedic surgery; Gentiva Safe Strides, which provides therapies for patients with balance issues; Gentiva Cardiopulmonary, which helps patients and their physicians manage heart and lung health in a home-base environment; and Gentiva Rehab Without Walls, which provides home and community-based neurorehabilitation therapies for patients with traumatic brain injury, cerebrovascular accident injury and acquired brain injury. The CareCentrix segment's operations provide administrative services and coordinate the delivery of home nursing services; acute and chronic infusion therapies; home medical equipment; respiratory products; orthotics and prosthetics; and services for managed care organizations and health plans. The other related services segment encompasses the firm's hospice; respiratory therapy and home medical equipment; infusion therapy; and consulting services businesses. In February 2006, the company acquired The Healthfield Group, Inc., a provider of home healthcare, hospice and related services throughout the Southeast, for $466 million. In June 2006 the company bought Lazarus House Hospice, Inc. and Carolina Vital Care, which provide hospice and home infusion services, for $4.5 million.

The company offers its employees medical, dental and vision insurance; life and disability insurance; a savings plan; an employee stock purchase plan; and tuition assistance.

FINANCIALS: **Sales and profits are in thousands of dollars—add 000 to get the full amount. 2007 Note: Financial information for 2007 was not available for all companies at press time.**

2007 Sales: $	2007 Profits: $	**U.S. Stock Ticker: GTIV**
2006 Sales: $1,106,588	2006 Profits: $20,776	**Int'l Ticker:** Int'l Exchange:
2005 Sales: $868,843	2005 Profits: $23,365	Employees: 15,200
2004 Sales: $845,764	2004 Profits: $26,488	Fiscal Year Ends: 12/31
2003 Sales: $814,029	2003 Profits: $56,766	Parent Company:

SALARIES/BENEFITS:

Pension Plan:	ESOP Stock Plan:	Profit Sharing:	Top Exec. Salary: $615,962	Bonus: $850,000
Savings Plan: Y	Stock Purch. Plan: Y		Second Exec. Salary: $359,607	Bonus: $255,000

OTHER THOUGHTS:

Apparent Women Officers or Directors: 3
Hot Spot for Advancement for Women/Minorities: Y

LOCATIONS: ("Y" = Yes)

West:	Southwest:	Midwest:	Southeast:	Northeast:	International:
Y	Y	Y	Y	Y	

Note: Financial information, benefits and other data can change quickly and may vary from those stated here.

GENZYME CORP

www.genzyme.com

Industry Group Code: 325412 **Ranks within this company's industry group:** Sales: 20 Profits: 32

Insurance/HMO/PPO:		Drugs:		Equipment/Supplies:		Hospitals/Clinics:		Services:		Health Care:	
Insurance:		Manufacturer:	Y	Manufacturer:	Y	Acute Care:		Diagnostics:		Home Health:	
Managed Care:		Distributor:		Distributor:		Sub-Acute:		Labs/Testing:		Long-Term Care:	
Utilization Management:		Specialty Pharmacy:		Leasing/Finance:		Outpatient Surgery:		Staffing:		Physical Therapy:	
Payment Processing:		Vitamins/Nutritionals:		Information Systems:		Physical Rehab. Ctr.:		Waste Disposal:		Physician Prac. Mgmt.:	
		Clinical Trials:	Y			Psychiatric Clinics:		Specialty Svcs.:			

TYPES OF BUSINESS:

Pharmaceuticals Discovery & Development
Genetic Disease Treatments
Surgical Products
Diagnostic Products
Genetic Testing Services
Oncology Products
Biomaterials
Medical Devices

BRANDS/DIVISIONS/AFFILIATES:

Renagel
Cerezyme
Fabrazyme
Aldurazyme
Thyrogen
Thymoglobulin
Carticel
AnorMED

CONTACTS:

Note: Officers with more than one job title may be intentionally listed here more than once.

Henri A. Termeer, CEO
Henri A. Termeer, Pres.
Michael S. Wyzga, CFO/Chief Acct. Officer/Exec. VP
Zoltan Csimma, Chief Human Resources Officer/Sr. VP
Alan E. Smith, Chief Scientific Officer/Sr. VP-Research
Thomas J. DesRosier, General Counsel/Sr. VP/Chief Patent Counsel
Mark Bamforth, Sr. VP-Corp. Oper. & Pharmaceuticals
Richard H. Douglas, Sr. VP-Corp. Dev.
Elliott D. Hillback, Jr., Sr. VP-Corp. Affairs
Evan M. Lebson, VP/Treas.
Mara G. Aspinall, Pres., Genetics
John Butler, Pres., Genzyme Renal
Ann Merrifield, Pres., Biosurgery
Donald E. Pogorzelski, Pres., Genzyme Diagnostics
Henri A. Termeer, Chmn.
Sandford D. Smith, Pres., Intl. Group

Phone: 617-252-7500	**Fax:** 617-252-7600
Toll-Free:	
Address: 500 Kendall St., Cambridge, MA 02142 US	

GROWTH PLANS/SPECIAL FEATURES:

Genzyme Corporation is a major biotech drug manufacturer operating through six major units: renal, therapeutics, transplant, biosurgery, diagnostics/genetics and oncology. The renal unit specializes in treatments for patients suffering from diseases including chronic renal failure. Its main products are Renagel, which reduces phosphorus levels in hemodialysis patients, and Hectorol, a treatment for secondary hyperparathyroidism. The therapeutics unit's products and services are used in the treatment of genetic disorders and other chronic debilitating diseases, including lysosomal storage disorders (LSDs). Its main products include Cerezyme/Ceredase for Type I Gaucher disease, Fabrazyme for Fabry disease, Myozyme for Pompe disease and Thyrogen, a diagnostic agent used in the follow-up treatment of patients with thyroid cancer. The transplant unit's products address pre-transplantation, prevention and treatment of acute rejection in organ transplantation, as well as other autoimmune disorders. Its products include two immunosuppressive polyclonal antibodies, Thymoglobulin and Lymphoglobulin. The biosurgery unit's portfolio of devices, biomaterials and biotherapeutics are used primarily in the orthopedic, general surgery and severe burn treatment markets. Products include Synvisc for the treatment of pain caused by osteoarthritis of the knee; and the Carticel line of products, repairing knee cartilage after trauma. The genetics unit develops, manufactures and distributes in vitro diagnostic products with an emphasis on point-of-care products for the in-hospital and out-of-hospital rapid test segment. Additionally, Genzyme operates an Other division that incorporates the company's diagnostic products, oncology, bulk pharmaceuticals and cardiovascular businesses. In late 2006, Genzyme acquired AnorMED a biotechnology company.

FINANCIALS:

Sales and profits are in thousands of dollars—add 000 to get the full amount. 2007 Note: Financial information for 2007 was not available for all companies at press time.

2007 Sales: $	2007 Profits: $	**U.S. Stock Ticker: GENZ**
2006 Sales: $3,187,013	2006 Profits: $-16,797	**Int'l Ticker:** Int'l Exchange:
2005 Sales: $2,734,842	2005 Profits: $441,489	Employees: 8,000
2004 Sales: $2,201,145	2004 Profits: $86,527	Fiscal Year Ends: 12/31
2003 Sales: $1,713,900	2003 Profits: $-67,600	Parent Company:

SALARIES/BENEFITS:

Pension Plan:	ESOP Stock Plan:	Profit Sharing:	Top Exec. Salary: $1,365,000	Bonus: $1,759,500
Savings Plan: Y	Stock Purch. Plan: Y		Second Exec. Salary: $650,000	Bonus: $445,000

OTHER THOUGHTS:

Apparent Women Officers or Directors: 2
Hot Spot for Advancement for Women/Minorities: Y

LOCATIONS: ("Y" = Yes)

West:	Southwest:	Midwest:	Southeast:	Northeast:	International:
Y	Y	Y	Y	Y	Y

GISH BIOMEDICAL INC www.gishbiomedical.com

Industry Group Code: 339113 **Ranks within this company's industry group:** Sales: Profits:

Insurance/HMO/PPO:		Drugs:		Equipment/Supplies:		Hospitals/Clinics:		Services:		Health Care:	
Insurance:		Manufacturer:		Manufacturer:	Y	Acute Care:		Diagnostics:		Home Health:	
Managed Care:		Distributor:		Distributor:		Sub-Acute:		Labs/Testing:		Long-Term Care:	
Utilization Management:		Specialty Pharmacy:		Leasing/Finance:		Outpatient Surgery:		Staffing:		Physical Therapy:	
Payment Processing:		Vitamins/Nutritionals:		Information Systems:		Physical Rehab. Ctr.:		Waste Disposal:		Physician Prac. Mgmt.:	
		Clinical Trials:				Psychiatric Clinics:		Specialty Svcs.:			

TYPES OF BUSINESS:

Equipment-Cardiac & Orthopedic Surgical Products
Disposable Surgical Devices

BRANDS/DIVISIONS/AFFILIATES:

CardioTech International
StatSat
Orthofuser
Vision
Hemed
CAPVRF44
GBS Coating

CONTACTS: *Note: Officers with more than one job title may be intentionally listed here more than once.*

Kelly D. Scott, CEO
Kelly D. Scott, Pres.
Leslie M. Taeger, CFO
Michael Szycher, Pres./CEO-CardioTech
John W. Galuchie Jr., Chmn.

Phone: 800-938-0531	**Fax:** 949-635-6296
Toll-Free: 866-221-9911	
Address: 22942 Arroyo Vista, Rancho Santa Margarita, CA 92688 US	

GROWTH PLANS/SPECIAL FEATURES:

Gish Biomedical, Inc., a subsidiary of CardioTec International, Inc., manufactures, assembles and sel medical devices used within open heart operatin procedures, such as custom tubing sets, all-inclusiv operating packs and oxygenators. During open-hea surgery, the patient's blood is diverted from the heart throug sterile plastic tubing and various other devices to a oxygenator device, which oxygenates the blood before it i returned to the patient. Such devices and components ar manufactured and assembled in the Gish clean roon sterilized and then shipped either to the hospital or to one c Gish's specialty distributors, which service such hospitals Gish produces the custom cardiovascular tubing system that transport the blood from the patient to the oxygenato the venous reservoir tools that are used to pool, filter an defoam blood prior to its introduction to the oxygenator; th company's Vision brand Oxygenator; the StatSat oxyge saturation monitor, which monitors the bloods oxygen level during surgery; and the arterial filters, which remove gaseou micro-emboli and debris from the patient's blood before reenters the body. In addition to the products that make u the circuit, Gish also manufactures cardiotomy reservoirs which are used to recover blood shed during open hea surgery; the cardioplegia delivery systems used to protec and preserve heart tissue; the critical care central venou access catheters and ports used for long-term vascula access; the Orthofuser-brand vacuum system used post operative orthopedic surgeries; and Gish Biocompatibl Surfaces Coatings, which is a biocompatible coating used t cover its disposable products. Some of Gish's clients includ the Loma Linda University Medical Center and the Toront General Hospital. In January 2007, CardioTech Internationa hired an investment banking firm to identify potentia purchasers of Gish and to manage its eventual sale.

FINANCIALS: **Sales and profits are in thousands of dollars—add 000 to get the full amount. 2007 Note: Financial information for 2007 was not available for all companies at press time.**

2007 Sales: $	2007 Profits: $	**U.S. Stock Ticker: Subsidiary**
2006 Sales: $	2006 Profits: $	**Int'l Ticker:** Int'l Exchange:
2005 Sales: $	2005 Profits: $	Employees: 122
2004 Sales: $	2004 Profits: $	Fiscal Year Ends: 3/31
2003 Sales: $	2003 Profits: $	Parent Company: CARDIOTECH INTERNATIONAL

SALARIES/BENEFITS:

Pension Plan:	ESOP Stock Plan:	Profit Sharing:	Top Exec. Salary: $180,000	Bonus: $28,650
Savings Plan: Y	Stock Purch. Plan:		Second Exec. Salary: $118,750	Bonus: $

OTHER THOUGHTS:

Apparent Women Officers or Directors: 2
Hot Spot for Advancement for Women/Minorities:

LOCATIONS: ("Y" = Yes)

West:	Southwest:	Midwest:	Southeast:	Northeast:	International:
Y					

GLAXOSMITHKLINE PLC www.gsk.com

ndustry Group Code: 325412 **Ranks within this company's industry group:** Sales: 3 Profits: 3

nsurance/HMO/PPO:		Drugs:		Equipment/Supplies:		Hospitals/Clinics:		Services:		Health Care:	
nsurance:		Manufacturer:	Y	Manufacturer:		Acute Care:		Diagnostics:		Home Health:	
lanaged Care:		Distributor:	Y	Distributor:		Sub-Acute:		Labs/Testing:		Long-Term Care:	
Jtilization Management:		Specialty Pharmacy:		Leasing/Finance:		Outpatient Surgery:		Staffing:		Physical Therapy:	
ayment Processing:		Vitamins/Nutritionals:		Information Systems:		Physical Rehab. Ctr.:		Waste Disposal:		Physician Prac. Mgmt.:	
		Clinical Trials:	Y			Psychiatric Clinics:		Specialty Svcs.:			

TYPES OF BUSINESS:

rescription Medications
sthma Drugs
espiratory Drugs
ntibiotics
ntivirals
ermatological Drugs
ver-the-Counter & Nutritional Products

BRANDS/DIVISIONS/AFFILIATES:

Lanoxin
Flovent
Paxil
Domantis, Ltd.
Zantac
Nicorette
PLIVA-Istraivacki Institut
Citrucel

CONTACTS: *Note: Officers with more than one job title may be intentionally listed here more than once.*

Jean-Pierre Garnier, CEO
Julian Heslop, CFO
Daniel Phelan, Sr. VP-Human Resources
Tadataka Yamada, Chmn., R&D
Ford Calhoun, CIO
David Pulman, Pres., Global Mfg. & Supply
Rupert Bondy, General Counsel/Sr. VP
David Stout, Pres., Pharm. Oper.
Jennie Younger, Sr. VP-Corp. Comm. & Partnerships
Marc Dunoyer, Pres., Pharmaceuticals, Japan
Chris Viehbacher, Pres., Pharmaceuticals U.S.
Andrew Witty, Pres., Pharmaceuticals, Europe
John Clarke, Pres., Consumer Healthcare
Christopher Gent, Chmn.
Russell Greig, Pres., Pharmaceuticals, Intl.

Phone: 44-20-8047-5000 **Fax:** 44-20-8047-7807
Toll-Free: 888-825-5249
Address: 980 Great West Rd., Brentford, Middlesex, TW8 9GS UK

GROWTH PLANS/SPECIAL FEATURES:

GlaxoSmithKline (GSK) is a leading research-based pharmaceutical company formed from the merger of Glaxo Wellcome and SmithKline Beecham. Its subsidiaries consist of global drug and health companies engaged in the creation, discovery, development, manufacturing and marketing of pharmaceuticals and other consumer health products. The firm's major markets are based in the U.S., Japan, U.K., Spain and Italy. GSK operates in three industry segments: pharmaceuticals, vaccines and consumer health care. Recently developed medications include Paxil for depression and anxiety; Lamictal for epilepsy and bipolar disorder; Ventolin for bronchitis; and Augmentin for bacterial infections. Additionally, GSK also designs prescription medications for the treatment of heart and circulatory conditions, cancer, HIV/AIDS and malaria. Consumer health care products include over-the-counter medication such as Citrucel and Nicorette; oral care products such as Aquafresh; and nutritional products such as Boost. GSK's vaccines are designed to treat life-threatening illnesses such as hepatitis A, diphtheria, influenza and bacterial meningitis. GSK has also recently developed a new therapeutic vaccine which prevents cancer patients from relapsing after recovery. Research and development operations takes place at 14 sites in five countries on clinical trials and new drug discovery technologies. Its seven centers focus on cardiovascular and urogenital systems; metabolic and viral disorders; microbial or musculoskeletal diseases; neurological and gastrointestinal problems; psychiatric conditions; respiratory diseases and biopharmaceutical products. In 2006 and early 2007, GlaxoSmithKline received approval from the FDA to distribute Tykerb in combination with Xeloda to treat breast cancer, Avandamet, a treatment for type 2 diabetes, and Wellbutrin XL. GSK is also in the process of acquiring Praecis Pharmaceuticals and have recently acquired both Domantis Ltd, a company which focuses on antibody therapies, and CNS, the manufacturer of Breathe Right nasal strips and Fiberchoice, in 2006.

U.S. employees of GSK are offered a competitive benefits package including health care and other insurance, an employee assistance program, dependent care resources and corporate discounts.

FINANCIALS: Sales and profits are in thousands of dollars—add 000 to get the full amount. 2007 Note: Financial information for 2007 was not available for all companies at press time.

2007 Sales: $	2007 Profits: $	**U.S. Stock Ticker: GSK**
2006 Sales: $45,595,800	2006 Profits: $10,793,000	**Int'l Ticker: GSK** Int'l Exchange: London-LSE
2005 Sales: $37,783,631	2005 Profits: $8,400,952	Employees: 110,000
2004 Sales: $34,863,347	2004 Profits: $7,015,930	Fiscal Year Ends: 12/31
2003 Sales: $17,251,000	2003 Profits: $1,949,000	Parent Company:

SALARIES/BENEFITS:

Pension Plan: Y	ESOP Stock Plan: Y	Profit Sharing:	Top Exec. Salary: $1,523,000	Bonus: $2,250,000
Savings Plan: Y	Stock Purch. Plan:		Second Exec. Salary: $949,136	Bonus: $

OTHER THOUGHTS:

Apparent Women Officers or Directors: 1
Hot Spot for Advancement for Women/Minorities:

LOCATIONS: ("Y" = Yes)

West:	Southwest:	Midwest:	Southeast:	Northeast:	International:
Y	Y	Y	Y	Y	Y

Note: Financial information, benefits and other data can change quickly and may vary from those stated here.

GLOBAL HEALTHCARE EXCHANGE www.ghx.com

Industry Group Code: 511217 **Ranks within this company's industry group:** Sales: Profits:

Insurance/HMO/PPO:		Drugs:		Equipment/Supplies:		Hospitals/Clinics:		Services:		Health Care:	
Insurance:		Manufacturer:		Manufacturer:		Acute Care:		Diagnostics:		Home Health:	
Managed Care:		Distributor:		Distributor:		Sub-Acute:		Labs/Testing:		Long-Term Care:	
Utilization Management:		Specialty Pharmacy:		Leasing/Finance:		Outpatient Surgery:		Staffing:		Physical Therapy:	
Payment Processing:		Vitamins/Nutritionals:		Information Systems:	Y	Physical Rehab. Ctr.:		Waste Disposal:		Physician Prac. Mgmt.:	
		Clinical Trials:				Psychiatric Clinics:		Specialty Svcs.:	Y		

TYPES OF BUSINESS:

Healthcare Supply Chain Management

BRANDS/DIVISIONS/AFFILIATES:

GHX Connect Plus
AllSource Product Data Repository
Contract Center
Market4Care
NoInk Communications
GHX Mobile Solutions

CONTACTS: *Note: Officers with more than one job title may be intentionally listed here more than once.*

Michael Mahoney, CEO
Bruce Johnson, Pres.
Kurt Blasena, Exec. VP-Sales
Leigh Anderson, CTO
Bill Carlson, VP-Mktg. & Prod. Mgmt.

Phone: 720-887-7000	**Fax:** 720-887-7200
Toll-Free: 800-968-7449	
Address: 11000 Westmoor Circle, Ste. 400, Westminster, CO 80021 US	

GROWTH PLANS/SPECIAL FEATURES:

Global Healthcare Exchange LLC, or GHX, is dedicated t making the supply chain for healthcare practitioners mo efficient. The firm offers software products that eliminate th operational errors that typically occur between tradin partners, enabling buyers and sellers to automate the purchasing processes and make more accurate and cheap orders. The company's proprietary products include th AllSource Product Data Repository, which allows businesse easy access to product data on all transactions; GH Connect Plus, which provides healthcare organizations market through which to make electronic transaction Contract Center, which allows new contract information to b processed automatically; and various other products that ar designed to help simplify the supply chain. All of thes exchange services support trading partner connectivity an provide electronic order validation and reporting. GHX products work in conjunction with a seven-step plan th promises to significantly enhance the supply chain b cleansing and correcting company data; becomin connected through GHX software; creating onlin requisitions and ordering; updating contract price monitoring orders along the supply chain; simplifyin accounts payable; and working with GHX to continuall update and improve all aspects of the business proces GHX has two Customer Relations Centers, one serving th U.S. and Canada and the other serving Europe. In Jun 2007, the company expanded its European offerings b completing the acquisition of Market4Care, a Netherland based provider of e-procurement and other supply chai services. Together, the two companies serve more than 90 hospitals and 250 suppliers in Europe. Also in recent new in March 2007 the company changed the name of NoIn Communications, which it had acquired in July 2006, to GH Mobile Solutions.

FINANCIALS: Sales and profits are in thousands of dollars—add 000 to get the full amount. 2007 Note: Financial information for 2007 was not available for all companies at press time.

2007 Sales: $	2007 Profits: $	**U.S. Stock Ticker: Private**
2006 Sales: $	2006 Profits: $	**Int'l Ticker:** Int'l Exchange:
2005 Sales: $	2005 Profits: $	Employees:
2004 Sales: $	2004 Profits: $	Fiscal Year Ends: 12/31
2003 Sales: $	2003 Profits: $	Parent Company:

SALARIES/BENEFITS:

Pension Plan:	ESOP Stock Plan:	Profit Sharing:	Top Exec. Salary: $	Bonus: $
Savings Plan:	Stock Purch. Plan:		Second Exec. Salary: $	Bonus: $

OTHER THOUGHTS:

Apparent Women Officers or Directors:
Hot Spot for Advancement for Women/Minorities:

LOCATIONS: ("Y" = Yes)

West:	Southwest:	Midwest:	Southeast:	Northeast:	International:
Y	Y	Y	Y	Y	Y

GNC CORPORATION

www.gnc.com

Industry Group Code: 446191 **Ranks within this company's industry group:** Sales: Profits:

Insurance/HMO/PPO:		Drugs:		Equipment/Supplies:		Hospitals/Clinics:		Services:		Health Care:	
Insurance:		Manufacturer:	Y	Manufacturer:		Acute Care:		Diagnostics:		Home Health:	
Managed Care:		Distributor:		Distributor:		Sub-Acute:		Labs/Testing:		Long-Term Care:	
Utilization Management:		Specialty Pharmacy:		Leasing/Finance:		Outpatient Surgery:		Staffing:		Physical Therapy:	
Payment Processing:		Vitamins/Nutritionals:	Y	Information Systems:		Physical Rehab. Ctr.:		Waste Disposal:		Physician Prac. Mgmt.:	
		Clinical Trials:				Psychiatric Clinics:		Specialty Svcs.:			

TYPES OF BUSINESS:

Nutritional Supplements, Retail
Fitness Equipment
Online Sales
Nutritional Supplements, Manufacturing

BRANDS/DIVISIONS/AFFILIATES:

General Nutrition Centers
Royal Numico
PharmAssure
GNC Live Well
Mega Men
Total Lean
Preventive Nutrition

CONTACTS: *Note: Officers with more than one job title may be intentionally listed here more than once.*

Bruce E. Barkus, CEO
Joseph Fortunato, COO/Sr. Exec. VP
Bruce E. Barkus, Pres.
Curtis Larrimer, CFO/Exec. VP
Susan Trimbo, Sr. VP-Scientific Affairs
Michael Locke, Sr. VP-Mfg.
Guru Ramanathan, Sr. VP-Scientific Affairs
Robert J. DiNicola, Chmn.

Phone: 412-288-4600 **Fax:** 412-288-4764
Toll-Free:
Address: 300 6th Ave., Pittsburgh, PA 15222 US

GROWTH PLANS/SPECIAL FEATURES:

GNC Corporation, the parent of General Nutrition Centers, is a leading specialty retailer of nutritional supplements in the U.S. The company operates more than 3,500 retail outlets and maintains approximately 1,300 franchise locations throughout the U.S. and in 48 international markets. The company's GNC Live Well store format offers a full range of supplements and expanded product lines, such as aromatherapy, bath and spa and a broad selection of self-care-related products. GNC's products are divided mainly into four groups: vitamins and minerals, which are available in liquid, tablet and powder form; sports nutrition products, which are designed to be taken in conjunction with a exercise or fitness plan; diet products, available under the Total Lean and Body Answers brands; and other wellness products, which include Gold Card membership packages, cosmetics, food items and health management products. Through a strategic alliance with Rite Aid Corporation, GNC operates over 1,000 store-within-a-store concepts within Rite Aid retail drug stores nationwide. GNC also manufactures Rite Aid private-label products. In addition, the companies have introduced a vitamin and supplement line under the PharmAssure brand name. Through a partnership with Drugstore.com, GNC has the exclusive online rights to sell GNC-brand products, as well as the PharmAssure brand of vitamins and nutritional supplements. The firm's products are sold under proprietary brands including Mega Men, Pro Performance, Total Lean and Preventive Nutrition, as well as under nationally recognized third-party brands including Muscletech, EAS and Atkins. GNC operates two manufacturing facilities in South Carolina and distribution centers in Pennsylvania, South Carolina and Arizona.

FINANCIALS: **Sales and profits are in thousands of dollars—add 000 to get the full amount. 2007 Note: Financial information for 2007 was not available for all companies at press time.**

2007 Sales: $
2006 Sales: $
2005 Sales: $1,318,000
2004 Sales: $1,344,700
2003 Sales: $1,429,500

2007 Profits: $
2006 Profits: $
2005 Profits: $18,400
2004 Profits: $41,700
2003 Profits: $

U.S. Stock Ticker: Private
Int'l Ticker: Int'l Exchange:
Employees: 14,251
Fiscal Year Ends: 12/31
Parent Company:

SALARIES/BENEFITS:

Pension Plan: ESOP Stock Plan: Profit Sharing: Top Exec. Salary: $542,321 Bonus: $
Savings Plan: Stock Purch. Plan: Second Exec. Salary: $399,519 Bonus: $

OTHER THOUGHTS:

Apparent Women Officers or Directors: 1
Hot Spot for Advancement for Women/Minorities:

LOCATIONS: ("Y" = Yes)

West:	Southwest:	Midwest:	Southeast:	Northeast:	International:
Y	Y	Y	Y	Y	Y

Note: Financial information, benefits and other data can change quickly and may vary from those stated here.

GROUP HEALTH COOPERATIVE OF PUGET SOUND

www.ghc.org

Industry Group Code: 524114 **Ranks within this company's industry group:** Sales: Profits:

Insurance/HMO/PPO:		Drugs:		Equipment/Supplies:		Hospitals/Clinics:		Services:		Health Care:	
Insurance:		Manufacturer:		Manufacturer:		Acute Care:	Y	Diagnostics:		Home Health:	
Managed Care:	Y	Distributor:		Distributor:		Sub-Acute:	Y	Labs/Testing:		Long-Term Care:	
Utilization Management:		Specialty Pharmacy:	Y	Leasing/Finance:		Outpatient Surgery:		Staffing:		Physical Therapy:	
Payment Processing:		Vitamins/Nutritionals:		Information Systems:		Physical Rehab. Ctr.:		Waste Disposal:		Physician Prac. Mgmt.:	
		Clinical Trials:	Y			Psychiatric Clinics:	Y	Specialty Svcs.:	Y		

TYPES OF BUSINESS:

Insurance-Medical & Health, HMOs & PPOs
HMO, PPO & POS Plans
Clinics & Long-Term Facilities
Medical Research
Pharmacies

BRANDS/DIVISIONS/AFFILIATES:

Group Health Options, Inc.
Group Health Permanente
Group Heatlh Center for Health Studies
Group Health Community Foundation
KPS Health Plans
Kaiser Permanente

CONTACTS: *Note: Officers with more than one job title may be intentionally listed here more than once.*

Scott Armstrong, CEO
Scott Armstrong, Pres.
Richard Magnuson, CFO/Exec. VP
Rick Woods, General Counsel/Exec. VP
Laura McMillan, Interim Exec. Dir.-Organization Strategic Planning
Pam MacEwan, Exec. VP-Public Affairs & Governance
Barbara Belt-Lloyd, Controller/Interim Treas.
Hugh Straley, Medical Dir.-Cooperative/Pres., Permanente
James Hereford, Exec. VP-Strategic Svcs. & Quality
Marc West, Exec. VP-Group Health Permanente
Peter Morgan, Exec. VP-Group Practice Div.
Ruth Ballweg, Chmn.

Phone: 206-448-5600	**Fax:** 206-448-4010
Toll-Free: 888-901-4636	
Address: 521 Wall St., Seattle, WA 98121 US	

GROWTH PLANS/SPECIAL FEATURES:

Group Health Cooperative of Puget Sound (GHCPS) is consumer-governed, not-for-profit health care system th provides both medical coverage and care. It and i subsidiaries and affiliates serve almost 570,000 membe throughout 20 Washington state counties and two Nor Idaho counties. The company's members participate HMO, PPO or point of service (POS) health plans. facilities include two hospitals, 25 primary care centers, s special care units, eight behavioral health clinics, 15 visic centers, five hearing centers and six clinics that specialize speech, language and learning services. It also contrac with 39 other hospitals and over 9,000 practitioners; and also offers pharmacy services and a one-year accredite pharmacy training residency. The firm's family of Grou Health organizations, which provide care to over 70% of th company's members, includes Group Health Options, Inc., wholly-owned subsidiary that offers coordinated-care plan mainly for employers, ranging from a define physicia network plan to pay per service plans that members woul pay out of pocket for any care they receive outside th network. Group Health Permanente is a multi-special medical group whose doctors and other clinicians provid care at company-operated medical facilities. Group Healt Center for Health Studies is a research center that conduct epidemiologic, health services and clinical research. Grou Health Community Foundation is a charitable foundatio promoting health among children and teens. Additionall KPS Health Plans offers coverage for individuals, scho districts, federal employees, families, seniors, groups an other associations. GHCPS's affiliates include Kais Permanente, which works with the company in areas such a marketing to regional and national customers, sharing be clinical practices and providing full-service memb reciprocity. Finally, the firm has an alliance to share medic centers and hospitals with Virginia Mason Medical Cent and the Everett Clinic.

FINANCIALS: Sales and profits are in thousands of dollars—add 000 to get the full amount. 2007 Note: Financial information for 2007 was not available for all companies at press time.

2007 Sales: $	2007 Profits: $	**U.S. Stock Ticker: Nonprofit**
2006 Sales: $	2006 Profits: $	**Int'l Ticker:** Int'l Exchange:
2005 Sales: $	2005 Profits: $	Employees: 9,708
2004 Sales: $	2004 Profits: $	Fiscal Year Ends: 12/31
2003 Sales: $1,966,100	2003 Profits: $155,700	Parent Company:

SALARIES/BENEFITS:

Pension Plan: Y	ESOP Stock Plan:	Profit Sharing:	Top Exec. Salary: $	Bonus: $
Savings Plan: Y	Stock Purch. Plan:		Second Exec. Salary: $	Bonus: $

OTHER THOUGHTS:

Apparent Women Officers or Directors: 2
Hot Spot for Advancement for Women/Minorities: Y

LOCATIONS: ("Y" = Yes)

West:	Southwest:	Midwest:	Southeast:	Northeast:	International:
Y					

Note: Financial information, benefits and other data can change quickly and may vary from those stated here.

GROUP HEALTH INCORPORATED

www.ghi.com

Industry Group Code: 524114 **Ranks within this company's industry group:** Sales: 22 Profits: 23

Insurance/HMO/PPO:		Drugs:		Equipment/Supplies:		Hospitals/Clinics:		Services:		Health Care:	
Insurance:	Y	Manufacturer:		Manufacturer:		Acute Care:		Diagnostics:		Home Health:	
Managed Care:	Y	Distributor:		Distributor:		Sub-Acute:		Labs/Testing:		Long-Term Care:	
Utilization Management:		Specialty Pharmacy:		Leasing/Finance:		Outpatient Surgery:		Staffing:		Physical Therapy:	
Payment Processing:		Vitamins/Nutritionals:		Information Systems:		Physical Rehab. Ctr.:		Waste Disposal:		Physician Prac. Mgmt.:	
		Clinical Trials:				Psychiatric Clinics:		Specialty Svcs.:			

TYPES OF BUSINESS:

Insurance-Medical & Health, HMOs & PPOs
Health Insurance

BRANDS/DIVISIONS/AFFILIATES:

GHI HMO
Health Insurance Plan of Greater New York (HIP)
EmblemHealth, Inc.

CONTACTS: *Note: Officers with more than one job title may be intentionally listed here more than once.*

Frank J. Branchini, CEO/Vice Chmn.
Aran Ron, COO
Aran Ron, Pres.
Michael Palmateer, CFO
George Babitsch, Sr. VP-Sales & Account Mgmt.
Mariann Drohan, VP-Human Resources
Robert Allen, VP-IT
Robert Allen, VP-Tech. Svcs.
Michael Palmateer, Sr. VP-Admin.
Jeffrey Chansler, General Counsel/Sr. VP
Thomas Dwyer, Sr. VP-Oper.
Martin Adelstein, VP-Labor & Bus. Dev.
John Demers, VP-Corp. Comm.
Michael Palmateer, Sr. VP-Finance/Corp. Treas.
Thomas Nemeth, Sr. VP-Labor Relations
Michael Della Iacono, VP-Finance/Treas.
Ilene Margolin, Sr. VP-Corp. Affairs
Maria Martins-Lopes, Chief Medical Officer/Sr. VP-Medical Affairs
James F. Gill, Chmn.

Phone: 212-615-0000	**Fax:** 212-563-8561
Toll-Free: 800-444-2333	
Address: 441 9th Ave., New York, NY 10001-1681 US	

GROWTH PLANS/SPECIAL FEATURES:

Group Health Incorporated (GHI) is a not-for-profit organization that offers health insurance and administrative services to over 2.6 million members in the state of New York. Founded in 1937, GHI provides affordable health care to a broad segment of the population. The company and its subsidiary, GHI HMO, offer a range of flexible plans including medical, dental, vision, hospital, prescription drug and managed mental health coverage options, in addition to administrative-services-only plans. Offerings include plans for small groups, with 2-50 employees; plans for large groups, with more than 50 employees; and individual and family plans for people without a group. The firm has locations in New York City, Albany, Buffalo, Lake Katrine and Syracuse. Recently, GHI and Health Insurance Plan of Greater New York (HIP) have agreed to a merger that will unite the two companies under the leadership of a governing foundation, which will include an equal number of directors from both companies. With a combined membership of more than 4 million in the metropolitan area, the merger will create the largest health insurer based in New York State. EmblemHealth, Inc. will become the parent company for both entities following the merger. With the merger, the two will become a for-profit organization; this conversion is awaiting approval from the New York State Department of Insurance.

FINANCIALS: **Sales and profits are in thousands of dollars—add 000 to get the full amount. 2007 Note: Financial information for 2007 was not available for all companies at press time.**

2007 Sales: $	2007 Profits: $	**U.S. Stock Ticker: Nonprofit**
2006 Sales: $2,741,540	2006 Profits: $33,754	**Int'l Ticker:** Int'l Exchange:
2005 Sales: $2,560,313	2005 Profits: $9,446	Employees: 2,400
2004 Sales: $2,456,663	2004 Profits: $-14,504	Fiscal Year Ends: 12/31
2003 Sales: $2,157,473	2003 Profits: $5,606	Parent Company:

SALARIES/BENEFITS:

Pension Plan:	ESOP Stock Plan:	Profit Sharing:	Top Exec. Salary: $	Bonus: $
Savings Plan:	Stock Purch. Plan:		Second Exec. Salary: $	Bonus: $

OTHER THOUGHTS:

Apparent Women Officers or Directors: 9
Hot Spot for Advancement for Women/Minorities: Y

LOCATIONS: ("Y" = Yes)

West:	Southwest:	Midwest:	Southeast:	Northeast:	International:
				Y	

Note: Financial information, benefits and other data can change quickly and may vary from those stated here.

GSI GROUP INC

www.gsig.com

Industry Group Code: 339113 **Ranks within this company's industry group:** Sales: 42 Profits: 53

Insurance/HMO/PPO:		Drugs:		Equipment/Supplies:		Hospitals/Clinics:		Services:		Health Care:	
Insurance:		Manufacturer:		Manufacturer:	Y	Acute Care:		Diagnostics:		Home Health:	
Managed Care:		Distributor:		Distributor:		Sub-Acute:		Labs/Testing:		Long-Term Care:	
Utilization Management:		Specialty Pharmacy:		Leasing/Finance:		Outpatient Surgery:		Staffing:		Physical Therapy:	
Payment Processing:		Vitamins/Nutritionals:		Information Systems:		Physical Rehab. Ctr.:		Waste Disposal:		Physician Prac. Mgmt.:	
		Clinical Trials:				Psychiatric Clinics:		Specialty Svcs.:			

TYPES OF BUSINESS:

Equipment-Laser Systems
Motion Control Components
Lasers-Dermatology & Ophthalmology

BRANDS/DIVISIONS/AFFILIATES:

GSI Lumonics

CONTACTS: *Note: Officers with more than one job title may be intentionally listed here more than once.*

Sergio Edelstein, CEO
Sergio Edelstein, Pres.
Robert L. Bowen, CFO/VP
Linda Palmer, VP-Human Resources
Kurt A. Pelsue, CTO/VP
Daniel J. Lyne, General Counsel/VP
Felix I. Stukalin, VP-Bus. Dev.
Linda Palmer, VP-Corp. Comm.
Richard B. Black, Chmn.

Phone: 978-439-5511	**Fax:** 978-663-0044
Toll-Free: 800-342-3757	
Address: 39 Manning Rd., Billerica, MA 01821 US	

GROWTH PLANS/SPECIAL FEATURES:

GSI Group, Inc., designs, develops, manufactures an markets components, lasers and laser-based advance manufacturing systems as enabling tools for a wide range applications in the medical, automotive, semiconducto electronics, light industrial and aerospace industries. Wi operations in nine countries, the firm sells to origin equipment manufacturers (OEMs) worldwide. Th company's component products include optical scanners an subsystems used by OEMs for materials processing, te and measurement, alignment, inspection, imaging, and rapi prototyping, a well as medical applications in dermatolog and ophthalmology. Components are also used in fil imaging subsystems for CAT scans and magnetic resonanc imaging systems. GSI's lasers are primarily used materials processing applications in light automotiv electronics, aerospace, medical and light industrial market Laser systems are also used in applications such as lase repair to improve yields in the production of dynamic rando access memory chips; permanent marking systems f silicon wafers and individual dies for traceability and quali control; circuit processing systems for linear and mixe signal devices; certain passive electronic components an printed circuit board manufacturing systems; and for ho drilling, solder paste inspection and component placeme inspection. In March 2007, the company received a $ million wafer repair systems order, from Inotera, for its gree laser based M 555 model.

The firm offers American employees tuition reimburseme paid memberships to professional associations; paid semin and conference fees; employee referral incentives; educati savings plans; and credit union membership.

FINANCIALS: **Sales and profits are in thousands of dollars—add 000 to get the full amount. 2007 Note: Financial information for 2007 was not available for all companies at press time.**

2007 Sales: $	2007 Profits: $	**U.S. Stock Ticker: GSIG**
2006 Sales: $428,616	2006 Profits: $16,254	**Int'l Ticker:** Int'l Exchange:
2005 Sales: $344,144	2005 Profits: $2,789	Employees: 2,029
2004 Sales: $288,131	2004 Profits: $3,992	Fiscal Year Ends: 12/31
2003 Sales: $185,561	2003 Profits: $-2,170	Parent Company:

SALARIES/BENEFITS:

Pension Plan:	ESOP Stock Plan:	Profit Sharing:	Top Exec. Salary: $500,000	Bonus: $370,000
Savings Plan: Y	Stock Purch. Plan: Y		Second Exec. Salary: $290,000	Bonus: $142,535

OTHER THOUGHTS:

Apparent Women Officers or Directors: 1
Hot Spot for Advancement for Women/Minorities:

LOCATIONS: ("Y" = Yes)

West:	Southwest:	Midwest:	Southeast:	Northeast:	International:
Y		Y		Y	Y

GTC BIOTHERAPEUTICS INC www.gtc-bio.com

ndustry Group Code: 325414 **Ranks within this company's industry group:** Sales: 4 Profits: 4

nsurance/HMO/PPO:		Drugs:		Equipment/Supplies:		Hospitals/Clinics:		Services:		Health Care:	
nsurance:		Manufacturer:	Y	Manufacturer:		Acute Care:		Diagnostics:		Home Health:	
Managed Care:		Distributor:		Distributor:		Sub-Acute:		Labs/Testing:		Long-Term Care:	
Utilization Management:		Specialty Pharmacy:		Leasing/Finance:		Outpatient Surgery:		Staffing:		Physical Therapy:	
Payment Processing:		Vitamins/Nutritionals:		Information Systems:		Physical Rehab. Ctr.:		Waste Disposal:		Physician Prac. Mgmt.:	
		Clinical Trials:				Psychiatric Clinics:		Specialty Svcs.:			

TYPES OF BUSINESS:

Recombinant Proteins
Drugs-Anticoagulants
Transgenic Animals

BRANDS/DIVISIONS/AFFILIATES:

Genzyme Transgenics Corp.
Atryn

CONTACTS: *Note: Officers with more than one job title may be intentionally listed here more than once.*

Geoffrey F. Cox, CEO
Geoffrey F. Cox, Pres.
John B. Green, CFO
Harry M. Meade, Sr. VP-R&D
Daniel S. Woloshen, General Counsel/Sr. VP
Gregory Liposky, Sr. VP-Oper.
Ashley Lawton, VP-Bus. Dev.
Thomas E. Newberry, VP-Corp. Comm.
John B. Green, Sr. VP-Finance/Treas.
Carol A. Ziomek, VP-Dev.
Suzanne Groet, VP-Therapeutic Protein Dev.
Richard A. Scotland, Sr. VP-Regulatory Affairs
Frederick J. Finnegan, VP-Commercial Dev.
Geoffrey F. Cox, Chmn.

Phone: 508-620-9700 **Fax:** 508-370-3797
Toll-Free:
Address: 175 Crossing Blvd., Framingham, MA 01702-9322 US

GROWTH PLANS/SPECIAL FEATURES:

GTC Biotherapeutics, Inc. (GTC) applies transgenic technology to develop recombinant proteins for human therapeutic uses. The company uses transgenic animals that express specific recombinant proteins in their milk. Its technology platform includes the ability to generate animals and provide for animal husbandry, breeding and milking, as well as the ability to purify the milk to a clarified intermediate bulk material that may undergo manufacturing to obtain a clinical grade product. The firm generates transgenic animals through microinjection and nuclear transfer, and it expects to rely primarily on nuclear transfer techniques in new program development work. GTC uses goats in most of its commercial development programs due to the relatively short gestation times and relatively high milk production volume of the animals. The company's leading product is ATryn for patients with hereditary antithrombin deficiency undergoing surgical procedures. Antithrombin is an important protein found in the bloodstream with anticoagulant and anti-inflammatory properties. The drug is currently in Phase 3 of clinical trials in the U.S., while it has been approved for use in the European Union. It is also in Phase 1 clinical trials for disseminated intravascular coagulation, which is an acquired deficiency of antithrombin that occurs in sepsis. In addition to its transgenic technologies, GTC is developing a recombinant human serum albumin, a malaria vaccine, and a CD137 antibody to solid tumors. The firm has development partnerships with companies including Abbott Labs, Bristol-Myers Squibb, Centocor, Elan Pharmaceuticals, Progenics and ImmunoGen. In January 2006, the company received a patent covering the production of therapeutic proteins in the milk of transgenic mammals. In August 2006, the European Commission approved GTC's product ATryn for marketing.

GTC offers its employees tuition reimbursement and health coverage.

FINANCIALS: **Sales and profits are in thousands of dollars—add 000 to get the full amount. 2007 Note: Financial information for 2007 was not available for all companies at press time.**

2007 Sales: $	2007 Profits: $	**U.S. Stock Ticker: GTCB**
2006 Sales: $6,128	2006 Profits: $-33,345	**Int'l Ticker:** Int'l Exchange:
2005 Sales: $4,152	2005 Profits: $-30,112	Employees: 153
2004 Sales: $6,626	2004 Profits: $-29,493	Fiscal Year Ends: 1/01
2003 Sales: $9,764	2003 Profits: $-29,537	Parent Company:

SALARIES/BENEFITS:

Pension Plan:	ESOP Stock Plan:	Profit Sharing:	Top Exec. Salary: $458,640	Bonus: $157,225
Savings Plan: Y	Stock Purch. Plan: Y		Second Exec. Salary: $294,840	Bonus: $76,688

OTHER THOUGHTS:

Apparent Women Officers or Directors: 2
Hot Spot for Advancement for Women/Minorities: Y

LOCATIONS: ("Y" = Yes)

West:	Southwest:	Midwest:	Southeast:	Northeast:	International:
				Y	

Note: Financial information, benefits and other data can change quickly and may vary from those stated here.

GYRUS GROUP PLC www.gyrusplc.com

Industry Group Code: 339113 **Ranks within this company's industry group:** Sales: 45 Profits: 46

Insurance/HMO/PPO:		Drugs:		Equipment/Supplies:		Hospitals/Clinics:		Services:		Health Care:	
Insurance:		Manufacturer:		Manufacturer:	Y	Acute Care:		Diagnostics:		Home Health:	
Managed Care:		Distributor:		Distributor:	Y	Sub-Acute:		Labs/Testing:		Long-Term Care:	
Utilization Management:		Specialty Pharmacy:		Leasing/Finance:		Outpatient Surgery:		Staffing:		Physical Therapy:	
Payment Processing:		Vitamins/Nutritionals:		Information Systems:		Physical Rehab. Ctr.:		Waste Disposal:		Physician Prac. Mgmt.:	
		Clinical Trials:				Psychiatric Clinics:		Specialty Svcs.:			

TYPES OF BUSINESS:

Supplies-Surgical Instruments
Ear, Nose & Throat Products
Urology & Gynecology Products

BRANDS/DIVISIONS/AFFILIATES:

PlasmaKinetic
Gyrus AMCI
Endowrist PL Dissecting Forceps
Gyrus North America Sales, Inc.
Gyrus International, Ltd.
Urology Solutions Pty Ltd.
Gyrus Australia Pty Ltd.

CONTACTS: *Note: Officers with more than one job title may be intentionally listed here more than once.*

Roy Davis, CEO
Simon Shaw, CFO
Linsey Williams, VP-Human Resources
Scott Sanders, VP-Prod. Dev./Procedures
Ron Honig, VP-Legal/Corp. Sec.
Craig Swandal, VP-Oper.
Robert Hoxie, Pres., ENT Div., Gyrus ACMI
Bob Gadsden, VP-Intellectual Property
Mark Jensen, VP-Regulatory Affairs & Quality Assurance
Brian Steer, Exec. Chmn.
Michael Geraghty, Pres., Int'l Div., Gyrus AMCI

Phone: 44-29-2077-6300	**Fax:** 44-29-2077-6301
Toll-Free:	
Address: Fortran Rd., St. Mellons, Cardiff, CF3 0LT UK	

GROWTH PLANS/SPECIAL FEATURES:

Gyrus Group plc develops and manufactures advanced surgical systems. Its products are based on its PlasmaKinetic technology, which uses radio frequencies to cut, vaporize and coagulate tissue or seal blood vessels. Gyrus operates through four global business divisions: Ear nose and throat (ENT), which provided approximately 18% of Gyrus' 2006 revenue; surgical, 24.6%; urology & gynecology 45%; and partnered technologies (PT), 12.3%. Gyrus AMCI runs all but PT. The ENT division provides surgical instruments, packing materials, scopes and implants for otology, rhinology, and head, neck, throat and upper airway surgery. The surgical segment focuses on providing equipment for laparoscopic surgery, a minimally invasive procedure that inserts slender surgical instruments and advanced camera systems through small incisions; and general surgery instruments. The urology and gynecology division focuses on endoscopic, similar to laparoscopic surgery for the prostate, bladder, kidney and uterine regions. The PT division develops, licenses and commercializes Gyrus' technology outside of its core areas by out-licensing to a number of marketing partners, including Johnson & Johnson's Depuy Mitek and Ethicon Endo-Surgery; Guidant; ConMed; and, most recently, Intuitive Surgical Inc. In May 2006, Gyrus Group announced that it had partnered with Intuitive Surgical for the development of new robotic surgery instrumentation. Under the agreement, Gyrus will receive a license fee and royalties on sales of Endowrist PL Dissecting Forceps for robot application using the da Vinci Surgical System. The firm also sells its products directly through two organizations: Gyrus North America Sales, Inc. and Gyrus International, Ltd. Its web site contains multiple educational resources for nurses, physicians and patients, including narrated online lessons, online PowerPoint presentations and links to web sites. Recently, the company acquired Urology Solutions Pty Limited, which it will rename Gyrus Australia Pty Limited, the exclusive distributor of the Gyrus's surgical products in Australia and New Zealand.

FINANCIALS: Sales and profits are in thousands of dollars—add 000 to get the full amount. 2007 Note: Financial information for 2007 was not available for all companies at press time.

2007 Sales: $
2006 Sales: $417,800
2005 Sales: $267,944
2004 Sales: $167,400
2003 Sales: $138,900

2007 Profits: $
2006 Profits: $25,800
2005 Profits: $11,183
2004 Profits: $15,114
2003 Profits: $10,600

U.S. Stock Ticker: GGYRF
Int'l Ticker: GYG Int'l Exchange: London-LSE
Employees: 1,434
Fiscal Year Ends: 12/31
Parent Company:

SALARIES/BENEFITS:

Pension Plan: ESOP Stock Plan: Profit Sharing: Top Exec. Salary: $609,818 Bonus: $304,909
Savings Plan: Stock Purch. Plan: Second Exec. Salary: $457,363 Bonus: $228,667

OTHER THOUGHTS:

Apparent Women Officers or Directors: 2
Hot Spot for Advancement for Women/Minorities:

LOCATIONS: ("Y" = Yes)

West:	Southwest:	Midwest:	Southeast:	Northeast:	International:
		Y	Y	Y	Y

HAEMONETICS CORPORATION www.haemonetics.com

ndustry Group Code: 339113 **Ranks within this company's industry group:** Sales: 43 Profits: 29

ısurance/HMO/PPO:		Drugs:		Equipment/Supplies:		Hospitals/Clinics:		Services:		Health Care:	
ısurance:		Manufacturer:		Manufacturer:	Y	Acute Care:		Diagnostics:		Home Health:	
Ianaged Care:		Distributor:		Distributor:		Sub-Acute:		Labs/Testing:		Long-Term Care:	
tilization Management:		Specialty Pharmacy:		Leasing/Finance:		Outpatient Surgery:		Staffing:		Physical Therapy:	
ayment Processing:		Vitamins/Nutritionals:		Information Systems:	Y	Physical Rehab. Ctr.:		Waste Disposal:		Physician Prac. Mgmt.:	
		Clinical Trials:				Psychiatric Clinics:		Specialty Svcs.:			

TYPES OF BUSINESS:

:quipment-Blood-Recovery Systems
iurgical Blood Salvage Equipment
3lood Component Therapy Equipment
ıutomated Blood Collection Equipment

BRANDS/DIVISIONS/AFFILIATES:

PCS System
ИCS System
ACS System
Cell Saver System
OrthoPAT System
cardioPAT System
SmartSuction System
Cymbal System

CONTACTS: *Note: Officers with more than one job title may be ntentionally listed here more than once.*

3rad Nutter, CEO
3rian Concannon, COO
3rad Nutter, Pres.
Christopher Lindop, CFO/VP-Bus. Dev.
Jlrich Eckert, VP-Sales & Mktg., Donor Plasma Div. Europe
Joseph Forish, VP-Human Resources
Robert Ebbeling, VP-Tech. Oper.
3ob Pike, VP-New Prod. Dev.
William Granville, VP-Worldwide Mfg.
James O'Shaughnessy, General Counsel
Robert Ebbeling, VP-Oper.
William Still, VP-Bus. Dev.
Lisa Lopez, VP-Corp. Affairs
Susan Hanlon, VP-Planning & Control
Tom Lawlor, Pres., Patient Div.
Peter Allen, Pres., Donor Div.
Pam Spear, VP-Quality Systems
Mark Popovsky, VP/Corp. Medical Dir.
Ronald A. Matricaria, Chmn.
Ryoji Sakai, Pres., Japan

Phone: 781-848-7100	**Fax:** 781-356-3558
Toll-Free: 800-225-5242	
Address: 400 Wood Rd., Braintree, MA 02184-9114 US	

GROWTH PLANS/SPECIAL FEATURES:

Haemonetics Corporation is a global medical devices company that manufactures automated systems for the collection, processing and surgical salvage of blood. Haemonetics markets its products to hospitals, commercial plasma fractionators and national health organizations in over 50 countries. The company's blood donor products include the PCS brand plasma systems, which automate the collection of plasma from donors who are often paid a fee for their donation; the MCS brand blood bank system, which automates the collection of platelets from volunteer donors; and the ACS brand blood bank system, which automates the process used to freeze, thaw and wash red blood cells. Haemonetics' patient products include the Cell Saver, OrthoPAT and cardioPAT brand blood salvage systems, which allow surgeons to collect the blood lost by a patient during or after surgery for transfusion; and the SmartSuction family of products used to clear blood and debris from the surgical field. The company's software and services division principally provides support to its donor division customers. Recently, the company acquired nanotechnology company Arryx, whose proprietary technology uses light to move and manipulate small objects. Applications of the technology include blood separation and processing. In March 2007, Haemonetics announced the launch of its Cymbal system, a new mobile blood collection system. The company acquired Infonale, a developer of information technology software and consulting services for optimizing hospital blood use, for $1.3 million in July. Haemonetics announced in August the formation of a new subsidiary, Haemonetics Software Solutions, Inc., to provide information technology solutions to the blood and plasma collection industries.

Haemonetics offers its employees an on-site child care center, a flexible spending program, an employee stock purchase plan, a 401(k) plan, a tuition reimbursement/educational assistance plan, employee assistance programs, a referral bonus program, a wellness program, company sponsored events and medical, dental and vision coverage.

FINANCIALS: **Sales and profits are in thousands of dollars—add 000 to get the full amount. 2007 Note: Financial information for 2007 was not available for all companies at press time.**

2007 Sales: $449,607	2007 Profits: $49,109	**U.S. Stock Ticker: HAE**
2006 Sales: $419,733	2006 Profits: $69,076	**Int'l Ticker:** Int'l Exchange:
2005 Sales: $383,600	2005 Profits: $39,600	Employees: 1,826
2004 Sales: $364,229	2004 Profits: $29,320	Fiscal Year Ends: 3/31
2003 Sales: $337,000	2003 Profits: $28,400	Parent Company:

SALARIES/BENEFITS:

Pension Plan:	ESOP Stock Plan:	Profit Sharing:	Top Exec. Salary: $518,077	Bonus: $
Savings Plan: Y	Stock Purch. Plan: Y		Second Exec. Salary: $382,854	Bonus: $200,000

OTHER THOUGHTS:

Apparent Women Officers or Directors: 5
Hot Spot for Advancement for Women/Minorities: Y

LOCATIONS: ("Y" = Yes)

West:	Southwest:	Midwest:	Southeast:	Northeast:	International:
			Y	Y	Y

HANGER ORTHOPEDIC GROUP INC www.hanger.com

Industry Group Code: 621340 **Ranks within this company's industry group:** Sales: 2 Profits: 2

Insurance/HMO/PPO:		Drugs:		Equipment/Supplies:		Hospitals/Clinics:		Services:		Health Care:	
Insurance:		Manufacturer:		Manufacturer:	Y	Acute Care:		Diagnostics:		Home Health:	
Managed Care:		Distributor:		Distributor:	Y	Sub-Acute:		Labs/Testing:		Long-Term Care:	
Utilization Management:		Specialty Pharmacy:		Leasing/Finance:		Outpatient Surgery:		Staffing:		Physical Therapy:	
Payment Processing:		Vitamins/Nutritionals:		Information Systems:		Physical Rehab. Ctr.:	Y	Waste Disposal:		Physician Prac. Mgmt.:	
		Clinical Trials:				Psychiatric Clinics:		Specialty Svcs.:			

TYPES OF BUSINESS:

Orthotic & Prosthetic Patient Care Centers
Orthotic & Prosthetic Devices & Components Distribution

BRANDS/DIVISIONS/AFFILIATES:

Southern Prosthetic Supply, Inc.
IN, Inc.
Innovative Neurotronics, Inc.
Linkia, LLC
WalkAide System

CONTACTS: *Note: Officers with more than one job title may be intentionally listed here more than once.*

Ivan R. Sabel, CEO
Thomas F. Kirk, COO
Thomas F. Kirk, Pres.
George E. McHenry, CFO
Hai Tran, Treas.
Richmond L. Taylor, Pres., Hanger Prosthetics & Orthotics, Inc.
Ronald N. May, Pres., Southern Prosthetic Supply, Inc.
Ivan R. Sabel, Chmn.

Phone: 301-986-0701	**Fax:** 301-986-0702
Toll-Free:	
Address: 2 Bethesda Metro Center, Ste. 1200, Bethesda, MD 20814 US	

GROWTH PLANS/SPECIAL FEATURES:

Hanger Orthopedic Group, Inc. owns and operates orthopedic and prosthetic (O&P) patient-care centers accounting for roughly 22% of the O&P patient-care market in the U.S. The company operates in two segments: patient care services, which provides its services through 61[?] patient-care centers and over 1,000 practitioners in 45 states and Washington, D.C.; and distribution, which distributes O&P components to the O&P market and the firm's patient care centers. In the orthotics business, Hanger Orthopedic designs, fabricates, fits and maintains standard and custom made braces and other devices (such as spinal, knee and sport-medicine braces) that provide external support to patients suffering from musculoskeletal disorders, such as ailments of the back, extremities or joints and injuries from sports or other activities. In the prosthetic business, the company designs, fabricates, fits and maintains custom made artificial limbs for patients who are without one or more limbs as a result of traumatic injuries, vascular diseases diabetes, cancer or congenital disorders. Subsidiary Southern Prosthetic Supply, Inc. distributes branded and private label O&P devices and components in the U.S., all of which are manufactured by third parties. Subsidiary Innovative Neurotronics, Inc. creates products for sale in the company's patient-care centers and to patients who have a loss of mobility due to strokes, multiple sclerosis or other similar conditions. Subsidiary Linkia, LLC develops programs to manage all aspects of O&P patient care for large private payors. Subsidiary IN, Inc.'s line of functional electrical stimulation products, the WalkAide System, is a medical device designed to counter the lack of ankle dorsiflexion (foot drop), in patients who sustained damage to upper motor neurons or pathways to the spinal cord. The WalkAide System electronically stimulates the appropriate nerves and muscles. In June 2007, Hanger Orthopedics acquired Paris O&P, Inc., a provider of O&P services with locations in Texas and Oklahoma.

FINANCIALS: Sales and profits are in thousands of dollars—add 000 to get the full amount. 2007 Note: Financial information for 2007 was not available for all companies at press time.

2007 Sales: $	2007 Profits: $	**U.S. Stock Ticker: HGR**
2006 Sales: $598,766	2006 Profits: $3,434	**Int'l Ticker:** Int'l Exchange:
2005 Sales: $578,241	2005 Profits: $17,753	Employees: 3,302
2004 Sales: $568,721	2004 Profits: $-23,394	Fiscal Year Ends: 12/31
2003 Sales: $547,903	2003 Profits: $16,239	Parent Company:

SALARIES/BENEFITS:

Pension Plan:	ESOP Stock Plan:	Profit Sharing:	Top Exec. Salary: $545,000	Bonus: $135,182
Savings Plan:	Stock Purch. Plan:		Second Exec. Salary: $463,500	Bonus: $107,781

OTHER THOUGHTS:

Apparent Women Officers or Directors: 1
Hot Spot for Advancement for Women/Minorities:

LOCATIONS: ("Y" = Yes)

West:	Southwest:	Midwest:	Southeast:	Northeast:	International:
Y	Y	Y	Y	Y	Y

Note: Financial information, benefits and other data can change quickly and may vary from those stated here.

HARBORSIDE HEALTHCARE CORP

www.harborsidehealthcare.com

Industry Group Code: 623110 **Ranks within this company's industry group:** Sales: Profits:

Insurance/HMO/PPO:		Drugs:		Equipment/Supplies:		Hospitals/Clinics:		Services:		Health Care:	
nsurance:		Manufacturer:		Manufacturer:		Acute Care:		Diagnostics:		Home Health:	
Managed Care:		Distributor:		Distributor:		Sub-Acute:	Y	Labs/Testing:		Long-Term Care:	Y
Utilization Management:		Specialty Pharmacy:		Leasing/Finance:		Outpatient Surgery:		Staffing:		Physical Therapy:	Y
Payment Processing:		Vitamins/Nutritionals:		Information Systems:		Physical Rehab. Ctr.:	Y	Waste Disposal:		Physician Prac. Mgmt.:	
		Clinical Trials:				Psychiatric Clinics:	Y	Specialty Svcs.:	Y		

TYPES OF BUSINESS:

Long-Term Health Care/Nursing Homes
Sub-Acute Care Facilities
Rehabilitation Services
Temporary Staffing Services

BRANDS/DIVISIONS/AFFILIATES:

SunBridge Healthcare Corp.
Sun Healthcare Group, Inc.

CONTACTS: *Note: Officers with more than one job title may be intentionally listed here more than once.*

Damian N. Dell'Anno, CEO
Damian N. Dell'Anno, COO
Damian N. Dell'Anno, Pres.
William H. Stephan, CFO/Sr. VP
Bruce J. Beardsley, Sr. VP-Acquisitions
Damian N. Dell'Anno, Chmn.

Phone: 949-255-7100 **Fax:** 949-255-7054
Toll-Free: 800-729-6600
Address: 18831 Von Karman, Ste. 400, Irvine, CA 92612 US

GROWTH PLANS/SPECIAL FEATURES:

Harborside Healthcare Corp., a subsidiary of SunBridge Healthcare Corp., which in its turn is a subsidiary of Sun Healthcare Group, Inc., is a provider of long-term care, post-acute care and other specialty medical services in the mid-Atlantic, Midwest and New England. The company operates 66 facilities serving more than 7,500 clients in nine states: Connecticut, Indiana, Kentucky, Maryland, Massachusetts, New Jersey, New Hampshire, Ohio and Rhode Island. The firm provides traditional skilled nursing care; a wide range of sub-acute care programs such as orthopedic, CVA/stroke, cardiac, pulmonary and wound care; as well as distinct programs for the provision of care to Alzheimer's and hospice patients. Harborside provides both short- and long-term programs. Short-term programs are designed primarily as transitional care for people who are returning home after a hospital stay. These programs focus on enabling patients to achieve their highest possible level of function and self-sufficiency through a multi-faceted approach to patient needs and care. The medical, social and rehabilitative needs of patients are addressed by a team of nurses, therapists, pharmacists, dieticians and social workers under the direction of a physician. Long term programs are focused primarily on the care of patients with Alzheimer's and other dementias. In addition, Harborside provides rehabilitation therapy services both at company-operated and non-affiliated facilities. Harborside also provides support services, including dietary services, social services, housekeeping and laundry services, pharmaceutical and medical supplies and routine rehabilitation therapy. In April 2007, Harborside was acquired by SunBridge Healthcare Corp., a subsidiary of Sun Healthcare Group, Inc.

The company offers its employees medical, dental, prescription drug and vision insurance; a 401(k) plan; life and disability insurance; and nursing tuition assistance.

FINANCIALS: **Sales and profits are in thousands of dollars—add 000 to get the full amount. 2007 Note: Financial information for 2007 was not available for all companies at press time.**

2007 Sales: $	2007 Profits: $	**U.S. Stock Ticker: Subsidiary**
2006 Sales: $	2006 Profits: $	**Int'l Ticker:** Int'l Exchange:
2005 Sales: $	2005 Profits: $	Employees: 8,000
2004 Sales: $	2004 Profits: $	Fiscal Year Ends:
2003 Sales: $	2003 Profits: $	Parent Company: SUNBRIDGE HEALTHCARE CORP

SALARIES/BENEFITS:

Pension Plan:	ESOP Stock Plan:	Profit Sharing:	Top Exec. Salary: $397,523	Bonus: $86,250
Savings Plan: Y	Stock Purch. Plan:		Second Exec. Salary: $281,259	Bonus: $45,000

OTHER THOUGHTS:

Apparent Women Officers or Directors:
Hot Spot for Advancement for Women/Minorities: Y

LOCATIONS: ("Y" = Yes)

West:	Southwest:	Midwest:	Southeast:	Northeast:	International:
Y		Y		Y	

HARVARD PILGRIM HEALTH CARE INC

www.harvardpilgrim.org

Industry Group Code: 524114 **Ranks within this company's industry group:** Sales: 23 Profits: 21

Insurance/HMO/PPO:		Drugs:		Equipment/Supplies:		Hospitals/Clinics:		Services:		Health Care:	
Insurance:	Y	Manufacturer:		Manufacturer:		Acute Care:		Diagnostics:		Home Health:	
Managed Care:	Y	Distributor:		Distributor:		Sub-Acute:		Labs/Testing:		Long-Term Care:	
Utilization Management:		Specialty Pharmacy:		Leasing/Finance:		Outpatient Surgery:		Staffing:		Physical Therapy:	
Payment Processing:		Vitamins/Nutritionals:		Information Systems:		Physical Rehab. Ctr.:		Waste Disposal:		Physician Prac. Mgmt.:	
		Clinical Trials:				Psychiatric Clinics:		Specialty Svcs.:			

TYPES OF BUSINESS:

Insurance-Medical & Health, HMOs & PPOs
Indemnity Insurance

BRANDS/DIVISIONS/AFFILIATES:

Harvard Pilgrim Health Care of New England
HPHC Insurance Company
First Seniority
Medicare Enhance
HPHConnect
Health Plans, Inc.
Benefit Plan Management, Inc.

CONTACTS: *Note: Officers with more than one job title may be intentionally listed here more than once.*

Charles D. Baker, CEO
Bruce M. Bullen, COO
Charles D. Baker, Pres.
Joseph C. Capezza, CFO
Vincent Capozzi, Sr. VP-Sales & Mktg.
Deborah A. Hicks, VP-Human Resources
Deborah A. Norton, CIO/Sr. VP
Vicki Coates, VP-Benefits, Products & Market Performance
Laura S. Peabody, General Counsel/Sr. VP
David Cochran, Sr. VP-Strategic Dev.
Marie Montgomery, VP-Corp. Acct./Controller
Roberta Herman, Sr. VP/Chief Medical Officer
William R. Breidenbach, Pres., Health Plans, Inc.
Lynn A. Bowman, VP-Customer Service
Beth-Ann Roberts, VP-Northern New England Oper.
Charles D. Baker, Chmn.

Phone: 617-745-1000 **Fax:** 617-509-7590
Toll-Free: 888-888-4742
Address: 93 Worcester St., Wellesley, MA 02481 US

GROWTH PLANS/SPECIAL FEATURES:

Harvard Pilgrim Health Care, Inc. is a not-for-profit health plan with approximately 800,000 members and a network of more than 22,000 providers and 130 hospitals. The firm provides health coverage in Massachusetts and Maine, as well as in New Hampshire through its Harvard Pilgrim Health Care of New England subsidiary. In addition, the firm is the parent company of HPHC Insurance Company, an indemnity insurance company in Massachusetts and New Hampshire. The firm offers a variety of plan choices, including HMOs, PPOs and point-of-service plans. The company also enrolls Medicare beneficiaries through its First Seniority programs as well as offering its HPHConnect web site for online benefits administration. Subsidiary Health Plans, Inc. specializes in administering customized self-insured or ASO (Administrative Services Only) plans for employers. Health Plans, Inc. is the largest third party administrator (TPA) in New England. Through a recently formed alliance with UnitedHealth Group, combining the company's network of doctors and hospitals with UnitedHealth's national network, the Harvard Pilgrim also offers a program for multi-site, multi-state employers that have a substantial number of employees in the company's region.

FINANCIALS: **Sales and profits are in thousands of dollars—add 000 to get the full amount. 2007 Note: Financial information for 2007 was not available for all companies at press time.**

2007 Sales: $	2007 Profits: $	**U.S. Stock Ticker: Nonprofit**
2006 Sales: $2,488,095	2006 Profits: $70,536	**Int'l Ticker:** Int'l Exchange:
2005 Sales: $2,235,843	2005 Profits: $73,807	Employees: 1,400
2004 Sales: $2,300,000	2004 Profits: $38,600	Fiscal Year Ends: 12/31
2003 Sales: $2,100,000	2003 Profits: $44,200	Parent Company:

SALARIES/BENEFITS:

Pension Plan:	ESOP Stock Plan:	Profit Sharing:	Top Exec. Salary: $	Bonus: $
Savings Plan: Y	Stock Purch. Plan:		Second Exec. Salary: $	Bonus: $

OTHER THOUGHTS:

Apparent Women Officers or Directors: 9
Hot Spot for Advancement for Women/Minorities: Y

LOCATIONS: ("Y" = Yes)

West:	Southwest:	Midwest:	Southeast:	Northeast:	International:
Y				Y	

Note: Financial information, benefits and other data can change quickly and may vary from those stated here.

HCA INC

www.hcahealthcare.com

Industry Group Code: 622110 **Ranks within this company's industry group:** Sales: 2 Profits: 1

Insurance/HMO/PPO:		Drugs:		Equipment/Supplies:		Hospitals/Clinics:		Services:		Health Care:	
Insurance:		Manufacturer:		Manufacturer:		Acute Care:	Y	Diagnostics:		Home Health:	
Managed Care:		Distributor:		Distributor:		Sub-Acute:	Y	Labs/Testing:		Long-Term Care:	
Utilization Management:		Specialty Pharmacy:		Leasing/Finance:		Outpatient Surgery:	Y	Staffing:		Physical Therapy:	
Payment Processing:		Vitamins/Nutritionals:		Information Systems:		Physical Rehab. Ctr.:	Y	Waste Disposal:		Physician Prac. Mgmt.:	
		Clinical Trials:				Psychiatric Clinics:	Y	Specialty Svcs.:			

TYPES OF BUSINESS:

Hospitals-General
Outpatient Surgery Centers
Sub-Acute Care
Psychiatric Hospitals
Rehabilitation Services
Hospital Management Services

BRANDS/DIVISIONS/AFFILIATES:

BAIN CAPITAL LLC
KKR & CO LP (KOHLBERG KRAVIS ROBERTS & CO)
MERRILL LYNCH & CO INC

CONTACTS: *Note: Officers with more than one job title may be intentionally listed here more than once.*

Jack O. Bovender, Jr., CEO
Richard M. Bracken, COO
Richard M. Bracken, Pres.
R. Milton Johnson, CFO/Exec. VP
John M. Steele, Sr. VP-Human Resources
Noel B. Williams, CIO/Sr. VP
Robert A. Waterman, General Counsel/Sr. VP
V. Carl George, VP-Dev.
David G. Anderson, Sr. VP-Finance/Treas.
Chuck J. Hall, Pres., Eastern Group
Jonathan B. Perlin, Chief Medical Officer/Sr. VP-Quality
Victor L. Campbell, Sr. VP
Rosalyn S. Elton, Sr. VP-Oper. Finance
Jack O. Bovender, Jr., Chmn.
James A. Fitzgerald, Jr., Sr. VP-Supply Chain Oper.

Phone: 615-344-2068	**Fax:**
Toll-Free:	
Address: 1 Park Plaza, I-4W, Nashville, TN 37203 US	

GROWTH PLANS/SPECIAL FEATURES:

HCA, Inc., formerly known as HCA Healthcare Co., owns and operates approximately 170 hospitals and approximately 113 outpatient surgery centers in 20 states, England and Switzerland. The company's acute care hospitals provide a full range of services, including internal medicine, general surgery, neurosurgery, orthopedics, obstetrics, cardiac care, diagnostic and emergency services, radiology, respiratory therapy, cardiology and physical therapy. The psychiatric hospitals provide therapeutic programs including child, adolescent and adult psychiatric care and adult and adolescent alcohol and drug abuse treatment and counseling. The outpatient health care facilities operated by HCA include surgery centers, diagnostic and imaging centers, comprehensive outpatient rehabilitation and physical therapy centers. The company's hospitals do not engage in extensive medical research and education programs; however, some facilities are affiliated with medical schools and may participate in the clinical rotation of medical interns and residents. In addition, HCA provides a variety of management services to health care facilities such as patient safety programs; ethics and compliance programs; national supply contracts; equipment purchasing and leasing contracts; and accounting, financial and clinical systems. Other services include governmental reimbursement assistance; construction planning and coordination; information technology systems; legal counsel; human resource services; and internal audit. In 2006, HCA was taken private in a buyout deal valued $33 billion (including the company's debt; without debt the buyout was worth $21 billion). The group participating in the HCA negotiations includes three private-equity investors: Bain Capital, LLC; KKR & Co. LP (Kohlberg, Kravis, Roberts & Co.); and Merrill Lynch & Co.'s Global Private Equity.

HCA offers its employees a day care flexible spending account; child care center discounts; an adoption assistance program; a ConSern student loan program; laser surgery discounts at LaserVision; a healthcare flexible spending account; and medical, dental and vision coverage.

FINANCIALS: **Sales and profits are in thousands of dollars—add 000 to get the full amount. 2007 Note: Financial information for 2007 was not available for all companies at press time.**

2007 Sales: $	2007 Profits: $	**U.S. Stock Ticker: Private**
2006 Sales: $25,477,000	2006 Profits: $1,036,000	**Int'l Ticker:** Int'l Exchange:
2005 Sales: $24,455,000	2005 Profits: $1,424,000	Employees: 186,000
2004 Sales: $23,502,000	2004 Profits: $1,246,000	Fiscal Year Ends: 12/31
2003 Sales: $21,808,000	2003 Profits: $1,332,000	Parent Company: BAIN CAPITAL LLC

SALARIES/BENEFITS:

Pension Plan: Y	ESOP Stock Plan:	Profit Sharing:	Top Exec. Salary: $1,404,959	Bonus: $
Savings Plan: Y	Stock Purch. Plan:		Second Exec. Salary: $817,667	Bonus: $

OTHER THOUGHTS:

Apparent Women Officers or Directors: 3
Hot Spot for Advancement for Women/Minorities: Y

LOCATIONS: ("Y" = Yes)

West:	Southwest:	Midwest:	Southeast:	Northeast:	International:
Y	Y	Y	Y	Y	Y

Note: Financial information, benefits and other data can change quickly and may vary from those stated here.

HEALTH CARE SERVICE CORPORATION www.hcsc.net

Industry Group Code: 524114 **Ranks within this company's industry group:** Sales: 6 Profits: 5

Insurance/HMO/PPO:		Drugs:		Equipment/Supplies:		Hospitals/Clinics:		Services:		Health Care:	
Insurance:	Y	Manufacturer:		Manufacturer:		Acute Care:		Diagnostics:		Home Health:	
Managed Care:	Y	Distributor:		Distributor:		Sub-Acute:		Labs/Testing:		Long-Term Care:	
Utilization Management:		Specialty Pharmacy:		Leasing/Finance:		Outpatient Surgery:		Staffing:		Physical Therapy:	
Payment Processing:	Y	Vitamins/Nutritionals:		Information Systems:		Physical Rehab. Ctr.:		Waste Disposal:		Physician Prac. Mgmt.:	
		Clinical Trials:				Psychiatric Clinics:		Specialty Svcs.:	Y		

TYPES OF BUSINESS:

Insurance-Medical & Health, HMOs & PPOs
Traditional Indemnity Plans
Medicare Supplemental Health
Life Insurance
Dental & Vision Insurance
Electronic Claims & Information Network
Workers' Compensation
Retirement Services

BRANDS/DIVISIONS/AFFILIATES:

Blue Cross and Blue Shield of Illinois
Blue Cross and Blue Shield of Texas
Blue Cross and Blue Shield of New Mexico
Preferred Financial Group
Colorado Bankers Life Insurance Company
Medical Life Insurance Company
Dental Network of America, Inc.
Health Information Network, Inc. (The)

CONTACTS: *Note: Officers with more than one job title may be intentionally listed here more than once.*

Raymond F. McCaskey, CEO
Raymond F. McCaskey, Pres.
Denise A. Bujack, CFO/Sr. VP
Patrick F. O'Connor, Sr. VP/Chief Human Resources Officer
John A. Oborn, CIO/Sr. VP
Deborah Dorman-Rodriguez, Chief Legal Officer/Sr. VP
Gail K. Boudreaux, Exec. VP-Oper.
Karen Chesrown, Sr. VP-Strategy
Robert Kieckhefer, VP-Public Affairs
Martin G. Foster, Pres., Texas Div.
Tara D. Gurber, Sr. VP-Audit
Elizabeth A. Watrin, Pres., New Mexico Div.
Ray A. Angeli, Sr. VP-Subscriber Services
Milton Carroll, Chmn.

Phone: 312-653-6000	**Fax:** 312-819-1220
Toll-Free:	
Address: 300 E. Randolph St., Chicago, IL 60601-5099 US	

GROWTH PLANS/SPECIAL FEATURES:

Health Care Service Corporation (HCSC) is a non-investor owned mutual insurance company that operates through its Blue Cross and Blue Shield divisions in Illinois, Texas, New Mexico and Oklahoma. It also has several subsidiaries to offer a variety of health and life insurance products and related services to employers and individuals. It provides PPOs, HMOs, POS plans, traditional indemnity and Medicare supplemental health plans to approximately 9.5 million members through Blue Cross and Blue Shield of Illinois (BCBSI), Blue Cross and Blue Shield of Texas (BCBST) and Blue Cross and Blue Shield of New Mexico (BCBSNM). Through its non-Blue Cross and Blue Shield subsidiaries, the company offers prescription drug plans, Medicare supplemental insurance, dental and vision coverage, life and disability insurance, workers compensation, retirement services and medical financial services. One such subsidiary, Preferred Financial Group, is made up of HSCS's various life insurance subsidiaries, including Fort Dearborn Life Insurance Company of Illinois (FDL) and Colorado Bankers Life Insurance Company. Another subsidiary, Dental Network of America, Inc., functions as a third-party administrator for all company dental programs and is registered in every state except Florida. It also offers a dental discount card program. The Health Information Network, Inc., a wholly-owned subsidiary, is an electronic claims and information network that acts as a clearinghouse for physicians, hospitals and other providers to file patient claims and other transactions electronically with their billing agents. Hallmark Services Corporation, another wholly-owned subsidiary, provides administration and claim adjudication services for individual policies to the direct markets divisions of BCBSI and BCBST.

HCSC has been recognized by DiversityInc as one of the top five U.S. companies, and it is the highest ranking health insurer on the magazine's Top 50 Companies for Diversity list.

FINANCIALS: Sales and profits are in thousands of dollars—add 000 to get the full amount. 2007 Note: Financial information for 2007 was not available for all companies at press time.

2007 Sales: $	2007 Profits: $	**U.S. Stock Ticker: Mutual Company**
2006 Sales: $12,971,600	2006 Profits: $1,115,400	**Int'l Ticker:** Int'l Exchange:
2005 Sales: $11,713,900	2005 Profits: $1,145,600	Employees: 14,000
2004 Sales: $10,629,100	2004 Profits: $1,049,400	Fiscal Year Ends: 12/31
2003 Sales: $9,140,400	2003 Profits: $614,000	Parent Company:

SALARIES/BENEFITS:

Pension Plan:	ESOP Stock Plan:	Profit Sharing:	Top Exec. Salary: $	Bonus: $
Savings Plan:	Stock Purch. Plan:		Second Exec. Salary: $	Bonus: $

OTHER THOUGHTS:

Apparent Women Officers or Directors: 6
Hot Spot for Advancement for Women/Minorities: Y

LOCATIONS: ("Y" = Yes)

West:	Southwest:	Midwest:	Southeast:	Northeast:	International:
Y	Y	Y		Y	

HEALTH GRADES INC www.healthgrades.com

Industry Group Code: 514199 **Ranks within this company's industry group:** Sales: 2 Profits: 2

Insurance/HMO/PPO:		Drugs:		Equipment/Supplies:		Hospitals/Clinics:		Services:		Health Care:	
Insurance:		Manufacturer:		Manufacturer:		Acute Care:		Diagnostics:		Home Health:	
Managed Care:		Distributor:		Distributor:		Sub-Acute:		Labs/Testing:		Long-Term Care:	
Utilization Management:		Specialty Pharmacy:		Leasing/Finance:		Outpatient Surgery:		Staffing:		Physical Therapy:	
Payment Processing:		Vitamins/Nutritionals:		Information Systems:		Physical Rehab. Ctr.:		Waste Disposal:		Physician Prac. Mgmt.:	
		Clinical Trials:				Psychiatric Clinics:		Specialty Svcs.:	Y		

TYPES OF BUSINESS:

Online Health Information
Health Providers Ratings Data
Consulting Services
Marketing Assistance Services

BRANDS/DIVISIONS/AFFILIATES:

CompareYourCare
Clinical Excellence Research & Consulting group

CONTACTS: *Note: Officers with more than one job title may be intentionally listed here more than once.*

Kerry R. Hicks, CEO
Kerry R. Hicks, Pres.
Allen Dodge, CFO/Exec. VP
Kirk Schreck, Sr. VP-Sales
Allen Silkin, Sr. VP-Internet Advertising
David G. Hicks, Exec. VP
Sarah P. Loughran, Exec. VP
Samantha Collier, Sr. VP-Medical Affairs/Chief Medical Officer
Tod Baker, Sr. VP-Internet Patient Acquisition
Kerry R. Hicks, Chmn.

Phone: 303-716-0041	**Fax:** 303-716-1298
Toll-Free:	
Address: 500 Golden Ridge Rd., Ste. 100, Golden, CO 80401 US	

GROWTH PLANS/SPECIAL FEATURES:

Health Grades, Inc. (HGI) is a health care ratings and consulting company that provides consumers with the means to assess and compare the quality or qualifications of health care providers including hospitals, nursing homes, home health agencies, hospice programs and fertility clinics. It currently provides ratings or profile information on over 5,000 hospitals, 700,000 physicians in over 120 specialties and 16,000 nursing homes. This information is available on the firm's web site free of charge to consumers, employers and health plans, with more detailed reports available for a fee. For hospitals with high ratings, HGI offers the opportunity to license its ratings and trademarks and provides assistance in marketing programs. The company also offers consulting services to hospitals that either want to build a reputation based on quality of care or are working to identify areas to improve quality. The firm's Health Management Suite of products is available to organizations to license under the Clinical Excellence Research & Consulting Guide, Physician Quality Guide, Nursing Home Quality Guide and Home Health Quality brands. HGI has an ongoing collaboration with the Leapfrog Group to analyze and report the findings of hospital patient safety surveys. Leapfrog's survey assesses the extent to which hospitals strive to implement patient safety practices and rewards for advances in safety. In addition to its other online databases, in March 2007 HGI launched the first physician malpractice database in the country that is the public. In July 2007, the company expanded and renamed its Hospital Quality consultancy group to the HealthGrades Clinical Excellence Research & Consulting group.

FINANCIALS: **Sales and profits are in thousands of dollars—add 000 to get the full amount. 2007 Note: Financial information for 2007 was not available for all companies at press time.**

2007 Sales: $	2007 Profits: $	**U.S. Stock Ticker: HGRD**
2006 Sales: $27,770	2006 Profits: $3,181	**Int'l Ticker:** Int'l Exchange:
2005 Sales: $20,808	2005 Profits: $4,140	Employees: 123
2004 Sales: $14,538	2004 Profits: $1,782	Fiscal Year Ends: 12/31
2003 Sales: $8,805	2003 Profits: $-1,284	Parent Company:

SALARIES/BENEFITS:

Pension Plan:	ESOP Stock Plan:	Profit Sharing:	Top Exec. Salary: $315,683	Bonus: $130,000
Savings Plan: Y	Stock Purch. Plan: Y		Second Exec. Salary: $214,665	Bonus: $26,000

OTHER THOUGHTS:

Apparent Women Officers or Directors: 1
Hot Spot for Advancement for Women/Minorities:

LOCATIONS: ("Y" = Yes)

West:	Southwest:	Midwest:	Southeast:	Northeast:	International:
Y					

Note: Financial information, benefits and other data can change quickly and may vary from those stated here.

HEALTH INSURANCE PLAN OF GREATER NEW YORK

www.hipusa.com

Industry Group Code: 524114 **Ranks within this company's industry group:** Sales: Profits:

Insurance/HMO/PPO:		Drugs:		Equipment/Supplies:		Hospitals/Clinics:		Services:		Health Care:	
Insurance:	Y	Manufacturer:		Manufacturer:		Acute Care:		Diagnostics:		Home Health:	
Managed Care:	Y	Distributor:		Distributor:		Sub-Acute:		Labs/Testing:		Long-Term Care:	
Utilization Management:		Specialty Pharmacy:		Leasing/Finance:		Outpatient Surgery:		Staffing:		Physical Therapy:	
Payment Processing:		Vitamins/Nutritionals:		Information Systems:		Physical Rehab. Ctr.:		Waste Disposal:		Physician Prac. Mgmt.:	
		Clinical Trials:				Psychiatric Clinics:		Specialty Svcs.:			

TYPES OF BUSINESS:

Insurance-Medical & Health, HMOs & PPOs
HMO

BRANDS/DIVISIONS/AFFILIATES:

ConnectiCare Holding Company
Vytra Health Plans
HIP Integrative Wellness
Group Health, Inc. (GHI)
PerfectHealth

CONTACTS: *Note: Officers with more than one job title may be intentionally listed here more than once.*

Anthony L. Watson, CEO
Daniel T. McGowan, COO
Daniel T. McGowan, Pres.
Michael D. Fullwood, CFO/Exec. VP
Dewitt M. Smith, Sr. VP-Mktg. & Sales
Fred Blickman, Sr. VP-Human Resources
John H. Steber, CIO
Pedro Villalba, CTO
Vincent Scicchitano, Sr. VP-Prod. & Customer Mgmt.
Michael D. Fullwood, General Counsel/Corp. Sec.
John H. Steber, Exec. VP-Oper.
Arthur J. Byrd, VP-Investor Rel.
Dominic F. D'Adamo, Sr. VP-Finance/Corp. Controller
Arthur J. Byrd, Treas.
Anthony L. Watson, Chmn.

Phone: 212-630-5000	**Fax:** 212-630-8747
Toll-Free: 800-447-8255	
Address: 55 Water St., New York, NY 10041-8190 US	

GROWTH PLANS/SPECIAL FEATURES:

Health Insurance Plan of Greater New York (HIP) is the largest HMO in New York City based on membership. HIP maintains contracts with 160 hospitals, including acute care institutions, in New York, Connecticut and Massachusetts, to provide services to members. HIP's total network, including subsidiaries, comprises nearly 43,000 physicians and other providers in over 72,000 locations in New York, Connecticut and Massachusetts. The company has acquired several businesses in its history including Vytra Health Plans, ConnectiCare and PerfectHealth, bringing HIP's total combined membership to approximately 1.4 million. HIP was the first health insurance company in the nation to translate its web site into Chinese and Korean in addition to Spanish, as well as being rated the number-one insurance company in the U.S. for the innovative use of technology by Information Week Magazine. In addition to HIP's comprehensive heath insurance options, the company provides programs and discounts for alternative medicine such as acupuncture, massage therapy and nutritional counseling, mental health services and chemical dependency treatment, pharmacy services, dental plans and women's wellness programs. HIP Integrative Wellness is an initiative supporting the belief that the best patient care will be attentive to the patient's spiritual, emotional and mental states as well as the physical. In November 2006, HIP and Group Health Incorporated were affiliated when EmblemHealth Inc. became the parent organization of both entities. Since then, GHI and HIP have submitted a plan to combine the two not-for-profit health benefits providers into a single for-profit publicly traded company.

FINANCIALS: **Sales and profits are in thousands of dollars—add 000 to get the full amount. 2007 Note: Financial information for 2007 was not available for all companies at press time.**

2007 Sales: $	2007 Profits: $	**U.S. Stock Ticker: Nonprofit**
2006 Sales: $	2006 Profits: $	**Int'l Ticker:** Int'l Exchange:
2005 Sales: $4,599,802	2005 Profits: $115,333	Employees: 1,800
2004 Sales: $3,654,183	2004 Profits: $215,260	Fiscal Year Ends: 12/31
2003 Sales: $3,369,900	2003 Profits: $274,800	Parent Company:

SALARIES/BENEFITS:

Pension Plan: Y	ESOP Stock Plan:	Profit Sharing:	Top Exec. Salary: $	Bonus: $
Savings Plan: Y	Stock Purch. Plan:		Second Exec. Salary: $	Bonus: $

OTHER THOUGHTS:

Apparent Women Officers or Directors: 9
Hot Spot for Advancement for Women/Minorities: Y

LOCATIONS: ("Y" = Yes)

West:	Southwest:	Midwest:	Southeast:	Northeast:	International:
				Y	

Note: Financial information, benefits and other data can change quickly and may vary from those stated here.

HEALTH MANAGEMENT ASSOCIATES INC www.hma-corp.com

Industry Group Code: 622110 **Ranks within this company's industry group:** Sales: 13 Profits: 11

Insurance/HMO/PPO:		Drugs:		Equipment/Supplies:		Hospitals/Clinics:		Services:		Health Care:	
Insurance:		Manufacturer:		Manufacturer:		Acute Care:	Y	Diagnostics:		Home Health:	
Managed Care:		Distributor:		Distributor:		Sub-Acute:		Labs/Testing:		Long-Term Care:	
Utilization Management:		Specialty Pharmacy:		Leasing/Finance:		Outpatient Surgery:		Staffing:		Physical Therapy:	
Payment Processing:		Vitamins/Nutritionals:		Information Systems:		Physical Rehab. Ctr.:		Waste Disposal:		Physician Prac. Mgmt.:	
		Clinical Trials:				Psychiatric Clinics:	Y	Specialty Svcs.:			

TYPES OF BUSINESS:

Acute Care Hospitals

BRANDS/DIVISIONS/AFFILIATES:

CONTACTS: *Note: Officers with more than one job title may be intentionally listed here more than once.*

Burke W. Whitman, CEO
Kelly E. Curry, COO/Exec. VP
Burke W. Whitman, Pres.
Robert E. Farnham, CFO/Sr. VP
Timothy R. Parry, General Counsel/Sr. VP/Corp. Sec.
Peter M. Lawson, Exec. VP-Oper.
Joseph C. Meek, Corp. Treas.
Jon P. Vollmer, Exec. VP-Oper.
John C. Merriwether, VP-Financial Rel.
Lisa Gore, Sr. VP-Clinical Affairs
William J. Schoen, Chmn.

Phone: 239-598-3104	**Fax:** 239-598-2705
Toll-Free:	
Address: 5811 Pelican Bay Blvd., Ste. 500, Naples, FL 34108 US	

GROWTH PLANS/SPECIAL FEATURES:

Health Management Associates, Inc. owns and operates acute care hospitals in non-urban communities. The company operates 60 hospitals, with a total of 8,589 licensed beds. The firm operates facilities in Alabama, Arkansas, Florida, Georgia, Kentucky, Mississippi, Missouri, North Carolina, Oklahoma, Pennsylvania, South Carolina, Tennessee, Texas, Virginia, Washington and West Virginia. Services provides by the hospitals include general surgery, internal medicine, obstetrics, emergency room care, radiology, oncology, diagnostic care, coronary care and pediatric care. They also provide outpatient services such as one-day surgery, laboratory, x-ray, respiratory therapy, cardiology and physical therapy. In addition, some hospitals provide specialty services in, among other areas, cardiology (e.g., open-heart surgery), neuron-surgery, oncology, radiation therapy, computer-assisted tomography scanning, magnetic resonance imaging, lithotripsy and full-service obstetrics. The facilities benefit from centralized corporate resources such as purchasing; information services; finance and control systems; legal services; facilities planning; physicians recruitment services; administrative personnel management; marketing; and public relations. Some of the company's hospitals provide services to retired and certain other military personnel and their families, pursuant to the Civilian Health and Medical Program of Uniformed Services (CHAMPUS). In June 2006, Health Management Associates acquired Gulf Coast Medical Center, a 189-bed general acute care hospital in Mississippi. In September 2006, the company sold its two psychiatric hospitals in Florida with a combined total of 184 licensed beds.

The company offers its employees medical, dental and vision insurance; flexible spending accounts; life insurance; a 401(k) plan; and disability and critical illness insurance.

FINANCIALS: **Sales and profits are in thousands of dollars—add 000 to get the full amount. 2007 Note: Financial information for 2007 was not available for all companies at press time.**

2007 Sales: $	2007 Profits: $	**U.S. Stock Ticker: HMA**
2006 Sales: $4,056,599	2006 Profits: $182,749	**Int'l Ticker:** Int'l Exchange:
2005 Sales: $3,479,568	2005 Profits: $353,077	Employees: 34,500
2004 Sales: $3,092,547	2004 Profits: $325,099	Fiscal Year Ends: 12/31
2003 Sales: $2,560,600	2003 Profits: $283,400	Parent Company:

SALARIES/BENEFITS:

Pension Plan:	ESOP Stock Plan:	Profit Sharing:	Top Exec. Salary: $800,000	Bonus: $
Savings Plan: Y	Stock Purch. Plan:		Second Exec. Salary: $600,000	Bonus: $600,000

OTHER THOUGHTS:

Apparent Women Officers or Directors: 2
Hot Spot for Advancement for Women/Minorities:

LOCATIONS: ("Y" = Yes)

West:	Southwest:	Midwest:	Southeast:	Northeast:	International:
Y	Y	Y	Y	Y	

Note: Financial information, benefits and other data can change quickly and may vary from those stated here.

HEALTH MANAGEMENT SYSTEMS INC www.hmsy.com

Industry Group Code: 522320 **Ranks within this company's industry group:** Sales: 3 Profits: 3

Insurance/HMO/PPO:		Drugs:		Equipment/Supplies:		Hospitals/Clinics:		Services:		Health Care:	
Insurance:		Manufacturer:		Manufacturer:		Acute Care:		Diagnostics:		Home Health:	
Managed Care:		Distributor:		Distributor:		Sub-Acute:		Labs/Testing:		Long-Term Care:	
Utilization Management:	Y	Specialty Pharmacy:		Leasing/Finance:		Outpatient Surgery:		Staffing:		Physical Therapy:	
Payment Processing:	Y	Vitamins/Nutritionals:		Information Systems:	Y	Physical Rehab. Ctr.:		Waste Disposal:		Physician Prac. Mgmt.:	Y
		Clinical Trials:				Psychiatric Clinics:		Specialty Svcs.:	Y		

TYPES OF BUSINESS:

Data Processing-Health Care
Information Management Services
Outsourcing Services
Billing & Claims Management

BRANDS/DIVISIONS/AFFILIATES:

HMS Holdings Corp
Benefits Solutions Practice Area

CONTACTS:

Note: Officers with more than one job title may be intentionally listed here more than once.

Robert M. Holster, CEO
William C. Lucia, COO
William C. Lucia, Pres.
Walter D. Hosp, CFO
Richard M. Lang, Chief Compliance Officer
Robert M. Holster, Chmn.

Phone: 212-685-4545	**Fax:** 212-857-5973
Toll-Free: 877-467-0184	
Address: 401 Park Ave. S., New York, NY 10016 US	

GROWTH PLANS/SPECIAL FEATURES:

Health Management Systems, Inc. (HMS), a wholly-owned subsidiary of HMS Holdings Corp., provides information-based revenue enhancement services to health care providers and payors. The company has provided services in over 30 states and for the federal Centers for Medicare and Medicaid Services. It serves benefit clients by increasing revenue, accelerating cash flow and reducing operating and administrative costs. The company offers hospitals and other health care providers a comprehensive array of technology-based revenue cycle services. These services include identifying third-party resources; submitting timely and accurate bills to third-party payers and patients; recovering and properly accounting for the amounts due; and securing the appropriate cost-based reimbursement from entitlement programs. Clients may use one or more of the services or outsource the entirety of their business office operations to Health Management Systems. HMS offers a broad range of services to state Medicaid and other government agencies that administer health care entitlement programs. The firm's services are designed to identify and recover amounts that should have been the responsibility of a third party or that were paid inappropriately. In June 2006, HMS acquired the assets of Public Consulting Group, Inc.'s Benefit Solutions Practice Area for $80 million cash; 2,016,000 shares of HMS Holding's common stock; and a contingent cash payment of up to $15 million if certain revenue targets are met. In September 2006, the company merged with Benefit Solutions Practice Area.

The company offers its employees benefits that include medical, dental and vision insurance; a 401(k) plan; and tuition reimbursement.

FINANCIALS:

Sales and profits are in thousands of dollars—add 000 to get the full amount. 2007 Note: Financial information for 2007 was not available for all companies at press time.

2007 Sales: $	2007 Profits: $	**U.S. Stock Ticker: Subsidiary**
2006 Sales: $87,940	2006 Profits: $5,325	**Int'l Ticker:** Int'l Exchange:
2005 Sales: $60,024	2005 Profits: $8,027	Employees: 493
2004 Sales: $50,451	2004 Profits: $7,711	Fiscal Year Ends:
2003 Sales: $74,400	2003 Profits: $2,300	Parent Company: HMS HOLDINGS CORP

SALARIES/BENEFITS:

Pension Plan:	ESOP Stock Plan:	Profit Sharing:	Top Exec. Salary: $400,000	Bonus: $400,000
Savings Plan: Y	Stock Purch. Plan:		Second Exec. Salary: $300,000	Bonus: $300,000

OTHER THOUGHTS:

Apparent Women Officers or Directors: 1
Hot Spot for Advancement for Women/Minorities:

LOCATIONS: ("Y" = Yes)

West:	Southwest:	Midwest:	Southeast:	Northeast:	International:
Y	Y	Y	Y	Y	

Note: Financial information, benefits and other data can change quickly and may vary from those stated here.

HEALTH NET INC

www.healthnet.com

Industry Group Code: 524114 **Ranks within this company's industry group:** Sales: 7 Profits: 11

Insurance/HMO/PPO:		Drugs:		Equipment/Supplies:		Hospitals/Clinics:		Services:		Health Care:	
Insurance:	Y	Manufacturer:		Manufacturer:		Acute Care:		Diagnostics:		Home Health:	
Managed Care:	Y	Distributor:		Distributor:		Sub-Acute:		Labs/Testing:		Long-Term Care:	
Utilization Management:	Y	Specialty Pharmacy:		Leasing/Finance:		Outpatient Surgery:		Staffing:		Physical Therapy:	
Payment Processing:		Vitamins/Nutritionals:		Information Systems:		Physical Rehab. Ctr.:		Waste Disposal:		Physician Prac. Mgmt.:	
		Clinical Trials:				Psychiatric Clinics:		Specialty Svcs.:	Y		

TYPES OF BUSINESS:

Insurance-Medical & Health, HMOs & PPOs
Utilization Management
Health Care Services Management
Administrative Services
Health Insurance Underwriting
Life Insurance Underwriting

BRANDS/DIVISIONS/AFFILIATES:

Decision Power
It's Your Life Wellsite
Salud con Health Net

CONTACTS:

Note: Officers with more than one job title may be intentionally listed here more than once.

Jay M. Gellert, CEO
Jay M. Gellert, Pres.
James Woys, Interm CFO/Pres., Gov't & Specialty Svcs.
Mark S. El-Tawil, Chief Senior Prod. Officer
Linda V. Tiano, General Counsel/Sr. VP/Sec.
David W. Olson, Sr. VP-Corp. Comm.
John P. Sivori, Sr. VP/Pres., Health Net Pharmaceutical Svcs.
Steven H. Nelson, Pres., Health Net of the Northeast, Inc.
Steven Sell, CEO/Pres., MHN
Stephen D. Lynch, Pres., Regional Health Plans
Roger F. Greaves, Chmn.

Phone: 818-676-6000 **Fax:** 818-676-8591
Toll-Free: 800-291-6911
Address: 21650 Oxnard St., Woodland Hills, CA 91367 US

GROWTH PLANS/SPECIAL FEATURES:

Health Net, Inc. is an integrated managed care organization that delivers managed health care services through health plans and government sponsored managed care plans. The firm's subsidiaries also offer products related to prescription drugs; managed health care product coordination for multi-region employers; and administrative services for medical groups and self-funded benefits programs. HealthNet's managed health care options include health benefits provided through a network of health maintenance organizations (HMOs), insured preferred provider organizations (PPOs) and point-of-service (POS) plans to approximately 6.6 million individuals in 27 states and Washington, D.C. These operations extend through group, individual, Medicare, Medicaid, TRICARE and Veterans Affairs programs. HealthNet's HMOs and PPOs contract approximately 48,000 primary care physicians and 144,000 specialist physicians. Health Net's behavioral health subsidiary provides mental health benefits to approximately 7.3 million individuals in all 50 states. The company owns health and life insurance companies licensed to sell exclusive provider organization (EPO), PPO, POS and indemnity products, as well as auxiliary non-health products such as life and accidental death and dismemberment, dental, vision, behavioral health and disability insurance, in 46 states and Washington, D.C. In 2006, approximately 55% of the company's commercial members were covered by HMOs; 42% were covered by POS and PPO products; and 3% by EPO and fee-for-service products including consumer-directed health plans. The firm also provides the Decision Power series of programs designed to directly involve patients in their health care decisions. It runs the It's Your Life Wellsite, similar to the Decision Power programs, but targeted at Medicare members. The Salud con Health Net is a project of its Californian branch designed to help uninsured Latino immigrants meet their health care needs. In April 2006, Health Net acquired the assets of Universal Care, a Long Beach, California-based health care company. The acquisition netted the company approximately 100,000 members.

FINANCIALS:

Sales and profits are in thousands of dollars—add 000 to get the full amount. 2007 Note: Financial information for 2007 was not available for all companies at press time.

2007 Sales: $	2007 Profits: $
2006 Sales: $12,908,350	2006 Profits: $329,313
2005 Sales: $11,940,533	2005 Profits: $229,785
2004 Sales: $11,646,393	2004 Profits: $42,604
2003 Sales: $10,959,000	2003 Profits: $234,000

U.S. Stock Ticker: HNT
Int'l Ticker: Int'l Exchange:
Employees: 9,725
Fiscal Year Ends: 12/31
Parent Company:

SALARIES/BENEFITS:

Pension Plan:	ESOP Stock Plan:	Profit Sharing:	Top Exec. Salary: $1,061,538	Bonus: $1,213,713
Savings Plan: Y	Stock Purch. Plan:		Second Exec. Salary: $545,197	Bonus: $

OTHER THOUGHTS:

Apparent Women Officers or Directors: 1
Hot Spot for Advancement for Women/Minorities:

LOCATIONS: ("Y" = Yes)

West:	Southwest:	Midwest:	Southeast:	Northeast:	International:
Y	Y			Y	

Note: Financial information, benefits and other data can change quickly and may vary from those stated here.

HEALTHAXIS INC

www.healthaxis.com

Industry Group Code: 511212 **Ranks within this company's industry group:** Sales: 8 Profits: 6

Insurance/HMO/PPO:		Drugs:		Equipment/Supplies:		Hospitals/Clinics:		Services:		Health Care:	
Insurance:		Manufacturer:		Manufacturer:		Acute Care:		Diagnostics:		Home Health:	
Managed Care:		Distributor:		Distributor:		Sub-Acute:		Labs/Testing:		Long-Term Care:	
Utilization Management:		Specialty Pharmacy:		Leasing/Finance:		Outpatient Surgery:		Staffing:		Physical Therapy:	
Payment Processing:		Vitamins/Nutritionals:		Information Systems:	Y	Physical Rehab. Ctr.:		Waste Disposal:		Physician Prac. Mgmt.:	
		Clinical Trials:				Psychiatric Clinics:		Specialty Svcs.:	Y		

TYPES OF BUSINESS:

Software-Health Care Administration
Benefit Administration Systems
Web-Enabled Administration Systems
Imaging Services
Outsourcing Services

BRANDS/DIVISIONS/AFFILIATES:

Application Service Provider
Insur-Admin
Insur-Claims
WebAxis-Employee/Member and Employer Self-service
WebAxis Broker
WebAxis-Enroll
Ultimate TPA

CONTACTS: *Note: Officers with more than one job title may be intentionally listed here more than once.*

John M. Carradine, CEO
John M. Carradine, Pres.
Ron Herbert, CFO
Brent Webb, General Counsel/Sec./Sr. VP
Bill Malone, VP-Oper.
Lawrence Thompson, Exec. VP
Roxanne Seale, Sr. VP-Application Solutions
James W. McLane, Chmn.

Phone: 972-443-5000 **Fax:** 972-443-5231
Toll-Free: 800-519-0679
Address: 7301 State Hwy. 161, Ste. 300, Irving, TX 75039 US

GROWTH PLANS/SPECIAL FEATURES:

Healthaxis, Inc. is a technology-enhanced, fully integrated solutions and services provider for health benefit administrators and health insurance claim processors. It offers software and related business services through its Application Service Provider (ASP) technology to help health insurance payers, third-party administrators (TPAs), preferred provider organizations (PPOs) and self-administered employer groups provide claims related services to members, employees and providers. Assisting these ASP technologies are Healthaxis' web-based capabilities and its (BPO) services. Healthaxis' products are divided into three categories: Benefit Administration and Claims Processing Systems; Web Connectivity Products; and Business Process Outsourcing (BPO) Services. Benefit administration, including enrollment, billing and premium collection, is provided by Insur-Admin. Insur-Claims is a paperless processing system for a variety of insurance plans, including health, dental, life, disability and executive reimbursement. Both systems utilize IBM-based hardware and software, and mainly market to TPAs. Web connectivity consists of the WebAxis suite of programs. WebAxis-Employee/Member and Employer Self-service is a solution that provides a wide range of information to members, including administrative and claims information regarding coverage, demographics, eligibility, claims status and provider directories. WebAxis Broker provides online quoting and proposal management for small group products, permitting insurance brokers and agents to interact with potential customers. WebAxis-Enroll provides online plan information, summary plan documents, online help, email capability for enrollment administrators, secure confirmation notices and administrating monitoring and reporting. BPO includes, among other things, the automated capture, imaging, storage and retrieval of paper and electronic claims, attachments, and related correspondence. Historically, each of the company's three product lines were sold a la carte, but in July 2006, Healthaxis introduced the Ultimate TPA solution, which bundled all the services needed by a typical TPA, offering it at a fixed price per employee per month.

FINANCIALS: **Sales and profits are in thousands of dollars—add 000 to get the full amount. 2007 Note: Financial information for 2007 was not available for all companies at press time.**

2007 Sales: $
2006 Sales: $16,674
2005 Sales: $15,705
2004 Sales: $16,162
2003 Sales: $20,851

2007 Profits: $
2006 Profits: $- 526
2005 Profits: $-2,251
2004 Profits: $-5,958
2003 Profits: $-4,264

U.S. Stock Ticker: HAXS
Int'l Ticker: Int'l Exchange:
Employees: 256
Fiscal Year Ends: 12/31
Parent Company:

SALARIES/BENEFITS:

Pension Plan: ESOP Stock Plan: Profit Sharing: Top Exec. Salary: $250,000 Bonus: $
Savings Plan: Y Stock Purch. Plan: Second Exec. Salary: $200,000 Bonus: $49,985

OTHER THOUGHTS:

Apparent Women Officers or Directors: 1
Hot Spot for Advancement for Women/Minorities:

LOCATIONS: ("Y" = Yes)

West:	Southwest:	Midwest:	Southeast:	Northeast:	International:
	Y				

Note: Financial information, benefits and other data can change quickly and may vary from those stated here.

HEALTHNOW NEW YORK www.healthnowny.com

Industry Group Code: 524114 **Ranks within this company's industry group:** Sales: Profits:

Insurance/HMO/PPO:		Drugs:		Equipment/Supplies:		Hospitals/Clinics:		Services:		Health Care:	
Insurance:	Y	Manufacturer:		Manufacturer:		Acute Care:		Diagnostics:		Home Health:	
Managed Care:	Y	Distributor:		Distributor:		Sub-Acute:		Labs/Testing:		Long-Term Care:	
Utilization Management:		Specialty Pharmacy:		Leasing/Finance:		Outpatient Surgery:		Staffing:		Physical Therapy:	
Payment Processing:		Vitamins/Nutritionals:		Information Systems:		Physical Rehab. Ctr.:		Waste Disposal:		Physician Prac. Mgmt.:	
		Clinical Trials:				Psychiatric Clinics:		Specialty Svcs.:			

TYPES OF BUSINESS:

Insurance-Medical & Health, HMOs & PPOs

BRANDS/DIVISIONS/AFFILIATES:

BlueCross BlueShield of Western New York
BlueShield of Northeastern New York
Community Blue
Traditional Blue
HealthNow
Upstate Medicare Part B Claims Processing

CONTACTS: *Note: Officers with more than one job title may be intentionally listed here more than once.*

Alphonso O'Neil-White, CEO
Alphonso O'Neil-White, Pres.
James H. Dickerson, CFO/Exec. VP
Stephen G. Jepson, Sr. VP-Corp. Sales
Ralph F. Volpe, VP-Human Resources
Gary J. Kerl, CIO/Sr. VP
Ralph F. Volpe, VP-Admin. Svcs.
Kenneth J. Sodaro, General Counsel/VP/Corp. Sec.
Nora K. McGuire, Sr. VP-Mktg. & Bus. Dev.
Alden F. Schutte, Sr. VP-Corp. Affairs
George L. Busch, VP-Finance
Cheryl A. Howe, Exec. VP-Mktg. Mgmt. & Health Svcs.
Jeffrey L. Adams, VP/Chief Actuary
David J. Uba, Sr. VP-Strategic Initiatives
Joseph J. Castiglia, Chmn.

Phone: 716-887-6900 **Fax:** 716-887-8981
Toll-Free: 800-856-0480
Address: 1901 Main St., Buffalo, NY 14240 US

GROWTH PLANS/SPECIAL FEATURES:

HealthNow New York, Inc. provides health insurance and related services to more than 900,000 members in New York State. The company operates through four divisions: BlueCross BlueShield of Western New York; BlueShield of Northeastern New York; HealthNow New York; and Upstate Medicare Part B Claims Processing. These divisions provide health insurance products and related services, including preferred provider organizations (PPO), health maintenance organization (HMO), points of service (POS) and indemnity plans under the Community Blue, Traditional Blue and HealthNow brands. In addition, the firm provides Medicare and Medicaid services through its upstate Medicare division and durable medical equipment regional carrier (DMERC).

The company offers its employees medical and dental insurance; flexible spending accounts; short- and long-term disability insurance; life and AD&D insurance; a 401(k) plan; tuition assistance; an employee assistance program; and wellness programs.

FINANCIALS: **Sales and profits are in thousands of dollars—add 000 to get the full amount. 2007 Note: Financial information for 2007 was not available for all companies at press time.**

2007 Sales: $	2007 Profits: $	**U.S. Stock Ticker: Private**
2006 Sales: $	2006 Profits: $	**Int'l Ticker:** Int'l Exchange:
2005 Sales: $	2005 Profits: $	Employees: 700
2004 Sales: $2,062,108	2004 Profits: $62,585	Fiscal Year Ends:
2003 Sales: $1,775,600	2003 Profits: $55,200	Parent Company:

SALARIES/BENEFITS:

Pension Plan:	ESOP Stock Plan:	Profit Sharing:	Top Exec. Salary: $	Bonus: $
Savings Plan:	Stock Purch. Plan:		Second Exec. Salary: $	Bonus: $

OTHER THOUGHTS:

Apparent Women Officers or Directors: 9
Hot Spot for Advancement for Women/Minorities: Y

LOCATIONS: ("Y" = Yes)

West:	Southwest:	Midwest:	Southeast:	Northeast:	International:
				Y	

HEALTHSOUTH CORP

www.healthsouth.com

Industry Group Code: 621490 **Ranks within this company's industry group:** Sales: 4 Profits: 16

Insurance/HMO/PPO:		Drugs:		Equipment/Supplies:		Hospitals/Clinics:		Services:		Health Care:	
Insurance:		Manufacturer:		Manufacturer:		Acute Care:	Y	Diagnostics:		Home Health:	
Managed Care:		Distributor:		Distributor:		Sub-Acute:		Labs/Testing:		Long-Term Care:	Y
Utilization Management:		Specialty Pharmacy:		Leasing/Finance:		Outpatient Surgery:		Staffing:		Physical Therapy:	Y
Payment Processing:		Vitamins/Nutritionals:		Information Systems:		Physical Rehab. Ctr.:	Y	Waste Disposal:		Physician Prac. Mgmt.:	
		Clinical Trials:				Psychiatric Clinics:		Specialty Svcs.:			

TYPES OF BUSINESS:

Inpatient Rehabilitation Facilities
Long-term Care Hospitals
Home Health Programs

BRANDS/DIVISIONS/AFFILIATES:

CONTACTS: *Note: Officers with more than one job title may be intentionally listed here more than once.*

Jay Grinney, CEO
Jay Grinney, Pres.
John L. Workman, CFO/Exec. VP
John P. Whittington, General Counsel/Exec. VP/Corp. Sec.
Mark J. Tarr, Exec. VP-Oper.
Jon F. Hanson, Chmn.

Phone: 205-967-7116	**Fax:** 205-969-6889
Toll-Free: 888-476-8849	
Address: 1 HealthSouth Pkwy., Birmingham, AL 35243 US	

GROWTH PLANS/SPECIAL FEATURES:

HealthSouth Corp. provides rehabilitative health care anc ambulatory surgery services in the U.S., owning roughly 97ε facilities. The inpatient division, which generated 58% o revenue in 2006, provides rehabilitation services to patients with physical disabilities due to various conditions such as head injury, spinal cord injury, certain orthopedic problems and neuromuscular disease. The segment operates inpatient rehabilitation facilities, long-term care hospitals anc home health programs. The facilities are located in 27 states, with a concentration in Texas, Pennsylvania, Florida Tennessee and Alabama. The company also has a facility ir Puerto Rico. The division operates 92 freestanding inpatien rehabilitation facilities and ten long-term acute care hospitals In addition, the division operates 11 inpatient rehabilitatior units, three outpatient facilities and two gamma knife radiosurgery centers through management contracts. The firm plans to focus solely on operating the inpatien rehabilitation facilities and growing the inpatient rehabilitatior business through bed expansion, consolidation in existinç markets (through joint venturing or acquisition), de-novc projects in existing and new markets and acquisitions in new markets. Although the initial focus will be to enhance its position in the inpatient rehabilitation industry, over the longer term HealthSouth plans to begin looking for growth opportunities in long-term acute care, home health anc hospice. In May 2007, HealthSouth sold its outpatien rehabilitation division to Select Medical Corp. In June 2007 the company sold its surgery division to TPG, Inc. In Augus 2007, the firm sold its diagnostic division to The Gores Group.

The company offers its employees medical, dental and visior insurance; flexible spending accounts; life and disability insurance; a 401(k) plan; a college savings plan; and ar employee assistance program.

FINANCIALS: **Sales and profits are in thousands of dollars—add 000 to get the full amount. 2007 Note: Financial information for 2007 was not available for all companies at press time.**

2007 Sales: $	2007 Profits: $	**U.S. Stock Ticker: HLS**
2006 Sales: $3,000,100	2006 Profits: $-647,200	**Int'l Ticker:** Int'l Exchange:
2005 Sales: $3,117,000	2005 Profits: $-445,994	Employees: 33,000
2004 Sales: $3,409,700	2004 Profits: $-174,470	Fiscal Year Ends: 12/31
2003 Sales: $3,909,421	2003 Profits: $-434,557	Parent Company:

SALARIES/BENEFITS:

Pension Plan:	ESOP Stock Plan:	Profit Sharing:	Top Exec. Salary: $980,110	Bonus: $765,075
Savings Plan: Y	Stock Purch. Plan:		Second Exec. Salary: $642,603	Bonus: $463,532

OTHER THOUGHTS:

Apparent Women Officers or Directors: 1
Hot Spot for Advancement for Women/Minorities:

LOCATIONS: ("Y" = Yes)

West:	Southwest:	Midwest:	Southeast:	Northeast:	International:
Y	Y	Y	Y	Y	Y

HEALTHSTREAM INC

www.healthstream.com

Industry Group Code: 611410 **Ranks within this company's industry group:** Sales: 1 Profits: 1

Insurance/HMO/PPO:		Drugs:		Equipment/Supplies:		Hospitals/Clinics:		Services:		Health Care:	
Insurance:		Manufacturer:		Manufacturer:		Acute Care:		Diagnostics:		Home Health:	
Managed Care:		Distributor:		Distributor:		Sub-Acute:		Labs/Testing:		Long-Term Care:	
Utilization Management:		Specialty Pharmacy:		Leasing/Finance:		Outpatient Surgery:		Staffing:		Physical Therapy:	
Payment Processing:		Vitamins/Nutritionals:		Information Systems:	Y	Physical Rehab. Ctr.:		Waste Disposal:		Physician Prac. Mgmt.:	
		Clinical Trials:				Psychiatric Clinics:		Specialty Svcs.:	Y		

TYPES OF BUSINESS:

Educational & Training Content
Internet-based Educational Programs

BRANDS/DIVISIONS/AFFILIATES:

HealthStream Learning Center
Authoring Pro
A.D.A.M., Inc.
HealthStream Express
Data Management and Research, Inc.
The Jackson Organization

CONTACTS: *Note: Officers with more than one job title may be intentionally listed here more than once.*

Robert A. Frist, Jr., CEO
Robert A. Frist, Jr., Pres.
Arthur E. Newman, Interm CFO
Kevin P. O'Hara, Sr. VP-Mktg.
Arthur E. Newman, Exec. VP-Human Resources
J. Edward Pearson, Sr. VP-HealthStream Research
Kevin P. O'Hara, Sr. VP-Prod. Mgmt. Group
Kevin P. O'Hara, General Counsel/Sec.
Arthur E. Newman, Exec. VP-Finance & Acct.
Arthur E. Newman, Exec. VP-Systems
Robert A. Frist, Jr., Chmn.

Phone: 615-301-3100	**Fax:** 615-301-3200
Toll-Free: 800-933-9293	
Address: 209 10th Ave. S., Ste. 450, Nashville, TN 37203 US	

GROWTH PLANS/SPECIAL FEATURES:

HealthStream, Inc. provides Internet-based training and services for the health care industry. The firm provides services to healthcare organizations (HCOs) throughout the U.S. and Canada focusing primarily on acute-care facilities, although it also serves pharmaceutical and medical device (PMD) companies. Within its HCO business unit, HealthStream focuses on expanding its web-based application service provider, e-learning and installed learning management products. The company's flagship HealthStream Learning Center (HLC) platform provides organizations with Internet-based training and continuing education services. Training material is hosted on a central data center that allows end users to access services online, eliminating the need for on-site installations. HLC also provides tools that enable administrators to configure and modify materials, track completion and predict training expenses. HealthStream has provided training to 1,400 healthcare organizations, and has approximately 1.45 million hospital-based subscribers currently enrolled in HLC. The company's largest customers include Guidant Corp., Merck & Co., Zimmer, HCA, Tenet Healthcare Corp., Triad Hospitals, LifePoint Hospitals and Ardent Health Services. In addition to its standard HLC subscription, the firm also offers the Authoring Pro upgrade, with an industry leading image library, owned by A.D.A.M.; Inc.; and it offers HealthStream Express, a streamlined version of HLC. Within its PMD business unit, the company focuses on providing services such as live and online educational and training activities aimed at health care professionals, as well as online training for medical industry sales representatives. Recently, HealthStream acquired Data Management and Research, Inc. (DMR) for about $10 million. DMR is a small company that offers quality and satisfaction surveys, data analyses of survey results and other research-based measurement tools quality and satisfaction surveys primarily to physicians, patients, employees and community members. In March 2007, the firm acquired The Jackson Organization, Research Consultants, Inc. (TJO) for approximately $12.6 million. TJO provides the same services and DMR.

FINANCIALS: **Sales and profits are in thousands of dollars—add 000 to get the full amount. 2007 Note: Financial information for 2007 was not available for all companies at press time.**

2007 Sales: $	2007 Profits: $	**U.S. Stock Ticker: HSTM**
2006 Sales: $31,783	2006 Profits: $2,500	**Int'l Ticker:** Int'l Exchange:
2005 Sales: $27,400	2005 Profits: $1,900	Employees: 160
2004 Sales: $20,100	2004 Profits: $-1,000	Fiscal Year Ends: 12/31
2003 Sales: $18,195	2003 Profits: $-3,412	Parent Company:

SALARIES/BENEFITS:

Pension Plan:	ESOP Stock Plan:	Profit Sharing:	Top Exec. Salary: $184,167	Bonus: $14,875
Savings Plan: Y	Stock Purch. Plan:		Second Exec. Salary: $182,083	Bonus: $12,750

OTHER THOUGHTS:

Apparent Women Officers or Directors:
Hot Spot for Advancement for Women/Minorities:

LOCATIONS: ("Y" = Yes)

West:	Southwest:	Midwest:	Southeast:	Northeast:	International:
Y			Y	Y	

HEALTHTRONICS INC www.healthtronics.com

Industry Group Code: 621490 **Ranks within this company's industry group:** Sales: 11 Profits: 9

Insurance/HMO/PPO:		Drugs:		Equipment/Supplies:		Hospitals/Clinics:		Services:		Health Care:	
Insurance:		Manufacturer:		Manufacturer:	Y	Acute Care:		Diagnostics:		Home Health:	
Managed Care:		Distributor:		Distributor:		Sub-Acute:		Labs/Testing:		Long-Term Care:	
Utilization Management:		Specialty Pharmacy:		Leasing/Finance:		Outpatient Surgery:		Staffing:	Y	Physical Therapy:	
Payment Processing:		Vitamins/Nutritionals:		Information Systems:		Physical Rehab. Ctr.:		Waste Disposal:		Physician Prac. Mgmt.:	Y
		Clinical Trials:				Psychiatric Clinics:		Specialty Svcs.:	Y		

TYPES OF BUSINESS:

Lithotripsy Services
Orthopedics Practice Management
Urologic Staffing

BRANDS/DIVISIONS/AFFILIATES:

Prime Medical Services, Inc.
HealthTronics Surgical Services, Inc.
LithoDiamond Ultra
MultiVantage
RevoLix
TotalRad Radiation Therapy Solutions

CONTACTS: *Note: Officers with more than one job title may be intentionally listed here more than once.*

Sam B. Humphries, CEO
Sam B. Humphries, Pres.
Ross A. Goolsby, CFO/Sr. VP
Richard A. Rusk, VP/Controller/Treas./Sec.
Christopher B. Schneider, Pres., Medical Products
James S. B. Whittenburg, Pres., Urology Svcs.
Mark Koeniguer, VP-Radiation Therapies
R. Steven Hicks, Chmn.

Phone: 512-328-2892	Fax: 512-328-8510
Toll-Free: 888-252-6575	
Address: 1301 Capital of Texas Hwy., Ste. B-200, Austin, TX 78746 US	

GROWTH PLANS/SPECIAL FEATURES:

HealthTronics, Inc., formed by the 2004 merger of Prim Medical Services, Inc. and HealthTronics Surgical Service Inc., is a health care service provider in three busines segments: urological services and products; medical device and services; and specialty vehicles. HealthTronic urological unit focuses on lithotripsy systems, which serve network of 3,000 physicians in 47 states. Lithotripsy is th non-invasive treatment of kidney stones using shockwave to break up the stones and allow them to pass painless from the body with a short recovery period, usually a matte of hours. The company's lithotripsy services includ scheduling, staffing, training, quality assuranc maintenance, regulatory compliance and contracting wi hospitals and surgery centers. In the medical devices an service sector, HealthTronics manufactures, sells an maintains lithotripters and related equipment, including th LithoDiamond Ultra lithotriper which combine electromagnetic and electrohydraulic therapy options. Th unit also distributes intra-operative X-ray imaging system such as MultiVantage for multipurpose surgical suites, an other mobile patient management tables. HealthTronics als has the RevoLix, minimally invasive line of laser products fo urological procedures, including the RevoLix Duo, one of th only products to combine lithotripsy and laser technologies i one. The company formerly operated AK Specialty Vehicle providing manufacturing services, installation, refurbishme and repair of medical devices such as magnetic resonanc imaging (MRI), cardiac catheterization, CT scanners an positron emission tomography, as well as non-medic devices for communications and broadcasting application for mobile medical services providers. In July 2006, the fir sold the division for $140 million to Oshkosh Truck Corp. I June 2007, it acquired a 35% interest in Keystone Mobi Partners, LP, a leading provider of lithotripsy services i Pennsylvania. In May 2007, it launched TotalRad Radiatio Therapy Solutions, part of its Urology Services division.

FINANCIALS: **Sales and profits are in thousands of dollars—add 000 to get the full amount. 2007 Note: Financial information for 2007 was not available for all companies at press time.**

2007 Sales: $	2007 Profits: $	**U.S. Stock Ticker: HTRN**
2006 Sales: $142,891	2006 Profits: $8,683	**Int'l Ticker:** Int'l Exchange:
2005 Sales: $152,267	2005 Profits: $9,188	Employees: 293
2004 Sales: $87,143	2004 Profits: $1,353	Fiscal Year Ends: 12/31
2003 Sales: $159,618	2003 Profits: $6,422	Parent Company:

SALARIES/BENEFITS:

Pension Plan:	ESOP Stock Plan:	Profit Sharing:	Top Exec. Salary: $279,996	Bonus: $146,403
Savings Plan:	Stock Purch. Plan:		Second Exec. Salary: $245,163	Bonus: $133,000

OTHER THOUGHTS:

Apparent Women Officers or Directors:
Hot Spot for Advancement for Women/Minorities:

LOCATIONS: ("Y" = Yes)

West:	Southwest:	Midwest:	Southeast:	Northeast:	International:
	Y		Y		Y

HEALTHWAYS INC www.americanhealthways.com

Industry Group Code: 621490 **Ranks within this company's industry group:** Sales: 7 Profits: 6

Insurance/HMO/PPO:		Drugs:		Equipment/Supplies:		Hospitals/Clinics:		Services:		Health Care:	
Insurance:		Manufacturer:		Manufacturer:		Acute Care:		Diagnostics:		Home Health:	
Managed Care:		Distributor:		Distributor:		Sub-Acute:		Labs/Testing:		Long-Term Care:	
Utilization Management:	Y	Specialty Pharmacy:		Leasing/Finance:		Outpatient Surgery:		Staffing:		Physical Therapy:	
Payment Processing:		Vitamins/Nutritionals:		Information Systems:		Physical Rehab. Ctr.:		Waste Disposal:		Physician Prac. Mgmt.:	
		Clinical Trials:				Psychiatric Clinics:		Specialty Svcs.:	Y		

TYPES OF BUSINESS:

Disease Management Programs
Ambulatory Surgery Centers
Arthritis Care
Osteoporosis Care
Cardiac Disease Management Services
Respiratory Disease Management Services
Online Disease Management
Outsourced Diabetes Treatment Programs

BRANDS/DIVISIONS/AFFILIATES:

CentreVu Customer Care Solution
Cardiac Healthways
Respiratory Healthways
Diabetes Healthways
MyHealthways
Axia Health Management, LLC

CONTACTS: *Note: Officers with more than one job title may be intentionally listed here more than once.*

Ben R. Leedle, CEO
James E. Pope, COO/Exec. VP
Ben R. Leedle, Pres.
Mary A. Chaput, CFO/Exec. VP
Donald B. Taylor, Exec. VP-Sales & Mktg.
Robert L. Chaput, CIO/Exec. VP
Robert E. Stone, Exec. VP/Chief Strategy Officer
Kriste Goad, Sr. Dir.-Corp. Comm
Mary D. Hunter, Exec. VP
Dexter W. Shurney, Chief Medical Officer
Thomas G. Cigarran, Chmn.
Matthew E. Kelliher, Exec. VP-Int'l Bus.

Phone: 615-665-1122 **Fax:** 615-665-7697
Toll-Free: 800-327-3822
Address: 3841 Green Hills Village Dr., Nashville, TN 37215-6104 US

GROWTH PLANS/SPECIAL FEATURES:

Healthways, Inc., formerly American Healthways, Inc., provides specialized, comprehensive care enhancement and disease management services to health plans, physicians and hospitals in all 50 states, Washington, D.C., Puerto Rico and Guam. Its programs are designed to improve health care quality at a lower cost by creating programs that help people with chronic diseases lead healthier lives by providing access to highly skilled nurses; making sure they understand and follow doctors' orders; are aware of and can recognize early warning signs associated with a major health episode; and are setting achievable goals for themselves, such as to exercise more, lose weight, quit smoking or otherwise improve their current health status. Comply programs include specialized support for people with diabetes, coronary artery disease, heart failure, asthma, chronic obstructive pulmonary disease, end-stage renal disease, cancer, chronic kidney disease, acid-related stomach disorders, hepatitis C, inflammatory bowel disease, irritable bowel syndrome, lower-back pain, osteoarthritis, osteoporosis, urinary incontinence and high-risk population management. Healthways also features MyHealthways, a web-based application that allows physicians, patients and care coordinators to actively monitor a chronic disease, receive customized plans of action or identify at-risk individuals through predictive modeling technology. In October 2006, Healthways and Axia Health Management, LLC signed a definitive agreement whereby Healthways will purchase Axia for $450 million. In March 2007, Healthways and Blue Cross Blue Shield of Massachusetts (BCBSMA) announced the expansion of their collaborative efforts, adding coronary artery disease (CAD) and chronic obstructive pulmonary disease (COPD) Care Support programs to the interventions currently offered to BCBSMA members.

Healthways offers its employees a complete benefits package including flexible spending accounts, tuition reimbursement, performance bonuses and a 401(k) savings plan.

FINANCIALS: **Sales and profits are in thousands of dollars—add 000 to get the full amount. 2007 Note: Financial information for 2007 was not available for all companies at press time.**

2007 Sales: $	2007 Profits: $	**U.S. Stock Ticker: HWAY**
2006 Sales: $412,308	2006 Profits: $37,151	**Int'l Ticker:** Int'l Exchange:
2005 Sales: $312,504	2005 Profits: $33,084	Employees: 2,855
2004 Sales: $245,410	2004 Profits: $26,058	Fiscal Year Ends: 8/31
2003 Sales: $165,500	2003 Profits: $18,500	Parent Company:

SALARIES/BENEFITS:

Pension Plan:	ESOP Stock Plan:	Profit Sharing:	Top Exec. Salary: $600,000	Bonus: $316,800
Savings Plan: Y	Stock Purch. Plan:		Second Exec. Salary: $375,000	Bonus: $148,500

OTHER THOUGHTS:

Apparent Women Officers or Directors: 3
Hot Spot for Advancement for Women/Minorities: Y

LOCATIONS: ("Y" = Yes)

West:	Southwest:	Midwest:	Southeast:	Northeast:	International:
Y	Y	Y	Y	Y	Y

HEARUSA INC

www.hearusa.com

Industry Group Code: 621490 **Ranks within this company's industry group:** Sales: 14 Profits: 13

Insurance/HMO/PPO:		Drugs:		Equipment/Supplies:		Hospitals/Clinics:		Services:		Health Care:	
Insurance:		Manufacturer:		Manufacturer:		Acute Care:		Diagnostics:		Home Health:	
Managed Care:		Distributor:		Distributor:	Y	Sub-Acute:		Labs/Testing:		Long-Term Care:	
Utilization Management:		Specialty Pharmacy:		Leasing/Finance:		Outpatient Surgery:		Staffing:		Physical Therapy:	
Payment Processing:		Vitamins/Nutritionals:		Information Systems:		Physical Rehab. Ctr.:		Waste Disposal:		Physician Prac. Mgmt.:	
		Clinical Trials:				Psychiatric Clinics:		Specialty Svcs.:	Y		

TYPES OF BUSINESS:

Hearing Care Centers
Hearing Benefits Management
Hearing Aids
Hearing Care Devices

BRANDS/DIVISIONS/AFFILIATES:

HEARx
HearUSA Hearing Care Network
Siemens Hearing Instruments

CONTACTS: *Note: Officers with more than one job title may be intentionally listed here more than once.*

Stephen J. Hansbrough, CEO
Kenneth Schofield, COO
Stephen J. Hansbrough, Pres.
Gino Chouinard, CFO/Exec. VP
Gene Fell, Sr. VP-Bus. Dev.
Paige Brough, Sr. VP-Corp. Comm.
Cindy Beyer, Sr. VP-Professional Svcs.
Donna Taylor, Sr. VP-Bus. Integration
Paul A. Brown, Chmn.

Phone: 561-478-8770 **Fax:** 561-478-9603
Toll-Free:
Address: 1250 Northpoint Pkwy., West Palm Beach, FL 33407 US

GROWTH PLANS/SPECIAL FEATURES:

HearUSA, Inc., formerly known as HEARx, owns an manages a network of approximately 173 HearUSA hearin care centers that provide a full range of audiological product and services for the hearing impaired. The company serve customers in Florida, New York, New Jersey Massachusetts, Ohio, Michigan, Minnesota, Missour California and Ontario, Canada. HearUSA also sponsors a network of approximately 1,600 credentialed audiologis providers that participate in selected hearing benef programs contracted by the company with employer groups health insurers and benefit sponsors in 49 states. Throug the network, the company can pursue national hearing car contracts and offer managed hearing benefits in area outside its center markets. HearUSA services over 40 benefit programs for hearing care with various healt maintenance organizations, preferred provider organizations insurers, benefit administrators and health care providers Each HearUSA center is staffed by a licensed audiologist o hearing instrument specialist, and most are located i shopping or medical centers. The centers offer a complet range of high quality hearing aids, with emphasis on th latest digital technology along with assessment an evaluation of hearing. In addition, HearUSA offers othe products related to hearing care, such as telephone an television amplifiers, telecaptioners and decoders, pock talkers, specially adapted telephones, alarm clock doorbells and fire alarms. HearUSA also offers onlin information about hearing loss, hearing aids, assistiv listening devices and the services offered by hearing healt care professionals. The company's website also offer online purchases of hearing-related products, such a batteries, hearing aid accessories and assistive listenin devices. In February 2006, the company extended it agreement with Siemens Hearing Instruments, th wholesaler of HearUSA's hearing aid products, to cover th next five years.

FINANCIALS: **Sales and profits are in thousands of dollars—add 000 to get the full amount. 2007 Note: Financial information for 2007 was not available for all companies at press time.**

2007 Sales: $	2007 Profits: $	**U.S. Stock Ticker: EAR**
2006 Sales: $88,786	2006 Profits: $-3,174	**Int'l Ticker:** Int'l Exchange:
2005 Sales: $76,672	2005 Profits: $-2,264	Employees: 654
2004 Sales: $68,750	2004 Profits: $-3,449	Fiscal Year Ends: 12/31
2003 Sales: $70,545	2003 Profits: $-1,109	Parent Company:

SALARIES/BENEFITS:

Pension Plan:	ESOP Stock Plan:	Profit Sharing:	Top Exec. Salary: $385,000	Bonus: $
Savings Plan: Y	Stock Purch. Plan:		Second Exec. Salary: $260,000	Bonus: $

OTHER THOUGHTS:

Apparent Women Officers or Directors: 3
Hot Spot for Advancement for Women/Minorities: Y

LOCATIONS: ("Y" = Yes)

West:	Southwest:	Midwest:	Southeast:	Northeast:	International:
Y		Y	Y	Y	Y

HEMACARE CORPORATION www.hemacare.com

Industry Group Code: 621991 **Ranks within this company's industry group:** Sales: 1 Profits: 1

Insurance/HMO/PPO:		Drugs:		Equipment/Supplies:		Hospitals/Clinics:		Services:		Health Care:	
Insurance:		Manufacturer:		Manufacturer:		Acute Care:		Diagnostics:		Home Health:	
Managed Care:		Distributor:		Distributor:	Y	Sub-Acute:		Labs/Testing:	Y	Long-Term Care:	
Utilization Management:		Specialty Pharmacy:		Leasing/Finance:		Outpatient Surgery:		Staffing:	Y	Physical Therapy:	
Payment Processing:		Vitamins/Nutritionals:		Information Systems:		Physical Rehab. Ctr.:		Waste Disposal:		Physician Prac. Mgmt.:	
		Clinical Trials:				Psychiatric Clinics:		Specialty Svcs.:	Y		

TYPES OF BUSINESS:

Management-Blood Collection Centers & Blood Banks
Blood Products
Stem-Cell Collection
Therapeutics
Temporary Equipment & Staffing

BRANDS/DIVISIONS/AFFILIATES:

Coral Blood Services, Inc.
Teragenix Corporation
HemaCare BioScience, Inc.

CONTACTS: *Note: Officers with more than one job title may be intentionally listed here more than once.*

Julian Steffenhagen, CEO
Teresa S. Sligh, Pres.
Robert S. Chilton, CFO/Exec. VP
Joshua Levy, Medical Dir.-HemaCare Corp.
David Ciavarella, Medical Dir.-Coral Blood Services
Jacquelyn Hedlund, Medical Dir.-Coral Blood Services
Julian Steffenhagen, Chmn.

Phone: 818-226-1968 **Fax:** 818-337-7520
Toll-Free:
Address: 15350 Sherman Way, Ste. 350, Van Nuys, CA 91406 US

GROWTH PLANS/SPECIAL FEATURES:

HemaCare Corporation and its wholly-owned subsidiary, Coral Blood Services, Inc., collects, processes and distributes blood and related services and products to hospitals and medical centers. The company divides its business into two categories: blood products and blood services. The blood products segment provides hospitals with significant portions of their blood supply needs. HemaCare's blood products operations specialize in the collection and distribution of apheresis platelets, focusing on single-donor platelets. The company operates and manages donor centers and mobile donor vehicles to collect transfusable blood products from donors, and also collects human-derived blood products which are utilized by health research related organizations. HemaCare's blood services operations provide hospitals with specialty-trained nurses and specialized equipment on a mobile basis. Therapeutic apheresis is the company's clinical treatment of autoimmune diseases and blood disorders, designed to remove selected or abnormal components or cells. Other services include stem cell collection and an assortment of therapeutic treatments, which are provided to patients with a variety of disorders. The company has entered into blood management programs (BMPs) with many of its hospital customers. In BMP arrangements, HemaCare provides its products and services, as well as donor testing, community blood drives and specialized collections, under multi-year contractual agreements. HemaCare believes its BMPs benefit hospitals in several ways, including greater reliability than local blood centers, overall reduction in blood procurement costs and access to experienced nurses and physicians. HemaCare serves over 160 hospitals in Southern California and the East Coast, and is accredited by the American Association of Blood Banks. In August 2006, the company acquired Florida-based Teragenix Corporation, subsequently renamed HemaCare BioScience, Inc., which sources, processes and distributes human biological specimens, manufactures quality control products and provides clinical trial management and support services.

The company offers employee benefits including employee assistance plans, tuition reimbursement and credit union membership.

FINANCIALS: Sales and profits are in thousands of dollars—add 000 to get the full amount. 2007 Note: Financial information for 2007 was not available for all companies at press time.

2007 Sales: $ | 2007 Profits: $
2006 Sales: $36,484 | 2006 Profits: $1,851
2005 Sales: $31,227 | 2005 Profits: $1,655
2004 Sales: $26,836 | 2004 Profits: $1,545
2003 Sales: $27,488 | 2003 Profits: $-4,679

U.S. Stock Ticker: HEMA
Int'l Ticker: Int'l Exchange:
Employees: 354
Fiscal Year Ends: 12/31
Parent Company:

SALARIES/BENEFITS:

Pension Plan: | ESOP Stock Plan: | Profit Sharing: Y | Top Exec. Salary: $289,000 | Bonus: $132,000
Savings Plan: Y | Stock Purch. Plan: Y | Second Exec. Salary: $225,000 | Bonus: $20,000

OTHER THOUGHTS:

Apparent Women Officers or Directors: 3
Hot Spot for Advancement for Women/Minorities: Y

LOCATIONS: ("Y" = Yes)

West:	Southwest:	Midwest:	Southeast:	Northeast:	International:
Y			Y	Y	

HENRY FORD HEALTH SYSTEMS www.henryfordhealth.org

Industry Group Code: 622110 **Ranks within this company's industry group:** Sales: Profits:

Insurance/HMO/PPO:		Drugs:		Equipment/Supplies:		Hospitals/Clinics:		Services:		Health Care:	
Insurance:	Y	Manufacturer:		Manufacturer:		Acute Care:	Y	Diagnostics:		Home Health:	Y
Managed Care:		Distributor:		Distributor:	Y	Sub-Acute:	Y	Labs/Testing:		Long-Term Care:	Y
Utilization Management:		Specialty Pharmacy:		Leasing/Finance:		Outpatient Surgery:	Y	Staffing:		Physical Therapy:	Y
Payment Processing:		Vitamins/Nutritionals:		Information Systems:		Physical Rehab. Ctr.:	Y	Waste Disposal:		Physician Prac. Mgmt.:	Y
		Clinical Trials:				Psychiatric Clinics:	Y	Specialty Svcs.:	Y		

TYPES OF BUSINESS:

Hospitals-General
Nursing Homes
Home Health Care
Medical Equipment
Insurance
Psychiatric Services
Research & Education
Osteopathy

BRANDS/DIVISIONS/AFFILIATES:

Health Alliance Plan of Michigan
Heart & Vascular Institute
Kingswood Hospital
Henry Ford Wyandotte Hospital
Henry Ford Hospital
Neuroscience Institute
Vattikuti Urology Institute
Josephine Ford Cancer Center

CONTACTS: *Note: Officers with more than one job title may be intentionally listed here more than once.*

Nancy M. Schlichting, CEO
Robert Riney, COO
Nancy M. Schlichting, Pres.
James M. Connelly, CFO
Constance Cronin, Chief Nursing Officer
Anthony Armada, Pres./CEO-Henry Ford Hospital & Health Network
Mark A. Kelley, CEO-Henry Ford Medical Group
Gary Rounding, Sr. VP-Philanthropy

Phone: 313-876-8700 **Fax:** 313-876-9243
Toll-Free: 800-436-7936
Address: 1 Ford Pl., Detroit, MI 48202-3450 US

GROWTH PLANS/SPECIAL FEATURES:

Henry Ford Health System, founded in 1915 by automobil manufacturer Henry Ford, is a collection of hospitals an other health care facilities in southeastern Michigan. Th system operates seven hospitals, including the Henry For Hospital, a 903-bed tertiary care hospital, education an research complex in Detroit; the Kingswood Hospital, a 10(bed facility providing inpatient treatment for acute episode of mental illness; the Henry Ford Bi-County Hospital, a 20: bed acute care hospital that is home to the olde osteopathic teaching program in the U.S.; the Henry For Wyandotte Hospital, a 344-bed teaching hospital offering wide range of services including surgery, cardiac car hospice care and 24-hour emergency care; the Henry For Cottage Hospital in Grosse Pointe Farms, which provide inpatient and outpatient physical rehabilitation and ment health services; Henry Ford Macomb Hospital, a 435-be hospital that provides comprehensive, acute care; and th Henry Ford West Bloomfield Hospital, the first stage of 300-bed full service hospital. The group also operate several specialty clinics including the Heart & Vascul Institute, the Josephine Ford Cancer Center, th Neuroscience Institute and the Vattikuti Urology Institute. I addition, the firm manages nursing homes, hospice need home health care, a medical equipment supplier and a healt insurance provider called Health Alliance Plan of Michiga with more than 530,000 members. Yet another unit, Th Henry Ford Medical Group, is one of the nation's large group practices, with 900 physicians and researchers in 4 specialties. The group serves the 25 Henry Ford medic centers in four Michigan counties.

Henry Ford Health System offers its employees a wide rang of benefits including adoption assistance, tuition assistanc domestic partner benefits, a child care center, a discou plan through Ford Motor Company, General Motors an Daimler Chrysler, banking services and a fitness center.

FINANCIALS: **Sales and profits are in thousands of dollars—add 000 to get the full amount. 2007 Note: Financial information for 2007 was not available for all companies at press time.**

2007 Sales: $	2007 Profits: $	**U.S. Stock Ticker: Nonprofit**
2006 Sales: $	2006 Profits: $	**Int'l Ticker:** Int'l Exchange:
2005 Sales: $	2005 Profits: $	Employees: 13,800
2004 Sales: $2,846,281	2004 Profits: $85,780	Fiscal Year Ends: 12/31
2003 Sales: $2,597,291	2003 Profits: $31,829	Parent Company:

SALARIES/BENEFITS:

Pension Plan: Y	ESOP Stock Plan:	Profit Sharing:	Top Exec. Salary: $	Bonus: $
Savings Plan:	Stock Purch. Plan:		Second Exec. Salary: $	Bonus: $

OTHER THOUGHTS:

Apparent Women Officers or Directors: 2
Hot Spot for Advancement for Women/Minorities:

LOCATIONS: ("Y" = Yes)

West:	Southwest:	Midwest:	Southeast:	Northeast:	International:
		Y			

HENRY SCHEIN INC

www.henryschein.com

ndustry Group Code: 421450 **Ranks within this company's industry group:** Sales: 2 Profits: 3

nsurance/HMO/PPO:		Drugs:		Equipment/Supplies:		Hospitals/Clinics:		Services:		Health Care:	
nsurance:		Manufacturer:		Manufacturer:		Acute Care:		Diagnostics:		Home Health:	
1anaged Care:		Distributor:		Distributor:	Y	Sub-Acute:		Labs/Testing:		Long-Term Care:	
Jtilization Management:		Specialty Pharmacy:		Leasing/Finance:		Outpatient Surgery:		Staffing:		Physical Therapy:	
'ayment Processing:		Vitamins/Nutritionals:		Information Systems:		Physical Rehab. Ctr.:		Waste Disposal:		Physician Prac. Mgmt.:	
		Clinical Trials:				Psychiatric Clinics:		Specialty Svcs.:			

TYPES OF BUSINESS:

Health Care Products Distribution
Dental Supplies Distribution
Veterinary Products Distribution
Electronic Catalogs

BRANDS/DIVISIONS/AFFILIATES:

Aruba
Dentrix
Easy Dental
AVImark
W. & J. Dunlop, Ltd.

CONTACTS: *Note: Officers with more than one job title may be intentionally listed here more than once.*

Stanley M. Bergman, CEO
James P. Breslawski, COO
James P. Breslawski, Pres.
Steven Paladino, CFO/Exec. VP
Gerald A. Benjamin, Chief Admin. Officer/Exec. VP
Mark E. Mlotek, Exec. VP-Bus. Dev.
Susan Vassallo, VP-Corp. Comm.
Neal Goldner, VP-Investor Rel.
Leonard A. David, Sr. VP/Chief Compliance Officer
Stanley Komaroff, Sr. Advisor
Michael Racioppi, Pres., Medical Group
Stanley M. Bergman, Chmn.
Michael Zack, Sr. VP/Pres., Int'l Group

Phone: 631-843-5500	**Fax:** 631-843-5658
Toll-Free:	
Address: 135 Duryea Rd., Melville, NY 11747 US	

GROWTH PLANS/SPECIAL FEATURES:

Henry Schein, Inc. is a distributor of healthcare products and services to office-based healthcare practitioners in North America and Europe. The company operates in two segments: healthcare distribution and technology. The healthcare distribution segment aggregates the dental, medical (including animal health) and international operating segments. Products distributed include consumable products; small equipment; laboratory products; large dental equipment; branded and generic pharmaceuticals; vaccines; surgical products; diagnostic tests; infection-control products; and vitamins. The technology segment provides software, technology and other value-added services to healthcare practitioners, primarily in the U.S. and Canada. Value-added solutions include practice-management software systems for dental and medical practitioners and animal health clinics. The lead practice-management software solutions include DENTRIX and Easy Dental for dental practices and AVImark for veterinary clinics. The technology group offerings also include financial services and continuing education for practitioners. Henry Schein offers a broad selection of more than 170,000 branded and Henry Schein private-brand products. The company markets its products and services to over 500,000 customers in more than 200 countries, including dental practitioners and dental laboratories; physician practices; and animal health clinics. The firm currently distributes over 35 million pieces of direct marketing material through the Aruba electronic catalog and ordering system. Henry Schein's web site provides an array of value-added features including instant customer registration, easy shopping and ordering and improved customer service and supply procurement capabilities. In June 2007, the company agreed to acquire Becker-Parkin Dental Supply Co.'s full-service and special markets business. In August 2007, the firm acquired W. & J. Dunlop, Ltd., a supplier of animal health products and services to veterinary clinics in the U.K.

The company offers its employees medical, dental and vision plans; a 401(k) plan; life and AD&D insurance; short- and long-term disability insurance; flexible spending accounts; tuition assistance; a college savings plan; and on-site wellness programs.

FINANCIALS: **Sales and profits are in thousands of dollars—add 000 to get the full amount. 2007 Note: Financial information for 2007 was not available for all companies at press time.**

2007 Sales: $	2007 Profits: $	**U.S. Stock Ticker: HSIC**
2006 Sales: $5,153,097	2006 Profits: $163,759	**Int'l Ticker:** Int'l Exchange:
2005 Sales: $4,635,929	2005 Profits: $139,759	Employees: 11,000
2004 Sales: $3,898,485	2004 Profits: $114,274	Fiscal Year Ends: 12/31
2003 Sales: $3,353,805	2003 Profits: $137,501	Parent Company:

SALARIES/BENEFITS:

Pension Plan:	ESOP Stock Plan:	Profit Sharing:	Top Exec. Salary: $1,000,000	Bonus: $1,300,000
Savings Plan: Y	Stock Purch. Plan:		Second Exec. Salary: $513,401	Bonus: $390,000

OTHER THOUGHTS:

Apparent Women Officers or Directors: 1
Hot Spot for Advancement for Women/Minorities:

LOCATIONS: ("Y" = Yes)

West:	Southwest:	Midwest:	Southeast:	Northeast:	International:
Y	Y	Y	Y	Y	Y

Note: Financial information, benefits and other data can change quickly and may vary from those stated here.

HIGHMARK INC www.highmark.com

Industry Group Code: 524114 **Ranks within this company's industry group:** Sales: 8 Profits: 10

Insurance/HMO/PPO:		Drugs:		Equipment/Supplies:		Hospitals/Clinics:		Services:		Health Care:	
Insurance:	Y	Manufacturer:		Manufacturer:		Acute Care:		Diagnostics:		Home Health:	
Managed Care:	Y	Distributor:		Distributor:		Sub-Acute:		Labs/Testing:		Long-Term Care:	
Utilization Management:		Specialty Pharmacy:		Leasing/Finance:		Outpatient Surgery:		Staffing:		Physical Therapy:	
Payment Processing:		Vitamins/Nutritionals:		Information Systems:		Physical Rehab. Ctr.:		Waste Disposal:		Physician Prac. Mgmt.:	
		Clinical Trials:				Psychiatric Clinics:		Specialty Svcs.:			

TYPES OF BUSINESS:

Insurance-Medical & Health, HMOs & PPOs
Administrative Services

BRANDS/DIVISIONS/AFFILIATES:

Blue Cross Blue Shield Association
Mountain State Blue Cross Blue Shield
Employee Benefit Data Services Co.
Highmark Caring Foundation
Keystone Health Plan West
Davis Vision, Inc.
HM Insurance Group, Inc.
United Concordia

CONTACTS: *Note: Officers with more than one job title may be intentionally listed here more than once.*

Kenneth R. Melani, CEO
Kenneth R. Melani, Pres.
Nanette DeTurk, CFO
S. Tyrone Alexander, VP-Human Resources
S. Tyrone Alexander, VP-Admin. Svcs.
Gary R. Truitt, General Counsel/Exec. VP/Corp. Sec.
Aaron A. Walton, Sr. VP-Corp. Affairs
Nanette DeTurk, Treas./Exec. VP
Elizabeth A. Farbacher, Sr. VP/Chief Audit Exec.
James M. Klingensmith, Exec. VP-Health Services
David M. O'Brien, Exec. VP-Gov't Svcs.
Robert C. Gray, VP-Subsidiary Svcs.
J. Robert Baum, Chmn.

Phone: 412-544-7000	**Fax:** 412-544-8368
Toll-Free:	
Address: 120 5th Ave., Pittsburgh, PA 15222 US	

GROWTH PLANS/SPECIAL FEATURES:

Highmark, an independent licensee of the Blue Cross Blu Shield Association, is one of the largest health insurers in th United States, providing health insurance to 4.6 millio customers, primarily in Pennsylvania. Insurance plar include medical, dental, vision, indemnity and casual insurance. The firm was created in 1996 by th consolidation of Pennsylvania Blue Shield, now calle Highmark Blue Shield, and a Blue Cross plan in wester Pennsylvania, now called Highmark Blue Cross Blue Shiel Subsidiaries offering the Blue Cross Blue Shield plar include Mountain State Blue Cross Blue Shield; Keyston Health Plan West; Employee Benefit Data Services Co Davis Vision, Inc.; HM Insurance Group, Inc.; Unite Concordia Companies, Inc.; Viva International Group; Ey Care Centers of America, Inc.; Industrial Manageme Consultants, Inc.; HM Health Insurance Company; Highma Medicare Services, Inc.; Highmark Foundation; and Standa Property Corporation. Through the Highmark Carin Foundation, Highmark offers free health care coverage children whose parents exceed the financial requirements f public aid but still cannot afford private insurance. Highma has recently been active in the promotion of Africa American health programs, with initiatives such as $250,000 grant toward diabetes, in July 2006, and $160,000 grant to Washington County Health Partners identify health issues for local African Americans, in Jun 2006. In March 2007, Highmark agreed to a propose combination with Independence Blue Cross to form a ne company.

Highmark offers its employees a 401(k) plan, a retireme plan, a tuition reimbursement program and health, dental an vision coverage.

FINANCIALS: **Sales and profits are in thousands of dollars—add 000 to get the full amount. 2007 Note: Financial information for 2007 was not available for all companies at press time.**

2007 Sales: $	2007 Profits: $	**U.S. Stock Ticker: Nonprofit**
2006 Sales: $11,083,800	2006 Profits: $398,300	**Int'l Ticker:** Int'l Exchange:
2005 Sales: $9,847,300	2005 Profits: $341,600	Employees: 18,500
2004 Sales: $9,118,400	2004 Profits: $310,500	Fiscal Year Ends: 12/31
2003 Sales: $8,104,800	2003 Profits: $75,700	Parent Company:

SALARIES/BENEFITS:

Pension Plan: Y	ESOP Stock Plan:	Profit Sharing:	Top Exec. Salary: $	Bonus: $
Savings Plan: Y	Stock Purch. Plan:		Second Exec. Salary: $	Bonus: $

OTHER THOUGHTS:

Apparent Women Officers or Directors: 3
Hot Spot for Advancement for Women/Minorities: Y

LOCATIONS: ("Y" = Yes)

West:	Southwest:	Midwest:	Southeast:	Northeast:	International:
				Y	

HILLENBRAND INDUSTRIES

www.hillenbrand.com

Industry Group Code: 339113 **Ranks within this company's industry group:** Sales: 18 Profits: 16

Insurance/HMO/PPO:		Drugs:		Equipment/Supplies:		Hospitals/Clinics:		Services:		Health Care:	
Insurance:	Y	Manufacturer:		Manufacturer:	Y	Acute Care:		Diagnostics:		Home Health:	
Managed Care:		Distributor:		Distributor:		Sub-Acute:		Labs/Testing:		Long-Term Care:	
Utilization Management:		Specialty Pharmacy:		Leasing/Finance:	Y	Outpatient Surgery:		Staffing:		Physical Therapy:	
Payment Processing:		Vitamins/Nutritionals:		Information Systems:		Physical Rehab. Ctr.:		Waste Disposal:		Physician Prac. Mgmt.:	
		Clinical Trials:				Psychiatric Clinics:		Specialty Svcs.:	Y		

TYPES OF BUSINESS:

Equipment-Hospital Beds & Related Products
Funeral Planning Financial Services
Burial Caskets & Related Products
Life Insurance Products
Specialized Therapy Products

BRANDS/DIVISIONS/AFFILIATES:

Batesville Casket Company
Forethought Financial Services
Forethought Federal Savings Bank
Forethought Life Insurance Company
Forethought Group, Inc. (The)
Arkansas National Life Insurance Company
Hill-Rom Company Inc
Basic Care

CONTACTS: *Note: Officers with more than one job title may be intentionally listed here more than once.*

Peter H. Soderberg, CEO
Peter H. Soderberg, Pres.
Gregory N. Miller, CFO/Chief Acct. Officer/VP
Bruce Bonnevier, VP-Human Resources
Patrick D. de Maynadier, General Counsel/VP/Corp. Sec.
Michael J. Grippo, Chief Bus. Dev. Officer
Blair A. Rieth, Jr., VP-Investor Rel.
Mark R. Lanning, VP/Treas.
Kimberly K. Dennis, VP-Shared Svcs.
Larry V. Baker, VP-Corp. Tax
Kenneth A. Camp, VP/CEO/Pres., Batesville Casket Co.
Stephen W. McMillen, VP-Exec. Leadership Dev.
Ray J. Hillenbrand, Chmn.

Phone: 812-934-7000	**Fax:** 812-934-7371
Toll-Free:	
Address: 700 State Rte. 46 E., Batesville, IN 47006-8835 US	

GROWTH PLANS/SPECIAL FEATURES:

Hillenbrand Industries, Inc. is a holding company for its two major operating businesses serving the health care and funeral services industries in the U.S. and abroad. The funeral services group consists of two companies, Batesville Casket Company and Forethought Financial Services. Batesville is among the world's leading casket makers and also sells cremation urns as well as related support services. It serves funeral directors operating licensed funeral homes in North America and certain export markets. Forethought provides funeral planning financial products and marketing services in the U.S. Its customers are licensed funeral homes, funeral professionals, licensed agents and other death care providers. Forethought also manages Forethought Federal Savings Bank, which gives individuals the opportunity to save for their own funeral arrangements, as well as Forethought Life Insurance Co., the Forethought Group, Inc. and Arkansas National Life Insurance Company. The health care group consists of Hill-Rom, Inc., a manufacturer of equipment for the health care market and a provider of specialized rental therapy products designed to assist with the problems of patient immobility. It serves acute, ambulatory and long-term health care facilities and home care patients worldwide. In addition to its domestic operations, Hill-Rom operates hospital bed, therapy bed and patient room manufacturing facilities in France. These products are sold and leased directly to hospitals and nursing homes throughout Europe.

FINANCIALS: **Sales and profits are in thousands of dollars—add 000 to get the full amount. 2007 Note: Financial information for 2007 was not available for all companies at press time.**

2007 Sales: $	2007 Profits: $	**U.S. Stock Ticker: HB**
2006 Sales: $1,962,900	2006 Profits: $221,200	**Int'l Ticker:** Int'l Exchange:
2005 Sales: $1,938,100	2005 Profits: $-96,300	Employees: 9,300
2004 Sales: $1,829,300	2004 Profits: $188,200	Fiscal Year Ends: 9/30
2003 Sales: $2,042,000	2003 Profits: $138,000	Parent Company:

SALARIES/BENEFITS:

Pension Plan: Y	ESOP Stock Plan:	Profit Sharing:	Top Exec. Salary: $425,205	Bonus: $678,960
Savings Plan: Y	Stock Purch. Plan:		Second Exec. Salary: $400,869	Bonus: $322,671

OTHER THOUGHTS:

Apparent Women Officers or Directors: 3
Hot Spot for Advancement for Women/Minorities: Y

LOCATIONS: ("Y" = Yes)

West:	Southwest:	Midwest:	Southeast:	Northeast:	International:
		Y	Y	Y	Y

HILL-ROM COMPANY INC www.hill-rom.com

Industry Group Code: 339113 **Ranks within this company's industry group:** Sales: Profits:

Insurance/HMO/PPO:		Drugs:		Equipment/Supplies:		Hospitals/Clinics:		Services:		Health Care:	
Insurance:		Manufacturer:		Manufacturer:	Y	Acute Care:		Diagnostics:		Home Health:	
Managed Care:		Distributor:		Distributor:	Y	Sub-Acute:		Labs/Testing:		Long-Term Care:	
Utilization Management:		Specialty Pharmacy:		Leasing/Finance:		Outpatient Surgery:		Staffing:		Physical Therapy:	
Payment Processing:		Vitamins/Nutritionals:		Information Systems:		Physical Rehab. Ctr.:		Waste Disposal:		Physician Prac. Mgmt.:	
		Clinical Trials:				Psychiatric Clinics:		Specialty Svcs.:			

TYPES OF BUSINESS:

Equipment-Hospital Beds & Related Products
Stretchers

BRANDS/DIVISIONS/AFFILIATES:

Hillenbrand Industries
TotalCare
TotalCare Sp02RT
PrimeAire
ZoneAire
PrimeAire
Acuair
Comfortline

CONTACTS: *Note: Officers with more than one job title may be intentionally listed here more than once.*

Peter Soderberg, CEO
Peter Soderberg, Pres.
Gregory N. Miller, CFO
Abel Ang, VP-Tech. Dev.
Abel Ang, VP-Int'l Bus.

Phone: 812-934-7777	**Fax:** 812-934-8189
Toll-Free:	
Address: 1069 State Route 46 E., Batesville, IN 47006 US	

GROWTH PLANS/SPECIAL FEATURES:

Hill-Rom Company, a subsidiary of Hillenbrand Industries sells, rents and services hospital products, including hospital beds; non-invasive therapeutic surfaces and devices stretchers and other transport systems; furniture communication and locating systems; and operating room accessories. The company provides therapy products fo acute care, homecare and long-term care, as well as a fu line of stretchers under the TranStar name and specialize mattresses. Other products include nurse call systems, feta monitoring information systems, siderail communications surgical table accessories, bedside cabinets, tables an mattresses. The company's architectural products includ customized, prefabricated modules that are either wal mounted or on freestanding columns and allow medica equipment such as gases, communication accessories an electrical services to be kept safely in patient rooms. Th firm primarily focuses on a line of electrically adjustabl hospital beds that can be adjusted to varied orthopedic an therapeutic contours and positions. Hospital bed model include the TotalCare Sp02RT bed, a pulmonary bed tha delivers rotation, percussion and vibration; the TotalCar bed, a bed designed for acute patients with little to n mobility; and the Affinity 4 bed, designed for the materni department. Hill-Rom provides therapy systems to hospitals long-term care facilities and homes through service center located in the U.S., Canada and Western Europe. Th company's products are sold directly and throug distributorships. Hill-Rom also rents beds, infusion pumps monitors and other equipment to hospitals, long-term car facilities and private homes. In August 2006, Hill-Ror announced the beginning of a five-year strategic alliance wit St. Louis-based Ascension Health. The deal hinges upo the reduction and elimination of occurrences within th patient care environment of adverse events, which include pressure sores, ventilator-associated pneumonia and patier falls.

The company offers its employees medical, dental and visio insurance; life, short- and long-term disability insurance; 401(k) plan; an employee assistance program; and tuitio reimbursement.

FINANCIALS: **Sales and profits are in thousands of dollars—add 000 to get the full amount. 2007 Note: Financial information for 2007 was not available for all companies at press time.**

2007 Sales: $	2007 Profits: $	**U.S. Stock Ticker: Subsidiary**
2006 Sales: $	2006 Profits: $	**Int'l Ticker:** Int'l Exchange:
2005 Sales: $	2005 Profits: $	Employees: 6,500
2004 Sales: $	2004 Profits: $	Fiscal Year Ends:
2003 Sales: $1,067,000	2003 Profits: $	Parent Company: HILLENBRAND INDUSTRIES

SALARIES/BENEFITS:

Pension Plan:	ESOP Stock Plan:	Profit Sharing:	Top Exec. Salary: $	Bonus: $
Savings Plan: Y	Stock Purch. Plan:		Second Exec. Salary: $	Bonus: $

OTHER THOUGHTS:

Apparent Women Officers or Directors:
Hot Spot for Advancement for Women/Minorities:

LOCATIONS: ("Y" = Yes)

West:	Southwest:	Midwest:	Southeast:	Northeast:	International:
Y		Y		Y	Y

HITACHI MEDICAL CORPORATION www.hitachi-medical.co.jp

Industry Group Code: 339113 **Ranks within this company's industry group:** Sales: Profits:

Insurance/HMO/PPO:		Drugs:		Equipment/Supplies:		Hospitals/Clinics:		Services:		Health Care:	
Insurance:		Manufacturer:		Manufacturer:	Y	Acute Care:		Diagnostics:		Home Health:	
Managed Care:		Distributor:		Distributor:		Sub-Acute:		Labs/Testing:		Long-Term Care:	
Utilization Management:		Specialty Pharmacy:		Leasing/Finance:		Outpatient Surgery:		Staffing:		Physical Therapy:	
Payment Processing:		Vitamins/Nutritionals:		Information Systems:		Physical Rehab. Ctr.:		Waste Disposal:		Physician Prac. Mgmt.:	
		Clinical Trials:				Psychiatric Clinics:		Specialty Svcs.:	Y		

TYPES OF BUSINESS:

Equipment-Medical Systems
Medical Imaging Systems

BRANDS/DIVISIONS/AFFILIATES:

ECHELON Vega
AIRIS Elite
ROBUSTO
POPULUS
Hitachi Medical Computer Systems, Inc.
Hitachi Medical Systems America, Inc.
Performance Controls, Inc.
Hitachi, Ltd.

CONTACTS: *Note: Officers with more than one job title may be intentionally listed here more than once.*

Yuzou Inakazu, Co-CEO
Yuzou Inakazu, Pres.
Kiyoshi Hamamatsu, Co-CEO/Sr. VP-Mktg. & Medical Info. Sys.
Norifumi Katsukura, Exec. Officer-Human Resources & Labor Affairs
Norifumi Katsukura, Exec. Officer-Legal Affairs & Risk Measures
Kazuyoshi Miki, VP-Dev., Quality Control & Intellectual Property
Kenichirou Kosugi, VP-Finance
Kenzou Sawaide, Exec. Officer-Domestic Sales & Svcs. Bus.
Etsuji Yamamoto, Exec. Officer-Mgmt. Support
Kenichi Kaneki, Exec. Officer-Environment & Export Control
Hideki Takahashi, VP-Int'l Sales
Yoshirou Kuwata, Chmn.
Masao Miyake, Exec. Officer-Int'l Bus.

Phone: 81-3-3526-8400 **Fax:**
Toll-Free:
Address: Akihabara UDX., 4-14-1, Soto-Kanda, Chiyoda-ku, Tokyo, Japan

GROWTH PLANS/SPECIAL FEATURES:

Hitachi Medical Corporation manufactures equipment for the medical industry. It operates two segments. The Medical Systems Segment produces various medical imaging systems, including magnetic resonance imaging (MRI), X-ray computerized tomography (CT), conventional X-ray and diagnostic ultrasound (US). Some of its brand names include the ECHELON Vega and AIRIS Elite MRI systems; the ROBUSTO four-slice CT system; and the digital POPULUS conventional X-ray system. The medical systems segment also produces nuclear medicines. This segment produced 91.5% of the company's 2007 sales. The Medical Information Systems Segment provides electronic medical charts and a medical checkup data management system. The medical information systems segment also produces medical image management systems. Subsidiary Hitachi Medical Computer Systems, Inc. produces a medical accounting system. The firm has regional branch offices in 17 major Japanese cities; four manufacturing facilities located in Kashiwa City, Osaka, Chiba Prefecture and Mobara City; and local sales and service offices in 46 Japanese locations. Some of the firm's international medical systems sales and service subsidiaries include Hitachi Medical Systems America, Inc.; Hitachi Medical Systems (Singapore) Pte, Ltd.; Hitachi Medical Systems Europe Holding AG; Hitachi Medical Systems (Beijing) Corporation; and Hitachi Medical (Guangzhou) Co., Ltd. It also has two medical systems components manufacturing subsidiaries: Hitachi Medical Systems (Suzhou) Corporation and Performance Controls, Inc. The company is 61.7% owned by Hitachi, Ltd., with the next largest shareholder, State Street Bank and Trust Company 55019 owning 2.8% of the company. Hitachi Medical Systems primarily sells its medical equipment to hospitals owned by Hitachi, Ltd. Its major clients include private, general, university, national and other public hospitals; private clinics; airline companies; and canned and bottled beverage companies.

FINANCIALS: **Sales and profits are in thousands of dollars—add 000 to get the full amount. 2007 Note: Financial information for 2007 was not available for all companies at press time.**

2007 Sales: $	2007 Profits: $	**U.S. Stock Ticker: Subsidiary**
2006 Sales: $	2006 Profits: $	**Int'l Ticker: 6910** Int'l Exchange: Tokyo-TSE
2005 Sales: $	2005 Profits: $	Employees:
2004 Sales: $	2004 Profits: $	Fiscal Year Ends: 3/31
2003 Sales: $	2003 Profits: $	Parent Company: HITACHI LTD

SALARIES/BENEFITS:

Pension Plan:	ESOP Stock Plan:	Profit Sharing:	Top Exec. Salary: $	Bonus: $
Savings Plan:	Stock Purch. Plan:		Second Exec. Salary: $	Bonus: $

OTHER THOUGHTS:

Apparent Women Officers or Directors:
Hot Spot for Advancement for Women/Minorities:

LOCATIONS: ("Y" = Yes)

West:	Southwest:	Midwest:	Southeast:	Northeast:	International:
		Y			Y

HITACHI MEDICAL SYSTEMS AMERICA www.hitachimed.com

Industry Group Code: 339113 **Ranks within this company's industry group:** Sales: Profits:

Insurance/HMO/PPO:		Drugs:		Equipment/Supplies:		Hospitals/Clinics:		Services:		Health Care:	
Insurance:		Manufacturer:		Manufacturer:		Acute Care:		Diagnostics:		Home Health:	
Managed Care:		Distributor:		Distributor:	Y	Sub-Acute:		Labs/Testing:		Long-Term Care:	
Utilization Management:		Specialty Pharmacy:		Leasing/Finance:		Outpatient Surgery:		Staffing:		Physical Therapy:	
Payment Processing:		Vitamins/Nutritionals:		Information Systems:		Physical Rehab. Ctr.:		Waste Disposal:		Physician Prac. Mgmt.:	
		Clinical Trials:				Psychiatric Clinics:		Specialty Svcs.:	Y		

TYPES OF BUSINESS:

Marketing-Medical Imaging Systems

BRANDS/DIVISIONS/AFFILIATES:

Hitachi Medical Corporation
Hitachi Ltd
ORIGIN
Echelon
CXR 4
CB MercuRay
Sceptre
ETG-4000

CONTACTS:

Note: Officers with more than one job title may be intentionally listed here more than once.

Donald Broomfield, CEO
Donald Broomfield, Pres.
Phil Chang, Manager-Mktg. Comm.
Douglas Thistlethwaite, Manager-Regulatory Affairs
William (Bill) Bishop, VP-New Bus. Dev.
Richard Kurz, Controller/VP
Sheldon Schaffer, VP/Gen. Manager-Magnetic Resonance
James Confer, VP-Service

Phone: 330-425-1313	**Fax:** 330-425-1410
Toll-Free: 800-800-3106	
Address: 1959 Summit Commerce Park, Twinsburg, OH 44087 US	

GROWTH PLANS/SPECIAL FEATURES:

Hitachi Medical Systems America, Inc. (HMSA), founded b Japanese company Hitachi Medical Corporation, which itself a subsidiary of Hitachi, Ltd., provides marketing an support for all of Hitachi's medical diagnostic imagin equipment in the U.S. Its most commonly marketed product are a line of MRI (Magnetic Resonance Imagining ultrasound and CT (Computed Tomography) system although it also markets optical tomography and PE (Positron Emission Tomography) systems. Its MRI system include the ORIGIN operating software and VERTE computer systems as well as other accessories and imag capture packages. Its six brands include MPR-7000, AIRIS Altaire and the newest product line, Echelon. HMSA's seve ultrasound imaging systems range from the simplistic EUB 405 Plus compact black and white system with minima features, up to the high-end HI VISION 8500 color, high resolution system. Its ultrasound products also includ probes ranging from those attached to a fingertip to thos used in endoscopic surgery; and include approximately 3 different models. HMSA's sole CT imaging system is th CXR 4 with features such as real-time image reconstructio and an operating system and networking capability based o Microsoft Windows. Other products include the C MercuRay digital X-ray scanner capable of 360 degre rotation allowing it to capture 3-D as well as 2-D images Some of HMSA's PET scanners feature CT imaging as wel and come in a variety of packages, such as the Sceptre cardiac configuration. Most of its PET products are sol under the Sceptre brand; but the company also markets th AVIA line of workstation interfaces. Finally, HMSA's optica tomography sole system, the ETG-4000, utilizes nea infrared light to provide real-time measurements and image of hemoglobin (the oxygen carrying molecule in red bloo cells) levels in the brain. The company provides assistanc for its marketed products including installation, site plannin systematic preventive maintenance and other services.

FINANCIALS:

Sales and profits are in thousands of dollars—add 000 to get the full amount. 2007 Note: Financial information for 2007 was not available for all companies at press time.

2007 Sales: $	2007 Profits: $	**U.S. Stock Ticker: Subsidiary**
2006 Sales: $	2006 Profits: $	**Int'l Ticker:** Int'l Exchange:
2005 Sales: $	2005 Profits: $	Employees:
2004 Sales: $	2004 Profits: $	Fiscal Year Ends: 3/31
2003 Sales: $	2003 Profits: $	Parent Company: HITACHI LTD

SALARIES/BENEFITS:

Pension Plan:	ESOP Stock Plan:	Profit Sharing:	Top Exec. Salary: $	Bonus: $
Savings Plan:	Stock Purch. Plan:		Second Exec. Salary: $	Bonus: $

OTHER THOUGHTS:

Apparent Women Officers or Directors:
Hot Spot for Advancement for Women/Minorities:

LOCATIONS: ("Y" = Yes)

West:	Southwest:	Midwest:	Southeast:	Northeast:	International:
		Y			

HLTH CORP

www.hlth.com

Industry Group Code: 522320 **Ranks within this company's industry group:** Sales: 2 Profits: 1

Insurance/HMO/PPO:		Drugs:		Equipment/Supplies:		Hospitals/Clinics:		Services:		Health Care:	
Insurance:		Manufacturer:		Manufacturer:	Y	Acute Care:		Diagnostics:		Home Health:	
Managed Care:		Distributor:		Distributor:		Sub-Acute:		Labs/Testing:		Long-Term Care:	
Utilization Management:		Specialty Pharmacy:		Leasing/Finance:		Outpatient Surgery:		Staffing:		Physical Therapy:	
Payment Processing:	Y	Vitamins/Nutritionals:		Information Systems:	Y	Physical Rehab. Ctr.:		Waste Disposal:		Physician Prac. Mgmt.:	
		Clinical Trials:				Psychiatric Clinics:		Specialty Svcs.:			

TYPES OF BUSINESS:

Business-to-Business Health Care Applications
Web-Based Health Care Information
Transaction Processing
Plastic Products
Information Technology Systems

BRANDS/DIVISIONS/AFFILIATES:

Emdeon Corporation
WebMD
Little Blue Book (The)
ACP Medicine
ACS Surgery: Principles of Practice
ViPS
Porex
Emdeon Business Services LLC

CONTACTS: *Note: Officers with more than one job title may be intentionally listed here more than once.*

Kevin M. Cameron, CEO
Mark D. Funston, CFO/Exec. VP
Charles A. Mele, General Counsel/Corp. Sec./Exec. VP
Wayne T. Gattinella, CEO/Pres., WebMD
Arthur Lehrer, CEO & Pres., ViPS
William G. Midgette, CEO-Porex
Martin J. Wygod, Chmn.

Phone: 201-703-3400	**Fax:** 201-703-3401
Toll-Free:	
Address: 669 River Dr., Ctr. 2, Elmwood Park, NJ 07407 US	

GROWTH PLANS/SPECIAL FEATURES:

HLTH Corporation, formerly Emdeon Corporation, provides web-based health care information and services to facilitate connectivity and transactions among physicians, patients, payers, suppliers and consumers. The company's subsidiary, WebMD, provides health information services for consumers, physicians, healthcare professionals, employers and health plans through its public and private online portals and health-focused publications. WebMD's operations include Public Online Portals, enabling individuals to obtain detailed information on a particular disease or condition, locate physicians, store individual healthcare information, assess their personal health status, receive periodic e-newsletters and alerts on topics of individual interest and participate in online communities with peers and experts; Private Online Portals, providing a platform for employers and health plans to provide their employees and plan members with access to personalized health and benefit information and decision support technology to assist in making benefit, provider and treatment choices; Publishing and Other Services provides complementary offline health content including The Little Blue Book, ACP Medicine, ACS Surgery: Principles of Practice and WebMD the Magazine. HLTH's ViPS segment provides healthcare data management, analytics, decision-support and process automation solutions to governmental, Blue Cross Blue Shield and commercial healthcare payers. ViPS operates through the Government Solutions Group and Healthpayer Solutions Group. HLTH's Porex segment develops, manufactures and distributes proprietary porous plastic products and components used in healthcare, industrial and consumer applications. HLTH owns 48% of EBS Master LLC, which owns Emdeon Business Services LLC (EBS). EBS provides revenue cycle management solutions and electronic transaction services that automate key business and administrative functions for healthcare payers and providers. In February 2007, EBS announced a new multi-payer electronic payment and remittance solution.

HLTH offers its employees flexible spending accounts; a tuition reimbursement program; an employee assistance program; 401(k) plan; and medical, dental and vision coverage plans.

FINANCIALS: **Sales and profits are in thousands of dollars—add 000 to get the full amount. 2007 Note: Financial information for 2007 was not available for all companies at press time.**

2007 Sales: $	2007 Profits: $	**U.S. Stock Ticker: HLTH**
2006 Sales: $1,098,608	2006 Profits: $767,739	**Int'l Ticker:** Int'l Exchange:
2005 Sales: $1,026,475	2005 Profits: $72,974	Employees: 2,260
2004 Sales: $918,097	2004 Profits: $39,334	Fiscal Year Ends: 12/31
2003 Sales: $963,980	2003 Profits: $-17,006	Parent Company:

SALARIES/BENEFITS:

Pension Plan:	ESOP Stock Plan:	Profit Sharing:	Top Exec. Salary: $975,000	Bonus: $3,530,000
Savings Plan: Y	Stock Purch. Plan:		Second Exec. Salary: $660,000	Bonus: $3,530,000

OTHER THOUGHTS:

Apparent Women Officers or Directors:
Hot Spot for Advancement for Women/Minorities:

LOCATIONS: ("Y" = Yes)

West:	Southwest:	Midwest:	Southeast:	Northeast:	International:
	Y	Y	Y	Y	

HOLOGIC INC

www.hologic.com

Industry Group Code: 339113 **Ranks within this company's industry group:** Sales: 41 Profits: 44

Insurance/HMO/PPO:		Drugs:		Equipment/Supplies:		Hospitals/Clinics:		Services:		Health Care:	
Insurance:		Manufacturer:		Manufacturer:	Y	Acute Care:		Diagnostics:		Home Health:	
Managed Care:		Distributor:		Distributor:		Sub-Acute:		Labs/Testing:		Long-Term Care:	
Utilization Management:		Specialty Pharmacy:		Leasing/Finance:		Outpatient Surgery:		Staffing:		Physical Therapy:	
Payment Processing:		Vitamins/Nutritionals:		Information Systems:		Physical Rehab. Ctr.:		Waste Disposal:		Physician Prac. Mgmt.:	
		Clinical Trials:				Psychiatric Clinics:		Specialty Svcs.:			

TYPES OF BUSINESS:

Medical Diagnostic & Imaging Equipment
Mammography Systems
X-Ray Bone Densitometers
Radiography Systems
Biopsy Systems

BRANDS/DIVISIONS/AFFILIATES:

LORAD
Discovery QDR
Sahara
Selenia
R2 Technology
MultiCare Platinum
Explorer
Suros Surgical Systems

CONTACTS: *Note: Officers with more than one job title may be intentionally listed here more than once.*

John W. Cumming, CEO
Robert Cascella, COO
Robert Cascella, Pres.
Glenn P. Muir, CFO/Exec. VP
John Pekarsky, Sr. VP-Sales & Strategic Accounts
Jay A. Stein, CTO
John W. Cumming, Chmn.

Phone: 781-999-7300	**Fax:**
Toll-Free:	
Address: 35 Crosby Dr., Bedford, MA 01730 US	

GROWTH PLANS/SPECIAL FEATURES:

Hologic, Inc. is a leading developer, manufacturer an supplier of diagnostic and medical imaging systems primaril serving the health care needs of women. The company' core women's health care business units are focused o mammography, breast care and osteoporosis assessmen Hologic's mammography and breast care business un includes a product line of film-based and digit mammography systems, such as its LORAD line of screen film mammography systems and the Selenia digit mammography system, computer-aided detection (CAD such as its recently acquired R2 Technology for CAD syste development, breast biopsy systems, such as its MultiCar Platinum prone breast biopsy table and the StereoLoc upright attachment, and breast biopsy and tissue extractio devices. The company's osteoporosis assessment busines unit primarily consists of dual-energy X-ray bon densitometry systems, including its Discovery QDR Serie and its Explorer Series bone densitometer, and Sahara, lightweight, portable ultrasound-based osteoporosi assessment product. In addition to its women's healthcar products, the company also develops, manufactures an supplies mini C-arm imaging products, distributes the Esaot extremity MRI system and manufactures and sells AE photoconductor materials for a variety of electrophotographi applications. Customers include hospitals, imaging clinics private practices and major pharmaceutical companies tha use its products in conducting clinical trials. In April 2006 Hologic acquired Suros Surgical Systems, a leader in th field of devices used for minimally invasive biopsy and tissu extraction, for about $240 million. In May 2007, the fir agreed to acquire Cytyc Corp. for $6.2 billion.

FINANCIALS: **Sales and profits are in thousands of dollars—add 000 to get the full amount. 2007 Note: Financial information for 2007 was not available for all companies at press time.**

2007 Sales: $	2007 Profits: $	**U.S. Stock Ticker: HOLX**
2006 Sales: $462,680	2006 Profits: $27,423	**Int'l Ticker:** Int'l Exchange:
2005 Sales: $287,684	2005 Profits: $28,256	Employees: 1,617
2004 Sales: $228,705	2004 Profits: $12,164	Fiscal Year Ends: 9/30
2003 Sales: $204,035	2003 Profits: $2,882	Parent Company:

SALARIES/BENEFITS:

Pension Plan:	ESOP Stock Plan:	Profit Sharing: Y	Top Exec. Salary: $486,328	Bonus: $775,020
Savings Plan: Y	Stock Purch. Plan: Y		Second Exec. Salary: $342,580	Bonus: $525,000

OTHER THOUGHTS:

Apparent Women Officers or Directors:
Hot Spot for Advancement for Women/Minorities:

LOCATIONS: ("Y" = Yes)

West:	Southwest:	Midwest:	Southeast:	Northeast:	International:
Y		Y		Y	Y

HOOPER HOLMES INC www.hooperholmes.com

Industry Group Code: 621511 **Ranks within this company's industry group:** Sales: 5 Profits: 8

Insurance/HMO/PPO:		Drugs:		Equipment/Supplies:		Hospitals/Clinics:		Services:		Health Care:	
Insurance:		Manufacturer:		Manufacturer:		Acute Care:		Diagnostics:		Home Health:	
Managed Care:		Distributor:		Distributor:		Sub-Acute:		Labs/Testing:	Y	Long-Term Care:	
Utilization Management:		Specialty Pharmacy:		Leasing/Finance:		Outpatient Surgery:		Staffing:		Physical Therapy:	
Payment Processing:		Vitamins/Nutritionals:		Information Systems:	Y	Physical Rehab. Ctr.:		Waste Disposal:		Physician Prac. Mgmt.:	
		Clinical Trials:				Psychiatric Clinics:		Specialty Svcs.:	Y		

TYPES OF BUSINESS:

Services-Testing (Health & Life Insurance Prospects)
Health Information Underwriting Services
Home Medical Examinations
Outsourced Information Services
Electronic Case Management

BRANDS/DIVISIONS/AFFILIATES:

Portamedic
Medicals Direct
Infolink
Heritage Labs International, LLC
BioSignia, Inc.

CONTACTS: *Note: Officers with more than one job title may be intentionally listed here more than once.*

James Calver, CEO
John L. Spenser, COO
James Calver, Pres.
Michael Shea, CFO/Sr. VP
Burt Wolder, Chief Mktg. Officer/Sr. VP
Richard D'Alesandro, Sr. VP-Admin. Svcs. Group
William F. Kracklauer, General Counsel/Sr. VP/Sec.
Chris Behling, Sr. VP-Bus. Dev.
Joseph A. Marone, VP/Controller
Ron Levesque, Pres., Portamedic
Chuck Groseth, Sr. VP/National Sales Mgr.
Mark Patterson, Pres., Heritage Labs
Steve Sherrill, Pres., Hooper Holmes Underwriting Solutions
Benjamin A. Currier, Chmn.

Phone: 908-766-5000 **Fax:**
Toll-Free:
Address: 170 Mt. Airy Rd., Basking Ridge, NJ 07920 US

GROWTH PLANS/SPECIAL FEATURES:

Hooper Holmes, Inc. provides risk assessment and medical claims management services. The company coordinates the activities of over 9,000 paramedical examiners through its network of branch and contract affiliate offices. Hooper Holmes operates through two divisions: the Health Information Division and the Claims Evaluation Division. The Health Information Division provides medical-related risk assessment information to life and health insurance carriers. These services include performing paramedical and medical examinations of individual insurance policy applicants throughout the U.S. under the Portamedic brand name, and in the U.K. under the Medicals Direct brand name; completing telephone interviews of applicants and collecting applicants' medical records under the Infolink name; testing the blood, urine and other specimens; and underwriting life insurance policies on an outsourced basis for life insurance companies. A paramedical exam typically consists of questions about an applicant's medical history, measurements of the applicant's height and weight, blood pressure and pulse. Blood and urine specimens are also collected, to be tested by a laboratory. The company's subsidiary Heritage Labs International, LLC, processes the blood and urine specimens obtained in connection with a portion of the paramedical examinations handled by Portamedic, as well as specimens provided by third-party health information service providers. Hooper Holmes' Claims Evaluation Division provides medical claims evaluation services to property and casualty insurance carriers, law firms, self-insurers and third-party administrators for use in processing personal injury accident claims. The core activity of this business consists of arranging for independent medical exams by a doctor for the purpose of rendering an objective opinion regarding the nature, origin, treatment and causal relationship of an injury. The company provides its claims evaluation services in connection with automobile, liability, disability and worker's compensation claims. In September 2007, Hooper Holmes announced a joint marketing agreement with BioSignia, Inc., a provider of healthcare solutions.

FINANCIALS: **Sales and profits are in thousands of dollars—add 000 to get the full amount. 2007 Note: Financial information for 2007 was not available for all companies at press time.**

2007 Sales: $	2007 Profits: $	**U.S. Stock Ticker: HH**
2006 Sales: $293,862	2006 Profits: $-85,181	**Int'l Ticker:** Int'l Exchange:
2005 Sales: $320,346	2005 Profits: $-96,623	Employees: 3,270
2004 Sales: $326,651	2004 Profits: $10,015	Fiscal Year Ends: 12/31
2003 Sales: $300,182	2003 Profits: $15,847	Parent Company:

SALARIES/BENEFITS:

Pension Plan:	ESOP Stock Plan:	Profit Sharing:	Top Exec. Salary: $383,333	Bonus: $400,000
Savings Plan:	Stock Purch. Plan:		Second Exec. Salary: $275,000	Bonus: $

OTHER THOUGHTS:

Apparent Women Officers or Directors:
Hot Spot for Advancement for Women/Minorities:

LOCATIONS: ("Y" = Yes)

West:	Southwest:	Midwest:	Southeast:	Northeast:	International:
Y	Y	Y	Y	Y	Y

HORIZON HEALTH CORPORATION www.horizonhealth.com

Industry Group Code: 621490 **Ranks within this company's industry group:** Sales: 9 Profits: 7

Insurance/HMO/PPO:		Drugs:		Equipment/Supplies:		Hospitals/Clinics:		Services:		Health Care:	
Insurance:		Manufacturer:		Manufacturer:		Acute Care:		Diagnostics:		Home Health:	
Managed Care:		Distributor:		Distributor:		Sub-Acute:		Labs/Testing:		Long-Term Care:	
Utilization Management:	Y	Specialty Pharmacy:		Leasing/Finance:		Outpatient Surgery:		Staffing:	Y	Physical Therapy:	Y
Payment Processing:		Vitamins/Nutritionals:		Information Systems:	Y	Physical Rehab. Ctr.:	Y	Waste Disposal:		Physician Prac. Mgmt.:	
		Clinical Trials:				Psychiatric Clinics:	Y	Specialty Svcs.:	Y		

TYPES OF BUSINESS:

Behavioral Health Clinical Services
Hospital Services
Contract Management Services
Employee Assistance Program Services

BRANDS/DIVISIONS/AFFILIATES:

Psychiatric Solutions, Inc.
Lighthouse Care Centers, LLC
Focus Healthcare, LLC
Kids Behavioral Health
Kingwood Pines Hospital

CONTACTS: *Note: Officers with more than one job title may be intentionally listed here more than once.*

Ken Newman, CEO
Ken Newman, Pres.
John E. Pitts, CFO
David K. Meyercord, Exec. VP-Admin.
David K. Meyercord, General Counsel
Donald W. Thayer, Exec. VP-Acquisitions & Dev.
Valerie Evans, Investor Rel.
John E. Pitts, Exec. VP-Finance
David K. White, Pres., Contract Mgmt. Svcs.
Frank J. Baumann, Pres., Hospital Svcs.
Cindy Sheriff, Pres., EAP Svcs.
Ken Newman, Chmn.

Phone: 972-420-8200 **Fax:** 972-420-8252
Toll-Free: 800-931-4646
Address: 2941 S. Lake Vista Dr., Lewisville, TX 75067 US

GROWTH PLANS/SPECIAL FEATURES:

Horizon Health Corp. is a health care services provider with a focus on its behavioral health clinical services. The company operates in three segments: hospital services, contract management services and employee assistance program services. Hospital services include behavioral health care facilities (residential or psychiatric treatment facilities) that offer a wide range of inpatient behavioral health care services for children, adolescents and adults. The firm works with mental health care professionals; psychiatrists; non-psychiatric physicians; emergency rooms; insurance and managed care organizations; company sponsored employee assistance programs; and law enforcement and community agencies that interact with individuals who many need treatment for behavioral illness or substance abuse. The contract management services include behavioral health contract management services and physical rehabilitation contract management services. The employee assistance programs services assist employees and their dependents with resolution of behavioral conditions or other personal concerns. In 2006, Horizon Health acquired the behavioral facilities of Lighthouse Care Centers, LLC and Focus Healthcare, LLC for roughly $91 million. In addition, the company purchased Kids Behavioral Health of Utah, Inc., a Utah corporation, for roughly $9.6 million and Kingwood Pines Hospital, a 78-bed behavioral health facility in Texas, for approximately $14.1 million. In June 2007, the company was acquired by Psychiatric Solutions, Inc. (PSI) for roughly $426 million. As a result, it became a wholly owned subsidiary of PSI.

Horizon Health offers employees a flexible benefit plan; medical, dental and pharmacy insurance; group and supplemental life insurance; a 401(k) plan; and an employee assistance plan.

FINANCIALS: Sales and profits are in thousands of dollars—add 000 to get the full amount. 2007 Note: Financial information for 2007 was not available for all companies at press time.

2007 Sales: $	2007 Profits: $	**U.S. Stock Ticker: Subsidiary**
2006 Sales: $275,000	2006 Profits: $12,100	**Int'l Ticker:** Int'l Exchange:
2005 Sales: $207,392	2005 Profits: $5,151	Employees: 2,804
2004 Sales: $180,323	2004 Profits: $10,775	Fiscal Year Ends: 8/31
2003 Sales: $166,300	2003 Profits: $9,600	Parent Company: PSYCHIATRIC SOLUTIONS INC

SALARIES/BENEFITS:

Pension Plan:	ESOP Stock Plan:	Profit Sharing:	Top Exec. Salary: $450,000	Bonus: $
Savings Plan: Y	Stock Purch. Plan:		Second Exec. Salary: $325,000	Bonus: $

OTHER THOUGHTS:

Apparent Women Officers or Directors: 2
Hot Spot for Advancement for Women/Minorities:

LOCATIONS: ("Y" = Yes)

West:	Southwest:	Midwest:	Southeast:	Northeast:	International:
Y	Y	Y	Y	Y	

Note: Financial information, benefits and other data can change quickly and may vary from those stated here.

HORIZON HEALTHCARE SERVICES INC www.horizon-bcbsnj.com

Industry Group Code: 524114 **Ranks within this company's industry group:** Sales: 15 Profits: 14

Insurance/HMO/PPO:		Drugs:		Equipment/Supplies:		Hospitals/Clinics:		Services:		Health Care:	
Insurance:	Y	Manufacturer:		Manufacturer:		Acute Care:		Diagnostics:		Home Health:	
Managed Care:	Y	Distributor:		Distributor:		Sub-Acute:		Labs/Testing:		Long-Term Care:	
Utilization Management:	Y	Specialty Pharmacy:		Leasing/Finance:		Outpatient Surgery:		Staffing:		Physical Therapy:	
Payment Processing:		Vitamins/Nutritionals:		Information Systems:		Physical Rehab. Ctr.:		Waste Disposal:		Physician Prac. Mgmt.:	
		Clinical Trials:				Psychiatric Clinics:		Specialty Svcs.:			

TYPES OF BUSINESS:

Insurance-Medical & Health, HMOs & PPOs
Workers' Compensation
Utilization Management
Insurance-Dental
Insurance-Behavioral Health
Insurance-Casualty
Insurance-Life

BRANDS/DIVISIONS/AFFILIATES:

Blue Cross Blue Shield
Horizon HMO
Magellan Behavioral Health
Horizon Healthcare Dental, Inc.
Horizon Casualty Services, Inc.
Horizon Healthcare Insurance Company of New York
Adherance Improvement Messaging
Horizon NJ Health

CONTACTS: *Note: Officers with more than one job title may be intentionally listed here more than once.*

William J. Marino, CEO
William J. Marino, Pres.
Robert J. Pures, CFO
Mark Barnard, Sr. VP-Info. Systems/CIO
Kathryn McKinnon, VP-Prod. Dev. & Underwriting
Robert J. Pures, Sr. VP-Admin.
John W. Campbel, General Counsel/Corp. Sec./Sr. VP
Donna Celestini, VP-Strategy & Dev.
Robert J. Pures, Treas.
Christy W. Bell, Sr. VP-Healthcare Mgmt.
Robert A. Marino, Sr. VP-Market Bus. Units
Patrick J. Geraghty, Sr. VP-Svcs.
Jim Albano, VP-Health Care Svcs.
Vincent J. Giblin, Chmn.

Phone: 973-466-4000 **Fax:** 973-466-4317
Toll-Free: 800-355-2583
Address: 3 Penn Plaza E., Newark, NJ 07101 US

GROWTH PLANS/SPECIAL FEATURES:

Horizon Healthcare Services, Inc., doing business as Horizon Blue Cross Blue Shield of New Jersey (HBCBSNJ), is the only licensed Blue Cross Blue Shield plan in New Jersey. The firm serves over 3.2 million members throughout north, south and central New Jersey. The firm's insurance plans include traditional indemnity, Horizon HMO, Horizon PPO, Horizon POS, Horizon MSA (a medical savings account) and Horizon Direct Access (an open access plan). The company also offers dental, Medicare supplement, behavioral health insurance and workers' compensation. Magellan Behavioral Health provides utilization reviews and management services to HBCBDNJ customers receiving mental health and substance abuse treatment. In addition, HBCBSNJ provides services through affiliates Horizon Healthcare Dental, Inc., which provides managed dental plans for individuals and groups; and Horizon Casualty Services, Inc., which provides workers' compensation, managed care, claims administration services and auto injury management services. The firm also operates through several subsidiaries that are not Blue Cross and Blue Shield licensed companies. Horizon Healthcare Insurance Company of New York provides managed care and traditional plans in New York State, a growing market for the company. Horizon Healthcare Insurance Agency, Inc. offers group life and employee benefit coverage, including accidental death and dismemberment, dependent life, premium conversions, weekly income, long-term disability, flexible spending accounts and group term life insurance. Horizon NJ Health, New Jersey's largest managed health care organization, serves the publicly insured Medicaid and NJ FamilyCare populations. Recently, the firm introduced a messaging system called Adherence Improvement Messaging program (AIM), used for electronic-prescribing, that will provide medication adherence information and specific clinical messages for asthma and hyperlipidemia patients. AIM will provide information to physicians to promote appropriate utilization of medications.

Along with medical benefits, Horizon BCBSNJ offers its employees flexible spending accounts, employee assistance, educational assistance, a credit union and child care.

FINANCIALS: **Sales and profits are in thousands of dollars—add 000 to get the full amount. 2007 Note: Financial information for 2007 was not available for all companies at press time.**

2007 Sales: $	2007 Profits: $	**U.S. Stock Ticker: Nonprofit**
2006 Sales: $6,730,317	2006 Profits: $180,066	**Int'l Ticker:** Int'l Exchange:
2005 Sales: $5,903,953	2005 Profits: $213,751	Employees: 4,400
2004 Sales: $5,500,000	2004 Profits: $	Fiscal Year Ends: 12/31
2003 Sales: $5,082,400	2003 Profits: $171,100	Parent Company:

SALARIES/BENEFITS:

Pension Plan: Y	ESOP Stock Plan:	Profit Sharing:	Top Exec. Salary: $	Bonus: $
Savings Plan: Y	Stock Purch. Plan:		Second Exec. Salary: $	Bonus: $

OTHER THOUGHTS:

Apparent Women Officers or Directors: 2
Hot Spot for Advancement for Women/Minorities:

LOCATIONS: ("Y" = Yes)

West:	Southwest:	Midwest:	Southeast:	Northeast:	International:
				Y	

Note: Financial information, benefits and other data can change quickly and may vary from those stated here.

HOSPIRA INC

www.hospira.com

Industry Group Code: 339113 **Ranks within this company's industry group:** Sales: 13 Profits: 14

Insurance/HMO/PPO:		Drugs:		Equipment/Supplies:		Hospitals/Clinics:		Services:		Health Care:	
Insurance:		Manufacturer:	Y	Manufacturer:		Acute Care:		Diagnostics:		Home Health:	
Managed Care:		Distributor:		Distributor:		Sub-Acute:		Labs/Testing:		Long-Term Care:	
Utilization Management:		Specialty Pharmacy:		Leasing/Finance:		Outpatient Surgery:		Staffing:		Physical Therapy:	
Payment Processing:		Vitamins/Nutritionals:		Information Systems:	Y	Physical Rehab. Ctr.:		Waste Disposal:		Physician Prac. Mgmt.:	
		Clinical Trials:				Psychiatric Clinics:		Specialty Svcs.:			

TYPES OF BUSINESS:

Pharmaceutical Development
Generic Pharmaceuticals
Medication Delivery Systems
Anesthetics
Injectable Medications
Diagnostic Imaging Agents
Drug Library Software
Contract Manufacturing

BRANDS/DIVISIONS/AFFILIATES:

Abbott Laboratories
One 2 One
Mayne Pharma Limited

CONTACTS: *Note: Officers with more than one job title may be intentionally listed here more than once.*

Christopher B. Begley, CEO
Terrence C. Kearney, COO
Thomas E. Werner, CFO
Edward A. Ogunro, Sr. VP-R&D/Chief Science Officer
Brian J. Smith, General Counsel/Sr. VP
Thomas E. Werner, Sr. VP-Finance
David A. Jones, Chmn.

Phone: 224-212-2000 **Fax:** 224-212-3350
Toll-Free: 877-946-7747
Address: 275 N. Field Dr., Lake Forest, IL 60045 US

GROWTH PLANS/SPECIAL FEATURES:

Hospira, Inc. is a global specialty pharmaceutical and medication delivery company. The company's primary operations involve the research and development of generic pharmaceuticals, pharmaceuticals based on proprietary pharmaceuticals whose patents have expired. It was established in 2003 by Abbott Laboratories in order to facilitate the company's planned spin-off in the manufacturing and sales of hospital products, including injectable pharmaceuticals and medication delivery systems. Operating independently since May 2004, Hospira oversees most of Abbott's former hospital products division and select operations formerly managed by Abbott's international segment. The company's activities include the development, manufacture and marketing of specialty injectable pharmaceuticals and medication delivery systems that deliver drugs and intravenous (I.V.) fluids. Additionally, the firm offers contract manufacturing services to proprietary pharmaceutical and biotechnology companies for formulation development, filling and finishing of injectable pharmaceuticals. Hospira's specialty injectable pharmaceutical products primarily consist of generic injectable pharmaceuticals including analgesics, anesthetics, anti-infectives, cardiovascular drugs, oncology drugs and others. Hospira's specialty injectable pharmaceutical products include Precedex, a proprietary sedative that is used in the intensive care setting. The firm's medication delivery systems offer management systems, which include electronic drug delivery pumps, safety software, administration sets and accessories, and related services; and infusion therapy solutions and products that are used to deliver I.V. fluids and medications to patients. Through its One 2 One manufacturing services group, Hospira provides contract manufacturing services for formulation development, filling and finishing of injectable drugs worldwide. The company works with its customers to develop stable injectable forms of their drugs, and Hospira fills and finishes those and other drugs into containers and packaging selected by the customer. The customer then sells the finished products under its own label. In early 2007, Hospira acquired Mayne Pharma Limited, and injectable pharmaceuticals manufacturer based in Australia.

FINANCIALS: Sales and profits are in thousands of dollars—add 000 to get the full amount. 2007 Note: Financial information for 2007 was not available for all companies at press time.

2007 Sales: $
2006 Sales: $2,688,505
2005 Sales: $2,626,696
2004 Sales: $2,645,036
2003 Sales: $2,400,200

2007 Profits: $
2006 Profits: $237,679
2005 Profits: $235,638
2004 Profits: $301,552
2003 Profits: $260,400

U.S. Stock Ticker: HSP
Int'l Ticker: Int'l Exchange:
Employees: 13,000
Fiscal Year Ends: 12/31
Parent Company:

SALARIES/BENEFITS:

Pension Plan: Y
Savings Plan: Y
ESOP Stock Plan:
Stock Purch. Plan:
Profit Sharing:
Top Exec. Salary: $766,154 Bonus: $1,038,423
Second Exec. Salary: $362,615 Bonus: $391,633

OTHER THOUGHTS:

Apparent Women Officers or Directors:
Hot Spot for Advancement for Women/Minorities:

LOCATIONS: ("Y" = Yes)

West:	Southwest:	Midwest:	Southeast:	Northeast:	International:
Y	Y	Y	Y	Y	Y

HUMAN GENOME SCIENCES INC www.hgsi.com

ndustry Group Code: 325412 **Ranks within this company's industry group:** Sales: 39 Profits: 42

nsurance/HMO/PPO:		Drugs:		Equipment/Supplies:		Hospitals/Clinics:		Services:		Health Care:	
nsurance:		Manufacturer:		Manufacturer:		Acute Care:		Diagnostics:		Home Health:	
lanaged Care:		Distributor:		Distributor:		Sub-Acute:		Labs/Testing:		Long-Term Care:	
tilization Management:		Specialty Pharmacy:		Leasing/Finance:		Outpatient Surgery:		Staffing:		Physical Therapy:	
ayment Processing:		Vitamins/Nutritionals:		Information Systems:		Physical Rehab. Ctr.:		Waste Disposal:		Physician Prac. Mgmt.:	
		Clinical Trials:	Y			Psychiatric Clinics:		Specialty Svcs.:			

TYPES OF BUSINESS:

Oncology, Immunology & Infectious Diseases Drugs

BRANDS/DIVISIONS/AFFILIATES:

LymphoStat-B
Albuferon
Abthrax

CONTACTS:

Note: Officers with more than one job title may be intentionally listed here more than once.

H. Thomas Watkins, CEO
H. Thomas Watkins, Pres.
Timothy C. Barabe, CFO/Sr. VP
Susan Bateson McKay, Sr. VP-Human Resources
David C. Stump, Exec. VP-R&D
James H. Davis, General Counsel/Exec. VP
Curan M. Simpson, Sr. VP-Oper.
Jerry Parrott, VP-Corp. Comm.
Barry A. Labinger, Chief Commercial Officer/Exec. VP
Argeris N. Karabelas, Chmn.

Phone: 301-309-8504	**Fax:** 301-309-8512
Toll-Free:	
Address: 14200 Shady Grove Rd., Rockville, MD 20850 US	

GROWTH PLANS/SPECIAL FEATURES:

Human Genome Sciences, Inc. (HGS) is a commercially focused drug development company with three products advancing into late-stage clinical development: Albuferon for chronic hepatitis, LymphoStat-B for systemic lupus erythematosus and ABthrax for anthrax disease. The company also has a pipeline of compounds in earlier stages of clinical development in oncology, immunology and infectious disease, including rheumatoid arthritis and HIV/AIDS. The firm's partners conduct clinical trials of additional drugs to treat cardiovascular, metabolic and central nervous system diseases and advanced a number of products derived from the company's technology to clinical development. The Albuferon collaborator is Novartis and the LymphoStat-B collaborator is GlaxoSmithKline. GlaxoSmithKline entered several small molecule drugs into clinical development including GSK480848, for the treatment of atherosclerosis; GSK462795, for the treatment of bone disease; and GSK649868, for the treatment of sleep disorders. HGS entered into collaboration agreements for the co-development and co-commercialization of its Albuferon and LymphoStat-B products. The company has roughly 560 U.S. patents covering genes and proteins. In February 2007, the company announced that it initiated a Phase III clinical trial of Albuferon in combination with ribavirin for treatment of chronic hepatitis C genotypes 2 and 3; and Phase III clinical trial of LymphoStat-B in patients with active systemic lupus erythematosus.

The company offers its employees medical, dental and vision insurance; flexible spending accounts; life and AD&D insurance; short- and long-term disability; a 401(k) plan; an employee stock purchase plan; and education assistance.

FINANCIALS:

Sales and profits are in thousands of dollars—add 000 to get the full amount. 2007 Note: Financial information for 2007 was not available for all companies at press time.

2007 Sales: $	2007 Profits: $	**U.S. Stock Ticker: HGSI**
2006 Sales: $25,755	2006 Profits: $-210,327	**Int'l Ticker:** Int'l Exchange:
2005 Sales: $19,113	2005 Profits: $-239,439	Employees: 880
2004 Sales: $3,831	2004 Profits: $-242,898	Fiscal Year Ends: 12/31
2003 Sales: $8,168	2003 Profits: $-185,324	Parent Company:

SALARIES/BENEFITS:

Pension Plan:	ESOP Stock Plan:	Profit Sharing:	Top Exec. Salary: $650,000	Bonus: $650,000
Savings Plan: Y	Stock Purch. Plan: Y		Second Exec. Salary: $460,000	Bonus: $391,000

OTHER THOUGHTS:

Apparent Women Officers or Directors: 1
Hot Spot for Advancement for Women/Minorities:

LOCATIONS: ("Y" = Yes)

West:	Southwest:	Midwest:	Southeast:	Northeast:	International:
				Y	

Note: Financial information, benefits and other data can change quickly and may vary from those stated here.

HUMANA INC

www.humana.com

Industry Group Code: 524114 **Ranks within this company's industry group:** Sales: 4 Profits: 8

Insurance/HMO/PPO:		Drugs:		Equipment/Supplies:		Hospitals/Clinics:		Services:		Health Care:	
Insurance:	Y	Manufacturer:		Manufacturer:		Acute Care:		Diagnostics:		Home Health:	
Managed Care:	Y	Distributor:		Distributor:		Sub-Acute:		Labs/Testing:		Long-Term Care:	
Utilization Management:		Specialty Pharmacy:		Leasing/Finance:		Outpatient Surgery:		Staffing:		Physical Therapy:	
Payment Processing:		Vitamins/Nutritionals:		Information Systems:		Physical Rehab. Ctr.:		Waste Disposal:		Physician Prac. Mgmt.:	
		Clinical Trials:				Psychiatric Clinics:		Specialty Svcs.:			

TYPES OF BUSINESS:

Insurance-Medical & Health, HMOs & PPOs
Insurance-Dental
Employee Benefit Plans
Insurance-Group Life
Wellness Programs

BRANDS/DIVISIONS/AFFILIATES:

Humana Military Services, Inc.
Humana Dental
HumanaOne
Humana Ventures
Humana Medicare
Sensei
Card Guard AG
CompBenefits Corp.

CONTACTS: *Note: Officers with more than one job title may be intentionally listed here more than once.*

Michael B. McCallister, CEO
James E. Murray, COO/Sr. VP
Michael B. McCallister, Pres.
James H. Bloem, CFO/Sr. VP/Treas.
Steven O. Moya, Chief Mktg. Officer/Sr. VP
Bonnie C. Hathcock, Chief Human Resources Officer/Sr. VP
Jonathan T. Lord, Chief Innovation Officer/Sr. VP
Bruce J. Goodman, Chief Svc. & Info. Officer/Sr. VP
Stefen F. Brueckner, VP-Senior Products
Arthur P. Hipwell, General Counsel/Sr. VP
Thomas J. Liston, Sr. VP-Strategy & Corp. Dev.
Tom Noland, Sr. VP-Corp. Comm.
Regina C. Nethery, VP-Investor Rel.
Steven E. McCulley, VP/Controller/Principal Acct. Officer
Michael Fedyna, Chief Actuary
P. Anthony (Tony) Hammond, VP-Health Svcs./Chief Medical Actuary
Heidi S. Margulis, Sr. VP-Gov't Rel.
Joan O. Lenahan, VP/Corp. Sec.
David A. Jones Jr., Chmn.
Bruce Perkins, Sr. VP-National Contracting & Puerto Rico Oper.

Phone: 502-580-1000	**Fax:** 502-580-3677
Toll-Free: 800-486-2620	
Address: 500 W. Main St., Louisville, KY 40202 US	

GROWTH PLANS/SPECIAL FEATURES:

Humana, Inc. is one of the largest publicly traded health benefits companies in the U.S., based on revenues. The company serves approximately 11.3 million members in the U.S. and Puerto Rico. It divides its business between government and commercial operations. Government operations consist of Medicare, TRICARE and Medicaid business. Its commercial operations, which are offered to both employer groups and individuals, consist of medical and specialty services. Its main business units are as follows Humana Military Healthcare Services, Inc. provides TRICARE services to 2.8 million military beneficiaries. Humana Dental covers 2.6 million customers, making it one of the largest dental carries in the U.S. HumanaOne offers insurance coverage to individuals. Humana Ventures is a capital investing branch of Humana. Finally, Humana Medicare offers plans for Medicare patients to help them with drug and medical coverage. Humana contracts with approximately 540,000 physicians, 5,300 hospitals, 263,000 other providers and dentists, in one of the largest networks in the U.S. The company also offers a wide variety of services to employers, such as workers' compensation, dental plans, group life plans and an administrative-services-only plan. Humana provides health benefits and related services to companies ranging from fewer than 10 to over 10,000 employees. Many of its products are offered through HMOs (health maintenance organizations), Private Fee-For-Service (PFFS) and preferred provider organizations (PPOs). Sensei, a joint venture with Card Guard AG, currently provides weight loss assistance via the Internet or mobile phones, with other programs targeting cardiovascular risk and other health problems in development. In June 2007, the firm agreed to acquire CompBenefits Corp., a company with over 4.8 million members which provides vision products and dental plans, for roughly $360 million.

Humana offers healthcare spending accounts; tuition reimbursement; paid holidays; medical and dental benefits; life insurance; and adoption assistance.

FINANCIALS: Sales and profits are in thousands of dollars—add 000 to get the full amount. 2007 Note: Financial information for 2007 was not available for all companies at press time.

2007 Sales: $	2007 Profits: $	**U.S. Stock Ticker: HUM**
2006 Sales: $21,416,537	2006 Profits: $487,423	**Int'l Ticker:** Int'l Exchange:
2005 Sales: $14,418,127	2005 Profits: $296,730	Employees: 22,300
2004 Sales: $13,104,325	2004 Profits: $269,947	Fiscal Year Ends: 12/31
2003 Sales: $12,226,311	2003 Profits: $228,934	Parent Company:

SALARIES/BENEFITS:

Pension Plan: Y	ESOP Stock Plan:	Profit Sharing:	Top Exec. Salary: $900,000	Bonus: $1,552,419
Savings Plan: Y	Stock Purch. Plan:		Second Exec. Salary: $591,370	Bonus: $849,892

OTHER THOUGHTS:

Apparent Women Officers or Directors: 4
Hot Spot for Advancement for Women/Minorities: Y

LOCATIONS: ("Y" = Yes)

West:	Southwest:	Midwest:	Southeast:	Northeast:	International:
Y	Y	Y	Y	Y	Y

I FLOW CORPORATION — www.iflo.com

ndustry Group Code: 339113 **Ranks within this company's industry group:** Sales: 81 Profits: 58

nsurance/HMO/PPO:		Drugs:		Equipment/Supplies:		Hospitals/Clinics:		Services:		Health Care:	
nsurance:		Manufacturer:		Manufacturer:	Y	Acute Care:		Diagnostics:		Home Health:	
Managed Care:		Distributor:		Distributor:	Y	Sub-Acute:		Labs/Testing:		Long-Term Care:	
tilization Management:		Specialty Pharmacy:		Leasing/Finance:		Outpatient Surgery:		Staffing:		Physical Therapy:	
ayment Processing:		Vitamins/Nutritionals:		Information Systems:		Physical Rehab. Ctr.:		Waste Disposal:		Physician Prac. Mgmt.:	
		Clinical Trials:				Psychiatric Clinics:		Specialty Svcs.:			

TYPES OF BUSINESS:

Medical Equipment-Mobile Infusion Systems
Anesthesia Kits
Rental Infusion Equipment

BRANDS/DIVISIONS/AFFILIATES:

On-Q PainBuster Post-Operative Pain Relief System
Soaker Catheter
SilverSoaker Catheter
C-bloc Continuous Nerve Block System
Block Medical de Mexico
Homepump Eclipse
Easypump
InfuSystem, Inc.

CONTACTS: *Note: Officers with more than one job title may be intentionally listed here more than once.*

Donald M. Earhart, CEO
James J. Dal Porto, COO/Exec. VP
Donald M. Earhart, Pres.
James R. Talevich, CFO
James J. Dal Porto, Corp. Sec.
James R. Talevich, Treas.
Donald M. Earhart, Chmn.

Phone: 929-206-2700	**Fax:** 949-206-2600
Toll-Free: 800-448-3569	
Address: 20202 Windrow Dr., Lake Forest, CA 92630 US	

GROWTH PLANS/SPECIAL FEATURES:

I-Flow Corporation designs, develops and markets technically advanced, low-cost ambulatory drug delivery systems. Its products are used both in hospitals, homes and alternate site settings, including freestanding surgery centers and physicians' offices. The firm's family of products is focused on two primary market segments: regional anesthesia and intravenous (IV) infusion therapy. I-Flow currently manufactures a line of compact, portable infusion pumps, catheters, needles and pain kits. I-Flow's acute pain kit product line includes the On-Q PainBuster Post-Operative Pain Relief System, the Soaker Catheter, the SilverSoaker Catheter and the C-bloc Continuous Nerve Block System. The company's On-Q systems offer continuous wound site pain management, which is considered to be one of the most ideal treatments for post-operative pain because fewer narcotics, which have negative side effects, are used than in traditional methods of post-operative pain management. I-Flow's product line of elastomeric pumps delivers medication from an elastic balloon that does not rely on gravity for proper delivery, making it both safe and simple enough for patients to use for self-administration of medication. The company's elastomeric line of products, including its Homepump Eclipse and Easypump, can be used for antibiotic therapy, pain management medications, chemotherapy and other medications. I-Flow's non-electric IV bag delivery systems, including its Paragon and Sidekick ambulatory infusion pumps, consist of a reusable mechanical infuser and specially designed administration sets. Subsidiary InfuSystem, Inc. provides infusion pumps for rent on a month-to-month basis to the cancer infusion therapy market. I-Flow also owns a subsidiary in Mexico, Block Medical de Mexico, which manufactures a substantial portion of the company's products. In October 2006 I-Flow signed an agreement to sell InfuSystem to HAPC, Inc. for $100 million. In June 2007, I-Flow announced forming a strategic alliance with GE Healthcare to conduct clinical trials and explore joint opportunities in the anesthesiology market.

FINANCIALS: **Sales and profits are in thousands of dollars—add 000 to get the full amount. 2007 Note: Financial information for 2007 was not available for all companies at press time.**

2007 Sales: $	2007 Profits: $	**U.S. Stock Ticker: IFLO**
2006 Sales: $93,582	2006 Profits: $13,674	**Int'l Ticker:** Int'l Exchange:
2005 Sales: $72,119	2005 Profits: $-8,405	Employees: 990
2004 Sales: $51,796	2004 Profits: $-17,110	Fiscal Year Ends: 12/31
2003 Sales: $47,043	2003 Profits: $ 457	Parent Company:

SALARIES/BENEFITS:

Pension Plan:	ESOP Stock Plan:	Profit Sharing:	Top Exec. Salary: $437,682	Bonus: $912,516
Savings Plan: Y	Stock Purch. Plan:		Second Exec. Salary: $277,599	Bonus: $608,343

OTHER THOUGHTS:

Apparent Women Officers or Directors:
Hot Spot for Advancement for Women/Minorities:

LOCATIONS: ("Y" = Yes)

West:	Southwest:	Midwest:	Southeast:	Northeast:	International:
Y		Y			Y

ICU MEDICAL INC

www.icumed.com

Industry Group Code: 339113 **Ranks within this company's industry group:** Sales: 62 Profits: 47

Insurance/HMO/PPO:		Drugs:		Equipment/Supplies:		Hospitals/Clinics:		Services:		Health Care:	
Insurance:		Manufacturer:		Manufacturer:	Y	Acute Care:		Diagnostics:		Home Health:	
Managed Care:		Distributor:		Distributor:		Sub-Acute:		Labs/Testing:		Long-Term Care:	
Utilization Management:		Specialty Pharmacy:		Leasing/Finance:		Outpatient Surgery:		Staffing:		Physical Therapy:	
Payment Processing:		Vitamins/Nutritionals:		Information Systems:		Physical Rehab. Ctr.:		Waste Disposal:		Physician Prac. Mgmt.:	
		Clinical Trials:				Psychiatric Clinics:		Specialty Svcs.:			

TYPES OF BUSINESS:

Equipment-Intravenous Connection Devices
Custom IV Systems

BRANDS/DIVISIONS/AFFILIATES:

CLAVE
CLC2000
1o2 Valve
Bio-Plexus, Inc.
Punctur-Guard
Orbit 90

CONTACTS:

Note: Officers with more than one job title may be intentionally listed here more than once.

George Lopez, CEO
George Lopez, Pres.
Francis O'Brien, CFO
Alison Burcar, VP-Mktg.
James Reitz, Dir.-Human Resources
Francis O'Brien, Corp. Sec.
Steven C. Riggs, VP-Oper.
Scott E. Lamb, Controller
Richard A. Costello, VP-Sales
Francis O'Brien, Treas.
George Lopez, Chmn.

Phone: 949-366-2183	**Fax:** 949-366-8368
Toll-Free: 800-824-7890	
Address: 951 Calle Amanecer, San Clemente, CA 92673 US	

GROWTH PLANS/SPECIAL FEATURES:

ICU Medical is a leader in the development, manufactur and sale of disposable medical connection systems for us in intravenous (I.V.) therapy applications. Its devices ar designed to protect health care workers and their patient from exposure to infectious diseases such as hepatitis B an C and HIV by accidental needlesticks. The firm is also leader in the production of custom I.V. systems and low-cos generic I.V. systems. The company's main product, th CLAVE, is a one-piece, needleless I.V. connection devic that annually represents about 40% of the company' revenue. The CLAVE allows protected, secure and steril I.V. connections without needles and without the failure prone mechanical valves used in other I.V. systems. It wa designed to reduce the need for needles in acute car hospitals, home health care, ambulatory surgical centers nursing homes, convalescent facilities, physicians' offices medical clinics and emergency centers. Principal product introduced in recent years are the CLC2000, which prevent the black-flow of blood into the catheter; the 1o2 Valve which is a one or two way drug delivery system; the Teg Connector, which is a new infection control connector for us with dialysis catheters; and the Punctur-Guard line of bloo collection needles, which reduce the risk of needlesticks b allowing the practitioner to blunt the needle while it is still i the vein. A key element in ICU's strategy has been th development and implementation of proprietary software fo custom product design, customer orders and order tracking combined with an innovative system to coordinate th manufacture of components in the U.S., assembly o components into sets in Mexico and Italy and internationa distribution of finished products. ICU sells approximatel 77% of its products to Hospire, with which it has a long-term fixed price medical supply contract.

FINANCIALS:

Sales and profits are in thousands of dollars—add 000 to get the full amount. 2007 Note: Financial information for 2007 was not available for all companies at press time.

2007 Sales: $	2007 Profits: $	**U.S. Stock Ticker: ICUI**
2006 Sales: $201,613	2006 Profits: $25,660	**Int'l Ticker:** Int'l Exchange:
2005 Sales: $157,532	2005 Profits: $20,274	Employees: 1,819
2004 Sales: $75,550	2004 Profits: $5,000	Fiscal Year Ends: 12/31
2003 Sales: $107,354	2003 Profits: $22,297	Parent Company:

SALARIES/BENEFITS:

Pension Plan:	ESOP Stock Plan:	Profit Sharing:	Top Exec. Salary: $500,000	Bonus: $625,000
Savings Plan: Y	Stock Purch. Plan: Y		Second Exec. Salary: $290,000	Bonus: $108,750

OTHER THOUGHTS:

Apparent Women Officers or Directors: 1
Hot Spot for Advancement for Women/Minorities:

LOCATIONS: ("Y" = Yes)

West:	Southwest:	Midwest:	Southeast:	Northeast:	International:
Y				Y	Y

Note: Financial information, benefits and other data can change quickly and may vary from those stated here.

IDEXX LABORATORIES INC www.idexx.com

Industry Group Code: 325413 **Ranks within this company's industry group:** Sales: 1 Profits: 1

Insurance/HMO/PPO:		Drugs:		Equipment/Supplies:		Hospitals/Clinics:		Services:		Health Care:	
Insurance:		Manufacturer:		Manufacturer:		Acute Care:		Diagnostics:	Y	Home Health:	
Managed Care:		Distributor:		Distributor:		Sub-Acute:		Labs/Testing:	Y	Long-Term Care:	
Utilization Management:		Specialty Pharmacy:	Y	Leasing/Finance:		Outpatient Surgery:		Staffing:		Physical Therapy:	
Payment Processing:		Vitamins/Nutritionals:		Information Systems:	Y	Physical Rehab. Ctr.:		Waste Disposal:		Physician Prac. Mgmt.:	
		Clinical Trials:				Psychiatric Clinics:		Specialty Svcs.:	Y		

TYPES OF BUSINESS:

Veterinary Laboratory Testing & Consulting
Point-of-Care Diagnostic Products
Veterinary Pharmaceuticals
Information Management Software
Food & Water Testing Products

BRANDS/DIVISIONS/AFFILIATES:

Colilert-18
SNAP
Parallux
Colisure
SURPASS
Vita-Tech Canada, Inc.

CONTACTS: *Note: Officers with more than one job title may be intentionally listed here more than once.*

Jonathan W. Ayers, CEO
Jonathan W. Ayers, Pres.
Merilee Raines, CFO/VP
William C. Wallen, Sr. VP/Chief Scientific Officer
Conan R. Deady, General Counsel/Sec./VP
Irene C. Kerr, VP-Worldwide Oper.
Merilee Raines, Treas.
James Polewaczyck, VP-Rapid Assay & Digital Radiography
Michael Williams, VP-Instrument Diagnostics
Thomas J. Dupree, VP-Companion Animal Group
S. Sam Fratoni, VP
Jonathan W. Ayers, Chmn.
Ali Naqui, VP-Dairy, Water, APAC & Latin America Oper.

Phone: 207-556-0300 **Fax:** 207-556-0346
Toll-Free: 800-548-6733
Address: 1 IDEXX Dr., Westbrook, ME 04092-2041 US

GROWTH PLANS/SPECIAL FEATURES:

IDEXX Laboratories, Inc. develops, manufacturesand distributes products and provides services for the veterinary and the food and water testing markets. The company operates in three business segments: products and services for the veterinary market, referred to as the Companion Animal Group; water quality products; and products for production animal health, referred to as the Production Animal Segment. The company also operated a smaller segment that comprises products for dairy quality, referred to as Dairy. Its primary business focus is on animal health. IDEXX's companion animal and equine veterinary offerings include in-clinic diagnostic tests and instrumentation, laboratory services, pharmaceuticals and veterinary practice information management software, as well as a range of single-use, hand-held test kits. The principal single-use tests, sold under the SNAP name, include a feline combination test, the SNAP Combo FIV antibody/FeLV antigen test, which enables veterinarians to test simultaneously for feline leukemia virus and feline immunodeficiency virus; a canine combination test, the SNAP 3Dx, which tests simultaneously for Lyme disease, Ehrlichia canis and heartworm; and a canine heartworm-only test. IDEXX has received FDA approval for its topical equine anti-inflammatory SURPASS. In addition, it also provides assay kits, software and instrumentation for accurate assessment of infectious disease in production animals, such as cattle, swine and poultry. The company currently offers commercial veterinary laboratory and consulting services in the U.S. through facilities located in Arizona, California, Colorado, Illinois, Maryland, Massachusetts, New Jersey, Oregon and Texas. The water quality segment's products include Colilert-18 and Colisure tests, which simultaneously detect total coliforms and E. coli in water. IDEXX's two principal products for use in testing for antibiotic residue in milk are the SNAP Beta-lactam test and the Parallux system. In 2007, the company acquired Vita-Tech Canada, Inc., the largest provider of reference laboratory testing services to veterinary offices in Canada.

FINANCIALS: **Sales and profits are in thousands of dollars—add 000 to get the full amount. 2007 Note: Financial information for 2007 was not available for all companies at press time.**

2007 Sales: $	2007 Profits: $	**U.S. Stock Ticker: IDXX**
2006 Sales: $739,117	2006 Profits: $93,678	**Int'l Ticker:** Int'l Exchange:
2005 Sales: $638,095	2005 Profits: $78,254	Employees: 3,900
2004 Sales: $549,181	2004 Profits: $78,332	Fiscal Year Ends: 12/31
2003 Sales: $475,992	2003 Profits: $57,090	Parent Company:

SALARIES/BENEFITS:

Pension Plan:	ESOP Stock Plan:	Profit Sharing:	Top Exec. Salary: $600,000	Bonus: $650,000
Savings Plan: Y	Stock Purch. Plan: Y		Second Exec. Salary: $350,000	Bonus: $255,000

OTHER THOUGHTS:

Apparent Women Officers or Directors: 2
Hot Spot for Advancement for Women/Minorities: Y

LOCATIONS: ("Y" = Yes)

West:	Southwest:	Midwest:	Southeast:	Northeast:	International:
Y	Y	Y	Y	Y	Y

IMMUCOR INC

www.immucor.com

Industry Group Code: 339113 **Ranks within this company's industry group:** Sales: 67 Profits: 37

Insurance/HMO/PPO:		Drugs:		Equipment/Supplies:		Hospitals/Clinics:		Services:		Health Care:	
Insurance:		Manufacturer:		Manufacturer:	Y	Acute Care:		Diagnostics:		Home Health:	
Managed Care:		Distributor:		Distributor:	Y	Sub-Acute:		Labs/Testing:		Long-Term Care:	
Utilization Management:		Specialty Pharmacy:		Leasing/Finance:		Outpatient Surgery:		Staffing:		Physical Therapy:	
Payment Processing:		Vitamins/Nutritionals:		Information Systems:		Physical Rehab. Ctr.:		Waste Disposal:		Physician Prac. Mgmt.:	
		Clinical Trials:				Psychiatric Clinics:		Specialty Svcs.:			

TYPES OF BUSINESS:

Equipment-Blood Testing
Automated Blood Bank Instruments
Blood Reagents

BRANDS/DIVISIONS/AFFILIATES:

ABS2000
ROSYS Plato
DIAS Plus
Galileo

CONTACTS:

Note: Officers with more than one job title may be intentionally listed here more than once.

Gioacchino (Nino) DeChirico, CEO
Gioacchino (Nino) De Chirico, Pres.
Michael C. Poynter, VP-Sales
Ralph A. Eatz, Chief Scientific Officer/Sr. VP
Phil Moise, General Counsel/Sec./VP
Didier L. Lanson, Dir.-European Oper.
Joseph E. Rosen, Chmn.
Jean-Jacques de Jaegher, VP-Int'l

Phone: 770-441-2051	**Fax:** 770-441-3807
Toll-Free: 800-829-2553	
Address: 3130 Gateway Dr., Norcross, GA 30091-5625 US	

GROWTH PLANS/SPECIAL FEATURES:

Immucor, Inc. develops, manufactures and sells a line o reagents and automated systems used primarily b hospitals, clinical laboratories and blood banks for tests tha detect and identify properties of the cell and serun components of human blood prior to a blood transfusion The company's blood bank systems include the ABS2000 the first FDA-cleared instrument for full automation of bloo typing and antibody screening assays; and ROSYS Plato which provides medium sized donor centers. Immucor has an ongoing agreement with Bio-Tek, a subsidiary o Lionheart Technologies, for the development of the ABS200 automated blood bank analyzer. The firm also distributes laboratory equipment designed to automate certain bloo testing procedures and is to be used in conjunction with its solid-phase, Capture products. Capture products include Capture-P, which detects platelet antibodies; Capture-R and Capture-R Select, involved in red cell antibody detection; and Capture-CMV and Capture-S, both infectious disease tests. Immucor's latest automated walk-away instrument for the hospital blood bank transfusion laboratory is the Galileo Echo. The product recently received clearance fo distribution from the Japanese and Canadian health ministries; and in June 2007, it received approval from the FDA in the U.S. The Galileo Echo can process over 300 antibody screenings using pooled cells and over 70 type screens per hour; it is significantly smaller and faster than the ABS2000. The forerunner of Echo, simply called Galileo, received 114 purchase orders in 2007, and has received 481 total orders, including 286 in Europe, 193 in North America and 2 in Japan; and of these, 423 are generating reagent revenues. In February 2006, Immucor announced that it had received a purchase order for two Galileo systems from Duke University Medical Center. In April 2006, it announced that the FDA had cleared its Capture-S and CMV Assays for use on the Galileo Echo.

FINANCIALS:

Sales and profits are in thousands of dollars—add 000 to get the full amount. 2007 Note: Financial information for 2007 was not available for all companies at press time.

2007 Sales: $223,678	2007 Profits: $60,068	**U.S. Stock Ticker: BLUD**
2006 Sales: $183,506	2006 Profits: $39,843	**Int'l Ticker:** Int'l Exchange:
2005 Sales: $144,786	2005 Profits: $23,910	Employees: 610
2004 Sales: $112,558	2004 Profits: $12,538	Fiscal Year Ends: 5/31
2003 Sales: $98,300	2003 Profits: $14,400	Parent Company:

SALARIES/BENEFITS:

Pension Plan:	ESOP Stock Plan:	Profit Sharing:	Top Exec. Salary: $404,384	Bonus: $
Savings Plan: Y	Stock Purch. Plan:		Second Exec. Salary: $368,528	Bonus: $

OTHER THOUGHTS:

Apparent Women Officers or Directors:
Hot Spot for Advancement for Women/Minorities:

LOCATIONS: ("Y" = Yes)

West:	Southwest:	Midwest:	Southeast:	Northeast:	International:
			Y		Y

IMS HEALTH INC www.imshealth.com

Industry Group Code: 541910 **Ranks within this company's industry group:** Sales: 1 Profits: 1

Insurance/HMO/PPO:		Drugs:		Equipment/Supplies:		Hospitals/Clinics:		Services:		Health Care:	
Insurance:		Manufacturer:		Manufacturer:		Acute Care:		Diagnostics:		Home Health:	
Managed Care:		Distributor:		Distributor:		Sub-Acute:		Labs/Testing:		Long-Term Care:	
Utilization Management:		Specialty Pharmacy:		Leasing/Finance:		Outpatient Surgery:		Staffing:		Physical Therapy:	
Payment Processing:	Y	Vitamins/Nutritionals:		Information Systems:	Y	Physical Rehab. Ctr.:		Waste Disposal:		Physician Prac. Mgmt.:	
		Clinical Trials:				Psychiatric Clinics:		Specialty Svcs.:	Y		

TYPES OF BUSINESS:

Market Research - Pharmaceuticals
Pharmaceutical Sales Tracking
Health Care Databases
Software-Sales Management & Market Research
Physician Profiling
Industry Audits
Prescription Tracking Reporting Services

BRANDS/DIVISIONS/AFFILIATES:

Drug Distribution Data (DDD) Service
ValueMedics

CONTACTS: *Note: Officers with more than one job title may be intentionally listed here more than once.*

David R. Carlucci, CEO
Giles V. J. Pajot, COO
David R. Carlucci, Pres.
Leslye G. Katz, CFO/Sr. VP
Bruce F. Boggs, Sr. VP-Global Mktg. & External Affairs
Robert H. Steinfeld, General Counsel/Sr. VP/Corp. Sec.
Murray L. Aitken, Sr. VP-Corp. Strategy
Stephen Phua, VP/General Mgr.-Asia Pacific
Tatsuyuki Saeki, Pres. & Representative Dir.-Japan
William J. Nelligan, Pres., IMS America
Giles V. J. Pajot, Exec. VP/Pres., Global Bus. Mgmt.
David R. Carlucci, Chmn.
Kevin Knightly, Pres., EMEA

Phone: 203-319-4700	**Fax:** 203-319-4701
Toll-Free:	
Address: 1499 Post Rd., Fairfield, CT 06824 US	

GROWTH PLANS/SPECIAL FEATURES:

IMS Health, Inc. is one of the world's leading providers of market intelligence to the pharmaceutical and health care industries. IMS provides products designed for sales force effectiveness, as well as products for portfolio optimization and launch/brand management. The firm's services include consultation with clients regarding pharmaceutical market trends and development of customized software applications and data warehouse tools. The firm's sales force effectiveness product offerings have produced as much as half of the firm's worldwide revenue. The firm's drug distribution data (DDD) service falls within the scope sales force effectiveness. The DDD allows clients to track the flow of sales for their products through various channels of distribution, including direct sales by pharmaceutical manufacturers and indirect sales through wholesalers and other sources. The firm's prescription tracking reporting services also work within the sales force effectiveness segment, helping companies effectively market to the drug prescribers. The portfolio optimization services encompass pharmaceutical and prescription audits, which in turn reveal a company's product sales broken down into therapeutic class, package size and dosage form. IMS's launch and brand management services offer consulting services to firms in each stage of a product/brand's lifecycle. The firm also provides services related to managed care and consumer health. Concerning consumer health, IMS is currently focused on providing over-the-counter (OTC) manufacturers insights into consumer purchasing dynamics and promotional impact. In 2007, the firm announced the acquisition of ValueMedics Research LLC, a healthcare research and consulting firm.

FINANCIALS: Sales and profits are in thousands of dollars—add 000 to get the full amount. 2007 Note: Financial information for 2007 was not available for all companies at press time.

2007 Sales: $	2007 Profits: $	**U.S. Stock Ticker: RX**
2006 Sales: $1,958,588	2006 Profits: $315,511	**Int'l Ticker:** Int'l Exchange:
2005 Sales: $1,754,791	2005 Profits: $284,091	Employees: 7,400
2004 Sales: $1,569,045	2004 Profits: $285,422	Fiscal Year Ends: 12/31
2003 Sales: $1,381,800	2003 Profits: $639,000	Parent Company:

SALARIES/BENEFITS:

Pension Plan:	ESOP Stock Plan:	Profit Sharing:	Top Exec. Salary: $801,250	Bonus: $1,041,625
Savings Plan: Y	Stock Purch. Plan: Y		Second Exec. Salary: $675,780	Bonus: $646,123

OTHER THOUGHTS:

Apparent Women Officers or Directors: 2
Hot Spot for Advancement for Women/Minorities: Y

LOCATIONS: ("Y" = Yes)

West:	Southwest:	Midwest:	Southeast:	Northeast:	International:
Y				Y	Y

INAMED CORP www.allerganandinamed.com

Industry Group Code: 339113 **Ranks within this company's industry group:** Sales: Profits:

Insurance/HMO/PPO:		Drugs:		Equipment/Supplies:		Hospitals/Clinics:		Services:		Health Care:	
Insurance:		Manufacturer:		Manufacturer:	Y	Acute Care:		Diagnostics:		Home Health:	
Managed Care:		Distributor:		Distributor:		Sub-Acute:		Labs/Testing:		Long-Term Care:	
Utilization Management:		Specialty Pharmacy:		Leasing/Finance:		Outpatient Surgery:		Staffing:		Physical Therapy:	
Payment Processing:		Vitamins/Nutritionals:		Information Systems:		Physical Rehab. Ctr.:		Waste Disposal:		Physician Prac. Mgmt.:	Y
		Clinical Trials:				Psychiatric Clinics:		Specialty Svcs.:			

TYPES OF BUSINESS:

Supplies-Prostheses
Breast Implants
Tissue Expanders
Facial Implants
Obesity Products

BRANDS/DIVISIONS/AFFILIATES:

INAMED Aesthetics
INAMED Health
INAMED International
Hydra Fill
Styl 150 One Stage BioDIMENSIONAL
Lap Band
Allergan Inc

CONTACTS: *Note: Officers with more than one job title may be intentionally listed here more than once.*

Nicholas L. Teti, CEO
Nicholas L. Teti, Pres.
Nicholas L. Teti, Chmn.

Phone: 805-683-6761	**Fax:** 805-692-5432
Toll-Free:	
Address: 5540 Ekwill St., Santa Barbara, CA 93111 US	

GROWTH PLANS/SPECIAL FEATURES:

INAMED Corp., a subsidiary of Allergan, Inc., is a globa surgical and medical device company engaged in the development, manufacturing and marketing of products fo the plastic and reconstructive surgery; aesthetic medicine and obesity markets. The company operates through two primary divisions, INAMED Aesthetics and INAMED Health as well maintaining partnerships with Biomatrix and Genzyme Biosurgery. INAMED Aesthetics offers a line of breast implants for augmentation and reconstruction surgeries following mastectomies, as well as collagen-based facial implants to correct facial wrinkles and improve lip definition. INAMED Health develops and markets medical devices to treat obesity using minimally invasive surgery. The company also offers a physician marketing program designed to assist in increasing incremental consultations, promote practice differentiation and optimize profitability. Products include The Style 150 – One Stage BioDIMENSIONAL reconstruction system for breast reconstruction and tissue expanders; Hydra Fill, a hyaluronic acid based face implant; and Lap Band, for treatment of severe obesity. INAMED International extends the company's sales, marketing and manufacturing presence to locations in Canada, Germany, France, Spain, Italy, Ireland, the U.K., Costa Rica, Japan and Australia.

The company offers its employees medical, dental, vision and prescription drug insurance; an employee assistance plan; life and AD&D insurance; short- and long-term disability insurance; travel accident insurance; a 401(k) plan; an employee stock purchase plan; and educational assistance.

FINANCIALS: **Sales and profits are in thousands of dollars—add 000 to get the full amount. 2007 Note: Financial information for 2007 was not available for all companies at press time.**

2007 Sales: $	2007 Profits: $	**U.S. Stock Ticker: Subsidiary**
2006 Sales: $	2006 Profits: $	**Int'l Ticker:** Int'l Exchange:
2005 Sales: $437,800	2005 Profits: $-26,200	Employees: 1,300
2004 Sales: $384,400	2004 Profits: $63,100	Fiscal Year Ends:
2003 Sales: $332,600	2003 Profits: $53,000	Parent Company: ALLERGAN INC

SALARIES/BENEFITS:

Pension Plan:	ESOP Stock Plan:	Profit Sharing:	Top Exec. Salary: $452,698	Bonus: $625,100
Savings Plan: Y	Stock Purch. Plan: Y		Second Exec. Salary: $296,068	Bonus: $315,000

OTHER THOUGHTS:

Apparent Women Officers or Directors:
Hot Spot for Advancement for Women/Minorities:

LOCATIONS: ("Y" = Yes)

West:	Southwest:	Midwest:	Southeast:	Northeast:	International:
Y					Y

INCYTE CORP

www.incyte.com

ndustry Group Code: 325412 **Ranks within this company's industry group:** Sales: 38 Profits: 37

nsurance/HMO/PPO:		Drugs:		Equipment/Supplies:		Hospitals/Clinics:		Services:		Health Care:	
nsurance:		Manufacturer:		Manufacturer:		Acute Care:		Diagnostics:		Home Health:	
Managed Care:		Distributor:		Distributor:		Sub-Acute:		Labs/Testing:		Long-Term Care:	
Jtilization Management:		Specialty Pharmacy:		Leasing/Finance:		Outpatient Surgery:		Staffing:		Physical Therapy:	
Payment Processing:		Vitamins/Nutritionals:		Information Systems:	Y	Physical Rehab. Ctr.:		Waste Disposal:		Physician Prac. Mgmt.:	
		Clinical Trials:				Psychiatric Clinics:		Specialty Svcs.:	Y		

TYPES OF BUSINESS:

Drug Discovery & Development
Genetic Information Research
Gene Expression Services

BRANDS/DIVISIONS/AFFILIATES:

Incyte Genomics
BioKnowledge Library (BKL)
CCR5 Antagonists
INCB9471
INCB13739
Dexelvucitabine

CONTACTS: *Note: Officers with more than one job title may be intentionally listed here more than once.*

Paul A. Friedman, CEO
Paul A. Friedman, Pres.
David C. Hastings, CFO/Exec. VP
Paula J. Swain, Exec. VP-Human Resources
Brian W. Metcalf, Chief Drug Discovery Scientist/Exec. VP
Patricia A. Schreck, General Counsel/Exec. VP
John A. Keller, Chief Bus. Officer/Exec. VP
Richard U. DeSchutter, Chmn.

Phone: 302-498-6700 **Fax:** 302-425-2750
Toll-Free:
Address: Rte. 141 & Henry Clay Rd., Bldg. E336, Wilmington, DE 19880 US

GROWTH PLANS/SPECIAL FEATURES:

Incyte Corp., formerly Incyte Genomics, discovers and develops small molecule drugs for the treatment of HIV, diabetes, oncology and inflammation. The company was historically involved with marketing and selling access to its proprietary genomic information database, the BioKnowledge Library (BKL), however it has since discontinued that service. The company currently has multiple products in its pipeline, all within preclinical, Phase I and Phase II clinical studies. For HIV, Incyte is developing CCR5 Antagonists, which belong to a new class of drugs called HIV Entry Inhibitors. The product works by blocking HIV before the virus enters the cell and begins the replication process. The lead product candidate is INCB9471, and currently is in Phase II clinical trials. Incyte's diabetes program relies on products that block the enzyme 11ßHSD1, which may potentially reduce insulin resistance and restore glycemic control in type 2 diabetes. The product INCB13739 is currently in Phase II clinical study. The cancer study program includes products which block epidermal growth factor receptor pathways, which are normally tightly regulated but become out of control in instances of cancer, especially solid tumors. Incyte currently has one product in Phase II clinical studies for cancer. In inflammation program uses CCR2 antagonists which block macrophage accumulation around multiple sclerosis related lesions. An excess of macrophages leads to loss of muscle control, vision, balance and sensation. The company has one product for inflammation in preclinical study. Incyte also is researching the use and control of Janus-associated Kinase Inhibitors (JAK), which may be useful in treating multiple inflammatory diseases, myeloproliferative disorders, and certain cancers. In April 2006, Incyte was forced to discontinue development of Dexelvucitabine, a previous lead candidate for the treatment of HIV, due to complications arising in patients undergoing the treatment.

FINANCIALS: **Sales and profits are in thousands of dollars—add 000 to get the full amount. 2007 Note: Financial information for 2007 was not available for all companies at press time.**

2007 Sales: $	2007 Profits: $	**U.S. Stock Ticker: INCY**
2006 Sales: $27,643	2006 Profits: $-74,166	**Int'l Ticker:** Int'l Exchange:
2005 Sales: $7,846	2005 Profits: $-103,043	Employees: 186
2004 Sales: $14,146	2004 Profits: $-164,817	Fiscal Year Ends: 12/31
2003 Sales: $47,092	2003 Profits: $-166,463	Parent Company:

SALARIES/BENEFITS:

Pension Plan:	ESOP Stock Plan:	Profit Sharing:	Top Exec. Salary: $543,577	Bonus: $393,120
Savings Plan:	Stock Purch. Plan:		Second Exec. Salary: $350,010	Bonus: $180,797

OTHER THOUGHTS:

Apparent Women Officers or Directors: 2
Hot Spot for Advancement for Women/Minorities: Y

LOCATIONS: ("Y" = Yes)

West:	Southwest:	Midwest:	Southeast:	Northeast:	International:
Y				Y	

INDEPENDENCE HOLDING CO www.independenceholding.com

Industry Group Code: 524113 **Ranks within this company's industry group:** Sales: 1 Profits: 1

Insurance/HMO/PPO:		Drugs:		Equipment/Supplies:		Hospitals/Clinics:		Services:		Health Care:	
Insurance:	Y	Manufacturer:		Manufacturer:		Acute Care:		Diagnostics:		Home Health:	
Managed Care:		Distributor:		Distributor:		Sub-Acute:		Labs/Testing:		Long-Term Care:	
Utilization Management:		Specialty Pharmacy:		Leasing/Finance:		Outpatient Surgery:		Staffing:		Physical Therapy:	
Payment Processing:		Vitamins/Nutritionals:		Information Systems:		Physical Rehab. Ctr.:		Waste Disposal:		Physician Prac. Mgmt.:	
		Clinical Trials:				Psychiatric Clinics:		Specialty Svcs.:			

TYPES OF BUSINESS:

Insurance Underwriting
Medical Stop-Loss
Group Health & Life Insurance

BRANDS/DIVISIONS/AFFILIATES:

Standard Security Life Insurance Company
Madison National Life Insurance Company, Inc.
Insurers Administrative Corporation
Health Plan Administrators
GroupLink, Inc.
IHC Health Solutions, Inc.
Community America Insurance Services, Inc.
Healthy Advantage

CONTACTS: *Note: Officers with more than one job title may be intentionally listed here more than once.*

Roy T. K. Thung, CEO
David Kettig, Co-COO/Sr. VP
Roy T. K. Thung, Pres.
Teresa A. Herbert, CFO/Sr. VP
Adam C. Vandervoort, General Counsel/VP/Sec.
Jeffrey Smedsrud, Chief Strategic Dev. Officer/Sr. VP
Colleen P. Maggi, Controller/VP
Scott Wood, Co-COO/Sr. VP
James Kenneally, VP-Corp. Dev.
Henry B. Spencer, VP-Investments
C. Winfield Swarr, Chief Underwriting Officer/VP
Edward Netter, Chmn.

Phone: 203-358-8000 **Fax:** 203-348-3103
Toll-Free:
Address: 96 Cummings Point Rd., Stamford, CT 06902 US

GROWTH PLANS/SPECIAL FEATURES:

Independence Holding Co. (IHC) is a holding company principally engaged in the life and health insurance business. The company operates through its wholly-owned insurance companies, Standard Security Insurance Company and Madison National Life Insurance Company, Inc.; and its marketing and administrative companies, including Insurers Administrative Corporation, Health Plan Administrators, GroupLink, Inc., IHC Health Solutions, Inc. and Community America Insurance Services, Inc. The company's employer medical stop-loss is its largest product line. Medical stop-loss insurance allows self-insured employers to manage the risk of excessive health insurance exposures by limiting aggregate and specific losses to a predetermined amount. Standard Security Life markets major medical stop-loss in all 50 states, the District of Columbia, the Virgin Islands and Puerto Rico. In addition, it also sells short-term statutory disability benefit product in New York State and certain life, annuity and blanket accident coverage sold primarily in New York State to volunteer emergency personnel. Madison National Life sells group life and disability, credit life and disability and individual life insurance in 49 states, Puerto Rico, the U.S. Virgin Islands and Puerto Rico. It also markets group life and disability products, primarily in the Midwest, credit life and disability, individual life and annuities to military and civilian government employees; and acquires block of life policies from other insurance companies. Independence American reinsures a significant portion of the medical stop-loss business written by Standard Security Life and Madison National Life. In 2007, Independence Holding launched Healthy Advantage, a small group self-funded health insurance.

FINANCIALS: **Sales and profits are in thousands of dollars—add 000 to get the full amount. 2007 Note: Financial information for 2007 was not available for all companies at press time.**

2007 Sales: $	2007 Profits: $	**U.S. Stock Ticker: IHC**
2006 Sales: $364,688	2006 Profits: $14,061	**Int'l Ticker:** Int'l Exchange:
2005 Sales: $296,417	2005 Profits: $17,301	Employees: 652
2004 Sales: $225,669	2004 Profits: $22,939	Fiscal Year Ends: 12/31
2003 Sales: $187,900	2003 Profits: $18,593	Parent Company:

SALARIES/BENEFITS:

Pension Plan:	ESOP Stock Plan:	Profit Sharing:	Top Exec. Salary: $370,690	Bonus: $380,000
Savings Plan:	Stock Purch. Plan:		Second Exec. Salary: $297,917	Bonus: $100,000

OTHER THOUGHTS:

Apparent Women Officers or Directors: 2
Hot Spot for Advancement for Women/Minorities:

LOCATIONS: ("Y" = Yes)

West:	Southwest:	Midwest:	Southeast:	Northeast:	International:
				Y	

INSTITUT STRAUMANN AG www.straumann.com

Industry Group Code: 339113 **Ranks within this company's industry group:** Sales: Profits:

Insurance/HMO/PPO:		Drugs:		Equipment/Supplies:		Hospitals/Clinics:		Services:		Health Care:	
Insurance:		Manufacturer:	Y	Manufacturer:	Y	Acute Care:		Diagnostics:		Home Health:	
Managed Care:		Distributor:		Distributor:		Sub-Acute:		Labs/Testing:		Long-Term Care:	
Utilization Management:		Specialty Pharmacy:		Leasing/Finance:		Outpatient Surgery:		Staffing:		Physical Therapy:	
Payment Processing:		Vitamins/Nutritionals:		Information Systems:		Physical Rehab. Ctr.:		Waste Disposal:		Physician Prac. Mgmt.:	
		Clinical Trials:				Psychiatric Clinics:		Specialty Svcs.:			

TYPES OF BUSINESS:

Dental Implants
Dental Tissue Regeneration
Dental Drugs, Manufacturing

BRANDS/DIVISIONS/AFFILIATES:

Straumann Dental Implant System
etkon
Daishin Implant System
Biora AB
Emdogain
SLActive
CARES
DenTech

CONTACTS: *Note: Officers with more than one job title may be intentionally listed here more than once.*

Gilbert Achermann, CEO
Marco Gadola, CFO
Mark Hill, Head-Corp. Comm.
Marianne Burgi, Head-Market & Product Support
Sandro Matter, Head-Products Div.
Rudolf Maag, Chmn.
Wolfgang Becker, Head-Sales, Europe

Phone: 41-61-965-11-11	**Fax:** 41-61-965-11-01
Toll-Free:	
Address: Peter Merian-Weg 12, Basel, CH-4052 Switzerland	

GROWTH PLANS/SPECIAL FEATURES:

Institut Straumann AG is the world's second-largest producer of dental implants and a major provider of dental tissue regeneration products. Based in Switzerland, Straumann maintains subsidiaries and distributors in countries throughout the world, with its most important markets being Germany and the U.S. The company is organized into two segments, the implants division and the biologics division. The implants division produces a range of products for the Straumann Dental Implant System, which includes implants, prosthetic components and instruments. Brand names include the TE implant and the SynOcta prosthetic product lines. The biologics division focuses on biotechnology for the reconstruction of dental bone and soft tissue. The company acquired Biora AB, the Swedish developer of Enamel Matrix Derivative (EMD) protein, as a major steppingstone in the expansion of its biologics activities. Its Emdogain gel for the treatment of periodontitis has firmly positioned the company in the market for periodontal tissue regeneration. Some of the company's most recent developments include SLActive, a new implant surface technology that decreases the healing time after surgery and increases general stability of the dental implants it is employed in; and Straumann Bone Ceramic, a synthetic bone graft substitute that actually augments the patient's jaw bone structure to be able to support advanced dental appliances. A new program, the Computer Aided Restoration Service (or CARES), offers an exceptionally precise way to design custom prostheses. Recent acquisitions of the company include etkon, a company focused on conventional and implant-based tooth restoration using CAD/CAM technology, and Daishin Implant System, the exclusive distributor of Straumann implant products and services in Japan.

FINANCIALS: **Sales and profits are in thousands of dollars—add 000 to get the full amount. 2007 Note: Financial information for 2007 was not available for all companies at press time.**

2007 Sales: $	2007 Profits: $	**U.S. Stock Ticker:**
2006 Sales: $	2006 Profits: $	**Int'l Ticker: STMN** Int'l Exchange: Zurich-SWX
2005 Sales: $387,056	2005 Profits: $97,363	Employees: 1,340
2004 Sales: $327,082	2004 Profits: $78,210	Fiscal Year Ends: 12/31
2003 Sales: $269,400	2003 Profits: $62,900	Parent Company:

SALARIES/BENEFITS:

Pension Plan:	ESOP Stock Plan:	Profit Sharing:	Top Exec. Salary: $	Bonus: $
Savings Plan:	Stock Purch. Plan:		Second Exec. Salary: $	Bonus: $

OTHER THOUGHTS:

Apparent Women Officers or Directors: 1
Hot Spot for Advancement for Women/Minorities:

LOCATIONS: ("Y" = Yes)

West:	Southwest:	Midwest:	Southeast:	Northeast:	International:
				Y	Y

Note: Financial information, benefits and other data can change quickly and may vary from those stated here.

INTEGRA LIFESCIENCES HOLDINGS CORPwww.integra-ls.com

Industry Group Code: 339113 **Ranks within this company's industry group:** Sales: 44 Profits: 43

Insurance/HMO/PPO:		Drugs:		Equipment/Supplies:		Hospitals/Clinics:		Services:		Health Care:	
Insurance:		Manufacturer:	Y	Manufacturer:	Y	Acute Care:		Diagnostics:		Home Health:	
Managed Care:		Distributor:		Distributor:		Sub-Acute:		Labs/Testing:		Long-Term Care:	
Utilization Management:		Specialty Pharmacy:		Leasing/Finance:		Outpatient Surgery:		Staffing:		Physical Therapy:	
Payment Processing:		Vitamins/Nutritionals:		Information Systems:		Physical Rehab. Ctr.:		Waste Disposal:		Physician Prac. Mgmt.:	
		Clinical Trials:				Psychiatric Clinics:		Specialty Svcs.:			

TYPES OF BUSINESS:

Medical Equipment Manufacturing
Implants & Biomaterials
Absorbable Medical Products
Tissue Regeneration Technology
Neurosurgery Products
Skin Replacement Products

BRANDS/DIVISIONS/AFFILIATES:

Integra NeuroSciences
Integra Plastic and Reconstructive Surgery
JARIT Surgical Instruments, Inc.
DuraGen Dural Graft Matrix
NeuraGen Nerve Guide
DenLite
LXY Healthcare
Kinetikos Medical, Inc.

CONTACTS: *Note: Officers with more than one job title may be intentionally listed here more than once.*

Stuart M. Essig, CEO
Gerard S. Carlozzi, COO/Exec. VP
Stuart M. Essig, Pres.
Maureen B. Bellantoni, CFO/Exec. VP
Deborah A. Leonetti, Sr. VP-Mktg.
Wilma J. Davis, Sr. VP-Human Resources
Simon J. Archibald, Chief Scientific Officer/VP-Clinical Affairs
Randy Gottlieb, CIO/VP
Linda Littlejohns, VP-Clinical Dev.
Donald R. Nociolo, Sr. VP-Mfg. Oper.
John B. Henneman, III, Chief Admin. Officer/Exec. VP/Corp. Sec.
Richard D. Gorelick, General Counsel/VP
John Bostjancic, VP-Corp. Dev.
John Bostjancic, VP-Investor Rel.
David B. Holtz, Sr. VP-Finance/Treas.
Howard Jamner, Chmn.-Jarit Surgical Instruments
Judith E. O'Grady, Sr. VP-Quality, Regulatory & Clinical Affairs
Jerry Corbin, VP/Corp. Controller
Robert D. Paltridge, Pres., Extremity Reconstruction
Richard E. Caruso, Chmn.
Zeev Hadass, VP-European Oper.

Phone: 609-275-0500 **Fax:** 609-275-5363
Toll-Free: 800-654-2873
Address: 311 C Enterprise Dr., Plainsboro, NJ 08536 US

GROWTH PLANS/SPECIAL FEATURES:

Integra Lifesciences Holdings Corporation develops manufactures and markets medical devices, implants and biomaterials for use in neurotrauma, neurosurgery, plastic and reconstructive surgery and general surgery. The company's two primary product lines include neurosurgical/orthopedic implants and medical/surgical implants. The Neuro/Ortho implants group provides dural grafts for the repair of dura mater, dermal regeneration and engineered wound dressing, implants for small bone and joint fixation; repair of peripheral nerves and hydrocephalus management. The MedSurg Equipment product group produces ultrasonic surgery systems for tissue ablation, cranial stabilization and brain retraction systems and instrumentation for use in general, neurosurgical, spinal and plastic and reconstructive surgery and dental procedures. Patented products of the company include the DuraGen Dural Graft Matrix, the NeuraGen Nerve Guide, the INTEGRA Dermal Regeneration Template and the INTEGRA Bilayer Matrix Wound Dressing, which incorporates Integra's proprietary absorbable implant technology. Products principally focus on injuries that involve the brain, cranium spine and central nervous system and the repair and reconstruction of soft tissue. Integra's products are marketed and sold through its subsidiaries, Integra NeuroSciences, Integra Plastic and Reconstructive Surgery, Jarit and Miltex Surgical Instruments, Inc. and other strategic alliances. Integra's sales teams are located throughout the United States, Canada, Germany, the U.K., the Belenux region and France. In August 2006, the firm acquired Kinetikos Medical, Inc., a developer and manufacturer of orthopedic implants and surgical devices for small bones and joints. In May 2007, Integra announced that it would acquire the assets of the pain management business of Physician Industries, Inc. for $4 million. The company also closed the acquisition of LXY Healthcare, a manufacturer of fiber optic headlight systems for the medical industry, and acquired the DenLite illuminated mirror product line from Welch Allyn, Inc. in 2007.

FINANCIALS: Sales and profits are in thousands of dollars—add 000 to get the full amount. 2007 Note: Financial information for 2007 was not available for all companies at press time.

2007 Sales: $
2006 Sales: $419,297
2005 Sales: $277,935
2004 Sales: $229,825
2003 Sales: $166,695

2007 Profits: $
2006 Profits: $29,407
2005 Profits: $37,194
2004 Profits: $17,197
2003 Profits: $26,861

U.S. Stock Ticker: IART
Int'l Ticker: Int'l Exchange:
Employees: 1,750
Fiscal Year Ends: 12/31
Parent Company:

SALARIES/BENEFITS:

Pension Plan:
Savings Plan: Y
ESOP Stock Plan:
Stock Purch. Plan: Y
Profit Sharing:
Top Exec. Salary: $500,000 Bonus: $500,000
Second Exec. Salary: $420,000 Bonus: $168,000

OTHER THOUGHTS:

Apparent Women Officers or Directors: 7
Hot Spot for Advancement for Women/Minorities: Y

LOCATIONS: ("Y" = Yes)

West:	Southwest:	Midwest:	Southeast:	Northeast:	International:
Y		Y		Y	Y

Note: Financial information, benefits and other data can change quickly and may vary from those stated here.

INTEGRAMED AMERICA INC www.integramed.com

Industry Group Code: 621111 **Ranks within this company's industry group:** Sales: 6 Profits: 5

Insurance/HMO/PPO:		Drugs:		Equipment/Supplies:		Hospitals/Clinics:		Services:		Health Care:	
Insurance:		Manufacturer:		Manufacturer:		Acute Care:		Diagnostics:		Home Health:	
Managed Care:		Distributor:	Y	Distributor:	Y	Sub-Acute:		Labs/Testing:		Long-Term Care:	
Utilization Management:		Specialty Pharmacy:		Leasing/Finance:		Outpatient Surgery:		Staffing:		Physical Therapy:	
Payment Processing:		Vitamins/Nutritionals:		Information Systems:	Y	Physical Rehab. Ctr.:		Waste Disposal:		Physician Prac. Mgmt.:	Y
		Clinical Trials:				Psychiatric Clinics:		Specialty Svcs.:	Y		

TYPES OF BUSINESS:

Fertility Treatments
Physician Practice Management-Reproductive Services
Treatment Financing Programs
Fertility-Related Pharmaceutical Distribution

BRANDS/DIVISIONS/AFFILIATES:

FertilityWeb
IntegraMed Pharmaceutical Services, Inc.
IntegraMed Financial Services
ARTWorks Clinical Information System
ARTWorks Practice Management Information System
FertilityPartners
FertilityMarKit
Vein Clinics of America

CONTACTS: *Note: Officers with more than one job title may be intentionally listed here more than once.*

Jay Higham, CEO
Jay Higham, Pres.
John W. Hlywak, Jr., CFO/Sr. VP
Scott Soifer, Sr. VP-Mktg.
Donald S. Wood, Sr. VP-Oper. Admin.
Claude White, General Counsel/VP/Corp. Sec.
Scott Soifer, VP-Dev.
Pamela Schumann, VP-Consumer Services
Joe Travia, Sr. VP-Oper., Eastern Region
Gerardo Canet, Chmn.

Phone: 914-253-8000 **Fax:** 914-253-8008
Toll-Free: 800-458-0044
Address: 2 Manhattanville Rd., 3rd Fl., Purchase, NY 10577 US

GROWTH PLANS/SPECIAL FEATURES:

IntegraMed America, Inc. offers products and services to patients and providers in the fertility industry. The company provides services to a network of 29 reproductive science centers including fertility clinics, embryologic laboratories and clinical research sites, which all provide conventional fertility and assisted reproductive technology (ART) services. Through these centers, Integramed performs approximately 20% of all in-vitro fertilization procedures in the U.S. The company's discrete service packages include FertilityWeb, a web site development, hosting and marketing service; FertilityPurchase, a group purchasing program; FertilityMarKit marketing and sales programs; ARTWorks Clinical Information System; ARTWorks Practice Management Information System; and FertilityPartners, its turnkey fertility center operation. FertilityPartners offers administrative services such as accounting, human resources and purchasing of supplies; servicing and financing patient accounts receivable; marketing and sales; and integrated information systems. In addition, the firm distributes pharmaceutical products and services directly to patients through subsidiary IntegraMed Pharmaceutical Services, Inc., which, through a partnership with Ivpcare, Inc., has access to programs such as CycleTrack and Education Matters. CycleTrack allows the firm to limit drug distribution to only the amount required by each individual patient, minimizing the cost to third-party payers and patients. Education Matters is a comprehensive patient education program that offers videos and written materials devoted to educating patients on the proper handling and administration of complex fertility products. Through IntegraMed Financial Services, the firm also provides patients with treatment financing programs, allowing them to select the option that best suits their financial situations from a full range of payment choices. In August 2007, IntegraMed acquired Vein Clinics of America, a private company focused exclusively on treating vein disease.

FINANCIALS: Sales and profits are in thousands of dollars—add 000 to get the full amount. 2007 Note: Financial information for 2007 was not available for all companies at press time.

2007 Sales: $	2007 Profits: $	**U.S. Stock Ticker: INMD**
2006 Sales: $126,438	2006 Profits: $3,224	**Int'l Ticker:** Int'l Exchange:
2005 Sales: $128,890	2005 Profits: $1,723	Employees: 949
2004 Sales: $107,653	2004 Profits: $1,186	Fiscal Year Ends: 12/31
2003 Sales: $93,690	2003 Profits: $1,044	Parent Company:

SALARIES/BENEFITS:

Pension Plan:	ESOP Stock Plan:	Profit Sharing:	Top Exec. Salary: $275,000	Bonus: $148,500
Savings Plan:	Stock Purch. Plan:		Second Exec. Salary: $234,000	Bonus: $105,750

OTHER THOUGHTS:

Apparent Women Officers or Directors: 3
Hot Spot for Advancement for Women/Minorities: Y

LOCATIONS: ("Y" = Yes)

West:	Southwest:	Midwest:	Southeast:	Northeast:	International:
Y	Y	Y	Y	Y	

INTERMOUNTAIN HEALTH CARE

www.intermountainhealthcare.org

Industry Group Code: 622110 **Ranks within this company's industry group:** Sales: Profits:

Insurance/HMO/PPO:		Drugs:		Equipment/Supplies:		Hospitals/Clinics:		Services:		Health Care:	
Insurance:	Y	Manufacturer:		Manufacturer:		Acute Care:	Y	Diagnostics:		Home Health:	Y
Managed Care:		Distributor:		Distributor:	Y	Sub-Acute:	Y	Labs/Testing:		Long-Term Care:	
Utilization Management:		Specialty Pharmacy:		Leasing/Finance:		Outpatient Surgery:	Y	Staffing:		Physical Therapy:	Y
Payment Processing:		Vitamins/Nutritionals:		Information Systems:		Physical Rehab. Ctr.:	Y	Waste Disposal:		Physician Prac. Mgmt.:	Y
		Clinical Trials:				Psychiatric Clinics:		Specialty Svcs.:	Y		

TYPES OF BUSINESS:

Hospitals-General
Surgical Centers
Emergency Air Transport
Pharmacies
Counseling Services
Rehabilitation Centers
Home Care
Health Insurance

BRANDS/DIVISIONS/AFFILIATES:

Life Flight
IHC Physician Group
IHC HomeCare
IHC Health Plans
IHC North Temple Clinic
Intermountain Medical Center Campus
SelectHealth

CONTACTS: *Note: Officers with more than one job title may be intentionally listed here more than once.*

William H. Nelson, CEO
William H. Nelson, Pres.
Bert Zimmerli, CFO
Marc Probst, CIO
Merrill Gappmayer, Chmn.

Phone: 801-442-2000	**Fax:** 801-442-3327
Toll-Free:	
Address: 36 S. State St., Fl. 22, Salt Lake City, UT 84111 US	

GROWTH PLANS/SPECIAL FEATURES:

Intermountain Health Care, Inc. (IHC) is a nonprofit health care provider for Utah and southeastern Idaho. The firm operates 21 hospitals, surgical centers and a minor emergency pediatric clinic. IHC also runs Life Flight, an emergency air transport system, a collection of physician clinics, pharmacies, trauma services, counseling, dialysis and rehabilitation centers. The IHC Physician Group has 400 full-time clinical and general practice doctors. The firm also runs a variety of subsidiaries for additional patient assistance. IHC HomeCare offers home nursing, a hospice center, pharmacy delivery and medical equipment and supplies for the elderly and infirm. Formerly IHC Health Plans, SelectHealth supplies medical, prescription and dental insurance to corporate and individual clients. IHC has completed construction for its new Intermountain Medical Center campus, a teaching and research hospital working with the Utah School of Medicine and local nursing college. The campus will include five specialized hospitals: a heart and lung hospital; a women's and newborn hospital; a cancer treatment hospital; an ambulatory and outpatient diagnostics hospital; and a tertiary inpatient hospital which includes critical care and trauma treatment.

IHC offers its employees a healthcare flexible spending account, employee assistance, a healthy balance program, on-site exercise facilities, free flu shots, a 401(k) plan, a 403(b) plan, a pension plan, tuition reimbursement, childcare discounts, adoption benefits, a dependent care flexible spending account, credit union membership and health and dental insurance.

FINANCIALS: **Sales and profits are in thousands of dollars—add 000 to get the full amount. 2007 Note: Financial information for 2007 was not available for all companies at press time.**

2007 Sales: $	2007 Profits: $	**U.S. Stock Ticker: Nonprofit**
2006 Sales: $	2006 Profits: $	**Int'l Ticker:** Int'l Exchange:
2005 Sales: $	2005 Profits: $	Employees:
2004 Sales: $	2004 Profits: $	Fiscal Year Ends: 12/31
2003 Sales: $3,266,700	2003 Profits: $893,200	Parent Company:

SALARIES/BENEFITS:

Pension Plan: Y	ESOP Stock Plan:	Profit Sharing:	Top Exec. Salary: $	Bonus: $
Savings Plan: Y	Stock Purch. Plan:		Second Exec. Salary: $	Bonus: $

OTHER THOUGHTS:

Apparent Women Officers or Directors:
Hot Spot for Advancement for Women/Minorities:

LOCATIONS: ("Y" = Yes)

West:	Southwest:	Midwest:	Southeast:	Northeast:	International:
Y					

INTUITIVE SURGICAL INC

www.intuitivesurgical.com

Industry Group Code: 339113 **Ranks within this company's industry group:** Sales: 49 Profits: 27

Insurance/HMO/PPO:		**Drugs:**		**Equipment/Supplies:**		**Hospitals/Clinics:**		**Services:**		**Health Care:**	
Insurance:		Manufacturer:		Manufacturer:	Y	Acute Care:		Diagnostics:		Home Health:	
Managed Care:		Distributor:		Distributor:		Sub-Acute:		Labs/Testing:		Long-Term Care:	
Utilization Management:		Specialty Pharmacy:		Leasing/Finance:		Outpatient Surgery:		Staffing:		Physical Therapy:	
Payment Processing:		Vitamins/Nutritionals:		Information Systems:		Physical Rehab. Ctr.:		Waste Disposal:		Physician Prac. Mgmt.:	
		Clinical Trials:				Psychiatric Clinics:		Specialty Svcs.:			

TYPES OF BUSINESS:

Endoscopic Surgery Products
Operative Surgical Robots

BRANDS/DIVISIONS/AFFILIATES:

da Vinci Surgical System
EndoWrist
SOCRATES
ZEUS
HERMES
AESOP

CONTACTS: *Note: Officers with more than one job title may be intentionally listed here more than once.*

Lonnie M. Smith, CEO
Gary S. Guthart, COO
Gary S. Guthart, Pres.
Marshall L. Mohr, CFO/Sr. VP
Rick Epstein, Sr. VP-Mktg.
Heather Hand, VP-Human Resources
Dave Rosa, VP-Prod. Dev.
Sal Brogna, VP-Eng.
Augusto V. Castello, VP-Mfg.
John F. (Rick) Runkel, General Counsel/Sr. VP
Aleks Cukic, VP-Bus. Dev. & Strategic Planning
Benjamin Gong, VP-Finance/Treas.
Jim Alecxih, VP-United States Sales
Colin Morales, VP-Customer Service
Frank D. Nguyen, VP-Intellectual Property & Licensing
Jerry McNamara, Sr. VP-Worldwide Sales & Mktg.
Dave Rosa, VP-Sales & Mktg. Int'l

Phone: 408-523-2100	**Fax:** 408-523-1390
Toll-Free: 888-868-4647	
Address: 950 Kifer Rd., Sunnyvale, CA 94086 US	

GROWTH PLANS/SPECIAL FEATURES:

Intuitive Surgical, Inc. is a leading manufacturer of operative surgical robotics. The firm designs and manufactures the da Vinci Surgical System, which consists of a surgeon's console, a patient-side cart, a high-performance vision system and Intuitive's proprietary wristed instruments. The system provides the surgeon with the control, range of motion, fine tissue manipulation capability and 3-D visualization characteristics of open surgery, while simultaneously allowing the surgeon to work through the small ports of minimally invasive surgery (MIS). The da Vinci Surgical System can be used to control Intuitive's endoscopic instruments. Surgeons operate while seated comfortably at a console viewing a bright and sharp 3-D image of the surgical field. In 2006, Intuitive enhanced the system with a number of additional features including a motorized patient cart; beginning in 2007 the system is available with high definition visualization. Intuitive also manufactures a variety of EndoWrist instruments, each of which incorporates a wrist joint for natural dexterity with tips customized for various surgical procedures. Other products include the AESOP Endoscopic Positioner, a surgical robot capable of positioning an endoscope in response to surgeon's commands; the ZEUS Surgical System, a robotic platform; the HERMES Control Center, a voice activated operating room control system; and the SOCRATES Telementoring System, an interactive telecollaborative system allowing a surgeon to mentor and collaborate with another surgeon during an operation. Intuitive no longer promotes the ZEUS and SOCRATES products, though it continues to support systems already installed at customer sites.

Intuitive offers its employees a dependent care plan; a medical expenses reimbursement plan; a commuter check program; an employee assistance program; an employee recognition program; a patent bonus program; on-site dental services; on-site dry cleaning and oil change services; discounts at local amusement parks and attractions; company events; and prescription, dental and vision coverage.

FINANCIALS: **Sales and profits are in thousands of dollars—add 000 to get the full amount. 2007 Note: Financial information for 2007 was not available for all companies at press time.**

2007 Sales: $	2007 Profits: $	**U.S. Stock Ticker: ISRG**
2006 Sales: $372,682	2006 Profits: $72,044	**Int'l Ticker:** Int'l Exchange:
2005 Sales: $227,338	2005 Profits: $94,134	Employees: 563
2004 Sales: $138,803	2004 Profits: $23,478	Fiscal Year Ends: 12/31
2003 Sales: $91,675	2003 Profits: $-9,623	Parent Company:

SALARIES/BENEFITS:

Pension Plan:	ESOP Stock Plan:	Profit Sharing:	Top Exec. Salary: $427,000	Bonus: $425,000
Savings Plan: Y	Stock Purch. Plan: Y		Second Exec. Salary: $343,750	Bonus: $275,000

OTHER THOUGHTS:

Apparent Women Officers or Directors: 1
Hot Spot for Advancement for Women/Minorities:

LOCATIONS: ("Y" = Yes)

West:	Southwest:	Midwest:	Southeast:	Northeast:	International:
Y					Y

Note: Financial information, benefits and other data can change quickly and may vary from those stated here.

INVACARE CORP www.invacare.com

Industry Group Code: 339113 **Ranks within this company's industry group:** Sales: 23 Profits: 97

Insurance/HMO/PPO:		Drugs:		Equipment/Supplies:		Hospitals/Clinics:		Services:		Health Care:	
Insurance:		Manufacturer:		Manufacturer:	Y	Acute Care:		Diagnostics:		Home Health:	
Managed Care:		Distributor:		Distributor:	Y	Sub-Acute:		Labs/Testing:		Long-Term Care:	
Utilization Management:		Specialty Pharmacy:		Leasing/Finance:		Outpatient Surgery:		Staffing:		Physical Therapy:	
Payment Processing:		Vitamins/Nutritionals:		Information Systems:		Physical Rehab. Ctr.:		Waste Disposal:		Physician Prac. Mgmt.:	
		Clinical Trials:				Psychiatric Clinics:		Specialty Svcs.:			

TYPES OF BUSINESS:

Supplies-Wheelchairs
Home Health Care Equipment
Home Respiratory Products
Medical Supplies

BRANDS/DIVISIONS/AFFILIATES:

Storm Series TDX
Pronto Series Power Wheelchair
SureStep
AT'm
HomeFill
Top End

CONTACTS: *Note: Officers with more than one job title may be intentionally listed here more than once.*

A. Malachi Mixon, III, CEO
Gerald B. Blouch, COO
Gerald B. Blouch, Pres.
Gregory C. Thompson, CFO/Sr. VP
Louis F.J. Slangen, Sr. VP-Global Sales & Mktg.
Joseph S. Usaj, Sr. VP-Human Resources
Joseph B. Richey, II, Sr. VP-Electronics & Design Eng.
Dale LaPorte, General Counsel
Dale LaPorte, Sr. VP-Bus. Dev.
Joseph B. Richey, II, Pres., Invacare Tech.
A. Malachi Mixon, III, Chmn.

Phone: 440-329-6000	**Fax:**
Toll-Free:	
Address: 1 Invacare Way, Elyria, OH 44036 US	

GROWTH PLANS/SPECIAL FEATURES:

Invacare Corp. is a leading manufacturer and distributor o health care products for the non-acute care environment including the home health care and retail markets. The firm sells its products to over 25,000 home health care and reta locations in the U.S., Australia, Canada, Europe, New Zealand and Asia. Invacare's product line includes powe and manual wheelchairs, motorized scooters, seating an positioning products, home care beds, mattress overlays home respiratory products, bathing equipment, lifts an slings and patient aids. Invacare's power wheelchair lin includes the Invacare, Storm Series and Pronto Series bran names. The Storm Series TDX line of power wheelchair offers power, stability and maneuverability. The Pront Series Power Wheelchairs with SureStep feature center wheel driven performance for maneuverability and intuitiv driving. Invacare's line of power wheelchairs also include fully customizable models. Invacare manufactures an markets a range of custom manual wheelchairs for everyday sports and recreational uses, marketed under the Invacar and Invacare Top End brand names. Invacare manufacture the AT'm portable power wheelchair for consumers needin light duty powered mobility with the ability to quickl disassemble and be transported even in a compact or mid size vehicle, as well as two portable, compact scooters. Th company's home respiratory products include oxyge concentrators, HomeFill oxygen transfilling systems, slee apnea products and aerosol therapy. In addition, the firm i a manufacturer and distributor of beds and furnishings for it non-acute care markets and numerous lines of brande medical supplies addressing ostomy, incontinence, diabete and wound care, among other health issues. The compan also manufactures, markets and distributes many accessor products, including spare parts, wheelchair cushions, arn rests, wheels and respiratory parts. New produc development has been given a strong emphasis as part o Invacare's strategy to gain market share and maintai competitive advantage.

Invacare offers its employees an educational assistanc program.

FINANCIALS: Sales and profits are in thousands of dollars—add 000 to get the full amount. 2007 Note: Financial information for 2007 was not available for all companies at press time.

2007 Sales: $	2007 Profits: $	**U.S. Stock Ticker: IVC**
2006 Sales: $1,498,035	2006 Profits: $-317,774	**Int'l Ticker:** Int'l Exchange:
2005 Sales: $1,529,732	2005 Profits: $48,852	Employees: 6,000
2004 Sales: $1,403,327	2004 Profits: $75,197	Fiscal Year Ends: 12/31
2003 Sales: $1,247,176	2003 Profits: $71,409	Parent Company:

SALARIES/BENEFITS:

Pension Plan:	ESOP Stock Plan:	Profit Sharing:	Top Exec. Salary: $1,074,450	Bonus: $
Savings Plan:	Stock Purch. Plan:		Second Exec. Salary: $674,200	Bonus: $

OTHER THOUGHTS:

Apparent Women Officers or Directors:
Hot Spot for Advancement for Women/Minorities:

LOCATIONS: ("Y" = Yes)

West:	Southwest:	Midwest:	Southeast:	Northeast:	International:
Y	Y	Y	Y	Y	Y

Note: Financial information, benefits and other data can change quickly and may vary from those stated here.

NVENTIV HEALTH INC www.ventiv.com

ndustry Group Code: 541613 **Ranks within this company's industry group:** Sales: 1 Profits: 1

nsurance/HMO/PPO:		Drugs:		Equipment/Supplies:		Hospitals/Clinics:		Services:		Health Care:	
nsurance:		Manufacturer:		Manufacturer:		Acute Care:		Diagnostics:		Home Health:	
lanaged Care:		Distributor:		Distributor:		Sub-Acute:		Labs/Testing:		Long-Term Care:	
tilization Management:		Specialty Pharmacy:		Leasing/Finance:		Outpatient Surgery:		Staffing:		Physical Therapy:	
ayment Processing:		Vitamins/Nutritionals:		Information Systems:	Y	Physical Rehab. Ctr.:		Waste Disposal:		Physician Prac. Mgmt.:	
		Clinical Trials:				Psychiatric Clinics:		Specialty Svcs.:	Y		

TYPES OF BUSINESS:

larketing-Life Sciences & Pharmaceuticals
ales & Marketing Outsourcing
linical Staffing
lealth Care Communications
dvertising Services
)ata Services
ales Force Deployment
linical & Statistical Research

BRANDS/DIVISIONS/AFFILIATES:

nVentiv Commercial Services
nVentiv Communications
nVentiv Clinical Services
ranklin Group (The)
harmaceutical Resource Solutions
SSW Worldwide
tonefly
ledFocus

CONTACTS: *Note: Officers with more than one job title may be ntentionally listed here more than once.*

ran Broshy, CEO
ohn Emery, CFO/Corp. Sec.
errell Herring, CEO/Pres., Ventiv Comm. Svcs.
lane Walter, CEO-inVentiv Communications
homas A. Hanley, Jr., CEO/Pres., Smith Hanley Holding Company
lichael Hlinak, Pres., inventive Clinical
)aniel M. Snyder, Chmn.

hone: 732-748-4666	**Fax:** 732-537-4912
oll-Free: 800-416-0555	
ddress: 200 Cottontail Ln., 8th Fl., Somerset, NJ 08873 US	

GROWTH PLANS/SPECIAL FEATURES:

inVentiv Health, Inc. is a clinical services and marketing services provider for the pharmaceutical and life sciences industry. inVentiv's services include sales and marketing; clinical staffing; planning and analytics; marketing support; professional development and training; and data collection and management. The company is structured into three business units: inVentiv Commercial Services, inVentiv Communications and inVentiv Clinical Services. inVentiv Commercial Services, formerly inVentiv Pharma Services, oversees most of the firm's services such as sales and marketing teams and recruitment of sales representatives in the commercial services area. Additional subsidiaries and acquisitions of this group include the Franklin Group, Pharmaceutical Resource Solutions and Promotech. inVentiv Communications provides advertising, business communications, branding, medical education and contract marketing services via subsidiaries GSW Worldwide, Palio, Navicor, Stonefly and Jeffrey Simbrow and Associates. inVentiv Clinical Services consists of subsidiaries Smith Hanley Associates, Smith Hanley Consulting Group and MedFocus (collectively Smith Hanley), HHI Clinical & Statistical Research Services and Anova Clinical Resources. This segment provides services related to recruitment, clinical staffing and data collection and management. inVentiv's clients include Sanofi-Aventis Group, Bayer Corporation, Bristol-Myers Squibb and Watson Pharmaceuticals, Inc. Daniel M. Snyder, owner of the Washington Redskins football team, retains a significant interest in inVentiv as the company's chairman. Recently, the company acquired the assets of The Maxwell Group (including its MedConference brand of on-demand virtual services) for 8.1 million in cash and stock. In 2007, the firm acquired Ignite (Incendia Health, Inc.), a medical advertising and interactive communications firm, for $20 million in cash and stock. In addition, the company acquired Chamberlain (a public relations firm in the healthcare industry) for $13 million. The new companies are included in the firm's inVentiv Communications segment.

inVentiv has its own training center and offers online courses to enrich its employees' skills and leadership.

FINANCIALS: **Sales and profits are in thousands of dollars—add 000 to get the full amount. 2007 Note: Financial information for 2007 was not available for all companies at press time.**

2007 Sales: $	2007 Profits: $	**U.S. Stock Ticker: VTIV**
2006 Sales: $766,245	2006 Profits: $51,235	**Int'l Ticker:** Int'l Exchange:
2005 Sales: $556,312	2005 Profits: $43,863	Employees: 5,200
2004 Sales: $352,184	2004 Profits: $31,132	Fiscal Year Ends: 12/31
2003 Sales: $224,453	2003 Profits: $5,776	Parent Company:

SALARIES/BENEFITS:

ension Plan:	ESOP Stock Plan:	Profit Sharing:	Top Exec. Salary: $535,137	Bonus: $600,000
avings Plan: Y	Stock Purch. Plan:		Second Exec. Salary: $345,000	Bonus: $345,000

OTHER THOUGHTS:

pparent Women Officers or Directors:
lot Spot for Advancement for Women/Minorities:

LOCATIONS: ("Y" = Yes)

West:	Southwest:	Midwest:	Southeast:	Northeast:	International:
Y	Y	Y	Y	Y	

INVERNESS MEDICAL INNOVATIONS INC

www.invernessmedical.com

Industry Group Code: 339113 **Ranks within this company's industry group:** Sales: 37 Profits: 91

Insurance/HMO/PPO:		Drugs:		Equipment/Supplies:		Hospitals/Clinics:		Services:		Health Care:	
Insurance:		Manufacturer:		Manufacturer:	Y	Acute Care:		Diagnostics:		Home Health:	
Managed Care:		Distributor:		Distributor:	Y	Sub-Acute:		Labs/Testing:		Long-Term Care:	
Utilization Management:		Specialty Pharmacy:		Leasing/Finance:		Outpatient Surgery:		Staffing:		Physical Therapy:	
Payment Processing:		Vitamins/Nutritionals:	Y	Information Systems:		Physical Rehab. Ctr.:		Waste Disposal:		Physician Prac. Mgmt.:	
		Clinical Trials:				Psychiatric Clinics:		Specialty Svcs.:			

TYPES OF BUSINESS:

Supplies-Over-the-Counter Health Care Products
Self-Test Diagnostic Products
Vitamins & Nutritional Supplements
Professional Diagnostic Products

BRANDS/DIVISIONS/AFFILIATES:

Fact plus
Accu-Clear
Inverness Medical Nutritionals Group
Stresstabs
SPD Swiss Precision Diagnostics GmbH
Cholestech Corp
Acceava
Clearview

CONTACTS: *Note: Officers with more than one job title may be intentionally listed here more than once.*

Ron Zwanziger, CEO
Ron Zwanziger, Pres.
David Teitel, CFO
Jerry McAleer, VP-R&D & Cardiology
Ellen Chiniara, General Counsel
Paul T. Hempel, Sr. VP-Leadership & Dev./Special Counsel
David Toohey, Pres., Professional Diagnostics
David Scott, Chief Scientific Officer
Hilde Eylenbosch, Pres., Consumer Diagnostics
John Yonkin, Pres., US Point of Care & Medical Nutritionals
Ron Zwanziger, Chmn.
Geoffrey Jenkins, VP-Worldwide Oper.

Phone: 781-647-3900 **Fax:** 781-647-3939
Toll-Free:
Address: 51 Sawyer Rd., Ste. 200, Waltham, MA 02453 US

GROWTH PLANS/SPECIAL FEATURES:

Inverness Medical Innovations, Inc. (IMI) develop manufactures and markets in-vitro diagnostic products f the over-the-counter pregnancy and fertility/ovulation te market and the professional rapid diagnostic test market The company's major reportable segments are consum diagnostic products, vitamins and nutritional supplemen and professional diagnostic products. Inverness' curre consumer diagnostic products primarily target the worldwi over-the-counter pregnancy and fertility/ovulation te market. The company's pregnancy and fertility/ovulatio tests, sold under the brand names Fact plus and Accu-Clea display visual results in approximately one minute or thre minutes depending on the product. Inverness markets wide variety of vitamins and nutritional supplements primari within the U.S. through its subsidiary Inverness Medic Nutritionals Group, including Stresstabs, a B-comple vitamin with added antioxidants; Ferro-Sequels, a tim release iron supplement; Protegra, an antioxidant vitami and mineral supplement; Posture-D, a calcium supplemen SoyCare, a soy supplement for menopause; ALLBEE, a li of B-complex vitamins; and Z-BEC, a zinc supplement wi B-complex vitamins and added antioxidants. Invernes professional diagnostics products consist primarily laboratory and point-of-care tests in the areas of women health, infectious disease, cardiovascular disease and drug of abuse, including Acceava, BinaxNOW, BioStar OI Clearview, Determine, Signify, SureStep, Inverness Medic TestPack and Wampole brand rapid membrane te products; Wampole brand enzyme linked immunosorbe assays (ELISA) tests; the AtheNA Multi-Lyte Test Syste indirect fluorescent antibody assays; and an Albumin Cob Binding clinical chemistry assay for detecting Ischemi Modified Albumin (IMA). In recent news, Invernes announced the formation of a 50/50 joint venture compa with The Procter & Gamble Company, SPD Swiss Precisio Diagnostics GmbH, for the development, manufactur marketing and sale of consumer diagnostics products. June 2007, the company acquired Cholestech Corporation.

FINANCIALS: **Sales and profits are in thousands of dollars—add 000 to get the full amount. 2007 Note: Financial information for 2007 was not available for all companies at press time.**

2007 Sales: $
2006 Sales: $569,454
2005 Sales: $421,900
2004 Sales: $374,000
2003 Sales: $296,712

2007 Profits: $
2006 Profits: $-16,842
2005 Profits: $-19,200
2004 Profits: $-17,300
2003 Profits: $9,560

U.S. Stock Ticker: IMA
Int'l Ticker: Int'l Exchange:
Employees: 2,561
Fiscal Year Ends: 12/31
Parent Company:

SALARIES/BENEFITS:

Pension Plan: Y ESOP Stock Plan: Profit Sharing: Top Exec. Salary: $550,000 Bonus: $550,000
Savings Plan: Y Stock Purch. Plan: Y Second Exec. Salary: $431,177 Bonus: $125,000

OTHER THOUGHTS:

Apparent Women Officers or Directors: 2
Hot Spot for Advancement for Women/Minorities:

LOCATIONS: ("Y" = Yes)

West:	Southwest:	Midwest:	Southeast:	Northeast:	International:
Y				Y	Y

Note: Financial information, benefits and other data can change quickly and may vary from those stated here.

IRIDEX CORP

www.iridex.com

ndustry Group Code: 339113 **Ranks within this company's industry group:** Sales: 96 Profits: 84

nsurance/HMO/PPO:		Drugs:		Equipment/Supplies:		Hospitals/Clinics:		Services:		Health Care:	
nsurance:		Manufacturer:		Manufacturer:	Y	Acute Care:		Diagnostics:		Home Health:	
Managed Care:		Distributor:		Distributor:		Sub-Acute:		Labs/Testing:		Long-Term Care:	
Jtilization Management:		Specialty Pharmacy:		Leasing/Finance:		Outpatient Surgery:		Staffing:		Physical Therapy:	
Payment Processing:		Vitamins/Nutritionals:		Information Systems:		Physical Rehab. Ctr.:		Waste Disposal:		Physician Prac. Mgmt.:	
		Clinical Trials:				Psychiatric Clinics:		Specialty Svcs.:			

TYPES OF BUSINESS:

Equipment-Laser Systems
Ophthalmological & Dermatological Laser Systems

BRANDS/DIVISIONS/AFFILIATES:

OcuLight TX
IRIS Medical IQ810 Laser System
OcuLight Symphony
OcuLight SL
OcuLight GL
EndoProbe
Laserscope
Gemini Laser System

CONTACTS: *Note: Officers with more than one job title may be intentionally listed here more than once.*

Barry G. Caldwell, CEO
Barry Caldwell, Pres.
Meryl A. Rains, CFO/VP
Donald J. Todd, Sr. VP-Mktg. & Customer Support
Larry Tannenbaum, Sr. VP-Admin.
Timothy Powers, VP-Oper.
Larry Tannenbaum, Chief Bus. Officer/Sr. VP
James L. Donovan, VP-Corp. Bus. Dev.
Theodore A. Boutacoff, Chmn.
Eduardo Arias, Sr. VP-Int'l Sales & Bus. Dev.

Phone: 650-940-4700	**Fax:** 650-940-4710
Toll-Free: 800-388-4747	
Address: 1212 Terra Bella Ave., Mountain View, CA 94043-1824 US	

GROWTH PLANS/SPECIAL FEATURES:

IRIDEX Corporation is a leading global provider of therapeutic based laser systems and delivery devices used to treat eye diseases in ophthalmology and skin conditions in dermatology. The company's family of OcuLight laser systems, which accounts for the majority of its revenues, is used for ophthalmic applications primarily in operating rooms. The OcuLight product family includes the OcuLight TX, IRIS Medical IQ810 Laser System, the OcuLight Symphony, OcuLight SL, OcuLight SLx, OcuLight GL and OcuLight GLx laser photocoagulation systems. IRIDEX's ophthalmology products are used in the treatment of serious eye diseases, including the three leading causes of irreversible blindness: diabetic retinopathy, glaucoma and age-related macular degeneration (AMD). IRIDEX's dermatology products treat skin conditions, primarily vascular and pigmented lesions. The company's dermatology laser systems include the DioLite XP and the VariLite Dual Wavelength Laser systems. The company's ophthalmic and dermatology laser system consists of small, portable laser consoles and delivery devices. While dermatologists almost always use the company's laser systems in their offices, ophthalmologists and plastic surgeons typically use the laser systems in hospital operating rooms and ambulatory surgery centers. Ophthalmologists use the company's laser with either an indirect laser ophthalmoscope or a disposable single-use EndoProbe. IRIDEX markets its products through a direct sales force in the U.S. and a network of 77 distributors that sells to 107 countries around the world. In January 2007, IRIDEX announced completing its acquisition of Laserscope's aesthetics business, including four patents, a license to an additional nine Laserscope patents and a license under Palomar hair removal patents, for $26 million. Laserscope aesthetic treatments encompass minimally invasive surgical techniques for hair removal, leg veins, wrinkle removal, acne damage, sun damage and skin rejuvenation. Laserscope's aesthetic products include the Gemini Laser System, Venus-i Laser Systems, Lyra-i Laser System, Aura-i Laser System and Solis IPL System.

FINANCIALS: **Sales and profits are in thousands of dollars—add 000 to get the full amount. 2007 Note: Financial information for 2007 was not available for all companies at press time.**

2007 Sales: $	2007 Profits: $	**U.S. Stock Ticker: IRIX**
2006 Sales: $35,904	2006 Profits: $-5,753	**Int'l Ticker:** Int'l Exchange:
2005 Sales: $37,029	2005 Profits: $1,671	Employees: 121
2004 Sales: $32,810	2004 Profits: $- 402	Fiscal Year Ends: 12/31
2003 Sales: $31,699	2003 Profits: $ 371	Parent Company:

SALARIES/BENEFITS:

Pension Plan:	ESOP Stock Plan:	Profit Sharing:	Top Exec. Salary: $300,000	Bonus: $
Savings Plan: Y	Stock Purch. Plan: Y		Second Exec. Salary: $254,776	Bonus: $5,000

OTHER THOUGHTS:

Apparent Women Officers or Directors: 1
Hot Spot for Advancement for Women/Minorities:

LOCATIONS: ("Y" = Yes)

West:	Southwest:	Midwest:	Southeast:	Northeast:	International:
Y	Y	Y	Y	Y	

IRIS INTERNATIONAL INC www.proiris.com

Industry Group Code: 339113 **Ranks within this company's industry group:** Sales: 85 Profits: 77

Insurance/HMO/PPO:		Drugs:		Equipment/Supplies:		Hospitals/Clinics:		Services:		Health Care:	
Insurance:		Manufacturer:		Manufacturer:	Y	Acute Care:		Diagnostics:		Home Health:	
Managed Care:		Distributor:		Distributor:		Sub-Acute:		Labs/Testing:		Long-Term Care:	
Utilization Management:		Specialty Pharmacy:		Leasing/Finance:		Outpatient Surgery:		Staffing:		Physical Therapy:	
Payment Processing:		Vitamins/Nutritionals:		Information Systems:	Y	Physical Rehab. Ctr.:		Waste Disposal:		Physician Prac. Mgmt.:	
		Clinical Trials:				Psychiatric Clinics:		Specialty Svcs.:	Y		

TYPES OF BUSINESS:

Equipment-Body Fluid Analysis
Automated Urinalysis Workstations
Digital Imaging Software, Research & Development

BRANDS/DIVISIONS/AFFILIATES:

iQ200 Automated Urine Microscopy Analyzer
Automated Intelligent Microscopy
Leucadia Technologies, Inc.
Iris Molecular Diagnostics
StatSpin, Inc.
Advanced Digital Imaging Research LLC

CONTACTS: *Note: Officers with more than one job title may be intentionally listed here more than once.*

Cesar M. Garcia, CEO
Cesar M. Garcia, Pres.
Peter L. Donato, CFO/VP
John Yi, VP-Oper.
Dino M. Alfano, Pres., Iris Diagnostics Division
Robert A. Mello, VP/Gen. Mgr.-Iris Sample Processing
Kenneth Castleman, Pres., Advanced Digital Imaging Research
Richard H. Williams, Chmn.

Phone: 818-709-1244	**Fax:** 818-700-9661
Toll-Free: 800-776-4747	
Address: 9172 Eton Ave., Chatsworth, CA 91311-5874 US	

GROWTH PLANS/SPECIAL FEATURES:

IRIS International, Inc. manufactures and markets automate urinalysis imaging systems and medical devices used hospitals and clinical reference laboratories worldwide. Th company's largest business unit, Diagnostic Divisio designs, manufactures and markets in-vitro diagnostic systems, consumables and supplies for urinalysis and boc fluids testing. The in-vitro diagnostics imaging systems ar based on patented Automated Intelligent Microscopy (AIN technology. The division's iQ200 Automated Urir Microscopy Analyzer is a user-friendly, bench top, fu automated analyzer capable of performing microscopy in flowing stream utilizing the company's neural network-base Automated Particle Recognition software to enable hig speed digital processing to classify and display images microscopic particles. The iQ200 microscopy analyze have the ability to be seamlessly connected to automate chemistry analyzers to constitute a fully integrated urinalys system performing both chemistry and microscop simultaneously on a urine sample, as well as the analysis certain body fluids. In April 2006, the company acquire molecular diagnostics company Leucadia Technologies, Inc now named Iris Molecular Diagnostics. A new molecul diagnostics product line will be based on the platfor technologies acquired, which includes ultra-sensitiv detection capabilities under the detection thresholds current immunoassay and molecular diagnostics method IRIS's second business unit, StatSpin, Inc., markets sma centrifuges, DNA processing stations and other equipme and accessories for rapid specimen processing. Advanc Digital Imaging Research LLC (ADIR), the company's thi business unit, does not generate revenue but assists in th advancement of proprietary imaging technology whi conducting government-sponsored research and contra development in imaging and pattern recognition. In Ma 2007, the company announced a decision to close its ADI subsidiary, as ADIR no longer qualifies for governme funding under new Small Business Administration guideline

IRIS offers its employees a 401(k) plan, an employee stoc purchase plan, a cafeteria plan, education reimburseme and medical, dental and vision insurance.

FINANCIALS: **Sales and profits are in thousands of dollars—add 000 to get the full amount. 2007 Note: Financial information for 2007 was not available for all companies at press time.**

2007 Sales: $	2007 Profits: $	**U.S. Stock Ticker: IRIS**
2006 Sales: $70,494	2006 Profits: $- 175	**Int'l Ticker:** Int'l Exchange:
2005 Sales: $62,780	2005 Profits: $6,131	Employees: 274
2004 Sales: $43,650	2004 Profits: $2,280	Fiscal Year Ends: 12/31
2003 Sales: $31,345	2003 Profits: $- 530	Parent Company:

SALARIES/BENEFITS:

Pension Plan:	ESOP Stock Plan:	Profit Sharing:	Top Exec. Salary: $373,449	Bonus: $84,375
Savings Plan: Y	Stock Purch. Plan: Y		Second Exec. Salary: $227,082	Bonus: $

OTHER THOUGHTS:

Apparent Women Officers or Directors:
Hot Spot for Advancement for Women/Minorities:

LOCATIONS: ("Y" = Yes)

West:	Southwest:	Midwest:	Southeast:	Northeast:	International:
Y	Y			Y	Y

JEAN COUTU GROUP INC (THE) www.jeancoutu.com

ndustry Group Code: 446110 **Ranks within this company's industry group:** Sales: 4 Profits: 4

surance/HMO/PPO:		Drugs:		Equipment/Supplies:		Hospitals/Clinics:		Services:		Health Care:	
surance:		Manufacturer:		Manufacturer:		Acute Care:		Diagnostics:		Home Health:	
anaged Care:		Distributor:	Y	Distributor:		Sub-Acute:		Labs/Testing:		Long-Term Care:	
ilization Management:		Specialty Pharmacy:		Leasing/Finance:		Outpatient Surgery:		Staffing:		Physical Therapy:	
ayment Processing:		Vitamins/Nutritionals:		Information Systems:		Physical Rehab. Ctr.:		Waste Disposal:		Physician Prac. Mgmt.:	
		Clinical Trials:				Psychiatric Clinics:		Specialty Svcs.:			

YPES OF BUSINESS:

rug Stores
eal Estate
harmacies

BRANDS/DIVISIONS/AFFILIATES:

X Information Centre Ltd.
IR MILES Rewards Program
JC Jean Coutu
outiques Passion Beaute

CONTACTS: *Note: Officers with more than one job title may be ntentionally listed here more than once.*

rancois J. Coutu, CEO
rancois J. Coutu, Pres./Vice-Chmn.
lain Lafortune, Sr. VP-Mktg. & Purchasing
enis Courcy, VP-Human Resources
ichel Boucher, CIO
ohanne Meloche, VP-Cosmetics, Exclusive Brands & Beauty Programs
enis Courcy, VP-Legal Affairs
ichard Mayrand, VP-Public Affairs & Pharmacy
ichael Murray, Dir.-Investor Rel.
ndre Belzile, Sr. VP-Finance & Corp. Affairs
ormand Messier, Sr. VP-Network Exploitation
im Lachapelle, Corp. Sec.
von Goyer, VP-Services & Promotions
arcel A. Raymond, VP-Control & Treasury
ean Coutu, Chmn.
ean-Pierre Normandin, VP-Distribution Ctr.

hone: 450-646-9611	**Fax:** 450-646-5649
oll-Free:	
ddress: 530 Beriault St., Longueil, QC J4G 1S8 Canada	

GROWTH PLANS/SPECIAL FEATURES:

The Jean Coutu Group (JCG) is a Canadian retailer of pharmaceuticals and over-the-counter drugs. Its RX Information Centre Ltd. subsidiary is responsible for the development and implementation of technological solutions to improve the efficiency of operations and quality of service. In June 2007, JCG completed the sale of all 1,854 of its U.S. Brooks and Eckerd drug stores, as well as its six U.S. distribution centers, to Rite Aid Corporation for approximately $2.3 billion in cash; and it will also receive a 31.7% common stock interest in Rite Aid as part of the transaction. During 2006, the company had closed 78 non-performing Eckerd drugstores and sold the former Eckerd headquarters in Largo, Florida for $24 million. The firm will continue on as franchisor and distributor for its network of 328 Canadian franchised PJC Jean Coutu drugstores, located in Quebec, New Brunswick and Ontario. Its drugstores filled 55.2 million prescriptions in 2007, averaging 3,187 per week, and the average drugstore has $10.3 million in annual sales. The firm supplies approximately 75% of the drugstores' products, including almost all prescription drugs. JCG also operates 38 Boutiques Passion Beaute stores, 11 of which were opened in 2007. Additionally, 53 of the company's stores are full service postal outlets; and all stores that were previously unequipped for digital photo processing were made capable during 2007. It is one of the only pharmacies in Quebec to offer the AIR MILES Rewards Program. In 2007, it began offering customers the chance to redeem reward miles for purchases. In 2007, JCG opened or relocated nine stores, and renovated or expanded 18 stores; and in 2008, it plans to open eight new drugstores, relocate 11 drugstores and complete 44 drugstore renovations as well as open 20 new Boutiques Passion Beaute stores.

FINANCIALS: **Sales and profits are in thousands of dollars—add 000 to get the full amount. 2007 Note: Financial information for 2007 was not available for all companies at press time.**

007 Sales: $1,146,970	2007 Profits: $140,800	**U.S. Stock Ticker: JCOUF**
006 Sales: $11,143,100	2006 Profits: $103,800	**Int'l Ticker: PJC.A** Int'l Exchange: Toronto-TSX
005 Sales: $9,617,363	2005 Profits: $104,378	Employees: 47,115
004 Sales: $3,042,967	2004 Profits: $132,683	Fiscal Year Ends: 5/31
003 Sales: $2,924,000	2003 Profits: $118,100	Parent Company:

ALARIES/BENEFITS:

ension Plan:	ESOP Stock Plan:	Profit Sharing:	Top Exec. Salary: $	Bonus: $
avings Plan:	Stock Purch. Plan:		Second Exec. Salary: $	Bonus: $

THER THOUGHTS:

pparent Women Officers or Directors: 4
ot Spot for Advancement for Women/Minorities: Y

LOCATIONS: ("Y" = Yes)

West:	Southwest:	Midwest:	Southeast:	Northeast:	International:
					Y

Note: Financial information, benefits and other data can change quickly and may vary from those stated here.

JEFFERSON HEALTH SYSTEM INC www.jeffersonhealth.org

Industry Group Code: 622110 **Ranks within this company's industry group:** Sales: 16 Profits: 8

Insurance/HMO/PPO:		Drugs:		Equipment/Supplies:		Hospitals/Clinics:		Services:		Health Care:	
Insurance:		Manufacturer:		Manufacturer:		Acute Care:	Y	Diagnostics:		Home Health:	
Managed Care:		Distributor:		Distributor:		Sub-Acute:	Y	Labs/Testing:		Long-Term Care:	
Utilization Management:		Specialty Pharmacy:		Leasing/Finance:		Outpatient Surgery:	Y	Staffing:		Physical Therapy:	
Payment Processing:		Vitamins/Nutritionals:		Information Systems:		Physical Rehab. Ctr.:	Y	Waste Disposal:		Physician Prac. Mgmt.:	
		Clinical Trials:				Psychiatric Clinics:	Y	Specialty Svcs.:			

TYPES OF BUSINESS:

Hospitals
Sub-Acute Care
Behavioral Health Services
Ambulatory Care Centers
Rehabilitation Services
Long-Term Care
Teaching Hospitals

BRANDS/DIVISIONS/AFFILIATES:

Albert Einstein Healthcare Network
Frankford Hospitals
Magee Rehabilitation
Main Line Health
Thomas Jefferson University Hospitals
Jefferson HealthCARE
Jefferson Radiation Oncology

CONTACTS:

Note: Officers with more than one job title may be intentionally listed here more than once.

Joseph T. Sebastianelli, CEO
Joseph T. Sebastianelli, Pres.
Kirk E. Gorman, CFO
David F. Simon, General Counsel/Sr. VP
Diane Salter, VP-Insurance
Alfred W. Putnam Jr., Chmn.

Phone: 610-255-6200	**Fax:** 610-225-6254
Toll-Free:	
Address: 259 N. Radnor-Chester Rd., Ste. 290, Radnor, PA 19087 US	

GROWTH PLANS/SPECIAL FEATURES:

Jefferson Health System, Inc. (JHS) is a nonprofit grou consisting of five member health care organizations in th greater Philadelphia, Pennsylvania area. The Albert Einste Healthcare Network operates six major facilities and number of outpatient centers, including a tertiary ca teaching hospital, a behavioral health center, two gener care centers, a nationally recognized rehabilitation facility, sub-acute care center and a long-term care residence f seniors. Frankford Hospitals' system includes three hospit campuses in Philadelphia and Bucks County, thre ambulatory care sites and several primary care satellites ar specialty practices. Magee Rehabilitation's hospital is one 16 federally designated model Regional Spinal Cord Inju Centers and is home to the nation's first brain inju rehabilitation program to be accredited by the Commissic on the Accreditation of Rehabilitation Facilities. The hospit provides inpatient and outpatient services for people wi spinal cord injuries, brain injuries, strokes, orthopedic injurie and amputations, as well as general rehabilitation ar ventilator services. Main Line Health, one of the foundir members of JHS, operates four hospitals and a number health centers in the suburbs of Philadelphia. Its clinic specialties include behavioral health, pediatrics, geriatric women's health and cancer, cardiac, pulmonary, orthoped and stroke care. The other founding member, Thoma Jefferson University Hospitals, operates two Philadelph teaching hospitals as well as Jefferson HealthCARE Voorhees, New Jersey and Jefferson Radiation Oncolog sites throughout the Delaware Valley. In 2007, the compar reached an agreement with Keystone Mercy Health Plan th includes new long-term hospital, physician, and ancilla provider contracts for the provision of healthcare services.

FINANCIALS:

Sales and profits are in thousands of dollars—add 000 to get the full amount. 2007 Note: Financial information for 2007 was not available for all companies at press time.

2007 Sales: $	2007 Profits: $	**U.S. Stock Ticker: Nonprofit**
2006 Sales: $3,202,500	2006 Profits: $237,700	**Int'l Ticker:** Int'l Exchange:
2005 Sales: $2,984,000	2005 Profits: $145,900	Employees: 27,000
2004 Sales: $2,732,100	2004 Profits: $81,200	Fiscal Year Ends: 6/30
2003 Sales: $2,499,900	2003 Profits: $	Parent Company:

SALARIES/BENEFITS:

Pension Plan:	ESOP Stock Plan:	Profit Sharing:	Top Exec. Salary: $	Bonus: $
Savings Plan:	Stock Purch. Plan:		Second Exec. Salary: $	Bonus: $

OTHER THOUGHTS:

Apparent Women Officers or Directors: 1
Hot Spot for Advancement for Women/Minorities:

LOCATIONS: ("Y" = Yes)

West:	Southwest:	Midwest:	Southeast:	Northeast:	International:
				Y	

JENNY CRAIG INC

www.jennycraig.com

Industry Group Code: 446190 **Ranks within this company's industry group:** Sales: Profits:

Insurance/HMO/PPO:		Drugs:		Equipment/Supplies:		Hospitals/Clinics:		Services:		Health Care:	
Insurance:		Manufacturer:		Manufacturer:		Acute Care:		Diagnostics:		Home Health:	
Managed Care:		Distributor:		Distributor:		Sub-Acute:		Labs/Testing:		Long-Term Care:	
Utilization Management:		Specialty Pharmacy:		Leasing/Finance:		Outpatient Surgery:		Staffing:		Physical Therapy:	
Payment Processing:		Vitamins/Nutritionals:		Information Systems:		Physical Rehab. Ctr.:		Waste Disposal:		Physician Prac. Mgmt.:	
		Clinical Trials:				Psychiatric Clinics:		Specialty Svcs.:	Y		

TYPES OF BUSINESS:

Weight Management Centers
Packaged Food
Video Production
Franchising
Online Sales & Services

BRANDS/DIVISIONS/AFFILIATES:

Nestle SA
Jenny Craig Platinum
Jenny Rewards
YourStyle
myJenny
Jenny Direct
Jenny Tuneup

CONTACTS: *Note: Officers with more than one job title may be intentionally listed here more than once.*

Patty Larchet, CEO
Jim Kelly, CFO
Scott Parker, VP-Mktg.
Chris Hilker, VP-Human Resources & Organizational Dev.
Lisa Talamini, VP-Research & Program Innovation
Shoukry Tiab, CIO/VP-IT
Lewis Shender, Chief Legal Officer
Dana Fisher, VP-Oper.
Lewis Shender, VP-New Bus. Dev.
Alan V. Dobies, VP-Corp. Svcs.
Doug Fisher, VP-Franchise Oper. & Dev.
Corrine Perritano, VP-Direct to Consumer Bus.

Phone: 760-696-4000 **Fax:** 760-696-4009
Toll-Free: 800-597-5366
Address: 5770 Fleet St., Carlsbad, CA 92008 US

GROWTH PLANS/SPECIAL FEATURES:

Jenny Craig, Inc. is a weight management company. The firm has 650 owned and franchised locations throughout the U.S., Canada, Australia, New Zealand and Puerto Rico. Jenny Craig offers clients personalized diet programs with the help of one-on-one consultations with weight loss counselors. Weight loss is achieved via personalized diet plans, which include Jenny's Cuisine food products and fresh foods prepared using Jenny Craig recipes; exercise plans; and counseling and support available online, by phone or in person at Jenny Craig centers. Program options include Jenny Craig Platinum, Jenny Craig Gold, Jenny Rewards and Jenny Tuneup. The company also offers Jenny Direct, an at-home program that delivers Jenny's Cuisine food items and provides once-a-week telephone consultations with a counselor. Once a weight goal is achieved, Jenny Craig offers weight maintenance programs with consultations and menu planning. Information is available for members on personal weight tracking, lifestyle planning and selected recipes through the company's myJenny online service. The web site also features a wide variety of popular food products such as Jenny's Cuisine breakfast, lunch, dinner and snack items, as well as sauces, dressings, cookbooks and exercise videos. The company also produces and markets DVDs, journals, CDs and workout accessories. The YourStyle program offers a flexible, customized weight management plan with a greater variety of menu choices. In January 2006, Jenny Craig partnered with Dr. Martha Beck, an internationally-recognized life coach, to create Touchstones for Success, a package combing a DVD, CD and five Touchstones, which feature inspirational thoughts. In June 2006, Nestle S.A. bought the company for $600 million.

The company offers its employees life and AD&D insurance; an employee assistance program; medical, dental, prescription and vision insurance; long-term disability insurance; and a 401(k) plan.

FINANCIALS: **Sales and profits are in thousands of dollars—add 000 to get the full amount. 2007 Note: Financial information for 2007 was not available for all companies at press time.**

2007 Sales: $	2007 Profits: $	**U.S. Stock Ticker: Subsidiary**
2006 Sales: $	2006 Profits: $	**Int'l Ticker:** Int'l Exchange:
2005 Sales: $	2005 Profits: $	Employees: 3,000
2004 Sales: $360,000	2004 Profits: $	Fiscal Year Ends:
2003 Sales: $280,000	2003 Profits: $	Parent Company: NESTLE SA

SALARIES/BENEFITS:

Pension Plan:	ESOP Stock Plan:	Profit Sharing:	Top Exec. Salary: $	Bonus: $
Savings Plan: Y	Stock Purch. Plan:		Second Exec. Salary: $	Bonus: $

OTHER THOUGHTS:

Apparent Women Officers or Directors: 4
Hot Spot for Advancement for Women/Minorities: Y

LOCATIONS: ("Y" = Yes)

West:	Southwest:	Midwest:	Southeast:	Northeast:	International:
Y	Y	Y	Y	Y	Y

JOHNS HOPKINS MEDICINE www.hopkinsmedicine.org

Industry Group Code: 622110 **Ranks within this company's industry group:** Sales: Profits:

Insurance/HMO/PPO:		Drugs:		Equipment/Supplies:		Hospitals/Clinics:		Services:		Health Care:	
Insurance:		Manufacturer:		Manufacturer:		Acute Care:	Y	Diagnostics:		Home Health:	Y
Managed Care:		Distributor:		Distributor:		Sub-Acute:	Y	Labs/Testing:		Long-Term Care:	
Utilization Management:		Specialty Pharmacy:		Leasing/Finance:		Outpatient Surgery:		Staffing:		Physical Therapy:	Y
Payment Processing:		Vitamins/Nutritionals:		Information Systems:		Physical Rehab. Ctr.:	Y	Waste Disposal:		Physician Prac. Mgmt.:	Y
		Clinical Trials:				Psychiatric Clinics:		Specialty Svcs.:	Y		

TYPES OF BUSINESS:

Medical Care
Medical Research
Medical School
Home Care Services
Physician Network Management

BRANDS/DIVISIONS/AFFILIATES:

Johns Hopkins University School of Medicine
Johns Hopkins Health System
Johns Hopkins Hospital and Outpatient Center
Johns Hopkins Bayview Medical Center
Johns Hopkins HealthCare
Johns Hopkins Bloomberg School of Public Health
Johns Hopkins School of Nursing

CONTACTS: *Note: Officers with more than one job title may be intentionally listed here more than once.*

Edward D. Miller, CEO
Richard A. Grossi, CFO/VP
Chi V. Dang, Vice Dean-Research
Stephanie Reel, VP-Info. Svcs.
Steven J. Thompson, Vice Dean-Admin.
Joanne E. Pollak, General Counsel/VP
Toby A. Gordon, VP-Strategic Planning & Market Research
Elaine Freeman, VP-Corp. Comm.
William R. Brody, Pres., Johns Hopkins University
Ronald R. Peterson, Pres., Johns Hopkins Hospital & Health System
Judy Reitz, VP-Quality Improvement
Joseph R. Coppola, VP-Corp. Security
C. Michael Armstrong, Chmn.

Phone: 410-955-5000	**Fax:** 410-955-4452
Toll-Free:	
Address: 720 Rutland Ave., Baltimore, MD 21205 US	

GROWTH PLANS/SPECIAL FEATURES:

Johns Hopkins Medicine is a nonprofit organization tha includes Johns Hopkins University School of Medicine an the Johns Hopkins Health System. The medical schoo consists of 32 academic departments from anesthesiology urology. Although the University is headquartered i Baltimore, Maryland, it has campuses in China, Italy an Singapore. In addition, John Hopkins Medicine als operates many other educational programs, including John Hopkins School of Nursing, Johns Hopkins Bloomber School of Public Health and graduate and continuin education. Johns Hopkins Health System provide comprehensive health care services, operating primaril through its three Maryland hospitals. The Johns Hopkin Hospital and Outpatient Center has been rated the bes hospital in the nation for over a decade, treating patient from around the world. Johns Hopkins Bayview Medica Center is a teaching hospital housing a neonatal intensiv care unit, sleep disorders center, area-wide trauma center regional burn center and a nationally regarded geriatric center on its 130-acre campus. The organization also offer a home care group that provides visits by nurses, physical occupational and speech therapists, home health aides an social workers; a network of physicians providing community based health care; three facilities at which faculty physician practice; and programs to assist patients and families from foreign countries or other U.S. cities with physicia appointments, lodging, transportation, interpreter services financial arrangements, day care centers and sightseeing Johns Hopkins HealthCare serves medical professionals an payers by providing eligibility database management member-physician services, claims adjudication, car management, patient outreach programs, decision suppor matrices, client-focused product development an physician/facility network development and management.

Johns Hopkins provides its professionals with a number o benefits including child/elder care, education benefits, a 403(b) retirement savings plan and Wellnet, which provide wellness services such as health assessment an motivational programs.

FINANCIALS: **Sales and profits are in thousands of dollars—add 000 to get the full amount. 2007 Note: Financial information for 2007 was not available for all companies at press time.**

2007 Sales: $	2007 Profits: $	**U.S. Stock Ticker: Nonprofit**
2006 Sales: $	2006 Profits: $	**Int'l Ticker:** Int'l Exchange:
2005 Sales: $	2005 Profits: $	Employees: 25,000
2004 Sales: $2,994,700	2004 Profits: $29,800	Fiscal Year Ends: 6/30
2003 Sales: $1,600,000	2003 Profits: $	Parent Company:

SALARIES/BENEFITS:

Pension Plan:	ESOP Stock Plan:	Profit Sharing:	Top Exec. Salary: $	Bonus: $
Savings Plan: Y	Stock Purch. Plan:		Second Exec. Salary: $	Bonus: $

OTHER THOUGHTS:

Apparent Women Officers or Directors: 6
Hot Spot for Advancement for Women/Minorities: Y

LOCATIONS: ("Y" = Yes)

West:	Southwest:	Midwest:	Southeast:	Northeast:	International:
				Y	Y

Note: Financial information, benefits and other data can change quickly and may vary from those stated here.

JOHNSON & JOHNSON www.jnj.com

ndustry Group Code: 325412 **Ranks within this company's industry group:** Sales: 1 Profits: 2

nsurance/HMO/PPO:		Drugs:		Equipment/Supplies:		Hospitals/Clinics:		Services:		Health Care:	
nsurance:		Manufacturer:	Y	Manufacturer:	Y	Acute Care:		Diagnostics:		Home Health:	
lanaged Care:		Distributor:	Y	Distributor:	Y	Sub-Acute:		Labs/Testing:		Long-Term Care:	
tilization Management:		Specialty Pharmacy:		Leasing/Finance:		Outpatient Surgery:		Staffing:		Physical Therapy:	
ayment Processing:		Vitamins/Nutritionals:		Information Systems:		Physical Rehab. Ctr.:		Waste Disposal:		Physician Prac. Mgmt.:	
		Clinical Trials:				Psychiatric Clinics:		Specialty Svcs.:			

TYPES OF BUSINESS:

ersonal Health Care & Hygiene Products
terilization Products
urgical Products
harmaceuticals
kin Care Products
aby Care Products
ontact Lenses
ledical Equipment

BRANDS/DIVISIONS/AFFILIATES:

isperdal
Mylanta
Band-Aid
ylenol
Monistat
McNeil Nutritionals, LLC
Hand Innovations
Conor Medsystems, Inc.

CONTACTS: *Note: Officers with more than one job title may be ntentionally listed here more than once.*

Villiam C. Weldon, CEO
ames T. Lenehan, Pres.
Dominic J. Caruso, CFO
Kaye Foster-Check, VP-Human Resources
Per A. Peterson, Chmn., R&D Pharmaceuticals Group
Russell C. Deyo, General Counsel/Chief Compliance Officer
Dominic J. Caruso, VP-Finance
Colleen A. Goggins, Worldwide Chmn., Consumer & Personal Care
Christine A. Poon, Worldwide Chmn., Medicine & Nutritionals
oseph C. Scodari, Chmn., Pharmaceuticals Group
Michael J. Dormer, Chmn.-Medical Devices
Villiam C. Weldon, Chmn.

Phone: 732-524-0400	Fax: 732-524-3300
Toll-Free:	
Address: One Johnson & Johnson Plaza, New Brunswick, NJ 08933 US	

GROWTH PLANS/SPECIAL FEATURES:

Johnson & Johnson, founded in 1886, is one of the world's most comprehensive and well-known manufacturers of health care products. The firm owns more than 250 companies in over 90 countries and markets its products in almost every country in the world. Johnson & Johnson's worldwide operations are divided into three segments: consumer, pharmaceutical, and medical devices and diagnostics. The company's principal consumer goods are personal care and hygiene products, including nonprescription drugs, adult skin and hair care, baby care, oral care, first aid and sanitary protection products. Major consumer brands include Mylanta, Band-Aid, Tylenol, Aveeno and Monistat. The pharmaceutical segment covers a wide spectrum of health fields, including antifungal, anti-infective, cardiovascular, dermatology, immunology, pain management, psychotropic and women's health. Among its pharmaceutical products are Risperdal, an antipsychotic used to treat schizophrenia, and Remicade for the treatment of Crohn's disease and rheumatoid arthritis. In the medical devices and diagnostics segment, Johnson & Johnson makes a number of products including suture and mechanical wound closure products, surgical instruments, disposable contact lenses, joint replacement products and intravenous catheters. Johnson & Johnson is pursuing nanotechnology applications in the biomedical fields primarily through research and funding agreements with other biotech companies, including Cordis. In early 2006, the company acquired Hand Innovations, Animas Corporation and Guidant Corporation. The $24 billion Guidant purchase will contribute an extensive line of life-saving technology for cardiac and vascular patients. In December 2006, Johnson & Johnson acquired Pfizer, Inc.'s Consumer Healthcare unit for $16.6 billion. In early 2007, Johnson & Johnson acquired Conor Medsystems, Inc., a cardiovascular device developer.

Johnson & Johnson offers its employees comprehensive heath and wellness. Some locations offer on-site child care centers and Nurture Space programs through which new mothers get counseling on how to return to work while breastfeeding.

FINANCIALS: **Sales and profits are in thousands of dollars—add 000 to get the full amount. 2007 Note: Financial information for 2007 was not available for all companies at press time.**

2007 Sales: $	2007 Profits: $	**U.S. Stock Ticker: JNJ**
2006 Sales: $53,324,000	2006 Profits: $11,053,000	**Int'l Ticker:** Int'l Exchange:
2005 Sales: $50,514,000	2005 Profits: $10,060,000	Employees: 122,200
2004 Sales: $47,348,000	2004 Profits: $8,180,000	Fiscal Year Ends: 12/31
2003 Sales: $41,862,000	2003 Profits: $7,197,000	Parent Company:

SALARIES/BENEFITS:

Pension Plan: Y	ESOP Stock Plan:	Profit Sharing:	Top Exec. Salary: $1,659,231	Bonus: $7,461,440
Savings Plan: Y	Stock Purch. Plan:		Second Exec. Salary: $1,023,846	Bonus: $2,574,880

OTHER THOUGHTS:

Apparent Women Officers or Directors: 3
Hot Spot for Advancement for Women/Minorities: Y

LOCATIONS: ("Y" = Yes)

West:	Southwest:	Midwest:	Southeast:	Northeast:	International:
Y	Y	Y	Y	Y	Y

KAISER PERMANENTE www.kaiserpermanente.org

Industry Group Code: 622110 **Ranks within this company's industry group:** Sales: 1 Profits:

Insurance/HMO/PPO:		Drugs:		Equipment/Supplies:		Hospitals/Clinics:		Services:		Health Care:	
Insurance:	Y	Manufacturer:		Manufacturer:		Acute Care:	Y	Diagnostics:		Home Health:	
Managed Care:	Y	Distributor:		Distributor:		Sub-Acute:	Y	Labs/Testing:		Long-Term Care:	
Utilization Management:		Specialty Pharmacy:		Leasing/Finance:		Outpatient Surgery:	Y	Staffing:		Physical Therapy:	
Payment Processing:		Vitamins/Nutritionals:		Information Systems:		Physical Rehab. Ctr.:		Waste Disposal:		Physician Prac. Mgmt.:	
		Clinical Trials:				Psychiatric Clinics:		Specialty Svcs.:			

TYPES OF BUSINESS:

Hospitals & Clinics
General & Specialty Hospitals
Outpatient Facilities
HMO
Health Insurance
Integrated Health Care System
Physician Networks

BRANDS/DIVISIONS/AFFILIATES:

Kaiser Foundation Health Plan, Inc.
Kaiser Foundation Hospitals
Permanente Medical Groups
KP HealthConnect
Coalition of Kaiser Permanente Unions (The)
Kaiser Permanente Healthcare Institute
National Labor College

CONTACTS: *Note: Officers with more than one job title may be intentionally listed here more than once.*

George C. Halvorson, CEO
Kathy Lancaster, CFO/Sr. VP
Thomas A. Curtin Jr., Sr. VP-Nat'l Sales & Account Mgmt.
Laurence G. O'Neil, Sr. VP-Human Resources
Robert M. Crane, Sr. VP-Research
J. Clifford Dodd, CIO/Sr. VP
J. Clifford Dodd, Chief Admin. Officer/Sr. VP
Steven Zatkin, General Counsel/Sr. VP
Arthur M. Southam, Exec. VP-Health Plan Oper.
Robert M. Crane, Sr. VP-Policy Dev.
Anna-Lisa Silvestre, VP-Online Svcs.
Jack Cochran, Exec. Dir.-The Permanente Federation
Raymond J. Baxter, Sr. VP-Community Benefit
Louise L. Liang, Sr. VP-Quality & Clinical Systems Support
Bernard J. Tyson, Sr. VP-Health Plan & Hospital Oper.
George C. Halvorson, Chmn.

Phone: 510-271-5800	**Fax:** 510-267-7524
Toll-Free:	
Address: 1 Kaiser Plz., Ste. 2600, Oakland, CA 94612-3673 US	

GROWTH PLANS/SPECIAL FEATURES:

Kaiser Permanente is a non-profit company dedicated providing integrated health care coverage. This natio leading company operates in Washington, D.C. and nir states: California, Colorado, Georgia, Hawaii, Marylan Ohio, Oregon, Virginia and Washington. It serves almost 8 million members, of which approximately 6.5 million are California. Kaiser has three main operating divisions: Kais Foundation Health Plan, Inc., which contracts with individua and groups to provide medical coverage; Kaiser Foundatic Hospitals and their subsidiaries, operating communi hospitals and outpatient facilities in several states; ar Permanente Medical Groups, the company's network physicians providing health care to its members. Th company resources include 32 medical centers, includir hospitals and outpatient facilities; 431 medical offices; ar 13,000 physicians. Kaiser Foundation Hospitals also fur medical and health-related research. The firm, as participant in the Medicare program, cares for approximate 880,000 Medicare members, making it the largest healt plan serving the Medicare program. The KP HealthConne program integrates clinical records with appointment registration and billing, thereby significantly improving ca delivery and patient satisfaction. In May 2007, the fir announced a joint donation of $450,000, made in conjunctio with the Coalition of Kaiser Permanente Unions, to th Maryland based National Labor College, in order to establis the Kaiser Permanente Healthcare Institute, which w educate labor leaders and union members in health ca issues, including courses on health care bargaining. February 2007, the firm's Northern California Division Research launched a massive program to investigate th links between environmental factors, such as air qualit water purity, lifestyles or habits, to specific diseases, such a cancer, diabetes, Alzheimer's disease and others.

Kaiser Permanente's employee health care coverag extends to spouses and domestic partners and unmarrie children; and it provides paid time off for vacation designated holidays, sick leave and what it calls life balanc days.

FINANCIALS: Sales and profits are in thousands of dollars—add 000 to get the full amount. 2007 Note: Financial information for 2007 was not available for all companies at press time.

2007 Sales: $	2007 Profits: $	**U.S. Stock Ticker: Nonprofit**
2006 Sales: $34,600,000	2006 Profits: $	**Int'l Ticker:** Int'l Exchange:
2005 Sales: $31,100,000	2005 Profits: $1,000,000	Employees: 156,000
2004 Sales: $26,600,000	2004 Profits: $1,600,000	Fiscal Year Ends: 12/31
2003 Sales: $25,300,000	2003 Profits: $996,000	Parent Company:

SALARIES/BENEFITS:

Pension Plan: Y	ESOP Stock Plan:	Profit Sharing:	Top Exec. Salary: $	Bonus: $
Savings Plan: Y	Stock Purch. Plan:		Second Exec. Salary: $	Bonus: $

OTHER THOUGHTS:

Apparent Women Officers or Directors: 3
Hot Spot for Advancement for Women/Minorities: Y

LOCATIONS: ("Y" = Yes)

West:	Southwest:	Midwest:	Southeast:	Northeast:	International:
Y		Y	Y	Y	

KENDLE INTERNATIONAL INC www.kendle.com

Industry Group Code: 325412 **Ranks within this company's industry group:** Sales: 33 Profits: 29

Insurance/HMO/PPO:		Drugs:		Equipment/Supplies:		Hospitals/Clinics:		Services:		Health Care:	
Insurance:		Manufacturer:		Manufacturer:		Acute Care:		Diagnostics:		Home Health:	
Managed Care:		Distributor:		Distributor:		Sub-Acute:		Labs/Testing:	Y	Long-Term Care:	
Utilization Management:		Specialty Pharmacy:		Leasing/Finance:		Outpatient Surgery:		Staffing:		Physical Therapy:	
Payment Processing:		Vitamins/Nutritionals:		Information Systems:	Y	Physical Rehab. Ctr.:		Waste Disposal:		Physician Prac. Mgmt.:	
		Clinical Trials:	Y			Psychiatric Clinics:		Specialty Svcs.:	Y		

TYPES OF BUSINESS:

Pharmaceutical Development-Clinical Trials
Statistical Analysis
Technical Writing
Regulatory Assistance
Consulting Services
Clinical Trial Software
Clinical Data Management
e-Learning

BRANDS/DIVISIONS/AFFILIATES:

eKendleCollege
TrialWare
TrialWeb
TrialBase
TrialView
TriaLine
eKendleCollege
Latin American CRO Int'l Clinical Research, Ltd.

CONTACTS:

Note: Officers with more than one job title may be intentionally listed here more than once.

Candace Kendle, CEO
Christopher Bergen, COO
Christopher Bergen, Pres.
Karl Brenkert, III, CFO/Sr. VP
Simon Higginbotham, Chief Mktg. Officer/VP
Karen L. Crone, VP-Global Human Resources
Gary Wedig, CIO
Anthony Forcellini, VP-Strategic Dev.
Anthony Forcellini, Treas.
Dennis Hurley, VP-Global Clinical Dev. Latin America
Martha Feller, VP-Global Clinical Dev. North America
Dieter Seitz-Tutter, VP-Global Clinical Dev. Europe
Cynthia L. Verst, VP-Late Phase
Candace Kendle, Chmn.

Phone: 513-381-5550 **Fax:** 513-381-5870
Toll-Free: 800-733-1572
Address: 1200 Carew Tower, 441 Vine St., Cincinnati, OH 45202 US

GROWTH PLANS/SPECIAL FEATURES:

Kendle International, Inc. is a leading global clinical research organization that provides a broad range of Phase I-IV global clinical development services to the biopharmaceutical industry. The company augments the research and development activities of biopharmaceutical companies by offering value-added clinical research services and proprietary information technology designed to reduce drug development time and expense. The firm operates in two segments: Early Stage, which handles all Phase I testing services; and Late Stage, which handles all Phase II-IV services. Kendle's services include clinical trial management, clinical data management, statistical analysis, technical writing and regulatory consulting and representation. It runs a state-of-the-art clinical pharmacology unit in the Netherlands, where it offers services for drugs undergoing clinical trials. The company's therapeutic expertise covers fields such as cardiovascular, dermatology, hematology, oncology, respiratory and women's health. Through its health care communications division, the firm provides organizational, meeting management and publication services to various professional associations and pharmaceutical companies. The firm's proprietary TrialWare product line includes a database management system, TrialBase; an interactive voice response patient randomization system, TriaLine; a validated medical imaging system, TrialView; a global project management system, TrialWatch; an Internet based collaborative tool, TrialWeb; and a late phase technology system, Trial4. Additionally, the company operates eKendleCollege, an online e-learning division that runs seminars and training programs, focusing on the organization of clinical trials. In 2006, Kendle acquired Latin America CRO International Clinical Research Limited, a late stage clinical research company with operations in Argentina, Brazil, Chile and Colombia. Later that year, the company acquired the late phase service business of Charles River Laboratories International, Inc.

Kendle offers its employees flexible work schedules, business-casual dress and continuing education through its corporate university and tuition reimbursement program, as well as the option to telecommute.

FINANCIALS:

Sales and profits are in thousands of dollars—add 000 to get the full amount. 2007 Note: Financial information for 2007 was not available for all companies at press time.

2007 Sales: $	2007 Profits: $	**U.S. Stock Ticker: KNDL**
2006 Sales: $373,936	2006 Profits: $8,530	**Int'l Ticker:** Int'l Exchange:
2005 Sales: $250,639	2005 Profits: $10,674	Employees: 3,050
2004 Sales: $215,868	2004 Profits: $3,572	Fiscal Year Ends: 12/31
2003 Sales: $209,657	2003 Profits: $-1,690	Parent Company:

SALARIES/BENEFITS:

Pension Plan:	ESOP Stock Plan:	Profit Sharing: Y	Top Exec. Salary: $344,578	Bonus: $50,170
Savings Plan: Y	Stock Purch. Plan: Y		Second Exec. Salary: $298,619	Bonus: $38,647

OTHER THOUGHTS:

Apparent Women Officers or Directors: 6
Hot Spot for Advancement for Women/Minorities: Y

LOCATIONS: ("Y" = Yes)

West:	Southwest:	Midwest:	Southeast:	Northeast:	International:
		Y		Y	Y

Note: Financial information, benefits and other data can change quickly and may vary from those stated here.

KIMBERLY CLARK CORP www.kimberly-clark.com

Industry Group Code: 322000 **Ranks within this company's industry group:** Sales: 1 Profits: 1

Insurance/HMO/PPO:		Drugs:		Equipment/Supplies:		Hospitals/Clinics:		Services:		Health Care:	
Insurance:		Manufacturer:		Manufacturer:	Y	Acute Care:		Diagnostics:		Home Health:	
Managed Care:		Distributor:		Distributor:		Sub-Acute:		Labs/Testing:		Long-Term Care:	
Utilization Management:		Specialty Pharmacy:		Leasing/Finance:		Outpatient Surgery:		Staffing:		Physical Therapy:	
Payment Processing:		Vitamins/Nutritionals:		Information Systems:		Physical Rehab. Ctr.:		Waste Disposal:		Physician Prac. Mgmt.:	
		Clinical Trials:				Psychiatric Clinics:		Specialty Svcs.:			

TYPES OF BUSINESS:

Personal Care Products-Paper
Consumer Tissue Products
Safety Products
Healthcare Products

BRANDS/DIVISIONS/AFFILIATES:

Kleenex
Scott
Huggies
Kotex
Depend
Pull-Ups
Poise
Wypall

CONTACTS: *Note: Officers with more than one job title may be intentionally listed here more than once.*

Thomas J. Falk, CEO
Mark A. Buthman, CFO/Sr. VP
Anthony J. Palmer, Chief Mktg. Officer/Sr. VP
Lizanne C. Gottung, Sr. VP-Human Resources
Robert W. Black, Chief Strategy Officer/Sr. VP
Robert E. Abernathy, Pres., Developing & Emerging Markets
Joanne Bauer, Pres., Healthcare Bus.
Steven R. Kalmanson, Pres., North Atlantic Consumer Prod.
Jan B. Spencer, Pres., Kimberly-Clark Professional
Thomas J. Falk, Chmn.

Phone: 972-281-1200	Fax: 972-281-1490
Toll-Free:	
Address: 351 Phelps Dr., Irving, TX 75038 US	

GROWTH PLANS/SPECIAL FEATURES:

Kimberly-Clark Corp. (KC) is a global health and hygier company. The firm is principally engaged in th manufacturing and marketing of a wide range of health ar hygiene products around the world. Most of these produc are made from natural or synthetic fibers using technologie in fibers, nonwovens and absorbency. KC operates in fo segments: personal care; consumer tissue; K-C profession & other; and healthcare. The personal care segme manufactures and markets disposable diapers, training ar youth pants, and swimpants; baby wipes; feminine ar incontinence care products; and related products. Produc in this segment are primarily for household use and are so under brand names such as Huggies, Pull-Ups, Litt Swimmer, GoodNites, Kotex, Lightdays, Depend and Pois The consumer tissue segment manufactures and marke facial and bathroom tissue; paper towels; napkins; an related products for household use. Products in this divisic are sold under brands such as Kleenex, Scott, Cottonell Viva, Andrex, Scottex, Hakle and Page. The K- professional & other segment manufactures and marke facial and bathroom tissue; paper towels; napkins; wiper and a range of safety products the for away-from-hom marketplace. Brand names in this segment includ Kimberly-Clark, Kleenex, Scott, WypAll, Kimtech, Kleengua and Kimcare. The healthcare segment manufactures an markets healthcare products such as surgical gown drapes; infection control products; sterilization wra disposable face masks and exam gloves; respirato products; and other disposable medical products. Produc in this division are sold under the Kimberly-Clark and Balla brand names. In November 2006, KC increased it ownership to 100% in its Brazilian affiliate Kimberly-Cla Industria e Comercio Ltda.

The company offers its employees medical and dent insurance; short- and long-term disability insurance; life an business travel insurance; an incentive investment plan; an a retirement contribution plan.

FINANCIALS: **Sales and profits are in thousands of dollars—add 000 to get the full amount. 2007 Note: Financial information for 2007 was not available for all companies at press time.**

2007 Sales: $	2007 Profits: $	**U.S. Stock Ticker: KMB**
2006 Sales: $16,746,900	2006 Profits: $1,499,500	**Int'l Ticker:** Int'l Exchange:
2005 Sales: $15,902,600	2005 Profits: $1,568,300	Employees: 55,000
2004 Sales: $15,083,200	2004 Profits: $1,800,200	Fiscal Year Ends: 12/31
2003 Sales: $14,348,000	2003 Profits: $1,694,200	Parent Company:

SALARIES/BENEFITS:

Pension Plan: Y	ESOP Stock Plan:	Profit Sharing:	Top Exec. Salary: $1,175,000	Bonus: $1,367,700
Savings Plan:	Stock Purch. Plan:		Second Exec. Salary: $618,000	Bonus: $476,362

OTHER THOUGHTS:

Apparent Women Officers or Directors: 4
Hot Spot for Advancement for Women/Minorities: Y

LOCATIONS: ("Y" = Yes)

West:	Southwest:	Midwest:	Southeast:	Northeast:	International:
Y	Y	Y	Y	Y	Y

KINDRED HEALTHCARE INC www.kindredhealthcare.com

ndustry Group Code: 623110 **Ranks within this company's industry group:** Sales: 1 Profits: 2

nsurance/HMO/PPO:		Drugs:		Equipment/Supplies:		Hospitals/Clinics:		Services:		Health Care:	
nsurance:		Manufacturer:		Manufacturer:		Acute Care:	Y	Diagnostics:		Home Health:	
Managed Care:		Distributor:		Distributor:		Sub-Acute:		Labs/Testing:		Long-Term Care:	Y
tilization Management:		Specialty Pharmacy:	Y	Leasing/Finance:		Outpatient Surgery:		Staffing:		Physical Therapy:	Y
Payment Processing:		Vitamins/Nutritionals:		Information Systems:		Physical Rehab. Ctr.:	Y	Waste Disposal:		Physician Prac. Mgmt.:	
		Clinical Trials:				Psychiatric Clinics:		Specialty Svcs.:			

TYPES OF BUSINESS:

Hospitals
Nursing Centers
nstitutional Pharmacies
Contract Rehabilitation Services

BRANDS/DIVISIONS/AFFILIATES:

Peoplefirst Rehabilitation
AmerisourceBergen Corp.
PharMerica Corp.

CONTACTS: *Note: Officers with more than one job title may be intentionally listed here more than once.*

Paul J. Diaz, CEO
Paul J. Diaz, Pres.
Richard A. Lechleiter, CFO/Exec. VP
Richard E. Chapman, CIO/Exec. VP
Richard E. Chapman, Chief Admin. Officer
M. Suzanne Riedman, General Counsel/Sr. VP
Gregory C. Miller, Sr. VP-Corp. Dev. & Financial Planning
Frank J. Battafarano, Exec. VP/Pres., Hospital Division
Lane M. Bowen, Exec. VP/Pres., Health Svcs. Division
William M. Altman, Sr. VP-Compliance & Gov't Programs
Joseph L. Landenwich, Sr. VP-Corp. Legal Affairs/Corp. Sec.
Edward J. Diaz, Exec. Chmn.

Phone: 502-596-7300	**Fax:** 502-596-4170
Toll-Free: 800-545-0749	
Address: 680 S. 4th St., Louisville, KY 40202 US	

GROWTH PLANS/SPECIAL FEATURES:

Kindred Healthcare, Inc. is a healthcare services company that operates hospitals, nursing centers, institutional pharmacies and a contract rehabilitation services business across the U.S. The company runs four operating divisions. The hospital division operates 81 long-term acute care hospitals with 6,419 licensed beds in 24 states. The firm treats medically complex patients, including the critically ill, suffering from multiple organ system failures, most commonly the cardiovascular, pulmonary, gastro-intestinal and cutaneous systems. A number of hospitals in this division offer outpatient services, which may include diagnostic services, rehabilitation therapy, CT scanning, one-day surgery, laboratory and X-ray. More than 70% of patients are over 65 years of age. The health service division operates 242 nursing centers with 30,664 licensed beds in 28 states. Through its nursing centers, Kindred Healthcare provides long-term care services; a full range of pharmacy, medical and clinical services; and routine services, including daily, dietary, social and recreational services. A number of nursing centers offer specialized programs for residents suffering from Alzheimer's disease and other dementias. The contract rehabilitation services business provides rehabilitative services under the name Peoplefirst Rehabilitation primarily in long-term care settings. In addition to standard physical, occupational and speech therapies, the company provides specialized care programs designed to deal with dementia and Alzheimer's disease, wound care, pain management and pulmonary therapies. The pharmacy division operates an institutional pharmacy business with 46 pharmacies in 26 states and a pharmacy management business servicing substantially all of the firm's hospitals. The segment purchases, repackages and dispenses pharmaceuticals, both prescription and non-prescription, in accordance with physician orders and delivers such medication to the healthcare facility for administration to patients. In July 2007, Kindred Healthcare and AmerisourceBergen Corp. announced the completion of the transaction that combines their respective institutional pharmacy businesses to create PharMerica Corp., a new, independent company.

FINANCIALS: **Sales and profits are in thousands of dollars—add 000 to get the full amount. 2007 Note: Financial information for 2007 was not available for all companies at press time.**

2007 Sales: $	2007 Profits: $	**U.S. Stock Ticker: KND**
2006 Sales: $4,266,661	2006 Profits: $78,711	**Int'l Ticker:** Int'l Exchange:
2005 Sales: $3,852,975	2005 Profits: $144,909	Employees: 55,000
2004 Sales: $3,421,411	2004 Profits: $70,580	Fiscal Year Ends: 12/31
2003 Sales: $3,284,019	2003 Profits: $-75,336	Parent Company:

SALARIES/BENEFITS:

Pension Plan:	ESOP Stock Plan:	Profit Sharing:	Top Exec. Salary: $847,906	Bonus: $1,432,779
Savings Plan:	Stock Purch. Plan:		Second Exec. Salary: $635,928	Bonus: $

OTHER THOUGHTS:

Apparent Women Officers or Directors: 3
Hot Spot for Advancement for Women/Minorities: Y

LOCATIONS: ("Y" = Yes)

West:	Southwest:	Midwest:	Southeast:	Northeast:	International:
Y	Y	Y	Y	Y	

KINETIC CONCEPTS INC

www.kci1.com

Industry Group Code: 339113 **Ranks within this company's industry group:** Sales: 24 Profits: 18

Insurance/HMO/PPO:		Drugs:		Equipment/Supplies:		Hospitals/Clinics:		Services:		Health Care:	
Insurance:		Manufacturer:		Manufacturer:	Y	Acute Care:		Diagnostics:		Home Health:	
Managed Care:		Distributor:		Distributor:	Y	Sub-Acute:		Labs/Testing:		Long-Term Care:	
Utilization Management:		Specialty Pharmacy:		Leasing/Finance:		Outpatient Surgery:		Staffing:		Physical Therapy:	
Payment Processing:		Vitamins/Nutritionals:		Information Systems:		Physical Rehab. Ctr.:		Waste Disposal:		Physician Prac. Mgmt.:	
		Clinical Trials:				Psychiatric Clinics:		Specialty Svcs.:			

TYPES OF BUSINESS:

Equipment-Specialized Mattresses & Beds
Kinetic Therapy Products
Therapeutic Support Surfaces
Wound Closure Devices
Circulatory Devices

BRANDS/DIVISIONS/AFFILIATES:

Roto Rest Delta
FirstStep
KinAir
AtmosAir
Vacuum Assisted Closure
BariAir Therapy System
TriaDyne
PediDyne

CONTACTS: *Note: Officers with more than one job title may be intentionally listed here more than once.*

Catherine M. Burzik, CEO
Catherine M. Burzik, Pres.
Martin J. Landon, CFO/VP
R. James Cravens, VP-Human Resources
Daniel C. Wadsworth, Jr., VP-Global R&D
David H. Ramsey, CIO/Sr. VP
Michael J. Burke, VP-Mfg. & Quality
Stephen D. Seidel, General Counsel/Sr. VP/Corp. Sec.
G. Frederick Rush, VP-Corp. Dev.
Mark Carbeau, Pres., KCI USA
Linwood Staub, Pres., Global V.A.C. Therapy
Daniel Ciaburri, Chief Medical Officer
Ronald W. Dollens, Chmn.
Jorg W. Menten, Pres., CKI Intl.

Phone: 210-524-9000	**Fax:** 210-255-6998
Toll-Free: 800-275-4524	
Address: 8023 Vantage Dr., San Antonio, TX 78230-4726 US	

GROWTH PLANS/SPECIAL FEATURES:

Kinetic Concepts, Inc. (KCI) is a global medical technolog company that designs, manufactures, markets and service proprietary products that can improve clinical outcomes b accelerating the healing process or preventing complication The company operates through a network of 141 U.S. ar 67 international service centers that work with over 2,60 medium-to-large hospitals, 3,900 acute care hospitals, 6,90 extended care organizations and 10,500 home health ca agencies. KCI's medical systems and therapeutic surface are used in four major clinical applications. Its wour healing and tissue repair systems incorporate Vacuu Assisted Closure technology, consisting of the therapy unit, foam dressing, an occlusive drape, a tube system connectir the dressing to the therapy unit and a canister. This negativ pressure therapy is used on serious trauma wounds, faile surgical closures, amputations, burns covering a larg portion of the body, serious pressure ulcers and other difficu wounds. For treatment of immobile patients with life threatening conditions, KCI offers the Prone Therapy, Kinet Prone Therapy and Kinetic Therapy systems, which rota the patient by up to 40 degrees on either side, using kinet therapy to promote pulmonary health. The company therapeutic surfaces for wound treatment and preventic treat pressure sores, burns, ulcers, skin grafts and other sk conditions. They also help prevent the formation of pressu sores in certain immobile individuals by reducing frictio between skin and bed and by using surfaces supported b air, foam, silicon beads or viscous fluid. These include th KinAir and FluidAir beds, FirstStep and TriCell overlays an AtmosAir seating surfaces. The TheraPulse framed bed and DynaPulse overlay also provide treatment through continuous pulsating action that improves patients capillar and lymphatic circulation. Finally, the company produce bariatric support surfaces and aids for obese patient including the BariAir Therapy System, which can serve as bed, chair, weigh scale and examination table.

FINANCIALS: Sales and profits are in thousands of dollars—add 000 to get the full amount. 2007 Note: Financial information for 2007 was not available for all companies at press time.

2007 Sales: $	2007 Profits: $	**U.S. Stock Ticker: KCI**
2006 Sales: $1,371,636	2006 Profits: $195,468	**Int'l Ticker:** Int'l Exchange:
2005 Sales: $1,208,556	2005 Profits: $122,155	Employees: 6,300
2004 Sales: $992,636	2004 Profits: $96,488	Fiscal Year Ends: 12/31
2003 Sales: $763,836	2003 Profits: $69,646	Parent Company:

SALARIES/BENEFITS:

Pension Plan:	ESOP Stock Plan:	Profit Sharing:	Top Exec. Salary: $667,500	Bonus: $459,000
Savings Plan: Y	Stock Purch. Plan: Y		Second Exec. Salary: $343,750	Bonus: $169,400

OTHER THOUGHTS:

Apparent Women Officers or Directors: 1
Hot Spot for Advancement for Women/Minorities:

LOCATIONS: ("Y" = Yes)

West:	Southwest:	Midwest:	Southeast:	Northeast:	International:
	Y				Y

KYPHON INC www.kyphon.com

ıdustry Group Code: 339113 **Ranks within this company's industry group:** Sales: 47 Profits: 38

ısurance/HMO/PPO:		Drugs:		Equipment/Supplies:		Hospitals/Clinics:		Services:		Health Care:	
ısurance:		Manufacturer:		Manufacturer:	Y	Acute Care:		Diagnostics:		Home Health:	
lanaged Care:		Distributor:		Distributor:		Sub-Acute:		Labs/Testing:		Long-Term Care:	
tilization Management:		Specialty Pharmacy:		Leasing/Finance:		Outpatient Surgery:		Staffing:		Physical Therapy:	
ayment Processing:		Vitamins/Nutritionals:		Information Systems:		Physical Rehab. Ctr.:		Waste Disposal:		Physician Prac. Mgmt.:	
		Clinical Trials:				Psychiatric Clinics:		Specialty Svcs.:			

TYPES OF BUSINESS:

ıurgical Equipment-Spinal
ıone Cement

BRANDS/DIVISIONS/AFFILIATES:

KyphX
KyphOs
KyphX HV-R
St. Francis Medical Technologies, Inc.
nnoSpine, Inc.
K-STOP IPD System
Discyphor Catheter System
Discyphor Introducer Needle

CONTACTS: *Note: Officers with more than one job title may be ntentionally listed here more than once.*

Richard W. Mott, CEO
Arthur T. Taylor, COO/VP
Richard W. Mott, Pres.
Maureen L. Lamb, CFO/VP
Stephen C. Hams, VP-Human Resources
Karen D. Talmadge, Exec. VP/Chief Science Officer
David M. Shaw, General Counsel/VP-Legal Affairs/Sec.
Rick S. Kline, VP-Oper.
Frank P. Grillo, VP-Mktg., Strategy & Bus. Dev.
Julie D. Tracy, Chief Comm. Officer/VP
Maureen L. Lamb, Treas.
Bradley W. Paddock, VP-U.S. Sales
Mary K. Hailey, VP-Health Care Policy & Govt. Rel.
Alexandre M. DiNello, VP-R&D
Elizabeth A. Rothwell, VP-Quality Assurance & Regulatory Affairs
James Treace, Chmn.
Robert A. Vandervelde, Pres., Int'l

Phone: 408-548-6500 **Fax:**
Toll-Free:
Address: 1221 Crossman Ave., Sunnyvale, CA 94089 US

GROWTH PLANS/SPECIAL FEATURES:

Kyphon, Inc. designs, manufactures and markets medical devices to treat and restore spinal anatomy and diagnose the source of low back pain using minimally invasive technology. Its devices are used primarily by spine specialists, including orthopedic surgeons and neurosurgeons, interventional radiologists, as well as interventional neuroradiologists who repair spinal fractures caused by osteoporosis, trauma, benign lesions and cancer. The firm's three product families are Spinal Fracture Management and Repair; Disc Disease Diagnosis and Therapies; and Spinal Motion Preservation. Kyphon's Spinal Fracture Management and Repair products consist of its KyphX instruments, which use its proprietary balloon technology and include bone access systems, inflatable bone tamps, inflation syringes, bone filler devices, bone biopsy devices and curettes. Kyphon's Disc Disease Diagnosis and Therapies products consist of the Discyphor Catheter System, which uses a balloon catheter to create access to an intervertebral disc, allowing for the injection of anesthetic or saline, the Discyphor Introducer Needle, which uses a disposable needle to create access to an intervertebral disc, and the Discyphor Spinal Needle, which uses a disposable spinal needle to perform provocative discography and facilitate the placement of the Discyphor Catheter. Kyphon's Spinal Motion Preservation products consist of its X-STOP Interspinous Process Decompression (IPD) System. Kyphon has trained approximately 10,400 physicians in North America, Europe and Asia Pacific in the use of its KyphX instruments, and these physicians had used these instruments in approximately 285,000 patients and 335,000 spinal fractures. In early 2006, Kyphon acquired InnoSpine, Inc., a privately held developer and manufacturer of low back pain diagnosis and treatment products. Kyphon agreed in December 2006 to acquire certain assets and property rights of Disc-O-Tech Medical Technologies, Ltd. In early 2007, Kyphon acquired St. Francis Medical Technologies, Inc., a private manufacturer of the X-STOP IPD System. In July 2007, the firm agreed to be acquired by Medtronic, Inc. for roughly $3.9 billion.

FINANCIALS: **Sales and profits are in thousands of dollars—add 000 to get the full amount. 2007 Note: Financial information for 2007 was not available for all companies at press time.**

2007 Sales: $	2007 Profits: $	**U.S. Stock Ticker: KYPH**
2006 Sales: $407,790	2006 Profits: $39,732	**Int'l Ticker:** Int'l Exchange:
2005 Sales: $306,082	2005 Profits: $29,836	Employees: 1,090
2004 Sales: $213,414	2004 Profits: $21,717	Fiscal Year Ends: 12/31
2003 Sales: $131,028	2003 Profits: $27,323	Parent Company:

SALARIES/BENEFITS:

Pension Plan:	ESOP Stock Plan:	Profit Sharing:	Top Exec. Salary: $461,250	Bonus: $474,966
Savings Plan: Y	Stock Purch. Plan:		Second Exec. Salary: $358,983	Bonus: $169,144

OTHER THOUGHTS:

Apparent Women Officers or Directors: 5
Hot Spot for Advancement for Women/Minorities: Y

LOCATIONS: ("Y" = Yes)

West:	Southwest:	Midwest:	Southeast:	Northeast:	International:
Y					Y

LABORATORY CORP OF AMERICA HOLDINGS

www.labcorp.com

Industry Group Code: 621511 **Ranks within this company's industry group:** Sales: 2 Profits: 2

Insurance/HMO/PPO:		Drugs:		Equipment/Supplies:		Hospitals/Clinics:		Services:		Health Care:	
Insurance:		Manufacturer:		Manufacturer:		Acute Care:		Diagnostics:	Y	Home Health:	
Managed Care:		Distributor:		Distributor:		Sub-Acute:		Labs/Testing:	Y	Long-Term Care:	
Utilization Management:		Specialty Pharmacy:		Leasing/Finance:		Outpatient Surgery:		Staffing:		Physical Therapy:	
Payment Processing:		Vitamins/Nutritionals:		Information Systems:		Physical Rehab. Ctr.:		Waste Disposal:		Physician Prac. Mgmt.:	
		Clinical Trials:				Psychiatric Clinics:		Specialty Svcs.:			

TYPES OF BUSINESS:

Clinical Laboratory Testing
Diagnostics
Urinalyses
Blood Cell Counts
Blood Chemistry Analysis
HIV Tests
Genetic Testing
Specialty & Niche Tests

BRANDS/DIVISIONS/AFFILIATES:

Dianon Systems, Inc.
Esoterix, Inc.
US Pathology Labs, Inc.

CONTACTS: *Note: Officers with more than one job title may be intentionally listed here more than once.*

David P. King, CEO
Don Hardison, COO/Exec. VP
David P. King, Pres.
Wesley R. Elingburg, CFO
Benjamin R. Miller, Exec. VP-Mktg. & Sales
Myla P. Lai-Goldman, Chief Scientific Officer
Andrew S. Walton, CIO
Bradford T. Smith, Chief Legal Officer/Corp. Sec.
Woodrow L. Cook, Exec. VP-Eastern Oper.
Andrew S. Walton, Exec. VP-Strategic Planning
Bradford T. Smith, Exec. VP-Corp. Affairs
Eric Lindblom, Sr. VP-Investor & Media Rel.
Wesley R. Elingburg, Exec. VP/Treas.
Myla P. Lai-Goldman, Medical Dir./Exec. VP
William B. Haas, Exec. VP-Esoteric Bus.
Benjamin R. Miller, Exec. VP-Managed Care
Allen W. Troub, Exec. VP-Western Oper.
Thomas P. Mac Mahon, Chmn.

Phone: 336-229-1127	**Fax:** 336-436-1205
Toll-Free: 800-334-5261	
Address: 358 S. Main St., Burlington, NC 27215 US	

GROWTH PLANS/SPECIAL FEATURES:

Laboratory Corporation of America Holdings (LabCorp) i one of the top two independent clinical laboratory companie in the U.S., offering more than 4,400 health-relate laboratory tests to the medical industry. The tests are use primarily in routine screening, patient diagnosis an monitoring and treatment of disease. Its laboratorie participated in the development of genomic application using polymerase chain reaction (PCR) technology an LabCorp was the first commercial laboratory to provide thi technology to health care providers. The company operate a nationwide network of 36 primary testing facilities and ove 1,700 service centers, consisting of branches, patient servic centers and STAT labs, which can perform routine test quickly and report results to the physician within 24 hours Some of its labs are operated by subsidiaries Diano Systems, Inc.; Esoterix, Inc.; and US Pathology Labs, Inc They are leading providers of anatomic pathology testin services. The most common tests performed by the firn include blood chemistry analysis, urinalyses, blood ce counts, Pap smears, HIV tests, microbiology cultures an substance abuse tests. The company processes an averag of approximately 370,000 specimens per day for ove 220,000 clients in all 50 states, Washington, D.C., Puert Rico and Canada. LabCorp also performs specialty an niche testing including infectious disease and allergy testin and a number of genetics testing services and forensi identity tests. The company provides clinical laborator testing for pharmaceutical companies conducting clinica research trials on new drugs. The expansion of its specialt and niche testing business is currently a primary growt strategy for the company. In June 2006, LabCorp formed a relationship with Duke University to work together ir advanced research studies in specified clinical testin applications in genomic medicine.

LabCorp offers its employees flexible spending accounts tuition reimbursement, adoption assistance, credit unior membership, an employee assistance program and a lega assistance program.

FINANCIALS: Sales and profits are in thousands of dollars—add 000 to get the full amount. 2007 Note: Financial information for 2007 was not available for all companies at press time.

2007 Sales: $	2007 Profits: $	**U.S. Stock Ticker: LH**
2006 Sales: $3,590,800	2006 Profits: $431,600	**Int'l Ticker:** Int'l Exchange:
2005 Sales: $3,327,600	2005 Profits: $386,200	Employees: 25,000
2004 Sales: $3,084,800	2004 Profits: $363,000	Fiscal Year Ends: 12/31
2003 Sales: $2,939,400	2003 Profits: $321,000	Parent Company:

SALARIES/BENEFITS:

Pension Plan: Y	ESOP Stock Plan:	Profit Sharing:	Top Exec. Salary: $989,526	Bonus: $2,041,500
Savings Plan:	Stock Purch. Plan:		Second Exec. Salary: $524,960	Bonus: $850,575

OTHER THOUGHTS:

Apparent Women Officers or Directors: 1
Hot Spot for Advancement for Women/Minorities:

LOCATIONS: ("Y" = Yes)

West:	Southwest:	Midwest:	Southeast:	Northeast:	International:
Y	Y	Y	Y	Y	Y

LAKELAND INDUSTRIES INC

www.lakeland.com

Industry Group Code: 339113 **Ranks within this company's industry group:** Sales: 80 Profits: 69

Insurance/HMO/PPO:		Drugs:		Equipment/Supplies:		Hospitals/Clinics:		Services:		Health Care:	
Insurance:		Manufacturer:		Manufacturer:	Y	Acute Care:		Diagnostics:		Home Health:	
Managed Care:		Distributor:		Distributor:		Sub-Acute:		Labs/Testing:		Long-Term Care:	
Utilization Management:		Specialty Pharmacy:		Leasing/Finance:		Outpatient Surgery:		Staffing:		Physical Therapy:	
Payment Processing:		Vitamins/Nutritionals:		Information Systems:		Physical Rehab. Ctr.:		Waste Disposal:		Physician Prac. Mgmt.:	
		Clinical Trials:				Psychiatric Clinics:		Specialty Svcs.:			

TYPES OF BUSINESS:

Safety Clothing
Reusable Industrial & Medical Apparel
Chemical Protection Clothing
Specialty Safety Gloves
Heat Resistant Clothing
Disposable Protective Garments

BRANDS/DIVISIONS/AFFILIATES:

Lakeland Protective Wear, Inc.
Fyrepel
MicroMax
Kutbuster
Mifflin Valley, Inc.

CONTACTS:

Note: Officers with more than one job title may be intentionally listed here more than once.

Christopher J. Ryan, CEO
Christopher J. Ryan, Pres.
Gary Pokrassa, CFO
Harvey Pride, Jr., Sr. VP-Mfg.
Christopher J. Ryan, General Counsel/Corp. Sec.
James M. McCormick, Treas./Controller
Gregory D. Willis, Exec. VP
Paul C. Smith, VP
Gregory Pontes, VP-Mfg.
Raymond J. Smith, Chmn.

Phone: 631-981-9700 **Fax:** 631-981-9751
Toll-Free: 800-645-9291
Address: 701 Koehler Ave., Ste. 7, Ronkonkoma, NY 11779-7410 US

GROWTH PLANS/SPECIAL FEATURES:

Lakeland Industries, Inc. manufactures and sells a comprehensive line of safety garments and accessories for the industrial safety and protective clothing industries in the U.S. The company's major product areas include disposable and limited-use protective clothing; specialty gloves and arm guards; reusable woven industrial and medical apparel; fire- and heat-protective clothing; and chemical protective suits for use by toxic waste clean-up teams, hazardous material clean-up teams and first responders to acts of terrorism. The firm's disposable and reusable garments protect the wearer from contaminants or irritants, such as chemicals, pesticides, fertilizers, paint, grease and dust; from viruses and bacteria; and from limited exposure to hazardous waste and toxic chemicals including acids, asbestos, lead and hydro-carbons (PCBs). Lakeland's products are also used to prevent human contamination of manufacturing processes in clean-room environments. Disposable clothing products include coveralls, lab coats, hoods, aprons, sleeves and smocks. Lakeland's heat protective gear is used by firefighters (under the Fyrepel brand), as well as for maintenance of extreme high-temperature industrial equipment (up to 1,500 degrees Fahrenheit ambient) and for crash and rescue operations. The company's high-end chemical protective suits protect wearers from highly concentrated and powerful chemical and biological toxins such as toxic wastes at Super Fund sites, accidental toxic chemical spills or biological discharges, the handling of chemical or biological warfare weapons and the cleaning and maintenance of chemical, petrochemical and nuclear facilities. Lakeland buys most of its raw materials for manufacturing from DuPont, including Kevlar and Tyvek.

FINANCIALS:

Sales and profits are in thousands of dollars—add 000 to get the full amount. 2007 Note: Financial information for 2007 was not available for all companies at press time.

2007 Sales: $	2007 Profits: $	**U.S. Stock Ticker: LAKE**
2006 Sales: $98,740	2006 Profits: $6,329	**Int'l Ticker:** Int'l Exchange:
2005 Sales: $95,320	2005 Profits: $5,016	Employees: 1,634
2004 Sales: $89,717	2004 Profits: $3,638	Fiscal Year Ends: 1/31
2003 Sales: $77,800	2003 Profits: $2,600	Parent Company:

SALARIES/BENEFITS:

Pension Plan:	ESOP Stock Plan:	Profit Sharing:	Top Exec. Salary: $400,000	Bonus: $35,000
Savings Plan: Y	Stock Purch. Plan:		Second Exec. Salary: $250,000	Bonus: $

OTHER THOUGHTS:

Apparent Women Officers or Directors:
Hot Spot for Advancement for Women/Minorities:

LOCATIONS: ("Y" = Yes)

West:	Southwest:	Midwest:	Southeast:	Northeast:	International:
		Y	Y	Y	Y

Note: Financial information, benefits and other data can change quickly and may vary from those stated here.

LASERSCOPE

www.laserscope.com

Industry Group Code: 339113 **Ranks within this company's industry group:** Sales: Profits:

Insurance/HMO/PPO:		Drugs:		Equipment/Supplies:		Hospitals/Clinics:		Services:		Health Care:	
Insurance:		Manufacturer:		Manufacturer:	Y	Acute Care:		Diagnostics:		Home Health:	
Managed Care:		Distributor:		Distributor:		Sub-Acute:		Labs/Testing:		Long-Term Care:	
Utilization Management:		Specialty Pharmacy:		Leasing/Finance:		Outpatient Surgery:		Staffing:		Physical Therapy:	
Payment Processing:		Vitamins/Nutritionals:		Information Systems:		Physical Rehab. Ctr.:		Waste Disposal:		Physician Prac. Mgmt.:	
		Clinical Trials:				Psychiatric Clinics:		Specialty Svcs.:			

TYPES OF BUSINESS:

Equipment-Medical Laser Systems
Energy Delivery Devices

BRANDS/DIVISIONS/AFFILIATES:

American Medical Systems Holdings Inc
Solis
Aura
Venus
GreenLight
800 Series
McKesson Corporation Medical Group
Iridex

CONTACTS: *Note: Officers with more than one job title may be intentionally listed here more than once.*

Eric M. Reuter, CEO
Eric M. Reuter, Pres.
Derek Bertocci, CFO
Dennis LaLumandiere, VP-Human Resources & Organizational Dev.
Ken Arnold, VP-R&D
Robert L. Mathews, Group VP-Prod. Dev.
Peter Hadrovic, VP-Legal Affairs/General Counsel/Sec.
Robert L. Mathews, Group VP-Oper.
Derek Bertocci, VP-Finance
Van A. Frazier, VP-Quality Assurance & Regulatory Affairs
Kester Nahen, VP-Application Research
Robert Mann, VP-Global Sales & Mktg., Surgical
Lloyd Diamond, VP-Mktg., Urology
Robert J. Pressley, Chmn.

Phone: 408-943-0636	**Fax:** 408-943-1462
Toll-Free: 800-356-7600	
Address: 3070 Orchard Dr., San Jose, CA 95134-2011 US	

GROWTH PLANS/SPECIAL FEATURES:

Laserscope designs, manufactures, sells and services medical laser systems and related devices primarily for medical offices, outpatient surgical centers and hospitals. The company is a pioneer in the development and commercialization of lasers and fiber-optic devices for a wide variety of applications. Laserscope's product portfolio consists of more than 300 products, including KTP, Nd:YAG, KTP/Nd:YAG and Erbium:Yag medical laser systems and related energy delivery devices. The firm's primary medical markets are aesthetic surgery and urology. Secondary markets include ear, nose and throat (ENT) surgery, general surgery, gynecology, neurosurgery and pulmonary/thoracic surgery. The company's systems for aesthetic treatments include the Solis, Lyra, Aura, Gemini and Venus laser systems which are used for hair removal, leg veins, spider-veins, age spots, acne and skin and acne scar resurfacing. The company's GreenLight laser system, utilized in urological treatments, combines a single-wavelength laser and an ADDStat disposable fiber-optic delivery device for photo-selective vaporization of the prostate, a procedure to treat benign prostatic hyperplasia. The 800 Series KTP/YAG Surgical Laser System is designed for use in hospitals. It is a high-power, dual-wavelength system with applications in urology, general surgery and other surgical specialties. Its KTP/532 beam surgically cuts, vaporizes and coagulates tissue with minimal disruption to adjacent areas. Cutting and vaporization are achieved with minimal bleeding, making the system effective for endoscopic as well as open surgical procedures. Laserscope also markets surgical instruments, disposables, kits, optical fibers and other accessories to support its laser systems. McKesson Corporation Medical Group distributes many of the firm's products in the U.S. In July 2006, the company was acquired by Kermit Merger Corp., a subsidiary of American Medical Systems Holdings, Inc. (AMS), for approximately $715 million. In January 2007, Iridex acquired certain assets of Laserscope's aesthetics business, including four patents and a license to nine more patents, for $26 million.

FINANCIALS: **Sales and profits are in thousands of dollars—add 000 to get the full amount. 2007 Note: Financial information for 2007 was not available for all companies at press time.**

2007 Sales: $
2006 Sales: $
2005 Sales: $127,124
2004 Sales: $93,770
2003 Sales: $57,427

2007 Profits: $
2006 Profits: $
2005 Profits: $22,550
2004 Profits: $14,739
2003 Profits: $2,517

U.S. Stock Ticker: Subsidiary
Int'l Ticker: Int'l Exchange:
Employees: 296
Fiscal Year Ends: 12/31
Parent Company: AMERICAN MEDICAL SYSTEMS HOLDINGS INC

SALARIES/BENEFITS:

Pension Plan:	ESOP Stock Plan:	Profit Sharing:	Top Exec. Salary: $280,000	Bonus: $276,244
Savings Plan: Y	Stock Purch. Plan: Y		Second Exec. Salary: $189,800	Bonus: $149,222

OTHER THOUGHTS:

Apparent Women Officers or Directors:
Hot Spot for Advancement for Women/Minorities:

LOCATIONS: ("Y" = Yes)

West:	Southwest:	Midwest:	Southeast:	Northeast:	International:
Y	Y	Y	Y	Y	Y

LCA-VISION INC www.lasikplus.com

ıdustry Group Code: 621490 **Ranks within this company's industry group:** Sales: 10 Profits: 4

ısurance/HMO/PPO:		Drugs:		Equipment/Supplies:		Hospitals/Clinics:		Services:		Health Care:	
ısurance:		Manufacturer:		Manufacturer:		Acute Care:		Diagnostics:		Home Health:	
ǀanaged Care:		Distributor:		Distributor:		Sub-Acute:		Labs/Testing:		Long-Term Care:	
tilization Management:		Specialty Pharmacy:		Leasing/Finance:		Outpatient Surgery:	Y	Staffing:		Physical Therapy:	
ayment Processing:		Vitamins/Nutritionals:		Information Systems:		Physical Rehab. Ctr.:		Waste Disposal:		Physician Prac. Mgmt.:	
		Clinical Trials:				Psychiatric Clinics:		Specialty Svcs.:			

TYPES OF BUSINESS:

ervices-Laser Vision Correction Surgery Centers
RK (photo-refractive keratectomy)
ASIK (Laser-In-Situ Keratomileusis)

BRANDS/DIVISIONS/AFFILIATES:

.asikPlus

CONTACTS: *Note: Officers with more than one job title may be ntentionally listed here more than once.*

teven C. Straus, CEO
\lan H. Buckey, CFO
lames H. Brenner, Chief Mktg. Officer
Stephen M. Jones, Sr. VP-Human Resources
\lan H. Buckey, Exec. VP-Finance
/ichael J. Celebrezze, Sr. VP-Finance/Treas.
:. Anthony Woods, Chmn.

Phone: 513-792-9292	**Fax:** 513-792-5620
Toll-Free: 800-688-4550	
Address: 7840 Montgomery Rd., Cincinnati, OH 45236 US	

GROWTH PLANS/SPECIAL FEATURES:

LCA-Vision, Inc. is a provider of fixed-site laser vision correction services at its LasikPlus vision centers. The company's vision centers help correct nearsightedness, farsightedness and astigmatism. Treatments are done by using one of two methods: PRK (photo-refractive keratectomy) and LASIK (Laser-In-Situ Keratomileusis). PRK removes the thin layer of cell covering the outer surface of the cornea (the epithelium) and treats it with excimer laser pulses. LASIK reshapes the cornea with an excimer laser by cutting a flap in the top of the cornea to expose the inner cornea. The corneal flap is then treated with excimer laser pulses according to the patient's prescription. The LASIK procedure now accounts for virtually all of the procedures performed by LCA, as recovery time is significantly shorter and patient discomfort is negligible. LCA currently uses three suppliers for fixed site excimer lasers: Bausch & Lomb, Advanced Medical Optics and Alcon. The company operates about 70 LasikPlus vision correction centers in the U.S. and also has a joint venture in Canada. The firm has performed more than 740,000 laser vision correction procedures since the company's inception. LCA has gradually transferred all of its facilities to closed-access, which means LCA maintains full operational and financial control over its business, directly employing its own ophthalmologists and taking on full responsibility for marketing and patient acquisition. The company also offers procedures using a new wavefront-guided LASIK system, a system that allows doctors to map out the exact surface of the cornea before surgery, and thus provide personalized, more accurate modifications to the cornea, with an end result of clearer vision.

The company offers its employees medical, death and disability protection and retirement savings plans.

FINANCIALS: **Sales and profits are in thousands of dollars—add 000 to get the full amount. 2007 Note: Financial information for 2007 was not available for all companies at press time.**

2007 Sales: $	2007 Profits: $	**U.S. Stock Ticker: LCAV**
2006 Sales: $256,927	2006 Profits: $38,296	**Int'l Ticker:** Int'l Exchange:
2005 Sales: $192,397	2005 Profits: $31,653	Employees: 700
2004 Sales: $127,122	2004 Profits: $32,029	Fiscal Year Ends: 12/31
2003 Sales: $81,423	2003 Profits: $7,269	Parent Company:

SALARIES/BENEFITS:

Pension Plan:	ESOP Stock Plan:	Profit Sharing:	Top Exec. Salary: $1,125,000	Bonus: $
Savings Plan: Y	Stock Purch. Plan:		Second Exec. Salary: $300,000	Bonus: $128,475

OTHER THOUGHTS:

Apparent Women Officers or Directors:
Hot Spot for Advancement for Women/Minorities:

LOCATIONS: ("Y" = Yes)

West:	Southwest:	Midwest:	Southeast:	Northeast:	International:
Y	Y	Y	Y	Y	Y

LIFE CARE CENTERS OF AMERICA www.lcca.com

Industry Group Code: 623110 **Ranks within this company's industry group:** Sales: Profits:

Insurance/HMO/PPO:		Drugs:		Equipment/Supplies:		Hospitals/Clinics:		Services:		Health Care:	
Insurance:		Manufacturer:		Manufacturer:		Acute Care:		Diagnostics:		Home Health:	Y
Managed Care:		Distributor:		Distributor:		Sub-Acute:	Y	Labs/Testing:		Long-Term Care:	Y
Utilization Management:		Specialty Pharmacy:		Leasing/Finance:		Outpatient Surgery:		Staffing:		Physical Therapy:	Y
Payment Processing:		Vitamins/Nutritionals:		Information Systems:		Physical Rehab. Ctr.:	Y	Waste Disposal:		Physician Prac. Mgmt.:	
		Clinical Trials:				Psychiatric Clinics:		Specialty Svcs.:	Y		

TYPES OF BUSINESS:

Assisted Living Facilities
Home Care
Respite Care
Alzheimer's Care
Hospice
Rehabilitation
Physical Therapy

BRANDS/DIVISIONS/AFFILIATES:

CONTACTS:

Note: Officers with more than one job title may be intentionally listed here more than once.

Cathy Murray, COO
Beecher Hunter, Pres.
Forrest L. Preston, Chmn.

Phone: 423-472-9585	**Fax:** 423-339-8350
Toll-Free: 800-554-9585	
Address: 3570 Keith St. NW, Cleveland, TN 37320 US	

GROWTH PLANS/SPECIAL FEATURES:

Life Care Centers of America (LCCA) operates over 260 skilled nursing, assisted living, retirement, home care and Alzheimer's centers in 28 states. Its assisted living centers promote independence and dignity while providing help with tasks such as dressing, bathing and grooming. The staff of these facilities also assists with medications and discretely monitors patients' health. Through American Lifestyles, LCCA operates 40 additional retirement communities for more affluent seniors. These offer fine accommodations, trained chefs and minimal assistance. Most of the firm's locations also provide Alzheimer's care, respite care, sub-acute medical care, wound care, adult day care, hospice and rehabilitation services such as physical, occupational and speech therapy. LCCA's senior living campuses provide various types of facilities in one location, offering retirement, assisted living and nursing care depending on the changing needs of the patients. The company's Life Care at Home agencies offer health and social services for people who prefer to stay at home yet require care that cannot be provided by family members. Services range from intermittent to live-in and may include administration of medication, physical therapy, occupational therapy, speech therapy and errands such as grocery shopping. Home Care facilities are located in Washington, Utah, Arizona, Colorado, Tennessee, Florida, Massachusetts and Rhode Island.

FINANCIALS:

Sales and profits are in thousands of dollars—add 000 to get the full amount. 2007 Note: Financial information for 2007 was not available for all companies at press time.

2007 Sales: $	2007 Profits: $	**U.S. Stock Ticker: Private**
2006 Sales: $	2006 Profits: $	**Int'l Ticker:** Int'l Exchange:
2005 Sales: $	2005 Profits: $	Employees:
2004 Sales: $	2004 Profits: $	Fiscal Year Ends:
2003 Sales: $	2003 Profits: $	Parent Company:

SALARIES/BENEFITS:

Pension Plan:	ESOP Stock Plan:	Profit Sharing:	Top Exec. Salary: $	Bonus: $
Savings Plan:	Stock Purch. Plan:		Second Exec. Salary: $	Bonus: $

OTHER THOUGHTS:

Apparent Women Officers or Directors: 1
Hot Spot for Advancement for Women/Minorities: Y

LOCATIONS: ("Y" = Yes)

West:	Southwest:	Midwest:	Southeast:	Northeast:	International:
Y	Y	Y	Y	Y	

Note: Financial information, benefits and other data can change quickly and may vary from those stated here.

LIFECELL CORPORATION www.lifecell.com

ndustry Group Code: 325414 **Ranks within this company's industry group:** Sales: 3 Profits: 3

nsurance/HMO/PPO:		Drugs:		Equipment/Supplies:		Hospitals/Clinics:		Services:		Health Care:	
nsurance:		Manufacturer:	Y	Manufacturer:	Y	Acute Care:		Diagnostics:		Home Health:	
lanaged Care:		Distributor:		Distributor:		Sub-Acute:		Labs/Testing:		Long-Term Care:	
tilization Management:		Specialty Pharmacy:		Leasing/Finance:		Outpatient Surgery:		Staffing:		Physical Therapy:	
ayment Processing:		Vitamins/Nutritionals:		Information Systems:		Physical Rehab. Ctr.:		Waste Disposal:		Physician Prac. Mgmt.:	
		Clinical Trials:				Psychiatric Clinics:		Specialty Svcs.:			

TYPES OF BUSINESS:

issue Replacement Products
kin Replacement Technology
one Grafting Technology
egenerative Medicine

BRANDS/DIVISIONS/AFFILIATES:

lloDerm
ymetra
epliform
raft Jacket
lloCraft DBM

CONTACTS: *Note: Officers with more than one job title may be ntentionally listed here more than once.*

aul G. Thomas, CEO
aul G. Thomas, Pres.
teven T. Sobieski, CFO
teven T. Sobieski, Sr. VP-Admin.
teven T. Sobieski, VP-Finance
ruce Lamb, Sr. VP-Dev. & Regulatory Affairs
isa N. Colleran, Sr. VP-Commercial Oper.
aul G. Thomas, Chmn.

Phone: 908-947-1100	Fax: 908-947-1200
Toll-Free:	
Address: 1 Millennium Way, Branchburg, NJ 08876 US	

GROWTH PLANS/SPECIAL FEATURES:

LifeCell Corporation specializes in regenerative medicine, developing and manufacturing products geared toward the repair, replacement and preservation of human tissues. The company has developed and patented several proprietary technologies, including a method for producing an acellular tissue matrix, a method for cell preservation through signal transduction and a method for freeze-drying biological cells and tissues without damage. Products are used in reconstructive, orthopedic and urogynecologic surgical procedures to repair soft tissue defects. The company's products include AlloDerm, for plastic reconstructive, general surgical, burn and periodontal procedures; Cymetra, a particulate form of AlloDerm suitable for injection; GraftJacket, for orthopedic applications and lower extremity wounds; AlloCraft DBM, for bone grafting procedures; and Repliform, for urogynecologic surgical procedures. The firm markets AlloDerm in the United States for plastic reconstructive, general surgical and burn applications and Cymetra to hospital-based surgeons through its direct sales and marketing organization. BioHorizons Implant Systems, Inc. is LifeCell's exclusive distributor in the U.S. and certain international markets of AlloDerm and AlloDerm GBR for use in periodontal applications. Boston Scientific Corp. is the exclusive worldwide sales and marketing agent of Repliform for use in urogynecology. Wright Medical Group is the exclusive distributor in the U.S. and certain international markets for GraftJacket. Stryker Corp. is the exclusive distributor in the U.S. for AlloCraft DBM.

The company offers its employees a 401(k); medical, dental and vision insurance; life and AD&D insurance; short- and long-term disability; an employee assistance program; and a college savings plan.

FINANCIALS: Sales and profits are in thousands of dollars—add 000 to get the full amount. 2007 Note: Financial information for 2007 was not available for all companies at press time.

2007 Sales: $	2007 Profits: $	**U.S. Stock Ticker: LIFC**
2006 Sales: $141,680	2006 Profits: $20,469	**Int'l Ticker:** Int'l Exchange:
2005 Sales: $94,398	2005 Profits: $12,044	Employees: 335
2004 Sales: $61,127	2004 Profits: $7,184	Fiscal Year Ends: 12/31
2003 Sales: $40,249	2003 Profits: $18,672	Parent Company:

SALARIES/BENEFITS:

Pension Plan:	ESOP Stock Plan:	Profit Sharing:	Top Exec. Salary: $477,750	Bonus: $390,417
Savings Plan: Y	Stock Purch. Plan:		Second Exec. Salary: $272,225	Bonus: $130,913

OTHER THOUGHTS:

Apparent Women Officers or Directors: 1
Hot Spot for Advancement for Women/Minorities:

LOCATIONS: ("Y" = Yes)

West:	Southwest:	Midwest:	Southeast:	Northeast:	International:
				Y	

LIFECORE BIOMEDICAL INC www.lifecore.com

Industry Group Code: 339113 **Ranks within this company's industry group:** Sales: 88 Profits: 67

Insurance/HMO/PPO:		Drugs:		Equipment/Supplies:		Hospitals/Clinics:		Services:		Health Care:	
Insurance:		Manufacturer:		Manufacturer:	Y	Acute Care:		Diagnostics:		Home Health:	
Managed Care:		Distributor:		Distributor:		Sub-Acute:		Labs/Testing:		Long-Term Care:	
Utilization Management:		Specialty Pharmacy:		Leasing/Finance:		Outpatient Surgery:		Staffing:		Physical Therapy:	
Payment Processing:		Vitamins/Nutritionals:		Information Systems:		Physical Rehab. Ctr.:		Waste Disposal:		Physician Prac. Mgmt.:	
		Clinical Trials:				Psychiatric Clinics:		Specialty Svcs.:			

TYPES OF BUSINESS:

Biomaterials & Medical Device Manufacturing
Bone Regeneration Products
Surgical Devices
Dental Implants

BRANDS/DIVISIONS/AFFILIATES:

Support Plus
Lifecore Prima Implant System

CONTACTS: *Note: Officers with more than one job title may be intentionally listed here more than once.*

Dennis J. Allingham, CEO
Dennis J. Allingham, Pres.
David M. Noel, CFO
Kipling Thacker, VP-New Bus. Dev.
David M. Noel, VP-Finance
Andre P. Decarie, VP-Mktg. & Sales, Oral Restorative Div.
Larry D. Hiebert, VP/General Mgr.-Hyaluronan Div.

Phone: 952-368-4300	**Fax:** 952-368-3411
Toll-Free:	
Address: 3515 Lyman Blvd., Chaska, MN 55318 US	

GROWTH PLANS/SPECIAL FEATURES:

Lifecore Biomedical, Inc. develops and manufactures biomaterials and medical devices with applications in various surgical markets. The company operates two divisions, the hyaluronan division and the oral restorative division. Its hyaluronan division is principally involved in the development and manufacture of products utilizing hyaluronan, a naturally occurring polysaccharide that is widely distributed in the extracellar matrix of connective tissues in both animals and humans. This division sells primarily to three medical segments: ophthalmic, orthopedic and veterinary. Lifecore also supplies hyaluronan to customers pursuing other medical applications, such as wound care, aesthetic surgery, medical device coatings, tissue engineering, drug delivery and pharmaceuticals. Lifecore's oral restorative division develops and markets precision surgical and prosthetic devices for the restoration of damaged or deteriorating dentition and associated support tissues. The company's dental implants are permanently implanted in the jaw for tooth replacement therapy as long-term support for crowns, bridges and dentures. It also offers bone regenerative products for the repair of bone defects resulting from periodontal disease and tooth loss. Additionally, the oral restorative division provides professional support services to its dental surgery clients through comprehensive education curricula, as provided in the company's various Support Plus programs and surgical courses. These professional continuing education programs are designed to train restorative clinicians and their auxiliary teams in the principles of tooth replacement therapy and practice management. Recently, the company announced the proprietary Lifecore Prima Implant System.

Lifecore offers its employees an employee assistance program and an on-site fitness center. Lifecore has been certified by the Minnesota Safety and Health Achievement and Recognition Program, a recognition of a higher standard of safety and health programs that goes beyond required OSHA standards.

FINANCIALS: **Sales and profits are in thousands of dollars—add 000 to get the full amount. 2007 Note: Financial information for 2007 was not available for all companies at press time.**

2007 Sales: $69,629	2007 Profits: $7,719	**U.S. Stock Ticker: LCBM**
2006 Sales: $63,097	2006 Profits: $7,040	**Int'l Ticker:** Int'l Exchange:
2005 Sales: $55,695	2005 Profits: $17,511	Employees: 241
2004 Sales: $47,036	2004 Profits: $ 707	Fiscal Year Ends: 6/30
2003 Sales: $42,400	2003 Profits: $- 400	Parent Company:

SALARIES/BENEFITS:

Pension Plan:	ESOP Stock Plan:	Profit Sharing:	Top Exec. Salary: $300,000	Bonus: $135,000
Savings Plan: Y	Stock Purch. Plan: Y		Second Exec. Salary: $175,632	Bonus: $29,450

OTHER THOUGHTS:

Apparent Women Officers or Directors:
Hot Spot for Advancement for Women/Minorities:

LOCATIONS: ("Y" = Yes)

West:	Southwest:	Midwest:	Southeast:	Northeast:	International:
		Y			Y

LIFEPOINT HOSPITALS INC www.lifepointhospitals.com

Industry Group Code: 622110 **Ranks within this company's industry group:** Sales: 22 Profits: 15

Insurance/HMO/PPO:		Drugs:		Equipment/Supplies:		Hospitals/Clinics:		Services:		Health Care:	
Insurance:		Manufacturer:		Manufacturer:		Acute Care:	Y	Diagnostics:		Home Health:	
Managed Care:		Distributor:		Distributor:		Sub-Acute:		Labs/Testing:		Long-Term Care:	
Utilization Management:		Specialty Pharmacy:		Leasing/Finance:		Outpatient Surgery:		Staffing:		Physical Therapy:	
Payment Processing:		Vitamins/Nutritionals:		Information Systems:		Physical Rehab. Ctr.:		Waste Disposal:		Physician Prac. Mgmt.:	
		Clinical Trials:				Psychiatric Clinics:		Specialty Svcs.:			

TYPES OF BUSINESS:

Acute Care Hospitals

BRANDS/DIVISIONS/AFFILIATES:

Havasu Regional Medical Center

CONTACTS:

Note: Officers with more than one job title may be intentionally listed here more than once.

William Carpenter III, CEO
William M. Gracey, COO
William Carpenter III, Pres.
David M. Dill, CFO
Penny Brake, VP-Investor Rel.
Owen G. Shell, Jr., Chmn.

Phone: 615-372-8500	**Fax:** 615-372-8575
Toll-Free:	
Address: 103 Powell Ct., Ste. 200, Brentwood, TN 37027 US	

GROWTH PLANS/SPECIAL FEATURES:

LifePoint Hospitals, Inc. is a holding company that owns and operates general acute care hospitals in non-urban communities in the U.S. The firm operates some 50 hospitals located in 19 states in Alabama, Arizona, California, Colorado, Florida, Indiana, Kansas, Kentucky, Louisiana, Mississippi, Nevada, New Mexico, South Carolina, Tennessee, Texas, Utah, Virginia, West Virginia and Wyoming. The company's hospitals typically provide the range of medical and surgical services commonly available in hospitals in non-urban markets. These services generally include general surgery, internal medicine, obstetrics, psychiatric care, emergency room care, radiology, oncology, diagnostic care, coronary care, rehabilitation services, pediatric services, and, in some hospitals, specialized services such as open-heart surgery, skilled nursing and neuro-surgery. In many markets, LifePoint also provides outpatient services such as one-day surgery, laboratory, x-ray, respiratory therapy, imaging, sports medicine and lithotripsy. The firm's hospitals do not engage in extensive medical research and medical education programs. However, two of its hospitals have an affiliation with medical schools, including the clinical rotation of medical students, and one owns and operates a school of health professions with a nursing program and a radiological technology program. In addition to providing access to capital resources, the company makes available management services to its hospitals, including education and training; human resources management; physician services management; accounting, financial, tax and reimbursement management; and risk management. In June 2006, the company acquired four hospitals from HCA, located in Virginia and West Virginia, for a purchase price of $239 million. In September 2006, LifePoint acquired Havasu Regional Medical Center in Arizona.

The company offers its employees medical, dental and vision insurance; life and disability insurance; an employee stock ownership plan; and a retirement plan.

FINANCIALS:

Sales and profits are in thousands of dollars—add 000 to get the full amount. 2007 Note: Financial information for 2007 was not available for all companies at press time.

2007 Sales: $	2007 Profits: $	**U.S. Stock Ticker: LPNT**
2006 Sales: $2,439,700	2006 Profits: $142,200	**Int'l Ticker:** Int'l Exchange:
2005 Sales: $1,841,500	2005 Profits: $79,000	Employees: 9,300
2004 Sales: $996,900	2004 Profits: $85,700	Fiscal Year Ends: 12/31
2003 Sales: $907,100	2003 Profits: $68,500	Parent Company:

SALARIES/BENEFITS:

Pension Plan: Y	ESOP Stock Plan:	Profit Sharing:	Top Exec. Salary: $598,558	Bonus: $525,250
Savings Plan:	Stock Purch. Plan: Y		Second Exec. Salary: $490,385	Bonus: $358,125

OTHER THOUGHTS:

Apparent Women Officers or Directors:
Hot Spot for Advancement for Women/Minorities: Y

LOCATIONS: ("Y" = Yes)

West:	Southwest:	Midwest:	Southeast:	Northeast:	International:
Y	Y	Y	Y	Y	

Note: Financial information, benefits and other data can change quickly and may vary from those stated here.

LIFESCAN INC

www.lifescan.com

Industry Group Code: 339113 **Ranks within this company's industry group:** Sales: Profits:

Insurance/HMO/PPO:		Drugs:		Equipment/Supplies:		Hospitals/Clinics:		Services:		Health Care:	
Insurance:		Manufacturer:		Manufacturer:	Y	Acute Care:		Diagnostics:		Home Health:	
Managed Care:		Distributor:		Distributor:		Sub-Acute:		Labs/Testing:		Long-Term Care:	
Utilization Management:		Specialty Pharmacy:		Leasing/Finance:		Outpatient Surgery:		Staffing:		Physical Therapy:	
Payment Processing:		Vitamins/Nutritionals:		Information Systems:	Y	Physical Rehab. Ctr.:		Waste Disposal:		Physician Prac. Mgmt.:	
		Clinical Trials:				Psychiatric Clinics:		Specialty Svcs.:			

TYPES OF BUSINESS:

Medical Testing Products
Blood Glucose Monitoring Products

BRANDS/DIVISIONS/AFFILIATES:

Johnson & Johnson
OneTouch
InDuo
OneTouch Ultra 2 Meter
OneTouch UltraSmart Meter
Unistik
DataLink Data Management System
OneTouch Gold

CONTACTS: *Note: Officers with more than one job title may be intentionally listed here more than once.*

Tom West, Pres.
Denise E. McEachern, VP-Regulatory & Dev. Affairs
John E. Klopp, Wolrdwide VP-Bus. Dev.

Phone: 408-263-9789 **Fax:** 408-942-6070
Toll-Free: 800-227-8862
Address: 1000 Gibraltar Dr., Milpitas, CA 95035 US

GROWTH PLANS/SPECIAL FEATURES:

LifeScan, Inc., a subsidiary of Johnson & Johnson, is a provider of systems and procedures for diabetic blood glucose monitoring for home and hospital use. The company's OneTouch technology eliminates wiping and timing procedures, making it easier for patients to test their own blood glucose levels. Two OneTouch systems, the Ultra 2 Meter and UltraSmart Meter, require less blood than other tests, are designed to be quick and easy to use and some provide the ability to take blood from an arm rather than fingertips. LifeScan's InDuo, a glucose monitoring and insulin dosing system, incorporating the ability to adjust insulin doses up or down depending on blood glucose measurements, is no longer sold, but the company continues to provide support to existing InDuo customers. The firm also sells OneTouch test strips, lancets and Diabetes Management Software, which tracks glucose values, weight, blood pressure and cholesterol and allows patients to customize medications by name and create meal schedules and insulin regimens. Institutional products include the SureStep testing system, Unistik lancing devices and the DataLink Data Management System, as well as an institutional version of the OneTouch system. The company has a diabetes membership club, OneTouch Gold, designed to cater to the dietary and physical health needs of people with diabetes. LifeScan has operations in Puerto Rico and Scotland.

FINANCIALS: **Sales and profits are in thousands of dollars—add 000 to get the full amount. 2007 Note: Financial information for 2007 was not available for all companies at press time.**

2007 Sales: $
2006 Sales: $
2005 Sales: $
2004 Sales: $1,701,000
2003 Sales: $1,004,000

2007 Profits: $
2006 Profits: $
2005 Profits: $
2004 Profits: $
2003 Profits: $

U.S. Stock Ticker: Subsidiary
Int'l Ticker: Int'l Exchange:
Employees: 2,500
Fiscal Year Ends:
Parent Company: JOHNSON & JOHNSON

SALARIES/BENEFITS:

Pension Plan: ESOP Stock Plan: Profit Sharing: Top Exec. Salary: $ Bonus: $
Savings Plan: Stock Purch. Plan: Second Exec. Salary: $ Bonus: $

OTHER THOUGHTS:

Apparent Women Officers or Directors: 1
Hot Spot for Advancement for Women/Minorities:

LOCATIONS: ("Y" = Yes)

West:	Southwest:	Midwest:	Southeast:	Northeast:	International:
Y					Y

Note: Financial information, benefits and other data can change quickly and may vary from those stated here.

LIFETIME HEALTHCARE COMPANIES (THE) www.lifethc.com

Industry Group Code: 524114 **Ranks within this company's industry group:** Sales: 17 Profits: 17

Insurance/HMO/PPO:		Drugs:		Equipment/Supplies:		Hospitals/Clinics:		Services:		Health Care:	
Insurance:	Y	Manufacturer:		Manufacturer:		Acute Care:		Diagnostics:		Home Health:	Y
Managed Care:		Distributor:		Distributor:	Y	Sub-Acute:	Y	Labs/Testing:		Long-Term Care:	
Utilization Management:		Specialty Pharmacy:		Leasing/Finance:		Outpatient Surgery:		Staffing:		Physical Therapy:	
Payment Processing:		Vitamins/Nutritionals:		Information Systems:		Physical Rehab. Ctr.:		Waste Disposal:		Physician Prac. Mgmt.:	
		Clinical Trials:				Psychiatric Clinics:		Specialty Svcs.:			

TYPES OF BUSINESS:

Insurance-Medical & Health, HMOs & PPOs
Insurance-Group Life
Insurance-Property/Casualty
Insurance-Long-Term Care
Health Care Services
Employee Benefits Services
Medical Centers
Medical Equipment Distribution

BRANDS/DIVISIONS/AFFILIATES:

Excellus BlueCross BlueShield
Univera Healthcare
MedAmerica Insurance Company
EBS Benefit Solutions
Genesee Region Home Care Association
RMSCO, Inc.
Support Services Alliance, Inc.
Lifetime Health Medical Group

CONTACTS: *Note: Officers with more than one job title may be intentionally listed here more than once.*

David H. Klein, CEO
David H. Klein, Pres.
Emil D. Duda, CFO/Sr. Exec. VP
Ginger Parysek, Sr. VP-Corp. Human Resources
David McDowell, CIO/Sr. VP
Robert Krenitsky, CTO
Christopher C. Booth, Sr. VP-Admin.
Christopher C. Booth, General Counsel/Sr. VP
Morris R. Levene, Sr. VP-Bus. Dev.
Geoffrey E. Taylor, VP-Corp. Comm.
Edward J. Wardrop, Treas.
Robert A. Toczynski, Chief Actuary
Jonathan S. Kaplan, Chief Medical Officer
Marie Phillipe, VP-Diversity
Valerie J. Rosenhoch, VP-Legislative & Regulatory Policy

Phone: 585-454-1700 **Fax:** 585-238-4233
Toll-Free:
Address: 165 Court St., Rochester, NY 14647 US

GROWTH PLANS/SPECIAL FEATURES:

Lifetime Healthcare Companies is a family of companies that provide health coverage and health-care services to more than 2 million New Yorkers. The company's main subsidiary, Excellus BlueCross BlueShield (EBB), serves more than 1.4 million members in New York. A not-for-profit health insurer, EBB offers personal health and dental, small business health and long-term care insurance plans. Other Lifetime affiliates include Univera Healthcare, which offers managed care, indemnity and dental plan options to both individuals and groups; MedAmerica Insurance Company, a provider of long-term care insurance; EBS Benefit Solutions, an employee benefits administration and consulting company; Genesee Region Home Care Association, which offers home health services, durable medical equipment, nursing and hospice services; RMSCO, Inc., an administrator of workers' compensation, disability and self-insured medical plans; and Support Services Alliance, Inc., which offers small businesses insurance products and business services. The Lifetime Health Medical Group provides primary care through a network of health centers and medical offices.

Lifetime's subsidiary companies offer their employees a range of benefits, which may include flexible spending accounts, tuition reimbursement and credit union membership.

FINANCIALS: **Sales and profits are in thousands of dollars—add 000 to get the full amount. 2007 Note: Financial information for 2007 was not available for all companies at press time.**

2007 Sales: $
2006 Sales: $4,814,077
2005 Sales: $4,489,043
2004 Sales: $4,053,705
2003 Sales: $4,301,685

2007 Profits: $
2006 Profits: $151,722
2005 Profits: $197,876
2004 Profits: $104,786
2003 Profits: $179,923

U.S. Stock Ticker: Nonprofit
Int'l Ticker: Int'l Exchange:
Employees: 6,200
Fiscal Year Ends: 12/31
Parent Company:

SALARIES/BENEFITS:

Pension Plan: ESOP Stock Plan: Profit Sharing: Top Exec. Salary: $ Bonus: $
Savings Plan: Stock Purch. Plan: Second Exec. Salary: $ Bonus: $

OTHER THOUGHTS:

Apparent Women Officers or Directors: 7
Hot Spot for Advancement for Women/Minorities: Y

LOCATIONS: ("Y" = Yes)

West:	Southwest:	Midwest:	Southeast:	Northeast:	International:
				Y	

Note: Financial information, benefits and other data can change quickly and may vary from those stated here.

LOGISTICARE INC

www.logisticare.com

Industry Group Code: 621111 **Ranks within this company's industry group:** Sales: 5 Profits:

Insurance/HMO/PPO:		Drugs:		Equipment/Supplies:		Hospitals/Clinics:		Services:		Health Care:	
Insurance:		Manufacturer:		Manufacturer:		Acute Care:		Diagnostics:		Home Health:	
Managed Care:		Distributor:		Distributor:		Sub-Acute:		Labs/Testing:		Long-Term Care:	
Utilization Management:		Specialty Pharmacy:		Leasing/Finance:		Outpatient Surgery:		Staffing:		Physical Therapy:	
Payment Processing:		Vitamins/Nutritionals:		Information Systems:		Physical Rehab. Ctr.:		Waste Disposal:		Physician Prac. Mgmt.:	
		Clinical Trials:				Psychiatric Clinics:		Specialty Svcs.:	Y		

TYPES OF BUSINESS:

Medical Transportation Management Services
Outsourced Logistics Services

BRANDS/DIVISIONS/AFFILIATES:

EMTrack
LogistiCAD

CONTACTS:
Note: Officers with more than one job title may be intentionally listed here more than once.

John L. Shermyen, CEO
Herman M. Schwarz, COO
Thomas Oram, CFO
Jenny Southern, Dir.-Human Resources
Albert Cortina, Chief Admin. Officer
Chinta Gaston, General Counsel
Lisa Leach, Dir.-Oper.
Ray P. Williams, Sr. VP-Public Affairs
Windy J. Brooks, Controller
Ed Domansky, Dir.-Corp. Comm.
Gloria Thompson-Robinson, Dir.-Administrative Svcs.

Phone: 770-907-7596	**Fax:** 770-907-7598
Toll-Free: 800-486-7647	
Address: 1800 Phoenix Blvd., Ste. 120, Atlanta, GA 30349 US	

GROWTH PLANS/SPECIAL FEATURES:

LogistiCare, Inc. is an outsourced scheduler of ambulance and patient transport services for insurance companies managed care organizations and government healtl agencies, with expertise in the area of non-emergenc medical transportation (NEMT). Instead of owning its ow vehicles, it manages call centers, patient eligibility screening scheduling, dispatch, billing and quality assurance. It als manages local transportation provider networks that includ operators of ambulances and special transportation for th disabled. LogisitiCare recruits and accredits local firms fo its network of providers; and in sum, it has contracts with 80 transportation providers, coordinating about 11 million trip per year. LogistiCare operates 11 network operation centers that are linked via T-1 lines in order to handle a ca volume of approximately 12,000 reservations and schedulin an average of 36,000 trips daily. All calls are recorde digitally and archived in the system database. The fir developed the integrated software system known a LogistiCAD in order to automatically coordinate all of thi data and generate scheduling, routing, quality assuranc reporting, transportation cost estimates and billin verification. It processes transportation requests an dispatches drivers through its network of carriers, using it proprietary EMTrack system that tracks all of the company' vehicles. LogistiCare is able to use its LogistiCAD system i conjunction with sophisticated GPS navigation to gai improved transportation access and service delivery in rur and remote areas. The company's government client include state Medicaid agencies, school boards and ADA paratransit authorities. Healthcare sector clients includ hospital systems and many of the nations largest manage care organizations. In August 2007, LogistiCare establishe a new call center in Mullins, South Carolina that will manag four regions of South Carolina's Medicaid non-emergenc medical transportation and schedule a projected 1.4 millio trips annually.

FINANCIALS:
Sales and profits are in thousands of dollars—add 000 to get the full amount. 2007 Note: Financial information for 2007 was not available for all companies at press time.

2007 Sales: $	2007 Profits: $	**U.S. Stock Ticker: Private**
2006 Sales: $252,000	2006 Profits: $	**Int'l Ticker:** Int'l Exchange:
2005 Sales: $255,000	2005 Profits: $	Employees: 900
2004 Sales: $220,000	2004 Profits: $	Fiscal Year Ends: 12/31
2003 Sales: $184,000	2003 Profits: $ 700	Parent Company:

SALARIES/BENEFITS:

Pension Plan:	ESOP Stock Plan:	Profit Sharing:	Top Exec. Salary: $	Bonus: $
Savings Plan:	Stock Purch. Plan:		Second Exec. Salary: $	Bonus: $

OTHER THOUGHTS:

Apparent Women Officers or Directors: 5
Hot Spot for Advancement for Women/Minorities: Y

LOCATIONS: ("Y" = Yes)

West:	Southwest:	Midwest:	Southeast:	Northeast:	International:
Y	Y	Y	Y	Y	

LONGS DRUG STORES CORPORATION www.longs.com

Industry Group Code: 446110 **Ranks within this company's industry group:** Sales: 5 Profits: 5

Insurance/HMO/PPO:		Drugs:		Equipment/Supplies:		Hospitals/Clinics:		Services:		Health Care:	
Insurance:		Manufacturer:		Manufacturer:		Acute Care:		Diagnostics:		Home Health:	
Managed Care:		Distributor:	Y	Distributor:		Sub-Acute:		Labs/Testing:		Long-Term Care:	
Utilization Management:	Y	Specialty Pharmacy:	Y	Leasing/Finance:		Outpatient Surgery:		Staffing:		Physical Therapy:	
Payment Processing:		Vitamins/Nutritionals:	Y	Information Systems:		Physical Rehab. Ctr.:		Waste Disposal:		Physician Prac. Mgmt.:	
		Clinical Trials:				Psychiatric Clinics:		Specialty Svcs.:			

TYPES OF BUSINESS:

Drug Stores
Mail-Service Pharmacy
Prescription Benefits Management
Photo Processing

BRANDS/DIVISIONS/AFFILIATES:

RxAmerica
American Diversified Pharmacies, Inc.
Network Pharmaceuticals, Inc.
Bayside Basics
Pacific Living
Walnut Grove
Holiday Place

CONTACTS: *Note: Officers with more than one job title may be intentionally listed here more than once.*

Warren F. Bryant, CEO
Karen Stout, COO/Exec. VP
Warren F. Bryant, Pres.
Steven F. McCann, CFO/Exec. VP
Linda M. Watt, Sr. VP-Human Resources
Michael M. Laddon, CIO/Sr. VP
Todd J. Vasos, Chief Merch. Officer/Sr. VP
William J. Rainey, General Counsel/Sr. VP/Corp. Sec.
Bruce E. Schwallie, Exec. VP-Bus. Dev. & Managed Care
Roger Chelemedos, Controller/Treas./Sr. VP
Warren F. Bryant, Chmn.

Phone: 925-937-1170	**Fax:** 925-210-6886
Toll-Free:	
Address: 141 N. Civic Dr., Walnut Creek, CA 94596 US	

GROWTH PLANS/SPECIAL FEATURES:

Longs Drug Stores Corporation, founded in 1938 by brothers Joe and Tom Long, is one of the largest drug store chains in North America, with approximately 509 stores throughout California, Hawaii, Nevada, Oregon, Washington and Colorado. Longs' retail drug stores sell prescription drugs and a wide assortment of nationally advertised brand name and private brand general merchandise, including over-the-counter medications, health and beauty products, cosmetics, photo and photo processing, convenience food, beverage items, greeting cards, housewares, automotive and sporting goods. The company's private brand offerings are sold under such names as Longs, Bayside Basics, Pacific Living, Walnut Grove and Holiday Place. Longs also offers a variety of immunizations and health screening services in many of its retail drug stores, such as blood, glucose, osteoporosis, stroke and cholesterol testing. The company's web site offers community health screening schedules, prescription refills and pharmacist access, coupons and education regarding a monthly health topic. The company's RxAmerica subsidiary provides comprehensive pharmacy benefit management services nationwide including prescription benefit plan design and implementation, claims administration and formulary management to third-party health plans and other organizations. Longs manages prescription benefit plans covering approximately 7.1 million lives with a network of pharmacies in all 50 states as well as Puerto Rico and the Virgin Islands. RxAmerica began offering prescription drug plans under Medicare Part D in 2006. Another subsidiary, American Diversified Pharmacies, Inc., operates a state-of-the-art mail-service pharmacy. In June 2006, the company purchased certain assets of Network Pharmaceuticals, Inc. including 21 retail pharmacies, one wholesale pharmacy and one closed door pharmacy for approximately $10 million, plus inventory. In January 2007, the company agreed to purchase four retail pharmacies from PharMerica, Inc., a recent spin-off of AmerisourceBergen Corporation. In April 2007, Longs agreed to exchange six stores with Rite Aid Corporation.

FINANCIALS: **Sales and profits are in thousands of dollars—add 000 to get the full amount. 2007 Note: Financial information for 2007 was not available for all companies at press time.**

2007 Sales: $	2007 Profits: $	**U.S. Stock Ticker: LDG**
2006 Sales: $4,670,303	2006 Profits: $73,884	**Int'l Ticker:** Int'l Exchange:
2005 Sales: $4,607,873	2005 Profits: $36,560	Employees: 22,000
2004 Sales: $4,526,524	2004 Profits: $29,764	Fiscal Year Ends: 1/28
2003 Sales: $4,426,300	2003 Profits: $6,700	Parent Company:

SALARIES/BENEFITS:

Pension Plan:	ESOP Stock Plan:	Profit Sharing: Y	Top Exec. Salary: $843,750	Bonus: $653,940
Savings Plan: Y	Stock Purch. Plan:		Second Exec. Salary: $428,269	Bonus: $199,735

OTHER THOUGHTS:

Apparent Women Officers or Directors: 2
Hot Spot for Advancement for Women/Minorities: Y

LOCATIONS: ("Y" = Yes)

West:	Southwest:	Midwest:	Southeast:	Northeast:	International:
Y					

LUMENIS LTD

www.lumenis.com

Industry Group Code: 339113 **Ranks within this company's industry group:** Sales: Profits:

Insurance/HMO/PPO:		Drugs:		Equipment/Supplies:		Hospitals/Clinics:		Services:		Health Care:	
Insurance:		Manufacturer:		Manufacturer:	Y	Acute Care:		Diagnostics:		Home Health:	
Managed Care:		Distributor:		Distributor:		Sub-Acute:		Labs/Testing:		Long-Term Care:	
Utilization Management:		Specialty Pharmacy:		Leasing/Finance:		Outpatient Surgery:		Staffing:		Physical Therapy:	
Payment Processing:		Vitamins/Nutritionals:		Information Systems:		Physical Rehab. Ctr.:		Waste Disposal:		Physician Prac. Mgmt.:	
		Clinical Trials:				Psychiatric Clinics:		Specialty Svcs.:			

TYPES OF BUSINESS:

Laser Surgery Products
Aesthetic Laser Products
Ophthalmic Laser Products
Veterinarian Laser Products
Dental Laser Products

BRANDS/DIVISIONS/AFFILIATES:

Intense Pulsed Light
Elora IPL
LightSheer
Selecta Duet
Aura PT
Opal PDT
Visudyne
Novartis AG

CONTACTS:

Note: Officers with more than one job title may be intentionally listed here more than once.

Dov Ofer, CEO
Zivi Nedivi, COO
Avner Raz, Pres.
Lauri A. Hanover, CFO/Sr. VP
Ruth Shaked, VP-Human Resources
Amnon Harari, Sr. VP-R&D
Igor Gradov, CTO/VP
William Weisel, General Counsel/Corp. Sec./VP
Robert Mann, Pres., Lumenis America
Kow (Alex) Tanaka, Pres., Lumenis Japan
Nelson Mendes, Pres., Lumenis Latin America/Caribbean
Zhai Qiying, Pres., Lumenis China/Asia Pacific
Harel Beit-On, Chmn.
Eckhard Lachenaur, Pres., Lumenis Europe

Phone: 972-4-959-9000	**Fax:** 972-4-959-9050
Toll-Free:	
Address: Yokneam Industrial Park, Yokneam, 20692 Israel	

GROWTH PLANS/SPECIAL FEATURES:

Lumenis, Ltd. is a world leader in laser and light-based technologies for medical and aesthetic applications. The company has more than 70,000 systems installed in doctors offices, clinics and operating rooms in over 100 countries. Approximately 48.4% of its 2006 revenues came from the Americas, and of that revenue 90% came from the U.S. 22.6% came from Europe; 14.9% came from China and Asia Pacific; and 14.1% came from Japan. The company has five main product areas: Aesthetic, which accounted for 34% of Lumenis' 2006 revenues; ophthalmic (eye-related), 19%; surgical, 22%; dental, 3%; and veterinary, 22%. Aesthetic applications include tattoo and hair removal; treating wrinkles; reducing the damage from sun, aging or environmental exposure; removing brown spots, sunspots, scars and stretch marks; and removing vascular lesions such as spider veins and other red spots. Products include Intense Pulsed Light (IPL) technology that generates high temperature broad band light pulses, including the Elora IPL skin treatment; and various laser systems including the LightSheer hair removal laser. Ophthalmic systems include the Selecta Duet and Aura PT photodisruptors that separate tissue or drill holes in the retina as part of a cataract or glaucoma treatment. It also produces the Opal PDT laser system that activates the drug Visudyne, provided by Novartis AG, which removes abnormal blood vessels without cutting. Surgical systems are generally lasers, and have a wide variety of applications including in dermatology, urology, neurosurgery, gastroenterology, orthopedic surgery and general surgery. The laser systems may be used to resurface skin, ablate (or remove) tissue, coagulate blood, vaporize tissue and even treat fungal infections. Dental applications typically involve drilling, cavity preparation, gum trimming and periodontal procedures; and the lasers can even whiten teeth. Veterinary surgical applications include the removal of cysts, tumors and warts; neutering; spaying; and declawing.

FINANCIALS:

Sales and profits are in thousands of dollars—add 000 to get the full amount. 2007 Note: Financial information for 2007 was not available for all companies at press time.

2007 Sales: $	2007 Profits: $	**U.S. Stock Ticker: LUME.PK**
2006 Sales: $	2006 Profits: $	**Int'l Ticker:** Int'l Exchange:
2005 Sales: $283,329	2005 Profits: $-14,666	Employees: 900
2004 Sales: $272,698	2004 Profits: $-12,004	Fiscal Year Ends: 12/31
2003 Sales: $287,200	2003 Profits: $-78,300	Parent Company:

SALARIES/BENEFITS:

Pension Plan:	ESOP Stock Plan:	Profit Sharing:	Top Exec. Salary: $265,261	Bonus: $520,000
Savings Plan:	Stock Purch. Plan:		Second Exec. Salary: $264,974	Bonus: $163,928

OTHER THOUGHTS:

Apparent Women Officers or Directors: 3
Hot Spot for Advancement for Women/Minorities: Y

LOCATIONS: ("Y" = Yes)

West:	Southwest:	Midwest:	Southeast:	Northeast:	International:
Y					Y

LUXOTTICA GROUP SPA

www.luxottica.it

Industry Group Code: 333314 **Ranks within this company's industry group:** Sales: 1 Profits: 1

Insurance/HMO/PPO:		**Drugs:**		**Equipment/Supplies:**		**Hospitals/Clinics:**		**Services:**		**Health Care:**	
Insurance:		Manufacturer:		Manufacturer:	Y	Acute Care:		Diagnostics:		Home Health:	
Managed Care:		Distributor:		Distributor:		Sub-Acute:		Labs/Testing:		Long-Term Care:	
Utilization Management:		Specialty Pharmacy:		Leasing/Finance:		Outpatient Surgery:		Staffing:		Physical Therapy:	
Payment Processing:		Vitamins/Nutritionals:		Information Systems:		Physical Rehab. Ctr.:		Waste Disposal:		Physician Prac. Mgmt.:	
		Clinical Trials:				Psychiatric Clinics:		Specialty Svcs.:	Y		

TYPES OF BUSINESS:

Lens/Eyeglass Frame Manufacturing
Vision Plan Provider
Lens/Eyeglass Frame Retailer
Eye Care Services

BRANDS/DIVISIONS/AFFILIATES:

Ray Ban
Vogue
Luxottica, S.r.l.
LensCrafters, Inc.
EyeMed Vision Care, LLC
FeatherWates SPF
D.O.C Optics
I.C. Optics, S.r.l.

CONTACTS: *Note: Officers with more than one job title may be intentionally listed here more than once.*

Andrea Guerra, CEO
Enrico Cavatorta, CFO
Fabio D'Angelantonio, Head-Group Mktg.
Nicola Pela, Head-Group Human Resources
Umberto Soccal, Group Chief IT Officer
Marco Vendramini, Group Chief Admin. Officer
Mario Lugli, General Counsel
Sabina Grossi, Head-Investor Rel.
Enrico Mistron, Controller
Frank Baynham, Exec. VP-Stores, Retail North America
Tom Coleman, Exec. VP-Retail Asia-Pacific
Crhis Beer, COO-Retail, Asia-Pacifica, Australia & New Zealand
George Minakakis, COO-Greater China
Leonardo Del Vecchio, Exec. Chmn.
Kerry Bradley, COO-Retail, North America

Phone: 39-02-863341	**Fax:** 39-0437-63223
Toll-Free:	
Address: Via C. Cantu, 2, Milan, 20123 Italy	

GROWTH PLANS/SPECIAL FEATURES:

Luxottica Group S.p.A. is one of the world's largest manufacturers and retailers of prescription and fashion eyeglass frames and sunglasses. Company-owned brands include Ray Ban, Vogue, Persol, Arnette, Killer Loop, Revo, Sferoflex and Luxottica. It licenses brands from Prada, Ungaro, Versace, Chanel, DKNY, Bvlgari, Moschino, Brooks Brothers, Miu Miu, Anne Klein and others. Some of the firm's subsidiaries include Luxottica, S.r.l.; Killer Loop Eyewear, S.r.l.; Tristar Optical Co., Ltd.; Collezione Rathschuler; Luxottica Leasing, SPA; Luxottica USA; LensCrafters, Inc.; Luxottica Luxembourg; and other retail and wholesale subsidiaries located worldwide. In 2006, Luxottica distributed approximately 18.6 million prescription frames and 24.8 million sunglasses in 5,100 models through its wholesale and retail networks in 120 countries worldwide. Luxottica is involved in the U.S. health care market through subsidiary EyeMed Vision Care, LLC. EyeMed offers members a vision plan including a network of optometrists, ophthalmologists and opticians; and Luxottica eyeglass frames. Luxottica manufactures one of the only prescription sunglass lenses, called FeatherWates SPF, to receive the Skin Cancer Foundation's Seal of Recommendation. In February 2006, Luxottica announced it had signed a ten-year eye-glasses licensing agreement, worth over $1.75 billion, with Polo Ralph Lauren Corp. In February 2007, the Group acquired the retail optical business of D.O.C Optics, with 100 stores in the American Midwest, for approximately $110 million. In March 2007, the company approved a partial de-merger of Luxottica S.r.l., intended to help streamline the subsidiary. Luxottica Group will retain the main assets of Luxottica including trademarks and some interests Luxottica had in the Group's retail division. Some other assets will be transferred to Group subsidiary I.C. Optics, S.r.l. In March 2007, the company acquired two sunglasses retail chains in South Africa with a total 65 stores, for approximately $13.96 million. In June 2007, the firm agreed to acquire Oakley, Inc. for $2.1 billion.

FINANCIALS: **Sales and profits are in thousands of dollars—add 000 to get the full amount. 2007 Note: Financial information for 2007 was not available for all companies at press time.**

2007 Sales: $	2007 Profits: $	**U.S. Stock Ticker: LUX**
2006 Sales: $5,175,835	2006 Profits: $405,345	**Int'l Ticker: LUX** Int'l Exchange: Milan-BI
2005 Sales: $5,260,312	2005 Profits: $411,959	Employees: 55,000
2004 Sales: $3,917,844	2004 Profits: $345,208	Fiscal Year Ends: 12/31
2003 Sales: $3,551,100	2003 Profits: $336,100	Parent Company:

SALARIES/BENEFITS:

Pension Plan:	ESOP Stock Plan:	Profit Sharing:	Top Exec. Salary: $1,152,808	Bonus: $780,042
Savings Plan:	Stock Purch. Plan:		Second Exec. Salary: $178,301	Bonus: $1,316,699

OTHER THOUGHTS:

Apparent Women Officers or Directors: 4
Hot Spot for Advancement for Women/Minorities: Y

LOCATIONS: ("Y" = Yes)

West:	Southwest:	Midwest:	Southeast:	Northeast:	International:
Y	Y	Y	Y	Y	Y

Note: Financial information, benefits and other data can change quickly and may vary from those stated here.

MAGELLAN HEALTH SERVICES INCwww.magellanhealth.com

Industry Group Code: 622210 **Ranks within this company's industry group:** Sales: 1 Profits: 1

Insurance/HMO/PPO:		Drugs:		Equipment/Supplies:		Hospitals/Clinics:		Services:		Health Care:	
Insurance:		Manufacturer:		Manufacturer:		Acute Care:		Diagnostics:		Home Health:	
Managed Care:	Y	Distributor:		Distributor:		Sub-Acute:		Labs/Testing:		Long-Term Care:	
Utilization Management:	Y	Specialty Pharmacy:		Leasing/Finance:		Outpatient Surgery:		Staffing:		Physical Therapy:	
Payment Processing:		Vitamins/Nutritionals:		Information Systems:	Y	Physical Rehab. Ctr.:		Waste Disposal:		Physician Prac. Mgmt.:	
		Clinical Trials:				Psychiatric Clinics:		Specialty Svcs.:	Y		

TYPES OF BUSINESS:

Managed Behavioral Health Care Plans
Psychiatric Hospitals
Residential Treatment Centers

BRANDS/DIVISIONS/AFFILIATES:

ICORE Healthcare, LLC
National Imaging Associates, Inc.
Managed Behavioral Healthcare

CONTACTS: *Note: Officers with more than one job title may be intentionally listed here more than once.*

Steven J. Shulman, CEO
Rene Lerer, COO
Rene Lerer, Pres.
Mark S. Demilio, CFO
Michael Majerik, Chief Sales & Mktg. Officer
Caskie Lewis-Clapper, Chief Human Resources Officer
Anthony M. Kotin, Chief Clinical Officer
Daniel N. Gregoire, General Counsel
Erin S. Somers, Sr. VP-Public Rel.
John J. Donahue, Chmn.-Nat'l Imaging Associates
Eric Reimer, CEO-Nat'l Imaging Associates
Raju L. Mantena, Pres., ICORE Healthcore, LLC.
Russell C. Petrella, Pres., Behavioral Health
Steven J. Shulman, Chmn.

Phone: 860-507-1900	**Fax:** 860-507-1990
Toll-Free: 800-410-8312	
Address: 55 Nod Rd., Avon, CT 06001 US	

GROWTH PLANS/SPECIAL FEATURES:

Magellan Health Services, Inc. mainly provides health-related services through six segments. Magellan's main business is Managed Behavioral Healthcare, running three segments. In general, its counseling, therapy and crisis intervention services are provided through third-party treatment providers including psychiatrists and psychologists; as well as through psychiatric hospitals, residential treatment centers and other treatment facilities. It provides risk-based products, where the company assumes all or a portion of the responsibility of treatment costs; administrative services only (ASO) products, where the company provides claims administration, utilization renewal or provider network management; and employee assistance programs (EAPs), where the company provides short outpatient counseling. The Health Plan segment, working with managed care companies and other health plans, has 7.7 million risk-based, 0.2 million EAP and 19.7 million ASO customers; and its combined 2006 revenue was $656 million. The Employer segment works with corporations, government agencies and labor unions; it has 0.1 million risk-based, 13.6 million EAP and 0.2 million ASO customers, and generated $128.7 million in revenue. The Public Sector segment works with Medicaid recipients through state and local governments; has 1.8 million risk-based and 0.2 million ASO customers; and generated $808.7 million in revenue. ICORE Healthcare, LLC, acquired in July 2006 for approximately $210 million added specialty pharmaceuticals; and National Imaging Associates, Inc., acquired in January 2006 for approximately $121 million, added radiology benefits management businesses to the company's offerings. The pharmaceutical segment contracts with 29 health plans and 10 pharmaceutical manufacturers; and the radiology segment manages the benefits of 17.3 million people. The company's last segment is corporate and other, which provides operational support functions such as sales, marketing and IT; and corporate support functions such as executive, finance, human resources and legal.

Magellan offers flexible spending accounts, tuition reimbursement, adoption assistance, a confidential employee assistance program, and a medical plan.

FINANCIALS: **Sales and profits are in thousands of dollars—add 000 to get the full amount. 2007 Note: Financial information for 2007 was not available for all companies at press time.**

2007 Sales: $	2007 Profits: $	**U.S. Stock Ticker: MGLN**
2006 Sales: $1,690,270	2006 Profits: $86,871	**Int'l Ticker:** Int'l Exchange:
2005 Sales: $1,808,003	2005 Profits: $130,589	Employees: 3,900
2004 Sales: $1,795,402	2004 Profits: $64,315	Fiscal Year Ends: 12/31
2003 Sales: $1,510,746	2003 Profits: $451,770	Parent Company:

SALARIES/BENEFITS:

Pension Plan:	ESOP Stock Plan: Y	Profit Sharing:	Top Exec. Salary: $1,071,200	Bonus: $1,839,000
Savings Plan: Y	Stock Purch. Plan: Y		Second Exec. Salary: $642,720	Bonus: $1,095,000

OTHER THOUGHTS:

Apparent Women Officers or Directors: 2
Hot Spot for Advancement for Women/Minorities:

LOCATIONS: ("Y" = Yes)

West:	Southwest:	Midwest:	Southeast:	Northeast:	International:
Y	Y	Y	Y	Y	

MALLINCKRODT INC

www.mallinckrodt.com

Industry Group Code: 325413 **Ranks within this company's industry group:** Sales: Profits:

Insurance/HMO/PPO:		Drugs:		Equipment/Supplies:		Hospitals/Clinics:		Services:		Health Care:	
Insurance:		Manufacturer:	Y	Manufacturer:	Y	Acute Care:		Diagnostics:		Home Health:	
Managed Care:		Distributor:		Distributor:		Sub-Acute:		Labs/Testing:		Long-Term Care:	
Utilization Management:		Specialty Pharmacy:		Leasing/Finance:		Outpatient Surgery:		Staffing:		Physical Therapy:	
Payment Processing:		Vitamins/Nutritionals:		Information Systems:		Physical Rehab. Ctr.:		Waste Disposal:		Physician Prac. Mgmt.:	
		Clinical Trials:				Psychiatric Clinics:		Specialty Svcs.:			

TYPES OF BUSINESS:

Imaging Agents & Radiopharmaceuticals
Diagnostics Products
Bulk Analgesic Pharmaceuticals
Generic Pharmaceuticals
Active Pharmaceutical Ingredients
Medical Devices
Respiratory Products

BRANDS/DIVISIONS/AFFILIATES:

Puritan-Bennett
Shiley
DAR
Nellcor
OptiMARK
OxiFirst
NeutroSpec
Covidien Ltd.

CONTACTS: *Note: Officers with more than one job title may be intentionally listed here more than once.*

Douglas A. McKinney, CFO
Lisa Britt, VP-Human Resources
Douglas A. McKinney, VP-Finance
Scott Drake, Pres., Respiratory Div.
Michael J. Collins, Pres., Pharmaceuticals Div.
Steven Hanley, Pres., Imaging Div.

Phone: 314-654-2000 **Fax:** 314-654-5381
Toll-Free: 800-325-8888
Address: 675 McDonnell Blvd., Hazelwood, MO 63042 US

GROWTH PLANS/SPECIAL FEATURES:

Mallinckrodt, Inc., a subsidiary of Covidien Ltd. (formerly Tyco Healthcare Group), develops and manufactures a wide range of medical products and devices, primarily used by hospitals for diagnostic and treatment purposes. It is a world leader in bulk analgesic pharmaceuticals and a leader in generic dosage pharmaceuticals. The company's imaging group produces a full line of imaging agents and radiopharmaceuticals, including ultrasound and MRI contrast agents, x-ray contrast media, catheters and injection systems. Through its respiratory segment, the firm offers a variety of products, including anesthesia, airway management and temperature management devices; medical gases; oxygen therapy and asthma management products; sleep diagnostics and therapy devices; and blood analysis products. Its products are sold under the Shiley, DAR, Nellcor and Puritan-Bennett brands. Mallinckrodt's pharmaceuticals division is focused on providing pain relief and addiction therapy, with a product line that includes codeine, morphine, methadone, naltrexone (for alcohol addiction) and methylphenidate (for attention deficit/hyperactivity disorder). It also supplies raw materials and active pharmaceutical ingredients, makes generic drugs and provides contract manufacturing and other services. Its Brand Pharmaceuticals business acquires and markets other companies' under-promoted products. The company is the developer of the OxiFirst fetal oxygen monitoring system, a new technology that enables obstetricians to monitor fetal oxygenation during labor and delivery. The firm's imaging division has developed OptiMARK, the first and only MRI contrast agent that is FDA-approved for administration by power injection.

FINANCIALS: **Sales and profits are in thousands of dollars—add 000 to get the full amount. 2007 Note: Financial information for 2007 was not available for all companies at press time.**

2007 Sales: $	2007 Profits: $	**U.S. Stock Ticker: Subsidiary**
2006 Sales: $	2006 Profits: $	**Int'l Ticker:** Int'l Exchange:
2005 Sales: $	2005 Profits: $	Employees: 11,000
2004 Sales: $	2004 Profits: $	Fiscal Year Ends: 9/30
2003 Sales: $	2003 Profits: $	Parent Company: COVIDIEN LTD

SALARIES/BENEFITS:

Pension Plan:	ESOP Stock Plan:	Profit Sharing:	Top Exec. Salary: $732,840	Bonus: $4,072,400
Savings Plan:	Stock Purch. Plan:		Second Exec. Salary: $322,793	Bonus: $1,095,600

OTHER THOUGHTS:

Apparent Women Officers or Directors: 1
Hot Spot for Advancement for Women/Minorities:

LOCATIONS: ("Y" = Yes)

West:	Southwest:	Midwest:	Southeast:	Northeast:	International:
Y		Y		Y	Y

MANOR CARE INC www.hcr-manorcare.com

Industry Group Code: 623110 **Ranks within this company's industry group:** Sales: 2 Profits: 1

Insurance/HMO/PPO:		Drugs:		Equipment/Supplies:		Hospitals/Clinics:		Services:		Health Care:	
Insurance:		Manufacturer:		Manufacturer:		Acute Care:		Diagnostics:		Home Health:	Y
Managed Care:		Distributor:		Distributor:		Sub-Acute:	Y	Labs/Testing:		Long-Term Care:	Y
Utilization Management:		Specialty Pharmacy:		Leasing/Finance:		Outpatient Surgery:		Staffing:		Physical Therapy:	
Payment Processing:		Vitamins/Nutritionals:		Information Systems:		Physical Rehab. Ctr.:	Y	Waste Disposal:		Physician Prac. Mgmt.:	
		Clinical Trials:				Psychiatric Clinics:		Specialty Svcs.:			

TYPES OF BUSINESS:

Long-Term Health Care/Nursing Homes
Home Health Care
Short-Term Care Facilities
Assisted Living Facilities
Rehabilitation Clinics

BRANDS/DIVISIONS/AFFILIATES:

HCR Manor Care
Springhouse
Heartland
HCR Manor Care Foundation
ManorCare
Arden Courts

CONTACTS: *Note: Officers with more than one job title may be intentionally listed here more than once.*

Paul A. Ormond, CEO
Stephen L. Guillard, COO/Exec. VP
Paul A. Ormond, Pres.
Steven M. Cavanaugh, CFO/VP
Richard A. Parr II, General Counsel/VP/Corp. Sec.
Spencer C. Moler, Controller/VP
Nancy A. Edwards, VP/Gen. Manager-Central Div.
John K. Graham, Group VP-Hospice & Home Care
Jeffrey A. Grillo, VP/Gen. Manager-Mid-Atlantic Div.
Lynn M. Hood, VP/Gen. Manager-Southeast Div.
Paul A. Ormond, Chmn.

Phone: 419-252-5500	**Fax:**
Toll-Free:	
Address: 333 N. Summit St., Toledo, OH 43604-2617 US	

GROWTH PLANS/SPECIAL FEATURES:

Manor Care, Inc. provides a range of health care services including skilled nursing care, assisted living, post-acute medical and rehabilitation care, hospice care, home health care and rehabilitation therapy. Manor Care operates 27[illegible] skilled nursing facilities and 65 assisted living facilities in 3[illegible] states, with 62% of its facilities located in Florida, Illinois Michigan, Ohio and Pennsylvania. These facilities primaril operate under the names Heartland, ManorCare Health Services and Arden Courts. Manor Care's long-term care services consist of skilled nursing centers, assisted living services, post-acute medical and rehabilitation care and Alzheimer's care. The skilled nursing centers use interdisciplinary teams of experienced medical professionals including registered nurses, licensed practical nurses and certified nursing assistants, to provide services prescribed by physicians, design Quality of Life programs to give the highest practicable level of functional independence to patients, provide physical, speech, respiratory and occupational therapy and provide quality nutrition services social services, activities and housekeeping and laundry services. Manor Care's assisted living services provide personal care services and assistance with general activitie of daily living such as dressing, bathing, meal preparation and medication management. Manor Care provides hospice and home health care through 116 offices in 25 states focusing on the physical, spiritual and psychosocial needs of individuals facing a life-limiting illness. Other health care services include outpatient rehabilitation therapy, which it provides in its 92 outpatient therapy clinics located in Midwestern and Mid-Atlantic states, Texas and Florida as well as through work sites, schools, hospitals and other health care settings. In July 2007, the firm agreed to be acquired and taken private by Carlyle Group for roughly $6.[illegible] billion.

Manor's employee benefits include tuition reimbursement access to a credit union, retirement benefits and medical dental, prescription drug and vision coverage.

FINANCIALS: **Sales and profits are in thousands of dollars—add 000 to get the full amount. 2007 Note: Financial information for 2007 was not available for all companies at press time.**

2007 Sales: $	2007 Profits: $	**U.S. Stock Ticker: HCR**
2006 Sales: $3,613,185	2006 Profits: $169,560	**Int'l Ticker:** Int'l Exchange:
2005 Sales: $3,417,290	2005 Profits: $160,955	Employees: 59,500
2004 Sales: $3,208,867	2004 Profits: $168,222	Fiscal Year Ends: 12/31
2003 Sales: $3,029,441	2003 Profits: $119,007	Parent Company:

SALARIES/BENEFITS:

Pension Plan: Y	ESOP Stock Plan:	Profit Sharing:	Top Exec. Salary: $1,000,550	Bonus: $2,864,500
Savings Plan: Y	Stock Purch. Plan:		Second Exec. Salary: $639,015	Bonus: $1,429,000

OTHER THOUGHTS:

Apparent Women Officers or Directors: 3
Hot Spot for Advancement for Women/Minorities: Y

LOCATIONS: ("Y" = Yes)

West:	Southwest:	Midwest:	Southeast:	Northeast:	International:
Y	Y	Y	Y	Y	

MARIAN HEALTH SYSTEMS www.marianhealthsystem.com

Industry Group Code: 622110 **Ranks within this company's industry group:** Sales: 17 Profits: 16

Insurance/HMO/PPO:		Drugs:		Equipment/Supplies:		Hospitals/Clinics:		Services:		Health Care:	
nsurance:		Manufacturer:		Manufacturer:		Acute Care:	Y	Diagnostics:		Home Health:	Y
Managed Care:		Distributor:		Distributor:		Sub-Acute:	Y	Labs/Testing:	Y	Long-Term Care:	Y
Utilization Management:		Specialty Pharmacy:		Leasing/Finance:		Outpatient Surgery:	Y	Staffing:		Physical Therapy:	Y
Payment Processing:		Vitamins/Nutritionals:		Information Systems:		Physical Rehab. Ctr.:	Y	Waste Disposal:		Physician Prac. Mgmt.:	
		Clinical Trials:				Psychiatric Clinics:	Y	Specialty Svcs.:			

TYPES OF BUSINESS:

Hospitals
Senior Communities
Long-Term Care
Home Care Services
Rehabilitation Services
Cancer Care
Dialysis Centers

BRANDS/DIVISIONS/AFFILIATES:

Sisters of the Sorrowful Mother
Saint Clair's Health System
Ministry Health Care
Affinity Health System
Saint John Health System
Via Christi Health System

CONTACTS: *Note: Officers with more than one job title may be intentionally listed here more than once.*

M. Therese Gottschalk, CEO
M. Therese Gottschalk, Pres.
Nicholas Desien, CEO/Pres., Ministry Health Care
Gary J. Blan, CEO/Pres., Saint Clare's Health System
Kevin P. Conlin, CEO/Pres., Via Christi Health System
M. Therese Gottschalk, CEO/Pres., St. John Health System

Phone: 918-742-9988 **Fax:**
Toll-Free:
Address: P.O. Box 4753, Tulsa, OK 74159 US

GROWTH PLANS/SPECIAL FEATURES:

Marian Health System is a vehicle through which the Sisters of the Sorrowful Mother minister healthcare to the needy. The company manages four health care systems in Kansas, New Jersey, Oklahoma and Wisconsin, and has decentralized management for each location to respond more efficiently to local needs. Marian has separated its organizations into four regional companies: the Saint Clair's Health System, Ministry Health Care, St. John Health System and Via Christi Health System. The Saint Clair's Health System has four hospitals and three senior assistance communities. Health care services include women's health, maternal-child care, emergency services, pediatrics, behavioral therapy and cancer care through an affiliation with Memorial Sloan-Kettering Cancer Center. The Ministry Health Care system includes eight hospitals, two medical centers, clinics, long-term care facilities, home care agencies, dialysis centers and many other programs and services in Wisconsin and Minnesota. The Affinity Health System, located in Wisconsin, runs one hospital, two medical centers, a rehabilitation center, a nursing home called Saint Elisabeth's and a convalescent center. The St. John Health System manages five health centers and six nursing homes and is a regional leader in radiology, cardiology, oncology, urology, wellness and physical rehabilitation. The Via Christi Health System, co-sponsored with the Sisters of St. Joseph of Wichita, has five hospitals and medical centers and 10 senior living communities.

FINANCIALS: **Sales and profits are in thousands of dollars—add 000 to get the full amount. 2007 Note: Financial information for 2007 was not available for all companies at press time.**

2007 Sales: $	2007 Profits: $	**U.S. Stock Ticker: Nonprofit**
2006 Sales: $3,144,406	2006 Profits: $84,095	**Int'l Ticker:** Int'l Exchange:
2005 Sales: $2,969,453	2005 Profits: $108,115	Employees: 4,011
2004 Sales: $2,855,369	2004 Profits: $111,294	Fiscal Year Ends: 9/30
2003 Sales: $2,765,665	2003 Profits: $68,304	Parent Company:

SALARIES/BENEFITS:

Pension Plan:	ESOP Stock Plan:	Profit Sharing:	Top Exec. Salary: $	Bonus: $
Savings Plan:	Stock Purch. Plan:		Second Exec. Salary: $	Bonus: $

OTHER THOUGHTS:

Apparent Women Officers or Directors: 1
Hot Spot for Advancement for Women/Minorities:

LOCATIONS: ("Y" = Yes)

West:	Southwest:	Midwest:	Southeast:	Northeast:	International:
	Y	Y		Y	

MARSH & MCLENNAN COMPANIES INC www.marshmac.com

Industry Group Code: 524210 **Ranks within this company's industry group:** Sales: 1 Profits: 1

Insurance/HMO/PPO:		Drugs:		Equipment/Supplies:		Hospitals/Clinics:		Services:		Health Care:	
Insurance:	Y	Manufacturer:		Manufacturer:		Acute Care:		Diagnostics:		Home Health:	
Managed Care:		Distributor:		Distributor:		Sub-Acute:		Labs/Testing:		Long-Term Care:	
Utilization Management:		Specialty Pharmacy:		Leasing/Finance:		Outpatient Surgery:		Staffing:		Physical Therapy:	
Payment Processing:		Vitamins/Nutritionals:		Information Systems:		Physical Rehab. Ctr.:		Waste Disposal:		Physician Prac. Mgmt.:	
		Clinical Trials:				Psychiatric Clinics:		Specialty Svcs.:	Y		

TYPES OF BUSINESS:

Insurance Brokerage
Consulting Services
Risk Management
Benefits Administration
Human Resources Services

BRANDS/DIVISIONS/AFFILIATES:

Marsh, Inc.
Guy Carpenter & Company, LLC
Marsh & McLennan Risk Capital Holdings
Kroll Inc
Mercer Inc
Oliver Wyman Group
Mercer Specialty Consulting
Putnam LLC

CONTACTS: *Note: Officers with more than one job title may be intentionally listed here more than once.*

Michael G. Cherkasky, CEO/Acting CEO-Marsh, Inc.
Michael G. Cherkasky, Pres.
Matthew B. Bartley, CFO
James Speros, Chief Mktg. Officer/Sr. VP
Michael A. Petrullo, Chief Admin. Officer/Sr. VP
Peter J. Beshar, General Counsel/Exec. VP
Michael A. Beber, Chief Strategic Dev. Officer/Sr. VP
Christine Walton, VP-Public Rel.
Mike Bischoff, VP-Investor Rel.
Alan W. Bieler, Treas.
M. Michele Burns, Chmn./CEO-Mercer, Inc.
Simon Freakley, CEO/Pres., Kroll Inc.
John Drzik, CEO/Pres., Oliver Wyman Group
David Spiller, CEO/Pres., Guy Carpenter & Company, LLC
Stephen R. Hardis, Chmn.
Mathis Cabiallavetta, Chmn.-MCC Int'l

Phone: 212-345-5000	**Fax:** 212-345-4838
Toll-Free:	
Address: 1166 Ave. of the Americas, New York, NY 10036-2774 US	

GROWTH PLANS/SPECIAL FEATURES:

Marsh and McLennan Companies, Inc. (MMC), one of th world's largest insurance brokerage firms, provides globa professional services with transactional capabilities to client in over 100 countries. The company operates thre segments: Risk and Insurance Services; Risk Consulting an Technology; and Consulting. The Risk and Insuranc segment, which generated 45% of MMC's operatin segments revenue, is primarily composed of two companie and their subsidiaries. Marsh, Inc., operating through 40 offices in 100 countries, provides risk managemen insurance broking, consulting and insurance progran management services; and Guy Carpenter & Company, LL provides reinsurance broking, catastrophe and financia modeling services and related advisory functions. Thi segment also owns investments in private equity funds an other firms through Marsh & McLennan Risk Capita Holdings. Risk Consulting and Technology, which generate 8% of revenues, consists of Kroll, Inc. and its subsidiaries Besides technology and consulting services, it provide security as well as corporate advisory and restructuring. It consulting services include finance and risk managemen The Consulting segment, which generated 35% of revenue operates through Mercer, Inc. and its two main subsidiaries Mercer Human Resource Consulting and Mercer Specialt Consulting. Mercer Human Resource offers consultation covering retirement and investments; health and benefits talent; and outsourcing. It has 16,700 colleagues in forty-on countries. Mercer Specialty offers consultations coverin management; organization design and change; an economics. It has 3,100 colleagues in over fifty countries Finally, the company formerly ran an Investmen Management segment, generating 12% of 2006 segmen revenue, operated through Putnam Investments Trust. I August 2007, the firm completed the sale of Putnan Investments to Great-West Lifeco, Inc., a unit of Powe Financial Corp., for $3.9 billion. Putnam Investment managed over 10 million shareholder accounts and over 30 institutional accounts.

The company provides an employee gifts matching program and health and welfare benefit programs.

FINANCIALS: **Sales and profits are in thousands of dollars—add 000 to get the full amount. 2007 Note: Financial information for 2007 was not available for all companies at press time.**

2007 Sales: $	2007 Profits: $	**U.S. Stock Ticker: MMC**
2006 Sales: $11,921,000	2006 Profits: $990,000	**Int'l Ticker:** Int'l Exchange:
2005 Sales: $11,578,000	2005 Profits: $404,000	Employees: 55,000
2004 Sales: $11,727,000	2004 Profits: $176,000	Fiscal Year Ends: 12/31
2003 Sales: $11,588,000	2003 Profits: $1,540,000	Parent Company:

SALARIES/BENEFITS:

Pension Plan: Y	ESOP Stock Plan:	Profit Sharing:	Top Exec. Salary: $1,000,000	Bonus: $2,650,000
Savings Plan: Y	Stock Purch. Plan: Y		Second Exec. Salary: $1,000,000	Bonus: $2,500,000

OTHER THOUGHTS:

Apparent Women Officers or Directors: 2
Hot Spot for Advancement for Women/Minorities:

LOCATIONS: ("Y" = Yes)

West:	Southwest:	Midwest:	Southeast:	Northeast:	International:
Y	Y	Y		Y	Y

Note: Financial information, benefits and other data can change quickly and may vary from those stated here.

MATRIA HEALTHCARE INC

www.matria.com

Industry Group Code: 621610 **Ranks within this company's industry group:** Sales: 7 Profits: 2

Insurance/HMO/PPO:		Drugs:		Equipment/Supplies:		Hospitals/Clinics:		Services:		Health Care:	
Insurance:		Manufacturer:		Manufacturer:		Acute Care:		Diagnostics:		Home Health:	Y
Managed Care:		Distributor:		Distributor:	Y	Sub-Acute:		Labs/Testing:		Long-Term Care:	
Utilization Management:	Y	Specialty Pharmacy:		Leasing/Finance:		Outpatient Surgery:		Staffing:		Physical Therapy:	
Payment Processing:		Vitamins/Nutritionals:		Information Systems:		Physical Rehab. Ctr.:		Waste Disposal:		Physician Prac. Mgmt.:	
		Clinical Trials:				Psychiatric Clinics:		Specialty Svcs.:	Y		

TYPES OF BUSINESS:

Disease Management Services
Home Health Care-Obstetrical
Blood Sampling & Testing Devices
High-Risk Maternity Care
Women & Children's Health
Medical Diagnostics

BRANDS/DIVISIONS/AFFILIATES:

Health Enhancement
Quality Oncology, Inc.
Miavita, LLC
WinningHabits, Inc.
CorSolutions Medical, Inc.

CONTACTS: *Note: Officers with more than one job title may be intentionally listed here more than once.*

Parker H. Petit, CEO
Richard M. Hassett, COO
Richard M. Hassett, Pres.
Jeffrey L. Hinton, CFO/Sr. VP
Steven Janicak, Chief Mktg. Officer
Martin L. Olson, Sr. VP-R&D/Informatics
Robert W. Kelley, Jr., VP-Tech.
Thornton A. Kuntz, Jr., Chief Admin. Officer/Sr. VP
Roberta L. McCaw, General Counsel/VP-Legal/Sec.
Ronald R. Loeppke, Chief Strategic Officer/Exec. VP
Richard A. Cockrell, VP-Investor Rel.
Joseph A. Blankenship, Corp. Controller/VP
Kenneth P. Yale, VP-Gov't Programs
Donald E. Fetterolf, Corp. VP-Health Intelligence
Yvonne V. Scoggins, Sr. VP-Bus. Analysis
Earl P. Rousseau, Pres., Health Enhancement
Parker H. Petit, Chmn.

Phone: 770-767-4500	**Fax:** 770-767-4521
Toll-Free: 800-456-4060	
Address: 1850 Parkway Pl., Marietta, GA 30067 US	

GROWTH PLANS/SPECIAL FEATURES:

Matria Healthcare, Inc. provides comprehensive, integrated programs and services focused on wellness, disease and condition management, productivity enhancement and informatics. The company calls this suite of services Health Enhancement, which has 50 service centers throughout the U.S. It primarily serves self-insured employers; private and government sponsored health plans; pharmaceutical companies; and patients. Approximately 57% of its 2006 revenue came from health plans, 34% from employers, 7% from government payors and 2% from administrative services only self-insured employer clients. Matria's disease management programs help patients with diabetes, emphysema, asthma, obesity, chronic pain, substance abuse, cancer, back pain, coronary artery disease, high-risk obstetrics, smoking cessation and asthma. Included in this list are its interactive online services such as smoking cessation aids and exercise programs. The firm also offers women's and children's health care with disease management services designed to assist physicians in the management of maternity patients. Services include risk assessment, patient education and management, infusion therapy, gestational diabetes management and other monitoring and clinical services as prescribed by the patient's physician. Some of its former acquisitions include Quality Oncology, Inc., provider of cancer disease management services; Miavita, LLC, an online provider of health and wellness programs; and WinningHabits, Inc., a provider of corporate wellness programs. It formerly offered a pharmacy as well as divesting Facet Technologies, Inc., and Dia Real, which designed its diabetes products, in September and October 2006, respectively. In January 2006, it acquired CorSolutions Medical, Inc., another leading provider of disease management services, and underwent a major restructuring, now managing all its business under the Health Enhancement segment.

The company offers employees educational assistance, adoption assistance and credit union membership.

FINANCIALS: **Sales and profits are in thousands of dollars—add 000 to get the full amount. 2007 Note: Financial information for 2007 was not available for all companies at press time.**

2007 Sales: $	2007 Profits: $	**U.S. Stock Ticker: MATR**
2006 Sales: $336,139	2006 Profits: $52,690	**Int'l Ticker:** Int'l Exchange:
2005 Sales: $179,231	2005 Profits: $13,963	Employees: 1,766
2004 Sales: $145,087	2004 Profits: $27,066	Fiscal Year Ends: 12/31
2003 Sales: $326,847	2003 Profits: $7,306	Parent Company:

SALARIES/BENEFITS:

Pension Plan:	ESOP Stock Plan:	Profit Sharing:	Top Exec. Salary: $544,576	Bonus: $315,000
Savings Plan: Y	Stock Purch. Plan: Y		Second Exec. Salary: $384,577	Bonus: $105,000

OTHER THOUGHTS:

Apparent Women Officers or Directors: 2
Hot Spot for Advancement for Women/Minorities: Y

LOCATIONS: ("Y" = Yes)

West:	Southwest:	Midwest:	Southeast:	Northeast:	International:
Y	Y	Y	Y	Y	Y

MAXYGEN INC www.maxygen.com

Industry Group Code: 325412 **Ranks within this company's industry group:** Sales: 40 Profits: 31

Insurance/HMO/PPO:		Drugs:		Equipment/Supplies:		Hospitals/Clinics:		Services:		Health Care:	
Insurance:		Manufacturer:	Y	Manufacturer:		Acute Care:		Diagnostics:		Home Health:	
Managed Care:		Distributor:		Distributor:		Sub-Acute:		Labs/Testing:	Y	Long-Term Care:	
Utilization Management:		Specialty Pharmacy:		Leasing/Finance:		Outpatient Surgery:		Staffing:		Physical Therapy:	
Payment Processing:		Vitamins/Nutritionals:		Information Systems:		Physical Rehab. Ctr.:		Waste Disposal:		Physician Prac. Mgmt.:	
		Clinical Trials:				Psychiatric Clinics:		Specialty Svcs.:	Y		

TYPES OF BUSINESS:

Drug Discovery & Development
Improved & Novel Pharmaceuticals
Research Services
Chemicals
Research & Development-Molecular Evolution

BRANDS/DIVISIONS/AFFILIATES:

MolecularBreeding
DNAShuffling
MaxyScan
Codexis, Inc.
Avidia
Maxy-G34
Maxy-alpha
InterMune

CONTACTS: *Note: Officers with more than one job title may be intentionally listed here more than once.*

Russell Howard, CEO
Elliot Goldstein, COO
Lawrence Briscoe, CFO/Sr. VP
Stuart Pollard, Chief Scientific Officer/Sr. VP
Michael Rabson, General Counsel/Sr. VP
Grant Yonehiro, Sr. VP-Oper.
Grant Yonehiro, Sr. VP-Global Bus. Dev.
Santosh Vetticaden, Chief Medical Officer
Isaac Stein, Chmn.

Phone: 650-298-5300	**Fax:** 650-364-2715
Toll-Free:	
Address: 301 Galveston Dr., Redwood City, CA 94063 US	

GROWTH PLANS/SPECIAL FEATURES:

Maxygen, Inc. is a biotechnology company that works on th discovery and development of improved protei pharmaceuticals for the treatment of diseases and seriou medical conditions. Technologies developed by Maxyge include MolecularBreeding, a process that mimics the natura events of evolution using DNAShuffling, a recombinatio process that generates a diverse library of novel DN sequences. MolecularBreeding allows the company t rapidly move from product concept to IND-ready dru candidate, lowering costs associated with research an expanding the potential for discovery. The company' MaxyScan screening systems than selects individu proteins with desired characteristics from gene variant within the library for additional experimentation. Maxyge currently has four product candidates in different clinic study phases: Maxy-G34, designed to treat neutropeni Maxy-alpha, for treatment of hepatitis C; Maxy VII, treatme of uncontrollable bleeding; and Maxy-Gamma, designed t treat pulmonary fibrosis. In addition to developing product Maxygen invests in HIV vaccines and Codexis, Inc, biotechnology company that improves the manufacturin process of small molecular pharmaceutical product Maxygen has also entered into several strategi collaborations with Roche to co-develop its MAXY-C product candidates for treatment of uncontrolled bleedin Maxygen is working with InterMune in order to develop an commercialize interferon gamma products. In October 200 Maxygen purchased Avidia from Amgen for $17.8 millio This newly acquired company will be used for th development of a new class of therapeutic peptides f treatment in the fields of autoimmunity, inflammation an oncology.

Maxygen offers its employees comprehensive medic insurance, service awards, concierge service, a credit unio annual Costco memberships, health club membership an tuition reimbursement. The company also pays 75% c employee mass transit costs and provides on-site bicycl lockers.

FINANCIALS: Sales and profits are in thousands of dollars—add 000 to get the full amount. 2007 Note: Financial information for 2007 was not available for all companies at press time.

2007 Sales: $	2007 Profits: $	**U.S. Stock Ticker: MAXY**
2006 Sales: $25,021	2006 Profits: $-16,482	**Int'l Ticker:** Int'l Exchange:
2005 Sales: $14,501	2005 Profits: $-18,436	Employees: 151
2004 Sales: $16,275	2004 Profits: $9,342	Fiscal Year Ends: 12/31
2003 Sales: $30,528	2003 Profits: $-44,964	Parent Company:

SALARIES/BENEFITS:

Pension Plan:	ESOP Stock Plan: Y	Profit Sharing:	Top Exec. Salary: $455,000	Bonus: $182,000
Savings Plan: Y	Stock Purch. Plan: Y		Second Exec. Salary: $366,261	Bonus: $181,130

OTHER THOUGHTS:

Apparent Women Officers or Directors: 1
Hot Spot for Advancement for Women/Minorities:

LOCATIONS: ("Y" = Yes)

West:	Southwest:	Midwest:	Southeast:	Northeast:	International:
Y					Y

Note: Financial information, benefits and other data can change quickly and may vary from those stated here.

MAYO FOUNDATION FOR MEDICAL EDUCATION AND RESEARCH

www.mayo.edu

ndustry Group Code: 622110 **Ranks within this company's industry group:** Sales: 10 Profits: 7

nsurance/HMO/PPO:		Drugs:		Equipment/Supplies:		Hospitals/Clinics:		Services:		Health Care:	
nsurance:		Manufacturer:		Manufacturer:		Acute Care:	Y	Diagnostics:	Y	Home Health:	
Aanaged Care:		Distributor:		Distributor:		Sub-Acute:	Y	Labs/Testing:	Y	Long-Term Care:	Y
Jtilization Management:		Specialty Pharmacy:		Leasing/Finance:		Outpatient Surgery:	Y	Staffing:		Physical Therapy:	
Payment Processing:		Vitamins/Nutritionals:		Information Systems:		Physical Rehab. Ctr.:		Waste Disposal:		Physician Prac. Mgmt.:	Y
		Clinical Trials:	Y			Psychiatric Clinics:		Specialty Svcs.:	Y		

TYPES OF BUSINESS:

Hospitals/Clinics-General & Specialty Hospitals
Physician Practice Management
Medical Research
Health Care Education

BRANDS/DIVISIONS/AFFILIATES:

Mayo Clinic
St. Marys Hospital
Rochester Medical Hospital
Mayo Eugenio Litta Children's Hospital
St. Luke's Hospital
Mayo Clinic Hospital
Mayo Health System
Mayo Clinic College of Medicine

CONTACTS: *Note: Officers with more than one job title may be intentionally listed here more than once.*

Denis A. Cortese, CEO
Denis A. Cortese, Pres.
Jeffrey W. Bolton, CFO
Abdul Bengali, Chmn.-IT
Shirley Weis, Chief Admin. Officer
Bert A. Getz, Chmn.

Phone: 507-284-2511	**Fax:** 507-284-0161
Toll-Free:	
Address: 200 1st St. SW, Rochester, MN 55905 US	

GROWTH PLANS/SPECIAL FEATURES:

The Mayo Foundation for Medical Education and Research is a not-for-profit health care organization providing medical treatment, physician management, health care education, research and other specialized medical services through a network of clinics and hospitals in the Midwest, Arizona and Florida. The three primary clinics, which house physician group practices, are located in Rochester, Minnesota; Jacksonville, Florida; and Scottsdale, Arizona. These clinics are accompanied by hospitals in each of the three cities. St. Marys Hospital, with 1,157 beds, Rochester Medical Hospital, with 794 beds and the 85-bed Mayo Eugenio Litta Children's Hospital are located in Rochester, Minnesota. St. Luke's Hospital in Florida has 289 private rooms, and Mayo Clinic Hospital in Arizona has 208 beds and emergency room/urgent care services. In total, the group includes 2,500 staff physicians and medical scientists, almost 900 clinical and research employees, 2,100 residents and students and 42,000 administrative and allied health staff, spread over all locations and facilities. The Mayo Health System is a provider network of clinics and hospitals serving 60 communities in Iowa, Minnesota and Wisconsin. The Mayo Clinic College of Medicine, operating through the foundation's clinics and hospitals, is broken into five segments: Mayo School of Graduate Medical Education, Mayo Graduate School, Mayo Medical School, Mayo School of Health Sciences and Mayo School of Continuing Medical Education.

For the third consecutive year, Mayo made Fortune Magazine's list of The100 Best Companies to Work For in 2006. Benefits offered to Mayo employees vary by location and include flexible spending accounts, tuition assistance, child care services, adoption reimbursement, a scholarship plan, relocation reimbursement and a variety of insurance options.

FINANCIALS: **Sales and profits are in thousands of dollars—add 000 to get the full amount. 2007 Note: Financial information for 2007 was not available for all companies at press time.**

2007 Sales: $	2007 Profits: $	**U.S. Stock Ticker: Nonprofit**
2006 Sales: $5,234,100	2006 Profits: $279,000	**Int'l Ticker:** Int'l Exchange:
2005 Sales: $5,802,300	2005 Profits: $	Employees: 53,208
2004 Sales: $5,353,800	2004 Profits: $	Fiscal Year Ends: 12/31
2003 Sales: $4,823,400	2003 Profits: $348,900	Parent Company:

SALARIES/BENEFITS:

Pension Plan: Y	ESOP Stock Plan:	Profit Sharing:	Top Exec. Salary: $	Bonus: $
Savings Plan: Y	Stock Purch. Plan:		Second Exec. Salary: $	Bonus: $

OTHER THOUGHTS:

Apparent Women Officers or Directors: 1
Hot Spot for Advancement for Women/Minorities:

LOCATIONS: ("Y" = Yes)

West:	Southwest:	Midwest:	Southeast:	Northeast:	International:
	Y	Y	Y		

MCKESSON CORPORATION www.mckesson.com

Industry Group Code: 422210 **Ranks within this company's industry group:** Sales: 1 Profits: 2

Insurance/HMO/PPO:		Drugs:		Equipment/Supplies:		Hospitals/Clinics:		Services:		Health Care:	
Insurance:		Manufacturer:		Manufacturer:		Acute Care:		Diagnostics:		Home Health:	
Managed Care:		Distributor:	Y	Distributor:	Y	Sub-Acute:		Labs/Testing:		Long-Term Care:	
Utilization Management:		Specialty Pharmacy:		Leasing/Finance:		Outpatient Surgery:		Staffing:		Physical Therapy:	
Payment Processing:	Y	Vitamins/Nutritionals:		Information Systems:	Y	Physical Rehab. Ctr.:		Waste Disposal:		Physician Prac. Mgmt.:	
		Clinical Trials:				Psychiatric Clinics:		Specialty Svcs.:	Y		

TYPES OF BUSINESS:

Pharmaceutical Solutions
Medical-Surgical Solutions
Provider Technologies

BRANDS/DIVISIONS/AFFILIATES:

McKesson U.S. Pharmaceutical
McKesson Canada
McKesson Health Solutions
McKesson Pharmacy Systems
McKesson Medication Management
ZEE Medical
Per-Se Technologies, Inc.
Physician Micro Systems, Inc.

CONTACTS: *Note: Officers with more than one job title may be intentionally listed here more than once.*

John H. Hammergren, CEO
John H. Hammergren, Pres.
Jeffrey C. Campbell, CFO/Exec. VP
Paul E. Kirincic, Exec. VP-Human Resources
Randall N. Spratt, CIO/Exec. VP
Laureen E. Seeger, General Counsel/Exec. VP/Sec.
Marc E. Owen, Exec. VP-Corp. Strategy & Bus. Dev.
Paul C. Julian, Exec. VP/ Pres., McKesson Distribution Solutions
Pamela Pure, Exec. VP/Pres., McKesson Technology Solutions
John H. Hammergren, Chmn.

Phone: 415-983-8300	**Fax:** 415-983-7160
Toll-Free:	
Address: 1 Post St., San Francisco, CA 94104 US	

GROWTH PLANS/SPECIAL FEATURES:

McKesson Corp. provides supply, information and car management products and services to the healthcar industry. The company operates in three segment pharmaceutical solutions, medical-surgical solutions an provider technologies. The pharmaceutical solution segment, responsible for 95% of revenue in 2007, distribute ethical and proprietary drugs and health and beauty car products throughout North America. This segment als provides medical management and specialty pharmaceutic solutions for biotech and pharmaceutical manufacturer patient and other services for payors; software an consulting and outsourcing services to pharmacies; an through Parata Systems, LLC, sells automate pharmaceutical dispensing systems for retail pharmacie The division consists of McKesson U.S. Pharmaceutica McKesson Canada, McKesson Health Solutions, McKesso Pharmacy Systems, McKesson Medication Management an McKesson Specialty Distribution. The medical-surgic solutions segment provides medical-surgical supp distribution, equipment, logistics and other services t healthcare providers that include physicians' offices, surge centers, extended care facilities, homecare and occupation health sites through a network of 29 distribution cente within the U.S. This segment includes ZEE Medical, provider of first aid, safety and training solutions. Th provider technologies segment delivers enterprise-wid patient care, clinical, financial, supply chain and strateg management software solutions; pharmacy automation f hospitals; as well as connectivity, outsourcing and othe services, to healthcare organizations throughout Nor America, the U.K. and other European countries. McKesso customers include hospitals, physicians, homeca providers, retail pharmacies and payors. In January 200 McKesson acquired Per-Se Technologies, Inc. In Februa 2007, the company purchased Physician Micro System Inc., a provider of integrated software for electronic heal records, medical billing and appointment scheduling. In Ju 2007, the firm agreed to acquire Awarix, Inc., an enterpris patient care visibility system provider.

The company offers its employees medical, dental and visio insurance; life and AD&D insurance; flexible spendin accounts; a 401(k) plan; an employee stock purchase pla and an employee assistance program.

FINANCIALS: **Sales and profits are in thousands of dollars—add 000 to get the full amount. 2007 Note: Financial information for 2007 was not available for all companies at press time.**

2007 Sales: $92,977,000	2007 Profits: $913,000	**U.S. Stock Ticker: MCK**
2006 Sales: $86,983,000	2006 Profits: $751,000	**Int'l Ticker:** Int'l Exchange:
2005 Sales: $79,096,000	2005 Profits: $-157,000	Employees: 31,800
2004 Sales: $69,210,000	2004 Profits: $646,500	Fiscal Year Ends: 3/31
2003 Sales: $57,120,800	2003 Profits: $555,400	Parent Company:

SALARIES/BENEFITS:

Pension Plan:	ESOP Stock Plan:	Profit Sharing:	Top Exec. Salary: $1,366,716	Bonus: $10,981,932
Savings Plan: Y	Stock Purch. Plan: Y		Second Exec. Salary: $830,829	Bonus: $4,450,000

OTHER THOUGHTS:

Apparent Women Officers or Directors: 5
Hot Spot for Advancement for Women/Minorities: Y

LOCATIONS: ("Y" = Yes)

West:	Southwest:	Midwest:	Southeast:	Northeast:	International:
Y	Y	Y	Y	Y	Y

Note: Financial information, benefits and other data can change quickly and may vary from those stated here.

MDS INC

www.mdsintl.com

Industry Group Code: 621511 **Ranks within this company's industry group:** Sales: 3 Profits: 3

Insurance/HMO/PPO:		Drugs:		Equipment/Supplies:		Hospitals/Clinics:		Services:		Health Care:	
Insurance:		Manufacturer:	Y	Manufacturer:		Acute Care:		Diagnostics:		Home Health:	
Managed Care:		Distributor:		Distributor:		Sub-Acute:		Labs/Testing:		Long-Term Care:	
Utilization Management:		Specialty Pharmacy:		Leasing/Finance:		Outpatient Surgery:		Staffing:		Physical Therapy:	
Payment Processing:		Vitamins/Nutritionals:		Information Systems:		Physical Rehab. Ctr.:		Waste Disposal:		Physician Prac. Mgmt.:	
		Clinical Trials:				Psychiatric Clinics:		Specialty Svcs.:	Y		

TYPES OF BUSINESS:

Drug Discovery & Development Services
Analytic Instruments & Technology
Imaging Agents
Medical & Surgical Supplies
Irradiation Systems
Health Care Product Distribution
Venture Capital

BRANDS/DIVISIONS/AFFILIATES:

MDS Nordion
MDS Sciex
MDS Diagnostic Services
MDS Pharma Services
MDS Capital Corp.
MDS Analytical Technologies
Molecular Devices Corporation

CONTACTS: *Note: Officers with more than one job title may be intentionally listed here more than once.*

Stephen P. DeFalco, CEO
Stephen P. DeFalco, Pres.
Douglas S. Prince, CFO
James M. Reid, Exec. VP-Global Human Resources
Thomas E. Gernon, CIO
Ken Horton, General Counsel
Kennith L. Horton, Exec. VP-Corp. Dev.
Sharon Mathers, Sr. VP-External Comm.
Sharon Mathers, Sr. VP-Investor Rel.
Douglas S. Prince, Exec. VP-Finance
Steve West, Pres., MDS Nordion
David Spaight, Pres., MDS Pharma Svcs.
Andrew W. Boorn, Pres., MDS Analytical Technologies
John Mayberry, Chmn.

Phone: 416-213-4082 **Fax:** 416-675-0688
Toll-Free: 888-637-7222
Address: 2700 Matheson Blvd. E., Mississauga, ON L4W 4V9 Canada

GROWTH PLANS/SPECIAL FEATURES:

MDS, Inc. is a global biotechnology firm operating in health, life sciences and venture capital areas, with operations in 28 countries around the world, including locations in North and South America, Europe, Asia and Africa. The life sciences segment includes MDS Pharma Services, MDS Analytical Technologies and MDS Nordion, providing drug discovery and development services; analytical instruments and technology solutions; and radioisotopes, radiation and related technologies. Customers include pharmaceutical and biotechnology companies, hospitals and health care professionals. MDS Pharma Services provides contract research services to pharmaceutical manufacturers and biotechnology companies, focusing particularly on pre-clinical and early clinical drug development. MDS Nordion's cobalt-60 irradiation systems are used to sterilize over much of the world's disposable medical supplies, to irradiate blood for blood transfusions and to destroy harmful bacteria on produce. MDS Analytical Technologies, which is the technological section of the company, has key markets in the US, Western Europe and Japan. MDS also owns 47% of MDS Capital Corp., which manages funds totaling over $1 billion. In November 2006, the company sold its 50% interest in Source Medical to its partner, Cardinal Health, Inc., for $79 million. In February 2007, MDS sold its Canadian laboratories service to Borealis Infrastructure Management Inc. for $1.3 billion. In March 2007, MDS acquired Molecular Devices Corporation for $615 million, and created a new segment called MDS Analytical Technologies, which is a merger between MDS Sciex and the newly acquired company.

MDS offers its employees a subsidized full-service cafeteria, an employee managed fitness center, health and wellness resources and many other benefits.

FINANCIALS: **Sales and profits are in thousands of dollars—add 000 to get the full amount. 2007 Note: Financial information for 2007 was not available for all companies at press time.**

2007 Sales: $	2007 Profits: $	**U.S. Stock Ticker: MDZ**
2006 Sales: $1,017,200	2006 Profits: $123,100	**Int'l Ticker: MDS** Int'l Exchange: Toronto-TSX
2005 Sales: $1,296,908	2005 Profits: $26,999	Employees: 8,800
2004 Sales: $1,447,000	2004 Profits: $42,000	Fiscal Year Ends: 10/31
2003 Sales: $1,364,000	2003 Profits: $36,000	Parent Company:

SALARIES/BENEFITS:

Pension Plan: Y	ESOP Stock Plan:	Profit Sharing:	Top Exec. Salary: $	Bonus: $
Savings Plan:	Stock Purch. Plan: Y		Second Exec. Salary: $	Bonus: $

OTHER THOUGHTS:

Apparent Women Officers or Directors: 1
Hot Spot for Advancement for Women/Minorities:

LOCATIONS: ("Y" = Yes)

West:	Southwest:	Midwest:	Southeast:	Northeast:	International:
Y	Y	Y	Y	Y	Y

Note: Financial information, benefits and other data can change quickly and may vary from those stated here.

MEDAVANT HEALTHCARE SOLUTIONS

www.medavanthealth.com

Industry Group Code: 522320 **Ranks within this company's industry group:** Sales: 5 Profits: 4

Insurance/HMO/PPO:		Drugs:		Equipment/Supplies:		Hospitals/Clinics:		Services:		Health Care:	
Insurance:		Manufacturer:		Manufacturer:		Acute Care:		Diagnostics:		Home Health:	
Managed Care:		Distributor:		Distributor:		Sub-Acute:		Labs/Testing:		Long-Term Care:	
Utilization Management:		Specialty Pharmacy:		Leasing/Finance:		Outpatient Surgery:		Staffing:		Physical Therapy:	
Payment Processing:		Vitamins/Nutritionals:		Information Systems:		Physical Rehab. Ctr.:		Waste Disposal:		Physician Prac. Mgmt.:	
		Clinical Trials:				Psychiatric Clinics:		Specialty Svcs.:	Y		

TYPES OF BUSINESS:

Medical Claims Processing
Communications Equipment Sales

BRANDS/DIVISIONS/AFFILIATES:

ProxyMed
PlanVista
medavanthealth.com
Phoenix
ClaimPassXL
PreScribe
Pilot
Navigator

CONTACTS: *Note: Officers with more than one job title may be intentionally listed here more than once.*

John G. Lettko, CEO
Gerard M. Hayden, Jr., CFO
Emily Pietrzak, Exec. VP-Sales
Allison Myers, Exec. VP-Human Resources
Adnane Khalil, VP-Tech.
Eric Arnson, Dir.-Prod. Mgmt.
Peter Fleming, III, General Counsel
Lonnie Hardin, Exec. VP-Bus. Oper.
Teresa D. Stubbs, VP-Corp. Comm.
David Richards, VP-Sales & Account Mgmt.
Teresa D. Stubbs, Exec. VP-Mktg.
James B. Hudak, Chmn.

Phone: 770-806-9918	**Fax:** 770-806-4799
Toll-Free: 800-882-0802	
Address: 1854 Shackleford Ct., Ste. 200, Norcross, GA 30093 US	

GROWTH PLANS/SPECIAL FEATURES:

MedAvant Healthcare Solutions (MHS), formerly ProxyMe is an independent medical claims clearinghouse. It provide connectivity, cost-containment services and related valu added products to physician offices, payers, medic laboratories, pharmacies and other health care institution The company maintains an open network for electroni transactions. MHS is organized into two segments acros six regional centers: transaction services and laborato communication solutions. The transaction services segme comprises transaction, cost containment, business proces outsourcing and other services principally betwee physicians and insurance companies and betwee physicians and pharmacies. The primary tool its variou customers use to process claims is an electronic connectio supplemented by a real-time web portal called myMedAva powered by the Phoenix platform. This system offers bo standard and premium services and other features such a verifying a patient's insurance, enrolling with payers, trackin a claim's progress with the payer and retrieving reports fro payers. The transaction services segment also operates preferred provider organization (PPO), called the Nationa Preferred Provider Network, and provides electroni prescription management through its online and deskto application tool, PreScribe. The laboratory communication segment is involved in the sale, lease and service communication devices, typically to laboratories. Its primar products include an intelligent printing technology for secur laboratory reports, the Fleet Management System online to for routine problem alerts and the recently released Pil wireless report transfer device. As a leader in the healthca technology industry, the firm works with 450,000 provider 42,000 pharmacies, 200 laboratories and 1,500 insuranc payer organizations, as a networks provider for preferre provider organizations. In June 2007, MedAvent launched front-end gateway solution for insurance payers, whic includes pre-receipt fraud and abuse detection, clinical cod editing, claim aggregation and real-time research tools. Th company expanded its business in October 2006 b acquiring Medical Resource, LLC and National Provide Network, Inc. for $5 million.

FINANCIALS: **Sales and profits are in thousands of dollars—add 000 to get the full amount. 2007 Note: Financial information for 2007 was not available for all companies at press time.**

2007 Sales: $	2007 Profits: $	**U.S. Stock Ticker: PILL**
2006 Sales: $65,462	2006 Profits: $-6,610	**Int'l Ticker:** Int'l Exchange:
2005 Sales: $77,519	2005 Profits: $-105,294	Employees: 336
2004 Sales: $90,246	2004 Profits: $-3,800	Fiscal Year Ends: 12/31
2003 Sales: $71,556	2003 Profits: $-5,000	Parent Company:

SALARIES/BENEFITS:

Pension Plan:	ESOP Stock Plan:	Profit Sharing:	Top Exec. Salary: $412,154	Bonus: $138,600
Savings Plan: Y	Stock Purch. Plan:		Second Exec. Salary: $210,000	Bonus: $52,500

OTHER THOUGHTS:

Apparent Women Officers or Directors: 3
Hot Spot for Advancement for Women/Minorities: Y

LOCATIONS: ("Y" = Yes)

West:	Southwest:	Midwest:	Southeast:	Northeast:	International:
Y		Y	Y	Y	

MEDCATH CORPORATION www.medcath.com

Industry Group Code: 622110 **Ranks within this company's industry group:** Sales: 26 Profits: 20

Insurance/HMO/PPO:		Drugs:		Equipment/Supplies:		Hospitals/Clinics:		Services:		Health Care:	
Insurance:		Manufacturer:		Manufacturer:		Acute Care:	Y	Diagnostics:	Y	Home Health:	
Managed Care:		Distributor:		Distributor:		Sub-Acute:		Labs/Testing:	Y	Long-Term Care:	
Utilization Management:		Specialty Pharmacy:		Leasing/Finance:		Outpatient Surgery:		Staffing:		Physical Therapy:	
Payment Processing:		Vitamins/Nutritionals:		Information Systems:		Physical Rehab. Ctr.:		Waste Disposal:		Physician Prac. Mgmt.:	
		Clinical Trials:				Psychiatric Clinics:		Specialty Svcs.:	Y		

TYPES OF BUSINESS:

Cardiac Care Hospitals
Management & Consulting Services
Cardiac Catheterization Labs

BRANDS/DIVISIONS/AFFILIATES:

St. Francis Healthcare Services

CONTACTS: *Note: Officers with more than one job title may be intentionally listed here more than once.*

O. Edwin French, CEO
Phil Mazzuca, COO
O. Edwin French, Pres.
James E. Harris, CFO/Exec. VP
Gary C. Bell, Chief Dev. Officer/Sr. VP
Arthur Parker, Treas./Sr. VP
Joan McCanless, Sr. VP/Chief Clinical Compliance Officer
John T. Casey, Chmn.

Phone: 704-708-6600	**Fax:** 704-708-5035
Toll-Free:	
Address: 10720 Sikes Pl., Ste. 300, Charlotte, NC 28277 US	

GROWTH PLANS/SPECIAL FEATURES:

MedCath Corporation is a healthcare provider focused primarily on the diagnosis and treatment of cardiovascular disease. MedCath owns and operates hospitals in partnership with physicians it believes have established reputations for clinical excellence. The company has also entered into partnerships with community hospital systems and manages the cardiovascular program of various hospitals operated by other parties. MedCath's 11 heart hospitals are freestanding, licensed general acute care hospitals capable of providing a full complement of health services, with qualified specialists in various specialties and a focus on cardiovascular care. These facilities have a total of 667 beds and are located in Arizona, Arkansas, California, Louisiana, New Mexico, Ohio, South Dakota and Texas. In addition, the company provides cardiovascular care services through 26 diagnostic and therapeutic facilities and through mobile cardiac catheterization laboratories. Physicians use mobile diagnostic facilities to evaluate the functioning of patients' hearts and coronary arteries and to serve areas that do not have the patient volume to support a full-time facility. MedCath has developed an innovative, standardized facility design and infrastructure specifically tailored to cardiovascular care. In February 2007, MedCath entered into a letter of intent to sell its 49% interest in the Heart Hospital of Lafayette. In May 2007, the company announced plans to begin a 120 bed general acute care expansion of its hospital in Lacombe, Louisiana. In August 2007, the company announced plans to build a 105 bed capacity general acute care hospital in Kingman, Arizona. Also in August, MedCath announced entering into a venture to manage the catheterization laboratories of St. Francis Healthcare Services of Wilmington, Delaware.

MedCath offers its employees a 401(k) plan, flexible spending accounts, tuition reimbursement, nurse scholarship programs, a legal plan, a college savings plan, payroll deducted auto and home insurance and medical, vision, dental and prescription drug coverage.

FINANCIALS: **Sales and profits are in thousands of dollars—add 000 to get the full amount. 2007 Note: Financial information for 2007 was not available for all companies at press time.**

2007 Sales: $	2007 Profits: $	**U.S. Stock Ticker: MDTH**
2006 Sales: $706,374	2006 Profits: $12,576	**Int'l Ticker:** Int'l Exchange:
2005 Sales: $672,001	2005 Profits: $8,791	Employees: 3,805
2004 Sales: $608,514	2004 Profits: $-3,623	Fiscal Year Ends: 9/30
2003 Sales: $542,986	2003 Profits: $-60,306	Parent Company:

SALARIES/BENEFITS:

Pension Plan:	ESOP Stock Plan:	Profit Sharing:	Top Exec. Salary: $394,212	Bonus: $243,750
Savings Plan: Y	Stock Purch. Plan:		Second Exec. Salary: $325,769	Bonus: $357,500

OTHER THOUGHTS:

Apparent Women Officers or Directors: 1
Hot Spot for Advancement for Women/Minorities:

LOCATIONS: ("Y" = Yes)

West:	Southwest:	Midwest:	Southeast:	Northeast:	International:
Y	Y	Y	Y		

MEDCO HEALTH SOLUTIONS www.medcohealth.com

Industry Group Code: 522320A **Ranks within this company's industry group:** Sales: 1 Profits: 2

Insurance/HMO/PPO:		Drugs:		Equipment/Supplies:		Hospitals/Clinics:		Services:		Health Care:	
Insurance:		Manufacturer:		Manufacturer:		Acute Care:		Diagnostics:		Home Health:	
Managed Care:	Y	Distributor:	Y	Distributor:		Sub-Acute:		Labs/Testing:		Long-Term Care:	
Utilization Management:		Specialty Pharmacy:	Y	Leasing/Finance:		Outpatient Surgery:		Staffing:		Physical Therapy:	
Payment Processing:		Vitamins/Nutritionals:		Information Systems:		Physical Rehab. Ctr.:		Waste Disposal:		Physician Prac. Mgmt.:	
		Clinical Trials:				Psychiatric Clinics:		Specialty Svcs.:	Y		

TYPES OF BUSINESS:

Pharmacy Benefits Management
Payment & Transaction Processing
Online Services

BRANDS/DIVISIONS/AFFILIATES:

Accredo Health Group, Inc.

CONTACTS: *Note: Officers with more than one job title may be intentionally listed here more than once.*

David B. Snow, Jr., CEO
Kenneth O. Klepper, COO
Kenneth O. Klepper, Pres.
JoAnn A. Reed, CFO/Sr. VP-Finance
Jack A. Smith, Chief Mktg. Officer/Sr. VP
Karin Princivalle, Sr. VP-Human Resources
John P. Driscoll, Sr. VP-Prod. Dev.
David S. Machlowitz, General Counsel/Sr. VP/Sec.
John P. Driscoll, Sr. VP-Bus. Dev.
Richard J. Rubino, Chief Acct. Officer/Sr. VP/Controller
Bryan D. Birch, Group Pres., Employer Accounts
Robert S. Epstein, Chief Medical Officer/Sr. VP-Medical Affairs
Brian T. Griffin, Group Pres., Health Plans
Glenn C. Taylor, Group Pres., Key Accounts
David B. Snow, Jr., Chmn.

Phone: 201-269-3400	**Fax:** 201-269-1109
Toll-Free:	
Address: 100 Parsons Pond Dr., Franklin Lakes, NJ 07417-2603 US	

GROWTH PLANS/SPECIAL FEATURES:

Medco Health Solutions, Inc. is a leading pharmacy benefit manager (PBM) in the U.S. PBM services include the desig and implementation of formularies, lists of preferred drug from which clients can choose; claims adjudication an administration for pharmacies; discounts on certa pharmaceuticals that have been negotiated with dru manufacturers; and other management and contr programs. Medco also runs a home drug business through network of nearly 60,000 retail pharmacies. Medco's ma order services, which dispensed approximately 89 millio prescriptions in 2006, consist of nine mail order pharmacie throughout the U.S., all of which are electronically networke through an integrated systems platform. The firm has clie businesses in all of the major industry segments, includin Blue Cross Blue Shield plans; managed care organization (HMOs and PPOs); insurance carriers; third-party bene plan administrators; employers; federal, state and loc government agencies; and union-sponsored benefit plan Medco has developed its own technology platform th includes automated home delivery pharmacies, specialize call center pharmacies and Internet applications. Th specific PBM services include benefit plan design service including formulary choice, mail incentive program coverage rules, cost-share decisions and plan limitations an exclusions; clinical management services such as clinic information and clinical decision support tools; and physicia and web-based services. Accredo Health Group, Inc., wholly-owned subsidiary which Medco acquired in 2005 fo $2.3 billion, is one of the nation's largest specialty pharmac operations. Its services include collection of drug utilizatio and patient compliance information; patient education an monitoring; reimbursement expertise; and overnight dru delivery.

FINANCIALS: Sales and profits are in thousands of dollars—add 000 to get the full amount. 2007 Note: Financial information for 2007 was not available for all companies at press time.

2007 Sales: $	2007 Profits: $	**U.S. Stock Ticker: MHS**
2006 Sales: $42,543,700	2006 Profits: $630,200	**Int'l Ticker:** Int'l Exchange:
2005 Sales: $37,870,900	2005 Profits: $602,000	Employees: 15,200
2004 Sales: $35,351,900	2004 Profits: $481,600	Fiscal Year Ends: 12/31
2003 Sales: $34,264,500	2003 Profits: $425,800	Parent Company:

SALARIES/BENEFITS:

Pension Plan: Y	ESOP Stock Plan:	Profit Sharing:	Top Exec. Salary: $1,183,224	Bonus: $
Savings Plan: Y	Stock Purch. Plan: Y		Second Exec. Salary: $673,158	Bonus: $

OTHER THOUGHTS:

Apparent Women Officers or Directors: 2
Hot Spot for Advancement for Women/Minorities: Y

LOCATIONS: ("Y" = Yes)

West:	Southwest:	Midwest:	Southeast:	Northeast:	International:
Y	Y	Y	Y	Y	

MEDICAL ACTION INDUSTRIES INC www.medical-action.com

Industry Group Code: 339113 **Ranks within this company's industry group:** Sales: 69 Profits: 61

Insurance/HMO/PPO:		Drugs:		Equipment/Supplies:		Hospitals/Clinics:		Services:		Health Care:	
Insurance:		Manufacturer:		Manufacturer:	Y	Acute Care:		Diagnostics:		Home Health:	
Managed Care:		Distributor:		Distributor:	Y	Sub-Acute:		Labs/Testing:		Long-Term Care:	
Utilization Management:		Specialty Pharmacy:		Leasing/Finance:		Outpatient Surgery:		Staffing:		Physical Therapy:	
Payment Processing:		Vitamins/Nutritionals:		Information Systems:		Physical Rehab. Ctr.:		Waste Disposal:		Physician Prac. Mgmt.:	
		Clinical Trials:				Psychiatric Clinics:		Specialty Svcs.:			

TYPES OF BUSINESS:

Supplies-Laparoscopy Sponges & Operating Room Towels
Disposable Surgical Products
Waste Containment Systems
Patient Bedside Utensils
Laboratory Products
Minor Procedure Kits & Trays
Sterilization Products
Dressings

BRANDS/DIVISIONS/AFFILIATES:

SOF KRIMP
SePro
Tubegauz
Medegen Medical Products, LLC

CONTACTS: *Note: Officers with more than one job title may be intentionally listed here more than once.*

Paul D. Meringolo, CEO
Paul D. Meringolo, Pres.
Manuel B. Losada, VP-Mktg. & Sales
Laurie Darnaby, Dir.-Human Resources
Carmine Morello, VP-IT
Richard G. Satin, General Counsel
Richard G. Satin, VP-Oper.
Victor Bacchioni, Corp. Controller
Anthony Gadzinski, Dir.-Alternate Care
Steven Carlson, Dir.-North American Mfg. Oper.
Adnan Syed, Dir.-E-Commerce & System Dev.
Peter Meringolo, Dir.-Intl. Mktg.
Paul D. Meringolo, Chmn.
Eric Liu, VP-Int'l Oper. & Global Dev.

Phone: 631-231-4600 **Fax:** 631-231-3075
Toll-Free: 800-645-7042
Address: 800 Prime Pl., Hauppauge, NY 11788 US

GROWTH PLANS/SPECIAL FEATURES:

Medical Action Industries, Inc. (MAI) develops, manufactures, markets and distributes a variety of disposable medical products to acute care facilities in both domestic and international markets. The company is currently expanding its end-user base to include physician, dental and veterinary offices, out-patient surgery centers and long-term care facilities. MAI specializes in the provision of medical products in six categories: patient bedside utensils; minor procedure kits and trays; containment systems for medical waste; operating room disposables and sterilization products; dressings and surgical sponges; and laboratory products. Patient bedside utensils include wash basins; bedpans; pitchers; urinals; denture cups; and perineal bottles. Minor procedure kits and trays products include central line dressing trays; suture removal trays; incision and drainage trays; razor and shave prep kits; and instruments and instrument trays, among others. Containment systems products include biohazardous waste containment bags; non-infectious medical waste bags; chemotherapy waste containment bags; sterility maintenance covers; and autoclavable bags, among others. Disposables and sterilization products include needle counters; sterilization indicators; disposable operating room towels; and surgical headwear and shoe covers. Dressings and surgical sponges include burn dressings; gauze sponges; conforming bandage rolls; and specialty sponges; along with proprietary SOF KRIMP bandage rolls and Tubegauz premium brand and SePro value brand elastic nets, which are tubular bandages. Laboratory products include petri dishes; specimen containers; calculi strainers; and culture tubes, among others. These products are marketed through an extensive network of independent distributors, direct sales personnel and manufacturers' representatives. MAI's manufacturing, packaging and warehousing activities are conducted in North Carolina, Tennessee, West Virginia and Colorado. In February 2007, MAI announced that it will close the Colorado facility of its recently acquired subsidiary, Medegen Medical Products, LLC, in March 2008.

FINANCIALS: **Sales and profits are in thousands of dollars—add 000 to get the full amount. 2007 Note: Financial information for 2007 was not available for all companies at press time.**

2007 Sales: $217,328	2007 Profits: $12,969	**U.S. Stock Ticker: MDCI**
2006 Sales: $150,942	2006 Profits: $11,461	**Int'l Ticker:** Int'l Exchange:
2005 Sales: $141,423	2005 Profits: $10,682	Employees: 385
2004 Sales: $127,601	2004 Profits: $9,434	Fiscal Year Ends: 3/31
2003 Sales: $104,800	2003 Profits: $8,200	Parent Company:

SALARIES/BENEFITS:

Pension Plan:	ESOP Stock Plan:	Profit Sharing:	Top Exec. Salary: $936,684	Bonus: $150,000
Savings Plan:	Stock Purch. Plan:		Second Exec. Salary: $300,721	Bonus: $

OTHER THOUGHTS:

Apparent Women Officers or Directors: 2
Hot Spot for Advancement for Women/Minorities:

LOCATIONS: ("Y" = Yes)

West:	Southwest:	Midwest:	Southeast:	Northeast:	International:
Y				Y	Y

Note: Financial information, benefits and other data can change quickly and may vary from those stated here.

MEDICAL INFORMATION TECHNOLOGY INC

www.meditech.com

Industry Group Code: 511212 **Ranks within this company's industry group:** Sales: 3 Profits: 2

Insurance/HMO/PPO:		Drugs:		Equipment/Supplies:		Hospitals/Clinics:		Services:		Health Care:	
Insurance:		Manufacturer:		Manufacturer:		Acute Care:		Diagnostics:		Home Health:	
Managed Care:		Distributor:		Distributor:		Sub-Acute:		Labs/Testing:		Long-Term Care:	
Utilization Management:		Specialty Pharmacy:		Leasing/Finance:		Outpatient Surgery:		Staffing:		Physical Therapy:	
Payment Processing:		Vitamins/Nutritionals:		Information Systems:	Y	Physical Rehab. Ctr.:		Waste Disposal:		Physician Prac. Mgmt.:	
		Clinical Trials:				Psychiatric Clinics:		Specialty Svcs.:			

TYPES OF BUSINESS:

Computer Software-Health Care

BRANDS/DIVISIONS/AFFILIATES:

MAGIC
Physician Care Manager
Data Repository
Patient Care and Patient Safety Management
Health Information Management
Patient Care Technologies, Inc.

CONTACTS: *Note: Officers with more than one job title may be intentionally listed here more than once.*

A. Neil Pappalardo, CEO
Howard Messing, COO
Howard Messing, Pres.
Barbara A. Manzolillo, CFO
Stu Lefthes, VP-Sales
Chris Anschuetz, VP-System Tech.
Robert Gale, Sr. VP-Prod. Dev.
Barbara A. Manzolillo, Treas.
Michelle O'Connor, VP-Prod. Dev.
Hoda Sayed-Friel, VP-Mktg.
Steve Koretz, VP-Implementation
Joanne Wood, VP-Client Svcs.
A. Neil Pappalardo, Chmn.

Phone: 781-821-3000	**Fax:** 781-821-2199
Toll-Free:	
Address: Meditech Cir., Westwood, MA 02090 US	

GROWTH PLANS/SPECIAL FEATURES:

Medical Information Technology, Inc. (MEDITECH) develo and markets information system software for the health ca industry. MEDITECH's software products automate a varie of hospital functions, as well as providing products for lon term care facilities; ambulatory care centers; acute-ca hospitals; emergency rooms; pharmacies; imaging; ar therapeutic service facilities and behavioral health facilitie The company's products can be operated stand-alone, integrated through the company's proprietary MAG operating system. MEDITECH specifies aggrega components for each hospital and suggests typic configurations from selected hardware vendors pertaining its software needs. The firm's software products includ Physician Care Manager, which allows doctors to revie patient information, manage orders, sign records ar document care through a single, unified desktop; Da Repository, which helps hospitals and doctors create repor quickly and simply using archived data; Patient Care ar Patient Safety Management software, which manages ord entry, provides bedside medication verification, handle operating room management, provides nursing interfac systems, creates enterprise medical records and provide patient education and discharge instructions; Heal Information Management software, which helps patien check into facilities and be verified quickly and accuratel and Supply Chain Management software, which allow facilities to keep track of inventory and order replaceme inventory when needed. In addition, MEDITECH's corpora software can consolidate a hospital's human resource staffing and scheduling; materials management; gener accounting; budget forecasting; and quality and materia management operations. In April 2007, the firm agreed acquire its long-time partner Patient Care Technologies, Inc which will become a subsidiary.

The company's facilities are equipped with ATMs and dr cleaning services for the convenience of employees, as we as a company golf course. The employee benefits packag includes medical and dental insurance; life and long ter disability insurance; a profit-sharing trust; travel stipend child and elder care referral services; educational assistanc and referral bonuses.

FINANCIALS: **Sales and profits are in thousands of dollars—add 000 to get the full amount. 2007 Note: Financial information for 2007 was not available for all companies at press time.**

2007 Sales: $	2007 Profits: $	**U.S. Stock Ticker: Private**
2006 Sales: $344,600	2006 Profits: $87,200	**Int'l Ticker:** Int'l Exchange:
2005 Sales: $304,568	2005 Profits: $77,676	Employees: 2,566
2004 Sales: $280,781	2004 Profits: $71,441	Fiscal Year Ends: 12/31
2003 Sales: $270,800	2003 Profits: $67,400	Parent Company:

SALARIES/BENEFITS:

Pension Plan: Y	ESOP Stock Plan:	Profit Sharing: Y	Top Exec. Salary: $360,000	Bonus: $721,736
Savings Plan:	Stock Purch. Plan: Y		Second Exec. Salary: $240,000	Bonus: $621,736

OTHER THOUGHTS:

Apparent Women Officers or Directors: 4
Hot Spot for Advancement for Women/Minorities: Y

LOCATIONS: ("Y" = Yes)

West:	Southwest:	Midwest:	Southeast:	Northeast:	International:
				Y	

MEDICAL MUTUAL OF OHIO www.medmutual.com

ndustry Group Code: 524114 **Ranks within this company's industry group:** Sales: Profits:

Insurance/HMO/PPO:		Drugs:		Equipment/Supplies:		Hospitals/Clinics:		Services:		Health Care:	
nsurance:	Y	Manufacturer:		Manufacturer:		Acute Care:		Diagnostics:		Home Health:	
lanaged Care:		Distributor:		Distributor:		Sub-Acute:		Labs/Testing:		Long-Term Care:	
Jtilization Management:		Specialty Pharmacy:		Leasing/Finance:		Outpatient Surgery:		Staffing:		Physical Therapy:	
ayment Processing:		Vitamins/Nutritionals:		Information Systems:		Physical Rehab. Ctr.:		Waste Disposal:		Physician Prac. Mgmt.:	
		Clinical Trials:				Psychiatric Clinics:		Specialty Svcs.:			

TYPES OF BUSINESS:

nsurance-Medical & Health, HMOs & PPOs
Vorkers' Compensation Insurance
.ife Insurance
Dental Insurance
/ision Insurance

BRANDS/DIVISIONS/AFFILIATES:

Blue Cross Blue Shield of Ohio
1st Medical Network, LLC
Consumers Life

CONTACTS: *Note: Officers with more than one job title may be ntentionally listed here more than once.*

Kent W. Clapp, CEO
Kent W. Clapp, Pres.
Susan Tyler, CFO/Exec. VP
Kenneth Sidon, CIO/Exec. VP
Don Olson, Manager-Media Rel.
Kenneth Sidon, Pres., Antares Mgmt. Solutions
Kent W. Clapp, Chmn.

Phone: 216-687-7000 **Fax:** 216-687-6044
Toll-Free: 800-700-2583
Address: 2060 E. 9th St., Cleveland, OH 44115 US

GROWTH PLANS/SPECIAL FEATURES:

Medical Mutual of Ohio, formerly Blue Cross Blue Shield of Ohio, is a not-for-profit health care company that provides health insurance to more than 3.9 million customers and 31,000 group customers in Ohio through individual and corporate plans. Medical Mutual insurance programs include HMOs, PPOs, POSs, indemnity and Medicare supplemental. It also provides dental, vision, life and workers' compensation insurance. Medical Mutual's website offers information on customers individual insurance policies as well as healthcare planning, special information on accounts for retirement and general health information. The company also offers a health and wellness section that gives resources for preventative information, smoking cessation and fitness. In April 2006, the company acquired a majority ownership in 1st Medical Network, LLC, a provider of health insurance based in Georgia. The purchase will allow Medical Mutual's fully-owned subsidiary, Consumers Life, to do business in Georgia.

The company offers its employees medical, dental and vision insurance; flexible spending accounts; a 401(k) plan; education assistance; and wellness benefits such as fitness center discounts.

FINANCIALS: **Sales and profits are in thousands of dollars—add 000 to get the full amount. 2007 Note: Financial information for 2007 was not available for all companies at press time.**

2007 Sales: $ | 2007 Profits: $
2006 Sales: $ | 2006 Profits: $
2005 Sales: $ | 2005 Profits: $
2004 Sales: $1,900,000 | 2004 Profits: $
2003 Sales: $1,600,000 | 2003 Profits: $

U.S. Stock Ticker: Nonprofit
Int'l Ticker: Int'l Exchange:
Employees: 2,500
Fiscal Year Ends: 12/31
Parent Company:

SALARIES/BENEFITS:

Pension Plan: | ESOP Stock Plan: | Profit Sharing: | Top Exec. Salary: $ | Bonus: $
Savings Plan: Y | Stock Purch. Plan: | | Second Exec. Salary: $ | Bonus: $

OTHER THOUGHTS:

Apparent Women Officers or Directors: 1
Hot Spot for Advancement for Women/Minorities: Y

LOCATIONS: ("Y" = Yes)

West:	Southwest:	Midwest:	Southeast:	Northeast:	International:
		Y			

MEDSTAR HEALTH www.medstarhealth.org

Industry Group Code: 622110 **Ranks within this company's industry group:** Sales: 19 Profits:

Insurance/HMO/PPO:		Drugs:		Equipment/Supplies:		Hospitals/Clinics:		Services:		Health Care:	
Insurance:		Manufacturer:		Manufacturer:		Acute Care:	Y	Diagnostics:		Home Health:	Y
Managed Care:		Distributor:		Distributor:		Sub-Acute:	Y	Labs/Testing:		Long-Term Care:	Y
Utilization Management:		Specialty Pharmacy:		Leasing/Finance:		Outpatient Surgery:		Staffing:		Physical Therapy:	
Payment Processing:		Vitamins/Nutritionals:		Information Systems:		Physical Rehab. Ctr.:	Y	Waste Disposal:		Physician Prac. Mgmt.:	Y
		Clinical Trials:				Psychiatric Clinics:		Specialty Svcs.:	Y		

TYPES OF BUSINESS:

Hospitals
Assisted Living Services
Home Health Services
Ambulatory Centers
Rehabilitation Centers
Nursing Homes
Physician Network Management
Research

BRANDS/DIVISIONS/AFFILIATES:

MedStar Physician Partners
MedStar Health Visiting Nurse Association
MedStar Diabetes Institute
MedStar Research Institute
Franklin Square Hospital Center
Good Samaritan Hospital
Georgetown University Hospital
Union Memorial Hospital

CONTACTS: *Note: Officers with more than one job title may be intentionally listed here more than once.*

John P. McDaniel, CEO
Kenneth A. Samet, COO
Kenneth A. Samet, Pres.
Michael J. Curran, CFO/Exec. VP-Finance
David P. Noe, VP-Corp. Human Resources
Catherine Szenczy, CIO/Sr.VP
Robert J. Ryan, General Counsel/Sr. VP
Christine M. Swearingen, Sr. VP-Corp. Strategy & Bus. Dev.
Erika Murray, Dir.-Corp. Public Rel. & Commnuity Affairs
Joel N. Bryan, VP/Corp. Treasurer
Michael C. Rogers, Exec. VP-Corp. Services
William L. Thomas, Exec. VP-Medical Affairs
Steven S. Cohen, Sr. VP-Integrated Oper.
Eric Wagner, VP-Managed Care
Edward J. Brody, Chmn.

Phone: 410-772-6500	**Fax:** 410-715-3905
Toll-Free: 877-772-6505	
Address: 5565 Sterrett Pl., 5th Fl., Columbia, MD 21044 US	

GROWTH PLANS/SPECIAL FEATURES:

MedStar Health is a not-for-profit, community-based healt care organization primarily composed of 25 integrate businesses, including seven major hospitals. The hospital reside in the Baltimore/Washington, D.C. area, and includ the following: Franklin Square Hospital Center, Goo Samaritan Hospital, Harbor Hospital and Union Memoria Hospital in Baltimore; and Washington Hospital Cente Georgetown University Hospital and National Rehabilitatio Hospital in Washington, D.C. MedStar serves rough 150,000 inpatients and over 1 million outpatients annual and has 2,700 licensed beds. The hospitals' service include primary, urgent and sub-acute care, medica education and research. MedStar also provides assiste living, home health, hospice and long-term care, an operates nursing homes, senior housing, adult day care rehabilitation and ambulatory centers. The organizatio manages MedStar Physician Partners, a comprehensiv physician network serving the region. Other subsidiarie include the MedStar Health Visiting Nurse Association, th MedStar Diabetes Institute and the MedStar Researc Institute. In 2007, Ensign Pharmacy changed its name t MedStar Pharmacy, after 23 years serving MedStar Healt hospitals. The goal of this name change is to better link th brands across all channels, as well as to reinforce th service MedStar offers the Baltimore/Washington, D.C region.

FINANCIALS: Sales and profits are in thousands of dollars—add 000 to get the full amount. 2007 Note: Financial information for 2007 was not available for all companies at press time.

2007 Sales: $	2007 Profits: $	**U.S. Stock Ticker: Nonprofit**
2006 Sales: $2,950,000	2006 Profits: $	**Int'l Ticker:** Int'l Exchange:
2005 Sales: $2,690,000	2005 Profits: $	Employees: 23,000
2004 Sales: $	2004 Profits: $	Fiscal Year Ends: 6/30
2003 Sales: $2,250,000	2003 Profits: $	Parent Company:

SALARIES/BENEFITS:

Pension Plan:	ESOP Stock Plan:	Profit Sharing:	Top Exec. Salary: $	Bonus: $
Savings Plan:	Stock Purch. Plan:		Second Exec. Salary: $	Bonus: $

OTHER THOUGHTS:

Apparent Women Officers or Directors: 4
Hot Spot for Advancement for Women/Minorities: Y

LOCATIONS: ("Y" = Yes)

West:	Southwest:	Midwest:	Southeast:	Northeast:	International:
				Y	

MEDTRONIC CARDIOVASCULAR www.medtronicvascular.com

dustry Group Code: 339113 **Ranks within this company's industry group:** Sales: Profits:

surance/HMO/PPO:		Drugs:		Equipment/Supplies:		Hospitals/Clinics:		Services:		Health Care:	
surance:		Manufacturer:		Manufacturer:	Y	Acute Care:		Diagnostics:		Home Health:	
anaged Care:		Distributor:		Distributor:		Sub-Acute:		Labs/Testing:		Long-Term Care:	
ilization Management:		Specialty Pharmacy:		Leasing/Finance:		Outpatient Surgery:		Staffing:		Physical Therapy:	
ayment Processing:		Vitamins/Nutritionals:		Information Systems:		Physical Rehab. Ctr.:		Waste Disposal:		Physician Prac. Mgmt.:	
		Clinical Trials:				Psychiatric Clinics:		Specialty Svcs.:			

YPES OF BUSINESS:

ledical Instruments-Stents & Catheters
oronary Products
eurovascular Products
eripheral Products
ndovascular Products

BRANDS/DIVISIONS/AFFILIATES:

ledtronic Vascular
ledtronic Cardiac Surgery
Driver
licro-Driver
neuRx AAA
ledtronic EDGE

CONTACTS: *Note: Officers with more than one job title may be ntentionally listed here more than once.*

Scott Ward, Pres.

Phone: 763-514-4000	Fax: 707-525-0114
Toll-Free: 800-328-2518	
Address: 3576 Unocal Pl., Santa Rosa, CA 95403 US	

GROWTH PLANS/SPECIAL FEATURES:

Medtronic CardioVascular, a subsidiary of Medtronic, Inc., produces medical devices, treatments and therapies for coronary artery, vascular and structural heart disease. The company, which was formed in April 2007 through the combination of Medtronic's Vascular and Cardiac Surgery subsidiaries, consists of four major divisions. The Coronary and Peripheral division focuses on the treatment of atherosclerosis through the development of minimally invasive catheter and stent-based technologies. Stints are used by surgeons to prop open diseased arteries in the heart following coronary surgery. Two of the company's primary products in this segment are the Driver modular stent, which is composed of cobalt-alloy in order to provide increased strength and the Micro-Driver coronary stent system, which was released in 2006 and is used in small vessels and tortuous anatomies. The Endovascular Innovations division works for the treatment of aortic and thoracic aneurysms by producing stent grafts, such as the AneuRx AAA stent graft system. The Structural Heart Disease division designs and manufactures products for the treatment of heart valve disease and atrial fibrillation. Finally, the Revascularization and Surgical Therapies division focuses on products for open heart and coronary bypass grafting. The company also offers the Medtronic EDGE, an education program that offers training events for the purpose of expanding the skills of cardiac surgeons. Some of the fields in which the programs specialize include complex mitral valve repair, advanced valve surgery, robotic surgical techniques, beating heart strategies, endovascular strategies and cardiac rhythm management.

Medtronic offers its employees a benefits package that includes medical and dental insurance, elder care assistance, adoption assistance, tuition reimbursement, an employee assistance program, massage therapy programs, a retirement plan, a stock purchase plan, sick childcare options and scholarships for the children of employees.

FINANCIALS: **Sales and profits are in thousands of dollars—add 000 to get the full amount. 2007 Note: Financial information for 2007 was not available for all companies at press time.**

2007 Sales: $	2007 Profits: $	**U.S. Stock Ticker: Subsidiary**
2006 Sales: $	2006 Profits: $	**Int'l Ticker:** Int'l Exchange:
2005 Sales: $	2005 Profits: $	Employees: 1,265
2004 Sales: $	2004 Profits: $	Fiscal Year Ends: 4/30
2003 Sales: $	2003 Profits: $	Parent Company: MEDTRONIC INC

SALARIES/BENEFITS:

Pension Plan: Y	ESOP Stock Plan:	Profit Sharing:	Top Exec. Salary: $	Bonus: $
Savings Plan: Y	Stock Purch. Plan: Y		Second Exec. Salary: $	Bonus: $

OTHER THOUGHTS:

Apparent Women Officers or Directors:
Hot Spot for Advancement for Women/Minorities:

LOCATIONS: ("Y" = Yes)

West:	Southwest:	Midwest:	Southeast:	Northeast:	International:
Y					

Note: Financial information, benefits and other data can change quickly and may vary from those stated here.

MEDTRONIC INC

www.medtronic.com

Industry Group Code: 339113 **Ranks within this company's industry group:** Sales: 2 Profits: 2

Insurance/HMO/PPO:		Drugs:		Equipment/Supplies:		Hospitals/Clinics:		Services:		Health Care:	
Insurance:		Manufacturer:		Manufacturer:	Y	Acute Care:		Diagnostics:		Home Health:	
Managed Care:		Distributor:		Distributor:		Sub-Acute:		Labs/Testing:		Long-Term Care:	
Utilization Management:		Specialty Pharmacy:		Leasing/Finance:		Outpatient Surgery:		Staffing:		Physical Therapy:	
Payment Processing:		Vitamins/Nutritionals:		Information Systems:		Physical Rehab. Ctr.:		Waste Disposal:		Physician Prac. Mgmt.:	
		Clinical Trials:				Psychiatric Clinics:		Specialty Svcs.:			

TYPES OF BUSINESS:

Equipment-Defibrillators & Pacing Products
Neurological Devices
Diabetes Management Devices
Ear, Nose & Throat Surgical Equipment
Pain Management Devices
Catheters & Stents
Cardiac Surgery Equipment

BRANDS/DIVISIONS/AFFILIATES:

Medtronic ENT
Medtronic Xomed
MimiMed Paradigm REAL-Time
Guardian REAL-Time
EnRhythm
INFUSE Bone Graft
DIAM Spinal Stabilization System
Continuous Glucose Monitoring

CONTACTS: *Note: Officers with more than one job title may be intentionally listed here more than once.*

William A. Hawkins III, CEO
Michael F. DeMane, Sr., COO
William A. Hawkins, III, Pres.
Gary Ellis, CFO/Sr. VP
Janet S. Fiola, VP-Human Resources
H. James Dallas, CIO/Sr. VP
Stephen N. Oesterle, Sr. VP-Medicine & Tech.
Terrance Carlson, General Counsel/Corp. Sec./Sr. VP
Susan Alpert, Sr. VP/Chief Quality & Regulatory Officer
Jean-Luc Butel, Sr. VP/Pres.-Asia Pacific
Oern R. Stuge, Sr. VP/Pres., Cardiac Surgery
Arthur D. Collins, Jr., Chmn.
Barry Wilson, Sr. VP-Int'l Rel.

Phone: 763-514-4000	**Fax:** 763-514-4879
Toll-Free: 800-328-2518	
Address: 710 Medtronic Pkwy. NE, Minneapolis, MN 55432 US	

GROWTH PLANS/SPECIAL FEATURES:

Medtronic, Inc. is a global leader in medical technology whose professed mission is alleviating pain, restoring health and extending life for millions of people around the world. The firm offers a wide range of products and therapies and holds market-leading positions in almost all major markets in which it competes. The firm operates in six business sectors: cardiac rhythm disease management; cardiac surgery; neurological, spinal; ear, nose and throat (ENT surgery; vascular disease; and diabetes. Medtronic is one of the world's largest suppliers of medical devices for cardiac rhythm management, including pacemakers and implantable cardiac defibrillators. The Cardiac Surgery division specializes in revascularization, heart valve repair and replacement, and blood management, offering cardiac surgeons a broad range of products for the operating room. The Neurological and Spinal division offers drug delivery systems, neurosurgical implant devices and therapeutic systems for chronic pain and neurological disorders. The ENT surgery unit operates under the name Medtronic Xomed, and is a leading manufacturer ENT surgical products. The Vascular Therapy division combines a variety of treatments for coronary vascular disease, including stents and angioplasty catheters. The Diabetes unit provides glucose monitors, insulin pumps and other products, as well as informational resources available on the firm's web site. In 2006, the firm released three new pacemakers and received FDA approval to conduct a number of trials, including the study of the INFUSE Bone Graft in a cervical spine fusion, as well as the DIAM Spinal Stabilization System, meant to prove that the DIAM system is optimal for patients with degenerative disc diseases. In 2007, the FDA approved the firm's Continuous Glucose Monitoring devices for children and teenagers. The FDA also approved Medtronic's INFUSE Bone Graft treatment for certain oral maxillofacial and dental regenerative bone grafting procedures. In July 2007, the firm agreed to acquire Kyphon, Inc. for roughly $3.9 billion.

FINANCIALS: **Sales and profits are in thousands of dollars—add 000 to get the full amount. 2007 Note: Financial information for 2007 was not available for all companies at press time.**

2007 Sales: $12,299,000	2007 Profits: $2,802,000	**U.S. Stock Ticker: MDT**
2006 Sales: $11,292,000	2006 Profits: $2,546,700	**Int'l Ticker:** Int'l Exchange:
2005 Sales: $10,054,600	2005 Profits: $1,803,900	Employees: 37,800
2004 Sales: $9,087,200	2004 Profits: $1,959,300	Fiscal Year Ends: 4/30
2003 Sales: $7,665,200	2003 Profits: $1,599,800	Parent Company:

SALARIES/BENEFITS:

Pension Plan:	ESOP Stock Plan:	Profit Sharing:	Top Exec. Salary: $1,175,000	Bonus: $1,827,125
Savings Plan: Y	Stock Purch. Plan: Y		Second Exec. Salary: $735,000	Bonus: $802,400

OTHER THOUGHTS:

Apparent Women Officers or Directors: 2
Hot Spot for Advancement for Women/Minorities:

LOCATIONS: ("Y" = Yes)

West:	Southwest:	Midwest:	Southeast:	Northeast:	International:
Y	Y	Y	Y	Y	Y

MEDTRONIC MINIMED INC www.minimed.com

Industry Group Code: 339113 **Ranks within this company's industry group:** Sales: Profits:

Insurance/HMO/PPO:		Drugs:		Equipment/Supplies:		Hospitals/Clinics:		Services:		Health Care:	
nsurance:		Manufacturer:		Manufacturer:	Y	Acute Care:		Diagnostics:		Home Health:	
Managed Care:		Distributor:		Distributor:		Sub-Acute:		Labs/Testing:		Long-Term Care:	
Utilization Management:		Specialty Pharmacy:		Leasing/Finance:		Outpatient Surgery:		Staffing:		Physical Therapy:	
Payment Processing:		Vitamins/Nutritionals:		Information Systems:		Physical Rehab. Ctr.:		Waste Disposal:		Physician Prac. Mgmt.:	
		Clinical Trials:				Psychiatric Clinics:		Specialty Svcs.:			

TYPES OF BUSINESS:

Equipment-Diabetes Management Products
Drug Delivery Microinfusion Systems
External Insulin Pumps & Related Products
Obesity Treatment

BRANDS/DIVISIONS/AFFILIATES:

Medtronic, Inc.
Medtronic CareLink Therapy Management System
Paradigm
CGMS System Gold
Guardian Continuous Glucose Monitor System
Transneuronix Inc.

CONTACTS: *Note: Officers with more than one job title may be intentionally listed here more than once.*

Bill Hawkins, CEO
Michael DeMane, COO
Bill Hawkins, Pres.
Gary Ellis, CFO
Carol McCormick, VP-Human Resources
H. James Dallas, CIO/Sr. VP
Stephen Oesterle, VP-Tech. & Medicine
Terrance Carlson, General Counsel
Susan Alpert, VP-Chief Quality & Regulatory Officer
Jean-Luc Butel, VP-Asia Pacific
Arthur D. Collins, Jr., Chmn.

Phone: 818-362-5958 **Fax:** 818-364-2246
Toll-Free: 800-933-3322
Address: 18000 Devonshire St., Northridge, CA 91325-1219 US

GROWTH PLANS/SPECIAL FEATURES:

Medtronic MiniMed Inc., a subsidiary of Medtronic, Inc., designs, develops, manufactures and markets advanced microinfusion systems for the delivery of a variety of drugs, with a primary focus on insulin for the intensive management of diabetes. The company sells external insulin pumps and related disposables, which are designed to deliver small quantities of insulin in a controlled, programmable profile. Medtronic MiniMed has also developed an implantable insulin pump and is developing continuous subcutaneous glucose monitoring systems. The firm's Paradigm insulin pump underwent its third generation of upgrades in 2004. This model includes the web-based Medtronic CareLink Therapy Management System, which charts trends in A1C, BG and carbohydrates to optimize therapy. Medtronic MiniMed plans to use the Paradigm platform to launch the world's first sensor-augmented insulin pump system. The firm also offers a line of therapy management software that turns pump, meter and logbook data into treatment reports. In addition, the CGMS System Gold is often prescribed by health professionals because it provides a clearer picture of blood sugar levels than fingersticks. The CGMS System Gold measures blood sugar levels every five minutes for a total of 288 readings a day. The company generally markets different insulin pump models to different areas of the world. For instance, Medicare/Medicaid patients in the U.S. are offered the Paradigm 512R/712R pumps; 508 or 508B lines are offered in Latin America and Asia Pacific; 512/712 models are offered in Western Europe, Australia, New Zealand and countries in the Middle East.

Medtronic MiniMed offers employees tuition reimbursement, flexible spending accounts, credit union membership and discounts on attractions and special events.

FINANCIALS: Sales and profits are in thousands of dollars—add 000 to get the full amount. 2007 Note: Financial information for 2007 was not available for all companies at press time.

2007 Sales: $	2007 Profits: $	**U.S. Stock Ticker: Subsidiary**
2006 Sales: $	2006 Profits: $	**Int'l Ticker:** Int'l Exchange:
2005 Sales: $	2005 Profits: $	Employees: 33,000
2004 Sales: $	2004 Profits: $	Fiscal Year Ends: 4/30
2003 Sales: $	2003 Profits: $	Parent Company: MEDTRONIC INC

SALARIES/BENEFITS:

Pension Plan:	ESOP Stock Plan:	Profit Sharing:	Top Exec. Salary: $	Bonus: $
Savings Plan: Y	Stock Purch. Plan: Y		Second Exec. Salary: $	Bonus: $

OTHER THOUGHTS:

Apparent Women Officers or Directors: 3
Hot Spot for Advancement for Women/Minorities: Y

LOCATIONS: ("Y" = Yes)

West:	Southwest:	Midwest:	Southeast:	Northeast:	International:
Y	Y	Y	Y	Y	Y

MEDTRONIC SOFAMOR DANEK www.sofamordanek.com

Industry Group Code: 339113 **Ranks within this company's industry group:** Sales: Profits:

Insurance/HMO/PPO:		Drugs:		Equipment/Supplies:		Hospitals/Clinics:		Services:		Health Care:	
Insurance:		Manufacturer:		Manufacturer:	Y	Acute Care:		Diagnostics:		Home Health:	
Managed Care:		Distributor:		Distributor:		Sub-Acute:		Labs/Testing:		Long-Term Care:	
Utilization Management:		Specialty Pharmacy:		Leasing/Finance:		Outpatient Surgery:		Staffing:		Physical Therapy:	
Payment Processing:		Vitamins/Nutritionals:		Information Systems:		Physical Rehab. Ctr.:		Waste Disposal:		Physician Prac. Mgmt.:	
		Clinical Trials:				Psychiatric Clinics:		Specialty Svcs.:			

TYPES OF BUSINESS:

Spinal Implants
Bone Grafts
Image Guidance & Surgical Navigation Devices

BRANDS/DIVISIONS/AFFILIATES:

INFUSE Bone Graft
CD Horizon Eclipse Spinal System
METRx MicroDiscectomy System
CD Horizon Sextant System
Medtronic, Inc.
MySpineTools.com
iScoliosis.com

CONTACTS: *Note: Officers with more than one job title may be intentionally listed here more than once.*

Peter Wehly, Pres.

Phone: 901-396-2695	**Fax:** 901-396-2699
Toll-Free: 800-876-3133	
Address: 1800 Pyramid Pl., Memphis, TN 38132 US	

GROWTH PLANS/SPECIAL FEATURES:

Medtronic Sofamor Danek, Inc., a subsidiary of Medtronic Inc., is a world leader in producing spinal devices instruments, computerized image guidance products and biomaterials. These products are utilized in the treatment of spinal disorders, such as herniated discs, congenital spine disorders, degenerative disc disease, tumors, fractures and stenosis. Sofamore Danek primarily produces a series of minimal-access spinal technologies (MAST) that allow safe reproducible access to the spine with minimal disruption of vital muscles and surrounding structures. These techniques involve the use of advanced navigation and instrumentation to allow surgeons to operate with smaller incisions and less tissue damage than traditional surgeries, thus reducing pain and blood loss and improving recovery periods. Products used to treat spinal disorders and deformities include rods and pedical screws, plating systems, and interbody devices like spinal cages, bone dowels and bone wedges, which can be used in spinal fusion of both the thoracolumbar (mid to lower vertebrae) and cervical (upper spine and neck) regions of the spine. Products include the CD Horizon Sextant System for multi-level spinal fusion; the METRx MicroDiscectomy System to treat herniated discs; the CD Horizon Eclipse Spinal System to correct curvature of the spine in scoliosis patients; and the INFUSE Bone Graft which contains a recombinant human bone morphogenetic protein that induces the body to grow its own bone, eliminating the need for a painful second surgery to harvest bone from elsewhere in the body. The company also provides physicians and patients with information through websites such as MySpineTools.com, Back.com, iScoliosis.com, and NeckReference.com. In July 2006, the FDA approved the company's DIAM Spinal Stabilization System for use in a clinical study.

Sofamor Danek offers employees on-site wellness screenings, massage therapy programs, on-site fitness centers, elder and child care assistance, adoption assistance and nursing rooms for new mothers.

FINANCIALS: **Sales and profits are in thousands of dollars—add 000 to get the full amount. 2007 Note: Financial information for 2007 was not available for all companies at press time.**

2007 Sales: $	2007 Profits: $	**U.S. Stock Ticker: Subsidiary**
2006 Sales: $	2006 Profits: $	**Int'l Ticker:** Int'l Exchange:
2005 Sales: $	2005 Profits: $	Employees:
2004 Sales: $	2004 Profits: $	Fiscal Year Ends: 4/30
2003 Sales: $	2003 Profits: $	Parent Company: MEDTRONIC INC

SALARIES/BENEFITS:

Pension Plan: Y	ESOP Stock Plan: Y	Profit Sharing:	Top Exec. Salary: $	Bonus: $
Savings Plan: Y	Stock Purch. Plan: Y		Second Exec. Salary: $	Bonus: $

OTHER THOUGHTS:

Apparent Women Officers or Directors:
Hot Spot for Advancement for Women/Minorities:

LOCATIONS: ("Y" = Yes)

West:	Southwest:	Midwest:	Southeast:	Northeast:	International:
			Y	Y	Y

Note: Financial information, benefits and other data can change quickly and may vary from those stated here.

MEDTRONIC XOMED SURGICAL PRODUCTS INC

www.xomed.com

Industry Group Code: 339113 **Ranks within this company's industry group:** Sales: Profits:

Insurance/HMO/PPO:		Drugs:		Equipment/Supplies:		Hospitals/Clinics:		Services:		Health Care:	
Insurance:		Manufacturer:		Manufacturer:	Y	Acute Care:		Diagnostics:		Home Health:	
Managed Care:		Distributor:		Distributor:		Sub-Acute:		Labs/Testing:		Long-Term Care:	
Utilization Management:		Specialty Pharmacy:		Leasing/Finance:		Outpatient Surgery:		Staffing:		Physical Therapy:	
Payment Processing:		Vitamins/Nutritionals:		Information Systems:		Physical Rehab. Ctr.:		Waste Disposal:		Physician Prac. Mgmt.:	
		Clinical Trials:				Psychiatric Clinics:		Specialty Svcs.:			

TYPES OF BUSINESS:

Supplies-Ear, Nose & Throat Surgery
Wound Dressings
Plastic Surgery Equipment
Endoscopy & Image Guidance Equipment

BRANDS/DIVISIONS/AFFILIATES:

Medtronic Inc
MeroPack
LandmarX Element
NIM-Response 2.0
Meniett
Visao
MicroFrance
Medtronic Ophthalmics

CONTACTS: *Note: Officers with more than one job title may be intentionally listed here more than once.*

Mike Nicoletta, COO
Bob Blankemeyer, Pres.
David Damm, VP-Domestic Sales
Michael Darragh, VP-Human Resources
Craig Drager, VP-R&D
Jamie A. Frias, VP-Legal Counsel
Gerald Bussell, VP-Global Oper.
Rob Jordheim, VP-Finance
Mark Fletcher, Pres., ENT Div.
John A. Williams, Corp. Controller/Assistant Treas.
Jonathan Lee, VP-Quality Assurance & Regulatory Affairs
Vince Racano, VP-Int'l Mktg.

Phone: 904-296-9600 **Fax:** 904-296-9666
Toll-Free: 800-874-5797
Address: 6743 Southpoint Dr. N., Jacksonville, FL 32216-0980 US

GROWTH PLANS/SPECIAL FEATURES:

Medtronic Xomed, Inc., a subsidiary of medical device manufacturer Medtronic, Inc., is a leading developer, manufacturer and marketer of surgical products for use by ear, nose and throat specialists. The company's products cover six areas: Rhinology, which are products having to do specifically with the nose; laryngology, covering the throat; otology/neurotology, ear-related and neurological products; general otolaryngology, covering all three ENT zones; instrumentation; and opthalmics, or eye related products. Rhinology products include the MeroPack bioresorbable nasal dressing that can absorb 14 times its weight in fluid; the LandmarX Element image-guided surgery system that provides fast set-up through auto recognition of instruments and other user friendly features; and other surgical equipment, primarily blades. Laryngological instruments consist primarily of endoscopic equipment for surgery or biopsy; and also include the NIM-Response 2.0 nerve integrity monitoring system designed to help surgeons monitor nerve and brain activity during surgery. Otological/neurotological products include the Meniett, a portable pressure pulse generator, which treats Meniere's disease; the Visao high-speed otologic drill; and other surgical implements, primarily picks, clamps, knives and other handheld equipment. General otolaryngology products consist of the XPS powered tonsillectomy and adenoidectomy blade set that features precise tissue removal capabilities which produces a faster operation as well as quicker recovery time. Its instrumentation is produced under the MicroFrance brand and includes a variety of surgical implements for rhinology, otology, laryngology and head and neck. Ophthalmic products are produced by Medtronic Ophthalmics, and include electo surgery, fluid management and other surgical instrumentation.

The company offers its employees medical and dental insurance coverage; life insurance; both short- and long-term disability coverage; on-site fitness centers; employee assistance and message therapy programs; childcare referral; flexible work schedules; tuition reimbursement; and adoption assistance programs.

FINANCIALS: **Sales and profits are in thousands of dollars—add 000 to get the full amount. 2007 Note: Financial information for 2007 was not available for all companies at press time.**

2007 Sales: $	2007 Profits: $	**U.S. Stock Ticker: Subsidiary**
2006 Sales: $	2006 Profits: $	**Int'l Ticker:** Int'l Exchange:
2005 Sales: $	2005 Profits: $	Employees:
2004 Sales: $	2004 Profits: $	Fiscal Year Ends: 4/30
2003 Sales: $	2003 Profits: $	Parent Company: MEDTRONIC INC

SALARIES/BENEFITS:

Pension Plan: Y	ESOP Stock Plan: Y	Profit Sharing:	Top Exec. Salary: $	Bonus: $
Savings Plan: Y	Stock Purch. Plan: Y		Second Exec. Salary: $	Bonus: $

OTHER THOUGHTS:

Apparent Women Officers or Directors: 1
Hot Spot for Advancement for Women/Minorities:

LOCATIONS: ("Y" = Yes)

West:	Southwest:	Midwest:	Southeast:	Northeast:	International:
Y	Y	Y	Y	Y	Y

MEMORIAL HERMANN HEALTHCARE SYSTEM

www.memorialhermann.org

Industry Group Code: 622110 **Ranks within this company's industry group:** Sales: Profits:

Insurance/HMO/PPO:		Drugs:		Equipment/Supplies:		Hospitals/Clinics:		Services:		Health Care:	
Insurance:		Manufacturer:		Manufacturer:		Acute Care:	Y	Diagnostics:	Y	Home Health:	Y
Managed Care:		Distributor:		Distributor:		Sub-Acute:	Y	Labs/Testing:	Y	Long-Term Care:	Y
Utilization Management:		Specialty Pharmacy:		Leasing/Finance:		Outpatient Surgery:	Y	Staffing:		Physical Therapy:	Y
Payment Processing:		Vitamins/Nutritionals:		Information Systems:		Physical Rehab. Ctr.:	Y	Waste Disposal:		Physician Prac. Mgmt.:	
		Clinical Trials:				Psychiatric Clinics:	Y	Specialty Svcs.:	Y		

TYPES OF BUSINESS:

Hospitals
Long-Term Care
Retirement & Nursing Homes
Wellness Centers
Rehabilitation Services
Home Health Services
Air Ambulance Services
Sports Medicine

BRANDS/DIVISIONS/AFFILIATES:

Memorial Hermann Garden Spa
Houston Health Hour Radio Show
Lindig Men's Health Center & Resource Library
Mind/Body Institute for Clinical Wellness
Memorial Hermann Heart & Vascular Institute
Memorial Hermann Children's Hospital
Fort Bend Hospital
Katy Hospital

CONTACTS: *Note: Officers with more than one job title may be intentionally listed here more than once.*

Daniel J. Wolterman, CEO
Daniel J. Wolterman, Pres.
Carrol E. Aulbaugh, Sr. VP-Finance
Craig Cordola, CEO-Children's Memorial Hermann Hospital
James R. Montague, Chmn.

Phone: 713-448-5555 **Fax:** 713-448-5665
Toll-Free:
Address: 7737 Southwest Fwy., Ste. 200, Houston, TX 77074 US

GROWTH PLANS/SPECIAL FEATURES:

Memorial Hermann Healthcare System is a leading provider of health care in greater Houston and southeast Texas. The system consists of nine acute care hospitals, one children's hospital, three vascular and heart hospitals, two long-term acute care hospitals, one rehabilitation hospital, a physician network for primary and specialty care, retirement living and nursing homes, a wellness center, one home health agency, an air ambulance service and more than a dozen affiliates spread across southeast Texas. The acute care hospitals include Memorial Hermann Children's Hospital, Fort Bend Hospital, Memorial Hermann Hospital, Katy Hospital, Memorial City Hospital, Northwest Hospital, Southeast Hospital, Southwest Hospital and Woodlands Hospital. Together these hospitals contain over 3,000 licensed beds and offer the full range of health care services, including a sports medicine center, residency programs, radiology, chemical dependency programs, nutrition programs, a vocational nursing program, infertility services, diabetes self-management programs and cancer treatment. The Memorial Hermann Garden Spa, Houston Health Hour Radio Show, Lindig Men's Health Center and Resource Library and the Mind/Body Institute for Clinical Wellness are also part of the system. In June 2007, Memorial announced that Triumph HealthCare will acquire Memorial Hermann Continuing Care Corporation's Long Term Acute Care operations.

Memorial Hermann provides residency programs, nursing internships, massage and spa therapy school and technical schools. It provides its employees with a comprehensive health care package, an employee assistance program, legal assistance, discounted auto and home insurance and tuition reimbursement.

FINANCIALS: **Sales and profits are in thousands of dollars—add 000 to get the full amount. 2007 Note: Financial information for 2007 was not available for all companies at press time.**

2007 Sales: $
2006 Sales: $
2005 Sales: $
2004 Sales: $
2003 Sales: $2,500,000

2007 Profits: $
2006 Profits: $
2005 Profits: $
2004 Profits: $
2003 Profits: $

U.S. Stock Ticker: Nonprofit
Int'l Ticker: Int'l Exchange:
Employees: 16,500
Fiscal Year Ends: 6/30
Parent Company:

SALARIES/BENEFITS:

Pension Plan: Y
Savings Plan:
ESOP Stock Plan:
Stock Purch. Plan:
Profit Sharing:
Top Exec. Salary: $ Bonus: $
Second Exec. Salary: $ Bonus: $

OTHER THOUGHTS:

Apparent Women Officers or Directors: 1
Hot Spot for Advancement for Women/Minorities:

LOCATIONS: ("Y" = Yes)

West:	Southwest:	Midwest:	Southeast:	Northeast:	International:
	Y				

MEMORIAL SLOAN KETTERING CANCER CENTER

www.mskcc.org

ndustry Group Code: 622110 **Ranks within this company's industry group:** Sales: 25 Profits: 17

nsurance/HMO/PPO:		Drugs:		Equipment/Supplies:		Hospitals/Clinics:		Services:		Health Care:	
nsurance:		Manufacturer:		Manufacturer:		Acute Care:	Y	Diagnostics:	Y	Home Health:	
lanaged Care:		Distributor:		Distributor:		Sub-Acute:		Labs/Testing:	Y	Long-Term Care:	
tilization Management:		Specialty Pharmacy:		Leasing/Finance:		Outpatient Surgery:		Staffing:		Physical Therapy:	
ayment Processing:		Vitamins/Nutritionals:		Information Systems:		Physical Rehab. Ctr.:	Y	Waste Disposal:		Physician Prac. Mgmt.:	
		Clinical Trials:				Psychiatric Clinics:		Specialty Svcs.:	Y		

TYPES OF BUSINESS:

ancer Center-Inpatient & Outpatient
ancer Research

BRANDS/DIVISIONS/AFFILIATES:

Memorial Hospital for Cancer & Allied Diseases
Sloan-Kettering Institute
Claire Tow Pediatric Pavilion
Bright Space

CONTACTS: *Note: Officers with more than one job title may be intentionally listed here more than once.*

Harold Varmus, CEO
Harold Varmus, Pres.
Ellen M. Sonet, VP-Mktg.
Dennis Dowdell, Jr, VP-Human Resources
Patricia Skarulis, CIO/VP-Info. Systems
Roger Parker, General Counsel/Sr. VP
Richard Naum, VP-Dev.
Anne Thomas, VP-Public Affairs
Michael Gutrick, Sr. VP-Finance
Thomas J. Fahey, Jr., Sr. VP-Clinical Program Dev.
Robert Wittee, Physician in Chief, Memorial Hospital
Thomas Kelly, Dir.-Sloan-Kettering Inst.
Douglas A. Warner, III, Chmn.

Phone: 212-639-2000 **Fax:** 212-639-3576
Toll-Free:
Address: 1275 York Ave., New York, NY 10021 US

GROWTH PLANS/SPECIAL FEATURES:

Memorial Sloan-Kettering Cancer Center (MSKCC), a not-for-profit organization, consists of two facilities, namely Memorial Hospital for Cancer and Allied Diseases and the Sloan-Kettering Institute. Memorial Hospital offers both inpatient and outpatient services. Its patient care consists of early detection, precise diagnosis and tailored treatment. Center experts are trained in using radiotherapy on tumor sites, conducting cancer surgery and developing chemotherapy drugs. The Sloan-Kettering Institute functions as the hospital's research arm, with specific focus on genetics, biochemistry, structural biology, computational biology, immunology and therapeutics. The institute provides research training in conjunction with the Weill Medical College of Cornell University and the Rockefeller University for PhD and MD students. The Institute's research areas include the study of cancer biology and genetics, with the intention of isolating molecular and genetic determinants of cancer predisposition, tumor development and metastasis. MSKCC also operates a Pediatric Day Hospital to provide advanced outpatient care in a family friendly environment, as well as the Breast Examination Center of Harlem (BECH), which provides breast and cervical cancer screening at no out-of-pocket expense to the women of Harlem. Recently, MSKCC also opened The Claire Tow Pediatric Pavilion, with new inpatient and outpatient facilities on one contiguous floor. In 2007, MSKCC, along with The Bright Horizons Foundation for Children, Abyssinian Development Corporation and Community Playthings, announced the opening of Harlem's first Bright Space center for homeless children at Abyssinian House, a Tier II transitional residence serving the families of Harlem.

Memorial Sloan-Kettering Cancer Center provides its employees with a flexible benefits program, including employee discounts, work/life balance programs and tuition reimbursement.

FINANCIALS: Sales and profits are in thousands of dollars—add 000 to get the full amount. 2007 Note: Financial information for 2007 was not available for all companies at press time.

2007 Sales: $
2006 Sales: $1,837,899
2005 Sales: $1,627,502
2004 Sales: $1,490,449
2003 Sales: $1,312,437

2007 Profits: $
2006 Profits: $78,741
2005 Profits: $51,594
2004 Profits: $52,359
2003 Profits: $422,700

U.S. Stock Ticker: Nonprofit
Int'l Ticker: Int'l Exchange:
Employees: 8,255
Fiscal Year Ends: 12/31
Parent Company:

SALARIES/BENEFITS:

Pension Plan: Y ESOP Stock Plan: Profit Sharing: Top Exec. Salary: $ Bonus: $
Savings Plan: Y Stock Purch. Plan: Second Exec. Salary: $ Bonus: $

OTHER THOUGHTS:

Apparent Women Officers or Directors: 3
Hot Spot for Advancement for Women/Minorities: Y

LOCATIONS: ("Y" = Yes)

West:	Southwest:	Midwest:	Southeast:	Northeast:	International:
				Y	

Note: Financial information, benefits and other data can change quickly and may vary from those stated here.

MENTOR CORP

www.mentorcorp.com

Industry Group Code: 339113 **Ranks within this company's industry group:** Sales: 54 Profits: 32

Insurance/HMO/PPO:		Drugs:		Equipment/Supplies:		Hospitals/Clinics:		Services:		Health Care:	
Insurance:		Manufacturer:		Manufacturer:	Y	Acute Care:		Diagnostics:		Home Health:	
Managed Care:		Distributor:		Distributor:	Y	Sub-Acute:		Labs/Testing:		Long-Term Care:	
Utilization Management:		Specialty Pharmacy:		Leasing/Finance:		Outpatient Surgery:		Staffing:		Physical Therapy:	
Payment Processing:		Vitamins/Nutritionals:		Information Systems:		Physical Rehab. Ctr.:		Waste Disposal:		Physician Prac. Mgmt.:	
		Clinical Trials:				Psychiatric Clinics:		Specialty Svcs.:			

TYPES OF BUSINESS:

Supplies-Plastic Surgery Products
Breast Implants
Liposuction

BRANDS/DIVISIONS/AFFILIATES:

Contour Profile Tissue Expander
Contour Profile
MemoryGel
BufferZone
Centerscope
Mentor UltraSculpt
Puragen
Prevell

CONTACTS: *Note: Officers with more than one job title may be intentionally listed here more than once.*

Joshua H. Levine, CEO
Edward S. Northup, COO/VP
Joshua H. Levine, Pres.
Loren L. McFarland, CFO/VP
Cathryn S. Ullery, VP-Human Resources
Loren L. McFarland, Treas.
Clarke Scherff, VP-Regulatory Compliance & Quality
Joseph E. Whitters, Chmn.

Phone: 805-879-6000	**Fax:** 805-964-2712
Toll-Free: 800-525-0245	
Address: 201 Mentor Dr., Santa Barbara, CA 93111 US	

GROWTH PLANS/SPECIAL FEATURES:

Mentor Corporation develops, manufactures, licenses and markets a broad range of products serving the plastic and reconstructive surgical markets in the U.S. and more than 60 other countries. The company's aesthetic products fall into three general categories: surgical breast implants; soft tissue aspiration or body contouring (liposuction); and facial rejuvenation products for skin restoration. Mentor's line of breast implant products includes Contour Profile, its saline-filled implant brand, and MemoryGel, its silicone gel-filled implant brand. MemoryGel received FDA approval for sale in November 2007, prior to which the company could only market it outside of the U.S. The company also markets the following proprietary breast products: the Contour Profile Tissue Expander lines of breast expanders, which prepare the tissue to later hold the implant; BufferZone, which is a self-sealing technology; and Centerscope, which is a line of injector port locators. All of these mammary prostheses are used in augmentation procedures to enhance breast size and shape, correct breast asymmetries, help restore fullness after breast feeding and reconstruct breasts following a mastectomy. With respect to body contouring, Mentor markets a complete line of liposuction products and disposable supplies, including its Mentor UltraSculpt technology, which allows surgeons to gently liquefy fat and remove it from surrounding tissue. This procedure is more accurate and produces far less physical trauma than conventional liposuction. The company also offers a line of extremity tissue expanders that are used in growing additional tissue for reconstruction and skin graft procedures. Finally, Mentor supplies dermal filters, such as Puragen and Prevell, and cosmeceutical products that help plastic surgeons and dermatologists correct for wrinkles and various other skin conditions. In June 2006, Mentor completed the sale of its surgical urology and its clinical and consumer healthcare business segments to Coloplast A/S for $463 million.

FINANCIALS: **Sales and profits are in thousands of dollars—add 000 to get the full amount. 2007 Note: Financial information for 2007 was not available for all companies at press time.**

2007 Sales: $301,974	2007 Profits: $290,614	**U.S. Stock Ticker: MNT**
2006 Sales: $268,272	2006 Profits: $62,357	**Int'l Ticker:** Int'l Exchange:
2005 Sales: $251,726	2005 Profits: $54,881	Employees: 950
2004 Sales: $218,437	2004 Profits: $54,779	Fiscal Year Ends: 3/31
2003 Sales: $382,400	2003 Profits: $55,900	Parent Company:

SALARIES/BENEFITS:

Pension Plan:	ESOP Stock Plan:	Profit Sharing:	Top Exec. Salary: $500,000	Bonus: $950,000
Savings Plan: Y	Stock Purch. Plan: Y		Second Exec. Salary: $300,000	Bonus: $450,000

OTHER THOUGHTS:

Apparent Women Officers or Directors: 2
Hot Spot for Advancement for Women/Minorities: Y

LOCATIONS: ("Y" = Yes)

West:	Southwest:	Midwest:	Southeast:	Northeast:	International:
Y	Y	Y			Y

MERCER INC

www.mercer.com

Industry Group Code: 541612 **Ranks within this company's industry group:** Sales: 1 Profits:

Insurance/HMO/PPO:		Drugs:		Equipment/Supplies:		Hospitals/Clinics:		Services:		Health Care:	
Insurance:		Manufacturer:		Manufacturer:		Acute Care:		Diagnostics:		Home Health:	
Managed Care:		Distributor:		Distributor:		Sub-Acute:		Labs/Testing:		Long-Term Care:	
Utilization Management:		Specialty Pharmacy:		Leasing/Finance:		Outpatient Surgery:		Staffing:		Physical Therapy:	
Payment Processing:		Vitamins/Nutritionals:		Information Systems:		Physical Rehab. Ctr.:		Waste Disposal:		Physician Prac. Mgmt.:	
		Clinical Trials:				Psychiatric Clinics:		Specialty Svcs.:	Y		

TYPES OF BUSINESS:

Consulting-Human Resources
Employee Benefits Consulting
Compensation Consulting
Investment Consulting
Outsourced Human Resources Services (BPO)
Employee Benefits Administration
Retirement Plan Administration
Absence Management

BRANDS/DIVISIONS/AFFILIATES:

Mercer HR
Mercer Investment Consulting
Mercer Retirement
Mercer Global Investments
Mercer Human Capital
Mercer HR Services
Marsh & McLennan Companies, Inc.

CONTACTS: *Note: Officers with more than one job title may be intentionally listed here more than once.*

M. Michele Burns, CEO
Patricia Milligan, Leader-Global Market Dev.
Steve Mele, Chief Human Resources Officer
Charles Salmans, Global Head-Public Rel.
M. Michele Burns, Chmn.

Phone: 212-345-7000 **Fax:** 212-345-7414
Toll-Free:
Address: 1166 Ave. of the Americas, New York, NY 10036 US

GROWTH PLANS/SPECIAL FEATURES:

Mercer, Inc. (Mercer HR) is a global provider of a broad range of human resource advice and solutions. Mercer HR also provides related financial advice, products and services in the retirement, health and benefits areas. The firm has four lines of business: Retirement & Investments; Health & Benefits; Talent; and Outsourcing. The Retirement & Investments segment is divided into three units: Mercer Retirement, Mercer Investment Consulting and Mercer Global Investments. Mercer Retirement offers consulting services in defined benefit and defined contribution plans, executive retirement plans, retiree medical benefits and the retiree benefits aspects of mergers and acquisitions. Mercer Investment Consulting offers customized guidance at each stage of an investment decision, risk management and investment monitoring process. Mercer Global Investments provides global, multi-manager investment solutions to institutional investors (primarily retirement plan sponsors and trustees) and individual investors (in Australia and prospectively in other countries), primarily for investment of their retirement plan assets. The Health & Benefits segment offers advice and solutions related to a broad spectrum of health and welfare related issues including health care strategy, health care funding, pharmacy, disease management and absentee management. The Talent segment works through subsidiary Mercer Human Capital to design, analyze and align clients' compensation and performance management systems, including both executive compensation and broad-based employee compensation programs. It also provides data, software and compensation administration services to help companies manage and operate their compensation and total rewards programs. The Outsourcing segment, through subsidiary Mercer HR Services, provides outsourced human resources administration, technology and business process solutions globally. The majority of Mercer HR's clients are Fortune 1000 and FTSE 100 companies. Mercer HR has offices in 41 countries around the globe, and the firm is a subsidiary of Marsh & McLennan Companies, Inc.

FINANCIALS: **Sales and profits are in thousands of dollars—add 000 to get the full amount. 2007 Note: Financial information for 2007 was not available for all companies at press time.**

2007 Sales: $	2007 Profits: $	**U.S. Stock Ticker: Subsidiary**
2006 Sales: $3,021,000	2006 Profits: $	**Int'l Ticker:** Int'l Exchange:
2005 Sales: $2,794,000	2005 Profits: $	Employees: 16,500
2004 Sales: $	2004 Profits: $	Fiscal Year Ends: 12/31
2003 Sales: $	2003 Profits: $	Parent Company: MARSH & MCLENNAN COMPANIES INC

SALARIES/BENEFITS:

Pension Plan:	ESOP Stock Plan:	Profit Sharing:	Top Exec. Salary: $	Bonus: $
Savings Plan:	Stock Purch. Plan:		Second Exec. Salary: $	Bonus: $

OTHER THOUGHTS:

Apparent Women Officers or Directors: 3
Hot Spot for Advancement for Women/Minorities: Y

LOCATIONS: ("Y" = Yes)

West:	Southwest:	Midwest:	Southeast:	Northeast:	International:
Y	Y	Y	Y	Y	Y

Note: Financial information, benefits and other data can change quickly and may vary from those stated here.

MERCK & CO INC

www.merck.com

Industry Group Code: 325412 **Ranks within this company's industry group:** Sales: 8 Profits: 7

Insurance/HMO/PPO:		Drugs:		Equipment/Supplies:		Hospitals/Clinics:		Services:		Health Care:	
Insurance:		Manufacturer:	Y	Manufacturer:		Acute Care:		Diagnostics:		Home Health:	
Managed Care:	Y	Distributor:		Distributor:		Sub-Acute:		Labs/Testing:		Long-Term Care:	
Utilization Management:		Specialty Pharmacy:		Leasing/Finance:		Outpatient Surgery:		Staffing:		Physical Therapy:	
Payment Processing:		Vitamins/Nutritionals:		Information Systems:		Physical Rehab. Ctr.:		Waste Disposal:		Physician Prac. Mgmt.:	
		Clinical Trials:				Psychiatric Clinics:		Specialty Svcs.:	Y		

TYPES OF BUSINESS:

Pharmaceuticals Development & Manufacturing
Cholesterol Drugs
Hypertension Drugs
Heart Failure Drugs
Allergy & Asthma Drugs
Animal Health Products
Vaccines
Preventative Drugs

BRANDS/DIVISIONS/AFFILIATES:

Merck Institute for Science Education
Sirna Therapeutics, Inc.
Singulair
Propecia
Cozaar
Fosamax
Gardasil
Vioxx

CONTACTS: *Note: Officers with more than one job title may be intentionally listed here more than once.*

Richard Clark, CEO
Richard Clark, Pres.
Peter Kellogg, CFO/Exec. VP
Mirian Graddick-Weir, Sr. VP-Human Resources
Peter Kim, Pres., Research Laboratories
Chris Scalet, CIO/Sr. VP-Svcs.
Willie Deese, Pres., Mfg. Div.
Bruce N. Kuhlik, General Counsel
Peter Kellogg, Exec. VP-Bus. Dev. & Licensing Activities
Peter Kellogg, Exec. VP-Investor Rel.
Judy Lewent, Chief-Finance
Kenneth C. Frazier, Pres., Global Human Health
Richard Clark, Chmn.
Per Wold-Olsen, Pres., Human Health, EMEA

Phone: 908-423-1000 **Fax:** 908-735-1253
Toll-Free:
Address: 1 Merck Dr., Whitehouse Station, NJ 08889-0100 US

GROWTH PLANS/SPECIAL FEATURES:

Merck & Co., Inc. is a leading research-driven pharmaceutical company that manufactures a broad range of products sold in approximately 150 countries. These products include therapeutic and preventative drugs generally sold by prescription and medications used to control and alleviate disease. As one of the world's largest pharmaceutical companies, Merck's line of big selling medicine includes drugs like Zocor for cholesterol; Fosamax for the prevention of osteoporosis; and Cozaar and Hyzaar for high blood pressure. The company also manufactures Propecia, a popular treatment for male pattern baldness, and Singulair, a seasonal allergy and asthma medicine, both of which are offered in tablet form. Merck's bestselling Vioxx product, an arthritis and pain medication, was discontinued in 2004 due to ongoing litigation. The withdrawal of this drug has serious negative implications for the company. Vioxx's return to the market hinges on an FDA review. In addition to medicines, the company manufactures vaccines such as Rotateq, designed to prevent gastroenteritis in infants and children; and Gardasil, a new product designed to reduce the probabilities of cancer. In May 2006, Merck agreed to acquire Abmaxis, Inc. and GlycoFi, Inc. At the end of December 2006, Merck acquired Sirna Therapeutics, Inc., which develops drugs based on RNA interference, for $1.1 billion. In 2006, five Merck products were approved by the FDA: Gardasil, a vaccine for HPV, which causes cervical cancer and warts; Januvia, which improves blood sugar control for patients with type 2 diabetes; Zostavax, a vaccine to prevent shingles; RotaTeq, a vaccine to prevent rotavirus gastroenteritis in infants; and Zolinza, which treats advanced cutaneous T-cell lymphoma.

Merck offers its employees on-site fitness facilities, day care and summer camp programs, tuition reimbursement and financial planning assistance.

FINANCIALS: **Sales and profits are in thousands of dollars—add 000 to get the full amount. 2007 Note: Financial information for 2007 was not available for all companies at press time.**

2007 Sales: $	2007 Profits: $	**U.S. Stock Ticker: MRK**
2006 Sales: $22,636,000	2006 Profits: $4,433,800	**Int'l Ticker:** Int'l Exchange:
2005 Sales: $22,011,900	2005 Profits: $4,631,300	Employees: 60,000
2004 Sales: $22,938,600	2004 Profits: $5,813,400	Fiscal Year Ends: 12/31
2003 Sales: $22,485,900	2003 Profits: $6,830,900	Parent Company:

SALARIES/BENEFITS:

Pension Plan: Y	ESOP Stock Plan:	Profit Sharing:	Top Exec. Salary: $1,183,334	Bonus: $1,800,000
Savings Plan: Y	Stock Purch. Plan:		Second Exec. Salary: $828,130	Bonus: $875,000

OTHER THOUGHTS:

Apparent Women Officers or Directors: 2
Hot Spot for Advancement for Women/Minorities: Y

LOCATIONS: ("Y" = Yes)

West:	Southwest:	Midwest:	Southeast:	Northeast:	International:
Y	Y	Y	Y	Y	Y

MERCK SERONO SA

www.serono.com

Industry Group Code: 325412 **Ranks within this company's industry group:** Sales: Profits:

Insurance/HMO/PPO:		Drugs:		Equipment/Supplies:		Hospitals/Clinics:		Services:		Health Care:	
Insurance:		Manufacturer:	Y	Manufacturer:		Acute Care:		Diagnostics:		Home Health:	
Managed Care:		Distributor:		Distributor:		Sub-Acute:		Labs/Testing:		Long-Term Care:	
Utilization Management:		Specialty Pharmacy:		Leasing/Finance:		Outpatient Surgery:		Staffing:		Physical Therapy:	
Payment Processing:		Vitamins/Nutritionals:		Information Systems:		Physical Rehab. Ctr.:		Waste Disposal:		Physician Prac. Mgmt.:	
		Clinical Trials:				Psychiatric Clinics:		Specialty Svcs.:			

TYPES OF BUSINESS:

Pharmaceuticals Development
Fertility Drugs
Neurology Drugs
Growth & Metabolism Drugs
Dermatology Drugs
Oncology Research

BRANDS/DIVISIONS/AFFILIATES:

GONAL-f
Ovidrel/Ovitrelle
Luveris
Crinone
Cetrotide
Rebif
Saizen
Merck KGaA

CONTACTS: *Note: Officers with more than one job title may be intentionally listed here more than once.*

Elmer Schnee, CEO/Dir.
Olaf Klinger, CFO
Francois Naef, Chief Admin. Officer
Michael Becker, Chmn.

Phone: 41-22-414-3000 **Fax:** 41-22-731-2179
Toll-Free:
Address: 9, chemin des Mines, Case postale 54, Geneva, CH-1211 20 Switzerland

GROWTH PLANS/SPECIAL FEATURES:

Merck Serono SA (SRA), formerly Serono SA, was formed in January 2007 when Merck KGaA acquired Serono in a $13 billion transaction. SRA is a global biotechnology company that focuses on product development in four therapeutic areas: reproductive health, growth and metabolism, multiple sclerosis and dermatology. The company currently markets GONAL-f, Ovitrelle, Luveris, Crinone and Cetrotide for female infertility; Rebif and Rebiject for multiple sclerosis; Saizen for growth hormone deficiency in children and Raptiva for psoriasis. SRA has also launched a web site, fertility.com, which addresses infertility issues and provides support for couples who are seeking or undergoing treatments. The firm markets its products in Europe, Asia, Latin America and North America and is involved in numerous worldwide partnerships with companies such as Amgen and Astrazeneca. It also established the SRA Biotech Center (SBC) for the sole purpose of manufacturing bulk pharmaceutical products under U.S., European, Japanese, Australian and Swiss pharmaceutical regulations. SRA operates in 44 countries and has a large network of research and development personnel at three global research institutes: SRA Pharmaceutical Institute in Geneva, Switzerland; SRA Research Institute in Boston; and an Italian facility dedicated to pharmacological research. Currently, SRA has eight biotechnology products on the market and more than 25 ongoing preclinical development projects. SRA research principally centers on genetics and functional genomics in order to identify new therapeutic proteins in areas such as the autoimmune/inflammatory system and oncology. SRA has also focused in particular on treatments for rheumatoid arthritis, osteoarthritis, lymphomas and leukemia. In 2007, SRA launched easypod, an electric growth hormone injection device used for the administration of Saizen. Since the company's recent acquisition, numerous changes will take place, which include the reorganization of its executive board and the modification of all of its logos and names in its global facilities.

FINANCIALS: Sales and profits are in thousands of dollars—add 000 to get the full amount. 2007 Note: Financial information for 2007 was not available for all companies at press time.

2007 Sales: $
2006 Sales: $
2005 Sales: $2,586,400
2004 Sales: $2,177,900
2003 Sales: $1,858,000

2007 Profits: $
2006 Profits: $
2005 Profits: $-105,300
2004 Profits: $494,200
2003 Profits: $390,000

U.S. Stock Ticker: Subsidiary
Int'l Ticker: SEO Int'l Exchange: Zurich-SWX
Employees: 4,900
Fiscal Year Ends: 12/31
Parent Company: MERCK KGAA

SALARIES/BENEFITS:

Pension Plan: Y ESOP Stock Plan: Y Profit Sharing: Y Top Exec. Salary: $ Bonus: $
Savings Plan: Stock Purch. Plan: Second Exec. Salary: $ Bonus: $

OTHER THOUGHTS:

Apparent Women Officers or Directors:
Hot Spot for Advancement for Women/Minorities:

LOCATIONS: ("Y" = Yes)

West:	Southwest:	Midwest:	Southeast:	Northeast:	International:
				Y	Y

Note: Financial information, benefits and other data can change quickly and may vary from those stated here.

MERIDIAN BIOSCIENCE INC www.meridianbioscience.com

Industry Group Code: 325413 **Ranks within this company's industry group:** Sales: 6 Profits: 4

Insurance/HMO/PPO:		Drugs:		Equipment/Supplies:		Hospitals/Clinics:		Services:		Health Care:	
Insurance:		Manufacturer:		Manufacturer:	Y	Acute Care:		Diagnostics:		Home Health:	
Managed Care:		Distributor:		Distributor:		Sub-Acute:		Labs/Testing:		Long-Term Care:	
Utilization Management:		Specialty Pharmacy:		Leasing/Finance:		Outpatient Surgery:		Staffing:		Physical Therapy:	
Payment Processing:		Vitamins/Nutritionals:		Information Systems:		Physical Rehab. Ctr.:		Waste Disposal:		Physician Prac. Mgmt.:	
		Clinical Trials:				Psychiatric Clinics:		Specialty Svcs.:			

TYPES OF BUSINESS:

Diagnostic Test Kits
Contract Manufacturing
Bulk Antigens, Antibodies & Reagents

BRANDS/DIVISIONS/AFFILIATES:

Biodesign
OEM Concepts
Viral Antigens
cGMP
ImmunoCard STAT EHEC

CONTACTS: *Note: Officers with more than one job title may be intentionally listed here more than once.*

William J. Motto, CEO
John A. Kraeutler, COO
John A. Kraeutler, Pres.
Melissa A. Lueke, CFO/VP
Todd W. Motto, VP-Sales & Mktg.
Kenneth J. Kozak, VP-R&D
Lawrence J. Baldini, Exec. VP-Info. Systems
Lawrence J. Baldini, Exec. VP-Oper.
Susan D. Rolih, VP-Regulatory Affairs & Quality Systems
William J. Motto, Chmn.
Antonio A. Interno, Sr. VP/Pres./Managing Dir.-Europe

Phone: 513-271-3700	**Fax:** 513-271-3762
Toll-Free:	
Address: 3471 River Hills Dr., Cincinnati, OH 45244 US	

GROWTH PLANS/SPECIAL FEATURES:

Meridian Biosciences, Inc. is a life science company that develops, manufactures, sells and distributes diagnostic test kits, primarily for certain respiratory, gastrointestinal, viral and parasitic infectious diseases; manufactures and distributes bulk antigens, antibodies and reagents; and contract manufactures proteins and other biologicals. The company operates in three segments: U.S. diagnostics, European diagnostics and life science. The U.S. diagnostics segment focuses on the development, manufacture, sale and distribution of diagnostic test kits, which utilize immunodiagnostic technologies that test samples of blood, urine, stool and other body fluids or tissue for the presence of antigens and antibodies of specific infectious diseases. Products also include transport media that store and preserve specimen samples from patient collection to laboratory testing. The European diagnostics segment focuses on the sale and distribution of diagnostic test kits. Its sales and distribution network consists of direct sales forces in Belgium, France, Holland and Italy; and independent distributors in other European, African and Middle Eastern countries. The life sciences segment focuses on the development, manufacture, sale and distribution of bulk antigens, antibodies and reagents, as well as contract development and manufacturing services. The segment is represented by four product-line brands: Biodesign, which represents monoclonal and polyclonal antibodies and assay reagents; OEM Concepts, which represents contract ascites and antibody production services; Viral Antigens, which represents viral proteins; and cGMP biologics, which represents contract development and manufacturing services for drug and vaccine discovery and development. Meridian's core diagnostic products generated 79% of revenue in 2006. In February 2007, the company received clearance from the FDA to market ImmunoCard STAT EHEC, a test for the diagnosis of E. coli infection.

The company offers its employees health, dental and life insurance; a 401(k) plan; stock options; an employee stock purchase plan; a profit-sharing plan; tuition reimbursement; and an employee assistance plan.

FINANCIALS: **Sales and profits are in thousands of dollars—add 000 to get the full amount. 2007 Note: Financial information for 2007 was not available for all companies at press time.**

2007 Sales: $	2007 Profits: $	**U.S. Stock Ticker: VIVO**
2006 Sales: $108,413	2006 Profits: $18,325	**Int'l Ticker:** Int'l Exchange:
2005 Sales: $92,965	2005 Profits: $12,565	Employees: 363
2004 Sales: $79,606	2004 Profits: $9,185	Fiscal Year Ends: 9/30
2003 Sales: $65,864	2003 Profits: $7,018	Parent Company:

SALARIES/BENEFITS:

Pension Plan:	ESOP Stock Plan:	Profit Sharing: Y	Top Exec. Salary: $456,155	Bonus: $490,875
Savings Plan: Y	Stock Purch. Plan: Y		Second Exec. Salary: $360,573	Bonus: $388,500

OTHER THOUGHTS:

Apparent Women Officers or Directors: 2
Hot Spot for Advancement for Women/Minorities: Y

LOCATIONS: ("Y" = Yes)

West:	Southwest:	Midwest:	Southeast:	Northeast:	International:
				Y	Y

MERIDIAN MEDICAL TECHNOLOGIES INC

www.meridianmeds.com

ndustry Group Code: 339113 **Ranks within this company's industry group:** Sales: Profits:

nsurance/HMO/PPO:		Drugs:		Equipment/Supplies:		Hospitals/Clinics:		Services:		Health Care:	
nsurance:		Manufacturer:		Manufacturer:	Y	Acute Care:		Diagnostics:		Home Health:	
Managed Care:		Distributor:		Distributor:		Sub-Acute:		Labs/Testing:		Long-Term Care:	
Jtilization Management:		Specialty Pharmacy:		Leasing/Finance:		Outpatient Surgery:		Staffing:		Physical Therapy:	
Payment Processing:		Vitamins/Nutritionals:		Information Systems:		Physical Rehab. Ctr.:		Waste Disposal:		Physician Prac. Mgmt.:	
		Clinical Trials:				Psychiatric Clinics:		Specialty Svcs.:			

TYPES OF BUSINESS:

Supplies-Allergic Reaction Auto-Injectors
Cardiopulmonary Diagnostics

BRANDS/DIVISIONS/AFFILIATES:

King Pharmaceuticals Inc
EpiPen
CardioPocket
Morphine Auto-Injector
CardioBeeper
AtroPen
Mark I Nerve Agent Antidote Kit

CONTACTS: *Note: Officers with more than one job title may be intentionally listed here more than once.*

Dennis P. O'Brien, Pres.
Paul Lippner, Dir.-Int'l Sales
Ted Marcuccio, VP-Bus. Dev. & Strategic Planning
Geoffrey Ritson, Manager-Int'l Sales, U.K.

Phone: 443-259-7800 **Fax:** 443-259-7801
Toll-Free: 800-638-8093
Address: 10240 Old Columbia Rd., Columbia, MD 21046 US

GROWTH PLANS/SPECIAL FEATURES:

Meridian Medical Technologies, Inc., a subsidiary of King Pharmaceuticals, Inc., is a worldwide developer of auto-injector drug delivery systems and manufacturer non-invasive cardiopulmonary diagnostic equipment. Meridian delivers technology for medicine in early intervention home health care and emergency medical technologies and also provides product development and manufacturing support to the pharmaceutical and biotechnology industries. The company's drug delivery systems unit participates in the rapidly developing home and emergency markets for drugs using innovative technology. The firm is an innovator in auto-injector technology and currently produces EpiPen, the leading epinephrine injection product for severe allergic reactions. Meridian markets a Morphine Auto-Injector as well as AtroPen, a pre-prepared injection of nerve agent antidote, and the Mark I Nerve Agent Antidote Kit. Meridian also markets CardioPocket (a pocket-size ECG transmitter) and CardioBeeper (a personal heart monitor). The company's principal customers are the U.S. armed forces and homeland defense first responders.

FINANCIALS: **Sales and profits are in thousands of dollars—add 000 to get the full amount. 2007 Note: Financial information for 2007 was not available for all companies at press time.**

2007 Sales: $ | 2007 Profits: $
2006 Sales: $ | 2006 Profits: $
2005 Sales: $ | 2005 Profits: $
2004 Sales: $ | 2004 Profits: $
2003 Sales: $ | 2003 Profits: $

U.S. Stock Ticker: Subsidiary
Int'l Ticker: Int'l Exchange:
Employees: 452
Fiscal Year Ends:
Parent Company: KING PHARMACEUTICALS INC

SALARIES/BENEFITS:

Pension Plan: ESOP Stock Plan: Profit Sharing: Top Exec. Salary: $395,833 Bonus: $140,000
Savings Plan: Stock Purch. Plan: Second Exec. Salary: $169,333 Bonus: $40,000

OTHER THOUGHTS:

Apparent Women Officers or Directors:
Hot Spot for Advancement for Women/Minorities:

LOCATIONS: ("Y" = Yes)

West:	Southwest:	Midwest:	Southeast:	Northeast:	International:
		Y		Y	Y

MERIT MEDICAL SYSTEMS INC

www.merit.com

Industry Group Code: 339113 **Ranks within this company's industry group:** Sales: 65 Profits: 60

Insurance/HMO/PPO:		Drugs:		Equipment/Supplies:		Hospitals/Clinics:		Services:		Health Care:	
Insurance:		Manufacturer:		Manufacturer:	Y	Acute Care:		Diagnostics:		Home Health:	
Managed Care:		Distributor:		Distributor:	Y	Sub-Acute:		Labs/Testing:		Long-Term Care:	
Utilization Management:		Specialty Pharmacy:		Leasing/Finance:		Outpatient Surgery:		Staffing:		Physical Therapy:	
Payment Processing:		Vitamins/Nutritionals:		Information Systems:		Physical Rehab. Ctr.:		Waste Disposal:		Physician Prac. Mgmt.:	
		Clinical Trials:				Psychiatric Clinics:		Specialty Svcs.:			

TYPES OF BUSINESS:

Disposable Products-Cardiology & Radiology

BRANDS/DIVISIONS/AFFILIATES:

Futura Safety Scalpel

CONTACTS: *Note: Officers with more than one job title may be intentionally listed here more than once.*

Fred P. Lampropoulos, CEO
Arlin D. Nelson, COO
Fred P. Lampropoulos, Pres.
Kent W. Stanger, CFO
Martin R. Stephens, VP-Sales
Kent W. Stanger, Corp. Sec.
Kent W. Stanger, Treas.
Fred P. Lampropoulos, Chmn.

Phone: 801-253-1600 **Fax:** 801-253-1652
Toll-Free: 800-356-3748
Address: 1600 W. Merit Pkwy., South Jordan, UT 84095 US

GROWTH PLANS/SPECIAL FEATURES:

Merit Medical Systems, Inc. develops, manufactures and distributes disposable proprietary medical products used in interventional diagnostic and therapeutic procedures, particularly in cardiology and radiology. The company's products are designed to assist physicians in diagnosing disease and intervening in the areas of radiology and cardiology. Products include coronary control syringes; inflation devices; specialty syringes; waste management products; high-pressure tubing and connectors; disposable blood pressure transducer and pressure monitoring tubing and accessories; disposable hemostasis valves, guide wire torque devices and accessories; drainage catheters and accessories; diagnostic angiographic pigtail catheters; guide catheters; percutaneous sheath introducers, obturators and vessel dialators; diagnostic guide wires; pressure infusor bags; and angiography needles and accessories. Sales are made primarily to U.S. hospitals through a direct sales force. In 2006, the U.S. domestic sales force made approximately 43% of U.S. sales directly to hospitals and roughly 15% of U.S. sales through other channels such as U.S. customs packagers and distributors. Original equipment manufacturers (OEMs) accounted for approximately 14% of 2006 revenue. About 28% of sales in 2006 were made in international markets. Merit has subsidiaries in Ireland, Germany, France, the U.K., Belgium, the Netherlands, Denmark and Sweden. In April 2006, Merit announced that it had acquired the manufacturing and sale capabilities of an auto-retractable safety scalpel currently branded as the Futura Safety Scalpel. In July 2007, the company acquired technology from Lightek Corp. for flexible radioplaque plastic laminate composition.

The company offers its employees medical and dental insurance; short- and long-term disability insurance; life and AD&D insurance; a 401(k) plan; an employee stock purchase plan; and an employee assistance program.

FINANCIALS: **Sales and profits are in thousands of dollars—add 000 to get the full amount. 2007 Note: Financial information for 2007 was not available for all companies at press time.**

2007 Sales: $	2007 Profits: $	**U.S. Stock Ticker: MMSI**
2006 Sales: $190,674	2006 Profits: $12,301	**Int'l Ticker:** Int'l Exchange:
2005 Sales: $166,585	2005 Profits: $15,778	Employees: 1,709
2004 Sales: $151,398	2004 Profits: $17,932	Fiscal Year Ends: 12/31
2003 Sales: $135,954	2003 Profits: $17,295	Parent Company:

SALARIES/BENEFITS:

Pension Plan:	ESOP Stock Plan:	Profit Sharing:	Top Exec. Salary: $456,400	Bonus: $200,300
Savings Plan: Y	Stock Purch. Plan: Y		Second Exec. Salary: $248,077	Bonus: $105,100

OTHER THOUGHTS:

Apparent Women Officers or Directors:
Hot Spot for Advancement for Women/Minorities: Y

LOCATIONS: ("Y" = Yes)

West:	Southwest:	Midwest:	Southeast:	Northeast:	International:
Y					Y

METROPOLITAN HEALTH NETWORKS www.metcare.com

Industry Group Code: 524114 **Ranks within this company's industry group:** Sales: 28 Profits: 25

Insurance/HMO/PPO:		Drugs:		Equipment/Supplies:		Hospitals/Clinics:		Services:		Health Care:	
Insurance:		Manufacturer:		Manufacturer:		Acute Care:		Diagnostics:		Home Health:	
Managed Care:	Y	Distributor:		Distributor:		Sub-Acute:		Labs/Testing:		Long-Term Care:	
Utilization Management:	Y	Specialty Pharmacy:		Leasing/Finance:		Outpatient Surgery:		Staffing:		Physical Therapy:	
Payment Processing:		Vitamins/Nutritionals:		Information Systems:		Physical Rehab. Ctr.:		Waste Disposal:		Physician Prac. Mgmt.:	
		Clinical Trials:				Psychiatric Clinics:		Specialty Svcs.:	Y		

TYPES OF BUSINESS:

Provider Service Network
HMO
Managed Care Risk Contracting
Disease Management
Pharmacy Benefits Management
Utilization Management

BRANDS/DIVISIONS/AFFILIATES:

MetHealth
Metcare
Metcare RX, Inc.
Medicare Advantage HMO
METCARE Health Plans, Inc.
AdvantageCare

CONTACTS: *Note: Officers with more than one job title may be intentionally listed here more than once.*

Michael M. Earley, CEO
Debra A. Finnel, COO
Debra A. Finnel, Pres.
Robert Sabo, CFO
Sharon Munroe, VP-Human Resources
Roman G. Fisher, CIO/Sr. VP
Roberto L. Palenzuela, General Counsel/Chief Compliance Officer
Maria A. Xirau, VP-Oper.
Jose A. Guethon, Chief Medical Officer-AdvantageCare
Brenton Hood, VP-Network Oper.
Lucille Soltesz, VP-Quality Mgmt.
Hymin Zucker, Chief Medical Officer-Metcare of Florida, Inc.
Michael M. Earley, Chmn.

Phone: 561-805-8500 **Fax:** 561-805-8501
Toll-Free: 888-663-8227
Address: 250 Australian Ave. S., Ste. 400, West Palm Beach, FL 33401 US

GROWTH PLANS/SPECIAL FEATURES:

Metropolitan Health Networks, Inc. (MHN) provides comprehensive healthcare services for approximately 25,600 Medicare patients and 3,800 Medicare Advantage beneficiaries through its provider service network (PSN) and its health maintenance organization (HMO) in South and Central Florida. Both of MHN's PSN and HMO operations are focused on individuals covered by Medicare, which covers the costs of hospitalization, medical care and other related health services for U.S. Citizens that are 65 years or older, qualified disabled persons and persons suffering from end-staged renal disease. In addition to its primary care practices, the PSN holds network contracts with Humana and 26 independent primary care physician practices and operates eight primary care physician practice and one medical oncology physician practice. Metropolitan's HMO operations are conducted through its wholly-owned subsidiary, Metcare Health Plans, Inc, which offers services to Medicare beneficiaries in six Florida counties under its AdvantageCare plan. The company also operates a managed care network and infrastructure of experts in disease, quality and utilization management, which involves the proper utilization of costs and care of high-risk patients, generating a standard of measurement for its overall patient care against the best medical practices and conducting a daily review of data created by encounters, referrals, hospital admissions and nursing home information.

The firm offers employees 2-tiered health insurance, education assistance, supplemental health benefits, a credit union and a Costco membership.

FINANCIALS: **Sales and profits are in thousands of dollars—add 000 to get the full amount. 2007 Note: Financial information for 2007 was not available for all companies at press time.**

2007 Sales: $	2007 Profits: $	**U.S. Stock Ticker: MDF**
2006 Sales: $228,216	2006 Profits: $ 473	**Int'l Ticker:** Int'l Exchange:
2005 Sales: $183,765	2005 Profits: $2,382	Employees: 204
2004 Sales: $158,070	2004 Profits: $18,822	Fiscal Year Ends: 12/31
2003 Sales: $143,874	2003 Profits: $4,402	Parent Company:

SALARIES/BENEFITS:

Pension Plan:	ESOP Stock Plan:	Profit Sharing:	Top Exec. Salary: $300,000	Bonus: $
Savings Plan: Y	Stock Purch. Plan:		Second Exec. Salary: $300,000	Bonus: $

OTHER THOUGHTS:

Apparent Women Officers or Directors: 3
Hot Spot for Advancement for Women/Minorities: Y

LOCATIONS: ("Y" = Yes)

West:	Southwest:	Midwest:	Southeast:	Northeast:	International:
			Y		

Note: Financial information, benefits and other data can change quickly and may vary from those stated here.

METTLER-TOLEDO INTERNATIONAL glo.mt.com

Industry Group Code: 334500 **Ranks within this company's industry group:** Sales: 1 Profits: 1

Insurance/HMO/PPO:		Drugs:		Equipment/Supplies:		Hospitals/Clinics:		Services:		Health Care:	
Insurance:		Manufacturer:		Manufacturer:	Y	Acute Care:		Diagnostics:		Home Health:	
Managed Care:		Distributor:		Distributor:		Sub-Acute:		Labs/Testing:		Long-Term Care:	
Utilization Management:		Specialty Pharmacy:		Leasing/Finance:		Outpatient Surgery:		Staffing:		Physical Therapy:	
Payment Processing:		Vitamins/Nutritionals:		Information Systems:		Physical Rehab. Ctr.:		Waste Disposal:		Physician Prac. Mgmt.:	
		Clinical Trials:				Psychiatric Clinics:		Specialty Svcs.:	Y		

TYPES OF BUSINESS:

Equipment-Measurement Instruments
Manufacturing-Laboratory Equipment
Manufacturing-Industrial Weighing Equipment
Manufacturing-Retail Weighing Equipment
Software
Product Inspections

BRANDS/DIVISIONS/AFFILIATES:

Rainin
SofTechnics, Inc.

CONTACTS: *Note: Officers with more than one job title may be intentionally listed here more than once.*

Robert F. Spoerry, CEO
Robert F. Spoerry, Pres.
William P. Donnelly, CFO
Olivier A. Filiol, Head-Global Sales, Mktg. & Service
Peter Burker, Head-Human Resources
Beat E. Luthi, Head-Laboratory Div.
William P. Donnelly, Head-Info. Systems
Joakim Weidemanis, Head-Prod. Inspection Div.
James T. Bellerjeau, General Counsel/Sec.
Mary T. Finnegan, Head-Investor Rel.
Mary T. Finnegan, Treas.
Ken A. Peters, Head-North America
Olivier A. Filliol, Head-Process Analytics Div.
Urs Widmer, Head-Industrial Div.
Hans-Peter von Arb, Head-Retail
Robert F. Spoerry, Chmn.
Karl M. Lang, Head-Asia/Pacific

Phone: 41-1-944-2211 **Fax:** 41-1-944-3090
Toll-Free:
Address: Im Langacher, Greifensee, Zurich CH-8606 Switzerland

GROWTH PLANS/SPECIAL FEATURES:

Mettler-Toledo International, Inc. is a leading provider o weighing equipment. Its five business segments are U.S Operations, Swiss Operations, Western European Operations, Chinese Operations and Other. In 2006 approximately 33.6% of the firm's revenue came from the U.S.; 3.3% came from Switzerland and 38.5% from the res of Europe; 8.1% came from China; and 16.5% came from the rest of the world. Its products and services are broken dow as follows. Laboratory instruments accounted for 44% o 2006 sales. They include laboratory balances that have a range from one ten-millionth of a gram to 32 kilograms Pipettes are sold under the Rainin brand name, and include tips and accessories. They are used in pharmaceutical biotech, clinical and academic settings. Titrators measure material properties such as weight, dimension and viscoelasticity (a type of malleability), as a function o temperature; and are often used by the food and beverage industry. The company also manufactures density and refractometry instruments that measure chemica concentrations in solutions; and other laboratory products such as pH meters. Mettler-Toledo also offers laboratory software to analyze data from its instrumentation. Its industrial instruments, 42% of 2006 sales, include vehicle scale systems that can handle weights up to 500 tons; are usable with both trucks and railcars; and provide accurate measurements in extreme environmental conditions. It provides industrial scales and balances that can handle loads from a few grams to several thousand kilograms, for applications ranging from chemical production to weighing mail and packages. It produces terminals and software to help automatically collect and analyze data. Mettler-Toledo also provides product inspections. Retail weighing solutions, 14% of 2006 sales, include stand-alone scales and balances with pricing and printing functions; and networks that integrate backroom, counter, self-service and checkout weighing functions. Subsidiary SofTechnics, Inc. provides retail inventory management software.

FINANCIALS: **Sales and profits are in thousands of dollars—add 000 to get the full amount. 2007 Note: Financial information for 2007 was not available for all companies at press time.**

2007 Sales: $
2006 Sales: $1,594,912
2005 Sales: $1,482,472
2004 Sales: $1,404,454
2003 Sales: $1,304,400

2007 Profits: $
2006 Profits: $157,532
2005 Profits: $108,902
2004 Profits: $107,957
2003 Profits: $95,800

U.S. Stock Ticker: MTD
Int'l Ticker: Int'l Exchange:
Employees: 9,100
Fiscal Year Ends: 12/31
Parent Company:

SALARIES/BENEFITS:

Pension Plan: Y ESOP Stock Plan: Profit Sharing: Top Exec. Salary: $918,279 Bonus: $1,431,414
Savings Plan: Stock Purch. Plan: Second Exec. Salary: $355,276 Bonus: $526,668

OTHER THOUGHTS:

Apparent Women Officers or Directors: 1
Hot Spot for Advancement for Women/Minorities:

LOCATIONS: ("Y" = Yes)

West:	Southwest:	Midwest:	Southeast:	Northeast:	International:
Y		Y	Y	Y	Y

Note: Financial information, benefits and other data can change quickly and may vary from those stated here.

MICROTEK MEDICAL HOLDINGS INC www.microtekmed.com

ndustry Group Code: 339113 **Ranks within this company's industry group:** Sales: 73 Profits: 65

nsurance/HMO/PPO:		Drugs:		Equipment/Supplies:		Hospitals/Clinics:		Services:		Health Care:	
nsurance:		Manufacturer:		Manufacturer:	Y	Acute Care:		Diagnostics:		Home Health:	
lanaged Care:		Distributor:		Distributor:		Sub-Acute:		Labs/Testing:		Long-Term Care:	
Jtilization Management:		Specialty Pharmacy:		Leasing/Finance:		Outpatient Surgery:		Staffing:		Physical Therapy:	
'ayment Processing:		Vitamins/Nutritionals:		Information Systems:		Physical Rehab. Ctr.:		Waste Disposal:		Physician Prac. Mgmt.:	
		Clinical Trials:				Psychiatric Clinics:		Specialty Svcs.:			

TYPES OF BUSINESS:

Supplies-Assorted Health Care Products
Disposable Products
Biohazard Disposal Products
Safety & Protection Products
Fluid Management Products
Nuclear Protective & Disposal Products

BRANDS/DIVISIONS/AFFILIATES:

Microtek Medical, Inc.
osorb
LTS-Plus
MediaPlast
OREX Technologies International
nternational Medical Products, B.V.
KMMS Holdings, Ltd.
Ecolab, Inc.

CONTACTS: *Note: Officers with more than one job title may be intentionally listed here more than once.*

Dan R. Lee, CEO
Mark J. Alvarez, COO
Dan R. Lee, Pres.
Roger (Jerry) Wilson, CFO
Roger (Jerry) Wilson, Sec.
Roger (Jerry) Wilson, Treas.
Dan R. Lee, Chmn.

Phone: 678-896-4400 **Fax:** 662-327-5921
Toll-Free: 800-824-3027
Address: 13000 Deerfield Pkwy., Ste. 300, Alpharetta, GA 30004 US

GROWTH PLANS/SPECIAL FEATURES:

Microtek Medical Holdings, Inc. (MMHI) is a leading manufacturer and marketer of infection control products, fluid control products and safety products to healthcare professionals. It conducts virtually all operations through Microtek Medical, Inc. (MMI), a subsidiary that develops, manufactures and sells infection control, fluid control and safety products to health care professionals for use in environments such as operating rooms and outpatient surgical centers. These consist primarily of disposable equipment drapes, specialty patient drapes, Iosorb and LTS-Plus biohazard encapsulation products, CleanOp cleaning kits, Venodyne pneumatic pumps, decanters and wound evacuation products. MMI also offers the MediaPlast line of fluid management products and ChillBuster portable patient warming system. The company engages in contract manufacturing and private labeling and is a supplier of OEM disposable medical devices. MMHI's OREX Technologies International (OTI) subsidiary develops and sells protective products for the nuclear power market, such as coveralls, hoods and booties. OTI's MICROBasix processing system is used to process and dispose of contaminated OREX products. Recently, the firm licensed all manufacturing and sales of its OREX materials and processing technology to Eastern Technologies, Inc. MMHI also recently acquired assets of Ortho/Plast, a marketer of orthopedic products, and of International Medical Products, B.V., a producer of various gynecological devices and wound care products. In March 2006, MMHI announced that it had acquired KMMS Holdings, Ltd. and its European manufacturing and distribution operations, which, collectively, are known as Samco. Headquartered in Malta and with distribution capabilities in Munich, Germany, Samco manufactures and sells a variety of disposable surgical products. In August 2007, the company agreed to be acquired by Ecolab, Inc. for approximately $287 million. If the merger is completed, Microtek will become a wholly-owned subsidiary of Ecolab.

Microtek employees are offered health, dental, disability and term life insurance.

FINANCIALS: **Sales and profits are in thousands of dollars—add 000 to get the full amount. 2007 Note: Financial information for 2007 was not available for all companies at press time.**

2007 Sales: $	2007 Profits: $	**U.S. Stock Ticker: MTMD**
2006 Sales: $141,577	2006 Profits: $7,915	**Int'l Ticker:** Int'l Exchange:
2005 Sales: $134,458	2005 Profits: $14,504	Employees: 1,873
2004 Sales: $126,581	2004 Profits: $9,921	Fiscal Year Ends: 12/31
2003 Sales: $98,664	2003 Profits: $16,023	Parent Company:

SALARIES/BENEFITS:

Pension Plan:	ESOP Stock Plan:	Profit Sharing:	Top Exec. Salary: $367,854	Bonus: $208,125
Savings Plan: Y	Stock Purch. Plan: Y		Second Exec. Salary: $232,181	Bonus: $85,906

OTHER THOUGHTS:

Apparent Women Officers or Directors:
Hot Spot for Advancement for Women/Minorities:

LOCATIONS: ("Y" = Yes)

West:	Southwest:	Midwest:	Southeast:	Northeast:	International:
	Y		Y		Y

Note: Financial information, benefits and other data can change quickly and may vary from those stated here.

MID ATLANTIC MEDICAL SERVICES INC www.mamsi.com

Industry Group Code: 524114 **Ranks within this company's industry group:** Sales: Profits:

Insurance/HMO/PPO:		Drugs:		Equipment/Supplies:		Hospitals/Clinics:		Services:		Health Care:	
Insurance:	Y	Manufacturer:		Manufacturer:		Acute Care:		Diagnostics:		Home Health:	Y
Managed Care:	Y	Distributor:		Distributor:		Sub-Acute:		Labs/Testing:		Long-Term Care:	
Utilization Management:		Specialty Pharmacy:		Leasing/Finance:		Outpatient Surgery:		Staffing:		Physical Therapy:	
Payment Processing:		Vitamins/Nutritionals:		Information Systems:		Physical Rehab. Ctr.:		Waste Disposal:		Physician Prac. Mgmt.:	
		Clinical Trials:				Psychiatric Clinics:		Specialty Svcs.:			

TYPES OF BUSINESS:

Insurance-Medical & Health, HMOs & PPOs
Health Insurance
Home Health Care Services
Dental Insurance
Vision Insurance
Term Life Insurance

BRANDS/DIVISIONS/AFFILIATES:

MAMSI Life & Health Insurance Company
Optimum Choice, Inc.
MD-Individual Practice Association, Inc.
Optimum Choice of the Carolinas, Inc.
HomeCall, Inc.
Alliance PPO, LLC
Mid Atlantic Psychiatric Services, Inc.
UnitedHealth Group

CONTACTS: *Note: Officers with more than one job title may be intentionally listed here more than once.*

Kevin Ruth, CEO
Robert E. Foss, CFO/Sr. VP
R. Larry Mauzy, CIO/Exec. VP

Phone: 301-762-8205	**Fax:** 301-838-5682
Toll-Free: 800-544-2853	
Address: 4 Taft Ct., Rockville, MD 20850-5310 US	

GROWTH PLANS/SPECIAL FEATURES:

Mid Atlantic Medical Services, Inc. (MAMSI) is a subsidiar of UnitedHealth Group, Inc., a health care company wit more than 50 million clients. MAMSI, along with it subsidiaries, comprises one of the largest managed car companies in the mid-Atlantic region of the U.S. Th company's health care plans offer a wide variety of product and health care coverage options through Preferred Provide Organizations (PPO), Health Maintenance Organization (HMO), Point of Services (POS) and indemnity products MAMSI provides home health care, prescription dru coverage, vision and dental coverage, term life insuranc and short-term disability insurance. The company serve approximately 1.9 million clients in Maryland, Washington D.C., Virginia, Delaware, West Virginia, northern Nort Carolina and southeast Pennsylvania. Within its network, it customers can call upon over 45,000 physicians, health car practitioners and facilities. MAMSI also offers eMAMSI, suite of Internet-based services for members, employers an physicians that includes childhood immunization reminders pregnancy education and cardiovascular disease prevention MAMSI operates three companies offing health benefits: MD Individual Practice Association, Inc.; Optimum Choice, Inc. MAMSI Life and Health Insurance Company. Additionally the firm runs Alliance PPO LLC and Alliance Recover Services Inc. for third party payers. For home healt companies, MAMSI also operates HomeCall, Inc.; FirstCal Inc.; HomeCall Pharmaceutical Services, Inc.; and HomeCa Hospice Services, Inc.

The company offers employees tuition reimbursement an credit union membership.

FINANCIALS: **Sales and profits are in thousands of dollars—add 000 to get the full amount. 2007 Note: Financial information for 2007 was not available for all companies at press time.**

2007 Sales: $	2007 Profits: $	**U.S. Stock Ticker: Subsidiary**
2006 Sales: $	2006 Profits: $	**Int'l Ticker:** Int'l Exchange:
2005 Sales: $	2005 Profits: $	Employees: 3,315
2004 Sales: $	2004 Profits: $	Fiscal Year Ends: 12/31
2003 Sales: $	2003 Profits: $	Parent Company: UNITEDHEALTH GROUP INC

SALARIES/BENEFITS:

Pension Plan:	ESOP Stock Plan:	Profit Sharing:	Top Exec. Salary: $818,226	Bonus: $778,602
Savings Plan: Y	Stock Purch. Plan:		Second Exec. Salary: $635,202	Bonus: $559,977

OTHER THOUGHTS:

Apparent Women Officers or Directors: 4
Hot Spot for Advancement for Women/Minorities: Y

LOCATIONS: ("Y" = Yes)

West:	Southwest:	Midwest:	Southeast:	Northeast:	International:
			Y	Y	

MILLENNIUM PHARMACEUTICALS INC www.mlnm.com

ndustry Group Code: 325412 **Ranks within this company's industry group:** Sales: 31 Profits: 35

nsurance/HMO/PPO:		Drugs:		Equipment/Supplies:		Hospitals/Clinics:		Services:		Health Care:	
nsurance:		Manufacturer:	Y	Manufacturer:		Acute Care:		Diagnostics:		Home Health:	
Managed Care:		Distributor:		Distributor:		Sub-Acute:		Labs/Testing:	Y	Long-Term Care:	
Jtilization Management:		Specialty Pharmacy:		Leasing/Finance:		Outpatient Surgery:		Staffing:		Physical Therapy:	
Payment Processing:		Vitamins/Nutritionals:		Information Systems:		Physical Rehab. Ctr.:		Waste Disposal:		Physician Prac. Mgmt.:	
		Clinical Trials:				Psychiatric Clinics:		Specialty Svcs.:	Y		

TYPES OF BUSINESS:

Pharmaceuticals Discovery & Development
Gene-Based Drug Discovery Platform
Small-Molecule Drugs
Diagnostic Products

BRANDS/DIVISIONS/AFFILIATES:

COR Therapeutics, Inc.
VELCADE
INTEGRILIN
Millennium University

CONTACTS: *Note: Officers with more than one job title may be intentionally listed here more than once.*

Deborah Dunsire, CEO
Kevin Starr, COO
Deborah Dunsire, Pres.
Marsha Fanucci, CFO/Sr. VP
Stephen M. Gansler, Sr. VP-Human Resources
Robert I. Tepper, VP-R&D
Laurie B. Keating, General Counsel
Anna Protopapas, VP-Corp. Dev.
Clare Midgley, VP-Global Corp. Affairs
Christophe Bianchi, Exec. VP-Commercial Oper.
Joseph Bolen, Chief Scientific Officer
Nancy Simonian, Chief Medical Officer
Peter Smith, Sr. VP-Non-Clinical Development Sciences
Kenneth Weg, Chmn.

Phone: 617-679-7000	**Fax:** 617-374-7788
Toll-Free: 800-390-5663	
Address: 40 Landsdowne St., Cambridge, MA 02139 US	

GROWTH PLANS/SPECIAL FEATURES:

Millennium Pharmaceuticals researches and manufactures small-molecule, biotherapeutic and predictive medicine products. The company integrates large-scale genetics, genomics, high-throughput screening and informatics into a drug discovery platform that accelerates the development of therapeutic and diagnostic products. The firm identifies important genes, determines their functions, validates drug and product development targets, formulates assays based on these targets and identifies product candidates. Millenium's research primarily emphasizes treatments for cancer and inflammation. It focuses on developing small-molecule drugs, typically formulated into pills for oral consumption, as well as proteins and monoclonal antibodies, usually only available as injections. The company licenses its platforms to various pharmaceutical and biotechnology firms in exchange for royalties from products developed with the technology. Millennium's VELCADE was one of the first proteasome inhibitors to earn FDA-approval for multiple myeloma, a cancer of the blood. Sales from the VELCADE product made up about 45% of the firm's 2006 revenue, and the company continues to focus its efforts on the product in other areas. The firm also receives a large share of its revenue from royalties culled from INTEGRILIN, a drug used to treat acute coronary syndrome, marketed by Schering-Plough.

The firm's Millennium University offers employees a variety of in-house workshops and off-site seminars designed to enhance career development.

FINANCIALS: Sales and profits are in thousands of dollars—add 000 to get the full amount. 2007 Note: Financial information for 2007 was not available for all companies at press time.

2007 Sales: $	2007 Profits: $	**U.S. Stock Ticker: MLNM**
2006 Sales: $486,830	2006 Profits: $-43,953	**Int'l Ticker:** Int'l Exchange:
2005 Sales: $558,308	2005 Profits: $-198,249	Employees: 947
2004 Sales: $448,206	2004 Profits: $-252,297	Fiscal Year Ends: 12/31
2003 Sales: $433,687	2003 Profits: $-483,687	Parent Company:

SALARIES/BENEFITS:

Pension Plan:	ESOP Stock Plan:	Profit Sharing:	Top Exec. Salary: $457,619	Bonus: $166,137
Savings Plan: Y	Stock Purch. Plan: Y		Second Exec. Salary: $392,512	Bonus: $157,338

OTHER THOUGHTS:

Apparent Women Officers or Directors: 5
Hot Spot for Advancement for Women/Minorities: Y

LOCATIONS: ("Y" = Yes)

West:	Southwest:	Midwest:	Southeast:	Northeast:	International:
Y				Y	Y

MINDRAY MEDICAL INTERNATIONAL LIMITED

www.mindray.com

Industry Group Code: 339113 **Ranks within this company's industry group:** Sales: 63 Profits: 36

Insurance/HMO/PPO:		Drugs:		Equipment/Supplies:		Hospitals/Clinics:		Services:		Health Care:	
Insurance:		Manufacturer:		Manufacturer:	Y	Acute Care:		Diagnostics:		Home Health:	
Managed Care:		Distributor:		Distributor:		Sub-Acute:		Labs/Testing:		Long-Term Care:	
Utilization Management:		Specialty Pharmacy:		Leasing/Finance:		Outpatient Surgery:		Staffing:		Physical Therapy:	
Payment Processing:		Vitamins/Nutritionals:		Information Systems:		Physical Rehab. Ctr.:		Waste Disposal:		Physician Prac. Mgmt.:	
		Clinical Trials:				Psychiatric Clinics:		Specialty Svcs.:			

TYPES OF BUSINESS:

Medical/Dental/Surgical Equipment & Supplies, Manufacturing

BRANDS/DIVISIONS/AFFILIATES:

PM-800 Series
Hypervisor VI
BC-2800 Series
BC-3000 Series
BS-300 Series
DP-8800 Series
DP-9900 Series
DC-6

CONTACTS: *Note: Officers with more than one job title may be intentionally listed here more than once.*

Xu Hang, Co-CEO
Li Xiting, Pres./Co-CEO
Joyce I-Yin Hsu, CFO
Cheng Minghe, Exec. VP-Sales & Mktg.
Yan Baiping, Exec. VP-R&D
Mu Lemin, Exec. VP-Admin.
Tim Fitzpatrick, General Counsel
Xu Hang, Chmn.

Phone: 86-755-2658-2888	**Fax:** 86-755-2658-2500
Toll-Free:	
Address: Mindray Building, Keji 12th Rd. S., Nanshan, Shenzhen 518057 China	

GROWTH PLANS/SPECIAL FEATURES:

Mindray Medical International Limited is a develope manufacturer and marketer of medical devices in China, wit a significant growing presence outside of China. Th company sells its products primarily to over 1,80 distributors, with 650 direct sales and sales suppo personnel selling to hospitals, clinics, government agencies ODM (Original Design Manufacturer) customers and OEM (Original Equipment Manufacturer) customers. Mindra offers products in three categories: patient monitorin devices, diagnostic laboratory instruments and ultrasoun imaging systems. Patient monitoring devices offered b Mindray include its PM-800 and -900 Series, a portabl device featuring a color display, arrhythmia analysis pacemaker detection and a built-in recorder; and it Hypervisor VI, a central monitoring system featuring a optional dual screen capable of displaying information on u to 32 beds, a maximum 64 patient monitoring by telemetr system, LAN or wireless LAN networking, bi-directiona communication between bedside monitors and centra station, a 240 hour trend table review, 720 alarm records an 20,000 patient records. Diagnostic laboratory instrument offered by Mindray include its BC-2800 and -3000 Serie hematology analyzers, featuring a 3-part differential, 1 parameters, complete automation, storage for 10,000 t 35,000 samples, a built-in thermal recorder, 30-60 sample per hour analyzing capability and a color display; and th BS-300 Series biochemistry analyzer, featuring complet automation, 300 test per hour capability, up to 50 on-boar chemistries, three independent probes and a refrigerate reagent compartment. Ultrasound imaging equipmer offered by Mindray includes its DP-8800, -9900 and -660 Series mobile systems featuring multi-purpose capability, 14-10 inch monitor and digital imaging. In September 2006 Mindray launched the first color Doppler diagnosti ultrasound system, its DC-6. In June 2007, the compan received 510(k) clearance from the FDA for its BC-320 automatic, three-part differential hematology analyzer and it Hypervisor VI.

Mindray offers its employees training through its Lifelon University of Employees.

FINANCIALS: **Sales and profits are in thousands of dollars—add 000 to get the full amount. 2007 Note: Financial information for 2007 was not available for all companies at press time.**

2007 Sales: $	2007 Profits: $	**U.S. Stock Ticker: MR**
2006 Sales: $194,126	2006 Profits: $46,358	**Int'l Ticker:** Int'l Exchange:
2005 Sales: $	2005 Profits: $	Employees: 2,744
2004 Sales: $	2004 Profits: $	Fiscal Year Ends: 12/31
2003 Sales: $	2003 Profits: $	Parent Company:

SALARIES/BENEFITS:

Pension Plan:	ESOP Stock Plan:	Profit Sharing:	Top Exec. Salary: $	Bonus: $
Savings Plan:	Stock Purch. Plan:		Second Exec. Salary: $	Bonus: $

OTHER THOUGHTS:

Apparent Women Officers or Directors: 1
Hot Spot for Advancement for Women/Minorities:

LOCATIONS: ("Y" = Yes)

West:	Southwest:	Midwest:	Southeast:	Northeast:	International:
				Y	Y

Note: Financial information, benefits and other data can change quickly and may vary from those stated here.

MINE SAFETY APPLIANCES CO www.msanet.com

ndustry Group Code: 339113 **Ranks within this company's industry group:** Sales: 30 Profits: 31

nsurance/HMO/PPO:		Drugs:		Equipment/Supplies:		Hospitals/Clinics:		Services:		Health Care:	
nsurance:		Manufacturer:		Manufacturer:	Y	Acute Care:		Diagnostics:		Home Health:	
lanaged Care:		Distributor:		Distributor:		Sub-Acute:		Labs/Testing:		Long-Term Care:	
tilization Management:		Specialty Pharmacy:		Leasing/Finance:		Outpatient Surgery:		Staffing:		Physical Therapy:	
ayment Processing:		Vitamins/Nutritionals:		Information Systems:		Physical Rehab. Ctr.:		Waste Disposal:		Physician Prac. Mgmt.:	
		Clinical Trials:				Psychiatric Clinics:		Specialty Svcs.:			

TYPES OF BUSINESS:

:quipment/Supplies-Manufacturer
iafety & Health Equipment
'ersonal Protective Products
Respiratory Protective Equipment
:ombat Helmets
hermal Imaging Cameras
iecurity Sensors & Systems

BRANDS/DIVISIONS/AFFILIATES:

'araclete Armor and Equipment, Inc.

CONTACTS: *Note: Officers with more than one job title may be ntentionally listed here more than once.*

ohn T. Ryan, III, CEO
Villiam M. Lambert, COO
Villiam M. Lambert, Pres.
)ennis L. Zeitler, CFO/Sr. VP
'aul R. Uhler, VP-Global Human Resources
itephen C. Plut, CIO/VP
Ronald N. Herring, Jr, VP-Global Prod. Dev.
)ouglas K. McClaine, General Counsel/VP
:erry M. Bove, VP-Global Oper.
oseph A. Bigler, Pres., MSA North America
ohn T. Ryan, III, Chmn.
Roberto Canizares, Exec. VP/Pres., MSA Int'l

'hone: 412-967-3000 **Fax:** 412-967-3451
'oll-Free: 800-672-2222
\ddress: 121 Gamma Dr., Pittsburgh, PA 15238 US

GROWTH PLANS/SPECIAL FEATURES:

Mine Safety Appliances Company (MSA) is primarily engaged in the development, manufacture and supply of sophisticated safety and health equipment. The company's safety products are used by workers around the world in fire service, homeland security, the military, construction services and other industries. MSA's principle product offerings fall under four distinct categories: respiratory protection; hand-held and permanent instruments; eye, face, hearing, and head protection; and body protection. The company produces numerous respiratory systems, such as Self Contained Breathing Apparatuses (SCBA); escape hoods, which allow workers to escape from dangerous gases; and filtering respirators, such as military full face gas masks, half-mask respirators, powered-air purifying respirators and pollen masks. MSA's hand-held and permanent instruments include gas detection instruments and thermal imaging cameras, which detect for the lack of oxygen in confined spaces or the presence of combustible or toxic gases. Hand-held thermal imaging cameras are used by firefighters to see victims through dense smoke and to detect a fires source. Eye, face, hearing, and head protection is used in work environments with hazards such as dust, metal fragments, chemicals, extreme glare, optical radiation, and items dropped from above. The company produces industrial hard hats, fire helmets, military helmets, hearing protection products, protective eyewear and face shields. MSA's body protection includes harnesses and lifelines and a ballistic body armor division that was expanded in September 2006 due to the acquisition of Paraclete Armor and Equipment, Inc. The company devotes significant resources to research and development, and produces safety products that exceed worldwide government and industry standards. MSA maintains manufacturing and research operations in 13 countries and products are sold in approximately 120 countries. The company was recently awarded two new ballistic helmet contracts: $15.5 million from the U.S. Army in March 2007; and $9.9 million from the Canadian military in June 2007.

FINANCIALS: **Sales and profits are in thousands of dollars—add 000 to get the full amount. 2007 Note: Financial information for 2007 was not available for all companies at press time.**

007 Sales: $	2007 Profits: $	**U.S. Stock Ticker: MSA**
006 Sales: $913,714	2006 Profits: $63,918	**Int'l Ticker:** Int'l Exchange:
005 Sales: $907,912	2005 Profits: $81,783	Employees: 4,900
004 Sales: $852,509	2004 Profits: $71,047	Fiscal Year Ends: 12/31
003 Sales: $698,197	2003 Profits: $65,267	Parent Company:

SALARIES/BENEFITS:

'ension Plan: Y	ESOP Stock Plan:	Profit Sharing:	Top Exec. Salary: $661,053	Bonus: $379,249
iavings Plan:	Stock Purch. Plan:		Second Exec. Salary: $352,661	Bonus: $158,219

OTHER THOUGHTS:

\pparent Women Officers or Directors:
lot Spot for Advancement for Women/Minorities:

LOCATIONS: ("Y" = Yes)

West:	Southwest:	Midwest:	Southeast:	Northeast:	International:
Y		Y		Y	Y

Note: Financial information, benefits and other data can change quickly and may vary from those stated here.

MINNTECH CORP www.minntech.com

Industry Group Code: 339113 **Ranks within this company's industry group:** Sales: Profits:

Insurance/HMO/PPO:		Drugs:		Equipment/Supplies:		Hospitals/Clinics:		Services:		Health Care:	
Insurance:		Manufacturer:		Manufacturer:	Y	Acute Care:		Diagnostics:		Home Health:	
Managed Care:		Distributor:		Distributor:		Sub-Acute:		Labs/Testing:		Long-Term Care:	
Utilization Management:		Specialty Pharmacy:		Leasing/Finance:		Outpatient Surgery:		Staffing:		Physical Therapy:	
Payment Processing:		Vitamins/Nutritionals:		Information Systems:		Physical Rehab. Ctr.:		Waste Disposal:		Physician Prac. Mgmt.:	
		Clinical Trials:				Psychiatric Clinics:		Specialty Svcs.:			

TYPES OF BUSINESS:

Supplies-Kidney Dialysis Products
Sterilants
Filtration & Separation Products

BRANDS/DIVISIONS/AFFILIATES:

Minntech Renal Systems
Minntech International
Minntech Fiberflo
Cantel Medical Corp.
Renalin 100 Cold Sterilant
RenaClear
RenaPak
Medivators Reprocessing Systems

CONTACTS: *Note: Officers with more than one job title may be intentionally listed here more than once.*

Roy Malkin, CEO
Roy Malkin, Pres.
John Gray, VP-Global Mktg.
Denise Bauer, VP-Human Resources
Michael Petersen, VP-R&D
Jim McMillen, VP-Mfg.
Kevin Finkle, VP-Admin.
Kevin Finkle, VP-Finance
John Gray, VP-Filtration Tech.
Paul E. Helms, Exec. VP
Craig Smith, VP-Quality Assurance
Nicholas Strout, VP-Int'l

Phone: 763-553-3300	**Fax:** 763-553-3387
Toll-Free: 800-328-3345	
Address: 14605 28th Ave. N., Minneapolis, MN 55447-4822 US	

GROWTH PLANS/SPECIAL FEATURES:

Minntech Corp., a subsidiary of Cantel Medical Corp develops, manufactures and markets medical supplies ar devices, sterilants and filtration and separation product The company operates across two segments, Ren Systems and Filtration Technologies. Minntech's ren systems segment's products are used primarily hemodialysis. Products used in dialysis are marketed und the trade name Minntech Renal Systems. In addition dialyzer reprocessing systems and hemodialys concentrates, the renal systems segment is a full servic provider of treatment supplies for clinics. The segment als boasts such backroom support products as the Renalog R Reprocessing Management Software, RenaClear Automate Header Cleaning System and Renalin 100. Minntech filtration technologies segment provides a total system approach designed to facilitate and improve the medic filtration process. The company utilizes as the co component for a variety of applications a unique polysulfor hollow fiber system featuring sterilants. These filtration ar separation products are marketed to the medica semiconductor, food and beverage and biopharmaceutic industries under the name Minntech Fiberflo. The firm ha also developed core technologies in electronics, fiber plastics and chemical solutions. The company has glob operations in the U.K., Japan and other areas in the As Pacific region and Latin America.

FINANCIALS: **Sales and profits are in thousands of dollars—add 000 to get the full amount. 2007 Note: Financial information for 2007 was not available for all companies at press time.**

2007 Sales: $	2007 Profits: $	**U.S. Stock Ticker: Subsidiary**
2006 Sales: $	2006 Profits: $	**Int'l Ticker:** Int'l Exchange:
2005 Sales: $	2005 Profits: $	Employees: 376
2004 Sales: $	2004 Profits: $	Fiscal Year Ends: 7/31
2003 Sales: $	2003 Profits: $	Parent Company: CANTEL MEDICAL CORP

SALARIES/BENEFITS:

Pension Plan:	ESOP Stock Plan:	Profit Sharing: Y	Top Exec. Salary: $293,750	Bonus: $198,750
Savings Plan: Y	Stock Purch. Plan:		Second Exec. Salary: $227,707	Bonus: $105,495

OTHER THOUGHTS:

Apparent Women Officers or Directors: 1
Hot Spot for Advancement for Women/Minorities:

LOCATIONS: ("Y" = Yes)

West:	Southwest:	Midwest:	Southeast:	Northeast:	International:
Y	Y	Y	Y	Y	Y

MINUTECLINIC

www.minuteclinic.com

ndustry Group Code: 621490 **Ranks within this company's industry group:** Sales: Profits:

nsurance/HMO/PPO:		Drugs:		Equipment/Supplies:		Hospitals/Clinics:		Services:		Health Care:	
nsurance:		Manufacturer:		Manufacturer:		Acute Care:		Diagnostics:		Home Health:	
⁄lanaged Care:		Distributor:		Distributor:		Sub-Acute:	Y	Labs/Testing:		Long-Term Care:	
Jtilization Management:		Specialty Pharmacy:		Leasing/Finance:		Outpatient Surgery:		Staffing:		Physical Therapy:	
⁊ayment Processing:		Vitamins/Nutritionals:		Information Systems:		Physical Rehab. Ctr.:		Waste Disposal:		Physician Prac. Mgmt.:	
		Clinical Trials:				Psychiatric Clinics:		Specialty Svcs.:			

TYPES OF BUSINESS:

n-store Clinics

BRANDS/DIVISIONS/AFFILIATES:

CVS Caremark Corporation

CONTACTS: *Note: Officers with more than one job title may be ntentionally listed here more than once.*

⁄lichael Howe, CEO
.inda Hall Whitman, COO
Kent Lillemoe, CFO
Stacy Hintermeister, VP-Mktg. & Sales
Julie Buske, VP-Human Resources
Cris Ross, CIO
Jenni Jones, VP-Oper.
Judy McClellan, VP-Bus. Dev.
James Woodburn, Chief Medical Officer
Neil J. Rolland, VP-Payer Rel.
Donna Haugland, Dir.-Recruitment & Hiring
Glen Nelson, Chmn.

Phone: 612-659-7111	**Fax:**
Toll-Free:	
Address: 333 Washington Ave. N., Ste. 5000, Minneapolis, MN 55401 US	

GROWTH PLANS/SPECIAL FEATURES:

MinuteClinic, a wholly-owned subsidiary of CVS Caremark Corporation, is a chain of quick service health care clinics that are located in grocery stores, pharmacies and office buildings. The clinics are open seven days a week and are staffed by certified nurse practitioners (CNPs) who can diagnose and prescribe medications on site with an average visit time of approximately 15 minutes. The company licenses small departments inside larger stores and staffs them with CNPs able to treat common health problems such as ear infections and strep throat. Additionally, the clinics can administer a variety of vaccines and treat a variety of skin conditions. Seriously ill patients are referred to a larger clinic or hospital. No appointments are needed to see a CNP, and patients can shop in the store while waiting to be seen. Treatments range from $28 to $110, generally less than seeing a doctor, and MinuteClinic accepts most major forms of insurance. Each MinuteClinic currently generates about 25-30 patient visits per day, 70% of which represent new pharmacy customers for the clinic's retail host. In July 2007, the company opened its 200th clinic. These clinics are operated in 22 states within drug stores such as CVS/pharmacy, Bartell Drug and Cub Foods. The company plans to construct a new clinic within every CVS/pharmacy in the country, with an anticipated 400 locations by the end of 2007.

MinuteClinic provides its employees with benefits that include medical, dental, disability and life insurance; flexible spending accounts; a 401(k) plan; professional liability insurance; employee assistance; continuing medical education; and it will cover the expenses for the employee's Drug Enforcement License. In addition, MinuteClinic does not charge employees or their immediate family for walk-in health care services at its clinics.

FINANCIALS: **Sales and profits are in thousands of dollars—add 000 to get the full amount. 2007 Note: Financial information for 2007 was not available for all companies at press time.**

2007 Sales: $	2007 Profits: $	**U.S. Stock Ticker: Subsidiary**
2006 Sales: $	2006 Profits: $	**Int'l Ticker:** Int'l Exchange:
2005 Sales: $	2005 Profits: $	Employees:
2004 Sales: $	2004 Profits: $	Fiscal Year Ends:
2003 Sales: $	2003 Profits: $	Parent Company: CVS CAREMARK CORPORATION

SALARIES/BENEFITS:

Pension Plan:	ESOP Stock Plan:	Profit Sharing:	Top Exec. Salary: $	Bonus: $
Savings Plan: Y	Stock Purch. Plan:		Second Exec. Salary: $	Bonus: $

OTHER THOUGHTS:

Apparent Women Officers or Directors: 7
Hot Spot for Advancement for Women/Minorities: Y

LOCATIONS: ("Y" = Yes)

West:	Southwest:	Midwest:	Southeast:	Northeast:	International:
Y	Y	Y	Y	Y	

MISONIX INC www.misonix.com

Industry Group Code: 339113 **Ranks within this company's industry group:** Sales: 95 Profits: 83

Insurance/HMO/PPO:		Drugs:		Equipment/Supplies:		Hospitals/Clinics:		Services:		Health Care:	
Insurance:		Manufacturer:		Manufacturer:	Y	Acute Care:		Diagnostics:		Home Health:	
Managed Care:		Distributor:		Distributor:		Sub-Acute:		Labs/Testing:		Long-Term Care:	
Utilization Management:		Specialty Pharmacy:		Leasing/Finance:		Outpatient Surgery:		Staffing:		Physical Therapy:	
Payment Processing:		Vitamins/Nutritionals:		Information Systems:		Physical Rehab. Ctr.:		Waste Disposal:		Physician Prac. Mgmt.:	
		Clinical Trials:				Psychiatric Clinics:		Specialty Svcs.:	Y		

TYPES OF BUSINESS:

Ultrasonic Medical Devices
Laboratory & Scientific Products

BRANDS/DIVISIONS/AFFILIATES:

Labcaire Systems, Ltd.
UKHIFU
Sonora Medical Systems, Inc.
Hearing Innovations, Inc.
Acousting Marketing Research, Inc.
Mystaire
Aura
Sonicator

CONTACTS: *Note: Officers with more than one job title may be intentionally listed here more than once.*

Michael A. McManus, Jr., CEO
Michael A. McManus, Jr., Pres.
Richard Zaremba, CFO/Sr. VP
Dan Voic, VP-R&D
Dan Voic, VP-Eng.
Frank Napoli, VP-Oper.
Ronald Manna, VP-Regulatory Affairs

Phone: 631-694-9555	**Fax:** 631-694-9412
Toll-Free: 800-694-9612	
Address: 1938 New Highway, Farmingdale, NY 11735 US	

GROWTH PLANS/SPECIAL FEATURES:

Misonix, Inc. designs, manufactures and markets ultrason medical devices. The company also develops and marke ultrasonic equipment for use in the scientific and industri markets; ductless fume enclosures for filtration of gaseo contaminates; and environmental control products for th abatement of air pollution. Misonix owns Labcaire System Ltd., a U.K.-based company, which designs, manufacture services and markets air-handling system for the protectio of personnel, products and the environment from airbor hazards. The company also has a 60% ownership UKHIFU, in Bristol, England, which distributes and service equipment for the ablation of cancerous tissue of th prostate. The firm's 90% owned subsidiary, Acous Marketing Research, Inc., which does business as Sono Medical Systems, Inc., is an ISO 9001 certified refurbisher ultrasound system and replacement transducers for th medical diagnostic ultrasound industry. Subsidiary Heari Innovations, Inc. is a development company with patente HiSonic ultrasonic technology for the treatment of profou deafness and tinnitus. Misonix's other revenue produci activities consist of the manufacture and sale of Sonicat ultrasonic liquid processor and cell disruptors; Aura ductle fume hood products; Mystaire scrubbers for the abatement air pollution; and Guardian autoscope reprocessi disinfecting and rinsing equipment. The company relies distributors such as Medline Industries, Inc.; Byro Aesculap, Inc.; and ACMI Corp., and independe distributors for the marketing of its medical products. Th firm relies on direct salespersons, distributors, manufacturi representatives and catalog listings for the marketing of laboratory and scientific products. In 2006, about 37% of n sales were to foreign markets.

FINANCIALS: Sales and profits are in thousands of dollars—add 000 to get the full amount. 2007 Note: Financial information for 2007 was not available for all companies at press time.

2007 Sales: $	2007 Profits: $	**U.S. Stock Ticker: MSON**
2006 Sales: $39,067	2006 Profits: $-3,759	**Int'l Ticker:** Int'l Exchange:
2005 Sales: $45,907	2005 Profits: $ 936	Employees: 207
2004 Sales: $39,059	2004 Profits: $1,718	Fiscal Year Ends: 6/30
2003 Sales: $34,900	2003 Profits: $1,000	Parent Company:

SALARIES/BENEFITS:

Pension Plan:	ESOP Stock Plan:	Profit Sharing:	Top Exec. Salary: $275,000	Bonus: $
Savings Plan:	Stock Purch. Plan:		Second Exec. Salary: $178,437	Bonus: $28,000

OTHER THOUGHTS:

Apparent Women Officers or Directors:
Hot Spot for Advancement for Women/Minorities:

LOCATIONS: ("Y" = Yes)

West:	Southwest:	Midwest:	Southeast:	Northeast:	International:
Y				Y	Y

MIV THERAPEUTICS INC www.mivtherapeutics.com

Industry Group Code: 339113 Ranks within this company's industry group: Sales: Profits: 87

Insurance/HMO/PPO:		Drugs:		Equipment/Supplies:		Hospitals/Clinics:		Services:		Health Care:	
Insurance:		Manufacturer:		Manufacturer:	Y	Acute Care:		Diagnostics:		Home Health:	
Managed Care:		Distributor:		Distributor:		Sub-Acute:		Labs/Testing:		Long-Term Care:	
Utilization Management:		Specialty Pharmacy:		Leasing/Finance:		Outpatient Surgery:		Staffing:		Physical Therapy:	
Payment Processing:		Vitamins/Nutritionals:		Information Systems:		Physical Rehab. Ctr.:		Waste Disposal:		Physician Prac. Mgmt.:	
		Clinical Trials:				Psychiatric Clinics:		Specialty Svcs.:			

TYPES OF BUSINESS:

Medical Equipment-Stents
Biocompatible Coatings
Drug-Eluting Stents
Research & Development

BRANDS/DIVISIONS/AFFILIATES:

MIVI Technologies, Inc.
DBS Holdings, Inc.
M-I Vascular, Inc.
SagaX Medical Technologies, Inc.
Sahajanand Medical Technologies PVT Ltd.
X-Act Inflation Device
Biosync Scientific
Vascore Medical (Suzhou) Co., Ltd.

CONTACTS:

Note: Officers with more than one job title may be intentionally listed here more than once.

Alan P. Lindsay, CEO
Mark Landy, Pres.
Patrick A. McGowan, CFO/Exec. VP
Arc Rajtar, VP-Oper.
Dov V. Shimon, CEO-SagaX Medical Tech., Inc.
Tom Troczynski, VP-Coating Tech.
Alan P. Lindsay, Chmn.

Phone: 604-301-9545	**Fax:** 604-301-9546
Toll-Free:	
Address: 8765 Ash St., Unit 1, Vancouver, BC V6P 6T3 Canada	

GROWTH PLANS/SPECIAL FEATURES:

MIV Therapeutics, Inc. is a research and development company that is currently pursuing the commercialization of next-generation biocompatible coatings called Hydroxylapatite (HAp) for stents and other cardiovascular medical devices. HAp is found in bone and tooth enamel and is easily and rapidly integrated within the human body without inducing thombogenicity, allergic or inflammatory reactions. HAp-coated coronary stents with a nanofilm coating allow insertion of a balloon catheter within the circulatory system with minimal inflammatory side effects. MIV is also developing drug-eluting stents with a thicker coating of HAp for peripheral stents, biodegradable implants, gene therapy and chemotherapeutic delivery systems. Porous HAp coatings can be loaded with a large quantity of drugs such as anti-inflammatories, immune system depressants, anti-thrombotic and anti-restenotic drugs, which make it one of the most widely used systems for coronary revascularization. In September 2006, the company acquired Vascore Medical (Suzhou) Co., Ltd., a China-based company that specializes in the manufacturing of advanced cardiovascular stents and medical devices. In February 2007, MIV acquired Biosync Scientific, an India-based company that designs and develops interventional cardiology products. Since the acquisition of BioSync, MIV has introduced eight new products for commercialization in Europe, India and Asia. Newly marketed products includes the GenX CrCo thin-strut coronary stent system, the X-Act Inflation Device, a haemostatic Y-connected adaptor kit, an insertion tool, a guide wire torquer and a high-pressure 3-way stopcock.

FINANCIALS:

Sales and profits are in thousands of dollars—add 000 to get the full amount. 2007 Note: Financial information for 2007 was not available for all companies at press time.

2007 Sales: $ 191	2007 Profits: $-10,499	**U.S. Stock Ticker: MIVT**
2006 Sales: $	2006 Profits: $-9,094	**Int'l Ticker:** Int'l Exchange:
2005 Sales: $	2005 Profits: $-6,609	Employees: 90
2004 Sales: $	2004 Profits: $-3,500	Fiscal Year Ends: 5/31
2003 Sales: $	2003 Profits: $-3,200	Parent Company:

SALARIES/BENEFITS:

Pension Plan:	ESOP Stock Plan:	Profit Sharing:	Top Exec. Salary: $185,244	Bonus: $
Savings Plan:	Stock Purch. Plan:		Second Exec. Salary: $101,941	Bonus: $

OTHER THOUGHTS:

Apparent Women Officers or Directors:
Hot Spot for Advancement for Women/Minorities:

LOCATIONS: ("Y" = Yes)

West:	Southwest:	Midwest:	Southeast:	Northeast:	International:
			Y		Y

Note: Financial information, benefits and other data can change quickly and may vary from those stated here.

MOLINA HEALTHCARE INC www.molinahealthcare.com

Industry Group Code: 524114 **Ranks within this company's industry group:** Sales: 26 Profits: 22

Insurance/HMO/PPO:		Drugs:		Equipment/Supplies:		Hospitals/Clinics:		Services:		Health Care:	
Insurance:		Manufacturer:		Manufacturer:		Acute Care:		Diagnostics:		Home Health:	
Managed Care:	Y	Distributor:		Distributor:		Sub-Acute:		Labs/Testing:		Long-Term Care:	
Utilization Management:		Specialty Pharmacy:		Leasing/Finance:		Outpatient Surgery:		Staffing:		Physical Therapy:	
Payment Processing:		Vitamins/Nutritionals:		Information Systems:		Physical Rehab. Ctr.:		Waste Disposal:		Physician Prac. Mgmt.:	
		Clinical Trials:				Psychiatric Clinics:		Specialty Svcs.:			

TYPES OF BUSINESS:

HMO-Low Income Patients
Medicaid HMO
SCHIP HMO

BRANDS/DIVISIONS/AFFILIATES:

Mercy CarePlus

CONTACTS: *Note: Officers with more than one job title may be intentionally listed here more than once.*

J. Mario Molina, CEO
Terry Bayer, COO
J. Mario Molina, Pres.
John C. Molina, CFO
Martha (Molina) Bernadett, Exec. VP-R&D
Mark L. Andrews, Chief Legal Officer/Corp. Sec.
James W. Howatt, Chief Medical Officer

Phone: 562-435-3666	**Fax:**
Toll-Free: 888-562-5442	
Address: 1 Golden Shore Dr., Long Beach, CA 90802 US	

GROWTH PLANS/SPECIAL FEATURES:

Molina Healthcare, Inc. is a multi-stage managed ca organization participating exclusively in governmen sponsored health care programs for low-income person such as the Medicaid program and the State Children Health Insurance Program (SCHIP), as well as a sma number of persons who are dually eligible under th Medicaid and Medicare programs. Molina conducts i business primarily through seven licensed health plans in th states of California, Michigan, New Mexico, Ohio, Texa Utah and Washington. The health plans are locally operate by the company's subsidiaries, each of which is licensed a a health maintenance organization (HMO). Approximately million members are enrolled in the company's health plan Molina's revenues are derived primarily from premiu revenues paid to its HMOs by the relevant state Medica authority, which are generally an agreed upon amount p member per month regardless of whether the membe utilizes any medical services in that month or whether the utilize services in excess of that amount. Each HM arranges for health care services for its members b contracting with health care providers in the releva communities or states, including contracting with primar care physicians, specialist physicians, physician group hospitals and other medical care providers. Molina' California HMO operates 19 of its own primary car community clinics. Molina is working on the development a predictive modeling capability that will support a mor proactive case and health management approach as well a a provider profiling capability to supply network physician with information and tools to assist them in makin appropriate, cost-effective referrals for specialty and hospit care. The company also develops specialized diseas management programs, educational programs an pharmacy management programs. In September 200 Molina acquired Mercy CarePlus, a Medicaid managed car organization based in St. Louis, Missouri for approximate $74 million.

FINANCIALS: **Sales and profits are in thousands of dollars—add 000 to get the full amount. 2007 Note: Financial information for 2007 was not available for all companies at press time.**

2007 Sales: $	2007 Profits: $	**U.S. Stock Ticker: MOH**
2006 Sales: $2,004,995	2006 Profits: $45,727	**Int'l Ticker:** Int'l Exchange:
2005 Sales: $1,650,058	2005 Profits: $27,596	Employees: 2,000
2004 Sales: $1,175,268	2004 Profits: $55,773	Fiscal Year Ends: 12/31
2003 Sales: $	2003 Profits: $	Parent Company:

SALARIES/BENEFITS:

Pension Plan:	ESOP Stock Plan:	Profit Sharing:	Top Exec. Salary: $751,923	Bonus: $
Savings Plan: Y	Stock Purch. Plan: Y		Second Exec. Salary: $656,923	Bonus: $

OTHER THOUGHTS:

Apparent Women Officers or Directors: 2
Hot Spot for Advancement for Women/Minorities:

LOCATIONS: ("Y" = Yes)

West:	Southwest:	Midwest:	Southeast:	Northeast:	International:
Y	Y	Y			

MOLNLYCKE HEALTH CARE GROUP AB www.molnlycke.com

Industry Group Code: 339113 **Ranks within this company's industry group:** Sales: Profits:

Insurance/HMO/PPO:		Drugs:		Equipment/Supplies:		Hospitals/Clinics:		Services:		Health Care:	
Insurance:		Manufacturer:	Y	Manufacturer:		Acute Care:		Diagnostics:		Home Health:	
Managed Care:		Distributor:		Distributor:		Sub-Acute:		Labs/Testing:		Long-Term Care:	
Utilization Management:		Specialty Pharmacy:		Leasing/Finance:		Outpatient Surgery:		Staffing:	Y	Physical Therapy:	
Payment Processing:		Vitamins/Nutritionals:		Information Systems:		Physical Rehab. Ctr.:		Waste Disposal:		Physician Prac. Mgmt.:	
		Clinical Trials:				Psychiatric Clinics:		Specialty Svcs.:	Y		

TYPES OF BUSINESS:

Single-Use Surgical & Wound Care Products Manufacturing
Supply Chain & Logistics Management Consulting
Operating Room Staffing

BRANDS/DIVISIONS/AFFILIATES:

BARRIER
Biogel
Xelma
Mepore
Molnlycke Health Care Wound Care Academy
SupplyPartner
Biogel Eclipse Indicator
HibiSCRUB

CONTACTS: *Note: Officers with more than one job title may be intentionally listed here more than once.*

Pierre Guyot, CEO
Pierre Guyot, Pres.
Steve Hamlett, CFO
Stefan Fransson, Sr. VP-IT
Rob Bennsion, Sr. VP-Legal, Regulatory & Quality Affairs/Sec.
Stefan Fransson, Sr. VP-Bus. Dev.
Christina Sterner,, Dir.-Comm.
Pierre Guyot, Acting Pres., Wound Care Div.
Bob Contreras, Pres., Surgical Div.
Gunnar Brock, Chmn.

Phone: 46-31-722-30-00	**Fax:** 46-31-722-34-00
Toll-Free:	
Address: Gamlestadsvagen 3C, Goteborg, SE-402 52 Sweden	

GROWTH PLANS/SPECIAL FEATURES:

Molnlycke Health Care Group AB manufactures single-use healthcare products. It has two main divisions. The Surgical division provides drapes, surgical powder free gloves, staff clothing, skin antiseptics, customized procedure trays and also various services. BARRIER, HibiAntisepticsTM, Biogel and Procedure Pak are some of its brand names. The Wound Care division products include the topical application Xelma, an extracellual matrix protein treatment for hard to heal wounds, such as leg ulcers; Mepore, one of the world's first self-adhesive bandages; the Mepitel and Mepiform soft silicone dressings; and Mesalt wet saline dressings. Molnlycke's services include offering staffing for operating rooms, including qualified nurses and other specialist staff; and consultations regarding supply chain optimization, cost identification and some professional education. As part of its educative efforts, the company maintains the Molnlycke Health Care Wound Care Academy, a combination library and Special Advisory Groups engaged in disseminating wound care educational materials and best practice documents to healthcare professionals. The firm also offers SupplyPartner, a service that monitors a customer's stock levels and tailors inventory shipments for that client's needs, all managed automatically, without the client needing to place orders. In March 2007, the firm launched the Biogel Eclipse Indicator, a double-layered puncture-indicating deproteinised natural rubber latex glove. The gloves' green layer under a straw-colored layer forms a green patch around a puncture in the presence of a fluid. In March 2007, Investor AB and Morgan Stanley Principle Investments jointly acquired the company from Apax Partners for approximately $3.95 billion. In July 2007, Molnlycke began offering the HibiSCRUB hospital-strength bodywash for home use by those visiting a hospital for elective surgery. The product, which remains effective for up to six hours after application, helps prevent new bacteria, common skin fungi and viral infections, and has been used by doctors and nurses for 40 years.

FINANCIALS: **Sales and profits are in thousands of dollars—add 000 to get the full amount. 2007 Note: Financial information for 2007 was not available for all companies at press time.**

2007 Sales: $	2007 Profits: $	**U.S. Stock Ticker: Private**
2006 Sales: $	2006 Profits: $	**Int'l Ticker:** Int'l Exchange:
2005 Sales: $	2005 Profits: $	Employees:
2004 Sales: $	2004 Profits: $	Fiscal Year Ends:
2003 Sales: $	2003 Profits: $	Parent Company: MORGAN STANLEY

SALARIES/BENEFITS:

Pension Plan:	ESOP Stock Plan:	Profit Sharing:	Top Exec. Salary: $	Bonus: $
Savings Plan:	Stock Purch. Plan:		Second Exec. Salary: $	Bonus: $

OTHER THOUGHTS:

Apparent Women Officers or Directors:
Hot Spot for Advancement for Women/Minorities:

LOCATIONS: ("Y" = Yes)

West:	Southwest:	Midwest:	Southeast:	Northeast:	International:
			Y	Y	Y

MOORE MEDICAL CORP www2.mooremedical.com

Industry Group Code: 421450 **Ranks within this company's industry group:** Sales: Profits:

Insurance/HMO/PPO:		Drugs:		Equipment/Supplies:		Hospitals/Clinics:		Services:		Health Care:	
Insurance:		Manufacturer:		Manufacturer:		Acute Care:		Diagnostics:		Home Health:	
Managed Care:		Distributor:	Y	Distributor:	Y	Sub-Acute:		Labs/Testing:		Long-Term Care:	
Utilization Management:		Specialty Pharmacy:		Leasing/Finance:		Outpatient Surgery:		Staffing:		Physical Therapy:	
Payment Processing:		Vitamins/Nutritionals:		Information Systems:		Physical Rehab. Ctr.:		Waste Disposal:		Physician Prac. Mgmt.:	
		Clinical Trials:				Psychiatric Clinics:		Specialty Svcs.:			

TYPES OF BUSINESS:

Distribution-Assorted Health Care Products

BRANDS/DIVISIONS/AFFILIATES:

McKesson Corporation

CONTACTS:

Note: Officers with more than one job title may be intentionally listed here more than once.

Gail Gagnon, Manager-Human Resources
Rick Frey, VP

Phone: 860-826-3600 **Fax:** 860-225-4440
Toll-Free:
Address: 389 John Downey Dr., New Britain, CT 06050 US

GROWTH PLANS/SPECIAL FEATURES:

Moore Medical Corp., a subsidiary of McKesson Corp., is a Internet-enabled, multi-channel, specialty direct markete and distributor of medical, surgical and pharmaceutic products to nearly 100,000 healthcare practices and facilitie in non-hospital settings nationwide. The company customers include physicians, emergency medic technicians, schools, correctional institutions, municipalitie occupational healthcare professionals and other special practice communities. Moore Medical markets to and serve its customers through direct mail, industry-specialize telephone support staff, field sales representatives and th Internet. The company purchases products primarily fro manufacturers and other distributors and does n manufacture or assemble any products, with the exception c medical and first-aid kits. The largest product suppliers fo the firm are 3M, Becton Dickinson, GlaxoSmithKlin Johnson & Johnson, Kendall Healthcare Products Co Laerdal Medical Corp., Microflex, Wyeth-Ayerst Lab Graham Medical Products and Welch Allyn. Moore Medic has distribution centers located in New Britain, Connecticu Visalia, California; and Jacksonville, Florida, as well a remote telesales and customer service centers in Scottsdal Arizona and Visalia, California.

FINANCIALS:

Sales and profits are in thousands of dollars—add 000 to get the full amount. 2007 Note: Financial information for 2007 was not available for all companies at press time.

2007 Sales: $	2007 Profits: $	**U.S. Stock Ticker: Subsidiary**
2006 Sales: $	2006 Profits: $	**Int'l Ticker:** Int'l Exchange:
2005 Sales: $	2005 Profits: $	Employees: 315
2004 Sales: $	2004 Profits: $	Fiscal Year Ends:
2003 Sales: $141,700	2003 Profits: $-1,500	Parent Company: MCKESSON CORPORATION

SALARIES/BENEFITS:

Pension Plan:	ESOP Stock Plan:	Profit Sharing:	Top Exec. Salary: $295,550	Bonus: $27,957
Savings Plan:	Stock Purch. Plan:		Second Exec. Salary: $225,000	Bonus: $20,192

OTHER THOUGHTS:

Apparent Women Officers or Directors: 1
Hot Spot for Advancement for Women/Minorities:

LOCATIONS: ("Y" = Yes)

West:	Southwest:	Midwest:	Southeast:	Northeast:	International:
Y	Y		Y	Y	

MORRISON MANAGEMENT SPECIALISTS INC

www.iammorrison.com

Industry Group Code: 722310 **Ranks within this company's industry group:** Sales: Profits:

Insurance/HMO/PPO:		Drugs:		Equipment/Supplies:		Hospitals/Clinics:		Services:		Health Care:	
Insurance:		Manufacturer:		Manufacturer:		Acute Care:		Diagnostics:		Home Health:	
Managed Care:		Distributor:		Distributor:		Sub-Acute:		Labs/Testing:		Long-Term Care:	
Utilization Management:		Specialty Pharmacy:		Leasing/Finance:		Outpatient Surgery:		Staffing:		Physical Therapy:	
Payment Processing:		Vitamins/Nutritionals:		Information Systems:		Physical Rehab. Ctr.:		Waste Disposal:		Physician Prac. Mgmt.:	
		Clinical Trials:				Psychiatric Clinics:		Specialty Svcs.:	Y		

TYPES OF BUSINESS:

Healthcare Food Services & Senior Dining
Food Service-Long Term Care Facilities
Human Resource Services

BRANDS/DIVISIONS/AFFILIATES:

Compass Group PLC
Morrison Healthcare Food Services
Morrison Senior Dining
Morrison Human Resource Services
Crothall Services

CONTACTS: *Note: Officers with more than one job title may be intentionally listed here more than once.*

Scott MacLellan, CEO
Scott MacLellan, Pres.
Anthony Mitchell, CFO
Forrest Coley, Dir.-Bus. Dev.
Scott MacLellan, Chmn.

Phone: 404-845-3330	**Fax:** 404-845-3333
Toll-Free:	
Address: 5801 Peachtree Dunwoody Rd., Atlanta, GA 30342 US	

GROWTH PLANS/SPECIAL FEATURES:

Morrison Management Specialists, Inc., a subsidiary of the U.K.-based foodservice Compass Group PLC, is a health care and senior living food service companies. The company is organized into two groups: Morrison Healthcare Food Services and Morrison Senior Dining, providing hospital culinary programs and senior living food services, respectively. Morrison Healthcare Food Services has contracts with approximately 450 acute care clients; meanwhile, Morrison Senior Dining currently works in approximately 370 senior living communities. The Atlanta-based company provides food service for some of the largest healthcare systems in 41 states. Some of the company's other clients include Silvercrest Extended Care, Fountains Retirement Communities and MedStar. In addition to providing food services, Morrison helps clients manage costs, integrate their systems and create appealing food service environments. Morrison has branched out into other areas, forming Morrison Human Resource Services, which provides employee training, worker's compensation administration and benefit and payroll administration. Morrison is also in a longstanding partnership with Crothall Services, another member of the Compass Group. Crothall handles complementary areas of health care facilities management.

FINANCIALS: **Sales and profits are in thousands of dollars—add 000 to get the full amount. 2007 Note: Financial information for 2007 was not available for all companies at press time.**

2007 Sales: $	2007 Profits: $	**U.S. Stock Ticker: Subsidiary**
2006 Sales: $	2006 Profits: $	**Int'l Ticker:** Int'l Exchange:
2005 Sales: $	2005 Profits: $	Employees: 14,000
2004 Sales: $	2004 Profits: $	Fiscal Year Ends:
2003 Sales: $	2003 Profits: $	Parent Company: COMPASS GROUP PLC

SALARIES/BENEFITS:

Pension Plan:	ESOP Stock Plan:	Profit Sharing:	Top Exec. Salary: $393,000	Bonus: $225,000
Savings Plan:	Stock Purch. Plan:		Second Exec. Salary: $199,238	Bonus: $80,000

OTHER THOUGHTS:

Apparent Women Officers or Directors:
Hot Spot for Advancement for Women/Minorities:

LOCATIONS: ("Y" = Yes)

West:	Southwest:	Midwest:	Southeast:	Northeast:	International:
			Y		

Note: Financial information, benefits and other data can change quickly and may vary from those stated here.

MYLAN LABORATORIES INC www.mylan.com

Industry Group Code: 325416 **Ranks within this company's industry group:** Sales: 4 Profits: 3

Insurance/HMO/PPO:		Drugs:		Equipment/Supplies:		Hospitals/Clinics:		Services:		Health Care:	
Insurance:		Manufacturer:	Y	Manufacturer:		Acute Care:		Diagnostics:		Home Health:	
Managed Care:		Distributor:	Y	Distributor:		Sub-Acute:		Labs/Testing:		Long-Term Care:	
Utilization Management:		Specialty Pharmacy:	Y	Leasing/Finance:		Outpatient Surgery:		Staffing:		Physical Therapy:	
Payment Processing:		Vitamins/Nutritionals:		Information Systems:		Physical Rehab. Ctr.:		Waste Disposal:		Physician Prac. Mgmt.:	
		Clinical Trials:				Psychiatric Clinics:		Specialty Svcs.:			

TYPES OF BUSINESS:

Drugs-Generic
Generic Pharmaceuticals
Branded Pharmaceuticals

BRANDS/DIVISIONS/AFFILIATES:

UDL Laboratories, Inc.
Mylan Pharmaceuticals, Inc.
Mylan Technologies, Inc.
Matrix Laboratories
Docpharma
nebivolol

CONTACTS: *Note: Officers with more than one job title may be intentionally listed here more than once.*

Robert J. Coury, CEO
Edward J. Borkowski, CFO
Rajiv Malik, Head-Global Tech. Oper.
Stuart A. Williams, Chief Legal Officer
David F. Mulder, Sr. VP-Corp. & Bus. Dev.
Patrick Fitzgerald, VP-Public Rel.
Patrick Fitzgerald, VP-Investor Rel.
Daniel C. Rizzo, Jr., Corp. Controller/VP
Robert J. Coury, Vice Chmn.
Harry A. Korman, Pres., Mylan Pharmaceuticals/Sr. VP
Carolyn Myers, Pres., Mylan Technologies/VP
Heather Bresch, Head-North American Oper.
Milan Puskar, Chmn.

Phone: 724-514-1800 **Fax:** 724-514-1870
Toll-Free:
Address: 1500 Corporate Dr., Ste. 400, Canonsburg, PA 15317 US

GROWTH PLANS/SPECIAL FEATURES:

Mylan Laboratories, Inc. develops, licenses, manufacture distributes and markets generic, branded and brande generic pharmaceutical products. Branded products a marketed under brand names through marketing program that are designed to generate physician and consum loyalty. Generic products are the chemical and therapeut equivalents of reference brand drugs. Branded gener products are the brands sold by a holder as generic, ofte through a licensing agreement with a generic company through a subsidiary, at the same time other gener competition enters the market. The company reports as tw segments: the Mylan segment and the Matrix segment. Th Mylan segment operates through three primary busines units: Mylan Pharmacuticals, Inc.; UDL Laboratories, Inc and Mylan Technologies, Inc. Mylan holds one of the lea market positions in new and refilled prescriptions dispense among all pharmaceutical companies in the U.S. Th company's portfolio of generic products includes over 17 products and covers a range of dosage forms includin immediate- and extended-release oral tablets and capsule as well as transdermal patches. Matrix is one of the world largest manufacturers of API's (active pharmaceutic ingredients). In Europe the segment operates throug Docpharma, a wholly-owned subsidiary. In 2006, th company announced an agreement with Forest Laboratorie Holdings, Ltd., a wholly owned subsidiary of Fore Laboratories Inc., for the commercialization, developme and distribution of Mylan's nebivolol compound in the U.S and Canada. Recently, the company acquired Matr Laboratories. In May 2007, the firm agreed to acquire th generic-drugs unit of Merck KGaA for $6.7 billion.

Mylan offers its employees healthcare coverage, life an disability insurance, an educational assistance program wellness benefits and time-off benefits, among others.

FINANCIALS: **Sales and profits are in thousands of dollars—add 000 to get the full amount. 2007 Note: Financial information for 2007 was not available for all companies at press time.**

2007 Sales: $1,611,819	2007 Profits: $217,284	**U.S. Stock Ticker: MYL**
2006 Sales: $1,257,164	2006 Profits: $184,542	**Int'l Ticker:** Int'l Exchange:
2005 Sales: $1,253,374	2005 Profits: $203,592	Employees: 6,400
2004 Sales: $1,374,617	2004 Profits: $334,609	Fiscal Year Ends: 3/31
2003 Sales: $1,269,200	2003 Profits: $272,400	Parent Company:

SALARIES/BENEFITS:

Pension Plan:	ESOP Stock Plan:	Profit Sharing:	Top Exec. Salary: $1,500,000	Bonus: $2,737,500
Savings Plan: Y	Stock Purch. Plan:		Second Exec. Salary: $523,591	Bonus: $

OTHER THOUGHTS:

Apparent Women Officers or Directors: 2
Hot Spot for Advancement for Women/Minorities: Y

LOCATIONS: ("Y" = Yes)

West:	Southwest:	Midwest:	Southeast:	Northeast:	International:
	Y	Y		Y	Y

NANOBIO CORPORATION www.nanobio.com

ndustry Group Code: 325412A **Ranks within this company's industry group:** Sales: Profits:

nsurance/HMO/PPO:		Drugs:		Equipment/Supplies:		Hospitals/Clinics:		Services:		Health Care:	
nsurance:		Manufacturer:	Y	Manufacturer:		Acute Care:		Diagnostics:		Home Health:	
Managed Care:		Distributor:		Distributor:		Sub-Acute:		Labs/Testing:		Long-Term Care:	
Jtilization Management:		Specialty Pharmacy:		Leasing/Finance:		Outpatient Surgery:		Staffing:		Physical Therapy:	
Payment Processing:		Vitamins/Nutritionals:		Information Systems:		Physical Rehab. Ctr.:		Waste Disposal:		Physician Prac. Mgmt.:	
		Clinical Trials:				Psychiatric Clinics:		Specialty Svcs.:	Y		

TYPES OF BUSINESS:

Drug Delivery Systems
Nanoemulsion Technology
Cold Sore Treatments
Drugs-Antimicrobial

BRANDS/DIVISIONS/AFFILIATES:

NanoStat
NanoHPX
NanoTxt

CONTACTS: *Note: Officers with more than one job title may be intentionally listed here more than once.*

Michael J. Nestor, CEO
David Peralta, COO
David Peralta, CFO
James Baker, Chief Scientific Officer
John Coffey, VP-Bus. Dev.
Mary R. Flack, VP-Clinical & Regulatory Affairs
James Baker, Chmn.

Phone: 734-302-4000	**Fax:** 734-302-9150
Toll-Free:	
Address: 2311 Green Rd., Ste. A, Ann Arbor, MI 48105 US	

GROWTH PLANS/SPECIAL FEATURES:

NanoBio Corporation is a biopharmaceutical company that develops and markets anti-infection products and mucosal vaccines. The company's main technology platform is NanoStat, which implements oil-in-water emulsions that are roughly 150-400 nanometers in size. Nanoemulsion particles can rapidly penetrate the skin through pores and hair shafts to the site of an infection, where it physically kills lipid-containing organisms by penetrating the outer membrane of pathogenic organisms. NanoStat emulsions have the added benefit of being selectively lethal to targeted microbes without affecting any surrounding skin and mucous membranes. NanoBio's current commercial product pipeline consists of five anti-infective pharmaceuticals and two mucosal vaccines. The firm's two leading anti-infective products are NB-001 (Phase III), a treatment for cold sores, and NB-002 (Phase II) for nail fungus, which are both in the clinical stages of development. NanoStat mucosal vaccines are designed to treat influenza, H5N1, hepatitis B, pneumonia, tuberculosis, small pox anthrax and other various viral and bacterial diseases. NanoBio also holds exclusive intellectual property rights for virucidal, fungicidal, sporicidal and bactericidal applications in a wide spectrum of products that include personal care products, medical products and anti-bioterrorism applications. NanoBio also maintains a research team to discover new applications and methods relating to Varicella zoster (a virus that causes shingles), vaginitis, ocular infections, influenza prophylaxis and drug delivery systems. In August 2006, the company received a $30 million equity investment from Perseus, LLC, which is aiding the firm in expanding its clinical product pipeline.

NanoBio offers employees health benefits, flexible spending accounts, an investment 401(k) plan and annual bonuses that are based on an employee performance ratings and the company's overall achievements.

FINANCIALS: **Sales and profits are in thousands of dollars—add 000 to get the full amount. 2007 Note: Financial information for 2007 was not available for all companies at press time.**

2007 Sales: $	2007 Profits: $	**U.S. Stock Ticker: Private**
2006 Sales: $	2006 Profits: $	**Int'l Ticker:** Int'l Exchange:
2005 Sales: $	2005 Profits: $	Employees:
2004 Sales: $	2004 Profits: $	Fiscal Year Ends: 12/31
2003 Sales: $	2003 Profits: $	Parent Company:

SALARIES/BENEFITS:

Pension Plan:	ESOP Stock Plan:	Profit Sharing: Y	Top Exec. Salary: $	Bonus: $
Savings Plan: Y	Stock Purch. Plan:		Second Exec. Salary: $	Bonus: $

OTHER THOUGHTS:

Apparent Women Officers or Directors:
Hot Spot for Advancement for Women/Minorities:

LOCATIONS: ("Y" = Yes)

West:	Southwest:	Midwest:	Southeast:	Northeast:	International:
		Y			

Note: Financial information, benefits and other data can change quickly and may vary from those stated here.

NATIONAL DENTEX CORP www.nationaldentex.com

Industry Group Code: 339113 **Ranks within this company's industry group:** Sales: 71 Profits: 71

Insurance/HMO/PPO:		Drugs:		Equipment/Supplies:		Hospitals/Clinics:		Services:		Health Care:	
Insurance:		Manufacturer:		Manufacturer:	Y	Acute Care:		Diagnostics:		Home Health:	
Managed Care:		Distributor:		Distributor:		Sub-Acute:		Labs/Testing:	Y	Long-Term Care:	
Utilization Management:		Specialty Pharmacy:		Leasing/Finance:		Outpatient Surgery:		Staffing:		Physical Therapy:	
Payment Processing:		Vitamins/Nutritionals:		Information Systems:		Physical Rehab. Ctr.:		Waste Disposal:		Physician Prac. Mgmt.:	
		Clinical Trials:				Psychiatric Clinics:		Specialty Svcs.:			

TYPES OF BUSINESS:

Dental Prosthetic Appliances
Dental Laboratories

BRANDS/DIVISIONS/AFFILIATES:

Green Dental Laboratories, Inc.
Keller Group, Inc.
Impact Dental Laboratory, Ltd.

CONTACTS: *Note: Officers with more than one job title may be intentionally listed here more than once.*

David L. Brown, CEO
David L. Brown, Pres.
Lynn D. Dine, VP-R&D
Richard G. Mariacher, VP-Tech. Svcs.
Donald H. Siegel, Sec.
Doug Baker, VP-Oper.
Richard F. Becker, Jr., Treas./Exec. VP
Tom Keller, VP-Oper.
Bill Keller, VP-Oper.
Dean Ribeiro, VP-Client Rel.
Josh Green, Exec. VP-Laboratory Oper.
David V. Harkins, Chmn.

Phone: 508-358-4422	**Fax:** 508-358-6199
Toll-Free:	
Address: 526 Boston Post Rd., Wayland, MA 01778 US	

GROWTH PLANS/SPECIAL FEATURES:

National Dentex Corp. designs, manufactures, markets an sells custom dental prosthetic appliances such as crowns bridges and dentures. The company owns and operates 4 dental laboratories and five branch laboratories locate throughout 31 states. The firm operates in three segments Green Dental, representing the operations of Green Denta Laboratories, Inc. located in Arkansas; Keller, representin the operations of Keller Group, Inc.; and NDX Laboratories which represents the company's remaining laboratories National Dentex's products are groups in three mai categories: restorative, which consist primarily of crowns an bridges; reconstructive, which consist primarily of partia dentures and full dentures; and cosmetic products, whic consist primarily of porcelain veneers and ceramic crowns The products are manufactured from materials such as hig noble, noble and predominantly base alloys, dental resins composites and porcelain. The company's products ar produced by trained technicians working primarily with wor orders and cases, such as impressions, models and occlusa registrations of a patient's teeth, provided by the over 24,00 dentists in the company's customer base. Each of th company's local dental laboratories markets and sells it products through its own direct sales force. The branc laboratories are smaller than the main laboratories and thu offer fewer products. When one of the branches is unable t fill an order, it sends it on to one of the full-servic laboratories. In October 2006, National Dentex acquire Impact Dental Laboratory, Ltd. of Canada and Keller Group Inc., a dental laboratory business, for about $20 million.

The company offers its employees medical and denta insurance; educational assistance; an employee stoc purchase plan; a profit sharing plan; stock options; and lif insurance.

FINANCIALS: **Sales and profits are in thousands of dollars—add 000 to get the full amount. 2007 Note: Financial information for 2007 was not available for all companies at press time.**

2007 Sales: $	2007 Profits: $	**U.S. Stock Ticker: NADX**
2006 Sales: $150,107	2006 Profits: $5,763	**Int'l Ticker:** Int'l Exchange:
2005 Sales: $135,843	2005 Profits: $7,089	Employees: 2,156
2004 Sales: $111,753	2004 Profits: $5,159	Fiscal Year Ends: 12/31
2003 Sales: $99,274	2003 Profits: $5,757	Parent Company:

SALARIES/BENEFITS:

Pension Plan:	ESOP Stock Plan:	Profit Sharing: Y	Top Exec. Salary: $350,000	Bonus: $
Savings Plan:	Stock Purch. Plan: Y		Second Exec. Salary: $220,000	Bonus: $15,000

OTHER THOUGHTS:

Apparent Women Officers or Directors: 1
Hot Spot for Advancement for Women/Minorities:

LOCATIONS: ("Y" = Yes)

West:	Southwest:	Midwest:	Southeast:	Northeast:	International:
Y	Y	Y	Y	Y	Y

NATIONAL HEALTHCARE CORP www.nhccare.com

ndustry Group Code: 623110 **Ranks within this company's industry group:** Sales: 5 Profits: 3

surance/HMO/PPO:		Drugs:		Equipment/Supplies:		Hospitals/Clinics:		Services:		Health Care:	
surance:	Y	Manufacturer:		Manufacturer:		Acute Care:		Diagnostics:		Home Health:	Y
anaged Care:	Y	Distributor:		Distributor:		Sub-Acute:	Y	Labs/Testing:		Long-Term Care:	Y
tilization Management:		Specialty Pharmacy:	Y	Leasing/Finance:		Outpatient Surgery:		Staffing:		Physical Therapy:	Y
ayment Processing:		Vitamins/Nutritionals:		Information Systems:		Physical Rehab. Ctr.:	Y	Waste Disposal:		Physician Prac. Mgmt.:	
		Clinical Trials:				Psychiatric Clinics:		Specialty Svcs.:	Y		

TYPES OF BUSINESS:

ong-Term & Home Health Care
ehabilitative Services
ledical Specialty Units
harmacy Operations
ssisted Living Projects
lanaged Care Contracts
utritional Support Services
eal Estate

BRANDS/DIVISIONS/AFFILIATES:

lational Health Realty, Inc.
lational Health Investors

CONTACTS: *Note: Officers with more than one job title may be ntentionally listed here more than once.*

Robert G. Adams, CEO
Robert G. Adams, Pres.
Iike Ussery, Sr. VP-Oper.
). Gerald Coggin, Sr. VP-Corporate Rel.
Donald K. Daniel, Controller/Sr. VP/Chief Acct. Officer
Charlotte A. Swafford, Sr. VP/Treasurer
V. Andrew Adams, Chmn.

Phone: 615-890-2020	**Fax:** 615-890-0123
Toll-Free:	
Address: 100 E. Vine St., Murfreesboro, TN 37130 US	

GROWTH PLANS/SPECIAL FEATURES:

National HealthCare Corporation (NHC) operates long-term health care centers and home health care programs primarily in the southeastern and Midwestern regions of the U.S. The majority of the company's revenue comes from its health care services, with the remainder coming from its National Health Realty and National Health Investors subsidiaries. NHC's health services include long-term health care centers, rehabilitative services, medical specialty units, pharmacy operations, assisted living projects, managed care contracts, hospice programs and homecare programs. The firm services about 75 long-term health care centers, 30 home care programs, 10 independent living centers and assisted living centers at 22 locations. NHC also maintains specialized care units such as Alzheimer's disease care units, sub-acute nursing units and a number of in-house pharmacies. The company's health care centers, operated by its subsidiaries, provide in-patient skilled and intermediate nursing care services and in-patient and out-patient rehabilitation services. Skilled nursing care consists of 24-hour nursing service by registered or licensed practical nurses and intermediate nursing care by non-licensed personnel. The health care centers provide rehabilitative care, including physical, occupational and speech therapies designed to aid the patient's recovery. Most of the company's retirement centers are constructed adjacent to NHC's health care properties. Apart from its health care services, NHC is engaged in management, accounting, and financial services; nutritional support services; advisory services; and insurance services. Its management and support services are provided to contracted centers, to which NHC provides operational support through the use of regional nurses, accounting and financial services, cash management, data processing, legal, consulting and services. In December 2006, the company entered into a merger agreement with its publicly held subsidiary, National Health Realty, Inc.

FINANCIALS: Sales and profits are in thousands of dollars—add 000 to get the full amount. 2007 Note: Financial information for 2007 was not available for all companies at press time.

2007 Sales: $	2007 Profits: $	**U.S. Stock Ticker: NHC**
2006 Sales: $562,958	2006 Profits: $36,740	**Int'l Ticker:** Int'l Exchange:
2005 Sales: $542,381	2005 Profits: $28,635	Employees: 11,000
2004 Sales: $521,829	2004 Profits: $23,972	Fiscal Year Ends: 12/31
2003 Sales: $472,864	2003 Profits: $19,952	Parent Company:

SALARIES/BENEFITS:

Pension Plan:	ESOP Stock Plan:	Profit Sharing:	Top Exec. Salary: $145,385	Bonus: $950,000
Savings Plan:	Stock Purch. Plan: Y		Second Exec. Salary: $124,231	Bonus: $600,000

OTHER THOUGHTS:

Apparent Women Officers or Directors: 1
Hot Spot for Advancement for Women/Minorities: Y

LOCATIONS: ("Y" = Yes)

West:	Southwest:	Midwest:	Southeast:	Northeast:	International:
		Y	Y	Y	

Note: Financial information, benefits and other data can change quickly and may vary from those stated here.

NATIONAL HOME HEALTH CARE CORP www.nhhc.net

Industry Group Code: 621610 **Ranks within this company's industry group:** Sales: 12 Profits: 10

Insurance/HMO/PPO:		Drugs:		Equipment/Supplies:		Hospitals/Clinics:		Services:		Health Care:	
Insurance:		Manufacturer:		Manufacturer:		Acute Care:		Diagnostics:		Home Health:	Y
Managed Care:		Distributor:		Distributor:		Sub-Acute:		Labs/Testing:		Long-Term Care:	
Utilization Management:		Specialty Pharmacy:		Leasing/Finance:		Outpatient Surgery:		Staffing:	Y	Physical Therapy:	Y
Payment Processing:		Vitamins/Nutritionals:		Information Systems:		Physical Rehab. Ctr.:		Waste Disposal:		Physician Prac. Mgmt.:	
		Clinical Trials:				Psychiatric Clinics:		Specialty Svcs.:	Y		

TYPES OF BUSINESS:

Home Health Care
Disease Management Services
Physical, Occupational & Speech Therapies
Staffing Services
Medical Social Services
Mental Health Services

BRANDS/DIVISIONS/AFFILIATES:

Health Acquisition Corp.
New England Home Care, Inc.
Medical Resources Home Health Corp.
Connecticut Staffing Works Corp.
Allen Health Care
Accredited Health Services, Inc.

CONTACTS: *Note: Officers with more than one job title may be intentionally listed here more than once.*

Steven Fialkow, CEO
Steven Fialkow, Pres.
Robert P. Heller, CFO
Steven Fialkow, Corp. Sec.
Robert P. Heller, Treas./VP-Finance
Frederick H. Fialkow, Chmn.

Phone: 914-722-9000	**Fax:** 914-722-9239
Toll-Free:	
Address: 700 White Plains Rd., Ste. 275, Scarsdale, NY 10583 US	

GROWTH PLANS/SPECIAL FEATURES:

National Home Health Care Corporation (NHHC) is a provider of home health care services. It operates 31 offices consisting of one parent corporate office, 21 offices that coordinate home health care services and nine satellite offices. The company has two Medicare provider numbers and is a Medicaid provider in each of the four states in which it operates. NHHC provides home health care services including monitoring, interventions and medication administration by registered nurses; technical procedures and medical dressing changes by licensed practical nurses; muscle strengthening and restoration of range of motion by physical and occupational therapists; communication and oral skill restoration by speech pathologists; acute and chronic illness assistance by medical social workers; personal care such as bathing assistance by home health aides; and private duty services such as continuous hourly nursing care and sitter services. NHHC boasts five principal operating subsidiaries: Health Acquisition Corp. (New York); New England Home Care, Inc., (Connecticut); Accredited Health Services, Inc. (New Jersey); Connecticut Staffing Works Corp. (Connecticut); and Medical Resources Home Health Corp. (Massachusetts). Doing business as Allen Health Care Services, Health Acquisition Corp., provides its services through registered nurses, personal care aides, home health aides and homemakers. New England Home Care provides full-service home health care 24 hours a day, seven days a week, with weekends, holidays and after-hours are supported by an on-call system. The company also offers specialty services such as adult/geriatric, pediatric, post-acute rehabilitation and behavioral health. Accredited Health Services provides home health aide services. Connecticut Staffing Works conducts health care staffing operations, providing temporary staffing to hospitals, skilled nursing facilities, long-term care centers, occupational health sites, juvenile detention centers, correctional facilities, group homes, schools and other institutions.

FINANCIALS: Sales and profits are in thousands of dollars—add 000 to get the full amount. 2007 Note: Financial information for 2007 was not available for all companies at press time.

2007 Sales: $	2007 Profits: $	**U.S. Stock Ticker: NHHC**
2006 Sales: $102,365	2006 Profits: $3,655	**Int'l Ticker:** Int'l Exchange:
2005 Sales: $98,461	2005 Profits: $3,567	Employees: 3,410
2004 Sales: $94,592	2004 Profits: $4,720	Fiscal Year Ends: 7/31
2003 Sales: $97,200	2003 Profits: $5,800	Parent Company:

SALARIES/BENEFITS:

Pension Plan:	ESOP Stock Plan:	Profit Sharing:	Top Exec. Salary: $545,475	Bonus: $39,198
Savings Plan: Y	Stock Purch. Plan:		Second Exec. Salary: $428,654	Bonus: $144,979

OTHER THOUGHTS:

Apparent Women Officers or Directors:
Hot Spot for Advancement for Women/Minorities:

LOCATIONS: ("Y" = Yes)

West:	Southwest:	Midwest:	Southeast:	Northeast:	International:
				Y	

NATIONAL MEDICAL HEALTH CARD SYSTEMS INC

www.nmhc.com

ndustry Group Code: 522320A **Ranks within this company's industry group:** Sales: 5 Profits: 4

surance/HMO/PPO:		Drugs:		Equipment/Supplies:		Hospitals/Clinics:		Services:		Health Care:	
surance:		Manufacturer:		Manufacturer:		Acute Care:		Diagnostics:		Home Health:	
anaged Care:		Distributor:		Distributor:		Sub-Acute:		Labs/Testing:		Long-Term Care:	
tilization Management:	Y	Specialty Pharmacy:	Y	Leasing/Finance:		Outpatient Surgery:		Staffing:		Physical Therapy:	
ayment Processing:		Vitamins/Nutritionals:		Information Systems:	Y	Physical Rehab. Ctr.:		Waste Disposal:		Physician Prac. Mgmt.:	
		Clinical Trials:				Psychiatric Clinics:		Specialty Svcs.:	Y		

TYPES OF BUSINESS:

ayment & Transaction Processing
harmacy Benefits Management
ealth Information Systems
ail-Order & Specialty Pharmacies

BRANDS/DIVISIONS/AFFILIATES:

NMHC Rx
ntegrail, Inc.
NMHCRX Mail Order, Inc.
scend Specialty Pharmacy Services, Inc.
Pharmaceutical Care Network
MedIntelligence

CONTACTS: *Note: Officers with more than one job title may be ntentionally listed here more than once.*

ames F. Smith, CEO
ames F. Smith, Pres.
Stuart Diamond, CFO
ery Baskin, Chief Mktg. Officer
Neil Carfagna, Chief Human Resources Officer
Bill Masters, CIO
onathan I. Friedman, Chief Legal Officer
ery Baskin, Exec. VP-Bus. Dev.
Mark A. Adkison, Chief Specialty Pharmacy Officer
ames Flanick, Chief Mail Service Pharmacy Officer
Robert Kordella, Chief Clinical Officer
Nathan J. Schultz, Chief Svcs. Officer
Thomas W. Erickson, Chmn.

Phone: 516-626-0007	**Fax:** 516-605-6981
Toll-Free: 800-251-3883	
Address: 26 Harbor Park Dr., Port Washington, NY 11050 US	

GROWTH PLANS/SPECIAL FEATURES:

National Medical Health Card Systems, Inc. (NMHC) provides pharmacy benefit management (PBM) services through a subsidiary, NMHC Rx. Its chief clients are corporations, labor organizations, third-party administrators; self-insured employer groups; workers' compensation plans; school districts and municipalities. NMHC's programs are designed to assist pharmacy benefit plan sponsors by monitoring the cost and quality of prescription drugs and other related services, which include claims management, drug analysis, physician profiling and benefit design consultation. It offers these drugs and services through a network of over 50,000 participating pharmacies. The company's program components are integrated and managed through proprietary system protocols. In addition, NMHC operates a health information company through subsidiary Integrail, Inc.; a mail-service pharmacy through subsidiary NMHCRX Mail Order, Inc.; and a specialty pharmacy, designed to handle patients with either high cost, self-injected medications or compounded prescriptions, through subsidiary Ascend Specialty Pharmacy Services, Inc.

FINANCIALS: Sales and profits are in thousands of dollars—add 000 to get the full amount. 2007 Note: Financial information for 2007 was not available for all companies at press time.

2007 Sales: $679,081	2007 Profits: $ 92	**U.S. Stock Ticker: NMHC**
2006 Sales: $862,853	2006 Profits: $9,657	**Int'l Ticker:** Int'l Exchange:
2005 Sales: $800,592	2005 Profits: $12,381	Employees: 465
2004 Sales: $651,098	2004 Profits: $7,953	Fiscal Year Ends: 6/30
2003 Sales: $573,300	2003 Profits: $6,400	Parent Company:

SALARIES/BENEFITS:

Pension Plan:	ESOP Stock Plan:	Profit Sharing:	Top Exec. Salary: $355,230	Bonus: $45,000
Savings Plan: Y	Stock Purch. Plan:		Second Exec. Salary: $230,884	Bonus: $16,675

OTHER THOUGHTS:

Apparent Women Officers or Directors:
Hot Spot for Advancement for Women/Minorities:

LOCATIONS: ("Y" = Yes)

West:	Southwest:	Midwest:	Southeast:	Northeast:	International:
Y	Y		Y	Y	

Note: Financial information, benefits and other data can change quickly and may vary from those stated here.

NEKTAR THERAPEUTICS www.nektar.com

Industry Group Code: 325412A **Ranks within this company's industry group:** Sales: 2 Profits: 3

Insurance/HMO/PPO:		Drugs:		Equipment/Supplies:		Hospitals/Clinics:		Services:		Health Care:	
Insurance:		Manufacturer:		Manufacturer:	Y	Acute Care:		Diagnostics:		Home Health:	
Managed Care:		Distributor:		Distributor:		Sub-Acute:		Labs/Testing:		Long-Term Care:	
Utilization Management:		Specialty Pharmacy:		Leasing/Finance:		Outpatient Surgery:		Staffing:		Physical Therapy:	
Payment Processing:		Vitamins/Nutritionals:		Information Systems:		Physical Rehab. Ctr.:		Waste Disposal:		Physician Prac. Mgmt.:	
		Clinical Trials:				Psychiatric Clinics:		Specialty Svcs.:			

TYPES OF BUSINESS:

Drug Delivery Systems
PEG-Based Delivery Systems
Molecular & Particle Engineering
Equipment-Inhalers

BRANDS/DIVISIONS/AFFILIATES:

Nektar PEGylation Technology
Nektar Pulmonary Technology
Macugen
PEGASYS
Exubera
Neulasta
Somavert
PEG-INTRON

CONTACTS: *Note: Officers with more than one job title may be intentionally listed here more than once.*

Howard W. Robin, CEO
Hoyoung Huh, COO/Head-Pegylation Bus. Unit
Howard W. Robin, Pres.
Louis Drapeau, CFO
Dorian Rinella, VP-Human Resources & Facilities
David Johnston, Sr. VP-R&D
Gil M. Labrucherie, General Counsel/Sec.
Christopher J. Searcy, Sr. VP-Corp. Dev.
Tim Warner, Sr. VP-Investor Rel./Corp. Affairs
Louis Drapeau, Sr. VP-Finance
Nevan Elam, Sr. VP/Head-Pulmonary Bus. Unit
John S. Patton, Chief Scientific Officer
David Tolley, Sr. VP/General Mgr.-Nektar Alabama
Robert B. Chess, Chmn.

Phone: 650-631-3100	**Fax:** 650-631-3150
Toll-Free:	
Address: 150 Industrial Rd., San Carlos, CA 94070 US	

GROWTH PLANS/SPECIAL FEATURES:

Nektar Therapeutics is a biopharmaceutical compan focused on developing technology for unmet medical needs The company focuses on applying its advanced drug deliver technologies to improve therapeutic molecules' efficacy safety and convenience and to enable the development c new molecules. The company creates differentiate products by applying its platform technologies to establishe or novel medicine. The firm creates potential breakthroug products by developing products in collaboration wit pharmaceutical and biotechnology companies that seek t improve and differentiate their products and by applying it technologies to already approved drugs to create an develop its own differentiated products. The company' leading technology platforms are Pulmonary Technology an PEGylation Technology. Pulmonary Technology make drugs inhaleable to deliver them to and through the lungs fc both systemic and local lung applications. PEGylatio Technology is a chemical process designed to enhance th performance of most drug classes with the potential t improve solubility and stability; increase drug half-life; reduc immune responses to an active drug; and improve th efficacy and/or safety of a molecule in certain instances These technologies are the platforms that form the basis o all of the company's products that have received FD approval. Leading products include Macugen treatment fo macular degeneration; PEGASYS for chronic Hepatitis C Somavert human growth hormone receptor antagonist Definity ultrasound contrast agent; Exubera inhaleabl insulin; PEG-INTRON for treating Hepatitis C; and Neulast for the treatment of neutropenia, a condition where the body produces too few white blood cells. Most of these have beer developed in collaboration with other pharmaceutica companies, including Amgen, Eyetech, Pfizer, Roche anc Schering-Plough. In September 2006, Nektar Therapeutics together with Zelos Therapeutics announced the initiation o a phase one clinical trial of an inhaled powder formulation o Zelos' parathyroid hormone.

FINANCIALS: Sales and profits are in thousands of dollars—add 000 to get the full amount. 2007 Note: Financial information for 2007 was not available for all companies at press time.

2007 Sales: $	2007 Profits: $	**U.S. Stock Ticker: NKTR**
2006 Sales: $217,718	2006 Profits: $-154,761	**Int'l Ticker:** Int'l Exchange:
2005 Sales: $126,279	2005 Profits: $-185,111	Employees: 793
2004 Sales: $114,270	2004 Profits: $-101,886	Fiscal Year Ends: 12/31
2003 Sales: $106,257	2003 Profits: $-65,890	Parent Company:

SALARIES/BENEFITS:

Pension Plan:	ESOP Stock Plan:	Profit Sharing:	Top Exec. Salary: $418,459	Bonus: $262,718
Savings Plan: Y	Stock Purch. Plan:		Second Exec. Salary: $336,589	Bonus: $119,968

OTHER THOUGHTS:

Apparent Women Officers or Directors: 2
Hot Spot for Advancement for Women/Minorities: Y

LOCATIONS: ("Y" = Yes)

West:	Southwest:	Midwest:	Southeast:	Northeast:	International:
Y			Y		Y

NEUROCRINE BIOSCIENCES INC www.neurocrine.com

ıdustry Group Code: 325412 **Ranks within this company's industry group:** Sales: 37 Profits: 40

ısurance/HMO/PPO:		Drugs:		Equipment/Supplies:		Hospitals/Clinics:		Services:		Health Care:	
ısurance:		Manufacturer:	Y	Manufacturer:		Acute Care:		Diagnostics:		Home Health:	
ıanaged Care:		Distributor:		Distributor:		Sub-Acute:		Labs/Testing:		Long-Term Care:	
tilization Management:		Specialty Pharmacy:		Leasing/Finance:		Outpatient Surgery:		Staffing:		Physical Therapy:	
ayment Processing:		Vitamins/Nutritionals:		Information Systems:		Physical Rehab. Ctr.:		Waste Disposal:		Physician Prac. Mgmt.:	
		Clinical Trials:				Psychiatric Clinics:		Specialty Svcs.:			

TYPES OF BUSINESS:

ᵖharmaceuticals Discovery & Development
ɔrugs-Neurological & Immune Disorder

BRANDS/DIVISIONS/AFFILIATES:

ndiplon
Jrocortin 2
GnRH Antagonist
CRF-R Antagonist

CONTACTS: *Note: Officers with more than one job title may be ntentionally listed here more than once.*

Gary A. Lyons, CEO
Kevin C. Gorman, COO
Gary A. Lyons, Pres.
Tim Coughlin, CFO
Carol Baum, VP-Mktg.
Richard Ranieri, Sr. VP-Human Resources
Dimitri E. Grigoriadis, VP-Research
Bill Wilson, VP-IT
Margaret E. Valeur-Jensen, General Counsel/Sr. VP/Corp. Sec.
Henry Pan, Exec. VP-Clinical Dev.
Haig Bozigian, Sr. VP-Pharmaceutical & Preclinical Dev.
Barbara Finn, VP-Regulatory Affairs & Quality Assurance
Chris O'Brien, Chief Medical Officer
Joseph A. Mollica, Chmn.
D. Bruce Campbell, Sr. VP-Int'l Dev.

Phone: 858-617-7600 **Fax:** 858-617-7601
Toll-Free:
Address: 12790 El Camino Real, San Diego, CA 92130 US

GROWTH PLANS/SPECIAL FEATURES:

Neurocrine Biosciences, Inc. (NBI) is a neuroimmunology company focused on the discovery and development of therapeutics to treat diseases and disorders of the central nervous and immune systems. The company's neuroscience, endocrine and immunology research segments provide a biological understanding of the molecular interactions of the central nervous, immune and endocrine systems. The firm currently has three active research programs, addressing anxiety, depression, gastrointestinal disorders, cachexia, pain, obesity, Parkinson's disease and insomnia. Indiplon, developed in partnership with Pfizer, is NBI's lead drug candidate. The company is working on a small-molecule Gonadotropin-Releasing Hormone (GnRH) receptor antagonist for the treatment of endometriosis. In January 2007, Neurocrine announced positive preliminary results from its second 'proof of concept', safety and efficacy Phase II clinical trial using its GnRH receptor antagonist in patients with endometriosis. In June 2007, Neurocrine resubmitted its New Drug Application (NDA) for indiplon 5 mg and 10 mg capsules for the treatment of insomnia in both adult and elderly patients to the U.S. Food and Drug Administration (FDA). Urocortin 2, which has finished Phase II testing, is being developed for congestive heart failure. The company is also in the process of developing a response to depression and anxiety through its research into the construction of a selective molecular antagonist to the Corticotropin Releasing Factor (CRF) type 1 receptor, which it believes is linked with these disorders.

NBI offers its employees medical and dental coverage; health and dependent care flexible spending accounts and long term care programs; a 401(k); stock options and bonuses based on performance; a 24-hour on-site workout room; a full service café; massage therapy and yoga sessions; and a number of recreational events including summer picnics, holiday parties, Friday afternoon gatherings and an annual bowling tournament.

FINANCIALS: **Sales and profits are in thousands of dollars—add 000 to get the full amount. 2007 Note: Financial information for 2007 was not available for all companies at press time.**

2007 Sales: $ | 2007 Profits: $
2006 Sales: $39,234 | 2006 Profits: $-107,205
2005 Sales: $123,889 | 2005 Profits: $-22,191
2004 Sales: $85,176 | 2004 Profits: $-45,773
2003 Sales: $139,078 | 2003 Profits: $-30,256

U.S. Stock Ticker: NBIX
Int'l Ticker: Int'l Exchange:
Employees: 588
Fiscal Year Ends: 12/31
Parent Company:

SALARIES/BENEFITS:

Pension Plan: | ESOP Stock Plan: Y | Profit Sharing: | Top Exec. Salary: $600,000 | Bonus: $
Savings Plan: Y | Stock Purch. Plan: Y | | Second Exec. Salary: $365,000 | Bonus: $

OTHER THOUGHTS:

Apparent Women Officers or Directors: 3
Hot Spot for Advancement for Women/Minorities: Y

LOCATIONS: ("Y" = Yes)

West:	Southwest:	Midwest:	Southeast:	Northeast:	International:
Y					

Note: Financial information, benefits and other data can change quickly and may vary from those stated here.

NEW YORK CITY HEALTH AND HOSPITALS CORPORATION

www.nyc.gov/html/hhc/html/home/home.shtml

Industry Group Code: 622110 **Ranks within this company's industry group:** Sales: 8 Profits: 22

Insurance/HMO/PPO:		Drugs:		Equipment/Supplies:		Hospitals/Clinics:		Services:		Health Care:	
Insurance:		Manufacturer:		Manufacturer:		Acute Care:	Y	Diagnostics:		Home Health:	Y
Managed Care:	Y	Distributor:		Distributor:		Sub-Acute:	Y	Labs/Testing:		Long-Term Care:	Y
Utilization Management:		Specialty Pharmacy:		Leasing/Finance:		Outpatient Surgery:		Staffing:		Physical Therapy:	
Payment Processing:		Vitamins/Nutritionals:		Information Systems:		Physical Rehab. Ctr.:		Waste Disposal:		Physician Prac. Mgmt.:	
		Clinical Trials:				Psychiatric Clinics:		Specialty Svcs.:			

TYPES OF BUSINESS:

Hospitals-General
Community Health Clinics
HMO
Long-Term Care Facilities
Home Health Care
Correctional Facility Health Services

BRANDS/DIVISIONS/AFFILIATES:

MetroPlus
HHC Health & Home Care

CONTACTS: *Note: Officers with more than one job title may be intentionally listed here more than once.*

Alan D. Aviles, CEO
Alan D. Aviles, Pres.
Richard A. Levy, General Counsel/Sr. VP
Frank J. Cirillo, Sr. VP-Oper.
LaRay Brown, Sr. VP-Planning & Community Health
Marlene Zurack, Sr. VP-Finance
Ramanathan Raju, Exec. VP-Medical & Professional Affairs
Phillip W. Robinson, Sr. VP-Facilities Dev.
Van Dunn, Sr. VP-Medical & Professional Affairs
Charlynn Goins, Chmn.

Phone: 212-788-3321	**Fax:** 212-788-0040
Toll-Free:	
Address: 125 Worth St., Ste. 514, New York, NY 10013 US	

GROWTH PLANS/SPECIAL FEATURES:

New York City Health and Hospitals Corporations (HHC) provides health care to all five boroughs of New York serving 1.3 million New Yorkers annually and caring for nearly 500,000 people with no health insurance. The company operates 11 acute care hospitals, six Diagnostic and Treatment Centers, more than 80 community health clinics (including Communicare Centers and Child Health Clinics), four long-term care facilities and a certified home health care agency. HHC also runs medical stations in New York correctional facilities. HHC Health and Home Care, a division of HHC, is a home health agency for Manhattan, Queens and the Bronx. Services include nursing, physical therapy, speech-language pathology, housekeepers, home health aides, personal care workers and medical supply. The company also runs MetroPlus, a health maintenance organization. HHC is beginning a major modernization of its facilities, which will total $1.3 billion, with new buildings already open for Kings County Hospital and Queens Hospital center, along with modernization projects underway for Harlem Hospital Center, Bellevue Hospital Center, Coney Island Hospital and Jacobi Medical Center, with smaller improvements being implemented at other facilities.

FINANCIALS: Sales and profits are in thousands of dollars—add 000 to get the full amount. 2007 Note: Financial information for 2007 was not available for all companies at press time.

2007 Sales: $	2007 Profits: $	**U.S. Stock Ticker: Government-Owned**
2006 Sales: $5,731,620	2006 Profits: $-1,638,815	**Int'l Ticker:** Int'l Exchange:
2005 Sales: $4,678,288	2005 Profits: $-28,542	Employees:
2004 Sales: $	2004 Profits: $	Fiscal Year Ends: 6/30
2003 Sales: $4,200,000	2003 Profits: $	Parent Company:

SALARIES/BENEFITS:

Pension Plan:	ESOP Stock Plan:	Profit Sharing:	Top Exec. Salary: $	Bonus: $
Savings Plan:	Stock Purch. Plan:		Second Exec. Salary: $	Bonus: $

OTHER THOUGHTS:

Apparent Women Officers or Directors: 2
Hot Spot for Advancement for Women/Minorities:

LOCATIONS: ("Y" = Yes)

West:	Southwest:	Midwest:	Southeast:	Northeast:	International:
				Y	

NEW YORK HEALTH CARE INC www.nyhc.com

Industry Group Code: 621610 **Ranks within this company's industry group:** Sales: 13 Profits: 12

Insurance/HMO/PPO:		Drugs:		Equipment/Supplies:		Hospitals/Clinics:		Services:		Health Care:	
Insurance:		Manufacturer:	Y	Manufacturer:		Acute Care:		Diagnostics:		Home Health:	Y
Managed Care:		Distributor:		Distributor:		Sub-Acute:		Labs/Testing:		Long-Term Care:	
Utilization Management:		Specialty Pharmacy:		Leasing/Finance:		Outpatient Surgery:		Staffing:		Physical Therapy:	Y
Payment Processing:		Vitamins/Nutritionals:	Y	Information Systems:		Physical Rehab. Ctr.:		Waste Disposal:		Physician Prac. Mgmt.:	
		Clinical Trials:				Psychiatric Clinics:		Specialty Svcs.:			

TYPES OF BUSINESS:

Biotherapeutic Agents-Gastrointestinal Treatments
Nursing & Assisted Living Services
Home Health Care

BRANDS/DIVISIONS/AFFILIATES:

BioBalance Corp.
PROBACTRIX

CONTACTS: *Note: Officers with more than one job title may be intentionally listed here more than once.*

Dennis M. O'Donnell, CEO
Jacob Rosenberg, CFO
Shalom Yurman, Dir.-Info. Svcs.
Anthony Acquaviva, Comptroller
Joseph Segel, CEO-Health Care Div.

Phone: 718-375-6700	**Fax:** 718-375-1555
Toll-Free:	
Address: 1850 McDonald Ave., Brooklyn, NY 11223 US	

GROWTH PLANS/SPECIAL FEATURES:

New York Health Care, Inc. (NYHC) is a healthcare company that operates through two business segments: a licensed home health care agency that provides nursing and assisted living services to homebound clients; and a manufacturer and marketer of proprietary biotherapeutic agents for the treatment of gastrointestinal disorders. The biotherapeutic segment works through the firm's BioBalance Corporation subsidiary. BioBalance is a development-stage specialty pharmaceutical company focused on the development of patented biotherapeutic agents for gastrointestinal disorders. These disorders include pouchitis, Irritable Bowel Syndrome (IBS), inflammatory bowel disease and diarrhea caused by antibiotics, chemotherapy or AIDS. Its sole product, PROBACTRIX, is under review by the FDA to be recognized as a medicinal food, which has much less stringent regulations than a drug. The firm's home care services continue to provide meal preparation, light housekeeping, standard nursing services, physical therapy and medicine administration. NYHC's staff is fluent in Spanish, Mandarin, Cantonese, Yiddish and Russian.

FINANCIALS: **Sales and profits are in thousands of dollars—add 000 to get the full amount. 2007 Note: Financial information for 2007 was not available for all companies at press time.**

2007 Sales: $	2007 Profits: $	**U.S. Stock Ticker: BBAL.OB**
2006 Sales: $45,558	2006 Profits: $-3,756	**Int'l Ticker:** Int'l Exchange:
2005 Sales: $44,723	2005 Profits: $-6,322	Employees: 1,783
2004 Sales: $42,286	2004 Profits: $-6,072	Fiscal Year Ends: 12/31
2003 Sales: $45,060	2003 Profits: $-22,052	Parent Company:

SALARIES/BENEFITS:

Pension Plan:	ESOP Stock Plan:	Profit Sharing:	Top Exec. Salary: $155,769	Bonus: $112,500
Savings Plan: Y	Stock Purch. Plan:		Second Exec. Salary: $288,560	Bonus: $271,340

OTHER THOUGHTS:

Apparent Women Officers or Directors:
Hot Spot for Advancement for Women/Minorities:

LOCATIONS: ("Y" = Yes)

West:	Southwest:	Midwest:	Southeast:	Northeast:	International:
				Y	

NEW YORK-PRESBYTERIAN HEALTHCARE SYSTEM

www.nypsystem.org

Industry Group Code: 622110 **Ranks within this company's industry group:** Sales: Profits:

Insurance/HMO/PPO:		Drugs:		Equipment/Supplies:		Hospitals/Clinics:		Services:		Health Care:	
Insurance:		Manufacturer:		Manufacturer:		Acute Care:	Y	Diagnostics:		Home Health:	
Managed Care:		Distributor:		Distributor:		Sub-Acute:	Y	Labs/Testing:		Long-Term Care:	Y
Utilization Management:		Specialty Pharmacy:		Leasing/Finance:		Outpatient Surgery:	Y	Staffing:		Physical Therapy:	Y
Payment Processing:		Vitamins/Nutritionals:		Information Systems:		Physical Rehab. Ctr.:	Y	Waste Disposal:		Physician Prac. Mgmt.:	
		Clinical Trials:				Psychiatric Clinics:	Y	Specialty Svcs.:	Y		

TYPES OF BUSINESS:

Hospitals
Nursing Homes
Rehabilitation Centers

BRANDS/DIVISIONS/AFFILIATES:

New York-Presbyterian Hospital
Weill Medical College-Cornell University
Columbia University College-Physicians & Surgeons

CONTACTS:

Note: Officers with more than one job title may be intentionally listed here more than once.

Herbert Pardes, CEO
Steven J. Corwin, COO/Exec. VP
Herbert Pardes, Pres.
Phyllis R. F. Lantos, CFO/Sr. VP/Treas.
G. Thomas Ferguson, Chief Human Resources Officer/Sr. VP
Aurelia G. Boyer, CIO/Sr. VP
Laurence Berger, VP-Admin.
Maxine Fass, General Counsel/Sr. VP/Chief Legal Officer
Emme Deland, Sr. VP-Strategy
Gary J. Zuar, Sr. VP-Finance
Wayne M. Osten, VP-System Dev.
Eliot J. Lazar, Chief Medical Officer/VP
John J. Mack, Chmn.

Phone: 212-305-2500	**Fax:** 212-746-8235
Toll-Free: 877-697-9355	
Address: 525 E. 68th St., New York, NY 10021-4870 US	

GROWTH PLANS/SPECIAL FEATURES:

The New York-Presbyterian Healthcare System is a not-for profit partnership of hospitals, specialty institutes an continuing care centers serving New York, New Jersey an Connecticut. In total the system includes 43 total facilitie (33 hospitals, two rehab hospitals, four nursing homes an four specialty institutes) all of which are affiliated with tw medical schools: Columbia University College of Physician and Surgeons and Weill Medical College of Corne University. The system had a combined 548,644 inpatien discharges last year, approximately 7 million outpatient visit and a total of over 11,000 licensed beds. NewYork Presbyterian Healthcare System operates 12 nursing homes health care clinics, and rehabilitation centers that it doesn' own. The system's flagship hospital and founder is New York-Presbyterian Hospital, which was formed from the merger of The Presbyterian Hospital and The New York Hospital, the second oldest hospital in the U.S., dating from 1771. New York-Presbyterian Hospital's five campuses are the primary teaching sites for both Columbia's and Cornell's medical colleges. The hospital has leading specialists in every field of medicine and several well-regarded centers o excellence, including AIDS care, aesthetic laser surgery gene therapy, reproductive medicine, trauma, vascula medicine and women's health.

The New York-Presbyterian Healthcare System employs more than 2,500 volunteers through the New York Wei Cornell Center, the Columbia University Center and the Aller Pavilion. Volunteers are used in every area, including ambulatory care clinics, radiology, adult recreation, chilc literacy and food services. Volunteers enjoy various benefits including tax deductions, discounted theater tickets and a letter of commendation to future employers.

FINANCIALS:

Sales and profits are in thousands of dollars—add 000 to get the full amount. 2007 Note: Financial information for 2007 was not available for all companies at press time.

2007 Sales: $	2007 Profits: $	**U.S. Stock Ticker: Nonprofit**
2006 Sales: $	2006 Profits: $	**Int'l Ticker:** Int'l Exchange:
2005 Sales: $	2005 Profits: $	Employees: 53,562
2004 Sales: $	2004 Profits: $	Fiscal Year Ends: 12/31
2003 Sales: $7,060,000	2003 Profits: $	Parent Company:

SALARIES/BENEFITS:

Pension Plan:	ESOP Stock Plan:	Profit Sharing:	Top Exec. Salary: $	Bonus: $
Savings Plan:	Stock Purch. Plan:		Second Exec. Salary: $	Bonus: $

OTHER THOUGHTS:

Apparent Women Officers or Directors: 4
Hot Spot for Advancement for Women/Minorities: Y

LOCATIONS: ("Y" = Yes)

West:	Southwest:	Midwest:	Southeast:	Northeast:	International:
				Y	

Note: Financial information, benefits and other data can change quickly and may vary from those stated here.

NMT MEDICAL INC www.nmtmedical.com

ndustry Group Code: 339113 **Ranks within this company's industry group:** Sales: 99 Profits: 70

surance/HMO/PPO:		Drugs:		Equipment/Supplies:		Hospitals/Clinics:		Services:		Health Care:	
surance:		Manufacturer:		Manufacturer:	Y	Acute Care:		Diagnostics:		Home Health:	
anaged Care:		Distributor:		Distributor:		Sub-Acute:		Labs/Testing:		Long-Term Care:	
tilization Management:		Specialty Pharmacy:		Leasing/Finance:		Outpatient Surgery:		Staffing:		Physical Therapy:	
ayment Processing:		Vitamins/Nutritionals:		Information Systems:		Physical Rehab. Ctr.:		Waste Disposal:		Physician Prac. Mgmt.:	
		Clinical Trials:				Psychiatric Clinics:		Specialty Svcs.:			

YPES OF BUSINESS:

quipment-Surgery
ardiovascular Implant Devices

BRANDS/DIVISIONS/AFFILIATES:

hildren's Medical Center Corporation
ardioSEAL
STARFlex
ligraine Intervention with STARFlex Technology II
BioSTAR

CONTACTS: *Note: Officers with more than one job title may be ntentionally listed here more than once.*

ohn A. Ahern, CEO
ohn A. Ahern, Pres.
ichard E. Davis, CFO/Exec. VP
ohn A. Ahern, Chmn.

hone: 617-737-0930	Fax: 617-737-0924
oll-Free: 800-666-6484	
Address: 27 Wormwood St., Boston, MA 02210-1625 US	

GROWTH PLANS/SPECIAL FEATURES:

NMT Medical, Inc. is a leading medical technology company that designs, develops, manufactures and markets proprietary implant technologies that allow interventional cardiologists to treat cardiac sources of migraine headaches, stroke and other potential brain attacks through minimally invasive, catheter-based procedures. The company's products provide alternative approaches to existing complex treatments; shorten procedures, hospitalization and recovery times; and lower overall treatment costs. NMT's cardiovascular business unit provides interventional cardiologists with proprietary, catheter-based implant technologies designed to minimize or prevent the risk of embolic events. It also serves the pediatric interventional cardiologist with a broad range of cardiac septal repair implants delivered with non-surgical catheter techniques. The company acquired the rights to CardioSEAL, a cardiac septal repair implant, from Children's Medical Center Corporation (CMCC), also known as Children's Hospital Boston; and under the licensing agreement, must pay CMCC royalties on all commercial sales of cardiac septal repair products. CardioSEAL is sold in the U.S., Canada and Europe. STARFlex, sold only in Europe, adds to CardioSEAL a self-adjusting, flexible spring system that adjusts automatically to allow the implant to lie flat against the septum. NMT is conducting a study, named Migraine Intervention with STARFlex Technology (MIST) II, testing the relationship between a cardiac defect known as patent foramen ovale (PFO) and migraines. It is evaluating the safety and effectiveness of STARFlex for treating and preventing migraine headaches in PFO defect patients. In July 2007, the company launched its newest product, BioSTAR, in Europe and Canada. BioSTAR is a collagen based material that helps seal PFO and other atrial level defects, and it is used in combination with STARFlex. The collagen not only helps speed the natural healing process, but acts as a delivery system for drugs, cells, proteins and genes; and approximately 90% to 95% of the product should be eventually absorbed.

FINANCIALS: **Sales and profits are in thousands of dollars—add 000 to get the full amount. 2007 Note: Financial information for 2007 was not available for all companies at press time.**

2007 Sales: $	2007 Profits: $	**U.S. Stock Ticker: NMTI**
2006 Sales: $28,151	2006 Profits: $5,883	**Int'l Ticker:** Int'l Exchange:
2005 Sales: $23,916	2005 Profits: $-7,882	Employees: 115
2004 Sales: $21,460	2004 Profits: $-1,909	Fiscal Year Ends: 12/31
2003 Sales: $22,961	2003 Profits: $-1,150	Parent Company:

SALARIES/BENEFITS:

Pension Plan:	ESOP Stock Plan:	Profit Sharing:	Top Exec. Salary: $400,000	Bonus: $
Savings Plan: Y	Stock Purch. Plan:		Second Exec. Salary: $300,000	Bonus: $135,000

OTHER THOUGHTS:

Apparent Women Officers or Directors:
Hot Spot for Advancement for Women/Minorities:

LOCATIONS: ("Y" = Yes)

West:	Southwest:	Midwest:	Southeast:	Northeast:	International:
				Y	

Note: Financial information, benefits and other data can change quickly and may vary from those stated here.

NOVAMED INC

www.novamed.com

Industry Group Code: 621490 **Ranks within this company's industry group:** Sales: 13 Profits: 11

Insurance/HMO/PPO:		Drugs:		Equipment/Supplies:		Hospitals/Clinics:		Services:		Health Care:	
Insurance:		Manufacturer:		Manufacturer:	Y	Acute Care:		Diagnostics:		Home Health:	
Managed Care:		Distributor:		Distributor:	Y	Sub-Acute:		Labs/Testing:		Long-Term Care:	
Utilization Management:		Specialty Pharmacy:		Leasing/Finance:		Outpatient Surgery:	Y	Staffing:		Physical Therapy:	
Payment Processing:		Vitamins/Nutritionals:		Information Systems:		Physical Rehab. Ctr.:		Waste Disposal:		Physician Prac. Mgmt.:	
		Clinical Trials:				Psychiatric Clinics:		Specialty Svcs.:	Y		

TYPES OF BUSINESS:

Outpatient Surgery
Eye-Care Services
Laser Vision Correction
Corrective Lenses Labs
Eye-Care Products Distribution
Purchasing and Supply Chain Services
Marketing Services

BRANDS/DIVISIONS/AFFILIATES:

NovaMed Eyecare, Inc.
NovaMed Management Services

CONTACTS: *Note: Officers with more than one job title may be intentionally listed here more than once.*

Thomas S. Hall, CEO
Thomas S. Hall, Pres.
Scott T. Macomber, CFO/Exec. VP
Robert D. Watson, VP-Mktg.
John W. Lawrence, Jr., General Counsel/Sr. VP
E. Michele Vickery, Exec. VP-Oper.
Thomas J. Chirillo, Sr. VP-Corp. Dev.
John P. Hart, Corp. Controller/VP
William Kennedy, Sr. VP-Bus. Dev.
Frank L. Soppa, VP-Optical Services Group
Jack M. Clark, Jr., Exec. VP/Chief Revenue Officer
Thomas S. Hall, Chmn.

Phone: 312-664-4100	**Fax:** 312-664-4250
Toll-Free: 800-388-4133	
Address: 980 N. Michigan Ave., Ste. 1620, Chicago, IL 60611 US	

GROWTH PLANS/SPECIAL FEATURES:

NovaMed, Inc. is a health care services company that strives to acquire, develop and operate ambulatory surgery centers (ASCs) in joint ownership with physicians throughout the U.S. Its facilities are comprised of 37 primarily practice based ASCs in 18 states. All but 10 of the locations are single-specialty ophthalmic surgical facilities where eye-care professionals perform surgical procedures, such as cataract and laser vision correction. NovaMed provides excimer lasers to eye-care professionals for use in laser vision correction surgery through fixed-site laser service agreements. The company continues to expand its ASC services into specialties such as orthopedics, gastroenterology, urology, pain management, plastic surgery and gynecology. In addition to its ASCs, NovaMed also owns and operates an optical products purchasing organization; a marketing products and services business which provides eye clinics with brochures, videos and advertising design services; and an optical laboratory business that specializes in surfacing and finishing corrective eyeglass lenses, and selling them to ophthalmologists, optometrists, opticians and optical retail chains. The firm offers its management services to two eye care practices by providing business, information technology, administrative and financial services in exchange for a management fee. NovaMed is constantly expanding its operations through new ambulatory surgery center acquisitions: in September 2006, it acquired an ASC located in Sandusky, Ohio; in October 2006, it acquired ASCs in Cleveland, Tennessee and Gainesville, Florida; in November 2006, it bought an ASC in Warrensburg, Missouri; in December 2006, it obtained an ASC in Sebring, Florida; and in June 2007, it purchased an ASC in Portage, Michigan.

FINANCIALS: **Sales and profits are in thousands of dollars—add 000 to get the full amount. 2007 Note: Financial information for 2007 was not available for all companies at press time.**

2007 Sales: $	2007 Profits: $	**U.S. Stock Ticker: NOVA**
2006 Sales: $108,434	2006 Profits: $5,737	**Int'l Ticker:** Int'l Exchange:
2005 Sales: $81,226	2005 Profits: $5,589	Employees: 666
2004 Sales: $63,648	2004 Profits: $4,459	Fiscal Year Ends: 12/31
2003 Sales: $55,506	2003 Profits: $3,491	Parent Company:

SALARIES/BENEFITS:

Pension Plan:	ESOP Stock Plan:	Profit Sharing:	Top Exec. Salary: $500,000	Bonus: $225,000
Savings Plan: Y	Stock Purch. Plan: Y		Second Exec. Salary: $265,308	Bonus: $83,633

OTHER THOUGHTS:

Apparent Women Officers or Directors:
Hot Spot for Advancement for Women/Minorities: Y

LOCATIONS: ("Y" = Yes)

West:	Southwest:	Midwest:	Southeast:	Northeast:	International:
Y	Y	Y	Y	Y	

NOVARTIS AG

www.novartis.com

Industry Group Code: 325412 **Ranks within this company's industry group:** Sales: 5 Profits: 4

Insurance/HMO/PPO:		Drugs:		Equipment/Supplies:		Hospitals/Clinics:		Services:		Health Care:	
Insurance:		Manufacturer:	Y	Manufacturer:	Y	Acute Care:		Diagnostics:		Home Health:	
Managed Care:		Distributor:		Distributor:		Sub-Acute:		Labs/Testing:		Long-Term Care:	
Utilization Management:		Specialty Pharmacy:		Leasing/Finance:		Outpatient Surgery:		Staffing:		Physical Therapy:	
Payment Processing:		Vitamins/Nutritionals:	Y	Information Systems:		Physical Rehab. Ctr.:		Waste Disposal:		Physician Prac. Mgmt.:	
		Clinical Trials:				Psychiatric Clinics:		Specialty Svcs.:			

TYPES OF BUSINESS:

Drugs-Diversified
Therapeutic Drug Discovery
Therapeutic Drug Manufacturing
Generic Drugs
Over-the-Counter Drugs
Ophthalmic Products
Nutritional Products
Veterinary Products

BRANDS/DIVISIONS/AFFILIATES:

CIBA Vision
Grand Laboratories, Inc.
ImmTech Biologics, Inc.
Novartis Institute for Biomedical Research, Inc.
Sandoz
Sabex
Gerber Products Co.
Chiron Corp.

CONTACTS: *Note: Officers with more than one job title may be intentionally listed here more than once.*

Daniel Vasella, CEO
Alex Gorsky, COO
Daniel Vasella, Pres.
Raymund Breu, CFO
Jurgen Brokatzky-Geiger, Dir.-Human Resources
Urs Barlocher, Dir.-Legal & Tax Affairs
Ann Bailey, Dir.-Public Affairs & Corp. Comm.
Thomas Ebeling, CEO, Pharmaceuticals
Paul Choffat, CEO, Consumer Health
Mark Fishman, Pres., Novartis Institute for Biomedical Research
Andreas Rummelt, CEO, Sandoz
Daniel Vasella, Chmn.

Phone: 41-61-324-1111 **Fax:** 41-61-324-8001
Toll-Free:
Address: Lichtstrasse 35, Basel, CH-4056 Switzerland

GROWTH PLANS/SPECIAL FEATURES:

Novartis AG (NVS) researches and develops pharmaceuticals as well as a large number of consumer and animal health products. NVS operates in four segments: pharmaceuticals; vaccines and diagnostics; consumer health; and Sandoz Generics. Through its pharmaceuticals division, NVS develops, manufactures and markets prescription medications in a variety of areas, which include treatments for cardiovascular diseases, neurological disorders, respiratory conditions, dermatological conditions and infectious diseases. NVS also provides specialty medications in the fields of oncology, hematology, transplantation, immunology and ophthalmics. The vaccines division produces a large number of vaccinations for influenza, meningitis, rabies and tick-borne encephalitis. In the consumer health sector, NVS manufactures over-the-counter medication such as Maalox and Triaminic, animal health products, medical nutrition products, infant products and CIBA Vision. CIBA Vision is a subsidiary of NVS which researches and develops eye care products, lens care products and ophthalmic surgical products. The animal health division also provides solutions for pest control and offers a number of medications for both pets and farm animals to prevent parasitic and bacterial infections. Another sector of consumer health includes Gerber Products Co., a popular brand providing both infant care and nutrition. Sandoz Generics, is engaged in developing and manufacturing generic pharmaceuticals and currently holds a product list of over 840 compounds in over 5,000 dosage forms. In late 2006, NVS agreed to sell its medical nutrition business to Nestle and also made plans in early 2007 to relocate its vaccines and diagnostics division headquarters to Cambridge, Massachusetts. Recently, the FDA issued its approval for distribution of Tekturna, a high blood pressure medication, and Procleix Tigris System, a blood screening for the West Nile virus. In March 2007, the FDA asked NVS to remove Zelnorm from the U.S. market.

Novartis offers its employees child care, elderly care support, tuition reimbursement and health and fitness programs.

FINANCIALS: **Sales and profits are in thousands of dollars—add 000 to get the full amount. 2007 Note: Financial information for 2007 was not available for all companies at press time.**

2007 Sales: $	2007 Profits: $	**U.S. Stock Ticker: NVS**
2006 Sales: $36,031,000	2006 Profits: $7,202,000	**Int'l Ticker: NOVN** Int'l Exchange: Zurich-SWX
2005 Sales: $31,005,000	2005 Profits: $6,141,000	Employees: 100,735
2004 Sales: $27,126,000	2004 Profits: $5,601,000	Fiscal Year Ends: 12/31
2003 Sales: $24,864,000	2003 Profits: $5,016,000	Parent Company:

SALARIES/BENEFITS:

Pension Plan: Y	ESOP Stock Plan:	Profit Sharing:	Top Exec. Salary: $	Bonus: $
Savings Plan:	Stock Purch. Plan:		Second Exec. Salary: $	Bonus: $

OTHER THOUGHTS:

Apparent Women Officers or Directors: 1
Hot Spot for Advancement for Women/Minorities:

LOCATIONS: ("Y" = Yes)

West:	Southwest:	Midwest:	Southeast:	Northeast:	International:
Y		Y	Y	Y	Y

Note: Financial information, benefits and other data can change quickly and may vary from those stated here.

NOVATION LLC (VHA INC)

www.novationco.com

Industry Group Code: 561400 **Ranks within this company's industry group:** Sales: Profits:

Insurance/HMO/PPO:		Drugs:		Equipment/Supplies:		Hospitals/Clinics:		Services:		Health Care:	
Insurance:		Manufacturer:		Manufacturer:		Acute Care:		Diagnostics:		Home Health:	
Managed Care:		Distributor:	Y	Distributor:	Y	Sub-Acute:		Labs/Testing:		Long-Term Care:	
Utilization Management:		Specialty Pharmacy:		Leasing/Finance:		Outpatient Surgery:		Staffing:		Physical Therapy:	
Payment Processing:		Vitamins/Nutritionals:		Information Systems:		Physical Rehab. Ctr.:		Waste Disposal:		Physician Prac. Mgmt.:	
		Clinical Trials:				Psychiatric Clinics:		Specialty Svcs.:	Y		

TYPES OF BUSINESS:

Medical Supplies Distributor
Pharmaceuticals Distributor
Supply Chain Management
Health Care Consulting
Health Care Publications

BRANDS/DIVISIONS/AFFILIATES:

Marketplace@Novation
NOVAPLUS
University HealthSystem Consortium
VHA, Inc.

CONTACTS: *Note: Officers with more than one job title may be intentionally listed here more than once.*

Joellyn Willis, Pres.
Alex Latham, VP-Info. Svcs.
Jill Witter, General Counsel
Jo Klein, VP-Strategy, Planning & Research
Kristin Lucido, Dir.-Public Rel.
Mike Woodhouse, Dir.-Financial Svcs.
Eldon Petersen, Group Sr. VP
Mick Hunt, VP-Pharmacy
Maryann S. Restino, VP-Contract & Program Svcs.
Kevin Stanley, VP-Contract & Program Svcs.
Larry Dooley, VP-Supplier Rel.

Phone: 972-581-5000	**Fax:** 972-581-5013
Toll-Free: 888-766-8283	
Address: 125 E. John Carpenter Fwy., Ste. 1400, Irving, TX 75062 US	

GROWTH PLANS/SPECIAL FEATURES:

Novation, LLC, a joint venture between Universit HealthSystem Consortium(UHC) and VHA, Inc., is a leadin medical supply chain management company. It supplie over 2,500 health care organizations, including VH hospitals, and UHC, one of the nation's leading healt benefits services. The company's NOVAPLUS private labe offers over 1,300 items. Novation, through over 60 suppliers, can provide up to 85% of the products that it clients use in their medical practices, including medical an surgical supplies, pharmaceuticals, diagnostic imagin machines, business products, laboratory products, dietar and food products and capital equipment. In addition Novation offers e-commerce services for its customers an suppliers, a health care management consultancy, a servic delivery team and a variety of publications Marketplace@Novation is a members-only, Internet-base service that allows health care suppliers to provide product at a lower price. Novation also provides contracting service to over 10,000 health care and education customers o Provista, a group purchasing and business solution organization jointly owned by VHA and UHC and formed t serve organizations that are not members of either alliance The company's health care consultancy service teache organizations how to reduce cost and increase safety. It service delivery division manages the relationships betwee various facilities and their suppliers and helps to implemen cost-reduction strategies. Novation also publishe newsletters, product shortages and recalls, industry news and the latest in clinical information. VHA owns approximately 75% of Novation.

FINANCIALS: Sales and profits are in thousands of dollars—add 000 to get the full amount. 2007 Note: Financial information for 2007 was not available for all companies at press time.

2007 Sales: $	2007 Profits: $	**U.S. Stock Ticker: Joint Venture**
2006 Sales: $	2006 Profits: $	**Int'l Ticker:** Int'l Exchange:
2005 Sales: $	2005 Profits: $	Employees:
2004 Sales: $	2004 Profits: $	Fiscal Year Ends: 12/31
2003 Sales: $	2003 Profits: $	Parent Company: VHA INC

SALARIES/BENEFITS:

Pension Plan:	ESOP Stock Plan:	Profit Sharing:	Top Exec. Salary: $	Bonus: $
Savings Plan:	Stock Purch. Plan:		Second Exec. Salary: $	Bonus: $

OTHER THOUGHTS:

Apparent Women Officers or Directors: 6
Hot Spot for Advancement for Women/Minorities: Y

LOCATIONS: ("Y" = Yes)

West:	Southwest:	Midwest:	Southeast:	Northeast:	International:
Y	Y	Y	Y	Y	

NOVO-NORDISK AS www.novonordisk.com

ndustry Group Code: 325412 **Ranks within this company's industry group:** Sales: 18 Profits: 18

nsurance/HMO/PPO:		Drugs:		Equipment/Supplies:		Hospitals/Clinics:		Services:		Health Care:	
nsurance:		Manufacturer:	Y	Manufacturer:	Y	Acute Care:		Diagnostics:		Home Health:	
Managed Care:		Distributor:		Distributor:		Sub-Acute:		Labs/Testing:		Long-Term Care:	
Jtilization Management:		Specialty Pharmacy:		Leasing/Finance:		Outpatient Surgery:		Staffing:		Physical Therapy:	
Payment Processing:		Vitamins/Nutritionals:		Information Systems:		Physical Rehab. Ctr.:		Waste Disposal:		Physician Prac. Mgmt.:	
		Clinical Trials:				Psychiatric Clinics:		Specialty Svcs.:	Y		

TYPES OF BUSINESS:

Drugs-Diabetes
Hormone Replacement Therapy
Growth Disorder Drugs
Hemophilia Drugs
Insulin Delivery Systems
Educational & Training Services

BRANDS/DIVISIONS/AFFILIATES:

NovoPen
FlexPen
Norditropin SimpleXx
NovoSeven
Activelle
Trisequens
Estrofem
Novo-Nordisk Research US

CONTACTS: *Note: Officers with more than one job title may be intentionally listed here more than once.*

Lars R. Sorensen, CEO
Kare Schultz, COO/Exec. VP
Lars R. Sorensen, Pres.
Jesper Brandgaard, CFO/Exec. VP
Mads K. Thomsen, Chief Science Officer/Exec. VP
Lise Kingo, Exec. VP/Chief of Staff
Sten Scheibye, Chmn.

Phone: 45-4444-8888 **Fax:** 45-4449-0555
Toll-Free:
Address: 2880 Novo Alle, Basgvaerd, DK-2880 Denmark

GROWTH PLANS/SPECIAL FEATURES:

Novo-Nordisk AS focuses on developing treatments for diabetes, hemostasis management, growth hormone therapy and hormone replacement therapy. With its affiliates, the company has employees in 79 countries, and it markets its products in 179 countries. The firm is a world leader in insulin manufacturing and has the broadest diabetes product line in the world. The NovoPen and FlexPen products are pen-like, multiple-dose injectors that allow patients to easily inject themselves with insulin or hormones. Novo-Nordisk's growth hormone replacement product, Norditropin SimpleXx, is a premixed liquid growth hormone designed to provide the most flexible and accurate dosing. The company's NovoSeven product, a treatment for hemophilia, is a recombinant coagulation factor that enables coagulation to proceed in the absence of natural factors. The firm also manufactures post-menopausal hormone replacement therapy products, including Activelle, Kliogest, Trisequens, Estrofem and Vagifem. In addition, the company offers educational services and training materials for both patients and health care professionals. The company has a licensing agreement with ZymoGenetics for microarrays. Novo-Nordisk also owns and operates a dedicated hemostasis research center in the U.S. The facility, Novo-Nordisk Research US, is the first in the country dedicated to life-threatening bleeding. In February 2007, Novo-Nordisk divested its ownership of Dako A/S, a cancer diagnosis company.

Novo-Nordisk offers its U.S. employees health, life, dental, auto and supplemental insurance, as well as tuition reimbursement.

FINANCIALS: Sales and profits are in thousands of dollars—add 000 to get the full amount. 2007 Note: Financial information for 2007 was not available for all companies at press time.

2007 Sales: $	2007 Profits: $	**U.S. Stock Ticker: NVO**
2006 Sales: $6,913,700	2006 Profits: $1,126,020	**Int'l Ticker: NOVO B** Int'l Exchange: Copenhagen-CSE
2005 Sales: $5,446,472	2005 Profits: $946,073	Employees: 22,500
2004 Sales: $5,324,285	2004 Profits: $859,229	Fiscal Year Ends: 12/31
2003 Sales: $4,501,000	2003 Profits: $824,000	Parent Company:

SALARIES/BENEFITS:

Pension Plan:	ESOP Stock Plan:	Profit Sharing:	Top Exec. Salary: $	Bonus: $
Savings Plan: Y	Stock Purch. Plan:		Second Exec. Salary: $	Bonus: $

OTHER THOUGHTS:

Apparent Women Officers or Directors: 2
Hot Spot for Advancement for Women/Minorities: Y

LOCATIONS: ("Y" = Yes)

West:	Southwest:	Midwest:	Southeast:	Northeast:	International:
Y	Y	Y	Y	Y	Y

NYER MEDICAL GROUP INC www.nyermedicalgroup.com

Industry Group Code: 421450 **Ranks within this company's industry group:** Sales: 7 Profits: 6

Insurance/HMO/PPO:		Drugs:		Equipment/Supplies:		Hospitals/Clinics:		Services:		Health Care:	
Insurance:		Manufacturer:		Manufacturer:		Acute Care:		Diagnostics:		Home Health:	
Managed Care:		Distributor:		Distributor:	Y	Sub-Acute:		Labs/Testing:		Long-Term Care:	
Utilization Management:		Specialty Pharmacy:	Y	Leasing/Finance:		Outpatient Surgery:		Staffing:		Physical Therapy:	
Payment Processing:		Vitamins/Nutritionals:		Information Systems:		Physical Rehab. Ctr.:		Waste Disposal:		Physician Prac. Mgmt.:	
		Clinical Trials:				Psychiatric Clinics:		Specialty Svcs.:			

TYPES OF BUSINESS:

Distribution-Medical Equipment
Home Health Supplies
Surgical/Laboratory Supplies
Fire, Police & Rescue Equipment
Drug Stores
Online Medical Supply Sales
Emergency Medical Services Supplies

BRANDS/DIVISIONS/AFFILIATES:

ADCO Surgical Supply, Inc.
ADCO South Medical Supplies, Inc.
Eaton Apothecary
D.A.W., Inc.
medicalmailorder.com
Connors Pharmacy

CONTACTS: *Note: Officers with more than one job title may be intentionally listed here more than once.*

Karen L. Wright, CEO
Karen L. Wright, Pres.
Karen L. Wright, VP-Oper.
Karen L. Wright, Treas./VP-Finance
Wayne Gunter, VP
Michael Curry, VP
David Dumochel, VP

Phone: 207-942-5273	**Fax:**
Toll-Free:	
Address: 1292 Hammond St., Bangor, ME 04401 US	

GROWTH PLANS/SPECIAL FEATURES:

Nyer Medical Group, Inc. (NMG) is a holding company tha operates medical supply subsidiaries and a chain o pharmacies. It boasts two wholly-owned subsidiaries anc one majority owned subsidiary: ADCO Surgical Supply, Inc. ADCO South Medical Supplies, Inc.; and D.A.W., Inc., 80% owned by NMG. Its ADCO Surgical Supply and ADCC South Medical Supplies subsidiaries sell surgical anc medical equipment and supplies, wholesale and retail, tc health care facilities throughout New England, Florida anc worldwide through its website medicalmailorder.com. ADCC derives 90% of its revenues from sales to institutiona customers (primarily nursing homes and physician offices) while the balance comes from its retail and home healt centers. ADCO and ADCO South provide over 4,50C combined stock items and special orders for non stock items Doing business as Eaton Apothecary, subsidiary D.A.W., Inc operates a chain of 15 pharmacy drug stores located in the greater Boston area and has contracts to manage three pharmacies owned by federally qualified health centers. Eaton additionally has contracts to provide pharmacy services to patients of three other federally qualified health centers. Pursuant to the contracts, Eaton maintains an inventory owned by the health centers for the purpose o dispensing prescriptions to health center patients. The vas majority of the prescriptions dispensed are dispensed to uninsured patients. The health centers then bill the Massachusetts Uncompensated Care Pool for the dispensed prescriptions. Eaton also operates three Medicine-On-Time medication management systems, which cater to elderly clients who are unable to manage their medication regimens and yet are not frail enough for nursing homes. In April 2006, Eaton acquired Connors Pharmacy in Gloucester, Massachusetts. In July 2007, Nyer announced that Eaton has added three new pharmacies, bringing its total number of pharmacies to 18.

FINANCIALS: Sales and profits are in thousands of dollars—add 000 to get the full amount. 2007 Note: Financial information for 2007 was not available for all companies at press time.

2007 Sales: $	2007 Profits: $	**U.S. Stock Ticker: NYER**
2006 Sales: $63,597	2006 Profits: $ 858	**Int'l Ticker:** Int'l Exchange:
2005 Sales: $61,184	2005 Profits: $ 224	Employees: 278
2004 Sales: $61,687	2004 Profits: $- 425	Fiscal Year Ends: 6/30
2003 Sales: $59,900	2003 Profits: $ 500	Parent Company:

SALARIES/BENEFITS:

Pension Plan:	ESOP Stock Plan:	Profit Sharing:	Top Exec. Salary: $148,930	Bonus: $8,710
Savings Plan: Y	Stock Purch. Plan:		Second Exec. Salary: $148,930	Bonus: $8,710

OTHER THOUGHTS:

Apparent Women Officers or Directors: 1
Hot Spot for Advancement for Women/Minorities:

LOCATIONS: ("Y" = Yes)

West:	Southwest:	Midwest:	Southeast:	Northeast:	International:
Y			Y	Y	

ODYSSEY HEALTHCARE INC

www.odsyhealth.com

ndustry Group Code: 621610 **Ranks within this company's industry group:** Sales: 6 Profits: 8

nsurance/HMO/PPO:		Drugs:		Equipment/Supplies:		Hospitals/Clinics:		Services:		Health Care:	
nsurance:		Manufacturer:		Manufacturer:		Acute Care:		Diagnostics:		Home Health:	
Managed Care:		Distributor:		Distributor:	Y	Sub-Acute:		Labs/Testing:		Long-Term Care:	Y
Jtilization Management:		Specialty Pharmacy:		Leasing/Finance:		Outpatient Surgery:		Staffing:		Physical Therapy:	Y
Payment Processing:		Vitamins/Nutritionals:		Information Systems:		Physical Rehab. Ctr.:		Waste Disposal:		Physician Prac. Mgmt.:	
		Clinical Trials:				Psychiatric Clinics:		Specialty Svcs.:	Y		

TYPES OF BUSINESS:

Hospice Care Services
Medical Supplies & Equipment

BRANDS/DIVISIONS/AFFILIATES:

CONTACTS:

Note: Officers with more than one job title may be intentionally listed here more than once.

Robert Lefton, CEO
Deborah A. Hoffpauir, COO/Sr. VP
Robert Lefton, Pres.
R. Dick Allison, CFO/Sr. VP
Brenda A. Belger, VP-Human Resources
W. Bradley Bickham, General Counsel/VP
Woodrin Grossman, Sr. VP-Strategy & Dev.
Kathleen A. Ventre, Dir.-Clinical Affairs
Richard R. Burnham, Chmn.

Phone: 214-922-9711	**Fax:** 214-922-9752
Toll-Free: 888-922-9711	
Address: 717 N. Harwood St., Ste. 1500, Dallas, TX 75201 US	

GROWTH PLANS/SPECIAL FEATURES:

Odyssey HealthCare, Inc. is a provider of hospice care from 81 Medicare-certified hospice programs in 30 states, with over 8,400 patients. Hospice services provide a wide range of care and services to terminally ill patients and their families. Odyssey assigns each of its patients to an interdisciplinary team that assesses the clinical, psychosocial and spiritual needs of the patient and his or her family; develops a plan of care; and delivers, monitors and coordinates that plan. This team typically includes a physician, a patient care manager, one or more nurses, one or more home health aides, a medical social worker, a chaplain, a homemaker and one or more specially trained volunteers. Odyssey provides symptom-relieving medication and medical supplies and equipment associated with the terminal illness, such as bandages, catheters, oxygen, hospital bed, wheelchair and walkers, at no cost to the patient. The company is dependent on the federal Medicare program, deriving roughly 92.7% of revenue from it in 2006. In 2006, Odyssey acquired one hospice program that it merged into its existing one in Valdosta, Georgia. In 2007, Odyssey acquired another small hospice program that it merged into its existing program in Athens, Georgia.

Odyssey offers its employees a 401(k) plan; an employee stock purchase plan; dental, vision, medical and life insurance; flexible spending accounts; tuition reimbursement; and short- and long- term disability insurance.

FINANCIALS:

Sales and profits are in thousands of dollars—add 000 to get the full amount. 2007 Note: Financial information for 2007 was not available for all companies at press time.

2007 Sales: $	2007 Profits: $	**U.S. Stock Ticker: ODSY**
2006 Sales: $409,831	2006 Profits: $19,729	**Int'l Ticker:** Int'l Exchange:
2005 Sales: $378,073	2005 Profits: $18,556	Employees: 5,033
2004 Sales: $340,180	2004 Profits: $34,996	Fiscal Year Ends: 12/31
2003 Sales: $274,309	2003 Profits: $31,207	Parent Company:

SALARIES/BENEFITS:

Pension Plan:	ESOP Stock Plan:	Profit Sharing:	Top Exec. Salary: $500,000	Bonus: $
Savings Plan: Y	Stock Purch. Plan: Y		Second Exec. Salary: $324,450	Bonus: $

OTHER THOUGHTS:

Apparent Women Officers or Directors: 3
Hot Spot for Advancement for Women/Minorities: Y

LOCATIONS: ("Y" = Yes)

West:	Southwest:	Midwest:	Southeast:	Northeast:	International:
Y	Y	Y	Y	Y	

Note: Financial information, benefits and other data can change quickly and may vary from those stated here.

OHIOHEALTH CORPORATION www.ohiohealth.com

Industry Group Code: 622110 **Ranks within this company's industry group:** Sales: Profits:

Insurance/HMO/PPO:		Drugs:		Equipment/Supplies:		Hospitals/Clinics:		Services:		Health Care:	
Insurance:	Y	Manufacturer:		Manufacturer:		Acute Care:	Y	Diagnostics:		Home Health:	Y
Managed Care:		Distributor:		Distributor:		Sub-Acute:		Labs/Testing:		Long-Term Care:	Y
Utilization Management:		Specialty Pharmacy:		Leasing/Finance:		Outpatient Surgery:	Y	Staffing:		Physical Therapy:	
Payment Processing:		Vitamins/Nutritionals:		Information Systems:		Physical Rehab. Ctr.:	Y	Waste Disposal:		Physician Prac. Mgmt.:	
		Clinical Trials:				Psychiatric Clinics:		Specialty Svcs.:			

TYPES OF BUSINESS:

Hospitals-General
Health Insurance
Home Health Care
Hospice Services
Long-Term Care
Surgery Centers
Rehabilitation Services

BRANDS/DIVISIONS/AFFILIATES:

HomeReach
WorkHealth
OhioHealth Group
HealthReach PPO
Doctors Hospital Nelsonville
Grant Medical Center
Hardin Memorial Hospital
Southern Ohio Medical Center

CONTACTS:

Note: Officers with more than one job title may be intentionally listed here more than once.

David Blom, CEO
Robert P. Millen, COO/Sr. VP
David Blom, Pres.
Mike Louge, CFO/Sr. VP
Debra P. Moore, Sr. VP-Human Resources
Michael Krouse, CIO
Mark Hopkins, Mgr.-Media Rel.
Bob Gilbert, System VP-Ambulatory Services
Mark R. Montoney, Chief Medical Officer
Jeff Kaplan, Sr. VP/Chief Advancement Officer
Cheryl Herbert, Pres., Dublin Methodist Hospital

Phone: 614-544-4455	**Fax:** 614-566-6938
Toll-Free:	
Address: 1087 Dennison Ave., Columbus, OH 43201 US	

GROWTH PLANS/SPECIAL FEATURES:

OhioHealth Corporation, founded in 1891, operates nine acute care hospitals in Ohio, alongside five affiliate hospitals. Together, its hospitals provide outpatient health care, surgery centers, home health services, long-term care facilities and hospice services. The company has partnerships with approximately 2,300 physicians and operates 2,000 acute care beds, with total admissions of approximately 108,000. OhioHealth also owns HomeReach, a home health care provider; WorkHealth, a workers compensation and rehabilitation services provider; and OhioHealth Group, a joint venture with the Medical Group of Ohio that manages HealthReach PPO. OhioHealth owns Doctors Hospital at Nelsonville, Doctors Hospital, Grant Medical Center, Hardin Memorial Hospital, Marion General Hospital, Riverside Methodist Hospital and Southern Ohio Medical Center, Grady Memorial Hospital and Dublin Methodist Hospital (opening in January 2008). In September, 2007, the company announced a physician at its Riverside Methodist Hospital became the world's first physician to treat a common form of peripheral arterial disease (PAD) with a new device that hopes to improve outcomes, speed recovery and may minimize the risk of complications.

FINANCIALS:

Sales and profits are in thousands of dollars—add 000 to get the full amount. 2007 Note: Financial information for 2007 was not available for all companies at press time.

2007 Sales: $	2007 Profits: $	**U.S. Stock Ticker: Nonprofit**
2006 Sales: $	2006 Profits: $	**Int'l Ticker:** Int'l Exchange:
2005 Sales: $	2005 Profits: $	Employees: 15,000
2004 Sales: $	2004 Profits: $	Fiscal Year Ends: 6/30
2003 Sales: $1,036,000	2003 Profits: $	Parent Company:

SALARIES/BENEFITS:

Pension Plan: Y	ESOP Stock Plan:	Profit Sharing:	Top Exec. Salary: $	Bonus: $
Savings Plan: Y	Stock Purch. Plan:		Second Exec. Salary: $	Bonus: $

OTHER THOUGHTS:

Apparent Women Officers or Directors: 2
Hot Spot for Advancement for Women/Minorities: Y

LOCATIONS: ("Y" = Yes)

West:	Southwest:	Midwest:	Southeast:	Northeast:	International:
		Y			

OMNICARE INC

www.omnicare.com

Industry Group Code: 446110A **Ranks within this company's industry group:** Sales: 1 Profits: 1

Insurance/HMO/PPO:		Drugs:		Equipment/Supplies:		Hospitals/Clinics:		Services:		Health Care:	
Insurance:		Manufacturer:	Y	Manufacturer:		Acute Care:		Diagnostics:		Home Health:	
Managed Care:		Distributor:	Y	Distributor:	Y	Sub-Acute:		Labs/Testing:	Y	Long-Term Care:	
Utilization Management:		Specialty Pharmacy:	Y	Leasing/Finance:		Outpatient Surgery:		Staffing:		Physical Therapy:	
Payment Processing:	Y	Vitamins/Nutritionals:		Information Systems:	Y	Physical Rehab. Ctr.:		Waste Disposal:		Physician Prac. Mgmt.:	
		Clinical Trials:				Psychiatric Clinics:		Specialty Svcs.:	Y		

TYPES OF BUSINESS:

Specialty Pharmacies
Infusion Therapy
Consulting Services
Pharmaceutical Research
Medical Records Services
Billing Services
Pharmaceutical Distribution
Software Information Systems

BRANDS/DIVISIONS/AFFILIATES:

Omnicare Clinical Research

CONTACTS: *Note: Officers with more than one job title may be intentionally listed here more than once.*

Joel F. Gemunder, CEO
Patrick E. Keefe, COO/Exec. VP
Joel F. Gemunder, Pres.
David W. Froesel, Jr., CFO/Sr. VP
Kirk Pompeo, Sr. VP-Sales & Mktg.
D. Michael Laney, VP-MIS
Mark G. Kobasuk, General Counsel/VP
Patrick E. Keefe, Exec. VP-Oper.
Tracy Finn, VP-Strategic Planning & Dev.
Paul W. Baldwin, VP-Public Affairs
Bradley S. Abbott, Controller/VP/Group Exec.-Corp. Financial Svcs.
Cheryl D. Hodges, Sr. VP/Corp. Sec.
Donald E. Amorosi, VP-Trade Rel.
Dale B. Evans, VP/CEO-Omnicare Clinical Research
W. Gary Erwin, Pres., Omnicare Senior Health Outcomes
Edward Hutton, Chmn.
Daniel J. Maloney, VP-Purchasing

Phone: 859-392-3300 **Fax:**
Toll-Free:
Address: 100 E. RiverCenter Blvd., Ste. 1600, Covington, KY 41101 US

GROWTH PLANS/SPECIAL FEATURES:

Omnicare, Inc. is a leading provider of geriatric pharmaceuticals and related geriatric pharmacy services to long-term care institutions such as skilled nursing facilities, assisted living facilities and retirement centers, as well as hospitals and other institutional health care facilities. The firm's main business segment, pharmacy services, provides pharmaceutical distribution, related pharmacy consulting, data management services and medical supplies to long-term care facilities. Services include purchasing, repackaging and dispensing pharmaceuticals, computerized medical record keeping and third-party billing for residents in the institutions. Omnicare also provides consultant pharmacist services, including evaluating monthly patient drug therapy, monitoring the drug distribution system within the nursing facility, assisting in compliance with state and federal regulations and providing proprietary clinical and health management programs. In addition, Omnicare's pharmacy services segment provides ancillary services, such as providing medications and nutrition for intravenous administration (infusion therapy services) and furnishing respiratory therapy services, medical supplies and equipment, clinical care planning, financial software information systems, pharmaceutical informatics services, mail order pharmacy and other pharmacy distribution and patient assistance services for specialty pharmaceuticals. Another business segment, contract research organization services, or CRO services, is a leading international provider of comprehensive product development and research services to client companies in the pharmaceutical, biotechnology, medical device and diagnostics industries. Subsidiary Omnicare Clinical Research has expertise in various fields including cardiovascular, anti-infectives, oncology, central nervous system and geriatrics areas.

FINANCIALS: **Sales and profits are in thousands of dollars—add 000 to get the full amount. 2007 Note: Financial information for 2007 was not available for all companies at press time.**

2007 Sales: $	2007 Profits: $	**U.S. Stock Ticker: OCR**
2006 Sales: $6,492,993	2006 Profits: $183,572	**Int'l Ticker:** Int'l Exchange:
2005 Sales: $5,292,782	2005 Profits: $226,491	Employees: 17,100
2004 Sales: $4,119,891	2004 Profits: $236,011	Fiscal Year Ends: 12/31
2003 Sales: $3,499,174	2003 Profits: $194,368	Parent Company:

SALARIES/BENEFITS:

Pension Plan: Y	ESOP Stock Plan:	Profit Sharing:	Top Exec. Salary: $1,600,000	Bonus: $
Savings Plan: Y	Stock Purch. Plan:		Second Exec. Salary: $472,000	Bonus: $

OTHER THOUGHTS:

Apparent Women Officers or Directors: 3
Hot Spot for Advancement for Women/Minorities: Y

LOCATIONS: ("Y" = Yes)

West:	Southwest:	Midwest:	Southeast:	Northeast:	International:
Y	Y	Y	Y	Y	Y

OPTICARE HEALTH SYSTEMS www.opticare.com

Industry Group Code: 621490 **Ranks within this company's industry group:** Sales: Profits:

Insurance/HMO/PPO:		Drugs:		Equipment/Supplies:		Hospitals/Clinics:		Services:		Health Care:	
Insurance:	Y	Manufacturer:		Manufacturer:		Acute Care:		Diagnostics:		Home Health:	
Managed Care:	Y	Distributor:		Distributor:		Sub-Acute:		Labs/Testing:		Long-Term Care:	
Utilization Management:		Specialty Pharmacy:		Leasing/Finance:		Outpatient Surgery:		Staffing:		Physical Therapy:	
Payment Processing:		Vitamins/Nutritionals:		Information Systems:		Physical Rehab. Ctr.:		Waste Disposal:		Physician Prac. Mgmt.:	
		Clinical Trials:				Psychiatric Clinics:		Specialty Svcs.:			

TYPES OF BUSINESS:

Managed Vision Care Plans

BRANDS/DIVISIONS/AFFILIATES:

Centene Corp

GROWTH PLANS/SPECIAL FEATURES:

OptiCare Managed Vision, a subsidiary of Centene Corp provides managed vision care plans to more than 3 millio people. The company collaborates with national and loc managed care organizations to design and administer ey care programs. The firm offers a wide range of bene options that cover routine eye exams, eyeglasses (lense and frames), contacts and prescription sunglasse OptiCare's offerings include discounts on routine eye exam and optical hardware; discounts on laser surgery in sele markets; complete coverage of routine exams with choice hardware allowances; and full medical surgical eye car carve outs. In July 2006, Centene Corp. acquired Opticare' managed vision business.

CONTACTS:

Note: Officers with more than one job title may be intentionally listed here more than once.

Juan Marrero, VP-Info. Systems
Larry Keely, Sr. VP-Oper.

Phone:	**Fax:**
Toll-Free: 800-334-3937	
Address: 112 Zebulon Ct., Rocky Mount, NC 27804 US	

FINANCIALS:

Sales and profits are in thousands of dollars—add 000 to get the full amount. 2007 Note: Financial information for 2007 was not available for all companies at press time.

2007 Sales: $	2007 Profits: $	**U.S. Stock Ticker: Subsidiary**
2006 Sales: $	2006 Profits: $	**Int'l Ticker:** Int'l Exchange:
2005 Sales: $	2005 Profits: $	Employees: 393
2004 Sales: $58,903	2004 Profits: $-8,340	Fiscal Year Ends: 12/31
2003 Sales: $125,702	2003 Profits: $-12,353	Parent Company: CENTENE CORPORATION

SALARIES/BENEFITS:

Pension Plan:	ESOP Stock Plan:	Profit Sharing:	Top Exec. Salary: $345,000	Bonus: $93,500
Savings Plan:	Stock Purch. Plan:		Second Exec. Salary: $150,000	Bonus: $50,000

OTHER THOUGHTS:

Apparent Women Officers or Directors:
Hot Spot for Advancement for Women/Minorities:

LOCATIONS: ("Y" = Yes)

West:	Southwest:	Midwest:	Southeast:	Northeast:	International:
				Y	

OPTION CARE INC

www.optioncare.com

Industry Group Code: 621610 **Ranks within this company's industry group:** Sales: 4 Profits: 6

Insurance/HMO/PPO:		Drugs:		Equipment/Supplies:		Hospitals/Clinics:		Services:		Health Care:	
Insurance:		Manufacturer:		Manufacturer:		Acute Care:		Diagnostics:		Home Health:	Y
Managed Care:		Distributor:	Y	Distributor:	Y	Sub-Acute:		Labs/Testing:		Long-Term Care:	
Utilization Management:		Specialty Pharmacy:	Y	Leasing/Finance:	Y	Outpatient Surgery:		Staffing:		Physical Therapy:	
Payment Processing:		Vitamins/Nutritionals:	Y	Information Systems:	Y	Physical Rehab. Ctr.:		Waste Disposal:		Physician Prac. Mgmt.:	
		Clinical Trials:				Psychiatric Clinics:		Specialty Svcs.:	Y		

TYPES OF BUSINESS:

Specialty Pharmacy Services
Home Health Care
Infusion Therapy
Home Health Equipment
Home Health Care Data Management
Software Products

BRANDS/DIVISIONS/AFFILIATES:

Walgreen Co
Option Care of New Jersey

CONTACTS: *Note: Officers with more than one job title may be intentionally listed here more than once.*

Rajat Rai, CEO
Rajat Raj, Pres.
Paul Mastrapa, CFO/Sr. VP
Joseph Bonaccorsi, General Counsel/Sr. VP/Corp. Sec.
John N. Kapoor, Chmn.

Phone: 847-465-2100 **Fax:**
Toll-Free:
Address: 485 E. Half Day Rd., Ste. 300, Buffalo Grove, IL 60089 US

GROWTH PLANS/SPECIAL FEATURES:

Option Care, Inc., a subsidiary of Walgreen Co., is a leading provider of specialty pharmacy services and home infusion pharmacy services to patients with acute or chronic conditions that can be treated at home, at one of the company's local ambulatory infusion centers or in a physician's office. Option Care was acquired by Walgreen Co. in September 2007. Option Care provides its services to patients on behalf of managed care organizations, government healthcare programs and biopharmaceutical manufacturers through two company-owned, high-volume distribution facilities, 58 company-owned and managed locations and 53 franchised locations throughout the U.S. Option Care's services include the distribution and administration of infused and injectible medications, patient care coordination, clinical and compliance management and reimbursement support. Home infusion therapies provided by Option Care include total parenteral nutrition, providing required nutrients to patients with digestive or gastro-intestinal problems; anti-infective therapy, providing medication for infections related to diseases such as osteomyelitis and urinary tract infections; pain management; enteral nutrition, providing nutritional formula by tube directly into the stomach or colon; and chemotherapy. Chronic diseases or conditions for which Option Care provides specialty pharmacy services include growth hormone deficiency, respiratory syncytial virus (RSV) prevention, hepatitis C virus, multiple sclerosis, hemophilia, immune deficiency, cancer and asthma. The company helps manage patients' conditions through counseling and education regarding their treatment and by providing ongoing monitoring to encourage patient compliance with the prescribed therapy, as well as providing services to help patients receive reimbursement benefits. In May 2006, Option Care announced the acquisition of its franchisee, Option Care of New Jersey.

Option Care offers its employees a stock purchase plan, a 401(k) plan, a flexible savings account, tuition reimbursement, ongoing training programs, clinical symposiums, Continuing Education courses and health, dental and vision insurance.

FINANCIALS: **Sales and profits are in thousands of dollars—add 000 to get the full amount. 2007 Note: Financial information for 2007 was not available for all companies at press time.**

2007 Sales: $	2007 Profits: $	**U.S. Stock Ticker: Subsidiary**
2006 Sales: $659,412	2006 Profits: $21,685	**Int'l Ticker:** Int'l Exchange:
2005 Sales: $504,578	2005 Profits: $20,618	Employees: 2,924
2004 Sales: $414,430	2004 Profits: $16,548	Fiscal Year Ends: 12/31
2003 Sales: $335,440	2003 Profits: $8,718	Parent Company: WALGREEN CO

SALARIES/BENEFITS:

Pension Plan:	ESOP Stock Plan:	Profit Sharing:	Top Exec. Salary: $380,000	Bonus: $108,000
Savings Plan: Y	Stock Purch. Plan: Y		Second Exec. Salary: $262,500	Bonus: $45,000

OTHER THOUGHTS:

Apparent Women Officers or Directors:
Hot Spot for Advancement for Women/Minorities:

LOCATIONS: ("Y" = Yes)

West:	Southwest:	Midwest:	Southeast:	Northeast:	International:
Y	Y	Y	Y	Y	

Note: Financial information, benefits and other data can change quickly and may vary from those stated here.

ORGANOGENESIS INC www.organogenesis.com

Industry Group Code: 325414 **Ranks within this company's industry group:** Sales: Profits:

Insurance/HMO/PPO:		Drugs:		Equipment/Supplies:		Hospitals/Clinics:		Services:		Health Care:	
Insurance:		Manufacturer:		Manufacturer:	Y	Acute Care:		Diagnostics:		Home Health:	
Managed Care:		Distributor:		Distributor:		Sub-Acute:		Labs/Testing:		Long-Term Care:	
Utilization Management:		Specialty Pharmacy:		Leasing/Finance:		Outpatient Surgery:		Staffing:		Physical Therapy:	
Payment Processing:		Vitamins/Nutritionals:		Information Systems:		Physical Rehab. Ctr.:		Waste Disposal:		Physician Prac. Mgmt.:	
		Clinical Trials:				Psychiatric Clinics:		Specialty Svcs.:			

TYPES OF BUSINESS:

Tissue Replacement Products
Wound Dressing Products

BRANDS/DIVISIONS/AFFILIATES:

Apligraf
FortaDerm Antimicrobial
FortaPerm
FortaGen
CuffPatch
Revitix
TestSkin & TestSkin II
BioSTAR

CONTACTS: *Note: Officers with more than one job title may be intentionally listed here more than once.*

Geoff MacKay, CEO
Gary S. Gillheeney, Sr., COO/Exec. VP
Geoff MacKay, Pres.
Gary S. Gillheeney, Sr., CFO/Exec. VP
Santino Costanzo, VP-Sales, Bio-active Wound Healing
Houda Damaha, Dir.-Human Resources
Vincent Ronfard, Chief Scientist Officer
Phillip Nolan, VP-Mfg. Oper.
Richard Shaw, VP-Finance
Dario Eklund, VP-Bio-Surgery & Bio-Aesthetics
Patrick Bilbo, VP-Clinical & Regulatory Affairs
Susan Chapman, Dir.-Production
Shannon Banks, Dir.-Project Mgmt.

Phone: 781-575-0775	**Fax:** 781-575-0440
Toll-Free:	
Address: 150 Dan Rd., Canton, MA 02021 US	

GROWTH PLANS/SPECIAL FEATURES:

Organogenesis, Inc. is a tissue-engineering firm tha designs, develops and manufactures medical product containing living cells or natural connective tissue Organogenesis specializes in bio-active wound healing, bio aesthetics and bio-surgery. Its bio-active wound healin products include: Apligraf, designed for the treatment o venous leg ulcers due to poor blood circulation and fo diabetic foot ulcers without tendon, muscle, capsule or bon exposure; Fortaderm Antimicrobial, a collagen base antimicrobial wound dressing that helps wounds heal b providing the dermal scaffolding or structure to help th body's own cells migrate to facilitate closure of the wound and VCT01, currently in late stage development, th company's next generation of bio-engineered skin substitute which is self assembled, bi-layered bio engineered skin. Bio aesthetics products include: Revitix, which utilizes th technology and living cells that make up Apligraf t rejuvenate skin; and TestSkin, along with TestSkin II, mode of human skin that mimic the key properties of actual ski used for simulating in a lab the reaction of skin whe exposed to various products/drugs. Bio-surgery product include: CuffPatch for rotator cuff surgery, which repairs th tendons that connect the upper arm bones to the should blade; FortaGen, used for tissue repair in cases of vagina prolapse (a condition caused by the protrusion (herniation) o a pelvic organ into the vaginal area); FortaPerm, used as sling to raise a dropped bladder neck, which causes stres urinary incontinence, the leakage of urine as a result o increased pressure (i.e., coughing, laughing, sneezing) upo the bladder, back into a position from which it is able to sh when pressure is applied; and BioSTAR, an implan technology for the treatment of cardiac sources of migrain headaches, strokes and other potential brain attacks, namel a common heart defect called a patent foramen ovale (PFO)

FINANCIALS: **Sales and profits are in thousands of dollars—add 000 to get the full amount. 2007 Note: Financial information for 2007 was not available for all companies at press time.**

2007 Sales: $	2007 Profits: $	**U.S. Stock Ticker: Private**
2006 Sales: $	2006 Profits: $	**Int'l Ticker:** Int'l Exchange:
2005 Sales: $	2005 Profits: $	Employees: 182
2004 Sales: $	2004 Profits: $	Fiscal Year Ends: 12/31
2003 Sales: $	2003 Profits: $	Parent Company:

SALARIES/BENEFITS:

Pension Plan:	ESOP Stock Plan:	Profit Sharing:	Top Exec. Salary: $277,420	Bonus: $56,000
Savings Plan: Y	Stock Purch. Plan:		Second Exec. Salary: $229,836	Bonus: $30,000

OTHER THOUGHTS:

Apparent Women Officers or Directors: 2
Hot Spot for Advancement for Women/Minorities: Y

LOCATIONS: ("Y" = Yes)

West:	Southwest:	Midwest:	Southeast:	Northeast:	International:
				Y	Y

ORTHOFIX INTERNATIONAL NV www.orthofix.com

ndustry Group Code: 339113 **Ranks within this company's industry group:** Sales: 50 Profits: 86

nsurance/HMO/PPO:		Drugs:		Equipment/Supplies:		Hospitals/Clinics:		Services:		Health Care:	
nsurance:		Manufacturer:		Manufacturer:	Y	Acute Care:		Diagnostics:		Home Health:	
lanaged Care:		Distributor:		Distributor:	Y	Sub-Acute:		Labs/Testing:		Long-Term Care:	
tilization Management:		Specialty Pharmacy:		Leasing/Finance:		Outpatient Surgery:		Staffing:		Physical Therapy:	
ayment Processing:		Vitamins/Nutritionals:		Information Systems:		Physical Rehab. Ctr.:		Waste Disposal:		Physician Prac. Mgmt.:	
		Clinical Trials:				Psychiatric Clinics:		Specialty Svcs.:			

TYPES OF BUSINESS:

ledical Equipment-Orthopedic
one Reconstruction Equipment
)rthopedic Fixation Devices

BRANDS/DIVISIONS/AFFILIATES:

)rthofix
ProCallus
)rthotrac
‹Caliber
)ASIS
EZBrace
Spinal-Stim
Blackstone Medical, Inc.

CONTACTS: *Note: Officers with more than one job title may be ntentionally listed here more than once.*

lan Milinazzo, CEO
lan Milinazzo, Pres.
homas Hein, CFO
ric Brown, Sr. VP-Sales
aymond Kolls, General Counsel/Sr. VP/Corp. Sec.
lichael Simpson, Sr. VP-Global Oper.
lichael Finegan, VP-Corp. Dev.
)an Yarbrough, Dir.-Investor Rel.
latt Lyons, CEO/Pres., Blackstone Medical
ill Lyons, Pres., Blackstone Biologics
radley R. Mason, VP/Pres., Breg, Inc.
honda Fellows, Sr. VP-Gov't Affairs/Privacy Officer
ames F. Gero, Chmn.
)liver Burckhardt, Pres., Int'l Div.

Phone: 0039-045-6719081 **Fax:** 0039-045-6719081
Toll-Free:
Address: Via delle Nazioni, 9, Bussolengo, VR-37012 Italy

GROWTH PLANS/SPECIAL FEATURES:

Orthofix International NV designs, manufactures and distributes medical equipment used principally by musculoskeletal medical specialists including minimally invasive surgical equipment, as well as non-surgical products. The company has multiple trademarked products including Orthofix, ProCallus, Orthotrac, XCaliber, OASIS, EZBrace, Spinal-Stim, Physio-Stim, Breg, Polar Care and Pain Care. These products are designed to address the lifelong bone-and-joint health needs of patients of all ages, helping them achieve a more active and mobile lifestyle. Orthopedic products account for approximately 90% of revenues and are divided into three market sectors: spine, bone reconstruction and trauma. Orthofix's most successful products are external and internal fixation devices used in fracture treatment, limb lengthening and bone reconstruction; non-invasive stimulation products used to bolster healing in spinal fusions and non-union fractures; and bracing products used for ligament injury prevention, pain management and protection of surgical repair for faster healing. Other products include a device for enhancing venous circulation, cold therapy products, pain management products, bone cement and devices for bone cement removal, and a bone substitute compound, as well as the bone growth stimulators Physio-Stim and Spinal-Stim. Orthofix has facilities in the U.S., the U.K., Italy, Mexico and the Seychelles and distributes products in the U.S., the U.K., Ireland, Italy, Germany, Switzerland, Austria, France, Belgium, Mexico and Brazil. In September 2006, the Orthofix completed the $333 million acquisition of Blackstone Medical, Inc., a company specializing in the design, development and marketing of spinal implant and related biologics products. Then in December 2006, Regeneration Technologies, Inc. signed an agreement to manufacture Blackstone spinal allograft implants.

FINANCIALS: Sales and profits are in thousands of dollars—add 000 to get the full amount. 2007 Note: Financial information for 2007 was not available for all companies at press time.

007 Sales: $	2007 Profits: $	**U.S. Stock Ticker: OFIX**
006 Sales: $365,359	2006 Profits: $-7,042	**Int'l Ticker:** Int'l Exchange:
005 Sales: $313,304	2005 Profits: $73,402	Employees: 1,324
004 Sales: $286,638	2004 Profits: $34,149	Fiscal Year Ends: 12/31
003 Sales: $203,707	2003 Profits: $24,730	Parent Company:

SALARIES/BENEFITS:

Pension Plan:	ESOP Stock Plan:	Profit Sharing:	Top Exec. Salary: $407,500	Bonus: $228,450
Savings Plan:	Stock Purch. Plan:		Second Exec. Salary: $270,375	Bonus: $115,197

OTHER THOUGHTS:

Apparent Women Officers or Directors: 1
Hot Spot for Advancement for Women/Minorities:

LOCATIONS: ("Y" = Yes)

West:	Southwest:	Midwest:	Southeast:	Northeast:	International:
Y			Y	Y	Y

OSTEOTECH INC www.osteotech.com

Industry Group Code: 339113 **Ranks within this company's industry group:** Sales: 78 Profits: 75

Insurance/HMO/PPO:		Drugs:		Equipment/Supplies:		Hospitals/Clinics:		Services:		Health Care:	
Insurance:		Manufacturer:		Manufacturer:	Y	Acute Care:		Diagnostics:		Home Health:	
Managed Care:		Distributor:		Distributor:		Sub-Acute:		Labs/Testing:		Long-Term Care:	
Utilization Management:		Specialty Pharmacy:		Leasing/Finance:		Outpatient Surgery:		Staffing:		Physical Therapy:	
Payment Processing:		Vitamins/Nutritionals:		Information Systems:		Physical Rehab. Ctr.:		Waste Disposal:		Physician Prac. Mgmt.:	
		Clinical Trials:				Psychiatric Clinics:		Specialty Svcs.:	Y		

TYPES OF BUSINESS:

Supplies-Processed Bone
Musculoskeletal System Repair Products & Services
Allograft Bone Tissue

BRANDS/DIVISIONS/AFFILIATES:

Grafton Demineralized Bone Matrix
D-Min Process
GraftCage Spacers
Plexur P
Novation LLC (VHA INC)

CONTACTS: *Note: Officers with more than one job title may be intentionally listed here more than once.*

Sam Owusu-Akyaw, CEO
Sam Owusu-Akyaw, Pres.
Mark H. Burroughs, CFO/Exec. VP
Chuck Lanza, VP-Sales
Martin Rexroad, VP-Human Resources
Donna A. Haag, VP-Info. Mgmt.
Robert W. Honneffer, Sr. VP-Oper.
Robert M. Wynalek, Pres., Domestic
Roman Hitchev, Managing Dir./Pres., OCBG/VP-Int'l
Greg Cannedy, VP-Quality Assurance & Regulatory Affairs
Greg Cannedy, VP-Good Tissue Practices
Kenneth P. Fallon, III, Chmn.
Richard Russo, Pres., Int'l
Donna Haag, VP-Supply Chain

Phone: 732-542-2800	**Fax:** 732-542-9312
Toll-Free:	
Address: 51 James Way, Eatontown, NJ 07724 US	

GROWTH PLANS/SPECIAL FEATURES:

Osteotech, Inc. develops and provides services and product primarily focused on the repair and healing of th musculoskeletal system and marketed to the orthopedi spinal, neurological, oral/maxillofacial, dental and gener surgery markets in the United States and Europe. The fir is a leading processor and developer of human bone an bone connective tissue, or allograft bone tissue, forms. Th allograft bone tissue is procured by independent tissu banks or other tissue recovery organizations, primari through the donation of tissue from deceased donors, and used for transplantation. Osteotech's five main operatin segments are the Demineralized Bone Matrix (DBM Segment, the Traditional Tissue Segment, the Spin Allograft Segment, the Hybrid/Synthetic Segment and th Client Services Segment. Osteotech has developed proprietary demineralization process, the D-Min Process, f cortical bone which yields Grafton DBM, a non-weig bearing form of allograft bone tissue which can be used aid in the formation of new bone through the processes osteoconduction and osteoinduction, and the Xpanse Bor Inserts. Cortical bone is believed to be the principal reservo for various proteins that are instrumental for osteoinductio In addition, based on studies completed by an independe testing laboratory specializing in viral inactivation studies, th D-Min Process has been validated to inactivate a panel viruses, including HIV-1, HIV-2, hepatitis B, hepatitis cytomeglia and polio. Once allograft bone tissue processed into tissue grafts, Osteotech markets ar distributes the grafts to surgeons and hospitals. Th Hybrid/Synthetics Segment includes revenue fro Osteotech's GraftCage Spacers. In February 200 Osteotech received FDA clearance for Plexur P, a osteoconductive, bone/polymer biocomposite. In May 200 the company entered into a single-source agreement wi Novation, LLC. Under the terms of this agreemer Osteotech will have the opportunity to provide Novation participating members with Osteotech's line of proprieta products.

FINANCIALS: Sales and profits are in thousands of dollars—add 000 to get the full amount. 2007 Note: Financial information for 2007 was not available for all companies at press time.

2007 Sales: $	2007 Profits: $	**U.S. Stock Ticker: OSTE**
2006 Sales: $99,241	2006 Profits: $1,907	**Int'l Ticker:** Int'l Exchange:
2005 Sales: $93,307	2005 Profits: $-21,117	Employees: 354
2004 Sales: $88,577	2004 Profits: $-5,283	Fiscal Year Ends: 12/31
2003 Sales: $94,433	2003 Profits: $10,867	Parent Company:

SALARIES/BENEFITS:

Pension Plan:	ESOP Stock Plan:	Profit Sharing:	Top Exec. Salary: $370,000	Bonus: $138,750
Savings Plan: Y	Stock Purch. Plan:		Second Exec. Salary: $292,750	Bonus: $84,200

OTHER THOUGHTS:

Apparent Women Officers or Directors: 1
Hot Spot for Advancement for Women/Minorities:

LOCATIONS: ("Y" = Yes)

West:	Southwest:	Midwest:	Southeast:	Northeast:	International:
				Y	Y

OUTLOOK POINTE CORP www.outlookpointe.com

ndustry Group Code: 623110 **Ranks within this company's industry group:** Sales: Profits:

surance/HMO/PPO:		Drugs:		Equipment/Supplies:		Hospitals/Clinics:		Services:		Health Care:	
nsurance:		Manufacturer:		Manufacturer:		Acute Care:		Diagnostics:		Home Health:	
lanaged Care:		Distributor:		Distributor:		Sub-Acute:		Labs/Testing:		Long-Term Care:	Y
tilization Management:		Specialty Pharmacy:		Leasing/Finance:		Outpatient Surgery:		Staffing:		Physical Therapy:	Y
ayment Processing:		Vitamins/Nutritionals:		Information Systems:		Physical Rehab. Ctr.:		Waste Disposal:		Physician Prac. Mgmt.:	
		Clinical Trials:				Psychiatric Clinics:		Specialty Svcs.:			

TYPES OF BUSINESS:

ssisted Living Facilities
Vellness Programs
hysical Therapy

BRANDS/DIVISIONS/AFFILIATES:

alanced Gold
alanced Care Corporation

CONTACTS:

Note: Officers with more than one job title may be ntentionally listed here more than once.

m Fields, CEO
im Fields, Pres.
redrick Zullinger, CFO

hone: 717-796-6100	Fax: 717-796-6150
oll-Free:	
ddress: 1215 Manor Dr., Mechanicsburg, PA 17055 US	

GROWTH PLANS/SPECIAL FEATURES:

Outlook Pointe Corp. develops, manages and operates assisted living facilities to meet the needs of upper-middle-, middle- and moderate-income populations in non-urban, secondary markets. The company operates 37 facilities in seven states: Arkansas, North Carolina, Ohio, Pennsylvania, Virginia, Tennessee and West Virginia. These facilities provide a care continuum consisting of preventative care and wellness, medical rehabilitation, dementia and Alzheimer's care and, in certain markets, extended care. Outlook Pointe's philosophy includes the belief that providing health care services coupled with wellness and preventative therapy will strengthen residents, improve their health and forestall the deterioration that generally accompanies aging, thus extending their lives and lengths of stay in assisted living facilities. Balanced Gold, the firm's wellness-oriented program, has been developed to address resident care needs proactively, stabilizing and improving residents' cognitive, emotional and physical well-being through participation in exercise classes, gardening, intellectually stimulating games, religious studies and social events. The company also offers physical, occupational and speech therapy services, which are available for both residents and outpatients, and Alzheimer's and dementia care according to patients' needs. In addition, Outlook Pointe provides adult day care and respite care. The company is owned by Balanced Care Corporation, which in turn is owned by IPBC Acquisition Corporation, a nursing home facility operator in Canada.

FINANCIALS:

Sales and profits are in thousands of dollars—add 000 to get the full amount. 2007 Note: Financial information for 2007 was not available for all companies at press time.

007 Sales: $	2007 Profits: $	**U.S. Stock Ticker: Subsidiary**
006 Sales: $	2006 Profits: $	**Int'l Ticker:** Int'l Exchange:
005 Sales: $	2005 Profits: $	Employees: 2,100
004 Sales: $	2004 Profits: $	Fiscal Year Ends: 6/30
003 Sales: $	2003 Profits: $	Parent Company: BALANCED CARE CORPORATION

SALARIES/BENEFITS:

ension Plan:	ESOP Stock Plan:	Profit Sharing:	Top Exec. Salary: $235,504	Bonus: $105,000
avings Plan:	Stock Purch. Plan:		Second Exec. Salary: $180,000	Bonus: $65,000

OTHER THOUGHTS:

pparent Women Officers or Directors:
lot Spot for Advancement for Women/Minorities:

LOCATIONS: ("Y" = Yes)

West:	Southwest:	Midwest:	Southeast:	Northeast:	International:
		Y	Y	Y	

OWENS & MINOR INC www.owens-minor.com

Industry Group Code: 421450 **Ranks within this company's industry group:** Sales: 1 Profits: 4

Insurance/HMO/PPO:		Drugs:		Equipment/Supplies:		Hospitals/Clinics:		Services:		Health Care:	
Insurance:		Manufacturer:		Manufacturer:		Acute Care:		Diagnostics:		Home Health:	
Managed Care:		Distributor:		Distributor:	Y	Sub-Acute:		Labs/Testing:		Long-Term Care:	
Utilization Management:		Specialty Pharmacy:		Leasing/Finance:		Outpatient Surgery:		Staffing:		Physical Therapy:	
Payment Processing:		Vitamins/Nutritionals:		Information Systems:		Physical Rehab. Ctr.:		Waste Disposal:		Physician Prac. Mgmt.:	
		Clinical Trials:				Psychiatric Clinics:		Specialty Svcs.:	Y		

TYPES OF BUSINESS:

Distribution-Medical & Surgical Equipment
Supply Chain Management

BRANDS/DIVISIONS/AFFILIATES:

Pandac
CostTrack
WISDOM
OM DIRECT
SurgiTrack

CONTACTS: *Note: Officers with more than one job title may be intentionally listed here more than once.*

Craig R. Smith, CEO
Craig R. Smith, Pres.
James L. Bierman, CFO
Erika T. Davis, Sr. VP-Human Resources
Richard W. Mears, CIO/Sr. VP
Grace R. den Hartog, General Counsel/Sr. VP/Corp. Sec.
Charles C. Colpo, Sr. VP-Oper.
Hugh F. Gouldthorpe, VP-Comm. & Quality
Richard F. Bozard, Treas./VP
Olwen Cape, VP/Controller
Mark Van Sumeren, Sr. VP-OM Solutions
G. Gilmer Minor, III, Chmn.

Phone: 804-723-7000	**Fax:** 804-723-7100
Toll-Free:	
Address: 9120 Lockwood Blvd., Mechanicsville, VA 23116 US	

GROWTH PLANS/SPECIAL FEATURES:

Owens & Minor, Inc. (OMI) is a distributor of medical an surgical supplies to the acute-care market, a healthca supply-chain management company and a national direct-t consumer supplier of testing and monitoring supplies fo diabetics. In its acute-care supply distribution, the compar distributes 180,000 finished medical and surgical product produced by over 1,200 suppliers to about 4,000 healthca provider customers from 50 distribution centers nationwid The firm's primary distribution customers are acute-ca hospitals and integrated healthcare networks, which accou for more than 90% of the company's revenue. Oth customers include the federal government, for which O serves as a vendor for medical and surgical supp distribution services for the U.S. Department of Defense. O a more limited basis, the company serves alternate ca providers including clinics, home healthcare organization nursing homes, physicians' offices, rehabilitation faciliti and surgery centers. The firm typically provides i distribution services under contractual arrangements wi terms ranging from three to five years. Most of OMI's sal consist of consumable goods such as disposable glove dressings; endoscopic products; intravenous product needles and syringes; sterile procedure trays; surgic products and gowns; urological products; and wound closu products. CostTrack separates product and process costs clearly reflect the cost of individual distribution activitie Pandac and SurgiTrack are both programs that help wi operating room equipment management. Online service and order forms are available through OM DIRECT an WISDOM. In September 2006, OMI acquired McKessc Corp.'s acute-care medical supply assets for $170 million.

The company offers its employees health, dental and visio insurance; life insurance; a 401(k) plan; a stock purchas plan; and education assistance.

FINANCIALS: **Sales and profits are in thousands of dollars—add 000 to get the full amount. 2007 Note: Financial information for 2007 was not available for all companies at press time.**

2007 Sales: $	2007 Profits: $	**U.S. Stock Ticker: OMI**
2006 Sales: $5,533,736	2006 Profits: $48,752	**Int'l Ticker:** Int'l Exchange:
2005 Sales: $4,822,414	2005 Profits: $64,420	Employees: 4,600
2004 Sales: $4,525,105	2004 Profits: $60,500	Fiscal Year Ends: 12/31
2003 Sales: $4,244,067	2003 Profits: $53,641	Parent Company:

SALARIES/BENEFITS:

Pension Plan:	ESOP Stock Plan:	Profit Sharing:	Top Exec. Salary: $717,307	Bonus: $
Savings Plan: Y	Stock Purch. Plan: Y		Second Exec. Salary: $415,768	Bonus: $

OTHER THOUGHTS:

Apparent Women Officers or Directors: 4
Hot Spot for Advancement for Women/Minorities: Y

LOCATIONS: ("Y" = Yes)

West:	Southwest:	Midwest:	Southeast:	Northeast:	International:
Y	Y	Y	Y	Y	

PACIFICARE HEALTH SYSTEMS INC www.pacificare.com

ndustry Group Code: 524114 Ranks within this company's industry group: Sales: Profits:

nsurance/HMO/PPO:		Drugs:		Equipment/Supplies:		Hospitals/Clinics:		Services:		Health Care:	
nsurance:	Y	Manufacturer:		Manufacturer:		Acute Care:		Diagnostics:		Home Health:	
lanaged Care:	Y	Distributor:		Distributor:		Sub-Acute:		Labs/Testing:		Long-Term Care:	
tilization Management:		Specialty Pharmacy:		Leasing/Finance:		Outpatient Surgery:		Staffing:		Physical Therapy:	
ayment Processing:		Vitamins/Nutritionals:		Information Systems:		Physical Rehab. Ctr.:		Waste Disposal:		Physician Prac. Mgmt.:	
		Clinical Trials:				Psychiatric Clinics:		Specialty Svcs.:	Y		

TYPES OF BUSINESS:

nsurance-Medical & Health, HMOs & PPOs
lanaged Care Products & Services
nsurance-Dental
ehavioral Health
Vellness Programs
lanagement Services
harmacy Benefit Management

BRANDS/DIVISIONS/AFFILIATES:

JnitedHealth Group Inc

CONTACTS: *Note: Officers with more than one job title may be ntentionally listed here more than once.*

Ioward G. Phantstiel, CEO
Gregory W. Scott, CFO/Exec. VP
Sharon D. Garrett, Exec. VP-Enterprise Svcs.
Ioward G. Phanstiel, Chmn.

Phone: 714-952-1121	**Fax:** 714-226-3581
Toll-Free: 800-624-8822	
Address: 5995 Plaza Dr., Cypress, CA 90630 US	

GROWTH PLANS/SPECIAL FEATURES:

PacifiCare Health Systems, Inc., a subsidiary of The UnitedHealth Group, Inc., is a managed health care services company that serves approximately 3 million health maintenance organization (HMO) members and 10 million specialty plan members and offers a variety of specialty managed health care products. The company's commercial plans offer products to employer groups and individuals, including HMO, preferred provider organization (PPO) and point-of-service (POS) plans. The company operates through a set of subsidiaries organized in the following way: dental, vision, pharmacy, behavioral health and Covantage. PacifiCare Dental and Vision Administrators, formerly California Dental Health Plan, offers a non-traditional form of benefits. Instead of the fee-for-service method of payment, these plans pay dentists on a per member per month basis. PrescriptionSolutions is PacifiCare's Pharmaceutical wholly-owned subsidiary. PacifiCare Behavioral Health serves over 4 million members of various health plans, union trusts, employers, school districts and municipalities. Finally, the subsidiary Covantage provides outsourced employee benefits administration services including: health and welfare, COBRA/HIPAA administration, FSA and personalized customer service. PacifiCare also offers Medicare risk management through SHUSA, a division that provides management services and best practices to HMOs and health care delivery systems.

The company offers its employees medical, dental and vision insurance; flexible spending accounts; life and AD&D insurance; short- and long-term disability insurance; a 401(k) plan; a stock purchase plan; and tuition reimbursement.

FINANCIALS: **Sales and profits are in thousands of dollars—add 000 to get the full amount. 2007 Note: Financial information for 2007 was not available for all companies at press time.**

2007 Sales: $	2007 Profits: $	**U.S. Stock Ticker: Subsidiary**
2006 Sales: $	2006 Profits: $	**Int'l Ticker:** Int'l Exchange:
2005 Sales: $	2005 Profits: $	Employees: 9,800
2004 Sales: $12,276,800	2004 Profits: $231,193	Fiscal Year Ends: 12/31
2003 Sales: $11,008,511	2003 Profits: $242,748	Parent Company: UNITEDHEALTH GROUP INC

SALARIES/BENEFITS:

Pension Plan:	ESOP Stock Plan:	Profit Sharing:	Top Exec. Salary: $976,155	Bonus: $2,000,000
Savings Plan: Y	Stock Purch. Plan: Y		Second Exec. Salary: $642,308	Bonus: $690,000

OTHER THOUGHTS:

Apparent Women Officers or Directors: 1
Hot Spot for Advancement for Women/Minorities: Y

LOCATIONS: ("Y" = Yes)

West:	Southwest:	Midwest:	Southeast:	Northeast:	International:
Y	Y				

PALOMAR MEDICAL TECHNOLOGIES INC www.palmed.com

Industry Group Code: 339113 **Ranks within this company's industry group:** Sales: 74 Profits: 35

Insurance/HMO/PPO:		Drugs:		Equipment/Supplies:		Hospitals/Clinics:		Services:		Health Care:	
Insurance:		Manufacturer:		Manufacturer:	Y	Acute Care:		Diagnostics:		Home Health:	
Managed Care:		Distributor:		Distributor:		Sub-Acute:		Labs/Testing:		Long-Term Care:	
Utilization Management:		Specialty Pharmacy:		Leasing/Finance:		Outpatient Surgery:		Staffing:		Physical Therapy:	
Payment Processing:		Vitamins/Nutritionals:		Information Systems:		Physical Rehab. Ctr.:		Waste Disposal:		Physician Prac. Mgmt.:	
		Clinical Trials:				Psychiatric Clinics:		Specialty Svcs.:			

TYPES OF BUSINESS:

Equipment-Laser Hair Removal Systems
Tattoo & Lesion Removal Systems
Aesthetic Laser Products

BRANDS/DIVISIONS/AFFILIATES:

EsteLux Pulsed Light System
MediLux Pulsed Light System
StarLux Pulsed Light and Laser System
RejuveLux
Active Contact Cooling
StarLux 500
Q-YAG 5

CONTACTS: *Note: Officers with more than one job title may be intentionally listed here more than once.*

Joseph P. Caruso, CEO
Joseph P. Caruso, Pres.
Paul S. Weiner, CFO/Treas./Sr. VP
Paul F. Wiener, Sr. VP-Sales & Mktg.
Gregory Altshuler, Sr. VP-Research
Michael H. Smotrich, CTO
Patricia A. Davis, General Counsel/Sr. VP/Corp. Sec.
Steven Armstrong, Sr. VP-Oper.
Douglas Baraw, Chief Acct. Officer/VP
Jeffrey Knight, VP-North American Sales & Mktg.
Louis P. Valente, Chmn.

Phone: 781-993-2300 **Fax:** 781-993-2330
Toll-Free: 800-725-6627
Address: 82 Cambridge St., Ste. 1, Burlington, MA 01803 US

GROWTH PLANS/SPECIAL FEATURES:

Palomar Medical Technologies, Inc. is focused on lasers an light-based products for use in dermatology and cosmet procedures. The company offers a range of products for ha removal, removal of vascular lesions, removal of leg vein removal of benign pigmented lesions, tattoo removal, acn removal, wrinkle removal, Pseudofolliculitis Barbae (PFE treatment, treatment of scars and skin tightening. Palomar principal products are its Lux platform, including the EsteLu Pulsed Light System, the MediLux Pulsed Light System, th StarLux Pulsed Light and Laser System. The EsteLu Pulsed Light System includes six handpieces which em pulses of intense light to treat unwanted hair, sunspot rosacea, actinic bronzing, spider veins, birthmark telangiectasias and acne. The LuxG handpiece delivers th RejuveLux process, a photofacial treatment that remove pigmented and vascular lesions to improve skin tone an texture. The LuxR handpiece can be used to remove hair o all skin types, including deep tans. The LuxB handpiec provides effective treatment of lighter pigmented lesions o fair skin as well as leg and spider veins, and the Lux handpiece treats pigmented lesions and mild to moderat acne. The MediLux Pulsed Light System provides increase power, a faster repetition rate and a snap-on connector. Th StarLux Laser and Pulsed Light System, with a single pow supply capable of operating both lasers and lamps, include increased power, Active Contact Cooling and a full col touch screen for easy operation. Palomar's patented Activ Contact Cooling technology sends a chilled water supp through the StarLux handpieces. In February 2007, Paloma launched its StarLux 500, providing 70% more power an increased functionality and speed of treatment. For tatto and pigmented lesion removal, Palomar sells the Q-YAG system, a Q-switched, frequency-doubled Neodymium las which incorporates the laser into the handpiece, making smaller and lighter than traditional systems.

FINANCIALS: Sales and profits are in thousands of dollars—add 000 to get the full amount. 2007 Note: Financial information for 2007 was not available for all companies at press time.

2007 Sales: $	2007 Profits: $	**U.S. Stock Ticker: PMTI**
2006 Sales: $126,544	2006 Profits: $52,977	**Int'l Ticker:** Int'l Exchange:
2005 Sales: $76,154	2005 Profits: $17,453	Employees: 225
2004 Sales: $54,432	2004 Profits: $10,633	Fiscal Year Ends: 12/31
2003 Sales: $34,773	2003 Profits: $3,369	Parent Company:

SALARIES/BENEFITS:

Pension Plan:	ESOP Stock Plan:	Profit Sharing:	Top Exec. Salary: $317,200	Bonus: $759,109
Savings Plan: Y	Stock Purch. Plan:		Second Exec. Salary: $228,800	Bonus: $547,553

OTHER THOUGHTS:

Apparent Women Officers or Directors: 1
Hot Spot for Advancement for Women/Minorities:

LOCATIONS: ("Y" = Yes)

West:	Southwest:	Midwest:	Southeast:	Northeast:	International:
				Y	

PAR PHARMACEUTICAL COMPANIES INCwww.parpharm.com

Industry Group Code: 325416 **Ranks within this company's industry group:** Sales: 5 Profits: 4

Insurance/HMO/PPO:		Drugs:		Equipment/Supplies:		Hospitals/Clinics:		Services:		Health Care:	
Insurance:		Manufacturer:	Y	Manufacturer:		Acute Care:		Diagnostics:		Home Health:	
Managed Care:		Distributor:		Distributor:		Sub-Acute:		Labs/Testing:		Long-Term Care:	
Utilization Management:		Specialty Pharmacy:		Leasing/Finance:		Outpatient Surgery:		Staffing:		Physical Therapy:	
Payment Processing:		Vitamins/Nutritionals:		Information Systems:		Physical Rehab. Ctr.:		Waste Disposal:		Physician Prac. Mgmt.:	
		Clinical Trials:				Psychiatric Clinics:		Specialty Svcs.:			

TYPES OF BUSINESS:

Drugs-Generic & Branded
Pharmaceutical Intermediates

BRANDS/DIVISIONS/AFFILIATES:

Pharmaceutical Resources, Inc.
Par Pharmaceutical, Inc.
Megace ES
Kali Laboratories, Inc.
FineTech Laboratories Ltd.
Optimer Pharmaceutials, Inc.

CONTACTS: *Note: Officers with more than one job title may be intentionally listed here more than once.*

Patrick G. LePore, CEO
Gerard A. Martino, COO/Exec. VP
Patrick G. LePore, Pres.
Veronica A. Lubatkin, CFO/Exec. VP
Thomas Haughey, General Counsel/Sec./Exec. VP
Paul V. Campanelli, Pres., Generic Products Div.
John A. MacPhee, Pres., Branded Products Div.
John D. Abernathy, Chmn.

Phone: 201-802-4000	**Fax:** 201-802-4600
Toll-Free:	
Address: 300 Tice Blvd., Woodcliff Lake, NJ 07677 US	

GROWTH PLANS/SPECIAL FEATURES:

Par Pharmaceutical Companies, Inc. (formerly Pharmaceutical Resources, Inc.) develops, manufactures and markets branded and generic pharmaceuticals through its principal subsidiary, Par Pharmaceutical, Inc. Products include treatments for central nervous system disorders, cardiovascular drugs, analgesics, anti-inflammatory products, anti-bacterials, anti-diabetics, antihistamines, anti-virals, cholesterol-lowering drugs and ovulation stimulants. Subsequent to the shipment of the company's first branded product, Megace ES, in late 2005, Par now operates in two segments: generic pharmaceuticals and branded pharmaceuticals. In the generic segment, the company's product line comprises generic prescription drugs consisting of 213 products representing various dosage strengths for 92 separate drugs. These are manufactured principally in the solid oral dosage form (tablet, caplet and two-piece hard shell capsule). Among these are generic versions of Advil, Daypro, Glucophage, Zantac, Clomid, Prozac, Halcion and Prilosec. Par's only product in the branded segment is Megace ES, which was given FDA approval in June 2005 for the treatment of anorexia, cachexia, or an unexplained, significant weight loss in patients with a diagnosis of AIDS. In 2006, Optimer Pharmaceutials, Inc. announced its Phase IIA clinical studies have indicated that PAR-101, another brand product, appears to be efficacious in the treatment of Clostridium difficile-associated diarrhea. With the recent acquisition of Kali Laboratories, Inc. Par more than doubled the size of its research and development capabilities. The company recently received FDA approval to market generic versions of Isotopin SR and Ultracet, for hypertension and pain respectively. The firm recently divested former subsidiary FineTech Laboratories Ltd. In 2007, Par announced the commencement of shipping of metoprolol succinate extended release 100mg and 200mg tablets, as well as the shipment of generic Zantac syrup.

PAR offers employees a 529 college savings plan, career growth opportunities, annual incentive programs and a flexible spending plan, along with health, dental and life insurance.

FINANCIALS: **Sales and profits are in thousands of dollars—add 000 to get the full amount. 2007 Note: Financial information for 2007 was not available for all companies at press time.**

2007 Sales: $	2007 Profits: $	**U.S. Stock Ticker: PRX**
2006 Sales: $725,168	2006 Profits: $6,741	**Int'l Ticker:** Int'l Exchange:
2005 Sales: $432,256	2005 Profits: $-15,309	Employees: 794
2004 Sales: $647,975	2004 Profits: $7,558	Fiscal Year Ends: 9/30
2003 Sales: $646,023	2003 Profits: $122,533	Parent Company:

SALARIES/BENEFITS:

Pension Plan:	ESOP Stock Plan:	Profit Sharing:	Top Exec. Salary: $620,400	Bonus: $395,505
Savings Plan: Y	Stock Purch. Plan: Y		Second Exec. Salary: $410,597	Bonus: $354,375

OTHER THOUGHTS:

Apparent Women Officers or Directors: 1
Hot Spot for Advancement for Women/Minorities:

LOCATIONS: ("Y" = Yes)

West:	Southwest:	Midwest:	Southeast:	Northeast:	International:
				Y	

Note: Financial information, benefits and other data can change quickly and may vary from those stated here.

PARTNERS HEALTHCARE SYSTEM www.partners.org

Industry Group Code: 622110 **Ranks within this company's industry group:** Sales: Profits:

Insurance/HMO/PPO:		Drugs:		Equipment/Supplies:		Hospitals/Clinics:		Services:		Health Care:	
Insurance:		Manufacturer:		Manufacturer:		Acute Care:	Y	Diagnostics:		Home Health:	Y
Managed Care:		Distributor:		Distributor:		Sub-Acute:		Labs/Testing:		Long-Term Care:	Y
Utilization Management:		Specialty Pharmacy:		Leasing/Finance:		Outpatient Surgery:		Staffing:		Physical Therapy:	
Payment Processing:		Vitamins/Nutritionals:		Information Systems:		Physical Rehab. Ctr.:		Waste Disposal:		Physician Prac. Mgmt.:	Y
		Clinical Trials:				Psychiatric Clinics:	Y	Specialty Svcs.:	Y		

TYPES OF BUSINESS:

Hospitals-General
Home & Long-Term Care
Medical Schools
Private Practices
Teaching Hospitals
Mental Health Hospitals

BRANDS/DIVISIONS/AFFILIATES:

Massachusetts General Hospital
Brigham & Women's Hospital
Partners Community HealthCare
Dana-Farber/Partners CancerCare
MGH Institute of Health Professions
Harvard Medical School
Newton-Wellesley Hospital
North Shore Medical Center

CONTACTS: *Note: Officers with more than one job title may be intentionally listed here more than once.*

James J. Mongan, CEO
Thomas P. Glynn, COO
James J. Mongan, Pres.
Dennis D. Colling, VP-Human Resources
John P. Glaser, CIO/VP
Robin M. Jacoby, Chief of Staff
Brent L. Henry, General Counsel/VP
Lynne J. Eickholt, VP-Bus. Planning & Market Dev.
Christopher H. Colecchi, VP-Research Ventures & Licensing
Matthew E. Fishman, VP-Community Health
Patrick Gilligan, VP-Managed Care Contracting & Finance
John M. Connors, Jr., Chmn.

Phone: 617-278-1000	**Fax:** 617-278-1049
Toll-Free:	
Address: Prudential Tower, 800 Boylston St., Ste. 1150, Boston, MA 02199-8001 US	

GROWTH PLANS/SPECIAL FEATURES:

Partners HealthCare is the largest health care system i Massachusetts. The firm was founded as the umbrell corporation for Massachusetts General Hospital and Brigha & Women's Hospital and has since grown to include primar physicians, specialist caregivers, acute care hospitals medical schools and long-term elderly care. Other compar members include Partners Community HealthCare, network of more than 1,000 physicians and 3,500 specialist serving more than 1.5 million patients; the Dana Farber/Partners CancerCare, a joint venture with Dan Farber Cancer Institute; MGH Institute of Health Profession and Harvard Medical School. Partners member hospital include the North Shore Medical Center; the McLea Hospital for the treatment of mental illness and chemic dependency; and Newton-Wellesley, the premier communit teaching hospital in Massachusetts. The firm also run Partners Continuing Care, an elderly care facility for hom and community care.

Along with medical, dental, vision and life coverage, Partner offers its employees spending accounts, child care, tuitio reimbursement, prescription drug coverage, a retiree medic savings account and work/life resources.

FINANCIALS: **Sales and profits are in thousands of dollars—add 000 to get the full amount. 2007 Note: Financial information for 2007 was not available for all companies at press time.**

2007 Sales: $	2007 Profits: $	**U.S. Stock Ticker: Nonprofit**
2006 Sales: $	2006 Profits: $	**Int'l Ticker:** Int'l Exchange:
2005 Sales: $	2005 Profits: $	Employees:
2004 Sales: $	2004 Profits: $	Fiscal Year Ends: 9/30
2003 Sales: $4,561,200	2003 Profits: $85,600	Parent Company:

SALARIES/BENEFITS:

Pension Plan: Y	ESOP Stock Plan:	Profit Sharing:	Top Exec. Salary: $	Bonus: $
Savings Plan: Y	Stock Purch. Plan:		Second Exec. Salary: $	Bonus: $

OTHER THOUGHTS:

Apparent Women Officers or Directors: 2
Hot Spot for Advancement for Women/Minorities:

LOCATIONS: ("Y" = Yes)

West:	Southwest:	Midwest:	Southeast:	Northeast:	International:
				Y	

PATTERSON COMPANIES INC www.pattersoncompanies.com

Industry Group Code: 421450 **Ranks within this company's industry group:** Sales: 4 Profits: 1

Insurance/HMO/PPO:		Drugs:		Equipment/Supplies:		Hospitals/Clinics:		Services:		Health Care:	
Insurance:		Manufacturer:		Manufacturer:	Y	Acute Care:		Diagnostics:		Home Health:	
Managed Care:		Distributor:		Distributor:	Y	Sub-Acute:		Labs/Testing:		Long-Term Care:	
Utilization Management:		Specialty Pharmacy:		Leasing/Finance:	Y	Outpatient Surgery:		Staffing:		Physical Therapy:	
Payment Processing:		Vitamins/Nutritionals:		Information Systems:	Y	Physical Rehab. Ctr.:		Waste Disposal:		Physician Prac. Mgmt.:	
		Clinical Trials:				Psychiatric Clinics:		Specialty Svcs.:	Y		

TYPES OF BUSINESS:

Dental Products & Related Services
Veterinary Products
Non-Wheelchair Assistive Products

BRANDS/DIVISIONS/AFFILIATES:

Patterson Dental Co.
Accu-Bite Dental Products, LLC
Webster Management LP
Patterson Medical Holdings, Inc.
Dale Surgical Professional Supply, Inc.
Metri Medical, Inc.
Sammons Preston Rolyan
Homecraft

CONTACTS: *Note: Officers with more than one job title may be intentionally listed here more than once.*

James W. Wiltz, CEO
James W. Wiltz, Pres.
R. Stephen Armstrong, CFO/Exec. VP
Matthew L. Levitt, General Counsel/Sec.
Gary D. Johnson, VP-Oper.
Lynn E. Askew, VP-Mgmt. Info. Systems
David P. Sproat, Pres., Patterson Medical
Scott P. Anderson, Pres., Patterson Dental
George L. Henriques, Pres., Webster Veterinary Supply, Inc.
Peter L. Frechette, Chmn.

Phone: 651-686-1600	**Fax:** 651-686-9331
Toll-Free: 800-328-5536	
Address: 1031 Mendota Heights Rd., St. Paul, MN 55120 US	

GROWTH PLANS/SPECIAL FEATURES:

Patterson Companies, Inc., formerly Patterson Dental Co., is a value-added products distributor in the markets of dental supply; companion pet and equine veterinary supply; and rehabilitation and non-wheelchair assistive products supply market. The company operates in three segments: dental supply, veterinary supply and rehabilitation supply. The dental supply segment, Patterson Dental, is one of the two largest distributors of dental products in North America. The division provides consumable products, including x-ray film, restorative materials, hand instruments and sterilization products; basic and advanced technology dental equipment; practice management and clinical software; patient education systems; and office forms and stationery. Patterson Dental also offers related services including dental equipment installation; maintenance and repair; dental office design; and equipment financing. The veterinary supply segment, Webster Veterinary, provides products for the diagnosis, treatment and/or prevention of diseases in companion pets and equine animals. Webster's more than 11,000 products are sold by about 175 field sales representatives. The segment also has an agency commission business with several pharmaceutical manufacturers. The rehabilitation supply segment, Patterson Medical, formerly AbilityOne Corp., distributes rehabilitation medical supplies and non-wheelchair assistive products. Patterson Medical operates as Sammons Preston Rolyan in North America and Homecraft in international markets. Subsidiaries include Patterson Dental Holdings, Inc.; Direct Dental Supply Co.; Webster Management LP; Patterson Medical Holdings, Inc.; Accu-Bite Dental Products, LLC; Williamston Industrial Center, LLC; Strategic Dental Marketing, Inc.; AbilityOne, Ltd.; Metro Medical, Inc.; and Dale Surgical Professional Supply, Inc. In June 2006, Patterson acquired Dale Professional Surgical Supply Co., Inc., a Long Island-based dealer and distributor of rehabilitation equipment.

The company offers its employees medical, dental and vision insurance; short- and long-term disability insurance; life and personal accident insurance; a 401(k) plan; an employee stock purchase plan; an employee stock ownership plan; education assistance; and an employee assistance program.

FINANCIALS: **Sales and profits are in thousands of dollars—add 000 to get the full amount. 2007 Note: Financial information for 2007 was not available for all companies at press time.**

2007 Sales: $2,798,398	2007 Profits: $208,336	**U.S. Stock Ticker: PDCO**
2006 Sales: $2,615,123	2006 Profits: $198,425	**Int'l Ticker:** Int'l Exchange:
2005 Sales: $2,421,457	2005 Profits: $183,698	Employees: 6,580
2004 Sales: $1,969,349	2004 Profits: $149,465	Fiscal Year Ends: 4/30
2003 Sales: $1,657,000	2003 Profits: $119,700	Parent Company:

SALARIES/BENEFITS:

Pension Plan:	ESOP Stock Plan: Y	Profit Sharing:	Top Exec. Salary: $557,338	Bonus: $250,250
Savings Plan: Y	Stock Purch. Plan: Y		Second Exec. Salary: $300,000	Bonus: $171,500

OTHER THOUGHTS:

Apparent Women Officers or Directors: 1
Hot Spot for Advancement for Women/Minorities:

LOCATIONS: ("Y" = Yes)

West:	Southwest:	Midwest:	Southeast:	Northeast:	International:
Y	Y	Y	Y	Y	Y

Note: Financial information, benefits and other data can change quickly and may vary from those stated here.

PDI INC

www.pdi-inc.com

Industry Group Code: 541613 **Ranks within this company's industry group:** Sales: 2 Profits: 2

Insurance/HMO/PPO:		Drugs:		Equipment/Supplies:		Hospitals/Clinics:		Services:		Health Care:	
Insurance:		Manufacturer:		Manufacturer:		Acute Care:		Diagnostics:		Home Health:	
Managed Care:		Distributor:		Distributor:		Sub-Acute:		Labs/Testing:		Long-Term Care:	
Utilization Management:		Specialty Pharmacy:		Leasing/Finance:		Outpatient Surgery:		Staffing:		Physical Therapy:	
Payment Processing:		Vitamins/Nutritionals:		Information Systems:		Physical Rehab. Ctr.:		Waste Disposal:		Physician Prac. Mgmt.:	
		Clinical Trials:				Psychiatric Clinics:		Specialty Svcs.:	Y		

TYPES OF BUSINESS:

Marketing & Advertising-Medical & Pharmaceutical Products
Contract Sales Organization
Pharmaceutical Sales Support
Marketing Research

BRANDS/DIVISIONS/AFFILIATES:

Pharmakon, LLC

CONTACTS:

Note: Officers with more than one job title may be intentionally listed here more than once.

Michael J. Marquard, CEO
Jeffrey Smith, CFO/Exec. VP
Nancy Connolly, Sr. VP-Sales Support Svcs.
Nancy McCarthy, Exec. VP-Human Resources
Jo Ann Saitta, Sr. VP-IT
Jeffrey Smith, Treas.
Kevin Connolly, Exec. VP/General Manager-Diversified Mktg. Svcs.
David Stievater, Sr. VP-Emerging Pharma
John P. Dugan, Chmn.

Phone: 201-258-8450 **Fax:** 201-258-8400
Toll-Free: 800-242-7494
Address: Saddle River Executive Ctr., 1 Route 17 S., Saddle River, NJ 07458 US

GROWTH PLANS/SPECIAL FEATURES:

PDI, Inc. is a diversified sales and marketing servic company serving the biopharmaceutical and life scienc industries. In addition, the company develops and execut continuing medical education activities to he pharmaceutical manufacturers meet their strateg educational goals. The firm operates in three segment sales, which represented about 85% of revenue in 200 marketing services, which includes Pharmakon, TV marketing research & consulting and vital issues in medici business units and which generated 15% of revenue in 200 and PDI products group. The firm provides product-speci programs designed to maximize profitability throughout product's lifecycle, from pre-launch through maturity. Th company is recognized for its knowledge in sales, bra management, product marketing, marketing researc medical education, medical affairs and managed market a trade relations. PDI creates and executes sales a marketing programs designed for clients' products, which promotes for fees or percentages of sales, as well products the company itself distributes, licenses or ow outright. Clients engage PDI on a contractual basis design and implement product detailing programs for bo prescription and over-the-counter products. The compa has designed and executed customized sales and marketi programs for many of the industry's largest compani including AstraZeneca, GlaxoSmithKline, Novartis, Pfiz and Allergan. The firm's medical education a communications group creates custom programs to inform clients' potential customers about the benefits of its clien products. Such programs may include teleconference audio seminars, publication planning and continuing medic education programs. In addition, PDI offers qualitative a quantitative marketing research to health care provider patients and managed care customers in the U.S. a globally. In January 2006, PDI announced that it ha entered a three-year agreement with Align Pharmaceutica to assist them with the commercialization of their ne product entries for the oncology market.

FINANCIALS:

Sales and profits are in thousands of dollars—add 000 to get the full amount. 2007 Note: Financial information for 2007 was not available for all companies at press time.

2007 Sales: $	2007 Profits: $
2006 Sales: $239,242	2006 Profits: $11,809
2005 Sales: $305,205	2005 Profits: $-19,454
2004 Sales: $345,797	2004 Profits: $21,132
2003 Sales: $317,448	2003 Profits: $12,258

U.S. Stock Ticker: PDII
Int'l Ticker: Int'l Exchange:
Employees: 1,100
Fiscal Year Ends: 12/31
Parent Company:

SALARIES/BENEFITS:

Pension Plan:	ESOP Stock Plan:	Profit Sharing:	Top Exec. Salary: $322,056	Bonus: $181,157
Savings Plan: Y	Stock Purch. Plan:		Second Exec. Salary: $267,279	Bonus: $168,386

OTHER THOUGHTS:

Apparent Women Officers or Directors: 3
Hot Spot for Advancement for Women/Minorities: Y

LOCATIONS: ("Y" = Yes)

West:	Southwest:	Midwest:	Southeast:	Northeast:	International:
		Y		Y	

Note: Financial information, benefits and other data can change quickly and may vary from those stated here.

PEDIATRIC SERVICES OF AMERICA INC

www.psahealthcare.com

Industry Group Code: 621610 **Ranks within this company's industry group:** Sales: 11 Profits: 5

Insurance/HMO/PPO:		Drugs:		Equipment/Supplies:		Hospitals/Clinics:		Services:		Health Care:	
Insurance:		Manufacturer:		Manufacturer:		Acute Care:		Diagnostics:		Home Health:	Y
Managed Care:		Distributor:		Distributor:	Y	Sub-Acute:		Labs/Testing:		Long-Term Care:	
Utilization Management:		Specialty Pharmacy:		Leasing/Finance:	Y	Outpatient Surgery:		Staffing:		Physical Therapy:	Y
Payment Processing:		Vitamins/Nutritionals:		Information Systems:		Physical Rehab. Ctr.:		Waste Disposal:		Physician Prac. Mgmt.:	
		Clinical Trials:				Psychiatric Clinics:		Specialty Svcs.:	Y		

TYPES OF BUSINESS:

Pediatric Health Care & Related Services
Case Management Services
Private Duty Nursing
Prescribed Pediatric Extended Care

BRANDS/DIVISIONS/AFFILIATES:

Maternal Child Health, Inc.

CONTACTS: *Note: Officers with more than one job title may be intentionally listed here more than once.*

Daniel J. Kohl, CEO
Daniel J. Kohl, Pres.
James M. McNeill, CFO/Sr. VP
Wesley E. Debnam, VP-Human Resources
Thomas D. Zeimet, VP-Info. Systems
John R. Hamilton III, General Counsel/Chief Risk Officer
Mark A. Kulik, VP-Bus. Dev.
Lori J. Reel, Chief Acct. Officer/VP-Acct.
Elizabeth A. Rubio, VP-Oper., Private Duty Nursing & PPEC
Jeffrey K Nickell, VP-Reimbursement
Dale Valentine, VP-Compliance
Michael Patrick Davidsom, VP-Oper., Respiratory Therapy Equipment & Svcs.

Phone: 770-441-1580	**Fax:** 770-263-9340
Toll-Free: 800-950-1580	
Address: 310 Technology Pkwy., Norcross, GA 30092 US	

GROWTH PLANS/SPECIAL FEATURES:

Pediatric Services of America, Inc. (PSA) provides home healthcare and related services for medically fragile and chronically ill infants and children. The company operates through a network of over 50 branch offices, including satellite offices and new branch offices, locates in 18 states. The firm operates in two segments: private duty nursing (PDN) and prescribed pediatric extended care (PPEC) services. PSA provides a broad range of pediatric healthcare services, including nursing, rehabilitation and therapy services in PPEC day treatment centers; well care services and special needs education services for pediatric patients; and case management services in order to assist the family and patient by coordinating the provision of services between the insurer or the other payor, the physician, the hospital and other healthcare providers. In November 2006, PSA sold its respiratory therapy equipment and services business to Lincare, Inc. In February 2007, the company acquired select pediatric assets of Maternal Child Health, Inc. In April 2007, PSA announced that it entered into a definitive agreement pursuant to which the company will become a privately-owned company. Portfolio Logic will acquire all of the outstanding common shares of PSA.

FINANCIALS: **Sales and profits are in thousands of dollars—add 000 to get the full amount. 2007 Note: Financial information for 2007 was not available for all companies at press time.**

2007 Sales: $	2007 Profits: $	**U.S. Stock Ticker: PSAI**
2006 Sales: $119,360	2006 Profits: $24,126	**Int'l Ticker:** Int'l Exchange:
2005 Sales: $114,146	2005 Profits: $5,666	Employees: 4,300
2004 Sales: $106,713	2004 Profits: $4,012	Fiscal Year Ends: 9/30
2003 Sales: $155,757	2003 Profits: $5,126	Parent Company:

SALARIES/BENEFITS:

Pension Plan:	ESOP Stock Plan:	Profit Sharing:	Top Exec. Salary: $364,000	Bonus: $218,400
Savings Plan:	Stock Purch. Plan:		Second Exec. Salary: $270,000	Bonus: $140,000

OTHER THOUGHTS:

Apparent Women Officers or Directors: 2
Hot Spot for Advancement for Women/Minorities:

LOCATIONS: ("Y" = Yes)

West:	Southwest:	Midwest:	Southeast:	Northeast:	International:
Y	Y	Y	Y	Y	

Note: Financial information, benefits and other data can change quickly and may vary from those stated here.

PEDIATRIX MEDICAL GROUP INC www.pediatrix.com

Industry Group Code: 621111 **Ranks within this company's industry group:** Sales: 2 Profits: 1

Insurance/HMO/PPO:		Drugs:		Equipment/Supplies:		Hospitals/Clinics:		Services:		Health Care:	
Insurance:		Manufacturer:		Manufacturer:		Acute Care:		Diagnostics:		Home Health:	
Managed Care:		Distributor:		Distributor:		Sub-Acute:		Labs/Testing:	Y	Long-Term Care:	
Utilization Management:		Specialty Pharmacy:		Leasing/Finance:		Outpatient Surgery:		Staffing:	Y	Physical Therapy:	
Payment Processing:		Vitamins/Nutritionals:		Information Systems:		Physical Rehab. Ctr.:		Waste Disposal:		Physician Prac. Mgmt.:	Y
		Clinical Trials:				Psychiatric Clinics:		Specialty Svcs.:	Y		

TYPES OF BUSINESS:

Hospital-Based Pediatrician Practice Management
Pediatric Intensive Care Unit Management
Neonatal Intensive Care Unit Management
Perinatal Physician Services
Staffing Services
Laboratory Services

BRANDS/DIVISIONS/AFFILIATES:

Obstetrix Medical Group
Pediatrix University
natalu.com
Pediatrix Screening, Inc.
Atlanta Neonatal Physician Group

CONTACTS: *Note: Officers with more than one job title may be intentionally listed here more than once.*

Roger J. Medel, CEO
Joseph M. Calabro, COO
Joseph M. Calabro, Pres.
Karl B. Wagner, CFO
Alan R. Spitzer, Sr. VP-R&D
Robert C. Bryant, CIO/Sr. VP
David Clark, Sr. VP-Oper.
John F. Rizzo, Sr. VP-Bus. Dev.
Robert J. Balcom, Regional Pres., Central Region
Eric Kurzweil, Regional Pres., Mountain Region
Frederick V. Miller, Regional Pres., Atlantic Region
Carlos A. Perez, Regional Pres., Caribbean Region

Phone: 954-384-0175	**Fax:** 954-838-9961
Toll-Free: 800-243-3839	
Address: 1301 Concord Terrace, Sunrise, FL 33323 US	

GROWTH PLANS/SPECIAL FEATURES:

Pediatrix Medical Group, Inc. is a provider of physicia services at more than 289 hospital-based neonatal intensiv care units and 80 affiliated maternal fetal medicin subspecialists. The company's principle mission is th provision of comprehensive clinical care to babies bor prematurely or with medical complications and to expectar mothers experiencing complicated pregnancies. Pediatrix' network includes approximately 914 affiliated physicians including 724 neonatal physician subspecialists who provid clinical care in 32 states and Puerto Rico. The company als works with other pediatric subspecialists, including 5 pediatric cardiologists, 36 pediatric intensivists and 1 pediatric hospitalists. Pediatrix operates through fou primary divisions: Obstetrix Medical Group specializes i maternal-fetal medicine, providing care for woman and the unborn babies during high risk pregnancies; Pediatri Screening operates the nation's largest independer laboratory specializing in newborn hearing and metaboli screening; Pediatrix University focuses on clinical researc and on offering neonatal medical education through its virtu classrooms and online journals; and America Anesthesiology, a recently opened division that acts as national group practice specializing in anesthesia services In addition to providing physician services at hospital-base pediatric intensive care units and pediatrics departments i hospitals, the company also staffs and manages perinata practices, which involve the operation of outpatient offices a well as the management of inpatient maternal-fetal care. I 2007, Pediatrix increased its operations through a series c acquisitions: in January, it acquired the San Francisc Neonatology Medical Group, which serves three hospitals i the San Francisco area; in March, it acquired Neonatolog Associates, a group practice based out of Munster, Indiana in July, it acquired the San Antonio Pediatric Cardiolog Practice, which provides physician services throughout sout central Texas; in August, it acquired the Seattle Ultrasoun Physician Group Practice; and in September, it expanded it new American Anesthesiology division through th acquisition of Fairfax Anesthesiology Associates, Inc.

FINANCIALS: **Sales and profits are in thousands of dollars—add 000 to get the full amount. 2007 Note: Financial information for 2007 was not available for all companies at press time.**

2007 Sales: $	2007 Profits: $	**U.S. Stock Ticker: PDX**
2006 Sales: $818,554	2006 Profits: $124,465	**Int'l Ticker:** Int'l Exchange:
2005 Sales: $693,700	2005 Profits: $87,509	Employees: 3,378
2004 Sales: $619,629	2004 Profits: $96,195	Fiscal Year Ends: 12/31
2003 Sales: $551,197	2003 Profits: $84,328	Parent Company:

SALARIES/BENEFITS:

Pension Plan:	ESOP Stock Plan:	Profit Sharing:	Top Exec. Salary: $675,000	Bonus: $715,500
Savings Plan: Y	Stock Purch. Plan: Y		Second Exec. Salary: $450,000	Bonus: $477,000

OTHER THOUGHTS:

Apparent Women Officers or Directors:
Hot Spot for Advancement for Women/Minorities:

LOCATIONS: ("Y" = Yes)

West:	Southwest:	Midwest:	Southeast:	Northeast:	International:
Y	Y	Y	Y	Y	Y

Note: Financial information, benefits and other data can change quickly and may vary from those stated here.

PERKINELMER INC www.perkinelmer.com

Industry Group Code: 334500 **Ranks within this company's industry group:** Sales: 2 Profits: 2

Insurance/HMO/PPO:		Drugs:		Equipment/Supplies:		Hospitals/Clinics:		Services:		Health Care:	
Insurance:		Manufacturer:		Manufacturer:	Y	Acute Care:		Diagnostics:		Home Health:	
Managed Care:		Distributor:		Distributor:		Sub-Acute:		Labs/Testing:		Long-Term Care:	
Utilization Management:		Specialty Pharmacy:		Leasing/Finance:		Outpatient Surgery:		Staffing:		Physical Therapy:	
Payment Processing:		Vitamins/Nutritionals:		Information Systems:		Physical Rehab. Ctr.:		Waste Disposal:		Physician Prac. Mgmt.:	
		Clinical Trials:				Psychiatric Clinics:		Specialty Svcs.:	Y		

TYPES OF BUSINESS:

Medical Equipment-Assorted Instruments
Mechanical Components
Optoelectronics
Pharmaceutical Manufacturing
Life Science Systems

BRANDS/DIVISIONS/AFFILIATES:

LANCE
AlphaScreen
Trim XE
Clinical & Analitical Service Solutions, Ltd.
Evotec Technologies GmbH
Euroscreen Products S.A.
Improvision, Ltd.
AequoScreen

CONTACTS: *Note: Officers with more than one job title may be intentionally listed here more than once.*

Gregory L. Summe, CEO
Robert F. Friel, COO
Robert F. Friel, Pres.
Jeffrey D. Capello, CFO/Sr. VP
Richard F. Walsh, Chief Admin. Officer/Sr. VP
Katherine A. O'Hara, General Counsel/Sr. VP/Sec.
Michael L. Battles, Chief Acct. Officer/VP
John A. Roush, Sr. VP/Pres., Optoelectronics
Gregory L. Summe, Chmn.

Phone: 781-663-6900	**Fax:** 203-944-4904
Toll-Free:	
Address: 940 Winter St., Waltham, MA 02451 US	

GROWTH PLANS/SPECIAL FEATURES:

PerkinElmer, Inc. is a provider of scientific instruments, consumables and services to the pharmaceutical, biomedical, academic research, environmental testing and general industrial markets, commonly referred to as the health sciences and photonics markets. The firm designs, manufactures, markets and services products and systems throughout 125 countries. The company operates in two business units: life and analytical sciences; and optoelectronics. The life and analytical sciences unit is a provider of drug discovery; genetic screening; and environmental and chemical analysis tools, including instruments, reagents, consumables and services. The unit also conducts pharmaceutical manufacturing. Principal products in this segment include chemical and biological reagents such as LANCE and assay technologies such as AlphaScreen. The optoelectronics segment provides a broad range of digital imaging, sensor and specialty lighting components used in the biomedical, consumer products and other specialty end markets. The division is a supplier of amorphous silicon digital x-ray detectors used in medical imaging and radiation therapy, and its optical sensor products are used in sample detection in life sciences instruments; luggage screening; laser printers; security and fire detection systems; HVAC controls; document sorting; and smart weaponry. New product releases by the segment include the Trim XE family of xenon flash products for digital still cameras and mobile phone camera applications. In June 2006, the company acquired Clinical & Analytical Service Solutions, Ltd., a scientific equipment asset and managed maintenance company serving the pharmaceutical, biotechnology and healthcare markets, for roughly $12.4 million. In January 2007, the firm acquired Evotec Technologies GmbH for $33 million and Euroscreen Products S.A., a developer of AequoScreen cellular assay platform, for $18.1 million. In April 2007, PerkinElmer acquired Improvision, Ltd., a U.K. provider of cellular imaging software and integrated hardware solutions.

FINANCIALS: **Sales and profits are in thousands of dollars—add 000 to get the full amount. 2007 Note: Financial information for 2007 was not available for all companies at press time.**

2007 Sales: $	2007 Profits: $	**U.S. Stock Ticker: PKI**
2006 Sales: $1,546,358	2006 Profits: $119,583	**Int'l Ticker:** Int'l Exchange:
2005 Sales: $1,473,831	2005 Profits: $268,108	Employees: 8,500
2004 Sales: $1,429,089	2004 Profits: $96,043	Fiscal Year Ends: 12/31
2003 Sales: $1,535,200	2003 Profits: $52,900	Parent Company:

SALARIES/BENEFITS:

Pension Plan:	ESOP Stock Plan:	Profit Sharing:	Top Exec. Salary: $998,077	Bonus: $2,806,100
Savings Plan:	Stock Purch. Plan:		Second Exec. Salary: $542,115	Bonus: $1,170,648

OTHER THOUGHTS:

Apparent Women Officers or Directors: 2
Hot Spot for Advancement for Women/Minorities: Y

LOCATIONS: ("Y" = Yes)

West:	Southwest:	Midwest:	Southeast:	Northeast:	International:
Y		Y		Y	Y

PER-SE TECHNOLOGIES INC www.per-se.com

Industry Group Code: 511212 **Ranks within this company's industry group:** Sales: Profits:

Insurance/HMO/PPO:		Drugs:		Equipment/Supplies:		Hospitals/Clinics:		Services:		Health Care:	
Insurance:		Manufacturer:		Manufacturer:		Acute Care:		Diagnostics:		Home Health:	
Managed Care:		Distributor:		Distributor:		Sub-Acute:		Labs/Testing:		Long-Term Care:	
Utilization Management:		Specialty Pharmacy:		Leasing/Finance:		Outpatient Surgery:		Staffing:		Physical Therapy:	
Payment Processing:		Vitamins/Nutritionals:		Information Systems:	Y	Physical Rehab. Ctr.:		Waste Disposal:		Physician Prac. Mgmt.:	Y
		Clinical Trials:				Psychiatric Clinics:		Specialty Svcs.:	Y		

TYPES OF BUSINESS:

Physician Practice Management
Business Management Outsourcing
Health Care Application Software
Online Data Exchange

BRANDS/DIVISIONS/AFFILIATES:

McKesson Corporation
Pharmacy Services
Physician Services
Hospital Services
NDCHealth

CONTACTS: *Note: Officers with more than one job title may be intentionally listed here more than once.*

Philip M. Pead, CEO
Chris E. Perkins, COO
Philip M. Pead, Pres.
Stephen Scheppmann, CFO
Philip Jordan, Chief Products Strategy
Paul J. Quiner, General Counsel/Sr. VP
G. Scott MacKenzie, Pres., Pharmacy Solutions
Patrick Leonard, Pres., Physician Solutions
David Mason, Pres., Hospital Solutions
Philip M. Pead, Chmn.

Phone: 770-237-4300	**Fax:** 770-237-6525
Toll-Free: 877-737-3773	
Address: 1145 Sanctuary Pkwy., Ste. 200, Alpharetta, GA 30004 US	

GROWTH PLANS/SPECIAL FEATURES:

Per-Se Technologies, Inc., a wholly-owned subsidiary o McKesson Corporation operating under the Provide Technology segment, provides integrated busines management outsourcing services, application software an Internet-enabled connectivity for the health care industry. It Physicians Services division provides business manageme outsourcing services to the hospital-affiliated physicia practice market, physicians in academic settings and othe large physician practices. Services in this segment focus o the management of revenue cycles and include clinical dat collection, data input, medical coding, billing, contrac management and cash collection. Per-Se also provide enterprise-wide financial, clinical and administrative softwar to acute health care organizations, including patient financi management software and patient and staff schedulin systems. The firm provides connectivity and busines intelligence solutions to health care providers and payers helping to reduce administrative costs and enhance revenu cycle management. Many of these physician services ar offered to hospitals and pharmacies, as part of th company's new business re-organization, which divide activities between Physician, Hospital and Pharmac Services. Of these, the Pharmacy Services division recentl underwent a major expansion due to the acquisition o NDCHealth, a provider of healthcare technology an information solutions. The Per-Se Exchange is one of th largest electronic clearinghouses in the health care industry In January 2007, the $1.8 billion acquisition of the compan by McKesson Corporation was completed. McKesson plans to fully integrate Per-Se into its Provider Technologies segment in the near future.

FINANCIALS: Sales and profits are in thousands of dollars—add 000 to get the full amount. 2007 Note: Financial information for 2007 was not available for all companies at press time.

2007 Sales: $	2007 Profits: $	**U.S. Stock Ticker: Subsidiary**
2006 Sales: $	2006 Profits: $	**Int'l Ticker:** Int'l Exchange:
2005 Sales: $372,718	2005 Profits: $38,659	Employees: 5,100
2004 Sales: $352,800	2004 Profits: $48,158	Fiscal Year Ends: 12/31
2003 Sales: $335,200	2003 Profits: $12,000	Parent Company: MCKESSON CORPORATION

SALARIES/BENEFITS:

Pension Plan:	ESOP Stock Plan:	Profit Sharing:	Top Exec. Salary: $519,752	Bonus: $355,437
Savings Plan: Y	Stock Purch. Plan:		Second Exec. Salary: $350,879	Bonus: $178,221

OTHER THOUGHTS:

Apparent Women Officers or Directors:
Hot Spot for Advancement for Women/Minorities:

LOCATIONS: ("Y" = Yes)

West:	Southwest:	Midwest:	Southeast:	Northeast:	International:
			Y		Y

PETMED EXPRESS INC www.1800petmeds.com

Industry Group Code: 453910 **Ranks within this company's industry group:** Sales: 1 Profits: 1

Insurance/HMO/PPO:		Drugs:		Equipment/Supplies:		Hospitals/Clinics:		Services:		Health Care:	
surance:		Manufacturer:		Manufacturer:		Acute Care:		Diagnostics:		Home Health:	
anaged Care:		Distributor:		Distributor:	Y	Sub-Acute:		Labs/Testing:		Long-Term Care:	
tilization Management:		Specialty Pharmacy:	Y	Leasing/Finance:		Outpatient Surgery:		Staffing:		Physical Therapy:	
ayment Processing:		Vitamins/Nutritionals:	Y	Information Systems:		Physical Rehab. Ctr.:		Waste Disposal:		Physician Prac. Mgmt.:	
		Clinical Trials:				Psychiatric Clinics:		Specialty Svcs.:			

TYPES OF BUSINESS:

Prescription & Non-Prescription Pet Drugs
Mail Order Pet Pharmacy
Veterinary Medications
Animal Vitamins & Nutraceuticals
Pet Care Products

BRANDS/DIVISIONS/AFFILIATES:

1-800-PetMeds
PetHealth101.com
Frontline Plus
Advantage
K9 Advantix
Heartguard Plus
Sentinel
Interceptor

CONTACTS: *Note: Officers with more than one job title may be intentionally listed here more than once.*

Menderes Akdag, CEO
Menderes Akdag, Pres.
Bruce S. Rosenbloom, CFO
Robert C. Schweitzer, Chmn.

Phone: 954-979-5995	**Fax:** 954-971-0544
Toll-Free: 800-738-6337	
Address: 1441 SW 29th Ave., Pompano Beach, FL 33069 US	

GROWTH PLANS/SPECIAL FEATURES:

PetMed Express, Inc. is a nationwide pet pharmacy that markets its products under the brand name 1-800-PetMeds through national television, online and direct mail advertising campaigns. The company markets prescription and non-prescription pet medications and health and nutritional supplements for dogs, cats and horses directly to consumers, which allows increased convenience, lower prices and quicker delivery. PetMed operates a call center and publishes a full-color catalog featuring approximately 400 products. The firm offers a broad selection of name-brand medications for dogs and cats, including Frontline Plus, Advantage, K9 Advantix, Heartguard Plus, Sentinel, Interceptor, Program, Revolution, Deramaxx and Rimadyl, at prices that are competitive with those charged by veterinarians and retailers. PetMed's non-prescription medications include flea and tick control, bone and joint care products, vitamins and nutritional supplements and hygiene products. Prescription medications include heartworm treatments, thyroid and arthritis medications, antibiotics and other proprietary medications and generic substitutes. The company is continuously researching new products and selecting new products to become part of its product lineup, which is instantly reflected on the PetMed web site along with new featured products and promotions. The group also maintains PetHealth101.com, a new web site that gives pet owners access to health information covering pet behavior, illnesses and natural and pharmaceutical remedies for pet problems. In addition to pet medications, the firm also produces grooming tools, odor controllers, beds, bowls, leashes, training aids and treats. Approximately 1.9 million customers have purchased from PetMed within the last two years, with approximately 50% of customers residing in California, Florida, Texas, New York, New Jersey, Pennsylvania and Virginia. PetMed inventories its products and fills all customer orders from its 50,000 square foot facility in Pompano Beach, Florida.

FINANCIALS: **Sales and profits are in thousands of dollars—add 000 to get the full amount. 2007 Note: Financial information for 2007 was not available for all companies at press time.**

2007 Sales: $162,246	2007 Profits: $43,066	**U.S. Stock Ticker: PETS**
2006 Sales: $137,583	2006 Profits: $12,063	**Int'l Ticker:** Int'l Exchange:
2005 Sales: $108,358	2005 Profits: $8,010	Employees: 216
2004 Sales: $93,994	2004 Profits: $5,813	Fiscal Year Ends: 3/31
2003 Sales: $54,975	2003 Profits: $3,258	Parent Company:

SALARIES/BENEFITS:

Pension Plan:	ESOP Stock Plan:	Profit Sharing:	Top Exec. Salary: $254,615	Bonus: $
Savings Plan:	Stock Purch. Plan:		Second Exec. Salary: $146,060	Bonus: $1,000

OTHER THOUGHTS:

Apparent Women Officers or Directors:
Hot Spot for Advancement for Women/Minorities:

LOCATIONS: ("Y" = Yes)

West:	Southwest:	Midwest:	Southeast:	Northeast:	International:
			Y		

PFIZER INC

www.pfizer.com

Industry Group Code: 325412 **Ranks within this company's industry group:** Sales: 2 Profits: 1

Insurance/HMO/PPO:		Drugs:		Equipment/Supplies:		Hospitals/Clinics:		Services:		Health Care:	
Insurance:		Manufacturer:	Y	Manufacturer:		Acute Care:		Diagnostics:		Home Health:	
Managed Care:		Distributor:		Distributor:		Sub-Acute:		Labs/Testing:		Long-Term Care:	
Utilization Management:		Specialty Pharmacy:		Leasing/Finance:		Outpatient Surgery:		Staffing:		Physical Therapy:	
Payment Processing:		Vitamins/Nutritionals:		Information Systems:		Physical Rehab. Ctr.:		Waste Disposal:		Physician Prac. Mgmt.:	
		Clinical Trials:				Psychiatric Clinics:		Specialty Svcs.:			

TYPES OF BUSINESS:

Drugs-Diversified
Prescription Pharmaceuticals
Veterinary Pharmaceuticals
Capsule Manufacturing

BRANDS/DIVISIONS/AFFILIATES:

Celebrex
Viagra
Zoloft
Zyrtec
Aricept
Lipitor
Relpax
Pharmacia Corporation

CONTACTS: *Note: Officers with more than one job title may be intentionally listed here more than once.*

Jeffrey B. Kindler, CEO
Frank D'Amelio, CFO
Mary McLeod, Leader-Worldwide Talent Dev. & Human Resources
John L. LaMattina, Sr. VP/Pres., Pfizer Global R&D
Greg Vahle, Sr. VP-Global Bus. Svcs.
Jonathan White, Sr. VP-Tech. & Bus. Innovation
Nick Saccomano, Sr. VP-Exploratory Science & Tech.
Joseph M. Feczko, Sr. VP/Chief Medical Officer
Nat Ricciardi, Pres., Pfizer Global Mfg.
Allen Waxman, Sr. VP/General Counsel
Ian Read, Sr. VP/Pres., Worldwide Pharmaceutical Oper.
Ed Harrigan, Sr. VP-Worldwide Bus. Dev.
Rich Bagger, Sr. VP-Worldwide Public Affairs & Policy
Amal Naj, Sr. VP-Worldwide Investor Dev. & Strategy
Bill Roche, VP-Finance, Strategic Mgmt. & Functional Support
David Shedlarz, Vice Chmn.
Andreas Fibig, Sr. VP/General Mgr.-Powers Bus. Unit
Oliver Brandicourt, Sr. VP/General Mgr.-Pratt Bus. Unit
Susan Silbermann, Sr. VP-Worldwide Commercial Dev.
Jeffrey B. Kindler, Chmn.
Jean Michel Halfon, Area Pres., Latin America, Africa, ME & Canada

Phone: 212-573-2323 **Fax:** 212-573-7851
Toll-Free:
Address: 235 E. 42nd St., New York, NY 10017-5755 US

GROWTH PLANS/SPECIAL FEATURES:

Pfizer, Inc. is a research-based global drug company that discovers, develops, manufactures and markets prescription medicines for humans and animals. The company operates in two business segments: Human Health and Animal Health. The Human Health segment includes treatments for cardiovascular and metabolic diseases (including Lipitor and Norvasc), central nervous system disorders (including Zoloft, Xanax and Neurontin), arthritis and pain (Celebrex), infectious and respiratory diseases (including Spiriva and Exubera), cancer (including Ellence, Sutent and Camptosar), eye disease, endocrine disorders (Genotropin) and allergies (notably Zyrtec), among others. The company's Viagra is the leading treatment for erectile dysfunction and one of the world's most recognized pharmaceutical brands. The Animal Health Segment discovers, develops and sells products for the prevention and treatment of diseases in livestock and companion animals. Its products include parasiticides (including Revolution), anti-inflammatories (Rimadyl), vaccines, antibiotics and related medicines. Pfizer's staff includes 12,000 medical researchers who support substantial research and development projects and investments, totaling $7.6 billion in 2006. Currently, the company holds about 169 new molecular entities, 73 product-line extensions and more than 400 compounds in discovery research. In a major development, Pfizer acquired Pharmacia Corporation making it the largest pharmaceutical company in the U.S., Europe, Japan and Latin America. In June 2006, Johnson & Johnson agreed to acquire Pfizer's consumer health division, maker of Benadryl, Listerine and many other over-the-counter health items, for $16.6 billion dollars. In early 2007 Pfizer announced it would eliminate 10,000 positions (10% of its workforce) over the next two years. This includes more than 20% of its European sales force and 2,200 U.S. sales representatives. Additionally, the firm plans to close up to five of its research laboratories.

Pfizer offers its employees free prescription drugs, tuition reimbursement, adoption assistance, a referral program, educational loans and four-year college scholarships for children of employees.

FINANCIALS: **Sales and profits are in thousands of dollars—add 000 to get the full amount. 2007 Note: Financial information for 2007 was not available for all companies at press time.**

2007 Sales: $
2006 Sales: $48,371,000
2005 Sales: $47,405,000
2004 Sales: $48,988,000
2003 Sales: $45,188,000

2007 Profits: $
2006 Profits: $19,337,000
2005 Profits: $8,085,000
2004 Profits: $11,361,000
2003 Profits: $3,910,000

U.S. Stock Ticker: PFE
Int'l Ticker: Int'l Exchange:
Employees: 106,000
Fiscal Year Ends: 12/31
Parent Company:

SALARIES/BENEFITS:

Pension Plan: Y ESOP Stock Plan: Profit Sharing: Top Exec. Salary: $2,270,500 Bonus: $
Savings Plan: Y Stock Purch. Plan: Second Exec. Salary: $1,220,300 Bonus: $1,383,000

OTHER THOUGHTS:

Apparent Women Officers or Directors: 25
Hot Spot for Advancement for Women/Minorities: Y

LOCATIONS: ("Y" = Yes)

West:	Southwest:	Midwest:	Southeast:	Northeast:	International:
Y	Y	Y	Y	Y	Y

PHARMACEUTICAL PRODUCT DEVELOPMENT INC

www.ppdi.com

Industry Group Code: 541710 **Ranks within this company's industry group:** Sales: 2 Profits: 1

Insurance/HMO/PPO:		Drugs:		Equipment/Supplies:		Hospitals/Clinics:		Services:		Health Care:	
Insurance:		Manufacturer:		Manufacturer:		Acute Care:		Diagnostics:		Home Health:	
Managed Care:		Distributor:		Distributor:		Sub-Acute:		Labs/Testing:	Y	Long-Term Care:	
Utilization Management:		Specialty Pharmacy:		Leasing/Finance:		Outpatient Surgery:		Staffing:		Physical Therapy:	
Payment Processing:		Vitamins/Nutritionals:		Information Systems:	Y	Physical Rehab. Ctr.:		Waste Disposal:		Physician Prac. Mgmt.:	
		Clinical Trials:	Y			Psychiatric Clinics:		Specialty Svcs.:	Y		

TYPES OF BUSINESS:

Contract Research
Drug Discovery & Development Services
Clinical Data Consulting Services
Medical Marketing & Information Support Services
Drug Development Software
Medical Device Development

BRANDS/DIVISIONS/AFFILIATES:

PPD Discovery
PPD Development
CSS Informatics
PPD Medical Communications
PPD Virtual

CONTACTS: *Note: Officers with more than one job title may be intentionally listed here more than once.*

Fredric N. Eshelman, CEO
Linda Baddour, CFO
Paul S. Covington, Exec. VP-Dev.
William Richardson, Sr. VP-Global Bus. Dev.
Linda Baddour, Treas.
Frederic N. Eshelman, Vice Chmn.
Mark Roseman, VP-Clinical Oper.
Andy Strayer, Sr. VP-Clinical Oper.-Americas & Asia
Randy Marchbanks, VP-Bus. Dev.-Americas
Ernest Mario, Chmn.
Sue Stansfield, Sr. VP-Clinical Oper. & Project Mgmt., Europe

Phone: 910-251-0081	**Fax:** 910-762-5820
Toll-Free:	
Address: 3151 S. 17th St., Wilmington, NC 28412 US	

GROWTH PLANS/SPECIAL FEATURES:

Pharmaceutical Product Development, Inc. (PPD) provides drug discovery and development services to pharmaceutical and biotechnology companies as well as academic and government organizations. PPD's services are primarily divided into two company segments: PPD Discovery and PPD Development. Through the combined services of these segments, PPD helps pharmaceutical companies through all stages of clinical testing. The stages of testing can be specifically divided into preclinical, phase I, phase II-IIIb and post-approval. In the preclinical stages of drug testing, PPD provides information concerning the pharmaceutical composition of a new drug, its safety, its formulaic design and how it will be administered to children and adults. During phase I of testing, PPD conducts healthy volunteer clinics, provides data management services and guides companies/laboratories through regulatory affairs. In phase II and III tests, PPD oversees the later stages of product development and government approval, providing project management and clinical monitoring. In the post-approval stage of a drug's development, PPD provides technology and marketing services aimed to maximize the new drug's lifecycle. PPD has experience conducting research and drug development in several areas, including antiviral studies, cardiovascular diseases, critical care studies, endocrine/metabolic studies, hematology/oncology studies, immunology studies and ophthalmology studies. The firm additionally conducts regional, national and global studies and research projects through offices in 28 countries worldwide. In 2006, PPD signed an agreement with PDL BioPharma, Inc., whereby the firm will perform molecular profiling to discover biomarkers. Additionally, CSS Informatics, the clinical and safety data management division of PPD, entered into an agreement with i-clinics, Ltd., a software provider of data acquisition and management systems. In early 2007, PPD opened a new facility in Lanarkshire, Scotland.

FINANCIALS: **Sales and profits are in thousands of dollars—add 000 to get the full amount. 2007 Note: Financial information for 2007 was not available for all companies at press time.**

2007 Sales: $	2007 Profits: $	**U.S. Stock Ticker: PPDI**
2006 Sales: $1,247,682	2006 Profits: $156,652	**Int'l Ticker:** Int'l Exchange:
2005 Sales: $1,037,090	2005 Profits: $119,897	Employees: 9,150
2004 Sales: $841,256	2004 Profits: $91,684	Fiscal Year Ends: 12/31
2003 Sales: $726,983	2003 Profits: $46,310	Parent Company:

SALARIES/BENEFITS:

Pension Plan:	ESOP Stock Plan:	Profit Sharing:	Top Exec. Salary: $688,733	Bonus: $475,000
Savings Plan: Y	Stock Purch. Plan:		Second Exec. Salary: $348,189	Bonus: $175,000

OTHER THOUGHTS:

Apparent Women Officers or Directors: 2
Hot Spot for Advancement for Women/Minorities: Y

LOCATIONS: ("Y" = Yes)

West:	Southwest:	Midwest:	Southeast:	Northeast:	International:
Y		Y	Y	Y	Y

PHARMACOPEIA DRUG DISCOVERY www.pharmacopeia.com

Industry Group Code: 541710 **Ranks within this company's industry group:** Sales: 4 Profits: 3

Insurance/HMO/PPO:		Drugs:		Equipment/Supplies:		Hospitals/Clinics:		Services:		Health Care:	
Insurance:		Manufacturer:		Manufacturer:		Acute Care:		Diagnostics:		Home Health:	
Managed Care:		Distributor:		Distributor:		Sub-Acute:		Labs/Testing:	Y	Long-Term Care:	
Utilization Management:		Specialty Pharmacy:		Leasing/Finance:		Outpatient Surgery:		Staffing:		Physical Therapy:	
Payment Processing:		Vitamins/Nutritionals:		Information Systems:	Y	Physical Rehab. Ctr.:		Waste Disposal:		Physician Prac. Mgmt.:	
		Clinical Trials:				Psychiatric Clinics:		Specialty Svcs.:	Y		

TYPES OF BUSINESS:

Drug Discovery Technology
Molecular Combinational Chemistry
Molecular Modeling & Simulation Software
Chemical Databases

BRANDS/DIVISIONS/AFFILIATES:

ECLiPS

CONTACTS: *Note: Officers with more than one job title may be intentionally listed here more than once.*

Leslie Browne, CEO
Leslie Browne, Pres.
Brian M. Posner, CFO
David M. Floyd, Chief Scientific Officer/Exec. VP
Stephen Costalas, General Counsel/Corp. Sec./Exec. VP
Simon Tomlinson, Sr. VP-Bus. Dev.
Brian Posner, Treas./Exec. VP
Maria Webb, VP-Preclinical Research, Biological & Pharm.
Rene Belder, VP-Clinical & Regulatory Affairs
Joseph Mollica, Chmn.

Phone: 609-452-3600 **Fax:** 609-452-3672
Toll-Free:
Address: 3000 Eastpark Blvd., Cranbury, NJ 08512 US

GROWTH PLANS/SPECIAL FEATURES:

Pharmacopeia Drug Discovery, Inc. is engaged in the design, development and marketing of products and services that are intended to improve and accelerate drug discovery and chemical development. The company serves a large number of patients suffering from unmet medical needs, often focusing on conditions such as rheumatoid arthritis, chronic obstructive pulmonary disease, oncology and metabolic diseases. Currently, Pharmacopeia has ongoing programs for each of those conditions, all of which are now in clinical Phase One. To investigate potential chemical compounds for development, the company uses a proprietary chemical encoding/decoding process called ECLiPS technology. It allows chemists to perform thousands of reactions at a time on polymer beads. In addition, Pharmacopeia utilizes an ultra-high-throughput screening platform that enables the screening of hundred of thousands to millions of compounds per week. Pharmacopeia has also developed proprietary software to support its drug discovery activities. Its customers typically fund the research and provide for significant milestone payments when chemicals have passed through the lead discovery and optimization phases and are ready for development. The revenue is concentrated mainly in the company's two largest collaborators, Schering-Plough and N.V. Organon. In early 2006, the company entered into a drug discovery and development alliance with GlaxoSmithKline. It also licensed certain rights to novel therapeutic candidates from Bristol-Meyers Squibb, specifically those related to the treatment of cardiovascular disease. Also in 2006, Pharmacopeia formed an alliance with Cephalon, Inc. to discover and develop new drugs, which afforded the firm an up-front program access fee of $15 million. In 2007, Schering-Plough initiated Phase One clinical trials of a drug developed in partnership with Pharmacopeia to potentially treat metabolic diseases.

Pharmacopeia offers its employees health, vision, dental and prescription drug coverage benefits; flexible spending accounts; group life insurance; short and long term disability coverage; and education reimbursement.

FINANCIALS: **Sales and profits are in thousands of dollars—add 000 to get the full amount. 2007 Note: Financial information for 2007 was not available for all companies at press time.**

2007 Sales: $
2006 Sales: $16,936
2005 Sales: $20,403
2004 Sales: $24,359
2003 Sales: $29,503

2007 Profits: $
2006 Profits: $-27,764
2005 Profits: $-17,138
2004 Profits: $-17,420
2003 Profits: $-2,848

U.S. Stock Ticker: PCOP
Int'l Ticker: Int'l Exchange:
Employees: 150
Fiscal Year Ends: 12/31
Parent Company:

SALARIES/BENEFITS:

Pension Plan: ESOP Stock Plan: Profit Sharing: Top Exec. Salary: $379,167 Bonus: $82,000
Savings Plan: Y Stock Purch. Plan: Y Second Exec. Salary: $285,542 Bonus: $90,000

OTHER THOUGHTS:

Apparent Women Officers or Directors: 3
Hot Spot for Advancement for Women/Minorities: Y

LOCATIONS: ("Y" = Yes)

West:	Southwest:	Midwest:	Southeast:	Northeast:	International:
				Y	

Note: Financial information, benefits and other data can change quickly and may vary from those stated here.

PHARMERICA CORP www.pharmerica.com

Industry Group Code: 446110A **Ranks within this company's industry group:** Sales: 2 Profits: 2

Insurance/HMO/PPO:		Drugs:		Equipment/Supplies:		Hospitals/Clinics:		Services:		Health Care:	
Insurance:		Manufacturer:		Manufacturer:		Acute Care:		Diagnostics:		Home Health:	
Managed Care:		Distributor:	Y	Distributor:		Sub-Acute:		Labs/Testing:		Long-Term Care:	
Utilization Management:		Specialty Pharmacy:		Leasing/Finance:		Outpatient Surgery:		Staffing:		Physical Therapy:	
Payment Processing:		Vitamins/Nutritionals:		Information Systems:		Physical Rehab. Ctr.:		Waste Disposal:		Physician Prac. Mgmt.:	
		Clinical Trials:				Psychiatric Clinics:		Specialty Svcs.:			

TYPES OF BUSINESS:

Specialty Pharmacy Operations

BRANDS/DIVISIONS/AFFILIATES:

Kindred Pharmacy Services, Inc.
PharMerica Long-Term Care
Kindred Healthcare Operating, Inc.
Kindred Healthcare Inc
AmerisourceBergen Corp

CONTACTS: *Note: Officers with more than one job title may be intentionally listed here more than once.*

Gregory S. Weishar, CEO
Michael J. Culotta, CFO/Exec. VP
Robert A. McKay, Sr. VP-Mktg. & Sales
Anthony A. Hernandez, Sr. VP-Human Resources
Richard Toole, CIO/Sr. VP
Thomas Caneris, General Counsel/Sec./Sr. VP
Berard Tomassetti, Chief Acct. Officer/Sr. VP
Janice D. Rutkowski, Chief Clinical Officer/Sr. VP
Thomas P. Mac Mahon, Chmn.

Phone: 502-263-7216 **Fax:**
Toll-Free:
Address: 1901 Campus Pl., Louisville, KY 40299 US

GROWTH PLANS/SPECIAL FEATURES:

PharMerica Corporation, formerly Safari Holding Corporation, was formed by the merging of the pharmacy businesses of AmerisourceBergen Corporation and Kindred Healthcare, Inc. (Kindred). The businesses were Kindred Pharmacy Services, Inc. (KPS) and PharMerica Long-Term Care (PharMerica LTC); and the merger was completed in July 2007. These two companies are now wholly-owned by PharMerica Corporation. The company operates over 120 institutional pharmacies serving 310,000 long-term care facility beds in 40 states. The company has entered into many agreements with AmerisourceBergen and Kindred to acquire products and services from them for a contracted length of time. The prime vendor agreement mandates that PharMerica purchase at least 95% of its pharmaceutical drugs from AmerisourceBergen for its first five years of operation, with a minimum purchase value of $1 billion in the first year of operations. It entered an IT services agreement with Kindred Healthcare Operating, Inc. (KHO), a wholly owned subsidiary of Kindred, wherein KHO will exclusively provide PharMerica certain IT services and support related to IT infrastructure and financial systems for its first five years of operations, including financial management systems and payroll service and support; and while some of these services will be supplied at cost, others will be supplied at cost plus 10%. The company will handle most other functions, such as order entry, billing, medical records management and human resources, internally. Kindred also agreed to provide PharMerica with basic transaction services such as employee benefit administration, risk management, tax and accounting for the first year of PharMerica's operations.

FINANCIALS: **Sales and profits are in thousands of dollars—add 000 to get the full amount. 2007 Note: Financial information for 2007 was not available for all companies at press time.**

2007 Sales: $
2006 Sales: $1,119,964
2005 Sales: $1,571,400
2004 Sales: $
2003 Sales: $

2007 Profits: $
2006 Profits: $16,757
2005 Profits: $
2004 Profits: $
2003 Profits: $

U.S. Stock Ticker: PMC
Int'l Ticker: Int'l Exchange:
Employees:
Fiscal Year Ends: 12/31
Parent Company:

SALARIES/BENEFITS:

Pension Plan: ESOP Stock Plan: Profit Sharing: Top Exec. Salary: $ Bonus: $
Savings Plan: Stock Purch. Plan: Second Exec. Salary: $ Bonus: $

OTHER THOUGHTS:

Apparent Women Officers or Directors:
Hot Spot for Advancement for Women/Minorities:

LOCATIONS: ("Y" = Yes)

West:	Southwest:	Midwest:	Southeast:	Northeast:	International:
Y	Y	Y	Y	Y	

PHILIPS MEDICAL SYSTEMS www.medical.philips.com

Industry Group Code: 339113 **Ranks within this company's industry group:** Sales: Profits:

Insurance/HMO/PPO:		Drugs:		Equipment/Supplies:		Hospitals/Clinics:		Services:		Health Care:	
Insurance:		Manufacturer:		Manufacturer:	Y	Acute Care:		Diagnostics:		Home Health:	
Managed Care:		Distributor:		Distributor:		Sub-Acute:		Labs/Testing:		Long-Term Care:	
Utilization Management:		Specialty Pharmacy:		Leasing/Finance:		Outpatient Surgery:		Staffing:		Physical Therapy:	
Payment Processing:		Vitamins/Nutritionals:		Information Systems:		Physical Rehab. Ctr.:		Waste Disposal:		Physician Prac. Mgmt.:	
		Clinical Trials:				Psychiatric Clinics:		Specialty Svcs.:	Y		

TYPES OF BUSINESS:

Manufacturing-Medical Equipment
Diagnostic & Treatment Equipment
Imaging Equipment
Equipment Repair & Maintenance

BRANDS/DIVISIONS/AFFILIATES:

Royal Philips Electronics NV
DigitalDiagnost
Integris Allura
SonoCT
Stentor, Inc.
Intermagnetics General Corp.

CONTACTS: *Note: Officers with more than one job title may be intentionally listed here more than once.*

Jouko Karvinen, CEO
Jouko Karvinen, Pres.
Brent Shafer, Exec. VP-Sales & Svcs.
Paul Smit, VP-Strategy & Bus. Dev.

Phone: 425-487-7479	**Fax:** 425-482-8834
Toll-Free: 800-722-7900	
Address: 22100 Bothell Everett Hwy., Bothell, WA 98041 US	

GROWTH PLANS/SPECIAL FEATURES:

Philips Medical Systems (PMS), a subsidiary of electronic giant Royal Philips Electronics, manufactures and distributes medical diagnostic and treatment equipment throughout the world. The company's products and business lines include x-ray, ultrasound, computed tomography (CT), positron emission tomography (PET), cardiac and monitoring systems (CMS), cardiovascular x-ray, magnetic resonance imaging (MRI) and nuclear medicine. PMS has clinical segments devoted to anesthesiology, cardiovascular, critical care, molecular imaging, oncology, radiology, surgery and women's health. Additionally, PMS offers clinical information technology for cardiology and radiology image and information management. The company offers its products under the brand names DigitalDiagnost, Integris Allura and SonoCT. Along with the sale of its equipment, PMS also provides equipment installation, refurbishing and maintenance. The company operates Philips Healthcare Informatics segment in order to provide customer with tailored image and information management services for the cardiology and radiology fields. This segment, which is composed of a number of subsidiary companies, offers a variety of clinical data management products, including several types of Radiology Information Systems (RIS) and Picture Archiving and Communication Systems (PACS). The company also has several affiliate companies: Medquist is a majority owned company that offers outsourced medical record transcription services; Philips Medical Capital is a financial services joint venture that offers financial solutions to healthcare facilities for Philips Medical products; and Tricell is a joint venture that works to develop a new generation of flat digital detectors for x-ray imaging systems. In June 2006, PMS completed its $1.4 billion acquisition of Intermagnetics General Corporation, a leading developer and manufacturer of superconducting magnets and radio-frequency coils used in MRI systems. Also, in August 2007 Philips agreed to acquire XIMIS, Inc., a provider of a next generation RIS. When this deal is completed, XIMIS will be incorporated into PMS's Healthcare Informatics business division.

FINANCIALS: **Sales and profits are in thousands of dollars—add 000 to get the full amount. 2007 Note: Financial information for 2007 was not available for all companies at press time.**

2007 Sales: $
2006 Sales: $
2005 Sales: $
2004 Sales: $
2003 Sales: $

2007 Profits: $
2006 Profits: $
2005 Profits: $
2004 Profits: $
2003 Profits: $

U.S. Stock Ticker: Subsidiary
Int'l Ticker: Int'l Exchange:
Employees: 30,600
Fiscal Year Ends: 12/31
Parent Company: ROYAL PHILIPS ELECTRONICS NV

SALARIES/BENEFITS:

Pension Plan: ESOP Stock Plan: Profit Sharing: Top Exec. Salary: $ Bonus: $
Savings Plan: Stock Purch. Plan: Second Exec. Salary: $ Bonus: $

OTHER THOUGHTS:

Apparent Women Officers or Directors:
Hot Spot for Advancement for Women/Minorities:

LOCATIONS: ("Y" = Yes)

West:	Southwest:	Midwest:	Southeast:	Northeast:	International:
Y			Y		Y

Note: Financial information, benefits and other data can change quickly and may vary from those stated here.

POLYMEDICA CORPORATION

www.polymedica.com

Industry Group Code: 339113 **Ranks within this company's industry group:** Sales: 39 Profits: 33

Insurance/HMO/PPO:		Drugs:		Equipment/Supplies:		Hospitals/Clinics:		Services:		Health Care:	
Insurance:		Manufacturer:	Y	Manufacturer:	Y	Acute Care:		Diagnostics:		Home Health:	
Managed Care:		Distributor:	Y	Distributor:	Y	Sub-Acute:		Labs/Testing:		Long-Term Care:	
Utilization Management:		Specialty Pharmacy:		Leasing/Finance:		Outpatient Surgery:		Staffing:		Physical Therapy:	
Payment Processing:		Vitamins/Nutritionals:		Information Systems:		Physical Rehab. Ctr.:		Waste Disposal:		Physician Prac. Mgmt.:	
		Clinical Trials:				Psychiatric Clinics:		Specialty Svcs.:			

TYPES OF BUSINESS:

Equipment-Insulin & Related Products
Diabetes Testing Supplies
Prescription Respiratory Products
Prescription Oral Medications
Urology & Suppository Products
Home Diagnostic Kits

BRANDS/DIVISIONS/AFFILIATES:

Liberty Diabetes
National Diabetic Pharmacies, LLC
IntelliCare, Inc.

CONTACTS: *Note: Officers with more than one job title may be intentionally listed here more than once.*

Patrick T. Ryan, CEO
Keith W. Jones, COO
Stephen C. Farrell, Pres.
Jonathan A. Starr, CFO
Devin J. Anderson, General Counsel/Sec.
Thomas O. Pyle, Chmn.

Phone: 781-486-8111	**Fax:** 781-938-6950
Toll-Free:	
Address: 701 Edgewater Dr., Ste. 360, Wakefield, MA 01880 US	

GROWTH PLANS/SPECIAL FEATURES:

PolyMedica Corporation is a leading provider of direct-to-consumer medical products, conducting business through two segments: Diabetes and Pharmacy. The larger segment, Diabetes, sells insulin, syringes and other products primarily to Medicare-eligible customers suffering from diabetes and related chronic diseases. These products are sold under the brand name Liberty. Also, the company began distribution of a second private-label AgaMatrix/Liberty brand blood glucose monitor in 2007 to complement its private label relationship with Abbott Diabetes Care. The pharmaceuticals segment provides prescription oral medications not covered by Medicare and sells prescription urology and suppository products, over-the-counter female urinary discomfort products and AZO home medical diagnostic kits. The company offers its pharmaceuticals through both prescription drug plans and Medicare Advantage prescription plans to approximately 943,000 existing Diabetes patients and their spouses. PolyMedica attracts new patients through direct mail and targeted television, internet and print advertising, in addition to physician referrals, business partner relationships, and the acquisition of competitors and by acting as a service provider to members of commercial health plans. PolyMedica's direct-mail program serves approximately 875,000 customers throughout the country. Following its recent acquisition of IntelliCare, Inc., PolyMedica provides healthcare communication services and technology solutions that enhance patient care communications by offering medical call and contact center services and technology solutions focused on electronic patient relationship management. In August 2007, PolyMedica entered into an agreement to be acquired by Medco Health Solutions, Inc. for approximately $1.5 billion.

FINANCIALS: **Sales and profits are in thousands of dollars—add 000 to get the full amount. 2007 Note: Financial information for 2007 was not available for all companies at press time.**

2007 Sales: $675,487	2007 Profits: $33,672	**U.S. Stock Ticker: PLMD**
2006 Sales: $491,515	2006 Profits: $60,398	**Int'l Ticker:** Int'l Exchange:
2005 Sales: $451,467	2005 Profits: $32,434	Employees: 2,180
2004 Sales: $419,694	2004 Profits: $37,932	Fiscal Year Ends: 3/31
2003 Sales: $356,200	2003 Profits: $25,600	Parent Company:

SALARIES/BENEFITS:

Pension Plan:	ESOP Stock Plan:	Profit Sharing:	Top Exec. Salary: $696,713	Bonus: $
Savings Plan: Y	Stock Purch. Plan:		Second Exec. Salary: $395,299	Bonus: $

OTHER THOUGHTS:

Apparent Women Officers or Directors:
Hot Spot for Advancement for Women/Minorities:

LOCATIONS: ("Y" = Yes)

West:	Southwest:	Midwest:	Southeast:	Northeast:	International:
	Y	Y	Y	Y	

PREMERA BLUE CROSS

www.premera.com

Industry Group Code: 524114 **Ranks within this company's industry group:** Sales: 20 Profits: 19

Insurance/HMO/PPO:		Drugs:		Equipment/Supplies:		Hospitals/Clinics:		Services:		Health Care:	
Insurance:	Y	Manufacturer:		Manufacturer:		Acute Care:		Diagnostics:		Home Health:	
Managed Care:	Y	Distributor:		Distributor:		Sub-Acute:		Labs/Testing:		Long-Term Care:	
Utilization Management:		Specialty Pharmacy:		Leasing/Finance:		Outpatient Surgery:		Staffing:		Physical Therapy:	
Payment Processing:		Vitamins/Nutritionals:		Information Systems:		Physical Rehab. Ctr.:		Waste Disposal:		Physician Prac. Mgmt.:	
		Clinical Trials:				Psychiatric Clinics:		Specialty Svcs.:			

TYPES OF BUSINESS:

Insurance-Medical & Health, HMOs & PPOs
Dental Insurance
Long-Term Care Insurance

BRANDS/DIVISIONS/AFFILIATES:

Dimension
Pike Market Medical Clinic
Out of Pocket Estimator

CONTACTS: *Note: Officers with more than one job title may be intentionally listed here more than once.*

H. R. Brereton (Gubby) Barlow, CEO
H. R. Brereton (Gubby) Barlow, Pres.
Kent Marquardt, CFO/Exec. VP
Heyward Donigan, Chief Mktg. Exec./Exec. VP
Barbara Masqusin, Sr. VP-Human Resources
Kirsten Simonitsch, CIO/Sr. VP
Yori Milo, Chief Legal Officer/Exec. VP-Corp. Svcs.
Karen Bartlett, Exec. VP-Oper.
Brian Ancell, Exec. VP-Health Care Svcs. & Strategic Dev.
Audrey Halvorson, Chief Actuary/Sr. VP
John L. Castiglia, Chief Medical Officer
Richard Maturi, Sr. VP-Health Care Delivery Systems
Jack McRae, Sr. VP-Congressional & Legislative Affairs
John Pierce, VP/General Counsel

Phone: 425-918-4000 **Fax:** 425-918-5575
Toll-Free: 800-722-1471
Address: 7001 220th SW, Mountlake Terrace, WA 98043 US

GROWTH PLANS/SPECIAL FEATURES:

Premera Blue Cross is a not-for-profit health insuranc provider for Washington and Alaska. Through a network c 21,000 health care providers and 120 hospitals, the firr serves 1.4 million members in Washington and 114,00 members in Alaska. Premera health plans include preferre provider organization (PPO) plans, exclusive provide organization (EPO) plans, Medicare supplemental, indemnit coverage, dental and long-term care. Premera also offers collection of products under the Dimension brand that allov business customers to tailor health plans with features fron HMOs, PPOs or managed indemnity plans. Employers the decide which doctor and hospital network to support alon with options for out-of-network coverage, deductibles, co pays and pharmacy benefits. In January 2007, Premera an the Pike Market Medical Clinic announced a planne collaboration to provide primary care to low-income Seattl residents. In April 2007, the company launched its Out c Pocket Estimator tool, which will provide patients with a estimate of their out of pocket costs based on their specifi benefits package.

Employees of Premera receive dependant car reimbursement accounts, an educational assistanc program, on-site training, an employee assistance progran and legal assistance.

FINANCIALS: **Sales and profits are in thousands of dollars—add 000 to get the full amount. 2007 Note: Financial information for 2007 was not available for all companies at press time.**

2007 Sales: $
2006 Sales: $3,093,741
2005 Sales: $3,061,269
2004 Sales: $2,990,780
2003 Sales: $2,879,816

2007 Profits: $
2006 Profits: $121,360
2005 Profits: $90,928
2004 Profits: $87,133
2003 Profits: $53,619

U.S. Stock Ticker: Nonprofit
Int'l Ticker: Int'l Exchange:
Employees: 3,000
Fiscal Year Ends: 12/31
Parent Company:

SALARIES/BENEFITS:

Pension Plan: ESOP Stock Plan: Profit Sharing: Top Exec. Salary: $ Bonus: $
Savings Plan: Y Stock Purch. Plan: Second Exec. Salary: $ Bonus: $

OTHER THOUGHTS:

Apparent Women Officers or Directors: 4
Hot Spot for Advancement for Women/Minorities: Y

LOCATIONS: ("Y" = Yes)

West:	Southwest:	Midwest:	Southeast:	Northeast:	International:
Y					

PREMIER INC

www.premierinc.com

Industry Group Code: 561400 **Ranks within this company's industry group:** Sales: Profits:

Insurance/HMO/PPO:		Drugs:		Equipment/Supplies:		Hospitals/Clinics:		Services:		Health Care:	
Insurance:	Y	Manufacturer:		Manufacturer:		Acute Care:		Diagnostics:		Home Health:	
Managed Care:		Distributor:		Distributor:	Y	Sub-Acute:		Labs/Testing:		Long-Term Care:	
Utilization Management:		Specialty Pharmacy:		Leasing/Finance:		Outpatient Surgery:		Staffing:		Physical Therapy:	
Payment Processing:		Vitamins/Nutritionals:		Information Systems:	Y	Physical Rehab. Ctr.:		Waste Disposal:		Physician Prac. Mgmt.:	
		Clinical Trials:				Psychiatric Clinics:		Specialty Svcs.:	Y		

TYPES OF BUSINESS:

Medical Supply Distribution
Supply Chain Management
Health Care Consulting
Insurance Services
IT Services

BRANDS/DIVISIONS/AFFILIATES:

Premier Sourcing Partners
Premier Insurance Management
Advisor Suite
SupplyFOCUS
Portfolio Analysis

CONTACTS: *Note: Officers with more than one job title may be intentionally listed here more than once.*

Richard A. Norling, CEO
Susan D. DeVore, COO
Richard A. Norling, Pres.
Ann Rhoads, CFO
Jena E. Abernathy, VP-Human Resources
Blair Childs, Sr. VP-Public Affairs
Stephanie C. Alexander, VP-Healthcare Informatics
Robert L. Dowdy, Pres., Premier Insurance Management Services
Margaret R. Reagan, VP-Premier Advocacy
Richard Umbdenstock, Chmn.

Phone: 858-481-2727	**Fax:** 858-481-8919
Toll-Free:	
Address: 12225 Camino Real, San Diego, CA 92130 US	

GROWTH PLANS/SPECIAL FEATURES:

Premier, Inc. is primarily a medical supply chain management and health care consulting company. The firm is a joint venture owned by more than 200 independent hospitals, with approximately 1,500 affiliated hospitals and clinics nationwide. Premier supplies solutions in three areas where quality and financial performance are intimately linked: The healthcare supply chain; performance measurement and improvement; and insurance and risk management. Premier conducts group purchases of more than $17 billion in medical supplies and equipment per year. These products include facilities, food and dietary, imaging, information technology, medical and surgical and pharmacy supplies. The company also supplies low-cost insurance and medical IT services through its Premier Insurance Management subsidiary and through partnership with the American Excess Insurance Exchange. In addition, Premier offers a wide range of consulting services including IT, risk management, financial, safety support, pharmaceutical analysis, patient satisfaction and employee retention services. The company's supply chain, clinical processes and outcomes and staffing effectiveness consulting services are offered through its Advisor Suite, SupplyFOCUS and Portfolio Analysis resources. In April 2007, the company acquired CareScience from Quovadx, Inc.

Premier offers its employees a comprehensive benefits package that includes tuition reimbursement.

FINANCIALS: **Sales and profits are in thousands of dollars—add 000 to get the full amount. 2007 Note: Financial information for 2007 was not available for all companies at press time.**

2007 Sales: $	2007 Profits: $	**U.S. Stock Ticker: Joint Venture**
2006 Sales: $	2006 Profits: $	**Int'l Ticker:** Int'l Exchange:
2005 Sales: $404,265	2005 Profits: $230,451	Employees:
2004 Sales: $379,877	2004 Profits: $158,105	Fiscal Year Ends: 6/30
2003 Sales: $392,262	2003 Profits: $204,580	Parent Company:

SALARIES/BENEFITS:

Pension Plan: Y	ESOP Stock Plan:	Profit Sharing:	Top Exec. Salary: $	Bonus: $
Savings Plan: Y	Stock Purch. Plan:		Second Exec. Salary: $	Bonus: $

OTHER THOUGHTS:

Apparent Women Officers or Directors: 6
Hot Spot for Advancement for Women/Minorities: Y

LOCATIONS: ("Y" = Yes)

West:	Southwest:	Midwest:	Southeast:	Northeast:	International:
Y		Y		Y	

PROVIDENCE HEALTH & SERVICES www.providence.org

Industry Group Code: 622110 **Ranks within this company's industry group:** Sales: Profits:

Insurance/HMO/PPO:		Drugs:		Equipment/Supplies:		Hospitals/Clinics:		Services:		Health Care:	
Insurance:		Manufacturer:		Manufacturer:		Acute Care:	Y	Diagnostics:		Home Health:	Y
Managed Care:		Distributor:		Distributor:		Sub-Acute:	Y	Labs/Testing:		Long-Term Care:	Y
Utilization Management:		Specialty Pharmacy:		Leasing/Finance:		Outpatient Surgery:	Y	Staffing:		Physical Therapy:	
Payment Processing:		Vitamins/Nutritionals:		Information Systems:		Physical Rehab. Ctr.:		Waste Disposal:		Physician Prac. Mgmt.:	
		Clinical Trials:				Psychiatric Clinics:	Y	Specialty Svcs.:	Y		

TYPES OF BUSINESS:

Hospitals-General
Assisted Living Facilities
Low Income Living Facilities
Counseling

BRANDS/DIVISIONS/AFFILIATES:

Providence St. Peter Hospital
Little Company of Mary
Sisters of Providence
Providence Alaska Medical Center
Little Company of Mary Hospital
Providence Holy Cross Medical Center
Providence Kodiak Island Medical Center
Nurse Advice

CONTACTS: *Note: Officers with more than one job title may be intentionally listed here more than once.*

John Koster, CEO
John Koster, Pres.
Mike Butler, CFO
John Kenagy, CIO/VP
Jan Jones, Sr. VP-Admin.
Jeff Rogers, General Counsel
Claudia Haglund, VP-Strategic Planning
Tom Johnson, Chief Comm. Officer
Al Parrish, Chief Exec./ VP-Alaska Region
Russ Danielson, Chief Exec./VP-Oregon Region
William P. Sexton, CEO-North Coast Service Area
Keith Marton, Chief Medical Quality Officer
Kay Stepp, Chmn.

Phone: 206-464-3355	**Fax:** 206-464-4683
Toll-Free:	
Address: 506 2nd Ave., Ste. 1200, Seattle, WA 98104 US	

GROWTH PLANS/SPECIAL FEATURES:

Providence Health & Services, the result of a recent merger between Providence Services and Providence Health System, is a not-for-profit collection of health facilities in the Pacific Northwest run by two Catholic religious orders: the Sisters of Providence and the Little Company of Mary. The hospitals in the group offer acute and primary care, home and hospice care, substance abuse programs, mental health treatment and various community outreach programs. Providence focuses on providing care for poor and vulnerable patients by providing medical care as well as spiritual support. In addition, the group runs an advocacy program on the federal and state levels focused on creating a more equitable, accessible health care system. Some hospitals under the system include Providence Alaska Medical Center and Providence Kodiak Island Medical Center in Alaska; Providence St. Peter Hospital and Providence Centralia Hospital in Washington; Providence Hood River Memorial Hospital, Providence Seaside Hospital and Providence Newberg Hospital in Oregon; and Little Company of Mary Hospital and Providence Holy Cross Medical Center in California. Providence provides its patients with a 24-hour Nurse Advice line, a physician referral program and online bill pay services. In 2006, six Providence hospitals were given awards for Excellence in Patient Care from CareScience, a firm which assesses patient care and outcomes based on sixteen clinical indicators. Also in 2006, Providence completed major renovations for the Providence St. Vincent Medical Center in Portland, Oregon.

Providence Health offers its employees tuition reimbursement, an employee assistance program, flexible savings accounts and a variety of insurance options.

FINANCIALS: **Sales and profits are in thousands of dollars—add 000 to get the full amount. 2007 Note: Financial information for 2007 was not available for all companies at press time.**

2007 Sales: $	2007 Profits: $	**U.S. Stock Ticker: Nonprofit**
2006 Sales: $	2006 Profits: $	**Int'l Ticker:** Int'l Exchange:
2005 Sales: $4,020,601	2005 Profits: $	Employees: 33,940
2004 Sales: $	2004 Profits: $238,577	Fiscal Year Ends: 12/31
2003 Sales: $3,780,200	2003 Profits: $176,600	Parent Company:

SALARIES/BENEFITS:

Pension Plan:	ESOP Stock Plan:	Profit Sharing:	Top Exec. Salary: $	Bonus: $
Savings Plan: Y	Stock Purch. Plan:		Second Exec. Salary: $	Bonus: $

OTHER THOUGHTS:

Apparent Women Officers or Directors: 4
Hot Spot for Advancement for Women/Minorities: Y

LOCATIONS: ("Y" = Yes)

West:	Southwest:	Midwest:	Southeast:	Northeast:	International:
Y					

PROXYMED INC www.proxymed.com

ıdustry Group Code: 621111 **Ranks within this company's industry group:** Sales: 7 Profits: 6

ısurance/HMO/PPO:		Drugs:		Equipment/Supplies:		Hospitals/Clinics:		Services:		Health Care:	
ısurance:		Manufacturer:		Manufacturer:		Acute Care:		Diagnostics:		Home Health:	
ıanaged Care:		Distributor:		Distributor:		Sub-Acute:		Labs/Testing:		Long-Term Care:	
tilization Management:		Specialty Pharmacy:		Leasing/Finance:		Outpatient Surgery:		Staffing:		Physical Therapy:	
ayment Processing:		Vitamins/Nutritionals:		Information Systems:	Y	Physical Rehab. Ctr.:		Waste Disposal:		Physician Prac. Mgmt.:	Y
		Clinical Trials:				Psychiatric Clinics:		Specialty Svcs.:	Y		

YPES OF BUSINESS:

ıedical Practice Management
ıedical Document Transaction Services
abcratory Communications

BRANDS/DIVISIONS/AFFILIATES:

ıedAdvent Healthcare Solutions
ʼhoenix
ıational Preferred Provider Network
ʼreScribe
ʼilot
ʼleet Management System
ıedical Resources, LLC
ıational Provider Network, Inc.

CONTACTS: *Note: Officers with more than one job title may be ntentionally listed here more than once.*

ohn G. Lettko, CEO
ohn G. Lettko, Pres.
ɜerard M. Hayden, Jr., CFO
ɪmily J. Pietrzak, Exec. VP-Sales & Acct. Mgmt.
ıllison W. Myers, Exec. VP-Human Resources
ıdnane Khalil, Exec. VP-Tech.
ɪric D. Arnson, Exec. VP-Prod. Mgmt.
ʼeter E. Fleming, III, General Counsel/Exec. VP/Sec.
.onnie W. Hardin, VP-Bus. Oper.
ɪric D. Arnson, Exec. VP-Bus. Mgmt.
ʼeresa D. Stubbs, Exec. VP-Comm.
ɜerard M. Hayden, Jr., Treas./Exec. VP
ʼeresa D. Stubbs, Exec. VP-Mktg.
ıames B. Hudak, Chmn.

Phone: 770-806-9918	**Fax:**
Toll-Free:	
Address: 1854 Shackleford Ct., Ste. 200, Norcross, GA 30093 JS	

GROWTH PLANS/SPECIAL FEATURES:

ProxyMed, Inc., doing business as MedAdvent Healthcare Solutions, is an information technology company. The company works with 450,000 healthcare providers, 42,000 pharmacies, 200 labs and 1,500 insurance payers through its real-time processing system, Phoenix. Since early 2007, Phoenix has been processing all of MedAdvent's 750,000 daily transactions, offering total visibility to its claims processing cycle. MedAdvent operates two segments. The Transaction Services segment includes claims processing such as verifying a patient's insurance. It operates a PPO (Preferred Provider Organization), called National Preferred Provider Network (NPPN), which is accessed by more than 7 million patients, 450,000 physicians, 4,000 acute care facilities and 65,000 ancillary care providers, and which generates revenues by charging participating payers a percentage of the savings they receive through NPPN. It also provides electronic prescription management through PreScribe, a desktop and online application that sends new prescriptions and refill requests to over 42,000 pharmacies nationwide. Providers pay a flat monthly fee, and pharmacy partners have the choice of paying a flat monthly fee or on a per transaction basis. The Laboratory Communications segment provides printing technology labs install in physician's offices allowing the secure transmittal of laboratory reports. The segment has a patent pending web-enabled device called Pilot that transfers lab reports to printers, personal computers or hand-held devices. Fleet Management System provides a lab with an online tool to monitor its printers in physician's offices, alerting it of routine problems such as lack of paper or paper jam. In February 2006, ProxyMed acquired Florida-based Zenecks, Inc., adding bill negotiation services for patients who use out-of-network providers. In October 2006, it acquired Medical Resources, LLC, and National Provider Network, Inc. (MRL), for a total consideration of $5 million, which added more direct contracts to providers and additional contract providers in six states to ProxyMed's NPPN services.

FINANCIALS: **Sales and profits are in thousands of dollars—add 000 to get the full amount. 2007 Note: Financial information for 2007 was not available for all companies at press time.**

2007 Sales: $	2007 Profits: $	**U.S. Stock Ticker: PILL**
2006 Sales: $65,462	2006 Profits: $-3,370	**Int'l Ticker:** Int'l Exchange:
2005 Sales: $77,519	2005 Profits: $-103,177	Employees: 336
2004 Sales: $90,246	2004 Profits: $-1,974	Fiscal Year Ends: 12/31
2003 Sales: $	2003 Profits: $	Parent Company:

SALARIES/BENEFITS:

Pension Plan:	ESOP Stock Plan:	Profit Sharing:	Top Exec. Salary: $412,154	Bonus: $138,600
Savings Plan:	Stock Purch. Plan:		Second Exec. Salary: $210,000	Bonus: $52,500

OTHER THOUGHTS:

Apparent Women Officers or Directors: 3
Hot Spot for Advancement for Women/Minorities: Y

LOCATIONS: ("Y" = Yes)

West:	Southwest:	Midwest:	Southeast:	Northeast:	International:
Y	Y	Y	Y	Y	

PSS WORLD MEDICAL INC

www.pssd.com

Industry Group Code: 421450 **Ranks within this company's industry group:** Sales: 5 Profits: 5

Insurance/HMO/PPO:		Drugs:		Equipment/Supplies:		Hospitals/Clinics:		Services:		Health Care:	
Insurance:		Manufacturer:		Manufacturer:		Acute Care:		Diagnostics:		Home Health:	
Managed Care:		Distributor:	Y	Distributor:	Y	Sub-Acute:		Labs/Testing:		Long-Term Care:	
Utilization Management:		Specialty Pharmacy:		Leasing/Finance:		Outpatient Surgery:		Staffing:		Physical Therapy:	
Payment Processing:		Vitamins/Nutritionals:		Information Systems:		Physical Rehab. Ctr.:		Waste Disposal:		Physician Prac. Mgmt.:	
		Clinical Trials:				Psychiatric Clinics:		Specialty Svcs.:			

TYPES OF BUSINESS:

Medical Supplies & Equipment Distribution
Pharmaceuticals Distribution

BRANDS/DIVISIONS/AFFILIATES:

Select Medical Products
Gulf South Medical Supply, Inc.

CONTACTS:

Note: Officers with more than one job title may be intentionally listed here more than once.

David A. Smith, CEO
Gary A. Corless, COO/Exec. VP
David A. Smith, Pres.
David M. Bronson, CFO/Exec. VP
John F. Sasen, Sr., Chief Mktg. Officer/Exec. VP
Bradley J. Hilton, Sr. VP-Oper.
Jeffrey H. Anthony, Sr. VP-Corp. Dev.
Robert C. Weiner, VP-Investor Rel.
Kevin P. English, Sr. VP-Finance
Edward Dienes, Sr. VP-Sales-Physician Sales & Service
Billy Ray Clemons, Jr., VP-Sales-Gulf South Medical Supply
David D. Klarner, Treas./VP
Steven J. Magiera, VP-Bus. Dev.
David A. Smith, Chmn.

Phone: 904-332-3000 **Fax:** 904-332-3213
Toll-Free:
Address: 4345 Southpoint Blvd., Jacksonville, FL 32216 US

GROWTH PLANS/SPECIAL FEATURES:

PSS World Medical, Inc. is a national distributor of medica products, equipment and pharmaceutical related products to alternate-site healthcare providers including physician offices; long-term care and assisted living facilities; home health care; and hospice providers through 41 distribution centers, which serve all 50 states. The company operates in two segments: the physician business and the elder care business. The physician business segment distributes over 84,000 products consisting of medical-surgical disposable supplies, pharmaceutical products, diagnostic equipment non-diagnostic equipment and healthcare information technology products to primary care office-based physicians. Its brand names include Select Medical Products. The segment has about 740 sales professionals. The elder care business segment, or Gulf South Medical Supply, Inc. distributes over 26,000 medical and related products including medical supplies; incontinent supplies and persona care items; enteral feeding supplies; and home medica equipment to the long-term and elder care industry. The segment also provides Medicare Part B reimbursable products and billing services, either on a fee-for-service or full-assignment basis. The division primarily serves the nursing home and home health care industries as well as the assisted living market segment. PSS also supplies hospital beds, patient-lifts, wheel chairs, oxygen-concentrators, walkers, patient aids and bath safety products. Many of the company's wholesalers are located overseas throughout China, Thailand, Malaysia, India and the Philippines. In May 2007, the company agreed to acquire Activus Healthcare Solutions, Inc., a distributor of medical supplies.

The company provides its employees with benefits including health, dental and vision insurance; life insurance; an employee assistance program; flexible spending accounts; short- and long-term disability insurance; and a 401(k) plan.

FINANCIALS:

Sales and profits are in thousands of dollars—add 000 to get the full amount. 2007 Note: Financial information for 2007 was not available for all companies at press time.

2007 Sales: $1,741,639	2007 Profits: $50,481	**U.S. Stock Ticker: PSSI**
2006 Sales: $1,619,417	2006 Profits: $44,257	**Int'l Ticker:** Int'l Exchange:
2005 Sales: $1,473,769	2005 Profits: $38,972	Employees: 3,349
2004 Sales: $1,349,917	2004 Profits: $27,539	Fiscal Year Ends: 3/31
2003 Sales: $1,177,900	2003 Profits: $-54,800	Parent Company:

SALARIES/BENEFITS:

Pension Plan:	ESOP Stock Plan:	Profit Sharing:	Top Exec. Salary: $676,000	Bonus: $848,083
Savings Plan: Y	Stock Purch. Plan:		Second Exec. Salary: $389,880	Bonus: $336,275

OTHER THOUGHTS:

Apparent Women Officers or Directors: 2
Hot Spot for Advancement for Women/Minorities:

LOCATIONS: ("Y" = Yes)

West:	Southwest:	Midwest:	Southeast:	Northeast:	International:
Y	Y	Y	Y	Y	

PSYCHIATRIC SOLUTIONS INC www.psysolutions.com

Industry Group Code: 622210 **Ranks within this company's industry group:** Sales: 3 Profits: 2

Insurance/HMO/PPO:		Drugs:		Equipment/Supplies:		Hospitals/Clinics:		Services:		Health Care:	
Insurance:		Manufacturer:		Manufacturer:		Acute Care:		Diagnostics:		Home Health:	
Managed Care:		Distributor:		Distributor:		Sub-Acute:		Labs/Testing:		Long-Term Care:	
Utilization Management:		Specialty Pharmacy:		Leasing/Finance:		Outpatient Surgery:		Staffing:		Physical Therapy:	
Payment Processing:		Vitamins/Nutritionals:		Information Systems:		Physical Rehab. Ctr.:		Waste Disposal:		Physician Prac. Mgmt.:	
		Clinical Trials:				Psychiatric Clinics:	Y	Specialty Svcs.:			

TYPES OF BUSINESS:

Clinics-Psychiatric
Substance Abuse Treatment
Clinic Management Services

BRANDS/DIVISIONS/AFFILIATES:

Horizon Health Corp.

CONTACTS:

Note: Officers with more than one job title may be intentionally listed here more than once.

Joey A. Jacobs, CEO
Terry Bridges, COO
Joey A. Jacobs, Pres.
Brent Turner, Exec. VP-Admin.
Chris Howard, General Counsel/Exec. VP/Sec.
Steven T. Davidson, Chief Dev. Officer
Brent Turner, Exec. VP-Finance
Jack E. Polson, Chief Acct. Officer/Exec. VP
Joey A. Jacobs, Chmn.

Phone: 615-312-5700 **Fax:** 615-312-5711
Toll-Free:
Address: 6640 Carothers Pkwy., Ste. 500, Franklin, TN 37067 US

GROWTH PLANS/SPECIAL FEATURES:

Psychiatric Solutions, Inc. is a provider of inpatient behavioral healthcare services in the U.S. The company operates 75 inpatient behavioral healthcare facilities with over 8,000 beds in 29 states, Puerto Rico and the U.S. Virgin Islands. The firm also manages, through contracts, inpatient behavioral healthcare units for private third parties. The inpatient behavioral healthcare facilities, which accounted for about 95% of revenue in 2006, offer a wide range of inpatient behavioral healthcare services for children, adolescents and adults through a combination of acute inpatient behavioral facilities and residential treatment centers. These facilities work closely with mental health professionals, including licensed professional counselors, therapists, and social workers; psychiatrists; non-psychiatric physicians; emergency rooms; school systems; insurance and managed care organizations; company-sponsored employee assistance programs; and law enforcement and community agencies that interact with individuals who may need treatment for mental illness or substance abuse. Many of Psychiatric Solutions' inpatient facilities have mobile assessment teams who travel to prospective clients in order to assess their condition and determine if they meet established criteria for inpatient care. Those clients not meeting the established criteria for inpatient care may qualify for outpatient care or a less intensive level of care provided by the facility. The acute inpatient behavioral facilities provide an intensive level of care, including 24-hour skilled nursing observation and care; daily interventions and oversight by a psychiatrist; and intensive, coordinated treatment by a physician-led team of mental health professionals. The residential treatment centers offer longer term treatment programs primarily for children and adolescent with long-standing chronic behavioral health problems. The inpatient management contracts accounted for about 5% of revenue in 2006. In June 2007, Psychiatric Solutions acquired Horizon Health Corp., which operates and manages inpatient behavioral healthcare facilities and units, for roughly $426 million.

FINANCIALS:

Sales and profits are in thousands of dollars—add 000 to get the full amount. 2007 Note: Financial information for 2007 was not available for all companies at press time.

2007 Sales: $	2007 Profits: $	**U.S. Stock Ticker: PSYS**
2006 Sales: $1,026,490	2006 Profits: $60,632	**Int'l Ticker:** Int'l Exchange:
2005 Sales: $715,324	2005 Profits: $27,154	Employees: 18,700
2004 Sales: $470,969	2004 Profits: $16,801	Fiscal Year Ends: 12/31
2003 Sales: $293,665	2003 Profits: $5,216	Parent Company:

SALARIES/BENEFITS:

Pension Plan:	ESOP Stock Plan:	Profit Sharing:	Top Exec. Salary: $890,865	Bonus: $1,204,200
Savings Plan:	Stock Purch. Plan:		Second Exec. Salary: $340,625	Bonus: $230,344

OTHER THOUGHTS:

Apparent Women Officers or Directors: 1
Hot Spot for Advancement for Women/Minorities:

LOCATIONS: ("Y" = Yes)

West:	Southwest:	Midwest:	Southeast:	Northeast:	International:
Y	Y	Y	Y	Y	

Note: Financial information, benefits and other data can change quickly and may vary from those stated here.

QUALITY SYSTEMS INC

www.qsii.com

Industry Group Code: 511212 **Ranks within this company's industry group:** Sales: 5 Profits: 3

Insurance/HMO/PPO:		Drugs:		Equipment/Supplies:		Hospitals/Clinics:		Services:		Health Care:	
Insurance:		Manufacturer:		Manufacturer:		Acute Care:		Diagnostics:		Home Health:	
Managed Care:		Distributor:		Distributor:		Sub-Acute:		Labs/Testing:		Long-Term Care:	
Utilization Management:		Specialty Pharmacy:		Leasing/Finance:		Outpatient Surgery:		Staffing:		Physical Therapy:	
Payment Processing:		Vitamins/Nutritionals:		Information Systems:	Y	Physical Rehab. Ctr.:		Waste Disposal:		Physician Prac. Mgmt.:	
		Clinical Trials:				Psychiatric Clinics:		Specialty Svcs.:			

TYPES OF BUSINESS:

Software-Practice Management

BRANDS/DIVISIONS/AFFILIATES:

Clinical Product Suite
NextGen Healthcare Information Systems, Inc.
Electronic Medical Records
Enterprise Practice Management
Enterprise Appointment Scheduling
Enterprise Master Patient Index
Image Control System
Managed Care Server

CONTACTS: *Note: Officers with more than one job title may be intentionally listed here more than once.*

Louis E. Silverman, CEO
Louis E. Silverman, Pres.
Paul Holt, CFO
Paul Holt, Corp. Sec.
Patrick B. Cline, Pres., NextGen Healthcare Information Systems
Gregory Flynn, Exec. VP-Quality Systems Div.
Alan Totah, Sr. VP-Regulatory Affairs & Quality Systems
Sheldon Razin, Chmn.

Phone: 949-255-2600	**Fax:** 949-255-2605
Toll-Free: 800-888-7955	
Address: 18191 Von Karman Ave., Ste. 450, Irvine, CA 92612 US	

GROWTH PLANS/SPECIAL FEATURES:

Quality Systems, Inc. develops and provides computer based practice management, medical records, and e business applications for medical and dental group practices practice networks, management service organizations ambulatory care centers, community health centers and medical and dental schools. The company is headquartered in Irvine, California and has major facilities in Horsham Pennsylvania and Atlanta, Georgia. Quality Systems operates through two divisions, QSI and the NextGen Healthcare Information, which both develop and market products designed to streamline patient records and administrative functions such as billing and scheduling. The company's QSI division focuses on developing, marketing and supporting software suites for dental and niche medical practices. Its Clinical Product Suite is a UNIX-based medical practice management software suite that incorporates clinical tools including periodontal charting and digital imaging of x-ray and inter-oral camera images. NextGen, the company's other operating division, develops and sells proprietary electronic medical records software and practice management systems. Its NextGen product line includes Electronic Medical Records, Enterprise Practice Management, Enterprise Appointment Scheduling, Enterprise Master Patient Index, Image Control System Managed Care Server, Electronic Data Interchange (EDI), System Interfaces, Internet Operability, patient-centric and provider-centric web portal solutions and a handheld product. The group's EDI/Connectivity products automate a number of manual, often paper-based or telephony intensive communications between patients and providers, like as insurance claim forwards. NextGen products utilize Microsoft Windows technology and can operate in a client-server environment as well as via private intranet, the Internet or in an ASP environment. In July 2006, the NextGen EMR was certified by the Certification Commission for Healthcare Information Technology for having met its requirements for ambulatory electronic health records.

FINANCIALS: **Sales and profits are in thousands of dollars—add 000 to get the full amount. 2007 Note: Financial information for 2007 was not available for all companies at press time.**

2007 Sales: $157,165	2007 Profits: $33,232	**U.S. Stock Ticker: QSII**
2006 Sales: $119,287	2006 Profits: $23,322	**Int'l Ticker:** Int'l Exchange:
2005 Sales: $89,000	2005 Profits: $16,100	Employees: 661
2004 Sales: $70,934	2004 Profits: $10,400	Fiscal Year Ends: 3/31
2003 Sales: $54,769	2003 Profits: $7,035	Parent Company:

SALARIES/BENEFITS:

Pension Plan:	ESOP Stock Plan:	Profit Sharing:	Top Exec. Salary: $420,833	Bonus: $320,000
Savings Plan: Y	Stock Purch. Plan:		Second Exec. Salary: $400,000	Bonus: $228,000

OTHER THOUGHTS:

Apparent Women Officers or Directors:
Hot Spot for Advancement for Women/Minorities:

LOCATIONS: ("Y" = Yes)

West:	Southwest:	Midwest:	Southeast:	Northeast:	International:
Y			Y	Y	

Note: Financial information, benefits and other data can change quickly and may vary from those stated here.

QUEST DIAGNOSTICS INC www.questdiagnostics.com

ndustry Group Code: 621511 **Ranks within this company's industry group:** Sales: 1 Profits: 1

nsurance/HMO/PPO:		Drugs:		Equipment/Supplies:		Hospitals/Clinics:		Services:		Health Care:	
nsurance:		Manufacturer:		Manufacturer:		Acute Care:		Diagnostics:	Y	Home Health:	
Managed Care:		Distributor:		Distributor:		Sub-Acute:		Labs/Testing:	Y	Long-Term Care:	
Jtilization Management:		Specialty Pharmacy:		Leasing/Finance:		Outpatient Surgery:		Staffing:		Physical Therapy:	
Payment Processing:		Vitamins/Nutritionals:		Information Systems:		Physical Rehab. Ctr.:		Waste Disposal:		Physician Prac. Mgmt.:	
		Clinical Trials:				Psychiatric Clinics:		Specialty Svcs.:			

TYPES OF BUSINESS:

Services-Testing & Diagnostics
Clinical Laboratory Testing
Clinical Trials Testing
Esoteric Testing Laboratories

BRANDS/DIVISIONS/AFFILIATES:

Cardio CRP
HEPTIMAX
Focus Diagnostics, Inc.
CF Complete
CellSearch
Bio-Intact PTH
Leumeta
LabOne

CONTACTS: *Note: Officers with more than one job title may be intentionally listed here more than once.*

Surya N. Mohapatra, CEO
Surya N. Mohapatra, Pres.
Robert A. Hagemann, CFO/Sr. VP
Robert E. Peters, VP-Mktg. & Sales
Michael E. Prevoznik, General Counsel/VP-Legal & Compliance
Gary Samuels, VP-Corp. Comm. & Media Rel.
Laura Park, VP-Investor Rel.
David M. Zewe, Sr. VP-Diagnostic Testing Oper.
Surya N. Mohapatra, Chmn.

Phone: 201-393-5000 **Fax:** 201-729-8920
Toll-Free: 800-222-0446
Address: 1290 Wall Street W., Lyndhurst, NJ 07071 US

GROWTH PLANS/SPECIAL FEATURES:

Quest Diagnostics, Inc. is one of the largest clinical laboratory testing companies in the U.S., offering a broad array of diagnostic testing and related services to the health care industry. The firm's operations consist of routine, esoteric and clinical trials testing. Quest operates through its national network of 2,000 patient service centers, principal laboratories in more than 35 major metropolitan areas along with approximately 150 rapid-response laboratories, as well as esoteric testing laboratories on both coasts. Routine tests measure various important bodily health parameters such as the functions of the kidney, heart, liver, thyroid and other organs. Tests in this category include blood cholesterol level tests, complete blood cell counts, pap smears, HIV-related tests, urinalyses, pregnancy and prenatal tests, and substance-abuse tests. Esoteric tests require more sophisticated equipment and technology, professional attention and highly skilled personnel. The firm's tests in this field include Cardio CRP and HEPTIMAX. Quest's two esoteric testing laboratories, which operate as Quest Diagnostics Nichols Institute located in San Juan Capistrano, California, are among the leading esoteric clinical testing laboratories in the world. Esoteric tests involve a number of medical fields including endocrinology, genetics, immunology, microbiology, oncology, serology and special chemistry. Clinical trial testing primarily involves assessing the safety and efficacy of new drugs to meet FDA requirements, with services including Bio-Intact PTH. In recent news, Quest received FDA clearance to market its Plexus HerpeSelect 1 and 2 IgG test kit. Additionally, the company acquired diagnostic testing company AmeriPath, Inc. for approximately $2 billion. In July 2007, Quest introduced a new diagnostic testing technique to help physicians diagnose genetic metabolic disorders such as phenylketonuria (PKU) and homocystinuria.

Quest offers employees educational assistance, adoption assistance, free lab testing, annual development training and credit union access.

FINANCIALS: **Sales and profits are in thousands of dollars—add 000 to get the full amount. 2007 Note: Financial information for 2007 was not available for all companies at press time.**

2007 Sales: $	2007 Profits: $	**U.S. Stock Ticker: DGX**
2006 Sales: $6,268,659	2006 Profits: $586,421	**Int'l Ticker:** Int'l Exchange:
2005 Sales: $5,456,726	2005 Profits: $546,277	Employees: 41,000
2004 Sales: $5,066,986	2004 Profits: $499,195	Fiscal Year Ends: 12/31
2003 Sales: $4,737,958	2003 Profits: $436,717	Parent Company:

SALARIES/BENEFITS:

Pension Plan:	ESOP Stock Plan:	Profit Sharing: Y	Top Exec. Salary: $1,023,000	Bonus: $100,000
Savings Plan: Y	Stock Purch. Plan: Y		Second Exec. Salary: $481,415	Bonus: $

OTHER THOUGHTS:

Apparent Women Officers or Directors: 3
Hot Spot for Advancement for Women/Minorities: Y

LOCATIONS: ("Y" = Yes)

West:	Southwest:	Midwest:	Southeast:	Northeast:	International:
Y	Y	Y	Y	Y	Y

Note: Financial information, benefits and other data can change quickly and may vary from those stated here.

QUIDEL CORP

www.quidel.com

Industry Group Code: 339113 **Ranks within this company's industry group:** Sales: 76 Profits: 51

Insurance/HMO/PPO:		Drugs:		Equipment/Supplies:		Hospitals/Clinics:		Services:		Health Care:	
Insurance:		Manufacturer:		Manufacturer:	Y	Acute Care:		Diagnostics:		Home Health:	
Managed Care:		Distributor:		Distributor:		Sub-Acute:		Labs/Testing:		Long-Term Care:	
Utilization Management:		Specialty Pharmacy:		Leasing/Finance:		Outpatient Surgery:		Staffing:		Physical Therapy:	
Payment Processing:		Vitamins/Nutritionals:		Information Systems:		Physical Rehab. Ctr.:		Waste Disposal:		Physician Prac. Mgmt.:	
		Clinical Trials:				Psychiatric Clinics:		Specialty Svcs.:			

TYPES OF BUSINESS:

Rapid Diagnosis Solutions
Point-of-Care Diagnostic Tests
Research Products

BRANDS/DIVISIONS/AFFILIATES:

QuickVue
QuickVue Advance
RapidVue
Metra

CONTACTS:

Note: Officers with more than one job title may be intentionally listed here more than once.

Caren L. Mason, CEO
Caren L. Mason, Pres.
John M. Radak, CFO
Thomas J. Foley, CTO
Robert J. Bujarski, General Counsel/Sr. VP/Sec.
Scott M. McLeod, Sr. VP-Oper.
Richard Tarbox, III, Sr. VP/Corp. Dev. Officer
Mark A. Pulido, Chmn.

Phone: 858-552-1100	**Fax:** 858-546-8955
Toll-Free: 800-874-1517	
Address: 10165 McKellar Ct., San Diego, CA 92121 US	

GROWTH PLANS/SPECIAL FEATURES:

Quidel Corp. develops, manufactures and markets rapi diagnostic solutions at the professional point-of-care i infectious diseases and reproductive health. The compan focuses on point-of-care testing solutions specificall developed for the physical office lab and acute care market globally. The firm's products are used for detecting an managing a variety of medical conditions and illnesses including pregnancy, infectious diseases, autoimmun disorders and osteoporosis. Quidel sells its products t professionals for use in physician offices, hospitals, clinica laboratories and wellness screening centers. In 2006, abou 83% of revenue was generated from sales of the influenza Group A Strep and pregnancy tests. In addition to the rapi diagnosis business, the company also develops researc products through its Specialty Products Group, with a emphasis on potential future rapid test applications. Th segment is currently responsible for more than 100 of th company's clinical and research products used worldwide i reference laboratories and in research applications a universities and biotechnology companies. The division' revenues, earnings and assets represent less than 10% c the overall operations. Brand names include QuickVue RapidVue, QuickVue Advance and Metra. Quidel markets it products in the U.S. through a network of national an regional distributors, supported by a direct sales force Internationally, the company sells and markets primarily i Japan and Europe by channeling products through distributc organizations and sales agents.

The company offers its employees benefits includin medical, dental and vision insurance; a 401(k) plan; lif insurance; an employee stock purchase plan; flexibl spending accounts; and an employee assistance program.

FINANCIALS:

Sales and profits are in thousands of dollars—add 000 to get the full amount. 2007 Note: Financial information for 2007 was not available for all companies at press time.

2007 Sales: $	2007 Profits: $	**U.S. Stock Ticker: QDEL**
2006 Sales: $106,015	2006 Profits: $21,718	**Int'l Ticker:** Int'l Exchange:
2005 Sales: $92,299	2005 Profits: $-9,259	Employees: 266
2004 Sales: $78,691	2004 Profits: $-6,287	Fiscal Year Ends: 12/31
2003 Sales: $95,105	2003 Profits: $19,651	Parent Company:

SALARIES/BENEFITS:

Pension Plan:	ESOP Stock Plan:	Profit Sharing:	Top Exec. Salary: $445,192	Bonus: $231,750
Savings Plan: Y	Stock Purch. Plan: Y		Second Exec. Salary: $330,338	Bonus: $139,776

OTHER THOUGHTS:

Apparent Women Officers or Directors: 2
Hot Spot for Advancement for Women/Minorities:

LOCATIONS: ("Y" = Yes)

West:	Southwest:	Midwest:	Southeast:	Northeast:	International:
Y					

QUINTILES TRANSNATIONAL CORP www.quintiles.com

Industry Group Code: 541710 **Ranks within this company's industry group:** Sales: Profits:

Insurance/HMO/PPO:		Drugs:		Equipment/Supplies:		Hospitals/Clinics:		Services:		Health Care:	
Insurance:		Manufacturer:		Manufacturer:		Acute Care:		Diagnostics:		Home Health:	
Managed Care:		Distributor:		Distributor:		Sub-Acute:		Labs/Testing:	Y	Long-Term Care:	
Utilization Management:		Specialty Pharmacy:		Leasing/Finance:		Outpatient Surgery:		Staffing:		Physical Therapy:	
Payment Processing:		Vitamins/Nutritionals:		Information Systems:		Physical Rehab. Ctr.:		Waste Disposal:		Physician Prac. Mgmt.:	
		Clinical Trials:	Y			Psychiatric Clinics:		Specialty Svcs.:	Y		

TYPES OF BUSINESS:

Contract Research
Pharmaceutical, Biotech & Medical Device Research
Consulting & Training Services
Sales & Marketing Services

BRANDS/DIVISIONS/AFFILIATES:

PharmaBio Development
Innovex
Pharma Services Holding, Inc.
Medical Action Communication
Q.E.D. Communications

CONTACTS: *Note: Officers with more than one job title may be intentionally listed here more than once.*

Dennis Gillings, CEO
John Ratliff, COO
Mike Troullis, Acting CFO
Stephen DeCherny, Pres., Global Clinical Research Org.
William Deam, CIO
Oppel Greef, Pres., Clinical Tech. Svcs.
Ron Wooten, Exec. VP-Corp. Dev.
Hywel Evans, Pres., Quintiles Global Commercialization
Derek Winstanly, Exec. VP-Strategic Bus. Partnerships
Dennis Gillings, Chmn.

Phone: 919-998-2000	**Fax:** 919-998-9113
Toll-Free:	
Address: 4709 Creekstone Dr., Ste. 200, Durham, NC 27703 US	

GROWTH PLANS/SPECIAL FEATURES:

Quintiles Transnational Corp. provides full-service contract research, sales and marketing services to the global pharmaceutical, biotechnology and medical device industries. The company is one of the world's top contract research organizations (CROs), and it provides a broad range of contract services to speed the process from development to peak sales of a new drug or medical device. Quintiles operates through offices in 50 countries, organized in three primary business segments: the product development group, the commercialization group and the PharmaBio Development group. The product development group provides a full range of drug development services from strategic planning and preclinical services to regulatory submission and approval. The commercial services group, which operates under the Innovex brand, engages in sales force deployment and strategic marketing services as well as consulting services and training for its customers. Within the group, Medical Action Communication uses proven science and marketing technique to advertise products to a potential audience; while Q.E.D. Communications works with product managers in tailoring promotional programs, sales training and testing. The PharmaBio development group works with the other service groups to enter into strategic transactions that it believes will position the company to explore new opportunities and areas for potential growth. PharmaBio also acquires the rights to market pharmaceutical products. In early 2007, Quintiles partnered with Onmark, a group purchasing organization for medical community-based oncology practices, to increase its number of patient recruits in the U.S.

Quintiles Transnational offers its employees a comprehensive benefits package including on-the-job training, recreational activities and community support activities.

FINANCIALS: **Sales and profits are in thousands of dollars—add 000 to get the full amount. 2007 Note: Financial information for 2007 was not available for all companies at press time.**

2007 Sales: $	2007 Profits: $	**U.S. Stock Ticker: Private**
2006 Sales: $	2006 Profits: $	**Int'l Ticker:** Int'l Exchange:
2005 Sales: $2,398,583	2005 Profits: $ 648	Employees: 16,000
2004 Sales: $1,956,254	2004 Profits: $-7,427	Fiscal Year Ends: 12/31
2003 Sales: $2,046,000	2003 Profits: $-7,430,000	Parent Company:

SALARIES/BENEFITS:

Pension Plan:	ESOP Stock Plan:	Profit Sharing:	Top Exec. Salary: $706,061	Bonus: $825,000
Savings Plan: Y	Stock Purch. Plan:		Second Exec. Salary: $471,224	Bonus: $709,000

OTHER THOUGHTS:

Apparent Women Officers or Directors:
Hot Spot for Advancement for Women/Minorities:

LOCATIONS: ("Y" = Yes)

West:	Southwest:	Midwest:	Southeast:	Northeast:	International:
Y	Y	Y	Y	Y	Y

QUOVADX INC

www.quovadx.com

Industry Group Code: 511212 **Ranks within this company's industry group:** Sales: 6 Profits: 8

Insurance/HMO/PPO:		Drugs:		Equipment/Supplies:		Hospitals/Clinics:		Services:		Health Care:	
Insurance:		Manufacturer:		Manufacturer:		Acute Care:		Diagnostics:		Home Health:	
Managed Care:		Distributor:		Distributor:		Sub-Acute:		Labs/Testing:		Long-Term Care:	
Utilization Management:		Specialty Pharmacy:		Leasing/Finance:		Outpatient Surgery:		Staffing:		Physical Therapy:	
Payment Processing:		Vitamins/Nutritionals:		Information Systems:	Y	Physical Rehab. Ctr.:		Waste Disposal:		Physician Prac. Mgmt.:	
		Clinical Trials:				Psychiatric Clinics:		Specialty Svcs.:	Y		

TYPES OF BUSINESS:

Health Care Information Management Software
Customer Relationship Management Software
Consulting Services

BRANDS/DIVISIONS/AFFILIATES:

Cloverleaf Integration Suite
Screen Rejuvenator
Business Process Management Services
Cash Accelerator Suite
Rogue Wave Software Inc
Insurenet Hub
Premier, Inc.
Battery Ventures

CONTACTS: *Note: Officers with more than one job title may be intentionally listed here more than once.*

Russell Fleischer, CEO
Mike Epplen, Sr. VP-Sales & Mktg.
May Hu, Sr. VP-R&D
Carolyn Jolley, Sr. VP-Svcs. & Support
Paul Bellamy, Sr. VP-Int'l Oper.

Phone:	**Fax:** 972-361-3094
Toll-Free: 800-723-3033	
Address: 3010 LBJ Freeway, Ste. 475, Dallas, TX 75234 US	

GROWTH PLANS/SPECIAL FEATURES:

Quovadx, Inc. specializes in private and public healthca interoperability for clinical and financial integration. I Cloverleaf Integration Suite offers multiple secu communications systems so hospitals and health system can connect with laboratories, pharmacies and health plan Some of these connections include secure servers and a encrypted messaging system. The suite also offers th Screen Rejuvenator component, which replaces simp green-screen text displays with graphical interfaces. Finall it offers the Business Process Management Service (BPMS) component, which offers a rules engine th coordinates human and computer-to-computer interaction a well as enterprise integration routing instructions. Quovadx Cash Accelerator Suite allows a company to monitor i revenue cycle electronically from a singe interface. includes the Insurenet Direct platform which automates th connections between healthcare organizations to payer eliminating clearinghouses' intermediary fees. The Insuren Hub interface offers connections with over 2,300 governme and commercial payers for companies that still need interact with clearinghouses. Quovadx also offe companies services designed to help assign covere individuals with unique identifiers. The company has 2,0C installation sites worldwide through 900 clients. In Marc 2007, Quovadx completed the sale of its CareScienc division, which provided care management and analytic resources to hospitals and health systems, to Premier, Inc for $34.9 million. For a sum of $136.7 million, the remaind of the company was acquired by and merged into Rogu Wave Holdings, Inc., a subsidiary of Battery Ventures V L.P., in July 2007. Rogue Wave, formerly a division Quovadx that provided reusable software components ar services to professional developers for enterprise-clas applications, was spun off by Battery into a separa company, Rogue Wave Software, Inc. The former Integrate Solutions division of Quovadx was merged with Quartzi Holdings, Inc., also a subsidiary of Battery Ventures, and now the sole operation of the company known as Quovad Inc.

FINANCIALS: **Sales and profits are in thousands of dollars—add 000 to get the full amount. 2007 Note: Financial information for 2007 was not available for all companies at press time.**

2007 Sales: $	2007 Profits: $	**U.S. Stock Ticker: Private**
2006 Sales: $84,120	2006 Profits: $-13,115	**Int'l Ticker:** Int'l Exchange:
2005 Sales: $83,103	2005 Profits: $-2,888	Employees: 365
2004 Sales: $82,800	2004 Profits: $-24,231	Fiscal Year Ends: 12/31
2003 Sales: $71,595	2003 Profits: $-14,694	Parent Company: BATTERY VENTURES

SALARIES/BENEFITS:

Pension Plan:	ESOP Stock Plan:	Profit Sharing:	Top Exec. Salary: $833,546	Bonus: $403,846
Savings Plan:	Stock Purch. Plan:		Second Exec. Salary: $711,534	Bonus: $285,000

OTHER THOUGHTS:

Apparent Women Officers or Directors: 2
Hot Spot for Advancement for Women/Minorities:

LOCATIONS: ("Y" = Yes)

West:	Southwest:	Midwest:	Southeast:	Northeast:	International:
Y	Y				Y

RADNET INC

www.radnet.com

ndustry Group Code: 621511 **Ranks within this company's industry group:** Sales: 7 Profits: 7

nsurance/HMO/PPO:		Drugs:		Equipment/Supplies:		Hospitals/Clinics:		Services:		Health Care:	
nsurance:		Manufacturer:		Manufacturer:		Acute Care:		Diagnostics:	Y	Home Health:	
Ianaged Care:		Distributor:		Distributor:		Sub-Acute:		Labs/Testing:		Long-Term Care:	
Jtilization Management:		Specialty Pharmacy:		Leasing/Finance:		Outpatient Surgery:		Staffing:		Physical Therapy:	
ayment Processing:		Vitamins/Nutritionals:		Information Systems:		Physical Rehab. Ctr.:		Waste Disposal:		Physician Prac. Mgmt.:	
		Clinical Trials:				Psychiatric Clinics:		Specialty Svcs.:			

TYPES OF BUSINESS:

)iagnostics Services
Iedical Imaging Centers

BRANDS/DIVISIONS/AFFILIATES:

RadNet Management, Inc.
Radiologix, Inc.
Primedex Health Systems, Inc.

CONTACTS:

Note: Officers with more than one job title may be intentionally listed here more than once.

Ioward G. Berger, CEO
Ioward G. Berger, Pres.
Iark D. Stolper, CFO/Exec. VP
effrey L. Linden, General Counsel/Exec. VP
Ioward G. Berger, Treas.
Stephen M. Forthuber, Exec. VP/COO-Eastern Oper.
Jorman R. Hames, VP/Sec.
Jorman R. Hames, COO-Western Oper.

Phone: 310-445-2800	Fax: 310-445-2980
Toll-Free:	
Address: 1510 Cotner Ave., Los Angeles, CA 90024 US	

GROWTH PLANS/SPECIAL FEATURES:

RadNet, Inc., formerly known as Primedex Health Systems, Inc., operates a network of 129 diagnostic imaging centers, more than double the size of its network in 2006. The centers are located primarily in California, the Mid Atlantic, Florida, Kansas and New York; the centers offer medical imaging services to the public, including MRI, CT, PET, ultrasound, mammography, nuclear medicine and general diagnostic radiology. Approximately 36 of the firm's facilities are single-modality sites, offering either X-ray or MRI. These facilities are usually located near its 93 multi-modality sites to help accommodate overflow in target demographic areas. The most common imaging procedures are x-ray, fluoroscopy, endoscopy and modalities such as CT scans and digital image processing. The centers also offer open MRI, allowing studies with patients not typically compatible with conventional MRI, such as infants and pediatric, claustrophobic or obese patients. RadNet Management, Inc. manages the centers. Patients are generally referred to the centers by their treating physicians and may be affiliated with an IPA, HMO, PPO or similar organizations. The company provides all of the equipment as well as non-medical operational, management, financial and administrative services for diagnostic imaging services. In November 2006, RadNet acquired Radiologix, Inc., a nationwide provider of imaging services, for roughly $221 million. The acquisition expanded RadNet's operations beyond California as well as opening new markets within the state.

FINANCIALS:

Sales and profits are in thousands of dollars—add 000 to get the full amount. 2007 Note: Financial information for 2007 was not available for all companies at press time.

2007 Sales: $	2007 Profits: $	**U.S. Stock Ticker: RDNT**
2006 Sales: $161,005	2006 Profits: $-6,894	**Int'l Ticker:** Int'l Exchange:
2005 Sales: $145,573	2005 Profits: $-3,570	Employees: 1,237
2004 Sales: $137,277	2004 Profits: $-14,731	Fiscal Year Ends: 10/31
2003 Sales: $140,259	2003 Profits: $-2,267	Parent Company:

SALARIES/BENEFITS:

Pension Plan:	ESOP Stock Plan:	Profit Sharing:	Top Exec. Salary: $450,000	Bonus: $
Savings Plan: Y	Stock Purch. Plan:		Second Exec. Salary: $350,000	Bonus: $

OTHER THOUGHTS:

Apparent Women Officers or Directors:
Hot Spot for Advancement for Women/Minorities:

LOCATIONS: ("Y" = Yes)

West:	Southwest:	Midwest:	Southeast:	Northeast:	International:
Y	Y	Y	Y	Y	

REABLE THERAPEUTICS INC

www.encoremed.com

Industry Group Code: 339113 **Ranks within this company's industry group:** Sales: Profits:

Insurance/HMO/PPO:		Drugs:		Equipment/Supplies:		Hospitals/Clinics:		Services:		Health Care:	
Insurance:		Manufacturer:		Manufacturer:	Y	Acute Care:		Diagnostics:		Home Health:	
Managed Care:		Distributor:		Distributor:	Y	Sub-Acute:		Labs/Testing:		Long-Term Care:	
Utilization Management:		Specialty Pharmacy:		Leasing/Finance:		Outpatient Surgery:		Staffing:		Physical Therapy:	
Payment Processing:		Vitamins/Nutritionals:		Information Systems:		Physical Rehab. Ctr.:		Waste Disposal:		Physician Prac. Mgmt.:	
		Clinical Trials:				Psychiatric Clinics:		Specialty Svcs.:			

TYPES OF BUSINESS:

Clinical Orthopedic Rehabilitation Products & Devices
Electrotherapy Products
Rehabilitation Products
Spinal Implants

BRANDS/DIVISIONS/AFFILIATES:

Chattanooga Group
Empi, Inc.
Blackstone Capital Partners
Cefar AB
Keramos
Reverse Shoulder Prosthesis

CONTACTS: *Note: Officers with more than one job title may be intentionally listed here more than once.*

Kenneth W. Davidson, CEO
Paul Chapman, COO
Paul Chapman, Pres.
William W. Burke, CFO/Exec. VP
Harry L. Zimmerman, General Counsel/Exec. VP
Jack F. Cahill, Exec. VP/Pres., Surgical Implant Div.
Scott A. Klosterman, Exec. VP/Pres., Orthopedic Rehabilitation Div.
Kenneth W. Davidson, Chmn.

Phone: 512-832-9500	**Fax:** 512-834-6300
Toll-Free: 800-834-6300	
Address: 9800 Metric Blvd., Austin, TX 78758 US	

GROWTH PLANS/SPECIAL FEATURES:

Encore Medical Corporation designs, manufactures, marke and distributes orthopedic devices, sports medicin equipment and other related products for the orthoped industry worldwide. Encore's products are used to tre patients with musculoskeletal conditions resulting fro degenerative diseases, deformities and acute injurie These products serve the needs of physical therapist orthopedic surgeons and other health care professional The company is divided into two operating segments: th surgical implant division and the orthopedic rehabilitatic division. The surgical division manufactures products f surgical implantation and reconstruction including hip, kne shoulder and spinal implants. The orthopedic rehabilitatic division manufactures rehabilitation products includir electrotherapy devices and accessories used to treat pa and restore and maintain muscle function; therapy table iontophoresis drug delivery systems; and other medic devices used in rehabilitation therapy for orthoped surgeons' patients. The division is comprised of hor rehabilitation, through the subsidiary Empi, Inc., and clinic rehabilitation, through Chattanooga Group. Empi offe patients devices that interfere with pain messages b effectively applying electrical stimulation. The Chattanoog Group is a world leader in the manufacture of rehabilitatic equipment for treating skeletal, muscular, neurological ar soft tissue disorders. Part of the company's new produc includes the Keramos ceramic-on-ceramic acetabular h implant; Reverse Shoulder Prosthesis; and electrothera and laser products. In November 2006, Encore Medic went private after being acquired by Blackstone Capi Partners and acquired Cefar AB of Sweden, a Europea provider of electrotherapy and rehabilitation devices.

The company offers its employees a wide range of benefi that include a 401(k) plan.

FINANCIALS: **Sales and profits are in thousands of dollars—add 000 to get the full amount. 2007 Note: Financial information for 2007 was not available for all companies at press time.**

2007 Sales: $	2007 Profits: $	**U.S. Stock Ticker: Private**
2006 Sales: $	2006 Profits: $	**Int'l Ticker:** Int'l Exchange:
2005 Sales: $293,726	2005 Profits: $12,330	Employees: 1,300
2004 Sales: $148,081	2004 Profits: $5,527	Fiscal Year Ends: 12/31
2003 Sales: $108,059	2003 Profits: $-2,517	Parent Company:

SALARIES/BENEFITS:

Pension Plan:	ESOP Stock Plan:	Profit Sharing:	Top Exec. Salary: $438,712	Bonus: $220,000
Savings Plan: Y	Stock Purch. Plan:		Second Exec. Salary: $298,976	Bonus: $150,000

OTHER THOUGHTS:

Apparent Women Officers or Directors:
Hot Spot for Advancement for Women/Minorities:

LOCATIONS: ("Y" = Yes)

West:	Southwest:	Midwest:	Southeast:	Northeast:	International:
	Y				

REGENCE GROUP (THE) www.regence.com

ıdustry Group Code: 524114 **Ranks within this company's industry group:** Sales: Profits:

ısurance/HMO/PPO:		Drugs:		Equipment/Supplies:		Hospitals/Clinics:		Services:		Health Care:	
ısurance:	Y	Manufacturer:		Manufacturer:		Acute Care:		Diagnostics:		Home Health:	
anaged Care:		Distributor:		Distributor:		Sub-Acute:		Labs/Testing:		Long-Term Care:	
tilization Management:		Specialty Pharmacy:		Leasing/Finance:		Outpatient Surgery:		Staffing:		Physical Therapy:	
ayment Processing:		Vitamins/Nutritionals:		Information Systems:		Physical Rehab. Ctr.:		Waste Disposal:		Physician Prac. Mgmt.:	
		Clinical Trials:				Psychiatric Clinics:		Specialty Svcs.:			

'YPES OF BUSINESS:

ısurance-Medical & Health, HMOs & PPOs
ife Insurance
isability Insurance

BRANDS/DIVISIONS/AFFILIATES:

BlueCross BlueShield
Regence BlueShield of Idaho
Regence BlueCross BlueShield of Oregon
Regence BlueCross BlueShield of Utah
Regence BlueShield of Washington
Regence Breakthru
ısuris Northwest Health
ıterM

CONTACTS: *Note: Officers with more than one job title may be ıtentionally listed here more than once.*

lark Ganz, CEO
lark Ganz, Pres.
teve Hooker, CFO/Sr. VP
Iohan Niar, Chief Mktg. Officer/Exec. VP
erry E. Barnett, Chief Legal Officer
ill Barr, Exec. VP-Oper.
eff Robertson, Chief Medical Officer
om Kennedy, Sr. VP-Health Care Svcs.
lary O. McWilliams, Pres., Regence BlueShield
cott Ideson, Pres., Regence BlueCross BlueShield of Utah

'hone: 503-225-5221	Fax: 503-225-5274
oll-Free:	
ıddress: 200 SW Market St., Portland, OR 97201 US	

GROWTH PLANS/SPECIAL FEATURES:

The Regence Group Plans provides health insurance and related services in Idaho, Oregon, Utah and Washington through the Blue Cross Blue Shield brand. The firm offers multiple health insurance policies, which cover a variety of medical and dental emergencies and routine visits. The company's main insurance subsidiaries are Regence BlueShield of Idaho, Regence BlueCross BlueShield of Oregon, Regence BlueCross BlueShield of Utah and Regence BlueShield of Washington. The four companies work interchangeably, offering coverage for customers across state lines. Altogether, the firm provides health insurance coverage to nearly 3 million people. The firm's business strategy relies on the strength of the BlueCross BlueShield name, as well as the financial stability that comes with owning four groups under one name. The company also provides life, disability and short-term medical insurance through its Regence Life and Health Insurance subsidiary. The company has about 39,000 providers on its networks, the majority of which are located in the state of Washington. BlueShield of Washington offers customers the Regence Breakthru plan, which includes unlimited office visits, generic prescription drugs paid for before the deductible, preventive care and vision exams and hardware. Regence also operates, Asuris Northwest Health, a wholly-owned, non-profit insurance subsidiary that offers health care plans other than Blue Cross Blue Shield, while still taking advantage of the Regence network of providers. In September 2007, Regence released its new Oregon-based InterM plan, which provides inexpensive, short term coverage those seeking a job, starting up a business, going back to school or waiting for a group plan to take effect.

Regence offers its employees a choice of medical and dental plans; legal and financial assistance; pre-tax commute reimbursement accounts; on-site fitness centers; child care; credit union access; a 401(k) plan and a retirement plan.

FINANCIALS: **Sales and profits are in thousands of dollars—add 000 to get the full amount. 2007 Note: Financial information for 2007 was not available for all companies at press time.**

007 Sales: $	2007 Profits: $	**U.S. Stock Ticker: Private**
006 Sales: $	2006 Profits: $	**Int'l Ticker:** Int'l Exchange:
005 Sales: $6,500,000	2005 Profits: $	Employees: 6,000
004 Sales: $	2004 Profits: $	Fiscal Year Ends: 12/31
003 Sales: $6,700,000	2003 Profits: $	Parent Company:

SALARIES/BENEFITS:

ension Plan: Y	ESOP Stock Plan:	Profit Sharing:	Top Exec. Salary: $	Bonus: $
avings Plan: Y	Stock Purch. Plan:		Second Exec. Salary: $	Bonus: $

OTHER THOUGHTS:

ıpparent Women Officers or Directors:
lot Spot for Advancement for Women/Minorities:

LOCATIONS: ("Y" = Yes)

West:	Southwest:	Midwest:	Southeast:	Northeast:	International:
Y					

Note: Financial information, benefits and other data can change quickly and may vary from those stated here.

REGENERON PHARMACEUTICALS INC www.regeneron.com

Industry Group Code: 325412 **Ranks within this company's industry group:** Sales: 35 Profits: 39

Insurance/HMO/PPO:		Drugs:		Equipment/Supplies:		Hospitals/Clinics:		Services:		Health Care:	
Insurance:		Manufacturer:	Y	Manufacturer:		Acute Care:		Diagnostics:		Home Health:	
Managed Care:		Distributor:		Distributor:		Sub-Acute:		Labs/Testing:		Long-Term Care:	
Utilization Management:		Specialty Pharmacy:		Leasing/Finance:		Outpatient Surgery:		Staffing:		Physical Therapy:	
Payment Processing:		Vitamins/Nutritionals:		Information Systems:		Physical Rehab. Ctr.:		Waste Disposal:		Physician Prac. Mgmt.:	
		Clinical Trials:				Psychiatric Clinics:		Specialty Svcs.:			

TYPES OF BUSINESS:

Drugs-Diversified
Protein-Based Drugs
Small-Molecule Drugs
Genetics & Transgenic Mouse Technologies

BRANDS/DIVISIONS/AFFILIATES:

VelocImmune
VelociGene
VelociMouse
VEGF Trap
VEGF Trap-Eye
IL-1 Trap

CONTACTS: *Note: Officers with more than one job title may be intentionally listed here more than once.*

Leonard S. Schleifer, CEO
Leonard S. Schleifer, Pres.
Murray A. Goldberg, CFO
George D. Yancopoulos, Exec. VP/Chief Scientific Officer
Randall G. Rupp, Sr. VP-Mfg. & Process Sciences
Murray A. Goldberg, Sr. VP-Admin.
Stuart A. Kolinski, General Counsel/Sr. VP/Sec.
Murray A. Goldberg, Sr. VP-Finance/Treas./Asst. Sec.
George D. Yancopoulos, Pres., Regeneron Research Laboratories
Neil Stahl, Sr. VP-R & D Sciences
P. Roy Vagelos, Chmn.

Phone: 914-345-7400	**Fax:** 914-347-2847
Toll-Free:	
Address: 777 Old Saw Mill River Rd., Tarrytown, NY 10591-6707 US	

GROWTH PLANS/SPECIAL FEATURES:

Regeneron Pharmaceuticals, Inc. is a biopharmaceutic company that discovers, develops and intends commercialize pharmaceutical drugs for the treatment serious medical conditions. The firm is currently focusing c the three clinical development programs: VEGF Trap oncology; VEGF Trap eye formulation (VEGF Trap-Eye) eye diseases using intraocular delivery; and IL-1 Trap various systemic inflammatory indications. The VEGF Tra oncology development program is being developed joint with the sanofi-aventis Group through a 2003 agreemer Regeneron's preclinical research programs are in the area of oncology and angiogenesis, ophthalmology, metabolic ar related diseases, muscle diseases and disorder inflammation and immune diseases, bone and cartilage, pa and cardiovascular diseases. The company expects that i next generation of product candidates will be based on i proprietary technologies for developing Traps and Huma Monoclonal Antibodies. Since its inception the company ha not generated any sales or profits from the commercializatic of any of its product candidates. Regeneron's proprieta technologies include VelociGene, VelociMouse an VelocImmune, among others. The VelociGene technolog allows precise DNA manipulation and gene staining, helpin to identify where a particular gene is active in the bod VelociMouse technology allows for the direct and immedia generation of genetically altered mice from ES cells, avoidin the lengthy process involved in generating and breedin knock-out mice from chimeras. VelocImmune is a nov mouse technology platform for producing fully huma monoclonal antibodies. In 2007, the company announced i entry into a licensing agreement with AstraZeneca f Regeneron's VelocImmune technology in its intern research programs to discover human monoclon antibodies.

FINANCIALS: **Sales and profits are in thousands of dollars—add 000 to get the full amount. 2007 Note: Financial information for 2007 was not available for all companies at press time.**

2007 Sales: $	2007 Profits: $	**U.S. Stock Ticker: REGN**
2006 Sales: $63,447	2006 Profits: $-102,337	**Int'l Ticker:** Int'l Exchange:
2005 Sales: $66,193	2005 Profits: $-95,446	Employees: 573
2004 Sales: $174,017	2004 Profits: $41,699	Fiscal Year Ends: 12/31
2003 Sales: $57,497	2003 Profits: $-107,458	Parent Company:

SALARIES/BENEFITS:

Pension Plan:	ESOP Stock Plan:	Profit Sharing:	Top Exec. Salary: $685,000	Bonus: $420,000
Savings Plan: Y	Stock Purch. Plan:		Second Exec. Salary: $544,300	Bonus: $335,000

OTHER THOUGHTS:

Apparent Women Officers or Directors:
Hot Spot for Advancement for Women/Minorities:

LOCATIONS: ("Y" = Yes)

West:	Southwest:	Midwest:	Southeast:	Northeast:	International:
				Y	

Note: Financial information, benefits and other data can change quickly and may vary from those stated here.

REHABCARE GROUP INC

www.rehabcare.com

Industry Group Code: 621340 **Ranks within this company's industry group:** Sales: 1 Profits: 1

Insurance/HMO/PPO:		Drugs:		Equipment/Supplies:		Hospitals/Clinics:		Services:		Health Care:	
Insurance:		Manufacturer:		Manufacturer:		Acute Care:	Y	Diagnostics:		Home Health:	
Managed Care:		Distributor:		Distributor:		Sub-Acute:	Y	Labs/Testing:		Long-Term Care:	
Utilization Management:		Specialty Pharmacy:		Leasing/Finance:		Outpatient Surgery:		Staffing:		Physical Therapy:	Y
Payment Processing:		Vitamins/Nutritionals:		Information Systems:		Physical Rehab. Ctr.:	Y	Waste Disposal:		Physician Prac. Mgmt.:	
		Clinical Trials:				Psychiatric Clinics:		Specialty Svcs.:	Y		

TYPES OF BUSINESS:

Contract Rehabilitation Services
Acute Care Facilities
Skilled Nursing Services
Outpatient Therapy Programs
Long-Term Acute Care Facilities

BRANDS/DIVISIONS/AFFILIATES:

Solara Hospital
Symphony Health Services, LLC

CONTACTS: *Note: Officers with more than one job title may be intentionally listed here more than once.*

John H. Short, CEO
John H. Short, Pres.
Jay Shreiner, CFO/Sr. VP
Dave Totaro, Sr. VP-Mktg.
Michael R. Garcia, Chief Human Resources Officer/Sr. VP
Sean Maloney, Sr. VP-Clinical R&D
Richard Escue, CIO
Alan Sauber, Sr. VP-Gov't & Regulatory Affairs
Pat Henry, Exec. VP-Oper.
Don Adam, Chief Dev. Officer/Exec. VP
Dave Totaro, Sr. VP-Comm.
Tom Davis, Exec. VP-Freestanding Hospitals Div.
Kenneth K. Adams, Chief Medical Officer/Pres., Medical Affairs
Peter Doerner, Group Sr. VP-Bus. Dev.
Mary Pat Welc, Sr. VP-Oper.
H. Edwin Trusheim, Chmn.

Phone: 314-863-7422 **Fax:** 314-863-0769
Toll-Free: 800-677-1238
Address: 7733 Forsyth Blvd., 23rd Fl., St. Louis, MO 63105 US

GROWTH PLANS/SPECIAL FEATURES:

RehabCare Group, Inc. is a leading provider of rehabilitation program management services in more than 1,400 hospitals, nursing homes, outpatient facilities and other long-term care facilities, up from 800 and 900 facilities served in previous years, located in 43 states. In partnership with healthcare providers, it provides post-acute program management, medical direction, physical therapy rehabilitation, quality assurance, compliance review, specialty programs and census development services. The company also owns and operates three long-term acute care hospitals (LTACHs) and seven rehabilitation hospitals. RehabCare also provides staffing services for therapists and nurses as well as healthcare management consulting services. Its management services cover inpatient rehabilitation facilities within hospitals, skilled nursing units, outpatient rehabilitation programs, home health, and freestanding skilled nursing, long-term care and assisted living facilities. Within the long-term acute care and rehabilitation hospitals it operates, the company provides total medical care to patients in need of rehabilitation and to patients with medically complex diagnoses. Of the company's 2006 revenues, approximately 53.9% came from contract therapy, 29.2% from hospital rehabilitation program management, 12.5% came from operating its hospitals and 4.4% came from other healthcare services. In March 2006, RehabCare abandoned its 25% equity holding in InteliStaf Holdings, Inc., a privately held healthcare staffing company, incurring a $2.8 million loss on the write off. In May 2006, RehabCare announced its acquisition of Solara Hospital of New Orleans, a 44-bed, long-term acute care hospital that features approximately 120 employees, for $5.4 million. In July 2006, the company acquired Symphony Health Services, LLC, a contract provider of therapy services, for $109.9 million.

RehabCare Group offers health care, dental and flexible benefit plans; life, disability, professional liability and long term care insurance; paid time off; and professional education assistance.

FINANCIALS: **Sales and profits are in thousands of dollars—add 000 to get the full amount. 2007 Note: Financial information for 2007 was not available for all companies at press time.**

2007 Sales: $	2007 Profits: $	**U.S. Stock Ticker: RHB**
2006 Sales: $614,793	2006 Profits: $7,280	**Int'l Ticker:** Int'l Exchange:
2005 Sales: $454,266	2005 Profits: $-16,982	Employees: 16,500
2004 Sales: $383,846	2004 Profits: $23,181	Fiscal Year Ends: 12/31
2003 Sales: $539,322	2003 Profits: $-13,699	Parent Company:

SALARIES/BENEFITS:

Pension Plan:	ESOP Stock Plan:	Profit Sharing:	Top Exec. Salary: $573,813	Bonus: $334,794
Savings Plan: Y	Stock Purch. Plan:		Second Exec. Salary: $329,054	Bonus: $124,520

OTHER THOUGHTS:

Apparent Women Officers or Directors: 1
Hot Spot for Advancement for Women/Minorities:

LOCATIONS: ("Y" = Yes)

West:	Southwest:	Midwest:	Southeast:	Northeast:	International:
Y	Y	Y	Y	Y	

RES CARE INC

www.rescare.com

Industry Group Code: 622210 **Ranks within this company's industry group:** Sales: 2 Profits: 3

Insurance/HMO/PPO:		Drugs:		Equipment/Supplies:		Hospitals/Clinics:		Services:		Health Care:	
Insurance:		Manufacturer:		Manufacturer:		Acute Care:		Diagnostics:		Home Health:	Y
Managed Care:		Distributor:		Distributor:		Sub-Acute:		Labs/Testing:		Long-Term Care:	Y
Utilization Management:		Specialty Pharmacy:		Leasing/Finance:		Outpatient Surgery:		Staffing:		Physical Therapy:	
Payment Processing:		Vitamins/Nutritionals:		Information Systems:		Physical Rehab. Ctr.:		Waste Disposal:		Physician Prac. Mgmt.:	
		Clinical Trials:				Psychiatric Clinics:	Y	Specialty Svcs.:	Y		

TYPES OF BUSINESS:

Community Services
Job Corps Training Services
Employment Training Services

BRANDS/DIVISIONS/AFFILIATES:

Armstrong Unicare
Armstrong Uniserve
Workforce Services Group

CONTACTS: *Note: Officers with more than one job title may be intentionally listed here more than once.*

Ralph G. Gronefeld, CEO
Ralph G. Gronefeld, Pres.
David W. Miles, CFO
Nina P. Seigle, Chief People Officer
George Watts, CIO
David S. Waskey, General Counsel/Chief Compliance Officer
Richard Tinsley, Chief Dev. Officer
Nel Taylor, Chief Comm. Officer
Vincent Doran, Pres., Employment & Training Svcs. Group
Paul G. Dunn, Pres., Arbor E&T
Paul G. Dunn, Exec. VP-Western Division of Workforce Svcs.
Michael J. Reibel, Sr. VP-Support Svcs.
Ronald G. Geary, Chmn.

Phone: 502-394-2100 **Fax:** 502-394-2206
Toll-Free:
Address: 10140 Linn Station Rd., Louisville, KY 40223 US

GROWTH PLANS/SPECIAL FEATURES:

Res-Care, Inc. is a human service company that provides residential, therapeutic, job training and educational supports to people with developmental or other disabilities, to youth with special needs, to adults who experience barriers to employment and to older people who need home care assistance. The company's programs include services provided in both residential and non-residential settings to adults and youths with intellectual, cognitive and other developmental disabilities, and youths who have special educational or support needs, are from disadvantaged backgrounds or have severe emotional disorders, including some who have entered the juvenile justice system. The firm also offers, through drop-in or live-in services, personal care, meal preparation, housekeeping and transportation to the elderly in their own homes. In addition, Res-Care provides services to welfare recipients, young people and people who have been laid off or have special barriers to employment, to transition into the workforce and become productive employees. The company operates in three segments: community services, job corps training services and employment training services. Through the community services segment, the firm offers programs for individual with developmental disabilities designed to encourage greater independence and the development or maintenance of daily living skills. The job corps training services segment operates 17 job corps centers that provide for the educational and vocational skills training, healthcare, employment counseling and other support necessary to enable disadvantaged youths to become responsible working adults. The employment training services segment operates 240 career centers, which offer job training and placement programs that assist welfare recipients and disadvantaged job seekers in finding employment and improving their careers prospects. The company provides services in 36 states, Washington, D.C., Canada and Puerto Rico. In 2006 the company acquired Armstrong Uniserve and Armstrong Unicare of Washington, an in-home personal care and respite services company; and Workforce Services Group, a job training company.

FINANCIALS: Sales and profits are in thousands of dollars—add 000 to get the full amount. 2007 Note: Financial information for 2007 was not available for all companies at press time.

2007 Sales: $
2006 Sales: $1,302,118
2005 Sales: $1,046,556
2004 Sales: $966,185
2003 Sales: $961,333

2007 Profits: $
2006 Profits: $36,243
2005 Profits: $21,222
2004 Profits: $21,507
2003 Profits: $13,387

U.S. Stock Ticker: RSCR
Int'l Ticker: Int'l Exchange:
Employees: 37,000
Fiscal Year Ends: 12/31
Parent Company:

SALARIES/BENEFITS:

Pension Plan: ESOP Stock Plan: Profit Sharing:
Savings Plan: Stock Purch. Plan:
Top Exec. Salary: $379,796 Bonus: $370,000
Second Exec. Salary: $309,994 Bonus: $155,000

OTHER THOUGHTS:

Apparent Women Officers or Directors: 2
Hot Spot for Advancement for Women/Minorities: Y

LOCATIONS: ("Y" = Yes)

West:	Southwest:	Midwest:	Southeast:	Northeast:	International:
Y	Y	Y	Y	Y	Y

RESMED INC

www.resmed.com

Industry Group Code: 339113 **Ranks within this company's industry group:** Sales: 35 Profits: 25

Insurance/HMO/PPO:		Drugs:		Equipment/Supplies:		Hospitals/Clinics:		Services:		Health Care:	
Insurance:		Manufacturer:		Manufacturer:	Y	Acute Care:		Diagnostics:		Home Health:	
Managed Care:		Distributor:		Distributor:	Y	Sub-Acute:		Labs/Testing:		Long-Term Care:	
Utilization Management:		Specialty Pharmacy:		Leasing/Finance:		Outpatient Surgery:		Staffing:		Physical Therapy:	
Payment Processing:		Vitamins/Nutritionals:		Information Systems:		Physical Rehab. Ctr.:		Waste Disposal:		Physician Prac. Mgmt.:	
		Clinical Trials:				Psychiatric Clinics:		Specialty Svcs.:			

TYPES OF BUSINESS:

Sleep Disordered Breathing Medical Equipment
Diagnosis & Treatment Products

BRANDS/DIVISIONS/AFFILIATES:

ResMed, Ltd.
Medizintechnik fur Arzt und Patient GmbH
SMI
Saime SA
Swift
S8 Elite
S8 Escape
S8 Compact

CONTACTS:

Note: Officers with more than one job title may be intentionally listed here more than once.

Peter C. Farrell, CEO
Kieran T. Gallahue, COO
Kieran T. Gallahue, Pres.
Brett Sandercock, CFO
David Pendarvis, Global General Counsel
David Pendarvis, Sr. VP-Organizational Dev.
Paul Eisen, Sr. VP-Asia Pacific
Robert Douglas, COO-Sydney
Lasse Beijer, COO-Europe
Keith Serzen, COO-Americas
Peter C. Farrell, Chmn.
Kieran T. Gallahue, Pres., ResMed Global

Phone: 858-746-2400 **Fax:** 858-746-2900
Toll-Free: 800-424-0737
Address: 14040 Danielson St., Poway, CA 92064 US

GROWTH PLANS/SPECIAL FEATURES:

ResMed, Inc. develops, manufactures and distributes medical equipment for treating, diagnosing and managing sleep disordered breathing (SDB) and other respiratory disorders. SDB includes obstructive sleep apnea (OSA) and other related respiratory disorders that occur during sleep. The company was originally founded to commercialize a Continuous Positive Airway Pressure (CPAP) treatment for OSA, which delivers pressurized air, typically through a nasal mask, to prevent collapse of the upper airway during sleep. Since the introduction of nasal CPAP, the company has developed a number of innovative products for SDB, including airflow generators, diagnostic products, mask systems, headgear and other accessories. The company's business strategy includes expanding into new clinical applications by seeking to identify new uses for its technologies. It also hopes to increase consumer awareness of the little-known condition, which may afflict up to 20% of Americans. Studies have established a link between OSA and stroke and congestive heart failure (CHF), and ResMed is in the process of developing a device for the treatment of Cheyne-Stokes breathing in CHF patients. The firm sells products in over 67 countries through a combination of wholly-owned subsidiaries and independent distributors. The company's international locations include Australia, Egypt, Austria, Finland, France, Germany, Italy, the Netherlands, Norway, Spain, Sweden, Switzerland, the U.K. and Brazil. Masks, accessories, motors and diagnosis products accounted for roughly 48% of net revenues in 2006. Through subsidiaries ResMed, Ltd., Medizintechnik fur Arzt und Patient GmbH, SMI and Saime SA, the company owns 220 U.S. patents and 325 foreign patents.

FINANCIALS:

Sales and profits are in thousands of dollars—add 000 to get the full amount. 2007 Note: Financial information for 2007 was not available for all companies at press time.

2007 Sales: $716,332	2007 Profits: $66,302	**U.S. Stock Ticker: RMD**
2006 Sales: $606,996	2006 Profits: $88,211	**Int'l Ticker:** Int'l Exchange:
2005 Sales: $425,505	2005 Profits: $64,785	Employees: 2,700
2004 Sales: $339,338	2004 Profits: $57,284	Fiscal Year Ends: 6/30
2003 Sales: $273,600	2003 Profits: $45,700	Parent Company:

SALARIES/BENEFITS:

Pension Plan:	ESOP Stock Plan:	Profit Sharing:	Top Exec. Salary: $553,750	Bonus: $590,146
Savings Plan:	Stock Purch. Plan:		Second Exec. Salary: $378,750	Bonus: $398,215

OTHER THOUGHTS:

Apparent Women Officers or Directors:
Hot Spot for Advancement for Women/Minorities: Y

LOCATIONS: ("Y" = Yes)

West:	Southwest:	Midwest:	Southeast:	Northeast:	International:
Y					Y

RESPIRONICS INC www.respironics.com

Industry Group Code: 339113 **Ranks within this company's industry group:** Sales: 27 Profits: 23

Insurance/HMO/PPO:		Drugs:		Equipment/Supplies:		Hospitals/Clinics:		Services:		Health Care:	
Insurance:		Manufacturer:		Manufacturer:	Y	Acute Care:		Diagnostics:		Home Health:	
Managed Care:		Distributor:		Distributor:		Sub-Acute:		Labs/Testing:		Long-Term Care:	
Utilization Management:		Specialty Pharmacy:		Leasing/Finance:		Outpatient Surgery:		Staffing:		Physical Therapy:	
Payment Processing:		Vitamins/Nutritionals:		Information Systems:		Physical Rehab. Ctr.:		Waste Disposal:		Physician Prac. Mgmt.:	
		Clinical Trials:				Psychiatric Clinics:		Specialty Svcs.:			

TYPES OF BUSINESS:

Equipment/Supplies-Respiratory Devices

BRANDS/DIVISIONS/AFFILIATES:

Sleep Well Ventures
Children's Medical Ventures
OxyTec Medical Corporation
OxyTec 900

CONTACTS:

Note: Officers with more than one job title may be intentionally listed here more than once.

John L. Miclot, CEO
Craig B. Reynolds, COO/Exec. VP
John L. Miclot, Pres.
Daniel J. Bevevino, CFO/VP
David P. White, Chief Medical Officer
Steven Fulton, General Counsel/VP
Susan A. Lloyd, VP-Respiratory Drug Delivery Div.
Derek Smith, Pres., Hospital Group
Donald Spence, Pres., Sleep & Home Respiratory Group
Gerald E. McGinnis, Chmn.
Geoffrey C. Waters, Pres., Int'l Div.

Phone: 724-387-5200	**Fax:**
Toll-Free: 800-345-6443	
Address: 1010 Murry Ridge Ln., Murrysville, PA 15668-8525 US	

GROWTH PLANS/SPECIAL FEATURES:

Respironics, Inc. is a leading developer, manufacturer ar marketer of medical devices that are used for the treatme of patients suffering from sleep and respiratory disorder The company's products comprise the following tw categories: Sleep and Home Respiratory Products, whic include sleep disordered breathing products, hom respiratory care products and Sleep Well Ventures product and Hospital Products, which include critical care product respiratory drug delivery products and Children's Medic Ventures products. Sleep disordered breathing produc include devices and accessories used in the home for th treatment of Obstructive Sleep Apnea (OSA); patie interface products, including nasal pillows and full fac masks; and products that are used to diagnose slee disorders in sleep labs and for patient testing in the hom Home respiratory care products include noninvasiv ventilation products that provide positive airway pressure b mask to supplement the patient's own breathing; portable li support ventilators used in the home on patients requirin continuous support; stationary and portable oxygen delive products; and oximetry products. Sleep Well Venture products target undiagnosed and untreated sleep and slee related movement disorders such as insomnia, circadia rhythm disorders and restless leg syndrome. Critical car products include noninvasive ventilators, patient mask accessories, patient monitoring technologies an spontaneous breathing trial products. Respiratory dru delivery products include methods of delivering drugs via th respiratory pathway to help treat chronic obstructiv pulmonary disease, asthma, pulmonary arterial hypertensio and cystic fibrosis. Children's Medical Ventures provid developmentally supportive products for premature and infants in the hospital or home, including apnea monitors an diagnostic and treatment tools for jaundice. In 200 Respironics acquired OxyTec Medical Corporation, whic recently developed the OxyTec 900, a portable oxyge concentrator.

Respironics offers its employees wellness programs, fitnes centers, flex time, service awards, recognition program patent awards, educational assistance and credit unio membership.

FINANCIALS:

Sales and profits are in thousands of dollars—add 000 to get the full amount. 2007 Note: Financial information for 2007 was not available for all companies at press time.

2007 Sales: $1,195,035	2007 Profits: $122,285	**U.S. Stock Ticker: RESP**
2006 Sales: $1,046,141	2006 Profits: $99,893	**Int'l Ticker:** Int'l Exchange:
2005 Sales: $911,500	2005 Profits: $84,400	Employees: 4,900
2004 Sales: $759,550	2004 Profits: $65,020	Fiscal Year Ends: 6/30
2003 Sales: $629,800	2003 Profits: $46,600	Parent Company:

SALARIES/BENEFITS:

Pension Plan:	ESOP Stock Plan:	Profit Sharing: Y	Top Exec. Salary: $634,616	Bonus: $490,000
Savings Plan: Y	Stock Purch. Plan: Y		Second Exec. Salary: $500,225	Bonus: $312,096

OTHER THOUGHTS:

Apparent Women Officers or Directors: 1
Hot Spot for Advancement for Women/Minorities:

LOCATIONS: ("Y" = Yes)

West:	Southwest:	Midwest:	Southeast:	Northeast:	International:
Y	Y		Y	Y	Y

REVOLUTION HEALTH GROUP LLC www.revolutionhealth.com

Industry Group Code: 514199 **Ranks within this company's industry group:** Sales: Profits:

Insurance/HMO/PPO:		Drugs:		Equipment/Supplies:		Hospitals/Clinics:		Services:		Health Care:	
Insurance:		Manufacturer:		Manufacturer:		Acute Care:		Diagnostics:		Home Health:	
Managed Care:		Distributor:		Distributor:		Sub-Acute:		Labs/Testing:		Long-Term Care:	
Utilization Management:		Specialty Pharmacy:		Leasing/Finance:		Outpatient Surgery:		Staffing:		Physical Therapy:	
Payment Processing:		Vitamins/Nutritionals:		Information Systems:		Physical Rehab. Ctr.:		Waste Disposal:		Physician Prac. Mgmt.:	
		Clinical Trials:				Psychiatric Clinics:		Specialty Svcs.:	Y		

TYPES OF BUSINESS:

Healthcare & Medical Information Provider

BRANDS/DIVISIONS/AFFILIATES:

Revolution LLC
RevolutionHealth.com
MayoClinic.com
RHG Insurance Services, LLC
Extended Health
TLContact, Inc.
CarePages.com

CONTACTS: *Note: Officers with more than one job title may be intentionally listed here more than once.*

Steve Case, CEO
Ron Peele, CFO
Joel Obourn, Chief Sales Officer
Martin R. Fisher, CTO
James Bramson, General Counsel
Michael Singer, Exec. VP-Corp. Dev.
Jay Silverstein, Pres., Employer/Employee Group
Jeffrey Gruen, Chief Medical Officer
Melanie Bowen, Gen. Manager-RevolutionHealth.com
Anna Slomovic, Chief Privacy Officer
Steve Case, Chmn.

Phone: 202-776-1407	**Fax:**
Toll-Free:	
Address: 1250 Connecticut Ave. NW, Ste. 600, Washington, DC 20036-2651 US	

GROWTH PLANS/SPECIAL FEATURES:

Revolution Health Group, LLC, part of the Revolution LLC group of companies founded by AOL co-founder Steve Case, primarily seeks to transform the attitudes of consumers in order to allow them to make more informed healthcare choices. For instance, the company's web site, RevolutionHealth.com, offers a symptom checker, powered by MayoClinic.com, allowing users to input symptoms and receive feedback suggesting whether or not their condition is likely to need medical treatment. In all, the web site offers 125 similar online tools as well as other healthcare information. Additionally, Revolution Health offers membership, primarily targeting businesses, offering telephone based assistance ranging from answering health questions to helping settle health insurance claims and scheduling appointments. Furthermore, affiliate RHG Insurance Services, LLC, a licensed insurance agency, provides health insurance through insurance companies they work with (since it is not itself an insurance company), receiving a commission from any insurance purchased through it. Revolution Health, working through affiliate Extended Health, allows consumers to browse and compare health insurance products, and even helps consumers contact trusted brokers. Many of the company's services are offered free of charge; and the company makes money primarily by offering advertising on its web site, through its membership options and through RHG Insurance Services. Some of the company's partnerships include Alternative Medicine Magazine; Psychology Today; Rodale Inc., publisher of Men's Health, Women's Health, Prevention, Runner's World and other magazines; and Harvard Health Publications, a division of Harvard Medical School. In April 2007, the firm acquired TLContact, Inc., operator of CarePages.com, a leading Internet service providing family and friends the opportunity to develop online communities to support communication when someone close to them is receiving care.

FINANCIALS: **Sales and profits are in thousands of dollars—add 000 to get the full amount. 2007 Note: Financial information for 2007 was not available for all companies at press time.**

2007 Sales: $	2007 Profits: $	**U.S. Stock Ticker: Private**
2006 Sales: $	2006 Profits: $	**Int'l Ticker:** Int'l Exchange:
2005 Sales: $	2005 Profits: $	Employees:
2004 Sales: $	2004 Profits: $	Fiscal Year Ends: 12/31
2003 Sales: $	2003 Profits: $	Parent Company:

SALARIES/BENEFITS:

Pension Plan:	ESOP Stock Plan:	Profit Sharing:	Top Exec. Salary: $	Bonus: $
Savings Plan:	Stock Purch. Plan:		Second Exec. Salary: $	Bonus: $

OTHER THOUGHTS:

Apparent Women Officers or Directors: 4
Hot Spot for Advancement for Women/Minorities: Y

LOCATIONS: ("Y" = Yes)

West:	Southwest:	Midwest:	Southeast:	Northeast:	International:
				Y	

RITE AID CORPORATION

www.riteaid.com

Industry Group Code: 446110 **Ranks within this company's industry group:** Sales: 3 Profits: 3

Insurance/HMO/PPO:		Drugs:		Equipment/Supplies:		Hospitals/Clinics:		Services:		Health Care:	
Insurance:		Manufacturer:		Manufacturer:		Acute Care:		Diagnostics:		Home Health:	
Managed Care:		Distributor:	Y	Distributor:		Sub-Acute:		Labs/Testing:		Long-Term Care:	
Utilization Management:		Specialty Pharmacy:	Y	Leasing/Finance:		Outpatient Surgery:		Staffing:		Physical Therapy:	
Payment Processing:		Vitamins/Nutritionals:		Information Systems:		Physical Rehab. Ctr.:		Waste Disposal:		Physician Prac. Mgmt.:	
		Clinical Trials:				Psychiatric Clinics:		Specialty Svcs.:			

TYPES OF BUSINESS:

Drug Stores
Pharmacy Benefits Management

BRANDS/DIVISIONS/AFFILIATES:

FLAVORx
Rite Aid Health Solutions
Brooks Eckerd

CONTACTS: *Note: Officers with more than one job title may be intentionally listed here more than once.*

Mary Sammons, CEO
Robert J. Easley, COO
Mary Sammons, Pres.
Kevin Twomey, CFO/Exec. VP
Mark Panzer, Chief Mktg. Officer/Sr. Exec. VP
Todd McCarty, Sr. VP-Human Resources
Don P. Davis, CIO/Sr. VP
Pierre Legault, Chief Admin. Officer
Robert Sari, General Counsel/Exec. VP
Christopher Hall, Sr. VP-Strategic Bus. Dev.
Karen Rugen, Sr. VP-Corp. Comm.
Doug Donley, Chief Acct. Officer/Sr. VP
Mark de Bruin, Exec. VP-Pharmacy
Brian Fiala, Exec. VP-Store Oper.
Tony Bellezza, Sr. VP/Chief Compliance Officer
John Learish, Sr. VP-Mktg.
Mary Sammons, Chmn.
Wilson A. Lester, Jr., Sr. VP-Supply Chain

Phone: 717-761-2633	**Fax:** 717-975-5871
Toll-Free: 800-748-3243	
Address: 30 Hunter Ln., Camp Hill, PA 17011 US	

GROWTH PLANS/SPECIAL FEATURES:

Rite Aid Corp. is third largest retail drug store chain in t U.S., behind Walgreens and CVS. The company operat over 5,000 drug stores in 31 states and Washington, D. Rite Aid stores sell prescription drugs, which accounted about 64% of revenue in 2007, and other merchandise su as non-prescription medications; health and beauty aic personal care items; cosmetics; household items; beverage convenience foods; greeting cards; seasonal merchandis and numerous other everyday products. Rite Aid offers ov 26,000 products, approximately 3,000 of which are under t Rite Aid private brand. Approximately 56% of Rite Aic stores are freestanding; 43% include a drive-throu pharmacy; 67% include one-hour photo shops; and 38 include a GNC store-within-Rite Aid-store. Rite Aic pharmacies offer a service in which FLAVORx flavoring c be added to all prescription and over-the-counter syrups a liquid medications. Customers can choose from 20 differe flavorings. Rite Aid pharmacies can print prescription bot labels in 11 languages and large typeface. The compan Rite Aid Health Solutions segment provides pharma benefit management services to employers, health plans a insurance companies. Rite Aid hopes to open 800 to 1,0 new stores nationwide through 2011. In June 2007, t company acquired 1,854 Brooks and Eckerd Stores and distribution centers from The Jean Coutu Group, Inc. $2.36 billion. The stores are located in 18 states, mainly the Eastern and Mid-Atlantic regions. All stores will be branded Rite Aid.

The company offers its employees health, dental and visi insurance; life and AD&D insurance; a 401(k) plan; a sto purchase plan; and an employee assistance program.

FINANCIALS: Sales and profits are in thousands of dollars—add 000 to get the full amount. 2007 Note: Financial information for 2007 was not available for all companies at press time.

2007 Sales: $17,507,719	2007 Profits: $26,826	**U.S. Stock Ticker: RAD**
2006 Sales: $17,270,968	2006 Profits: $1,273,006	**Int'l Ticker:** Int'l Exchange:
2005 Sales: $16,816,439	2005 Profits: $302,478	Employees: 69,700
2004 Sales: $16,600,449	2004 Profits: $83,311	Fiscal Year Ends: 2/28
2003 Sales: $15,800,900	2003 Profits: $-112,100	Parent Company:

SALARIES/BENEFITS:

Pension Plan:	ESOP Stock Plan:	Profit Sharing:	Top Exec. Salary: $1,000,000	Bonus: $1,543,631
Savings Plan: Y	Stock Purch. Plan: Y		Second Exec. Salary: $775,000	Bonus: $877,297

OTHER THOUGHTS:

Apparent Women Officers or Directors: 5
Hot Spot for Advancement for Women/Minorities: Y

LOCATIONS: ("Y" = Yes)

West:	Southwest:	Midwest:	Southeast:	Northeast:	International:
Y	Y	Y	Y	Y	

ROCHE HOLDING LTD www.roche.com

dustry Group Code: 325412 **Ranks within this company's industry group:** Sales: 6 Profits: 5

surance/HMO/PPO:		Drugs:		Equipment/Supplies:		Hospitals/Clinics:		Services:		Health Care:	
surance:		Manufacturer:	Y	Manufacturer:		Acute Care:		Diagnostics:	Y	Home Health:	
anaged Care:		Distributor:		Distributor:		Sub-Acute:		Labs/Testing:		Long-Term Care:	
ilization Management:		Specialty Pharmacy:		Leasing/Finance:		Outpatient Surgery:		Staffing:		Physical Therapy:	
ayment Processing:		Vitamins/Nutritionals:		Information Systems:		Physical Rehab. Ctr.:		Waste Disposal:		Physician Prac. Mgmt.:	
		Clinical Trials:				Psychiatric Clinics:		Specialty Svcs.:			

YPES OF BUSINESS:

harmaceuticals Manufacturing
ntibiotics
agnostics
ancer Drugs
rology Products
V/AIDS Treatments
ansplant Drugs

BRANDS/DIVISIONS/AFFILIATES:

enentech
. Hoffmann-La Roche, Ltd.
leve
ennie
amiflu
erceptin
hugai Pharmaceuticals
ioveris Corporation

CONTACTS: *Note: Officers with more than one job title may be tentionally listed here more than once.*

everin Schwan, CEO
rich Hunziker, CFO
ascal Soriot, Head-Strategic Mktg.
ottlieb Keller, VP-Human Resources
onathan Knowles, Dir.-Global Research
duard E. Holdener, Dir.-Global Pharma Dev./Chief Medical Officer
ascal Soriot, Head-Commercial Oper.
olf D. Schlapfer, Head-Global Corp. Comm.
illiam M. Burns, CEO-Roche Pharmaceuticals
eter Hug, Head-Pharma Partnering
samu Nagayama, Pres./CEO-Chugai
anz B. Humer, Chmn.

hone: 41-61-688-1111	**Fax:** 41-61-691-9391
oll-Free:	
ddress: Grenzacherstrasse 124, Basel, 4070 Switzerland	

GROWTH PLANS/SPECIAL FEATURES:

Roche Holding, Ltd. is one of the world's largest health care companies, occupying an industry-leading position in the global diagnostics market and ranking as one of the top producers of pharmaceuticals, with particular market penetration in the areas of cancer drugs, virology and transplantation medicine. Group operations currently extend to some 150 countries, with additional alliances and research and development agreements with corporate and institutional partners furthering Roche's collective reach. Among the company's related corporate interests are majority ownership holdings in Genentech and Japanese pharmaceutical firm Chugai. Roche's products include the cancer drugs Avastin, Bondronat, Xeloda, Herceptin and Mabthera/Rituxan; the antibiotic Rocephin; the HIV/AIDS treatments Viracept, Fortovase and Fuzeon; and Tamiflu, which is used to prevent and treat influenza. Roche has invested heavily in diagnostics, both through internal resource development and through selective acquisitions. Roche companies control proprietary diagnostic technologies across a range of areas, including advanced DNA tests, leading consumer diabetes monitoring devices and applied sciences methodologies for laboratory research. As part of the recent mobilization of Tamiflu, the company recently came to an agreement with Gilead, which will coordinate the commercialization and manufacture of drug, important in the case of a flu pandemic. In early 2007, Roche granted GlaxoSmithKline Consumer Healthcare the non-prescription rights to the anti-obesity drug orlistat; these global rights exclude the U.S. and Japan. In April 2007, the firm agreed to acquire BioVeris Corp., a diagnostic company located in the U.S., for $600 million. The acquisition will strengthen Roche's position in the immunochemistry market.

FINANCIALS: **Sales and profits are in thousands of dollars—add 000 to get the full amount. 2007 Note: Financial information for 2007 was not available for all companies at press time.**

007 Sales: $	2007 Profits: $	**U.S. Stock Ticker: RHHBY**
006 Sales: $34,851,500	2006 Profits: $7,116,030	**Int'l Ticker: RO** Int'l Exchange: Zurich-SWX
005 Sales: $27,385,668	2005 Profits: $5,189,777	Employees: 68,218
004 Sales: $22,767,021	2004 Profits: $5,446,567	Fiscal Year Ends: 12/31
003 Sales: $25,132,100	2003 Profits: $2,470,500	Parent Company:

SALARIES/BENEFITS:

ension Plan:	ESOP Stock Plan:	Profit Sharing:	Top Exec. Salary: $	Bonus: $
avings Plan:	Stock Purch. Plan:		Second Exec. Salary: $	Bonus: $

OTHER THOUGHTS:

pparent Women Officers or Directors: 2
ot Spot for Advancement for Women/Minorities: Y

LOCATIONS: ("Y" = Yes)

West:	Southwest:	Midwest:	Southeast:	Northeast:	International:
Y	Y	Y	Y	Y	Y

Note: Financial information, benefits and other data can change quickly and may vary from those stated here.

ROTECH HEALTHCARE INC www.rotech.com

Industry Group Code: 339113 **Ranks within this company's industry group:** Sales: 38 Profits: 98

Insurance/HMO/PPO:		Drugs:		Equipment/Supplies:		Hospitals/Clinics:		Services:		Health Care:	
Insurance:		Manufacturer:		Manufacturer:		Acute Care:		Diagnostics:		Home Health:	
Managed Care:		Distributor:		Distributor:	Y	Sub-Acute:		Labs/Testing:		Long-Term Care:	
Utilization Management:		Specialty Pharmacy:		Leasing/Finance:		Outpatient Surgery:		Staffing:		Physical Therapy:	
Payment Processing:		Vitamins/Nutritionals:		Information Systems:		Physical Rehab. Ctr.:		Waste Disposal:		Physician Prac. Mgmt.:	
		Clinical Trials:				Psychiatric Clinics:		Specialty Svcs.:			

TYPES OF BUSINESS:

Home Medical Equipment
Respiratory Equipment

BRANDS/DIVISIONS/AFFILIATES:

CONTACTS:

Note: Officers with more than one job title may be intentionally listed here more than once.

Philip L. Carter, CEO
Michael R. Dobbs, COO
Philip L. Carter, Pres.
Steve Alsene, CFO
Rebecca L. Myers, Chief Legal Officer/Corp. Sec.
Arthur J. Reimers, Chmn.

Phone: 407-822-4600 **Fax:** 407-297-6217
Toll-Free: 877-603-7840
Address: 2600 Technology Dr., Ste. 300, Orlando, FL 32804 US

GROWTH PLANS/SPECIAL FEATURES:

Rotech Healthcare, Inc. is a provider of home medic equipment and related products and services in the U.S with an offering of respiratory therapy and durable hom medical equipment and related services. The compar provides equipment and services in 48 states throug approximately 500 operating centers located primarily in no urban markets. The firm supplies its equipment and service principally to older patients with breathing disorders, such a chronic obstructive pulmonary diseases, or COPD (whic include chronic bronchitis and emphysema), obstructiv sleep apnea and other cardiopulmonary disorders. Rotech revenues are derived principally from respiratory equipme rental and related services, making up about 89% Rotech's revenues. Respiratory equipment includes oxyge concentrator, liquid oxygen systems, portable oxyge systems, ventilator therapy systems, nebulizer equipme and sleep disorder breathing therapy systems for rental sale. Rotech also rents and sells durable medic equipment, including hospital beds, wheelchairs, walker patient aids and ancillary supplies, which generate abo 11% of revenues annually.

FINANCIALS:

Sales and profits are in thousands of dollars—add 000 to get the full amount. 2007 Note: Financial information for 2007 was not available for all companies at press time.

2007 Sales: $
2006 Sales: $498,751
2005 Sales: $533,182
2004 Sales: $535,329
2003 Sales: $581,221

2007 Profits: $
2006 Profits: $-534,099
2005 Profits: $5,546
2004 Profits: $36,010
2003 Profits: $8,413

U.S. Stock Ticker: ROHI
Int'l Ticker: Int'l Exchange:
Employees: 4,900
Fiscal Year Ends: 12/31
Parent Company:

SALARIES/BENEFITS:

Pension Plan: ESOP Stock Plan: Profit Sharing:
Savings Plan: Stock Purch. Plan:

Top Exec. Salary: $920,000 Bonus: $398,666
Second Exec. Salary: $520,000 Bonus: $225,333

OTHER THOUGHTS:

Apparent Women Officers or Directors: 1
Hot Spot for Advancement for Women/Minorities:

LOCATIONS: ("Y" = Yes)

West:	Southwest:	Midwest:	Southeast:	Northeast:	International:
Y	Y	Y	Y	Y	

SAFEGUARD HEALTH ENTERPRISES INC www.safeguard.net

Industry Group Code: 524114A **Ranks within this company's industry group:** Sales: Profits:

Insurance/HMO/PPO:		Drugs:		Equipment/Supplies:		Hospitals/Clinics:		Services:		Health Care:	
Insurance:	Y	Manufacturer:		Manufacturer:		Acute Care:		Diagnostics:		Home Health:	
Managed Care:	Y	Distributor:		Distributor:		Sub-Acute:		Labs/Testing:		Long-Term Care:	
Utilization Management:		Specialty Pharmacy:		Leasing/Finance:		Outpatient Surgery:		Staffing:		Physical Therapy:	
Payment Processing:		Vitamins/Nutritionals:		Information Systems:		Physical Rehab. Ctr.:		Waste Disposal:		Physician Prac. Mgmt.:	
		Clinical Trials:				Psychiatric Clinics:		Specialty Svcs.:			

TYPES OF BUSINESS:

HMO/PPO
Vision & Life Insurance Products
Administrative Services
Dental & Vision Benefit Plans
Employee Assistance Programs

BRANDS/DIVISIONS/AFFILIATES:

Health Net Vision, Inc.
SafeGuard Health Plans, Inc.
Health Net Dental, Inc.
SmileSaver

CONTACTS: *Note: Officers with more than one job title may be intentionally listed here more than once.*

James E. Buncher, CEO
Stephen J. Baker, COO
Stephen J. Baker, Pres.
Dennis L. Gates, CFO/Sr. VP
Kenneth E. Keating, VP-Mktg.
James E. Buncher, Chmn.

Phone: 949-425-4300 **Fax:** 949-425-4586
Toll-Free:
Address: 95 Enterprise, Ste. 100, Aliso Viejo, CA 92656-2605 US

GROWTH PLANS/SPECIAL FEATURES:

SafeGuard Health Enterprises, Inc. provides dental benefit plans, including HMO, PPO and indemnity plans, to government and private sector employers, associations and individuals. The company also offers vision benefit plans, administrative services and employee assistance programs. It operates through a group of subsidiaries. SafeGuard has group contracts with over 4,500 employer or association groups and delivers dental or vision services to approximately 1.8 million covered individuals in California, Texas, Nevada and Florida. Its dental HMO plans typically cover basic dental procedures, such as examinations, x-rays, cleanings and fillings, as well as more extensive procedures provided by a general dentist, such as root canals and crowns. They also cover procedures performed by specialists contracted with the company, including oral surgery, periodontics and orthodontics. PPO/indemnity plans generally cover the same procedures as HMO plans, but require subscribers to make a co-insurance payment at the time of each service. The firm's defined benefit dental plans reimburse subscribers and dependents a fixed amount for each procedure performed. Currently, the company has an agreement with MetLife to provide dual option dental benefit plans to employers in California. Most recently, SafeGuard has acquired GE's dental and vision health maintenance business in California, including the SmileSaver brand; increased business in Nevada by partnering with managed care firm NevadaCare; and struck up contracts in Harris County, Texas, the largest county employer in the state. In late 2006, the firm began offering its vision product in Nevada. In August 2007, the firm agreed to be acquired by MetLife, Inc.; terms of the transaction were not disclosed.

FINANCIALS: **Sales and profits are in thousands of dollars—add 000 to get the full amount. 2007 Note: Financial information for 2007 was not available for all companies at press time.**

2007 Sales: $ | 2007 Profits: $
2006 Sales: $ | 2006 Profits: $
2005 Sales: $ | 2005 Profits: $
2004 Sales: $ | 2004 Profits: $
2003 Sales: $104,891 | 2003 Profits: $7,813

U.S. Stock Ticker: Private
Int'l Ticker: Int'l Exchange:
Employees: 360
Fiscal Year Ends: 12/31
Parent Company:

SALARIES/BENEFITS:

Pension Plan: ESOP Stock Plan: Profit Sharing: Top Exec. Salary: $250,000 Bonus: $25,000
Savings Plan: Stock Purch. Plan: Second Exec. Salary: $220,000 Bonus: $20,000

OTHER THOUGHTS:

Apparent Women Officers or Directors:
Hot Spot for Advancement for Women/Minorities:

LOCATIONS: ("Y" = Yes)

West:	Southwest:	Midwest:	Southeast:	Northeast:	International:
Y	Y		Y		

SANOFI-AVENTIS

www.sanofi-synthelabo.fr

Industry Group Code: 325412 **Ranks within this company's industry group:** Sales: 4 Profits: 6

Insurance/HMO/PPO:		Drugs:		Equipment/Supplies:		Hospitals/Clinics:		Services:		Health Care:	
Insurance:		Manufacturer:	Y	Manufacturer:		Acute Care:		Diagnostics:		Home Health:	
Managed Care:		Distributor:		Distributor:		Sub-Acute:		Labs/Testing:		Long-Term Care:	
Utilization Management:		Specialty Pharmacy:		Leasing/Finance:		Outpatient Surgery:		Staffing:		Physical Therapy:	
Payment Processing:		Vitamins/Nutritionals:		Information Systems:		Physical Rehab. Ctr.:		Waste Disposal:		Physician Prac. Mgmt.:	
		Clinical Trials:				Psychiatric Clinics:		Specialty Svcs.:			

TYPES OF BUSINESS:

Pharmaceuticals Development & Manufacturing
Over-the-Counter Drugs
Cardiovascular Drugs
CNS Drugs
Oncology Drugs
Diabetes Drugs
Generics
Vaccines

BRANDS/DIVISIONS/AFFILIATES:

Aprovel
Plavix
Allegra
Depakine
Stilnox
Sanofi-Pasteur
Eloxatin
Sanofi-Synthelabo

CONTACTS: *Note: Officers with more than one job title may be intentionally listed here more than once.*

Gerard Le Fur, CEO
Jean-Claude Leroy, CFO/Exec. VP
Heinz Werner Meier, Sr. VP-Human Resources
Donna Vitter, General Counsel
Oliver Jacquesson, VP-Bus. Dev.
Michael Labie, Sr. VP-Corp. Comm.
Mark Cluzel, Sr. VP-Science & Medical Affairs
Hanspeter Spek, Exec. VP-Pharm. Oper.
Gilles Lhernould, VP-Industrial Oper.
David Williams, Sr. VP-Vaccines
Jean-Francois Dehecq, Chmn.
Greg Irace, Sr. VP-Pharm. Oper. USA

Phone: 33-1-53-77-4000	**Fax:** 33-1-53-77-4622
Toll-Free:	
Address: 174 Ave. de France, Paris, 75013 France	

GROWTH PLANS/SPECIAL FEATURES:

Sanofi-Aventis (SNY) is an international pharmaceutic group engaged in the research, development, manufacturi and marketing of primarily prescription pharmaceutic products. The company was created by the $67-billi merger of Sanofi-Synthelabo and Aventis in 2004, creati one of the largest pharmaceutical companies in the worl SNY conducts research and produces major pharmaceutic products in seven major therapeutic areas: cardiovascul diseases, thrombosis, metabolic disorders, oncology, centr nervous system (CNS) disorders and vaccines. The firm cardiovascular medications include the blood pressu medication, Aprovel and the anti-clotting agent, Plavix. the field of oncology, SNY manufactures products whi include Eloxatin, a treatment for colon-rectal cancer, a Taxotere as medication for breast cancer patients. CN medications include Stilnox, the world's leading prescripti insomnia medication, and Depakine, a treatment f epilepsy. Products in the internal medicine sector inclu the antihistamine, Allegra, as well as Xatral, a treatment f enlarged prostrates. SNY's subsidiary company, Sano Pasteur, produces more than 20 different vaccines that a distributed in over 150 countries. SNY operates on 300 site in 100 countries and its research and development sect markets at least 15 to 20 compounds per year. The researc department aims to explore new molecular ar physiopathological approaches in order to develop bett formulations of its pharmaceutical products. In late 200 SNY sold all of its interests in Rhodia to BNP Paribas. Th FDA also approved new indications for formerly develope drugs, which allows patients with acute ST-segme elevation myocardial infarction to use Plavix and head ar neck cancer patients to take the prescribed drug, Taxotere.

FINANCIALS: **Sales and profits are in thousands of dollars—add 000 to get the full amount. 2007 Note: Financial information for 2007 was not available for all companies at press time.**

2007 Sales: $	2007 Profits: $	**U.S. Stock Ticker: SNY**
2006 Sales: $38,722,100	2006 Profits: $6,003,540	**Int'l Ticker: SAN** Int'l Exchange: Paris-Euronext
2005 Sales: $37,272,700	2005 Profits: $3,538,800	Employees: 100,298
2004 Sales: $20,377,000	2004 Profits: $-4,890,000	Fiscal Year Ends: 12/31
2003 Sales: $10,118,000	2003 Profits: $2,610,000	Parent Company:

SALARIES/BENEFITS:

Pension Plan:	ESOP Stock Plan:	Profit Sharing:	Top Exec. Salary: $	Bonus: $
Savings Plan:	Stock Purch. Plan: Y		Second Exec. Salary: $	Bonus: $

OTHER THOUGHTS:

Apparent Women Officers or Directors: 3
Hot Spot for Advancement for Women/Minorities: Y

LOCATIONS: ("Y" = Yes)

West:	Southwest:	Midwest:	Southeast:	Northeast:	International:
Y	Y	Y	Y	Y	Y

SCHERING-PLOUGH CORP www.sch-plough.com

dustry Group Code: 325412 **Ranks within this company's industry group:** Sales: 14 Profits: 17

surance/HMO/PPO:		Drugs:		Equipment/Supplies:		Hospitals/Clinics:		Services:		Health Care:	
surance:		Manufacturer:	Y	Manufacturer:		Acute Care:		Diagnostics:		Home Health:	
anaged Care:		Distributor:		Distributor:		Sub-Acute:		Labs/Testing:		Long-Term Care:	
ilization Management:		Specialty Pharmacy:		Leasing/Finance:		Outpatient Surgery:		Staffing:		Physical Therapy:	
ayment Processing:		Vitamins/Nutritionals:		Information Systems:		Physical Rehab. Ctr.:		Waste Disposal:		Physician Prac. Mgmt.:	
		Clinical Trials:				Psychiatric Clinics:		Specialty Svcs.:			

YPES OF BUSINESS:

rugs-Diversified
nti-Infective & Anti-Cancer Drugs
ermatologicals
ardiovascular Drugs
nimal Health Products
ver-the-Counter Drugs
oot & Sun Care Products
enomics Research

BRANDS/DIVISIONS/AFFILIATES:

IASONEX
CLARINEX
AVELOX
EVITRA
Afrin
inactin
Akzo Nobel N.V.
Organon Biosciences N.V.

CONTACTS: *Note: Officers with more than one job title may be intentionally listed here more than once.*

red Hassan, CEO
Robert J. Bertolini, CFO/Exec. VP
. Ron Cheeley, Sr. VP-Global Human Resources
homas P. Koestler, Exec. VP/Pres., Schering-Plough Research Institute
homas Sabatino, Jr., Exec. VP/General Counsel
Carrie S. Cox, Exec. VP/Pres., Global Pharmaceuticals
ori Queisser, Sr. VP-Global Compliance & Bus. Practices
Raul E. Kohan, Group Dir.-Global Specialty Oper.
Brent Saunders, Sr. VP/Pres., Consumer Health Care
red Hassan, Chmn.

Phone: 908-298-4000	Fax: 908-298-7653
Toll-Free:	
Address: 2000 Galloping Hill Rd., Kenilworth, NJ 07033-0530 US	

GROWTH PLANS/SPECIAL FEATURES:

Schering-Plough Corporation (SGP) develops, manufactures and markets global health care products which are divided into three sectors: prescription pharmaceuticals, consumer products and animal health products. The SGP prescription pharmaceuticals segment produces both primary and specialty care advanced drug therapies. In the primary sector, SGP manufactures allergy/respiratory medication such as NASONEX and CLARINEX; antibiotics such as AVELOX and LEVITRA for male erectile dysfunction disorder. In the specialty care sector, notable products produced by this company include anti-inflammatory, anti-viral and antifungal medications as well as treatments in the fields of oncology and coronary care. SGP's consumer products division markets a number of over-the-counter drugs, foot care and sun care products. These products include Dr. Scholl's foot care products; Lotrimin and Tinactin antifungal cream; Afrin nasal decongestant spray; Correctol laxative tablets and Coppertone sun care products. SGP Animal Health manufactures a broad range of pharmaceuticals and biological products for pets and livestock. Animal health products include antibiotics such as Nuflor; Banamine, an anti-inflammatory drug; and a broad range of vaccines, parasiticides, sutures, bandages and nutritional products. The company's research sector, Schering-Plough Research Institute, has pioneered many new advances in biotechnology and immunology in support of drug discovery and the enhancement of existing prescription products. SGP currently markets its products in the U.S., Canada, Europe, Latin America and Asia. In late 2007, this company will acquire Organon Biosciences N.V. as well as the human and health care sectors of Akzo Nobel N.V. In 2006, SGP gained approval from both the FDA and the European Union to market NOFAXIL, a treatment for Oropharyngeal Candidiasis. SGP also began restructuring its current facilities in Latin American and the expansion of its discovery operations in Cambridge, Massachusetts.

FINANCIALS: **Sales and profits are in thousands of dollars—add 000 to get the full amount. 2007 Note: Financial information for 2007 was not available for all companies at press time.**

2007 Sales: $	2007 Profits: $	**U.S. Stock Ticker: SGP**
2006 Sales: $10,594,000	2006 Profits: $1,143,000	**Int'l Ticker:** Int'l Exchange:
2005 Sales: $9,508,000	2005 Profits: $269,000	Employees: 33,500
2004 Sales: $8,272,000	2004 Profits: $-947,000	Fiscal Year Ends: 12/31
2003 Sales: $8,334,000	2003 Profits: $-92,000	Parent Company:

SALARIES/BENEFITS:

Pension Plan: Y	ESOP Stock Plan:	Profit Sharing:	Top Exec. Salary: $1,556,250	Bonus: $3,861,600
Savings Plan:	Stock Purch. Plan:		Second Exec. Salary: $937,500	Bonus: $1,448,300

OTHER THOUGHTS:

Apparent Women Officers or Directors: 2
Hot Spot for Advancement for Women/Minorities: Y

LOCATIONS: ("Y" = Yes)

West:	Southwest:	Midwest:	Southeast:	Northeast:	International:
Y	Y	Y	Y	Y	Y

Note: Financial information, benefits and other data can change quickly and may vary from those stated here.

SCHICK TECHNOLOGIES INC

www.schicktech.com

Industry Group Code: 339113 **Ranks within this company's industry group:** Sales: Profits:

Insurance/HMO/PPO:		Drugs:		Equipment/Supplies:		Hospitals/Clinics:		Services:		Health Care:	
Insurance:		Manufacturer:		Manufacturer:	Y	Acute Care:		Diagnostics:		Home Health:	
Managed Care:		Distributor:		Distributor:		Sub-Acute:		Labs/Testing:		Long-Term Care:	
Utilization Management:		Specialty Pharmacy:		Leasing/Finance:		Outpatient Surgery:		Staffing:		Physical Therapy:	
Payment Processing:		Vitamins/Nutritionals:		Information Systems:		Physical Rehab. Ctr.:		Waste Disposal:		Physician Prac. Mgmt.:	
		Clinical Trials:				Psychiatric Clinics:		Specialty Svcs.:			

TYPES OF BUSINESS:

Equipment-Medical & Dental Digital Imaging Products
Dental X-Ray Devices

BRANDS/DIVISIONS/AFFILIATES:

CDR
CDR Wireless
CDRPan
accuDEXA
Sirona Dental Systems

CONTACTS:

Note: Officers with more than one job title may be intentionally listed here more than once.

Jeffrey T. Slovin, CEO
Jeffrey T. Slovin, Pres.
Michael Stone, Exec. VP-Sales & Mktg.
Stan Manelkern, VP-Eng.
Will Autz, VP-Mfg.
Ronald Rosner, VP-Admin.
Zvi N. Raskin, General Counsel/Corp. Sec.
William Rogers, VP-Oper.
Eli Schick, Dir.-Investor Rel.
Ronald Rosner, Dir.-Finance
William K. Hood, Chmn.

Phone: 718-937-5765	**Fax:** 718-937-5962
Toll-Free:	
Address: 30-00 47th Ave., Long Island City, NY 11101 US	

GROWTH PLANS/SPECIAL FEATURES:

Schick Technologies, Inc., the U.S. arm of Sirona Dental Systems, Inc., designs, develops and manufactures digital radiographic imaging systems and devices for the dental and medical markets. The firm's products, which are based on proprietary digital imaging technologies, create instant high resolution radiographs with reduced levels of radiation. The CDR system, which has become a leading product in the field over the past decade, uses an intra-oral sensor to produce instant, full-size, high-resolution dental x-ray images on a color computer monitor without the use of film or the need for chemical development, while reducing the radiation dose by up to 80% compared to conventional x-rays. The firm also manufactures and sells CDR Wireless, a wireless radiography sensor for use with an existing CDR system and CDRPan, a digital panoramic imaging device. In the field of medical radiography, the company manufactures and sells the accuDEXA bone densitometer, which assesses bone mineral density and fracture risk. Core products are based primarily on proprietary active-pixel sensor imaging technology, in addition to enhanced charged coupled device technology. In June 2006, Schick was subsumed beneath Sirona Dental Systems, Inc., a German producer of imaging products, in what was called a reverse merger. The acquisition allows Sirona to expand in the U.S. through the existing Schick structure, which is now publicly traded.

FINANCIALS:

Sales and profits are in thousands of dollars—add 000 to get the full amount. 2007 Note: Financial information for 2007 was not available for all companies at press time.

2007 Sales: $	2007 Profits: $	**U.S. Stock Ticker: Subsidiary**
2006 Sales: $	2006 Profits: $	**Int'l Ticker:** Int'l Exchange:
2005 Sales: $52,418	2005 Profits: $12,072	Employees: 139
2004 Sales: $39,393	2004 Profits: $18,109	Fiscal Year Ends: 9/30
2003 Sales: $29,817	2003 Profits: $11,825	Parent Company: SIRONA DENTAL SYSTEMS

SALARIES/BENEFITS:

Pension Plan:	ESOP Stock Plan:	Profit Sharing:	Top Exec. Salary: $313,561	Bonus: $243,750
Savings Plan: Y	Stock Purch. Plan:		Second Exec. Salary: $243,578	Bonus: $187,500

OTHER THOUGHTS:

Apparent Women Officers or Directors:
Hot Spot for Advancement for Women/Minorities:

LOCATIONS: ("Y" = Yes)

West:	Southwest:	Midwest:	Southeast:	Northeast:	International:
				Y	

SENTARA HEALTHCARE www.sentara.com

Industry Group Code: 622110 **Ranks within this company's industry group:** Sales: Profits:

Insurance/HMO/PPO:		Drugs:		Equipment/Supplies:		Hospitals/Clinics:		Services:		Health Care:	
Insurance:	Y	Manufacturer:		Manufacturer:		Acute Care:	Y	Diagnostics:	Y	Home Health:	Y
Managed Care:	Y	Distributor:		Distributor:		Sub-Acute:	Y	Labs/Testing:	Y	Long-Term Care:	Y
Utilization Management:		Specialty Pharmacy:		Leasing/Finance:		Outpatient Surgery:	Y	Staffing:		Physical Therapy:	Y
Payment Processing:		Vitamins/Nutritionals:		Information Systems:		Physical Rehab. Ctr.:	Y	Waste Disposal:		Physician Prac. Mgmt.:	
		Clinical Trials:				Psychiatric Clinics:	Y	Specialty Svcs.:	Y		

TYPES OF BUSINESS:

Hospitals-General
Health Insurance
Primary Care Practices
Home Health Care
Air Medical Transport
Rehabilitation Services
Physical Therapy Services
Organ Transplants

BRANDS/DIVISIONS/AFFILIATES:

Nightingale
Life Care
Mobile Meals
Sentara Bayside
Sentara CarePlex
Sentara Leigh
Sentara Norfolk General
Sentara Virginia Beach

CONTACTS: *Note: Officers with more than one job title may be intentionally listed here more than once.*

David L. Bernd, CEO
Howard Kern, COO
Howard Kern, Pres.
Robert A. Broermann, CFO/Sr. VP
Bertram Reese, CIO/VP
Gary R. Yates, Chief Medical Officer
David R. Maizel, VP-Sentara Medical Group
Vicky G. Gray, VP-System Dev.
Mary L. Blunt, Pres., Sentara Life Care Corp.
William K. Butler, II, Chmn.

Phone: 757-455-7000 **Fax:** 757-455-7164
Toll-Free: 800-736-8272
Address: 6015 Poplar Hall Dr., Norfolk, VA 23502 US

GROWTH PLANS/SPECIAL FEATURES:

Sentara Healthcare, founded in 1888, is a not-for-profit health care provider in Virginia and North Carolina that operates more than 87 care sites, including seven acute care hospitals, over 1,700 licensed beds, three outpatient care campuses, seven nursing centers, three assisted living centers and five advanced imaging centers. The firm's primary care and multi-specialty physician group includes approximately 230 physicians. Hospitals include Sentara Norfolk General, Sentara Leigh, Sentara Virginia Beach General, Sentara Bayside, Sentara CarePlex, Sentara Obici and Sentara Williamsburg Regional Medical Center (opened in August 2006). The company also offers home health and hospice services, physical therapy and rehabilitation services, ground and air medical transport, mobile diagnostic vans and two on-site fitness facilities. Its air transport system, Nightingale, is southeastern Virginia's only air ambulance service. Sentara offers a full range of health coverage plans including commercial plans, a Medicaid HMO and workers' compensation. The firm also operates the region's comprehensive solid organ transplant center, which has conducted more than 1,600 total heart and kidney transplants, including 200 heart transplants. Long-term life assistance, provided through the Life Care division, includes an adult day care center, the Mobile Meals program and the only program for all-inclusive care for the elderly (PACE) in the state. Sentara is the only health care system to have been ranked in the nation's top 10 facilities in Modern Healthcare magazine all nine years the survey has been conducted. In recent news, the Sentara Bayside Hospital Sleep Disorder Center added two sleep study rooms. In September 2007, the Sentara Obici Hospital's Sleep Disorders Center received full accreditation from the American Academy of Sleep Medicine.

Sentara offers its employees health care spending accounts, a tuition assistance program, an employee assistance program, discounts at Sentara facilities and area businesses and access to the Sentara Hampton Health and Fitness Center.

FINANCIALS: **Sales and profits are in thousands of dollars—add 000 to get the full amount. 2007 Note: Financial information for 2007 was not available for all companies at press time.**

2007 Sales: $	2007 Profits: $	**U.S. Stock Ticker: Nonprofit**
2006 Sales: $	2006 Profits: $	**Int'l Ticker:** Int'l Exchange:
2005 Sales: $	2005 Profits: $	Employees: 15,000
2004 Sales: $1,500,000	2004 Profits: $	Fiscal Year Ends: 4/30
2003 Sales: $1,530,000	2003 Profits: $	Parent Company:

SALARIES/BENEFITS:

Pension Plan: Y	ESOP Stock Plan:	Profit Sharing:	Top Exec. Salary: $	Bonus: $
Savings Plan: Y	Stock Purch. Plan:		Second Exec. Salary: $	Bonus: $

OTHER THOUGHTS:

Apparent Women Officers or Directors: 2
Hot Spot for Advancement for Women/Minorities:

LOCATIONS: ("Y" = Yes)

West:	Southwest:	Midwest:	Southeast:	Northeast:	International:
				Y	

Note: Financial information, benefits and other data can change quickly and may vary from those stated here.

SEPRACOR INC

www.sepracor.com

Industry Group Code: 325412 **Ranks within this company's industry group:** Sales: 26 Profits: 24

Insurance/HMO/PPO:		Drugs:		Equipment/Supplies:		Hospitals/Clinics:		Services:		Health Care:	
Insurance:		Manufacturer:	Y	Manufacturer:		Acute Care:		Diagnostics:		Home Health:	
Managed Care:		Distributor:		Distributor:		Sub-Acute:		Labs/Testing:		Long-Term Care:	
Utilization Management:		Specialty Pharmacy:		Leasing/Finance:		Outpatient Surgery:		Staffing:		Physical Therapy:	
Payment Processing:		Vitamins/Nutritionals:		Information Systems:		Physical Rehab. Ctr.:		Waste Disposal:		Physician Prac. Mgmt.:	
		Clinical Trials:				Psychiatric Clinics:		Specialty Svcs.:			

TYPES OF BUSINESS:

Pharmaceuticals Discovery & Development
Respiratory Treatments
Central Nervous System Disorder Treatments

BRANDS/DIVISIONS/AFFILIATES:

XOPENEX
LUNESTA
ALLEGRA
CLARINEX
XUSA/XYZAL
BROVANA

CONTACTS: *Note: Officers with more than one job title may be intentionally listed here more than once.*

Adrian Adams, CEO
William J. O'Shea, COO
Adrian Adams, Pres.
David P. Southwell, CFO
Mark H. N. Corrigan, Exec. VP-R&D
Robert F. Scumaci, Exec. VP-Tech. Oper.
Robert F. Scumaci, Exec. VP-Admin.
Andrew I. Koven, General Counsel/Exec. VP/Corp. Sec.
David P. Southwell, Exec. VP-Corp. Planning & Dev.
Robert F. Scumaci, Exec. VP-Finance
David P. Southwell, Exec. VP-Licensing
W. James O'Shea, Vice Chmn.
Timothy J. Barberich, Chmn.

Phone: 508-481-6700	**Fax:** 508-357-7499
Toll-Free: 800-245-5961	
Address: 84 Waterford Dr., Marlborough, MA 01752 US	

GROWTH PLANS/SPECIAL FEATURES:

Sepracor, Inc. is a research-based pharmaceutical compan whose goal is to discover, develop and market products tha are directed toward serving unmet medical needs particularly in the treatment of respiratory and centra nervous system disorders. The company also develops an markets improved versions of widely prescribed drugs These versions, known as improved chemical entities feature enhancements such as reduced side effects increased therapeutic efficacy, improved dosage forms and in some cases, additional indications. Serpacor's lea product is XOPENEX, an inhalation solution used i nebulizers for patients with asthma or chronic obstructiv pulmonary disease (COPD). BROVANA (arformotero tartrate) was approved in October 2006 as a long term twice-daily treatment for COPD. The product is administere by nebulizer. The company also markets LUNEST (eszopiclone) for the treatment of insomnia in adults Sepracor has entered into a license agreement with Eisa Co. Ltd. for the development and manufacture of LUNEST in Japan, which is scheduled to finish clinical trials in Japa by 2010. In addition, the company has designed treatment for asthma, depression and restless legs syndrome Sepracor markets its own and other companies' product through its sales force, co-promotion agreements and out-licensing partnerships. Due to the firm's patents relating to the chemicals desloratadine, fexofenadine and levocetirizine Sepracor has out-licensing agreements with Schering-Plough for CLARINEX, Aventis for ALLEGRA and UCE Farchim SA for its XUSAL/XYZAL products, all of which are allergy medications. In April 2007, the company commercially launched its newly approved prescription drug, BROVANA.

Sepracor offers its employees tuition reimbursement, adoption reimbursement, back-up childcare and a comprehensive health plan.

FINANCIALS: **Sales and profits are in thousands of dollars—add 000 to get the full amount. 2007 Note: Financial information for 2007 was not available for all companies at press time.**

2007 Sales: $	2007 Profits: $	**U.S. Stock Ticker: SEPR**
2006 Sales: $1,196,534	2006 Profits: $184,562	**Int'l Ticker:** Int'l Exchange:
2005 Sales: $820,928	2005 Profits: $3,927	Employees: 2,470
2004 Sales: $380,877	2004 Profits: $-296,910	Fiscal Year Ends: 12/31
2003 Sales: $344,040	2003 Profits: $-135,936	Parent Company:

SALARIES/BENEFITS:

Pension Plan:	ESOP Stock Plan:	Profit Sharing:	Top Exec. Salary: $875,000	Bonus: $525,000
Savings Plan: Y	Stock Purch. Plan: Y		Second Exec. Salary: $525,000	Bonus: $236,250

OTHER THOUGHTS:

Apparent Women Officers or Directors:
Hot Spot for Advancement for Women/Minorities:

LOCATIONS: ("Y" = Yes)

West:	Southwest:	Midwest:	Southeast:	Northeast:	International:
				Y	

SHIRE PLC

www.shire.com

Industry Group Code: 325412 **Ranks within this company's industry group:** Sales: 24 Profits: 21

Insurance/HMO/PPO:		Drugs:		Equipment/Supplies:		Hospitals/Clinics:		Services:		Health Care:	
Insurance:		Manufacturer:	Y	Manufacturer:		Acute Care:		Diagnostics:		Home Health:	
Managed Care:		Distributor:		Distributor:		Sub-Acute:		Labs/Testing:		Long-Term Care:	
Utilization Management:		Specialty Pharmacy:		Leasing/Finance:		Outpatient Surgery:		Staffing:		Physical Therapy:	
Payment Processing:		Vitamins/Nutritionals:		Information Systems:		Physical Rehab. Ctr.:		Waste Disposal:		Physician Prac. Mgmt.:	
		Clinical Trials:				Psychiatric Clinics:		Specialty Svcs.:			

TYPES OF BUSINESS:

Drugs-Diversified
Drug Delivery Technology
Small-Molecule Drugs

BRANDS/DIVISIONS/AFFILIATES:

Adderall
Daytrana
Carbatrol
Pentasa
Colazide
Replagal
Elaprase
Vyvanse

CONTACTS: *Note: Officers with more than one job title may be intentionally listed here more than once.*

Matthew Emmens, CEO
Angus Russell, CFO
Eliseo Salinas, Chief Scientific Officer/Exec. VP-Global R&D
Anita Graham, Chief Admin. Officer/Exec. VP-Corp. Bus. Svcs.
Tatjana May, General Counsel/Exec. VP-Global Legal Affairs/Sec.
Barbara Deptula, Exec. VP-Bus. Dev.
Clea Rosenfeld, VP-Investor Rel.
Joseph Rus, Exec. VP-Market Alliance & New Market Dev.
Mike Cola, Pres., Specialty Pharmaceuticals
David D. Pendergast, Pres., Human Genetic Therapies
Eric Rojas, Dir.-Investor Rel. North America
Matthew Emmens, Chmn.

Phone: 44-1256-894-000	**Fax:** 44-1256-894-708
Toll-Free:	
Address: Hampshire Int'l Business Park, Chineham, Basingstoke, Hampshire RG24 8EP UK	

GROWTH PLANS/SPECIAL FEATURES:

Shire plc is an international specialty pharmaceutical company with a strategic focus on four therapeutic areas: attention deficit and hyperactivity disorder (ADHD), human genetic therapies (HGT), gastrointestinal and renal diseases. Shire's main product for the treatment of ADHD is Adderall XR, designed to provide a day-long treatment with one morning dose. Daytrana, a transdermal delivery system for the once daily treatment of ADHD, is the first and only patch medication approved by the FDA for the pediatric treatment of ADHD. Carbatrol is the company's epilepsy treatment product. For the treatment of ulcerative colitis, Shire markets Pentasa and Colazide. Shire's HGT products include Replagal for the treatment of Fabry disease, a rare genetic disorder resulting from the deficiency of an enzyme involved in the breakdown of fats, and Elaprase for the treatment of Hunter syndrome, a rare genetic disorder interfering with the processing of certain waste substances in the body. For renal disease Shire markets Fosrenol, a phosphate binder for use in end-stage renal failure patients receiving dialysis. For the treatment of myeloproliferative disorders, a group of diseases in which one or more blood cell types are overproduced, Shire markets Agrylin in the United States and Xagrid in Europe. Other products marketed by Shire include Reminyl, CalciChew, Lodine, Solaraze and Vaniqa. The company additionally receives royalties on antiviral products for HIV and Hepatitis B based on certain of its patents. In February 2007, the firm agreed to acquire New River Pharmaceuticals for roughly $2.6 billion. Shire's newest ADHD medication, Vyvanse, was made available in the U.S. in July 2007.

Shire offers its employees business travel accident insurance, flexible spending account arrangements, an employee assistance program, a wellness/work-life program, a health and fitness subsidy, wellness rooms, adoption assistance, parenting leave and educational assistance.

FINANCIALS: **Sales and profits are in thousands of dollars—add 000 to get the full amount. 2007 Note: Financial information for 2007 was not available for all companies at press time.**

2007 Sales: $	2007 Profits: $	**U.S. Stock Ticker: SHPGY**
2006 Sales: $1,796,500	2006 Profits: $278,200	**Int'l Ticker: SHP.L** Int'l Exchange: London-LSE
2005 Sales: $1,599,300	2005 Profits: $-578,400	Employees: 2,868
2004 Sales: $1,363,200	2004 Profits: $263,300	Fiscal Year Ends: 12/31
2003 Sales: $1,237,101	2003 Profits: $276,051	Parent Company:

SALARIES/BENEFITS:

Pension Plan:	ESOP Stock Plan:	Profit Sharing:	Top Exec. Salary: $1,105,000	Bonus: $1,985,000
Savings Plan: Y	Stock Purch. Plan: Y		Second Exec. Salary: $701,000	Bonus: $971,000

OTHER THOUGHTS:

Apparent Women Officers or Directors: 4
Hot Spot for Advancement for Women/Minorities: Y

LOCATIONS: ("Y" = Yes)

West:	Southwest:	Midwest:	Southeast:	Northeast:	International:
				Y	Y

Note: Financial information, benefits and other data can change quickly and may vary from those stated here.

SHL TELEMEDICINE LTD www.shl-telemedicine.com

Industry Group Code: 513300D **Ranks within this company's industry group:** Sales: Profits:

Insurance/HMO/PPO:		Drugs:		Equipment/Supplies:		Hospitals/Clinics:		Services:		Health Care:	
Insurance:		Manufacturer:		Manufacturer:	Y	Acute Care:		Diagnostics:	Y	Home Health:	
Managed Care:		Distributor:		Distributor:		Sub-Acute:		Labs/Testing:		Long-Term Care:	
Utilization Management:		Specialty Pharmacy:		Leasing/Finance:		Outpatient Surgery:		Staffing:		Physical Therapy:	
Payment Processing:		Vitamins/Nutritionals:		Information Systems:	Y	Physical Rehab. Ctr.:		Waste Disposal:		Physician Prac. Mgmt.:	
		Clinical Trials:				Psychiatric Clinics:		Specialty Svcs.:	Y		

TYPES OF BUSINESS:

Services-Cardiovascular Disease Diagnostics & Therapy
Personal Telemedicine Systems
Medical Call Center Services
Cardiac Testing Services
Remote Cardiac Monitoring
Nuclear Cardiology Diagnostics
Outpatient Diagnostic Imaging
Ambulance Services

BRANDS/DIVISIONS/AFFILIATES:

Raytel Medical Corporation
PHTS
MC Interactives
CardioVision
Telepress
LidoPen
CardioPocket
Watchman

CONTACTS: *Note: Officers with more than one job title may be intentionally listed here more than once.*

Erez Alroy, Co-CEO
Yoram Alroy, Pres.
Arie Roth, Chief Medical Mgr.
Irit Alroy, Exec. VP-Tech. Dev.
Reuven Kaplan, VP-Oper., Israel
Erez Nachtomy, Exec. VP-Bus. Dev.
Haim Brosh, Exec. VP-Finance
Yariv Alroy, Co-CEO
Robert E. Sass, Gen. Mgr.-Raytel Cardiac Services
Jeff M. Flanegin, Pres., Raytel Diagnostic Services
Yoram Alroy, Chmn.
Eyal Lewin, Mng. Dir.-Personal Telemedicine Svcs. Germany

Phone: 972-3-561-2212	**Fax:** 972-3-624-2414
Toll-Free:	
Address: 90 Igal Alon St., Tel Aviv, 67891 Israel	

GROWTH PLANS/SPECIAL FEATURES:

SHL Telemedicine, Ltd. primarily develops and markets advanced personal telemedicine systems that transmit medical data from an individual to a medical call center, but it also provides medical call center services. SHL operates in Israel, in the U.S. through its Raytel Medical Corporation subsidiary and in select European markets, namely Germany, through Personal Healthcare Telemedicine Services (PHTS). Raytel offers remote pacemaker monitoring and other cardiac diagnostic services and operates outpatient diagnostic imaging facilities and cardiovascular diagnostic facilities. Raytel serves over 165,000 patients and 10,000 doctors annually. PHTS focuses on providing personal telemedicine services related to ailments of the heart in markets including Germany and Italy. SHL's client base consists of more than 300,000 customers, providing a reliable recurring revenue stream. Services are provided through a call center staffed with nurses under the supervision of physicians. Subscribers who do not call the center within pre-arranged time periods are automatically contacted, ensuring consistent monitoring patterns and on-going interaction with clients. Some of the firm's services and products include MC Interactives, a medical record database management application; CardioVision, a software package that serves as the backbone of the remote emergency cardiac diagnostic service; Telepress, a blood pressure reader/transmitter; LidoPen, a lidocaine auto-injector; CardioPocket, an electrocardiogram (ECG) heart monitoring transmitter wallet; Watchman, an emergency communication system built into a wristwatch; CardioBeeper, a heart monitoring handheld ECG transmitter; TeleWeight high-precision medical scales; and TeleBreather, a pulmonary data transmitter. SHL also operates a fleet of private ambulances in Israel. Royal Philips Electronics and the Alroy Group both have an 18.6% stake in the company. In 2006, Raytel Medical sold the operations of three of its imaging centers, closed two and the remaining imaging centers were closed or sold during the first half of 2007. In September 2007, the firm launched a new wireless arrhythmia device.

FINANCIALS: **Sales and profits are in thousands of dollars—add 000 to get the full amount. 2007 Note: Financial information for 2007 was not available for all companies at press time.**

2007 Sales: $	2007 Profits: $	**U.S. Stock Ticker:**
2006 Sales: $	2006 Profits: $	**Int'l Ticker: SHLTN** Int'l Exchange: Zurich-SWX
2005 Sales: $	2005 Profits: $	Employees: 1,389
2004 Sales: $	2004 Profits: $	Fiscal Year Ends: 9/30
2003 Sales: $	2003 Profits: $	Parent Company:

SALARIES/BENEFITS:

Pension Plan:	ESOP Stock Plan:	Profit Sharing:	Top Exec. Salary: $	Bonus: $
Savings Plan:	Stock Purch. Plan:		Second Exec. Salary: $	Bonus: $

OTHER THOUGHTS:

Apparent Women Officers or Directors: 1
Hot Spot for Advancement for Women/Minorities:

LOCATIONS: ("Y" = Yes)

West:	Southwest:	Midwest:	Southeast:	Northeast:	International:
		Y		Y	Y

SIEMENS AG

www.siemens.com

Industry Group Code: 334210 **Ranks within this company's industry group:** Sales: 1 Profits: 1

Insurance/HMO/PPO:		Drugs:		Equipment/Supplies:		Hospitals/Clinics:		Services:		Health Care:	
Insurance:		Manufacturer:		Manufacturer:	Y	Acute Care:		Diagnostics:	Y	Home Health:	
Managed Care:		Distributor:		Distributor:		Sub-Acute:		Labs/Testing:		Long-Term Care:	
Utilization Management:		Specialty Pharmacy:		Leasing/Finance:		Outpatient Surgery:		Staffing:		Physical Therapy:	
Payment Processing:		Vitamins/Nutritionals:		Information Systems:	Y	Physical Rehab. Ctr.:		Waste Disposal:		Physician Prac. Mgmt.:	
		Clinical Trials:				Psychiatric Clinics:		Specialty Svcs.:			

TYPES OF BUSINESS:

Telecommunications Equipment Manufacturer
Energy & Power Plant Systems & Consulting
IT Systems & Consulting
Lighting & Optical Systems
Automation Systems
Transportation & Logistics Systems
Photovoltaic Equipment
Medical and Health Care Services and Equipment

BRANDS/DIVISIONS/AFFILIATES:

CTI Molecular Imaging
BenQ
Exergy, Inc.
Siemens USA
Acuson
Siemens Medical Solutions Diagnostics
Dematic
Nokia Siemens Networks

CONTACTS: *Note: Officers with more than one job title may be intentionally listed here more than once.*

Peter H. Loescher, CEO
Joe Kaeser, CFO
Jürgen Radomski, Chief Personnel Officer
Hermann Requardt, Head-Corp. Tech.
Eduardo Montes, Head-Comm.
Ralf P. Thomas, Controller/VP
Dominik Asam, Pres., Siemens Financial Services GmbH
Uriel J. Sharef, Dir.-Power Generation
Klaus Patzak, VP-Financial Reporting & Controlling
Dennis Sadlowski, Pres./CEO-Siemens Energy & Automation, Inc.
Gerhard Cromme, Chmn.

Phone: 49-89-636-3300	**Fax:** 49-89-636-342-42
Toll-Free:	
Address: Wittelsbacherplatz 2, Munich, D-80333 Germany	

GROWTH PLANS/SPECIAL FEATURES:

Siemens AG is one of the largest electrical engineering and manufacturing companies in the world. Based in Germany, the firm sells products and services to 190 countries around the globe, including all 50 states in the United States, its largest single source of income. Siemens' product lines include equipment for information and communication; automation and control; power; transportation; medical; and lighting technologies, each with its own group within the company. The information and communications group is further separated into network and mobile branches. The network segment includes Internet protocol solutions, broadband and optical networks. The mobile segment provides infrastructure technologies, mobile end-user devices (cordless and cell phones), wireless modules and other applications. Siemens' automation and control group supplies industrial automation and building technology. With its U.S. partner Exergy, Inc., it plans and builds geothermal power plants with an electrical power output of up to 5 megawatts. The company also builds and installs waste heat systems and is one of the world's top 10 solar cell manufacturers. Siemens' transportation business is a leader in rail system and automotive electronics. Lighting operations include products for the general, automotive and photo-optic markets. In addition to products and technologies, the company provides IT consulting, operations and maintenance services. The company is researching integration of MEMS switches into its optical networking products. In recent news, Siemens acquired CTI Molecular Imaging for $1 billion. In 2006, Siemens acquired Bayer's diagnostics division for roughly $5.73 billion. In 2007, the firm's automation and drives group agreed to acquire UGS Corp. for $3.5 billion. Recently, Siemens partnered with Nokia to form Nokia Siemens Networks. In July 2007, the firm agreed to sell its VDO (automotive) unit to Continental AG for $15.8 billion, and simultaneously agreed to acquire Dade Behring, Inc. for $7 billion.

Employees of Siemens receive tuition, flexible schedules and scholarship programs for their children.

FINANCIALS: **Sales and profits are in thousands of dollars—add 000 to get the full amount. 2007 Note: Financial information for 2007 was not available for all companies at press time.**

2007 Sales: $	2007 Profits: $	**U.S. Stock Ticker: SI**
2006 Sales: $113,740,000	2006 Profits: $3,950,360	**Int'l Ticker: SIE** Int'l Exchange: Frankfurt-Euronext
2005 Sales: $90,670,000	2005 Profits: $2,702,000	Employees: 475,000
2004 Sales: $93,455,000	2004 Profits: $4,233,000	Fiscal Year Ends: 9/30
2003 Sales: $86,467,000	2003 Profits: $2,848,000	Parent Company:

SALARIES/BENEFITS:

Pension Plan: Y	ESOP Stock Plan:	Profit Sharing:	Top Exec. Salary: $	Bonus: $
Savings Plan: Y	Stock Purch. Plan:		Second Exec. Salary: $	Bonus: $

OTHER THOUGHTS:

Apparent Women Officers or Directors:
Hot Spot for Advancement for Women/Minorities:

LOCATIONS: ("Y" = Yes)

West:	Southwest:	Midwest:	Southeast:	Northeast:	International:
Y	Y	Y	Y	Y	Y

Note: Financial information, benefits and other data can change quickly and may vary from those stated here.

SIEMENS MEDICAL SOLUTIONS www.medical.siemens.com

Industry Group Code: 339113 **Ranks within this company's industry group:** Sales: 3 Profits:

Insurance/HMO/PPO:		Drugs:		Equipment/Supplies:		Hospitals/Clinics:		Services:		Health Care:	
Insurance:		Manufacturer:		Manufacturer:	Y	Acute Care:		Diagnostics:		Home Health:	
Managed Care:		Distributor:		Distributor:		Sub-Acute:		Labs/Testing:		Long-Term Care:	
Utilization Management:		Specialty Pharmacy:		Leasing/Finance:		Outpatient Surgery:		Staffing:		Physical Therapy:	
Payment Processing:		Vitamins/Nutritionals:		Information Systems:	Y	Physical Rehab. Ctr.:		Waste Disposal:		Physician Prac. Mgmt.:	
		Clinical Trials:				Psychiatric Clinics:		Specialty Svcs.:	Y		

TYPES OF BUSINESS:

Medical Equipment Manufacturing
Information Systems
Management Consulting
Ultrasound Systems
Hearing Aids

BRANDS/DIVISIONS/AFFILIATES:

Siemens AG
Soarian
TRIANO
Sonoline
Acuson
Somatom Sensation 16
Dade Behring Holdings Inc
Siemens Medical Solutions Diagnostics

CONTACTS: *Note: Officers with more than one job title may be intentionally listed here more than once.*

Peter Loscher, CEO
Peter Loscher, Pres.
Joe Kaeser, CFO/VP
Jurgen Radomski, Head-Personnel
Hermann Requardt, Head-Tech. Svcs.
Anthony Bihl, CEO-Siemens Medical Solutions Diagnostics
Sid Aroesty, COO-Siemens Medical Solutions Diagnostics
Jochen Schmitz, CFO-Siemens Medical Solutions Diagnostics

Phone: 49-91-31-840	**Fax:** 49-91-31-8437-54
Toll-Free:	
Address: Henkestrasse 127, Erlangen, 91052 Germany	

GROWTH PLANS/SPECIAL FEATURES:

Siemens Medical Solutions (SMS), a business segment o Siemens AG, is one of the largest suppliers to the healt care industry with operations in over 138 countries. SM and its subsidiaries, including Siemens Medical Systems i the U.S., offer innovative medical technologies, health car information systems, management consulting and suppo services. The firm manufactures and markets a wide rang of medical equipment including MRI systems, radiatio therapy equipment and patient monitoring systems. Wi 75% of all of the company's products less than five years ol the firm devotes 10% of its budget to research an development and launches numerous new products ever year. SMS's ultrasound division is the world's large supplier of ultrasound systems and also offers genera imaging systems. The company produces imagin equipment for cardiology, gynecology, radiology and urolog under the Sonoline and Acuson brand-name product line Through its health services division, the firm offer information technology support to doctors, hospitals an clinics. Through its hearing instruments division, SM makes a variety of hearing aids. Some of SMS's product include the Somatom Sensation 16 spiral CT scanner, a imaging system that enables previously unavailabl applications such as virtual flight through the heart o intestine, and TRIANO, the firm's newest generation hearin aid, made up of a combination of three microphones tha permit directional hearing. In January 2007, Siemen Medical Solutions acquired Gesellschaft fü Systemforschung und Dienstleistungen in Gesundheitswesen mbH, headquartered in Berlin. In Jul 2007, the company acquired Dade Behring, Inc., a leadin clinical laboratory diagnostics company.

SMS offers its employees work/life initiatives including chil care discounts, emergency child care, mothers' rooms financial planning resources, tuition reimbursement an flexible spending accounts.

FINANCIALS: **Sales and profits are in thousands of dollars—add 000 to get the full amount. 2007 Note: Financial information for 2007 was not available for all companies at press time.**

2007 Sales: $	2007 Profits: $	**U.S. Stock Ticker: Subsidiary**
2006 Sales: $11,121,700	2006 Profits: $	**Int'l Ticker:** Int'l Exchange:
2005 Sales: $10,309,236	2005 Profits: $1,163,063	Employees: 33,000
2004 Sales: $8,423,794	2004 Profits: $1,246,014	Fiscal Year Ends: 9/30
2003 Sales: $	2003 Profits: $	Parent Company: SIEMENS AG

SALARIES/BENEFITS:

Pension Plan: Y	ESOP Stock Plan:	Profit Sharing:	Top Exec. Salary: $	Bonus: $
Savings Plan: Y	Stock Purch. Plan:		Second Exec. Salary: $	Bonus: $

OTHER THOUGHTS:

Apparent Women Officers or Directors:
Hot Spot for Advancement for Women/Minorities:

LOCATIONS: ("Y" = Yes)

West:	Southwest:	Midwest:	Southeast:	Northeast:	International:
				Y	Y

SIEMENS MEDICAL SOLUTIONS DIAGNOSTICS

www.dpcweb.com

ndustry Group Code: 325413 **Ranks within this company's industry group:** Sales: Profits:

nsurance/HMO/PPO:		Drugs:		Equipment/Supplies:		Hospitals/Clinics:		Services:		Health Care:	
nsurance:		Manufacturer:		Manufacturer:	Y	Acute Care:		Diagnostics:		Home Health:	
lanaged Care:		Distributor:		Distributor:		Sub-Acute:		Labs/Testing:		Long-Term Care:	
tilization Management:		Specialty Pharmacy:		Leasing/Finance:		Outpatient Surgery:		Staffing:		Physical Therapy:	
ayment Processing:		Vitamins/Nutritionals:		Information Systems:	Y	Physical Rehab. Ctr.:		Waste Disposal:		Physician Prac. Mgmt.:	
		Clinical Trials:				Psychiatric Clinics:		Specialty Svcs.:			

YPES OF BUSINESS:

upplies-Immunodiagnostic Kits
onisotopic Diagnostic Tests
mmunoassay Analyzers
llergy Testing

BRANDS/DIVISIONS/AFFILIATES:

MMULITE
MMULITE 1000
Bayer Diagnostics
MMULITE Turbo
Sample Management System
MMULITE 2500
3gAllergy
Diagnostic Products Corp.

CONTACTS:

Note: Officers with more than one job title may be ntentionally listed here more than once.

Anthony P. Bihl, CEO
Sidney A. Aroesty, COO
Jochen Schmitz, CFO

Phone: 310-645-8200	Fax: 310-645-9999
Toll-Free: 800-768-6699	
Address: 5210 Pacific Concourse Dr., Los Angeles, CA 90045-5900 US	

GROWTH PLANS/SPECIAL FEATURES:

Siemens Medical Solutions Diagnostics (SMSD), formed from the 2006 acquisition and subsumption of Diagnostic Products Corp. (DPC) and Bayer Diagnostics, is a wholly-owned subsidiary of Siemens Medical Solutions USA, Inc. SMSD offers a broad portfolio of performance-driven diagnostics solutions that provide more effective ways to assist in the diagnosis, monitoring and management of disease. Its products and services offer the right balance of science, technology and practicality across the healthcare continuum to provide healthcare professionals with the vital information they need to deliver better, more personalized healthcare to patients around the world. With the acquisition of DPC and Bayer, SMSD has bridged the gap between in-vivo and in-vitro diagnostics to become the first full service diagnostics company. By bringing together medical imaging, laboratory diagnostics and healthcare and healthcare information technology, SMSD offers a unique set of solutions that provide clinical, operational and financial outcomes. The portfolio of SMSD includes products and services designed to optimize efficiency, improve workflow, help ensure patient safety and provide the highest levels of productivity and flexibility. Its broad spectrum of immunoassay, chemistry, hematology, molecular, urinalysis, diabetes and blood gas testing systems, in conjunction with automation, informatics and consulting solutions, serve the needs of laboratories of any size. SMSD's proprietary products include: the IMMULITE, ADVIA, RapidLab and Clinitek families of products, along with the DCA 2000+, the MicroMix 5, 3gAllergy and SMS products. In 2007, Siemens Medical Solutions USA agreed to acquire Dade Behring, Inc., a leading clinical laboratory diagnostics company. In April 2006, Diagnostic Products Corp. (DPC) was acquired by Siemens Medical Solutions USA, Inc. for approximately $1.86 billion.

FINANCIALS:

Sales and profits are in thousands of dollars—add 000 to get the full amount. 2007 Note: Financial information for 2007 was not available for all companies at press time.

2007 Sales: $	2007 Profits: $	**U.S. Stock Ticker: Subsidiary**
2006 Sales: $	2006 Profits: $	**Int'l Ticker:** Int'l Exchange:
2005 Sales: $481,100	2005 Profits: $67,200	Employees: 2,495
2004 Sales: $446,800	2004 Profits: $61,700	Fiscal Year Ends: 12/31
2003 Sales: $381,386	2003 Profits: $61,795	Parent Company: SIEMENS MEDICAL SOLUTIONS

SALARIES/BENEFITS:

Pension Plan:	ESOP Stock Plan:	Profit Sharing:	Top Exec. Salary: $600,000	Bonus: $
Savings Plan:	Stock Purch. Plan:		Second Exec. Salary: $450,000	Bonus: $30,000

OTHER THOUGHTS:

Apparent Women Officers or Directors: 1
Hot Spot for Advancement for Women/Minorities:

LOCATIONS: ("Y" = Yes)

West:	Southwest:	Midwest:	Southeast:	Northeast:	International:
Y				Y	Y

Note: Financial information, benefits and other data can change quickly and may vary from those stated here.

SIERRA HEALTH SERVICES INC www.sierrahealth.com

Industry Group Code: 524114 **Ranks within this company's industry group:** Sales: 27 Profits: 18

Insurance/HMO/PPO:		Drugs:		Equipment/Supplies:		Hospitals/Clinics:		Services:		Health Care:	
Insurance:	Y	Manufacturer:		Manufacturer:		Acute Care:		Diagnostics:		Home Health:	
Managed Care:	Y	Distributor:		Distributor:		Sub-Acute:		Labs/Testing:		Long-Term Care:	
Utilization Management:	Y	Specialty Pharmacy:		Leasing/Finance:		Outpatient Surgery:		Staffing:		Physical Therapy:	
Payment Processing:		Vitamins/Nutritionals:		Information Systems:		Physical Rehab. Ctr.:		Waste Disposal:		Physician Prac. Mgmt.:	
		Clinical Trials:				Psychiatric Clinics:		Specialty Svcs.:			

TYPES OF BUSINESS:

Insurance-Medical & Health, HMOs & PPOs
Testing & Diagnostic Services
Health Insurance
Administrative Services
Workers' Compensation Management
Behavioral Health Care Services
Hospice Health Programs
Substance Abuse Programs

BRANDS/DIVISIONS/AFFILIATES:

Southwest Medical Associates
Health Plan of Nevada, Inc.
Sierra Healthcare Options
Northern Nevada Health Netwrok
Behavioral Healthcare Options, Inc.
Family Care Health Services
Family Home Hospice
Sierra Health & Life Insurance Company, Inc.

CONTACTS: *Note: Officers with more than one job title may be intentionally listed here more than once.*

Anthony M. Marlon, CEO
Jonathon W. Bunker, COO
Jonathon W. Bunker, Pres.
Mark R. Briggs, CFO/Sr. VP
Donald J. Giancursio, Sr. VP-Sales
Daniel A. Kruger, VP-Human Resources
Robert L. Schaich, CIO
Frank E. Collins, Sr. VP-Legal & Admin.
Darren Sivertsen, Sr. VP-Oper.
Mark R. Briggs, Treas.
Christine A. Peterson, Chief Medical Officer
Anthony M. Marlon, Chmn.

Phone: 702-242-7000	**Fax:** 702-242-7960
Toll-Free:	
Address: 2724 N. Tenaya Way, Las Vegas, NV 89128 US	

GROWTH PLANS/SPECIAL FEATURES:

Sierra Health Services, Inc. provides and delivers managed care benefit plans for individuals, government programs and employers. The company's subsidiaries include health maintenance organizations, managed indemnity plans (HMO), workers' compensation medical management programs, a third-party administrative services program for employer-funded health benefit plans and an administrator of managed care federal contracts for the U.S. Department of Defense's TRICARE program. Sierra Health Services also offers behavioral health care services and hospice health programs. The company has a significant presence in Nevada, where its Southwest Medical Associates subsidiary is the largest multi-specialty medical group in the state. Southwest operates through over 200 providers and at 14 locations with a particular focus on Las Vegas. Another subsidiary, Health Plan of Nevada, Inc. is the state's largest HMO, with a range of benefit plans including point-of-service, individual coverage for self-employed workers and a Medicare program known as Senior Dimensions. Through subsidiary Sierra Healthcare Options, the firm offers administrative service products, including utilization review and PPO services, to large employer groups that are usually self-insured. Moreover, Sierra provides ancillary products and services that complement its managed health care programs, which include outpatient surgical care, diagnostic testing, x-rays, vision services and mental health and substance abuse services. Other Sierra subsidiaries include Northern Nevada Health Network, Behavior Healthcare Options, Family Health Care Services, Sierra Nevada Administrators and Family Home Hospice. In June 2007, the proposed $4.2 billion acquisition of the company by UnitedHealth Group, Inc. was approved by the local government and by the Sierra Health Service shareholders.

Sierra offers its employees a variety of internal training and development programs designed to enhance computer skills, management techniques and general professional development.

FINANCIALS: **Sales and profits are in thousands of dollars—add 000 to get the full amount. 2007 Note: Financial information for 2007 was not available for all companies at press time.**

2007 Sales: $	2007 Profits: $	**U.S. Stock Ticker: SIE**
2006 Sales: $1,718,892	2006 Profits: $140,471	**Int'l Ticker:** Int'l Exchange:
2005 Sales: $1,385,036	2005 Profits: $120,017	Employees: 2,900
2004 Sales: $1,575,554	2004 Profits: $122,737	Fiscal Year Ends: 12/31
2003 Sales: $1,485,079	2003 Profits: $62,326	Parent Company:

SALARIES/BENEFITS:

Pension Plan:	ESOP Stock Plan:	Profit Sharing:	Top Exec. Salary: $1,480,769	Bonus: $1,750,000
Savings Plan: Y	Stock Purch. Plan: Y		Second Exec. Salary: $423,077	Bonus: $550,000

OTHER THOUGHTS:

Apparent Women Officers or Directors: 1
Hot Spot for Advancement for Women/Minorities: Y

LOCATIONS: ("Y" = Yes)

West:	Southwest:	Midwest:	Southeast:	Northeast:	International:
Y	Y				

SIGMA ALDRICH CORP www.sigmaaldrich.com

Industry Group Code: 325000 **Ranks within this company's industry group:** Sales: 4 Profits: 3

Insurance/HMO/PPO:		Drugs:		Equipment/Supplies:		Hospitals/Clinics:		Services:		Health Care:	
Insurance:		Manufacturer:		Manufacturer:	Y	Acute Care:		Diagnostics:		Home Health:	
Managed Care:		Distributor:		Distributor:		Sub-Acute:		Labs/Testing:		Long-Term Care:	
Utilization Management:		Specialty Pharmacy:		Leasing/Finance:		Outpatient Surgery:		Staffing:		Physical Therapy:	
Payment Processing:		Vitamins/Nutritionals:		Information Systems:		Physical Rehab. Ctr.:		Waste Disposal:		Physician Prac. Mgmt.:	
		Clinical Trials:				Psychiatric Clinics:		Specialty Svcs.:			

TYPES OF BUSINESS:

Chemicals Manufacturing
Biotechnology Equipment
Pharmaceutical Ingredients
Fine Chemicals
Chromatography Products

BRANDS/DIVISIONS/AFFILIATES:

Research Essentials
Research Specialties
Research Biotech
SAFC
Iropharm
Advanced Separation Technologies, Inc.
Epichem Group, Ltd.

CONTACTS: *Note: Officers with more than one job title may be intentionally listed here more than once.*

Jai Nagarkatti, CEO
Jai Nagarkatti, Pres.
Mike Hogan, CFO
Doug Rau, VP-Human Resources
Carl Turza, CIO
Mike Hogan, Chief Admin. Officer/Sec.
Karen Miller, Controller
Giles Cottier, Pres., Research Essentials
Dave Julien, Pres., Research Specialties
Kirk Richter, Treas.
Steven Walton, VP-Quality & Safety
David R. Harvey, Chmn.

Phone: 314-771-5765 **Fax:** 314-771-5757
Toll-Free: 800-521-8956
Address: 3050 Spruce St., St. Louis, MO 63103 US

GROWTH PLANS/SPECIAL FEATURES:

Sigma Aldrich Corp. is a life science and high technology company that develops, manufactures, purchases and distributes a broad range of biochemicals and organic chemicals. The company offers roughly 100,000 chemicals (including 45,000 chemicals manufactured in-house) and 30,000 equipment products used for scientific and genomic research; biotechnology; pharmaceutical development; the diagnosis of disease; and pharmaceutical and high technology manufacturing. Sigma Aldrich operates in four segments: Research Essentials, which sells biological buffers, cell culture reagents, biochemicals, chemicals, solvents and other reagents and kits; Research Specialties, which provides organic chemicals, biochemicals, analytical reagents, chromatography consumables, reference materials and high-purity products; Research Biotech, which supplies immunochemical, molecular biology, cell signaling and neuroscience biochemicals and kits used in biotechnology, genomic, proteomic and other life science research applications; and SAFC (Fine Chemicals), which offers large-scale organic chemicals and biochemicals used in development and production by pharmaceutical, biotechnology, industrial and diagnosis companies. The company operates in 35 countries, selling its products in over 165 countries and servicing over 1 million customers. Customers include commercial laboratories; pharmaceutical and industrial companies; universities; diagnostics, chemical and biotechnology companies and hospitals; non-profit organizations; and governmental institutions. In 2006, Sigma Aldrich acquired Honeywell International's Iropharm unit, a custom chemical synthesis business located in Arklow, Ireland, increasing SAFC's API and pharmaceutical intermediates manufacturing capabilities; and Advanced Separation Technologies, Inc., a chiral chromatography business in NJ. In February 2007, Sigma Aldrich acquired Epichem Group, Ltd., a U.K.-based company, for roughly $60 million.

FINANCIALS: **Sales and profits are in thousands of dollars—add 000 to get the full amount. 2007 Note: Financial information for 2007 was not available for all companies at press time.**

2007 Sales: $
2006 Sales: $1,797,500
2005 Sales: $1,666,500
2004 Sales: $1,409,200
2003 Sales: $1,298,146

2007 Profits: $
2006 Profits: $276,800
2005 Profits: $258,300
2004 Profits: $232,900
2003 Profits: $193,102

U.S. Stock Ticker: SIAL
Int'l Ticker: Int'l Exchange:
Employees: 7,299
Fiscal Year Ends: 12/31
Parent Company:

SALARIES/BENEFITS:

Pension Plan: ESOP Stock Plan: Profit Sharing: Top Exec. Salary: $600,000 Bonus: $416,874
Savings Plan: Stock Purch. Plan: Second Exec. Salary: $430,000 Bonus: $222,955

OTHER THOUGHTS:

Apparent Women Officers or Directors: 1
Hot Spot for Advancement for Women/Minorities:

LOCATIONS: ("Y" = Yes)

West:	Southwest:	Midwest:	Southeast:	Northeast:	International:
		Y			Y

Note: Financial information, benefits and other data can change quickly and may vary from those stated here.

SIGNATURE EYEWEAR INC www.signatureeyewear.com

Industry Group Code: 333314 **Ranks within this company's industry group:** Sales: 2 Profits: 2

Insurance/HMO/PPO:		Drugs:		Equipment/Supplies:		Hospitals/Clinics:		Services:		Health Care:	
Insurance:		Manufacturer:		Manufacturer:	Y	Acute Care:		Diagnostics:		Home Health:	
Managed Care:		Distributor:		Distributor:	Y	Sub-Acute:		Labs/Testing:		Long-Term Care:	
Utilization Management:		Specialty Pharmacy:		Leasing/Finance:		Outpatient Surgery:		Staffing:		Physical Therapy:	
Payment Processing:		Vitamins/Nutritionals:		Information Systems:		Physical Rehab. Ctr.:		Waste Disposal:		Physician Prac. Mgmt.:	
		Clinical Trials:				Psychiatric Clinics:		Specialty Svcs.:			

TYPES OF BUSINESS:

Optical Instruments & Lens Manufacturing
Prescription Eyeglass & Sunglass Frames

BRANDS/DIVISIONS/AFFILIATES:

Signature Eyewear Collection
Intuition
Lifescape
Laura Ashley Eyewear
bebe eyes
Hart Schaffner & Marx Eyewear
Dakota Smith
HUMMER Eyegear

CONTACTS: *Note: Officers with more than one job title may be intentionally listed here more than once.*

Michael Prince, CEO
Michael Prince, CFO
Sheptanya Page, Dir.-Human Resources
Kevin D. Seifert, VP-Oper.
Jill Gardner, VP-Design
Richard M. Torre, Chmn.
Raul Khantzis, VP-Int'l Sales

Phone: 310-330-2700	**Fax:** 310-330-2765
Toll-Free: 800-765-3937	
Address: 498 N. Oak St., Inglewood, CA 90302 US	

GROWTH PLANS/SPECIAL FEATURES:

Signature Eyewear, Inc. (SEI) and its subsidiaries design, market and distribute prescription eyeglass frames and sunglasses. The company's frame styles are developed by its in-house design team, which works in close collaboration with many frame manufacturers throughout the world to develop unique styles. Once the factory develops a prototype, the designer presents the style to the licensor for approval. Once approved, Signature then contracts with the factory to manufacture the style. By these methods, Signature is able to choose the strengths of a variety of factories worldwide and to avoid reliance on any one factory. To assure quality, Signature's designers continue to work closely with the factory at each stage of a style's manufacturing process. The company operates primarily within the exclusive licenses for Laura Ashley Eyewear, bebe eyes, Nicole Miller Eyewear, Hart Schaffner Marx Eyewear, Hummer Eyegear, Dakota Smith and Cutter & Buck Eyewear. The company also produces frames under the Signature Eyewear Collections label, which allows the company to produce good quality, low cost styles by omitting the extra licensing fees and the time-consuming license approval process. SEI distributes its products to independent optical retailers in the U.S.; internationally through exclusive distributors and a direct sales force in Western Europe; and through its account managers to major optical retail chains, including Pearle Vision, LensCrafters and U.S. Vision. In March 2007, the company entered into a four-year license agreement to design and distribute women's optical and sun eyewear under the Carmen Marc Valvo name.

FINANCIALS: **Sales and profits are in thousands of dollars—add 000 to get the full amount. 2007 Note: Financial information for 2007 was not available for all companies at press time.**

2007 Sales: $	2007 Profits: $	**U.S. Stock Ticker: SEYE**
2006 Sales: $23,162	2006 Profits: $ 683	**Int'l Ticker:** Int'l Exchange:
2005 Sales: $25,050	2005 Profits: $1,606	Employees: 102
2004 Sales: $23,609	2004 Profits: $- 371	Fiscal Year Ends: 10/31
2003 Sales: $25,140	2003 Profits: $3,455	Parent Company:

SALARIES/BENEFITS:

Pension Plan:	ESOP Stock Plan:	Profit Sharing:	Top Exec. Salary: $275,000	Bonus: $
Savings Plan: Y	Stock Purch. Plan:		Second Exec. Salary: $110,800	Bonus: $15,000

OTHER THOUGHTS:

Apparent Women Officers or Directors: 1
Hot Spot for Advancement for Women/Minorities: Y

LOCATIONS: ("Y" = Yes)

West:	Southwest:	Midwest:	Southeast:	Northeast:	International:
Y					Y

SIMCERE PHARMACEUTICAL GROUP www.simcere.com

Industry Group Code: 325412 **Ranks within this company's industry group:** Sales: 34 Profits: 28

Insurance/HMO/PPO:		Drugs:		Equipment/Supplies:		Hospitals/Clinics:		Services:		Health Care:	
Insurance:		Manufacturer:	Y	Manufacturer:		Acute Care:		Diagnostics:		Home Health:	
Managed Care:		Distributor:		Distributor:		Sub-Acute:		Labs/Testing:		Long-Term Care:	
Utilization Management:		Specialty Pharmacy:		Leasing/Finance:		Outpatient Surgery:		Staffing:		Physical Therapy:	
Payment Processing:		Vitamins/Nutritionals:		Information Systems:		Physical Rehab. Ctr.:		Waste Disposal:		Physician Prac. Mgmt.:	
		Clinical Trials:				Psychiatric Clinics:		Specialty Svcs.:			

TYPES OF BUSINESS:

Branded Generic Pharmaceuticals
Drug Research

BRANDS/DIVISIONS/AFFILIATES:

Endu
Bicun
Zailin
Yingtaiqing
Anqi
Biqi
Simcere Medgenn Bio-Pharmaceutical Co., Ltd.

CONTACTS: *Note: Officers with more than one job title may be intentionally listed here more than once.*

Jinsheng Ren, CEO
Frank Zhigang Zhao, CFO
Yat Ming Chu, VP-Mktg. & Sales
Xiaojin Yin, VP-R&D
Jindong Zhou, VP-Mfg.
Haibo Qian, Sec.
Eric Wang Lam Cheung, VP-Investor Rel.
Jinsheng Ren, Chmn.

Phone: 86-25-8556-6666 **Fax:** 85-25-8547-1729
Toll-Free:
Address: No. 699-18 Xuan Wu Ave., Xuan Wu District, Nanjing, Jiangsu Province 210042 China

GROWTH PLANS/SPECIAL FEATURES:

Simcere Pharmaceutical Group is a Chinese manufacturer and supplier of branded generic pharmaceuticals. The company manufactures and sells 35 pharmaceutical products and is the exclusive distributor of three additional pharmaceutical products marketed under the firm's brand name. The firm's products are used for treatment of a wide range of diseases such as cancer; cerebrovascular and cardiovascular diseases; infections; arthritis; diarrhea; allergies; respiratory conditions; and urinary conditions. Simcere Pharmaceutical's products include Bicun, an anti-stroke medication and first synthetic free radical scavenger sold in China; Zailin, a generic amoxicillin granule antibiotic; Endu, an anticancer medication and first recombinant human endostatin injection in China; Yingtaiqing, a generic diclofenac sodium sustained-release capsule for inflammation and pain relief; Anqi, a generic amoxicillin with clavulanate potassium antibiotic; and Biqi, an OTC generic smectite powder for diarrhea. In addition, the Chinese FDA has approved the manufacture and sale of 100 other company products. Simcere Pharmaceutical has three manufacturing bases, two nationwide sales and marketing subsidiaries and one research and development center. In February 2006, the company established a joint laboratory for drug discovery with Tsinghua University. In September 2006, the company acquired 80% of Shandong Simcere Medgenn Bio-Pharmaceutical Co., Ltd. for roughly $26 million and launched Endu, also known as Endostar, its patented anti-cancer drug, the first recombinant human endostatin to be successfully commercialized. In April 2007, the firm started to trade on the New York Stock Exchange. In June 2007, Simcere Pharmaceutical entered into an agreement to acquire an additional 10% interest in Shandong Simcere Medgenn Bio-Pharmaceutical Co., Ltd. for roughly $3.5 million.

The company offers its employees benefits that include medical insurance and a housing plan.

FINANCIALS: **Sales and profits are in thousands of dollars—add 000 to get the full amount. 2007 Note: Financial information for 2007 was not available for all companies at press time.**

2007 Sales: $	2007 Profits: $	**U.S. Stock Ticker: SCR**
2006 Sales: $121,800	2006 Profits: $22,100	**Int'l Ticker:** Int'l Exchange:
2005 Sales: $91,300	2005 Profits: $12,700	Employees: 1,838
2004 Sales: $68,100	2004 Profits: $5,600	Fiscal Year Ends: 12/31
2003 Sales: $	2003 Profits: $	Parent Company:

SALARIES/BENEFITS:

Pension Plan:	ESOP Stock Plan:	Profit Sharing:	Top Exec. Salary: $	Bonus: $
Savings Plan:	Stock Purch. Plan:		Second Exec. Salary: $	Bonus: $

OTHER THOUGHTS:

Apparent Women Officers or Directors:
Hot Spot for Advancement for Women/Minorities:

LOCATIONS: ("Y" = Yes)

West:	Southwest:	Midwest:	Southeast:	Northeast:	International:
					Y

Note: Financial information, benefits and other data can change quickly and may vary from those stated here.

SISTERS OF MERCY HEALTH SYSTEMS www.mercy.net

Industry Group Code: 622110 **Ranks within this company's industry group:** Sales: 14 Profits: 18

Insurance/HMO/PPO:		Drugs:		Equipment/Supplies:		Hospitals/Clinics:		Services:		Health Care:	
Insurance:		Manufacturer:		Manufacturer:		Acute Care:	Y	Diagnostics:		Home Health:	
Managed Care:		Distributor:		Distributor:		Sub-Acute:	Y	Labs/Testing:		Long-Term Care:	Y
Utilization Management:		Specialty Pharmacy:		Leasing/Finance:		Outpatient Surgery:	Y	Staffing:		Physical Therapy:	
Payment Processing:		Vitamins/Nutritionals:		Information Systems:		Physical Rehab. Ctr.:		Waste Disposal:		Physician Prac. Mgmt.:	
		Clinical Trials:				Psychiatric Clinics:		Specialty Svcs.:	Y		

TYPES OF BUSINESS:

Hospitals-General
Outpatient Care
Health Classes
Long-Term Care
Community Service & Outreach

BRANDS/DIVISIONS/AFFILIATES:

Mercy Health Plans
Sisters of Mercy-St. Louis Regional Community
Mercy Ministries of Laredo

CONTACTS:

Note: Officers with more than one job title may be intentionally listed here more than once.

John Sullivan, CEO
John Sullivan, Pres.
James R. Jaacks, CFO/Sr. VP
Anthony Kinslow, VP-Human Resources
Mike McCurry, CIO/VP
Philip Wheeler, General Counsel/VP
Myra K. Aubuchon, VP-Planning
Vance Moore, VP-Resource Optimization/Pres., ROi
Myra K. Aubuchon, Sr. VP
Jolene Goedken, VP-Medical Svcs.
Glenn Mitchell, VP-Clinical Safety
Joseph M. Sullivan, Chmn.

Phone: 314-579-6100	**Fax:** 314-628-3723
Toll-Free:	
Address: 14528 S. Outer Forty, Ste. 100, Chesterfield, MO 63017 US	

GROWTH PLANS/SPECIAL FEATURES:

Sisters of Mercy Health Systems (Mercy), established in 1986, is one of the nine largest Catholic health care systems in the U.S. It operates outpatient clinics, physician practices hospitals, health plants, human services and community outreach programs in seven states: Arkansas, Louisiana Kansas, Mississippi, Missouri, Oklahoma and Texas. The organization's members include a heart hospital, outpatient care facilities, skilled nursing services providers, long-term residential care facilities, stand-alone clinics and over 4,000 licensed beds in eighteen acute care hospitals. It runs Mercy Health Plans, an HMO and third-party administrator in communities served by Mercy. The group also operates an active advocacy program for issues of social justice especially in the field of health care, providing participants with updates on issues of concern and the means of contacting elected officials. Mercy also offers a variety of free or inexpensive classes at its hospitals including a healing-through-the-arts program, babysitter skills, massage classes, infant care and CPR/first aid classes, as well as substance abuse and terminal illness support groups. It is sponsored by the Sisters of Mercy-St. Louis Regional Community. The Sisters of Mercy were founded nearly 200 years ago by Catherine McAuley, a nun who devoted her life and a large fortune to caring for Dublin's poor, and Mercy shares McAuley's vision. With outreach programs in Louisiana, Texas, Mississippi and Belize, Mercy allocates money for subsidized care, community outreach ministries and charity care. It operates Mercy Ministries of Laredo, an outpatient program that provides culturally sensitive services from 14 sites in the Laredo, Texas, area. Services include women's and children's health, health education, a diabetes center, a domestic violence shelter, and medication assistance and nutritional assistance programs.

Mercy offers education assistance for certified nurse assistants to obtain full nursing degrees.

FINANCIALS:

Sales and profits are in thousands of dollars—add 000 to get the full amount. 2007 Note: Financial information for 2007 was not available for all companies at press time.

2007 Sales: $	2007 Profits: $	**U.S. Stock Ticker: Nonprofit**
2006 Sales: $3,579,454	2006 Profits: $45,708	**Int'l Ticker:** Int'l Exchange:
2005 Sales: $3,246,696	2005 Profits: $55,460	Employees: 29,500
2004 Sales: $3,012,669	2004 Profits: $97,731	Fiscal Year Ends: 6/30
2003 Sales: $2,721,900	2003 Profits: $	Parent Company:

SALARIES/BENEFITS:

Pension Plan:	ESOP Stock Plan:	Profit Sharing:	Top Exec. Salary: $	Bonus: $
Savings Plan:	Stock Purch. Plan:		Second Exec. Salary: $	Bonus: $

OTHER THOUGHTS:

Apparent Women Officers or Directors: 4
Hot Spot for Advancement for Women/Minorities: Y

LOCATIONS: ("Y" = Yes)

West:	Southwest:	Midwest:	Southeast:	Northeast:	International:
	Y	Y	Y		Y

SKILLED HEALTHCARE GROUP INC

www.skilledhealthcaregroup.com

Industry Group Code: 623110 **Ranks within this company's industry group:** Sales: Profits:

Insurance/HMO/PPO:		Drugs:		Equipment/Supplies:		Hospitals/Clinics:		Services:		Health Care:	
Insurance:		Manufacturer:		Manufacturer:		Acute Care:		Diagnostics:		Home Health:	
Managed Care:		Distributor:		Distributor:		Sub-Acute:		Labs/Testing:		Long-Term Care:	Y
Utilization Management:		Specialty Pharmacy:		Leasing/Finance:		Outpatient Surgery:		Staffing:		Physical Therapy:	Y
Payment Processing:		Vitamins/Nutritionals:		Information Systems:		Physical Rehab. Ctr.:		Waste Disposal:		Physician Prac. Mgmt.:	
		Clinical Trials:				Psychiatric Clinics:		Specialty Svcs.:	Y		

TYPES OF BUSINESS:

Operating Skilled Nursing & Assisted Living Facilities
Rehabilitation Therapy
Hospice Care

BRANDS/DIVISIONS/AFFILIATES:

Skilled Healthcare, LLC
Express Recovery
Hallmark Rehabilitation, Inc.
Hospice Care of the West
Laurel Healthcare Providers, LLC

CONTACTS: *Note: Officers with more than one job title may be intentionally listed here more than once.*

Boyd Hendrickson, CEO
Jose Lynch, COO
John E. King, CFO/Treas.
Roland Rapp, Chief Admin. Officer
Roland Rapp, General Counsel/Sec.
Chris Felfe, Sr. VP-Finance/Chief Acct. Officer
Mark Wortley, Exec. VP/Pres., Ancillary Subsidiaries
Susan Whittle, Sr. VP/Chief Compliance Officer
Boyd Hendrickson, Chmn.

Phone: 949-282-5800 **Fax:**
Toll-Free:
Address: 27442 Portola Pkwy., Ste. 200, Foothill Ranch, CA 92610 US

GROWTH PLANS/SPECIAL FEATURES:

Skilled Healthcare Group, Inc. is a holding company with interests in skilled nursing and assisted living facilities, both operated by subsidiary Skilled Healthcare, LLC. Its subsidiaries own approximately 73% of these facilities. Its skilled nursing facilities, located in California, Nevada, Kansas, Missouri and Texas, have approximately 7,600 beds. They typically target high-acuity patients, often admitted to recover from strokes, cardiovascular ailments, joint replacements and other neurological, muscular or skeletal conditions. Its nursing facilities also often include an Express Recovery program that targets patients recovering form joint replacement surgery as well as cardiac and respiratory ailments; and features an extensive rehabilitation therapy regimen, a separate entrance, and typically consists of 12-36 beds. The company's 12 assisted living facilities have 794 licensed beds, and provide simple services such as meals, activities and security but not a level of nursing care available in the nursing homes. The firm operates subsidiary Hallmark Rehabilitation, Inc., which contracts with nursing homes to provide rehabilitation therapy services typically to high-acuity patients. Skilled Healthcare endeavors to meet the spiritual, physical and mental needs of terminally ill patients and their families through Hospice Care of the West, providing counseling, education, clinical and palliative care (which can offer pain relief but no cure). Skilled Healthcare, LLC also offers administrative and consulting services to the group's various activities. These services include payroll, IT support, clinical consulting and income tax preparation. In September 2007, the company acquired a hospice company and 10 skilled nursing facilities, whose collective beds totaled 1,180, located in Albuquerque, New Mexico, for approximately $51.5 million, from certain affiliates of Laurel Healthcare Providers, LLC.

FINANCIALS: **Sales and profits are in thousands of dollars—add 000 to get the full amount. 2007 Note: Financial information for 2007 was not available for all companies at press time.**

2007 Sales: $ | 2007 Profits: $
2006 Sales: $ | 2006 Profits: $
2005 Sales: $ | 2005 Profits: $
2004 Sales: $ | 2004 Profits: $
2003 Sales: $ | 2003 Profits: $

U.S. Stock Ticker: SKH
Int'l Ticker: Int'l Exchange:
Employees:
Fiscal Year Ends: 12/31
Parent Company: ONEX CORPORATION

SALARIES/BENEFITS:

Pension Plan: ESOP Stock Plan: Profit Sharing: Top Exec. Salary: $ Bonus: $
Savings Plan: Stock Purch. Plan: Second Exec. Salary: $ Bonus: $

OTHER THOUGHTS:

Apparent Women Officers or Directors: 1
Hot Spot for Advancement for Women/Minorities:

LOCATIONS: ("Y" = Yes)

West:	Southwest:	Midwest:	Southeast:	Northeast:	International:
Y	Y	Y			

Note: Financial information, benefits and other data can change quickly and may vary from those stated here.

SMITH & NEPHEW PLC www.smith-nephew.com

Industry Group Code: 339113 **Ranks within this company's industry group:** Sales: 12 Profits: 8

Insurance/HMO/PPO:		Drugs:		Equipment/Supplies:		Hospitals/Clinics:		Services:		Health Care:	
Insurance:		Manufacturer:		Manufacturer:	Y	Acute Care:		Diagnostics:		Home Health:	
Managed Care:		Distributor:		Distributor:		Sub-Acute:		Labs/Testing:		Long-Term Care:	
Utilization Management:		Specialty Pharmacy:		Leasing/Finance:		Outpatient Surgery:		Staffing:		Physical Therapy:	
Payment Processing:		Vitamins/Nutritionals:		Information Systems:		Physical Rehab. Ctr.:		Waste Disposal:		Physician Prac. Mgmt.:	
		Clinical Trials:				Psychiatric Clinics:		Specialty Svcs.:			

TYPES OF BUSINESS:

Medical Device Manufacturing-Orthopedics
Reconstructive Joint Implants
Endoscopy Products
Wound Management Products

BRANDS/DIVISIONS/AFFILIATES:

Smith & Nephew Group
GENESIS II
SUPARTZ
TRIVEX
Allevyn
Versajet
Iodosorb
EXOGEN 4000+

CONTACTS: *Note: Officers with more than one job title may be intentionally listed here more than once.*

David Illingworth, CEO
David Illingworth, Pres.
Adrian Hennah, CFO
Elizabeth Bolgiano, Group Dir.-Human Resources
Peter Arnold, Group Dir.-Tech.
Jim Ralston, Chief Legal Officer
Sarah Byrne-Quinn, Group Dir.-Strategy & Bus. Dev.
Liz Hewitt, Group Dir.-Corporate Affairs
Michael Frazzette, Pres., Endoscopy
Joe Woody, Pres., Advanced Wound Mgmt.
Mark Augusti, Pres., Orthopaedic Trauma & Clinical Therapies
Joseph DeVivo, Pres., Orthopaedic Reconstruction Div.
John Buchanan, Chmn.
Howard Miller, Pres., North American Bus., Advanced Wound Mgmt.

Phone: 44-20-7401-7646	**Fax:** 44-20-7930-3353
Toll-Free:	
Address: 15 Adam St., London, WC2N 6LA UK	

GROWTH PLANS/SPECIAL FEATURES:

Smith & Nephew PLC, founded in 1856, develops and markets advanced medical devices that help healthcare professionals treat patients effectively, and operates in 31 countries. It is the parent company of the Smith & Nephew Group, an international medical devices business organized into four global business units: Orthopedic Reconstruction; Orthopedic Trauma & Clinical Therapies; Endoscopy; and Advanced Wound Management. Orthopedic products include reconstructive joint implants; trauma products that help repair broken bones; and other pain relieving and healing products. Reconstructive joint implants include hip, knee and shoulder joints as well as ancillary products like bone cement used in reconstructive surgery. Product lines include the GENESIS II and PROFIX knee replacements, SUPARTZ joint fluid therapy, and EXOGEN ultrasound bone healing system. Smith & Nephew's Endoscopy unit, headquartered in Andover, Massachusetts, develops and markets a range of minimally invasive surgery techniques and educational programs to repair soft tissues, articulating joints, spinal discs and vascular structures. It focuses principally on arthroscopy. Arthroscopy is the minimally invasive surgery of joints, in particular the knee, hip and shoulder. Products include fluid management systems, cameras, scopes, light sources, radiofrequency ablation devices, powered shaver systems, soft tissue reattachment devices, blades and tissue regeneration products. It has developed a new technique for removing varicose veins, called TRIVEX. The Advanced Wound Management unit supplies products for chronic and acute wounds. Chronic wounds, such as pressure, leg or diabetic foot ulcers, are generally difficult to heal; and acute wounds, such as burns and post operative wounds, are generally life threatening, with potential scarring and infection. Its products include Allevyn foam dressings; Acticoad, dressings that contain silver; the Versajet hydrosurgery system; and Iodosorb, a dressing and ointment that contains iodine. In July 2006, the FDA approved Smith and Nephew's EXOGEN 4000+ Bone Healing System, which promotes the natural bone healing process.

FINANCIALS: **Sales and profits are in thousands of dollars—add 000 to get the full amount. 2007 Note: Financial information for 2007 was not available for all companies at press time.**

2007 Sales: $	2007 Profits: $	**U.S. Stock Ticker: SNN**
2006 Sales: $2,779,000	2006 Profits: $745,000	**Int'l Ticker: SN** Int'l Exchange: London-LSE
2005 Sales: $2,552,000	2005 Profits: $333,000	Employees: 8,830
2004 Sales: $2,301,000	2004 Profits: $245,000	Fiscal Year Ends: 12/31
2003 Sales: $2,102,500	2003 Profits: $264,100	Parent Company:

SALARIES/BENEFITS:

Pension Plan:	ESOP Stock Plan:	Profit Sharing:	Top Exec. Salary: $	Bonus: $
Savings Plan:	Stock Purch. Plan:		Second Exec. Salary: $	Bonus: $

OTHER THOUGHTS:

Apparent Women Officers or Directors: 2
Hot Spot for Advancement for Women/Minorities:

LOCATIONS: ("Y" = Yes)

West:	Southwest:	Midwest:	Southeast:	Northeast:	International:
			Y	Y	Y

SMITHS GROUP PLC

www.smiths-group.com

Industry Group Code: 333000 **Ranks within this company's industry group:** Sales: 1 Profits: 1

Insurance/HMO/PPO:		Drugs:		Equipment/Supplies:		Hospitals/Clinics:		Services:		Health Care:	
Insurance:		Manufacturer:		Manufacturer:	Y	Acute Care:		Diagnostics:		Home Health:	
Managed Care:		Distributor:		Distributor:		Sub-Acute:		Labs/Testing:		Long-Term Care:	
Utilization Management:		Specialty Pharmacy:		Leasing/Finance:		Outpatient Surgery:		Staffing:		Physical Therapy:	
Payment Processing:		Vitamins/Nutritionals:		Information Systems:		Physical Rehab. Ctr.:		Waste Disposal:		Physician Prac. Mgmt.:	
		Clinical Trials:				Psychiatric Clinics:		Specialty Svcs.:			

TYPES OF BUSINESS:

Machinery, Manufacturing
Medical Devices, Manufacturing

BRANDS/DIVISIONS/AFFILIATES:

John Crane
Interconnect
Flexible Technologies
Kelvin Hughes Limited
Smiths Aerospace
Smiths Detection
Smiths Medical
GE Detection

CONTACTS: *Note: Officers with more than one job title may be intentionally listed here more than once.*

Keith O. Butler-Wheelhouse, CEO
John Langston, Dir.-Finance
David P. Lillycrop, General Counsel
Russell Plumley, Dir.-Investor Rel.
Paul R. Cox, Group Mgr. Dir.-Specialty Engineering
John Ferrie, Group Mgr. Dir.-Aerospace
Donald H. Brydon, Chmn.

Phone: 44-20-8458-3232 **Fax:** 44-20-8457-8346
Toll-Free:
Address: 765 Finchley Rd., London, NW11 8DS UK

GROWTH PLANS/SPECIAL FEATURES:

Smiths Group plc is a global technology company with four main divisions: Aerospace; Detection; Medical; and Specialty Engineering. Smiths Aerospace is a transatlantic aerospace systems and equipment company which supplies precision components to all major aero-engine manufacturers. Smiths Detection provides security equipment for the detection and identification of explosives; chemical and biological agents; weapons; and contraband. This equipment is used by military forces, airport security, customs officers, and emergency services. Smiths Medical focuses on critical care and medication delivery, which include airway management; pain management; needle safety; temperature monitoring; hospital and ambulatory infusion; insulin infusion; vascular access; and in-vitro fertilization. Smiths Specialty Engineering is itself divided into four business areas: John Crane, which manufactures mechanical seals and related products for the petrochemical and transportation industries; Interconnect, which manufactures electronic connectors, coaxial, cable and connector assemblies, antennae, as well as lightning and surge protectors; Flexible Technologies provides flexible hose and ducting for commercial and consumer air moving products and for conveying gas, liquid and airborne solids in industrial processes; and Kelvin Hughes Limited, which designs and manufactures marine navigational systems as well as nautical charts. In January 2007, Smiths agreed to sell Smiths Aerospace to General Electric Company (GE) for $4.8 billion. In a separate deal, Smiths Detection and General Electric will establish a joint venture, GE Detection, aimed at the homeland security market.

FINANCIALS: **Sales and profits are in thousands of dollars—add 000 to get the full amount. 2007 Note: Financial information for 2007 was not available for all companies at press time.**

2007 Sales: $	2007 Profits: $	**U.S. Stock Ticker:**
2006 Sales: $6,564,200	2006 Profits: $45,100	**Int'l Ticker: SMIN** Int'l Exchange: London-LSE
2005 Sales: $5,302,900	2005 Profits: $388,100	Employees: 31,324
2004 Sales: $4,974,800	2004 Profits: $387,500	Fiscal Year Ends:
2003 Sales: $	2003 Profits: $	Parent Company:

SALARIES/BENEFITS:

Pension Plan:	ESOP Stock Plan:	Profit Sharing:	Top Exec. Salary: $	Bonus: $
Savings Plan:	Stock Purch. Plan:		Second Exec. Salary: $	Bonus: $

OTHER THOUGHTS:

Apparent Women Officers or Directors:
Hot Spot for Advancement for Women/Minorities:

LOCATIONS: ("Y" = Yes)

West:	Southwest:	Midwest:	Southeast:	Northeast:	International:
Y	Y	Y	Y	Y	Y

SOLUCIENT LLC www.solucient.com

Industry Group Code: 511212 **Ranks within this company's industry group:** Sales: Profits:

Insurance/HMO/PPO:		Drugs:		Equipment/Supplies:		Hospitals/Clinics:		Services:		Health Care:	
Insurance:		Manufacturer:		Manufacturer:		Acute Care:		Diagnostics:		Home Health:	
Managed Care:		Distributor:		Distributor:		Sub-Acute:		Labs/Testing:		Long-Term Care:	
Utilization Management:	Y	Specialty Pharmacy:		Leasing/Finance:		Outpatient Surgery:		Staffing:		Physical Therapy:	
Payment Processing:		Vitamins/Nutritionals:		Information Systems:	Y	Physical Rehab. Ctr.:		Waste Disposal:		Physician Prac. Mgmt.:	
		Clinical Trials:				Psychiatric Clinics:		Specialty Svcs.:			

TYPES OF BUSINESS:

Computer Software-Health Care
Research Databases
Decision Support Systems

BRANDS/DIVISIONS/AFFILIATES:

Veronis Suhler Stevenson Partners
VNU N.V.
VHA, Inc.
InpatientView
HealthViewPlus
AstroSachs
ProviderView
Market Planner Plus (The)

CONTACTS: *Note: Officers with more than one job title may be intentionally listed here more than once.*

Nancy P. Nelson, CEO
Gregg Bennett, Pres.
Thomas P. (Tom) Wilkas, CFO
Christopher Clemmensen, VP-Mktg.
Gary Pickens, Chief Research Officer
Matthew J. Bates, Sr. VP-Tech.
Ken Whitaker, Sr. VP-Prod. Dev.
Bill Needham, VP-Prod. Eng.
Andra Heller, General Counsel
Jonathan Greifenkamp, VP-Finance
Jean Chenoweth, Sr. VP-Performance Improvement
Matthew J. Bates, VP-Prod. & Solutions
Kaveh Safavi, Chief Medical Officer
Charles E. Leonard, Chmn.

Phone: 847-475-7526	**Fax:** 847-475-7830
Toll-Free: 800-366-7526	
Address: 1800 Sherman Ave., Evanston, IL 60201 US	

GROWTH PLANS/SPECIAL FEATURES:

Solucient, LLC is an information products company servin the healthcare industry. It is a market leader in developin and marketing integrated clinical information systems an products that healthcare managers use to expedite th performance of their organizations. Solucient is a joi venture of Veronis Suhler Stevenson Partners, VNU N.V and VHA, Inc. It has products ranging from standardize databases to highly focused decision support systems, whic assist customers in evaluating the efficacy and economics health care delivery. Solucient maintains the health car industry's leading database, which contains more than 2 million discharges, representing 77.5% of all discharge The company's client base of more than 5,500 custome includes over 2,900 hospitals and eight of the ten large pharmaceutical manufacturers. Solucient offers a range information products used in all areas of health car including providers, pharmaceuticals, managed care an employers. Providers, such as hospitals, rely on Solucient measure and analyze the cost and quality of medic interventions, thereby improving strategic decision-makin Solucient offers the pharmaceutical segment of the heal care industry data management, planning and direct-t consumer information. Companies also employ Solucient databases and products to analyze potential markets for the products. Managed care organizations use the firm targeted claim analysis systems to avoid overpayments providers, and organizations use Solucient's information an analysis of medical resource usage and outcomes to low medical costs and understand health care resource use. addition, Solucient offers benefit plan and health care clai information, which allows employers to improv performance, decision-making and managemen Solucient's product titles include InpatientVie HealthViewPlus, Astro Sachs, ProviderView and the Mark Planner Plus. In February 2006, Solucient announced it ha partnered with Continuum Health Partners, Inc., a non-pro healthcare system in New York City. Solucient will improv Continuum's operational information systems.

The company offers its employees flexible spendin accounts.

FINANCIALS: **Sales and profits are in thousands of dollars—add 000 to get the full amount. 2007 Note: Financial information for 2007 was not available for all companies at press time.**

2007 Sales: $	2007 Profits: $	**U.S. Stock Ticker: Subsidiary**
2006 Sales: $	2006 Profits: $	**Int'l Ticker:** Int'l Exchange:
2005 Sales: $	2005 Profits: $	Employees: 500
2004 Sales: $90,000	2004 Profits: $	Fiscal Year Ends: 12/31
2003 Sales: $50,000	2003 Profits: $	Parent Company: THOMSON CORPORATION (THE)

SALARIES/BENEFITS:

Pension Plan:	ESOP Stock Plan:	Profit Sharing:	Top Exec. Salary: $	Bonus: $
Savings Plan: Y	Stock Purch. Plan:		Second Exec. Salary: $	Bonus: $

OTHER THOUGHTS:

Apparent Women Officers or Directors: 2
Hot Spot for Advancement for Women/Minorities: Y

LOCATIONS: ("Y" = Yes)

West:	Southwest:	Midwest:	Southeast:	Northeast:	International:
Y		Y		Y	Y

SONIC INNOVATIONS INC www.sonici.com

ndustry Group Code: 339113 **Ranks within this company's industry group:** Sales: 70 Profits: 80

nsurance/HMO/PPO:		Drugs:		Equipment/Supplies:		Hospitals/Clinics:		Services:		Health Care:	
nsurance:		Manufacturer:		Manufacturer:	Y	Acute Care:		Diagnostics:		Home Health:	
lanaged Care:		Distributor:		Distributor:		Sub-Acute:		Labs/Testing:		Long-Term Care:	
tilization Management:		Specialty Pharmacy:		Leasing/Finance:		Outpatient Surgery:		Staffing:		Physical Therapy:	
ayment Processing:		Vitamins/Nutritionals:		Information Systems:		Physical Rehab. Ctr.:		Waste Disposal:		Physician Prac. Mgmt.:	
		Clinical Trials:				Psychiatric Clinics:		Specialty Svcs.:			

TYPES OF BUSINESS:

learing Aids
)iagnostic Equipment

BRANDS/DIVISIONS/AFFILIATES:

)igital Signal Processing
latura Pro
latura 2
ribute
)uartet
nnova
alance

CONTACTS: *Note: Officers with more than one job title may be ntentionally listed here more than once.*

amuel Westover, CEO
amuel Westover, Pres.
lichael Halloran, CFO/VP
ichard Scott, VP-Worldwide Mktg.
erry DaBell, VP-R&D
hristie Mitchell, VP-Mfg. Oper.
rent Shimada, VP-Admin.
rent Shimada, General Counsel
effrey Geigel, VP-North American Sales
ictor Bray, VP/Chief Audiology Officer
ndrew Raguskus, Exec. Chmn.

hone: 801-365-2800 **Fax:** 801-365-3000
oll-Free: 888-678-4327
ddress: 2795 E. Cottonwood Pkwy., Ste. 660, Salt Lake City, T 84121 US

GROWTH PLANS/SPECIAL FEATURES:

Sonic Innovations, Inc. designs, develops, manufactures and markets digital hearing aids. The company's patented digital signal processing (DSP) platform is one of the smallest single-chip platforms ever installed in a hearing aid. The DSP platform contains a set of algorithms that pre-process incoming sound and present it to the impaired cochlea in a way that helps to restore natural loudness perception and preserves cues necessary for speech understanding. This platform also processes sound at a faster rate than other digital hearing aids; has the ability to filter out unnecessary background noise; and can isolate the direction of sound in such a way that sound in front of the listener is emphasized. The DSP chip contains up to 16 independent compression channels programmable with one-decibel accuracy, enhancing the naturalness of sound and allowing for a personalized product. Sonic Innovations operates in three segments: North America, which includes owned operations in the U.S. and Canada; Europe, which includes owned operations in Germany, Denmark, the Netherlands, Austria, Switzerland and England; and rest-of-world, which includes an owned operation in Australia. The company's Balance, Innova, Natura Pro, Natura 2, Tribute and Quartet product lines conform to the six common models for hearing aids: behind-the-ear, in-the-ear, in-the-canal, half-shell, mini-canal and completely-in-the-canal. Outside the U.S., Sonic sells finished hearing aids and hearing aid kits primarily to distributors. Its Danish subsidiary distributes hearing aids and tinnitus products in Europe. The company holds 41 patents and patent applications in process. In addition to hearing aids, the firm produces diagnostic equipment such as audiometers, tympanometers and otoacoustic emission devices. The products allow patients to be tested in under 30 minutes, with an Otogram report summing up the patient's hearing requirements.

FINANCIALS: **Sales and profits are in thousands of dollars—add 000 to get the full amount. 2007 Note: Financial information for 2007 was not available for all companies at press time.**

007 Sales: $	2007 Profits: $	**U.S. Stock Ticker: SNCI**
006 Sales: $150,492	2006 Profits: $-1,580	**Int'l Ticker:** Int'l Exchange:
005 Sales: $99,126	2005 Profits: $-19,608	Employees: 639
004 Sales: $97,688	2004 Profits: $ 411	Fiscal Year Ends: 12/31
003 Sales: $87,690	2003 Profits: $ 376	Parent Company:

SALARIES/BENEFITS:

ension Plan:	ESOP Stock Plan:	Profit Sharing:	Top Exec. Salary: $331,116	Bonus: $205,246
avings Plan:	Stock Purch. Plan:		Second Exec. Salary: $254,346	Bonus: $

OTHER THOUGHTS:

pparent Women Officers or Directors: 2
ot Spot for Advancement for Women/Minorities:

LOCATIONS: ("Y" = Yes)

West:	Southwest:	Midwest:	Southeast:	Northeast:	International:
Y					Y

Note: Financial information, benefits and other data can change quickly and may vary from those stated here.

SPAN AMERICA MEDICAL SYSTEMS INC

www.spanamerica.com

Industry Group Code: 339113 **Ranks within this company's industry group:** Sales: 92 Profits: 74

Insurance/HMO/PPO:		Drugs:		Equipment/Supplies:		Hospitals/Clinics:		Services:		Health Care:	
Insurance:		Manufacturer:		Manufacturer:	Y	Acute Care:		Diagnostics:		Home Health:	
Managed Care:		Distributor:	Y	Distributor:	Y	Sub-Acute:		Labs/Testing:		Long-Term Care:	
Utilization Management:		Specialty Pharmacy:		Leasing/Finance:		Outpatient Surgery:		Staffing:		Physical Therapy:	
Payment Processing:		Vitamins/Nutritionals:		Information Systems:		Physical Rehab. Ctr.:		Waste Disposal:		Physician Prac. Mgmt.:	
		Clinical Trials:				Psychiatric Clinics:		Specialty Svcs.:			

TYPES OF BUSINESS:

Supplies-Therapeutic Mattresses
Polyurethane Foam Products
Wound Management Products
Intravenous Catheters
Skin Care Products

BRANDS/DIVISIONS/AFFILIATES:

Geo-Matt
Geo-Mattress
PressureGuard
Span-Aids
Isch-Dish
Sacral Dish
Selan
PJ Noyes Company

CONTACTS: *Note: Officers with more than one job title may be intentionally listed here more than once.*

James D. Ferguson, CEO
James D. Ferguson, Pres.
Richard C. Coggins, CFO
Clyde A. Shew, VP-Medical Sales & Mktg.
James R. O'Reagan, VP-R&D
James R. O'Reagan, VP-Eng.
Richard C. Coggins, Corp. Sec.
Robert E. Ackley, VP-Oper.
Richard C. Coggins, Treas.
Wanda J. Totton, VP-Quality Control
Thomas D. Henrion, Chmn.

Phone: 864-288-8877	**Fax:** 864-288-8692
Toll-Free: 800-888-6752	
Address: 70 Commerce Dr., Greenville, SC 29615 US	

GROWTH PLANS/SPECIAL FEATURES:

Span-America Medical Systems, Inc. manufactures a
distributes a variety of polyurethane foam products for t
medical and custom products markets, includi
polyurethane foam mattress overlays, powered and no
powered therapeutic replacement mattresses and patie
positioning and seating products. Span-America markets
products to all health care settings, including acute ca
hospitals, long-term care facilities and home health ca
providers, primarily in North America. The compa
produces a variety of foam mattress overlays, includi
convoluted foam pads and its patented Geo-Matt overla
The Geo-Matt design includes numerous individual foa
cells that are cut to exacting tolerances on compute
controlled equipment to create a clinically effective mattre
surface. These products are designed to provide patien
with greater comfort and to assist in treating patients w
have or are susceptible to developing pressure ulce
Span-America's overlay products are mattress pads rath
than complete mattresses and are marketed as le
expensive alternatives to more complex replaceme
mattresses. The company's Geo-Mattress products a
single-density or multi-layered foam mattresses topped w
the same patented Geo-Matt surface used in its overlay
Span-America's more complex non-powered replaceme
mattresses consist of products from the PressureGua
series and combine a polyurethane foam shell and static a
cylinders. The company's specialty line of positioners is so
primarily under the trademark Span-Aids and consists
over 300 different foam items that aid in relieving the bas
patient positioning problems of elevation, immobilizatio
muscle contracture, foot drop and foot or leg rotatio
Seating products made specifically as an aid to wou
healing include the Isch-Dish and Sacral Dish pressure reli
cushions. Span-America also markets the Selan line of sk
care creams and lotions under a license agreement with
Noyes Company as well as custom bedding and foa
products and the Secure I.V. line of short peripher
intravenous safety catheters.

FINANCIALS: **Sales and profits are in thousands of dollars—add 000 to get the full amount. 2007 Note: Financial information for 2007 was not available for all companies at press time.**

2007 Sales: $	2007 Profits: $	**U.S. Stock Ticker: SPAN**
2006 Sales: $51,557	2006 Profits: $3,055	**Int'l Ticker:** Int'l Exchange:
2005 Sales: $48,439	2005 Profits: $2,439	Employees: 289
2004 Sales: $49,929	2004 Profits: $1,985	Fiscal Year Ends: 9/30
2003 Sales: $41,575	2003 Profits: $1,399	Parent Company:

SALARIES/BENEFITS:

Pension Plan:	ESOP Stock Plan:	Profit Sharing:	Top Exec. Salary: $244,512	Bonus: $77,457
Savings Plan: Y	Stock Purch. Plan:		Second Exec. Salary: $169,583	Bonus: $53,721

OTHER THOUGHTS:

Apparent Women Officers or Directors: 1
Hot Spot for Advancement for Women/Minorities:

LOCATIONS: ("Y" = Yes)

West:	Southwest:	Midwest:	Southeast:	Northeast:	International:
Y			Y	Y	

SPECIALTY LABORATORIES INC www.specialtylabs.com

dustry Group Code: 621511 **Ranks within this company's industry group:** Sales: Profits:

surance/HMO/PPO:		Drugs:		Equipment/Supplies:		Hospitals/Clinics:		Services:		Health Care:	
surance:		Manufacturer:		Manufacturer:		Acute Care:		Diagnostics:		Home Health:	
anaged Care:		Distributor:		Distributor:		Sub-Acute:		Labs/Testing:	Y	Long-Term Care:	
ilization Management:		Specialty Pharmacy:		Leasing/Finance:		Outpatient Surgery:		Staffing:		Physical Therapy:	
yment Processing:		Vitamins/Nutritionals:		Information Systems:		Physical Rehab. Ctr.:		Waste Disposal:		Physician Prac. Mgmt.:	
		Clinical Trials:				Psychiatric Clinics:		Specialty Svcs.:			

YPES OF BUSINESS:

inical Laboratory Tests
ssays

RANDS/DIVISIONS/AFFILIATES:

meriPath, Inc.
ataPassport
ataPassport MD

ONTACTS: *Note: Officers with more than one job title may be entionally listed here more than once.*

none: 661-799-6543	Fax: 661-799-6634
oll-Free: 800-421-7110	
ddress: 27027 Tourney Rd., Valencia, CA 91355 US	

GROWTH PLANS/SPECIAL FEATURES:

Specialty Laboratories, Inc. (SL), a subsidiary of AmeriPath, Inc., is a research-based clinical laboratory, predominantly focused on developing and performing esoteric clinical laboratory tests, referred to as assays. The firm offers a comprehensive menu of more than 2,500 assays, many of which it developed through internal research and development efforts and which are used to diagnose, evaluate and monitor patients in the areas of endocrinology; genetics; infectious diseases; neurology; pediatrics; urology; allergy and immunology; cardiology and coagulation; hepatology; microbiology; oncology; rheumatology; women's health; dermatopathology; gastroenterology; nephrology; pathology; and toxicology. Assays include procedures in the areas of molecular diagnostics, protein chemistry, cellular immunology and advanced microbiology. Commonly ordered assays include viral and bacterial detection and drug therapy monitoring assays; autoimmune panels; and complex cancer evaluations. In addition, SL owns proprietary information technology that accelerates and automates test ordering and results reporting with customers. Current information technology products include DataPassport client interface module, designed to take advantage of Internet-based technologies; and DataPassportMD, a web-based laboratory order entry and resulting system. The company's primary customers are hospitals, independent clinical laboratories and physicians.

The company offers its employees health and vision plans; a 401(k) plan; short- and long-term disability plans; a health and dependent care account; an employee assistance program; and an education reimbursement program.

FINANCIALS: **Sales and profits are in thousands of dollars—add 000 to get the full amount. 2007 Note: Financial information for 2007 vas not available for all companies at press time.**

07 Sales: $	2007 Profits: $	**U.S. Stock Ticker: Subsidiary**
06 Sales: $	2006 Profits: $	**Int'l Ticker:** Int'l Exchange:
05 Sales: $	2005 Profits: $	Employees: 689
04 Sales: $134,803	2004 Profits: $-12,950	Fiscal Year Ends: 12/31
03 Sales: $119,653	2003 Profits: $-6,361	Parent Company: AMERIPATH INC

ALARIES/BENEFITS:

ension Plan:	ESOP Stock Plan:	Profit Sharing:	Top Exec. Salary: $422,908	Bonus: $
avings Plan: Y	Stock Purch. Plan:		Second Exec. Salary: $262,000	Bonus: $

THER THOUGHTS:

pparent Women Officers or Directors: 3
ot Spot for Advancement for Women/Minorities: Y

LOCATIONS: ("Y" = Yes)

West:	Southwest:	Midwest:	Southeast:	Northeast:	International:
Y					

SPECTRANETICS CORP www.spectranetics.com

Industry Group Code: 339113 **Ranks within this company's industry group:** Sales: 87 Profits: 78

Insurance/HMO/PPO:		Drugs:		Equipment/Supplies:		Hospitals/Clinics:		Services:		Health Care:	
Insurance:		Manufacturer:		Manufacturer:	Y	Acute Care:		Diagnostics:		Home Health:	
Managed Care:		Distributor:		Distributor:		Sub-Acute:		Labs/Testing:		Long-Term Care:	
Utilization Management:		Specialty Pharmacy:		Leasing/Finance:		Outpatient Surgery:		Staffing:		Physical Therapy:	
Payment Processing:		Vitamins/Nutritionals:		Information Systems:		Physical Rehab. Ctr.:		Waste Disposal:		Physician Prac. Mgmt.:	
		Clinical Trials:				Psychiatric Clinics:		Specialty Svcs.:			

TYPES OF BUSINESS:

Equipment-Laser Systems
Coronary & Vascular Blockage Treatments

BRANDS/DIVISIONS/AFFILIATES:

LACI
CLiRpath 2.5 Turbo Catheter
CLeaRS
Spectranetics Laser Sheath
Lead Locking Device
FAMILI

CONTACTS: *Note: Officers with more than one job title may be intentionally listed here more than once.*

John G. Schulte, CEO
Jonathan (Will) McGuire, COO
John G. Schulte, Pres.
Guy A. Childs, CFO/VP
Stephen D. Okland, Jr., VP-Sales & Mktg.
Wade A. Bowe, VP-Catheter Dev.
Wade A. Bowe, VP-Catheter Mfg.
Lawrence E. Martel, Jr., VP-Oper.
Larry O. Adighije, VP-Bus. Dev. & Strategy
Donald Fletcher, VP-Quality Assurance & Regulatory Compliance
Kelly W. Elliot, VP-Clinical Affairs & Regulatory Submissions
Emile J. Geisenheimer, Chmn.
Shar Matin, VP/Managing Dir.-Spectranetics, BV

Phone: 719-633-8333	**Fax:** 719-633-8791
Toll-Free: 800-231-0978	
Address: 96 Talamine Ct., Colorado Springs, CO 80907-5186 US	

GROWTH PLANS/SPECIAL FEATURES:

Spectranetics Corp. mainly develops, manufactures, marke and distributes a proprietary excimer laser system that trea coronary and vascular conditions. Spectranetics has t only excimer laser system approved in the U.S., Canad Japan and Europe for use in multiple, minimally invasi cardiovascular procedures. The system includes a CVX-3 laser unit and disposable laser catheters for use with t laser. Its laser catheters contain hundreds of small diamete flexible fiber-optic strands that can access difficult to rea peripheral and coronary anatomy and produce even distributed laser energy at the tip of the catheter. Excim lasers deliver a relatively cool ultraviolet light in sho controlled energy pulses to ablate, or remove, tissue. T system is used in atherectomy procedures that open clogg or obstructed arteries, as well as to remove infecte defective or abandoned lead wires from patients w pacemakers or implantable cardiac defibrillators (ICD). currently has 623 installed laser systems, of which 488 a located in the U.S. Spectranetics recently received FD approval for the use of its Laser Angioplasty for Critical Lim Ischemia (LACI) system, designed to treat patients sufferi from total blockages in their leg arteries. In recent years, t firm began marketing the CLiRpath 2.5 Turbo Catheter f treatment of total occlusions of the superior femoral arte Approximately 94% of its 2006 worldwide revenue ca from disposable catheter sales, service and laser rental; 80 came from disposable catheter sales alone. It al manufactures the CLeaRS pacemaker or ICD lead remov product line, which includes the Spectranetics Laser Shea and Lead Locking Device. The company is engaged in t FDA-approved extended Flow in Acute Myocardial Infarcti after Laser Intervention (FAMILI) trial, a feasibility test aimi to rapidly restore blood flow in heart attack patients.

Spectranetics offers its employees bereavement leav flexible spending accounts and an employee assistan program.

FINANCIALS: **Sales and profits are in thousands of dollars—add 000 to get the full amount. 2007 Note: Financial information for 2007 was not available for all companies at press time.**

2007 Sales: $	2007 Profits: $	**U.S. Stock Ticker: SPNC**
2006 Sales: $63,490	2006 Profits: $-1,447	**Int'l Ticker:** Int'l Exchange:
2005 Sales: $43,212	2005 Profits: $1,038	Employees: 311
2004 Sales: $34,708	2004 Profits: $2,952	Fiscal Year Ends: 12/31
2003 Sales: $27,869	2003 Profits: $ 929	Parent Company:

SALARIES/BENEFITS:

Pension Plan:	ESOP Stock Plan:	Profit Sharing:	Top Exec. Salary: $355,192	Bonus: $242,034
Savings Plan: Y	Stock Purch. Plan: Y		Second Exec. Salary: $208,077	Bonus: $141,187

OTHER THOUGHTS:

Apparent Women Officers or Directors: 1
Hot Spot for Advancement for Women/Minorities:

LOCATIONS: ("Y" = Yes)

West:	Southwest:	Midwest:	Southeast:	Northeast:	International:
Y					Y

SPECTRUM HEALTH

www.spectrum-health.org

Industry Group Code: 622110 **Ranks within this company's industry group:** Sales: Profits:

Insurance/HMO/PPO:		Drugs:		Equipment/Supplies:		Hospitals/Clinics:		Services:		Health Care:	
Insurance:		Manufacturer:		Manufacturer:		Acute Care:	Y	Diagnostics:	Y	Home Health:	
Managed Care:	Y	Distributor:		Distributor:		Sub-Acute:	Y	Labs/Testing:	Y	Long-Term Care:	Y
Utilization Management:		Specialty Pharmacy:		Leasing/Finance:		Outpatient Surgery:	Y	Staffing:		Physical Therapy:	Y
Payment Processing:		Vitamins/Nutritionals:		Information Systems:		Physical Rehab. Ctr.:	Y	Waste Disposal:		Physician Prac. Mgmt.:	
		Clinical Trials:				Psychiatric Clinics:	Y	Specialty Svcs.:			

TYPES OF BUSINESS:

Hospitals-General
Trauma Center
Neonatal Center
Burn Center
Poison Center
HMO
Long-Term Care
Children's Hospital

BRANDS/DIVISIONS/AFFILIATES:

Renucci Hospitality House
DeVos Children's Hospital
Kent Community Campus
Priority Health
Spectrum Health Laboratory Outreach Services
Van Andel Institute

CONTACTS:

Note: Officers with more than one job title may be intentionally listed here more than once.

Richard C. Breon, CEO
Richard C. Breon, Pres.
Michael P. Freed, CFO/Exec. VP
Patrick O'Hare, CIO/Sr. VP
Bruce Rossman, Mgr.-Media Relations

Phone: 616-391-1774	**Fax:** 616-391-2780
Toll-Free: 866-989-7999	
Address: 100 Michigan St. NE, Grand Rapids, MI 49503 US	

GROWTH PLANS/SPECIAL FEATURES:

Spectrum Health's health system serves western Michigan with more than 140 service areas and a total of 2,000 beds, including a Level 1 trauma center, a neonatal center, a burn center, a poison center and the Renucci Hospitality House. The firm also operates seven acute care hospitals that provide diagnostic, outpatient, inpatient and emergency care, including the Helen DeVos Children's Hospital, the only children's hospital in west Michigan, and Kent Community Campus, which provides long-term care for patients recovering from major illnesses and complex medical conditions. In addition to Spectrum's primary care locations, the firm operates over 100 outpatient sites for diagnostics, treatment, imaging services, surgery, rehabilitation and laboratory services. Spectrum also operates a continuing care division with 307 beds that provides a complete continuum of specialized services for adults and seniors recovering from illness and complex medical conditions, including subacute care, long-term acute care, rehabilitation, outpatient, residential and home care, as well as specialized units for patients with brain or spinal cord injuries. Spectrum Health Laboratory Outreach Services, with 400 employees and 21 board-certified pathologists, provides CT Scanning, diagnostic imaging, an endoscopy center, forensic pathology, interventional radiology, mammography, MRI, neurodiagnostics, nuclear medicine, PET imaging, ultrasound, vascular imaging, X-Ray and fluoroscopy services. The company's operations also include Priority Health, an HMO which serves more than 470,000 members throughout Michigan. In recent news, Spectrum announced forming a $6 million joint venture with the Van Andel Institute to provide molecular technologies for investigating such diseases as cancer, heart disease and mental illness at the DNA, RNA and protein levels. In August 2007, Spectrum became one of the first to offer Birmingham Hip Resurfacing, an alternative to hip replacement.

FINANCIALS:

Sales and profits are in thousands of dollars—add 000 to get the full amount. 2007 Note: Financial information for 2007 was not available for all companies at press time.

2007 Sales: $	2007 Profits: $	**U.S. Stock Ticker: Nonprofit**
2006 Sales: $	2006 Profits: $	**Int'l Ticker:** Int'l Exchange:
2005 Sales: $1,931,899	2005 Profits: $73,425	Employees: 14,400
2004 Sales: $1,678,721	2004 Profits: $35,961	Fiscal Year Ends: 6/30
2003 Sales: $1,537,600	2003 Profits: $	Parent Company:

SALARIES/BENEFITS:

Pension Plan:	ESOP Stock Plan:	Profit Sharing:	Top Exec. Salary: $	Bonus: $
Savings Plan:	Stock Purch. Plan:		Second Exec. Salary: $	Bonus: $

OTHER THOUGHTS:

Apparent Women Officers or Directors:
Hot Spot for Advancement for Women/Minorities:

LOCATIONS: ("Y" = Yes)

West:	Southwest:	Midwest:	Southeast:	Northeast:	International:
		Y			

Note: Financial information, benefits and other data can change quickly and may vary from those stated here.

SRI/SURGICAL EXPRESS INC www.sterilerec.com

Industry Group Code: 339113 **Ranks within this company's industry group:** Sales: 79 Profits: 81

Insurance/HMO/PPO:		Drugs:		Equipment/Supplies:		Hospitals/Clinics:		Services:		Health Care:	
Insurance:		Manufacturer:		Manufacturer:		Acute Care:		Diagnostics:		Home Health:	
Managed Care:		Distributor:		Distributor:	Y	Sub-Acute:		Labs/Testing:		Long-Term Care:	
Utilization Management:		Specialty Pharmacy:		Leasing/Finance:		Outpatient Surgery:		Staffing:		Physical Therapy:	
Payment Processing:		Vitamins/Nutritionals:		Information Systems:		Physical Rehab. Ctr.:		Waste Disposal:		Physician Prac. Mgmt.:	
		Clinical Trials:				Psychiatric Clinics:		Specialty Svcs.:	Y		

TYPES OF BUSINESS:

Supplies-Surgery
Surgical Delivery Services

BRANDS/DIVISIONS/AFFILIATES:

CONTACTS:

Note: Officers with more than one job title may be intentionally listed here more than once.

Wallace D. Ruiz, CFO/Sr. VP
Jon McGuire, Sr. VP-Strategic Sourcing
Jack A. Hamilton, Sr. VP-Process Eng. & Quality Assurance
Charles W. Federico, Chmn.

Phone: 813-891-9550	**Fax:** 813-818-9076
Toll-Free:	
Address: 12425 Race Track Rd., Tampa, FL 33626 US	

GROWTH PLANS/SPECIAL FEATURES:

SRI Surgical Express, Inc. provides daily processing assembly and delivery of reusable and disposable products and instruments that hospital customers require for surgery. Reusable products include gowns; back table and Mayo stand covers; towels; procedure and patient drapes; and basin sets. The company provides daily delivery, retrieval, processing, inspection, assembly and sterilization of reusable textiles from ten processing service facilities located across the U.S. The firm also offers off-site and on-site instrument processing. This service provides customized surgical instrument sets on a per-procedure fee basis. SRI's integrated closed-loop process starts with daily delivery of reusable and disposable surgical supplies and instruments to the healthcare provider. At the same time, the company picks up the reusable textiles, basins and instruments used in surgery and returns them to the processing facility. Used products arriving at its processing facility are sorted, cleaned, inspected, packaged, sterilized and subsequently, shipped back to the healthcare providers. This service uses two of the most technologically advanced reusable textiles for gowns and drapes: a Gore surgical barrier fabric, which is breathable yet liquid-proof and provides a viral and bacterial barrier; and an advanced microfiber polyester surgical fabric which is liquid- and bacteria-resistant. The firm serves approximately 350 hospitals and care centers. In February 2006, SRI announced a multi-year exclusive agreement to distribute Owens & Minor's Implant Tracking System to the tissue banking industry. Using barcode technology, Owens & Minor's Implant Tracking System enables clinicians to track bone and tissue implants, monitor expiration dates on implants and rapidly identify implant recipients in case of recalls.

FINANCIALS:

Sales and profits are in thousands of dollars—add 000 to get the full amount. 2007 Note: Financial information for 2007 was not available for all companies at press time.

2007 Sales: $	2007 Profits: $	**U.S. Stock Ticker: STRC**
2006 Sales: $98,831	2006 Profits: $-1,953	**Int'l Ticker:** Int'l Exchange:
2005 Sales: $91,734	2005 Profits: $ 393	Employees: 808
2004 Sales: $91,310	2004 Profits: $-4,998	Fiscal Year Ends: 12/31
2003 Sales: $86,474	2003 Profits: $- 499	Parent Company:

SALARIES/BENEFITS:

Pension Plan:	ESOP Stock Plan:	Profit Sharing:	Top Exec. Salary: $350,000	Bonus: $29,868
Savings Plan:	Stock Purch. Plan:		Second Exec. Salary: $262,500	Bonus: $22,444

OTHER THOUGHTS:

Apparent Women Officers or Directors:
Hot Spot for Advancement for Women/Minorities:

LOCATIONS: ("Y" = Yes)

West:	Southwest:	Midwest:	Southeast:	Northeast:	International:
Y	Y	Y	Y	Y	

SSL INTERNATIONAL PLC

www.ssl-international.com

Industry Group Code: 339113 **Ranks within this company's industry group:** Sales: 33 Profits:

Insurance/HMO/PPO:		Drugs:		Equipment/Supplies:		Hospitals/Clinics:		Services:		Health Care:	
Insurance:		Manufacturer:	Y	Manufacturer:	Y	Acute Care:		Diagnostics:		Home Health:	
Managed Care:		Distributor:		Distributor:		Sub-Acute:		Labs/Testing:		Long-Term Care:	
Utilization Management:		Specialty Pharmacy:		Leasing/Finance:		Outpatient Surgery:		Staffing:		Physical Therapy:	
Payment Processing:		Vitamins/Nutritionals:		Information Systems:		Physical Rehab. Ctr.:		Waste Disposal:		Physician Prac. Mgmt.:	
		Clinical Trials:				Psychiatric Clinics:		Specialty Svcs.:			

TYPES OF BUSINESS:

Health Care Products
Condoms
Footcare Products
Oral Analgesics
Cough Medicine
Mother & Baby Products

BRANDS/DIVISIONS/AFFILIATES:

Durex
Scholl
Syndol
Meltus
Sauber
Mister Baby
Schering-Plough Corp
Qingdao London Durex Co Ltd

CONTACTS:

Note: Officers with more than one job title may be intentionally listed here more than once.

Gary Watts, CEO
Antony Mannion, Sec.
Jan Young, Head-Comm.
Mark Moran, Group Dir.-Finance
Paul Doherty, Head-Corp. Affairs
Gerald Corbett, Chmn.
Ian Adamson, Managing Dir.-Europe
Mike Pilkington, Group Dir.-Supply Chain

Phone: 44-20-7367-5760 **Fax:** 44-20-7367-5790
Toll-Free:
Address: 35 New Bridge St., London, EC4V 6BW UK

GROWTH PLANS/SPECIAL FEATURES:

SSL International plc manufactures and distributes health care products under the Durex, Scholl, Syndol, Meltus, Sauber, Full Marks and Mister Baby brands. The firm sells its products in more than 130 countries and has manufacturing operations in Thailand, Spain and the U.K., as well as joint-venture manufacturing in India and China. The Durex brand comprises a range of condoms, lubricants and sensual massagers. Durex condoms have approximately 30% market share worldwide. The Scholl brand offers both foot care and footwear worldwide and includes products for blisters and corns, foot odor and aching feet, as well as exfoliating and moisturizing foot skincare products; footwear represents approximately 45% of this brands revenues. It is provided through a licensing agreement with Dr. Scholl's copyright owners, Schering-Plough HealthCare Products, Inc. Under the terms of the agreement, new products developed by either party will be available for sale through the other party. Syndol is the U.K.'s fastest-growing adult oral analgesic (pain reliever) that is also effective at relieving muscle tension. Meltus offers both child- and adult-strength cough medicine and has recently been reintroduced to the U.K. market. Sauber makes and markets compression hosiery and women's deodorant products for southern European markets. Mister Baby offers a range of mother and baby products, such as bottles and toys, also sold in southern Europe. The firm has recently sold several of its subsidiaries, including its medical and industrial gloves division; Silipos, which consisted of gel-based products for prosthetic, orthopedic and skin care applications; and the Regent Infection Control business. SSL also recently expanded the Durex family of products with Durex Play and Durex Tingle lubricants. In 2006, SSL announced plans to gain sole control over its joint venture, Qingdao London Durex Co Ltd, by purchasing the remaining shares in the company from Qingdao Double Butterfly Group Company Limited.

FINANCIALS:

Sales and profits are in thousands of dollars—add 000 to get the full amount. 2007 Note: Financial information for 2007 was not available for all companies at press time.

2007 Sales: $	2007 Profits: $	**U.S. Stock Ticker: SLSLF**
2006 Sales: $783,800	2006 Profits: $	**Int'l Ticker: SSL** Int'l Exchange: London-LSE
2005 Sales: $546,890	2005 Profits: $23,005	Employees: 4,780
2004 Sales: $982,800	2004 Profits: $-14,600	Fiscal Year Ends: 3/31
2003 Sales: $982,000	2003 Profits: $39,000	Parent Company:

SALARIES/BENEFITS:

Pension Plan:	ESOP Stock Plan:	Profit Sharing:	Top Exec. Salary: $	Bonus: $
Savings Plan:	Stock Purch. Plan:		Second Exec. Salary: $	Bonus: $

OTHER THOUGHTS:

Apparent Women Officers or Directors:
Hot Spot for Advancement for Women/Minorities:

LOCATIONS: ("Y" = Yes)

West:	Southwest:	Midwest:	Southeast:	Northeast:	International:
			Y		Y

Note: Financial information, benefits and other data can change quickly and may vary from those stated here.

SSM HEALTH CARE SYSTEM INC www.ssmhc.com

Industry Group Code: 622110 **Ranks within this company's industry group:** Sales: Profits:

Insurance/HMO/PPO:		Drugs:		Equipment/Supplies:		Hospitals/Clinics:		Services:		Health Care:	
Insurance:		Manufacturer:		Manufacturer:		Acute Care:	Y	Diagnostics:		Home Health:	Y
Managed Care:	Y	Distributor:		Distributor:		Sub-Acute:	Y	Labs/Testing:		Long-Term Care:	Y
Utilization Management:		Specialty Pharmacy:		Leasing/Finance:		Outpatient Surgery:		Staffing:		Physical Therapy:	
Payment Processing:		Vitamins/Nutritionals:		Information Systems:		Physical Rehab. Ctr.:	Y	Waste Disposal:		Physician Prac. Mgmt.:	
		Clinical Trials:				Psychiatric Clinics:		Specialty Svcs.:			

TYPES OF BUSINESS:

Hospitals-General
Nursing Homes
HMO
Hospice Services

BRANDS/DIVISIONS/AFFILIATES:

Franciscan Sisters of Mary
Premier Medical Insurance Group, Inc.
First Physicians Medical Group
Jefferson City Medical Group
SSM DePaul Medical Group
SSM Medical Group
SSM St. Charles Medical Group
Crossroads Regional Medical Center

CONTACTS: *Note: Officers with more than one job title may be intentionally listed here more than once.*

Mary Jean Ryan, CEO
William C. Schoenhard, COO/Exec. VP
Mary Jean Ryan, Pres.
Steven M. Barney, Sr. VP-Human Resources
Thomas K. Langston, CIO/VP
William P. Thomson, VP-Strategy
Suzy Farren, VP-Corp. Comm.
Kris A. Zimmer, Sr. VP-Finance
Dixie L. Platt, Sr. VP-Mission & External Rel.
James Sanger, Regional Pres.
Mary Stamonn-Harrison, Regional Pres.
Ronald L. Levy, Regional Pres.

Phone: 314-994-7800	**Fax:** 314-994-7900
Toll-Free:	
Address: 477 N. Lindbergh Blvd., St. Louis, MO 63141 US	

GROWTH PLANS/SPECIAL FEATURES:

SSM Health Care (SSMHC), sponsored by the Francisca Sisters of Mary, is one of the largest Catholic health system in the country. The firm owns, manages and is affiliated wit 20 acute care hospitals and three nursing homes in Missour Illinois, Wisconsin and Oklahoma, with more than 5,00 physicians and 24,000 employees providing a range c services from rehabilitation, pediatrics and home health t hospice, residential and skilled nursing care. The company' health related businesses include information and suppo services such as materials management and home care SSMHC also owns an interest in Premier Medical Insuranc Group, Inc., one of Wisconsin's largest health maintenanc organizations. Five medical groups are associated with th company: First Physicians, Jefferson City, SSM DePau SSM Medical and SSM St. Charles Clinic. SSMHC has bee active for more than 125 years, beginning in 1877 when fiv Catholic nuns fleeing religious persecution in German settled in St. Louis, Missouri in the midst of a smallpo epidemic and established a community hospital.

FINANCIALS: **Sales and profits are in thousands of dollars—add 000 to get the full amount. 2007 Note: Financial information for 2007 was not available for all companies at press time.**

2007 Sales: $	2007 Profits: $	**U.S. Stock Ticker: Nonprofit**
2006 Sales: $	2006 Profits: $	**Int'l Ticker:** Int'l Exchange:
2005 Sales: $	2005 Profits: $	Employees: 23,300
2004 Sales: $2,126,529	2004 Profits: $69,641	Fiscal Year Ends: 12/31
2003 Sales: $1,990,020	2003 Profits: $69,475	Parent Company:

SALARIES/BENEFITS:

Pension Plan:	ESOP Stock Plan:	Profit Sharing:	Top Exec. Salary: $	Bonus: $
Savings Plan:	Stock Purch. Plan:		Second Exec. Salary: $	Bonus: $

OTHER THOUGHTS:

Apparent Women Officers or Directors: 4
Hot Spot for Advancement for Women/Minorities: Y

LOCATIONS: ("Y" = Yes)

West:	Southwest:	Midwest:	Southeast:	Northeast:	International:
		Y	Y		

ST JUDE CHILDRENS RESEARCH HOSPITAL www.stjude.org

ıdustry Group Code: 622110 **Ranks within this company's industry group:** Sales: Profits:

ısurance/HMO/PPO:		**Drugs:**		**Equipment/Supplies:**		**Hospitals/Clinics:**		**Services:**		**Health Care:**	
ısurance:		Manufacturer:		Manufacturer:		Acute Care:	Y	Diagnostics:		Home Health:	
ıanaged Care:		Distributor:		Distributor:		Sub-Acute:		Labs/Testing:		Long-Term Care:	
ıtilization Management:		Specialty Pharmacy:		Leasing/Finance:		Outpatient Surgery:		Staffing:		Physical Therapy:	
ıayment Processing:		Vitamins/Nutritionals:		Information Systems:		Physical Rehab. Ctr.:		Waste Disposal:		Physician Prac. Mgmt.:	
		Clinical Trials:				Psychiatric Clinics:		Specialty Svcs.:	Y		

TYPES OF BUSINESS:

ıediatric Care
ıediatric Cancer Research & Treatment

BRANDS/DIVISIONS/AFFILIATES:

ıLSAC
ıure4Kids
ınternational Outreach Program

CONTACTS: *Note: Officers with more than one job title may be intentionally listed here more than once.*

ıVilliam E. Evans, CEO
ıohn Nash, COO
ıichael Canarios, CFO
ıames Downing, Scientific Dir.

Phone: 901-495-3300	**Fax:** 901-495-4011
Toll-Free: 800-822-6344	
Address: 332 N. Lauderdale, Memphis, TN 38105 US	

GROWTH PLANS/SPECIAL FEATURES:

St. Jude Children's Research Hospital, located in Memphis, Tennessee, is one of the world's premier centers for research and treatment of pediatric cancers and other catastrophic diseases. St. Jude's fundraising arm, ALSAC (American Lebanese Syrian Associated Charities) is also a leading health care charity in the country. ALSAC covers the cost of treatment not covered by insurance and all costs of treatment for those who have no insurance, including lodging, travel and food. Founded in 1962 by entertainer Danny Thomas, St. Jude currently sees about 4,900 patients yearly from across the U.S. and from more than 70 countries. St. Jude has also developed groundbreaking treatments that have dramatically increased survival rates for brain tumors, solid tumors, Hodgkin disease, non-Hodgkin lymphoma and many other catastrophic diseases. The hospital pioneered a treatment for acute lymphoblastic leukemia, the most common form of childhood leukemia, dramatically raising the cure rate from 4% in 1962 to over 90% today. Current research at the hospital is focused on work in bone-marrow transplantation, gene therapy, biochemistry of cancerous cells, radiation treatment, blood diseases, hereditary diseases and the psychological effects of catastrophic illness. St. Jude operates the International Outreach Program, a program that provides developing countries with the resources and technology to better treat catastrophic childhood diseases. The hospital also maintains Cure4Kids, a medical education and collaboration web site for doctors, scientists and health care workers who treat children with such diseases. In 2007, the hospital announced a partnership with Rady Children's Hospital in San Diego and the University of California, San Diego.

St. Jude offers a wide range of employee benefits including tuition reimbursement, flexible spending accounts, an on-site credit union and free shuttle service. In addition, the hospital offers internship and work programs for students preparing for careers in health care, social work or pastoral care.

FINANCIALS: **Sales and profits are in thousands of dollars—add 000 to get the full amount. 2007 Note: Financial information for 2007 was not available for all companies at press time.**

2007 Sales: $	2007 Profits: $	**U.S. Stock Ticker: Nonprofit**
2006 Sales: $	2006 Profits: $	**Int'l Ticker:** Int'l Exchange:
2005 Sales: $	2005 Profits: $	Employees: 2,500
2004 Sales: $640,516	2004 Profits: $	Fiscal Year Ends: 6/30
2003 Sales: $450,835	2003 Profits: $17,900	Parent Company:

SALARIES/BENEFITS:

Pension Plan: Y	ESOP Stock Plan:	Profit Sharing:	Top Exec. Salary: $	Bonus: $
Savings Plan:	Stock Purch. Plan:		Second Exec. Salary: $	Bonus: $

OTHER THOUGHTS:

Apparent Women Officers or Directors: 9
Hot Spot for Advancement for Women/Minorities: Y

LOCATIONS: ("Y" = Yes)

West:	Southwest:	Midwest:	Southeast:	Northeast:	International:
			Y		

Note: Financial information, benefits and other data can change quickly and may vary from those stated here.

ST JUDE MEDICAL INC

www.sjm.com

Industry Group Code: 339113 **Ranks within this company's industry group:** Sales: 11 Profits: 9

Insurance/HMO/PPO:		Drugs:		Equipment/Supplies:		Hospitals/Clinics:		Services:		Health Care:	
Insurance:		Manufacturer:		Manufacturer:	Y	Acute Care:		Diagnostics:		Home Health:	
Managed Care:		Distributor:		Distributor:	Y	Sub-Acute:		Labs/Testing:		Long-Term Care:	
Utilization Management:		Specialty Pharmacy:		Leasing/Finance:		Outpatient Surgery:		Staffing:		Physical Therapy:	
Payment Processing:		Vitamins/Nutritionals:		Information Systems:		Physical Rehab. Ctr.:		Waste Disposal:		Physician Prac. Mgmt.:	
		Clinical Trials:	Y			Psychiatric Clinics:		Specialty Svcs.:	Y		

TYPES OF BUSINESS:

Cardiovascular Medical Devices
Cardiac Rhythm Management Devices
Cardiac Surgery Devices
Cardiology Devices
Atrial Fibrillation Devices

BRANDS/DIVISIONS/AFFILIATES:

Atlas II ICD
Atlas II HF CRT-D

CONTACTS: *Note: Officers with more than one job title may be intentionally listed here more than once.*

Daniel J. Starks, CEO
Daniel J. Starks, Pres.
John C. Heinmiller, CFO/Exec. VP
Paul Bae, VP-Human Resources
William J. McGarry, CIO/VP-IT
Thomas R. Northenscold, VP-Admin.
Pamela S. Krop, General Counsel/VP/Sec.
Angela D. Craig, VP-Corp. Rel.
Mark D. Carlson, Chief Medical Officer/Sr. VP-Clinical Affairs
Christopher G. Chavez, Pres., Neuromodulation Division
Eric S. Fain, Pres., Cardiac Rhythm Mgmt. Division
George J. Fazio, Pres., Cardiovascular Division
Daniel J. Starks, Chmn.
Denis M. Gestin, Pres., SJM Europe

Phone: 651-483-2000	**Fax:** 651-482-8318
Toll-Free: 800-328-9634	
Address: 1 Lillehei Plaza, St. Paul, MN 55117 US	

GROWTH PLANS/SPECIAL FEATURES:

St. Jude Medical, Inc. develops, manufactures an distributes cardiovascular medical devices for global cardia rhythm management, cardiac surgery, cardiology and atri fibrillation therapy and implantable neuromodulation device for the management of chronic pain. The company operate in four segments: cardiac rhythm management, whos products include tachycardia implantable cardiovert defribrillator systems and bradycardia pacemaker system cardiovascular, whose products include vascular closur devices, guidewires, hemostasis introducers, mechanic and tissue heart valves and valve repair product neuromodulation, whose products include neurostimulatio devices; and atrial fibrillation, whose products includ electrophysiology introducers and catheters, advance cardiac mapping and navigation systems and ablatio systems. St. Jude's Neuromodulation Division focuses it efforts on the related therapy areas. Neuromodulation is th delivery of very small, precise doses of electric current c drugs directly to nerve sites and is aimed at treating patien suffering from chronic pain or other disabling nervous syster disorders. The firm markets and sells its products through direct sales force and independent distributors. The principa geographic markets for its products are the U.S., Europe an Japan. St. Jude also sells products in Canada, Lati America, Australia, New Zealand and the Asia-Pacific regior The cardiac rhythm management products generate roughly 62% of revenue in 2006. In July 2006, St. Jud announced it had received FDA approval for two device intended for the treatment of patients with potentially leth heart arrhythmias and heart failure, Atlas II ICD (implantabl cardioverter defibrillator) and Atlas II HF CRT-D (cardia resynchronization therapy defibrillator).

The company offers its employees medical, dental and visio insurance; flexible spending accounts; a 401(k) plan; a employee stock purchase plan; discretionary profit sharing access to a credit union; disability insurance; life insurance; physical fitness program; a matching gift program; and tuitio reimbursement.

FINANCIALS: **Sales and profits are in thousands of dollars—add 000 to get the full amount. 2007 Note: Financial information for 2007 was not available for all companies at press time.**

2007 Sales: $	2007 Profits: $	**U.S. Stock Ticker: STJ**
2006 Sales: $3,302,447	2006 Profits: $548,251	**Int'l Ticker:** Int'l Exchange:
2005 Sales: $2,915,280	2005 Profits: $393,490	Employees: 11,000
2004 Sales: $2,294,173	2004 Profits: $409,934	Fiscal Year Ends: 12/31
2003 Sales: $1,932,500	2003 Profits: $339,400	Parent Company:

SALARIES/BENEFITS:

Pension Plan:	ESOP Stock Plan:	Profit Sharing: Y	Top Exec. Salary: $975,000	Bonus: $1,009,125
Savings Plan: Y	Stock Purch. Plan: Y		Second Exec. Salary: $580,000	Bonus: $500,250

OTHER THOUGHTS:

Apparent Women Officers or Directors: 4
Hot Spot for Advancement for Women/Minorities: Y

LOCATIONS: ("Y" = Yes)

West:	Southwest:	Midwest:	Southeast:	Northeast:	International:
Y	Y	Y	Y	Y	Y

STAAR SURGICAL CO www.staar.com

ndustry Group Code: 339113 **Ranks within this company's industry group:** Sales: 89 Profits: 90

Insurance/HMO/PPO:		Drugs:		Equipment/Supplies:		Hospitals/Clinics:		Services:		Health Care:	
nsurance:		Manufacturer:		Manufacturer:	Y	Acute Care:		Diagnostics:		Home Health:	
Managed Care:		Distributor:		Distributor:		Sub-Acute:		Labs/Testing:		Long-Term Care:	
Utilization Management:		Specialty Pharmacy:		Leasing/Finance:		Outpatient Surgery:		Staffing:		Physical Therapy:	
Payment Processing:		Vitamins/Nutritionals:		Information Systems:		Physical Rehab. Ctr.:		Waste Disposal:		Physician Prac. Mgmt.:	
		Clinical Trials:				Psychiatric Clinics:		Specialty Svcs.:			

TYPES OF BUSINESS:

Equipment-Ophthalmic Surgery
ntraocular Lenses

BRANDS/DIVISIONS/AFFILIATES:

Collamer
Visian ICL
Visian Toric ICL
Canon Staar
Preloaded Injector
SonicWAVE Phacoemulsification System
Cruise Control
AquaFlow

CONTACTS: *Note: Officers with more than one job title may be intentionally listed here more than once.*

David Bailey, CEO
David Bailey, Pres.
Deborah Andrews, CFO/VP
Nick Curtis, Sr. VP-Sales
Craig Felberg, VP-R&D and Clinical
Charles S. Kaufman, General Counsel/VP/Corp. Sec.
Paul Hambrick, VP-Oper.
Guenther Roepstorff, Pres., Domilens GmbH
Rob Lally, VP-Quality Assurance & Regulatory Affairs
Robin Hughes, VP-Mktg.
Don M. Bailey, Chmn.

Phone: 626-303-7902	**Fax:** 626-359-8402
Toll-Free:	
Address: 1911 Walker Ave., Monrovia, CA 91016 US	

GROWTH PLANS/SPECIAL FEATURES:

STAAR Surgical Co. develops, produces and markets medical devices used by ophthalmologists and other eye care professionals to improve or correct vision in patients with refractive conditions, cataracts and glaucoma. The company's main product is a line of both one-piece and three-piece foldable silicone and Collamer intraocular lenses (IOLs), used after cataract extraction. The lens is folded and implanted into the eye behind the iris and in front of the natural lens using minimally invasive techniques. This procedure is performed with topical anesthesia on an outpatient basis, with visual recovery within one to 24 hours. It has developed two implantable Collamer lenses (ICLs), the Visian ICL and Visian Toric ICL, to treat astigmatic abnormalities, myopia (near-sightedness) and hypermyopia (far-sightedness). These products are sold in more than 40 countries. Through its Japanese joint venture company, Canon Staar, the firm has released the Preloaded Injector system for deploying intraocular lenses in the eye in international markets, although the Preloaded Injector is still awaiting approval in the U.S. Sales of IOLs accounted for approximately 46% of STAAR's 2006 revenues, while ICLs accounted for 22%. The SonicWAVE Phacoemulsification System is an alternative to surgery, using ultrasound for cataract removal. Its Cruise Control filter enables faster, cleaner phacoemulsification procedures. STAARVISC II is a viscoelastic material that maintains the shape of the eye during surgery. AquaFlow is collagen glaucoma drainage device. Sales of these other cataract products accounted for 31% of 2006 sales. These products are designed to improve patient outcomes, minimize patient risk and discomfort and simplify ophthalmic procedures and post-operative care. Products are sold worldwide, primarily to ophthalmologists, surgical centers, hospitals, managed care providers, health maintenance organizations and group purchasing organizations.

The company offers medical, dental, life, long-term disability and vision insurance and paid vacations.

FINANCIALS: **Sales and profits are in thousands of dollars—add 000 to get the full amount. 2007 Note: Financial information for 2007 was not available for all companies at press time.**

2007 Sales: $	2007 Profits: $	**U.S. Stock Ticker: STAA**
2006 Sales: $56,282	2006 Profits: $-15,044	**Int'l Ticker:** Int'l Exchange:
2005 Sales: $51,303	2005 Profits: $-11,175	Employees: 284
2004 Sales: $51,685	2004 Profits: $-11,332	Fiscal Year Ends: 12/31
2003 Sales: $50,458	2003 Profits: $-8,357	Parent Company:

SALARIES/BENEFITS:

Pension Plan:	ESOP Stock Plan:	Profit Sharing:	Top Exec. Salary: $400,583	Bonus: $80,000
Savings Plan: Y	Stock Purch. Plan:		Second Exec. Salary: $366,824	Bonus: $101,740

OTHER THOUGHTS:

Apparent Women Officers or Directors: 1
Hot Spot for Advancement for Women/Minorities:

LOCATIONS: ("Y" = Yes)

West:	Southwest:	Midwest:	Southeast:	Northeast:	International:
Y					Y

Note: Financial information, benefits and other data can change quickly and may vary from those stated here.

STERICYCLE INC

www.stericycle.com

Industry Group Code: 562000 **Ranks within this company's industry group:** Sales: 1 Profits: 1

Insurance/HMO/PPO:		Drugs:		Equipment/Supplies:		Hospitals/Clinics:		Services:		Health Care:	
Insurance:		Manufacturer:		Manufacturer:		Acute Care:		Diagnostics:		Home Health:	
Managed Care:		Distributor:		Distributor:		Sub-Acute:		Labs/Testing:		Long-Term Care:	
Utilization Management:		Specialty Pharmacy:		Leasing/Finance:		Outpatient Surgery:		Staffing:		Physical Therapy:	
Payment Processing:		Vitamins/Nutritionals:		Information Systems:		Physical Rehab. Ctr.:		Waste Disposal:	Y	Physician Prac. Mgmt.:	
		Clinical Trials:				Psychiatric Clinics:		Specialty Svcs.:			

TYPES OF BUSINESS:

Medical Waste Treatment

BRANDS/DIVISIONS/AFFILIATES:

Sterile Technologies Group
Direct Return
Steri-Safe
Steri-Tub
Bio Systems
Sterile Technologies, Ltd.

CONTACTS: *Note: Officers with more than one job title may be intentionally listed here more than once.*

Mark C. Miller, CEO
Richard T. Kogler, COO/Exec. VP
Mark C. Miller, Pres.
Frank ten Brink, CFO/Exec. VP
Frank ten Brink, Chief Admin. Officer
Richard L. Foss, Exec. VP-Corp. Dev.
Michael J. Collins, Pres., Return Management Svcs.
Shan Sacranie, Exec. VP-Int'l

Phone: 847-367-5910 **Fax:** 847-367-9493
Toll-Free: 800-643-0240
Address: 28161 N. Keith Dr., Lake Forest, IL 60045 US

GROWTH PLANS/SPECIAL FEATURES:

Stericycle, Inc. specializes in managing medical waste b helping the healthcare industry comply with a series c Federal regulations, most prominently, the Medical Wast Tracking Act of 1988. Through its national networks of 7 processing or combined processing and collection sites an 104 additional transfer sites, the firm is able to serve th United States, Canada, Mexico, Argentina, the Unite Kingdom and Ireland. In order to dispose of medical waste Stericycle utilizes various technologies, includin autoclaving, an electro-thermal-deactivation system (ETD) chemical treatment and incineration. While Stericycle' customers are mainly hospitals, clinics, acute care facilitie and dental offices, it also serves pharmacies an manufacturer of pharmaceuticals in dealing with expired o surplus products. The company generally provides it customers with its own waste containers, such as the plasti Steri-Tub and Bio Systems containers, to avoid needle stick and leakages; then it scans all containers on arrival a treatment facilities to detect radioactive materials. Afte treatment, the residual ash is passed on to a third-part landfill and the containers are returned to customers Stericycle utilizes its own branded methodologies, whic include Steri-Safe, a compliance program designed t familiarize clients with regulatory policy; and Direct Return, a pharmaceutical returns and product recall managemen service under the Stericycle Pharmaceutical Services unit The company serves approximately 351,700 customer worldwide, of which approximately 8,600 are large-quantit generators, such as hospitals, blood banks an pharmaceutical manufacturers, and approximately 343,10 are small-quantity generators, such as outpatient clinics medical and dental offices, long-term and sub-acute car facilities and retail pharmacies. In 2006, Stericycle acquire 16 new waste disposal centers, including the Ireland an U.K.-based Sterile Technologies, Ltd., which sold fo approximately $131 million.

The company offers its employees medical, dental and visio insurance; flexible spending accounts; an employe assistance program; and a tuition reimbursement program.

FINANCIALS: **Sales and profits are in thousands of dollars—add 000 to get the full amount. 2007 Note: Financial information for 2007 was not available for all companies at press time.**

2007 Sales: $
2006 Sales: $789,637
2005 Sales: $609,457
2004 Sales: $516,228
2003 Sales: $

2007 Profits: $
2006 Profits: $105,270
2005 Profits: $67,154
2004 Profits: $78,178
2003 Profits: $

U.S. Stock Ticker: SRCL
Int'l Ticker: Int'l Exchange:
Employees: 5,254
Fiscal Year Ends: 12/31
Parent Company:

SALARIES/BENEFITS:

Pension Plan: ESOP Stock Plan: Profit Sharing: Top Exec. Salary: $297,052 Bonus: $512,415
Savings Plan: Y Stock Purch. Plan: Y Second Exec. Salary: $222,789 Bonus: $217,219

OTHER THOUGHTS:

Apparent Women Officers or Directors:
Hot Spot for Advancement for Women/Minorities:

LOCATIONS: ("Y" = Yes)

West:	Southwest:	Midwest:	Southeast:	Northeast:	International:
Y	Y	Y	Y	Y	Y

STERIS CORP

www.steris.com

ndustry Group Code: 339113 **Ranks within this company's industry group:** Sales: 26 Profits: 28

ısurance/HMO/PPO:		**Drugs:**		**Equipment/Supplies:**		**Hospitals/Clinics:**		**Services:**		**Health Care:**	
ısurance:		Manufacturer:		Manufacturer:	Y	Acute Care:		Diagnostics:		Home Health:	
Ianaged Care:		Distributor:		Distributor:		Sub-Acute:		Labs/Testing:		Long-Term Care:	
tilization Management:		Specialty Pharmacy:		Leasing/Finance:		Outpatient Surgery:		Staffing:		Physical Therapy:	
ayment Processing:		Vitamins/Nutritionals:		Information Systems:		Physical Rehab. Ctr.:		Waste Disposal:		Physician Prac. Mgmt.:	
		Clinical Trials:				Psychiatric Clinics:		Specialty Svcs.:	Y		

TYPES OF BUSINESS:

ıealthcare Products & Related Services
ife Sciences Products
;terilization Services

BRANDS/DIVISIONS/AFFILIATES:

STERIS Isomedix Services
STERIS SYSTEM 1
Finn-Aqua
Amsco
Reliance
Basil
Detach
Lyovac

CONTACTS: *Note: Officers with more than one job title may be intentionally listed here more than once.*

Walter M. Rosebrough Jr., CEO
Walter M. Rosebrough Jr., Pres.
Peter A. Burke, CTO/Sr. VP
Mark D. McGinley, General Counsel/Sr. VP/Sec.
Timothy L. Chapman, Sr. VP-Bus. Strategy
William L. Aamoth, Corp. Treas.
Charles L. Immel, Sr. VP/Pres., Healthcare
Robert E. Moss, Sr. VP/Pres., Steris Isomedix Svcs.
Gerald J. Reis, Sr. VP/Pres., Life Sciences
Patrick J. McCullagh, VP-Global Quality Systems Eng. &Regulatory Affairs
John P. Wareham, Chmn.

Phone: 440-354-2600	**Fax:** 440-392-8972
Toll-Free: 800-548-4873	
Address: 5960 Heisley Rd., Mentor, OH 44060 US	

GROWTH PLANS/SPECIAL FEATURES:

Steris Corp. is a provider of infection prevention and surgical products and services, focused primarily on the critical markets of healthcare, pharmaceutical and research. The company offers capital products such as sterilizers and surgical tables; consumable products such as detergents and skin care products; and services, including equipment installation and maintenance, as well as the bulk sterilization of single-use medical devices. The firm operates in three segments: healthcare, life sciences and STERIS Isomedix Services. The healthcare segment, which accounted for about 71% of 2007 revenues, manufactures and sells capital equipment and accessories used in surgical and critical environments; emergency departments; gastrointestinal and sterile processing environments; and in infection control processes. This segment also provides various equipment maintenance programs and repair services to support effective operation of health care equipment. The health care segment includes products such as the company's STERIS SYSTEM 1, a complete system for sterile processing at or near the site of patient care. The life sciences segment, responsible for roughly 18% of 2007 revenue, manufactures and sells capital equipment, cleaning chemistries and service solutions to global pharmaceutical companies; private and public research facilities; government; military; industrial; transportation; and food and beverage customers. Systems and products offered include brand names such as Finn-Aqua and Amsco sterilizers; Reliance and Basil washers; Detach automated cage and bedding processing systems; Vaporized Hydrogen Peroxide (VHP) bio-decontamination systems; and Lyovac freeze dryers; as well as consumable products for contamination prevention, surface cleaning and sterility assurance. STERIS Isomedix Services, which contributed about 11% of 2007 revenue, performs sterilization services on a contract basis through 21 facilities in North America, where the company sterilizes medical devices and other products in bulk prior to their delivery to the end user.

FINANCIALS: **Sales and profits are in thousands of dollars—add 000 to get the full amount. 2007 Note: Financial information for 2007 was not available for all companies at press time.**

2007 Sales: $1,197,407	2007 Profits: $82,155	**U.S. Stock Ticker: STE**
2006 Sales: $1,160,285	2006 Profits: $70,289	**Int'l Ticker:** Int'l Exchange:
2005 Sales: $1,081,674	2005 Profits: $85,980	Employees: 5,100
2004 Sales: $1,031,908	2004 Profits: $94,243	Fiscal Year Ends: 3/31
2003 Sales: $972,100	2003 Profits: $79,400	Parent Company:

SALARIES/BENEFITS:

Pension Plan:	ESOP Stock Plan:	Profit Sharing:	Top Exec. Salary: $722,843	Bonus: $443,586
Savings Plan:	Stock Purch. Plan:		Second Exec. Salary: $308,449	Bonus: $107,500

OTHER THOUGHTS:

Apparent Women Officers or Directors:
Hot Spot for Advancement for Women/Minorities:

LOCATIONS: ("Y" = Yes)

West:	Southwest:	Midwest:	Southeast:	Northeast:	International:
Y	Y	Y	Y	Y	Y

Note: Financial information, benefits and other data can change quickly and may vary from those stated here.

STRYKER CORP

www.stryker.com

Industry Group Code: 339113 **Ranks within this company's industry group:** Sales: 8 Profits: 6

Insurance/HMO/PPO:		Drugs:		Equipment/Supplies:		Hospitals/Clinics:		Services:		Health Care:	
Insurance:		Manufacturer:		Manufacturer:	Y	Acute Care:		Diagnostics:		Home Health:	
Managed Care:		Distributor:		Distributor:		Sub-Acute:		Labs/Testing:		Long-Term Care:	
Utilization Management:		Specialty Pharmacy:		Leasing/Finance:		Outpatient Surgery:		Staffing:		Physical Therapy:	
Payment Processing:		Vitamins/Nutritionals:		Information Systems:	Y	Physical Rehab. Ctr.:		Waste Disposal:		Physician Prac. Mgmt.:	
		Clinical Trials:				Psychiatric Clinics:		Specialty Svcs.:			

TYPES OF BUSINESS:

Equipment-Orthopedic Implants
Powered Surgical Instruments
Endoscopic Systems
Patient Care & Handling Equipment
Outpatient Physical Therapy Services
Imaging Software

BRANDS/DIVISIONS/AFFILIATES:

Stryker Orthopaedics
Stryker Trauma
Stryker Spine
Stryker Leibinger Micro Implants
Stryker Biotech
Stryker Instruments
eTrauma
Sightline Technologies

CONTACTS: *Note: Officers with more than one job title may be intentionally listed here more than once.*

Stephen (Steve) MacMillan, CEO
Stephen (Steve) MacMillan, Pres.
Dean H. Bergy, CFO/VP
Michael W. Rude, VP-Human Resources
Curtis E. Hall, General Counsel/VP
Bryant S. Zanko, VP-Bus. Dev.
J. Patrick Anderson, VP-Corp. Affairs
Katherine A. Owen, VP-Investor Rel. & Strategy
James B. Praeger, Controller
James E. Kemler, VP/Group Pres., Biotech/Spine/Osteosynthesis/Dev.
Stephen S. Johnson, VP/Group Pres., MedSurg
James R. Lawson, Exec. VP
Bronwen R. Taylor, Chief Compliance Officer
John W. Brown, Chmn.
Luciano Cattanio, VP/Group Pres., Intl.

Phone: 269-385-2600	**Fax:** 269-385-1062
Toll-Free:	
Address: 2825 Airview Blvd., Kalamazoo, MI 49002 US	

GROWTH PLANS/SPECIAL FEATURES:

Stryker Corporation, founded in 1941, develop manufactures and markets specialty surgical and medic products, including orthopedic implants, powered surgic instruments, endoscopic systems and patient care ar handling equipment for the global market. Stryker als provides outpatient physical therapy services in the U. The firm's products are produced by two segment Orthopaedic Implants and MedSurg equipment. Th Orthopaedic Implant segment's products are designed ar manufactured by subsidiaries Stryker Orthopaedics, Stryk Trauma, Stryker Spine, Stryker Leibinger Micro Implants ar Stryker Biotech. They include reconstructive implants f knee, hip, elbow, shoulder and other joint surgeries; nailin plating and external fixation systems to mend traum injuries; spine implants; micro implants for craniomaxillofaci and hand surgery; bone cement; and OP-1, a natural prote that induces bone formation. Stryker MedSurg Equipme provides powered surgical instruments, surgical navigatic systems, endoscopic products, medical video imagir equipment and hospital beds and stretchers. These device are produced by Stryker Instruments, Stryker Endoscopy an Stryker Medical. The company formerly operate Physiotherapy Associates, which provided physica occupational and speech therapy services. Approximate 57% of its 2006 sales were from Orthopaedic Implants, 38 from MedSurg equipment, 5% other. 66% of the firm's sale are domestic, with the remaining 34% international. Stryke maintains administrative, sales, warehousing and distributio sites in 39 countries in Europe, Asia, Africa, Canada an Latin America; and exports products to numerou international destinations. Recently, the firm acquire eTrauma, a provider of image management and viewin software for the orthopedic market. In March 2006, Stryke acquired Sightline Technologies, a private company based i Israel that develops endoscopes. In June 2007 Physiotherapy Associates was sold for $150 million to Wate Street Healthcare Partners.

Stryker's employee benefits include adoption assistance tuition reimbursement; holiday gatherings and recreationa activities; and medical, dental, prescription, life, disability an vision insurance.

FINANCIALS: Sales and profits are in thousands of dollars—add 000 to get the full amount. 2007 Note: Financial information for 2007 was not available for all companies at press time.

2007 Sales: $
2006 Sales: $5,405,600
2005 Sales: $4,871,500
2004 Sales: $4,262,300
2003 Sales: $3,625,300

2007 Profits: $
2006 Profits: $777,700
2005 Profits: $643,600
2004 Profits: $440,000
2003 Profits: $453,500

U.S. Stock Ticker: SYK
Int'l Ticker: Int'l Exchange:
Employees: 18,806
Fiscal Year Ends: 12/31
Parent Company:

SALARIES/BENEFITS:

Pension Plan:
Savings Plan: Y
ESOP Stock Plan:
Stock Purch. Plan: Y
Profit Sharing:
Top Exec. Salary: $900,000 Bonus: $877,500
Second Exec. Salary: $781,045 Bonus: $161,052

OTHER THOUGHTS:

Apparent Women Officers or Directors: 1
Hot Spot for Advancement for Women/Minorities:

LOCATIONS: ("Y" = Yes)

West:	Southwest:	Midwest:	Southeast:	Northeast:	International:
Y	Y	Y		Y	Y

Note: Financial information, benefits and other data can change quickly and may vary from those stated here.

SUN HEALTHCARE GROUP www.sunh.com

Industry Group Code: 623110 **Ranks within this company's industry group:** Sales: 4 Profits: 4

Insurance/HMO/PPO:		Drugs:		Equipment/Supplies:		Hospitals/Clinics:		Services:		Health Care:	
Insurance:		Manufacturer:		Manufacturer:		Acute Care:	Y	Diagnostics:		Home Health:	Y
Managed Care:		Distributor:		Distributor:		Sub-Acute:	Y	Labs/Testing:	Y	Long-Term Care:	Y
Utilization Management:		Specialty Pharmacy:		Leasing/Finance:		Outpatient Surgery:		Staffing:	Y	Physical Therapy:	Y
Payment Processing:		Vitamins/Nutritionals:		Information Systems:		Physical Rehab. Ctr.:	Y	Waste Disposal:		Physician Prac. Mgmt.:	
		Clinical Trials:				Psychiatric Clinics:		Specialty Svcs.:			

TYPES OF BUSINESS:

Long-Term Care
Sub-Acute Care
Assisted Living Services
Temporary Medical Staffing
Mobile Radiology
Medical Laboratory Services
Home Health Care Services
Physical Therapy

BRANDS/DIVISIONS/AFFILIATES:

SunDance Rehabilitation Corp.
CareerStaff Unlimited, Inc.
SunPlus Home Health Services
Harborside Healthcare Corporation

CONTACTS: *Note: Officers with more than one job title may be intentionally listed here more than once.*

Richard K. Matros, CEO
L. Bryan Shaul, CFO/Exec. VP
Heidi J. Fisher, Sr. VP-Human Resources
Michael Newman, General Counsel/Exec. VP
Michael Polgardy, Treas.
Sheila Hagg-Rickert, Sr. VP-Risk Mgmt.
Chauncey J. Hunker, Sr. VP/Corp. Compliance Officer
Tracy Gregg, Pres., SunDance Rehabilitation Corp.
Richard Peranton, Pres., CareerStaff Unlimited
Richard K. Matros, Chmn.

Phone: 505-821-3355	**Fax:**
Toll-Free: 800-729-6600	
Address: 101 Sun Ave. N.E., Albuquerque, NM 87109 US	

GROWTH PLANS/SPECIAL FEATURES:

Sun Healthcare Group, Inc., through its subsidiaries, is a nationwide provider of long-term, sub-acute and related specialty healthcare services primarily to the senior population in the U.S. The firm operates in three principal business segments: inpatient services, rehabilitation therapy services and medical staffing services. Its core business is providing inpatient services, primarily through 118 skilled nursing facilities, 13 assisted and independent living facilities, seven mental health facilities and three specialty acute care hospitals with 15,447 licensed beds located in 19 states. These facilities provide inpatient skilled nursing and custodial services including daily nursing, therapeutic rehabilitation, social services, housekeeping, dietary and administrative services for individuals requiring certain assistance for activities in daily living. Specialized care is available for patients with Alzheimer's disease. The firm's rehabilitation services are provided at over 382 facilities in 32 states through SunDance Rehabilitation Corporation. These services include speech pathology, physical therapy and occupational therapy. Sun Healthcare's medical staffing services, through CareerStaff Unlimited, Inc., provides licensed therapists skilled in physical, occupational and speech therapy; nurses; pharmacists, pharmacist technicians and medical imaging technicians; physicians; and related medical personnel. CareerStaff customers include hospitals, skilled nursing facilities, schools and prisons. In December 2006, Sun Healthcare completed the sale of its subsidiary SunPlus Home Health Services, Inc. to AccentCare Home Health, Inc. for $19.5 million. In April 2007, Sun Healthcare completed the acquisition of Harborside Healthcare Corporation, a private healthcare company based in Boston, Massachusetts operating 73 skilled nursing facilities, one assisted living facility and one independent living facility, for $349.4 million.

FINANCIALS: **Sales and profits are in thousands of dollars—add 000 to get the full amount. 2007 Note: Financial information for 2007 was not available for all companies at press time.**

2007 Sales: $	2007 Profits: $	**U.S. Stock Ticker: SUNH**
2006 Sales: $1,045,637	2006 Profits: $27,118	**Int'l Ticker:** Int'l Exchange:
2005 Sales: $765,782	2005 Profits: $24,761	Employees: 19,350
2004 Sales: $700,863	2004 Profits: $-18,627	Fiscal Year Ends: 12/31
2003 Sales: $834,043	2003 Profits: $ 354	Parent Company:

SALARIES/BENEFITS:

Pension Plan:	ESOP Stock Plan:	Profit Sharing:	Top Exec. Salary: $757,692	Bonus: $1,034,375
Savings Plan: Y	Stock Purch. Plan:		Second Exec. Salary: $446,373	Bonus: $500,625

OTHER THOUGHTS:

Apparent Women Officers or Directors: 3
Hot Spot for Advancement for Women/Minorities: Y

LOCATIONS: ("Y" = Yes)

West:	Southwest:	Midwest:	Southeast:	Northeast:	International:
Y	Y	Y	Y	Y	

SUNRISE MEDICAL INC www.sunrisemedical.com

Industry Group Code: 339113 **Ranks within this company's industry group:** Sales: Profits:

Insurance/HMO/PPO:		Drugs:		Equipment/Supplies:		Hospitals/Clinics:		Services:		Health Care:	
Insurance:		Manufacturer:		Manufacturer:	Y	Acute Care:		Diagnostics:		Home Health:	
Managed Care:		Distributor:		Distributor:		Sub-Acute:		Labs/Testing:		Long-Term Care:	
Utilization Management:		Specialty Pharmacy:		Leasing/Finance:		Outpatient Surgery:		Staffing:		Physical Therapy:	
Payment Processing:		Vitamins/Nutritionals:		Information Systems:		Physical Rehab. Ctr.:		Waste Disposal:		Physician Prac. Mgmt.:	
		Clinical Trials:				Psychiatric Clinics:		Specialty Svcs.:	Y		

TYPES OF BUSINESS:

Medical Supplies-Wheelchairs
Home Respiratory Devices
Ambulatory & Bath Safety Aids
Therapeutic Mattresses & Support Surfaces
Patient-Room Beds & Furnishings
Speech Communication Devices

BRANDS/DIVISIONS/AFFILIATES:

Quickie
Zippie
Quickie Chameleon
DeVilbiss Manufacturing
DynaVox
Sunrise Medical Education
Mighty Lite Wheelchair

CONTACTS: *Note: Officers with more than one job title may be intentionally listed here more than once.*

Kathryn McDougal, Mgr.-Ambassador Program
John Kirkpatrick, VP-Global Bus. Systems
Michael N. Hammes, Chmn.

Phone: 760-930-1500 **Fax:** 760-930-1585
Toll-Free: 800-333-4000
Address: 2382 Faraday Ave., Ste. 200, Carlsbad, CA 92008 US

GROWTH PLANS/SPECIAL FEATURES:

Sunrise Medical, Inc. designs, manufactures and market medical products that address the recovery, rehabilitatio and respiratory needs of patients in institutional and hom care settings. The company's family of products i comprised of many brands in the homecare industr including Quickie, Sopur, Jay, DeVilbiss, Hoyer, Guardiar Coopers, Oxford and Joerns. Its products include custon manual and power wheelchairs and related seating systems ambulatory, bathing and lifting products; health care beds and furniture and therapeutic mattresses. Sunrise's broa range of wheelchairs includes the Quickie line, designed fo all purposes, including for sports such as tennis an basketball. The Mighty Lite Wheelchair line is designed fo children. Additionally, the company's DeVilbis Manufacturing subsidiary manufactures and markets a broa array of home respiratory products, including aerosc products, oxygen concentrators and sleep therapy products Through the DynaVox division, Sunrise markets speec communication devices. These devices feature dynami touch-screen technology, predictive natural languag software and a life-like voice synthesizer to speak for peopl with speech disorders. The Sunrise Medical Educatio department conducts seminars around the country tha provide technical and clinical information for respirator therapists, nurses, physicians and physical therapists. Th company has sales organization and distributors in over 9(countries.

FINANCIALS: Sales and profits are in thousands of dollars—add 000 to get the full amount. 2007 Note: Financial information for 2007 was not available for all companies at press time.

2007 Sales: $ 2007 Profits: $
2006 Sales: $ 2006 Profits: $
2005 Sales: $ 2005 Profits: $
2004 Sales: $ 2004 Profits: $
2003 Sales: $ 2003 Profits: $

U.S. Stock Ticker: Private
Int'l Ticker: Int'l Exchange:
Employees: 4,470
Fiscal Year Ends:
Parent Company:

SALARIES/BENEFITS:

Pension Plan: ESOP Stock Plan: Profit Sharing: Top Exec. Salary: $ Bonus: $
Savings Plan: Stock Purch. Plan: Second Exec. Salary: $ Bonus: $

OTHER THOUGHTS:

Apparent Women Officers or Directors: 1
Hot Spot for Advancement for Women/Minorities:

LOCATIONS: ("Y" = Yes)

West:	Southwest:	Midwest:	Southeast:	Northeast:	International:
Y	Y	Y	Y	Y	Y

SUNRISE SENIOR LIVING

www.sunrise-sl.com

Industry Group Code: 623110 **Ranks within this company's industry group:** Sales: Profits:

Insurance/HMO/PPO:		Drugs:		Equipment/Supplies:		Hospitals/Clinics:		Services:		Health Care:	
Insurance:		Manufacturer:		Manufacturer:		Acute Care:		Diagnostics:		Home Health:	
Managed Care:		Distributor:		Distributor:		Sub-Acute:		Labs/Testing:		Long-Term Care:	Y
Utilization Management:		Specialty Pharmacy:		Leasing/Finance:		Outpatient Surgery:		Staffing:		Physical Therapy:	
Payment Processing:		Vitamins/Nutritionals:		Information Systems:		Physical Rehab. Ctr.:		Waste Disposal:		Physician Prac. Mgmt.:	
		Clinical Trials:				Psychiatric Clinics:		Specialty Svcs.:	Y		

TYPES OF BUSINESS:

Long-Term Health Care
Assisted Living Centers
Independent Living Centers
Nursing Homes

BRANDS/DIVISIONS/AFFILIATES:

Sunrise Assisted Living
Aston Gardens
Trinity Hospice, Inc.

CONTACTS: *Note: Officers with more than one job title may be intentionally listed here more than once.*

Paul J. Klaassen, CEO
Tiffany L. Tomasso, COO
Thomas B. Newell, Pres.
Richard J. Nadeau, CFO
Jeffery M. Jasnoff, Sr. VP-Human Resources
John F. Gaul, General Counsel
Julie A. Pangelinan, Chief Acct. Officer
Teresa M. Klaassen, Chief Cultural Officer/Exec. VP
Christian Slavin, Exec. VP/Pres., Sunrise Properties
Michael B. Lanahan, Chmn.-Greystone Div.
Paul J. Klaassen, Chmn.

Phone: 703-273-7500	**Fax:** 703-744-1601
Toll-Free: 888-434-4648	
Address: 7902 Westpark Dr., McLean, VA 22102 US	

GROWTH PLANS/SPECIAL FEATURES:

Sunrise Senior Living, formerly Sunrise Assisted Living, Inc., offers a full range of services tailored to its individual resident needs, typically in apartment-like assisted living environments. The firm operates more than 453 senior living communities in 37 states, the U.K., Germany and Canada, with a resident capacity of approximately 53,000; and it has 38 more communities under construction. Upon move-in, Sunrise assists the resident in determining the level of care required and developing an individualized service plan, including selection of resident accommodations and the appropriate level of care. The services provided range from basic care, consisting of assistance with activities of daily living; to reminiscence care, which consists of programs and services to help cognitively impaired residents, including residents with Alzheimer's disease. The firm targets sites for development located in major metropolitan areas and their surrounding suburban communities, considering factors such as population, age demographics and estimated level of market demand. The company often revitalizes existing senior living centers and operates the home for a third-party owner. It owns or has interest in about half of the properties where it maintains services. In June 2006, the firm acquired six senior living communities operated under the Aston Gardens brand name. In September 2006, the company acquired Trinity Hospice, Inc. for $76 million. In August 2007, the company changed its meal options, no longer using trans fat oils in its food, as well as offering Davidson's Safest Choice Pasteurized Shell Eggs, allowing the company to offer poached and sunny side up eggs that are safe for adults over the age of 50 to eat without risk of salmonella and other food borne illnesses.

Sunrise offers employees flexible spending accounts; a scholarship program; tuition assistance; a meal discount program; a dental and vision care plan; life insurance; and scholarship program.

FINANCIALS: **Sales and profits are in thousands of dollars—add 000 to get the full amount. 2007 Note: Financial information for 2007 was not available for all companies at press time.**

2007 Sales: $	2007 Profits: $	**U.S. Stock Ticker: SRZ**
2006 Sales: $	2006 Profits: $	**Int'l Ticker:** Int'l Exchange:
2005 Sales: $1,819,479	2005 Profits: $79,742	Employees:
2004 Sales: $1,446,471	2004 Profits: $50,687	Fiscal Year Ends: 12/31
2003 Sales: $1,188,300	2003 Profits: $62,200	Parent Company:

SALARIES/BENEFITS:

Pension Plan:	ESOP Stock Plan:	Profit Sharing:	Top Exec. Salary: $463,742	Bonus: $
Savings Plan: Y	Stock Purch. Plan: Y		Second Exec. Salary: $360,688	Bonus: $446,000

OTHER THOUGHTS:

Apparent Women Officers or Directors: 2
Hot Spot for Advancement for Women/Minorities:

LOCATIONS: ("Y" = Yes)

West:	Southwest:	Midwest:	Southeast:	Northeast:	International:
Y	Y	Y	Y	Y	Y

SUTTER HEALTH

www.sutterhealth.org

Industry Group Code: 622110 **Ranks within this company's industry group:** Sales: 6 Profits: 4

Insurance/HMO/PPO:		Drugs:		Equipment/Supplies:		Hospitals/Clinics:		Services:		Health Care:	
Insurance:		Manufacturer:		Manufacturer:		Acute Care:	Y	Diagnostics:		Home Health:	Y
Managed Care:		Distributor:		Distributor:		Sub-Acute:	Y	Labs/Testing:		Long-Term Care:	Y
Utilization Management:		Specialty Pharmacy:		Leasing/Finance:		Outpatient Surgery:	Y	Staffing:		Physical Therapy:	
Payment Processing:		Vitamins/Nutritionals:		Information Systems:		Physical Rehab. Ctr.:		Waste Disposal:		Physician Prac. Mgmt.:	
		Clinical Trials:				Psychiatric Clinics:		Specialty Svcs.:	Y		

TYPES OF BUSINESS:

Hospitals-General
Neonatal Care
Pregnancy & Birth
Training Programs
Medical Research Facilities
Home Health Services
Hospice Networks
Long-Term Care

BRANDS/DIVISIONS/AFFILIATES:

Samuel Merritt College
Sutter Institute for Medical Research
Sutter Health Institute for Research and Education
Palo Alto Medical Foundation
California Pacific Medical Center

CONTACTS:

Note: Officers with more than one job title may be intentionally listed here more than once.

Patrick Fry, CEO
Patrick Fry, Pres.
Robert Reed, CFO/Sr. VP
Jon Manis, CIO
Peter S. Anderson, Sr. VP-Strategy & Bus. Dev.
Bill Gleeson, VP-Comm.
Svend Ryge, Treas./VP
Karen Garner, Mgr.-Comm.
Gordon Hunt, Chief Medical Officer
Jim Gray, Chmn.

Phone: 916-733-8800	**Fax:** 916-286-6841
Toll-Free:	
Address: 2200 River Plaza Dr., Sacramento, CA 95833 US	

GROWTH PLANS/SPECIAL FEATURES:

Sutter Health, Inc. is one of the nation's largest not-for-profit health care systems. Through its affiliates, the firm serves 100 northern California communities as well as locations in Oregon and Hawaii. The firm operates 26 hospitals, 10 neonatal ICU's, eight cardiac centers and 10 cancer centers; many of the group's hospitals operate charitable foundations and it has 3,500 affiliated doctors and over 5,500 volunteers. Sutter also operates physician and nurse training programs including the Samuel Merritt College for nursing and health professional training; clinical trial locations; home health companies; hospice and occupational health networks; comprehensive outpatient clinics; and long-term care centers. It is a regional leader in labor and delivery, neonatology, orthopedics, pediatrics and cancer care services. In 2006, Sutter conducted over 39,000 births; and gave more than 327,000 home health visits, 195,000 hospice visits and 2.48 million outpatient visits. Specialty services include pregnancy information and classes; cancer survival and heart health services; visiting nurse and hospice care; and direct medical billing services. It operates research institutes including Sutter Institute for Medical Research; Sutter Health Institute for Research and Education; Palo Alto Medical Foundation; and California Pacific Medical Center. Recently, Sutter Health became the first health network in its area to implement two eICU (electronic ICU) centers. The centers allow more comprehensive and consistent monitoring of ICU patients by feeding monitoring data to a central location. In June 2007, the Sutter Health network, including physicians, hospitals and other service providers, donated $1 million to the California Regional Health Information Organization in order to improve electronic access to medical records statewide.

Sutter offers employees flexible spending accounts; tuition reimbursement and continuing education units; telecommuting, job sharing and flextime options; an employee assistance program; medical, dental, vision, life and long-term disability insurance; short-term disability and extended sick leave; and paid vacations and holidays.

FINANCIALS:

Sales and profits are in thousands of dollars—add 000 to get the full amount. 2007 Note: Financial information for 2007 was not available for all companies at press time.

2007 Sales: $	2007 Profits: $	**U.S. Stock Ticker: Nonprofit**
2006 Sales: $7,258,000	2006 Profits: $587,000	**Int'l Ticker:** Int'l Exchange:
2005 Sales: $6,643,000	2005 Profits: $442,000	Employees: 43,139
2004 Sales: $6,280,000	2004 Profits: $428,000	Fiscal Year Ends: 12/31
2003 Sales: $5,672,000	2003 Profits: $465,000	Parent Company:

SALARIES/BENEFITS:

Pension Plan: Y	ESOP Stock Plan:	Profit Sharing:	Top Exec. Salary: $	Bonus: $
Savings Plan: Y	Stock Purch. Plan:		Second Exec. Salary: $	Bonus: $

OTHER THOUGHTS:

Apparent Women Officers or Directors: 1
Hot Spot for Advancement for Women/Minorities: Y

LOCATIONS: ("Y" = Yes)

West:	Southwest:	Midwest:	Southeast:	Northeast:	International:
Y					

Note: Financial information, benefits and other data can change quickly and may vary from those stated here.

SYBRON DENTAL SPECIALTIES INC www.sybrondental.com

Industry Group Code: 339113 **Ranks within this company's industry group:** Sales: Profits:

Insurance/HMO/PPO:		Drugs:		Equipment/Supplies:		Hospitals/Clinics:		Services:		Health Care:	
Insurance:		Manufacturer:		Manufacturer:	Y	Acute Care:		Diagnostics:		Home Health:	
Managed Care:		Distributor:		Distributor:		Sub-Acute:		Labs/Testing:		Long-Term Care:	
Utilization Management:		Specialty Pharmacy:		Leasing/Finance:		Outpatient Surgery:		Staffing:		Physical Therapy:	
Payment Processing:		Vitamins/Nutritionals:		Information Systems:		Physical Rehab. Ctr.:		Waste Disposal:		Physician Prac. Mgmt.:	
		Clinical Trials:				Psychiatric Clinics:		Specialty Svcs.:			

TYPES OF BUSINESS:

Dental Products
Orthodontic Products
Infection Control Products

BRANDS/DIVISIONS/AFFILIATES:

Danaher Corp
Kerr
Belle
Metrex
Ormco
Pinnacle
Demetron
Oraltronics Dental Implant Technology GmbH

CONTACTS: *Note: Officers with more than one job title may be intentionally listed here more than once.*

Floyd W. Pickrell, Jr., CEO
Daniel E. Even, COO
Floyd W. Pickrell, Jr., Pres.
Mark C. Yorba, CIO
Mark C. Yorba, VP-Tech.
Stephen J. Tomassi, General Counsel
Frances Zee, VP-Regulatory Affairs & Quality Assurance

Phone: 714-516-7400	**Fax:** 714-516-7543
Toll-Free: 800-537-7824	
Address: 1717 W. Collins Ave., Orange, CA 92867 US	

GROWTH PLANS/SPECIAL FEATURES:

Sybron Dental Specialties, Inc., a subsidiary of Danaher Corporation, is a leading manufacturer of consumable products for the dental and orthodontic professions. The firm operates in three business segments: professional dental, which develops, manufactures, markets and distributes a comprehensive line of products to the dental industry worldwide; orthodontics, which engineers and distributes orthodontic and endodontic products used in root canal therapy; and infection control products, including surface disinfectants, cleaners, detergents and hand-hygiene products. Sybron's subsidiaries include Kerr Corporation; Kerr Italia S.p.A; Ormco Corporation; Ormodent Group; Allesee Orthodontic Appliances, Inc.; Innova LifeSciences Corporation; Pinnacle Products, Inc.; KerrHAwe S.A.; Metrx Research Corporation; and Oraltronics Dental Implant Technology GmbH. The company's business strategy includes product innovation, ongoing cost reduction and selective acquisitions.

FINANCIALS: **Sales and profits are in thousands of dollars—add 000 to get the full amount. 2007 Note: Financial information for 2007 was not available for all companies at press time.**

2007 Sales: $	2007 Profits: $	**U.S. Stock Ticker: Subsidiary**
2006 Sales: $	2006 Profits: $	**Int'l Ticker:** Int'l Exchange:
2005 Sales: $649,666	2005 Profits: $76,685	Employees: 4,117
2004 Sales: $573,976	2004 Profits: $62,112	Fiscal Year Ends: 9/30
2003 Sales: $526,391	2003 Profits: $57,452	Parent Company: DANAHER CORP

SALARIES/BENEFITS:

Pension Plan:	ESOP Stock Plan:	Profit Sharing:	Top Exec. Salary: $625,000	Bonus: $1,057,375
Savings Plan: Y	Stock Purch. Plan:		Second Exec. Salary: $290,000	Bonus: $37,465

OTHER THOUGHTS:

Apparent Women Officers or Directors: 1
Hot Spot for Advancement for Women/Minorities:

LOCATIONS: ("Y" = Yes)

West:	Southwest:	Midwest:	Southeast:	Northeast:	International:
Y		Y		Y	Y

SYMMETRY MEDICAL INC www.symmetrymedical.com

Industry Group Code: 339113 **Ranks within this company's industry group:** Sales: 55 Profits: 49

Insurance/HMO/PPO:		Drugs:		Equipment/Supplies:		Hospitals/Clinics:		Services:		Health Care:	
Insurance:		Manufacturer:		Manufacturer:	Y	Acute Care:		Diagnostics:		Home Health:	
Managed Care:		Distributor:		Distributor:		Sub-Acute:		Labs/Testing:		Long-Term Care:	
Utilization Management:		Specialty Pharmacy:		Leasing/Finance:		Outpatient Surgery:		Staffing:		Physical Therapy:	
Payment Processing:		Vitamins/Nutritionals:		Information Systems:		Physical Rehab. Ctr.:		Waste Disposal:		Physician Prac. Mgmt.:	
		Clinical Trials:				Psychiatric Clinics:		Specialty Svcs.:	Y		

TYPES OF BUSINESS:

Orthopedic Implants
Aerospace Market Products & Services
Medical Cases

BRANDS/DIVISIONS/AFFILIATES:

Symmetry Jet
Symmetry Othy
Symmetry PolyVac
Symmetry Thornton
Symmetry UltreXX
Total Solutions
Riley Medical Inc.
Clamonta, Ltd.

CONTACTS: *Note: Officers with more than one job title may be intentionally listed here more than once.*

Brian Moore, CEO
Brian Moore, Pres.
Fred Hite, CFO/Sr. VP
D. Darin Martin, Sr. VP-Quality Assurance/Regulatory Affairs
Michael W. Curtis, Sr. VP/General Manager-Medical Products, USA
Frank Turner, Chmn.
Richard J. Senior, Sr. VP/General Manager-Europe

Phone: 574-268-2252	**Fax:** 574-267-4551
Toll-Free:	
Address: 220 W. Market St., Warsaw, IN 46580 US	

GROWTH PLANS/SPECIAL FEATURES:

Symmetry Medical, Inc. is an independent provider of implants and related instruments and cases to global orthopedic device manufacturers. The company designs, develops and produces these products for companies in other segments of the medical device market, including the dental, osteobiologic and endoscopy segments. The firm also provides limited specialized products and services to non-healthcare markets, such as the aerospace market. Symmetry Medical's primary products and services are comprised of implants, including forged, cast and machined products for the global orthopedic device market; instruments used in the placement and removal or orthopedic implants and other surgical procedures; cases, including plastic, metal and hybrid used to organize, secure and transport medical devices for orthopedic, endoscopy, dental and other surgical procedures; and other specialized products and services for non-healthcare markets, primarily the aerospace market. The subsidiary Symmetry Jet forges, creates and fully finishes orthopedic implants; Symmetry Othy is a supplier of custom and standard surgical instruments internationally; and Symmetry PolyVac manufactures metal, plastic and hybrid medical cases in New Hampshire and France. Symmetry Thornton, based in Sheffield, England, has supplied orthopedic components for over 100 years, specializing in precision forging, casting, rapid prototyping, machining and full finishing for implants. Symmetry UltreXX manufacturers and supplies precision spinal and trauma instruments and implants to original equipment manufacturers internationally. Symmetry Medical offers all of its products under the Othy, UltreXX and Total Solutions brands. In 2006, the company acquired Riley Medical, Inc. (a manufacturer of standard and custom cases, trays and containers to the medical device industry) for $45 million and Everest Metal Finishing, LLC and its affiliate, Everest Metal International, Ltd., for $8.8 million. In 2007, the firm acquired Whedon, Ltd., the holding company of Clamonta, Ltd., for $10 million and TNCO, Inc., a specialty medical instrument company, for $7 million.

FINANCIALS: **Sales and profits are in thousands of dollars—add 000 to get the full amount. 2007 Note: Financial information for 2007 was not available for all companies at press time.**

2007 Sales: $	2007 Profits: $	**U.S. Stock Ticker: SMA**
2006 Sales: $253,569	2006 Profits: $24,149	**Int'l Ticker:** Int'l Exchange:
2005 Sales: $263,766	2005 Profits: $31,800	Employees: 1,795
2004 Sales: $205,391	2004 Profits: $11,695	Fiscal Year Ends: 12/31
2003 Sales: $122,029	2003 Profits: $5,905	Parent Company:

SALARIES/BENEFITS:

Pension Plan:	ESOP Stock Plan:	Profit Sharing:	Top Exec. Salary: $375,000	Bonus: $50,000
Savings Plan:	Stock Purch. Plan:		Second Exec. Salary: $246,867	Bonus: $36,800

OTHER THOUGHTS:

Apparent Women Officers or Directors:
Hot Spot for Advancement for Women/Minorities:

LOCATIONS: ("Y" = Yes)

West:	Southwest:	Midwest:	Southeast:	Northeast:	International:
		Y		Y	Y

Note: Financial information, benefits and other data can change quickly and may vary from those stated here.

SYNOVIS LIFE TECHNOLOGIES INC www.synovislife.com

ndustry Group Code: 339113 **Ranks within this company's industry group:** Sales: 90 Profits: 79

nsurance/HMO/PPO:		Drugs:		Equipment/Supplies:		Hospitals/Clinics:		Services:		Health Care:	
nsurance:		Manufacturer:		Manufacturer:	Y	Acute Care:		Diagnostics:		Home Health:	
Managed Care:		Distributor:		Distributor:		Sub-Acute:		Labs/Testing:		Long-Term Care:	
Utilization Management:		Specialty Pharmacy:		Leasing/Finance:		Outpatient Surgery:		Staffing:		Physical Therapy:	
Payment Processing:		Vitamins/Nutritionals:		Information Systems:		Physical Rehab. Ctr.:		Waste Disposal:		Physician Prac. Mgmt.:	
		Clinical Trials:				Psychiatric Clinics:		Specialty Svcs.:	Y		

TYPES OF BUSINESS:

Surgical & Interventional Treatment Products
Implantable Biomaterials

BRANDS/DIVISIONS/AFFILIATES:

Synovis Surgical Innovations
Synovis Micro Companies Alliance
Synovis Interventional Solutions
Microvascular Anastomotis Coupler
Peri-Strips
Veritas
Tissue-Guard
4Closure Surgical Fascia Closure System

CONTACTS: *Note: Officers with more than one job title may be intentionally listed here more than once.*

Richard W. Kramp, CEO
Richard W. Kramp, Pres.
Brett A. Reynolds, CFO
B. Nicholas Oray, VP-R&D
Brett A. Reynolds, Corp. Sec.
Brett A. Reynolds, VP-Finance
Michael K. Campbell, Pres., Micro Companies Alliance, Inc.
Mary L. Frick, VP-Regulatory Affairs & Quality Assurance
Mary L. Frick, VP-Clinical Affairs
Timothy M. Scanlan, Chmn.

Phone: 651-796-7300	**Fax:** 651-642-9018
Toll-Free: 800-255-4018	
Address: 2575 University Ave. W., St. Paul, MN 55114 US	

GROWTH PLANS/SPECIAL FEATURES:

Synovis Life Technologies, Inc. is a diversified medical device company engaged in developing, manufacturing and bringing to market products for the surgical and interventional treatment of disease. The company operates in two business segments: the surgical business and the interventional business. The surgical business develops, through subsidiaries Synovis Innovations and Synovis Micro Companies Alliance, manufactures, markets and sells implantable biomaterial products, devices for microsurgery and surgical tools. Biometrical products include Peri-Strips, a biomaterial stapling buttress used as reinforcement at the surgical stable line to reduce the risk of potentially fatal leaks; Tissue-Guard, used to repair and replace damaged tissue in cardiac, vascular, thoracic, abdominal and neuron surgeries; and Veritas, for use in pelvic floor reconstruction, stress urinary incontinence treatment, vaginal and rectal prolapse repair, hernia repair as well as soft tissue repair. A device for microsurgery includes the Microvascular Anastomotic Coupler, which enables microsurgeons in numerous surgical specialties, including plastic and reconscructive. The interventional business, through subsidiary Synovis Interventional Solutions, develops, engineers, prototypes and manufactures coils, helices, stylets, guidewires and other complex micro-wire, polymer and micro-machined metal components used in minimally invasive devices for cardiac rhythm management, neurostimulation, vascular and other procedures. In addition, the interventional business designs and develops proprietary technology platforms that can be adapted for customers. In April 2007, Synovis acquired 4Closure Surgical Fascia Closure System, a device and operating method for closure of puncture in the fascia, a layer of connective tissue on the inner surface of the chest or abdominal wall, from Fascia Closure Systems, LLC.

FINANCIALS: **Sales and profits are in thousands of dollars—add 000 to get the full amount. 2007 Note: Financial information for 2007 was not available for all companies at press time.**

2007 Sales: $	2007 Profits: $	**U.S. Stock Ticker: SYNO**
2006 Sales: $55,835	2006 Profits: $-1,481	**Int'l Ticker:** Int'l Exchange:
2005 Sales: $60,256	2005 Profits: $ 883	Employees: 390
2004 Sales: $55,044	2004 Profits: $1,278	Fiscal Year Ends: 10/31
2003 Sales: $57,989	2003 Profits: $4,973	Parent Company:

SALARIES/BENEFITS:

Pension Plan:	ESOP Stock Plan:	Profit Sharing:	Top Exec. Salary: $375,000	Bonus: $15,000
Savings Plan: Y	Stock Purch. Plan:		Second Exec. Salary: $225,000	Bonus: $4,500

OTHER THOUGHTS:

Apparent Women Officers or Directors: 2
Hot Spot for Advancement for Women/Minorities: Y

LOCATIONS: ("Y" = Yes)

West:	Southwest:	Midwest:	Southeast:	Northeast:	International:
		Y			

Note: Financial information, benefits and other data can change quickly and may vary from those stated here.

TAKE CARE HEALTH SYSTEMS LLC www.takecarehealth.com

Industry Group Code: 621490 **Ranks within this company's industry group:** Sales: Profits:

Insurance/HMO/PPO:		Drugs:		Equipment/Supplies:		Hospitals/Clinics:		Services:		Health Care:	
Insurance:		Manufacturer:		Manufacturer:		Acute Care:		Diagnostics:		Home Health:	
Managed Care:		Distributor:		Distributor:		Sub-Acute:	Y	Labs/Testing:		Long-Term Care:	
Utilization Management:		Specialty Pharmacy:		Leasing/Finance:		Outpatient Surgery:		Staffing:		Physical Therapy:	
Payment Processing:		Vitamins/Nutritionals:		Information Systems:		Physical Rehab. Ctr.:		Waste Disposal:		Physician Prac. Mgmt.:	
		Clinical Trials:				Psychiatric Clinics:		Specialty Svcs.:			

TYPES OF BUSINESS:

Health Clinics

BRANDS/DIVISIONS/AFFILIATES:

Take Care Health Centers
Brooks Eckerd
Wallgreen Co

CONTACTS:

Note: Officers with more than one job title may be intentionally listed here more than once.

Peter Miller, CEO
Peter Miller, Pres.
Jeffrey J. Petrick, CFO
Margery Geers, Chief People Officer
Patrick Lucas, CIO
Charles Peck, Chief Medical Officer
Sandra Festa Ryan, Chief Nurse Practitioner
Hal F. Rosenbluth, Chmn.

Phone: 484-351-3200 **Fax:** 484-351-3800
Toll-Free: 866-825-3227
Address: 300 Barr Harbor Dr., Ste. 550, Conshohocken, PA 19428 US

GROWTH PLANS/SPECIAL FEATURES:

Take Care Health Systems LLC, a wholly-owned subsidiar of Walgreens Co., operates the Take Care nurse practitioner-based system, a chain of quick service healt care clinics. Take Care Health Centers are placed withi retail pharmacies, giving patients easy access to quality car and allowing them to fill prescriptions quickly. Take Car Health Centers are also found in professional health car practices; they are fully equipped with exam rooms an patient information kiosks. These Centers are staffed b certified nurse practitioners who can diagnose and prescrib medications on-site within retail pharmacies withou appointments. Take Care licenses small departments insid drugstores and staffs them with nurse practitioners able t treat common health problems such as minor injuries, ea infections and strep throat. The Centers can also perforn physicals, basic diagnostic testing and vaccinations Seriously ill patients are referred to a nearby full clinic c hospital. The firm currently has 46 clinics within Walgreen stores throughout Kansas, Illinois, Wisconsin and Missou and it has 10 within Eckerd Pharmacy stores i Pennsylvania. Take Care has 14 more Walgreens-base clinics scheduled to open in coming months. Within th company's clinics, advanced information systems manag the patients' records, collect information about symptom during consultations and provide suggestions abou diagnoses. When a prescription is issued, it is automaticall sent to the in-store pharmacy or to the drug store of th patient's choice. The firm was purchased by Walgreens Co in May 2007 with plans to construct more than 400 additiona in-store clinics by the end of 2008. In 2007 the firm signe contracts to be added as providers for the followin insurance companies: CIGNA HealthCare, University o Pittsburgh Medical Center (UPMC) Health Plan and Aetna.

FINANCIALS:

Sales and profits are in thousands of dollars—add 000 to get the full amount. 2007 Note: Financial information for 2007 was not available for all companies at press time.

2007 Sales: $ — 2007 Profits: $
2006 Sales: $ — 2006 Profits: $
2005 Sales: $ — 2005 Profits: $
2004 Sales: $ — 2004 Profits: $
2003 Sales: $ — 2003 Profits: $

U.S. Stock Ticker: Subsidiary
Int'l Ticker: Int'l Exchange:
Employees:
Fiscal Year Ends:
Parent Company: WALGREEN CO

SALARIES/BENEFITS:

Pension Plan: ESOP Stock Plan: Profit Sharing: Top Exec. Salary: $ Bonus: $
Savings Plan: Stock Purch. Plan: Second Exec. Salary: $ Bonus: $

OTHER THOUGHTS:

Apparent Women Officers or Directors: 2
Hot Spot for Advancement for Women/Minorities: Y

LOCATIONS: ("Y" = Yes)

West:	Southwest:	Midwest:	Southeast:	Northeast:	International:
Y		Y		Y	

Note: Financial information, benefits and other data can change quickly and may vary from those stated here.

TAKEDA PHARMACEUTICAL COMPANY LTD www.takeda.com

Industry Group Code: 325412 **Ranks within this company's industry group:** Sales: 15 Profits: 11

Insurance/HMO/PPO:		Drugs:		Equipment/Supplies:		Hospitals/Clinics:		Services:		Health Care:	
Insurance:		Manufacturer:		Manufacturer:		Acute Care:		Diagnostics:		Home Health:	
Managed Care:		Distributor:	Y	Distributor:		Sub-Acute:		Labs/Testing:		Long-Term Care:	
Utilization Management:		Specialty Pharmacy:		Leasing/Finance:		Outpatient Surgery:		Staffing:		Physical Therapy:	
Payment Processing:		Vitamins/Nutritionals:		Information Systems:		Physical Rehab. Ctr.:		Waste Disposal:		Physician Prac. Mgmt.:	
		Clinical Trials:	Y			Psychiatric Clinics:		Specialty Svcs.:			

TYPES OF BUSINESS:

Pharmaceuticals Discovery & Development
Over-the-Counter Drugs
Vitamins
Chemicals
Agricultural & Food Products

BRANDS/DIVISIONS/AFFILIATES:

Takeda America Holdings, Inc.
Takeda Research Investment, Inc.
TAP Pharmaceutical Products Inc.
Takeda Europe Research and Development Center Ltd.
Takeda Ireland Limited
Boie-Takeda Chemicals, Inc.
Paradigm Therapeutics Ltd.
Prevacid

CONTACTS: *Note: Officers with more than one job title may be intentionally listed here more than once.*

Yasuchika Hasegawa, Pres.
Tsutomu Miura, Gen. Mgr.-Ethical Prod. Mktg. Dept.
Tsudoi Miyoshi, Gen. Mgr.-Human Resources Dept.
Hiroshi Shinha, Gen. Mgr.-Legal Dept.
Yasuhiko Yamanaka, Gen. Mgr.-Corp. Strategy & Planning Dept.
Toyoji Yoshida, Gen. Mgr.-Corp. Comm. Dept.
Hiroaki Ogata, Gen. Mgr.-Bus. Dev. & Global Licensing Dept.
Hiroshi Sakiyama, Gen. Mgr.-Tokyo Branch
Teruo Sakurada, Gen. Mgr.-Osaka Branch
Hiroshi Ohtsuki, Pres., Consumer Healthcare Company
Kunio Takeda, Chmn.
Naohisa Takeda, Gen. Mgr.-Dept. of Europe & Asia

Phone: 81-6-6204-2111 **Fax:** 81-6-6204-2880
Toll-Free:
Address: 1-1, Doshomachi 4-chome, Chuo-ku,, Osaka, 540-8645 Japan

GROWTH PLANS/SPECIAL FEATURES:

Takeda Pharmaceutical Company Ltd., based in Japan, is an international research-based company focused on pharmaceuticals. One of the largest pharmaceutical companies in Japan, it operates three research centers and an international marketing network that includes 13 overseas bases in the U.S., Europe and Asia. Takeda discovers, develops, manufactures and markets pharmaceutical products in two categories: ethical and consumer health care drugs. Ethical drugs, as the firm denominates them, constitute about 81.5% of company sales. This segment includes the anti-prostatic cancer agent leuprolide acetate, marketed as Lupron Depot, Enantone, Prostap and Leuplin; the anti-peptic ulcer agent lansoprazole, marketed as Prevacid, Ogast, Takepron and other names; the anti-hypertensive agent candesartan cilexetil, marketed as Blopress, Kenzen and Amias; and the anti-diabetic agent pioglitazone hydrochloride, marketed as Actos. The company's consumer health care division focuses on the over-the-counter drug market. Takeda's main consumer brands include Alinamin, a vitamin B1 derivative; Benza, a cold remedy; and Hicee, a vitamin C preparation. Outside Japan, Takeda's subsidiaries include development, production, and sales and marketing companies, as well as holding companies in the U.S. and Europe. Overseas markets account for 44.3% of total sales. The company also operates subsidiaries with the agro, food, urethane chemicals and bulk vitamin businesses. Within research and development, Takeda focuses on the life-style related diseases, oncology, urologic diseases, central nervous system diseases and gastroenterology life cycle management. The company pursues alliances with other pharmaceutical manufacturers, biotechnology companies, universities and other research institutions to efficiently introduce key technologies. Takeda's plans are to increase sales of its four international strategic products (Leuprorelin, Lansoprazole, Candesartan and Pioglitazone); to expand its overseas operations by reinforcing infrastructures, and to restructure its non-pharmaceutical businesses. In March 2007, Takeda announced its intentions to acquire Paradigm Therapeutics Ltd.

FINANCIALS: **Sales and profits are in thousands of dollars—add 000 to get the full amount. 2007 Note: Financial information for 2007 was not available for all companies at press time.**

2007 Sales: $	2007 Profits: $	**U.S. Stock Ticker: TKPHF**
2006 Sales: $10,360,744	2006 Profits: $2,677,342	**Int'l Ticker: 4502** Int'l Exchange: Tokyo-TSE
2005 Sales: $10,441,300	2005 Profits: $2,579,600	Employees: 15,069
2004 Sales: $10,284,200	2004 Profits: $2,700,300	Fiscal Year Ends: 3/31
2003 Sales: $8,728,500	2003 Profits: $2,267,600	Parent Company:

SALARIES/BENEFITS:

Pension Plan:	ESOP Stock Plan:	Profit Sharing:	Top Exec. Salary: $	Bonus: $
Savings Plan:	Stock Purch. Plan:		Second Exec. Salary: $	Bonus: $

OTHER THOUGHTS:

Apparent Women Officers or Directors:
Hot Spot for Advancement for Women/Minorities:

LOCATIONS: ("Y" = Yes)

West:	Southwest:	Midwest:	Southeast:	Northeast:	International:
Y		Y			Y

TEAM HEALTH

www.teamhealth.com

Industry Group Code: 621111 **Ranks within this company's industry group:** Sales: Profits:

Insurance/HMO/PPO:		**Drugs:**		**Equipment/Supplies:**		**Hospitals/Clinics:**		**Services:**		**Health Care:**	
Insurance:		Manufacturer:		Manufacturer:		Acute Care:		Diagnostics:		Home Health:	
Managed Care:		Distributor:		Distributor:		Sub-Acute:		Labs/Testing:		Long-Term Care:	
Utilization Management:		Specialty Pharmacy:		Leasing/Finance:		Outpatient Surgery:		Staffing:	Y	Physical Therapy:	
Payment Processing:		Vitamins/Nutritionals:		Information Systems:		Physical Rehab. Ctr.:		Waste Disposal:		Physician Prac. Mgmt.:	
		Clinical Trials:				Psychiatric Clinics:		Specialty Svcs.:	Y		

TYPES OF BUSINESS:

Hospital Staffing
Emergency Department Administration
Pediatrics
Radiology & Teleradiology Services
Urgent Care
Blackstone Group LP (The)

BRANDS/DIVISIONS/AFFILIATES:

Daniel & Yeager
Spectrum Healthcare Resources
After Hours Pediatrics
Florida Acute Care Specialists

CONTACTS:

Note: Officers with more than one job title may be intentionally listed here more than once.

Lynn Massingale, CEO
Gregory Roth, COO
Gregory Roth, Pres.
David Jones, CFO
Michael Shea, Sr. VP-Mktg.
Robert Joyner, General Counsel/Exec. VP
Michael Shea, Sr. VP-Bus. Dev.
Steve Sherlin, Chief Compliance Officer
Gar LaSalle, Chief Medical Officer
Kit Crews, Sr. VP-Mergers & Acquisitions
Lynn Massingale, Chmn.

Phone: 865-693-1000	**Fax:** 865-539-8003
Toll-Free: 800-818-1498	
Address: 1900 Winston Rd., Ste. 300, Knoxville, TN 37919 US	

GROWTH PLANS/SPECIAL FEATURES:

Team Health, Inc., a private company owned by the Blackstone Group, provides clinical outsourcing services such as emergency department administration and staffing. In addition, the company offers services that include emergency, hospital and intensivist medicine; radiology and teleradiology services; pediatrics; military hospital staffing; locum tenens; medical call center services; occupational medicine; and urgent care. The firm has more than 6,000 health care professionals, including 5,000 physicians, who serve at 500 hospitals and affiliated clinics in 44 states and Puerto Rico, both permanently and as temporary assistance. The health care professionals are trained in a variety of different areas, specializing in anesthesia, emergency medicine, radiology, urgent care and pediatrics. Clients of the firm include civilian and military hospitals; surgical centers; imaging centers; and private clinics, which are concentrated mainly in Florida, the Midwest and California, the regions where Team Health is most active. The Team Health network operates through a series of specialty affiliates, organized regionally. For instance, Daniel & Yeager provide locum tenens, otherwise known as temporary workers; Spectrum Healthcare Resources offers military medical staffing; and After Hours Pediatrics provides urgent care facilities for infants, children and young adults, in concert with local pediatricians. In July 2006, Team Health acquired Florida Acute Care Specialists.

The company offers its employees health, dental and vision insurance; life and prescription drug insurance; long- and short-term disability insurance; a 401(k) plan; flexible spending accounts; and an employee assistance program.

FINANCIALS:

Sales and profits are in thousands of dollars—add 000 to get the full amount. 2007 Note: Financial information for 2007 was not available for all companies at press time.

2007 Sales: $	2007 Profits: $	**U.S. Stock Ticker: Private**
2006 Sales: $	2006 Profits: $	**Int'l Ticker:** Int'l Exchange:
2005 Sales: $	2005 Profits: $	Employees: 5,000
2004 Sales: $1,572,200	2004 Profits: $-49,200	Fiscal Year Ends:
2003 Sales: $1,479,000	2003 Profits: $-2,800	Parent Company: BLACKSTONE GROUP LP (THE)

SALARIES/BENEFITS:

Pension Plan:	ESOP Stock Plan:	Profit Sharing:	Top Exec. Salary: $	Bonus: $
Savings Plan: Y	Stock Purch. Plan:		Second Exec. Salary: $	Bonus: $

OTHER THOUGHTS:

Apparent Women Officers or Directors:
Hot Spot for Advancement for Women/Minorities:

LOCATIONS: ("Y" = Yes)

West:	Southwest:	Midwest:	Southeast:	Northeast:	International:
Y	Y	Y	Y	Y	Y

TECHNE CORP www.techne-corp.com

ndustry Group Code: 325413 **Ranks within this company's industry group:** Sales: 3 Profits: 2

nsurance/HMO/PPO:		Drugs:		Equipment/Supplies:		Hospitals/Clinics:		Services:		Health Care:	
nsurance:		Manufacturer:	Y	Manufacturer:	Y	Acute Care:		Diagnostics:		Home Health:	
Managed Care:		Distributor:		Distributor:	Y	Sub-Acute:		Labs/Testing:		Long-Term Care:	
Jtilization Management:		Specialty Pharmacy:		Leasing/Finance:		Outpatient Surgery:		Staffing:		Physical Therapy:	
Payment Processing:		Vitamins/Nutritionals:		Information Systems:		Physical Rehab. Ctr.:		Waste Disposal:		Physician Prac. Mgmt.:	
		Clinical Trials:				Psychiatric Clinics:		Specialty Svcs.:			

TYPES OF BUSINESS:

Biotechnology Products
Reagents, Antibodies & Assay Kits
Hematology Products

BRANDS/DIVISIONS/AFFILIATES:

Research and Diagnostic Systems, Inc.
R&D Systems Europe, Ltd.
R&D Systems GmbH
Whole Blood Flow Cytometry Control
Whole Blood Glucose/Hemoglobin Control
Fortron Bio Science, Inc.
BiosPacific, Inc.

CONTACTS: *Note: Officers with more than one job title may be intentionally listed here more than once.*

Thomas E. Oland, CEO
Thomas E. Oland, Pres.
Gergory J. Melson, CFO
Lea Simoane, Dir.-Human Resources
Richard A. Krzyzek, VP-Research
Gregory J. Melson, VP-Finance
Marcel Veronneau, VP-Hematology Oper.
Thomas E. Oland, Treas.
Roger C. Lucas, Vice Chmn.
Thomas E. Oland, Chmn.

Phone: 612-379-8854	**Fax:** 612-379-6580
Toll-Free: 800-343-7475	
Address: 614 McKinley Pl. NE, Minneapolis, MN 55413-2610 US	

GROWTH PLANS/SPECIAL FEATURES:

Techne Corp. is a holding company that operates via two subsidiaries: Research and Diagnostic Systems, Inc. (R&D Systems) and R&D Systems Europe, Ltd. (R&D Europe). R&D Systems manufactures biological products in two major segments hematology controls, which are used in clinical and hospital laboratories to monitor the accuracy of blood analysis instruments; and biotechnology products, which including purified proteins and antibodies that are sold exclusively to the research market and assay kits that are sold to the research and clinical diagnostic markets. R&D Europe distributes biotechnology products throughout Europe and also operates a sales office in France and its German sales subsidiary, R&D Systems GmbH. In recent years, R&D Systems has also expanded its product portfolio to include enzymes and intracellular cell signaling reagents such as proteases, kinases and phosphatases for diseases such as cancer, Alzheimer's ,arthritic, autoimmunity, diabetes, hypertension, obesity, AIDS and SARS. Techne also produces controls and calibrators for a variety of medical brands such as Abbott Diagnostics, Beckman Coulter, Bayer Technicon and Sysmex. In the hematology sector, the company's Whole Blood Flow Cytometry Control is used to identify and quantify white blood cells by their surface antigens while linearity and reportable range controls assess the linearity of hematology analyzers for white blood cells, red blood ells, platelets and reticulocytes. R&D Systems is currently engaged in ongoing research and development in all of its major product lines and is particularly focused on the release of new cytokines, antibodies and cytokine assay kits for the coming year.

FINANCIALS: Sales and profits are in thousands of dollars—add 000 to get the full amount. 2007 Note: Financial information for 2007 was not available for all companies at press time.

2007 Sales: $223,482	2007 Profits: $85,111	**U.S. Stock Ticker: TECH**
2006 Sales: $202,617	2006 Profits: $73,351	**Int'l Ticker:** Int'l Exchange:
2005 Sales: $178,700	2005 Profits: $66,100	Employees: 681
2004 Sales: $161,257	2004 Profits: $52,928	Fiscal Year Ends: 6/30
2003 Sales: $145,000	2003 Profits: $45,400	Parent Company:

SALARIES/BENEFITS:

Pension Plan:	ESOP Stock Plan:	Profit Sharing: Y	Top Exec. Salary: $254,000	Bonus: $
Savings Plan: Y	Stock Purch. Plan: Y		Second Exec. Salary: $251,400	Bonus: $45,755

OTHER THOUGHTS:

Apparent Women Officers or Directors: 2
Hot Spot for Advancement for Women/Minorities: Y

LOCATIONS: ("Y" = Yes)

West:	Southwest:	Midwest:	Southeast:	Northeast:	International:
		Y			Y

Note: Financial information, benefits and other data can change quickly and may vary from those stated here.

TELEFLEX INC

www.teleflex.com

Industry Group Code: 336300 **Ranks within this company's industry group:** Sales: 1 Profits: 1

Insurance/HMO/PPO:		Drugs:		Equipment/Supplies:		Hospitals/Clinics:		Services:		Health Care:	
Insurance:		Manufacturer:		Manufacturer:	Y	Acute Care:		Diagnostics:		Home Health:	
Managed Care:		Distributor:		Distributor:		Sub-Acute:		Labs/Testing:		Long-Term Care:	
Utilization Management:		Specialty Pharmacy:		Leasing/Finance:		Outpatient Surgery:		Staffing:		Physical Therapy:	
Payment Processing:		Vitamins/Nutritionals:		Information Systems:		Physical Rehab. Ctr.:		Waste Disposal:		Physician Prac. Mgmt.:	
		Clinical Trials:				Psychiatric Clinics:		Specialty Svcs.:			

TYPES OF BUSINESS:

Diversified Manufacturing
General & Specialized Surgical Products
Instrument Management Services
Sterilization Services
Automotive Products & Controls
Marine Products & Controls
Industrial Products & Services
Hospital Products & Equipment

BRANDS/DIVISIONS/AFFILIATES:

Teleflex Aerospace
Teleflex Medical
Teleflex Automotive
Southwest Wire Rope
Telflex Industrial
Teleflex Marine
Teleflex Power Systems
Arrow International, Inc.

CONTACTS: *Note: Officers with more than one job title may be intentionally listed here more than once.*

Jeffrey P. Black, CEO
Jeffrey P. Black, Pres.
Kevin K. Gordon, CFO/Exec. VP
Randal Gaboriault, CIO/VP-Strategic Dev.
Laurence G. Miller, Sr. VP/General Counsel/Corp. Sec.
Kevin K. Gordon, VP-Corp. Dev.
Julie McDowell, VP-Corp. Comm.
C. Jeffrey Jacobs, Treas.
Vince Northfield, Pres., Commercial
Gregg Winter, VP-Taxes
John B. Suddarth, Pres., Teleflex Aerospace
R. Ernest Wasser, Pres., Medical
Jeffrey P. Black, Chmn.

Phone: 610-948-5100 **Fax:** 610-948-0811
Toll-Free:
Address: 155 S. Limerick Rd., Limerick, PA 19468 US

GROWTH PLANS/SPECIAL FEATURES:

Teleflex, Inc. manufactures specialty products for the commercial, medical and aerospace industries. The firm is comprised of Teleflex Aerospace, Teleflex Automotive, Southwest Wire Rope, Teleflex Industrial, Teleflex Marine, Teleflex Medical and Teleflex Power Systems. The company is split into three sectors: commercial (47% of net revenue in 2006), medical (33% of 2006 revenue) and aerospace (20% of 2006 revenue). The commercial sector designs and manufactures motion control and vehicle management systems in both the automotive and nautical fields. The medical sector develops and produces disposable medical products, surgical instruments and specialty medical devices. Its hospital supply division, Rusch International, offers products such as catheters, endotracheal tubes, laryngoscopes, facemasks, tracheotomy tubes, stents and precision tubing and wire products. The aerospace segment provides repair and products for turbine engines and manufactures cargo-handling systems. Commercial aviation contributes 89% of net revenue in the aerospace sector. The company has recently made a number of major acquisitions. In November 2006, Teleflex acquired Ecotrans Technologies, Inc., a supplier of anti-idling and emissions solutions for the railway industry; additionally in November 2006, Teleflex acquired the assets of Taut, Inc., a provider of tools used in minimally invasive surgeries. In April 2007, the firm acquired all of the assets of Southern Wire Corporation, a leading distributor of wire rope cables. Also in April 2007, Teleflex acquired the assets of HDJ Company, Inc. and its wholly-owned subsidiary, Specialized Medical Devices, Inc., which provides medical manufacturing services. In July 2007, Teleflex agreed to acquire Arrow International, Inc., a leading supplier of specialized medical supplies for $2 billion; the company will become integrated with Teleflex Medical. In July 2007, Teleflex sold its Aerospace Manufacturing Group, a part of its aerospace division, to GKN plc.

Teleflex, Inc offers employees a variety of benefits including health and life insurance, disability coverage, retirement/401(k) plans and a tuition assistance program.

FINANCIALS: Sales and profits are in thousands of dollars—add 000 to get the full amount. 2007 Note: Financial information for 2007 was not available for all companies at press time.

2007 Sales: $	2007 Profits: $	**U.S. Stock Ticker: TFX**
2006 Sales: $2,646,757	2006 Profits: $139,430	**Int'l Ticker:** Int'l Exchange:
2005 Sales: $2,514,552	2005 Profits: $138,817	Employees: 19,800
2004 Sales: $2,390,411	2004 Profits: $9,517	Fiscal Year Ends: 12/31
2003 Sales: $2,060,896	2003 Profits: $109,103	Parent Company:

SALARIES/BENEFITS:

Pension Plan: Y	ESOP Stock Plan:	Profit Sharing:	Top Exec. Salary: $850,000	Bonus: $489,330
Savings Plan: Y	Stock Purch. Plan: Y		Second Exec. Salary: $440,001	Bonus: $453,028

OTHER THOUGHTS:

Apparent Women Officers or Directors: 1
Hot Spot for Advancement for Women/Minorities: Y

LOCATIONS: ("Y" = Yes)

West:	Southwest:	Midwest:	Southeast:	Northeast:	International:
Y	Y	Y	Y	Y	Y

TENET HEALTHCARE CORPORATION www.tenethealth.com

Industry Group Code: 622110 **Ranks within this company's industry group:** Sales: 4 Profits: 21

Insurance/HMO/PPO:		Drugs:		Equipment/Supplies:		Hospitals/Clinics:		Services:		Health Care:	
Insurance:		Manufacturer:		Manufacturer:		Acute Care:	Y	Diagnostics:		Home Health:	
Managed Care:		Distributor:		Distributor:		Sub-Acute:	Y	Labs/Testing:		Long-Term Care:	
Utilization Management:		Specialty Pharmacy:		Leasing/Finance:		Outpatient Surgery:	Y	Staffing:		Physical Therapy:	Y
Payment Processing:		Vitamins/Nutritionals:		Information Systems:		Physical Rehab. Ctr.:	Y	Waste Disposal:		Physician Prac. Mgmt.:	
		Clinical Trials:				Psychiatric Clinics:		Specialty Svcs.:			

TYPES OF BUSINESS:

Hospitals-General
Specialty Care Facilities
Outpatient Centers

BRANDS/DIVISIONS/AFFILIATES:

Coastal Carolina Medical Center

CONTACTS: *Note: Officers with more than one job title may be intentionally listed here more than once.*

Trevor Fetter, CEO
Stephen L. Newman, COO
Trevor Fetter, Pres.
Biggs C. Porter, CFO
Cathy Kusaka Fraser, Sr. VP-Human Resources
Stephen F. Brown, CIO/Exec. VP
E. Peter Urbanowicz, General Counsel
Stephen L. Newman, Interim Dir.-Clinical Quality Department
Audrey T. Andrews, Chief Compliance Officer
Edward Kangas, Chmn.

Phone: 469-893-2200	**Fax:** 469-893-8600
Toll-Free:	
Address: 13737 Noel Road, Dallas, TX 75240 US	

GROWTH PLANS/SPECIAL FEATURES:

Tenet Healthcare Corp. specializes in the provision of health care services, primarily through the operation of general hospitals. All of Tenet's operations are conducted through its subsidiaries. The company's 64 general hospitals (of which 53 are owned by subsidiaries and 11 by third parties and leased by the firm's subsidiaries), a cancer hospital and two critical access hospitals contain 16,310 licensed beds, serving both urban and rural communities in 12 states. The firm's operations are structured into five regions: the California region, which includes the hospitals in California and Nebraska; the Central-Northeast region, which include the hospitals in Missouri, Pennsylvania and Tennessee; the Southern States region, which includes the hospitals in Alabama, Georgia, Louisiana, North Carolina and South Carolina; the Texas region, which includes the hospitals in Texas; and the Florida region, which includes the hospitals in Florida. The majority of the Tenet's beds are concentrated in California, Florida and Texas. Each of the company's general hospitals offers acute care services, operating and recovery rooms, radiology services, respiratory therapy services, clinical laboratories and pharmacies; most also offer intensive care, critical care or coronary care units, physical therapy and orthopedic, oncology and outpatient services. In addition, some of the hospitals offer specialty procedures such as heart, lung, liver and kidney transplants; gamma-knife brain surgery; and bone marrow transplants. The company's subsidiaries also own or lease physician practices, captive insurance companies and various other ancillary health care businesses, including outpatient surgery centers, diagnostic imaging centers and occupational and rural health care clinics. In July 2007, Tenet acquired Coastal Carolina Medical Center, a 41-bed acute care hospital, for $35 million.

The company offers its employees medical, dental and vision insurance; life and AD&D insurance; a 401(k) plan; an employee stock purchase plan; and an employee assistance program.

FINANCIALS: **Sales and profits are in thousands of dollars—add 000 to get the full amount. 2007 Note: Financial information for 2007 was not available for all companies at press time.**

2007 Sales: $	2007 Profits: $	**U.S. Stock Ticker: THC**
2006 Sales: $8,701,000	2006 Profits: $-803,000	**Int'l Ticker:** Int'l Exchange:
2005 Sales: $8,614,000	2005 Profits: $-724,000	Employees: 68,952
2004 Sales: $8,768,000	2004 Profits: $-2,806,000	Fiscal Year Ends: 12/31
2003 Sales: $13,212,000	2003 Profits: $-1,477,000	Parent Company:

SALARIES/BENEFITS:

Pension Plan:	ESOP Stock Plan:	Profit Sharing:	Top Exec. Salary: $1,081,000	Bonus: $1,051,340
Savings Plan: Y	Stock Purch. Plan: Y		Second Exec. Salary: $728,077	Bonus: $560,675

OTHER THOUGHTS:

Apparent Women Officers or Directors: 4
Hot Spot for Advancement for Women/Minorities: Y

LOCATIONS: ("Y" = Yes)

West:	Southwest:	Midwest:	Southeast:	Northeast:	International:
Y	Y	Y	Y	Y	

Note: Financial information, benefits and other data can change quickly and may vary from those stated here.

TEVA PHARMACEUTICAL INDUSTRIES www.tevapharm.com

Industry Group Code: 325416 **Ranks within this company's industry group:** Sales: 1 Profits: 1

Insurance/HMO/PPO:		Drugs:		Equipment/Supplies:		Hospitals/Clinics:		Services:		Health Care:	
Insurance:		Manufacturer:	Y	Manufacturer:		Acute Care:		Diagnostics:		Home Health:	
Managed Care:		Distributor:		Distributor:		Sub-Acute:		Labs/Testing:		Long-Term Care:	
Utilization Management:		Specialty Pharmacy:		Leasing/Finance:		Outpatient Surgery:		Staffing:		Physical Therapy:	
Payment Processing:		Vitamins/Nutritionals:		Information Systems:		Physical Rehab. Ctr.:		Waste Disposal:		Physician Prac. Mgmt.:	
		Clinical Trials:				Psychiatric Clinics:		Specialty Svcs.:			

TYPES OF BUSINESS:

Drugs-Generic
Active Pharmaceutical Ingredients

BRANDS/DIVISIONS/AFFILIATES:

Teva Pharmaceuticals USA
Pharmachemie BV
Copaxone
Ivax Corporation

CONTACTS: *Note: Officers with more than one job title may be intentionally listed here more than once.*

Shlomo Yanai, CEO
Shlomo Yanai, Pres.
Dan S. Suesskind, CFO
Judith Vardi, VP-Israel Pharmaceutical Sales
Bruria Sofrin, VP-Human Resources
Ben-Zion Weiner, Chief R&D Officer
Shmuel Ben Zvi, VP-IT/Planning & Economics
Rodney Kasan, CTO/VP
Uzi Karniel, General Counsel/Corp. Sec.
Itzhak Krinsky, VP-Bus. Dev.
Doron Blachar, VP-Finance
George S. Barrett, VP-N. America/CEO/Pres., Teva North America
Amir Elstein, VP-Global Specialty Pharmaceutical Prod.
Gerard Van Odlijk, VP/CEO/Pres., Teva Pharmaceuticals Europe B.V.
Jacob Winter, VP-Global Generic Resources
Eli Hurvitz, Chmn.
Chaim Hurvitz, VP-Int'l

Phone: 972-3-926-7267	**Fax:** 972-3-923-4050
Toll-Free:	
Address: 5 Basel St., Petach Tikva, 49131 Israel	

GROWTH PLANS/SPECIAL FEATURES:

Teva Pharmaceutical Industries, Ltd., based in Israel, is a global pharmaceutical company that produces, distributes and sells pharmaceutical products internationally. Teva has additional manufacturing and marketing facilities in North America and Europe. Eighty percent of the firm's sales are in North America and Europe. The firm focuses on human pharmaceuticals (HP) and active pharmaceutical ingredients (API). The HP segment produces generic drugs in all major therapeutics in a variety of dosage forms, including capsules, tablets, creams, ointments and liquids. The API segment which accounts for 90% of total sales, distributes ingredients to manufacturers worldwide, in addition to supporting its own pharmaceutical products. Teva also manufactures innovative drugs in niche markets through its research and development efforts. Subsidiary Teva Pharmaceuticals USA is a dominant figure in the manufacture and distribution of generic drugs in the U.S. In addition, subsidiary Pharmachemie BV has the largest market share in generics in the Netherlands. The firm's two chief products are Copaxone, a branded treatment for MS, currently marketed and sold in 42 countries including the U.S., and Azilect, a new treatment for Parkinson's marketed in Israel, the U.S., Canada, Europe and Turkey. The firm's R&D activities focus on the development of innovative molecules for treatment of multiple sclerosis; other neurological and neurodegenerative diseases (Alzheimer's, Parkinson's and ALS); auto-immune and inflammatory diseases (Lupus and psoriasis); and diseases in the field of oncology (Hermato-oncological applications and Glioma). In January 2006, Teva acquired Ivax Corporation, a U.S.-based multinational generics company. The results of this purchase and the subsequent merger boosted Teva's operations to cover over 50 markets and expanded operations to 44 plants, 15 research centers and 18 API sites.

FINANCIALS: **Sales and profits are in thousands of dollars—add 000 to get the full amount. 2007 Note: Financial information for 2007 was not available for all companies at press time.**

2007 Sales: $	2007 Profits: $	**U.S. Stock Ticker: TEVA**
2006 Sales: $8,408,000	2006 Profits: $546,000	**Int'l Ticker: TEVA** Int'l Exchange: Tel Aviv-TASE
2005 Sales: $5,250,000	2005 Profits: $1,072,000	Employees: 26,670
2004 Sales: $4,799,000	2004 Profits: $-331,800	Fiscal Year Ends: 12/31
2003 Sales: $3,276,400	2003 Profits: $691,000	Parent Company:

SALARIES/BENEFITS:

Pension Plan: Y	ESOP Stock Plan:	Profit Sharing:	Top Exec. Salary: $	Bonus: $
Savings Plan: Y	Stock Purch. Plan: Y		Second Exec. Salary: $	Bonus: $

OTHER THOUGHTS:

Apparent Women Officers or Directors: 6
Hot Spot for Advancement for Women/Minorities: Y

LOCATIONS: ("Y" = Yes)

West:	Southwest:	Midwest:	Southeast:	Northeast:	International:
Y	Y	Y	Y	Y	Y

TEXAS HEALTH RESOURCES www.texashealth.org

ndustry Group Code: 622110 **Ranks within this company's industry group:** Sales: Profits:

nsurance/HMO/PPO:		Drugs:		Equipment/Supplies:		Hospitals/Clinics:		Services:		Health Care:	
nsurance:		Manufacturer:		Manufacturer:		Acute Care:	Y	Diagnostics:		Home Health:	
Aanaged Care:		Distributor:		Distributor:		Sub-Acute:	Y	Labs/Testing:		Long-Term Care:	Y
Jtilization Management:		Specialty Pharmacy:		Leasing/Finance:		Outpatient Surgery:		Staffing:		Physical Therapy:	
ayment Processing:		Vitamins/Nutritionals:		Information Systems:		Physical Rehab. Ctr.:	Y	Waste Disposal:		Physician Prac. Mgmt.:	
		Clinical Trials:				Psychiatric Clinics:	Y	Specialty Svcs.:	Y		

TYPES OF BUSINESS:

Hospitals-General
Medical Research
Retirement Community

BRANDS/DIVISIONS/AFFILIATES:

Harris Methodist Health System
Presbyterian Healthcare Resources
Arlington Memorial Hospital
Texas Health Research Institute
Presbyterian Village North

CONTACTS: *Note: Officers with more than one job title may be intentionally listed here more than once.*

Douglas D. Hawthorne, CEO
Douglas D. Hawthorne, Pres.
Ronald R. Long, CFO/Exec. VP-Resource Dev. & Deployment
Bonnie Bell, Exec. VP-People & Culture
Stephen C. Hanson, Exec. VP-Oper.
Dave Ashworth, VP-Strategy
Oscar L. Amparan, Pres., Harris Methodist Fort Worth Hospital
Barclay E. Berdan, Sr. Exec. VP-System Alignment & Performance
Michael Deegan, Exec. VP/Chief Clinical & Quality Officer
Mark Merrill, Pres., Presbyterian Hospital of Dallas

Phone: 817-462-7900	Fax: 817-462-6996
Toll-Free: 888-442-7747	
Address: 611 Ryan Plaza Dr., Ste. 900, Arlington, TX 76011 US	

GROWTH PLANS/SPECIAL FEATURES:

Texas Health Resources (THR) is one of the largest faith-based, nonprofit health care delivery systems in the U.S. The firm serves more than 6.3 million people in the Dallas-Ft. Worth area through three hospital systems. THR was formed in 1997 through the merger of Harris Methodist Health System, Presbyterian Healthcare System and Arlington Memorial Hospital Foundation, Inc. Together, the company has 13 hospitals and 27 health care sites with more than 2,600 hospital beds that are watched by more than 3,600 physicians. Arlington Memorial Hospital is an acute-care, full-service, 369-bed hospital in northern Texas with more than 550 staffed physicians. Harris Methodist Hospitals is a collection of six hospitals serving four counties. Harris Methodist H.E.B. Hospital includes a 50-bed psychiatric and behavioral health unit. The Presbyterian Healthcare system serves four Texas counties with six hospitals. The firm's Texas Health Research Institute (THRI) subsidiary conducts medical research, offers educational programs and develops projects for the prevention, diagnosis and treatment of diseases. Through THRI the company operates Presbyterian Institute for Minimally Invasive Technology (PIMIT), a program dedicated to the research and development of minimally invasive technologies and the training of health care professionals in such technologies. The group also operates Presbyterian Village North, a continuing care retirement community in north Dallas that offers independent living, assisted living, nursing care and Alzheimer care.

THR offers its employees health coverage, wellness programs, income protection, a dependent care spending account, on-site child care, on-site sick child care, adoption assistance, a 401(k) plan, credit union membership, tuition reimbursement and a nurse training program.

FINANCIALS: **Sales and profits are in thousands of dollars—add 000 to get the full amount. 2007 Note: Financial information for 2007 was not available for all companies at press time.**

2007 Sales: $	2007 Profits: $	**U.S. Stock Ticker: Nonprofit**
2006 Sales: $	2006 Profits: $	**Int'l Ticker:** Int'l Exchange:
2005 Sales: $	2005 Profits: $	Employees: 17,700
2004 Sales: $	2004 Profits: $	Fiscal Year Ends: 12/31
2003 Sales: $1,900,000	2003 Profits: $	Parent Company:

SALARIES/BENEFITS:

Pension Plan:	ESOP Stock Plan:	Profit Sharing:	Top Exec. Salary: $	Bonus: $
Savings Plan: Y	Stock Purch. Plan:		Second Exec. Salary: $	Bonus: $

OTHER THOUGHTS:

Apparent Women Officers or Directors: 1
Hot Spot for Advancement for Women/Minorities:

LOCATIONS: ("Y" = Yes)

West:	Southwest:	Midwest:	Southeast:	Northeast:	International:
	Y				

THERAGENICS CORP www.theragenics.com

Industry Group Code: 339113 **Ranks within this company's industry group:** Sales: 91 Profits: 68

Insurance/HMO/PPO:		Drugs:		Equipment/Supplies:		Hospitals/Clinics:		Services:		Health Care:	
Insurance:		Manufacturer:		Manufacturer:	Y	Acute Care:		Diagnostics:		Home Health:	
Managed Care:		Distributor:		Distributor:		Sub-Acute:		Labs/Testing:		Long-Term Care:	
Utilization Management:		Specialty Pharmacy:		Leasing/Finance:		Outpatient Surgery:		Staffing:		Physical Therapy:	
Payment Processing:		Vitamins/Nutritionals:		Information Systems:		Physical Rehab. Ctr.:		Waste Disposal:		Physician Prac. Mgmt.:	
		Clinical Trials:				Psychiatric Clinics:		Specialty Svcs.:			

TYPES OF BUSINESS:

Medical Devices
Surgical Products

BRANDS/DIVISIONS/AFFILIATES:

TheraSeed
CE Mark
CP Medical Corp.
Galt Medical Corp.

CONTACTS: *Note: Officers with more than one job title may be intentionally listed here more than once.*

M. Christine Jacobs, CEO
M. Christine Jacobs, Pres.
Frank J. Tarallo, CFO
Bruce W. Smith, Exec. VP-Strategy & Bus. Dev.
Frank J. Tarallo, Treas.
James R. Eddings, Pres., Galt Medical
Patrick J. Ferguson, Pres., CP Medical
R. Michael O'Bannon, Exec. VP-Organizational Dev.
M. Christine Jacobs, Chmn.

Phone: 770-271-0233	**Fax:** 770-831-5294
Toll-Free:	
Address: 5203 Bristol Industrial Way, Buford, GA 30518 US	

GROWTH PLANS/SPECIAL FEATURES:

Theragenics Corp. is a medical device company serving the cancer treatment and surgical markets. The company operates in two segments: the brachytherapy seed business and the surgical products business. The brachytherapy business segment produces, markets and sells TheraSeed the firm's premier palladium-103 prostrate cancer treatment device; I-seed, its iodone-125 based prostrate cancer treatment device; and other related products and services. Theragenics is the world's largest producer of palladium-103, the radioactive isotope that supplies the therapeutic radiation for its TheraSeed device. TheraSeed, marketed in Europe with the brand name CE Mark, is an implant the size of a grain of rice that is used primarily in treating localized prostate cancer with a one-time, minimally invasive procedure. The implant emits radiation within the immediate prostate area, killing the tumor while sparing surrounding organs from significant radiation exposure. Physicians, hospitals and other healthcare providers, primarily located in the United States, utilize the TheraSeed device. The majority of TheraSeed sales are channeled through one third-party distributor. The surgical products business segment consists of wound closure and vascular access products. Wound closure include sutures, needles and other surgical products with applications in, among other areas, urology, veterinary, cardiology, orthopedics, plastic surgery and dental. Vascular access includes introducers and guidewires used in the interventional radiology, interventional cardiology and vascular surgery markets. Theragenics subsidiaries, CP Medical Corp. and Galt Medical Corp. accounted for roughly 36% of revenue in 2006. In August 2006, Theragenics acquired Galt Medical Corp., a private manufacturer of disposable medical devices utilized for vascular access, for roughly $32.7 million.

The company offers its employees medical, dental and life insurance; short- and long-term disability protection; a 401(k) plan; an employee stock purchase plan; and an on-site wellness center.

FINANCIALS: **Sales and profits are in thousands of dollars—add 000 to get the full amount. 2007 Note: Financial information for 2007 was not available for all companies at press time.**

2007 Sales: $	2007 Profits: $	**U.S. Stock Ticker: TGX**
2006 Sales: $54,096	2006 Profits: $6,865	**Int'l Ticker:** Int'l Exchange:
2005 Sales: $44,270	2005 Profits: $-29,006	Employees: 315
2004 Sales: $33,338	2004 Profits: $-4,310	Fiscal Year Ends: 12/31
2003 Sales: $35,600	2003 Profits: $- 300	Parent Company:

SALARIES/BENEFITS:

Pension Plan:	ESOP Stock Plan:	Profit Sharing:	Top Exec. Salary: $493,000	Bonus: $270,000
Savings Plan: Y	Stock Purch. Plan: Y		Second Exec. Salary: $255,000	Bonus: $127,100

OTHER THOUGHTS:

Apparent Women Officers or Directors: 2
Hot Spot for Advancement for Women/Minorities: Y

LOCATIONS: ("Y" = Yes)

West:	Southwest:	Midwest:	Southeast:	Northeast:	International:
Y	Y		Y		

THERMO FISHER SCIENTIFIC INC www.thermofisher.com

Industry Group Code: 421450 **Ranks within this company's industry group:** Sales: 3 Profits: 2

Insurance/HMO/PPO:		Drugs:		Equipment/Supplies:		Hospitals/Clinics:		Services:		Health Care:	
Insurance:		Manufacturer:		Manufacturer:	Y	Acute Care:		Diagnostics:	Y	Home Health:	
Managed Care:		Distributor:		Distributor:		Sub-Acute:		Labs/Testing:	Y	Long-Term Care:	
Utilization Management:		Specialty Pharmacy:		Leasing/Finance:		Outpatient Surgery:		Staffing:		Physical Therapy:	
Payment Processing:		Vitamins/Nutritionals:		Information Systems:		Physical Rehab. Ctr.:		Waste Disposal:		Physician Prac. Mgmt.:	
		Clinical Trials:				Psychiatric Clinics:		Specialty Svcs.:	Y		

TYPES OF BUSINESS:

Laboratory Equipment & Supplies Distribution
Contract Manufacturing
Equipment Calibration & Repair
Clinical Trial Services
Laboratory Workstations
Clinical Consumables
Diagnostic Reagents
Custom Chemical Synthesis

BRANDS/DIVISIONS/AFFILIATES:

Fisher Scientific International
Thermo Electron Group
Qualigens Fine Chemicals

CONTACTS: *Note: Officers with more than one job title may be intentionally listed here more than once.*

Marijin E. Dekkers, CEO
Marijin E. Dekkers, Pres.
Peter M. Wilver, CFO
Stephen G. Sheehan, Sr. VP-Human Resources
Seth H. Hoogasian, General Counsel/Sec./Sr. VP
Kenneth J. Apicerno, VP-Investor Rel./Treas.
Peter E. Hornstra, VP/Chief Acct. Officer
Marc N. Casper, Exec. VP
Guy Broadbent, Sr. VP
Alan J. Malus, Sr. VP
Fredric T. Walder, Sr. VP-Customer Excellence
Joseph R. Massaro, Sr. VP-Global Bus. Svcs.

Phone: 781-622-1000	**Fax:** 781-622-1207
Toll-Free: 800-678-5599	
Address: 81 Wyman St., Waltham, MA 02454 US	

GROWTH PLANS/SPECIAL FEATURES:

Thermo Fisher Scientific Inc., formerly Fisher Scientific International, is a distributor of products and services principally to the scientific-research and clinical laboratory markets. It serves over 350,000 customers in biotechnology and pharmaceutical companies; colleges and universities; medical-research institutions; hospitals; reference, quality-control, process-control and research and development labs in various industries; and government agencies. Thermo Fisher offers an array of products and services, from biochemicals, cell-culture media and proprietary RNAi technology to rapid diagnostic tests, safety products and other consumable supplies. The company's services include pharmaceutical services for Phase III and IV clinical trials, laboratory instrument calibration and repair, contract manufacturing, custom chemical synthesis, combinatorial chemistry, specialized packaging and supply chain management. Thermo Fisher's laboratory workstations segment engages in the manufacture and sale of laboratory furniture and fume hoods and also provides laboratory design services. The company was formed by the 2006 acquisition of Fisher Scientific International by Thermo Electron Grooup for $10.6 billion. In July 2007, Thermo Fisher announced plans to acquire Qualigens Fine Chemicals, a division of GlaxoSmithKine Pharmaceuticals Ltd., based in India.

Thermo Fisher offers its employees health and dental insurance and a 401(k) plan.

FINANCIALS: **Sales and profits are in thousands of dollars—add 000 to get the full amount. 2007 Note: Financial information for 2007 was not available for all companies at press time.**

2007 Sales: $
2006 Sales: $3,791,617
2005 Sales: $2,633,027
2004 Sales: $2,205,995
2003 Sales: $1,899,400

2007 Profits: $
2006 Profits: $168,935
2005 Profits: $223,218
2004 Profits: $361,837
2003 Profits: $200,000

U.S. Stock Ticker: TMO
Int'l Ticker: Int'l Exchange:
Employees: 30,500
Fiscal Year Ends: 12/31
Parent Company: THERMO ELECTRON CORP

SALARIES/BENEFITS:

Pension Plan: ESOP Stock Plan: Profit Sharing: Top Exec. Salary: $1,036,539 Bonus: $2,135,000
Savings Plan: Y Stock Purch. Plan: Second Exec. Salary: $614,615 Bonus: $950,667

OTHER THOUGHTS:

Apparent Women Officers or Directors:
Hot Spot for Advancement for Women/Minorities:

LOCATIONS: ("Y" = Yes)

West:	Southwest:	Midwest:	Southeast:	Northeast:	International:
Y		Y	Y	Y	Y

THORATEC CORPORATION www.thoratec.com

Industry Group Code: 339113 **Ranks within this company's industry group:** Sales: 59 Profits: 73

Insurance/HMO/PPO:		Drugs:		Equipment/Supplies:		Hospitals/Clinics:		Services:		Health Care:	
Insurance:		Manufacturer:		Manufacturer:	Y	Acute Care:		Diagnostics:		Home Health:	
Managed Care:		Distributor:		Distributor:		Sub-Acute:		Labs/Testing:		Long-Term Care:	
Utilization Management:		Specialty Pharmacy:		Leasing/Finance:		Outpatient Surgery:		Staffing:		Physical Therapy:	
Payment Processing:		Vitamins/Nutritionals:		Information Systems:		Physical Rehab. Ctr.:		Waste Disposal:		Physician Prac. Mgmt.:	
		Clinical Trials:				Psychiatric Clinics:		Specialty Svcs.:			

TYPES OF BUSINESS:

Medical Equipment-Ventricular Assistance Devices
Circulatory Support Products
Vascular Graft Products
Point-of-Care Diagnostic Products

BRANDS/DIVISIONS/AFFILIATES:

Thoratec VAD
International Technidyne Corp.
Thermo Cardiosystems
Thoratec IVAD
HeartMate
Vectra
TLC-II
IRMA TRUpoint Blood Analysis System

CONTACTS: *Note: Officers with more than one job title may be intentionally listed here more than once.*

Gary F. Burbach, CEO
Gary F. Burbach, Pres.
David V. Smith, CFO/Exec. VP
Steve Brandt, VP-Sales
Glen Sunnergren, VP-Human Resources
David J. Farrar, VP-Research & Scientific Affairs
Laxmi N. Peri, VP-Tech.
Laxmi N. Peri, VP-Prod. Dev.
David A. Lehman, General Counsel/VP
Patrick Schmitz, VP-Oper.
Jon R. Shear, VP-Bus. Dev.
Donald A. Middlebrook, VP-Regulatory Affairs & Quality Assurance
Jeffrey W. Nelson, Pres., Cardiovascular Div.
Douglas M. Petty, VP-Mktg.
Robin R. Bostic, VP-Reimbursement
Neil Dimick, Chmn.

Phone: 925-847-8600	**Fax:** 925-847-8574
Toll-Free: 800-528-2577	
Address: 6035 Stoneridge Dr., Pleasanton, CA 94588 US	

GROWTH PLANS/SPECIAL FEATURES:

Thoratec Corp. is the leading manufacturer of circulator support products for the treatment of heart failure (HF). HI is a disorder in which the heart loses its ability to pump bloo efficiently; approximately 23 million people worldwide suffe from HF, with 2 million new cases diagnosed each yea Thoratec was the first company to receive approval from th FDA to commercially market a ventricular assist devic (VAD) to treat patients with late-stage HF. These VADs, th firm's primary products, are used to perform some or all c the heart's pumping function. Thoratec offers the wides range of products to serve this market. The firm's VAD have treated approximately 11,000 patients, can b implanted or worn outside the body and are suitable for th treatment of patients of varying sizes and ages for differer durations. The company is pursuing approval to use it VADs in other applications, including as an alternative t maximum drug therapy. Its operations comprise tw divisions: Cardiovascular and International Technidyn Corporation (ITC), a wholly owned subsidiary. Th Cardiovascular segment contains circulatory suppo products, which are products for the short- and long-terr treatment of HF. In addition, this segment has develope small diameter grafts using proprietary materials to addres the vascular access market. The grafts are sold for use i hemodialysis. ITC produces a family of single-use ski incision devices used to provide blood samples, as well a point-of-care products, including blood diagnostic tes systems. Thoratec's HeartMate II, a continuous flow devic designed to provide long-term cardiac support for advanced stage HF patients, is currently in a Phase II pivotal trial.

Thoratec offers its employees education assistance and referral program.

FINANCIALS: Sales and profits are in thousands of dollars—add 000 to get the full amount. 2007 Note: Financial information for 2007 was not available for all companies at press time.

2007 Sales: $	2007 Profits: $	**U.S. Stock Ticker: THOR**
2006 Sales: $214,133	2006 Profits: $3,973	**Int'l Ticker:** Int'l Exchange:
2005 Sales: $201,712	2005 Profits: $13,198	Employees: 934
2004 Sales: $172,341	2004 Profits: $3,564	Fiscal Year Ends: 1/02
2003 Sales: $149,916	2003 Profits: $-2,182	Parent Company:

SALARIES/BENEFITS:

Pension Plan:	ESOP Stock Plan:	Profit Sharing:	Top Exec. Salary: $344,712	Bonus: $149,733
Savings Plan: Y	Stock Purch. Plan: Y		Second Exec. Salary: $305,000	Bonus: $577,060

OTHER THOUGHTS:

Apparent Women Officers or Directors: 1
Hot Spot for Advancement for Women/Minorities: Y

LOCATIONS: ("Y" = Yes)

West:	Southwest:	Midwest:	Southeast:	Northeast:	International:
Y		Y		Y	Y

TLC VISION CORPORATION www.tlcv.com

ndustry Group Code: 621490 **Ranks within this company's industry group:** Sales: 8 Profits: 8

nsurance/HMO/PPO:		Drugs:		Equipment/Supplies:		Hospitals/Clinics:		Services:		Health Care:	
nsurance:		Manufacturer:		Manufacturer:		Acute Care:		Diagnostics:		Home Health:	
lanaged Care:		Distributor:		Distributor:		Sub-Acute:		Labs/Testing:		Long-Term Care:	
Jtilization Management:		Specialty Pharmacy:		Leasing/Finance:		Outpatient Surgery:	Y	Staffing:		Physical Therapy:	
ayment Processing:		Vitamins/Nutritionals:		Information Systems:	Y	Physical Rehab. Ctr.:		Waste Disposal:		Physician Prac. Mgmt.:	
		Clinical Trials:				Psychiatric Clinics:		Specialty Svcs.:			

TYPES OF BUSINESS:

ye Clinics
aser Vision Correction Services
lood Filtration Equipment
lanagement Software & Systems

BRANDS/DIVISIONS/AFFILIATES:

LCVision
ISS, Inc.

CONTACTS: *Note: Officers with more than one job title may be ntentionally listed here more than once.*

ames C. Wachtman, CEO
teven P. Rasche, CFO
lichael F. McEnaney, Chief Mktg. Officer/Exec. VP
ikki Bradley, Exec. VP-Human Resources
lenry Lynn, VP-Info. Systems
rian L. Andrew, General Counsel
ames J. Hyland, VP-Investor Rel.
ikki Bradley, Exec. VP-Clinical Svcs. & Quality Assurance
ames B. Tiffany, Pres., Midwest Surgical Services
Varren Rustand, Chmn.

hone: 905-602-2020	**Fax:** 905-602-2025
oll-Free: 800-852-1033	
ddress: 5280 Solar Dr., Ste. 300, Mississauga, ON L4W 5M8 anada	

GROWTH PLANS/SPECIAL FEATURES:

TLC Vision Corporation is a diversified eye care service company dedicated to improving lives through better vision by providing eye doctors with the tools and technologies needed to deliver high quality patient care. The majority of the company's revenues come from laser refractive surgery, which involves using an excimer laser to treat common refractive vision disorders such as myopia (nearsightedness), hyperopia (farsightedness) and astigmatism by reshaping the corona of the eye. TLC owns and manages approximately 80 refractive centers across the U.S. and Canada, with over 300 fixed and mobile laser equiptment access sites. The majority of the company's excimer lasers are manufactured by VISX. TLC physicians use excimer lasers to perform most forms of eye surgery, using photorefractive keratectomy (PRK), phototherapeutic keratectomy (PTK), laser in-situ keratomileusis (LASIK), CustomLASIK, astigmatic keratotomy (AK) or laser assisted sub-epithelial keratectomy (LASEK). TLC physicians might also use in Conductive Keratoplasty (CK), which uses radio frequencies instead of an excimer laser, or INTACS, which corrects nearsightedness by implanting rings in the cornea to reshape it rather than surgically altering the cornea. More than 90% of the excimer laser procedures performed at the company's eye care centers are LASIK treatments. TLC uses its proprietary management and administrative software in all of the company's eye clinics. The software provides surgical candidates with current information on affiliated doctors throughout North America, directs candidates to the closest eye care center, tracks calls and procedures, coordinates patients and doctor scheduling, produces financial and surgical outcome reporting and offers online consumer consultation, which allows consumers to book their consultation appointment. Also, through its MSS, Inc. subsidiary, the company furnishes hospitals and other facilities with mobile or fixed site access to cataract surgery equipment, supplies and technicians. In June 2007, TLC opened new TLC Laser Eye Centers in Portland, Oregon and in Chicago, Illinois.

FINANCIALS: **Sales and profits are in thousands of dollars—add 000 to get the full amount. 2007 Note: Financial information for 2007 was not available for all companies at press time.**

007 Sales: $	2007 Profits: $	**U.S. Stock Ticker: TLCV**
006 Sales: $281,800	2006 Profits: $11,500	**Int'l Ticker: TLC** Int'l Exchange: Toronto-TSX
005 Sales: $260,025	2005 Profits: $6,885	Employees: 281
004 Sales: $247,247	2004 Profits: $43,708	Fiscal Year Ends: 12/31
003 Sales: $195,680	2003 Profits: $-9,399	Parent Company:

SALARIES/BENEFITS:

ension Plan:	ESOP Stock Plan:	Profit Sharing:	Top Exec. Salary: $375,000	Bonus: $47,000
avings Plan: Y	Stock Purch. Plan: Y		Second Exec. Salary: $250,000	Bonus: $25,000

OTHER THOUGHTS:

pparent Women Officers or Directors: 2
lot Spot for Advancement for Women/Minorities:

LOCATIONS: ("Y" = Yes)

West:	Southwest:	Midwest:	Southeast:	Northeast:	International:
Y	Y	Y	Y	Y	Y

TOSHIBA CORPORATION www.toshiba.com

Industry Group Code: 334111 **Ranks within this company's industry group:** Sales: 1 Profits: 1

Insurance/HMO/PPO:		Drugs:		Equipment/Supplies:		Hospitals/Clinics:		Services:		Health Care:	
Insurance:		Manufacturer:		Manufacturer:	Y	Acute Care:		Diagnostics:		Home Health:	
Managed Care:		Distributor:		Distributor:		Sub-Acute:		Labs/Testing:		Long-Term Care:	
Utilization Management:		Specialty Pharmacy:		Leasing/Finance:		Outpatient Surgery:		Staffing:		Physical Therapy:	
Payment Processing:		Vitamins/Nutritionals:		Information Systems:	Y	Physical Rehab. Ctr.:		Waste Disposal:		Physician Prac. Mgmt.:	
		Clinical Trials:				Psychiatric Clinics:		Specialty Svcs.:			

TYPES OF BUSINESS:

Electronics Manufacturing
Computers & Accessories
Telecommunications Equipment
Semiconductors
Consumer Electronics
Medical & Industrial Equipment
Satellite Radio
Internet Services

BRANDS/DIVISIONS/AFFILIATES:

Mobile Communications Company
Digital Media Network Company
Personal Computer and Network Company
Semiconductor Company
Industrial and Power Systems and Services Company
Social Network and Infrastructure Systems Company
Data Imaging Solutions
Contact Office Solutions, Inc.

CONTACTS: *Note: Officers with more than one job title may be intentionally listed here more than once.*

Atsutoshi Nishida, CEO
Atsutoshi Nishida, Pres.
Takeshi Nakagawa, Corp. Sr. Exec. VP
Sadazumi Ryu, Corp. Sr. Exec. VP
Shigeo Koguchi, Corp. Sr. Exec. VP
Masao Namiki, Sr. VP/CEO-Social Infrastructure Group
Tadashi Okamura, Chmn.

Phone: 81-3-3457-4511	**Fax:** 81-3-3456-1631
Toll-Free:	
Address: 1-1, Shibaura 1-chome, Minato-ku, Tokyo, 105-8001 Japan	

GROWTH PLANS/SPECIAL FEATURES:

Toshiba, a world leader in the design and manufacture o technology, is active in three key domains: Digital Products which contributes 39% of net sales and has 94 consolidate subsidiaries, and includes personal computers, accessories mobile phones, AV equipment, digital and flat panel TVs an portable personal equipment; Electronic Devices, 21.37% and 45 consolidated subsidiaries, such as semiconductors electron tubes, optoelectronic devices, liquid crystal displays batteries and printed circuits boards; and Socia Infrastructure systems, 28.98% and 122 consolidate subsidiaries, which includes industrial apparatuses, powe generating equipment, transportation equipment, socia automation equipment, telecommunication systems broadcasting systems, elevators, escalators and medica systems. Additionally, the company has operations in hom appliances, which contributes 10.58% and has 5 consolidated subsidiaries. Toshiba is also provides Interne services and is launching a satellite radio business. Th company has seven in-house companies: Mobil Communications Company; Digital Media Networ Company; Personal Computer and Network Compan Semiconductor Company; Industrial Systems Compan Power Systems Company; and Social Network an Infrastructure Systems Company. The company expende $3.152 billion on research and development in 200 Toshiba has over 648 subsidiaries and affiliated companie throughout the world. In 2006, the firm agreed to acquir Westinghouse from British Nuclear Fuels plc, which will allo Toshiba to become a leader in nuclear power generation. I recent news, the company announced in April 2007 that has agreed to transfer its interest in Toshiba Entertainmen Inc., to Hakuhodo DY Media Partners Inc. Toshib Entertainment will become a wholly owned subsidiary o Hakuhodo. Additionally, in May 2007 the compan announced that it has entered into an agreement for the joi development of WiMAX base stations in the Japanese an global markets with Nortel.

Toshiba offers its American employees flexible spendin accounts, credit union access, theme park discounts, a employee purchase plan, wellness events and an employe referral program.

FINANCIALS: **Sales and profits are in thousands of dollars—add 000 to get the full amount. 2007 Note: Financial information for 2007 was not available for all companies at press time.**

2007 Sales: $	2007 Profits: $	**U.S. Stock Ticker: TOSBF**
2006 Sales: $53,945,200	2006 Profits: $664,900	**Int'l Ticker: 6502** Int'l Exchange: Tokyo-TSE
2005 Sales: $54,264,400	2005 Profits: $428,100	Employees: 190,708
2004 Sales: $52,815,600	2004 Profits: $272,900	Fiscal Year Ends: 3/31
2003 Sales: $47,191,800	2003 Profits: $154,400	Parent Company:

SALARIES/BENEFITS:

Pension Plan:	ESOP Stock Plan:	Profit Sharing:	Top Exec. Salary: $	Bonus: $
Savings Plan:	Stock Purch. Plan:		Second Exec. Salary: $	Bonus: $

OTHER THOUGHTS:

Apparent Women Officers or Directors:
Hot Spot for Advancement for Women/Minorities:

LOCATIONS: ("Y" = Yes)

West:	Southwest:	Midwest:	Southeast:	Northeast:	International:
Y	Y			Y	Y

Note: Financial information, benefits and other data can change quickly and may vary from those stated here.

OWERS PERRIN www.towersperrin.com

dustry Group Code: 541612 **Ranks within this company's industry group:** Sales: 2 Profits:

surance/HMO/PPO:		Drugs:		Equipment/Supplies:		Hospitals/Clinics:		Services:		Health Care:	
surance:		Manufacturer:		Manufacturer:		Acute Care:		Diagnostics:		Home Health:	
anaged Care:		Distributor:		Distributor:		Sub-Acute:		Labs/Testing:		Long-Term Care:	
lization Management:		Specialty Pharmacy:		Leasing/Finance:		Outpatient Surgery:		Staffing:		Physical Therapy:	
yment Processing:		Vitamins/Nutritionals:		Information Systems:		Physical Rehab. Ctr.:		Waste Disposal:		Physician Prac. Mgmt.:	
		Clinical Trials:				Psychiatric Clinics:		Specialty Svcs.:	Y		

YPES OF BUSINESS:

uman Resources Consulting
enefit Plan & Compensation Consulting
ctuarial & Management Consulting
einsurance Consulting
uman Resources Outsourcing
uman Resources Consulting

RANDS/DIVISIONS/AFFILIATES:

llinghast
owers Perrin Reinsurance
xcellerateHRO

ONTACTS: *Note: Officers with more than one job title may be entionally listed here more than once.*

ark Mactas, CEO
obert G. Hogan, COO
aureen Breakiron-Evans, CFO
ny Candito, VP-Mktg.
ny Candito, VP-Human Resources
ny Candito, CIO
ny Candito, Chief Admin. Officer
icia Guinn, Managing Dir.-Tillinghast
mes K. Foreman, Managing Dir.-HR Svcs.
ark Mactas, Chmn.
on Lowman, Managing Dir.-Global Markets

hone: 203-326-5400	**Fax:** 203-326-5499
oll-Free:	
ddress: 1 Stamford Plaza, 263 Tresser Blvd., Ste. 700, amford, CT 06901-3226 US	

GROWTH PLANS/SPECIAL FEATURES:

Towers Perrin is an international provider of human resources, benefit plan and compensation consultation, operating out of more than 70 offices in 24 countries. The firm has worked with three-quarters of the world's 500 largest companies and three-quarters of the Fortune 1000 U.S. companies. Towers Perrin's services include third-party administration for retirement, health and welfare plans and compensation administration; human resources consulting, including communication training; employee hiring research; and rewards and performance management. The company is divided into three sections: HR services, reinsurance and the subsidiary Tillinghast. The HR services business provides international human resources consulting and related services. Services include assistance with employee benefits, compensation, and communication and change management. Towers Perrin's reinsurance business provides intermediary services and consulting expertise for reinsurance through a blend of risk transfer vehicles. The firm helps with reinsurance strategy and program review; claims management and program administration; catastrophe exposure management; contract negotiation and placement; and market security issues. Tillinghast provides global actuarial and management consulting to insurance and financial services companies and advises other organizations on risk financing and self-insurance including mergers, acquisitions and restructuring; financial and regulatory reporting; risk, capital and value management; products, markets and distribution; and financial modeling software solutions. Recent acquisitions by the company include employee research firm ISR and MGMC, Inc., a company providing compensation surveys and advisory services to the financial services industry.

Towers Perrin offers its employees a pay-for-performance approach, enabling employees who excel to realize higher rewards.

FINANCIALS: **Sales and profits are in thousands of dollars—add 000 to get the full amount. 2007 Note: Financial information for 2007 was not available for all companies at press time.**

07 Sales: $	2007 Profits: $	**U.S. Stock Ticker: Private**
06 Sales: $2,200,000	2006 Profits: $	**Int'l Ticker:** Int'l Exchange:
05 Sales: $2,000,000	2005 Profits: $	Employees:
04 Sales: $1,700,000	2004 Profits: $	Fiscal Year Ends: 12/31
03 Sales: $1,500,000	2003 Profits: $	Parent Company:

ALARIES/BENEFITS:

ension Plan: Y	ESOP Stock Plan:	Profit Sharing:	Top Exec. Salary: $	Bonus: $
avings Plan:	Stock Purch. Plan:		Second Exec. Salary: $	Bonus: $

THER THOUGHTS:

pparent Women Officers or Directors: 1
ot Spot for Advancement for Women/Minorities:

LOCATIONS: ("Y" = Yes)

West:	Southwest:	Midwest:	Southeast:	Northeast:	International:
Y	Y	Y	Y	Y	Y

TRANSCEND SERVICES INC www.transcendservices.com

Industry Group Code: 514210 **Ranks within this company's industry group:** Sales: 1 Profits: 1

Insurance/HMO/PPO:		Drugs:		Equipment/Supplies:		Hospitals/Clinics:		Services:		Health Care:	
Insurance:		Manufacturer:		Manufacturer:		Acute Care:		Diagnostics:		Home Health:	
Managed Care:		Distributor:		Distributor:		Sub-Acute:		Labs/Testing:		Long-Term Care:	
Utilization Management:		Specialty Pharmacy:		Leasing/Finance:		Outpatient Surgery:		Staffing:		Physical Therapy:	
Payment Processing:		Vitamins/Nutritionals:		Information Systems:		Physical Rehab. Ctr.:		Waste Disposal:		Physician Prac. Mgmt.:	
		Clinical Trials:				Psychiatric Clinics:		Specialty Svcs.:	Y		

TYPES OF BUSINESS:

Data Processing Services
Internet-Based Medical Transcription Services

BRANDS/DIVISIONS/AFFILIATES:

BeyondTXT
OTP Technologies, Inc.

CONTACTS: *Note: Officers with more than one job title may be intentionally listed here more than once.*

Larry G. Gerdes, CEO
Susan McGrogan, COO
Larry G. Gerdes, Pres.
Lance Cornell, CFO
Jeffrey McKee, Sr. VP-Sales & Mktg.
Lance Cornell, Corp. Sec.
Lance Cornell, Treas.
Larry G. Gerdes, Chmn.

Phone: 404-836-8000	**Fax:** 404-836-8009
Toll-Free: 800-555-8727	
Address: 945 E. Paces Ferry Rd., Ste. 1475, Atlanta, GA 30326 US	

GROWTH PLANS/SPECIAL FEATURES:

Transcend Services, Inc. provides medical transcriptic services. Customers include hospitals, hospital system multi-specialty clinics and physician group practice Transcend provides services to over 160 hospitals ar clinics, with typical customers providing an average annu revenue of about $200,000, and several larger custome contributing annual revenues exceeding $1 million. Th company offers two primary options to its customers: f customers without transcription technology availabl Transcend offers BeyondTXT; alternatively, Transcend ca access a customer's existing system to provide transcriptic services. BeyondTXT is a web-enabled voice and da distribution technology that allows a physician to dicta reports into several dictation products on the market, such a handheld devices, or even over the phone, includir hospital- or clinic-based transcription stations, home phon or even cell phones. This information is captured digitally the firm's central voice hub in Atlanta, Georgia, where th digital files are compressed, encrypted and stored. Th audio recordings are then accessed by home-based medic transcription professionals through the Internet, who eith transcribe the physicians' voice recordings directly or edit a electronic document created by BeyondTXT's voic recognition tool. After transcription, documents are returne to the Atlanta hub over the Internet, and they are distribute securely to end-users such as hospital information system via fax, printers or the Internet. Documents are general produced and delivered within 24 hours, but may b delivered in as little as four hours for premium prices. I operations run around the clock, every day of the year. July 2006, it began subcontracting with two offshore medic transcription firms, which was processing 7% of Transcend volume by December 2006. In January 2007, the compar acquired some assets of OTP Technologies, Inc., a Chicag area medical transcription company.

Transcend Services offers medical, dental and vision plan life insurance; and paid time off.

FINANCIALS: **Sales and profits are in thousands of dollars—add 000 to get the full amount. 2007 Note: Financial information for 2007 was not available for all companies at press time.**

2007 Sales: $	2007 Profits: $	**U.S. Stock Ticker: TRCR**
2006 Sales: $32,912	2006 Profits: $2,047	**Int'l Ticker:** Int'l Exchange:
2005 Sales: $25,817	2005 Profits: $- 817	Employees: 877
2004 Sales: $15,197	2004 Profits: $ 299	Fiscal Year Ends: 12/31
2003 Sales: $14,663	2003 Profits: $1,020	Parent Company:

SALARIES/BENEFITS:

Pension Plan:	ESOP Stock Plan:	Profit Sharing:	Top Exec. Salary: $235,000	Bonus: $35,000
Savings Plan: Y	Stock Purch. Plan: Y		Second Exec. Salary: $160,000	Bonus: $35,000

OTHER THOUGHTS:

Apparent Women Officers or Directors: 1
Hot Spot for Advancement for Women/Minorities:

LOCATIONS: ("Y" = Yes)

West:	Southwest:	Midwest:	Southeast:	Northeast:	International:
Y	Y		Y		

Note: Financial information, benefits and other data can change quickly and may vary from those stated here.

TRIAD HOSPITALS INC www.triadhospitals.com

ıdustry Group Code: 622110 **Ranks within this company's industry group:** Sales: 9 Profits: 10

surance/HMO/PPO:		Drugs:		Equipment/Supplies:		Hospitals/Clinics:		Services:		Health Care:	
surance:		Manufacturer:		Manufacturer:		Acute Care:	Y	Diagnostics:		Home Health:	
lanaged Care:		Distributor:		Distributor:		Sub-Acute:	Y	Labs/Testing:		Long-Term Care:	
tilization Management:		Specialty Pharmacy:		Leasing/Finance:		Outpatient Surgery:	Y	Staffing:		Physical Therapy:	
ayment Processing:		Vitamins/Nutritionals:		Information Systems:		Physical Rehab. Ctr.:	Y	Waste Disposal:		Physician Prac. Mgmt.:	
		Clinical Trials:				Psychiatric Clinics:	Y	Specialty Svcs.:	Y		

TYPES OF BUSINESS:

lospitals-General
mbulatory Surgery Centers
lanagement & Consulting Services

BRANDS/DIVISIONS/AFFILIATES:

Quorum Health Group
Community Health Systems, Inc.

CONTACTS: *Note: Officers with more than one job title may be ıtentionally listed here more than once.*

ames Shelton, CEO

Phone: 214-473-7000	Fax: 214-473-9411
'oll-Free: 800-238-6006	
Address: 5800 Tennyson Pkwy., Plano, TX 75024 US	

GROWTH PLANS/SPECIAL FEATURES:

Triad Hospitals, Inc., a wholly-owned subsidiary of Community Health Systems, Inc., manages hospitals and surgery centers located in small cities and selected high-growth urban markets in the southwestern, western and south-central areas of the U.S. Triad's hospital facilities include approximately 50 general acute care hospitals and 10 ambulatory surgery centers located in the states of Alabama, Alaska, Arizona, Arkansas, Indiana, Louisiana, Mississippi, Nevada, New Mexico, Ohio, Oklahoma, Oregon, South Carolina, Tennessee, Texas and West Virginia. Triad's general acute care hospitals typically provide a full range of services commonly available in hospitals, such as internal medicine, general surgery, cardiology, oncology, neurosurgery, orthopedics, obstetrics, diagnostic and emergency services. These hospitals also provide outpatient and ancillary health care services such as outpatient surgery, laboratory services, radiology, cardiology, and respiratory and physical therapy. In addition, some of Triad's general acute care hospitals have a number of licensed psychiatric beds and provide psychiatric nursing services. Triad is also a minority investor in three joint ventures that own seven general acute care hospitals in Georgia and Nevada. Through its wholly-owned subsidiary, Quorum Health Resources, LLC (QHR), Triad provides management and consulting services, including ethics and compliance programs, national supply and equipment purchasing and leasing contracts, accounting, personnel management and internal audit access to over 200 independent general acute care hospitals located throughout the U.S. In July 2007 the $6.8 billion acquisition and merger of the company by Community Health Systems, Inc. was completed. Triad stock ceased to trade as of July 2007.

FINANCIALS: Sales and profits are in thousands of dollars—add 000 to get the full amount. 2007 Note: Financial information for 2007 was not available for all companies at press time.

007 Sales: $	2007 Profits: $	**U.S. Stock Ticker: Subsidiary**
006 Sales: $5,537,900	2006 Profits: $207,900	**Int'l Ticker:** Int'l Exchange:
005 Sales: $4,747,300	2005 Profits: $229,400	Employees: 42,000
004 Sales: $4,218,000	2004 Profits: $132,000	Fiscal Year Ends: 12/31
003 Sales: $3,865,900	2003 Profits: $95,200	Parent Company: COMMUNITY HEALTH SYSTEMS INC

SALARIES/BENEFITS:

Pension Plan:	ESOP Stock Plan:	Profit Sharing:	Top Exec. Salary: $1,508,558	Bonus: $1,141,875
Savings Plan:	Stock Purch. Plan:		Second Exec. Salary: $514,679	Bonus: $258,789

OTHER THOUGHTS:

Apparent Women Officers or Directors:
lot Spot for Advancement for Women/Minorities: Y

LOCATIONS: ("Y" = Yes)

West:	Southwest:	Midwest:	Southeast:	Northeast:	International:
Y	Y	Y	Y	Y	

Note: Financial information, benefits and other data can change quickly and may vary from those stated here.

TRINITY HEALTH COMPANY www.trinity-health.org

Industry Group Code: 622110 **Ranks within this company's industry group:** Sales: Profits:

Insurance/HMO/PPO:		Drugs:		Equipment/Supplies:		Hospitals/Clinics:		Services:		Health Care:	
Insurance:		Manufacturer:		Manufacturer:		Acute Care:	Y	Diagnostics:		Home Health:	Y
Managed Care:	Y	Distributor:		Distributor:		Sub-Acute:	Y	Labs/Testing:		Long-Term Care:	Y
Utilization Management:		Specialty Pharmacy:		Leasing/Finance:		Outpatient Surgery:		Staffing:		Physical Therapy:	
Payment Processing:		Vitamins/Nutritionals:		Information Systems:		Physical Rehab. Ctr.:		Waste Disposal:		Physician Prac. Mgmt.:	
		Clinical Trials:				Psychiatric Clinics:		Specialty Svcs.:	Y		

TYPES OF BUSINESS:

Hospitals
Assisted Living Facilities
Hospice Programs
Senior Housing Communities
Management & Consulting Services
HMO
Building & Design Services

BRANDS/DIVISIONS/AFFILIATES:

Catholic Health Ministries
Trinity Health International
Trinity Health Plans
Care Choice
Trinity Design
Genesis

CONTACTS: *Note: Officers with more than one job title may be intentionally listed here more than once.*

Joseph R. Swedish, CEO
Joseph R. Swedish, Pres.
Edward G. Chadwick, CFO/Sr. VP
Paul Browne, CIO/Sr. VP
Maria Szymanski, Chief Dev. Officer
Joy A. Gorzeman, Sr. VP-Patient Care Svcs. & Chief Nursing Officer
Michael A. Slubowski, Pres., Hospital & Health Networks
Catherine DeClercq, VP-Governance & Sponsorship
Michael Holper, Sr. VP-Organizational Integrity & Internal Audit
William Kreykes, Chmn.
Louis J. Fierens, II, Sr. VP-Supply Chain & Capital Projects Mgmt.

Phone: 248-489-5004	**Fax:** 248-489-6039
Toll-Free:	
Address: 27870 Cabot Dr., Novi, MI 48377-2920 US	

GROWTH PLANS/SPECIAL FEATURES:

Trinity Health Company, sponsored by Catholic Healt Ministries, is the country's fourth-largest Catholic healt system, with over 7,000 physicians and more than 6,50 acute-care and non-acute-care beds in 44 hospitals. Th firm also has 379 outpatient facilities, numerous assiste living facilities, home health services, hospice programs an senior housing communities in seven states. Trinity operate in California, Idaho, Indiana, Iowa, Maryland, Michigan, Ohi and internationally. The company's Trinity Healt International subsidiary provides management, training consulting and technical assistance to health car organizations and governments in more than 40 countrie around the world through more than 160 projects. Othe subsidiaries include Trinity Health Plans, which operate Care Choice HMOs in six southeast Michigan counties, an Trinity Design, which offers health care facility building an design services. In 2006, Trinity announced its eight successful hospital system activation of HealthQuest an Cerner PowerChart applications in support of clinica documentation and CPOE. CPOE is one component of $315 million initiative called Genesis, a major element c Trinity Health's process improvement initiative to implemer an integrate registration and electronic health record syster throughout the organization. Trinity is one of the first mult state health systems to engage in a large-scale initiative t increase efficiency and improve quality of care, usin computerized tools to support clinical process improvements In January 2007, the company's Mercy Medical Center Siou City facility acquired Oakland Memorial Hospital in Oaklanc Nebraska.

Trinity Health offers employees flexible spending accounts tuition reimbursement and adoption assistance.

FINANCIALS: **Sales and profits are in thousands of dollars—add 000 to get the full amount. 2007 Note: Financial information for 2007 was not available for all companies at press time.**

2007 Sales: $	2007 Profits: $	**U.S. Stock Ticker: Nonprofit**
2006 Sales: $	2006 Profits: $	**Int'l Ticker:** Int'l Exchange:
2005 Sales: $5,714,675	2005 Profits: $329,462	Employees: 44,950
2004 Sales: $5,286,500	2004 Profits: $240,167	Fiscal Year Ends: 6/30
2003 Sales: $4,956,700	2003 Profits: $-235,900	Parent Company:

SALARIES/BENEFITS:

Pension Plan: Y	ESOP Stock Plan:	Profit Sharing:	Top Exec. Salary: $	Bonus: $
Savings Plan: Y	Stock Purch. Plan:		Second Exec. Salary: $	Bonus: $

OTHER THOUGHTS:

Apparent Women Officers or Directors: 4
Hot Spot for Advancement for Women/Minorities: Y

LOCATIONS: ("Y" = Yes)

West:	Southwest:	Midwest:	Southeast:	Northeast:	International:
Y		Y		Y	Y

Note: Financial information, benefits and other data can change quickly and may vary from those stated here.

TRUSTMARK COMPANIES www.trustmarkinsurance.com

ıdustry Group Code: 522320A **Ranks within this company's industry group:** Sales: 6 Profits:

ısurance/HMO/PPO:		Drugs:		Equipment/Supplies:		Hospitals/Clinics:		Services:		Health Care:	
ısurance:	Y	Manufacturer:		Manufacturer:		Acute Care:		Diagnostics:		Home Health:	
ɫanaged Care:		Distributor:		Distributor:		Sub-Acute:		Labs/Testing:		Long-Term Care:	
ɫtilization Management:		Specialty Pharmacy:		Leasing/Finance:		Outpatient Surgery:		Staffing:		Physical Therapy:	
ayment Processing:		Vitamins/Nutritionals:		Information Systems:		Physical Rehab. Ctr.:		Waste Disposal:		Physician Prac. Mgmt.:	
		Clinical Trials:				Psychiatric Clinics:		Specialty Svcs.:			

TYPES OF BUSINESS:

:mployee Benefits Management

BRANDS/DIVISIONS/AFFILIATES:

:oreSource
'rustmark Group
'rustmark Voluntary Benefit Solutions
ɜtarmark
'rustmark Affinity Markets

CONTACTS: *Note: Officers with more than one job title may be ıtentionally listed here more than once.*

ɔavid M. McDonough, CEO
ɔavid M. McDonough, Pres.
. Grover Thomas, Jr., Chmn.

'hone: 847-615-1500 **Fax:** 847-615-3910
'oll-Free:
ıddress: 400 Field Dr., Lake Forest, IL 60045 US

GROWTH PLANS/SPECIAL FEATURES:

The Trustmark Companies offer health and life insurance and benefits administration services to employer groups through five major operating divisions. These subsidiaries are CoreSource, Trustmark Group Insurance, Trustmark Affinity Markets, Starmark and Trustmark Voluntary Benefit Solutions. CoreSource is one of the nation's largest employee benefit administrators, managing health care for over 2.5 million people across the U.S. It serves self-insured employers with claims administration, case management, provider network development, information management, fraud detection, COBRA administration and prescription drug benefit administration. Trustmark Group Insurance serves the health and life insurance needs of employers with between 51 and 500 employees. The company provides standard and custom medical, dental, life and disability plans; administrative services; stop loss insurance; experience rated refunds; and minimum premium plans. Trustmark Affinity Markets serves insurance policies to associations and other affiliated organizations. Starmark provides substantially the same services as Trustmark Group, for businesses with two to 50 employees. Trustmark Voluntary Benefit Solutions offers voluntary dental, universal life, disability and critical illness plans through businesses and credit unions.

FINANCIALS: Sales and profits are in thousands of dollars—add 000 to get the full amount. 2007 Note: Financial information for 2007 was not available for all companies at press time.

007 Sales: $	2007 Profits: $	**U.S. Stock Ticker: Mutual Company**
006 Sales: $100,900	2006 Profits: $	**Int'l Ticker:** Int'l Exchange:
005 Sales: $1,120,100	2005 Profits: $	Employees: 2,358
004 Sales: $1,170,000	2004 Profits: $	Fiscal Year Ends: 12/31
003 Sales: $1,130,500	2003 Profits: $15,700	Parent Company:

SALARIES/BENEFITS:

'ension Plan:	ESOP Stock Plan:	Profit Sharing:	Top Exec. Salary: $	Bonus: $
ɜavings Plan:	Stock Purch. Plan:		Second Exec. Salary: $	Bonus: $

OTHER THOUGHTS:

ıpparent Women Officers or Directors:
ɫot Spot for Advancement for Women/Minorities:

LOCATIONS: ("Y" = Yes)

West:	Southwest:	Midwest:	Southeast:	Northeast:	International:
Y	Y	Y	Y	Y	

TUFTS ASSOCIATED HEALTH PLANS www.tuftshealthplan.com

Industry Group Code: 524114 **Ranks within this company's industry group:** Sales: Profits:

Insurance/HMO/PPO:		Drugs:		Equipment/Supplies:		Hospitals/Clinics:		Services:		Health Care:	
Insurance:	Y	Manufacturer:		Manufacturer:		Acute Care:		Diagnostics:		Home Health:	
Managed Care:	Y	Distributor:		Distributor:		Sub-Acute:		Labs/Testing:		Long-Term Care:	
Utilization Management:		Specialty Pharmacy:		Leasing/Finance:		Outpatient Surgery:		Staffing:		Physical Therapy:	
Payment Processing:		Vitamins/Nutritionals:		Information Systems:		Physical Rehab. Ctr.:		Waste Disposal:		Physician Prac. Mgmt.:	
		Clinical Trials:				Psychiatric Clinics:		Specialty Svcs.:			

TYPES OF BUSINESS:

Insurance-Medical & Health, HMOs & PPOs
Administrative Services

BRANDS/DIVISIONS/AFFILIATES:

Tufts Associated Health Maintenance Organization
Secure Horizons
Tufts Benefit Administrators, Inc.
Tufts Total Health Plan
Tufts Preferred Provider Option

CONTACTS: *Note: Officers with more than one job title may be intentionally listed here more than once.*

James Roosevelt Jr., CEO
Thomas A. Croswell, COO
James Roosevelt Jr., Pres.
J. Andy Hilbert, CFO/Sr. VP
Robert D. Egan, Sr. VP-Mktg.
Lois Dehls Cornell, Sr. VP-Human Resources
Patricia Trebino, CIO
Robert D. Egan, Sr. VP-Prod. Dev.
Lois Dehls Cornell, General Counsel
Patricia Trebino, Sr. VP-Oper.
Allen J. Hinkle, Chief Medical Officer/Sr. VP
Brian P. Pagliaro, Sr. VP-Sales & Client Svcs.

Phone: 617-972-9400	**Fax:**
Toll-Free:	
Address: 705 Mount Auburn St., Watertown, MA 02472 US	

GROWTH PLANS/SPECIAL FEATURES:

Tufts Associated Health Plans provides to its collection o subsidiaries, including Tufts Associated Health Maintenanc Organization (TAHMO) and Tufts Insurance Compan administrative, management, advertising and marketin services. TAHMO has over 635,000 customers and offe health care coverage, including health maintenanc organization (HMO), preferred provider organization (PPO point-of-service (POS) and other plans, to corporation groups and individuals through employer groups. Th company has 80 community and teaching hospitals and ove 22,000 physicians in its network. Other health insuranc subsidiaries include Secure Horizons, a health pla specifically designed for seniors as a Medicare supplement plan, offering comprehensive health benefits includin preventive care; and the Tufts Total Health Plan for PO plans that offer a choice between two levels of coverag Tufts Insurance Company supplies life insurance to mor than 800,000 customers. Tufts Benefit Administrators, In offers third-party administrative services for the Tuf Preferred Provider Option and indemnity plans. In Augu 2007, the firm purchased the former Western Electr building from Prospectus, Inc. for roughly $86.5 million.

The company offers its employees a 401(k) plan; medic and dental insurance; employee discounts; flexible spendin accounts; life and disability insurance; and tuitio reimbursement. In March 2006, Tufts was ranked third o over 500 health plans for both HMO and POS products. was ranked second among managed care organization i New England.

FINANCIALS: **Sales and profits are in thousands of dollars—add 000 to get the full amount. 2007 Note: Financial information for 2007 was not available for all companies at press time.**

2007 Sales: $	2007 Profits: $	**U.S. Stock Ticker: Private**
2006 Sales: $	2006 Profits: $	**Int'l Ticker:** Int'l Exchange:
2005 Sales: $1,900,000	2005 Profits: $78,600	Employees: 2,500
2004 Sales: $2,100,000	2004 Profits: $28,100	Fiscal Year Ends:
2003 Sales: $2,300,000	2003 Profits: $56,900	Parent Company:

SALARIES/BENEFITS:

Pension Plan:	ESOP Stock Plan:	Profit Sharing:	Top Exec. Salary: $	Bonus: $
Savings Plan: Y	Stock Purch. Plan:		Second Exec. Salary: $	Bonus: $

OTHER THOUGHTS:

Apparent Women Officers or Directors: 2
Hot Spot for Advancement for Women/Minorities:

LOCATIONS: ("Y" = Yes)

West:	Southwest:	Midwest:	Southeast:	Northeast:	International:
				Y	

JNIPRISE INCORPORATED www.uniprise.com

ıdustry Group Code: 522320A **Ranks within this company's industry group:** Sales: Profits:

ısurance/HMO/PPO:		Drugs:		Equipment/Supplies:		Hospitals/Clinics:		Services:		Health Care:	
surance:		Manufacturer:		Manufacturer:		Acute Care:		Diagnostics:		Home Health:	
anaged Care:	Y	Distributor:		Distributor:		Sub-Acute:		Labs/Testing:		Long-Term Care:	
tilization Management:	Y	Specialty Pharmacy:		Leasing/Finance:		Outpatient Surgery:		Staffing:		Physical Therapy:	
ayment Processing:	Y	Vitamins/Nutritionals:		Information Systems:		Physical Rehab. Ctr.:		Waste Disposal:		Physician Prac. Mgmt.:	
		Clinical Trials:				Psychiatric Clinics:		Specialty Svcs.:			

'YPES OF BUSINESS:

mployee Benefits Management
lectronic Billing & Payment Systems

BRANDS/DIVISIONS/AFFILIATES:

JnitedHealth Group
:lectronic Benefit Administration Solutions
:ustomer Reporting System
nyuhc.com
Plan
Spectra
Ovations
Definity Health SM

CONTACTS: *Note: Officers with more than one job title may be ıtentionally listed here more than once.*

racy Bahl, CEO
avid Astar, COO
homas Tran, CFO/Sr. VP
aryl Richard, VP-Mktg.
aurie Zaugg, VP-Human Capital
aryl Richard, VP-Comm.
incent Kerr, Exec. VP-Network & Clinical Solutions
like Tarino, CEO-Definity Health

Phone: 860-702-5000	Fax: 860-702-5835
Toll-Free:	
Address: 450 Columbus Blvd., Hartford, CT 06115-0450 US	

GROWTH PLANS/SPECIAL FEATURES:

Uniprise Incorporated, a subsidiary of UnitedHealth Group, manages the benefit programs of some of the nation's leading businesses. It is the only company in the health benefits industry to focus solely on large employers, counting over half of the country's largest 100 companies as customers. The firm offers UnitedHealth products and services through the following divisions: health care solutions, dental care, vision care, retiree solutions and disability insurance. Uniprise's health care solutions program provides various plans, including DefinitySM; UnitedHealthcare Choice and Choice Plus; Managed Indemnity; UnitedHealthcare Select (EPO); UnitedHealthcare Select Plus (POS); and UnitedHealthcare Options (PPO). Uniprise's dental care includes a series of plans that allow its clients' employees flexibility in choosing a dentist. For vision care, the company offers benefits through Spectra, a division of UnitedHealth Group whose national network totals over 20,000 providers. Uniprise offers a variety of retiree solutions for active employees, through its DefinitySM Health Reimbursement Account; for early retirees, through self and fully-insured arrangements, scheduled benefit or high deductible plans and zero-dollar employer subsidy plans; and for medicare-eligible retirees, through Medicare supplement plans, Medicare Advantage plans and Medicare Part D programs. The company's disability insurance programs are offered through Unimerica Insurance Company and include short-term disability, long-term disability and voluntary disability. The company also offers as services like Electronic Benefit Administration Solutions; the Customer Reporting System; electronic billing and payment systems; and myuhc.com. Through myuhc.com, customers can identify, select and locate physicians; check the status of claims; request new ID cards; and verify eligibility. The firm's iPlan controls benefit costs, encourages good health and provides employees with choices and control. Uniprise's single, unified delivery platform allows it to process over 180 million claims each year and serve over 72 million telephone callers annually.

Uniprise employees receive medical and dental coverage and commuter and education expense reimbursement.

FINANCIALS: **Sales and profits are in thousands of dollars—add 000 to get the full amount. 2007 Note: Financial information for 2007 was not available for all companies at press time.**

:007 Sales: $	2007 Profits: $	**U.S. Stock Ticker: Subsidiary**
'006 Sales: $	2006 Profits: $	**Int'l Ticker:** Int'l Exchange:
:005 Sales: $3,850,000	2005 Profits: $799,000	Employees:
:004 Sales: $3,370,000	2004 Profits: $677,000	Fiscal Year Ends: 12/31
:003 Sales: $3,107,000	2003 Profits: $	Parent Company: UNITEDHEALTH GROUP INC

SALARIES/BENEFITS:

Pension Plan:	ESOP Stock Plan: Y	Profit Sharing:	Top Exec. Salary: $	Bonus: $
Savings Plan: Y	Stock Purch. Plan: Y		Second Exec. Salary: $	Bonus: $

OTHER THOUGHTS:

Apparent Women Officers or Directors: 1
Hot Spot for Advancement for Women/Minorities:

LOCATIONS: ("Y" = Yes)

West:	Southwest:	Midwest:	Southeast:	Northeast:	International:
				Y	

UNITED SURGICAL PARTNERS www.unitedsurgical.com

Industry Group Code: 621111 **Ranks within this company's industry group:** Sales: 4 Profits: 2

Insurance/HMO/PPO:		Drugs:		Equipment/Supplies:		Hospitals/Clinics:		Services:		Health Care:	
Insurance:		Manufacturer:		Manufacturer:		Acute Care:		Diagnostics:		Home Health:	
Managed Care:		Distributor:		Distributor:		Sub-Acute:		Labs/Testing:		Long-Term Care:	
Utilization Management:		Specialty Pharmacy:		Leasing/Finance:		Outpatient Surgery:	Y	Staffing:		Physical Therapy:	
Payment Processing:		Vitamins/Nutritionals:		Information Systems:		Physical Rehab. Ctr.:		Waste Disposal:		Physician Prac. Mgmt.:	Y
		Clinical Trials:				Psychiatric Clinics:		Specialty Svcs.:			

TYPES OF BUSINESS:

Outpatient Surgical Facility Management

BRANDS/DIVISIONS/AFFILIATES:

Global Healthcare Partners Limited
Holly House Hospital
Highgate Hospital
Parkside Hospital
Parkside Oncology Clinic
Surgis, Inc.
Welsh, Carson, Anderson & Stowe

CONTACTS: *Note: Officers with more than one job title may be intentionally listed here more than once.*

William H. Wilcox, CEO
Niels P. Vernegaard, COO/Exec. VP
William H. Wilcox, Pres.
Mark A. Kopser, CFO/Sr. VP
John J. Wellik, Sr. VP-Admin.
Joseph B. Cagle, General Counsel/VP
Jonathan R. Bond, Sr. VP-Oper.
Brett P. Brodnax, Chief Dev. Officer/Exec. VP
Richard J. Sirchio, VP-Investor Rel.
John J. Wellik, Sr. VP-Acct./Sec.
David Zarin, M.D., Sr. VP-Medical Affairs
Luke D. Johnson, Sr. VP-Oper./Pres., Ortholink Physicians Corp.
Desmond Shiels, Pres., Global Healthcare Partners U.K.
Mark C. Garvin, Sr. VP-Oper.
Donald E. Steen, Chmn.
Patricia McCann, Managing Dir.-Global Healthcare Partners U.K.

Phone: 972-713-3500	**Fax:** 972-713-3550
Toll-Free:	
Address: 15305 Dallas Pkwy., Ste. 1600, Addison, TX 75001-3500 US	

GROWTH PLANS/SPECIAL FEATURES:

United Surgical Partners International, Inc. (USPI) owns an operates 152 short stay surgical facilities, including surger centers and private surgical hospitals, in the U.S.; and fou private surgical hospitals in the U.K., all in the greate London area. Of its domestic facilities, 90 are jointly owne with not-for-profit healthcare systems; and all of its domesti facilities include physician owners. The U.K facilities ar managed and wholly owned by subsidiary Global Healthcar Partners Limited. USPI hopes to attract more physicia affiliations by focusing on physician satisfaction throug staffing, scheduling and clinical systems and protocols tha increase productivity. USPI also pursues strategi relationships with not-for-profit hospitals and health car systems by allowing them to outsource their non-emergenc surgical procedures to the company's facilities. In the U.S the firm generally offers physicians the opportunity t purchase equity interests in its facilities. USPI operate surgery centers in Alabama, Arizona, California, Florida Georgia, Illinois, Maryland, Michigan, Missouri, Nevada, Ne Jersey, New Mexico, New York, Ohio, Oklahoma Pennsylvania, Tennessee, Texas, Virginia and Wyoming Surgery Hospitals are located in Arizona, Louisiana Oklahoma and Texas. U.K. locations include 55-bed Holl House Hospital in Essex; 28-bed Highgate Hospital, 70-be Parkside Hospital and Parkside Oncology Clinic all in Nort London. In April 2006, USPI acquired Surgis, Inc., privately held surgery center company based in Nashville TN. In April 2007, the firm was acquired by private equit firm Welsh, Carson, Anderson & Stowe for approximatel $1.8 billion.

FINANCIALS: **Sales and profits are in thousands of dollars—add 000 to get the full amount. 2007 Note: Financial information for 2007 was not available for all companies at press time.**

2007 Sales: $	2007 Profits: $	**U.S. Stock Ticker: Private**
2006 Sales: $578,825	2006 Profits: $34,246	**Int'l Ticker:** Int'l Exchange:
2005 Sales: $469,601	2005 Profits: $47,294	Employees: 5,500
2004 Sales: $383,186	2004 Profits: $86,175	Fiscal Year Ends: 12/31
2003 Sales: $446,269	2003 Profits: $29,876	Parent Company: WELSH CARSON ANDERSON & STOWE

SALARIES/BENEFITS:

Pension Plan:	ESOP Stock Plan:	Profit Sharing:	Top Exec. Salary: $544,583	Bonus: $158,837
Savings Plan: Y	Stock Purch. Plan: Y		Second Exec. Salary: $314,167	Bonus: $80,178

OTHER THOUGHTS:

Apparent Women Officers or Directors: 2
Hot Spot for Advancement for Women/Minorities:

LOCATIONS: ("Y" = Yes)

West:	Southwest:	Midwest:	Southeast:	Northeast:	International:
Y	Y	Y	Y	Y	Y

UNITEDHEALTH GROUP INC www.unitedhealthgroup.com

Industry Group Code: 524114 **Ranks within this company's industry group:** Sales: 1 Profits: 1

Insurance/HMO/PPO:		Drugs:		Equipment/Supplies:		Hospitals/Clinics:		Services:		Health Care:	
Insurance:		Manufacturer:		Manufacturer:		Acute Care:		Diagnostics:		Home Health:	
Managed Care:	Y	Distributor:		Distributor:		Sub-Acute:		Labs/Testing:		Long-Term Care:	
Utilization Management:	Y	Specialty Pharmacy:		Leasing/Finance:		Outpatient Surgery:		Staffing:		Physical Therapy:	
Payment Processing:		Vitamins/Nutritionals:		Information Systems:		Physical Rehab. Ctr.:		Waste Disposal:		Physician Prac. Mgmt.:	
		Clinical Trials:				Psychiatric Clinics:		Specialty Svcs.:	Y		

TYPES OF BUSINESS:

Medical Insurance
Wellness Plans
Dental & Vision Insurance

BRANDS/DIVISIONS/AFFILIATES:

Americhoice Corporation
Uniprise Incorporated
Golden Rule Insurance Company
Ingenix
Definity Health
Mid Atlantic Medical Services Inc
Pacificare Health Systems Inc
Dental Benefits Providers

CONTACTS: *Note: Officers with more than one job title may be intentionally listed here more than once.*

Stephen J. Hemsley, CEO
Stephen J. Hemsley, Pres.
G. Mike Mikan, CFO/Exec. VP
Lori Sweere, Exec. VP-Human Capital
Thomas L. Strickland, Chief Legal Officer/Exec. VP
Don Nathan, Chief Comm. Officer/Sr. VP
Eric S. Rangen, Chief Acct. Officer/Sr. VP
Anthony Welters, Exec. VP/Head-Public & Social Markets Group
David s. Wichmann, Exec. VP/Pres., Individual & Employer Market Group
Reed V. Tuckson, Exec. VP/Chief-Medical Affairs
Jeannine M. Rivet, Exec. VP
Richard T. Burke, Chmn.

Phone: 952-936-1300	**Fax:** 952-936-7430
Toll-Free: 800-328-5979	
Address: 9900 Bren Rd. E., Minnetonka, MN 55343 US	

GROWTH PLANS/SPECIAL FEATURES:

UnitedHealth Group, Inc. is a diversified health and well-being company, serving about 70 million Americans. The company provides individuals with access to healthcare services and resources through more than 520,000 physicians and other care providers and 4,700 hospitals across the United States. The firm operates in four segments: Uniprise, healthcare services, specialized care services and Ingenix. The Uniprise segment delivers healthcare and well-being services nationwide to large national employers, individual consumer and other healthcare organizations through three business units: Uniprise strategic solutions, Definity Health and Exante financial services. The healthcare services segment consists of UnitedHealthcare, Ovations and AmeriChoice businesses. The specialized care services companies offer specialty health and wellness and ancillary benefits, services and resources to specific customer markets nationwide. These products and services include employee benefit offerings, provider networks and related resources focusing on behavioral health and substance abuse; dental; vision; disease management; complex and chronic illness; and care facilitation. The companies also offer solutions in the areas of complementary and alternative care; employee assistance; short-term disability; life insurance; work/life balance; and health-related information. The Ingenix segment offers database and data management services; software products; publications; consulting services; outsourced services; and pharmaceutical development and consulting services nationwide and internationally. Ingenix's customers include more than 5,000 hospitals; 250,000 physicians; 1,500 payers and intermediaries; more than 200 Fortune 500 companies; and more than 150 life sciences companies. In March 2007, UnitedHealth agreed to acquire Sierra Health Services, Inc. for $2.6 billion.

The company offers its employees medical, vision and dental insurance; flexible spending accounts; life and AD&D insurance; short- and long-term disability insurance; a 401(k) plan; an employee stock purchase plan; and tuition reimbursement.

FINANCIALS: **Sales and profits are in thousands of dollars—add 000 to get the full amount. 2007 Note: Financial information for 2007 was not available for all companies at press time.**

2007 Sales: $	2007 Profits: $	**U.S. Stock Ticker: UNH**
2006 Sales: $71,542,000	2006 Profits: $4,159,000	**Int'l Ticker:** Int'l Exchange:
2005 Sales: $46,425,000	2005 Profits: $3,083,000	Employees: 58,000
2004 Sales: $38,217,000	2004 Profits: $2,411,000	Fiscal Year Ends: 12/31
2003 Sales: $28,823,000	2003 Profits: $1,825,000	Parent Company:

SALARIES/BENEFITS:

Pension Plan:	ESOP Stock Plan:	Profit Sharing:	Top Exec. Salary: $2,146,923	Bonus: $
Savings Plan: Y	Stock Purch. Plan: Y		Second Exec. Salary: $1,019,615	Bonus: $2,875,000

OTHER THOUGHTS:

Apparent Women Officers or Directors: 3
Hot Spot for Advancement for Women/Minorities: Y

LOCATIONS: ("Y" = Yes)

West:	Southwest:	Midwest:	Southeast:	Northeast:	International:
Y	Y	Y	Y	Y	

Note: Financial information, benefits and other data can change quickly and may vary from those stated here.

UNIVERSAL HEALTH SERVICES INC www.uhsinc.com

Industry Group Code: 621490 **Ranks within this company's industry group:** Sales: 3 Profits: 3

Insurance/HMO/PPO:		Drugs:		Equipment/Supplies:		Hospitals/Clinics:		Services:		Health Care:	
Insurance:		Manufacturer:		Manufacturer:		Acute Care:	Y	Diagnostics:	Y	Home Health:	
Managed Care:		Distributor:		Distributor:		Sub-Acute:		Labs/Testing:		Long-Term Care:	
Utilization Management:		Specialty Pharmacy:		Leasing/Finance:		Outpatient Surgery:	Y	Staffing:		Physical Therapy:	
Payment Processing:		Vitamins/Nutritionals:		Information Systems:		Physical Rehab. Ctr.:		Waste Disposal:		Physician Prac. Mgmt.:	
		Clinical Trials:				Psychiatric Clinics:	Y	Specialty Svcs.:	Y		

TYPES OF BUSINESS:

Acute Care Hospitals
Radiation Oncology Centers
Behavioral Health Hospitals
Surgical Hospitals

BRANDS/DIVISIONS/AFFILIATES:

Texoma Healthcare System
TexomaCare

CONTACTS: *Note: Officers with more than one job title may be intentionally listed here more than once.*

Alan B. Miller, CEO
Alan B. Miller, Pres.
Steve G. Filton, CFO/Sr. VP
Bruce R. Gilbert, General Counsel
Cheryl K. Ramagano, Treas.
Charles F. Boyle, Controller
Richard C. Wright, VP
Debra K. Osteen, Sr. VP
Richard C. Wright, VP
Alan B. Miller, Chmn.

Phone: 610-768-3300	**Fax:** 610-768-3336
Toll-Free:	
Address: 367 S. Gulph Rd., King of Prussia, PA 19406 US	

GROWTH PLANS/SPECIAL FEATURES:

Universal Health Services, Inc. (UHS) owns and operates through its subsidiaries, acute care hospitals, behaviora health centers, surgical hospitals, ambulatory surger centers and radiation oncology centers. UHS has under it corporate mantle 31 acute care hospitals and 110 behaviora health centers located in 32 states, Washington, D.C. an Puerto Rico. Four of the company's acute care facilities i Louisiana were severely damaged and remain closed an non-operational as a result of Hurricane Katrina. As part c its ambulatory treatment centers division, the firm manage or owns outright or in partnerships with physicians, 1 surgical hospitals and surgery and radiation oncolog centers located in 6 states and Puerto Rico. Service provided by UHS' hospitals include general surgery, interna medicine, obstetrics, emergency room care, radiology oncology, diagnostic care, coronary care, pediatric service and behavioral health services. UHS also provides non medical services to its facilities including a variety c management services such as central purchasing information services, finance and control systems, facilitie planning, physician recruitment services, administrative personnel management, marketing and public relations. I January 2007, the company acquired certain assets o Texoma Healthcare System located in Texas, including a 234-bed acute-care hospital, a 60-bed behavioral healt hospital, a 21-bed freestanding rehabilitation hospital an TexomaCare, a 34-physician group practice.

The company offers its employees medical, dental and visio insurance; life and AD&D insurance; short- and long-tern disability insurance; a 401(k) plan; an employee stoc purchase plan; and flexible spending accounts.

FINANCIALS: Sales and profits are in thousands of dollars—add 000 to get the full amount. 2007 Note: Financial information for 2007 was not available for all companies at press time.

2007 Sales: $	2007 Profits: $	**U.S. Stock Ticker: UHS**
2006 Sales: $4,191,300	2006 Profits: $259,458	**Int'l Ticker:** Int'l Exchange:
2005 Sales: $3,935,480	2005 Profits: $240,845	Employees: 36,300
2004 Sales: $3,637,490	2004 Profits: $169,492	Fiscal Year Ends: 12/31
2003 Sales: $3,643,566	2003 Profits: $199,269	Parent Company:

SALARIES/BENEFITS:

Pension Plan:	ESOP Stock Plan:	Profit Sharing:	Top Exec. Salary: $1,228,204	Bonus: $6,566,000
Savings Plan: Y	Stock Purch. Plan: Y		Second Exec. Salary: $410,682	Bonus: $70,000

OTHER THOUGHTS:

Apparent Women Officers or Directors: 3
Hot Spot for Advancement for Women/Minorities: Y

LOCATIONS: ("Y" = Yes)

West:	Southwest:	Midwest:	Southeast:	Northeast:	International:
Y	Y		Y	Y	

UNIVERSAL HOSPITAL SERVICES INC www.uhs.com

Industry Group Code: 532400 **Ranks within this company's industry group:** Sales: 1 Profits: 1

Insurance/HMO/PPO:		Drugs:		Equipment/Supplies:		Hospitals/Clinics:		Services:		Health Care:	
Insurance:		Manufacturer:		Manufacturer:		Acute Care:		Diagnostics:		Home Health:	
Managed Care:		Distributor:		Distributor:	Y	Sub-Acute:		Labs/Testing:		Long-Term Care:	
Utilization Management:		Specialty Pharmacy:		Leasing/Finance:		Outpatient Surgery:		Staffing:		Physical Therapy:	
Payment Processing:		Vitamins/Nutritionals:		Information Systems:		Physical Rehab. Ctr.:		Waste Disposal:		Physician Prac. Mgmt.:	
		Clinical Trials:				Psychiatric Clinics:		Specialty Svcs.:	Y		

TYPES OF BUSINESS:

Medical Equipment Outsourcing & Services
Technical & Professional Services
Medical Equipment Sales & Remarketing

BRANDS/DIVISIONS/AFFILIATES:

Bear Stearns Cos Inc (The)

CONTACTS: *Note: Officers with more than one job title may be intentionally listed here more than once.*

Gary Blackford, CEO
Timothy Kuck, COO/Exec. VP
Gary D. Blackford, Pres.
Rex Clevenger, CFO/Exec. VP
Jeffrey Singer, Exec. VP-Sales & Mktg.
Walter Chesley, Sr. VP-Human Resources & Dev.
David Lawson, Sr. VP-Info. & Strategic Resources
Diana Vance-Bryan, General Counsel/Sr. VP
Scott Madson, Controller/Chief Acct. Officer
Steve Heintze, Sr. VP-Nat'l Acct.
Darren Thieding, VP-Sales Oper.
Phil Zeller, VP-Asset Optimization
Kenneth Harvey, VP-Sales-East Region
Gary Blackford, Chmn.

Phone: 952-893-3200	**Fax:** 952-893-0704
Toll-Free: 800-847-7368	
Address: 7700 France Ave. S., Ste. 275, Edina, MN 55435 US	

GROWTH PLANS/SPECIAL FEATURES:

Universal Hospital Services, Inc. (UHS) is a provider of medical equipment outsourcing and services to the healthcare industry in the U.S. The company operates in three segments: medical equipment outsourcing; technical and professional services; and medical equipment sales and remarketing. The medical equipment outsourcing segment, which accounted for roughly 79% of revenue in 2006, provides customers with the use of movable medical equipment and maintains the equipment for customers by performing preventative maintenance, repairs, cleaning and testing, and maintaining certain reporting records. The firm owns roughly 173,000 pieces of movable medical equipment, primarily in the categories of respiratory therapy, newborn care, critical care, patient monitors and specialty beds and pressure area management. UHS provides outsourcing services to more than 3,600 acute care hospitals in the US. The technical and professional services segment, which accounted for about 13.5% of revenue in 2006, offers a range of inspection, preventative maintenance, repair, logistic and consulting services through a team of over 250 technicians and professionals. The medical equipment sales and remarketing segment buys, sources, remarkets and disposes pre-owned medical equipment for its customers; provides sales and distribution of specialty medical equipment; and offers its customers disposable items that are used on a single-use basis. The company remarkets used medical equipment to hospitals, alternate care providers, veterinarians and equipment brokers. UHS provides its services to over 2,600 acute care hospitals and 2,900 alternate care providers through business locations around the world. In April 2007, the firm acquired the ICMS division of Intellamed, Inc. for roughly $14.5 million. In June 2007, UHS was bought by Bear Stearns Merchant Banking (BSMB), the private equity affiliate of The Bear Stearns Companies, Inc. The company is now owned by BSMB and the UHS management.

FINANCIALS: **Sales and profits are in thousands of dollars—add 000 to get the full amount. 2007 Note: Financial information for 2007 was not available for all companies at press time.**

2007 Sales: $	2007 Profits: $	**U.S. Stock Ticker: Private**
2006 Sales: $225,100	2006 Profits: $ 100	**Int'l Ticker:** Int'l Exchange:
2005 Sales: $215,900	2005 Profits: $-1,600	Employees: 1,274
2004 Sales: $199,600	2004 Profits: $-3,600	Fiscal Year Ends: 12/31
2003 Sales: $171,000	2003 Profits: $-19,500	Parent Company: BEAR STEARNS COS INC (THE)

SALARIES/BENEFITS:

Pension Plan:	ESOP Stock Plan:	Profit Sharing:	Top Exec. Salary: $234,862	Bonus: $151,600
Savings Plan:	Stock Purch. Plan:		Second Exec. Salary: $175,784	Bonus: $118,000

OTHER THOUGHTS:

Apparent Women Officers or Directors: 2
Hot Spot for Advancement for Women/Minorities:

LOCATIONS: ("Y" = Yes)

West:	Southwest:	Midwest:	Southeast:	Northeast:	International:
Y	Y	Y	Y	Y	

US ONCOLOGY INC

www.usoncology.com

Industry Group Code: 621111 **Ranks within this company's industry group:** Sales: 1 Profits: 3

Insurance/HMO/PPO:		Drugs:		Equipment/Supplies:		Hospitals/Clinics:		Services:		Health Care:	
Insurance:		Manufacturer:		Manufacturer:		Acute Care:		Diagnostics:		Home Health:	
Managed Care:		Distributor:		Distributor:		Sub-Acute:		Labs/Testing:		Long-Term Care:	
Utilization Management:		Specialty Pharmacy:	Y	Leasing/Finance:		Outpatient Surgery:	Y	Staffing:		Physical Therapy:	
Payment Processing:		Vitamins/Nutritionals:		Information Systems:		Physical Rehab. Ctr.:		Waste Disposal:		Physician Prac. Mgmt.:	Y
		Clinical Trials:				Psychiatric Clinics:		Specialty Svcs.:	Y		

TYPES OF BUSINESS:

Cancer Treatment
Oncology Pharmaceutical Services
Outpatient Cancer Center Operations
Research & Development Services

BRANDS/DIVISIONS/AFFILIATES:

Welsh, Carson, Anderson & Stowe

CONTACTS: *Note: Officers with more than one job title may be intentionally listed here more than once.*

R. Dale Ross, CEO
Bruce Broussard, Pres.
Rick McCook, CFO/Exec. VP
Leo Sands, Chief Admin. Officer/Exec.VP
Phillip H. Watts, General Counsel
Atul Dhir, Pres., Cancer Information Research Group
Atul Dhir, Pres., Cancer Info. Research Group
Altul Dhir, Exec. VP-BioPharmaceutical Svcs.
R. Dale Ross, Chmn.

Phone: 832-601-8766 **Fax:**
Toll-Free:
Address: 16825 Northchase Dr., Ste. 1300, Houston, TX 77060 US

GROWTH PLANS/SPECIAL FEATURES:

U.S. Oncology, Inc., owned by private equity firm Welsh Carson, Anderson & Stowe, is a cancer management company that provides management services under long term agreements to oncology practices. The firm's outpatient care centers provide amenities and support services for cancer patients and doctors, with a total of 460 sites of outpatient service in 32 states, including 85 cancer centers. The company has affiliated physicians in all aspects of diagnosis and outpatient treatment of cancer, including medical oncology, radiation, gynecologic oncology, stem cell transplantation, diagnostic radiology and clinical research. With more than 850 affiliated physicians, U.S. Oncology delivers care to more than half a million cancer patients each year. The company has two primary product offerings: Comprehensive Strategic Alliances and Oncology Pharmaceutical Services. Comprehensive Strategic Alliances offer oncology practices access to capital for diversification and expansion, construction of cancer centers, staff training and assistance in the addition of radiation therapy and diagnostic imaging technology. Oncology Pharmaceutical Services offers community-based oncology practices services to increase practice success, including bio-pharmaceutical contracting services and oncology drug management services. The clinical research group focuses on improving cancer survival rates, enhancing the patient's quality of life, reducing the cost of care and developing new approaches for diagnosis, treatment and post-treatment monitoring. The company assists in a number of aspects in the conduct of clinical trials, including protocol development, data coordination, institutional review, board coordination and contract review and negotiation.

The company offers its employees a 401(k) plan; medical, prescription and dental insurance; life and AD&D insurance; short- and long-term disability insurance; and a cafeteria plan.

FINANCIALS: Sales and profits are in thousands of dollars—add 000 to get the full amount. 2007 Note: Financial information for 2007 was not available for all companies at press time.

2007 Sales: $
2006 Sales: $2,811,400
2005 Sales: $2,518,600
2004 Sales: $2,259,800
2003 Sales: $1,965,725

2007 Profits: $
2006 Profits: $26,200
2005 Profits: $19,100
2004 Profits: $48,100
2003 Profits: $70,656

U.S. Stock Ticker: Private
Int'l Ticker: Int'l Exchange:
Employees: 8,600
Fiscal Year Ends:
Parent Company: WELSH CARSON ANDERSON & STOWE

SALARIES/BENEFITS:

Pension Plan: ESOP Stock Plan: Profit Sharing: Top Exec. Salary: $701,217 Bonus: $400,680
Savings Plan: Y Stock Purch. Plan: Second Exec. Salary: $390,247 Bonus: $140,700

OTHER THOUGHTS:

Apparent Women Officers or Directors:
Hot Spot for Advancement for Women/Minorities:

LOCATIONS: ("Y" = Yes)

West:	Southwest:	Midwest:	Southeast:	Northeast:	International:
Y	Y	Y	Y	Y	

US PHYSICAL THERAPY INC

www.usph.com

Industry Group Code: 621490 **Ranks within this company's industry group:** Sales: 12 Profits: 10

Insurance/HMO/PPO:		Drugs:		Equipment/Supplies:		Hospitals/Clinics:		Services:		Health Care:	
Insurance:		Manufacturer:		Manufacturer:		Acute Care:		Diagnostics:		Home Health:	
Managed Care:		Distributor:		Distributor:		Sub-Acute:		Labs/Testing:		Long-Term Care:	
Utilization Management:		Specialty Pharmacy:		Leasing/Finance:		Outpatient Surgery:		Staffing:		Physical Therapy:	Y
Payment Processing:		Vitamins/Nutritionals:		Information Systems:		Physical Rehab. Ctr.:	Y	Waste Disposal:		Physician Prac. Mgmt.:	
		Clinical Trials:				Psychiatric Clinics:		Specialty Svcs.:			

TYPES OF BUSINESS:

Occupational & Physical Therapy Clinics

BRANDS/DIVISIONS/AFFILIATES:

STAR Physical Therapy

CONTACTS:

Note: Officers with more than one job title may be intentionally listed here more than once.

Chris Reading, CEO
Glenn D. McDowell, COO
Chris Reading, Pres.
Larry McAfee, CFO/Exec. VP
Daniel C. Arnold, Chmn.

Phone: 713-297-7000 **Fax:** 713-297-7090
Toll-Free: 800-580-6285
Address: 1300 W. Sam Houston Pkwy. S, Ste. 300, Houston, TX 77042 US

GROWTH PLANS/SPECIAL FEATURES:

U.S. Physical Therapy, Inc. (UPT) operates outpatient physical therapy and occupational therapy clinics that provide pre- and post-operative care and treatment or orthopedic-related disorders, sports-injuries, preventive care, rehabilitation of injured workers and neurological-related injuries. The company operates through subsidiary clinic partnerships, in which the firm generally owns a 1% general partnership interest and 64% limited partnership interest in the managing therapists of the clinics own the remaining limited partnership interest in the majority of the clinics. To a lesser extent, UPT operates some clinics, through wholly-owned subsidiaries, under profit sharing arrangements with therapists. The company operates over some 300 outpatient physical and occupational therapy clinics in 41 states. Each clinic's staff typically includes one or more licensed physical or occupational therapists along with assistants, aides, exercise physiologists and athletic trainers. The clinics initially perform an evaluation of each patient, which is then followed by a treatment plan specific to the injury as prescribed by the patient's physician. The treatment plan may include a number of procedures, including therapeutic exercise, manual therapy techniques, ultrasound, electrical stimulation, hot packs, iontophoresis, education on management of daily life skills and home exercise programs. A clinic's business primarily comes from referrals by local physicians. In September 2007, the company acquired a majority interest in STAR Physical Therapy, a multi-partner outpatient rehabilitation practice with operations in southeastern U.S.

The company offers its employees medical, dental and vision insurance; life and AD&D insurance; disability insurance; a 401(k) plan; and education assistance.

FINANCIALS:

Sales and profits are in thousands of dollars—add 000 to get the full amount. 2007 Note: Financial information for 2007 was not available for all companies at press time.

2007 Sales: $	2007 Profits: $	**U.S. Stock Ticker: USPH**
2006 Sales: $135,194	2006 Profits: $6,296	**Int'l Ticker:** Int'l Exchange:
2005 Sales: $126,256	2005 Profits: $8,791	Employees: 1,506
2004 Sales: $111,709	2004 Profits: $6,678	Fiscal Year Ends: 12/31
2003 Sales: $105,513	2003 Profits: $7,331	Parent Company:

SALARIES/BENEFITS:

Pension Plan:	ESOP Stock Plan:	Profit Sharing:	Top Exec. Salary: $338,750	Bonus: $75,000
Savings Plan: Y	Stock Purch. Plan:		Second Exec. Salary: $338,750	Bonus: $75,000

OTHER THOUGHTS:

Apparent Women Officers or Directors:
Hot Spot for Advancement for Women/Minorities:

LOCATIONS: ("Y" = Yes)

West:	Southwest:	Midwest:	Southeast:	Northeast:	International:
Y	Y	Y	Y	Y	

UTAH MEDICAL PRODUCTS INC www.utahmed.com

Industry Group Code: 339113 **Ranks within this company's industry group:** Sales: 98 Profits: 64

Insurance/HMO/PPO:		Drugs:		Equipment/Supplies:		Hospitals/Clinics:		Services:		Health Care:	
Insurance:		Manufacturer:		Manufacturer:	Y	Acute Care:		Diagnostics:		Home Health:	
Managed Care:		Distributor:		Distributor:	Y	Sub-Acute:		Labs/Testing:		Long-Term Care:	
Utilization Management:		Specialty Pharmacy:		Leasing/Finance:		Outpatient Surgery:		Staffing:		Physical Therapy:	
Payment Processing:		Vitamins/Nutritionals:		Information Systems:		Physical Rehab. Ctr.:		Waste Disposal:		Physician Prac. Mgmt.:	
		Clinical Trials:				Psychiatric Clinics:		Specialty Svcs.:			

TYPES OF BUSINESS:

Equipment-Obstetrics & Gynecology
Disposable Products
Electrosurgical Systems
Neonatal Intensive Care Equipment

BRANDS/DIVISIONS/AFFILIATES:

Intran
Intran Plus
Disposa-Hood
Deltran
Gesco

CONTACTS: *Note: Officers with more than one job title may be intentionally listed here more than once.*

Kevin L. Cornwell, CEO
Kevin L. Cornwell, Pres.
Paul O. Richins, CFO/VP
Paul O. Richins, Chief Admin. Officer
Paul O. Richins, Treas.
Kevin L. Cornwell, Chmn.

Phone: 801-566-1200	**Fax:** 801-566-2062
Toll-Free: 800-533-4984	
Address: 7043 S. 300 W., Midvale, UT 84047 US	

GROWTH PLANS/SPECIAL FEATURES:

Utah Medical Products, Inc. (UTMD) produces predominatel proprietary disposable medical devices for hospital use. markets medical devices used in critical care, especially i neonatal intensive care units (NICU) and labor and deliver department in hospitals, as well as outpatient clinics an physicians' offices. UTMD's products include obstetric products, such as fetal monitoring accessories and vacuum assisted delivery systems; NICU products; and gynecology urology and electrosurgery products. The firm's main feta monitoring accessories include Intran, the first disposable intrauterine pressure catheter that places the pressur transducer at the pressure source within the uterine cavity and Intran Plus which also has refined tip design, a zer switch, and a dedicated amnio lumen which provide immediate access to amniotic fluid. For NICUs, the firr manufactures the Disposa-Hood, an infant respiratory hood the Deltran infant blood pressure monitoring system; an Gesco umbilical vessel catheters. UTMD's products are sol directly to end users in the U.S. domestic market by th company's own direct sales representatives and independer manufacturers' representatives, as well as being sol through specialty distributors, national hospital distributio companies and other medical device manufacturers Internationally, products are sold through other medica device companies and through independent medica products distributors. UTMD has representation in all majo developed countries through approximately 136 internationa distributors. Of UTMD's 2006 sales, 6% came from sales to other manufactures and 94% from direct sales and othe distribution networks; and 23% of total sales came fron international markets.

UTMD offers employees stock options; paid vacation an holidays; paid jury duty, military, family and bereavemen leave; medical, vision, dental and prescription drug plans paid life, disability, accidental death and dismembermen insurance; worker's compensation and unemploymen insurance; educational financial assistance; and credit unior membership. It also provides free flu shots, discountec entertainment event tickets, an annual holiday party and a summer picnic.

FINANCIALS: Sales and profits are in thousands of dollars—add 000 to get the full amount. 2007 Note: Financial information for 2007 was not available for all companies at press time.

2007 Sales: $	2007 Profits: $	**U.S. Stock Ticker: UTMD**
2006 Sales: $28,753	2006 Profits: $8,168	**Int'l Ticker:** Int'l Exchange:
2005 Sales: $27,692	2005 Profits: $7,547	Employees: 210
2004 Sales: $26,485	2004 Profits: $10,220	Fiscal Year Ends: 12/31
2003 Sales: $27,137	2003 Profits: $20,761	Parent Company:

SALARIES/BENEFITS:

Pension Plan:	ESOP Stock Plan:	Profit Sharing:	Top Exec. Salary: $256,100	Bonus: $261,250
Savings Plan: Y	Stock Purch. Plan: Y		Second Exec. Salary: $90,280	Bonus: $15,873

OTHER THOUGHTS:

Apparent Women Officers or Directors:
Hot Spot for Advancement for Women/Minorities:

LOCATIONS: ("Y" = Yes)

West:	Southwest:	Midwest:	Southeast:	Northeast:	International:
Y					Y

VALEANT PHARMACEUTICALS INTERNATIONAL

www.valeant.com

ndustry Group Code: 325412 **Ranks within this company's industry group:** Sales: 28 Profits: 36

nsurance/HMO/PPO:		Drugs:		Equipment/Supplies:		Hospitals/Clinics:		Services:		Health Care:	
nsurance:		Manufacturer:	Y	Manufacturer:		Acute Care:		Diagnostics:		Home Health:	
lanaged Care:		Distributor:		Distributor:		Sub-Acute:		Labs/Testing:		Long-Term Care:	
tilization Management:		Specialty Pharmacy:		Leasing/Finance:		Outpatient Surgery:		Staffing:		Physical Therapy:	
ayment Processing:		Vitamins/Nutritionals:	Y	Information Systems:		Physical Rehab. Ctr.:		Waste Disposal:		Physician Prac. Mgmt.:	
		Clinical Trials:				Psychiatric Clinics:		Specialty Svcs.:	Y		

TYPES OF BUSINESS:

Prescription & Non-Prescription Pharmaceuticals
leurology Drugs
)ermatology Drugs
nfectious Diseases Drugs

BRANDS/DIVISIONS/AFFILIATES:

Efudex/Efudix
)ermatix
Oxsoralen-Ultra
nfergen
/irazole
Kinerase
Mestinon
Librax

CONTACTS: *Note: Officers with more than one job title may be intentionally listed here more than once.*

Timothy C. Tyson, CEO
Timothy C. Tyson, Pres.
Peter J. Blott, CFO/Exec. VP
Geoffrey M. Glass, CIO/Sr. VP
Wesley P. Wheeler, Pres., Global Prod. Dev.
Eileen C. Pruette, General Counsel/Exec. VP
Jeff Misakian, VP-Investor Rel.
Martin N. Mercer, Exec. VP-Int'l
Wesley P. Wheeler, Pres., North America
Robert A. Ingram, Chmn.
Charles J. Bramlage, Pres., Europe

Phone: 949-461-6000 **Fax:** 949-461-6609
Toll-Free: 800-548-5100
Address: 1 Enterprise, Aliso Viejo, CA 92656 US

GROWTH PLANS/SPECIAL FEATURES:

Valeant Pharmaceuticals International is a global pharmaceutical company that develops, manufactures and markets a broad spectrum of prescription and non-prescription pharmaceuticals. The company focuses principally in the therapeutic areas of neurology, dermatology and infectious diseases. The firm's products also treat, among others, neuromuscular disorders, cancer, cardiovascular disease, diabetes and psychiatric disorders. Valeant's products are sold through three pharmaceutical segments: North America; International, composed of the Latin America, Asia and Australasia regions; and EMEA, Europe, Middle East and Africa. The company's specialty pharmaceuticals product portfolio comprises roughly 370 branded products with approximately 2,200 stock keeping units. Products in the neurology field include Mestinon, Librax, Migranal, Tasmar and Zelapar; in the dermatology, Efudex, Kinerase, Oxsoralen-Ultra and Dermatrix; and addressing infectious diseases, Infergen and Virazole. Valeant's research and development program focuses on preclinical and clinical development of identified molecules. The company is developing product candidates, including two clinical stage programs: taribavirin and retigabine. The firm's marketing and promotion efforts focus on the Promoted Products, which consists of products sold in more than 100 markets around the world with primary focus on the U.S., Mexico, Poland, Canada, Germany, Spain, Italy, the U.K. and France. In January 2006, Valeant acquired the U.S. and Canadian rights to the hepatitis C treatment drug Infergen from Intermune, Inc. In October 2006, the company signed a distribution agreement with Intendis GmbH for rights to certain dermatological products in the U.K., which include the distribution rights to Finacea, a topical treatment for rosacea. In December 2006, the firm sold its HIV and cancer development programs and certain discovery and preclinical assets to Ardea Biosciences. In January 2007, Valeant licensed the development and commercialization rights to the hepatitis B compound pradefovir to Schering-Plough.

FINANCIALS: **Sales and profits are in thousands of dollars—add 000 to get the full amount. 2007 Note: Financial information for 2007 was not available for all companies at press time.**

2007 Sales: $	2007 Profits: $	**U.S. Stock Ticker: VRX**
2006 Sales: $907,238	2006 Profits: $-56,565	**Int'l Ticker:** Int'l Exchange:
2005 Sales: $823,886	2005 Profits: $-188,143	Employees: 3,443
2004 Sales: $684,251	2004 Profits: $-154,653	Fiscal Year Ends: 12/31
2003 Sales: $685,953	2003 Profits: $-55,640	Parent Company:

SALARIES/BENEFITS:

Pension Plan:	ESOP Stock Plan:	Profit Sharing:	Top Exec. Salary: $860,000	Bonus: $645,000
Savings Plan:	Stock Purch. Plan:		Second Exec. Salary: $434,718	Bonus: $256,481

OTHER THOUGHTS:

Apparent Women Officers or Directors: 3
Hot Spot for Advancement for Women/Minorities: Y

LOCATIONS: ("Y" = Yes)

West:	Southwest:	Midwest:	Southeast:	Northeast:	International:
Y					Y

VARIAN MEDICAL SYSTEMS INC www.varian.com

Industry Group Code: 339113 **Ranks within this company's industry group:** Sales: 22 Profits: 13

Insurance/HMO/PPO:		Drugs:		Equipment/Supplies:		Hospitals/Clinics:		Services:		Health Care:	
Insurance:		Manufacturer:		Manufacturer:	Y	Acute Care:		Diagnostics:		Home Health:	
Managed Care:		Distributor:		Distributor:		Sub-Acute:		Labs/Testing:		Long-Term Care:	
Utilization Management:		Specialty Pharmacy:		Leasing/Finance:		Outpatient Surgery:		Staffing:		Physical Therapy:	
Payment Processing:		Vitamins/Nutritionals:		Information Systems:	Y	Physical Rehab. Ctr.:		Waste Disposal:		Physician Prac. Mgmt.:	
		Clinical Trials:				Psychiatric Clinics:		Specialty Svcs.:			

TYPES OF BUSINESS:

Oncology Systems
X-Ray Equipment
Software Systems
Security & Inspection Products

BRANDS/DIVISIONS/AFFILIATES:

Clinac
Ginzton Technology Center
PortalVision
Millennium

CONTACTS: *Note: Officers with more than one job title may be intentionally listed here more than once.*

Timothy E. Guertin, CEO
Timothy E. Guertin, Pres.
Elisha W. Finney, CFO/Sr. VP
Wendy S. Reitherman, VP-Human Resources
John W. Kuo, General Counsel/VP/Corp. Sec.
J. A. Thorson, VP-Bus. Dev.
Spencer R. Sias, VP-Corp. Comm.
Spencer R. Sias, VP-Investor Rel.
Franco N. Palomba, Treas./VP
Tai-Yun Chen, Controller/VP
Robert H. Kluge, VP/Pres., X-Ray Prod.
Dow R. Wilson, Exec. VP/Pres., Oncology Systems
George A. Zdasiuk, VP/CTO-Ginzton Tech. Center
Richard M. Levy, Chmn.

Phone: 650-493-4000	**Fax:** 650-842-5196
Toll-Free:	
Address: 3100 Hansen Way, Palo Alto, CA 94304 US	

GROWTH PLANS/SPECIAL FEATURES:

Varian Medical Systems, Inc. designs, manufactures, sell and services advanced equipment and software products fo treating cancer with radiation. The company also designs manufactures, sells and services X-ray tubes for origina equipment manufacturers (OEMs); replacement X-ray tubes flat panel digital image detectors for filmless X-rays fo medical, dental veterinary, scientific and industria applications; and linear accelerators for security an inspection purposes. The firm operates in three segments oncology systems, X-ray products and other. The oncolog systems segment provides software and hardware fo treating cancer with radiation, including linear accelerators treatment simulation and verification products; informatio management and treatment planning software; advance brachytherapy products and software; and other accessor products and services. The Clinac series of medical linea accelerators treats cancer by producing electrons and x-rays in shaped beams that target tumors and other abnormalitie in a patient. The Millennium series of multi-leaf collimators are used with a linear accelerator to define the size, shape and intensity of the radiation beams generated by the linea accelerator. PortalVision, an electronic portal imaging product verifies a patient's treatment position, a critica component for accurate delivery of radiotherapy treatment The X-ray products segment manufactures and sells X-ra imaging components and subsystems, namely X-ray tubes for use in a range of applications including compute tomography, or CT, scanning; radioscopic/fluoroscopi imaging; mammography; special procedures and industria applications and flat panel detectors for digital X-ray image capture, which is an alternative to image intensifier tubes fo fluoroscopy and X-ray film for radiography. The othe segment includes the security and inspection products business, which provides Linatron X-ray accelerators to OEMs; and technologies developed by the Ginzton Technology Center, including digital X-ray imaging technology; volumetric and functional imaging; improved X-ray sources; and technology for security and cargo screening applications.

FINANCIALS: **Sales and profits are in thousands of dollars—add 000 to get the full amount. 2007 Note: Financial information for 2007 was not available for all companies at press time.**

2007 Sales: $	2007 Profits: $	**U.S. Stock Ticker: VAR**
2006 Sales: $1,597,800	2006 Profits: $245,100	**Int'l Ticker:** Int'l Exchange:
2005 Sales: $1,382,600	2005 Profits: $206,600	Employees: 3,900
2004 Sales: $1,235,523	2004 Profits: $167,700	Fiscal Year Ends: 9/30
2003 Sales: $1,041,600	2003 Profits: $130,900	Parent Company:

SALARIES/BENEFITS:

Pension Plan:	ESOP Stock Plan:	Profit Sharing:	Top Exec. Salary: $681,766	Bonus: $319,801
Savings Plan:	Stock Purch. Plan:		Second Exec. Salary: $629,359	Bonus: $561,076

OTHER THOUGHTS:

Apparent Women Officers or Directors: 4
Hot Spot for Advancement for Women/Minorities: Y

LOCATIONS: ("Y" = Yes)

West:	Southwest:	Midwest:	Southeast:	Northeast:	International:
Y					

VCA ANTECH INC www.vcaantech.com

ndustry Group Code: 541940 **Ranks within this company's industry group:** Sales: 1 Profits: 1

nsurance/HMO/PPO:		Drugs:		Equipment/Supplies:		Hospitals/Clinics:		Services:		Health Care:	
nsurance:		Manufacturer:		Manufacturer:	Y	Acute Care:		Diagnostics:	Y	Home Health:	
Managed Care:		Distributor:		Distributor:	Y	Sub-Acute:		Labs/Testing:	Y	Long-Term Care:	
Jtilization Management:		Specialty Pharmacy:		Leasing/Finance:		Outpatient Surgery:		Staffing:		Physical Therapy:	
Payment Processing:		Vitamins/Nutritionals:		Information Systems:		Physical Rehab. Ctr.:		Waste Disposal:		Physician Prac. Mgmt.:	
		Clinical Trials:				Psychiatric Clinics:		Specialty Svcs.:	Y		

TYPES OF BUSINESS:

Animal Health Care Services
Veterinary Diagnostic Laboratories
Full-Service Animal Hospitals
Veterinary Equipment
Ultrasound Imaging

BRANDS/DIVISIONS/AFFILIATES:

Antech Diagnostics
Zoasis.com
VCA Animal Hospitals
Sound Technologies, Inc.
Healthy Pet Corp.

CONTACTS:

Note: Officers with more than one job title may be intentionally listed here more than once.

Robert (Bob) Antin, CEO
Arthur J. Antin, COO/Sr. VP
Robert (Bob) Antin, Pres.
Tomas W. Fuller, CFO
William C. Seckinger, VP-Mktg.
Tomas W. Fuller, Corp. Sec./VP
Neil Tauber, Sr. VP-Dev.
Dawn R. Olsen, Principal Acct. Officer/Controller/VP
Todd Tams, Chief Medical Officer, VCA Animal Hospitals
Robert (Bob) Antin, Chmn.

Phone: 310-571-6500 **Fax:** 310-571-6700
Toll-Free: 800-966-1822
Address: 12401 W. Olympic Blvd., Los Angeles, CA 90064-1022 US

GROWTH PLANS/SPECIAL FEATURES:

VCA Antech, Inc. (VCA) provides animal health care services and operates one of the largest networks of veterinary diagnostic laboratories and freestanding, full-service animal hospitals in the U.S. The firm's veterinary diagnostic laboratories, run by the Antech Diagnostics division, provides 300 different testing services as well as consulting services to veterinarians, who use these services in the detection, diagnosis, evaluation, monitoring, treatment and prevention of diseases and other conditions. The division operates 33 laboratories, of which those in large metropolitan areas and other primary hubs offer 24-hour service; approximately 9% of the company's total 2006 laboratory revenue came from servicing its own hospitals, and 71% came from major metropolitan areas. The laboratories provide testing daily to over 15,000 animal hospitals and zoos in all 50 states, as well as government agencies, and it offers clients access to results online through zoasis.com. The VCA Animal Hospitals division operates 379 animal hospitals in 37 states, offering a full range of general medical and surgical services for animals, as well as specialized treatments including advanced diagnostic services, internal medicine, oncology, ophthalmology, dermatology and cardiology. The division, which has most of its hospitals located in California, Florida and Illinois, is supported by 1,600 veterinarians. VCA animal hospitals typically have an annual revenue between $1 million and $2 million, have three to five full-time veterinarians on staff, and are open 10-15 hours per day, six or seven days a week. Subsidiary Sound Technologies, Inc., the company's medical technology segment, sells medical imaging, primarily ultrasound and digital radiography, equipment and related software and services. In June 2007, the company acquired Healthy Pet Corp. for $152.9 million. The acquisition brings the total number of animal hospitals controlled by the company up to 435 in 38 states.

FINANCIALS:

Sales and profits are in thousands of dollars—add 000 to get the full amount. 2007 Note: Financial information for 2007 was not available for all companies at press time.

2007 Sales: $	2007 Profits: $	**U.S. Stock Ticker: WOOF**
2006 Sales: $983,313	2006 Profits: $105,529	**Int'l Ticker:** Int'l Exchange:
2005 Sales: $839,666	2005 Profits: $67,816	Employees: 8,000
2004 Sales: $674,089	2004 Profits: $63,572	Fiscal Year Ends: 12/31
2003 Sales: $544,665	2003 Profits: $43,423	Parent Company:

SALARIES/BENEFITS:

Pension Plan:	ESOP Stock Plan:	Profit Sharing:	Top Exec. Salary: $683,617	Bonus: $825,000
Savings Plan: Y	Stock Purch. Plan:		Second Exec. Salary: $508,846	Bonus: $472,500

OTHER THOUGHTS:

Apparent Women Officers or Directors: 1
Hot Spot for Advancement for Women/Minorities:

LOCATIONS: ("Y" = Yes)

West:	Southwest:	Midwest:	Southeast:	Northeast:	International:
Y	Y	Y	Y	Y	

Note: Financial information, benefits and other data can change quickly and may vary from those stated here.

VENTANA MEDICAL SYSTEMS INC www.ventanamed.com

Industry Group Code: 339113 **Ranks within this company's industry group:** Sales: 58 Profits: 41

Insurance/HMO/PPO:		Drugs:		Equipment/Supplies:		Hospitals/Clinics:		Services:		Health Care:	
Insurance:		Manufacturer:		Manufacturer:	Y	Acute Care:		Diagnostics:		Home Health:	
Managed Care:		Distributor:		Distributor:		Sub-Acute:		Labs/Testing:		Long-Term Care:	
Utilization Management:		Specialty Pharmacy:		Leasing/Finance:		Outpatient Surgery:		Staffing:		Physical Therapy:	
Payment Processing:		Vitamins/Nutritionals:		Information Systems:		Physical Rehab. Ctr.:		Waste Disposal:		Physician Prac. Mgmt.:	
		Clinical Trials:				Psychiatric Clinics:		Specialty Svcs.:			

TYPES OF BUSINESS:

Instrument-Reagent Systems
Discovery Systems
Clinical Systems
Consumable Products

BRANDS/DIVISIONS/AFFILIATES:

Symphony
HER2 Silver in situ Hybridization
Discovery XT
BenchMark XT
BenchMark LT

CONTACTS: *Note: Officers with more than one job title may be intentionally listed here more than once.*

Chris Gleeson, CEO
Chris Gleeson, Pres.
Lawrence L. Mehren, CFO/Sr. VP
Denise van Zijll, VP-Human Resources/EH&S
Phil Miller, Sr. VP-Life Sciences R&D
Timothy B. Johnson, Sr. VP-Mfg. Oper.
Mark D. Tucker, General Counsel/Sr. VP
Timothy B. Johnson, Sr. VP-Corp. Dev.
Kendall B. Hendrick, Sr. VP-Systems Discovery & Dev.
Thomas M Grogan, Chief Medical Officer
Jack Schuler, Chmn.
Hany Massarany, Sr. VP-Global Oper.

Phone: 520-887-2155	**Fax:** 520-229-4207
Toll-Free: 800-227-2155	
Address: 1910 Innovation Park Dr., Tucson, AZ 85755 US	

GROWTH PLANS/SPECIAL FEATURES:

Ventana Medical Systems, Inc. develops, manufactures and markets instruments-reagent systems that automate slide staining in anatomical pathology and drug discovery laboratories worldwide. The company's clinical systems are tools for anatomical pathology labs in analyzing human tissue to assist in the diagnosis and treatment of cancer and infectious diseases. The firm's discovery systems are used by pharmaceutical and biotechnology companies to accelerate the discovery of new drug targets and to evaluate the of safety new drug compounds. In addition to instruments, Ventana markets consumable products including reagents and other accessories required to operate its instruments. Ventana also offers staining systems and associated reagents for automated cellular and tissue analyses. The company launched a new staining system in 2006, the Symphony, which uses a proprietary chemistry and staining process to produce and H&E (haematoxylin and eosin) stain slides with clarity and discrimination of micro anatomic detail. The company's customers include hospital-based anatomical pathology labs, independent reference labs, the drug discovery labs of pharmaceutical companies, biotechnology companies, government labs, medical research centers and reseller serving these units. In March 2007, Ventana launched HER2 Silver in situ Hybridization technology, which allows for the detection of the HER2 gene and chromosome 17.

Ventana offers its employees medical, dental, vision, life and accident insurance; an employee assistance plan; short- and long-term disability; a 401(k) plan; an employee stock purchase plan; an education assistance program; business travel accident insurance; and a 529 CollegeBound fund.

FINANCIALS: Sales and profits are in thousands of dollars—add 000 to get the full amount. 2007 Note: Financial information for 2007 was not available for all companies at press time.

2007 Sales: $	2007 Profits: $	**U.S. Stock Ticker: VMSI**
2006 Sales: $238,223	2006 Profits: $31,578	**Int'l Ticker:** Int'l Exchange:
2005 Sales: $199,132	2005 Profits: $25,488	Employees: 952
2004 Sales: $166,102	2004 Profits: $21,289	Fiscal Year Ends: 12/31
2003 Sales: $132,380	2003 Profits: $5,972	Parent Company:

SALARIES/BENEFITS:

Pension Plan:	ESOP Stock Plan:	Profit Sharing:	Top Exec. Salary: $367,500	Bonus: $
Savings Plan: Y	Stock Purch. Plan: Y		Second Exec. Salary: $273,269	Bonus: $58,800

OTHER THOUGHTS:

Apparent Women Officers or Directors: 1
Hot Spot for Advancement for Women/Minorities:

LOCATIONS: ("Y" = Yes)

West:	Southwest:	Midwest:	Southeast:	Northeast:	International:
	Y				Y

VISION SERVICE PLAN www.vsp.com

Industry Group Code: 524114A **Ranks within this company's industry group:** Sales: Profits:

Insurance/HMO/PPO:		Drugs:		Equipment/Supplies:		Hospitals/Clinics:		Services:		Health Care:	
Insurance:	Y	Manufacturer:		Manufacturer:	Y	Acute Care:		Diagnostics:		Home Health:	
Managed Care:		Distributor:		Distributor:		Sub-Acute:		Labs/Testing:		Long-Term Care:	
Utilization Management:		Specialty Pharmacy:		Leasing/Finance:	Y	Outpatient Surgery:		Staffing:		Physical Therapy:	
Payment Processing:		Vitamins/Nutritionals:		Information Systems:		Physical Rehab. Ctr.:		Waste Disposal:		Physician Prac. Mgmt.:	
		Clinical Trials:				Psychiatric Clinics:		Specialty Svcs.:			

TYPES OF BUSINESS:

Insurance-Supplemental and Specialty Health
Vision Insurance
Optical Frames
Laboratory Products & Materials, Optometry

BRANDS/DIVISIONS/AFFILIATES:

Sight for Students
Get Focused
VSP Optical Laboratories
Altair
Eyefinity

CONTACTS: *Note: Officers with more than one job title may be intentionally listed here more than once.*

Rob Lynch, CEO
Rob Lynch, Pres.
Patricia Cochran, CFO
Ric Steere, VP-Sales
Elaine Leuchars, VP-Human Resources
Steve Scott, VP-IT
Thomas Fessler, General Counsel/VP-Legal Div.
Gary Brooks, Sr. VP-Oper.
Robert Bass, Treas.
Kate Renwick-Espinosa, VP-Mktg.
Don Price, VP-Provider Rel.
Cheryl Johnson, VP-Health Care Svcs.
Dan L. Mannen, Chmn.

Phone: 916-851-5000 **Fax:** 916-851-4858
Toll-Free: 800-852-7600
Address: 3333 Quality Dr., Rancho Cordova, CA 95670 US

GROWTH PLANS/SPECIAL FEATURES:

Vision Service Plan (VSP) is a major eye care benefit provider in for the United States. The plan boasts over 47 million members served by more than 26,000 vision professionals and doctors, located in both rural and metropolitan areas throughout the nation. VSP offers benefit plans that vary from general eye care and eye glasses to laser vision correction. The firm has contracts with over 22,000 clients, including 228 Fortune 500 companies and approximately 100 health plans. The firm has offices in Arizona, California, Colorado, Connecticut, Florida, Georgia, Hawaii, Illinois, Indiana, Kansas, Maryland, Massachusetts, Minnesota, Missouri, New Jersey, North Carolina, Ohio, Pennsylvania, South Carolina, Texas and Washington. VSP has assisted 250,000 children through its Sight for Students program, which provides vision exams and glasses to low-income and uninsured children. The program was founded by General Colin Powell, and currently manages a $40 million budget to support low-income and uninsured children. The Get Focused program is VSP's national eye care awareness campaign, designed to promote eye education and regular eye exams. VSP also offers loans to assist eye doctors to buy existing practices, buy into partnerships or make down payments on private practices in California, Ohio, Texas and Colorado, through its VSP Optical Laboratories subsidiary. The VSP family of companies also consists of Altair Eyewear, which is a private label optical frame company that that sells exclusively to VSP eyecare professionals; and Eyefinity, which is an independent e-commerce business that offers professionals products and lab materials, and that has relationships with over 18,000 private eyecare practices. In September 2007, VSP entered into a joint venture with Perfect Optics, an optical laboratory near San Diego, California.

VSP offers its employees benefits including a bonus program, an employee assistance program and credit union membership.

FINANCIALS: **Sales and profits are in thousands of dollars—add 000 to get the full amount. 2007 Note: Financial information for 2007 was not available for all companies at press time.**

2007 Sales: $
2006 Sales: $
2005 Sales: $2,200,000
2004 Sales: $
2003 Sales: $1,970,000

2007 Profits: $
2006 Profits: $
2005 Profits: $
2004 Profits: $
2003 Profits: $

U.S. Stock Ticker: Private
Int'l Ticker: Int'l Exchange:
Employees: 1,900
Fiscal Year Ends: 12/31
Parent Company:

SALARIES/BENEFITS:

Pension Plan: ESOP Stock Plan: Profit Sharing: Top Exec. Salary: $ Bonus: $
Savings Plan: Y Stock Purch. Plan: Second Exec. Salary: $ Bonus: $

OTHER THOUGHTS:

Apparent Women Officers or Directors: 6
Hot Spot for Advancement for Women/Minorities: Y

LOCATIONS: ("Y" = Yes)

West:	Southwest:	Midwest:	Southeast:	Northeast:	International:
Y	Y	Y	Y	Y	

VITAL SIGNS INC

www.vital-signs.com

Industry Group Code: 339113 **Ranks within this company's industry group:** Sales: 61 Profits: 42

Insurance/HMO/PPO:		Drugs:		Equipment/Supplies:		Hospitals/Clinics:		Services:		Health Care:	
Insurance:		Manufacturer:		Manufacturer:	Y	Acute Care:		Diagnostics:		Home Health:	
Managed Care:		Distributor:		Distributor:	Y	Sub-Acute:		Labs/Testing:		Long-Term Care:	
Utilization Management:		Specialty Pharmacy:		Leasing/Finance:		Outpatient Surgery:		Staffing:		Physical Therapy:	
Payment Processing:		Vitamins/Nutritionals:		Information Systems:		Physical Rehab. Ctr.:		Waste Disposal:		Physician Prac. Mgmt.:	
		Clinical Trials:				Psychiatric Clinics:		Specialty Svcs.:			

TYPES OF BUSINESS:

Supplies-Respiratory & Critical Care
Single-Patient-Use Medical Products
Anesthesia Products
Home Care Products

BRANDS/DIVISIONS/AFFILIATES:

Futall AB
Vital Signs Sweden AB
Disposa-View
Sleep Services of America, Inc.
Greenlight II
Do You Snore, LLC
Southern Medical Equipment, Inc.
Advanced Sleep Technologies of Georgia, Inc.

CONTACTS: *Note: Officers with more than one job title may be intentionally listed here more than once.*

Terence D. Wall, CEO
Barry Wicker, COO
Terence D. Wall, Pres.
William Craig, CFO/Exec. VP
Mark Jefferson, VP-Mktg. & Sales
Jay Sturm, VP-Human Resources
Alan Furler, VP-R&D
Alex J. Chanin, CIO
Benn Vennesland, VP-Mfg. Oper.
Jay Sturm, General Counsel
John Easom, VP-Global Bus. Dev. & Planning
Anthony Martino, VP-Quality & Regulatory Affairs
Terence D. Wall, Chmn.

Phone: 973-790-1330	**Fax:** 973-790-3307
Toll-Free: 800-932-0760	
Address: 20 Campus Rd., Totowa, NJ 07512 US	

GROWTH PLANS/SPECIAL FEATURES:

Vital Signs, Inc. designs, manufactures and markets disposable medical products in its five business segments anesthesia, respiratory/critical care, sleep disorder interventional cardiology/radiology and pharmaceutical technology services. The company's anesthesia products include facemasks, breathing circuits, general anesthesia systems, disposable pressure infusers and single-use fiber optic laryngoscope systems. Respiratory and critical care products include manual resuscitators, blood pressure cuffs disposable arterial blood gas syringes and collection systems, heated humidification systems, continuous positive airway pressure systems, humidifiers and nebulizers and pediatric emergency systems. Vital Signs operates 56 sleep laboratories and centers to diagnose obstructive sleep apnea and also manufactures and sells products to treat these sleeping conditions. The cardiology/radiology business operates as Thomas Medical Products, which develops and manufactures precision devices such as percutaneous valved introducers, peelaway valved introducers, guiding sheaths and delivery sheaths to facilitate access to the cardiovascular system. Pharmaceutical technology services provides regulatory consulting services for clients in order to develop and validate systems for manufacturing, IT infrastructure, research and development, facilities, laboratory and quality assurance departments. The firm sells its products through national distributors and its own sales offices to over 70 countries worldwide. In early 2007, Vital Signs signed letters of intent to acquire a CPAP (continuous positive airway pressure) dealer located in the Mid-Atlantic region and a sleep lab company located in the southeastern U.S. In April 2007, the firm's subsidiary, Sleep Services of America, Inc., acquired the assets of Do You Snore, LLC, Southern Medical Equipment, Inc., and Advanced Sleep Technologies of Georgia, Inc.

FINANCIALS: **Sales and profits are in thousands of dollars—add 000 to get the full amount. 2007 Note: Financial information for 2007 was not available for all companies at press time.**

2007 Sales: $	2007 Profits: $	**U.S. Stock Ticker: VITL**
2006 Sales: $204,058	2006 Profits: $30,117	**Int'l Ticker:** Int'l Exchange:
2005 Sales: $194,037	2005 Profits: $26,389	Employees: 1,211
2004 Sales: $183,991	2004 Profits: $22,053	Fiscal Year Ends: 9/30
2003 Sales: $182,163	2003 Profits: $14,222	Parent Company:

SALARIES/BENEFITS:

Pension Plan:	ESOP Stock Plan:	Profit Sharing:	Top Exec. Salary: $350,000	Bonus: $57,750
Savings Plan: Y	Stock Purch. Plan:		Second Exec. Salary: $193,000	Bonus: $70,405

OTHER THOUGHTS:

Apparent Women Officers or Directors:
Hot Spot for Advancement for Women/Minorities:

LOCATIONS: ("Y" = Yes)

West:	Southwest:	Midwest:	Southeast:	Northeast:	International:
		Y		Y	Y

WALGREEN CO

www.walgreens.com

ndustry Group Code: 446110 **Ranks within this company's industry group:** Sales: 1 Profits: 1

nsurance/HMO/PPO:		Drugs:		Equipment/Supplies:		Hospitals/Clinics:		Services:		Health Care:	
nsurance:		Manufacturer:		Manufacturer:		Acute Care:		Diagnostics:		Home Health:	
Managed Care:		Distributor:	Y	Distributor:		Sub-Acute:		Labs/Testing:		Long-Term Care:	
Jtilization Management:		Specialty Pharmacy:	Y	Leasing/Finance:		Outpatient Surgery:		Staffing:		Physical Therapy:	
Payment Processing:		Vitamins/Nutritionals:		Information Systems:		Physical Rehab. Ctr.:		Waste Disposal:		Physician Prac. Mgmt.:	
		Clinical Trials:				Psychiatric Clinics:		Specialty Svcs.:	Y		

TYPES OF BUSINESS:

Drug Stores
Mail-Order Pharmacy Services
Pharmacy Benefit Management
Health Care Maintenance Services
Online Pharmacy Services
Photo Restoration Services

BRANDS/DIVISIONS/AFFILIATES:

Intercom Plus
Walgreens Mail Service
WHP Health Initiatives, Inc.
Walgreen's Health Services
Walgreen Advance Care, Inc.
C&M Pharmacy
Medmark Specialty Pharmacy
Take Care Health Systems LLC

CONTACTS: *Note: Officers with more than one job title may be intentionally listed here more than once.*

Jeffrey A. Rein, CEO
Gregory D. Wasson, COO
Gregory D. Wasson, Pres.
William M. Rudolphsen, CFO/Sr. VP
George Riedl, Exec. VP-Mktg.
Kenneth R. Weigand, Sr. VP-Human Resources
Dana I. Green, General Counsel/Sr. VP/Corp. Sec.
Mark A. Wagner, Exec. VP-Store Oper.
John W. Gleeson, Chief Strategy Officer/Sr. VP
John W. Spina, Treas./Sr. VP-Corp. Strategy
Trent E. Taylor, Exec. VP/Pres., Walgreens Health Services
Donald C. Huonker, Sr. VP-Pharmacy Svcs.
Kevin P. Walgreen, Sr. VP-Store Oper.
R. Bruce Bryant, Sr. VP-Store Oper.
Jeffrey A. Rein, Chmn.
J. Randolph Lewis, Sr. VP-Dist. & Logistics

Phone: 847-914-2500 **Fax:** 847-940-2804
Toll-Free:
Address: 200 Wilmot Rd., Deerfield, IL 60015 US

GROWTH PLANS/SPECIAL FEATURES:

Walgreen Co. operates the largest chain of U.S. drug stores based on sales. The company has 5,461 drugstores in 45 U.S. states and Puerto Rico, 12 full-service distribution centers and three mail service facilities. Walgreen currently opens approximately 450 new stores per year and expects to increase its total store count to 7,000 by 2010. The company's pharmacy business fills 529 million prescriptions annually. To coordinate its operations, the firm uses Intercom Plus, a proprietary computer system for filling prescriptions, linking all stores into a single network. Walgreen operates several health care-related businesses, such as Walgreens Mail Service, formerly Walgreens Healthcare Plus, Inc., a mail-order drug company; WHP Health Initiatives, Inc., a pharmacy benefits management company; Walgreens Health Services, a managed care business; and Walgreens Advance Care, Inc., a retailer of health care maintenance services. A large percentage of the company's stores have drive-through pharmacies, and most stores offer one-hour photo processing, in addition to cosmetics, toiletries, liquor, beverages and tobacco. In 2006, the company began to offer online digital photo services and a print cartridge refill service. The firm also accepts prescription refill orders online through its web site. Prescription sales account for approximately 64.3% of total sales and continue to increase each year. Part of the firm's strategy is to build large, free-standing retail buildings on prominent, high traffic corners. In 2006, the company added C&M Pharmacy, Medmark Specialty Pharmacy, Happy Harry's Pharmacy and Home Pharmacy in California to its pharmacy operations. In May 2007, Walgreen acquired Take Care Health Systems, an operator of convenient care clinics. In July 2007, the firm agreed to acquire Option Care, Inc., with over 100 locations in 34 states, for roughly $760 million.

Employees at the corporate staff level enjoy an on-site Walgreens store, cafeteria, employee discounts and rideshare programs.

FINANCIALS: Sales and profits are in thousands of dollars—add 000 to get the full amount. 2007 Note: Financial information for 2007 was not available for all companies at press time.

2007 Sales: $ — 2007 Profits: $
2006 Sales: $47,409,000 — 2006 Profits: $1,750,600
2005 Sales: $42,201,600 — 2005 Profits: $1,559,500
2004 Sales: $37,508,200 — 2004 Profits: $1,360,200
2003 Sales: $32,505,400 — 2003 Profits: $1,175,700

U.S. Stock Ticker: WAG
Int'l Ticker: Int'l Exchange:
Employees: 195,000
Fiscal Year Ends: 8/31
Parent Company:

SALARIES/BENEFITS:

Pension Plan: ESOP Stock Plan: Profit Sharing: Top Exec. Salary: $1,516,667 Bonus: $884,286
Savings Plan: Y Stock Purch. Plan: Y Second Exec. Salary: $883,333 Bonus: $500,005

OTHER THOUGHTS:

Apparent Women Officers or Directors: 2
Hot Spot for Advancement for Women/Minorities:

LOCATIONS: ("Y" = Yes)

West:	Southwest:	Midwest:	Southeast:	Northeast:	International:
Y	Y	Y	Y	Y	Y

WARNER CHILCOTT PLC

www.warnerchilcott.com

Industry Group Code: 325412 **Ranks within this company's industry group:** Sales: Profits:

Insurance/HMO/PPO:		Drugs:		Equipment/Supplies:		Hospitals/Clinics:		Services:		Health Care:	
Insurance:		Manufacturer:	Y	Manufacturer:		Acute Care:		Diagnostics:		Home Health:	
Managed Care:		Distributor:		Distributor:		Sub-Acute:		Labs/Testing:		Long-Term Care:	
Utilization Management:		Specialty Pharmacy:		Leasing/Finance:		Outpatient Surgery:		Staffing:		Physical Therapy:	
Payment Processing:		Vitamins/Nutritionals:		Information Systems:		Physical Rehab. Ctr.:		Waste Disposal:		Physician Prac. Mgmt.:	
		Clinical Trials:				Psychiatric Clinics:		Specialty Svcs.:			

TYPES OF BUSINESS:

Pharmaceuticals Development & Manufacturing
Contraceptives
Hormone Therapies
Vitamins
Dermatology Treatments

BRANDS/DIVISIONS/AFFILIATES:

Loestrin 24
Estrostep
femhrt
Ovcon
Estrace
Taclonex
Dovonex
Doryx

CONTACTS: *Note: Officers with more than one job title may be intentionally listed here more than once.*

Roger Boissonneault, CEO
Roger Boissonneault, Pres.
Paul Herendeen, CFO/Exec. VP
Herman Ellman, Sr. VP-Clinical Dev.
Leland H. Cross, Sr. VP-Tech. Oper.
Izumi Hara, General Counsel/Sr. VP/Corp. Sec.
Anthony D.Bruno, Exec. VP-Corp. Dev.
W. Carlton Reichel, Pres., Pharmaceuticals
Alvin Howard, Sr. VP-Regulatory Affairs

Phone: 973-442-3200	**Fax:** 973-442-3283
Toll-Free: 800-521-8813	
Address: 100 Enterprise Dr., Rockaway, NJ 07866 US	

GROWTH PLANS/SPECIAL FEATURES:

Warner Chilcott (WC) is a specialty pharmaceutical company that focuses on developing, manufacturing and marketing branded prescription pharmaceutical products in women's healthcare and dermatology. Its franchises are comprised of complementary portfolios of established, branded development stage and new products, including recently launched products Loestrin 24 and Taclonex. Its women's healthcare franchise is anchored by its strong presence in the hormonal contraceptive and hormone therapy categories and its dermatology franchise is built on its established positions in the markets for psoriasis and acne therapies. In April 2006, it launched Loestrin 24 Fe, an oral contraceptive with a novel patented 24-day dosing regimen, with the goal of growing the market share position it achieved with its Ovcon and Estrostep products in the hormonal contraceptive market. The company also has a significant presence in the hormone therapy market, primarily through its products femhrt and Estrace Cream. In dermatology, its psoriasis product Dovonex enjoys the leading position in the U.S. for the non-steroidal topical treatment of psoriasis. WC strengthened and extended its position in the market for psoriasis therapies with the April 2006 launch of Taclonex, the first once-a-day topical psoriasis treatment that combines betamethasone dipropionate, a corticosteroid, with calcipotriene, the active ingredient in Dovonex. The company's product Doryx is the leading branded oral tetracycline in the U.S. for the treatment of acne. Recently, the company launched Dorys delayed-release tablets. In 2007, WC announced collaborations with various entities, including: Foamix; Watson Pharmaceuticals; LEO Pharma; and Paratek.

FINANCIALS: **Sales and profits are in thousands of dollars—add 000 to get the full amount. 2007 Note: Financial information for 2007 was not available for all companies at press time.**

2007 Sales: $	2007 Profits: $	**U.S. Stock Ticker: Private**
2006 Sales: $	2006 Profits: $	**Int'l Ticker:** Int'l Exchange:
2005 Sales: $	2005 Profits: $	Employees: 960
2004 Sales: $	2004 Profits: $	Fiscal Year Ends: 12/31
2003 Sales: $432,300	2003 Profits: $96,200	Parent Company:

SALARIES/BENEFITS:

Pension Plan:	ESOP Stock Plan:	Profit Sharing:	Top Exec. Salary: $	Bonus: $
Savings Plan:	Stock Purch. Plan:		Second Exec. Salary: $	Bonus: $

OTHER THOUGHTS:

Apparent Women Officers or Directors:
Hot Spot for Advancement for Women/Minorities:

LOCATIONS: ("Y" = Yes)

West:	Southwest:	Midwest:	Southeast:	Northeast:	International:
				Y	Y

WATSON PHARMACEUTICALS INC www.watson.com

Industry Group Code: 325416 **Ranks within this company's industry group:** Sales: 2 Profits: 5

Insurance/HMO/PPO:		Drugs:		Equipment/Supplies:		Hospitals/Clinics:		Services:		Health Care:	
Insurance:		Manufacturer:	Y	Manufacturer:		Acute Care:		Diagnostics:		Home Health:	
Managed Care:		Distributor:		Distributor:		Sub-Acute:		Labs/Testing:		Long-Term Care:	
Utilization Management:		Specialty Pharmacy:		Leasing/Finance:		Outpatient Surgery:		Staffing:		Physical Therapy:	
Payment Processing:		Vitamins/Nutritionals:		Information Systems:		Physical Rehab. Ctr.:		Waste Disposal:		Physician Prac. Mgmt.:	
		Clinical Trials:				Psychiatric Clinics:		Specialty Svcs.:			

TYPES OF BUSINESS:

Generic Pharmaceuticals
Branded Drugs
Urology Drugs
Anti-Hypertensive Drugs
Psychiatric Drugs
Pain Management Drugs
Dermatology Drugs
Nephrology Drugs

BRANDS/DIVISIONS/AFFILIATES:

Watson Laboratories
Watson Pharma
Rugby
Ferrlecit
Trelstar Depot
Oxytrol
Anda
Andrx Corp.

CONTACTS:

Note: Officers with more than one job title may be intentionally listed here more than once.

Allen Chao, CEO
Susan Skara, Sr. VP-Human Resources
Charles D. Ebert, Sr. VP-R&D
Thomas R. Giordano, CIO/Sr. VP
David A. Buchen, General Counsel/Sr. VP/Sec.
Edward F. Heimers, Jr., Exec. VP/Pres., Brand Division
David C. Hsia, Sr. VP-Scientific Affairs
Gordon Munro, Sr. VP-Quality Assurance
Thomas R. Russillo, Exec. VP/Pres., U.S. Generics Division
Allen Chao, Chmn.

Phone: 951-493-5300 **Fax:** 973-355-8301
Toll-Free:
Address: 311 Bonnie Cir., Corona, CA 92880 US

GROWTH PLANS/SPECIAL FEATURES:

Watson Pharmaceuticals, Inc. manufactures and distributes over 25 branded and over 150 generic pharmaceutical products. The company offers generic versions of popular brand-name pharmaceuticals including Zyban, Wellbutrin, Lorcet, Vicodin, Percocet, Ocycontin, Nicorette, Lortab, Triphasil and Demulen. The firm markets its generic products through a network of 25 sales and marketing professionals under the Watson Laboratories and Watson Pharma labels. Over-the-counter products are sold under the Rugby label or private label. Generic products accounted for roughly 77% of net sales in 2006. Watson Pharmaceuticals' brand business segment develops, manufactures, markets, sells and distributes products primarily through two sales and marketing groups: specialty groups and nephrology. The specialty products include urology, anti-hypertensive, psychiatry, pain management and dermatology products and a genital warts treatment. Brand names include Trelstar Depot, Trelstar LA and Oxytrol. The nephrology product line consists of products for the treatment of iron deficiency anemia. The primary product is Ferrlecit, indicated for patients undergoing hemodialysis in conjunction with erythropoietin therapy. The company markets its brand products through 333 sales professionals and offers trademarked off-patent products to physicians, hospitals and healthcare professionals. Brand products accounted for roughly 19% of total revenue in 2006. The company's distribution business consists of Anda, Anda Pharmaceuticals and Valmed. During 2006, Watson Pharmaceuticals entered into an agreement with Solvay Pharmaceuticals for the promotion of AndroGel to urologists in the U.S. In November 2006, the company acquired Andrx Corp., a pharmaceutical products distributor, for roughly $1.9 billion. In June 2007, the firm received FDA approval forbypropion hydrochloride tablets, the generic equivalent to Wellbutrin XL tablets, for the treatment of major depressive disorder.

The company offers its employees medical, dental and vision insurance; a 401(k) plan; life and AD&D insurance; domestic partner coverage; business travel accident insurance; short- and long-term disability; pet insurance; and tuition reimbursement.

FINANCIALS:

Sales and profits are in thousands of dollars—add 000 to get the full amount. 2007 Note: Financial information for 2007 was not available for all companies at press time.

2007 Sales: $	2007 Profits: $	**U.S. Stock Ticker: WPI**
2006 Sales: $1,979,244	2006 Profits: $-445,005	**Int'l Ticker:** Int'l Exchange:
2005 Sales: $1,646,203	2005 Profits: $138,557	Employees: 5,830
2004 Sales: $1,640,551	2004 Profits: $150,018	Fiscal Year Ends: 12/31
2003 Sales: $1,457,722	2003 Profits: $202,864	Parent Company:

SALARIES/BENEFITS:

Pension Plan:	ESOP Stock Plan:	Profit Sharing:	Top Exec. Salary: $937,692	Bonus: $993,000
Savings Plan: Y	Stock Purch. Plan:		Second Exec. Salary: $420,038	Bonus: $

OTHER THOUGHTS:

Apparent Women Officers or Directors: 2
Hot Spot for Advancement for Women/Minorities: Y

LOCATIONS: ("Y" = Yes)

West:	Southwest:	Midwest:	Southeast:	Northeast:	International:
Y		Y	Y	Y	Y

WEBMD HEALTH CORP

www.webmd.com

Industry Group Code: 514199 **Ranks within this company's industry group:** Sales: 1 Profits: 1

Insurance/HMO/PPO:		Drugs:		Equipment/Supplies:		Hospitals/Clinics:		Services:		Health Care:	
Insurance:		Manufacturer:		Manufacturer:		Acute Care:		Diagnostics:		Home Health:	
Managed Care:		Distributor:		Distributor:		Sub-Acute:		Labs/Testing:		Long-Term Care:	
Utilization Management:		Specialty Pharmacy:		Leasing/Finance:		Outpatient Surgery:		Staffing:		Physical Therapy:	
Payment Processing:		Vitamins/Nutritionals:		Information Systems:		Physical Rehab. Ctr.:		Waste Disposal:		Physician Prac. Mgmt.:	
		Clinical Trials:				Psychiatric Clinics:		Specialty Svcs.:	Y		

TYPES OF BUSINESS:

Health Care Internet Portals
Publishing

BRANDS/DIVISIONS/AFFILIATES:

WebMD Health Holdings, Inc.
WebMD Health Network
Medscape
Little Blue Book (The)
WebMD Magazine
Subimo, LLC

CONTACTS: *Note: Officers with more than one job title may be intentionally listed here more than once.*

Wayne T. Gattinella, CEO
Anthony Vuolo, COO
Wayne T. Gattinella, Pres.
Mark D. Funston, CFO/Exec. VP
Douglas W. Wamsley, General Counsel/Exec. VP/Corp. Sec.
Nan-Kirsten Forte, Exec. VP-Consumer Svcs.
Steven Zatz, Exec. VP-Professional Svcs.
Craig Froude, Exec. VP-WebMD Health Svcs.
Martin J. Wygood, Chmn.

Phone: 212-624-3700	**Fax:** 212-624-3800
Toll-Free:	
Address: 111 8th Ave., New York, NY 10011 US	

GROWTH PLANS/SPECIAL FEATURES:

WebMD Health Corp., formerly a unit of Emdeon Corp known as WebMD Health Holdings, Inc., is a provider o health information services to consumers; physicians an other healthcare professionals; employers; and health plan through public and private online portals and health-focuse publications. The public online service, referred to as th WebMD Health Network, offers WebMD Health, th company's primary public portal, and Medscape fron WebMD, a public portal for physicians and health car professionals. WebMD Health provides health and wellnes articles and features, and decision-support services to hel consumers make informed decisions about health car providers, health risks and treatment options. Availabl information and interactive tools include detailed data o specific diseases or conditions, symptom analysis, physicia location and individual health care data storage. Medscap from WebMD assists physicians and health car professionals in improving clinical knowledge with origina content such as daily news, commentary, conferenc coverage and continuing medical education. The WebMD Health Network has an approximate monthly average of 3 million unique users per month. The firm generates revenu from its public offerings primarily through advertising sale and sponsorships. Private portals offered by WebMD enabl employees and health plan members to learn about benefits providers and treatment decisions, customized to a user' health insurance plan. Revenue is generated from th private side though content and technology licensed t employers such as American Airlines, Microsoft, PepsiCo Blue Cross Blue Shield of Massachusetts, Cigna and Empir Blue Cross and Blue Shield. In addition, the company has a publishing segment that produces publications such as Th Little Blue Book, a physician directory; and WebMD th Magazine, a consumer magazine distributed free of charg to physician office waiting rooms. In December 2006 WebMD acquired Subimo, LLC, a healthcare decisio support applications provider, for $60 million.

FINANCIALS: **Sales and profits are in thousands of dollars—add 000 to get the full amount. 2007 Note: Financial information for 2007 was not available for all companies at press time.**

2007 Sales: $	2007 Profits: $	**U.S. Stock Ticker: WBMD**
2006 Sales: $253,881	2006 Profits: $4,546	**Int'l Ticker:** Int'l Exchange:
2005 Sales: $168,938	2005 Profits: $7,745	Employees: 1,025
2004 Sales: $134,148	2004 Profits: $6,461	Fiscal Year Ends: 12/31
2003 Sales: $110,152	2003 Profits: $-7,425	Parent Company:

SALARIES/BENEFITS:

Pension Plan:	ESOP Stock Plan:	Profit Sharing:	Top Exec. Salary: $975,000	Bonus: $3,530,000
Savings Plan:	Stock Purch. Plan:		Second Exec. Salary: $560,000	Bonus: $340,000

OTHER THOUGHTS:

Apparent Women Officers or Directors: 1
Hot Spot for Advancement for Women/Minorities:

LOCATIONS: ("Y" = Yes)

West:	Southwest:	Midwest:	Southeast:	Northeast:	International:
				Y	

WEIGHT WATCHERS INTERNATIONAL INC

www.weightwatchers.com

Industry Group Code: 446190 **Ranks within this company's industry group:** Sales: 1 Profits: 1

Insurance/HMO/PPO:		Drugs:		Equipment/Supplies:		Hospitals/Clinics:		Services:		Health Care:	
Insurance:		Manufacturer:		Manufacturer:		Acute Care:		Diagnostics:		Home Health:	
Managed Care:		Distributor:		Distributor:		Sub-Acute:		Labs/Testing:		Long-Term Care:	
Utilization Management:		Specialty Pharmacy:		Leasing/Finance:		Outpatient Surgery:		Staffing:		Physical Therapy:	
Payment Processing:		Vitamins/Nutritionals:		Information Systems:		Physical Rehab. Ctr.:		Waste Disposal:		Physician Prac. Mgmt.:	
		Clinical Trials:				Psychiatric Clinics:		Specialty Svcs.:	Y		

TYPES OF BUSINESS:

Weight Management Programs
Franchising
Branded Diet Products

BRANDS/DIVISIONS/AFFILIATES:

Weight Watchers Corporate Solutions
Weight Watchers eTools
Weight Watchers Online
FlexPoints

CONTACTS: *Note: Officers with more than one job title may be intentionally listed here more than once.*

David P. Kirchhoff, CEO
Thilo Semmelbauer, COO
David P. Kirchhoff, Pres.
Ann Sardini, CFO/VP
Jeffrey A. Fiarman, General Counsel/Exec. VP/Sec.
Raymond Debbane, Chmn.

Phone: 212-589-2700	**Fax:** 212-589-2601
Toll-Free:	
Address: 11 Madison Ave., 17th Fl., New York, NY 10010 US	

GROWTH PLANS/SPECIAL FEATURES:

Weight Watchers International, Inc. is a global provider of weight management services, with a presence in 28 countries around the world. The company hosts weekly meetings that promote weight loss through diet, exercise, behavior modification and group support. Each week, over 1.5 million people attend approximately 50,000 Weight Watchers meetings around the world, which are run by roughly 15,000 classroom leaders. Weight Watchers uses a combination of company-owned operations and franchised operations. The firm also offers Weight Watchers Corporate Solutions, a line of weight loss products that can be customized to suit the employees in any company. This at-work program addresses the weight-loss needs of working people by holding classes at their place of employment. The company's web site offers Internet subscription weight management products to consumers and maintains an interactive presence for the Weight Watchers brand. Customers can subscribe to Weight Watchers Online, which provides interactive and personalized resources that allow users to follow its weight management plans via the Internet; and Weight Watchers eTools, the Internet weight management companion for Weight Watchers meetings members who want to interactively manage the day-to-day aspects of their weight management plans on the Internet. The company offers these two products in the U.S., the U.K., Canada, Germany, Australia and New Zealand. FlexPoints is the firm's proprietary system for tracking and maintaining food amounts. For self-help dieters, Weight Watchers also offers an at-home kit, which is a complete mail-order system including the full set of program materials used in meetings.

FINANCIALS: **Sales and profits are in thousands of dollars—add 000 to get the full amount. 2007 Note: Financial information for 2007 was not available for all companies at press time.**

2007 Sales: $	2007 Profits: $	**U.S. Stock Ticker: WTW**
2006 Sales: $1,233,300	2006 Profits: $209,800	**Int'l Ticker:** Int'l Exchange:
2005 Sales: $1,151,300	2005 Profits: $174,400	Employees: 47,000
2004 Sales: $1,024,900	2004 Profits: $183,100	Fiscal Year Ends: 12/31
2003 Sales: $943,932	2003 Profits: $143,941	Parent Company:

SALARIES/BENEFITS:

Pension Plan:	ESOP Stock Plan:	Profit Sharing:	Top Exec. Salary: $742,156	Bonus: $464,775
Savings Plan:	Stock Purch. Plan:		Second Exec. Salary: $356,924	Bonus: $205,855

OTHER THOUGHTS:

Apparent Women Officers or Directors: 1
Hot Spot for Advancement for Women/Minorities: Y

LOCATIONS: ("Y" = Yes)

West:	Southwest:	Midwest:	Southeast:	Northeast:	International:
Y	Y	Y	Y	Y	Y

Note: Financial information, benefits and other data can change quickly and may vary from those stated here.

WELCH ALLYN INC

www.welchallyn.com

Industry Group Code: 339113 **Ranks within this company's industry group:** Sales: Profits:

Insurance/HMO/PPO:		Drugs:		Equipment/Supplies:		Hospitals/Clinics:		Services:		Health Care:	
Insurance:		Manufacturer:		Manufacturer:	Y	Acute Care:		Diagnostics:		Home Health:	
Managed Care:		Distributor:		Distributor:		Sub-Acute:		Labs/Testing:		Long-Term Care:	
Utilization Management:		Specialty Pharmacy:		Leasing/Finance:		Outpatient Surgery:		Staffing:		Physical Therapy:	
Payment Processing:		Vitamins/Nutritionals:		Information Systems:	Y	Physical Rehab. Ctr.:		Waste Disposal:		Physician Prac. Mgmt.:	
		Clinical Trials:				Psychiatric Clinics:		Specialty Svcs.:	Y		

TYPES OF BUSINESS:

Equipment-Mobile Patient Monitoring Systems
Cardiac Defibrillators
Diagnostic and Therapeutic Devices
Precision Lamps
Image-Based Data Collection Systems
Training Services
Equipment Sales and Rentals
Remote Imaging Services

BRANDS/DIVISIONS/AFFILIATES:

Wm. Noah Allyn International Center
Everest VIT
HHP

CONTACTS: *Note: Officers with more than one job title may be intentionally listed here more than once.*

Julie A. Shimer, CEO
Julie A. Shimer, Pres.
Kevin Cahill, CFO/Exec. VP
Dan Fisher, Sr. VP-Human Resources
Darrell A. Clapper, Sr. VP-Global Oper.
Steve Meyer, Exec. VP-Ambulatory Cary & Americas
Doug Linquest, Exec. VP-Acute Care & Asia
Darrell A. Clapper, Sr. VP-Supply Chain

Phone: 315-685-4100 **Fax:** 315-685-2546
Toll-Free: 800-535-6663
Address: 4341 State St. Rd., Skaneateles Falls, NY 13153-0220 US

GROWTH PLANS/SPECIAL FEATURES:

Welch Allyn, Inc. manufactures medical equipment including diagnostic and therapeutic devices, cardiac defibrillators patient monitoring systems and miniature precision lamps Products and applications include eye and ear care; medica index and referencing; laryngoscopes; lighting; and monitoring devices. These are used for dental health inpatient care, pediatrics, general and family medicine women's health, ambulatory surgery, emergency care extended care, internal medicine and veterinary care. The firm operates numerous manufacturing, sales and distribution facilities throughout the world, in such places as Singapore, Malaysia, Japan, Australia, the U.K., Madrid South Africa, the Netherlands, Italy, Ireland and France. It also operates alternative businesses through subsidiaries The Wm. Noah Allyn International Center for Training and Sales Development, known as the Lodge, is a faculty training and retreat center in Skaneateles Falls, New York. Another subsidiary, HHP, formerly Hand Held Products, designs and manufactures image-based data collection systems for transportation, postal services, warehousing, manufacturing and retail customers. Everest VIT, a full-service remote imaging company, offers technology-based training and inspection by experienced, certified technicians as well as equipment sales and rentals. Welch Allyn's lighting products division uses several proprietary manufacturing techniques.

Welch Allyn's employee benefits include travel insurance, child and elder care, legal assistance, counseling, free health screenings, on-site fitness facilities and wellness incentives.

FINANCIALS: Sales and profits are in thousands of dollars—add 000 to get the full amount. 2007 Note: Financial information for 2007 was not available for all companies at press time.

2007 Sales: $	2007 Profits: $	**U.S. Stock Ticker: Private**
2006 Sales: $	2006 Profits: $	**Int'l Ticker:** Int'l Exchange:
2005 Sales: $	2005 Profits: $	Employees:
2004 Sales: $	2004 Profits: $	Fiscal Year Ends: 12/31
2003 Sales: $	2003 Profits: $	Parent Company:

SALARIES/BENEFITS:

Pension Plan:	ESOP Stock Plan:	Profit Sharing:	Top Exec. Salary: $	Bonus: $
Savings Plan:	Stock Purch. Plan:		Second Exec. Salary: $	Bonus: $

OTHER THOUGHTS:

Apparent Women Officers or Directors: 1
Hot Spot for Advancement for Women/Minorities:

LOCATIONS: ("Y" = Yes)

West:	Southwest:	Midwest:	Southeast:	Northeast:	International:
Y		Y	Y	Y	Y

WELLCARE GROUP OF COMPANIES www.wellcare.com

Industry Group Code: 524114 **Ranks within this company's industry group:** Sales: 19 Profits:

Insurance/HMO/PPO:		Drugs:		Equipment/Supplies:		Hospitals/Clinics:		Services:		Health Care:	
Insurance:		Manufacturer:		Manufacturer:		Acute Care:		Diagnostics:		Home Health:	
Managed Care:	Y	Distributor:		Distributor:		Sub-Acute:		Labs/Testing:		Long-Term Care:	
Utilization Management:		Specialty Pharmacy:		Leasing/Finance:		Outpatient Surgery:		Staffing:		Physical Therapy:	
Payment Processing:		Vitamins/Nutritionals:		Information Systems:		Physical Rehab. Ctr.:		Waste Disposal:		Physician Prac. Mgmt.:	
		Clinical Trials:				Psychiatric Clinics:		Specialty Svcs.:			

TYPES OF BUSINESS:

Insurance-Medical & Health, HMOs & PPOs

BRANDS/DIVISIONS/AFFILIATES:

WellCare

CONTACTS:

Note: Officers with more than one job title may be intentionally listed here more than once.

Todd Farha, CEO
Todd Farha, Pres.
Paul Behrens, CFO/Sr. VP
Rupesh Shah, Sr. VP-Market Expansion
Gretchen Demartini, VP-Human Resources
Anil Kottoor, CIO/Sr. VP
Thaddeus Bereday, General Counsel/Sr. VP
Jeffrey Potter, VP-Corp. Dev.
Donna Burtanger, Dir.-Corp. Comm.
Ace Hodgin, Sr. VP/Chief Medical Officer
Adam Miller, COO-Prescription Drug Plans
Michael Cotton, COO-Georgia
Dan Parietti, Pres., New York
Todd Farha, Chmn.

Phone: 813-290-6200	**Fax:** 813-262-2802
Toll-Free: 800-795-3432	
Address: 8735 Henderson Rd., Tampa, FL 33614 US	

GROWTH PLANS/SPECIAL FEATURES:

The WellCare Group of Companies manages government-sponsored healthcare programs, such as Medicaid, Medicare and State Children's Health Insurance Programs (S-CHIP). The group offers a variety of Medicare and Medicaid plans, including prescription drug plans and health plans for families, children, the aged, blind and disabled. Medicaid is a government program that provides medical assistance to low income and disabled people in the U.S. WellCare makes 2-3 year contracts with state and federal government agencies to provide selected members with fixed premiums. The plans that the group offers provide members with access to medical benefits that range from primary care and preventative programs to full hospitalization and tertiary care. Similarly, the group offers government sponsored Medicare through its MCC (Medicare coordinated care) plans and PFFS (private-fee-for-service) plans to eligible persons age 65 and over for a variety of hospital, medical insurance and prescription drug benefits. WellCare provides its members with an enhanced level of services relative to the original Medicare fee-for-service coverage, ranging from reduced out-of-pocket expenses to prescription drug coverage. In addition to Medicare and Medicaid, the group also has plans for S-CHIP, which is a federal and state matching program designed to expand health insurance to children whose families earn too much to qualify for traditional Medicaid, yet not enough to afford private health insurance. The total group of companies is made up of over 25,000 physician partners and 60,000 pharmacies that serve approximately 2.25 million members nationwide. Through its licensed subsidiaries it operates Medicaid plans in eight states and MCC plans in six states. The group also operates stand-alone Medicare proscription drug plans in all 50 states. In January 2007, WellCare ceased offering its Medicaid plans in Indiana, but began offering PFFS plans to Medicare beneficiaries in 39 states.

FINANCIALS:

Sales and profits are in thousands of dollars—add 000 to get the full amount. 2007 Note: Financial information for 2007 was not available for all companies at press time.

2007 Sales: $	2007 Profits: $	**U.S. Stock Ticker: WCG**
2006 Sales: $3,762,926	2006 Profits: $	**Int'l Ticker:** Int'l Exchange:
2005 Sales: $1,879,539	2005 Profits: $139,187	Employees: 2,000
2004 Sales: $1,395,203	2004 Profits: $49,250	Fiscal Year Ends: 12/31
2003 Sales: $1,046,000	2003 Profits: $23,500	Parent Company:

SALARIES/BENEFITS:

Pension Plan:	ESOP Stock Plan:	Profit Sharing:	Top Exec. Salary: $400,000	Bonus: $400,000
Savings Plan:	Stock Purch. Plan:		Second Exec. Salary: $282,269	Bonus: $200,000

OTHER THOUGHTS:

Apparent Women Officers or Directors: 1
Hot Spot for Advancement for Women/Minorities: Y

LOCATIONS: ("Y" = Yes)

West:	Southwest:	Midwest:	Southeast:	Northeast:	International:
		Y	Y	Y	

WELLPOINT INC www.wellpoint.com

Industry Group Code: 524114 **Ranks within this company's industry group:** Sales: 2 Profits: 2

Insurance/HMO/PPO:		Drugs:		Equipment/Supplies:		Hospitals/Clinics:		Services:		Health Care:	
Insurance:	Y	Manufacturer:		Manufacturer:		Acute Care:		Diagnostics:		Home Health:	
Managed Care:	Y	Distributor:		Distributor:		Sub-Acute:		Labs/Testing:		Long-Term Care:	
Utilization Management:		Specialty Pharmacy:		Leasing/Finance:		Outpatient Surgery:		Staffing:		Physical Therapy:	
Payment Processing:	Y	Vitamins/Nutritionals:		Information Systems:		Physical Rehab. Ctr.:		Waste Disposal:		Physician Prac. Mgmt.:	
		Clinical Trials:				Psychiatric Clinics:		Specialty Svcs.:	Y		

TYPES OF BUSINESS:

Health Insurance
Workers' Compensation Plans
Point-of-Service Plans
Dental Plans
Pharmaceutical Plans
Managed Care Services
Actuarial Services

BRANDS/DIVISIONS/AFFILIATES:

WellPoint Behavioral Health
Unicare
BLUE CROSS OF CALIFORNIA
BLUE CROSS AND BLUE SHIELD OF GEORGIA INC
WellPoint Dental Services
HealthLink, Inc.
WellPoint Pharmacy Management
American Imaging Management

CONTACTS: *Note: Officers with more than one job title may be intentionally listed here more than once.*

Angela F. Braly, CEO
Angela F. Braly, Pres.
Wayne S. DeVeydt, CFO/Exec. VP
Randy L. Brown, Exec. VP/Chief Human Resources Officer
Shamla Naidoo, Chief Info. Security Officer/VP
Alice F. Rosenblatt, Exec. VP-Integration Planning
Jamie S. Miller, Chief Acct. Officer/Sr. VP
Mark L. Boxer, Pres./CEO-Oper., Tech. & Gov't Svcs. Bus. Unit
Joan E. Herman, Pres./CEO-Specialty, Senior & State-Sponsored Bus.
Randall J. Lewis, Exec. VP-Internal Audit & Chief Compliance Officer
Samuel R. Nussbaum, Exec. VP/Chief Medical Officer
Larry C. Glasscock, Chmn.

Phone: 317-532-6000	**Fax:** 317-488-6028
Toll-Free:	
Address: 120 Monument Cir., Indianapolis, IN 46204 US	

GROWTH PLANS/SPECIAL FEATURES:

WellPoint, Inc. (formerly WellPoint Health Networks) is a health benefits company, serving over 34 million medical members. The company is an independent licensee of the Blue Cross and Blue Shield Association, an association of independent health benefit plans, and also serves customers as Unicare. The firm offers network-based managed care plans to the large and small employer, individual, Medicaid and senior markets. The managed care plans include preferred provider organizations, health maintenance organizations, point-of-service plans, traditional indemnity plans and other hybrid plans including consumer-driven health plans, hospital only and limited benefit products. In addition, WellPoint provides managed care services to self-funded customers, including claims processing, underwriting, stop loss insurance, actuarial services, provider network access, medical cost management and other administrative services. The company also provides specialty and other products and services including life and disability insurance benefits; pharmacy benefit management; specialty pharmacy; dental; vision; behavioral health benefit services; long-term care insurance; and flexible spending accounts. About 93% of operating revenue in 2006 was derived from premium income and roughly 7% from administrative fees and other revenues. The firm markets its products through a network of independent agents and brokers and through its in-house sales force. Subsidiaries include Blue Cross of California and Blue Cross Blue Shield of Georgia, as well as non-Blue Cross subsidiaries such as Healthlink, PrecisionRx, WellPoint Behavioral Health, WellPoint Dental Services and WellPoint Workers' Compensation Managed Care Services. Subsidiary WellPoint Pharmacy Management markets clinical management programs, drug formulary management, benefit design consultation, pharmacy network management, local network contract development, manufacturer discount programs and prescription drug databases. In August 2007, WellPoint acquired American Imaging Management, a radiology benefit management and technology provider.

WellPoint offers employees tuition assistance; a 401(k) plan; an employee stock purchase plan; retiree medical spending accounts; life insurance; long-term disability insurance; and financial education.

FINANCIALS:

Sales and profits are in thousands of dollars—add 000 to get the full amount. 2007 Note: Financial information for 2007 was not available for all companies at press time.

2007 Sales: $	2007 Profits: $	**U.S. Stock Ticker: WLP**
2006 Sales: $56,953,000	2006 Profits: $3,094,900	**Int'l Ticker:** Int'l Exchange:
2005 Sales: $44,541,300	2005 Profits: $2,463,800	Employees: 42,000
2004 Sales: $20,707,900	2004 Profits: $960,100	Fiscal Year Ends: 12/31
2003 Sales: $20,101,500	2003 Profits: $935,200	Parent Company:

SALARIES/BENEFITS:

Pension Plan:	ESOP Stock Plan:	Profit Sharing:	Top Exec. Salary: $1,290,385	Bonus: $2,013,206
Savings Plan: Y	Stock Purch. Plan: Y		Second Exec. Salary: $703,295	Bonus: $666,190

OTHER THOUGHTS:

Apparent Women Officers or Directors: 10
Hot Spot for Advancement for Women/Minorities: Y

LOCATIONS: ("Y" = Yes)

West:	Southwest:	Midwest:	Southeast:	Northeast:	International:
Y	Y	Y	Y	Y	

WEST PHARMACEUTICAL SERVICES INC

www.westpharma.com

ndustry Group Code: 322210 **Ranks within this company's industry group:** Sales: 1 Profits: 1

Insurance/HMO/PPO:		Drugs:		Equipment/Supplies:		Hospitals/Clinics:		Services:		Health Care:	
nsurance:		Manufacturer:		Manufacturer:	Y	Acute Care:		Diagnostics:		Home Health:	
Managed Care:		Distributor:		Distributor:		Sub-Acute:		Labs/Testing:		Long-Term Care:	
Jtilization Management:		Specialty Pharmacy:		Leasing/Finance:		Outpatient Surgery:		Staffing:		Physical Therapy:	
Payment Processing:		Vitamins/Nutritionals:		Information Systems:		Physical Rehab. Ctr.:		Waste Disposal:		Physician Prac. Mgmt.:	
		Clinical Trials:				Psychiatric Clinics:		Specialty Svcs.:			

TYPES OF BUSINESS:

njectable Drug Delivery Systems Components
Plastic Packaging Systems Components
Elastomer & Metal Components

BRANDS/DIVISIONS/AFFILIATES:

Flip-Off

CONTACTS: *Note: Officers with more than one job title may be intentionally listed here more than once.*

Donald E. Morel, CEO
Steven A. Ellers, COO
Steven A. Ellers, Pres.
William J. Federici, CFO/VP
Richard D. Luzzi, VP-Human Resources
John R. Gailey, General Counsel/VP/Sec.
Michael A. Anderson, VP/Treas.
Robert S. Hargesheimer, Pres., Tech Group
Donald A. McMillan, Pres., North America-Pharmaceutical Systems Div.
Joseph E. Abbott, VP-Corp. Controller
Donald E. Morel, Chmn.
Robert J. Keating, Pres., Europe & Asia Pacific-Pharmaceutical Div.

Phone: 610-594-2900 | **Fax:** 610-594-3000
Toll-Free:
Address: 101 Gordon Dr., Lionville, PA 19341 US

GROWTH PLANS/SPECIAL FEATURES:

West Pharmaceutical Services, Inc. manufactures components and systems for injectable drug delivery and plastic packaging and delivery system components for the healthcare, personal care and consumer products markets. The company's products include stoppers and seals for vials; and components used in syringes, intravenous delivery systems, blood collection systems and blood diagnostic systems. The firm operates in two segments: pharmaceutical systems and the tech group. The pharmaceutical systems segment designs, manufactures and sells a variety of elastomer and metal components used in parenteral drug delivery for the branded pharmaceutical, generic and biopharmaceutical industries. Products include elastomeric stoppers and discs; secondary closures for pharmaceutical vials, called Flip-Off aluminum seals; elastomeric syringe plungers, stoppers for blood collection systems, flashback bulbs and sleeve stoppers; elastomer and co-molded elastomer/plastic components for infusion sets; baby bottle nipple and pacifier bulbs; needle shields and tip caps; and dropper bulbs. The tech group segment serves the medical, pharmaceutical, diagnostic and healthcare markets with custom contract-manufacturing services. It also designs and manufactures unique components for surgical, ophthalmic, diagnostic and drug delivery systems such as contact lens storage kits, pill dispensers, safety needle syringes, and disposable blood collection systems and components. Sales outside of the U.S. account for roughly 49% of net sales.

The company offers its employees medical, life, dental and disability insurance; a 401(k) plan; a retirement plan; an employee stock purchase plan; an employee assistance program; an education assistance program; and flexible spending accounts.

FINANCIALS: **Sales and profits are in thousands of dollars—add 000 to get the full amount. 2007 Note: Financial information for 2007 was not available for all companies at press time.**

2007 Sales: $ | 2007 Profits: $
2006 Sales: $913,300 | 2006 Profits: $67,100
2005 Sales: $699,700 | 2005 Profits: $45,600
2004 Sales: $541,600 | 2004 Profits: $19,400
2003 Sales: $490,700 | 2003 Profits: $31,900

U.S. Stock Ticker: WST
Int'l Ticker: Int'l Exchange:
Employees: 6,323
Fiscal Year Ends: 12/31
Parent Company:

SALARIES/BENEFITS:

Pension Plan: Y | ESOP Stock Plan: | Profit Sharing: | Top Exec. Salary: $664,059 | Bonus: $916,004
Savings Plan: Y | Stock Purch. Plan: Y | | Second Exec. Salary: $388,145 | Bonus: $340,678

OTHER THOUGHTS:

Apparent Women Officers or Directors:
Hot Spot for Advancement for Women/Minorities:

LOCATIONS: ("Y" = Yes)

West:	Southwest:	Midwest:	Southeast:	Northeast:	International:
	Y	Y	Y	Y	Y

WRIGHT MEDICAL GROUP INC

www.wmt.com

Industry Group Code: 339113 **Ranks within this company's industry group:** Sales: 53 Profits: 56

Insurance/HMO/PPO:		Drugs:		Equipment/Supplies:		Hospitals/Clinics:		Services:		Health Care:	
Insurance:		Manufacturer:		Manufacturer:	Y	Acute Care:		Diagnostics:		Home Health:	
Managed Care:		Distributor:		Distributor:		Sub-Acute:		Labs/Testing:		Long-Term Care:	
Utilization Management:		Specialty Pharmacy:		Leasing/Finance:		Outpatient Surgery:		Staffing:		Physical Therapy:	
Payment Processing:		Vitamins/Nutritionals:		Information Systems:		Physical Rehab. Ctr.:		Waste Disposal:		Physician Prac. Mgmt.:	
		Clinical Trials:				Psychiatric Clinics:		Specialty Svcs.:			

TYPES OF BUSINESS:

Orthopedic Implants
Reconstructive Joint Devices
Biologics Materials

BRANDS/DIVISIONS/AFFILIATES:

Wright Medical Technology, Inc.
Advance Medial Pivot Knee
Conserve Hip System
Perfecta Hip System
Guardian Limb Salvage System
Allomatrix
Graftjacket Regenerative Tissue
A-Class

CONTACTS: *Note: Officers with more than one job title may be intentionally listed here more than once.*

Gary D. Henley, CEO
Gary D. Henley, Pres.
John K. Bakewell, CFO/Exec. VP
Cary P. Hagan, VP-Mktg.
Jeffrey G. Roberts, VP-R&D
Jeffrey G. Roberts, CTO/Sr. VP
Kyle M. Joines, VP-Mfg.
Jason P. Hood, General Counsel/VP/Corp. Sec.
Timothy E. Davis, Jr., VP-Bus. Dev.
Lance A. Berry, Controller/VP
Karen L. Harris, VP-Int'l Sales & Distribution
Joyce B. Jones, VP/Treas.
John T. Treace, VP-Biologics & Extremity Mktg.
Eric A. Stookey, VP-North American Sales
F. Barry Bays, Chmn.
Paul R. Kosters, Pres., EMEA
William J. Flannery, Logistics & Materials

Phone: 901-867-9971 **Fax:** 901-867-9534
Toll-Free: 800-238-7117
Address: 5677 Airline Rd., Arlington, TN 38002 US

GROWTH PLANS/SPECIAL FEATURES:

Wright Medical Group, Inc. is an international orthopedi device company that designs, manufactures and market reconstructive joint devices and bio-orthopedic material through its operating subsidiaries and Wright Medic Technology, Inc. The company's reconstructive joint device replace knees, hips and joints while bio-orthopedic and othe biologics materials replace damaged or diseased bones an tissue to stimulate natural growth. Wright particular focuses its interests on the higher-growth sectors advanced bearing surfaces, modular necks and bon conserving implants within the hip market and the integratio of its biologics products within reconstructive joi procedures and other orthopedic applications. The firm products include brand names such as the Advance Medi Pivot Knee, which is designed to approximate the motion of healthy knee by using a unique spherical medial feature, an the Conserve family of products, which provides a bon conserving alternative to conventional total hip reconstructio for patients diagnosed with avascular necrosis (AVN). Othe product brands include The Perfecta Hip System, th Guardian Limb Salvage System, the Lineage Acetabul System, the Osteoset bone graft substitute, Allomatri injectable putty and Graftjacket Regenerative Tissu Extremity products for the hand, wrist, elbow, shoulder, fo and ankle include the EVOLVE Modular Radial Hea System, the CHARLOTTE Foot and Ankle System, th LOCON-T and LOCON-V:S Distal Radius Plating System and the MICRONAIL intramedullary wrist fracture repa system. In 2007, the company announced that it would clos down its manufacturing, distribution and administrativ facility in Toulon, France. Wright also acquired the etern fixation product line of R&R Medical, Inc., which consists of variety of foot and ankle-focused external fixation device and the reconstructive foot surgery line from Darc International, Inc.

FINANCIALS: **Sales and profits are in thousands of dollars—add 000 to get the full amount. 2007 Note: Financial information for 2007 was not available for all companies at press time.**

2007 Sales: $	2007 Profits: $
2006 Sales: $338,938	2006 Profits: $14,411
2005 Sales: $319,137	2005 Profits: $21,065
2004 Sales: $297,539	2004 Profits: $24,022
2003 Sales: $248,932	2003 Profits: $17,397

U.S. Stock Ticker: WMGI
Int'l Ticker: Int'l Exchange:
Employees: 1,060
Fiscal Year Ends: 12/31
Parent Company:

SALARIES/BENEFITS:

Pension Plan:	ESOP Stock Plan:	Profit Sharing:	Top Exec. Salary: $290,875	Bonus: $
Savings Plan: Y	Stock Purch. Plan: Y		Second Exec. Salary: $241,750	Bonus: $

OTHER THOUGHTS:

Apparent Women Officers or Directors: 3
Hot Spot for Advancement for Women/Minorities: Y

LOCATIONS: ("Y" = Yes)

West:	Southwest:	Midwest:	Southeast:	Northeast:	International:
			Y		Y

WYETH

www.wyeth.com

ndustry Group Code: 325412 **Ranks within this company's industry group:** Sales: 10 Profits: 9

nsurance/HMO/PPO:		Drugs:		Equipment/Supplies:		Hospitals/Clinics:		Services:		Health Care:	
nsurance:		Manufacturer:	Y	Manufacturer:	Y	Acute Care:		Diagnostics:		Home Health:	
Managed Care:		Distributor:	Y	Distributor:	Y	Sub-Acute:		Labs/Testing:		Long-Term Care:	
tilization Management:		Specialty Pharmacy:		Leasing/Finance:		Outpatient Surgery:		Staffing:		Physical Therapy:	
ayment Processing:		Vitamins/Nutritionals:		Information Systems:		Physical Rehab. Ctr.:		Waste Disposal:		Physician Prac. Mgmt.:	
		Clinical Trials:				Psychiatric Clinics:		Specialty Svcs.:			

TYPES OF BUSINESS:

)rugs-Diversified
Vholesale Pharmaceuticals
nimal Health Care Products
iologicals
'accines
)ver-the-Counter Drugs
Vomen's Health Care Products
lutritional Supplements

BRANDS/DIVISIONS/AFFILIATES:

Chap Stick
Premarin
Dimetapp
Advil
Robitussin
Preparation H
Centrum
Vyeth K.K.

CONTACTS: *Note: Officers with more than one job title may be ntentionally listed here more than once.*

Robert Essner, CEO
ernard Poussot, COO
ernard Poussot, Pres.
Rene Lewin, VP-Human Resources
effrey Keisling, CIO
awrence Stein, General Counsel/Sr. VP
homas Hofstaetter, Sr. VP-Bus. Dev.
Marilyn Rhudy, VP-Public Affairs
ustin Victoria, VP-Investor Rel.
ohn Kelly, VP-Finance Oper.
ames Pohlman, VP-Corp. Strategic Initiatives
oseph Mahady, Sr. VP
Robert Ruffolo, Sr. VP
Robert E. Landry, Jr., Treas.
Robert Essner, Chmn.

Phone: 973-660-5000	Fax: 973-660-7026
Toll-Free:	
Address: 5 Giralda Farms, Madison, NJ 07940-0874 US	

GROWTH PLANS/SPECIAL FEATURES:

Wyeth is a global leader in pharmaceuticals, consumer health care products and animal health care products. The firm discovers, develops, manufactures, distributes and sells a diversified line of products arising from three divisions: pharmaceuticals, consumer health care and animal care. The pharmaceuticals segment is itself divided into women's health care, neuroscience, vaccines and infectious disease, musculoskeletal, internal medicine, hemophilia and immunology and oncology. The division sells branded and generic pharmaceuticals, biological and nutraceutical products as well as animal biological products and pharmaceuticals. Its branded products include Premarin, Prempro, Premphase, Triphasil, Ativan, Effexor, Altace, Inderal, Zoton, Protonix and Enbrel. The consumer health care segment's products include analgesics, cough/cold/allergy remedies, nutritional supplements, lip balm and hemorrhoidal, antacid, asthma and other relief items sold over-the-counter. The segment's well-known over-the-counter products include Advil, cold medicines Robitussin and Dimetapp and nutritional supplement Centrum, as well as Chap Stick, Caltrate, Preparation H and Solgar. The company's animal health care products include vaccines, pharmaceuticals, endectocides (dewormers that control both internal and external parasites) and growth implants under the brand names LymeVax, Duramune and Fel-O-Vax. The company recently upped its stake in Wyeth/Takeda Pharmaceutical Company Limited joint venture Wyeth K.K. to 80%, after the purchase of an additional 10 percent stake in 2006.

FINANCIALS: **Sales and profits are in thousands of dollars—add 000 to get the full amount. 2007 Note: Financial information for 2007 was not available for all companies at press time.**

007 Sales: $	2007 Profits: $	**U.S. Stock Ticker: WYE**
006 Sales: $20,350,655	2006 Profits: $4,196,706	**Int'l Ticker:** Int'l Exchange:
005 Sales: $18,755,790	2005 Profits: $3,656,298	Employees: 50,060
004 Sales: $17,358,028	2004 Profits: $1,233,997	Fiscal Year Ends: 12/31
003 Sales: $15,850,600	2003 Profits: $2,051,600	Parent Company:

SALARIES/BENEFITS:

Pension Plan: Y	ESOP Stock Plan:	Profit Sharing:	Top Exec. Salary: $1,590,000	Bonus: $2,700,000
Savings Plan: Y	Stock Purch. Plan:		Second Exec. Salary: $840,000	Bonus: $1,260,000

OTHER THOUGHTS:

Apparent Women Officers or Directors: 1
Hot Spot for Advancement for Women/Minorities:

LOCATIONS: ("Y" = Yes)

West:	Southwest:	Midwest:	Southeast:	Northeast:	International:
Y	Y	Y	Y	Y	Y

YOUNG INNOVATIONS INC

www.ydnt.com

Industry Group Code: 339113 **Ranks within this company's industry group:** Sales: 83 Profits: 55

Insurance/HMO/PPO:		Drugs:		Equipment/Supplies:		Hospitals/Clinics:		Services:		Health Care:	
Insurance:		Manufacturer:		Manufacturer:	Y	Acute Care:		Diagnostics:		Home Health:	
Managed Care:		Distributor:		Distributor:		Sub-Acute:		Labs/Testing:		Long-Term Care:	
Utilization Management:		Specialty Pharmacy:		Leasing/Finance:		Outpatient Surgery:		Staffing:		Physical Therapy:	
Payment Processing:		Vitamins/Nutritionals:		Information Systems:		Physical Rehab. Ctr.:		Waste Disposal:		Physician Prac. Mgmt.:	
		Clinical Trials:				Psychiatric Clinics:		Specialty Svcs.:			

TYPES OF BUSINESS:

Dental Instruments
X-Ray Equipment
Toothbrushes & Toothpastes
Ultrasonic Systems

BRANDS/DIVISIONS/AFFILIATES:

D-Lish
Festival
Spartan
Panoramic
ProCare
Athena Champion
Healthsonics
Obtura

CONTACTS: *Note: Officers with more than one job title may be intentionally listed here more than once.*

Alfred E. Brennan, CEO
Arthur L. Herbst, Jr., Pres.
Christine R. Boehning, CFO
Christine R. Boehning, Sec./VP
Daniel J. Tarullo, VP
Stephen Yaggy, VP
George E. Richmond, Chmn.

Phone: 314-344-0010	**Fax:** 314-344-0021
Toll-Free: 800-325-1881	
Address: 13705 Shoreline Ct. E., Earth City, MO 63045 US	

GROWTH PLANS/SPECIAL FEATURES:

Young Innovations, Inc. develops, manufactures an markets supplies and equipment used to facilitate th practice of dentistry and to promote oral health. The firr organized its products in five groups. The preventive grou includes prophylaxis (prophy) angles; prophy pastes fluorides; handpieces and components and microapplicators The infection control group includes surface disinfectants evacuation system cleaners; gloves and masks; ultrasoni cleaning systems; and instrument disinfectants. Th diagnostic group contains panoramic dental X-ray system and supplies such as Panoramic PC-1000 system an Panoramic PC-1000/Laser-1000; digital products; an supplies and service. The home care group markets hom care kits, toothbrushes and fluorides. The endodontic grou sells products for tooth root, dental pulp and surroundin tissue problems such as obturation products and ultrasoni systems. The company's products are primarily marketed t dental professionals, principally dentists, endodontists orthodontists, dental hygienists and dental assistants. Bran names include D-Lish, Festival, ProCare, Athena Champior Healthsonics, Obtura, Panoramic and Spartan. The firr markets its products primarily in the US. Young Innovatio also markets its products in several international markets including Canada, Europe, South America, Central Americ and the Pacific Rim. International sales represented les than 10% of total net sales in 2006. The company' manufacturing and distribution facilities are located i Missouri, California, Indiana, Tennessee, Texas, Canada Wisconsin and Ireland. In August 2006, Young Innovation acquired Microbrush, Inc. and Microbrush International, Ltd a dental microapplicators provider.

FINANCIALS: **Sales and profits are in thousands of dollars—add 000 to get the full amount. 2007 Note: Financial information for 2007 was not available for all companies at press time.**

2007 Sales: $	2007 Profits: $	**U.S. Stock Ticker: YDNT**
2006 Sales: $90,805	2006 Profits: $14,799	**Int'l Ticker:** Int'l Exchange:
2005 Sales: $84,766	2005 Profits: $15,338	Employees: 400
2004 Sales: $79,201	2004 Profits: $13,934	Fiscal Year Ends: 12/31
2003 Sales: $76,156	2003 Profits: $13,201	Parent Company:

SALARIES/BENEFITS:

Pension Plan:	ESOP Stock Plan:	Profit Sharing:	Top Exec. Salary: $382,692	Bonus: $
Savings Plan:	Stock Purch. Plan:		Second Exec. Salary: $307,115	Bonus: $

OTHER THOUGHTS:

Apparent Women Officers or Directors: 1
Hot Spot for Advancement for Women/Minorities:

LOCATIONS: ("Y" = Yes)

West:	Southwest:	Midwest:	Southeast:	Northeast:	International:
Y	Y	Y			Y

ZIMMER HOLDINGS INC

www.zimmer.com

ndustry Group Code: 339113 **Ranks within this company's industry group:** Sales: 10 Profits: 5

nsurance/HMO/PPO:		Drugs:		Equipment/Supplies:		Hospitals/Clinics:		Services:		Health Care:	
ısurance:		Manufacturer:		Manufacturer:	Y	Acute Care:		Diagnostics:		Home Health:	
lanaged Care:		Distributor:		Distributor:		Sub-Acute:		Labs/Testing:		Long-Term Care:	
tilization Management:		Specialty Pharmacy:		Leasing/Finance:		Outpatient Surgery:		Staffing:		Physical Therapy:	
ayment Processing:		Vitamins/Nutritionals:		Information Systems:		Physical Rehab. Ctr.:		Waste Disposal:		Physician Prac. Mgmt.:	
		Clinical Trials:				Psychiatric Clinics:		Specialty Svcs.:			

TYPES OF BUSINESS:

)rthopedic Supplies
iurgical Supplies & Systems
oint Implants
Knee & Hip Replacement Systems
racture Management Products

BRANDS/DIVISIONS/AFFILIATES:

lexGen
/erSys
/I/DN Intermedullary Fixation
Pulsavac Plus Wound Debridement System
.T.S. Tourniquet System
Ausculoskeletal Management Systems, LLC

CONTACTS: *Note: Officers with more than one job title may be ntentionally listed here more than once.*

)avid C. Dvorak, CEO
)avid C. Dvorak, Pres.
ames T. Crines, CFO/Exec. VP
iheryl L. Conley, Chief Mktg. Officer/Pres., Americas & Global Mktg.
Renee Rogers, VP-Global Human Resources
Cheryl R. Blanchard, Sr. VP-R&D/Chief Scientific Officer
Chad F. Phipps, General Counsel/Sr. VP/Sec.
Richard C. Stair, VP-Global Oper.
iean O'Hara, Mgr.-Investor Rel.
ames T. Crines, Exec. VP-Finance
erek Davis, VP-Finance/Controller/Chief Acct. Officer
on E. Kramer, Pres., US Sales
aura C. O'Donnell, Chief Compliance Officer
itephen H. L. Ooi, Pres., Asia Pacific
. Raymond Elliott, Chmn.
runo A. Melzi, Chmn.-Europe, Africa & Middle East
Richard C. Stair, VP-Logistics

hone: 574-267-6131	**Fax:** 574-372-4988
oll-Free: 800-613-6131	
ddress: 1800 W. Center St., Warsaw, IN 46581 US	

GROWTH PLANS/SPECIAL FEATURES:

Zimmer Holdings, Inc. designs, develops, manufactures and markets reconstructive orthopedic implants, including joint and dental; spinal implants; trauma products; and related orthopedic surgical products. The company also provides hospital-focused consulting services to help member institutions design, implement and manage orthopedic programs. Through its subsidiaries, the firm has operations in 24 countries and markets products in over 100 countries. Zimmer's main products are hip and knee replacements, fracture management products and various surgical products. The NexGen line is a line of knee replacement system surgery products for stabilization and revision procedures. The VerSys hip system is a family of hip products that offer design-specific options for varying patient needs. Fracture management products are used primarily to reattach or stabilize damaged bone or tissue to support the body's natural healing process. The M/DN Intramedullary Fixation, an intramedullary nailing system with multiple screw options for the internal fixation of long bone fractures, incorporates implants and instruments to align and fix fractures of the tibia, femur and humerus. The company's surgical products include the Pulsavac Plus Wound Debridement System and the A.T.S. Tourniquet System. The firm's primary customers include musculoskeletal surgeons, neurosurgeons, oral surgeons, dentists, hospitals, distributors, healthcare dealers and healthcare purchasing organizations or buying groups. In June 2006, Zimmer acquired Musculoskeletal Management Systems, LLC, more commonly knows as The Human Motion Institute, a hospital efficiency consulting business focused on orthopedics. In August 2007, the firm agreed to acquire ORTHOsoft, Inc., a computer navigation provider for orthopedic surgery.

Zimmer offers its employees medical, dental and vision insurance; flexible spending accounts; life and AD&D insurance; disability income protection plans; a savings and investment program; an employee stock purchase program; and tuition reimbursement.

FINANCIALS: **Sales and profits are in thousands of dollars—add 000 to get the full amount. 2007 Note: Financial information for 2007 was not available for all companies at press time.**

007 Sales: $	2007 Profits: $	**U.S. Stock Ticker: ZMH**
006 Sales: $3,495,400	2006 Profits: $834,500	**Int'l Ticker:** Int'l Exchange:
005 Sales: $3,286,100	2005 Profits: $732,500	Employees: 6,900
004 Sales: $2,980,900	2004 Profits: $541,800	Fiscal Year Ends: 12/31
003 Sales: $1,901,000	2003 Profits: $346,300	Parent Company:

SALARIES/BENEFITS:

ension Plan:	ESOP Stock Plan:	Profit Sharing:	Top Exec. Salary: $750,000	Bonus: $1,140,416
avings Plan: Y	Stock Purch. Plan: Y		Second Exec. Salary: $510,000	Bonus: $464,730

OTHER THOUGHTS:

pparent Women Officers or Directors: 4
ot Spot for Advancement for Women/Minorities: Y

LOCATIONS: ("Y" = Yes)

West:	Southwest:	Midwest:	Southeast:	Northeast:	International:
Y		Y	Y	Y	Y

ZLB BEHRING LLC www.zlbbehring.com

Industry Group Code: 339113 **Ranks within this company's industry group:** Sales: Profits:

Insurance/HMO/PPO:		Drugs:		Equipment/Supplies:		Hospitals/Clinics:		Services:		Health Care:	
Insurance:		Manufacturer:	Y	Manufacturer:	Y	Acute Care:		Diagnostics:		Home Health:	
Managed Care:		Distributor:		Distributor:		Sub-Acute:		Labs/Testing:		Long-Term Care:	
Utilization Management:		Specialty Pharmacy:		Leasing/Finance:		Outpatient Surgery:		Staffing:		Physical Therapy:	
Payment Processing:		Vitamins/Nutritionals:		Information Systems:		Physical Rehab. Ctr.:		Waste Disposal:		Physician Prac. Mgmt.:	
		Clinical Trials:				Psychiatric Clinics:		Specialty Svcs.:			

TYPES OF BUSINESS:

Plasma Products
Coagulants
Anticoagulants
Immunoglobulins
Surgical Wound Healers
Plasma Expanders
Plasma Collection
Medical Devices

BRANDS/DIVISIONS/AFFILIATES:

CSL Limited
Mix2Vial Alternative Transfer Device
Monoclate-P
Mononine
Stimate
Helixate FS
Vivaglobin
Zemaira

CONTACTS: *Note: Officers with more than one job title may be intentionally listed here more than once.*

Peter Turner, Pres.
Kathy Quay, Sr. VP-Human Resources
Roland Martin, Sr. VP-Global R&D
Paul Hermecz, Sr. VP/CIO
Greg Boss, General Counsel/Sr. VP
Paul R. Perreault, Exec. VP-Worldwide Commercial Oper.
Paul Walton, Sr. VP-Bus. Dev.
Dennis Jackman, Sr. VP-Public Affairs
Randy Furby, Sr. VP/General Mgr., Kankakee Plant
Karen Etchberger, Sr. VP-Global Quality
Gordon Naylor, Sr. VP- ZLB Plasma Services
Alan Anderson, VP-Western Europe
Kathryn Munro, Sr. VP-Supply Chain

Phone: 610-878-4155	**Fax:** 610-878-4913
Toll-Free:	
Address: 1020 First Ave., King of Prussia, PA 19406 US	

GROWTH PLANS/SPECIAL FEATURES:

ZLB Behring, a subsidiary of CSL Limited, specializes in th manufacture of plasma-based products. The firm's produ line includes drugs that treat hemophilia and othe coagulation disorders, immunoglobulins that prevent an treat immune disorders, anticoagulants, surgical wour healers and plasma expanders for shock, burns an circulatory disorders. ZLB Behring also operates one of th world's largest, fully owned plasma collection network Patented products include coagulators; critical care an immune mediated products; and Alpha-1 inhibitor Coagulator products include Humate-P, Monoclate-I Mononine, Stimate and Helixate FS, for the treatment classical hemophilia. Critical care products includ Albuminar-5, Albuminar-25 and Albumin (Human) U.S.P., 5 and 25%. Immune mediated disorders are treated wi Carimune NF Nanofiltered and Gammar-P I.V. The firm Alpha-1 inhibitor, Zemaira, treats chronic augmentation an provides maintenance therapy in individuals with alpha proteinase inhibitor deficiency and clinical evidence emphysema. ZLB Behring recently introduced the Mix2Vi Alternative Transfer Device, a plastic, needle-less devic with a built-in filter that simplifies the reconstituting medicines. In January 2006, the FDA approved ZL Behring's Vivaglobin human normal immunoglobuli Vivaglobin is a new treatment option for patients who suff intolerable side effects from IV treatment. In April 2006, ZL Behring announced that it has been granted a license by th FDA to produce Alpha-1 Proteinase Inhibitor, Zemaira, in new facility in its Kankakee, Illinois manufacturing complex.

FINANCIALS: **Sales and profits are in thousands of dollars—add 000 to get the full amount. 2007 Note: Financial information for 2007 was not available for all companies at press time.**

2007 Sales: $	2007 Profits: $	**U.S. Stock Ticker: Subsidiary**
2006 Sales: $	2006 Profits: $	**Int'l Ticker:** Int'l Exchange:
2005 Sales: $2,244,567	2005 Profits: $315,767	Employees:
2004 Sales: $1,037,503	2004 Profits: $	Fiscal Year Ends: 12/31
2003 Sales: $	2003 Profits: $	Parent Company: CSL LIMITED

SALARIES/BENEFITS:

Pension Plan:	ESOP Stock Plan:	Profit Sharing:	Top Exec. Salary: $	Bonus: $
Savings Plan:	Stock Purch. Plan:		Second Exec. Salary: $	Bonus: $

OTHER THOUGHTS:

Apparent Women Officers or Directors: 3
Hot Spot for Advancement for Women/Minorities: Y

LOCATIONS: ("Y" = Yes)

West:	Southwest:	Midwest:	Southeast:	Northeast:	International:
		Y		Y	Y

ZOLL MEDICAL CORP

www.zoll.com

ndustry Group Code: 339113 **Ranks within this company's industry group:** Sales: 57 Profits: 62

nsurance/HMO/PPO:		Drugs:		Equipment/Supplies:		Hospitals/Clinics:		Services:		Health Care:	
nsurance:		Manufacturer:		Manufacturer:	Y	Acute Care:		Diagnostics:		Home Health:	
Managed Care:		Distributor:		Distributor:		Sub-Acute:		Labs/Testing:		Long-Term Care:	
Jtilization Management:		Specialty Pharmacy:		Leasing/Finance:		Outpatient Surgery:		Staffing:		Physical Therapy:	
Payment Processing:		Vitamins/Nutritionals:		Information Systems:	Y	Physical Rehab. Ctr.:		Waste Disposal:		Physician Prac. Mgmt.:	
		Clinical Trials:				Psychiatric Clinics:		Specialty Svcs.:			

TYPES OF BUSINESS:

Cardiac Resuscitation Devices
Disposable Electrodes
Data Management Systems

BRANDS/DIVISIONS/AFFILIATES:

RescueNet
CodeNet
LifeCor, Inc.
AED Pro
AED Plus
LifeVest

CONTACTS: *Note: Officers with more than one job title may be intentionally listed here more than once.*

Richard A. Packer, CEO
Richard A. Packer, Pres.
A. Ernest Whiton, CFO
Ward M. Hamilton, VP-Mktg.
Donald R. Boucher, VP-R&D
A. Ernest Whiton, VP-Admin.
Stephen Korn, General Counsel/VP/Corp. Sec.
Edward T. Dunn, VP-Oper.
John P. Bergeron, VP/Treas.
Steven K. Flora, VP-North American Sales
Richard A. Packer, Chmn.
Alex N. Moghadam, VP-Int'l Oper.

Phone: 978-421-9655	**Fax:** 978-421-0025
Toll-Free: 800-348-9011	
Address: 269 Mill Rd., Chelmsford, MA 01824 US	

GROWTH PLANS/SPECIAL FEATURES:

Zoll Medical Corp. develops technologies and software that helps clinicians, emergency medical services (EMS) personnel and lay rescuers advance and improve the practice of resuscitation. The company provides technology that addresses various clinical interventions that are part of resuscitation efforts. The firm's products consist of professional defibrillators, which include the M Series, E Series, the new R series and the Life Vest wearable defibrillator; automated external defibrillators (AED) that assist with manual CPR efforts, which include the AED Pro and the AED Plus; disposable electrodes used with Zoll's line of defibrillators; the AutoPulse Non-invasive Cardiac Support Pump, used to automate the process of delivering chest compressions; documentations and information management, which include RescueNet for EMS personnel and CodeNet for hospitals; and fluid replacement utilizing the Zoll Infuser, also known as the Power Infuser, in the military. The company and its subsidiaries currently hold roughly 85 U.S. and 30 foreign patents, which relate to pacing, defibrillation, CPR and other resuscitation therapies. In April 2006, Zoll Medical acquired Lifecor, Inc., a company devoted to the production of external defibrillator systems.

FINANCIALS: **Sales and profits are in thousands of dollars—add 000 to get the full amount. 2007 Note: Financial information for 2007 was not available for all companies at press time.**

2007 Sales: $	2007 Profits: $	**U.S. Stock Ticker: ZOLL**
2006 Sales: $248,849	2006 Profits: $11,140	**Int'l Ticker:** Int'l Exchange:
2005 Sales: $211,340	2005 Profits: $1,963	Employees: 1,080
2004 Sales: $211,785	2004 Profits: $8,956	Fiscal Year Ends: 9/30
2003 Sales: $184,603	2003 Profits: $12,850	Parent Company:

SALARIES/BENEFITS:

Pension Plan:	ESOP Stock Plan:	Profit Sharing:	Top Exec. Salary: $350,000	Bonus: $375,000
Savings Plan:	Stock Purch. Plan:		Second Exec. Salary: $305,000	Bonus: $29,000

OTHER THOUGHTS:

Apparent Women Officers or Directors:
Hot Spot for Advancement for Women/Minorities:

LOCATIONS: ("Y" = Yes)

West:	Southwest:	Midwest:	Southeast:	Northeast:	International:
Y				Y	Y

Note: Financial information, benefits and other data can change quickly and may vary from those stated here.

ADDITIONAL INDEXES

CONTENTS:

INDEX OF FIRMS NOTED AS HOT SPOTS FOR ADVANCEMENT FOR WOMEN & MINORITIES

PHARMACEUTICAL PRODUCT DEVELOPMENT INC
PHARMACOPEIA DRUG DISCOVERY
PREMERA BLUE CROSS
PREMIER INC
PROVIDENCE HEALTH & SERVICES
PROXYMED INC
QUEST DIAGNOSTICS INC
RES CARE INC
RESMED INC
REVOLUTION HEALTH GROUP LLC
RITE AID CORPORATION
ROCHE HOLDING LTD
SANOFI-AVENTIS
SCHERING-PLOUGH CORP
SHIRE PLC
SIERRA HEALTH SERVICES INC
SIGNATURE EYEWEAR INC
SISTERS OF MERCY HEALTH SYSTEMS
SOLUCIENT LLC
SPECIALTY LABORATORIES INC
SSM HEALTH CARE SYSTEM INC
ST JUDE CHILDRENS RESEARCH HOSPITAL
ST JUDE MEDICAL INC
SUN HEALTHCARE GROUP
SUTTER HEALTH
SYNOVIS LIFE TECHNOLOGIES INC
TAKE CARE HEALTH SYSTEMS LLC
TECHNE CORP
TELEFLEX INC
TENET HEALTHCARE CORPORATION
TEVA PHARMACEUTICAL INDUSTRIES
THERAGENICS CORP
THORATEC CORPORATION
TRIAD HOSPITALS INC
TRINITY HEALTH COMPANY
UNITEDHEALTH GROUP INC
UNIVERSAL HEALTH SERVICES INC
VALEANT PHARMACEUTICALS INTERNATIONAL
VARIAN MEDICAL SYSTEMS INC
VISION SERVICE PLAN
WATSON PHARMACEUTICALS INC
WEIGHT WATCHERS INTERNATIONAL INC
WELLCARE GROUP OF COMPANIES
WELLPOINT INC
WRIGHT MEDICAL GROUP INC
ZIMMER HOLDINGS INC
ZLB BEHRING LLC

INDEX OF SUBSIDIARIES, BRAND NAMES AND AFFILIATIONS

Brand or subsidiary, followed by the name of the related corporation

INDEX OF SUBSIDIARIES, BRAND NAMES AND AFFILIATIONS, CONT.

INDEX OF SUBSIDIARIES, BRAND NAMES AND AFFILIATIONS, CONT.

INDEX OF SUBSIDIARIES, BRAND NAMES AND AFFILIATIONS, CONT.

INDEX OF SUBSIDIARIES, BRAND NAMES AND AFFILIATIONS, CONT.

INDEX OF SUBSIDIARIES, BRAND NAMES AND AFFILIATIONS, CONT.

INDEX OF SUBSIDIARIES, BRAND NAMES AND AFFILIATIONS, CONT.

INDEX OF SUBSIDIARIES, BRAND NAMES AND AFFILIATIONS, CONT.

INDEX OF SUBSIDIARIES, BRAND NAMES AND AFFILIATIONS, CONT.

INDEX OF SUBSIDIARIES, BRAND NAMES AND AFFILIATIONS, CONT.

INDEX OF SUBSIDIARIES, BRAND NAMES AND AFFILIATIONS, CONT.

INDEX OF SUBSIDIARIES, BRAND NAMES AND AFFILIATIONS, CONT.

INDEX OF SUBSIDIARIES, BRAND NAMES AND AFFILIATIONS, CONT.

INDEX OF SUBSIDIARIES, BRAND NAMES AND AFFILIATIONS, CONT.

INDEX OF SUBSIDIARIES, BRAND NAMES AND AFFILIATIONS, CONT.

INDEX OF SUBSIDIARIES, BRAND NAMES AND AFFILIATIONS, CONT.

INDEX OF SUBSIDIARIES, BRAND NAMES AND AFFILIATIONS, CONT.

INDEX OF SUBSIDIARIES, BRAND NAMES AND AFFILIATIONS, CONT.

INDEX OF SUBSIDIARIES, BRAND NAMES AND AFFILIATIONS, CONT.

INDEX OF SUBSIDIARIES, BRAND NAMES AND AFFILIATIONS, CONT.

INDEX OF SUBSIDIARIES, BRAND NAMES AND AFFILIATIONS, CONT.

INDEX OF SUBSIDIARIES, BRAND NAMES AND AFFILIATIONS, CONT.

INDEX OF SUBSIDIARIES, BRAND NAMES AND AFFILIATIONS, CONT.

INDEX OF SUBSIDIARIES, BRAND NAMES AND AFFILIATIONS, CONT.

INDEX OF SUBSIDIARIES, BRAND NAMES AND AFFILIATIONS, CONT.

INDEX OF SUBSIDIARIES, BRAND NAMES AND AFFILIATIONS, CONT.